# COGNITIVE PSYCHOLOGY

The only means of strengthening one's intellect
is to make up one's mind about nothing—to
let the mind be a thoroughfare for all thoughts.
Not a select party.

(John Keats)

# Cognitive Psychology
## A Student's Handbook

### Fourth Edition

Michael W. Eysenck
*(Royal Holloway, University of London, UK)*

Mark Keane
*(University College Dublin, Ireland)*

**Psychology Press**
Taylor & Francis Group
HOVE AND NEW YORK

First published 2000 by Psychology Press Ltd
27 Church Road, Hove, East Sussex, BN3 2FA

http://www.psypress.co.uk

Simultaneously published in the USA and Canada
by Taylor & Francis Inc
325 Chestnut Street, Suite 800, Philadelphia, PA 19106

Psychology Press is part of the Taylor & Francis Group

Reprinted 2000, 2001

Reprinted 2002 (twice) by Psychology Press Ltd
27 Church Road, Hove, East Sussex, BN3 2FA
29 West 35th Street, New York, NY 10001

*British Library Cataloguing in Publication Data*
A catalogue record for this book is available from the British Library

ISBN 0-86377-550-0 (hbk)
ISBN 0-86377-551-9 (pbk)

Cover design by Hybert Design, Waltham St Lawrence, Berkshire
Typeset in Hong Kong by Graphicraft Limited
Printed and bound in Great Britain by Biddles Ltd, Guildford and King's Lynn

# Contents

# Preface

Cognitive psychology has changed in several exciting ways in the few years since the third edition of this textbook. Of all the changes, the most dramatic has been the huge increase in the number of studies making use of sophisticated techniques (e.g., PET scans) to investigate human cognition. During the 1990s, such studies probably increased tenfold, and are set to increase still further during the early years of the third millennium. As a result, we now have four major approaches to cognitive psychology: experimental cognitive psychology based mainly on laboratory experiments; cognitive neuropsychology, which points up the effects of brain damage on cognition; cognitive science, with its emphasis on computational modelling; and cognitive neuroscience, which uses a wide range of techniques to study brain functioning. It is a worthwhile (but challenging) business to try to integrate information from these four approaches, and that it is exactly what we have tried to do in this book. As before, our busy professional lives have made it essential for us to work hard to avoid chaos. For example, the first author wrote several parts of the book in China, and other parts were written in Mexico, Poland, Russia, Israel, and the United States. The second author followed Joyce's ghost, writing parts of the book between Dublin and Trieste.

I (Michael Eysenck) would like to express my profound gratitude to my wife Christine, to whom this book (in common with the previous edition) is appropriately dedicated. I am also very grateful to our three children (Fleur, William, and Juliet) for their tolerance and understanding, just as was the case with the previous edition of this book. However, when I look back to the writing of the third edition of this textbook, it amazes me how much they have changed over the last five years.

Since I (Mark Keane) first collaborated on *Cognitive Psychology: A Student's Handbook* in 1990 my professional life has undergone considerable change, from a post-doc in psychology to Professor of Computer Science. My original motivation in writing this text was to influence the course of cognitive psychology as it was then developing, to encourage its extension in a computational direction. Looking back over the last 10 years, I am struck by the slowness of change in the introduction of these ideas. The standard psychology undergraduate degree does a very good job at giving students the tools for the empirical exploration of the mind. However, few courses give students the tools for the theoretical elaboration of the topic. In this respect, the discipline gets a "could do better" rather than an "excellent" on the mark sheet.

We are very grateful to several people for reading an entire draft of this book, and for offering valuable advice on how it might be improved. They include Ruth Byrne, Liz Styles, Trevor Harley, and Robert Logie. We would also like to thank those who commented on various chapters: John Towse, Steve Anderson, James Hampton, Fernand Gobet, Evan Heit, Alan Parkin, David Over, Ken Manktelow, Ken Gilhooly, Peter Ayton, Clare Harries, George Mather, Mark Georgeson, Gerry Altmann, Nick Wade, Mick Power, David Hardman, John Richardson, Vicki Bruce, Gillian Cohen, and Jonathan St.B.T. Evans.

*Michael Eysenck and Mark Keane*

# 1

# Introduction

## COGNITIVE PSYCHOLOGY AS A SCIENCE

In the years leading up to the millennium, people made increased efforts to understand each other and their own inner, mental space. This concern was marked with a tidal wave of research in the field of cognitive psychology, and by the emergence of cognitive science as a unified programme for studying the mind.

In the popular media, there are numerous books, films, and television programmes on the more accessible aspects of cognitive research. In scientific circles, cognitive psychology is currently a thriving area, dealing with a bewildering diversity of phenomena, including topics like attention, perception, learning, memory, language, emotion, concept formation, and thinking.

In spite of its diversity, cognitive psychology is unified by a common approach based on an analogy between the mind and the digital computer; this is the information-processing approach. This approach is the dominant paradigm or theoretical orientation (Kuhn, 1970) within cognitive psychology, and has been for some decades.

## Historical roots of cognitive psychology

The year 1956 was critical in the development of cognitive psychology. At a meeting at the Massachusetts Institute of Technology, Chomsky gave a paper on his theory of language, George Miller presented a paper on the magic number seven in short-term memory (Miller, 1956), and Newell and Simon discussed their very influential computational model called the General Problem Solver (discussed in Newell, Shaw, & Simon, 1958; see also Chapter 15). In addition, the first systematic attempt to consider concept formation from a cognitive perspective was reported (Bruner, Goodnow, & Austin, 1956).

The field of Artificial Intelligence was also founded in 1956 at the Dartmouth Conference, which was attended by Chomsky, McCarthy, Minsky, Newell, Simon, and Miller (see Gardner, 1985). Thus, 1956 witnessed the birth of both cognitive psychology and cognitive science as major disciplines. Books devoted to aspects of cognitive psychology began to appear (e.g., Broadbent, 1958; Bruner et al., 1956). However, it took several years before the entire information-processing viewpoint reached undergraduate courses (Lachman, Lachman, & Butterfield, 1979; Lindsay & Norman, 1977).

## Information processing: Consensus

Broadbent (1958) argued that much of cognition consists of a sequential series of processing stages. When a stimulus is presented, basic perceptual processes occur, followed by attentional processes that transfer some of the products of the initial perceptual processing to a short-term memory store. Thereafter, rehearsal serves to maintain information in the short-term memory store, and some of the information is transferred to a long-term memory store. Atkinson and Shiffrin (1968; see also Chapter 6) put forward one of the most detailed theories of this type.

This theoretical approach provided a simple framework for textbook writers. The stimulus input could be followed from the sense organs to its ultimate storage in long-term memory by successive chapters on perception, attention, short-term memory, and long-term memory. The crucial limitation with this approach is its assumption that stimuli impinge on an inactive and unprepared organism. In fact, processing is often affected substantially by the individual's past experience, expectations, and so on.

We can distinguish between *bottom-up processing* and *top-down processing*. Bottom-up or stimulus-driven processing is directly affected by stimulus input, whereas top-down or conceptually driven processing is affected by what the individual contributes (e.g., expectations determined by context and past experience). As an example of top-down processing, it is easier to read the word "well" in poor handwriting if it is presented in the sentence context, "I hope you are quite ____ ", than when it is presented on its own. The sequential stage model deals primarily with bottom-up or stimulus-driven processing, and its failure to consider top-down processing adequately is its greatest limitation.

During the 1970s, theorists such as Neisser (1976) argued that nearly all cognitive activity consists of interactive bottom-up and top-down processes occurring together (see Chapter 4). Perception and remembering might seem to be exceptions, because perception depends heavily on the precise stimuli presented (and thus on bottom-up processing), and remembering depends crucially on stored information (and thus on top-down processing). However, perception is influenced by the perceiver's expectations about to-be-presented stimuli (see Chapters 2, 3, and 4), and remembering is influenced by the precise environmental cues to memory that are available (see Chapter 6).

By the end of the 1970s, most cognitive psychologists agreed that the information-processing paradigm was the best way to study human cognition (see Lachman et al., 1979):

- People are autonomous, intentional beings interacting with the external world.
- The mind through which they interact with the world is a general-purpose, symbol-processing system ("symbols" are patterns stored in long-term memory which "designate or 'point to' structures outside themselves"; Simon & Kaplan, 1989, p. 13).
- Symbols are acted on by processes that transform them into other symbols that ultimately relate to things in the external world.
- The aim of psychological research is to specify the symbolic processes and representations underlying performance on all cognitive tasks.
- Cognitive processes take time, and predictions about reaction times can often be made.
- The mind is a limited-capacity processor having structural and resource limitations.
- The symbol system depends on a neurological substrate, but is not wholly constrained by it.

Many of these ideas stemmed from the view that human cognition resembles the functioning of computers. As Herb Simon (1980, p. 45) expressed it, "It might have been necessary a decade ago to argue for the commonality of the information processes that are employed by such disparate systems as computers and human nervous systems. The evidence for that commonality is now overwhelming." (See Simon, 1995, for an update of this view.)

The information-processing framework is continually developing as information technology develops. The computational metaphor is always being extended as computer technology develops. In the 1950s and 1960s, researchers mainly used the general properties of the computer to understand the mind (e.g., that it had a central processor and memory registers). Many different programming languages had been developed by the 1970s, leading to various aspects of computer software and languages being used (e.g., Johnson-Laird, 1977, on analogies to language understanding). After that, as massively parallel machines were developed, theorists returned to the notion that cognitive theories should be based on the parallel processing capabilities of the brain (Rumelhart, McClelland, & the PDP Research Group, 1986).

## Information processing: Diversity

Cognitive science is a trans-disciplinary grouping of cognitive psychology, artificial intelligence, linguistics, philosophy, neuroscience, and anthropology. The common aim of these disciplines is the understanding of the mind. To simplify matters, we will focus mainly on the relationship between cognitive psychology and artificial intelligence.

At the risk of oversimplification, we can identify four major approaches within cognitive psychology:

- *Experimental cognitive psychology*: it follows the experimental tradition of cognitive psychology, and involves no computational modelling.
- *Cognitive science*: it develops computational models to understand human cognition.
- *Cognitive neuropsychology*: it studies patterns of cognitive impairment shown by brain-damaged patients to provide valuable information about normal human cognition.
- *Cognitive neuroscience*: it uses several techniques for studying brain functioning (e.g., brain scans) to understand human cognition.

There are various reasons why these distinctions are less neat and tidy in reality than we have implied. First, terms such as cognitive science and cognitive neuroscience are sometimes used in a broader and more inclusive way than we have done. Second, there has been a rapid increase in recent years in studies that combine elements of more than one approach. Third, some have argued that experimental cognitive psychologists and cognitive scientists are both endangered species, given the galloping expansion of cognitive neuropsychology and cognitive neuroscience.

In this book, we will provide a synthesis of the insights emerging from all four approaches. The approach taken by experimental cognitive psychologists has been in existence for several decades, so we will focus mainly on the approaches of cognitive scientists, cognitive neuropsychologists, and cognitive neuroscientists in the following sections. Before doing so, however, we will consider some traditional ways of obtaining evidence about human cognition.

## Empirical methods

In most of the research discussed in this book, cognitive processes and structures were inferred from participants' behaviour (e.g., speed and/or accuracy of performance) obtained under well controlled conditions. This approach has proved to be very useful, and the data thus obtained have been used in the development and subsequent testing of most theories in cognitive psychology. However, there are two major potential problems with the use of such data:

1. Measures of the speed and accuracy of performance provide only *indirect* information about the internal processes and structures of central interest to cognitive psychologists.
2. Behavioural data are usually gathered in the artificial surroundings of the laboratory. The ways in which people behave in the laboratory may differ greatly from the ways they behave in everyday life (see Chapter 19).

Cognitive psychologists do not rely solely on behavioural data to obtain useful information from their participants. An alternative way of studying cognitive processes is by making use of *introspection*, which is defined by the *Oxford English Dictionary* as "examination or observation of one's own mental processes". Introspection depends on conscious experience, and each individual's conscious experience is personal and private. In spite of this, it is often assumed that introspection can provide useful evidence about some mental processes.

Nisbett and Wilson (1977) argued that introspection is practically worthless, supporting their argument with examples. In one study, participants were presented with a display of five essentially identical pairs of stockings, and decided which pair was the best. After they had made their choice, they indicated *why* they had chosen that particular pair. Most participants chose the right-most pair, and so their decisions were actually affected by relative spatial position. However, the participants strongly denied that spatial position had played any part in their decision, referring instead to slight differences in colour, texture, and so on among the pairs of stockings as having been important.

Nisbett and Wilson (1977, p. 248) claimed that people are generally unaware of the processes influencing their behaviour: "When people are asked to report how a particular stimulus influenced a particular response, they do so not by consulting a memory of the mediating process, but by applying or generating causal theories about the effects of that type of stimulus on that type of response." This view was supported by the discovery that an individual's introspections about what is determining his or her behaviour are often no more accurate than the guesses made by others.

The limitations of introspective evidence are becoming increasingly clear. For example, consider research on *implicit learning*, which involves learning complex material without the ability to verbalise what has been learned. There is reasonable evidence for the existence of implicit learning (see Chapter 7). There is even stronger evidence for *implicit memory*, which involves memory in the absence of conscious recollection. Normal and brain-damaged individuals can exhibit excellent memory performance even when they show no relevant introspective evidence (see Chapter 7).

Ericsson and Simon (1980, 1984) argued that Nisbett and Wilson (1977) had overstated the case against introspection. They proposed various criteria for distinguishing between valid and invalid uses of introspection:

- It is preferable to obtain introspective reports during the performance of a task rather than retrospectively, because of the fallibility of memory.
- Participants are more likely to produce accurate introspections when *describing* what they are attending to, or thinking about, than when required to *interpret* a situation or their own thought processes.
- People cannot usefully introspect about several kinds of processes (e.g., neuronal processes; recognition processes).

Careful consideration of the studies that Nisbett and Wilson (1977) regarded as striking evidence of the worthlessness of introspection reveals that participants generally provided retrospective interpretations about information that had probably never been fully attended to. Thus, their findings are consistent with the proposed guidelines for the use of introspection (Crutcher, 1994; Ericsson & Simon, 1984).

In sum, introspection is sometimes useful, but there is no conscious awareness of many cognitive processes or their products. This point is illustrated by the phenomena of implicit learning and implicit memory, but numerous other examples of the limitations of introspection will be presented throughout this book.

## COGNITIVE SCIENCE

Cognitive scientists develop computational models to understand human cognition. A decent computational model can show us that a given theory can be specified and allow us to predict behaviour in new situations. Mathematical models were used in experimental psychology long before the emergence of the information-processing paradigm (e.g., in IQ testing). These models can be used to make predictions, but often lack an explanatory component. For example, committing three traffic violations is a good predictor of whether a person is a bad risk for car insurance, but it is not clear why. One of the major benefits of the computational models developed in cognitive science is

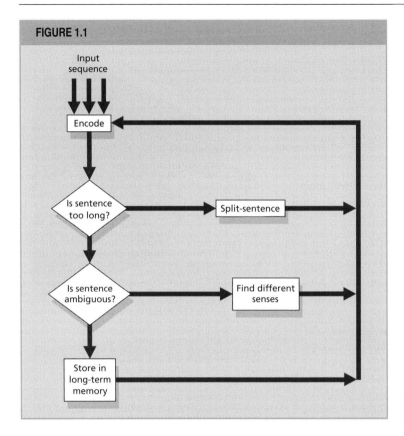

**FIGURE 1.1**

A flowchart of a bad theory about how we understand sentences.

that they can provide both an explanatory and predictive basis for a phenomenon (e.g., Keane, Ledgeway, & Duff, 1994; Costello & Keane, 2000). We will focus on computational models in this section, because they are the hallmark of the cognitive science approach.

## Computational modelling: From flowcharts to simulations

In the past, many experimental cognitive psychologists stated their theories in vague verbal statements. This made it hard to decide whether the evidence fitted the theory. In contrast, cognitive scientists produce computer programs to represent cognitive theories with all the details made explicit. In the 1960s and 1970s, cognitive psychologists tended to use flowcharts rather than programs to characterise their theories. Computer scientists use flowcharts as a sort of plan or blueprint for a program, before they write the detailed

code for it. Flowcharts are more specific than verbal descriptions, but can still be underspecified if not accompanied by a coded program.

An example of a very inadequate flowchart is shown in Figure 1.1. This is a flowchart of a bad theory about how we understand sentences. It assumes that a sentence is encoded in some form and then stored. After that, a decision process (indicated by a diamond) determines if the sentence is too long. If it is too long, then it is broken up and we return to the encode stage to re-encode the sentence. If it is ambiguous, then its two senses are distinguished, and we return to the encode stage. If it is not ambiguous, then it is stored in long-term memory. After one sentence is stored, we return to the encode stage to consider the next sentence.

In the days when cognitive psychologists only used flowcharts, sarcastic questions abounded, such as, "What happens in the boxes?" or "What goes down the arrows?". Such comments point to genuine criticisms. We need to know what is meant by "encode sentence", how long is "too long", and how sentence ambiguity is tested. For example, after deciding that only a certain length of sentence is acceptable, it may turn out that it is impossible to decide whether the sentence portions are ambiguous without considering the entire sentence. Thus, the boxes may look all right at a superficial glance, but real contradictions may appear when their contents are specified.

In similar fashion, exactly what goes down the arrows is critical. If one examines all the arrows converging on the "encode sentence" box, it is clear that more needs to be specified. There are four different kinds of thing entering this box: an encoded sentence from the environment; a sentence that has been broken up into bits by the "split-sentence" box; a sentence that has been broken up into several senses; and a command to consider the next sentence. Thus, the "encode" box has to perform several specific operations. In addition, it may have to record the fact that an item is either a sentence or a possible meaning of a sentence. Several other complex processes have to be specified within the "encode" box to handle these tasks, but the flowchart sadly fails to addresses these issues. The gaps in the flowchart show some similarities with those in the formula shown in Figure 1.2.

Not all theories expressed as flowcharts possess the deficiencies of the one described here. However, implementing a theory as a program is a good method for checking that it contains no hidden assumptions or vague terms. In the previous example, this would involve specifying the form of the input sentences, the nature of the storage mechanisms, and the various decision processes (e.g., those about sentence length and ambiguity). These computer programs are written in artificial intelligence programming languages, usually LISP (Norvig, 1992) or PROLOG (Shoham, 1993).

There are many issues surrounding the use of computer simulations and the ways in which they do and do not simulate cognitive processes (Cooper, Fox, Farrington, & Shallice, 1996; Costello & Keane, 2000; Palmer & Kimchi, 1986). Palmer and Kimchi (1986) argued that it should be possible to decompose a theory successively

**FIGURE 1.2**

"I THINK YOU SHOULD BE MORE EXPLICIT HERE IN STEP TWO."

The problem of being specific. Copyright © 1977 by Sidney Harris in American Scientist Magazine. Reproduced with permission of the author.

through a number of levels (from descriptive statement to flowchart to specific functions in a program) until one reaches a written program. In addition, they argued that it should be possible to draw a line at some level of decomposition, and say that everything above that line is psychologically plausible or meaningful, whereas everything below it is not. This issue of separating psychological aspects of the program from other aspects arises because there will always be parts of the program that have little to do with the psychological theory, but which are there simply because of the particular programming language being used and the machine on which the program is running. For example, in order to see what the program is doing, it is necessary to have print commands in the program which show the outputs of various stages in the computer's screen. However, no-one would argue that such print commands form part of the psychological model. Cooper et al. (1996) argue that psychological theories should not be

**Three issues surrounding computer simulation:**
- Is it possible to decompose a theory until one reaches the level of a written program?
- Is it possible to separate psychological aspects of a program from other aspects?
- Are there differences in reaction time between programs and human participants?

described using natural language at all, but that a formal specification language should be used. This would be a very precise language, like a logic, that would be directly executable as a program.

Other issues arise about the relationship between the performance of the program and the performance of human participants (Costello & Keane, 2000). For example, it is seldom meaningful to relate the speed of the program doing a simulated task to the reaction time taken by human participants, because the processing times of programs are affected by psychologically irrelevant features. Programs run faster on more powerful computers, or if the program's code is interpreted rather than compiled. However, the various materials that are presented to the program should result in differences in program operation time that correlate closely with differences in participants' reaction times in processing the same materials. At the very least, the program should be able to reproduce the same outputs as participants when given the same inputs.

## Computational modelling techniques

The general characteristics of computational models of cognition have been discussed at some length. It is now time to deal with some of the main types of computational model that have been used in recent years. Three main types are outlined briefly here: semantic networks; production systems; and connectionist networks.

### Semantic networks

Consider the problem of modelling what we know about the world (see Chapter 9). There is a long tradition from Aristotle and the British empiricist school of philosophers (Locke, Hume, Mill, Hartley, Bain) which proposes that all knowledge is in the form of associations. Three main principles of association have been proposed:

- Contiguity: two things become associated because they occurred together in time.
- Similarity: two things become associated because they are alike.
- Contrast: two things become associated because they are opposites.

There is a whole class of cognitive models owing their origins to these ideas; they are called associative or semantic or declarative networks. *Semantic networks* have the following general characteristics:

- Concepts are represented by linked nodes that form a network.
- These links can be of various kinds; they can represent very general relations (e.g., *is-associated-with* or *is-similar-to*) or specific, simple relations like *is-a* (e.g., John is-a policeman), or more complete relations like *play*, *hit*, *kick*.
- The nodes themselves and the links among nodes can have various activation strengths representing the similarity of one concept to another. Thus, for example, a dog and a cat node may be connected by a link with an activation of 0.5, whereas a dog and a pencil may be connected by a link with a strength of 0.1.
- Learning takes the form of adding new links and nodes to the network or changing the activation values on the links between nodes. For example, in learning that two concepts are similar, the activation of a link between them may be increased.
- Various effects (e.g., memory effects) can be modelled by allowing activation to spread throughout the network from a given node or set of nodes.
- The way in which activation spreads through a network can be determined by a variety of factors For example, it can be affected by the

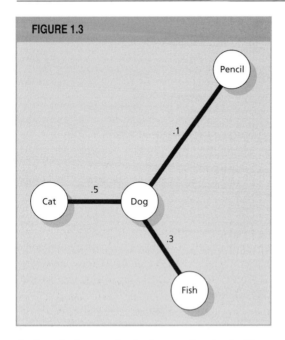

**FIGURE 1.3**

A schematic diagram of a simple semantic network with nodes for various concepts (i.e., dog, cat), and links between these nodes indicating the differential similarity of these concepts to each other.

number of links between a given node and the point of activation, or by the amount of time that has passed since the onset of activation.

Part of a very simple network model is shown in Figure 1.3. It corresponds closely to the semantic network model proposed by Collins and Loftus (1975). Such models have been successful in accounting for a various findings. Semantic priming effects in which the word "dog" is re-cognised more readily if it is preceded by the word "cat" (Meyer & Schvaneveldt, 1971) can be easily modelled using such networks (see Chapter 12). Ayers and Reder (1998) have used semantic net-works to understand misinformation effects in eyewitness testimony (see Chapter 8). At their best, semantic networks are both flexible and elegant modelling schemes.

## Production systems

Another popular approach to modelling cognition involves *production systems*. These are made up of productions, where a production is an "IF . . . THEN" rule. These rules can take many forms, but an example that is very useful in everyday life is, "If the green man is lit up, then cross the road". In a typical production system model, there is a long-term memory that contains a large set of these IF . . . THEN rules. There is also a working memory (i.e., a system holding information that is currently being processed). If information from the environment that "the green man is lit up" reaches working memory, it will match the IF-part of the rule in long-term memory, and trigger the THEN-part of the rule (i.e., cross the road).

Production systems have the following characteristics:

- They have numerous IF . . . THEN rules.
- They have a working memory containing information.
- The production system operates by matching the contents of working memory against the IF-parts of the rules and executing the THEN-parts.
- If some information in working memory matches the IF-part of many rules, there may be a *conflict-resolution strategy* selecting one of these rules as the best one to be executed.

Consider a very simple production system operating on lists of letters involving As and Bs (see Figure 1.4). The system has two rules:

1. IF a list in working memory has an A at the end THEN replace the A with AB.
2. IF a list in working memory has a B at the end THEN replace the B with an A.

If we give this system different inputs in the form of different lists of letters, then different things happen. If we give it CCC, this will be stored in working memory but will remain un-changed, because it does not match either of the IF-parts of the two rules. If we give it A, then it will be notified by the rules after the A is stored in working memory. This A is a list of one item and as such it matches rule 1. Rule 1 has the effect of replacing the A with AB, so that when the THEN-part is executed, working memory will

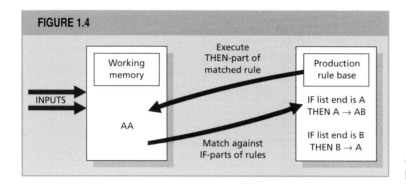

**FIGURE 1.4**

A schematic diagram of a simple production system.

contain an AB. On the next cycle, AB does not match rule 1 but it does match rule 2. As a result, the B is replaced by an A, leaving an AA in working memory. The system will next produce AAB, then AAAB, and so on.

Many aspects of cognition can be specified as sets of IF . . . THEN rules. For example, chess knowledge can readily be represented as a set of productions based on rules such as, "If the Queen is threatened, then move the Queen to a safe square". In this way, people's basic knowledge of chess can be modified as a collection of productions, and gaps in this knowledge as the absence of some productions. Newell and Simon (1972) first established the usefulness of production system models in characterising cognitive processes like problem solving and reasoning (see Chapter 14). However, these models have a wider applicability. Anderson (1993) has modelled human learning using production systems (see Chapter 14), and others have used them to model reinforcement behaviour in rats, and semantic memory (Holland et al., 1986).

*Connectionist networks*

Connectionist networks, neural networks, or parallel distributed processing models as they are variously called, are relative newcomers to the computational modelling scene. All previous techniques were marked by the need to program explicitly all aspects of the model, and by their use of explicit symbols to represent concepts. *Connectionist networks*, on the other hand, can to some extent program themselves, in that they can

"learn" to produce specific outputs when certain inputs are given to them. Furthermore, connectionist modellers often reject the use of explicit rules and symbols and use distributed representations, in which concepts are characterised as patterns of activation in the network (see Chapter 9).

Early theoretical proposals about the feasibility of learning in neural-like networks were made by McCulloch and Pitts (1943) and by Hebb (1949). However, the first neural network models, called Perceptrons, were shown to have several limitations (Minsky & Papert, 1988). By the late 1970s, hardware and software develpments in computing offered the possibility of constructing more complex networks overcoming many of these original limitations (e.g., Rumelhart, McClelland, & the PDP Research Group, 1986; McClelland, Rumelhart, & the PDP Research Group, 1986).

Connectionist networks typically have the following characteristics (see Figure 1.5):

- The network consists of elementary or neuron-like *units* or *nodes* connected together so that a single unit has many links to other units.
- Units affect other units by exciting or inhibiting them.
- The unit usually takes the weighted sum of all of the input links, and produces a single output to another unit if the weighted sum exceeds some threshold value.
- The network as a whole is characterised by the properties of the units that make it up, by the way they are connected together, and by the rules used to change the strength of connections among units.

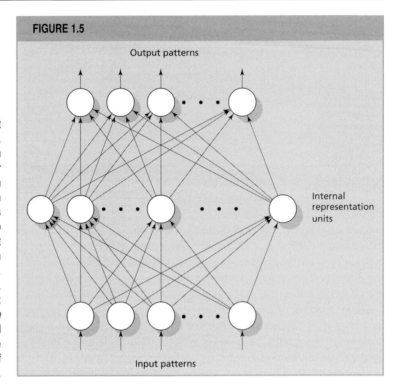

**FIGURE 1.5**

Output patterns

Internal representation units

Input patterns

A multi-layered connectionist network with a layer of input units, a layer of internal representation units or hidden units, and a layer of output units. Input patterns can be encoded, if there are enough hidden units, in a form that allows the appropriate output pattern to be generated from a given input pattern. Reproduced with permission from David E. Rumelhart & James L. McClelland, Parallel distributed processing: *Explorations in the microstructure of cognition (Vol. 1)*, published by the MIT Press, © 1986, the Massachusetts Institute of Technology.

- Networks can have different structures or layers; they can have a layer of input links, intermediate layers (of so-called "hidden units"), and a layer of output units.
- A representation of a concept can be stored in a distributed manner by a pattern of activation throughout the network.
- The same network can store many patterns without them necessarily interfering with each other if they are sufficiently distinct.
- An important learning rule used in networks is called *backward propagation of errors* (*BackProp*).

In order to understand connectionist networks fully, let us consider how individual units act when activation impinges on them. Any given unit can be connected to several other units (see Figure 1.6). Each of these other units can send an excitatory or an inhibitory signal to the first unit. This unit generally takes a weighted sum of all these inputs. If this sum exceeds some threshold, it produces an output. Figure 1.6 shows a simple diagram of just such a unit, which takes the inputs from a

number of other units and sums them to produce an output if a certain threshold is exceeded.

These networks can model cognitive behaviour without recourse to the kinds of explicit rules found in production systems. They do this by storing patterns of activation in the network that associate various inputs with certain outputs. The models typically make use of several layers to deal with complex behaviour. One layer consists of input units that encode a stimulus as a pattern of activation in those units. Another layer is an output layer, which produces some response as a pattern of activation. When the network has learned to produce a particular response at the output layer following the presentation of a particular stimulus at the input layer, it can exhibit behaviour that looks "as if" it had learned a rule of the form "IF such-and-such is the case THEN do so-and-so". However, no such rules exist explicitly in the model.

Networks learn the association between different inputs and outputs by modifying the weights on the links between units in the net. In Figure 1.6, we see that the weight on the links to a unit, as

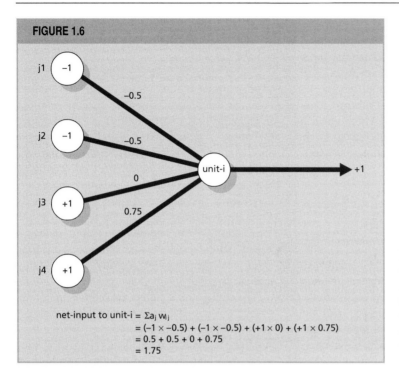

**FIGURE 1.6**

net-input to unit-i = $\Sigma a_j w_{ij}$
= $(-1 \times -0.5) + (-1 \times -0.5) + (+1 \times 0) + (+1 \times 0.75)$
= $0.5 + 0.5 + 0 + 0.75$
= $1.75$

Diagram showing how the inputs from a number of units are combined to determine the overall input to unit-i. Unit-i has a threshold of 1; so if its net input exceeds 1 then it will respond with +1, but if the net input is less than 1 then it will respond with −1.

well as the activation of other units, plays a crucial role in computing the response of that unit. Various learning rules modify these weights in systematic ways. When we apply such learning rules to a network, the weights on the links are modified until the net produces the required output patterns given certain input patterns.

One such learning rule is called "backward propagation of errors" or BackProp. BackProp allows a network to learn to associate a particular input pattern with a given output pattern. At the start of the learning period, the network is set up with random weights on the links among the units. During the early stages of learning, after the input pattern has been presented, the output units often produce the incorrect pattern or response. BackProp compares the imperfect pattern with the known required response, noting the errors that occur. It then back-propagates activation through the network so that the weights between the units are adjusted to produce the required pattern. This process is repeated with a particular stimulus pattern until the network produces the required response pattern. Thus, the model can

be made to learn the behaviour with which the cognitive scientist is concerned, rather than being explicitly programmed to do so.

Networks have been used to produce very interesting results. Several examples will be discussed throughout the text (see, for examples, Chapters 2, 10, and 16), but one concrete example will be mentioned here. Sejnowski and Rosenberg (1987) produced a connectionist network called NETtalk, which takes an English text as its input and produces reasonable English speech output. Even though the network is trained on a limited set of words, it can pronounce the words from new text with about 90% accuracy. Thus, the network seems to have learned the "rules of English pronunciation", but it has done so without having explicit rules that combine and encode sounds.

Connectionist models such as NETtalk have great "Wow!" value, and are the subject of much research interest. Some researchers might object to our classification of connectionist networks as merely one among a number of modelling techniques. However, others have argued that connectionism represents an alternative to the information-processing paradigm (Smolensky, 1988; Smolensky, Legendre, & Miyata, 1993). Indeed, if one examines the fundamental tenets of the information-processing framework, then connectionist schemes violate one or two. For example, symbol manipulation of the sort found in production systems does not seem to occur in connectionist networks. We will return to the complex issues raised by connectionist networks later in the book.

# COGNITIVE NEUROPSYCHOLOGY

Cognitive neuropsychology is concerned with the patterns of cognitive performance in brain-damaged patients. Those aspects of cognition that are intact or impaired are identified, with this information being of value for two main reasons. First, the cognitive performance of brain-damaged patients can often be explained by theories within cognitive psychology. Such theories specify the processes or mechanisms involved in normal cognitive functioning, and it should be possible in principle to account for many of the cognitive impairments of brain-damaged patients in terms of selective damage to some of those mechanisms.

Second, it may be possible to use information from brain-damaged patients to *reject* theories proposed by cognitive psychologists, and to propose new theories of normal cognitive functioning. According to Ellis and Young (1988, p. 4), a major aim of cognitive neuropsychology:

> is to draw conclusions about normal, intact cognitive processes from the patterns of impaired and intact capabilities seen in brain-injured patients . . . the cognitive neuropsychologist wishes to be in a position to assert that observed patterns of symptoms could not occur if the normal, intact cognitive system were not organised in a certain way.

The intention is that there should be bi-directional influences of cognitive psychology on cognitive neuropsychology, and of cognitive

neuropsychology on cognitive psychology. Historically, the former influence was the greater one, but the latter has become more important.

Before discussing the cognitive neuropsychological approach in more detail, we will discuss a concrete example of cognitive neuropsychology in operation. Atkinson and Shiffrin (1968) argued that there is an important distinction between a short-term memory store and a long-term memory store, and that information enters into the long-term store through rehearsal and other processing activities in the short-term store (see Chapter 6). Relevant evidence was obtained by Shallice and Warrington (1970). They studied a brain-damaged patient, KF, who seemed to have severely impaired short-term memory, but essentially intact long-term memory.

The study of this patient served two important purposes. First, it provided evidence to support the theoretical distinction between two memory systems. Second, it pointed to a real deficiency in the theoretical model of Atkinson and Shiffrin (1968). If, as this model suggests, long-term learning and memory depend on the short-term memory system, then it is surprising that someone with a grossly deficient short-term memory system also has normal long-term memory.

The case of KF shows very clearly the potential power of cognitive neuropsychology. The study of this one patient provided strong evidence that the dominant theory of memory at the end of the 1960s was seriously deficient. This is no mean achievement for a study on one patient!

## Cognitive neuropsychological evidence

How do cognitive neuropsychologists set about the task of understanding how the cognitive system functions? A crucial goal is the discovery of *dissociations*, which occur when a patient performs normally on one task but is impaired on a second task. In the case of KF, a dissociation was found between performance on short-term memory tasks and on long-term memory tasks. Such evidence can be used to argue that normal individuals possess at least two separate memory systems.

There is a potential problem in drawing sweeping conclusions from single dissociations.

A patient may perform poorly on one task and well on a second task simply because the first task is more complex than the second, rather than because the first task involves specific skills that have been affected by brain damage. The solution to this problem is to look for double dissociations. A *double dissociation* between two tasks (1 and 2) is shown when one patient performs normally on task 1 and at an impaired level on task 2, and another patient performs normally on task 2 and at an impaired level on task 1. If a double dissociation can be shown, then the results cannot be explained in terms of one task being harder than the other.

In the case of short-term and long-term memory, such a double dissocation has been shown. KF had impaired short-term memory but intact long-term memory, whereas amnesic patients have severely deficient long-term memory but intact short-term memory (see Chapter 7). These findings suggest there are two distinct memory systems which can suffer damage separately from each other.

If brain damage were usually very limited in scope, and affected only a single cognitive process or mechanism, then cognitive neuropsychology would be a fairly simple enterprise. In fact, brain damage is often rather extensive, so that several cognitive systems are all impaired to a greater or lesser extent. This means that much ingenuity is needed to make sense of the tantalising glimpses of human cognition provided by brain-damaged patients.

## Theoretical assumptions

Most cognitive neuropsychologists subscribe to the following assumptions (with the exception of the last one):

- The cognitive system exhibits *modularity*, i.e., there are several relatively independent cognitive processes or modules, each of which functions to some extent in isolation from the rest of the processing system; brain damage typically impairs only some of these modules.
- There is a meaningful relationship between the organisation of the physical brain and that of the mind; this assumption is known as *isomorphism*.

- Investigation of cognition in brain-damaged patients can tell us much about cognitive processes in normal individuals; this assumption is closely bound up with the other assumptions.
- Most patients can be categorised in terms of *syndromes*, each of which is based on co-occurring sets of symptoms.

### Syndromes

The traditional approach within neuropsychology made much use of syndromes. It was claimed that certain sets of symptoms or impairments are usually found together, and each set of co-occurring symptoms was used to define a separate syndrome (e.g., amnesia; dyslexia). This syndrome-based approach allows us to impose some order on the numerous brain-damaged patients who have been studied by assigning them to a fairly small number of categories. It is also of use in identifying those areas of the brain mainly responsible for cognitive function such as language, because we can search for those parts of the brain damaged in all those patients having a given syndrome.

In spite of its uses, the syndrome-based approach has substantial problems. It exaggerates the similarities among different patients allegedly suffering from the same syndrome. In addition, those symptoms or impairments said to form a syndrome may be found in the same patients solely because the underlying cognitive processes are anatomically adjacent.

There have been attempts to propose more specific syndromes or categories based on our theoretical understanding of cognition. However, the discovery of new patients with unusual patterns of deficits, and the occurrence of theoretical advances, mean that the categorisation system is constantly changing. As Ellis (1987) pointed out, "a syndrome thought at time $t$ to be due to damage to a single unitary module is bound to have fractionated by time $t + 2$ years into a host of awkward subtypes."

How should cognitive neuropsychologists react to these problems? Some cognitive neuropsychologists (e.g., Parkin, 1996) argue that it makes sense to carry out group studies in which patients with the same syndrome are considered together. He introduced what he called the "significance implies homogeneity [uniformity] rule". According to this rule, "if a group of subjects exhibits significant hetereogeneity [variability] then they will not be capable of generating statistically significant group differences" (Parkin, 1996, p. 16). The potential problem with this rule is that a group of patients can show a significant effect even though a majority of the individual patients fail to show the effect.

Ellis (1987) argued that cognitive neuropsychology should proceed on the basis of intensive single-case studies in which individual patients are studied on a wide range of tasks. An adequate theory of cognition should be as applicable to the individual case as to groups of individuals, and so single-case studies provide a perfectly adequate test of cognitive theories. The great advantage of this approach is that there is no need to make simplifying assumptions about which patients do and do not belong to the same syndrome.

Another argument for single-case studies is that it is often not possible to find a group of patients showing very similar cognitive deficits. As Shallice (1991, p. 432) pointed out, "as finer and finer aspects of the cognitive architecture are investigated in attempts to infer normal function, neuropsychology will be forced to resort more and more to single-case studies."

Ellis (1987) may have overstated the value of single-case studies. If our theoretical understanding of an area is rather limited, it may make sense to adopt the syndrome-based approach until the major theoretical issues have been clarified. Furthermore, many experimental cognitive psychologists disapprove of attaching great theoretical significance to findings from individuals who may

not be representative even of brain-damaged patients. As Shallice (1991, p. 433) argued:

> A selective impairment found in a particular task in some patient could just reflect: the patient's idiosyncratic strategy, the greater difficulty of that task compared with the others, a premorbid lacuna [gap] in that patient, or the way a reorganised system but not the original normal system operates.

A reasonable compromise position is to carry out a number of single-case studies. If a theoretically crucial dissociation is found in a single patient, then there are various ways of interpreting the data. However, if the same dissociation is obtained in a number of individual patients, it is less likely that all the patients had atypical cognitive systems prior to brain damage, or that they have all made use of similar compensatory strategies.

## Modularity

The whole enterprise of cognitive neuropsychology is based on the assumption that there are numerous *modules* or cognitive processors in the brain. These modules function relatively independently, so that damage to one module does not directly affect other modules. Modules are anatomically distinct, so that brain damage will often affect some modules while leaving others intact. Cognitive neuropsychology may help the discovery of these major building blocks of cognition. A double dissociation indicates that two tasks make use of different modules or cognitive processors, and so a series of double dissociations can be

| Syndrome-based approach vs. single-case studies | |
|---|---|
| *Syndrome-based approach* | *Single-case studies* |
| *Advantages* | *Advantages* |
| Provides a means of imposing order and categorising patients. | Avoids oversimplifying assumptions. |
| Allows identification of cognitive functions of brain areas. | No need to find groups of patients with very |
| Useful while major theoretical issues remain to be clarified. | similar cognitive deficits. |
| *Disadvantages* | *Disadvantages* |
| Oversimplification based on theoretical assumptions. | Evidence lacks generalisability and can even be |
| Exaggeration of similarities among patients. | misleading. |

used to provide a sketch-map of our modular cognitive system.

The notion of modularity was emphasised by Fodor (1983), who identified the following distinguishing features of modules:

- Informational encapsulation: each module functions independently from the functioning of other modules.
- Domain specificity: each module can process only one kind of input (e.g., words; faces).
- Mandatory or compulsory operation: the functioning of a module is not under any form of voluntary control.
- Innateness: modules are inborn.

Fodor's ideas have been influential. However, many psychologists have criticised mandatory operation and innateness as criteria for modularity. Some modules may operate automatically, but there is little evidence to suggest that they all do. It is implausible to assume the innateness of modules underlying skills such as reading and writing, as these are skills that the human race has developed only comparatively recently.

From the perspective of cognitive neuropsychologists, these criticisms do not pose any special problems. If the assumptions of information encapsulation and domain specificity remain tenable, then data from brain-damaged patients can continue to be used in the hunt for cognitive modules. This would still be the case even if it turned out that several modules or cognitive processors were neither mandatory nor innate.

It is not only cognitive neuropsychologists who subscribe to the notion of modularity. Most experimental cognitive psychologists, cognitive scientists, and cognitive neuroscientists also believe in modularity. The four groups differ mainly in terms of their preferred methods for showing modularity.

## Isomorphism

Cognitive neuropsychologists assume there is a meaningful relationship between the way in which the brain is organised at a physical level and the way in which the mind and its cognitive modules are organised. This assumption has been called

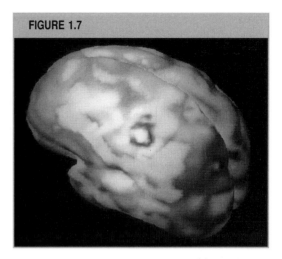

FIGURE 1.7

PET scans can be used to show localisation of function within the brain. This three-dimensional PET scan shows the metabolic activity within the brain during a hand exercise. The exercise involved moving the fingers of the right hand. The front of the brain is at the left. The most active area appears white; this is the motor cortex in the cerebral cortex where movement is coordinated. Photo credit: Montreal Neurological Institute/McGill University/CNRI/Science Photo Library.

*isomorphism*, meaning that two things (e.g., brain and mind) have the same shape or form. Thus, it is expected that each module will have a different physical location within the brain. If this expectation is disconfirmed, then cognitive neuropsychology and cognitive neuroscience will become more complex enterprises.

An assumption that is related to isomorphism is that there is localisation of function, meaning that any specific function or process occurs in a given location within the brain (Figure 1.7). The notion of localisation of function seems to be in conflict with the connectionist account, according to which a process (e.g., activation of a concept) can be distributed over a wide area of the brain. There is as yet no definitive evidence to support one view over the other.

## Evaluation

Are the various theoretical assumptions underlying cognitive neuropsychology correct? It is hard to tell. Modules do not actually "exist", but are convenient theoretical devices used to clarify our understanding. Therefore, the issue of whether the theoretical assumptions are valuable or not is probably best resolved by considering the extent to which cognitive neuropsychology is successful in increasing our knowledge of cognition. In other words, the proof of the pudding is in the eating. Farah (1994) argued that the evidence does not support what she termed the locality assumption, according to which damage to one module has only "local" effects. According to Farah (1994, p. 101), "The conclusion that the locality assumption may be false is a disheartening one. It undercuts much of the special appeal of neuropsychological architecture."

One of the most serious problems with cognitive neuropsychology stems from the difficulty in carrying out group studies. This has led to the increasing use of single-case studies. Such studies are sometimes very revealing. However, they can provide misleading evidence if the patient had specific cognitive deficits prior to brain damage, or if he or she has developed unusual compensatory strategies to cope with the consequences of brain damage.

## COGNITIVE NEUROSCIENCE

Some cognitive psychologists argue that we can understand cognition by relying on observations of people's performance on cognitive tasks and ignoring the neurophysiological processes occurring within the brain. For example, Baddeley (1997, p. 7) expressed some scepticism about the relevance of neurophysiological processes to the development of psychological theories:

A theory giving a successful account of the neurochemical basis of long-term memory . . . would be unlikely to offer an equally elegant and economical account of the psychological characteristics of memory. While it may in principle one day be possible to map one theory onto the other, it will still be useful to have *both* a psychological and a physiological theory . . . Neurophysiology

and neurochemistry are interesting and important areas, but at present they place relatively few constraints on psychological theories and models of human memory.

Why was Baddeley doubtful that neurophysiological evidence could contribute much to psychological understanding? The main reason was that psychologists and neurophysiologists tend to focus on different levels of analysis. In the same way that a carpenter does not need to know that wood consists mainly of atoms moving around rapidly in space, so it is claimed that cognitive psychologists do not need to know the fine-grain neurophysiological workings of the brain.

A different position was advocated by Churchland and Sejnowski (1991, p. 17), who suggested:

It would be convenient if we could understand the nature of cognition without understanding the nature of the brain itself. Unfortunately, it is difficult, if not impossible, to theorise effectively on these matters in the absence of neurobiological constraints. The primary reason is that computational space is consummately vast, and there are many conceivable solutions to the problems of how a cognitive operation could be accomplished. Neurobiological data provide essential constraints on computational theories, and they consequently provide an efficient means for narrowing the search space. Equally important, the data are also richly suggestive in hints concerning what might really be going on.

In line with these proposals, there are some psychological theories that are being fairly closely constrained by findings in the neurosciences (see Hummel & Holyoak, 1997, and Chapter 15).

Neurophysiologists have provided several kinds of valuable information about the brain's structure and functioning. In principle, it is possible to establish *where* in the brain certain cognitive processes occur, and *when* these processes occur. Such information can allow us to determine the order in which different parts of the brain become active when someone is performing a task. It also

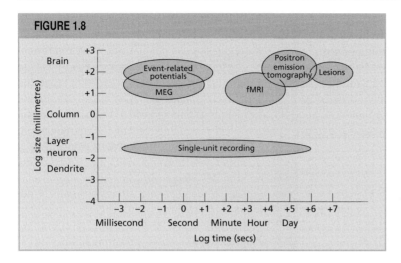

**FIGURE 1.8**

The spatial and temporal ranges of some techniques used to study brain functioning. Adapted from Churchland and Sejnowski (1991).

allows us to find out whether two tasks involve the same parts of the brain in the same way, or whether there are important differences. As we will see, this can be very important theoretically.

The various techniques for studying brain functioning differ in their spatial and temporal resolution (Churchland & Sejnowski, 1991). Some techniques provide information about the single-cell level, whereas others tell us about activity over much larger groups of cells. In similar fashion, some techniques provide information about brain activity on a millisecond-by-millisecond basis (which corresponds to the timescale for thinking), whereas others indicate brain activity only over much longer time periods such as minutes or hours.

Some of the main techniques will be discussed to give the reader some idea of the weapons available to cognitive neuroscientists. The spatial and temporal resolutions of some of these techniques are shown in Figure 1.8. High spatial and temporal resolutions are advantageous if a very detailed account of brain functioning is required, but low spatial and temporal resolutions can be more useful if a more general view of brain activity is required.

## Single-unit recording

*Single-unit recording* is a fine-grain technique developed over 40 years ago to permit the study of single neurons. A micro-electrode about one 10,000th of a millimetre in diameter is inserted into the brain of an animal to obtain a record of extracellular potentials. A stereotaxic apparatus is used to fix the animal's position, and to provide the researcher with precise information about the location of the electrode in three-dimensional space. Single-unit recording is a very sensitive technique, as electrical charges of as little as one-millionth of a volt can be detected.

The best known application of this technique was by Hubel and Wiesel (1962, 1979). They used it with cats and monkeys to study the neurophysiology of basic visual processes. Hubel and Wiesel found there were simple and complex cells in the primary visual cortex, but there were many more complex cells. These two types of cells both respond maximally to straight-line stimuli in a particular orientation (see Chapter 4). The findings of Hubel and Wiesel were so clear-cut that they constrained several subsequent theories of visual perception, including that of Marr (1982; see Chapter 2).

### Evaluation

The single-unit recording technique has the great value that it provides detailed information about brain functioning at the neuronal level, and is thus more fine-grain than other techniques (see Figure 1.8). Another advantage is that information about neuronal activity can be obtained over a very wide range of time periods from small fractions of a second up to several hours or days. A major limitation is that it is an invasive technique, and so would be unpleasant to use with humans. Another limitation is that it can only provide information about activity at the neuronal level, and so other techniques are needed to assess the functioning of larger areas of the cortex.

## Event-related potentials (ERPs)

The electroencephalogram (EEG) is based on recordings of electrical brain activity measured at the surface of the scalp. Very small changes in electrical activity within the brain are picked up by scalp electrodes. These changes can be shown on the screen of a cathode-ray tube by means of an oscilloscope. A key problem with the EEG is that there tends to be so much spontaneous or background brain activity that it obscures the impact of stimulus processing on the EEG recording.

A solution to this problem is to present the same stimulus several times. After that, the segment of EEG following each stimulus is extracted and lined up with respect to the time of stimulus onset. These EEG segments are then simply averaged together to produce a single waveform. This method produces *event-related potentials* (ERPs) from EEG recordings, and allows us to distinguish genuine effects of stimulation from background brain activity.

ERPs are particularly useful for assessing the timing of certain cognitive processes. For example, some attention theorists have argued that attended and unattended stimuli are processed differently at an early stage of processing, whereas others have claimed that they are both analysed fully in a similar way (see Chapter 5). Studies using ERPs have provided good evidence in favour of the former position. For example, Woldorff et al. (1993) found that ERPs were greater to attended than unattended auditory stimuli about 20–50 milliseconds after stimulus onset.

### Evaluation

ERPs provide more detailed information about the time course of brain activity than do most other techniques, and they have many medical applications (e.g., diagnosis of multiple sclerosis). However, ERPs do not indicate with any precision which regions of the brain are most involved in processing. This is due in part to the fact that the presence of skull and brain tissue distorts the electrical fields emerging from the brain. Furthermore, ERPs are mainly of value when the stimuli are simple and the task involves basic processes (e.g., target detection) occurring at a certain time after stimulus onset. As a result of these constraints (and the necessity of presenting the same stimulus several times) it would not be feasible to study most complex forms of cognition (e.g., problem solving; reasoning) with the use of ERPs.

## Positron emission tomography (PET)

Of all the new methods, the one that has attracted the most media interest is *positron emission tomography* or the PET scan. The technique is based on the detection of positrons, which are atomic particles emitted by some radioactive substances. Radioactively labelled water is injected into the body, and rapidly gathers in the brain's blood vessels. When part of the cortex becomes active, the labelled water moves rapidly to that place. A scanning device next measures the positrons emitted from the radioactive water. A computer then translates this information into pictures of the activity levels of different parts of the brain. It may sound dangerous to inject a radioactive substance into someone. However, only tiny amounts of radioactivity are involved.

Raichle (1994b) has described the typical way in which PET has been used by cognitive neuroscientists. It is based on a subtractive logic. Brain activity is assessed during an experimental task, and is also assessed during some control or baseline condition (e.g., before the task is presented). The brain activity during the control condition is then subtracted from that during the experimental task. It is assumed that this allows us to identify those parts of the brain that are active only during the performance of the task. This technique has been used in several studies designed to locate the parts of the brain most involved in *episodic memory*, which is long-term memory involving conscious recollection of the past (see Chapter 7).

There is more activity in the right prefrontal cortex when participants are trying to retrieve episodic memories than when they are trying to retrieve other kinds of memories (see Wheeler, Stuss, & Tulving, 1997, for a review).

*Evaluation*

One of the major advantages of PET is that it has reasonable spatial resolution, in that any active area within the brain can be located to within about 3 or 4 millimetres. It is also a fairly versatile technique, in that it can be used to identify the brain areas involved in a wide range of different cognitive activities.

PET has several limitations. First, the temporal resolution is very poor. PET scans indicate the total amount of activity in each region of the brain over a period of 60 seconds or longer, and so cannot reveal the rapid changes in brain activity accompanying most cognitive processes. Second, PET provides only an indirect measure of neural activity. As Anderson, Holliday, Singh, and Harding (1996, p. 423) pointed out, "changes in regional cerebral blood flow, reflected by changes in the spatial distribution of intravenously administered positron emitted radioisotopes, are assumed to reflect changes in neural activity." This assumption may be more applicable at early stages of processing. Third, it is an invasive technique, because participants have to be injected with radioactively labelled water. Fourth, it can be hard to interpret the findings from use of the subtraction technique. For example, it may seem plausible to assume that those parts of the brain active during retrieval of episodic memories but not other kinds of memories are directly involved in episodic memory retrieval. However, the participants may have been more motivated to retrieve such memories than other memories, and so some of the brain activity may reflect the involvement of motivational rather than memory systems.

## Magnetic resonance imaging (MRI and fMRI)

What happens in *magnetic resonance imaging* (MRI) is that radio waves are used to excite atoms in the brain. This produces magnetic changes which are detected by an 11-ton magnet surrounding

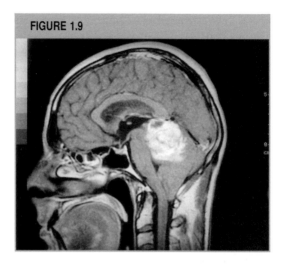

FIGURE 1.9

MRI scan showing a brain tumour. The tumour appears in bright contrast to the surrounding brain tissue. Photo credit: Simon Fraser/Neuroradiology Department, Newcastle General Hospital/Science Photo Library.

the patient. These changes are then interpreted by a computer and turned into a very precise three-dimensional picture. MRI scans (Figure 1.9) can be used to detect very small brain tumours. MRI scans can be obtained from numerous different angles. However, they only tell us about the *structure* of the brain rather than about its *functions*.

The MRI technology has been applied to the measurement of brain activity to provide *functional MRI* (fMRI). Neural activity in the brain produces increased blood flow in the active areas, and there is oxygen and glucose within the blood. According to Raichle (1994a, p. 41), "the amount of oxygen carried by haemoglobin (the molecule that transports oxygen . . . ) affects the magnetic properties of the haemoglobin . . . MRI can detect the functionally induced changes in blood oxygenation in the human brain." The approach based on fMRI provides three-dimensional images of the brain with areas of high activity clearly indicated. It is more useful than PET, because it provides more precise spatial information, and shows changes over shorter periods of time. However, it shares with PET a reliance on the subtraction technique in which brain activity during a control task or situation is subtracted from brain activity during the experimental task.

A study showing the usefulness of fMRI was reported by Tootell et al. (1995b). It involves the so-called waterfall illusion, in which lengthy viewing of a stimulus moving in one direction (e.g., a waterfall) is followed immediately by the illusion that stationary objects are moving in the opposite direction. There were two key findings. First, the gradual reduction in the size of the waterfall illusion over the first 60 seconds of observing the stationary stimulus was closely paralleled by the reduction in the area of activation observed in the fMRI. Second, most of the brain activity produced by the waterfall illusion was in V5, which is an area of the visual cortex known to be much involved in motion perception (see Chapter 2). Thus, the basic brain processes underlying the waterfall illusion are similar to those underlying normal motion perception.

### Evaluation

Raichle (1994a, p. 350) argued that fMRI has several advantages over other techniques:

> The technique has no known biological risk except for the occasional subject who suffers claustrophobia in the scanner (the entire body must be inserted into a relatively narrow tube). MRI provides both anatomical and functional information, which permits an accurate anatomical identification of the regions of activation in each subject. The spatial resolution is quite good, approaching the 1–2 millimetre range.

One limitation with fMRI is that it provides only an *indirect* measure of neural activity. As Anderson et al. (1996, p. 423) pointed out, "With fMRI, neural activity is reflected by changes in the relative concentrations of oxygenated and deoxygenated haemoglobin in the vicinity of the activity." Another limitation is that it has poor temporal resolution of the order of several seconds, so we cannot track the time course of cognitive processes. A final limitation is that it relies on the subtraction technique, and this may not accurately assess brain activity directly involved in the experimental task.

## Magneto-encephalography (MEG)

In recent years, a new technique known as *magneto-encephalography* or MEG has been developed. It involves using a superconducting quantum interference device (SQUID), which measures the magnetic fields produced by electrical brain activity. The evidence suggests that it can be regarded as "a direct measure of cortical neural activity" (Anderson et al., 1996, p. 423). It provides very accurate measurement of brain activity, in part because the skull is virtually transparent to magnetic fields. Thus, magnetic fields are little distorted by intervening tissue, which is an advantage over the electrical activity assessed by the EEG.

Anderson et al. used MEG in combination with MRI to study the properties of an area of the visual cortex known as V5 (see Chapter 2). They found with MEG that motion-contrast patterns produced large responses from V5, but that V5 did not seem to be responsive to colour. These data, in conjunction with previous findings from PET and fMRI studies, led Anderson et al. (1996, p. 429) to conclude that "these findings provide strong support for the hypothesis that a major function of human V5 is the rapid detection of objects moving relative to their background." In addition, Anderson et al. obtained evidence that V5 was active approximately 20 milliseconds after V1 (the primary visual cortex) in response to motion-contrast patterns. This is more valuable information than simply establishing that V1 and V5 are both active during this task, because it helps to clarify the *sequence* in which different brain areas contribute towards visual processing.

### Evaluation

MEG possesses several valuable features. First, the magnetic signals reflect neural activity reasonably directly. In contrast, PET and fMRI signals reflect blood flow, which is assumed in turn to reflect neural activity. Second, MEG supplies fairly detailed information at the millisecond level about the time course of cognitive processes. This matters because it makes it possible to work out the sequence of activation in different areas of the cortex.

| Techniques used by cognitive neuroscientists | | |
|---|---|---|
| Method | Strengths | Weaknesses |
| Single-unit recording | Fine-grain detail. Information obtained over a wide range of time periods. | Invasive. Only neuronal-level information is obtained. |
| ERPs | Detailed information about the time course of brain activity. | Lack precision in identifying specific areas of the brain. Can only be used to study basic cognitive processes. |
| PET | Active areas can be located to within 3–4 mm. Can identify a wide range of cognitive activities. | Cannot reveal rapid changes in brain activity. Provides only an indirect measure of neural activity. Findings from a subtraction technique can be hard to interpret. |
| MRI and fMRI | No known biological risk. Obtains accurate anatomical information. fMRI provides good information about timing. | Indirect measure of neural activity. Cannot track the time course of most cognitive processes. |
| MEG | Provides a reasonably direct measure of neural activity. Gives detailed information about the time course of cognitive processes. | Irrelevant sources of magnetism may interfere with measurement. Does not give accurate information about brain areas active at a given time. |

There are some major technical problems associated with the use of MEG. The magnetic field generated by the brain when thinking is about 100 million times weaker than the Earth's magnetic field, and a million times weaker than the magnetic fields around overhead power cables, and it is very hard to prevent irrelevant sources of magnetism from interfering with the measurement of brain activity. Superconductivity requires temperatures close to absolute zero, which means the SQUID has to be immersed in liquid helium at four degrees above the absolute zero of −273°C. However, these technical problems have been largely (or entirely) resolved. The major remaining disadvantage is that MEG does not provide structural or anatomical information. As a result, it is necessary to obtain an MRI as well as MEG data in order to locate the active brain areas.

## Section summary

All the techniques used by cognitive neuroscientists possess strengths and weaknesses. Thus, it is often desirable to use a number of different techniques to study any given aspect of human cognition. If similar findings are obtained from two techniques, this is known as converging evidence. Such evidence is of special value, because it suggests that the techniques are not providing distorted information. For example, studies using PET, fMRI, and MEG (e.g., Anderson et al., 1996; Tootell et al., 1995a, b) all indicate clearly that area V5 is much involved in motion perception.

It can also be of value to use two techniques differing in their particular strengths. For example, the ERP technique has good temporal resolution but poor spatial resolution, whereas the opposite is the case with fMRI. Their combined use offers the prospect of discovering the detailed time course *and* location of the processes involved in a cognitive task.

The techniques used within cognitive neuroscience are most useful when applied to areas of the brain that are organised in functionally discrete ways (S. Anderson, personal communication). For example, as we have seen, there is evidence that area V5 forms such an area for motion perception. It is considerably less clear that higher-order cognitive functions are organised in a similarly neat and tidy fashion. As a result, the various techniques discussed in this section may prove less informative when applied to such functions.

You may have got the impression that cognitive neuroscience consists mainly of various techniques for studying brain functioning. However, there is more than that to cognitive neuroscience. As Rugg (1997, p. 5) pointed out, "The distinctiveness [of cognitive neuroscience] arises from a lack of commitment to a single 'level' of explanation, and the resulting tendency for explanatory models to combine functional and physiological concepts." Various examples of this explanatory approach are considered during the course of this book.

## OUTLINE OF THIS BOOK

One problem with writing a textbook of cognitive psychology is that virtually all the processes and structures of the cognitive system are interdependent. Consider, for example, the case of a student *reading* a book to prepare for an examination. The student is *learning*, but there are several other processes going on as well. *Visual perception* is involved in the intake of information from the printed page, and there is *attention* to the content of the book (although attention may be captured by irrelevant stimuli). In order for the student to profit from the book, he or she must possess considerable *language skills*, and must also have rich *knowledge representations* that are relevant to the material in the book. There may be an element of *problem solving* in the student's attempts to relate what is in the book to the possibly conflicting information he or she has learned elsewhere. Furthermore, what the student learns will depend on his or her *emotional state*. Finally, the acid test of whether the learning has been effective and has produced *long-term memory* comes during the examination itself, when the material contained in the book must be *retrieved*.

The words italicised in the previous paragraph indicate some of the main ingredients of human cognition, and form the basis of our coverage of cognitive psychology. In view of the interdependent functioning of all aspects of the cognitive system, there is an emphasis in this book on the ways in which each process (e.g., perception) depends on other processes and structures (e.g., attention; long-term memory; stored representations). This should aid the task of making sense of the complexities of the human cognitive system.

## CHAPTER SUMMARY

- Cognitive psychology as a science. Cognitive psychology is unified by a common approach based on an analogy between the mind and the computer. This information-processing approach views the mind as a general-purpose, symbol-processing system of limited capacity. There are four main types of cognitive psychologists: experimental cognitive psychologists; cognitive scientists; cognitive neuropsychologists; and cognitive neuroscientists, who use various techniques to study brain functioning.
- Cognitive science. Cognitive scientists focus on computational models, in which theoretical assumptions have to be made explicit. These models are expressed in computer programs, which should produce the same outputs as people when given the same inputs. Three of the main types of computational model are semantic networks, production systems, and connectionist networks. Semantic networks consist of concepts, which are linked by various relations (e.g., is-similar-to). They are useful for modelling the structure of people's conceptual knowledge. Production systems are made up of productions in the form of "IF . . . THEN" rules. Connectionist networks differ from previous approaches in that they can "learn" from experience, for example, through the backward propagation of errors. Such networks often have several structures or layers (e.g., input units; intermediate or hidden units; and output units). Concepts are stored in a distributed manner.
- Cognitive neuropsychology. Cognitive neuropsychologists assume that the cognitive system is modular, that there is isomorphism between the organisation of the physical brain and the mind, and that the study of brain-damaged patients can tell us much about normal human cognition. The notion of syndromes has lost popularity, because syndromes typically exaggerate the similarity

of the symptoms shown by patients having allegedly the same condition. It can be hard to interpret the findings from brain-damaged patients for various reasons: patients may develop compensatory strategies after brain damage; the brain damage may affect several modules; patients may have had specific cognitive impairments *before* the brain damage.

- Cognitive neuroscience. Cognitive neuroscientists use various techniques for studying the brain, with these techniques varying in their spatial and temporal resolution. Important techniques include single-unit recording, event-related potentials, positron emission tomography, functional magnetic resonance imaging, and magneto-encephalography. Critics argue that neurophysiological findings are often at a different level of analysis from the one of most value to cognitive psychologists. In addition, such findings often fail to place significant constraints on psychological theorising.

## FURTHER READING

- Ellis, R., & Humphreys, G. (1999). *Connectionist psychology: A text with readings*. Hove, UK: Psychology Press. Connectionism has become very influential within cognitive science, and this approach is discussed very thoroughly in this book.
- Gazzaniga, M.S., Ivry, R.B., & Mangun, G.R. (1998). *Cognitive neuroscience: The biology of the mind*. New York: W.W. Norton & Co. This is a comprehensive book in which the relevance of the cognitive neuroscience approach to the major areas of cognitive psychology is considered in detail.
- McLeod, P., Plunkett, K., & Rolls, E.T. (1998). *Introduction to connectionist modelling of cognitive processes*. Oxford: Oxford University Press. The principles and applications of connectionism are presented, and this book should even enable you to build your own connectionist models!
- Rugg, M.D. (1997). *Cognitive neuroscience*. Hove, UK: Psychology Press. Several experts discuss the ways in which cognitive neuroscience has benefited their area of research.
- Wilson, R.A., & Keil, F. (1999). *The MIT encyclopaedia of the cognitive sciences*. Cambridge, MA: MIT Press. This enormous book has extensive coverage by experts of computational intelligence, the neurosciences, and cognitive psychology.

# 2

# Visual Perception: Basic Processes

## INTRODUCTION

This chapter and the following two deal with visual perception. We can perhaps best begin with a consideration of the concept of "perception". Roth (1986, p. 81) provided a representative definition: "The term perception refers to the means by which information acquired via the sense organs is transformed into experiences of objects, events, sounds, tastes, etc."

Visual perception seems so simple and effortless that we tend to take it for granted. In fact, it is very complex, and several processes are involved in transforming and interpreting sensory information. Some of the complexities of visual perception only became clear when workers in artificial intelligence tried to program computers to "perceive" the environment. Even when the environment was artificially simplified (e.g., consisting only of white solids) and the task was apparently easy (e.g., deciding how many objects there are), computers required very complicated programming to succeed. It is still the case that

no computers can match more than a fraction of the skills of visual perception possessed by nearly every adult human.

The experimental, computational, neuropsychological, and neuroscience approaches have all been influential in increasing our understanding of visual perception. In addition, neuroscience studies have played a larger role in vision research than in most other areas of cognitive psychology. A substantial proportion of the human cortex is devoted to visual processing, and so this emphasis on the neuroscientific approach is justified.

This chapter is concerned with some of the basic processes involved in visual perception. Higher-level processes are considered in Chapter 4, with major theoretical orientations and motion perception being dealt with in Chapter 3.

## PERCEPTUAL ORGANISATION

One of the most basic issues in visual perception is to account for *perceptual segregation*, i.e., our ability to work out which parts of the visual information presented to us belong together and thus form separate objects. One of the first systematic attempts to study perceptual segregation and the perceptual organisation to which it gives rise was made by the Gestaltists. They were a group of German psychologists (including Koffka, Köhler, and Wertheimer) who emigrated to the United States between the two World Wars. Their fundamental principle of perceptual organisation was the law of Prägnanz: "Of several geometrically possible organisations that one will actually occur which possesses the best, simplest and most stable shape" (Koffka, 1935, p. 138).

## Gestaltist approach

Although the law of Prägnanz was their key organisational principle, the Gestaltists also proposed several other laws. Most of these laws (see Figure 2.1) can be subsumed under the law of Prägnanz. The fact that three horizontal arrays of dots rather than vertical groups are perceived in Figure 2.1a indicates that visual elements tend to be grouped together if they are close to each other (the law of proximity). Figure 2.1b illustrates the law of similarity, which states that elements will be grouped together perceptually if

they are similar to each other. Vertical columns rather than horizontal rows are seen because the elements in the vertical columns are the same, whereas those in the horizontal rows are not. We see two crossing lines in Figure 2.1c, because according to the law of good continuation we group together those elements requiring the fewest changes or interruptions in straight or smoothly curving lines. Figure 2.1d illustrates the law of closure, according to which missing parts of a figure are filled in to complete the figure. Thus, a circle is seen even though it is incomplete.

Most Gestalt laws were derived from the study of static two-dimensional figures. However, Gestaltists also put forward the law of common fate, according to which visual elements that seem to move together are grouped together. This was shown in an interesting experiment by Johansson (1973; see Chapter 3). He attached lights to each of the joints of an actor who wore dark clothes, and then filmed him as he moved around in a dark room. Observers saw only a meaningless display of lights when the actor was at rest. However, they perceived a moving human figure when he walked around, although they could actually see only the lights. Other Gestalt-like phenomena (apparent motion; perceived causality) are also discussed in Chapter 3.

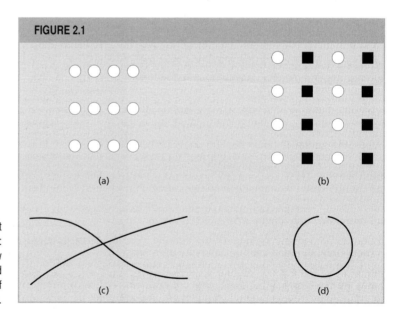

**FIGURE 2.1**

Examples of some of the Gestalt laws of perceptual organisation: (a) the law of proximity; (b) the law of similarity; (c) the law of good continuation; and (d) the law of closure.

FIGURE 2.2

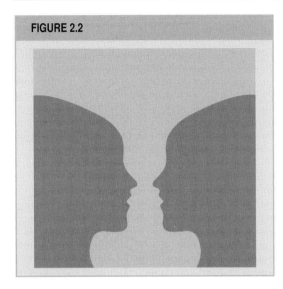

An ambiguous drawing which can be seen either as two faces or as a goblet.

The Gestaltists emphasised the importance of *figure–ground segregation* in perceptual organisation. One object or part of the visual field is identified as the figure, whereas the rest of the visual field is of less interest and so forms the ground. The laws of perceptual organisation permit this segregation into figure and ground to happen. According to the Gestaltists, the figure is perceived as having a distinct form or shape, whereas the ground lacks form. In addition, the figure is perceived as being in front of the ground, and the contour separating the figure from the ground is seen as belonging to the figure.

You can check the validity of these claims about figure and ground by looking at reversible figures such as the faces–goblet figure (see Figure 2.2). When the goblet is the figure, it seems to be in front of a black background, whereas the faces are in front of a white background when they form the figure.

Evidence that there is more attention to, and processing of, the figure than of the ground was reported by Weisstein and Wong (1986). They flashed vertical lines and slightly tilted lines onto the faces–goblet figure, and gave their participants the task of deciding whether the line was vertical. Performance on this task was three times better when the line was presented to what the participants perceived as the figure than to the ground.

The Gestaltists tried to explain their laws of perceptual organisation by their doctrine of *isomorphism*. According to this doctrine, the experience of visual organisation is mirrored by a precisely corresponding process in the brain. It was assumed that there are electrical "field forces" in the brain which help to produce the experience of a stable perceptual organisation when we look at our visual environment.

Unfortunately, the Gestaltists knew very little about the workings of the brain, and their pseudo-physiological ideas have not survived. Much damage was done to the theory by Lashley, Chow, and Semmes (1951) in a study on two chimpanzees. They placed four gold foil "conductors" in the visual area of one of the chimpanzees, and 23 gold pins vertically through the cortex of the other chimpanzee. Lashley et al. argued persuasively that the unpleasant things they had done to these chimpanzees would have severely disrupted any electrical field forces. In fact, the perceptual abilities of their chimpanzees were hardly affected. This suggests that electrical field forces are of much less significance than the Gestaltists claimed.

### Evaluation

The Gestalt approach led to the discovery of several important aspects of perceptual organisation. As Rock and Palmer (1990, p. 50) pointed out, "the laws of grouping have withstood the test of time. In fact, not one of them has been refuted, and no new ones have been added." However, they suggested two new laws of grouping themselves:

1.  The law of common region, according to which observers tend to group together elements that are contained within the same perceived region or area.
2.  The law of connectedness, according to which there is a tendency "to perceive any uniform, connected region—such as a spot, line or more extended area—as a single unit (Rock & Palmer, 1990, p. 50).

The Gestaltists relied heavily on introspective reports, or the "look at the figure and see for yourself" method. More convincing evidence was provided by Pomerantz and Garner (1973). Their participants were presented with stimuli consisting of two brackets arranged in various ways. The task was to sort the stimuli into two piles as fast as possible depending on whether the left-hand bracket was "(" or ")". The participants were instructed to ignore the right-hand bracket, but found it impossible to do this when the two brackets were groupable (e.g., because both brackets were similar in orientation or were close to each other). As a result, there were slower sorting times for groupable stimuli than for non-groupable ones.

The Gestaltists produced *descriptions* of interesting perceptual phenomena, but failed to provide adequate *explanations*. They assumed that observers use the various laws of perceptual grouping without the need for relevant perceptual learning, but did not provide any supporting evidence.

The Gestaltists argued that grouping of perceptual elements occurs *early* in visual processing. This assumption was tested by Rock and Palmer (1990). They presented luminous beads on parallel strings in the dark. The beads were closer to each other in the vertical direction than the horizontal one. As the law of proximity predicts, the beads were perceived as forming columns. When the display was tilted backwards, the beads were closer to each other horizontally than vertically in the two-dimensional retinal image, but remained closer to each vertically in three-dimensional space. What did the observers report? They saw the beads organised in vertical columns. As Rock and Palmer (1990, p. 51) concluded, "Grouping was based on perceived proximity in three-dimensional space rather than on actual proximity on the retina. Grouping by proximity must therefore occur after depth perception." Thus, grouping happens later in processing than was assumed by the Gestaltists.

According to the Gestaltists, the various laws of grouping operate in a bottom-up way to produce perceptual organisation. According to this position, information about the object or objects in the visual field is *not* used to determine how the visual field is segmented. Contrary evidence

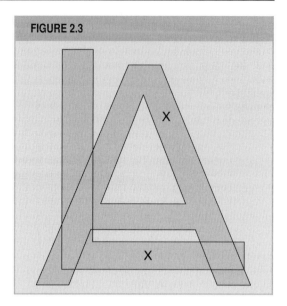

**FIGURE 2.3**

Overlapping transparent letters of the type used by Vecera and Farah (1997).

was reported by Vecera and Farah (1997). They presented two overlapping transparent letters (see Figure 2.3). The participants' task was to decide as rapidly as possible whether two *x*s in the figure were on the same shape. The key manipulation was whether the letters were presented in the upright position or upside down.

Vecera and Farah found that performance was significantly faster with upright letters than with upside down ones. This occurred because the two shapes to be segmented were much more familiar in the upright condition. Thus, as Vecera and Farah (1997, p. 1293) concluded, "top-down activation can partly guide the segmentation process." These findings suggest that the Gestaltists may have exaggerated the role of bottom-up processes in segmentation.

## Subsequent theories

The Gestaltists emphasised the importance of the law of Prägnanz, according to which the perceptual world is organised into the simplest and best shape. However, they lacked any effective means of assessing what shape is the simplest and best, and so relied on subjective impression. Restle

(1979) proposed an interesting way of clarifying the notion of simplicity. He studied the ways in which dots moving across a display are perceived. The most complicated approach would be to treat each dot as completely separate from all the others, and to calculate its starting position, speed, and direction of movement, and so on. In contrast, it is possible to treat the moving dots as belonging to groups, especially if they move together in the same direction and at the same speed. Restle was able to calculate precisely how much processing would be involved. Whatever grouping of moving dots in a display involved the least calculation generally corresponded to what was actually perceived.

Julesz (1975) pointed out that most of the stimuli used by the Gestaltists and their followers were very limited in that they were based mainly on lines and shapes. He studied the effects of brightness and colour on perceptual organisation. A visual display was perceived as consisting of two regions if the average brightness in each region differed considerably. However, a display was not perceived as divided into two regions if the detailed pattern of brightnesses in each region was different but there was only a modest difference in the average brightness. In similar fashion, a visual display consisting of coloured squares is perceived as forming two regions if the average wavelength of light in each region is clearly different. Two regions are less likely to be perceived if there are different patterns of colours in each region, but the average wavelength differs only slightly (e.g., mostly red and green squares in one region, and mostly yellow and blue squares in the other region).

Julesz (1975) found that there are some exceptions to the notion that average brightness or wavelength is crucial in determining whether a display is perceived as consisting of two regions. Another important factor is granularity, which refers to the way in which the elements in a region are distributed. At one extreme, all the elements could be evenly distributed within the field; at the other extreme, they could all be clumped together. Julesz found that a display in which the overall brightness is the same throughout the display but the granularity is greater in one half than the other will be perceived as consisting of two regions (see Figure 2.4).

The Gestaltists de-emphasised the complexities involved when laws of grouping are in conflict. This issue was addressed by Quinlan and Wilton (1998). For example, they presented a display such as the one shown in Figure 2.5a, in which there

**FIGURE 2.4**

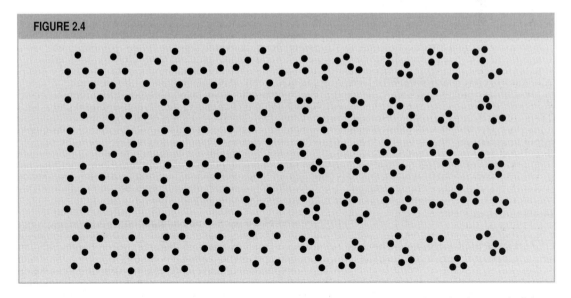

Even though the average brightness in the left and right areas is the same, there is a distinct boundary between the left and right halves of the figure because of a change in granularity. Adapted from Julesz (1975).

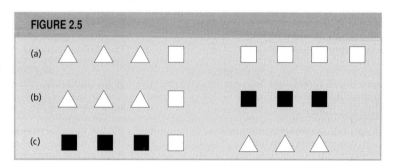

**FIGURE 2.5**

(a) display involving a conflict between proximity and similarity; (b) display with a conflict between shape and colour; (c) a different display with a conflict between shape and colour. All adapted from Quinlan and Wilton (1998).

is a conflict between proximity and similarity. About half the participants grouped the stimuli by proximity and half by similarity. Quinlan and Wilton also used more complex displays like those in Figure 2.5b and 2.5c. Their findings led them to propose the following notions:

- The visual elements in a display are initially grouped or clustered on the basis of proximity.
- Additional processes are used if elements that have provisionally been clustered together differ in one or more features (within-cluster mismatch).
- If there is a within-cluster mismatch on features but a between-cluster match, e.g., Figure 2.5a, then participants choose between grouping based on proximity or on similarity.
- If there are within-cluster and between-cluster mismatches, then proximity is ignored, and grouping is often based on colour. In the case of the displays shown in Figure 2.5b and 2.5c, most participants grouped on the basis of common colour rather than common shape.

Quinlan and Wilton (1998) have made an interesting contribution. However, what remains to be done is to provide a detailed theoretical account of the processes involved when conflicts between laws of grouping need to be resolved.

## DEPTH AND SIZE PERCEPTION

One of the major accomplishments of visual perception is the way in which the two-dimensional retinal image is transformed into perception of a three-dimensional world. The term "depth perception" is used in two rather different senses (Sekuler & Blake, 1994). First, there is *absolute distance*, which refers to the distance away from the observer that an object is located. Second, there is *relative distance*. This refers to the distance between two objects. It is used, for example, when fitting a slice of bread into a toaster. Judgements of relative distance are generally more accurate than judgements of absolute distance.

In real life, cues to depth are often provided by movement, either of the observer or of objects in the visual environment. However, the major focus here will be on cues to depth that are available even if the observer and the objects in the environment are static. These cues can conveniently be divided into monocular, binocular, oculomotor cues. *Monocular cues* are those that only require the use of one eye, although they can be used readily when someone has both eyes open. Such cues clearly exist, because the world still retains a sense of depth with one eye closed. *Binocular cues* are those that involve both eyes being used together. Finally, *oculomotor cues* are kinaesthetic, depending on sensations of muscular contraction of the muscles around the eye.

### Monocular cues

There are various monocular cues to depth. They are sometimes called *pictorial cues*, because they have been used by artists trying to create the impression of three-dimensional scenes while painting on two-dimensional canvases. One such cue is *linear perspective*. Parallel lines pointing directly away from us seem progressively closer

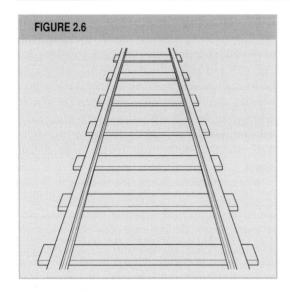

A texture gradient formed by a railway track.

Kanizsa's (1976) illusory square.

together as they recede into the distance (e.g., railway tracks or the edges of a motorway). This convergence of lines can create a powerful impression of depth in a two-dimensional drawing.

Another aspect of perspective is known as *aerial perspective*. Light is scattered as it travels through the atmosphere, especially if the atmosphere is dusty. As a result, more distant objects lose contrast and seem somewhat hazy. There is evidence (e.g., Fry, Bridgman, & Ellerbrock, 1949) that reducing the contrast of objects makes them appear to be more distant.

Another cue related to perspective is *texture*. Most objects (e.g., cobble-stoned roads; carpets) possess texture, and textured objects slanting away from us have what Gibson (e.g., 1979) described as a texture gradient. This can be defined as an gradient (rate of change) of texture density as you look from the front to the back of a slanting object. If you were unwise enough to stand between the rails of a railway track and look along it, the details would become less clear as you looked into the distance. In addition, the distance between the connections would appear to reduce (see Figure 2.6). Evidence that texture gradient can be a useful cue to depth in the absence of other depth cues was provided by Todd and Akerstrom (1987).

A further cue is *interposition*, in which a nearer object hides part of a more distant object from view. Some evidence of how powerful interposition can be is provided by Kanizsa's (1976) illusory square (see Figure 2.7). There is a strong impression of a white square in front of four black circles, in spite of the fact that most of the contours of the white square are missing. Thus, the visual system makes sense of the four sectored black discs by perceiving an illusory interpolated white square.

Another cue to depth is provided by *shading*. Flat, two-dimensional surfaces do not cast shadows, and so the presence of shading generally provides good evidence for the presence of a three-dimensional object. Ramachandran (1988) presented observers with a visual display consisting of numerous very similar shaded circular patches, some of which were illuminated by one light source and the remainder of which were illuminated by a different light source. The observers incorrectly assumed that the visual display was lit by a single light source above the display. This led them to assign different depths to different parts of the display (i.e., some "dents" were seen as bumps).

The sun was easily the major source of light until fairly recently in our evolutionary history, and this might explain why people assume that visual scenes are generally illuminated from above. Howard, Bergstrøm, and Masao (1990) pointed out that the notion of "above" is ambiguous, in that it can be above with reference to gravity (as is assumed in the explanation just given), or it can be above with reference to the position of the person's head. Accordingly, they persuaded their participants to view displays like those of Ramachandran (1988) with their heads upside down! The perceived source of light was determined with reference to head position rather than gravity, indicating that the location of the sun is not relevant to decisions about the direction of illumination. However, head orientation is normally upright, and so the assumption that the sun is above is probably closely associated with head position.

Another cue to depth is provided by *familiar size*. It is possible to use the retinal image size of an object to provide an accurate estimate of its distance, but only when you know the object's actual size. Ittelson (1951) had participants look at playing cards through a peep-hole that restricted them to monocular vision and largely eliminated cues to depth other than familiar size. There were three playing cards (normal size, half-size, and double-size), and they were presented one at a time at a distance of 2.28 metres from the observer. On the basis of familiar size, the judged distance of the normal card should have been 2.28 metres, that of the half-size card 4.56 metres, and that of the double-size card 1.14 metres. The actual judged distances were 2.28 metres, 4.56 metres, and 1.38 metres, indicating that familar size can be a powerful determinant of distance judgements.

Another cue to depth is *image blur*. As Mather (1997, p. 1147) pointed out, "if one image region contains sharply focused texture, and another contains blurred texture, then the two regions may be perceived at different depths, even in the absence of other depth cues." He discussed some of his findings on ambiguous stimuli consisting of two regions of texture (one sharp and one blurred), which were separated by a wavy boundary. When the boundary was sharp, the sharp texture was seen as nearer, whereas the opposite was the case when the boundary was blurred. Thus, the boundary is seen as part of the nearer region.

The final monocular cue we will discuss is *motion parallax*, which refers to the movement of an object's image over the retina. Consider, for example, two objects moving left to right across the line of vision at the same speed, but one object is much further away from the observer than is the other. In that case, the image cast by the nearer object would move much further across the retina than would the image cast by the more distant object.

Motion parallax is also involved if there are two stationary objects at different distances from the observer, and the observer moves sideways. It would again be the case that the image of the nearer object would travel a greater distance across the retina. Some of the properties of motion parallax can be seen through the windows of a moving train. Look into the far distance, and you will notice that the apparent speed of objects passing by seems faster the nearer they are to you.

Convincing evidence that motion parallax can generate depth information in the absence of all other cues was obtained by Rogers and Graham (1979). Their participants looked at a display containing about 2000 random dots with only one eye. When there was relative movement of a section of the display (motion parallax) to simulate the movement produced by a three-dimensional surface, the participants reported a three-dimensional surface standing out in depth from its surroundings. As Rogers and Graham (1979, p. 134) concluded, "it has been clearly demonstrated that parallax information can be a subtle and powerful cue to the shape and relative depth of three-dimensional surfaces."

## Binocular and oculomotor cues

The pictorial cues we have discussed could all be used as well by one-eyed people as by those with normal vision. Depth perception also depends on oculomotor cues, based on perceiving contractions of the muscles around the eyes. One such cue is *convergence*, which refers to the fact that the eyes turn inwards to focus on an object to a greater extent with a very close object than with one that is further away. Another oculomotor cue is *accommodation*, which refers to the variation in optical power produced by a thickening of the lens of the eye when focusing on a close object.

Depth perception also depends on binocular cues, which are only available when both eyes are used. *Stereopsis* involves binocular cues. It is stereoscopic vision depending on the differences in the images projected on the retinas of the two eyes. Convergence, accommodation, and stereopsis are only effective in facilitating depth perception over relatively short distances.

There has been some controversy about the usefulness of convergence as a cue to distance. The findings have tended to be negative when real objects are used, but more promising findings have been obtained with use of the "wallpaper illusion" (Logvinenko & Belopolskii, 1994). In the wallpaper illusion, there is underestimation of the apparent distance of a repetitive pattern when the fixation point is shifted towards the observer, and overestimation when the fixation point moves away from the observer. It has generally been assumed that convergence of the eyes explains the wallpaper illusion, but Logvinenko and Belopolskii cast doubt on that assumption. It is possible to perceive two illusory patterns at two different apparent distances at once, which would be impossible if the phenomenon depended entirely on convergence. In addition, participants can move their gaze around (and so change convergence) without any loss of the illusion. Such findings led Logvinenko and Belopolskii (1994, p. 216) to conclude as follows:

In view of the fact that the wallpaper illusion is commonly assumed to be the main evidence for convergence as a cue to distance, we conclude that convergence does not supply sufficient information for the perception of distance.

Accommodation is also of limited use. Its potential value as a depth cue is limited to the region of space immediately in front of you. However, distance judgements based on accommodation are rather inaccurate even when the object is at close range (e.g., Kunnapas, 1968).

The importance of stereopsis was shown clearly by Wheatstone (1838), who is generally regarded as the inventor of the stereoscope. What happens in a stereoscope is that separate pictures or drawings are presented to an observer in such a way that each eye receives essentially the information it would receive if the object or objects depicted were actually presented. The simulation of the disparity in the images presented to the two eyes produces a strong depth effect.

One might think that stereopsis is a straightforward phenomenon. In fact, it has proved very hard to work out in detail how two separate images turn into a single percept. In general terms, we must somehow establish *correspondences* between the information presented to one eye and that presented to the other eye. At one time, it was believed that the forms or objects presented to one eye were recognised independently, and that they were then fused into a single percept. However, this does not seem likely. Crucial evidence was obtained by Julesz (1971), who made use of random-dot stereograms. Each member of such a stereogram seems to consist of a random mixture of black and white dots, i.e., neither member seems to contain a recognisable form. However, when the stereogram is viewed in a stereoscope, an object (e.g., a square) can be clearly seen.

If stereopsis does not result from a matching of the forms from each image, how does it happen? Part of the answer was obtained by Frisby and Mayhew (1976). They made use of a process known as filtering to remove certain spatial frequencies (these are determined by the closeness together of alternating dark and light bars; see Chapter 4). Stereopsis remained when only high spatial frequencies (fine details) were removed from both halves of a stereogram, or when only low spatial frequencies (coarse, blurred structures) were removed from both. However, when high spatial frequencies were removed from one half and low spatial frequencies from the other, stereopsis was lost, and only one half of the stereogram could be seen at any one time. Thus, some overlap of spatial frequencies between the two halves of a stereogram is necessary for stereopsis.

Marr and Poggio (1976) proposed three rules that might be useful in matching up information from the two eyes:

- *Compatibility constraint*: elements from the input to each eye are matched with each other only if they are compatible (e.g., having the same colour; edges having the same orientation).
- *Uniqueness constraint*: each element in one image is allowed to match with only one element in the other image.
- *Continuity constraint*: matches between two points or elements are preferred where the disparities between the two images are similar to the disparities between nearby matches on the same surface.

These three constraints were incorporated into a theory that was able to produce appropriate solutions to random-dot stereograms (Marr & Poggio, 1976). However, Frisby (1986) pointed out that the continuity constraint is the least adequate. For example, if an object slants steeply away from the observer, then nearby matching points will not have very similar disparities. As a result, there may be a failure to match corresponding points with each other.

Mayhew and Frisby (1981) argued that stereopsis is very much bound up with the elaboration of descriptions in the raw primal sketch (see Chapter 4). This contrasts with the view of Marr and Poggio (1976), which is that stereopsis is rather separate from other aspects of visual processing. Mayhew and Frisby (1981) put forward a *figural continuity constraint*: most erroneous possible matches can be eliminated by considering the pattern of light-intensity changes in the area close to that of the potential match.

The emphasis in most theories of stereopsis has been on the basic visual processes involved. However, cognitive factors can be important. A case in point is Gregory's "hollow face" illusion (Figure 2.8). In this illusion, observers looking at a hollow mask of a face from a distance of a few feet report seeing a normal face (see also Chapter 3). Stereoscopic information is ignored in favour of expectations about human faces based on previous experience.

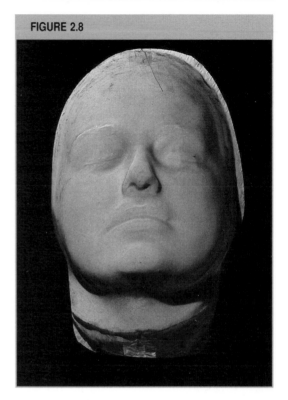

FIGURE 2.8

The hollow face illusion.

## Integrating cue information

We generally have access to several different depth cues. In order to have a complete understanding of depth perception, we need to know how information from the various cues is combined and integrated. For example, what do we do if two depth cues provide conflicting evidence? One possibility is that we make use of information from both cues to reach a compromise solution, but another possibility is that we accept the evidence from one cue and ignore the other.

Some of the major issues of cue combination were studied by Bruno and Cutting (1988). They identified three possible strategies that might be used by observers who had information available from two or more depth cues:

- *Additivity*: all the information from different cues is simply added together.

- *Selection*: information from a single cue is used, with information from the other cue or cues being ignored.
- *Multiplication*: information from different cues interacts in a multiplicative fashion.

Bruno and Cutting studied relative distance in studies in which three untextured parallel flat surfaces were arranged in depth. The observers viewed the displays monocularly, and there were four sources of information about depth: relative size; height in the projection plane; interposition; and motion parallax. The findings supported the additivity notion (Bruno & Cutting, 1988, p. 161): "Information is gathered by separate visual subsystems . . . and it is added together in the simplest manner." There is growing evidence that many visual processes operate in parallel (see the section entitled "Brain systems"), and the notion of additivity is entirely consistent with such evidence. However, it should be noted that the visual system may well make use of weighted addition. In other words, information from different depth cues is combined, but more weight is attached to some cues than to others.

It is advantageous to have a visual system that combines information from different depth cues in an additive fashion. Any depth cue provides inaccurate information under some circumstances, and so relying exclusively on any one cue would often lead to error. In contrast, taking equal account of all the available information (or using weighted addition) is often the best way of ensuring that depth perception is accurate. Another advantage of having additive, independent mechanisms involved in depth perception can be seen in infants, because each mechanism can develop in its own time without having to wait for other mechanisms to develop before it can be used. As Bruno and Cutting (1988) pointed out, infants can use motion parallax before the age of three months, even though many of the other mechanisms involved in depth perception have not developed at that stage.

Bruno and Cutting (1988) did not study what happens when two cues provide *conflicting* information about depth. However, it follows from their general theoretical orientation that observers would combine information from both cues in their depth perception. Support for this position was obtained by Rogers and Collett (1989). They set up a complex display in which binocular disparity and motion parallax cues provided conflicting information about depth, and found that the conflict was resolved by taking both cues into account.

The evidence indicates that observers typically use information from all the available depth cues when trying to judge relative or absolute distance. However, there are some exceptions. Woodworth and Schlosberg (1954) described a situation in which two normal playing cards of the same size were attached vertically to stands, with one card being closer to the observer than the other (see Figure 2.9). The observer viewed the two cards monocularly, and the further card looked more distant. In the next phase of the study, a corner was clipped from the nearer card, and the two cards were arranged so that in the observer's retinal image the edges of the more distant card exactly fitted the cutout edges of the nearer card. With monocular vision, the more distant card seemed to be in front of, and partially obscuring, the nearer card. In this case, the cue of interposition (which normally provides very powerful evidence about relative depth) completely overwhelmed the cue of familiar size.

## Size constancy

*Size constancy* is the tendency for any given object to appear the same size whether its size in the retinal image is large or small. For example, if you see someone walking towards you, their retinal image increases progressively, but their size seems to remain the same. Reasonable or high levels of size constancy have been obtained in numerous studies (see Goldstein, 1996).

Most research on size constancy has been carried out in the laboratory, and Brunswik (1956) argued that it was important to study size constancy in the external environment. Accordingly, he asked a student to walk around outdoors and to provide estimates of the sizes of numerous objects. She did this very successfully, and there was a correlation of +.99 between object size

**FIGURE 2.9**

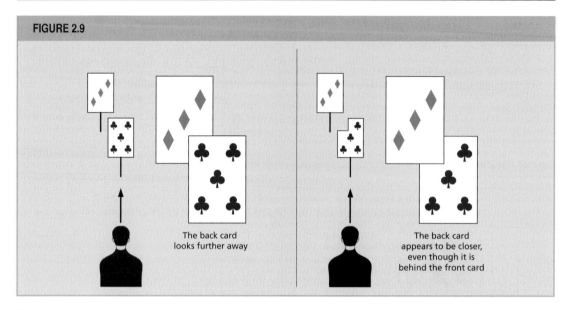

The back card looks further away

The back card appears to be closer, even though it is behind the front card

The two stages of the playing card experiment, as discussed by Woodsworth and Schlosberg (1954). When the first set-up is viewed, the card at the back looks further away, which it is. However, when the front card has been clipped and the position of the card rearranged, the back card looks as if it overlaps the front card. The cue of familiar size, telling the viewer that the smaller card must be further away from the bigger card, is overridden by the cue of interposition, suggesting that the card that appears to obscure part of the other one must be nearer to the viewer, despite its size.

and judged size. This high level of performance did not depend simply on the use of information about retinal size. Brunswik found that the correlation between actual object size and retinal image size was +.7 across all objects, but it fell to only +.1 when small objects were excluded from the analysis.

There is a potential problem with Brunswik's study. It is not clear whether the student's estimated sizes of objects reflected what she *saw* or what she *knew* to be the case. For example, a large oak tree a long way from us may look fairly small, even though we know that it is probably rather large.

Why do we show size constancy? A key reason is that we take account of an object's apparent distance when judging its size. For example, an object may be judged to be large even though its retinal image is very small if it is a long way away. The fact that size constancy is often not shown when we look at objects on the ground from the top of a tall building or from a plane may occur because it is hard to judge distance accurately. These ideas are incorporated into the

size–distance invariance hypothesis (Kilpatrick & Ittelson, 1953), according to which for a given size of retinal image, the perceived size of an object is proportional to its perceived distance.

Evidence consistent with the size–distance invariance hypothesis was reported by Holway and Boring (1941). Participants sat at the intersection of two hallways. The test circle was presented in one hallway, and the comparison circle was presented in the other one. The test circle could be of various sizes and at various distances, and the participants' task was to adjust the comparison circle so that it was the same size as the test circle. Their performance was very good when depth cues were available. However, it became poor when depth cues were removed by placing curtains in the hallway and requiring the participants to look through a peephole. Lichten and Lurie (1950) went a step further and removed all depth cues by using screens that only allowed the observers to see the test circles. In those circumstances, the participants relied totally on retinal image size in their judgements of object size.

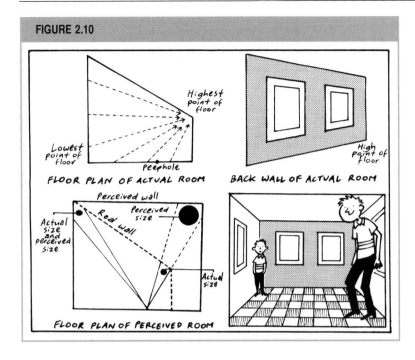

**FIGURE 2.10**

The Ames Room.

If size judgements depend on perceived distance, then size constancy should not be found when the perceived distance of an object is very different from its actual distance. The Ames room provides a good example (see Figure 2.10). It has a peculiar shape: the floor slopes, and the rear wall is not at right angles to the adjoining walls. In spite of this, the Ames room creates the same retinal image as a normal rectangular room when viewed through a peephole. The fact that one end of the rear wall is much further from the viewer is disguised by making it much higher. The cues suggesting that the rear wall is at right angles to the viewer are so strong that observers mistakenly assume that two adults standing in the corners by the rear wall are at the same distance from them. This leads them to estimate the size of the nearer adult as being much greater than that of the adult who is further away.

*Evaluation*

Perceived size and size constancy do typically depend in part on perceived distance. However, the relationship between perceived distance and perceived size is influenced by the kind of size judgements that observers are asked to make. Kaneko and Uchikawa (1997) argued that the instructions given to observers in previous studies were not always clear. They distinguished between perceived linear size (what the actual size of the object seems to be) and perceived angular size (the apparent retinal size of the object). Kaneko and Uchikawa (1997) manipulated depth cues such as binocular disparity. Overall, they found much more evidence for size constancy with linear-size instructions than with angular-size instructions. There was a closer approximation to size constancy with linear-size instructions when depth could be perceived more accurately, but this was less so with angular-size instructions. Thus, the size–distance invariance hypothesis is more applicable to judgements of linear size than of angular size.

Size judgements can depend on factors other than perceived distance. For example, we can use information about familiar size to make accurate assessments of size regardless of whether the retinal image is very large or very small. Evidence of the importance of familiar size was obtained by Schiffman (1967). Observers viewed familiar objects at various distances in the presence or absence of depth cues. Their size estimates were accurate even when depth cues were not available, because they made use of their knowledge of familiar size.

There is also evidence that the horizon is sometimes used in size estimation. The horizon is generally sufficiently far away that, "the line connecting the point of observation with the horizon is parallel to the ground" (Bertamini, Yang, & Proffitt, 1998, p. 673). As a result, an object that is on the line between a standing observer and the horizon is about 1.50 to 1.75 metres tall. Bertamini et al. (1998) obtained size judgements from standing and sitting observers. These judgements were most accurate when the objects being judged were at about eye-level height, suggesting that the horizon can be used as a reference point for size estimation.

In sum, size constancy depends on various factors including perceived distance, size familiarity, the horizon, and so on. As yet, we do not have a theory providing a coherent account of how these factors combine to produce size judgements.

## COLOUR PERCEPTION

Why has colour vision developed? After all, if you see an old black-and white film on television, it is perfectly easy to make sense of the moving images presented to your eyes. There are two main reasons why colour vision is of value to us (Sekuler & Blake, 1994):

- *Detection*: colour vision helps us to distinguish between an object and its background.
- *Discrimination*: colour vision makes it easier for us to make fine discriminations among objects (e.g., between ripe and unripe fruit).

In order to understand how we can discriminate about five million different colours, we need to start with the retina. There are two types of visual receptor cells in the retina: cones and rods. There are about six million cones, and they are mostly found in the fovea or central part of the retina. The cones are specialised for colour vision and for sharpness of vision. There are about 125 million rods, and they are concentrated in the outer regions of the retina. Rods are specialised for vision in dim light and for the detection of movement. Many of these differences stem from the fact that a retinal ganglion cell receives input from only a few cones but from hundreds of rods. As a result, only rods produce much activity in retinal ganglion cells in poor lighting conditions.

### Young–Helmholtz theory

Cone receptors contain light-sensitive photopigment which allows them to respond to light. According to the component or trichromatic theory put forward by Thomas Young and developed by Hermann von Helmholtz, there are three separate sets of fibres differing in the light wavelengths to which they respond most strongly. Subsequent research led to these sets of fibres becoming identified with cone receptors. One type of cone receptor is most sensitive to short-wavelength light, and is most responsive to stimuli that are perceived as blue. A second type of cone receptor is most sensitive to medium-wavelength light, and responds greatly to stimuli that are seen as green. The third type of cone receptor responds most to long-wavelength light such as that coming from stimuli distinguished as red.

How do we see other colours? According to the theory, many stimuli activate two or even all three cone types. The perception of yellow is based on the second and third cone types, and white light involves the activation of all three cone types.

Dartnall, Bowmaker, and Mollon (1983) obtained support for this theory using a technique known as *microspectrophotometry*. This revealed that there are three types of cones or receptors responding maximally to different wavelengths of light (see Figure 2.11). Each cone type absorbs a wide range of wavelengths, and so it would be wrong to equate one cone type with perception of blue, one with green, and one with red. Cicerone and Nerger (1989) found there are about

**FIGURE 2.11**

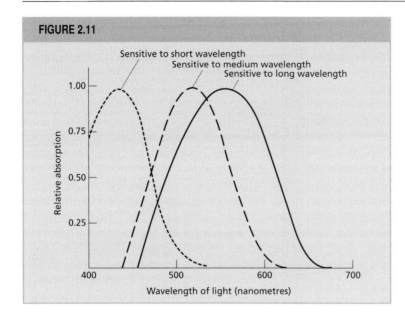

Three types of colour receptors or cones identified by microspectrophotometry. From Dartnall et al. (1983).

4 million long-wavelength cones, over 2 million medium-wavelength cones, and under 1 million short-wavelength cones.

Most individuals suffering from colour deficiency are not completely colour-blind, because they can distinguish some colours. The most common type of colour blindness is *red–green deficiency*, in which blue and yellow can be seen but red and green cannot. There are other, rarer forms of colour deficiency, such as an inability to perceive blue or yellow, combined with the ability to see red and green. According to the Young–Helmholtz theory, the obvious way to try to explain the fact that red–green deficiency is the commonest form of colour blindness is to argue that the medium- and long-wavelength cone types are more likely to be damaged or missing than are the short-wavelength cones. That is actually the case (Sekuler & Blake, 1994). There are rarer cases in which the short-wavelength cones are missing, and this disrupts perception of blue and yellow. However, this is not a complete account of colour deficiency, as we will see shortly.

The Young–Helmholtz theory fails to explain *negative afterimages*. If you stare at a square of a given colour for several seconds, and then shift your gaze to a white surface, you will see a negative afterimage in the complementary colour.

For example, a green square produces a red afterimage, whereas a blue square produces a yellow afterimage.

## Opponent-process theory

Ewald Hering (1878) put forward an opponent-process theory that handles some findings that cannot be explained by the Young–Helmholtz theory. Hering's key assumption was that there are three types of opponent processes in the visual system. One type of process produces perception of green when it responds in one way and of red when it responds in the opposite way. A second type of process produces perception of blue or yellow in the same fashion. The third type of process produces the perception of white at one extreme and of black at the other.

Evidence consistent with opponent-process theory was reported by Abramov and Gordon (1994). They presented observers with single wavelengths, and asked them to indicate the percentage of blue, green, yellow, and red they perceived. According to Hering's theory, it is not possible to see blue and yellow together, or to see red and green together, but the other colour combinations can occur. That is what Abramov and Gordon (1994) found.

Opponent-process theory helps to explain colour deficiency and negative afterimages. Red–green deficiency occurs when the high- or medium-wavelength cones are damaged or missing, and so the red–green channel cannot be used. In similar fashion, individuals lacking the short-wavelength cones cannot make effective use of the yellow–blue channel, and so their perception of these colours is disrupted. Negative afterimages can be explained by assuming that prolonged viewing of a given colour (e.g., red) produces one extreme of activity in the relevant opponent process. When attention is then directed to a white surface, the opponent process moves to its other extreme, and this produces the negative afterimage. Thus, the operation of opponent processes can account for negative afterimages.

DeValois and DeValois (1975) obtained physio-logical evidence in monkeys that was broadly consistent with Hering's theory. They discovered what they called opponent cells. These are cells located in the lateral geniculate nucleus that show increased activity to some wavelengths of light but decreased activity to others. For some cells, the transition point between increased and decreased activity occurred between the green and the red parts of the spectrum. As a result,

they were called red–green cells. Other cells had a transition point between the yellow and blue parts of the sprectrum, and so they were called blue–yellow cells.

## Synthesis

The Young–Helmholtz and Hering theories are both partially correct. Hurvich (1981; see Atkinson et al., 1993) argued that it is both possible and desirable to combine the two theories. According to this two-stage theory, signals from the three cone types identified by the Young–Helmholtz theory are sent to the opponent cells described within the opponent-process theory. The details of what is involved are shown in Figure 2.12. The short-wavelength cones send excitatory signals to the blue–yellow opponent cells, and the long-wavelength cones send inhibitory signals. If the strength of the excitatory signals is greater than that of the inhibitory ones, blue is seen; if the opposite is the case, then yellow is seen.

The medium-wavelength cones send excitatory signals to the green–red opponent cells, and the long-wavelength cones send inhibitory signals. Green is seen if the excitatory signals are stronger than the inhibitory ones, and red is seen if that is

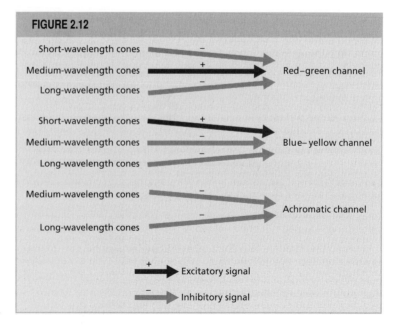

FIGURE 2.12

Two-stage theory of colour vision.

not the case. There is support for the theory from individuals suffering from the various forms of deficient colour perception discussed earlier.

## Colour constancy

*Colour constancy* is the tendency for a surface or object to appear to have the same colour when the illumination varies. The phenomenon of colour constancy indicates that colour vision does not depend only on the wavelengths of the light reflected from objects. If that were the case, then the same object would, for example, appear redder in artificial light than in natural light. In fact, we generally show reasonable colour constancy in such circumstances.

Zeki (1993, p. 12) argued forcefully that it is very important to understand colour constancy:

Why did colour constancy play such a subsidiary role in enquiries on colour vision? . . . until only very recently, it has been treated as a departure from the general rule, although it is in fact the central problem of colour vision . . . That general rule supposes that there is a precise and simple relationship between the wavelength composition of the light reaching the eye from every point on a surface and the colour of that point.

Why do we show colour constancy? One factor is *chromatic adaptation*, in which sensitivity to light of any given colour decreases over time. For example, if you are standing outside after dark, you may be struck by the yellowness of the artificial lights in people's houses. However, if you have been in a room illuminated by artificial light for some time, the light does not seem yellow. Chromatic adaptation has the effect of reducing the distorting effects of any given illumination on colour constancy.

One reason why we show colour constancy is because of familiarity. We know that letterboxes are bright red, and so they look the same colour whether they are illuminated by the sun or by artificial street lighting. For example, Delk and Fillenbaum (1965) presented various shapes cut out of the same orange-red cardboard. The shapes of objects that are typically red (e.g., heart; apple) were perceived as slightly redder than the shapes of other objects (e.g., mushrooms). However, it is hard with such evidence to distinguish between genuine perceptual effects and response or reporting bias.

These findings do not explain colour constancy for unfamiliar objects. Some insight into the factors involved in colour constancy was obtained by Land (1977). He presented his participants with two displays (known as Mondrians) consisting of rectangular shapes of different colours. He then adjusted the lighting of the displays so that two differently coloured rectangles (one from each display) reflected exactly the same wavelengths of light. However, the two rectangles were seen by Land's participants in their actual colours, showing strong evidence of colour constancy in the absence of familiarity. Finally, Land found that the two rectangles looked exactly the same (and so colour constancy broke down) when everything else in the two displays was blocked out.

What was happening in Land's study? According to Land's (1977, 1986) retinex theory, we decide the colour of a surface by *comparing* its ability to reflect short, medium, and long wavelengths against that of adjacent surfaces. Colour constancy breaks down when such comparisons cannot be made. More specifically, it is assumed within retinex theory that "the logarithm of the ratio of the light of a given wavelength reflected from a surface (the numerator), and the average of light of the same wavelength reflected from its surround (the denominator) is taken . . . The process is done independently three times for the three wavelengths [red, green, and blue light]" (Tovée, 1996, p. 107).

Zeki (1983) identified part of the physiological system involved in colour constancy. He found in a study on monkeys that certain cells in area V4 (discussed in the section entitled "Brain systems") responded strongly to a red patch in a multi-coloured display illuminated mainly by red light. These cells did not respond when the red patch was replaced by a green, blue, or white patches, even though the dominant reflected wavelength was red. Thus, these cells seem to respond to the *actual* colour of a surface rather than simply to the wavelengths reflected from it.

## Evaluation

As is predicted by retinex theory, the perception of an object's colour depends on some kind of *comparison* of the wavelengths of light reflected from that object and from other objects in the visual field. However, retinex theory does not provide a complete account of colour perception and colour constancy. For example, the theory does not indicate the precise ways in which neurons such as colour-opponent cells might be involved in colour perception. In addition, it does not directly address the role of familiar colour in influencing colour constancy.

It would seem to be predicted by retinex theory that colour constancy will be complete provided that observers can see the surroundings of a shape or object. However, that is often not the case. As Bramwell and Hurlbert (1996) pointed out, the extent to which colour constancy is obtained varies across studies from about 20% to 130%. One reason why colour constancy is often far from complete is because of limitations in the method of asymmetric matching by adjustment that is generally used. With this method, participants view two scenes under different lighting conditions, and adjust the colour of part of one scene to match that of the other scene. This is an unnatural task, because in everyday life we tend simply to decide whether a colour is the same as, or different from, that seen under different lighting conditions.

Bramwell and Hurlbert (1996) devised a more natural task involving same–different judgements of colour, and found greater colour constancy than is normally found. However, it was still not perfect.

Further evidence that retinex theory provides an incomplete account of colour constancy was produced by Jakobsson et al. (1997). They presented two-dimensional visual displays consisting of vertical stripes in two shades of grey. There was yellow-orange illumination of the upper half of the display, and bluish illumination of the lower half. What was seen by observers alternated between two different three-dimensional percepts of the two-dimensional display:

1. Horizontally folded percept: the central horizontal border between the two illuminations seemed to push out towards the observer, and there was almost complete colour constancy.
2. Vertically folded percept: the display seemed to be folded along the edges between successive grey stripes. There was no colour constancy, because the top half of the display looked yellow-orange and the bottom half looked blue. In other words, colour differences that were due to lighting were wrongly attributed to the display itself.

How can we explain these peculiar results? Jakobsson et al. (1997) argued that what they called the AMBEGUJAS phenomenon occurs because the observers make the wrong assumption that there is a single illuminant. The crucial point, however, is that Land's (1977, 1986) retinex theory cannot account for the findings. According to that

| Retinex theory | |
|---|---|
| *Strengths* | *Weaknesses* |
| • Demonstrated colour constancy for unfamiliar objects, a crucial step in understanding colour vision. <br> • Showed the importance of comparison of light wavelengths in colour vision. | • Account of colour constancy is incomplete. <br> • Task used lacks ecological validity. <br> • Does not show how familiar colour influences colour constancy. <br> • Cannot account for findings involving horizontally or vertically folded percepts. |

theory, the observers had adequate information to show colour constancy. Thus, neither the lack of colour constancy in the vertically folded percept or the alternating percepts of the display can be predicted from retinex theory. However, retinex theory is a 2-D model, and so it is perhaps unsurprising that it cannot handle some of the findings when more complex 3-D factors are considered.

## BRAIN SYSTEMS

In order to understand visual perception, it is useful to consider some of the major brain systems (see Gazzaniga, Ivry, & Mangun, 1998, or Tovée, 1996). It is important to note that an oversimplified view is presented here. There are more than 30 visual areas in the cortex, and over half of the area of the cortex responds to visual stimuli. Goldstein (1996, p. 97) provided a useful overview of the visual system:

As we travel farther from the retina, neurons require more specific stimuli to fire. Retinal ganglion cells respond to just about any stimulus, whereas end-stopped cells respond only to bars of a certain length that are moving in a particular direction . . . this specialisation increases even further as we move into other visual areas of the cortex.

The great majority of ganglion cells in the primate retina are M (magnocellular or large-bodied) and P (parvocellular or small-bodied) cells. The axons of these ganglion cells come together to form the optic nerve, which projects to the lateral geniculate nucleus. The lateral geniculate nucleus is organised into six layers, each of which receives input from one eye. Layers 1 and 2 receive inputs from large M ganglion cells, whereas layers 3–6 receive inputs from the smaller P ganglion cells.

Some indication of the functions of the lateral geniculate nucleus was obtained by Schiller,

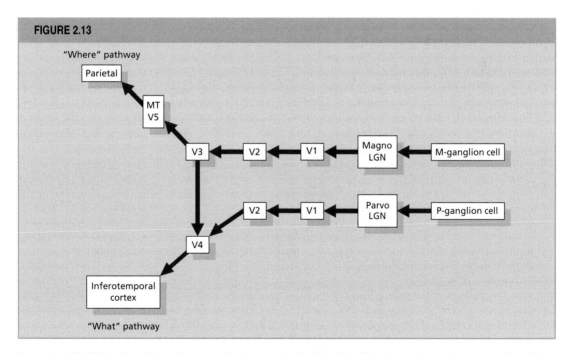

FIGURE 2.13

A very simplified illustration of the pathways and brain areas involved in vision. There is much more interconnectivity within the brain (VI onwards) than is shown, and there are additional unshown brain areas involved in vision. Adapted from Goldstein (1996).

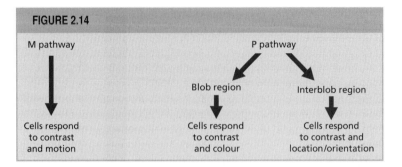

**FIGURE 2.14**

M pathway

P pathway

Blob region

Interblob region

Cells respond to contrast and motion

Cells respond to contrast and colour

Cells respond to contrast and location/orientation

Logothetis, and Charles (1990). They destroyed parts of the magno or parvo layers in monkeys. Magno lesions greatly impaired movement detection, whereas parvo lesions produced loss of the ability to perceive colour, fine textures, and detailed objects.

Neurons from the P layers and from the M layers mainly project to the primary visual cortex or V1 (see Figure 2.13). The P and M pathways are not totally segregated, because there seems to be an input from the M pathway into the P pathway (Nealey & Maunsell, 1994). There is good evidence that the P pathway has two divisions. When cytochrome oxidase is applied to the surface of V1, it becomes concentrated in areas of high metabolic activity. The areas associated with high metabolic activity are called *blobs*, whereas the areas of lower activity are called *interblobs*. These areas correspond to separate divisions within the P pathway. Cells in all three pathways (the M pathway; blob regions of the P pathway; interblob regions of the P pathway) respond strongly to contrast. Cells in the M pathway also respond strongly to motion, those in the blob regions of the P pathway respond strongly to colour, and those in the interblob regions respond strongly to location and orientation (Figure 2.14).

There seem to be three repeating substructures in area V2, consisting of thick stripes, thin stripes, and interstripes. The thick stripes represent the continuation of the M pathway, the thin stripes are a continuation of the P-blob pathway, and the interstripes are an extension of the P-interblob pathway.

After V2, there are two visual pathways proceeding further into the cortex, with these pathways corresponding to the magno and parvo layers. These are the parietal and temporal pathways, respectively (see Figure 2.13). We will be considering these pathways in more detail shortly and in the next chapter. For now, it should be noted that the parietal pathway is mainly concerned with movement processing, whereas the temporal pathway is concerned with colour and form processing.

The research of cognitive neuroscientists on the visual system was summarised by Zeki (1992, 1993). According to his functional specialisation theory, different parts of the cortex are specialised for different visual functions. This contrasts with the traditional view, according to which there was a unitary visual processing system.

Some of the main areas of the visual cortex in the macaque monkey are shown in Figure 2.15. The retina connects primarily to what is known as the primary visual cortex or area V1. The importance of area V1 is shown by the fact that lesions at any point along the pathway to it from the retina lead to total blindness within the affected part of V1. However, areas V2 to V5 are also of major significance in visual perception. Here are the main functions that Zeki (1992, 1993) ascribed to these areas:

- V1 and V2: these areas are involved at an early stage of visual perception. They contain different groups of cells responsive to colour and form, and may be said to "contain pigeonholes into which the different signals are assembled before being relayed to the specialised visual areas" (Zeki, 1992, p. 47). Research on cells in V1 by Hubel and Wiesel (e.g., 1968) is discussed in Chapter 4.

**FIGURE 2.15**

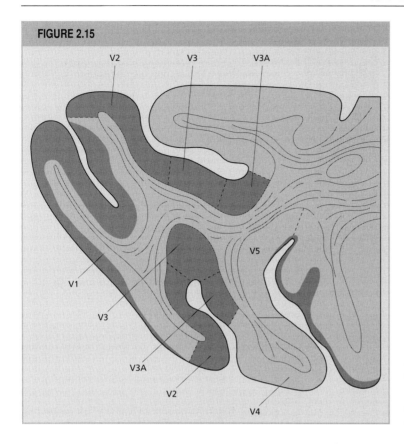

A cross-section of the visual cortex of the macaque monkey. From Zeki (1992). Reproduced with permission. © 1992 by Scientific American, Inc. All rights reserved.

- V3 and V3A: cells in these areas are responsive to form (especially the shapes of objects in motion) but not to colour.
- V4: the overwhelming majority of cells in this area are responsive to colour; many are also responsive to line orientation.
- V5: this area is specialised for visual motion (Zeki found in studies with macaque monkeys that all the cells in this area are responsive to motion, but are not responsive to colour).

A central assumption made by Zeki (1992, 1993) was that colour, form, and motion are processed in anatomically separate parts of the visual cortex. Much of the original evidence came from studies of monkeys. However, there is now considerable evidence from humans that Zeki's assumption is broadly correct, although form processing occurs in several different areas. Some of this evidence is considered next.

## Colour processing

The notion that different areas of the cortex are involved in colour and motion processing received support in a study by Cavanaugh, Tyler, and Favreau (1984). They presented a moving grating consisting of alternating red and green bars possessing equiluminance or equal brightness. The observers reported either that the bars did not seem to be moving, or there was only a modest impression of movement. Theoretically, it was assumed that the moving display only affected the colour processing system. It did not stimulate the motion processing system, because that system responds only to differences in brightness.

Evidence that area V4 is specialised for colour processing was reported by Lueck et al. (1989). They presented coloured or grey squares and rectangles to observers. PET scans indicated that

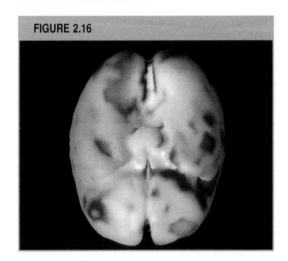

FIGURE 2.16

PET scans use radioactively-labelled substances introduced into the blood to view metabolic activity in three-dimensions, and this is a PET scan of the brain seen from below during visual activity. The frontal lobe is at lower centre. The most active area is the visual cortex within the occipital lobe at the back of the brain (at upper centre), showing the brain's visual centre.
Photo credit: Montreal Neurological Institute/McGill University/CNRI/Science Photo Library.

there was about 13% more blood flow within area V4 with the coloured stimuli, but other areas were not more affected by colour (Figure 2.16). Zeki (1993) carried out a similar study, and found that V1 and V4 were both activated more by the coloured displays.

If area V4 is specialised for colour processing, then patients with damage mostly limited to that area should show little or no colour perception, combined with fairly normal form and motion perception. This is the case in some patients with *achromatopsia*. However, many of them do have problems with object recognition as well as an inability to identify colours by name.

In spite of the fact that patients with achromatopsia complain that the world seems devoid of colour, some aspects of colour processing are preserved. Heywood, Cowey, and Newcombe (1994) studied MS, a patient with achromatopsia. He performed very poorly on an oddity task, on which he had to select the odd colour from a set of stimuli having the same shape. However, he performed well on a similar task on which he

had to select the odd form out of a set of stimuli (e.g., one cross and two squares), a task that could only be performed accurately by using colour information. As Køhler and Moscovitch (1997, p. 326) concluded, "MS is able to process information about colour implicitly when the actual perceptual judgement concerns form, but is unable to use this information explicitly when the judgement concerns colour."

Shuren et al. (1996) studied EH, a man who had developed achromatopsia as a result of a stroke. Use of MRI confirmed that area V4 was damaged. However, Shuren et al. (1996) were mainly interested in testing Farah's (1989) hypothesis that imagery involves use of the same stored representations as visual perception. This hypothesis led them to predict that EH would have impaired performance on imagery tasks involving colour (e.g., working out which two out of three named objects had the same colour). In fact, EH performed at normal levels on these imagery tasks. Shuren et al. (1996) concluded that EH probably had intact stored colour representations of objects, which permitted him to use colour imagery. However, connections between the visual input and these stored representations had been destroyed by the stroke, and so he had no colour perception.

It has often been assumed that the area of human cortex involved in colour processing corresponds to V4 in monkeys. However, a cautionary note may be in order. Schiller and Lee (1991) found that lesions to monkey V4 do not produce the permanent great impairment of colour perception seen in human patients with achromatopsia. Such findings led Tovée (1996, p. 110) to conclude: "Although an area in human cerebral cortex has been located that is selective for colour, it may not be the homologue [same structure] of monkey V4."

## Form processing

Several areas are involved in form processing in humans, including areas V3, V4, and IT (see Figure 2.13). However, the cognitive neuroscience approach to form perception has focused mainly on IT (inferotemporal cortex). Tanaka (1992) took recordings from individual neurons in IT while numerous objects were presented to monkeys to discover which objects produced the greatest response. After that, he presented features of the most effective stimulus in order to find out the crucial features to which each neuron was responding. Tanaka found that there were elaborate cells in IT that seemed to respond maximally to simple shapes.

Several other researchers have followed this line of research. For example, Sary, Vogels, and Orban (1993) found that the responses of elaborate cells in IT were unaffected by the size and orientation of the visual stimulus. The cells in IT are organised into functional columns, with all the cells in any one column responding to similar stimuli. It seems as if the simple shapes involved may form a "visual alphabet" of perhaps 600 shapes, from which object representations can be constructed. However, neuronal responding in IT may be more complex than has been suggested so far, with some cells responding best to their preferred shape plus the absence of some other shape (Young, 1995).

Some of the most interesting research has focused on responses to faces. There are numerous cells in IT that are responsive to faces, but show virtually no response to other stimuli. For example, Rolls and Tovée (1995) carried out a study on monkeys in which 23 faces and 45 other stimuli were presented. Any one cell showed strong responses to a few faces, coupled with little responding to the other faces or to the non-faces.

It might be expected that some brain-damaged patients would suffer from severely impaired form vision but fairly normal colour and motion processing. However, Zeki (1992, p. 47) claimed that, "no one has ever reported a complete and specific loss of form vision". He argued that the reason for this might be that a lesion that was large enough to destroy areas V3, V4, and IT would probably destroy area V1 as well. As a result, the patient would suffer from total blindness rather than simply loss of form perception.

## Motion processing

There is convincing evidence from cognitive neuroscience that area V5 is involved in motion

processsing. For example, Anderson et al. (1996) used magneto-encephalography (MEG) and MRI (see Chapter 1) to assess brain activity in response to motion stimuli. They reported that "human V5 is located near the occipito-temporal border in a minor sulcus [groove] immediately below the superior temporal sulcus" (Anderson et al., 1996, p. 428). This finding was consistent with previous findings using other techniques. For example, the special involvement of V5 in motion processing has been found in PET studies (e.g., Zeki et al., 1991) and in studies using functional MRI (e.g., Tootell et al., 1995a).

There is additional evidence about the importance of area V5 in motion processing in studies on brain-damaged patients suffering from *akinetopsia*. In this condition, stationary objects can generally be perceived fairly normally but objects in motion become invisible. Zihl, von Cramon, and Mai (1983) studied LM, a woman with akinetopsia who had suffered brain damage in both hemispheres. Shipp et al. (1994) used a high-resolution MRI scan to show that LM has bilateral damage to V5. She was good at locating stationary objects by sight, she had good colour discrimination, and her binocular visual functions (e.g., stereoscopic depth perception) were normal, but her motion perception was grossly deficient. According to Zihl et al. (1983):

She had difficulty . . . in pouring tea or coffee into a cup because the fluid appeared to be frozen, like a glacier. In addition, she could not stop pouring at the right time since she was unable to perceive the movement in the cup (or a pot) when the fluid rose . . . In a room where more than two people were walking she felt very insecure . . . because "people were suddenly here or there but I have not seen them moving".

LM's condition did not improve over time. However, she developed various ways of trying to cope with her lack of motion perception. For example, she stopped looking at people talking to her, because she found it disturbing that their lips did not seem to move (Zihl et al., 1991).

Striking evidence of the involvement of V5 in motion perception was reported by Beckers and Zeki (1995). They used transcranial magnetic stimulation to produce temporary inactivation of V5. The result was what appeared to be complete akinetopsia.

Van Essen and Gallant (1994) argued that V5 in primates seems to consist of two subdivisions. One subdivision is concerned with the motion of objects, and the other deals with the effects of our own movement through the environment. Neurons in the latter area are responsive to changes in the retinal size of objects. They are also responsive to the rotation of the retinal image of an object, as would occur when we tilt our head.

Zeki (1993) argued that area V3 is involved in processing dynamic form and in obtaining three-dimensional structure from motion. Evidence supporting this was obtained by de Jong et al. (1994). They presented moving dots that either simulated the forward motion of an observer over flat ground or moved in a random way. PET scans revealed that V3 was much more active in the former condtion.

## Blindsight

According to Zeki (1992, 1993), area V1 (the primary visual cortex) plays a central role in visual perception. Nearly all signals from the retina pass through this area before proceeding to the other areas specialised for different aspects of visual processing. Patients with partial or total damage of this area show a loss of vision in part or all of the visual field. However, in spite of this loss of conscious vision, some of these patients can make accurate judgements and discriminations about visual stimuli presented to the "blind" area. Such patients are said to show *blindsight*.

The most thoroughly studied patient with blindsight was DB, who was tested by Weiskrantz (e.g., 1986). DB's perceptual problems stemmed from an operation designed to reduce the number of severe migraines from which he suffered. Following the operation, DB was left with an area of blindness in the lower left quadrant of the visual field. However, he was able to detect whether or not a visual stimulus had been presented to the blind area, and he could also identify its location.

In spite of DB's performance, he seemed to have no conscious visual experience. According to Weiskrantz et al. (1974, p. 721), "When he was shown his results [by presenting them to the right visual field] he expressed surprise and insisted several times that he thought he was just 'guessing.' When he was shown a video film of his reaching and judging orientation of lines, he was openly astonished." However, it is hard to be sure that DB had no conscious visual experience, and the reports of other patients are sometimes confused on this issue. For example, patient EY "sensed a definite pinpoint of light", although "it does not actually look like a light. It looks like nothing at all" (Weiskrantz, 1980).

Weiskrantz, Barbur, and Sahraie (1995) argued that any residual conscious vision in blindsight patients is very different from conscious vision in normal individuals. They argued that it is characterised by "a contentless kind of awareness, a feeling of something happening, albeit not normal seeing" (Weiskrantz et al., 1995, p. 6122). They asked their patient to detect the direction of motion of a stimulus, and also to indicate whether he had any awareness of what was being presented. On "aware" trials, his detection performance tended to be better when the stimulus was moving faster. However, his performance on "unaware" trials did not depend on stimulus speed. As Weiskrantz (1995, p. 149) concluded, the patient's "unaware mode is not just a pale shadow of his aware mode".

Additional evidence that blindsight does not depend on conscious visual experience was reported by Rafal et al. (1990). They found that blindsight patients performed at chance when given the task of detecting a light presented to the blind area of the visual field. However, their speed of reaction to a light presented to the intact part of the visual field was slowed down when a light was presented to the blind area at the same time. Thus, a light that did not produce any conscious awareness nevertheless received sufficient processing to disrupt visual performance on another task.

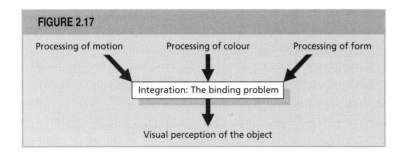

FIGURE 2.17

Processing of motion    Processing of colour    Processing of form

Integration: The binding problem

Visual perception of the object

What brain systems underlie blindsight? Køhler and Moscovitch (1997) discussed findings from several patients who had had an entire cerebral hemisphere removed. These patients showed evidence of blindsight for stimulus detection, stimulus localisation, form discrimination, and motion detection. These findings led Køhler and Moscovitch (1997, p. 322) to conclude: "The results . . . suggest that subcortical rather than cortical regions may mediate blindsight on tasks that involve these visual functions".

Fendrich, Wessinger, and Gazzaniga (1992) favoured an alternative position. According to conventional assessment, their patient had no conscious awareness of visual stimuli within a large area. However, when they used a more sensitive method, they discovered that the patient could report visual stimuli presented to certain small regions of the visual field. They concluded that their patient had preserved "islands" of function within the cortex that permitted him to show the phenomenon of blindsight. However, it is unlikely that this is true of most other blindsight patients.

Another possibility is that there is a "fast" pathway that proceeds directly to V5 without passing through V1 (primary visual cortex). Evidence supporting this view was reported by ffytche, Guy, and Zeki (1995). They obtained visual event-related potentials for moving stimuli, and found that V5 became active before, or at the same time as, V1. Blindsight patients may use this pathway even if V1 is totally destroyed.

## Integration of information

As Gazzaniga et al. (1998) indicated, "Visual perception is a divide-and-conquer strategy. Rather than have each visual area represent all attributes of an object, each area provides its own limited analysis. Processing is distributed and specialised." This functional specialisation poses difficulties of integration, in that information about an object's motion, colour, and form needs to be combined (Figure 2.17).

The difficult task of integrating information about objects in the visual field is known as the "binding" problem. As yet, little is known of how the brain solves the binding problem. One approach is based on oscillation-binding theory (Engel, Koenig, & Kreiter, 1992). Neurons sometimes exhibit oscillatory activity, in which there are alternating bursts of high and low rates of firing. According to the theory, neurons will tend to oscillate in a synchronised way when they are responding to the same object, and this can help to produce an integrated percept of an object.

Tovée (1996) raises various problems with oscillation-binding theory. Oscillation only seems to occur with moving stimuli, and so the theory cannot apply to static stimuli. In addition, the evidence suggests that oscillations develop too slowly and last for too long for them to contribute to object perception. Tovée argued that there may be less of a binding problem than has sometimes been supposed. The fact that there is only high visual acuity for stimuli presented to the fovea of the retina (combined with attentional focusing) creates "almost a tunnel vision effect, where only the visual information from the centre of the visual field is fully sampled and analysed" (Tovée, 1996, p. 177). The different features of an object are probably integrated or combined "in a subsequent higher integrative cortical area" (Tovée, 1996, p. 179).

## CHAPTER SUMMARY

- Perceptual organisation. The Gestaltists put forward several laws of perceptual organisation, including the law of proximity, the law of similarity, the law of good continuation, the law of closure, and the law of common fate. These laws assist in figure–ground segregation. The Gestaltists tried unsuccessfully to explain visual organisation in terms of electrical field forces in the brain. The Gestaltists provided descriptions rather than explanations, and did not manage to define precisely what is meant by a simple perceptual organisation. Their assumption that grouping of perceptual elements occurs very early in processing may be incorrect. Restle showed some of the ways in which perceptual grouping can economise on perceptual processing. The Gestaltists focused on lines and shapes, but Julesz found that perceptual grouping can also depend on brightness, colour, and granularity.

- Depth and size perception. Monocular cues to depth include linear perspective, aerial perspective, texture, shading, familiar size, and motion parallax. Convergence and accommodation are oculomotor cues, but are of limited usefulness. Stereopsis involves binocular cues, and involves establishing correspondences between the information presented to one eye and that presented to the other eye. Information from the various depth cues is generally combined in an additive way. Size constancy depends mainly on perceived distance, but familiar size is also important. When perceived distance is misjudged (e.g., the Ames room), then size judgements are inaccurate.

- Colour perception. Colour vision helps us to detect objects and to make finediscriminations among objects. According to the Young–Helmholtz theory, there are three types of nervous fibres (now known as cone receptors) differing in the light wavelengths to which they respond most strongly. This theory does not account fully for deficient colour vision or for negative after-images. Hering argued that there are three types of opponent processes in the visual system: green–red; blue–yellow; and white–black. A synthesis of the Young–Helmholtz and Hering theories accounts reasonably well for colour perception. According to retinex theory, colour constancy depends on comparisons between the light wavelength reflected from a surface and from its surround. However, colour constancy is often less complete than would be predicted by retinex theory. Colour constancy also depends on the fact that many objects have a familiar colour, and on chromatic adaptation.

- Brain systems. Colour, motion, and form are processed in anatomically separate parts of the visual cortex. Visual perception is based on a divide-and-conquer strategy based on functional specialisation. PET scans and studies on patients with achromatopsia reveal the key role of area V4 in colour processing. However, this may not correspond precisely with V4 in monkeys. Studies using MRI, MEG, and PET have indicated the involvement of area V5 in motion processing. This is supported by studies on patients suffering from akinetopsia, a condition that can be produced temporarily by transcortical magnetic stimulation to make V5 inactive. Area V3 is also involved in motion perception, especially processing of dynamic form and obtaining three-dimensional structure from motion. Several areas, including V3, V4, and IT, are involved in form perception. Some patients with damage to V1 show blindsight. The existence of blindsight in patients who have had an entire cerebral hemisphere removed suggests that blindsight can involve subcortical areas. The task of combining information about an object from different brain areas is a complex one, and may involve attentional processes.

## FURTHER READING

- Gazzaniga, M.S., Ivry, R.B., & Mangun, G.R. (1998). *Cognitive neuroscience: The biology of the mind*. New York: W.W. Norton. The basic pathways and brain areas involved in visual perception are discussed fully in Chapter 4 of this book.
- Køhler, S., & Moscovitch, M. (1997). Unconscious visual processing in neuropsychological syndromes: A survey of the literature and evaluation of models of consciousness. In M. Rugg (Ed.), *Cognitive neuroscience*. Hove, UK: Psychology Press. Various disorders of visual perception are discussed in detail in this chapter.
- Tovée, M.J. (1996). *An introduction to the visual system*. Cambridge: Cambridge University Press. Most of the topics discussed in this chapter are dealt with from various perspectives, and there is detailed coverage of the cognitive neuroscience approach.
- Wilson, R.A., & Keil, F. (1999). *The MIT encyclopaedia of the cognitive sciences*. Cambridge, MA: MIT Press. Basic processes in visual perception are discussed in a number of contributions to this encyclopaedia.

# Perception, Movement, and Action

## INTRODUCTION

Some of the main contemporary cognitive theories of perception were discussed in the previous two chapters. Most of these theories are based on the assumption that perception is a complex achievement. Most theorists assume that several kinds of information processing are required to transform the mosaic of light intensities on the retina into accurate and detailed perception of the visual environment. In other words, perception is *indirect* in that it depends on numerous internal processes. Those (e.g., Bruner, 1957; Gregory, 1970) who have emphasised internal processes not stemming directly from the stimulus input are sometimes known as *constructivist theorists*.

Gibson (1950, 1966, 1979) developed an approach to visual perception in apparent conflict with most cognitive and computational theories. His is a theory of *direct* perception: the information provided by the visual environment is allegedly sufficient to permit the individual to move around and to interact directly with that environment without the involvement of internal processes and representations.

Those theorists who argue that perception is indirect often claim that top-down or conceptually driven processes are of importance. In contrast, Gibson and other direct theorists typically emphasise the role of bottom-up or data-driven processes in perception. It is important to consider these viewpoints, because they illuminate some major issues relating to the nature of perception.

| Direct and indirect theories of perception | |
| --- | --- |
| *Direct processing theories* | *Indirect/constructivist processing theories* |
| • No internal representations involved<br>• Driven by bottom-up processes | • Dependent on internal processes<br>• Driven by top-down processes as well as bottom-up processes |

Gibson's direct theory involves an ecological approach, because of his insistence that we should study perception as it operates in the real world. In addition, he argued that perception and action are closely intertwined. Perception provides valuable information in the organisation of action, and action and movement by the organism facilitate accurate perception. Some of these issues will be addressed later.

## CONSTRUCTIVIST THEORIES

Helmholtz (1821–1894) argued that the inadequate information provided by the senses is augmented by *unconscious inferences*, which add meaning to sensory information. He assumed these inferences were unconscious, because we typically have no awareness that we are making inferences while perceiving. A good example of unconscious inference is the "hollow face" illusion (Gregory, 1973, see Chapter 2). The face is hollow, but the shading and other cues are consistent with a solid face. As a result of our expectations, we see a solid face. We continue to do so even when we "know" the face is hollow, indicating that conscious knowledge is not influencing perception.

The approach advocated by Helmholtz, which we will call the constructivist approach, remains influential. Theorists such as Bruner (1957), Neisser (1967), and Gregory (1972, 1980) all subscribe to assumptions resembling those originally proposed by Helmholtz:

- Perception is an active and constructive process; it is "something more than the direct registration of sensations . . . other events intervene between stimulation and experience" (Gordon, 1989, p. 124).
- Perception is not directly given by the stimulus input, but occurs as the end-product of the interactive influences of the presented stimulus and internal hypotheses, expectations, and knowledge, as well as motivational and emotional factors.
- Perception is influenced by hypotheses and expectations that are sometimes incorrect, and so it is prone to error.

The flavour of this theoretical approach was captured by Gregory (1972). He claimed that perceptions are constructions, "from floating fragmentary scraps of data signalled by the senses and drawn from the brain memory banks, themselves constructions from the snippets of the past." Thus, the frequently inadequate information supplied to the sense organs is used as the basis for making inferences or forming hypotheses about the external environment.

Contextual information can be used in making inferences about a visual stimulus. Palmer (1975) presented a scene (e.g., a kitchen) in pictorial form, followed by the very brief presentation of the picture of an object. This object was appropriate to the context (e.g., loaf) or inappropriate (e.g., mailbox). There was also a further condition in which no contextual scene was presented. The probability of identifying the object correctly was greatest when it was appropriate to the context, intermediate when there was no context, and lowest when it was inappropriate.

According to constructivist theorists, the formation of incorrect hypotheses or expectations leads to errors of perception. Ittelson (1952) argued that the perceptual hypotheses formed may be very inaccurate if a visual display appears familiar but is actually novel. An example of this is the well known Ames distorted room (see Chapter 2). The room is actually of a peculiar shape, but when viewed from a particular point it gives rise to the same retinal image as a conventional rectangular room.

It is perhaps not surprising that observers decide that the room is like a normal one. However, what is puzzling is that they maintain this belief even when someone inside the room walks backwards and forwards along the rear wall, apparently growing and shrinking as he or she proceeds! The reason for the apparent size changes is that the rear wall is not at right angles to the viewing point: one corner is actually much further away from the observer than the other corner. As might be expected by constructivist theorists, there is a greater likelihood of the room being perceived as having an odd shape and the person walking inside it remaining the same size when

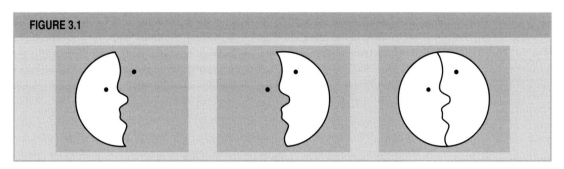

**FIGURE 3.1**

Examples of the type of stimuli used by Schafer and Murphy (1943).

that person is the spouse or close relative of the observer.

Another illustration of the possible pitfalls involved in relying too heavily on expectations or hypotheses comes in a classic study by Bruner, Postman, and Rodrigues (1951). Their participants expected to see conventional playing cards, but some were incongruous (e.g., black hearts). When these incongruous cards were presented briefly, participants sometimes reported seeing brown or purple hearts. Here we have an almost literal blending of stimulus information (bottom-up processing) and stored information (top-down processing). However, there are potential problems with reporting bias in this study.

## Motivation and emotion

A central assumption of the constructivist approach is that perception is not determined entirely by external stimuli. As a result, it is assumed that current motivational and emotional states may influence people's perceptual hypotheses and thus their visual perception. Consider, for example, a study by Schafer and Murphy (1943). They prepared drawings consisting of an irregular line drawn vertically through a circle so that either half of the circle could be seen as the profile of a face (Figure 3.1). During initial training, each face was presented separately. One face in each pair was associated with financial reward, whereas the other face was associated with financial punishment. When the original combined drawings were then presented briefly, participants were much

more likely to report perceiving the previously rewarded face than the previously punished one. Smith and Hochberg (1954) found in a similar study that delivering a shock when one of the two profile faces was presented decreased its tendency to be perceived later.

Bruner and Goodman (1947) studied motivational factors by asking rich and poor children to estimate the sizes of coins. The poor children overestimated the size of every coin more than did the rich children. Although this finding may reflect the greater value of money to poor children, a simpler explanation is that the rich children had more familiarity with coins, and so were more accurate in their size estimates. Ashley, Harper, and Runyon (1951) introduced an ingenious modification to the experimental design used by Bruner and Goodman (1947). They hypnotised adult participants into believing they were rich or poor, and found that the size estimates of coins were consistently larger when the participants were in the "poor" state.

Several other studies seem to show effects of motivation and emotion on perception. However, it is important to distinguish between effects on perception and on response. For example, it is well established from work on operant conditioning by Skinner and others that reward and punishment both influence the likelihood of making any given response. Thus, it is possible that reward and punishment in the study by Schafer and Murphy (1943) affected participants' *responses* without necessarily affecting actual visual perception.

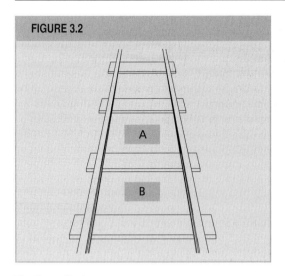

The Ponzo illusion.

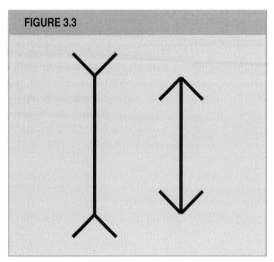

The Müller-Lyer illusion.

## Visual illusions

According to Gregory (1970, 1980), many classic visual illusions can be explained by assuming that previous knowledge derived from the perception of three-dimensional objects is applied inappropriately to the perception of two-dimensional figures. For example, people typically see a given object as having a constant size by taking account of its apparent distance (see Chapter 2). *Size constancy* means that an object is perceived as having the same size whether it is looked at from a short or a long distance away. This constancy contrasts with the size of the retinal image, which becomes progressively smaller as an object recedes into the distance. Gregory's (1970, 1980) misapplied size-constancy theory argues that this kind of perceptual processing is applied wrongly to produce several illusions.

The basic ideas in the theory can be understood with reference to the Ponzo illusion (see Figure 3.2). The long lines in the Figure look like railway lines or the edges of a road receding into the distance. Thus, the top horizontal line can be seen as further away from us than the bottom horizontal line. As rectangles A and B are the same size in the retinal image, the more distant rectangle (A) must actually be larger than the nearer one.

Misapplied size-constancy theory can also explain the Müller-Lyer illusion; see Figure 3.3). The vertical lines in the two figures are the same length. However, the vertical line on the left looks longer than the one in the figure on the right. According to Gregory (1970), the Müller-Lyer figures can be thought of as simple perspective drawings of three-dimensional objects. The left figure looks like the inside corners of a room, whereas the right figure is like the outside corners of a building. Thus, the vertical line in the left figure is in some sense further away from us than its fins, whereas the vertical line in the right figure is closer to us than its fins. Because the size of the retinal image is the same for both vertical lines, the principle of size constancy tells us that the line that is further away (i.e., the one in the left figure) must be longer. This is precisely the Müller-Lyer illusion. However, this explanation only works on the assumption that all fin tips of both figures are in the same plane, and it is not at all clear why perceivers would make this assumption (Georgeson, personal communication).

Gregory argued that figures such as the Ponzo and the Müller-Lyer are treated in many ways as three-dimensional objects. Why, then, do they seem flat and two-dimensional? According to Gregory, cues to depth are used *automatically* whether or not the figures are seen to be lying on a flat surface. As Gregory predicted, the two-dimensional Müller-Lyer figures appear three-dimensional when presented as luminous models in a darkened room.

It seems likely that the depth cues of two-dimensional drawings would be less effective than those of photographs. Supporting evidence was reported by Leibowitz et al. (1969). They found that the extent of the Ponzo illusion was significantly greater with a photograph than with a drawing.

Gregory's misapplied size-constancy theory is ingenious. However, Gregory's claim that luminous Müller-Lyer figures are seen three-dimensionally by everyone is incorrect. It is puzzling that the Müller-Lyer illusion remains when the fins on the two figures are replaced by other attachments (e.g., circles). Such evidence was interpreted by Matlin and Foley (1997) as supporting the *incorrect comparison theory*, according to which our perception of visual illusions is influenced by parts of the figure not being judged. Thus, for example, the vertical lines in the Müller-Lyer illusion may seem longer or shorter than their actual length simply because they form part of a large or small object.

Evidence in line with incorrect comparison theory was reported by Coren and Girgus (1972). The size of the Müller-Lyer illusion was greatly reduced when the fins were in a different colour from the vertical lines. Presumably this made it easier to ignore the fins.

DeLucia and Hochberg (1991) obtained convincing evidence that Gregory's theory is incomplete. They used a three-dimensional display consisting of three 2-foot high fins on the floor. It was obvious that all the fins were at the same distance from the viewer, but the typical Müller-Lyer effect was obtained. You can check this out by placing three open books in a line so that the ones on the left and the right are open to the right and the one in the middle is open to the left. The spine of the book in the middle should be the same distance from the spines of the other two books. In spite of this, the distance between the spine of the middle book and the spine of the book on the right should look longer (see Figure 3.4).

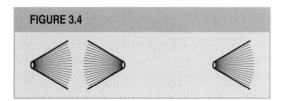

**FIGURE 3.4**

The Müller-Lyer illusion created with the use of three books.

Many visual illusions are reduced or eliminated when the participants have to take some form of appropriate action with respect to the figure. For example, Gentilucci et al. (1996) carried out a study with the Müller-Lyer illusion (see Figure 3.3). The participants were asked to point to various parts of the illusion. There were small effects of the illusion on hand movements, but these effects were much smaller than those obtained in the normal perceptual judgements. It is not clear on Gregory's theory why the Müller-Lyer illusion should be reduced in the pointing condition.

Similar findings were reported by Aglioti, Goodale, and De Souza (1995) with the Ebbinghaus illusion (see Figure 3.5). In this illusion, the central circle surrounded by smaller circles looks larger than a central circle of the same size surrounded by larger circles. Aglioti et al. (1995) constructed a three-dimensional version of this illusion, and obtained the usual illusion effect. More interestingly, when the participants reached to pick up one of the central discs, the maximum grip aperture of their reaching hand was almost entirely determined by the actual size of the disc. Thus, no illusion was apparent in the size of the hand grip. The findings remain the same, even when the participants cannot compare their hand opening with the disc as they reach for it (Haffenden & Goodale, 1998). A theoretical account of such findings is provided later in the chapter.

### Evaluation

The constructivist approach has led to the discovery of a wide range of interesting perceptual phenomena. Processes resembling those postulated by constructivist theorists probably underlie most

**FIGURE 3.5**

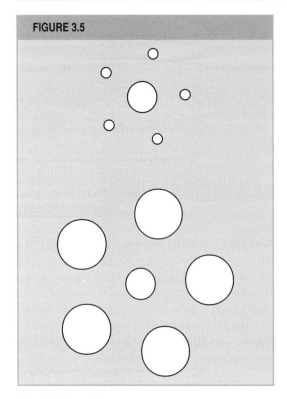

The Ebbinghaus illusion.

importance, many studies supporting the constructivist approach (e.g., Bruner et al., 1951; Palmer, 1975) involved presenting visual stimuli very briefly. Brief presentation reduces the impact of bottom-up processes, allowing more scope for top-down processes (e.g., hypotheses) to operate.

Third, it is not always clear what hypotheses would be formed by observers. Let us return to the study (Ittelson, 1951) in which someone walks backwards and forwards along the rear wall of the Ames room. Observers could interpret what they are seeing by hypothesising that the room is distorted and the person remains the same size, or by assuming that the room is normal but the person grows and shrinks. The former hypothesis strikes the authors as more plausible, but observers favour the latter.

Fourth, constructivist theorists such as Gregory have not succeeded in providing satisfactory explanations of most visual illusions. The classic visual illusions seem to depend on a range of factors, and so the search for a general theory (e.g., misapplied size constancy) is likely to prove fruitless.

## DIRECT PERCEPTION

Gibson's direct perception approach can be regarded as a bottom-up theory: he claimed there is much more information potentially available in sensory stimulation than is generally realised. However, he emphasised the role played in perception by movement of the individual within his or her environment, so his is not a bottom-up theory in the sense of an observer passively receiving sensory stimulation. Indeed, Gibson (1979) called his theory an *ecological approach* to emphasise that the primary function of perception is to facilitate interactions between individual and environment.

Some of Gibson's main theoretical assumptions are as follows:

• The pattern of light reaching the eye is an *optic array*; this structured light contains all

of these phenomena. However, many theorists disagree strongly with the constructivist viewpoint. They are unconvinced of the central assumption that perceivers resemble the great detective Sherlock Holmes as they struggle to make sense of the limited "fragmentary scraps of data" available to them. Some of the major problems for the constructivist approach will now be discussed.

First, this approach appears to predict that perception will often be in error, whereas in fact perception is typically accurate. If we are constantly using hypotheses and expectations to interpret sensory data, why is it that these hypotheses and expectations are correct nearly all the time? Presumably the environment provides much more information than the "fragmentary scraps" assumed by constructivist theorists.

Second, many of the experiments and demonstrations carried out by constructivist theorists involve artificial or unnatural stimuli. Of particular the visual information from the environment striking the eye.

- This optic array provides unambiguous or invariant information about the layout of objects in space. This information comes in many forms, including texture gradients, optic flow patterns, and affordances (all described later).
- Perception involves "picking up" the rich information provided by the optic array directly via resonance with little or no information processing involved.

Gibson was given the task in the Second World War of preparing training films describing the problems experienced by pilots taking off and landing. This led him to wonder exactly what information pilots have available to them while performing these manoeuvres. There is an *optic flow pattern* (Gibson, 1950), which can be illustrated by considering a pilot approaching the landing strip. The point towards which the pilot is moving (the *focus of expansion* or pole) appears motionless, with the rest of the visual environment apparently moving away from that point. The further away any part of the landing strip is from that point, the greater is its apparent speed of movement. Over time, aspects of the environment at some distance from the pole pass out of the visual field and are replaced by new aspects emerging at the pole. A shift in the centre of the outflow indicates there has been a change in the direction of the plane.

According to Gibson (1950), optic flow fields provide pilots with unambiguous information about their direction, speed, and altitude. Gibson was so impressed by the wealth of sensory information available to pilots in optic flow fields that he devoted himself to an analysis of the kinds of information available in sensory data under other conditions. For example, he argued that *texture gradients* provide very useful information. As we saw in Chapter 2, objects slanting away from you have a gradient (rate of change) of texture density as you look from the near edge to the far edge. Gibson (1966, 1979) claimed that observers "pick up" this information from the optic array, and so some aspects of depth are perceived directly.

The optic flow pattern and texture density illustrate some of the information that provides an observer with an unambiguous spatial layout of the environment. In more general terms, Gibson (1966, 1979) argued that certain higher-order characteristics of the visual array (invariants) remain unaltered when observers move around their environment. The fact that they remain the same over different viewing angles makes invariants of particular importance. The lack of apparent movement of the point towards which we are moving is one invariant feature of the optic array. Another invariant is useful in terms of maintaining size constancy: the ratio of an object's height to the distance between its base and the horizon is invariant regardless of its distance from the viewer. This invariant is known as the horizon ratio relation. Other invariants are discussed later.

## Meaning: Affordances

How can the Gibsonian approach handle the problem of meaning? Gibson (1979) claimed that all the potential uses of objects (their *affordances*) are directly perceivable. For example, a ladder "affords" ascent or descent, and a chair "affords" sitting. The notion of affordances was even applied (implausibly) to postboxes (Gibson, 1979, p. 139): "The postbox . . . affords letter-mailing to a letter-writing human in a community with a postal system. This fact is perceived when the postbox is identified as such." Most objects give rise to more than one affordance, with the particular affordance that influences behaviour depending on the perceiver's current psychological state. Thus, a hungry person will perceive the affordance of edibility when presented with an orange and so eat it, whereas an angry person may detect the affordance of a projectile and throw the orange at someone.

Gibson assumed that most perceptual learning has occurred during the history of mankind, and so does not need to occur during the individual's lifetime. However, we have to learn which affordances will satisfy particular goals, and we need to learn to attend to the appropriate aspects of the visual environment. According to Gibson's theory (Gordon, 1989, p. 161), "The most important contribution of learning to perception is to educate attention."

The notion of affordances forms part of Gibson's attempt to show that all the information needed to make sense of the visual environment is directly present in the visual input, and it illustrates the close relationship between perception and action. If he had not proposed the notion of affordances, or something very similar, then Gibson would have been forced to admit that the meaning of objects is stored in long-term memory.

## Resonance

How exactly do human perceivers manage to "pick up" the invariant information supplied by the visual world? According to Gibson, there is a process of *resonance*, which he explained by analogy to the workings of a radio. When a radio set is turned on, there may be only a hissing sound. However, if it is tuned properly, speech or music will be clearly audible. In Gibson's terms, the radio is now resonating with the information contained in the electromagnetic radiation.

This analogy suggests that perceivers can pick up information from the environment in a relatively automatic way if they are attuned to it. The radio operates in a holistic way, in the sense that damage to any part of its circuitry would prevent it working. In a similar way, Gibson assumed that the nervous system works in a holistic way when perceiving.

## Evaluation

The ecological approach to perception has proved successful in some ways. First, Gibson's views have had a major impact at the philosophical level. According to Gibson (1979, p. 8):

> The words "animal" and "environment" make an inseparable pair. Each term implies the other. No animal could exist without an environment surrounding it. Equally, though not so obvious, an environment implies an animal (or at least an organism) to be surrounded.

As Gordon (1989, p. 176) expressed it:

> Direct perceptionists can be said to have restored the environment to its central place in the study of perception . . . organisms did not evolve in a world of simple isolated stimuli.

Second, Gibson was right that visual stimuli provide much more information than had previously been thought to be the case. Traditional laboratory research had generally involved static observers looking at impoverished visual displays, often with chin rests being used to prevent head movements. Not surprisingly, such research had failed to reveal the richness of the information available in the everyday environment. In contrast, Gibson correctly emphasised that we spend much of our time in motion, and that the consequent moment-by-moment changes in the optic array provide much useful information (see later in the chapter).

Third, Gibson was correct in arguing that inaccurate perception often depends on the use of very artificial situations. However, the notion that visual illusions are merely unusual trick figures dreamed up by psychologists to baffle ordinary decent folk does not apply to all of them. Some visual illusions produce effects similar to those found in normal perception. Consider, for example, the vertical–horizontal illusion shown in Figure 3.6. The two lines are actually the same length, but

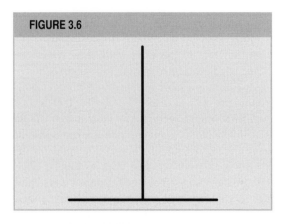

**FIGURE 3.6**

The vertical–horizontal illusion.

the vertical line appears longer than the horizontal one. This tendency to overestimate vertical extents relative to horizontal ones can readily be shown with real objects by taking a teacup, saucer, and two similar spoons. Place one spoon horizontally in the saucer and the other spoon vertically in the cup, and you should find that the vertical spoon looks much longer.

Fourth, the numerous laboratory studies apparently providing support for constructivist theories do not necessarily cast doubts on Gibson's direct theory. As Cutting (1986, p. 238) pointed out:

> Given that most visual stimuli in experiments are pictures (virtual rather than real objects) and that Gibson stated that picture perception is indirect, most psychological experiments have never been relevant to the direct/indirect distinction as he construed it.

On the negative side, Gibson's direct theory of perception has attracted many criticisms. First, the processes involved in identifying invariants in the environment, in discovering affordances, in "resonance", and so on, are much more complicated than was implied by Gibson. In the words of Marr (1982, p. 30), the major shortcoming of Gibson's analysis:

> results from a failure to realise two things. First, the detection of physical invariants, like image surfaces, is exactly and precisely an information-processing problem, in modern terminology. And second, he vastly under-rated the sheer difficulty of such detection.

Second, Gibson's theoretical approach applies much more to some aspects of perception than to others. The distinction between "seeing" and "seeing as" is useful in addressing this issue (Bruce et al., 1996). According to Fodor and Pylyshyn (1981, p. 189):

> What you see when you see a thing depends upon what the thing you see is. But what you see the thing as depends upon what you know about what you are seeing.

This sounds like mumbo jumbo. However, Fodor and Pylyshyn illustrated the point by considering someone called Smith who is lost at sea. Smith sees the Pole Star, but what matters for his survival is whether he sees it as the Pole Star or as simply an ordinary star. If it is the former, then this will be useful for navigational purposes; if it is the latter, then he remains as lost as ever. Gibson's approach is relevant to "seeing", but has little to say about "seeing as".

Third, Gibson's argument that there is no need to postulate internal representations (e.g., memories; $2\frac{1}{2}$-D sketches) to understand perception is flawed. Bruce et al. (1996) cited the work of Menzel (1978) as an example of the problems flowing from Gibson's argument. Chimpanzees were carried around a field, and shown the locations of 20 pieces of food buried in the ground. When each chimpanzee was released, it moved around the field efficiently picking up the pieces of food. As there was no information in the light reaching the chimpanzees to guide their search, they must have made use of memorial representations of the locations of the pieces of food.

| Gibson's direct theory of perception | |
|---|---|
| *Strengths* | *Weaknesses* |
| • Important at a philosophical level. Equal emphasis on organism and environment. | • Processes involved in perception are more complicated than Gibson implied. |
| • Gibson showed that visual stimuli provide more information than was previously thought. | • Theoretical approach does not apply as effectively to all aspects of perception. |
| • Artificial studies by constructivists do not necessarily invalidate Gibson's theory. | • Studies have found that perception involves memory and internal representations. |

## THEORETICAL INTEGRATION

One of the differences between constructivist theories and Gibson's approach is that top-down processes in perception are emphasised by constructivist theorists, whereas Gibson argued that bottom-up processes are of paramount importance. In fact, the relative importance of top-down and bottom-up processes depends on various factors. Visual perception may be largely determined by bottom-up processes when the viewing conditions are good, but involves top-down processes as the viewing conditions deteriorate because of very brief presentation times or lack of stimulus clarity. In line with this analysis, Gibson focused on visual perception under optimal viewing conditions, whereas constructivist theorists often use sub-optimal viewing conditions.

### Indirect vs. direct theories

We will now broaden out our discussion to consider the fundamental distinction between indirect and direct theories of perception. Most of the approaches to perception discussed in this book (e.g., the constructivist approach; the theories of Marr and Biederman) are indirect theories, whereas Gibson put forward a direct theory. What are the key differences between indirect and direct theories? According to Bruce et al. (1996), the following differences are central:

- Indirect theorists argue that perception involves the formation of an internal representation, whereas Gibson argued that this is not necessary.
- Indirect theorists assume that memory in the form of stored knowledge of the world is of central importance to perception, but Gibson denied this.
- Most indirect theorists argue that we need to understand the *interrelationships* of perceptual processing at different levels. In contrast, Gibson argued there are separate ecological and physiological levels of explanation, and he focused almost exclusively on the ecological level.

Why isn't the role of hypotheses and expectations included as one of the key differences between indirect and direct theories? After all, that is an important difference between the constructivist and Gibsonian approaches. The reason is that many indirect theorists (e.g., Marr; Biederman) have assumed that hypotheses and expectations play only a minor role in visual perception, even though they assume that stored knowledge is of crucial importance.

The indirect approach is more generally applicable to most human visual perception. According to Bruce et al. (1996, p. 374), "Perception of other people, familiar objects, and almost everything we perceive . . . requires additional kinds of representation of the perceived object." Gibson's assumption that stored knowledge is not involved in visual perception is highly dubious, and would invalidate nearly all the research discussed in Chapter 4! An illustration of the problems associated with Gibson's assumption was provided by Bruce et al. (1996, p. 377): "We find it unconvincing to explain a person returning after 10 years to their grandparents' home and seeing that a tree has been cut down as having detected directly an event specified by a transformation in the optic array."

### Reconciliation

The indirect and direct theories are very different, because the theorists concerned have been pursuing very different goals. This can be seen if we consider the distinction between perception for recognition and perception for action (Milner & Goodale, 1995, 1998; discussed more fully later in the chapter). Evidence from cognitive neuroscience and from cognitive neuropsychology has supported the distinction. This evidence has suggested that there is a ventral stream of processing more involved in perception for recognition and a dorsal stream more involved in perception for action (see later in this chapter), although perception for whatever purpose is typically based on both streams of processing. Most perception theorists (including Gregory, Marr, and Biederman) have focused on perception for recognition, whereas Gibson emphasised perception for action.

| A simplified account of Milner and Goodale's theoretical view based on dorsal and ventral streams of visual processing | |
|---|---|
| *Behaviourist approach* | *Reconstructive approach* |
| • Visually guided actions are central.<br>• Governed by the dorsal stream.<br>• Perception for action. | • Internal representations are central.<br>• Governed by the ventral stream.<br>• Perception for recognition. |
| • There is substantial communication and co-operation between the two systems. | |

There have been several demonstrations of the partial separateness of these two visual systems. For example, as we saw earlier, visual illusions clearly present when the task involves the perception-for-recognition (or ventral) system are much reduced when the task involves the perception-for-action (or dorsal) system (e.g., Aglioti et al., 1995; Gentilucci et al., 1996).

Goodale and Humphrey (1998, pp. 201–202) provided a detailed account of the relevance of the distinction between dorsal and ventral steams of visual processing to major theoretical positions:

The preoccupation with visually guided actions that characterises behaviourist approaches to vision [and Gibson's approach] has meant that most of the visual mechanisms that are being studied are those found in the dorsal stream. In contrast, the reconstructive approach (e.g., Marr, 1982) . . . is a "passive" approach in which the representation is central and the external behaviour of the external world is largely ignored. Reconstruction of the external world is exactly the kind of activity which we believe is carried out by the ventral stream.

Where does that leave the relationship between these major approaches? According to Goodale and Humphrey (1998, p. 181), "Marrian or 'reconstructive' approaches and Gibsonian or 'purposive-animate-behaviourist' approaches need not be seen as mutually exclusive, but rather as complementary in their emphasis on different aspects of visual function."

There are two important final points. First, the fact that there are two separate processing systems does *not* mean that they always function independently of each other. In fact, the two systems are interconnected and there is generally extensive communication and cooperation between them. Second, the descriptions by Milner and Goodale (1995, 1998, see later in this chapter) of the processing occurring within the dorsal and ventral streams are oversimplified, and will be subject to revision.

## MOTION, PERCEPTION, AND ACTION

Most research on visual perception used to involve a motionless observer viewing one or more static objects. Such research lacked *ecological validity* or relevance to our everyday experiences. We reach for objects, and we walk, run, or drive through the environment. At other times, we are stationary, but other living creatures or objects in the environment are in movement relative to us. The brain systems involved in motion perception are discussed in Chapter 2.

Gibson's theorising increased interest in issues such as visually guided action and the perception of movement. In the words of Greeno (1994, p. 341), Gibson believed that, "perception is a system that picks up information that supports coordination of the agent's actions with the systems that the environment provides."

We will start with the role of eye movements in visual perception. We are generally very efficient at deciding whether changes in the retinal image reflect movements made by ourselves or objects in the environment, or whether they simply reflect eye movements. After that, we consider the visual processes involved in facilitating human movement or action. Finally, we consider how we perceive object motion. Related issues sometimes arise in these last two areas. For example, the processes involved in perceiving how long it will be before we collide with an object in front of us may be rather similar whether we are moving at 30 mph (48 kilometres an hour) towards it, or it is moving at the same speed towards us.

The central issue is whether Gibson (1979) was correct in assuming that we interact directly with the environment, making use of invariant information. Directly available information (e.g., about optic flow patterns) is used in some of our interactions with the environment, but it remains controversial whether this is generally the case.

## Eye movements

Our eyes move about three or four times a second, and these eye movements generally produce substantial effects on the retinal image. In spite of that, we normally perceive the environment as stable and unmoving. There are several ways in which our visual systems could achieve this stability. One possibility is that the visual system monitors actual changes in the extra-ocular muscles controlling eye movements, and then uses that information to interpret changes in the retinal image. However, it would be important for information about eye-muscle movements to be used *before* the retinal image changed (or at the same time), because otherwise the altered retinal image might be misinterpreted.

The second possibility was favoured by Helmholtz (1866). He proposed an outflow theory, in which image movement is interpreted by using information about intended movement sent to the eye muscles. The fact that the visual world appears to move when the side of the eyeball is pressed supports this theory. There is movement within the retinal image unaccompanied by commands to the eye muscles, and so it is perceived as genuine. Sekuler and Blake (1994, p. 267) spelled out some of the details: "Perceived direction [of an object] develops from a comparison between two quantities, the command signals to the extraocular [outside the eye] muscles and the

accompanying retinal image motion. To derive perceived direction, simply subtract the retinal image motion from the command signal." As predicted, when the eyeball is pressed in one direction, the visual environment seems to move in the opposite direction.

One way of testing outflow theory is to study the effects of immobilising the eyes by means of a paralysing drug. According to the theory, the visual world should appear to move in the opposite direction when participants given such a drug try unsuccessfully to produce eye movements. This prediction has been supported (e.g., Matin et al., 1982). However, Stevens et al. (1976) obtained a slightly different effect. Their participant (John Stevens) reported that attempted eye movements following muscle paralysis produced a kind of relocation of the visual world but without movement.

Evidence for Helmholtz's theory was reported by Duhamel, Colby, and Goldberg (1992). They found that the parietal cortex in the monkey brain is of major importance to an understanding of how the visual system handles eye movements. Duhamel et al. (1992, p. 91) concluded as follows: "At the time a saccade [rapid, jerky eye movement] is planned, the parietal representation of the visual world undergoes a shift analogous to the shift of the image on the retina." Thus, visual processing in the parietal cortex anticipates the next eye movement in the period between its planning and execution.

In spite of the successes of outflow theory, it cannot be the whole story. As Tresilian (1994b, p. 336) remarked, outflow theory "predicts that if the eyes are stationary in the head, as the head rotates, the resulting image motion will be interpreted as motion of the environment, yet everyone knows that this does not happen." What probably happens is that we do not rely exclusively on information about intended eye movements in order to perceive a stable environment. Movement of the entire retinal image is probably attributed to movement of the head or eye, whereas movement of part of the retinal image is interpreted as movement of an external object. In addition, information about head movements is used in the same way as eye-movement information to permit us to see the environment as stable. The parietal lobe seems to be the site at which information about eye movements and head movements is integrated (see Andersen et al., 1997, for a review).

## VISUALLY GUIDED ACTION

From an ecological perspective, it is of central importance to focus on how we move around the environment. If we are to avoid premature death, we have to ensure we are not hit by cars when crossing the road; we must avoid falling over the edges of cliffs; and when driving we must avoid hitting cars coming the other way. Visual perception plays a major role in facilitating human locomotion and ensuring our safety. Some of the main processes involved are discussed in this section of the chapter.

### Heading: Optic flow patterns

When we want to reach some goal (e.g., a gate at the end of a field), we need to control our heading, or point towards which we are moving. Gibson (1950) emphasised the importance of *optic flow patterns*. When someone is moving forwards, the point towards which he or she is looking (the *focus of expansion*) appears motionless. In contrast, the visual field around that point seems to be expanding. Graziano, Andersen, and Snowden (1994) identified neurons in the medial superior temporal area that responded most to patterns of dots expanding outwards, and these neurons may provide the physiological basis for the perception of optic flow patterns.

As optic flow provides relatively precise information about the direction in which someone is heading, it follows from Gibson's (1950) theoretical position that heading judgements should be fairly accurate. In fact, heading errors of between 5° and 10° were reported in most early research (e.g., Warren, 1976). With that low level of accuracy, it is doubtful whether optic flow could provide adequate information for the control of locomotion.

Warren, Morris, and Kalish (1988) argued that there were some limitations with previous research. Heading judgements were generally obtained by requiring the participants to point, and this may be an insensitive measure. Accordingly, Warren et al. used a rather different task. They produced films consisting of moving dots, with each film simulating the optic flow pattern that would be produced if someone were moving in a given direction. The participants' task was to decide whether the person seemed to be heading to the left or to the right of a stationary target positioned at the horizon of the display. The mean error with this measure of heading accuracy averaged was about 1.2°. As Warren et al. (1988, p. 659) concluded, "optical flow can provide an adequate basis for the control of locomotion and other visually guided behaviour."

*Theoretical accounts*

Various aspects of optic flow might be of crucial importance to the perception of heading. Gibson (1950) proposed a global radial outflow hypothesis, according to which it is the overall or global outflow pattern that specifies the direction of heading. Alternatively, there is the local focus of outflow hypothesis (discussed by Warren et al., 1988), according to which the direction of heading is determined by locating the one element in the flow field that is stationary (the focus of expansion).

The focus of expansion is of most value when the individual in motion is looking directly at where he or she is going. However, car drivers often look at the line in the centre of the road or at the kerb instead. According to Lee (1980), drivers are more likely to use general optic flow information than the focus of expansion. When the driver is on course, the optic flow lines and the edges of the road will coincide. If the two do not match, then the driver is in danger of leaving the road.

Evidence against the local focus of outflow hypothesis was provided by Warren et al. (1988). They found that heading judgements were very accurate even when there was no stationary element in the visual environment.

## Evaluation

Optic flow patterns generally and the focus of expansion specifically may contribute towards our ability to head in the right direction. However, Gibson's approach does not take account of the fact that movement on the retina is determined by eye and head movements as well as by the optic flow pattern. As a result, the focus of expansion on the retina does not correspond with the point towards which someone is heading when eye movements lead the individual to be looking in a slightly different direction (Loppe & Rauscheck, 1994).

Cutting, Springer, Braren, and Johnson (1992) adopted a different approach. They assumed that eye movements are useful in the control of heading, whereas Gibsonian approaches have regarded eye movements as an unwanted nuisance. Eye movements that track an object provide valuable information, because objects closer to the observer than the fixated object appear to move faster in the visual field and in the opposite direction to objects further away. This so-called *differential motion parallax* applies to all objects except those directly in line with the point at which the individual is heading. Cutting et al. (1992) hypothesised that eye movements are controlled by differential motion parallax, and this helps to ensure the accuracy of heading behaviour.

The evidence for this hypothesis is mixed. In support, Cutting et al. (1992) found that their participants exhibited worse judgements of direction of heading when the information provided by differential motion parallax was misleading. However, Warren and Hannon (1988) found that eye movements are not necessary in order to judge heading direction accurately. Cutting et al. (1992) admitted that differential motion parallax is not valuable for car drivers or pilots, and that instead the optic flow pattern may be used.

## Time to contact

There are numerous situations in which we want to know when we are going to reach some object (e.g., the car immediately in front of us). We could make these calculations by estimating the initial distance away of the object (e.g., car; ball), estimating our speed, and then combining these two estimates into an overall estimate of the time to contact by dividing distance by speed. However, there are two possible sources of error in such calculations, and it is fairly complex to combine the two kinds of information.

Lee (1980) argued that it is not necessary to perceive either the distance or speed of an object we are approaching to work out the time to contact, provided we are approaching it with constant velocity. Time to contact can be calculated using only a single variable, namely the rate of expansion of the object's retinal image: the faster the image is expanding, the less time there is to contact. Lee used this notion to propose a measure of time to contact called T or tau, and which is defined as the inverse of the rate of expansion of the retinal image of the object: T = 1/(rate of expansion of object's retinal image). This theory is in general agreement with Gibson's approach, because it is assumed that information about time to contact is directly available.

According to Lee, information about tau is used when an object is approaching us as well as when we are approaching an object. It is also used in various sports when we need to be prepared to catch or hit an approaching ball, when long-jumpers approach the take-off board, and so on. For the present, we are concerned with time to contact when a person is moving towards an object. Later in the chapter, we will turn to the issue of time to contact when it is the object that is in movement.

Cavallo and Laurent (1988) tested Lee's (1976) theory in a study in which experienced drivers and beginners indicated when they expected a collision with a stationary obstacle to occur. Cavallo and Laurent manipulated how easy it was to assess speed by comparing normal and restricted visual fields, and they manipulated ease of distance assessment by comparing binocular and monocular vision. Their findings did *not* indicate that the rate of expansion of the obstacle's retinal image was the major determinant of time-to-contact judgements. Accuracy of time-to-contact estimation was greater when speed and distance were relatively easy to assess. The beginners made use of both speed and distance information in their estimates, whereas experienced drivers made more use of distance than of speed information.

Research on US Air Force pilots by Kruk and Regan (1983) may be relevant to Lee's (1976) theory. They assessed the pilots' sensitivity to change in the size of a square which changed size in an unpredictable way. As calculation of tau involves making use of information about size expansion, sensitivity to size changes is an indirect measure of sensitivity to tau. Kruk and Regan also assessed the pilots' ability to land a plane smoothly using a cockpit simulator. The pilots who produced the smoothest landings had the greatest sensitivity to size changes. It is thus possible that individual differences in pilots' landing abilities reflect their sensitivity to tau.

## Walking and running

Walking and running seem like very simple and automatic activities requiring only limited visual information. In fact, a considerable amount of visual monitoring of the environment is often needed. Anyone who has walked over rough ground at night under poor lighting conditions will probably remember that it can be a hard and uncomfortable experience.

Hollands et al. (1995) studied the eye movements of walkers walking on irregularly positioned stepping stones. The typical pattern was that there was an eye movement towards the next landing place of each leg before it was lifted into the air. Thus, the participants seemed to plan the complete movement of each leg before starting to move it.

Some of the processes involved in running were studied by Lee, Lishman, and Thomson (1982). They took films of female long-jumpers during their run-up. Jumps are disqualified if the long-jumper oversteps the take-off board, so precise positioning of the feet is important. Most coaches and athletes used to assume that expert long-jumpers develop a stereotyped stride pattern that is repeated on each run-up, and which relies very little on visual information. In contrast, Lee et al. (1982, p. 456) argued there are two major processes involved: (1) control consists "in regulating just one kinetic [relating to motion] parameter,

the vertical impulse of the step—keeping it constant during the approach phase and then adjusting it to regulate flight time in order to strike the board"; and (2) tau is used late in the run-up, because time-to-arrival at the board "is specified directly by a single optical parameter, the inverse of the rate of dilation of the image of the board."

Lee et al. (1982) obtained evidence in favour of their theoretical position. The athletes showed reasonable consistency in their stride patterns during most of the run-up, but there was a marked increase in the variability of stride lengths over the last three strides. This seemed to be due to alterations in the leap or vertical thrust of the take-off, which affected the flight length for each leg. This allowed the athletes' last stride to land appropriately with respect to the take-off board. According to Lee et al., these adjustments are visually guided by tau and they concluded that most of a long-jumper's run-up is determined by internal processes, with visual processes assuming great importance only in the last few strides.

In subsequent research, Warren, Young, and Lee (1986) trained athletes to place their feet on irregularly spaced targets while running on a treadmill. They confirmed the importance of varying flight length as a strategy for placing the feet in the desired place.

Berg, Wade, and Greer (1994) pointed out that Lee et al. (1982) had used only three jumpers, and had tested them under non-competitive conditions. However, Berg et al.'s findings with expert long-jumpers under competitive conditions were comparable to those of Lee et al. (1982). They also found that novice long-jumpers had similar run-up patterns, suggesting that using tau to regulate stride pattern occurs naturally.

## Car driving

Car driving is a skill that is not normally acquired until at least the late teens. In addition, it involves making decisions about steering, braking, and so on while the driver is moving at speed. These considerations suggest that drivers need to develop special strategies for using visual information. In the specific case of braking, it might be imagined that drivers would be influenced by the speed of their car, the speed of the car in front, and the distance between the two cars. However, Lee (1976) argued that decisions about decelerating or braking are based on the rate of angular expansion of either the car in front or its rear lights. He reported evidence consistent with this hypothesis, but did not show that other factors are not involved. Stewart, Cudworth, and Lishman (1993) argued that the driver's speed and the apparent distance of an obstacle also influenced braking behaviour.

Land and Lee (1994) recorded information about drivers' direction of gaze and the angle of the steering wheel as they approached and drove through bends. Immediately before they turned the steering wheel, drivers fixated on the inside edge (tangent point) of the approaching bend even though they were unaware of doing so. Why do they do this? According to Land and Lee, drivers may use the visual angle between the tangent point and the direction of heading to decide how much to turn the steering wheel.

*Evaluation*

The notion that we can estimate time to contact accurately on the basis of fairly simple information related to the rate of expansion of the retinal image is appealing. It is of theoretical interest because tau appears to be a good example of the kind of high-level invariant emphasised by Gibson. At the empirical level, research carried out in several situations has provided support for Lee's (1976) theoretical position.

However, there are various problems with the tau-based approach. First, as Cumming (1994, p. 355) pointed out, "It is very difficult to determine experimentally whether human subjects use tau to estimate time-to-contact directly. Furthermore, none of the experiments . . . excludes the possibility that other strategies are used for timing the actions studied."

Second, there has been a failure to consider alternative factors that might influence time-to-contact judgements. As Wann (1996, p. 1040) pointed out, "Recent trends in perceptual research have tended to ignore depth cues as reliable information for the control of action." In the specific

case of car drivers, they may use information about their own speed and about the distance between them and the car in front to work out time to contact.

Third, tau provides information about the time to contact or reach the eyes of the observer. In many situations (e.g., driving a car), this information is insufficient. For example, a driver who used tau to brake in order to avoid an obstacle might find that the front of his or her car has been smashed in (Cumming, 1994)!

Fourth, it is only a starting point to argue that tau is calculated in order to establish time to contact. What remains to be discovered are the precise processes involved in its calculation.

## Running to catch

In the previous section, we considered how people move through a stationary visual environment. More complex issues are raised when the crucial part of the visual environment is also moving. The example we will consider is that of a fielder at rounders, cricket, or baseball who has to run several metres at high speed to catch a ball. This ability is more surprising than you might imagine. The fielder only has information about the trajectory or flight path of the ball as seen from his or her perspective (this is the *optical trajectory*), and that trajectory is influenced by various factors such as wind resistance.

At a general level, Oudejans et al. (1996) found that fielders obtain very valuable information as they run towards the ball. They used a machine that shot tennis balls from behind a screen. The participants were only allowed to see the ball moving for one second, during which they either ran towards the ball or remained stationary. Those who ran towards the ball perceived the catchability of the ball much more accurately than did the stationary participants.

What information is used by fielders in motion towards a ball? McLeod and Dienes (1996) filmed expert fielders as they ran forwards or backwards to catch balls projected from a machine. They found that the fielders "ran at a speed that kept the acceleration of the tangent of the angle of elevation to the ball at 0" (McLeod & Dienes,

1996, p. 531). The tangent of the angle of elevation corresponds to the ratio of the height of the ball above ground to the horizontal distance of the fielder from it. Running so as to keep the rate of change of the tangent constant involves shortening one's horizontal distance from the ball in proportion to the rate at which it is dropping out of the sky, so as to intercept it at ground level. Use of this measure does not allow fielders to know in advance where or when the ball will land, but ensures that they arrive at the right place at the right time.

The McLeod–Dienes approach *only* relates to balls moving in the direction of the fielder, and does not cover the more common cases in which the ball is struck to the left or the right of the fielder. There are also other limitations and problems. As McLeod and Dienes (1996, p. 542) drily remarked:

> Our data do not indicate how the computational problem of keeping $d^2$ (tan alpha) $dt^2$ at zero is solved. Scepticism about the conclusion might stem from the feeling that $d^2$ (tan alpha)/$dt^2$ does not seem a particularly likely quantity for the nervous system to represent.

McBeath, Shaffer, and Kaiser (1995) produced a more general solution to the problem of how fielders catch balls. According to them, fielders run along a curved path designed to keep the optical trajectory (flight path as perceived by an observer) as straight as possible. Fielders following this strategy would arrive at the right place just in time to catch the ball, but would not know ahead of time where the ball would drop. Fielders using this strategy do not allow the ball to curve optically towards the ground, and they achieve this by continuously moving more directly under the ball.

McBeath et al. (1995) obtained support for their theory from two students who used shoulder-mounted cameras, and who were filmed trying to catch balls. According to McBeath et al.'s analysis, fielders should generally catch balls on the run rather than arriving in the catching area ahead of time. Less information about curvature of flight

is available to fielders when the ball is coming straight at them, and thus it should paradoxically be harder to catch the ball in such circumstances. Both of these predictions were confirmed.

## Evaluation

The theoretical approaches of McLeod and Dienes (1996) and of McBeath et al. (1995) have definite strengths. They show that fielders can make use of some invariant feature of the information potentially available to them to run into the optimal position to catch a ball. However, there are some unresolved issues. First, the research evidence is consistent with the theoretical approaches, but strong support is lacking. For example, it would be valuable to show that experimental manipulations of the key theoretical variables in artificial situations led fielders to make systematic errors. Second, the internal processes allowing individuals to calculate the measures allegedly involved remain unspecified. It is likely to prove difficult to show how anyone manages to calculate $d^2$ (tan alpha)/$dt^2$ in the stressful circumstances of a competitive cricket match or baseball game. Third, more research is needed to resolve the differences between the two theoretical approaches we have discussed.

## What and where systems

Several theorists (e.g. Mishkin & Ungerleider, 1982) have argued that vision is used for two crucial functions (refer back to Figure 2.13). First, there is object perception (*what* is it?). Second, there is spatial perception (*where* is it?). There is good evidence (at least in macaque monkeys) that rather different brain systems underlie each of these functions:

1. There is a ventral pathway running from the primary visual area in the cortex to the inferior temporal cortex; this pathway is specialised for object perception (i.e., what is it?).
2. There is a dorsal pathway running from the primary visual area in the cortex to the posterior parietal cortex; this pathway is specialised for spatial perception (i.e., where is it?).

Some of the original research in this area was reported by Mishkin and Ungerleider (1982). They used a situation in which there were two food wells, each of which was covered by a lid. There was food in one of the wells, and monkeys were allowed to lift one lid in order to find it. Food was either associated with a specific lid pattern (object information) or with whichever food well was closer to a small model tower (spatial information). Monkeys whose inferior temporal lobes were removed had problems in using object information but not spatial information. In contrast, monkeys whose parietal lobes were removed experienced difficulty in using spatial information but not object information.

Neuroimaging evidence was reported by Haxby et al. (1994). They used two tasks with normal participants. There was an object-recognition task that involved deciding which of two faces matched a target face. There was also a spatial task that involved deciding which of two figures consisting of a dot and two lines was a rotated version of the target figure. PET data indicated that the occipital region of the cortex was activated as participants performed both tasks. However, the pattern of activation differed elsewhere in the cortex. The object-recognition task produced heightened activation in the inferior and medial temporal cortex, whereas the spatial task led to increased activation in the parietal cortex. These patterns of activation are as predicted by the theory.

Milner and Goodale (1995, 1998) have developed and extended these theoretical ideas in several ways. They drew a distinction between vision for perception and vision for action (see earlier in the chapter). Both these systems use object and spatial information. However, they do so in different ways, with different representations being used for recognition and for visually guided action. According to Milner and Goodale, the dorsal pathway may be of greatest value in providing an answer to the question "How do I interact with that object?". That contrasts with Mishkin and Ungerleider (1982), who claimed that the dorsal pathway provides information to answer the question "Where is that object?".

Some of the most convincing evidence for the notion of separate visual systems for perception and for action has come from the study of brain-damaged patients. It was predicted that there would be a double dissociation: some patients would have reasonably intact vision for perception but severely impaired vision for action, and others would show the opposite pattern.

Half of the double dissociation consists of patients with *optic ataxia*. According to Georgopoulos (1997, p. 142), such patients "do not usually have impaired vision or impaired hand or arm movements, but show a severe impairment in visually guided reaching in the absence of perceptual disturbance in estimating distance." For example, consider a study by Perenin and Vighetto (1988). Patients with optic ataxia experienced great difficulty in rotating their hands appropriately when given the task of reaching towards and into a large oriented slot in front of them.

Which parts of the brain are damaged in optic ataxia? The answer varies from patient to patient. However, "The brain damage in cases of optic ataxia has been localised in the parietal cortex . . . , its underlying white matter and/or the posterior part of the corpus callosum" (Georgopoulos, 1997, p. 142).

The other half of the double dissociation consists of some patients with *visual agnosia* (see Chapter 4). This is a condition in which there are severe problems with object recognition. DF is the most studied patient having visual agnosia coupled with fairly good spatial perception. In spite of having reasonable visual acuity, DF was unable to identify any of a series of a selection of drawings of common objects. However, as was pointed out by Milner, Carey, and Harvey (1991), DF "had little difficulty in everyday activity such as opening doors, shaking hands, walking around furniture, and eating meals . . . she could accurately reach out and grasp a pencil orientated at different angles."

In a study by Goodale and Milner (1992), DF held a card in her hand, and looked at a circular block into which a slot had been cut. When she was asked to orient the card so that it would fit into the slot, she was unable to do so, suggesting that she has very poor perceptual skills. However, DF performed well when she was asked to move her hand forward and inset the card into the slot.

Carey, Harvey, and Milner (1996) obtained additional evidence of DF's ability to use visual information to guide her actions. She was given the task of picking up rectangular shapes differing in width and orientation. She was able to do this as well as normal individuals. However, DF did not show normal grasping behaviour when trying to pick up more complex objects (e.g., crosses) in which two different orientations are present together.

Which areas of the visual cortex are intact and damaged in DF? MRI indicated that most of the primary visual cortex is still intact. According to Milner and Goodale (1998, p. 8), it is reasonable to assume that, "the ventral stream is severely damaged and/or disconnected in DF (an assumption that is quite consistent with her pattern of brain damage)."

*Evaluation*

There are three exciting theoretical implications of research in this area. First, as Milner and Goodale (1998, p. 2) pointed out, "Standard accounts of vision implicitly assume that the purpose of the visual system is to construct some sort of internal model of the world outside." Thus, it is common to focus on vision for perception and to de-emphasise vision for action.

Second, Milner and Goodale (1998) argued that many visual illusions (e.g., geometric illusions) occur because of the processing of the visual input by the ventral system. According to Milner and Goodale (1998, p. 10), "the dorsal system, by and large, is not deceived by such optical illusions." Thus, it is predicted that the dorsal pathway or "where" system allows us to make accurate eye and hand movements with respect to illusory figures that we misperceive. For example, Wong and Mack (1981) re-presented a target stimulus after a 500-millisecond interval in the same location as before. The surrounding frame had been moved, so that the participants had the illusion that the target's position had changed. However, their eye movements were directed accurately to the actual position of the target. Similar findings have been obtained with other visual illusions. Gentilucci et al. (1996) obtained similar findings

with the Müller-Lyer illusion (see Figure 3.3). The participants were asked to point to various parts of the illusion. There were small effects of the illusion on hand movements, but these effects were much smaller than those obtained in perceptual judgements of the Müller-Lyer illusion (see earlier in the chapter).

Third, as Milner and Goodale (1995, 1998) implied, it is likely that vision for action makes use of rather different information than does vision for perception. Vision for action (based on the dorsal pathway) uses short-lasting, viewpoint-dependent representations, that is, the representations are influenced by the angle of viewing. In contrast, vision for perception (based on the ventral pathway) may use long-lasting, viewpoint-independent representations, that is, the representations rely on stored knowledge and are not influenced by the angle of viewing (see Chapter 4). According to Milner and Goodale (1998, p. 12), the dorsal system

> is designed to guide actions purely in the here and now, and its products are consequently useless for later reference . . . it is only through knowledge gained via the ventral stream that we can exercise insight, hindsight and foresight about the visual world.

What about future research? The theoretical approach so far has focused on the differences and separateness of the dorsal and ventral streams. Accordingly, "One of the important questions that remains to be answered is how the two streams interact both with each other and with other brain regions in the production of purposive behaviour" (Milner & Goodale, 1998, p. 12).

## PERCEPTION OF OBJECT MOTION

Perception of object motion is important for various reasons. It allows us to avoid colliding with moving objects. However, it also facilitates detection of small or camouflaged objects, and it can also permit us to identify an object's three-dimensional shape (known as the *kinetic depth effect*). A simple example of the kinetic depth effect was provided by Wallach and O'Connell (1953). A wire hanger is twisted into a random three-dimensional shape, and a light shining on it produces a shadow on a piece of paper. If the wire hanger is motionless, it is impossible to work out the three-dimensional shape of the wire hanger from the shadow. However, if the hanger rotates, its three-dimensional shape is readily perceived.

Several studies of the kinetic depth effect have used random-dot surfaces taken from three-dimensional objects. Three-dimensional structures can be perceived accurately even when only two different random-dot surfaces taken from the same object are presented alternately (see Todd & Norman, 1991). This is an impressive achievement, especially as computational analyses have suggested that a minimum of three distinct views should be required to identify an object's three-dimensional structure (e.g., Huang & Lee, 1989).

The focus in the first part of this section is on the perception of objects' motion. Two issues will be addressed. The first one is how we decide when an object moving in our direction will reach us. The second issue is how we are able to perceive biological movement even when only provided with impoverished information.

In the second part of this section, we consider two illusory phenomena related to object motion. The first phenomenon is *apparent movement*, and occurs when movement is perceived even though the observer is presented with a series of static images. Apparent movement is seen every time you see a film. The second phenomenon is known as *perceived causality*. Suppose, for example, you see one square move and collide with a second square, which then starts to move away. Most people report that it looks as if the first square has caused the second one to move.

## Time to contact

We saw earlier that people moving through an environment (e.g., long-jumpers) seem to make use of information about the rate of expansion of an object's retinal image to predict the time to contact. The measure generally used is tau, which

is the inverse of the rate of object expansion (Lee, 1980). There has been much research interest in trying to see whether the same is true when an object moves towards a more or less motionless observer.

Schiff and Detwiler (1979) obtained evidence that tau, rather than perceived distance or perceived velocity, is used to calculate time to contact. Adults were reasonably accurate at predicting when an object on a film would have hit them. Their accuracy was little affected by whether the object was filmed against a blank or a textured background, suggesting that information about the rate of expansion of the retinal image is sufficient to decide when an object will arrive.

Lee et al. (1983) studied the relevance of tau to performance in a situation in which participants had to jump up and punch balls dropped from various heights above them. The speed of a dropping ball increases over time, but the calculation of tau ignores such changes in velocity. It follows that the actual time to contact will be less than tau. The key finding was that the participants' leg and arm movements were determined more closely by tau than by the actual time to contact. However, tau was still useful, because its value predicts time to contact reasonably well in the last 250 milliseconds prior to contact.

Lee (1980) assumed that the rate of expansion of an object's retinal image is the crucial factor influencing judgements of time to contact. It would thus be valuable to manipulate the rate of expansion as directly as possible. Savelsbergh, Whiting, and Bootsma (1991) achieved this by requiring participants to catch a deflating ball that was swinging towards them on a pendulum. The rate of expansion of the retinal image is less for a deflating than for a non-deflating ball. Thus, on Lee's theory, participants should assume that the deflating ball would take longer to reach them than was actually the case. The peak grasp closure was 5 milliseconds later with the deflating ball, which is in line with prediction. Similar findings were reported by Savelsbergh et al. (1993).

The findings of Savelsbergh et al. (1991, 1993) have been regarded as the most convincing evidence that tau is used to calculate time to contact.

However, Wann (1996) argued persuasively that this is not the case. Strict application of the tau hypothesis to the data of Savelsbergh et al. (1993) indicated that the peak grasp closure should have occurred about 230 milliseconds later to the deflating ball than to the non-deflating ball. In fact, the average difference was only about 30 milliseconds. As Wann (1996, p. 1043) concluded, "The results of Savelsbergh et al. point to it [tau] being only one component in a multiple-source evaluation process."

Tau provides a measure of the time to contact with the observer's eyes, and does not indicate accurately when an object will reach his or her outstretched hand. It would seem to follow that interception of a rolling ball would be more accurate if the ball were moving directly towards participants rather than off to one side. However, Tresilian (1994a) obtained precisely the opposite findings, suggesting that other factors (e.g., angular position and velocity of the ball relative to the participant) influence performance.

*Evaluation*

Tau is not the *only* source of information used by observers. For example, Peper et al. (1994) had participants judge whether a ball had passed within arm's reach. The judgements were usually accurate, except when the ball was larger or smaller than expected. In those circumstances, the observers systematically misjudged the distance between themselves and the ball. Thus, familiar size can influence judgements of object motion relevant to an individual observer.

Convincing evidence that tau is not the only variable used in catching a ball was obtained by Wann and Rushton (1995). They used a virtual reality setup, which allowed them to manipulate tau and binocular disparity separately. The participants' task was to grasp a moving virtual ball with their hand. Tau and binocular disparity were both used to determine the timing of the participants' grasping movements. Whichever variable predicted an earlier arrival of the ball had more influence on grasping behaviour.

Another problem was identified by Cumming (1994). He pointed out that the value of tau would

be the same for two different objects provided that their size, distance, and approach velocity were all in a fixed ratio. Tau on its own would be insufficient to estimate time to contact, because the two objects would always be at different distances from the observer throughout their flight.

Tresilian (1995) argued that the tau hypothesis may be of most relevance when the moving target is viewed briefly, when a response needs to be made rapidly, and when the perceiver is well practised. When these conditions do not apply, then perceivers may use various cognitive processes to determine time to contact instead of, or in addition, to tau.

In sum, several sources of visual information can be used to facilitate the task of catching a moving ball or other object. Tau may be the most important variable, but familiar size, binocular disparity, angular position, and velocity of the object relative to the participant are other important variables.

## Biological movement

Most people are very good at interpreting the movements of other people, and can decide very rapidly whether someone is walking, running, limping, or whatever. How successful would we be at interpreting *biological movement* if the visual information available to us were greatly reduced? Johansson (1975) addressed this issue by attaching lights to actors' joints (e.g., wrists, knees, ankles). The actors were dressed entirely in black so that only the lights were visible, and they were then filmed as they moved around in the dark (Figure 3.7). Reasonably accurate perception of a moving person could be achieved even with only six lights and a short segment of film. Most observers could describe accurately the posture and movements of the actors, and it almost seemed as if their arms and legs could be seen.

Subsequent research has indicated that observers can make very precise discriminations when viewing point-light displays. Cutting and Kozlowski (1977) found that observers were reasonably good at identifying themselves and others known to them from point-light displays. Kozlowski and

**FIGURE 3.7**

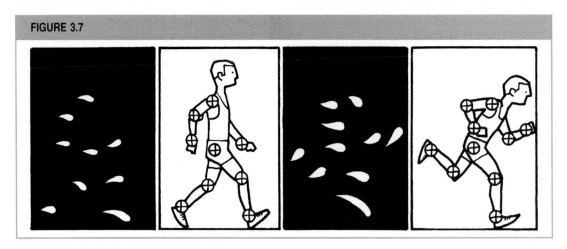

Johansson (1975) attached lights to an actor's joints. While the actor stood still in a darkened room, observers could not make sense of the arrangement of lights. However, as soon as he started to move around, they were able to perceive the lights as defining a human figure.

Cutting (1978) discovered that observers were correct about 65% of the time when guessing the sex of someone walking. Judgements were better when joints in both the upper and lower body or only the lower body were illuminated, presumably because good judgements depend on some overall bodily feature or features.

Some of the most interesting findings with point-light displays were reported by Runeson and Frykholm (1983). In one experiment, they asked the actors to lift a box weighing four kilograms and to carry it to a table, while trying to give the impression that the box weighed 6.5, 11.5, or 19 kilograms. Observers detected the actors' intentions from the pattern of lights, and so their perception of the weight of the box did not vary across conditions.

In another experiment, Runeson and Frykholm (1983) showed films of actors throwing sandbags to targets at different distances. The observers were good at judging how far the actors had intended to throw the bags, even though there were no lights on the bags. Finally, Runeson and Frykholm (1983) asked the actors to carry out a sequence of actions naturally or as if they were a member of the opposite sex. Observers guessed the gender of the actor correctly 85.5% of the time when he or she acted naturally, and there was only a modest

reduction to 75.5% correct in the deception condition.

*Theoretical accounts*

Does our ability to perceive biological motion accurately involve complex cognitive processes? Much of the evidence suggests that it does not. For example, Fox and McDaniel (1982) presented two different motion displays side by side to infants. One display consisted of dots representing someone running on the spot, and the other showed the same activity but presented upside down. Infants four months of age spent most of their time looking at the display that was the right way up, suggesting that they were able to detect biological motion.

More evidence suggesting that the detection of biological motion occurs straightforwardly was reported by Johansson, von Hofsten, and Jansson (1980). Observers who saw the moving lights for only one-fifth of a second perceived biological movement with no apparent difficulty.

These findings are consistent with Johansson's (1975) view that the ability to perceive biological motion is innate. However, it is clearly possible that four-month-old infants have learned from experience how to perceive biological motion. Runeson and Frykholm (1983) argued for a Gibsonian position, according to which aspects of biological motion provide invariant information. These invariants can be perceived with the impoverished information available from point-light displays, and can be identified even when there are deliberate attempts to deceive observers.

There have been various attempts to identify the invariant or invariants that might be used by observers to make accurate sex judgements. Cutting, Proffitt, and Kozlowski (1978) pointed out that men tend to show relatively greater side to side motion (or swing) of the shoulders than of the hips, whereas women show the opposite. The reason for this is that men typically have broad shoulders and narrow hips in comparison to women. The shoulders and hips move in opposition to each other, that is, when the right shoulder is forward, the left hip is forward. One can identify the *centre of moment* in the upper body, which is the neutral reference point around which the shoulders and hips swing. The position of the centre of moment is determined by the relative sizes of the shoulders and hips, and is typically lower in men than in women. Cutting et al. (1978) found that the centre of moment correlated well with the sex judgements made by observers.

Cutting (1978) extended these findings. He used artificial moving dot displays (i.e., the lights were not attached to people) in which only the centre of moment was varied. Judgements of the sex of "male" and "female" walkers were correct over 80% of the time, suggesting the importance of centre of moment. However, Cutting used a greater range of variation in the centre of moment than would be found in real human beings, and the general artificiality of his situation suggests some caution in generalising his findings to real-life situations.

Mather and Murdoch (1994) also used artifical point-light displays. Most previous studies had involved movement across the line of sight, but the "walkers" in their displays appeared to be walking either towards or away from the camera. There are two correlated cues that may be used by observers to decide whether they are looking at a man or a woman in point-light displays:

1. Structural cues based on the tendency of men to have broad shoulders and narrow hips, whereas women have the opposite tendency; these structural cues form the basis of the centre of moment.
2. Dynamic cues based on the tendency for men to show relatively greater body sway with the upper body than with the hips when walking, whereas woman show the opposite.

Sex judgements were based much more on dynamic cues than on structural ones when the two cues were in conflict. Thus, the centre of moment may be less important than was assumed by Cutting (e.g., 1978).

## Apparent motion

Anyone who has been to the cinema or watched television has experienced *apparent motion*. What is presented to the viewer is a rapid series of still images, but what is perceived is the illusion of continuous motion. Films are presented at a rate of 24 frames per second; this is known as the sample rate. Bruce et al. (1996, p. 187) made an important point about the relationship between apparent motion and real motion: "When the sample rate is high enough there is every reason to believe that 'real' (smooth) and 'apparent' (sampled) motion perception are effectively the same thing."

Apparent motion was shown under laboratory conditions by Wertheimer (1912), who was one of the Gestaltists (see Chapter 2). Two vertical lines in different spatial locations were presented alternately. When the delay between successive presentations was about one-twentieth of a second, observers often reported that there was one line that moved smoothly from place to place.

One of the main issues that needs to be resolved by the visual system in apparent motion is that of *correspondence*. This involves deciding which parts of successive still images belong to the same object in motion. Correspondence could be achieved by comparing each small part of successive images, but this would be very cumbersome with complex displays. For example, apparent motion can be created by using two large random-dot patterns which are identical except that dots in a square central position in one pattern are shifted to the left in the other pattern (discussed by Ramachandran & Anstis, 1986). When these two patterns are superimposed and presented in rapid alternation, a central square seems to move from side to side. As there are thousands of dots in each display, it seems improbable that the visual system meticulously compares each and every dot.

According to Ramachandran and Anstis (1986), the visual system focuses on certain features of a display when trying to detect correspondence. For example, the visual system seems good at detecting correspondences between areas of brightness and darkness (areas of low spatial frequency). A white square on a black background was presented for one-tenth of a second, and was replaced by a display with an outline square of the same size but coloured black on the left and a white circle on the left. The white square seemed to move towards the circle rather than towards the black square, suggesting that "the visual system tends to match areas of similar brightness in preference to matching sharp outlines" (Ramachandran & Anstis, 1986, p. 82).

The visual system prefers to perceive apparent motion in ways that would make sense in the real world. For example, we take account of the fact that objects in motion typically proceed along a straight path (the rule of inertia). This was shown in a two-stage experiment (Ramachandran & Anstis, 1986). In the first stage, two dots were presented rapidly at diagonal corners of an imaginary square, and were then replaced by identical dots in the opposite diagonal corners. About half the observers perceived two dots moving horizontally, with the other observers seeing the dots moving vertically. In the second stage, all the observers perceived two dots moving horizontally. The reason was that the display was embedded in the centre of a larger display in which two rows of dots moved horizontally creating an impression of linear movement in the larger display.

Ramachandran and Anstis (1986) argued that the visual system makes use of two other rules which affect decisions about correspondences or matches between successive images: the rule of rigidity and the rule of occlusion. According to the rule of rigidity, it is assumed that objects are rigid. Thus, if part of an object moves, all the rest of it moves as well. According to the rule of occlusion, an object continues to exist when it is hidden (or occluded) behind an intervening object. The relevance of these rules to apparent motion was shown using displays like those shown in Figure 3.8. The two displays were superimposed and then presented alternately. Four pie-shaped wedges are added and four are taken away, but what is seen is a white square moving right and left, occluding and uncovering discs in the background. This effect illustrates use of the rule of rigidity, because the dots within the square seem to move with it, even though in fact they remain stationary. The rule of occlusion is involved, because observers assume that the four circles remain intact, but that parts of them are occluded or partially obscured some of the time.

## Theoretical accounts

The rules used by observers to detect correspondence and perceive apparent motion are largely based on their knowledge of regularities in the world and of the properties of objects. However, Ramachandran and Anstis (1986) argued that only relatively low-level processes are needed to produce the various effects they obtained. The experiments they described all involved rapid rates of stimulus presentation, and they claimed that it is unlikely that higher-level cognitive processes could have operated at those speeds. Ramachandran and Anstis also referred to neurobiological research (see Chapter 2) indicating that some nerve cells are sensitive to the motion of images with low spatial frequencies. These nerve cells may play a part in detecting correspondences at an early stage of visual processing.

Other theorists have argued that there is more than one kind of apparent motion. For example, Braddick (1980) proposed that apparent motion sometimes depends on the stimulation of low-level direction-selective cells. There is good evidence (Regan, Beverley, & Cynader, 1979) for direction-selective cells in the visual cortex responding mainly to a particular direction of movement. Particularly impressive evidence for their existence was obtained by Salzman et al. (1992). They

FIGURE 3.8

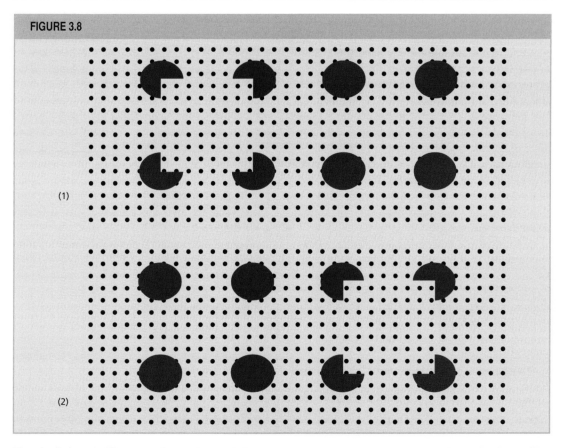

The stimuli shown in (1) are superimposed on, and alternated with, those shown in (2), creating the impression that a white square is moving right and left. Adapted from Ramachandran and Anstis (1986).

studied the perceived direction of movement in random-dot displays in monkeys. Electrical stimulation of direction-selective cells biased the monkeys' perception of motion. When cells responding to rightward movement were stimulated, this increased the probability of the display appearing to move in a rightward direction.

According to Braddick (1980), apparent motion of the central square when two large random-dot patterns are superimposed and alternated (see earlier description) involves low-level, direction-selective cells. He referred to this as "short-range" motion. However, he assumed that apparent motion of line stimuli (e.g., Wertheimer, 1912, discussed earlier) may involve higher-level, more cognitive processes, and he termed this "long-range" motion.

Braddick (1980) discussed evidence indicating important differences between apparent motion with random-dot and line displays. Apparent motion with random-dot displays requires the stimuli to be much closer together than is the case to perceive apparent motion with line displays, and there need to be much shorter intervals of time between stimuli (under 100 milliseconds versus 300 milliseconds, respectively). In addition, apparent motion with random-dot displays is not observed when the two stimuli are presented to different eyes, but is still perceived with line displays.

A different kind of evidence that apparent motion can be produced in more than one way was reported by Shiffrar and Freyd (1990). In part of their experiment, observers were presented in rapid succession with two photographs of a man with his hand held out and his palm facing forward. In one photograph, his hand was twisted as far left as possible, and in the other photograph it was twisted as far right as possible. There was a rotation of wrist of about 270° between the two photographs. Apparent motion could be seen either in the longer (270°) but biologically possible direction, or in the shorter (90°) but biologically impossible direction. When there was rapid alternation of the photographs, the shorter rotation was perceived. However, the longer and more plausible rotation was perceived when the rate of alternation was slower.

What do these findings mean? Shiffrar (1994) speculated that they can be understood in terms of the distinction between the dorsal (where is it?) and ventral (what is it?) streams of processing. It is only at the slower rate of alternation that it was possible to access knowledge from the ventral stream about hands and about what is physically possible.

There are various problems with the distinction between short-range and long-range motion (see Mather, 1994, for a review). For example, the spatial range of so-called short-range motion is almost certainly much greater when visual stimuli are presented a long way away from the fovea or central part of the retina, and this helps to undermine the distinction between short-range and long-range motion. As Wandell (1995, p. 365) concluded, "The long- and short-range motion classification is still widely used . . . But I suspect the classification will not last."

## Perception of causality

Michotte (1946) carried out a series of studies on *perceived causality*. In some studies, observers watched as one square moved towards a second square, with the first square stopping and the second square moving off at a slower rate than the first one as they came into contact. According to Michotte (1946), observers perceived that the first square had caused the motion of the second square (the "launching effect"). The perception of causality disappeared when there was a time

interval between the contact and the second square moving off, or if the second square moved off in a different direction to that of the first square. Another effect was termed "entraining". This occurred when one object moved towards a second object, and then the two objects moved off together at the same speed until they stopped together. It seemed to the observers as if the first object were carrying the second one or pushing it. The launching and entraining effects did not seem to be affected by the nature of the objects involved. In addition, the effects were observed even when the two objects were very different from each other.

It has proved hard to replicate Michotte's (1946) findings, perhaps because he often relied on rather small numbers of highly practised participants. Beasley (1968) found that only 65% of participants reported the impression of causality with the launching display, and that figure fell to 45% for the entraining effect. In strong contrast to Michotte's findings, Beasley (1968) found that 45% of participants reported causal impressions when the second object moved off at a 90° angle to the direction of motion of the first object. Finally, Beasley (1968) found that the perception of causality was influenced by the nature of the objects used, which is directly contrary to Michotte's findings.

### Theoretical accounts

Michotte (1946) put forward a Gestaltist view of perceived causality, according to which it occurs naturally when specific motion sequences are seen. He argued that causality is perceived in a rather direct way which does not rely on inferences or other cognitive processes. In addition, Michotte claimed that the perception of causality is innately determined. However, if Michotte is correct, it is hard to understand why many people fail to show the predicted effects.

If the perception of causality is direct, then we might expect to find it even in infants. Leslie and Keeble (1987) obtained evidence that six-month-old infants could perceive the launching effect. This finding suggests that fairly basic processes are involved in the perception of causality. Oakes (1994) obtained similar findings from seven-month-olds using simple displays, but these infants failed to perceive causality in more complex displays.

Michotte's (1946) assumption that the perception of causality does not involve the use of inferences was tested by Schlottmann and Shanks (1992). They arranged matters so that a change of colour by the second object *always* predicted its movement, whereas impact of the first object on the second object was less predictive. The participants learned to draw the correct inference that the change of colour in the second object was necessary for its movement of the second object, but this did not influence their causal impressions. However, when the first object collided with the second object, which changed colour and moved off, the observers claimed that it looked as if the first object caused the second one to move.

What do these findings mean? Schlottmann and Shanks (1992, p. 340) concluded as follows: "The results support the distinction that Michotte advocated between causal knowledge that arises from inference and that which is directly given in perception." This conclusion was supported by finding that 85% of the participants regarded their inference judgements and their ratings of perceived causality as independent of each other.

Schlottmann and Anderson (1993) studied the launching effect. They manipulated the gap between the two objects, the time period between the collision and the second object moving, and the ratio of the speeds of the two objects. They identified two successive processes, which they termed "valuation" and "integration". Valuation involves assigning weights to the various aspects of the moving display, and there were substantial individual differences in this form of processing. Integration involves combining or integrating information from these various aspects, and there were great similarities in this process across participants. Schlottmann and Anderson (1993, p. 797) concluded as follows: "The averaging integration model may correspond to the invariant perceptual structure of phenomenal causality, as proposed by Michotte. The valuation operation, on the other hand, can accommodate individual differences that may have experiential components, as suggested by his critics."

## Evaluation

Michotte was correct in assuming that causality can be perceived in a fairly direct way owing little to experience or to inferences. However, the perception of causality is more complex than he assumed. The existence of substantial individual differences in the perception of causality suggests that learning and experience play a greater role than was admitted by Michotte. It is hard to disagree with the conclusion of Schlottmann and Anderson (1993, p. 799):

> In adult cognition . . . the perceptual illusion of phenomenal causality must function together with acquired knowledge about causality in the physical world. Thus, ways are needed that can make effective progress on the innate-*plus*-learned question.

## CHAPTER SUMMARY

- Constructivist theories. According to constructivist theorists, perception is an active and constructive process depending on hypotheses and expectations. Evidence that perception is influenced by motivational and emotional factors supports the constructivist approach. This approach has been applied to visual illusions in the misapplied size-constancy theory, but other theories (e.g., incorrect comparison theory) have been used to explain such illusions. Constructivist theories are most applicable to the perception of degraded or briefly presented stimuli, but they seem to predict more errors in normal perception than are actually found.

- Direct perception. Gibson proposed an ecological theory of direct perception, according to which the optic array contains invariant information about the layout of objects in the visual environment. We pick up this invariant information by means of resonance, and meaning is dealt with by assuming that affordances are directly perceivable. Gibson was correct in assuming that the visual input provides a rich source of information. However, he underestimated the complexity of the processes involved in visual perception, and his notion of affordances is inadequate as a way of understanding the role of meaning in perception.

- Theoretical integration. Indirect theorists (e.g., the constructivists; Marr; Biederman) differ from direct theorists in assuming that perception involves the formation of internal representations, and that it depends on stored knowledge. A key reason why indirect and direct theories of perception are so different is because the former theories focus on perception for recognition, whereas the latter focus on perception for action. Thus, the two approaches can be regarded as complementary rather than as mutually exclusive. However, indirect theories provide a more generally adequate account.

- Motion, perception, and action. A central issue running through much research on motion, perception, and action is whether Gibson was correct in assuming that we interact with the environment in a direct way making use of invariant information. According to Helmholtz's outflow theory, movement within the retinal image is interpreted by making use of information about intended movement sent to the eye muscles. This theory explains why the visual world seems to move when the side of the eyeball is pressed.

- Visually guided action. It has been claimed that the optic flow pattern and/or the focus of expansion provide the information needed to account for accurate heading behaviour. However, movement on the retina is determined by eye and head movements as well as by the optic flow pattern. It is possible that differential motion parallax is used to determine heading behaviour. Time to contact can be assessed by using tau. However, it can also be assessed by estimating speed and distance. Studies on walking, running, and jumping are consistent with the tau hypothesis. Tau is a good example of the kind of high-level invariant emphasised by Gibson. However, there is no compelling evidence in favour of the tau hypothesis, and other factors (e.g., depth cues) have been ignored. There is also the issue of identifying the internal processes involved in the calculation of tau. Research on running to catch a ball suggests that catchers have a strategy for arriving at the right place just in time to catch the ball; this strategy may involve keeping the optical trajectory straight. The findings are consistent with the use of this strategy.

- Perception of object motion. There is evidence that tau is used to calculate time to contact when an object moves towards a more or less motionless observer. However, tau on its own is not always sufficient to assess time to contact, and other kinds of information (e.g., knowledge of familiar size) are also used. Observers can make very accurate judgements of biological movement when presented with point-light displays. Accurate sex judgements in studies on biological movement may depend on structural cues (e.g., the centre of moment) or an dynamic cues (e.g., body sway of the upper body and hips). Apparent motion is generally perceived in ways that would make sense in the real world. At low sample rates, decisions about correspondences or matches between successive images in apparent motion are based in part on the rules of inertia, rigidity, and occlusion. The distinction between short-range and long-range motion may be important. Perception of causality even with meaningless shapes is commonly found in certain circumstances. Michotte argued that perceived causality is innately determined, and does not depend on inferences. The factors producing perception of causality are more numerous and complex than Michotte assumed.

## FURTHER READING

- Bruce, V., Green, P.R., & Georgeson, M.A. (1996). *Visual perception: Physiology, psychology, and ecology (3rd Ed.)*. Hove, UK: Psychology Press. Several chapters of this book are of relevance. However, Chapter 17, with its excellent discussion of direct and indirect theories of perception, is of special value.
- Gazzaniga, M.S., Ivry, R.B., & Mangun, G.R. (1998). *Cognitive neuroscience: The biology of the mind*. New York: W.W. Norton. There is clear coverage of some of the issues discussed here in Chapter 5 of this book.
- Goldstein, E.B. (1996). *Sensation and perception (4th Ed.)*. New York: Brooks/Cole. There is good basic coverage of movement perception in Chapter 7 of this textbook.
- Milner, A.D., & Goodale, M.A. (1995). *The visual brain in action*. Oxford: Oxford University Press. Various theoretically exciting views on visual perception and action are discussed at length in this innovative book.

# Object Recognition

## INTRODUCTION

Throughout the waking day we are bombarded with information from the visual environment. Mostly we make sense of that information, which usually involves identifying or recognising the objects that surround us. Object recognition typically occurs so effortlessly that it is hard to believe it is actually a rather complex achievement.

The complexities of object recognition can be grasped by discussing the processes involved. First, there are usually numerous different overlapping objects in the visual environment, and we must somehow decide where one object ends and the next starts. This is difficult, as can be seen if we consider the visual environment of the first author as he is word-processing these words. There are well over 100 objects visible in the room in front of him and in the garden outside. Over 90% of these objects overlap, and are overlapped by, other objects.

Second, objects can be recognised accurately over a wide range of viewing distances and orientations. For example, there is a small table directly in front of the first author. He is confident that the table is round, although its retinal image is elliptical. The term "constancy" refers to the fact that the apparent size and shape of an object do not change despite large variations in the size and shape of the retinal image.

Third, we recognise that an object is, say, a chair without any apparent difficulty. Chairs vary enormously in their visual properties (e.g., colour, size, shape), and it is not immediately obvious how we manage to allocate such diverse visual stimuli to the same category. The discussion of the representation of concepts (e.g., Rosch et al., 1976) in Chapter 10 is relevant here.

**Key processes involved in object recognition**
- Overlapping: deciding where one object ends and another begins
- Accurate recognition of objects over varying distances and orientations
- Allocating diverse visual stimuli to the same category of objects

In spite of the complexities of object recognition, we can generally go beyond simply identifying objects in the visual environment. For example, we can normally describe what an object would look like if viewed from a different angle, and we know its uses and functions.

All in all, there is more to object recognition than might initially be supposed. This chapter is devoted to the task of unravelling some of the mysteries of object recognition in normal and brain-damaged individuals.

## PATTERN RECOGNITION

Given the complexities in recognising three-dimensional objects, it is sensible to start by considering the processes involved in the *pattern recognition* (identification or categorisation) of two-dimensional patterns. Much of this research has addressed the question of how alphanumeric patterns (alphabetical and numerical symbols) are recognised. A key issue here is the flexibility of the human perceptual system. For example, we can recognise the letter "A" rapidly and accurately across considerable variations in orientation, in typeface, in size, and in writing style. Why is pattern recognition so successful? Advocates of template theories and feature theories have proposed different answers to this question. However,

they agree that, at a very general level, pattern recognition involves matching information from the visual stimulus with information stored in memory.

### Template theories

The basic idea behind template theories is that there is a miniature copy or template stored in long-term memory corresponding to each of the visual patterns we know. A pattern is recognised on the basis of which template provides the closest match to the stimulus input. This kind of theory is very simple, but it is not very realistic in view of the enormous variations in visual stimuli allegedly matching the same template.

One modest improvement to the basic template theory is to assume that the visual stimulus undergoes a normalisation process (i.e., producing an internal representation in a standard position, size, and so on) before the search for a matching template begins. Normalisation would help pattern recognition for letters and digits, but it is improbable that it would consistently produce matching with the appropriate template.

Another way of trying to improve template theory would be to assume that there is more than one template for each letter and numeral. This would permit accurate matching of stimulus and template across a wider range of stimuli, but only at the cost of making the theory much more unwieldy.

Template theories are ill equipped to account for the adaptability shown by people when recognising alphanumeric stimuli. The limitations of template theories are especially obvious when the stimulus belongs to an ill defined category for which no single template could possibly suffice (e.g., buildings).

### Feature theories

According to feature theories, a pattern consists of a set of specific features or attributes. For example, a face could be said to possess various features: a nose, two eyes, a mouth, a chin, and so on. The process of pattern recognition is assumed to begin with the extraction of the features from the

**FIGURE 4.1**

| LIST 1 | LIST 2 |
|--------|--------|
| IMVXEW | ODUGQR |
| WVMEIX | GRODUQ |
| VXWIEM | DUROQG |
| MIEWVX | RGOUDQ |
| WEIMXV | RQGOUD |
| IWVXEM | UGQDRO |
| IXEZVW | GUQZOR |
| VWEMXI | ODGRUQ |
| MIVEWX | DRUQGO |
| WXEIMV | UQGORD |

Illustrative lists to study letter search; the distractors in List 2 share fewer features with the target letter Z than do the distractors in List 1.

**FIGURE 4.2**

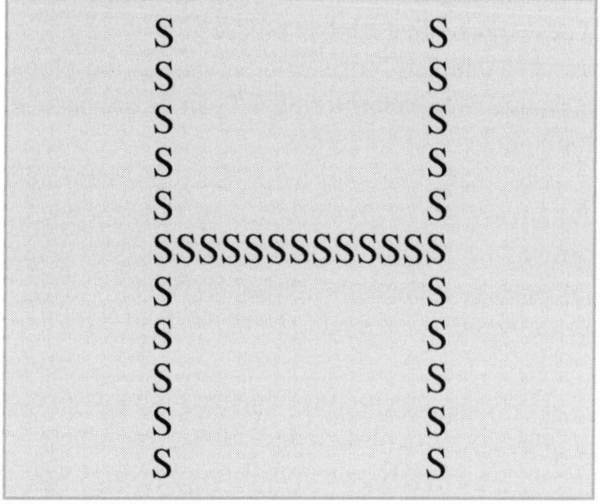

The kind of stimulus used by Navon (1977) to demonstrate the importance of global features in perception.

presented visual stimulus. This set of features is then combined, and compared against information stored in memory.

In the case of an alphanumeric pattern such as "A", feature theorists might argue that its crucial features are two straight lines and a connecting cross-bar. This kind of theoretical approach has the advantage that visual stimuli varying greatly in size, orientation, and minor details may nevertheless be identifiable as instances of the same pattern.

*Experimental evidence*

The feature-theory approach has received support in studies of visual search, in which a target letter has to be identified as rapidly as possible (see also Chapter 5). Neisser (1964) compared the time taken to detect the letter "Z" when the distractor letters consisted of straight lines (e.g., W, V) or contained rounded features (e.g., O, G) (see Figure 4.1). Performance was faster in the latter condition, presumably because

the distractors shared fewer features with the target letter Z.

Feature theories are based on the assumption that visual processing proceeds from a detailed analysis of a pattern or object to a global or general analysis. However, there is evidence suggesting that global processing often precedes more specific processing. Navon (1977) presented his participants with stimuli such as the one shown in Figure 4.2. In one of his studies, participants had to decide as rapidly as possible on some trials whether the large letter was an "H" or an "S"; on other trials, they had to decide whether the small letters were Hs or Ss. Performance speed with the small letters was greatly slowed when the large letter was different from the small letters. In contrast, decision speed with the large letter was unaffected by the nature of the small letters. According to Navon (1977, p. 354), these findings indicate that, "perceptual processes are temporally organised so that they proceed from global structuring towards more and more fine-grained analysis. In other words, a scene is decomposed rather than built up."

Some of the available evidence is inconsistent with Navon's conclusion. Kinchla and Wolfe (1979) used stimuli of a similar nature to those of Navon (1977), but of variable size. When the large letter was very large, processing of the small letters preceded processing of the large letter. They argued that global processing occurs prior to more detailed processing only when the global structure of a pattern or object can be ascertained by a single eye fixation.

The main problem with research stemming from Navon's (1977) study is that it has not proved possible to identify precisely *where* in the visual processing system the global advantage occurs. In the words of Kimchi (1992, p. 36):

> There seems to be evidence, though not entirely conclusive, that global advantage occurs at early perceptual processing. Certain findings suggest that the mechanisms underlying the effect may be sensory, but other findings are suggestive of attentional mechanisms.

### Cognitive neuroscience

Cognitive neuroscientists have obtained evidence of some relevance to feature theories. If the presentation of a visual stimulus leads initially to detailed processing of its basic features, then we might be able to identify cells in the cortex involved in such processing. However, the existence of cells specialised for responding to specific aspects of visual stimuli may be consistent with feature theories, but does *not* demonstrate that they are correct.

Hubel and Wiesel (e.g., 1979), used single-unit recordings to study individual neurons (see Chapter 1). They found that many cells responded in two different ways to a spot of light depending on which part of the cell was affected:

1. An "on" response, with an increased rate of firing while the light was on.
2. An "off" response, with the light causing a decreased rate of firing.

Many retinal ganglion cells, lateral geniculate cells, and layer IV primary visual cortex cells can be divided into on-centre cells and off-centre cells. On-centre cells produce the on-response to a light in the centre of their receptive field and an off-response to a light in the periphery; the opposite is the case with off-centre cells.

Hubel and Wiesel (e.g., 1979) discovered the existence of two types of neurons in the receptive fields of the primary visual cortex: simple cells and complex cells. Simple cells have "on" and "off" regions, with each region being rectangular in shape. Simple cells play an important role in detection. They respond most to dark bars in a light field, light bars in a dark field, or to straight edges between areas of light and dark. Any given simple cell only responds strongly to stimuli of a particular orientation, and so the responses of these cells could be relevant to feature detection.

There are many more complex cells than simple cells. They resemble simple cells in that they respond maximally to straight-line stimuli in a particular orientation. However, there are significant differences:

1. Complex cells have larger receptive fields.
2. The rate of firing of a complex cell to any given stimulus depends very little on its position within the cell's receptive field; in contrast, simple cells are divided into "on" and "off" regions.
3. Most complex cells respond well to moving contours, whereas simple cells respond only to stationary or slowly moving contours.

There is also evidence for the existence of hypercomplex cells. These cells respond most to rather more complex patterns than do simple or complex cells. For example, some respond maximally to corners, whereas others repond to other various specific angles.

It is important to note that cortical cells provide ambiguous information, because they respond in the same way to different stimuli. For example, a cell that responds maximally to a horizontal line moving slowly may respond moderately to a horizontal line moving rapidly and to a nearly horizontal line moving slowly. Thus, as Sekuler and Blake (1994, p. 134) pointed out, "Neurons in the visual cortex cannot really be called 'feature detectors', . . . because individual cells cannot signal the presence of a particular visual feature with certainty."

Hubel and Wiesel (1962) argued that processing in the visual cortex is based on straight lines and edges. An alternative view is based on gratings, which are patterns consisting of alternating lighter and darker bars. Of particular importance are *sinusoidal gratings*, in which there are gradual intensity changes between adjacent bars. According to Sekuler and Blake (1994), gratings possess four properties:

1. Spatial frequency: the spacing of bars as imaged on the retina.
2. Contrast: the difference in intensity of light and dark bars.
3. Orientation: the angle at which the bars of the grating are presented.
4. Spatial phase: the position of the grating with respect to some landmark (e.g., edge of a display).

It is possible to construct any desired visual pattern by manipulating each of these four properties of gratings.

Campbell and Robson (1968) assumed that the visual system contains sets of neurons (or channels) that respond to different spatial frequencies of gratings, and this assumption formed the basis of their multi-channel model. They obtained some support for their model by presenting people with compound gratings, which were formed by combining a number of simple sinusoidal gratings. The visual system responded differently to each of the components of these compound gratings, presumably because the channels appropriate to each component were being activated. Subsequent research indicated that most cells in the primary visual cortex respond more strongly to sinusoidal gratings than to lines and edges (see Pinel, 1997).

The emphasis on spatial frequency led to the development of the *contrast sensitivity function*, which indicates an individual's ability to detect targets of various spatial frequencies. Evidence that the contrast sensitivity function is a valuable measure was reported by Ginsburg, Evans, Sekuler, and Harp (1982). Pilots flew simulated missions in an aircraft simulator in conditions of reduced visibility, and sometimes had to abort a landing because the runway was blocked. Ginsburg et al. (1982) assessed the pilots' visual acuity, which is an assessment of the smallest detail that can be detected. The pilots' flying performance was not related to visual acuity. However, those pilots with the highest contrast sensitivities noticed that the runway was blocked from a greater distance than did those with the lowest contrast sensitivities.

Harvey, Roberts, and Gervais (1983) presented individual letters very briefly, and asked their participants to name them. Some letters (e.g., "K" and "N") having several features in common were not confused, which is contrary to the prediction of feature theory. In contrast, letters with similar spatial frequencies tended to be confused, even if they shared few common features. These findings suggest that spatial frequency is more important than features in the representation of letters within the visual system.

## Evaluation

Stimulus features play a role in pattern recognition. However, feature theories leave much that is of importance out of account. First, they de-emphasise the effects of context and of expectations on pattern recognition. Weisstein and Harris (1974) used a task involving detection of a line embedded either in a briefly flashed three-dimensional form or in a less coherent form. According to feature theorists, the target line should always activate the same feature detectors, and so the coherence of the form in which it is embedded should not affect detection. In fact, target detection was best when the target line was part of a three-dimensional form. Weisstein and Harris (1974) called this the "object-superiority effect", and this effect is inconsistent with many feature theories.

Second, pattern recognition does not depend solely on listing the features of a stimulus. For example, the letter "A" consists of two oblique uprights and a dash, but these three features can be presented in such a way that they are not perceived as an A: \ / –. In order to understand pattern recognition, we need to consider the *relationships* among features as well as simply the features themselves.

Third, the limitations of feature theories are clearer with three-dimensional than with two-dimensional stimuli. The fact that observers can generally recognise three-dimensional objects even when some of the major features are hidden from view is hard to account for on a theory that emphasises the role of features in recognition.

Fourth, global processing often precedes feature processing (e.g., Navon, 1977). Additional evidence comes from research on face processing (discussed later).

## MARR'S COMPUTATIONAL THEORY

Marr (1982) put forward a computational theory of the processes involved in object recognition. He proposed a series of *representations* (i.e.,

descriptions) providing increasingly detailed information about the visual environment. Marr identified three major kinds of representation (see Figure 4.3):

- Primal sketch: this provides a two-dimensional description of the main light-intensity changes in the visual input, including information about edges, contours, and blobs.
- $2\frac{1}{2}$-D sketch: this incorporates a description of the depth and orientation of visible surfaces, making use of information provided by shading, texture, motion, binocular disparity, and so on; like the primal sketch, it is observer-centred or viewpoint-dependent.
- 3-D model representation: this describes three-dimensionally the shapes of objects and their relative positions in a way that is independent of the observer's viewpoint (viewpoint-invariant).

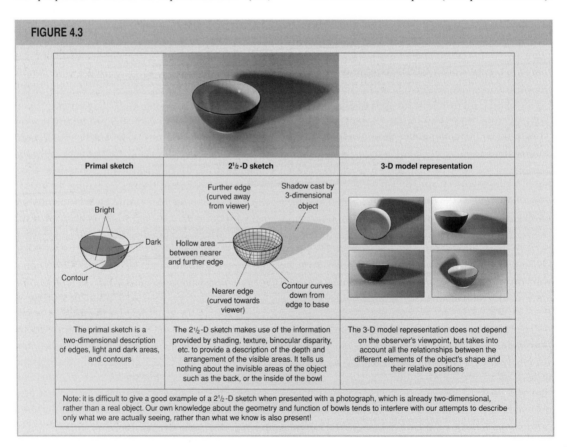

**FIGURE 4.3**

|  | Primal sketch | $2\frac{1}{2}$-D sketch | 3-D model representation |
|---|---|---|---|
|  | The primal sketch is a two-dimensional description of edges, light and dark areas, and contours | The $2\frac{1}{2}$-D sketch makes use of the information provided by shading, texture, binocular disparity, etc. to provide a description of the depth and arrangement of the visible areas. It tells us nothing about the invisible areas of the object such as the back, or the inside of the bowl | The 3-D model representation does not depend on the observer's viewpoint, but takes into account all the relationships between the different elements of the object's shape and their relative positions |

Note: it is difficult to give a good example of a $2\frac{1}{2}$-D sketch when presented with a photograph, which is already two-dimensional, rather than a real object. Our own knowledge about the geometry and function of bowls tends to interfere with our attempts to describe only what we are actually seeing, rather than what we know is also present!

Marr's three kinds of representations of the visual environment. Photographs by Bipinchandra J. Mistry.

## Primal sketch

According to Marr (1982), we can identify two versions of the primal sketch: the raw primal sketch and the full primal sketch. Both sketches are symbolic, meaning that they represent the image as a list of symbols. The *raw primal sketch* contains information about light-intensity changes in the visual scene, and the *full primal sketch* makes use of this information to identify the number and outline shapes of visual objects. Why are two separate primal sketches created? Part of the answer is that light-intensity changes can occur for various reasons. The intensity of light reflected from a surface depends on the angle at which light strikes it, and is reduced by shadows falling on the surface. In addition, there can be substantial differences in light intensity reflected from an object due to variations in its texture. Thus, the light-intensity changes incorporated into the raw primal sketch provide a fallible guide to object shapes and edges.

The raw primal sketch is formed from what is known as a *grey-level representation* of the retinal image. This representation is based on the light intensities in each very small area of the image; these areas are called *pixels* (picture elements). The intensity of light reflecting from any given pixel fluctuates continuously, and so there is a danger that the grey-level representation will be distorted by these momentary fluctuations. One approach is to average the light-intensity values of neighbouring pixels. This smoothing process can eliminate "noise", but it can produce a blurring effect in which valuable information is lost.

The usual answer to this problem is to assume that several representations of the image are formed which vary in their degree of blurring. Information from these image representations is then combined to form the raw primal sketch. According to Marr and Hildreth (1980), the raw primal sketch consists of four different tokens: edge-segments; bars; terminations; and blobs. Each of these tokens is based on a different pattern of light-intensity change in the blurred representations. One of the limitations of the approach of Marr and Hildreth is that it does not make full use of the intensity-change information contained in the grey-level representation (Watt, 1988).

## Full primal sketch

Various processes need to be applied to the raw primal sketch to identify its underlying structure or organisation. This is needed, because the information contained in the raw primal sketch is typically ambiguous and compatible with several underlying structures. Marr (1976) found that it was valuable to make use of two rather general principles when designing a program to achive perceptual organisation:

1. The principle of explicit naming.
2. The principle of least commitment.

According to the former principle, it is useful to give a name or symbol to a set of grouped elements. The reason is that the name or symbol can be used over and over again to describe other sets of grouped elements, all of which can then form a much larger grouping. According to the principle of least commitment, ambiguities are resolved only when there is convincing evidence as to the appropriate solution. This principle is useful, because mistakes at an early stage of processing can lead on to several other mistakes.

With respect to the principle of explicit naming, Marr's program assigned place tokens to small regions of the raw primal sketch, such as the position of a blob or edge, or the termination of a longer blob or edge. Various edge points in the raw primal sketch are incorporated into a single place token on the basis of Gestalt-like notions such as proximity, figural continuity, and closure (see Chapter 2). Place tokens are then grouped together in various ways, in part on the basis of the grouping principles advocated by the Gestaltists. Some examples of the ways in which place tokens are combined are:

- Clustering: place tokens that are close together can be combined to form higher-order place tokens.
- Curvilinear aggregation: place tokens that are aligned in the same direction will be joined to produce a contour.

## Section summary

Marr provided one of the first detailed accounts of the initial processes in visual perception. As such, it has been very influential. Marr's (1976, 1982) visual processing program for the full primal sketch was reasonably successful. One reason why the grouping principles applied to place tokens work is because they reflect what is generally the case in the real world. For example, visual elements that are close together are likely to belong to the same object, as are elements that are similar. The program works well although it typically does not rely on object knowledge or expectations when deciding what goes with what. However, there were cases of ambiguity when the program could not specify the contour or perceptual organisation until supplied with additional information.

Marr (1982) assumed that grouping is based on two-dimensional representations. However, grouping can also be based on three-dimensional representations (e.g., Rock & Palmer, 1990, see Chapter 2). Enns and Rensick (1990) found that their participants immediately perceived which in a display of block figures was the "odd-man-out". They were able to do this even though the figures differed only in their three-dimensional orientation. This suggests that three-dimensional or depth information can be used to group stimuli.

## $2\frac{1}{2}$-D sketch

According to Marr (1982), various stages are involved in the transformation of the primal sketch into the $2\frac{1}{2}$-D sketch. The first stage involves the construction of a *range map* ("local point-by-point depth information about surfaces in the scene", Frisby, 1986, p. 164). After this, higher-level descriptions (e.g., of convex and concave junctions between two or more surfaces) are produced by combining information from related parts of the range map. More is known of the processes involved in constructing a range map than in proceeding from that to the $2\frac{1}{2}$-D sketch itself.

What kinds of information are used in changing the primal sketch into the $2\frac{1}{2}$-D sketch? Use is made of shading, motion, texture, shape, and binocular disparity (see Chapter 2).

## 3-D model representation

The $2\frac{1}{2}$-D sketch apparently provides a poor basis for identifying an object, mainly because it is viewpoint-centred. This means that the representation of an object will vary considerably depending on the angle from which it is viewed, and this variability greatly complicates object recognition. As a result, the 3-D model representation (which contains viewpoint-invariant information) is produced. This representation remains the same regardless of the viewing angle.

Marr and Nishihara (1978) identified three desirable criteria for a 3-D representation:

- Accessibility: the representation can be constructed easily.
- Scope and uniqueness: "scope" is the extent to which the representation is applicable to all the shapes in a given category, and "uniqueness" means that all the different views of an object produce the same standard representation.
- Stability and sensitivity: "stability" indicates that a representation incorporates the similarities among objects, and "sensitivity" means it incorporates salient differences.

Marr and Nishihara proposed that the primitive units for describing objects should be cylinders having a major axis. These primitive units are hierarchically organised, with high-level units providing information about object shape and low-level units providing more detailed information. Why did Marr and Nishihara adopt this axis-based approach? They argued that the main axes of an object are usually easy to establish regardless of the viewing position, whereas other object characteristics (e.g., precise shape) are not.

We can illustrate Marr and Nishihara's theoretical approach by considering the hierarchical organisation of the human form (see Figure 4.4). The human form can be decomposed into a series of cylinders at different levels of generality. It was assumed that this overall 3-D description is stored in memory, and enables us to recognise appropriate visual stimuli as humans regardless of the angle of viewing.

**FIGURE 4.4**

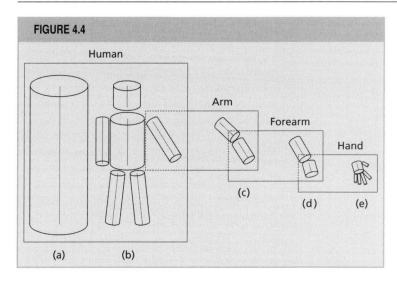

The hierarchical organisation of the human figure (from Marr & Nishihara, 1978) at various levels: (a) axis of the whole body; (b) axes at the level of arms, legs, and head; (c) arm divided into upper and lower arm; (d) a lower arm with separate hand; and (e) the palm and fingers of a hand.

According to Marr and Nishihara (1978), object recognition involves matching the 3-D model representation constructed from a visual stimulus against a catalogue of 3-D model representations stored in memory. To do this, it is necessary to identify the major axes of the visual stimulus. Marr and Nishihara proposed that concavities (areas where the contour points into the object) are identified first. With the human form, for example, there is a concave area in each armpit. These concavities are used to divide the visual image into segments (e.g., arms; legs; torso; head). Finally, the main axis of each segment is found.

There are some advantages associated with this emphasis on concavities and axis-based representations. First, the identification of concavities plays an important role in object recognition. Consider, for example, the faces–goblet ambiguous figure (look back at Figure 2.2), which was studied by Hoffman and Richards (1984). When one of the faces is seen, the concavities help the identification of the forehead, nose, lips, and chin. In contrast, when the goblet is seen, the concavities serve to define its base, stem, and bowl.

Second, it is possible to calculate the lengths and arrangement of axes of most visual objects regardless of the viewing angle. Third, information about axes can help object recognition. As Humphreys and Bruce (1989) pointed out, humans can be readily distinguished from gorillas on the basis of the relative lengths of the axes of the segments or cones corresponding to arms and legs: our legs are longer than our arms, whereas the opposite is true of gorillas.

## Biederman's recognition-by-components theory

Biederman (1987, 1990) put forward a theory of object recognition extending that of Marr and Nishihara (1978). The central assumption of his recognition-by-components theory is that objects consist of basic shapes or components known as "geons" (geometric ions). Examples of geons are blocks, cylinders, spheres, arcs, and wedges. According to Biederman (1987), there are about 36 different geons. This may seem suspiciously few to provide descriptions of all the objects we can recognise and identify. However, we can identify enormous numbers of spoken English words even though there are only about 44 phonemes in the English language. The reason is that these phonemes can be arranged in almost endless different orders. The same is true of geons. Part of the reason for the richness of the object descriptions provided by geons stems from the different possible spatial relationships among them. For example, a cup can be described by an arc connected to the side of a cylinder, and a bucket can

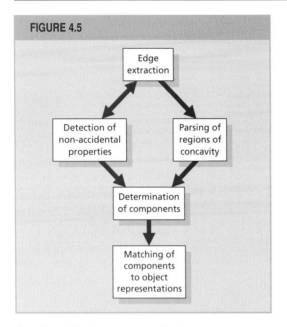

**FIGURE 4.5**

An outline of Biederman's recognition-by-components theory. Adapted from Biederman (1987).

be described by the same two geons, but with the arc connected to the top of the cylinder.

In order to understand recognition-by-components theory more fully, refer to Figure 4.5. The stage we have discussed so far is that of the determination of the components or geons of a visual object and their relationships. When this information is available, it is matched with stored object representations or structural models containing information about the nature of the relevant geons, their orientations, sizes, and so on. In general terms, the identification of any given visual object is determined by whichever stored object representation provides the best fit with the component- or geon-based information obtained from the visual object.

As can be seen in Figure 4.5, only part of Biederman's theory has been presented so far. What has been omitted is any analysis of how an object's components or geons are determined. The first step is edge extraction, which was described by Biederman (1987, p. 117) in the following way: "[There is] an early edge extraction stage, responsive to differences in surface characteristics namely, luminance, texture, or colour, provides a line drawing description of the object."

The next step is to decide how a visual object should be segmented to establish the number of parts of components of which it consists. Biederman (1987) agreed with Marr and Nishihara (1978) that the concave parts of an object's contour are of particular value in accomplishing the task of segmenting the visual image into parts.

The other major element is to decide which edge information from an object possesses the important characteristic of remaining invariant across different viewing angles. According to Biederman (1987), there are five such invariant properties of edges:

- Curvature: points on a curve.
- Parallel: sets of points in parallel.
- Co-termination: edges terminating at a common point.
- Co-linearity: points in a straight line.

According to the theory, the components or geons of a visual object are constructed from these invariant properties. Thus, for example, a cylinder has curved edges and two parallel edges connecting the curved edges, whereas a brick has three parallel edges and no curved edges. Biederman (1987, p. 116) argued that the five properties:

have the desirable properties that they are invariant over changes in orientation and can be determined from just a few points on each edge. Consequently, they allow a primitive [component or geon] to be extracted with great tolerance for variations of viewpoint, occlusion [obstruction], and noise.

An important part of Biederman's theory with respect to the invariant properties is what he called the "non-accidental" principle. According to this principle, regularities in the visual image reflect actual (or non-accidental) regularities in the world rather than depending on accidental characteristics of a given viewpoint. Thus, for example, it is assumed that a two-dimensional symmetry in the visual image indicates symmetry in the three-dimensional object. Use of the non-accidental principle helps object recognition, but occasionally leads to error. For example, a straight line in a visual image usually reflects a straight edge in the world, but it might not (e.g., a bicycle viewed end-on).

Some visual illusions can be explained by assuming that we use the non-accidental principle. For example, consider the Ames distorted room (described in Chapter 2). It is actually of a most peculiar shape, but when viewed from a particular point it gives rise to the same retinal image as a conventional rectangular room. Of particular relevance here, misleading properties such as symmetry and parallelism can be derived from the visual image of the Ames room, and may underlie the illusion.

Biederman's (1987) theory makes it clear how objects can be recognised in normal viewing conditions. However, we can generally recognise objects when the conditions are sub-optimal (e.g., an intervening object obscures part of the target object). According to Biederman (1987), there are various reasons why we are able to achieve object recognition in such conditions:

- The invariant properties (e.g., curvature; parallel lines) can still be detected even when only parts of edges can be seen.
- Provided that the concavities of a contour are visible, there are mechanisms allowing the missing parts of a contour to be restored.
- There is normally a considerable amount of redundant information available for recognising complex objects, and so they can still be identified when some of the geons or components are missing (e.g., a giraffe could be identified from its neck even if its legs were hidden from view).

Any adequate theory of object recognition needs to address the *binding problem*. A version of this problem arises when we are presented with several objects at the same time, and have to decide which features or geons belong to which objects. An attempt to solve this problem was made by Hummel and Biederman (1992), who proposed a connectionist model of Biederman's (1987) geon theory. This model is a seven-layer connectionist network taking as its input a line drawing of an object and producing as its output a unit representing its identity. According to Ellis and Humphreys (1999, p. 157), "The binding mechanism they employ . . . depends on synchrony in the activation of units in the network. In crude terms, units whose activation varies together are bound together, therefore so are the features they represent." More specifically, units that typically belong to the same object are connected by fast enabling links, which help to ensure that related units are all activated at the same time.

Hummel and Biederman (1992) carried out various simulation studies with their connectionist model, and showed that it provided an efficient and accurate mechanism for binding. However, it is not necessarily the case that people solve the binding problem in a similar way.

### Experimental evidence

A study by Biederman, Ju, and Clapper (1985) was designed to test the notion that complex objects can be detected even when some of the components or geons are missing. Line drawings of complex objects having six or nine components were presented briefly. Even when only three or four of their components were present, participants displayed about 90% accuracy in identifying the objects.

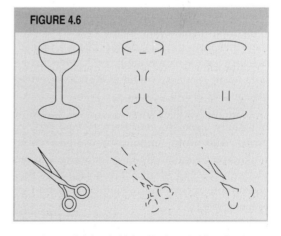

FIGURE 4.6

Intact figures (left-hand side), with degraded line drawings either preserving (middle column) or not preserving (far-right column) parts of the contour providing information about concavities. Adapted from Biederman (1987).

Biederman (1987) discussed one of his studies in which participants were presented with degraded line drawings of objects (see Figure 4.6). Object recognition was much harder to achieve when parts of the contour providing information about concavities were omitted than when other parts of the contour were deleted. This confirms the notion that information about concavities is important for object recognition.

According to Biederman's theory, object recognition depends on edge information rather than on surface information (e.g., colour). To test this, participants were presented with line drawings or full-colour photographs of common objects for between 50 and 100 ms (Biederman, 1987). Performance was comparable with the two types of stimuli: mean identification times were 11 ms faster with the coloured objects, but the error rate was slightly higher. Even objects for which colour would seem to be important (e.g., bananas) showed no benefit from being presented in colour.

Joseph and Proffitt (1996) pointed out that many studies have found that colour does help object recognition, especially for objects (e.g., cherries) having a characteristic colour. They replicated this finding. They also found that colour *knowledge* can be more important than colour *perception* in object recognition. For example, their participants took a relatively long time to decide that an orange-coloured asparagus was not celery, because the stored colours for asparagus and celery are very similar. Somewhat surprisingly, they took less time to decide that an orange-coloured asparagus was not a carrot, even though the visually presented colour of the asparagus was the same as that of carrots.

Biederman (1987) argued that the input image is initially organised into its constituent parts or geons, with geons forming the building blocks of object recognition. However, as we saw earlier, global processing of an entire object often precedes more specific processing of its parts (see Kimchi, 1992).

In sum, there is some experimental support for the kind of theory proposed by Biederman (1987). However, the central theoretical assumptions have not been tested directly. For example, there is no convincing evidence that the 36 components or geons proposed by Biederman do actually form the building blocks of object recognition.

*Evaluation*

As Humphreys and Riddoch (1994) pointed out, many theories of object recognition (e.g., those of Marr and Nishihara, and of Biederman) propose that object recognition depends on a series of processes as follows:

- Coding of edges.
- Grouping or encoding into higher-order features.
- Matching to stored structural knowledge.
- Access to semantic knowledge.

These theories have the great advantage over earlier theories of being more realistic about the complexities of recognising three-dimensional objects. However, they are still rather limited. First, these theories are reasonably effective when applied to objects having readily identifiable constituent parts, but they are much less so when applied to objects that do not (e.g., clouds).

Second, Biederman (1987) argued that edge-based extraction processes provide enough information to permit object recognition. As we have seen, evidence for this hypothesis was reported by Biederman and Ju (1988), who found that object recognition was as good with line drawings as with colour photographs. However, Sanocki et al. (1998) pointed out that such evidence only supports the hypothesis provided that line drawings consist only of edges that are present in the original stimulus. In fact, line drawings are usually idealised versions of the original edge information (e.g., edges that are irrelevant to the object are often omitted). Sanocki et al. (1998) also pointed out that edge-extraction processes are more likely to lead to accurate object recognition when objects are presented on their own rather than in the context of other objects. The reason is that it can be hard to decide which edges belong to which objects when several objects are presented together.

Sanocki et al. (1998) obtained strong support for the view that edge information is often insufficient to allow object recognition. Their

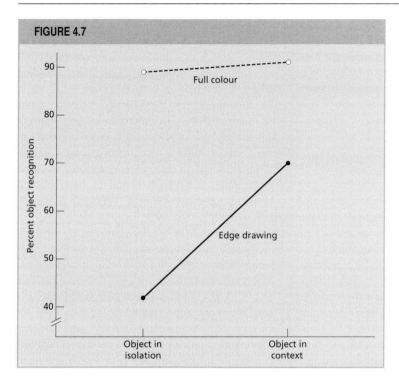

**FIGURE 4.7**

Object recognition as a function of stimulus type (edge drawings vs. colour photographs) and presence vs. absence of context. Data from Sanocki et al. (1998).

participants were presented for 1 second each with objects shown in the form of edge drawings or full-colour photographs, and these objects were presented in isolation or in context. Object recognition was much worse with the edge drawings than with the colour photographs, and this was especially the case when objects were presented in context (see Figure 4.7). Sanocki et al. (1998, p. 346) concluded as follows:

> Edge information is far from being suffici-
> ent for object recognition. The results call
> into question psychological and computer
> vision models [e.g., Biederman, 1987] that
> use local edge extractors as their only low-
> level process.

Third, Marr and Nishihara (1978), Biederman (1987, 1990), and others have emphasised the notion that object recognition involves matching an object-centred representation that is independent of the observer's viewpoint with object information stored in long-term memory. This theoretical view was explored by Biederman and Gerhardstein

(1993). They argued that object naming would be primed as well by two different views of an object as by two identical views, provided that the same object-centred structural description could be constructed from both views. Their findings supported the prediction, but other findings (e.g., Tarr & Bülthoff, 1995, 1998) do not (see later discussion).

Fourth, the theories put forward by Marr and Nishihara (1978), Biederman (1987), and others only account for fairly unsubtle perceptual discriminations, such as deciding whether the animal in front of us is a dog or cow. These theories have little to say about subtle perceptual discriminations *within* classes of objects. For example, the same geons are used to describe almost any cup, but we can readily identify the cup we normally use.

Fifth, the theories have de-emphasised the important role played by context in object recognition. For example, Palmer (1975) presented a picture of a scene (e.g., a kitchen), followed by the very brief presentation of the picture of an object. This object was sometimes appropriate to the context (e.g., a loaf), or it was inappropriate (e.g., mailbox or drum). There was also a further condition in which no contextual scene was presented. The context had a systematic effect on the probability of identifying the object correctly, with the probability being greater when the object was appropriate to the context, intermediate when there was no context, and lowest when the object was inappropriate to the context.

## Viewpoint-dependent and viewpoint-invariant theories

Theories of object recognition can be categorised as viewpoint-invariant or viewpoint-dependent. According to viewpoint-invariant theories (e.g., Biederman, 1987), ease of object recognition is *not* affected by the observer's viewpoint. In contrast, viewpoint-dependent theories (e.g., Tarr, 1995; Tarr & Bülthoff, 1995, 1998) assume that changes in viewpoint reduce the speed and/or accuracy of object recognition. According to such theories, "object representations are collections of views that depict the appearance of objects from specific viewpoints" (Tarr & Bülthoff, 1995). Object recognition is easier when the view of an object seen by an observer corresponds to one of the stored views of that object than when it does not.

Several findings support each type of theory. Research by Tarr supporting viewpoint-dependent theories was discussed by Tarr and Bülthoff (1995). Tarr gave participants extensive practice at recognising novel objects from certain specified viewpoints. The objects were then presented from various novel viewpoints. The findings across several studies were very consistent: "Response times and error rates for naming a familiar object in an unfamiliar viewpoint increased with rotation distance between the unfamiliar viewpoint and the nearest familiar viewpoint" (Tarr & Bülthoff, 1995, p. 1500). These findings are as predicted by viewpoint-dependent theories.

Phinney and Siegel (1999) pointed out that viewpoint-invariant theories (e.g., Biederman, 1987) typically assume that object recognition is based on stored three-dimensional representations of objects. In contrast, viewpoint-dependent theories often assume that object recognition involves multiple stored two-dimensional representations. Phinney and Siegel presented their participants with two random-dot stimuli separated by 1 second, and asked them to decide whether the shapes of the two stimuli were the same. Some of the stimuli contained only two-dimensional cues, whereas others contained only three-dimensional cues. The key finding was that object recognition could be supported by two-dimensional or by three-dimensional cues. Of most theoretical importance, the findings indicate that, "there is an internal storage of an object's representations in three dimensions, a tenet [belief] that has been rejected by viewpoint-based theories" (Phinney & Siegel, 1999, p. 725).

There seem to be some circumstances in which viewpoint-invariant mechanisms are used in object recognition, and others in which viewpoint-dependent mechanisms are used. According to Tarr and Bülthoff (1995), viewpoint-invariant mechanisms are more important when the task involves making easy categorical discriminations (e.g., between cars and bicycles). In contrast, viewpoint-dependent mechanisms are more important when the task requires hard within-category discriminations (e.g., between different makes of car). Indeed, Tarr and Bülthoff (1998, pp. 4–5) concluded that, "almost every behavioural study that has reported viewpoint-dependent recognition has also used tasks in which subjects must discriminate between visually-similar objects, not object classes."

Evidence consistent with this general approach was reported by Tarr et al. (1998). They considered recognition of the same 3-D objects under various conditions across nine experiments. Performance was close to viewpoint-invariant when the recognition task was easy (e.g., detailed feedback on each trial), but it was viewpoint-dependent when the task was difficult (e.g., no feedback provided).

## COGNITIVE NEUROPSYCHOLOGY APPROACH

Brain-damaged patients suffer from a very wide range of perceptual difficulties, and it would not be possible to discuss all forms of perceptual disorder relating to object recognition in this chapter. Instead, we will focus on some of the

| Three perceptual disorders | | |
|---|---|---|
| *Visual agnosia* | *Optic aphasia* | *Category-specific anomia* |
| Impaired object recognition although visual information reaches the cortex. | Impaired ability to name visually presented objects although use of object can be mimed. | Selectively impaired ability to name certain categories of objects. |
| Subdivided into: *Apperceptive agnosia* Deficits in perceptual processing. | | |
| *Associative agnosia* Impaired visual memory or access to semantic knowledge. | | |

main disorders: visual agnosia; optic aphasia; and category-specific anomia. Patients having specific problems with face recognition are discussed later in the chapter.

*Visual agnosia* is the term used to describe patients who have severely impaired object recognition, in spite of the fact that visual information reaches the cortex. In addition, patients with visual agnosia are able to recognise objects by using other sense modalities (e.g., touch; hearing). We can distinguish between two forms of visual agnosia:

1. *Apperceptive agnosia*: in this condition, object recognition is impaired because of severe deficits in perceptual processing.
2. *Associative agnosia*: in this condition, perceptual processes are intact, and object recognition is poor because of impaired visual memories of objects or impaired access to semantic knowledge about objects from these memories.

*Optic aphasia* refers to a condition in which there are particular problems in naming visually presented objects even though the same objects can be named when handled. A distinction has been drawn between optic aphasia and visual agnosia, because optic aphasics have the ability to mime the appropriate use of visually presented objects that they cannot name. This has sometimes been interpreted as meaning that optic aphasics have normal access to semantic information about visually presented objects. However, the evidence suggests

that such patients have some problems in accessing semantic information about objects (see Ellis & Humphreys, 1999). Schinder, Benson, and Scharre (1994, p. 455) argued that there were only minor differences between optic aphasia and visual agnosia, with the two conditions "differing primarily in the degree of callosal disconnection." More specifically, there is more damage to the corpus callosum (which connects the two hemispheres) in optic aphasics than in visual agnosics.

*Category-specific anomia* is a condition in which there is a selective impairment in naming certain categories of objects. The typical pattern in cases of category-specific anomia is that object naming is considerably worse for living things than for non-living things (e.g., Farah & Wallace, 1992).

## Visual agnosia

Much of the research in this area has centred on visual agnosia, and our coverage of the experimental evidence focuses on this disorder. Connectionist models designed to account for some of the major perceptual disorders have recently been put forward, and are discussed in the next major section of the chapter.

Two tests used to assess apperceptive agnosia are the Gollin picture test and the incomplete letters task. In the Gollin picture test, the participants are presented with a series of increasingly complete drawings of an object. Patients with apperceptive agnosia require more complete drawings than normal individuals to identify the objects. The incomplete letters task involves presenting letters in fragmented form and asking the participants to identify them. Patients with apperceptive agnosia are worse than normals at this task. Patients with apperceptive agnosia perform worse than those with associative agnosia on tests involving matching and copying objects that patients cannot name (see Køhler & Moscovitch, 1997).

Warrington and Taylor (1978) argued that the key problem in apperceptive agnosia is an inability to achieve object constancy, which involves being able to identify objects regardless of viewing conditions. They tested this hypothesis using pairs of photographs, one of which was a conventional or usual view and the other of which was an unusual view. For example, the usual view of a flat-iron was photographed from above, whereas the unusual view showed only the base of the iron and part of the handle. When the photographs were shown one at a time, the patients were reasonably good at identifying the objects when they were shown in the usual or conventional view, but were very poor at identifying the same objects shown from an unusual angle.

Warrington and Taylor (1978) obtained more dramatic evidence of the perceptual problems of these patients when they presented pairs of photographs together, and asked the patients to decide whether the same object was depicted in both photographs. The patients performed poorly on this task, indicating that they found it hard to identify an object shown from an unusual angle even when they knew what it might be on the basis of their identification of the accompanying usual view.

The findings obtained by Warrington and Taylor can be explained by assuming that the patients found it hard to transform unusual views of objects into appropriate 3-D model representations as described by Marr (1982). However, the view of an object can be unusual in at least two ways. It can be unusual because the object is foreshortened, thus making it hard to determine its principal axis of elongation, or because a distinctive feature of the object is hidden from view.

These possibilities were compared by Humphreys and Riddoch (1984, 1985). They used photographs in which some of the unusual views

were based on obscuring a distinctive feature, whereas others were based on foreshortening. The participants either had to name the object in a photograph, or they had to decide which two out of three photographs were of the same object.

In four patients having right posterior cerebral lesions, Humphreys and Riddoch (1984, 1985) found that they performed poorly with the foreshortened photographs but not with those lacking a distinctive feature. Marr and Nishihara (1978) argued that foreshortening makes it especially hard to attain a 3-D model representation, and so the findings are generally consistent with their theoretical position.

Patients with associative agnosia have problems in naming objects. However, they are fairly good at copying and matching objects they cannot name. For example, they can match photographs of objects taken from unusual angles. Some associative agnosics can discriminate on the object decision task between perceptually similar objects such as pictures of real objects and artificial objects created by switching the parts of real objects (e.g., Sheridan & Humphreys, 1993).

Some patients with associative agnosia show the phenomenon of category specificity, meaning that they have special problems in recognising certain categories of objects. For example, Warrington and Shallice (1984) studied a patient, JBR, who suffered from severe associative agnosia. He had much greater problems in identifying pictures of living than of non-living things, having success rates of about 6% and 90%, respectively. The findings from other studies indicate that the pattern shown by JBR is much more common than the opposite pattern, i.e., worse recognition of non-living than of living things. However, Warrington and McCarthy (1994) did report on one patient who showed consistently worse performance with drawings of objects than with drawings of animals. The task involved deciding which of five drawings was most closely associated with the target drawing.

How can we account for these findings? The greater difficulty in recognising living than non-living things can be explained by assuming that pictures of living things are more similar to each other than are pictures of non-living things, and are thus harder to recognise. Evidence consistent with this view was reported by Gaffan and Heywood (1993). They asked normal individuals to name pictures of living and non-living things that were presented for only 20 ms each. The key finding was that all the participants performed much worse on living than on non-living things, indicating that living things are harder to recognise.

The findings of Gaffan and Heywood (1993) do not explain why a few patients with associative agnosia have greater difficulty in object recognition for non-living objects than living ones. Perhaps different brain areas contain at least some of the semantic knowledge used in recognising living and non-living objects. A theory of this type was put forward by Farah and McClelland (1991), and is discussed in the next section.

An interesting case of agnosia was reported by Humphreys and Riddoch (1987). They studied HJA, who could not recognise most objects after suffering a stroke. However, he produced accurate drawings of objects he could not recognise, and he could draw objects from memory. His perceptual problems seem to centre around the fact that he found it very hard to *integrate* visual information about the parts of objects in order to see the objects themselves. In HJA's own words: "I have come to cope with recognising many common objects, if they are standing alone . . . When objects are placed together, though, I have more difficulties. To recognise one sausage on its own is far from picking one out from a dish of cold foods in a salad" (Humphreys & Riddoch, 1987).

Evidence that HJA had a serious problem in grouping or organising visual information was obtained by Humphreys et al. (1992). The task of searching for an inverted T target among a homogeneous set of distractors (Ts) is easy for most people. However, HJA's performance was very slow and error-prone, presumably because he found in very hard to group the distractors together.

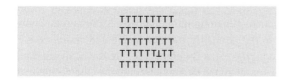

HJA is not the only agnosic patient to have problems with integrating visual information. For example, Behrmann, Moscovitch, and Winocur (1994) studied CK, a man who suffered head injury in a car crash. CK was reasonably good at copying a figure consisting of three touching geometric shapes (two diamonds and a circle). Nearly all normal individuals would copy this figure object by object. What CK did was to follow the outer boundary of the whole figure, which meant that he often moved on to the next shape before completing his drawing of the last one. As Gazzaniga, Ivry, and Mangun (1998, p. 193) concluded, "An inability to integrate features into a coherent whole may be the hallmark of many agnosic patients."

In sum, as Humphreys and Riddoch (1993) pointed out, the distinction between apperceptive agnosia and associative agnosia is oversimplified. According to them, visual object recognition involves a series of stages: feature coding; feature integration; accessing stored structural object descriptions; and accessing semantic knowledge about objects. Problems with visual object recognition can occur because of impairments at any of these stages. This is a more complex (but realistic) position than the simple distinction between apperceptive and associative agnosia.

## COGNITIVE SCIENCE APPROACH

Several theorists have put forward computer models designed to clarify the processes involved in object recognition and other higher-level perceptual processes. Some theorists have not only put forward computer models of perception, but have also assessed the effects of "lesions" or damage to the models on perceptual processing. The intention is to mimic the effects of brain damage to the human perceptual system. We will be considered two such models. The first computer model is designed to reveal some of the processes of object recognition, and has been lesioned to mimic the effects of visual agnosia. The second computer model focuses on various higher-level perceptual processes, and has been lesioned to mimic the effects of various human perceptual disorders.

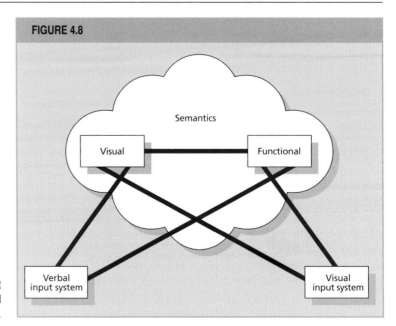

FIGURE 4.8

The architecture of a connectionist model proposed by Farah and McClelland (1991).

## Farah and McClelland (1991) model

Farah and McClelland (1991) produced a computational model based on a connectionist network. The model consists of two peripheral input systems (visual and verbal) and a semantic system. When an object is presented visually, this produces a unique pattern of activation within the visual input system. When the name of an object is presented, there is a unique pattern of activation within the verbal input system. There are no connections between the visual and verbal systems (see Figure 4.8). How is the model able to name objects? According to Farah and McClelland (1991), the visual and verbal systems are linked by a semantic system, and object naming involves information proceeding from the visual system to the semantic system and on to the verbal system.

One of the key features of the computer model is that the semantic system is divided into visual and functional or semantic units. There are three times as many of the former as of the latter, and all the units in the semantic system are interconnected. The visual units possess information about the visual characteristics of objects (e.g., bananas are yellow; people have two legs). In contrast, the functional units possess semantic information

about the uses of objects or about appropriate ways of interacting with them (e.g., food is to be eaten; chairs are for sitting on). Why are there three times as many visual units as functional units within the semantic system? Human participants were provided with dictionary definitions of living and non-living objects, and asked to classify the descriptors as visual or functional. Three times more of the descriptors were classified as visual than as functional. Of particular importance, the ratio of visual to functional descriptors was 7.7:1 for non-living objects, but only 1.4:1 for non-living objects. This difference between living and non-living objects was built into the semantic system of the model.

The computational model was tested by training it on object recognition (linking the visual and verbal representations) of 10 living and 10 non-living objects. Its performance was perfect after only 40 training trials. After that, Farah and McClelland (1991) simulated the effects of visual associative agnosia by means of "lesions" to the semantic system. This involved deactivating some of the semantic units. Damage to the visual units in the semantic system had much more severe consequences for object recognition of living than of non-living objects. Damage to the functional units had much less effect. It produced only a small reduction in object recognition, and that was limited to non-living objects.

*Evaluation*

The computational model of Farah and McClelland (1991) has various strengths. First, it provides a simple account of key processes involved in object recognition. Second, the model explains the double dissociation that has been found, with some patients having greater object recognition with living than with non-living objects, whereas some have the opposite pattern. Third, it also helps to explain why there are many more patients who have impaired ability to recognise living objects than those who have problems in recognising non-living objects.

On the negative side, the processes involved in object recognition are more complex than is suggested by the model. In addition, it is not clear that the semantic system is organised neatly into visual and functional sub-systems. It is possible that it is organised in part on a categorical basis, with different categories (e.g., animals; fruits) being stored in different regions of the brain. This possibility was explored by Damasio et al. (1996) who asked brain-damaged participants to name famous faces, animals, and tools. Different areas of the left hemisphere of the brain were associated with impaired object recognition for the three types of objects. As Damasio et al. (1996, pp. 499–500) concluded, "Abnormal retrieval of words for persons was correlated with damage clustered in the left TP [temporal pole]; abnormal retrieval of words for animals was correlated with damage in left IT [inferotemporal region]; and abnormal retrieval of words for tools correlated with damage in posterolateral IT [inferotemporal region]." These areas of the brain are shown in Figure 4.9.

Damasio et al. then gave the same object-naming task to normal participants. PET data showed that different areas of the left hemisphere were activated, depending on whether the participants were naming famous faces, animals, or tools. Most strikingly, the areas involved were the same as those identified from the study on brain-damaged patients. However, it is certain that

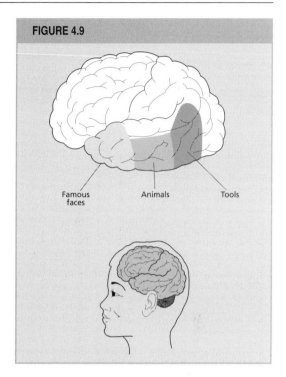

**FIGURE 4.9**

Famous faces    Animals    Tools

Areas of the left hemisphere associated with impaired object recognition for famous faces, animals, and tools. Adapted from Damasio et al. (1996).

several other areas of the brain are also involved in object recognition.

There is another problem with the model of Farah and McClelland (1991). According to the model, the visual and perceptual units in the semantic system are all *interconnected*. It follows that patients with severely impaired visual memory for objects should also have poor memory for functional information when provided with object names. In fact, some patients have intact functional memory for objects combined with very poor visual object memory (e.g., Riddoch & Humphreys, 1993).

## Humphreys et al. (1995) model

Humphreys, Lamote, and Lloyd-Jones (1995) produced an interactive activation and competition model of object recognition and naming, which has also been applied to visual agnosia. The model contains pools of units of four kinds (see Figure 4.10):

**FIGURE 4.10**

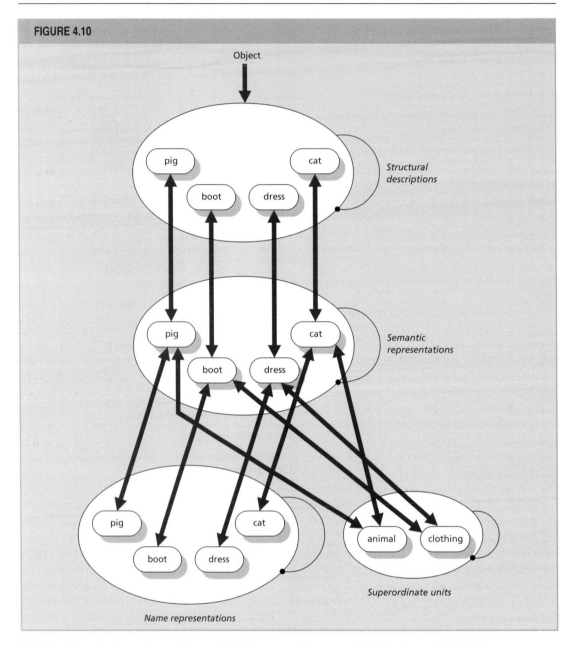

The interactive activation and competition model of object recognition proposed by Humphreys et al. (1995).

1. Stored structural descriptions of objects.
2. Semantic representations.
3. Name representations.
4. Superordinate units or category labels.

Activation from the structural units proceeds initially to semantic units before proceeding to name representations. There are bi-directional excitatory connections between related units at adjacent levels of the model. In addition, there are mutually inhibitory connections between units within each level. According to the model, the structural descriptions of objects visually similar to the object actually presented are activated to some extent. Of particular importance, it is assumed that living things are typically more visually similar to other members of the same category than is the case with non-living things.

## Evidence

According to the model, living things should generally be named more slowly than non-living things, but should be categorised more rapidly. Why is this so? Living things are more visually similar to each other than are non-living things. This causes more activation of irrelevant structural representations and name representations, which inhibits naming living things and slows performance. In contrast, the additional activation of irrelevant representations from the same category as the presented object for living objects increases activation of the appropriate category label and so speeds up categorisation. Both predictions were confirmed in simulations of the model, and correspond to findings on people (Humphreys et al., 1995).

Humphreys, Riddoch, and Quinlan (1988) found that objects with common names were named faster than objects with less common names, and that this frequency effect was greater for non-living things than for living things. Humphreys et al. (1995) found that their model produced the same pattern of findings. According to the model, the activation from semantic representations to name representations is greater for objects with more common names, and this produces the overall frequency effect. The greater activation of irrelevant structural and name representations when living objects are presented reduces this advantage.

Associative agnosics typically show worse identification of living things than of non-living things, but are reasonably good at categorising objects (e.g., Sheridan & Humphreys, 1993). When the model was "lesioned" in various places, this reduced its ability to name objects and especially living objects. The greater effect on living objects occurred because the presentation of a living object tends to activate the structural representations of various visually similar objects, and this makes naming more difficult.

Patients with category-specific anomia have selective impairment in the ability to name certain categories of objects (typically living objects), in spite of being able to access much semantic information about objects (e.g., Farah & Wallace, 1992). Humphreys et al. (1995) tried to mimic the effects of category-specific anomia by "lesioning" connections between the semantic and name representations in their model. They found that the model showed worse naming performance for living things than for non-living things, in line with the evidence from patients. The model is an interactive one, with the consequence that the greater activation of irrelevant structural representations when living objects are seen has knock-on effects that influence naming.

## Evaluation

The interactive activation and competition model of Humphreys et al. (1995) provides accounts of object recognition in both normal individuals and in those with various visual disorders. This is an advance on the model of Farah and McClelland (1991), which was designed only to simulate performance in patients suffering from visual disorders. It is also an advance on the earlier model in that it provides a detailed process model which can be applied to object recognition, object naming, and object categorisation.

There is another key advantage of the Humphreys et al. (1995) model. It is better equipped to handle the existence of patients with intact functional or semantic information for objects when presented with their names but greatly impaired visual information about objects (see earlier). In the Humphreys et al. (1995) model, visual or structural information is stored separately from functional (or semantic) information, and functional or semantic information is closer than visual or structural information to name information. Thus, it is entirely possible for object names to activate functional but not visual information.

Humphreys et al. (1995) found that "lesions" to the connections between structural descriptions and semantic representations in their model produced a pattern in which access to visual information when an object was presented was essentially intact but there was impaired access to semantic

FIGURE 4.11

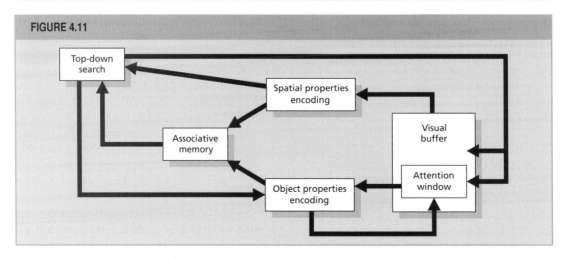

Kosslyn et al.'s theory of high-level vision. Adapted from Kosslyn et al. (1990).

information. This corresponds to the pattern found in some studies on patients with optic aphasia (e.g., Hillis & Caramazza, 1995). For example, such patients are good at at the difficult task of distinguishing between pictures of real objects and of artificial objects formed by combining parts from different real objects, even though they only seem to have partial access to semantic information. As Ellis and Humpreys (1999, p. 558) pointed out, these findings are problematical for other models: "Models such as those of Farah and McClelland (1991), which do not separate different forms of stored knowledge, find it more difficult to account for such a pattern of dissociation in which one ability stays intact."

The model does not provide a convincing explanation of those patients who have poorer naming and access to semantic information with non-living than with living things (e.g., Warrington & McCarthy, 1994). However, Ellis and Humphreys (1999, p. 554) argued that, "the effects can be accounted for if the lesion is not global but more selective, affecting the stored units and connections for the representations of non-living relative to living things."

## General theory of high-level vision

Kosslyn et al. (1990) put forward an ambitious theory of high-level vision (visual processing involving the use of previously stored information). Evidence about brain functioning was used in its formation, and a computer simulation model was constructed to consider what components are necessary for high-level visual processing. This computer simulation model was also used to consider the results of different kinds of damage to the visual system.

The outline of the theory is shown in Figure 4.11. There are various sub-systems within the overall visual perceptual system, and each of these sub-systems consists of a parallel distributed network. In terms of the flow of information, the starting point is information resembling that in Marr's (1982) $2\frac{1}{2}$-D sketch (i.e., edge, depth, and orientation information) being delivered to the *visual buffer*. There is more information available in the visual buffer than can be passed on to the later stages of visual processing, and so there needs to be an *attention window* to handle this problem.

One of the central assumptions of the theory is that the encoding of object information (i.e., "what" information) and of spatial information (i.e., "where" information) occurs in separate sub-systems. There is much support for this assumption (see Chapter 3). It is assumed that the spatial information supplied to the *spatial properties sub-system* from the visual buffer is retinotopic (location is specified relative to the retina). One of the main features of this sub-system is to transform this retinotopic representation, in which location is represented relative to objects in space. The object properties sub-system identifies the non-accidental properties of the input on the basis of edge, texture, colour, and intensity information in ways similar to those proposed by Biederman (1987). Kosslyn et al. (1990) left it open whether this sub-system produces viewpoint-centred or object-centred object representations.

The *associative memory sub-system* is responsible for integrating spatial and object information supplied by the spatial properties and object properties sub-systems. This information is compared against appropriate stored information in order to produce object recognition. This is an ongoing process: as spatial and object information accumulates in associative memory, a hypothesis of the object's identity is generated. Finally, *top-down search* tests the hypothesis. It can be used to look up in associative memory the properties the hypothesised object should have, or it can produce a shift in attention if this is needed for object recognition.

## Computer simulation

The implications of damage to parts of the visual processing system were assessed by Kosslyn et al. (1990) using computer simulation. Two-dimensional stimulus arrays representing either a face or a fox were placed in the visual buffer, and limited arrays consisting of one-ninth of the original array were passed on via the attention window to the other sub-systems. Four different tasks were then given to the computer simulation program:

1. What is this?
2. Who is this? (for faces only)
3. Are they the same? (for two pictures presented in succession)
4. What is here? (for two pictures presented together)

The most striking finding of the computer simulation was that many perceptual problems can be caused by several different kinds of lesion or damage. One example is *visual agnosia* (involving deficient ability to recognise visual objects in spite

of intact naming and attentional abilities), which was defined by poor performance on the first task listed earlier combined with intact performance on the third task. There were 34 different types of damage that produced this particular deficit. In similar fashion, there is *prosopagnosia* (difficulties in face recognition, see next section), which was defined by being able to identify a face as a face (first task) but being unable to identify correctly which face it was (second task). This pattern of performance was produced by 16 different types of damage.

Why can some disorders of visual perception be produced in numerous different ways? The main reason is because of the interconnected nature of the visual processing system shown in Figure 4.11. For example, damage within the object properties sub-system means there is an impoverished output from that sub-system to the associative memory sub-system. As a result, the associative memory sub-system cannot function effectively, even though it may be intact.

Kosslyn et al. (1990) also discussed a condition known as *simultanagnosia*, in which only one object at a time can be perceived (see also Chapter 5). The computer simulation revealed that this condition arose only through partial damage to that part of the spatial properties sub-system responsible for producing a spatiotopic representation. It could thus be predicted that simultanagnosia should be rarer than most other forms of perceptual deficit, and that is indeed the case.

## Evaluation

The theory proposed by Kosslyn et al. (1990) has three major strengths. First, it was the first theory to propose computational processing sub-systems underlying high-level vision that are in line with available knowledge of brain systems. Second, it provides a useful framework for cognitive neuro-psychologists in their efforts to make theoretical sense of the data from brain-damaged patients. Third, the theory is one of the few in which attentional and perceptual phenomena are integrated.

On the negative side, the theory is at too great a level of generality. As a result, there is little clarification of the detailed processes operating within each sub-system. This lack of specificity is perhaps especially noticeable so far as associative memory and top-down search are concerned. In both cases, it is much clearer *what* is accomplished by the particular sub-system than *how* it is accomplished.

## FACE RECOGNITION

There are various reasons for devoting a separate section of this chapter to face recognition. First, as face recognition is the most common way of identifying people we know, the ability to recognise faces is of great significance in our everyday lives. Second, face recognition differs in various ways from other forms of object recognition. Third, we now know a considerable amount about the processes involved in face recognition. Fourth, there is a theoretically interesting condition known as *prosopagnosia*. Prosopagnosic patients are unable to recognise familiar faces, and this can even extend to their own faces in a mirror. However, they generally have few problems in recognising other familiar objects. This inability to recognise faces occurs even though prosopagnosic patients can still recognise familiar people from their voices and names.

### Bruce and Young's (1986) model of face recognition

Influential models of face recognition were put forward by Bruce and Young (1986) and Burton and Bruce (1993). There are eight components in the Bruce and Young (1986) model (see Figure 4.12):

- Structural encoding: this produces various representations or descriptions of faces.
- Expression analysis: people's emotional states can be inferred from their facial features.
- Facial speech analysis: speech perception can be aided by observation of a speaker's lip movements.
- Directed visual processing: specific facial information may be processed selectively.
- Face recognition units: they contain structural information about known faces.

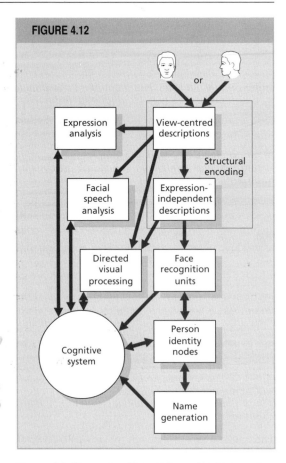

**FIGURE 4.12**

The model of face recognition put forward by Bruce and Young (1986).

- Person identity nodes: they provide information about individuals (e.g., their occupation, interests).
- Name generation: a person's name is stored separately.
- Cognitive system: this contains additional information (e.g., that actors and actresses tend to have attractive faces); this system also influences which of the other components receive attention.

The recognition of familiar faces depends mainly on structural encoding, face recognition units, person identity nodes, and name generation. In contrast, the processing of unfamiliar faces involves structural encoding, expression analysis, facial speech analysis, and directed visual processing.

## Experimental evidence

Bruce and Young (1986) assumed that familiar and unfamiliar faces are processed differently. If it were possible to find patients who showed good recognition of familiar faces but poor recognition of unfamiliar faces, and other patients who showed the opposite pattern, this double dissociation would suggest that the processes involved in the recognition of familiar and unfamiliar faces are different.

Malone et al. (1982) tested one patient who showed reasonable ability to recognise photographs of famous statesmen (14 out of 17 correct), but who was very impaired at matching unfamiliar faces. A second patient performed normally at matching unfamiliar faces, but had great difficulties in recognising photographs of famous people (only 5 out of 22 correct).

According to the model, the name generation component can be accessed only via the appropriate person identity node. As a result, we should never be able to put a name to a face without at the same time having available other information about that person (e.g., his or her occupation). Young, Hay, and Ellis (1985) asked participants to keep a diary record of the specific problems they experienced in face recognition. There were 1008 incidents altogether, but participants never reported putting a name to a face while knowing nothing else about that person. In contrast, there were 190 occasions on which a participant could remember a fair amount of information about a person, but not their name.

Cognitive neuropsychological evidence is also relevant. Practically no brain-damaged patients can put names to faces without knowing anything else about the person, but several patients show the opposite pattern. For example, Flude, Ellis, and Kay (1989) studied a patient, EST, who was able to retrieve the occupations for 85% of very familiar people when presented with their faces, but could recall only 15% of their names.

According to the model, another kind of problem should be fairly common. If the appropriate face recognition unit is activated, but the person identity node is not, there should be a feeling of familiarity coupled with an inability to think of any relevant information about the person. In the set of incidents collected by Young et al. (1985), this was reported on 233 occasions.

Reference back to Figure 4.12 suggests further predictions. When we look at a familiar face, familiarity information from the face recognition unit should be accessed first, followed by information about that person (e.g., occupation) from the person identity node, followed by that person's name from the name generation component. Thus, familiarity decisions about a face should be made faster than decisions based on person identity nodes. As predicted, Young, McWeeny, Hay, and Ellis (1986b) found that the decision as to whether a face was familiar was made faster than the decision as to whether it was the face of a politician.

It also follows from the model that decisions based on person identity nodes should be made faster than those based on the name generation component. Young, McWeeny, Hay, and Ellis (1986a) found that participants were much faster to decide whether a face belonged to a politician than they were to produce the person's name.

## Evaluation

The model of Bruce and Young (1986) provides a coherent account of the various kinds of information about faces, and the ways in which these kinds of information are related to each other. Another significant strength is that differences in the processing of familiar and unfamiliar faces are spelled out.

There are various limitations with the model. First, the account given of the processing of unfamiliar faces is much less detailed than that of familiar faces. Second, the cognitive system is vaguely specified. Third, some evidence is inconsistent with the assumption that names can be accessed only via relevant autobiographical information stored at the person identity node. An amnesic patient, ME, could match the faces and names of 88% of famous people for whom she was unable to recall any autobiographical information (de Haan, Young, & Newcombe, 1991).

Fourth, it is important for the theory that some patients show better recognition for familiar faces than unfamiliar faces, whereas others show the opposite pattern. This double dissociation was obtained by Malone et al. (1982), but has proved difficult to replicate. For example, Young et al. (1993) studied 34 brain-damaged men, and assessed their familiar face identification, unfamiliar face matching, and expression analysis. Five of the patients had a selective impairment of expression analysis, but there was much weaker evidence of selective impairment of familiar or unfamiliar face recognition. Young et al. (1993) argued that previous research may have produced misleading conclusions because of methodogical limitations.

## Interactive activation and competition model

Burton and Bruce (1993) developed the Bruce and Young (1986) model. Their interactive activation and competition model adopted a connectionist approach (see Figure 4.13). The face recognition units (FRUs) and the name recognition units (NRUs) contain stored information about specific faces and names, respectively. Person identity nodes (PINs) are gateways into semantic information, and can be activated by verbal input about people's names as well as by facial input. As a result, they provide information about the familiarity of individuals based on either verbal or facial information. Finally, the semantic information units (SIUs) contain name and other information about individuals (e.g., occupation; nationality).

### Experimental evidence

The model has been applied to associative priming effects that have been found with faces. For example, the time taken to decide whether a face is familiar is reduced when the face of a related person is shown immediately beforehand (e.g., Bruce & Valentine, 1986). According to the model, the first face activates SIUs, which feed back activation to the PIN of that face and related faces. This then speeds up the familiarity decision for the second face. As PINs can be activated by both names and faces, it follows that associative priming for familiarity decisions on faces should be found when the name of a person (e.g., Prince

Philip) is followed by the face of a related person (e.g., Queen Elizabeth). Precisely this has been found (e.g., Bruce & Valentine, 1986).

One of the differences between the interactive activation and competition model and Bruce and Young's (1986) model concerns the storage of name and autobiographical information. These kinds of information are both stored in SIUs in the Burton and Bruce (1993) model, whereas name information can only be accessed *after* autobiographical information in the Bruce and Young (1986) model. The fact that the amnesic patient ME (discussed earlier) could match names to faces in spite of being unable to access autobiographical information is more consistent with the Burton and Bruce (1993) model. In similar fashion, Cohen (1990) found that faces produced better recall of names than of occupations when the names were meaningful and the occupations were meaningless. This could not happen according to the Bruce and Young (1986) model, but poses no problems for the Burton and Bruce (1993) model.

The interactive activation and competition model can also be applied to the findings from patients with prosopagnosia. These findings are discussed later in the chapter.

## Configurational information

When we recognise a face shown in a photograph, there are two major kinds of information we might use: (1) information about the individual features (e.g., eye colour); or (2) information about the configuration or overall arrangement of the features. Many approaches to face recognition are based on a feature approach. For example, police forces often make use of Identikit, or Photofit, to aid face recognition in eyewitnesses. Photofit involves constructing a face resembling that of the criminal on a feature-by-feature basis (Figure 4.14).

Evidence that the configuration of facial features also needs to be considered was reported by Young, Hellawell, and Hay (1987). They constructed faces from photographs by combining the top halves and bottom halves of different famous faces. When the two halves were closely aligned, participants experienced great difficulty in naming the top halves. However, their performance was

**FIGURE 4.13**

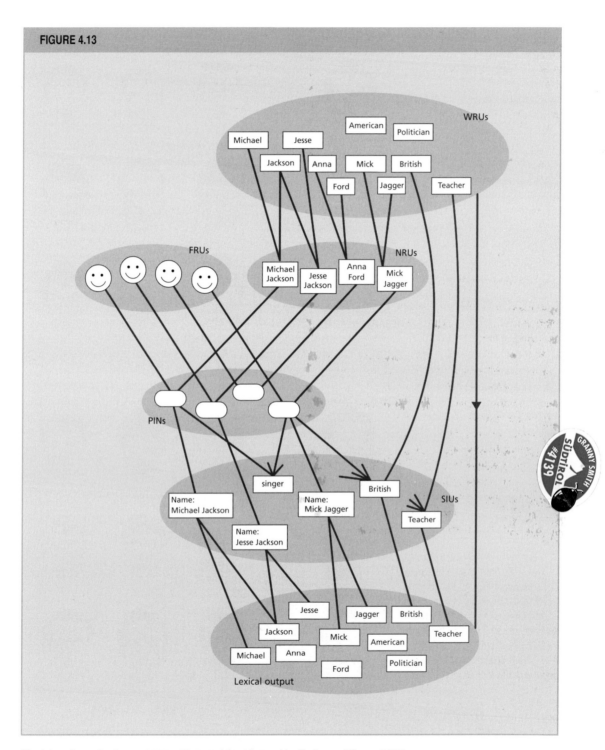

The interactive activation and competition model put forward by Burton and Bruce (1993).
WRUs = word recognition units; FRUs = face recognition units; NRUs = name recognition units;
PINs = person identity nodes; SIUs = semantic units.

**FIGURE 4.14**

Examples of attempted Photofit reconstruction. Each row shows a target face (at the left) and reconstructions of it made by different observers, from memory, immediately after viewing the target (Ellis, Shepherd, & Davies, 1975). Reproduced from The British Journal of Psychology © The British Psychological Society.

much better when the two halves were not closely aligned. Presumably close alignment produced a new configuration which interfered with face recognition.

Searcy and Bartlett (1996) reported convincing evidence that face processing is not solely configurational. Facial distortions in photographs were produced in two different ways:

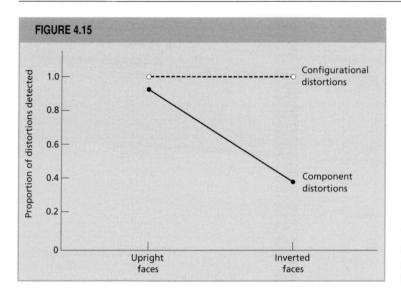

**FIGURE 4.15**

Detection of component and configurational distortions in upright and inverted faces. Based on data in Searcy and Bartlett (1996).

1.  Configural distortions (e.g., moving the eyes up and the mouth down).
2.  Component distortions (e.g., blurring the pupils of the eyes to produce cataracts, blackening teeth, and discolouring remaining teeth).

The photographs were then presented upright or inverted, and the participants gave them grotesqueness ratings on a 7-point scale. The findings suggest that component distortions are readily detected in both upright and inverted faces, whereas configural distortions are often not detected in inverted faces (see Figure 4.15). Thus, configurational and component processing can both be used with upright faces, but the processing of inverted faces is largely limited to component processing.

Most research on face recognition has used photographs or other two-dimensional stimuli. There are at least two potential limitations of such research. First, viewing an actual three-dimensional face provides more information for the observer than does viewing a two-dimensional representation. Second, people's faces are normally mobile, registering emotional states, agreement or disagreement with what is being said, and so on. None of these dynamic changes over time is available in a photograph. The importance of these changes was shown by Bruce and Valentine (1988). Small illuminated lights were spread over a face, which was then filmed in the dark so that only the lights could be seen. Participants showed some ability to determine the sex and the identity of each face on the basis of the movements of the lights, and they were very good at identifying expressive movements (such as smiling or frowning).

## Prosopagnosia

Patients with prosopagnosia cannot recognise familiar faces even though they can recognise other familiar objects. This might occur simply because more precise discriminations are required to distinguish between one specific face and another specific face than to distinguish between other kinds of objects (e.g., a chair and a table). An alternative view is that there are specific processing mechanisms that are only used for face recognition, and which are not involved in object recognition.

Farah (1994a) obtained evidence that prosopagnosic patients can be good at making precise discriminations for stimuli other than faces. She studied LH, who developed prosopagnosia as a result of a car crash. LH and control participants were presented with various faces and pairs of spectacles, and were then given a recognition-memory test. LH performed at about the same level as the normal controls in terms of recognition performance for pairs of spectacles. However, LH was at a great disadvantage to the controls on the test of face recognition (see Figure 4.16).

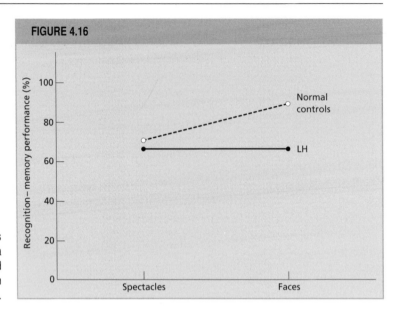

**FIGURE 4.16**

Recognition memory for faces and pairs of spectacles in a prosopagnosic patient (LH) and normal controls. Data from Farah (1994a).

The notion that face processing involves specific mechanisms would be strengthened if it were possible to show a *double dissociation*, with some patients having normal face recognition but visual agnosia for objects. Such patients have been identified (e.g., Moscovitch, Winocur, & Behrmann, 1997). If face processing involves specific mechanisms, then one might expect that there would be somewhat separate brain regions associated with face and object recognition. Farah and Aguirre (1999) carried out a meta-analysis of relevant PET and fMRI studies, and found that much of the evidence was inconsistent. However, Kanwisher, McDermott, and Chun (1997) obtained clear findings when they used fMRI to compare brain activity in response to faces, scrambled faces, houses, and hands. They found that there was face-specific activation in parts of the right fusiform gyrus, and these findings have been replicated by others (see Farah & Aguirre, 1999, for details).

## Implicit knowledge and connectionist models

Most (but not all) prosopagnosics possess some implicit knowledge about the familiarity of faces, face identity, and semantic information that is accessed through faces (e.g., occupation). For example, Bauer and Verfaellie (1988) asked a prosopagnosic patient to select the names corresponding to presented famous faces. The patient had no explicit knowledge about the faces, because his performance was at chance level. However, there were greater electrodermal responses when the names matched the faces than when they did not, indicating the existence of relevant implicit knowledge.

More evidence that prosopagnosic patients have implicit knowledge about faces was reported by De Haan, Young, and Newcombe (1987). They asked PH to classify names according to whether they belonged to politicians or not, and a famous distractor face was presented along with each name. PH was unable to classify the faces as belonging to politicians or non-politicians. However, his classification times for the names were longer when the distractor face came from a different occupational category to the name. This latter finding points to the existence of implicit knowledge about the famous individuals whose faces were presented.

Some prosopagnosic patients do not seem to possess implicit knowledge about faces. What is different about these patients? According to Køhler and Moscovitch (1997, p. 346), "Prosopagnosic patients who do not show implicit knowledge are those who have a perceptual impairment in analysing incoming information about the physical characteristics of faces."

Burton and Bruce's (1993) interactive activation and competition model (discussed earlier) provides a connectionist account of prosopagnosia and the use of implicit knowledge. Burton et al. (1991) simulated prosopagnosia by reducing the weights on the connections from the face recognition units (FRUs) to the person identity nodes (PINs). This reduced the activation of PINs to faces, and meant that faces were often not identified or recognised as familiar.

Burton et al. (1991) found that their "lesioned" model was able to make use of implicit knowledge in a similar way to prosopagnosic patients. Presentation of a face produced some activation of its PIN and the relevant SIUs, and this facilitated performance on tasks requiring the use of implicit knowledge.

*Evaluation*

The connectionist model of Burton and Bruce (1993) accounts for many of the basic phenomena associated with prosopagnosia. However, it has problems with some of the findings reported by Young and de Haan (1988). They found that their prosopagnosic patient showed evidence of using implicit knowledge about faces by learning face–name pairings faster when they were correct than when they were incorrect, but did not learn correct face–occupation pairings faster than incorrect ones. According to the model, faces partially activate relevant semantic knowledge, and so both types of correct pairings should have been learned more readily than incorrect pairings.

## Farah's two-process model

Farah (1990, 1994a) put forward a two-process model of object recognition of relevance to understanding face recognition. The model distinguishes between the following processes or forms of analysis:

1. Holistic analysis, in which the configuration or overall structure of an object is processed.
2. Analysis by parts, in which processing focuses on the constituent parts of an object.

Farah (1990) argued that holistic analysis and analysis by parts are involved in the recognition of most objects. However, face recognition depends mainly on holistic analysis, and reading words or text mostly involves analytic processing. Evidence supporting the notion that face recognition depends more than object recognition on holistic analysis was reported by Farah (1994a). The participants were presented initially with drawings of faces or houses, and were told to associate a name with each face and each house. Then the participants were presented either with whole faces and houses or with only a single feature (e.g., mouth; front door). Their task was to decide whether a given feature belonged to the individual whose name they had been given previously.

The findings are shown in Figure 4.17. Recognition performance for facial features was much better when the whole face was presented than when only a single feature was presented. In contrast, recognition for house features was very similar in whole and single-feature conditions. These findings suggest that holistic analysis is much more important for face recognition than for object recognition.

Farah (1994a) obtained additional support for her model by studying the *face inversion effect*. In this effect, the ability to recognise faces is significantly poorer when they are presented in an inverted (upside-down) way than when presented normally. Farah (1994a) found that normal individuals showed the face inversion effect. However, the prosopagnosic patient, LH, showed the opposite effect, having better face recognition for inverted faces (see Figure 4.18). How can we explain these findings? According to Farah (1994a), the face inversion effect occurs because the holistic or configural processing that normal individuals apply to faces presented normally cannot easily be used with inverted faces. However, prosopagnosic patients have very limited ability to use holistic or configural processing, and so their ability to recognise faces does not show the face inversion effect.

The theoretical and empirical approach of Farah (1990, 1994) was developed by Farah et al. (1998). They argued that the notion of holistic processing can be defined in various ways. Their preferred

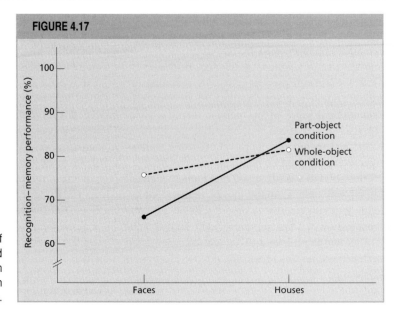

**FIGURE 4.17**

Recognition memory for features of houses and faces when presented with whole houses or faces or with only features. Data from Farah (1994a).

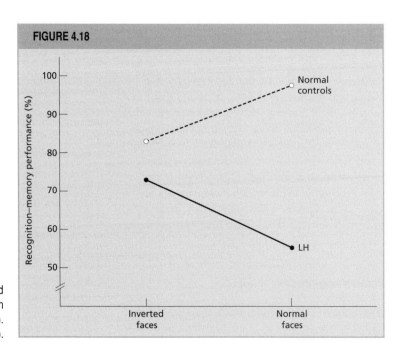

**FIGURE 4.18**

Face recognition for normal and inverted faces in normals and in a prosopagnosic patient (LH). Data from Farah (1994a).

definition was as follows: "it [holistic processing] involves relatively little part decomposition" (Farah et al., 1998, p. 484). What that means is that faces are generally recognised as wholes, and explicit representations of parts of the face (e.g., nose; mouth) play little or no part.

At the empirical level, Farah et al. (1998) pointed out that the previous research discussed by Farah (1990, 1994a) had shown that faces are stored in *memory* in a holistic form, but had not shown that faces are *perceived* holistically. They filled this gap in a series of studies. The participants were presented with a face, followed by a mask, followed by a second face. The task was to decide whether the second face was the same as the first. The key manipulation was the nature of the mask, which consisted either of parts of a face arranged randomly or of a whole face. The crucial prediction was as follows: "If faces are recognised as a whole and part representation plays a relatively small role in face recognition, then a mask made up of face parts should be less detrimental than a mask consisting of a whole face."

What did Farah et al. (1998) find? As predicted, face-recognition performance was better when part masks were used than when whole masks were used. This finding suggests that faces were processed holistically. In other conditions, the effects of part and whole masks on word and house recognition were assessed. The beneficial effects of part masks over whole masks were less with house stimuli than with faces, and there were no beneficial effects at all with word stimuli. Thus, as predicted, there seemed to be less holistic processing of object (house) and word stimuli than of faces.

### Brain damage

Farah (1990) discussed some evidence based on patients suffering from one or more of the following: *prosopagnosia*; *visual agnosia* (in which object recognition is disrupted in spite of the fact that visual information reaches the visual cortex); and *alexia* (problems with reading in spite of good ability to comprehend spoken language and good object recognition). According to the theory, prosopagnosia involves impaired holistic or configurational processing, alexia involves impaired analytic processing, and visual agnosia involves impaired holistic and analytic processing. It should be noted that Farah (1990) did not distinguish between apperceptive agnosia and associative agnosia.

Farah (1990) was interested in the co-occurrence of these three conditions in 87 patients. What would we expect from her theory? First, patients with visual agnosia (having impaired holistic and analytic processing) should also suffer from prosopagnosia or alexia, or both. This prediction was confirmed. There were 21 patients with all three conditions, 15 patients with visual agnosia

and alexia, 14 patients with visual agnosia and prosopagnosia, but only 1 patient who may have had visual agnosia on its own.

Second, and most importantly, there was a double dissociation between prosopagnosia and alexia. There were 35 patients who suffered from prosopagnosia without having alexia, and there are numerous reports in the literature of patients with alexia without prosopagnosia. Thus, the processes and brain systems underlying face recognition seem to be different from those underlying word recognition.

This conclusion receives support from attempts to identify the brain areas damaged in prosopagnosia and alexia using MRI and other neuroimaging techniques. Most prosopagnosic patients have damage to the occipital and/or temporal lobes of the cortex. In contrast, alexia "is typically associated with lesions of the left hemisphere, particularly lesions encompassing the angular gyrus in the posterior region of the parietal lobe" (Gazzaniga et al., 1998, pp. 202–203).

Third, it is assumed within the theory that reading and object recognition both involve analytic processing. Thus, it is predicted that patients with alexia (who have problems with analytic processing) should be impaired in their object recognition. This contrasts with the conventional view that patients with "pure" alexia have impairments only to reading abilities. This issue was studied by Behrmann, Nelson, and Sekuler (1998) in six patients who seemd to have "pure" alexia. Their key finding was that five out of six patients with this condition were significantly slower than normal participants to name visually complex pictures. These findings are in line with the prediction from Farah's theory.

### Evaluation

There is reasonable evidence from the research of Farah (1990, 1994) and elsewhere to suggest that the processes typically involved in face recognition differ somewhat from those involved in object recognition and reading. The two-process model describes some of the major similarities and differences in processing across these three types of stimuli.

On the negative side, Farah's approach is at a very general level that incorporates various over-simplifications. For example, Farah argued that faces are processed holistically, but there is evidence of a left-hemisphere system that is involved in processing faces more analytically in terms of their features (Parkin & Williamson, 1986). As Humphreys and Riddoch (1993) pointed out, the case of HJA (discussed earlier) provides evidence against Farah's theory. HJA can read common words well, but is extremely poor at recognising faces, suggesting that he has problems with holistic processing. However, when asked on the object decision test to decide whether objects are real or artificial, he performed better when they were presented as silhouettes rather than as line drawings. This last finding suggests that HJA has reasonably good ability to process holistically, which is difficult to handle within Farah's theoretical approach.

Finally, Farah's failure to distinguish between apperceptive and associative agnosia seems ill advised. For example, consider the case of HO, who had had herpes simplex encephalitis. His performance was essentially perfect on the un-usual views test (see earlier) and he performed well on the object decision test (Steward, Parkin, & Hunkin, 1992). However, he could name only 50% of objects on a naming task, and he did not know the functions of most objects. HO's problems are clearly related to associative agnosia rather than to apperceptive agnosia.

## CHAPTER SUMMARY

- Pattern recognition. Template theorists argue that stimuli are matched against miniature copies or templates of previously presented patterns. Unless the implausible assumption is made that there is an almost infinite number of templates to handle all possibilities, template theories seem inadequate to account for the versatility of perceptual processing. Feature theorists emphasise that any stimulus consists of specific features, and that feature analysis plays a crucial role in pattern recognition. The effects of context and of expectations are de-emphasised in most feature theories, as are the inter-relationships among features. A more adequate way of accounting for pattern recognition is provided by theories based on structural descriptions, which specify the structural arrangement of the constituent parts of a pattern.
- Object recognition. According to Marr, three main kinds of representation are involved in object recognition. The primal sketch makes use of information about light-intensity changes to identify the outline shapes of visual objects. This is followed by the $2\frac{1}{2}$-D sketch, which incorporates a description of the depth and orientation of visible surfaces. It is observer-centred or viewpoint-dependent, whereas the subsequent 3-D model representation is viewpoint-invariant and provides a three-dimensional description of objects. Biederman developed this approach, assuming that objects consist of basic shapes known as geons. An object's geons are determined by edge extraction processes focusing on invariant properties of edges (e.g., curvature), and the resulting geonal description is viewpoint-invariant. Edge information is often insufficient to permit object recognition, and surface information (e.g., colour) is often more involved in object recognition than predicted by Biederman. The theories of Marr and of Biederman were designed to account for easy categorical discriminations, and viewpoint-invariant processes are less important for hard within-category discriminations.
- Cognitive neuropsychology approach. Visual agnosia can be sub-divided into apperceptive agnosia and associative agnosia. Some agnosic patients have problems in integrating information from the parts of objects. Many agnosic patients have greater problems in identifying pictures of living than of non-living objects, perhaps because pictures of living objects are more similar to each

other. However, a few patients show the opposite pattern, suggesting that some of the semantic knowledge about living and non-living objects is stored in different regions of the brain.

- Cognitive science approach. Cognitive scientists have proposed connectionist models, which they have then "lesioned" to mimic the effects of brain damage on perception. The model of Farah and McClelland (1991), learned object recognition effectively, and it mimicked the double dissociation between object recognition for living and non-living objects found in patients with associative agnosia. However, the strong interconnectedness of visual and functional information in the model does not allow it to account for certain forms of visual disorder. Humphreys et al. (1995) put forward an interactive activation and competition model that accounts reasonably well for normal object recognition and for various perceptual disorders. Kosslyn et al. (1990) put forward a computer model of higher-level perceptual processes consisting of several sub-systems. Lesions to various parts of the model mimicked perceptual disorders such as visual agnosia, prosopagnosia, and simultanagnosia. This model does not identify the detailed processes involved in perception.
- Face recognition. Several kinds of information can be extracted from faces, with important differences existing between familiar and unfamiliar faces. It is very rare for anyone to put a name to a face without knowing anything else about the person. There is good evidence for configural processing of faces, but there is also component processing (especially of inverted faces). Prosopagnosic patients cannot recognise familiar faces, but generally possess some implicit knowledge about them. The available evidence suggests that the difficulties of prosopagnosic patients occur because of damage to specific face-processing mechanisms rather than a general inability to make precise discriminations. Farah's two-process model distinguishes between holistic analysis and analysis by parts. Face recognition involves mainly holistic analysis, whereas reading involves mainly analysis by parts, and object recognition involves both processes.

## FURTHER READING

- Ellis, R., & Humphreys, G. (1999). *Connectionist psychology: A text with readings*. Hove, UK: Psychology Press. There is an interesting discussion of connectionist approaches to various disorders of visual perception in Chapter 8 of this book.
- Gazzaniga, M.S., Ivry, R.B., & Mangun, G.R. (1998). *Cognitive neuroscience: The biology of the mind*. New York: W.W. Norton & Co. Chapter 5 of this book deals at length with neuroimaging and neuropsychological evidence relating to object recognition.
- Køhler, S., & Moscovitch, M. (1997). Unconscious visual processing in neuropsychological syndromes: A survey of the literature and evaluation of models of consciousness. In M.D. Rugg (Ed.), *Cognitive neuroscience*. Hove, UK: Psychology Press. This chapter contains interesting accounts of some of the major types of perceptual problems resulting from brain injury.
- Wilson, R.A., & Keil, F. (1999). *The MIT encyclopaedia of the cognitive sciences*. Cambridge, MA: MIT Press. Several chapters in this up-to-date book are devoted to aspects of visual perception, including object recognition.

# 5

# Attention and Performance Limitations

## INTRODUCTION

As Pashler (1998, p. 1) pointed out, "Attention has long posed a major challenge for psychologists." Historically, the concept of "attention" was treated as important by many philosophers and psychologists in the late 19th century. However, it fell into disrepute, because the behaviourists regarded all internal processes with the utmost suspicion. Attention became fashionable again following the publication of Broadbent's book *Perception and Communication* in 1958, and has remained an important topic ever since.

Attention is most commonly used to refer to selectivity of processing. This was the sense emphasised by William James (1890, pp. 403–404):

Everyone knows what attention is. It is the taking possession of the mind, in clear and vivid form, of one out of what seem several simultaneously possible objects or trains of thought. Focalisation, concentration, of consciousness are of its essence.

What is the relationship between attention and consciousness? Baars (1997) argued that access to consciousness is controlled by attentional mechanisms. Consider, for example, sentences such as, "We look in order to see" or "We listen in order to hear". According to Baars (1997, p. 364), "The distinction is between selecting an experience and being conscious of the selected event. In everyday language, the first word of each pair ["look"; "listen"] involves attention; the second word ["see"; "hear"] involves consciousness." In other words, attention resembles choosing a television channel and consciousness resembles the picture on the screen.

William James (1890) distinguished between "active" and "passive" modes of attention. Attention is active when controlled in a top-down way by the individual's goals, whereas it is passive when controlled in a bottom-up way by external stimuli (e.g., a loud noise). According to Yantis (1998, p. 252), "Stimulus-driven attentional control is both faster and more potent than goal-driven attentional control." The reason is that it typically requires processing effort to decide which stimulus is most relevant to the current goal.

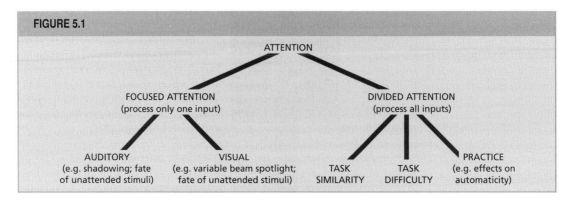

The ways in which different topics in attention are related to each other.

We have implied that there is a unitary attentional system. However, this is improbable. As Allport (1993, pp. 203–204) pointed out:

It seems no more plausible that there should be one unique mechanism, or computational resource, as the causal basis of all attentional phenomena than that there should be a unitary causal basis of thought, or perception, or of any other traditional category of folk psychology . . . Reference to attention (or to the central executive, or even to the anterior attention system) as an unspecified causal mechanism explains nothing.

There is a crucial distinction between focused and divided attention (see Figure 5.1). *Focused attention* is studied by presenting people with two or more stimulus inputs at the same time, and instructing them respond to only one. Work on focused attention can tell us how effectively people select certain inputs rather than others, and it enables us to study the nature of the selection process and the fate of unattended stimuli. *Divided attention* is also studied by presenting at least two stimulus inputs at the same time, but with instructions that *all* stimulus inputs must be attended to and responded to. Studies of divided attention provide useful information about an individual's processing limitations, and may tell us something about attentional mechanisms and their capacity.

The distinction between focused and divided attention can be related to some of the distinctions discussed earlier. Individuals typically *decide* whether to engage in focused or divided attention. Thus, the use of focused or divided attention is often determined by goal-driven or top-down attentional control processes.

There are *three* important limitations of attentional research. First, although we can attend to either the external environment or the internal environment (i.e., our own thoughts and information in long-term memory), most research has been concerned only with the former. Why is this? Researchers can identify and control environmental stimuli in ways that are impossible with internal determinants of attention.

Second, what we attend to in the real world is largely determined by our current goals. As Allport (1989, p. 664) pointed out, "What is important to recognise . . . is not the location of some imaginary boundary between the provinces of attention and motivation but, to the contrary, their essential interdependence." In most research, on the other hand, what participants attend to is determined by the experimental instructions rather than by their motivational states.

Third, as Tipper, Lortie, and Baylis (1992) noted, in the real world we generally attend to three-dimensional people and objects, and decide what actions might be suitable with respect to them. In the laboratory, the emphasis is on "experiments that briefly present static 2D displays and require arbitrary responses. It is clear that such experimental situations are rarely encountered in our usual interactions with the environment" (Tipper et al., 1992, p. 902).

## FOCUSED AUDITORY ATTENTION

The British scientist Colin Cherry was working in an electronics research laboratory at the Massachusetts Institute of Technology, but became involved in psychological research. What fascinated Cherry was the "cocktail party" problem: how are we able to follow just one conversation when several people are all talking at once? Cherry (1953) found that this ability involves using physical differences (e.g., sex of speaker; voice intensity; speaker location) to maintain attention to a chosen auditory message. When Cherry presented two messages in the same voice to both ears at once (thereby eliminating these physical differences), listeners found it very hard to separate out the two messages on the basis of meaning alone.

Cherry also carried out studies in which one auditory message had to be shadowed (i.e., repeated back out loud) while a second auditory message was played to the other ear. Very little information seemed to be extracted from the second or non-attended message. Listeners seldom noticed when that message was spoken in a foreign language or in reversed speech. In contrast, physical changes (e.g., a pure tone) were nearly always detected. The conclusion that unattended auditory information receives practically no processing was supported by other evidence. For example, there was very little memory for unattended words even when they were presented 35 times each (Moray, 1959).

### Broadbent's theory

Broadbent (1958) felt the findings from the shadowing task were important. He was also impressed by data from a memory task in which three pairs of digits were presented dichotically, i.e., three digits were heard one after the other by one ear, at the same time as three different digits were

presented to the other ear. Most participants chose to recall the digits ear by ear rather than pair by pair. Thus, if 496 were presented to one ear and 852 to the other ear, recall would be 496852 rather than 489562.

Broadbent (1958) accounted for the various findings as follows (see Figure 5.2):

- Two stimuli or messages presented at the same time gain access in parallel (at the same time) to a sensory buffer.
- One of the inputs is then allowed through a filter on the basis of its physical characteristics, with the other input remaining in the buffer for later processing.
- This filter prevents overloading of the limited-capacity mechanism beyond the filter; this mechanism processes the input thoroughly (e.g., in terms of its meaning).

This theory handles Cherry's basic findings, with unattended messages being rejected by the filter and thus receiving minimal processing. It also accounts for performance on Broadbent's dichotic task, because the filter selects one input on the basis of the most prominent physical characteristic distinguishing the two inputs (i.e., the ear of arrival). However, it is assumed incorrectly that the unattended message is always rejected at an early stage of processing. The original shadowing experiments used participants with very little experience of shadowing messages, so nearly all their available processing resources had to be allocated to shadowing. Underwood (1974) asked participants to detect digits presented on either the shadowed or the non-shadowed message. Naive participants detected only 8% of the digits on the non-shadowed message, but an experienced researcher in the area (Neville Moray) detected 67% of them.

In most of the early work on the shadowing task, the two messages were rather similar (i.e., they were both auditorily presented verbal messages). Allport, Antonis, and Reynolds (1972) found the degree of *similarity* between the two messages had a major impact on memory for the non-shadowed message. When shadowing of auditorily presented passages was combined with auditory presentation of words, memory for the words was very poor. However, when shadowing was combined with picture presentation, memory for the pictures was very good (90% correct). If two inputs are dissimilar, they can both be processed more fully than was allowed for on Broadbent's filter theory.

In the early studies, it was concluded that there was no processing of the meaning of unattended messages because the participants had no conscious awareness of their meaning. However, meaning may be processed without awareness. Von Wright, Anderson, and Stenman (1975) presented two lists of words auditorily, with instructions to shadow one list and ignore the other. When a word that had previously been associated with electric shock was presented on the non-attended list, there was sometimes a physiological reaction (galvanic skin response). The same effect was produced by presenting a word very similar in sound or meaning to the shocked word. Thus, information on the unattended message was sometimes processed for sound and meaning, even though the participants were not consciously aware that a word related to the previously shocked word had been presented.

*Evaluation*

Broadbent's (1958) proposed an *inflexible* system of selective attention that cannot account for the great variability in the amount of analysis of the non-shadowed message. The same inflexibility of the filter theory is shown in its assumption that the filter selects information on the basis of physical features. This assumption is supported by the tendency of participants to recall dichotically

presented digits ear by ear. However, Gray and Wedderburn (1960) made use of a version of the dichotic task in which "Who 6 there" might be presented to one ear as "4 goes 1" was presented to the other ear. The preferred order of report was determined by meaning (e.g., "who goes there" followed by "4 6 1"). The fact that selection can be based on the meaning of presented information is inconsistent with filter theory.

## Alternative theories

Treisman (1960) found with the shadowing task that the participants sometimes said a word that had been presented on the unattended channel. This is known as "breakthrough", and typically occurs when the word on the unattended channel is highly probable in the context of the message on the attended channel. Even in those circumstances, however, Treisman (1960) only observed breakthrough on 6% of trials.

Findings such as those of Treisman (1960) led Treisman (1964) to propose a theory in which the filter reduces or attenuates the analysis of unattended information (see Figure 5.2). Whereas Broadbent had suggested that there was a bottleneck early in processing, Treisman claimed that the location of the bottleneck was more flexible. She proposed that stimulus analysis proceeds systematically through a hierarchy starting with analyses based on physical cues, syllabic pattern, and specific words, and moving on to analyses based on individual words, grammatical structure, and meaning. If there is insufficient processing capacity to permit full stimulus analysis, then tests towards the top of the hierarchy are omitted.

Another important aspect of the theory proposed by Treisman (1964) was that the thresholds of all stimuli (e.g., words) consistent with current expectations are lowered. As a result, partially processed stimuli on the unattended channel sometimes exceed the threshold of conscious awareness. This aspect of the theory helps to account for the phenomenon of breakthrough.

Treisman's theory accounted for the extensive processing of unattended sources of information that had proved embarrassing for Broadbent. However, the same facts were also explained by

FIGURE 5.2

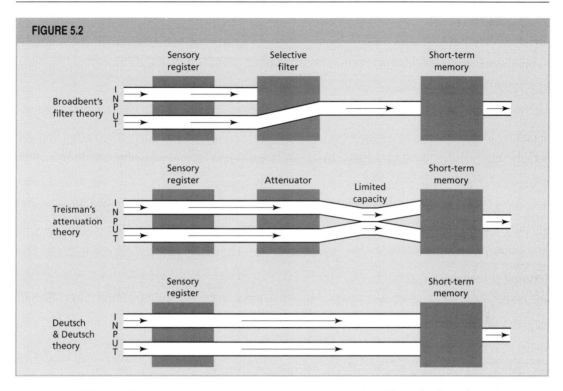

A comparison of Broadbent's theory (top); Treisman's theory (middle); and Deutsch and Deutsch's theory (bottom).

Deutsch and Deutsch (1963). They argued that all stimuli are fully analysed, with the most important or relevant stimulus determining the response (see Figure 5.2). This theory places the bottleneck in processing much nearer the response end of the processing system than did Treisman's attenuation theory. As a result, the theory proposed by Deutsch and Deutsch (1963) is often called late-selection theory, whereas the theories of Broadbent (1958) and Treisman (1964) are termed early-selection theories.

Treisman and Geffen (1967) had participants shadow one of two auditory messages, and tap when they detected a target word in either message. According to Treisman's theory, there should be attenuated analysis of the non-shadowed message, and so fewer targets should be detected on that message. According to Deutsch and Deutsch, there is complete perceptual analysis of all stimuli, and so there should be no difference in detection rates between the two messages. In fact, detection rates were much higher on the shadowed than the non-shadowed message (87% vs. 8%, respectively).

According to Deutsch and Deutsch (1967), only important inputs lead to responses. As the task used by Treisman and Geffen (1967) required their participants to make two responses (i.e., shadow and tap) to target words in the shadowed message, but only one response (i.e., tap) to targets in the non-shadowed message, the shadowed targets were more important than the non-shadowed ones.

Treisman and Riley (1969) responded by carrying out a study in which exactly the same response was made to all targets. Participants stopped shadowing and tapped when they detected a target in either message. Many more target words were detected on the shadowed message than the non-shadowed one.

Neurophysiological studies provide support for early-selection theories (see Luck, 1998, for a review). Woldorff et al. (1993) used the task of detecting auditory targets presented to the attended ear, with fast trains of non-targets being presented

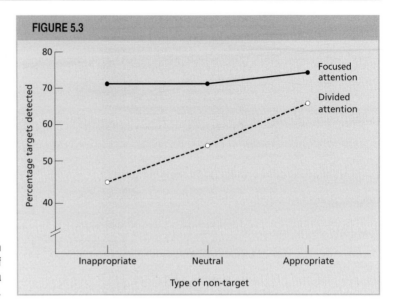

FIGURE 5.3

Effects of attention condition (divided vs. focused) and of type of non-target on target detection. Data from Johnston and Wilson (1980).

to each ear. Event-related potentials (ERPs; see Chapter 1) were recorded from attended and un-attended stimuli. There were greater ERPs to attended stimuli 20–50 milliseconds after stimulus onset. Thus, there is more processing of attended than unattended auditory stimuli starting from the initial activation of the auditory cortex.

## Johnston and Heinz's theory

Johnston and Heinz (1978) proposed a flexible model of attention incorporating the following assumptions:

- The more stages of processing that take place prior to selection, the greater the demands on processing capacity.
- Selection occurs as early in processing as possible to minimise demands on capacity.

Johnston and Wilson (1980) tested these assumptions. Pairs of words were presented together dichotically (i.e., one word to each ear), and the task was to identify target words consisting of members of a designated category. The targets were ambiguous words having two distinct meanings. If the category was "articles of clothing", then "socks" would be a possible target word. Each target word was accompanied by a non-target word biasing the appropriate meaning of the target (e.g., "smelly"), or a non-target word biasing the inappropriate meaning (e.g., "punches"), or by a neutral non-target word (e.g., "Tuesday").

When participants did not know which ear targets would arrive at (divided attention), appropriate non-targets facilitated the detection of targets and inappropriate non-targets impaired performance (see Figure 5.3). Thus, when attention had to be divided, the non-target words were processed for meaning. When participants knew all the targets would be presented to the left ear, the type of non-target word had no effect on target detection. Thus, non-targets were not processed for meaning in this focused attention condition, and so the amount of processing received by non-target stimuli is only as much as is necessary for task performance.

## Section summary

The analysis of unattended auditory inputs can be greater than was originally thought. However, the full analysis theory of Deutsch and Deutsch (1963) seems dubious. The most reasonable account of focused auditory attention may be along the lines suggested by Treisman (1964), with reduced or attenuated processing of sources of information outside focal attention. The extent of such processing is probably flexible, being determined in part by task demands (Johnston & Heinz, 1978). Styles (1997, p. 28) made a telling point: "Discovering precisely where selection occurs is only one small part of the issues surrounding attention, and finding *where* selection takes place may not help us to understand *why* or *how* this happens.

## FOCUSED VISUAL ATTENTION

Over the past 25 years, most researchers have studied visual rather than auditory attention. Why is this? Probably the main reason is that it is generally easier to control the presentation times of visual stimuli than of auditory stimuli.

Some of the issues we will be discussing in this section of the chapter have been considered from the cognitive neuropsychological perspective. Three attentional disorders have been studied fairly thoroughly: neglect; extinction; and Balint's syndrome (see Driver, 1998, for a review). *Neglect* is typically found after brain damage in the right parietal lobe, and is often the result of a stroke. Neglect patients with right-hemisphere damage do not notice, or fail to respond to, objects presented to their left (or contralesional) side. For example, when neglect patients draw an object or copy a drawing, they typically leave out everything on the left side of it. According to Driver (1998, p. 308), "The essential problem in neglect may be that while the patient can, in principle, look or attend toward the contralesional side, they usually fail to do so spontaneously." In addition, neglect patients can also show neglect on tasks involving images rather than visual perception (Bisiach & Luzzati, 1978). It is important to note that "neglect is not a single disorder but a range of disorders which can occur in varying degrees within any patient" (Parkin, 1996, p. 91).

It might be thought that neglect occurs because stimuli on one side of the visual field are not processed perceptually. However, most of the evidence indicates that that is not typically the case. For example, Marshall and Halligan (1988) presented a neglect patient with two drawings of a house that were identical, except that the house presented to the left visual field had flames coming out of one of its windows. The patient was unable to report any differences between the two drawings, but indicated that she would prefer to live in the house on the right.

How can we explain neglect? According to Parkin (1996, p. 108), "At the moment the most convincing class of theories concerning neglect are those that propose some form of attentional deficit. Essentially these theories suggest that there is an imbalance in the amount of attention allocated to left and right . . . However, the idea that a single theory of neglect will emerge is highly unlikely because of the diversity of defects being discovered." Posner's attentional theory of neglect is discussed later.

*Extinction* is a phenomenon frequently found in neglect patients. A *single* stimulus on either side of the visual field can be judged normally. However, when *two* stimuli are presented together, the one farther towards the side of the visual field away from the damage tends to go undetected. Some patients only show extinction when the two objects presented simultaneously are the same.

*Balint's syndrome* is associated with lesions in both hemispheres involving the posterior parietal lobe or parieto-occipital junction. It is characterised by various attentional problems. These include fixed gazing, gross misreaching for objects, and *simultanagnosia*, in which only one object can be attended to at a time. As Martin (1998, p. 228) noted, "A patient with Balint's syndrome might focus quite narrowly on the tip of a cigarette in his or her mouth and be unable to see a match offered a short distance away."

Convincing evidence that Balint's patients can only attend to one object at a time was reported by Humphreys and Riddoch (1993). When Balint's patients were presented with a mixture of red and green circles, they were generally unable to report seeing both colours. Presumably this happened because the patients could only attend to a single circle at a time. However, when the red and green circles were joined by lines (so that each object contained red and green), the patients' performance was much better.

## Spotlight or zoom lens?

According to Pashler (1998, p. 4), "the findings with visual stimuli have closely paralleled those with auditory stimuli". This similarity is clear when we consider research on focused attention. In some ways, focused visual attention resembles a spotlight. Everything within a fairly small region of the visual field can be seen clearly, but it is much harder to see anything not falling within the beam of the attentional spotlight. Attention can be shifted by moving the spotlight, and the simplest assumption is that the attentional spotlight moves at a constant rate (see Yantis, 1998). A more complex view of focused visual attention was put forward by Eriksen and St. James (1986). According to their zoom-lens model, attention is directed to a given region of the visual field. However, the area of focal attention can be increased or decreased in line with task demands.

Posner (1980) favoured the spotlight notion. He argued that there can be *covert attention*, in which the attentional spotlight shifts to a different spatial location in the absence of an eye movement. In his studies, the participants responded as rapidly as possible when they detected the onset of a light. Shortly before the onset of the light, they were presented with a central cue (arrow pointing to the left or right) or a peripheral cue (brief illumination of a box outline). These cues were mostly valid (i.e., they indicated where the target light would appear), but sometimes they were invalid (i.e., they provided misleading information about the location of the target light).

Posner's (1980) key findings were that valid cues produced faster responding to light onset than did neutral cues (a central cross), whereas invalid cues produced slower responding than neutral cues. The findings were comparable for central and peripheral cues, and were obtained in the absence of eye movements. When the cues were valid on only a small fraction of trials, they were ignored when they were central cues but affected performance when they were peripheral cues.

These findings led Posner (1980) to distinguish between two systems:

1. An endogenous system, which is controlled by the participant's intentions and is involved when central cues are presented.
2. An exogenous system, which automatically shifts attention and is involved when peripheral cues are presented.

Some evidence does not support the spotlight notion. Kwak, Dagenbach, and Egeth (1991) presented their participants with two letters at a time, and asked them to decide whether they were the same. The decision times were the same whether the letters were close together or far apart. This is inconsistent with the notion that visual attention is like a spotlight moving at a given rate.

Evidence in favour of the zoom-lens model was reported by LaBerge (1983). Five-letter words were presented. A probe requiring rapid response was occasionally presented instead of, or immediately after, the word. The probe could appear in the spatial position of any of the five letters of the word. In one condition, an attempt was made to focus the participants' attention on the middle letter of the five-letter word by asking them to categorise that letter. In another condition, the participants were required to categorise the entire word. It was expected that this would lead the participants to adopt a broader attentional beam.

The findings on speed of detection of the probe are shown in Figure 5.4. LaBerge (1983) assumed that the probe was responded to faster when it fell within the central attentional beam than when it did not. On this assumption, the attentional spotlight can have either a very narrow (letter task) or rather broad (word task) beam.

Eriksen and St. James (1986) also obtained support for the zoom-lens model. Their participants performed a task on a target stimulus whose location was indicated beforehand. Performance was impaired by the presence of distracting visual stimuli. However, the area over which interference effects were found was less when the participants had longer forewarning of the target stimulus. Presumably visual attention zoomed in more precisely on the area around the target stimulus over time.

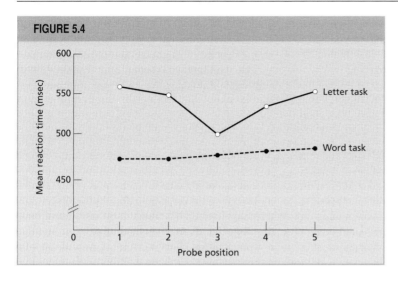

**FIGURE 5.4**

Mean reaction time to the probe as a function of probe position. The probe was presented at the time that a letter string would have been presented. Data from LaBerge (1983).

## Evaluation

As the zoom-lens model predicts, the size of the visual field within focal attention can vary substantially. However, focused visual attention is more complex than is implied by the model. For example, consider a study by Juola, Bowhuis, Cooper, and Warner (1991). A target letter (L or R) which had to be identified was presented in one of three rings having the same centre: an inner, a middle, and an outer ring. The participants fixated the centre of the display, and were given a cue that mostly provided accurate information as to the ring in which the target would be presented. If visual attention is like a spotlight or zoom lens, speed and accuracy of performance would be greatest for targets presented in the inner ring. In fact, performance was best when the target appeared in the ring that had been cued. This suggests that visual attention can be allocated in an O-shaped pattern to include only the outer or the middle ring.

There is a more fundamental objection to the spotlight and zoom-lens models. It is assumed within both models that visual attention is directed towards a given region in the visual field. However, visual attention is often directed to *objects* rather than to a particular *region*. Consider, for example, a study by Neisser and Becklen (1975). They superimposed two moving scenes on top of each other. Their participants could easily attend to one scene while ignoring the other. These findings suggest that objects within the visual environment can be the main focus of attention.

According to the spotlight approach, it might be expected that visual attention in patients with neglect and extinction would be limited only in area. However, this is not so. Marshall and Halligan (1994) presented a patient with neglect in the left visual field with ambiguous displays, each of which could be seen as a black shape against a white background or as a white shape on a black background. There was a jagged edge dividing the two shapes at the centre of each display. The patient was able to copy this jagged edge when asked to draw the shape on the left side of the display, but could not copy exactly the same edge when asked to draw the shape on the right side. Thus, the patient attended to objects rather than simply to a region of visual space.

Ward, Goodrich, and Driver (1994) studied two patients with extinction in the left visual field. Two stimuli were presented at once, and they either formed a good perceptual group (e.g., "[ and ]") or they did not (e.g., "[ and o"). The patients were much better at detecting the stimuli on the left side of the visual field when they belonged to a good perceptual group. Thus, visual attention in extinction patients is affected by grouping factors as well as by location.

What conclusion can we draw from studies such as those of Marshall and Halligan (1994) and Ward et al. (1994)? According to Driver (1998, p. 315), "The spatial extent of both normal and pathological [abnormal or diseased] attention is substantially modulated by grouping processes. Clearly, human covert attention is rather more sophisticated than a simple 'spotlight' metaphor implies."

## Unattended visual stimuli

There is generally rather limited processing of unattended auditory stimuli. What happens to unattended visual stimuli? Neurophysiological evidence suggests there is reduced processing of such stimuli. Luck (1998) discussed several studies in which the participants fixated a central point while attending to the left or the right visual field. A rapid succession of bars was presented to both fields, and the task involved detecting targets (smaller bars) in the attended visual field. Event-related potentials (ERPs; see Chapter 1) are larger to attended than to unattended stimuli. The ERPs to the two types of stimuli begin to differ with the first positive wave (P1), which starts about 75 milliseconds after stimulus onset.

Heinze et al. (1994) used a similar procedure to the one just described, and obtained PET scans as well as ERPs. They replicated the greater P1 to attended than to unattended visual stimuli. However, according to Luck (1998, p. 274), their key finding was that, "visual attention influences sensory processing in extrastriate visual cortex within 100 ms of stimulus onset, consistent with early-selection models of attention."

Evidence suggesting that there is very little processing of unattended visual stimuli was reported by Francolini and Egeth (1980). Circular arrays of red and black letters or numerals were presented, and the task was to count the number of red items and to ignore the black items. Performance speed was reduced when the *red* items consisted of numerals conflicting with the answer,

but there was no interference effect from the *black* items. These findings suggest there was little or no processing of the to-be-ignored black items.

The findings of Driver and Tipper (1989) contradicted this conclusion. They used the same task as Francolini and Egeth (1980), but focused on whether conflicting numerical values had been presented on the *previous* trial. There was an interference effect, and it was of the same size from red and black items. The finding that performance on any given trials was affected by the numerical values of to-be-ignored items from the previous trial means those items must have been processed. This is the phenomenon of *negative priming*. In this phenomenon, the processing of a target stimulus is inhibited if that stimulus or one very similar to it was an unattended or distracting stimulus on the previous trial.

Further evidence that there is often more processing of unattended visual stimuli than initially seems to be the case has been reported with neglect patients. McGlinchey-Berroth et al. (1993) asked such patients to decide which of two drawings matched a drawing presented immediately beforehand to the left or the right visual field. Neglect patients performed well when the initial drawing was presented to the right visual field, but at chance level when it was presented to the left visual field (see Figure 5.5). The latter finding suggests that stimuli in the left visual field were not processed. However, a very different conclusion emerged from a second study, in which neglect patients had to decide whether letter strings formed words. Decision times were faster on "yes" trials when the letter string was preceded by a semantically related object rather than an unrelated object. This effect was the same size regardless of whether the object was presented to the left or the right visual field (see Figure 5.5), indicating that there is some processing of left-field stimuli by neglect patients.

### Section summary

Neurophysiological evidence suggests there is reduced processing of unattended visual stimuli. The fact that processing of, and responding to, attended visual stimuli is often unaffected by unattended

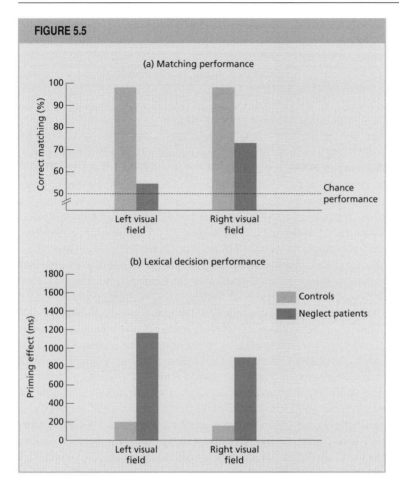

**FIGURE 5.5**

(a) Matching performance

(b) Lexical decision performance

Effects of prior presentation of a drawing to the left or right visual field on matching performance and lexical decision in neglect patients. Data from McGlinchey-Berroth et al. (1993).

stimuli suggests there is very little processing of such stimuli. However, when sensitive measures are used, there is strong evidence for some processing of the meaning of unattended stimuli by normals and by neglect patients. For example, normals exhibit a phenomenon known as negative priming.

## Visual search

One of the main ways we use focused visual attention in our everyday lives is in visual search (see Chapter 3). For example, we search through the books in a library looking for the one we want, or we look for a friend in a crowded room. An attempt to study the processes involved has been made by using visual search tasks. The

participants are presented with a visual display containing a variable number of items (the set or display size). A target (e.g., red G) is presented on half the trials, and the task is to decide as rapidly as possible whether the target is present in the display. Theory and research on this task are discussed next.

### Feature integration theory

The most influential approach to visual search is the feature integration theory put forward by Treisman (eg., 1988, 1992). She drew a distinction between the features of objects (e.g., colour, size, lines of particular orientation) and the objects themselves. Her theory based on this distinction includes the following assumptions:

- There is a rapid initial parallel process in which the visual features of objects in the environment are processed together; this is not dependent on attention.
- There is then a serial process in which features are combined to form objects.
- The serial process is slower than the initial parallel process, especially when the set size is large.
- Features can be combined by focused attending to the location of the object, in which case focused attention provides the "glue" forming unitary objects from the available features.
- Feature combination can be influenced by stored knowledge (e.g., bananas are usually yellow).
- In the absence of focused attention or relevant stored knowledge, features from different objects will be combined randomly, producing "illusory conjunctions".

Treisman and Gelade (1980) had previously obtained support for this theory. Their participants searched for a target in a visual display having a set or display size of between 1 and 30 items. The target was either an object (a green letter T), or consisted of a single feature (a blue letter or an S). When the target was a green letter T, all the non-targets shared one feature with the target (i.e., they were either the brown letter T or the green letter X). The prediction was that focused attention would be needed to detect the object target (because it was defined by a combination of features), but would not be required to detect single-feature targets.

The findings were as predicted (see Figure 5.6). Set or display size had a large effect on detection speed when the target was defined by a combination or conjunction of features (i.e., a green letter T), presumably because focused attention was required. However, there was very little effect of display size when the target was defined by a single feature (i.e., a blue letter or an S).

According to feature integration theory, lack of focused attention can produce illusory conjunctions. Treisman and Schmidt (1982) confirmed this prediction. There were numerous illusory conjunctions when attention was widely distributed, but not when the stimuli were presented to focal attention. Balint's patients have problems with visual attention generally, especially with the accurate location of visual stimuli. Accordingly, it might be expected they would be liable to illusory conjunctions. Friedman-Hill, Robertson, and Treisman (1995) studied a Balint's patient. He made a remarkably large number of illusory

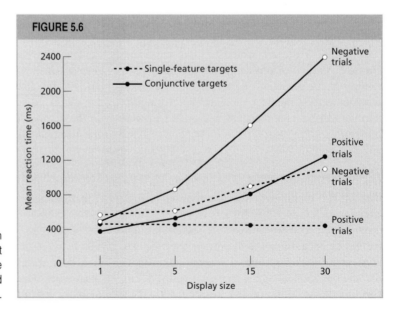

**FIGURE 5.6**

Performance speed on a detection task as a function of target definition (conjunctive vs. single feature) and display size. Adapted from Treisman and Gelade (1980).

conjunctions, miscombining the shape of one stimulus with the colour of another.

Treisman and Sato (1990) developed feature integration theory. They argued that the degree of *similarity* between the target and the distractors influences visual search time. They found that visual search for an object target defined by more than one feature was typically limited to those distractors having at least one of the target's features. For example, if you were looking for a blue circle in a display containing blue triangles, red circles, and red triangles, you would ignore red triangles. This contrasts with the views of Treisman and Gelade (1980), who argued that none of the stimuli would be ignored.

Treisman (1993) put forward a more complex version of feature integration theory, in which there are four kinds of attentional selection. First, there is selection by location involving a relatively broad or narrow attention window. Second, there is selection by features. Features are divided into surface-defining features (e.g., colour; brightness; relative motion) and shape-defining features (e.g., orientation; size). Third, there is selection on the basis of object-defined locations. Fourth, there is selection at a late stage of processing which determines the object file that controls the individual's response. Thus, attentional selectivity can operate at various levels depending on the particular demands of the current task.

## Guided search theory

Guided search theory was put forward by Wolfe (1998). It represents a substantial refinement of feature integration theory. There is an overall similarity, in that it is assumed within guided search theory that visual search initially involves efficient feature-based processing, followed by less efficient search processes. However, Wolfe (1998) replaced Treisman and Gelade's (1980) assumption that the initial processing is necessarily parallel and subsequent processing is serial with the notion that processes are more or less efficient. He did so because of the diverse findings in the literature: "Results of visual search experiments run from flat to steep RT [reaction time] × set size functions with no evidence of a dichotomous

division [division into two] . . . The continuum of search slopes does make it implausible to think that the search tasks, themselves, can be neatly classified as serial or parallel" (Wolfe, 1998, p. 20). Thus, there should be no effect of set or display size on detection times if parallel processing is used, but a substantial effect of set size if serial processing is used, but most actual findings fall between these two extremes.

According to guided search theory, the initial processing of basic features produces an activation map, in which each of the items in the visual display has its own level of activation. Suppose that someone is searching for red, horizontal targets. Feature processing would activate all red objects and all horizontal objects. Attention is then directed towards items on the basis of their level of activation, starting with those with the highest level of activation. This assumption allows us to understand why search times are longer when some of the non-targets share one or more features with the target stimuli (e.g., Duncan & Humphreys, 1989).

A great problem with the original version of feature integration theory is that targets in large displays are typically found faster than would be predicted. The activation-map notion provides a plausible way in which visual search can be made more efficient by ignoring stimuli not sharing any features with the target stimulus.

What are the basic features in visual search, and how can they be identified? According to Wolfe (1998, p. 23), the answer to the second question is as follows: "If a stimulus supports both efficient search *and* effortless segmentation [grouping], then it is probably safe to include it in the ranks of basic features." Wolfe (1998, p. 40) provided the following answer to the first question: "There appear to be about eight to ten basic features: colour, orientation, motion, size, curvature, depth, vernier offset [small irregularity in a line segment], gloss, and, perhaps, intersection."

## Attentional engagement theory

Duncan and Humphreys (1989, 1992) put forward attentional engagement theory. This was designed in part to explain why visual search is often faster and more efficient than would be expected on the original version of feature integration theory. They made two key predictions:

- Search times will be slower when the similarity between the target and the non-targets is increased.
- Search times will be slower when there is reduced similarity among non-targets. Thus, the slowest search times are obtained when non-targets are dissimilar to each other, but similar to the target.

Evidence that visual search can be very rapid when non-targets are all the same was obtained by Humphreys, Riddoch,and Quinlan (1985). Participants detected inverted T targets against a background of Ts the right way up. Detection speed was hardly affected by the number of non-targets. According to feature integration theory, the fact that the target was defined by a combination or conjunction of features (i.e., a vertical line and a horizontal line) means that visual search should have been greatly affected by the number of non-targets.

Duncan and Humpreys (1989, 1992) made the following theoretical assumptions:

- There is an initial parallel stage of perceptual segmentation and analysis based on all items.
- There is a later stage of processing in which selected information is entered into visual short-term memory; this corresponds to selective attention.
- The speed of visual search depends on how easily the target item enters visual short-term memory.
- Items well matched to the description of the target item are most likely to be selected for visual short-term memory; thus, non-targets that are similar to the target slow the search process.
- Items that are perceptually grouped (e.g., because they are very similar) will be selected (or rejected) together for visual short-term memory. Thus, dissimilar non-targets cannot be rejected together, and this slows the search process.

In the study by Treisman and Gelade (1980), there were long search times to detect a green letter T in a display containing brown Ts and green Xs (see Figure 5.6). Treisman and Gelade (1980) argued that this occurred because of the need for focal attention to produce the necessary conjunction of features. In contrast, Duncan and Humphreys (1989, 1992) claimed that the slow performance resulted from the high similarity between the target and non-target stimuli (the latter shared one of the features of the target stimulus) and the dissimilarity among the non-target stimuli (the two different non-targets shared no features).

Humphreys and Müller (1993) produced a connectionist model based on attentional engagement theory. This model, known as SERR (SEarch via Recursive Rejection), was based on the assumption that grouping and search processes operate in a parallel fashion. Müller, Humphreys, and Donnelly (1994) compared the predictions of SERR against those of feature integration theory. The participants had to detect T-type targets as rapidly as possible, with the distractors consisting of Ts at various different orientations. In one condition, there were two or more identical targets, and the participants had to respond as soon as they detected one or them. The time taken to detect targets in this condition was faster than the fastest time taken to detect the target in another condition in which there was only a single target in the display. This finding follows from the SERR model with its emphasis on parallel processing, but is very hard for serial processing theories to explain.

## Evaluation

Feature integration theory has influenced theoretical approaches to visual search in various ways. First, it is generally agreed that two successive processes are involved. Second, it is accepted that the first process is fast and efficient, whereas the second process is slower and less efficient. Third, the notion that different visual features are processed independently or separately seems attractive in view of the evidence that distinct areas of the visual cortex are specialised for processing different features (Zeki, 1993, see Chapter 2).

There were four key weaknesses with early versions of feature integration theory. First, as Wolfe (1998) pointed out, the assumption that visual search is either entirely parallel or serial is much too strong and disproved by the evidence. Second, the search for targets consisting of a conjunction or combination of features is faster than predicted by feature integration theory. Some of the factors involved are incorporated into guided search theory and attentional engagement theory. For example, search for conjunctive targets can be speeded up if non-targets can be grouped together or if non-targets share no features with targets.

Third, it was originally assumed within feature integration theory that the effect of set or display size on visual search depends mainly on the nature of the target (single feature or conjunctive feature). In fact, other factors (e.g., grouping of non-targets) also play a role.

Fourth, Treisman and Schmidt (1982) assumed that features are completely "free-floating" in the absence of focused attention. As a result, *any* features can combine together into illusory conjunctions. In fact, most illusory conjunctions occur between items that are close together rather than far apart (Ashby, Prinzmetal, Ivry, & Maddox, 1996). This led Ashby et al. (1996) to develop location uncertainty theory, according to which illusory conjunctions occur "because of uncertainty about the location of visual features" (p. 165).

Another issue with research on visual search concerns its relevance to the real world. As Wolfe (1998, p. 56) pointed out:

> In the real world, distractors are very heterogeneous [diverse]. Stimuli exist in many size scales in a single view. Items are probably defined by conjunctions of many features. You don't get several hundred trials with the same targets and distractors . . . A truly satisfying model of visual search will need . . . to account for the range of real-world visual behaviour.

## Disorders of visual attention

Posner and Petersen (1990) proposed a theoretical framework within which various disorders of visual attention can be understood. They argued that three separate abilities are involved in controlling the attentional spotlight:

- *Disengagement* of attention from a given visual stimulus.
- *Shifting* of attention from one target stimulus to another.
- *Engaging* or locking attention on a new visual stimulus.

These three abilities are all functions of the posterior attention system. In addition, there is an anterior attention system. This is involved in co-ordinating the different aspects of visual attention, and resembles the central executive component of the working memory system (see Chapter 6). According to Posner and Petersen (1990, p. 10), there is "a hierarchy of attentional systems in which the anterior system can pass control to the posterior system when it is not occupied with processing other material."

Posner (1995) developed some of these ideas. The anterior attentional system based in the frontal lobes was regarded as controlling stimulus selection and the allocation of mental resources. The posterior attentional system is influenced by the anterior system and controls lower-level aspects of attention, such as the disengagement of attention. There is some evidence that the anterior attentional system may be more complex than was assumed by Posner (1995). For example, Stuss et al. (1999) found that damage to the left frontal lobe produced a different pattern of disturbance of attention than did damage to the right frontal lobe. These findings suggest that there may be more than one anterior attentional system.

### Disengagement of attention

Posner, Walker, Friedrich, and Rafal (1984) presented cues to the locations of forthcoming targets to neglect patients. The patients generally coped fairly well with this task, even when the cue and the target were both presented to the impaired visual field. However, when the cue was presented to the unimpaired visual field and the target was presented to the impaired visual field, the patients' performance was very poor. These findings suggest that the patients found it very hard to disengage their attention from visual stimuli presented to the unimpaired side of visual space. Thus, problems with disengagement play a significant role in producing the symptoms shown by neglect patients.

Patients with neglect have suffered damage to the parietal region of the brain (Posner et al., 1984). A different kind of evidence that the parietal area is important in attention was reported by Petersen, Corbetta, Miezin, and Shulman (1994). PET scans indicated that there was much activation within the parietal area when attention shifted from one spatial location to another.

Problems with disengaging attention are also found in Balint's syndrome patients suffering from simultanagnosia. In this condition (mentioned earlier), only one object (out of two or more) can be seen at any one time, even when the objects are close together. As most of these patients have full visual fields, it seems that the attended visual object exerts a "hold" on attention that makes disengagement difficult. However, neglected stimuli are processed to some extent. Coslett and Saffran (1991) observed strong effects of semantic relatedness between two briefly presented words in a patient with simultanagnosia.

## Shifting of attention

Posner, Rafal, Choate, and Vaughan (1985) looked at problems of shifting attention by studying patients suffering from progressive supranuclear palsy. Such patients have damage to the midbrain, so they find it very hard to make voluntary eye movements, especially in the vertical direction. These patients responded to visual targets, and there were sometimes cues to the locations of forthcoming targets. There was a short, intermediate, or long interval between the cue and the target. At all intervals, valid cues (cues providing accurate information about target location) speeded up responding to the targets when the targets were presented to the left or the right of the cue. However, only cues at the long interval aided responding when the targets were presented above or below the cues. Thus, the patients had

difficulty in shifting their attention in the vertical direction.

Attentional deficits apparently associated with shifting of attention have been studied in patients with Balint's syndrome. These patients have difficulty in reaching for stimuli using visual guidance. Humphreys and Riddoch (1993) presented two Balint's patients with 32 circles in a display. The circles were either all the same colour, or half were one colour and the other half a different colour. The circles were either close together or spaced, and the task was to decide whether they were all the same colour. On trials where there were circles of two colours, one of the patients (SA) performed much better when the circles were close together than when they were spaced (79% vs. 62%, respectively). The other patient (SP) performed equivalently in both conditions (62% vs. 59%, respectively). Apparently some patients with Balint's syndrome (e.g., SA) find it hard to shift attention within the visual field.

## Engaging attention

Rafal and Posner (1987) studied problems of engaging attention in patients with damage to the pulvinar nucleus of the thalamus. These patients were given the task of responding to visual targets that were preceded by cues. The patients responded faster when the cues were valid than when they were invalid, regardless of whether the target stimulus was presented to the same side as the brain damage or to the opposite side. However, they responded rather slowly following both kinds of cues when the target stimulus was presented to the side of the visual field opposite to that of the brain damage. According to Rafal and Posner (1987), these findings reflect a problem the patients have in engaging attention to such stimuli.

Additional evidence that the pulvinar nucleus of the thalamus is involved in controlling focused attention was obtained by LaBerge and Buchsbaum (1990). PET scans indicated increased activation in the pulvinar nucleus when participants were told to ignore a given stimulus. Thus, the pulvinar nucleus is involved in preventing attention from being focused on an unwanted stimulus as well as in directing attention to significant stimuli.

## Section summary

As Posner and Petersen (1990, p. 28) pointed out, the findings indicate that "the parietal lobe first disengages attention from its present focus, then the midbrain area acts to move the index of attention to the area of the target, and the pulvinar nucleus is involved in reading out data from the indexed locations". An important implication is that the attentional system is rather complex. As Allport (1989, p. 644) expressed it, "spatial attention is a distributed function in which many functionally differentiated structures participate, rather than a function controlled uniquely by a single centre". This increased understanding of the complexities of attention has arisen in large part because of the study of brain-damaged patients.

## DIVIDED ATTENTION

What happens when people try to do two things at once? The answer clearly depends on the nature of the two "things". Sometimes the attempt is successful, as when an experienced motorist drives a car and holds a conversation at the same time, or a tennis player notes the position of his or her opponent while running at speed and preparing to make a stroke. At other times, as when someone tries to rub their stomach with one hand while patting their head with the other, there can be a complete disruption of performance.

Hampson (1989) made the key point that focused and divided attention are more similar than might have been expected. Factors such as use of different modalities which aid focused or selective attention generally also make divided attention easier. According to Hampson (1989, p. 267), "anything which minimises interference between processes, or keeps them 'further apart' will allow them to be dealt with more readily either selectively or together."

Theoretically, breakdowns of performance when two tasks are combined shed light on the limitations of the human information-processing system. Some theorists (e.g., Norman & Shallice, 1986) argue that such breakdowns reflect the limited capacity of a single multi-purpose central processor or executive sometimes described as "attention". Other theorists are more impressed by our apparent ability to perform two fairly complex tasks at the same time without disruption or interference. Such theorists favour the notion of several specific processing resources, arguing that there will be no interference between two tasks provided that they make use of different processing resources.

More progress has been made empirically than theoretically. It is possible to predict fairly accurately whether or not two tasks can be combined successfully, but the accounts offered by different theorists are very diverse. Accordingly, we will discuss some of the factual evidence before moving on to the murkier issue of how the data are to be explained.

## Factors determining dual-task performance

### Task similarity

When we think of pairs of activities that are performed well together in everyday life, the examples that come to mind usually involve two rather dissimilar activities (e.g., driving and talking; reading and listening to music). As we have seen, when people shadow or repeat back prose passages while learning auditorily presented words, their subsequent recognition-memory performance for the words is at chance level (Allport et al., 1972). However, the same authors found that memory was excellent when the to-be-remembered material consisted of pictures.

Various kinds of similarity need to be distinguished. Wickens (1984) reviewed the evidence and concluded that two tasks interfere to the extent that they have the same stimulus modality (e.g., visual or auditory), make use of the same stages of processing (input, internal processing, and output), and rely on related memory codes (e.g., verbal or visual). Response similarity is also important. McLeod (1977) asked participants to perform a continuous tracking task with manual responding together with a tone-identification task. Some participants responded vocally to the tones, whereas others responded with the hand not involved in the tracking task. Performance on the tracking task was worse with high response similarity (manual responses on both tasks) than with low response similarity (manual responses on one task and vocal ones on the other).

Similarity of stimulus modality has probably been studied most thoroughly. Treisman and Davies (1973) found two monitoring tasks interfered with each much more when the stimuli on both tasks were in the same sense modality (visual or auditory) than when they were in different modalities.

It is often very hard to measure similarity. How similar are piano playing and poetry writing, or driving a car and watching a football match? Only when there is a better understanding of the processes involved in the performance of such tasks will sensible answers be forthcoming.

*Practice*

Common sense suggests that the old saying "Practice makes perfect" is especially applicable to dual-task performance. For example, learner drivers find it almost impossible to drive and hold a conversation, whereas expert drivers find it fairly easy. Support for this commonsensical position was obtained by Spelke, Hirst, and Neisser (1976) in a study on two students called Diane and John. These students received five hours' training a week for four months on a variety of tasks. Their first task was to read short stories for comprehension while writing down words to dictation. They found this very hard initially, and their reading speed and handwriting both suffered considerably. After six weeks of training, however, they could read as rapidly and with as much comprehension when taking dictation as when only reading, and the quality of their handwriting had also improved.

In spite of this impressive dual-task performance, Spelke et al. were still not satisfied. Diane and John could recall only 35 out of the thousands of words they had written down at dictation. Even when 20 successive dictated words formed a sentence or came from a single semantic category, the two students were unaware of that. With further training, however, they learned to write down the names of the categories to which the dictated

words belonged while maintaining normal reading speed and comprehension.

Spelke et al. (1976, p. 229) wondered whether the popular notion that we have limited processing capacity is accurate, basing themselves on the dramatic findings with John and Diane: "People's ability to develop skills in specialised situations is so great that it may never be possible to define general limits on cognitive capacity." However, there are alternative ways of interpreting their findings. Perhaps the dictation task was performed rather automatically, and so placed few demands on cognitive capacity, or there might have been a rapid alternation of attention between reading and writing. Hirst et al. (1980) claimed that writing to dictation was not done automatically, because the students understood what they were writing. They also claimed that reading and dictation could only be performed together with success by alternation of attention if the reading material were simple and highly redundant. However, they found that most participants could still read and take dictation effectively when less redundant reading matter was used.

Do the studies by Spelke et al. (1976) and by Hirst et al. (1980) show that two complex tasks can be performed together without disruption? One of the participants used by Hirst et al. was tested at dictation *without* reading, and made fewer than half the number of errors that occurred when reading at the same time. Furthermore, the reading task gave the participants much flexibility in terms of when they attended to the reading matter, and such flexibility means that there may well have been some alternation of attention between tasks.

There are other cases of apparently successful performance of two complex tasks, but the requisite skills were always highly practised. Expert pianists can play from seen music while repeating back or shadowing heard speech (Allport et al., 1972), and an expert typist can type and shadow at the same time (Shaffer, 1975). These studies are often regarded as providing evidence of completely successful task combination. However, there are signs of interference when the data are inspected closely (Broadbent, 1982).

Why might practice aid dual-task performance? First, participants may develop new strategies for performing the tasks to minimise task interference. Second, the demands that a task makes on attentional or other central resources may be reduced with practice. Third, although a task initially requires the use of several specific processing resources, practice may reduce the number of resources required. These possibilities are considered in more detail later.

## Task difficulty

The ability to perform two tasks together depends on their difficulty, and there are several studies showing the expected pattern of results. For example Sullivan (1976) used the tasks of shadowing an auditory message and detecting target words on a non-shadowed message at the same time. When the shadowing task was made harder by using a less redundant message, fewer targets were detected on the non-shadowed message. However, it is hard to define "task difficulty" with any precision.

The demands for resources of two tasks performed together might be thought to equal the sums of the demands of the two tasks when performed separately. However, the necessity to perform two tasks together often introduces new demands of co-ordination and avoidance of interference. Duncan (1979) asked his participants to respond to closely successive stimuli, one requiring a left-hand response and the other a right-hand response. The relationship between each stimulus and response was either corresponding (e.g., rightmost stimulus calling for response of the rightmost finger) or crossed (e.g., leftmost stimulus calling for response of the rightmost finger). Performance was poor when the relationship was corresponding for one stimulus but crossed for the other. In these circumstances, the participants were sometimes confused, with their errors being largely those expected if the inappropriate stimulus–response relationship had been selected.

## Bottleneck theories

Welford (1952) argued that there is a bottleneck in the processing system making it hard (or impossible) for two decisions about the appropriate responses to two different stimuli to be made at the same time. Much of the supporting evidence comes from studies of the *psychological refractory period*. In these studies, there are two stimuli (e g., two lights) and two responses (e.g., button presses), and the task is to respond to each stimulus as rapidly as possible. When the second stimulus is presented very shortly after the first one, there is generally a marked slowing of the response to the second stimulus: this is known as the psychological refractory period effect (see Welford, 1952).

It could be argued that the psychological refractory period occurs simply because people are not used to responding to two immediately successive stimuli. However, Pashler (1993) discussed one of his studies in which the effect was still observable after more than 10,000 practice trials.

Another objection to the notion that the delay in responding to the second stimulus reflects a bottleneck in processing is that the effect is due to similarity of stimuli and/or similarity of responses. According to the bottleneck theory, the psychological refractory period effect should be present even when the two stimuli and responses differ greatly. In contrast, the effect should disappear if similarity is crucial. Pashler (1990) used a tone requiring a vocal response and a visual letter requiring a button-push response. Some participants were told the order in which the stimuli would be presented, whereas the others were not. In spite of a lack of either stimulus or response similarity, there was a psychological refractory period effect, and it was greater when the order of stimuli was known than when it was not (see Figure 5.7). Thus, the findings provided strong support for the bottleneck position.

Pashler (1998, p. 177) ended his review with the following conclusion:

If there were no fundamental constraint preventing central stages of multiple tasks from being carried out simultaneously, one might expect that exceptions to PRP [psychological refractory period] interference would be encountered frequently But in fact, . . . only a handful of exceptions have been noted

**FIGURE 5.7**

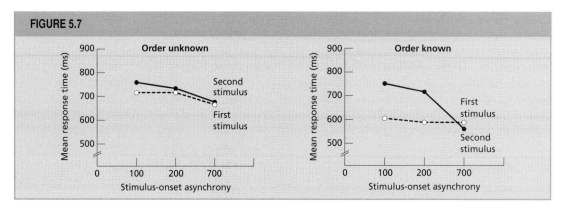

Response times to the first and second stimuli as a function of time between the onset of the stimuli (stimulus-onset asynchrony) and whether or not the order of the stimuli was known beforehand. Adapted from Pashler (1990).

. . . These exceptions have generally been interpreted as indicating that certain specific neural pathways are capable of bypassing the central bottleneck.

Earlier we discussed studies (e.g., Hirst et al., 1980; Spelke et al., 1976) in which two complex tasks were performed remarkably well together. Such findings make it hard to argue for the existence of a bottleneck in processing. However, studies on the psychological refractory period have the advantage of very precise assessment of the time taken to respond to any given stimulus. The coarse-grained measures obtained in studies such as those of Spelke et al. (1976) and Hirst et al. (1980) may simply be too insensitive to permit detection of bottlenecks.

It has been assumed so far that there is a single bottleneck, but there may be multiple bottlenecks. Pashler (1998, p. 175) addressed this issue: "At present, . . . a single bottleneck seems sufficient to account for the response delays observed in 'standard' PRP designs involving pairs of choice RT [response time] tasks. In fact, results from these paradigms are difficult to square with the existence of multiple bottlenecks."

Pashler et al. (1994) studied *split-brain patients*, in whom the connections between the cortical hemispheres have been surgically cut. One stimulus–response task was presented to one hemisphere and the other was presented to the other hemisphere. If the bottleneck is located in the cortex,

then it might be expected that these patients would not show the psychological refractory period effect. In fact, they had a normal effect, suggesting that sub-cortical structures underlie the effect.

The evidence from studies of the psychological refractory period indicates that there is a bottleneck, and that some processing is serial. However, the size of the psychological refractory period is typically not very large, and suggests that most processes do not operate in a serial way. As Pashler (1998, p. 184) pointed out, "The idea of obligatory serial central processing is quite consistent with a great deal of parallel processing."

## Central capacity theories

A simple way of accounting for many dual-task findings is to assume there is some central capacity (e.g. central executive) which can be used flexibly across a wide range of activities. This central processor has strictly limited resources, and is sometimes known as attention or effort. The extent to which two tasks can be performed together depends on the demands that each task makes on those resources. If the combined demands of the two tasks do not exceed the total resources of the central capacity, then the two tasks will not interfere with each other. However, if the resources are insufficient, then performance disruption is inevitable.

One of the best known of the capacity theories was put forward by Kahneman (1973). He argued that attentional capacity is limited but the capacity can vary somewhat. More specifically, it is greater when task difficulty is high than when it is low, and it increases in conditions of high effort or motivation. Increased effort tends to produce physiological arousal, and this can be assessed in various ways (e.g., pupillary dilation).

There are various problems with Kahneman's (1973) theory. He did not define his key terms very clearly, referring to a "a nonspecific input, which may be variously labelled 'effort', 'capacity', or 'attention'." Another problem is that it is assumed that effort and attentional capacity are determined in part by task difficulty, but it is very hard to determine the difficulty of a task with any precision.

Bourke, Duncan, and Nimmo-Smith (1996) tested predictions of central capacity theory. They selected four tasks that were designed to be as different as possible:

1.  Random generation: generating letters at random.
2.  Prototype learning: working out the features of two patterns or prototypes from seeing various exemplars.
3.  Manual task: screwing a nut down to the bottom of a bolt and back up to the top, and then down to the bottom of a second bolt and back up, and so on.
4.  Tone task: detecting the occurrence of a target tone.

The participants were given two of these tasks to perform together, with one task being identified as more important than the other. The basic argument was as follows: if there is a central or general capacity, then the task making most demands on this capacity will interfere most with all three of the other tasks. In contrast, the task making fewest demands on this capacity will intefere least with all the other tasks.

What did Bourke et al. (1996) find? First, these very different tasks did interfere with each other. Second, the random generation task interfered the most overall with the performance of the other tasks, and the tone task interfered the least. Third, and of greatest importance, the random

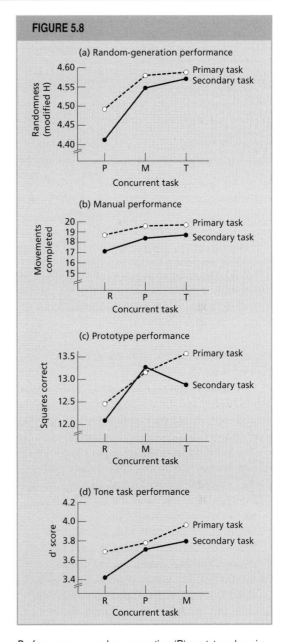

**FIGURE 5.8**

(a) Random-generation performance

(b) Manual performance

(c) Prototype performance

(d) Tone task performance

Performance on random generation (R), prototype learning (P), manual (M), and tone (T) tasks as a function of concurrent task. Adapted from Bourke et al. (1996).

generation task consistently interfered most with the prototype, manual, and tone tasks, and it did so whether it was the primary or the secondary task (see Figure 5.8). The tone task consistently interfered least with each of the other three tasks. Thus,

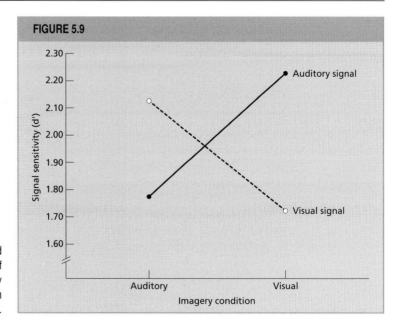

**FIGURE 5.9**

Sensitivity (d′) to auditory and visual signals as a function of concurrent imagery modality (auditory vs. visual). Adapted from Segal and Fusella (1970).

the findings accorded with the predictions of a general capacity theory.

The main limitation of the study by Bourke et al. (1996) is that it did not clarify the nature of the central capacity. As they admitted (1996, p. 544),

The general factor may be a limited pool of processing resource that needs to be invested for a task to be performed. It may be a limited central executive that coordinates or monitors other processes and is limited in how much it can deal with at one time. It may also represent a general limit of the entire cognitive system on the amount of information that can be processed at a given time. The method developed here deals only with the existence of a general factor in dual-task decrements, not its nature.

*Evaluation*

Central capacity theories cannot explain all the findings. According to such theories, the crucial determinant of dual-task performance is the difficulty level of the two tasks, with difficulty being defined in terms of the demands placed on the resources of the central capacity. However, the effects of task difficulty are often swamped by those of task similarity. For example, Segal and Fusella (1970) combined image construction (visual or auditory) with signal detection (visual or auditory). The auditory image task impaired detection of auditory signals more than did the visual task (see Figure 5.9), suggesting that the auditory image task was more demanding than the visual image task. However, the auditory image task was less disruptive than the visual image task when each task was combined with a task requiring detection of visual signals, suggesting the opposite conclusion. In this study, task similarity was clearly a much more important factor than task difficulty.

Allport (1989, p. 647) argued that such findings, "point to a multiplicity of attentional functions, dependent on a multiplicity of specialised subsystems. No one of these subsystems appears uniquely 'central'." It is possible to "explain" dual-task performance by assuming that the resources of some central capacity have been exceeded, and to account for a lack of interference by assuming that the two tasks did not exceed those resources. However, in the absence of any independent assessment of central processing capacity, this is simply a re-description of the findings rather than an explanation.

## Modular theories

The views of central capacity theorists can be compared with those of cognitive neuropsychologists, who assume that the processing system is modular (i.e., consisting of numerous fairly independent processors or modules). Evidence for modularity comes from the study of language in brain-damaged patients (see Chapters 12 and 13). If the processing system consists of specific processing mechanisms, then it is clear why the degree of similarity between two tasks is so important: similar tasks compete for the same specific processing mechanisms or modules, and thus produce interference, whereas dissimilar tasks involve different modules, and so do not interfere.

Allport (1989) and others have argued that dual-task performance can be accounted for in terms of modules or specific processing resources. However, there are significant problems with this theoretical approach. First, it does not provide an adequate explanation of findings on the psychological refractory period effect. Second, there is no consensus regarding the nature or number of these processing modules. Third, most modular theories cannot be falsified. Whatever the findings, it is always possible to account for them by assuming the existence of appropriate specific modules. Fourth, if there were several modules operating in parallel, there would be substantial problems in terms of co-ordinating their outputs to produce coherent behaviour

## Synthesis theories

Some theorists (e.g., Baddeley, 1986; Eysenck, 1982) favour an approach based on a synthesis of the central capacity and modular notions. According to them, there is a hierarchical structure. The central processor or central executive is at the top of the hierarchy, and is involved in the co-ordination and control of behaviour. Below this level are specific processing mechanisms operating relatively independently of each other.

One of the problems with the notion that there are several specific processing mechanisms and one general processing mechanism is that there does not appear to be a unitary attentional system.

As we saw in the earlier discussion of cognitive neuropsychological findings, it seems that somewhat separate mechanisms are involved in disengaging, shifting, and engaging attention. If there is no general processing mechanism, then it may be unrealistic to assume that the processing system possesses a hierarchical structure.

## AUTOMATIC PROCESSING

A key phenomenon in studies of divided attention is the dramatic improvement that practice often has on performance. The commonest explanation for this phenomenon is that some processing activities become automatic as a result of prolonged practice. There is reasonable agreement on the criteria for automatic processes:

- They are fast.
- They do not reduce the capacity for performing other tasks (i.e., they demand zero attention).
- They are unavailable to consciousness.
- They are unavoidable (i.e., they always occur when an appropriate stimulus is presented, even if that stimulus is outside the field of attention).

As Hampson (1989, p. 264) pointed out, "Criteria for automatic processes are easy to find, but hard to satisfy empirically." For example, the requirement that automatic processes should not need attention means that they should have no influence on the concurrent performance of an attention-demanding task. This is rarely the case (see Pashler, 1998). There are also problems with the unavoidability criterion. The *Stroop effect*, in which the naming of the colours in which words are printed is slowed down by using colour words (e.g., the word YELLOW printed in red), has often been regarded as involving unavoidable and automatic processing of the colour words. However, Kahneman and Henik (1979) found that the Stroop effect was much larger when the distracting information (i.e., the colour name) was in the same location as the to-be-named colour

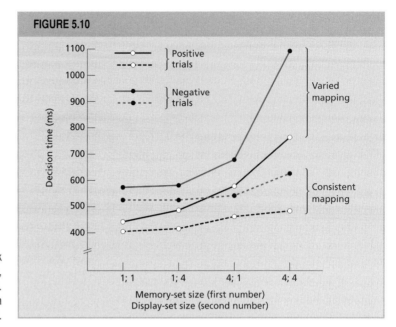

**FIGURE 5.10**

Response times on a decision task as a function of memory-set size, display-set size, and consistent vs. varied mapping. Data from Shiffrin and Schneider (1977).

rather than in an adjacent location. Thus, the processes producing the Stroop effect are not entirely unavoidable, and so are not completely automatic.

Few processes are fully automatic in the sense of conforming to all the criteria, with a much larger number of processes being only partially automatic. Later in this section we consider a theoretical approach (that of Norman & Shallice, 1986) which distinguishes between fully automatic and partially automatic processes.

## Shiffrin and Schneider's theory

Shiffrin and Schneider (1977) and Schneider and Shiffrin (1977) argued for a theoretical distinction between controlled and automatic processes. According to them:

- Controlled processes are of limited capacity, require attention, and can be used flexibly in changing circumstances.
- Automatic processes suffer no capacity limitations, do not require attention, and are very hard to modify once they have been learned.

Schneider and Shiffrin made use of a task in which participants memorised one, two, three, or four letters (the memory set), were then shown a visual display containing one, two, three, or four letters, and finally decided as rapidly as possible whether any one of the items in the visual display was the same as any one of the items in the memory set. The crucial manipulation was the type of mapping used. With consistent mapping, only consonants were used as members of the memory set, and only numbers were used as distractors in the visual display (or vice versa). Thus, if a participant were given only consonants to memorise, then he or she would know that any consonant detected in the visual display must be an item from the memory set. With varied mapping, a mixture of numbers and consonants was used to form the memory set and to provide distractors in the visual display.

There were striking effects of the mapping manipulation (see Figure 5.10). The numbers of items in the memory set and visual display greatly affected decision speed in the varied mapping conditions, but not in the consistent mapping conditions. According to Schneider and Shiffrin

(1977), a controlled search process was used with varied mapping. This involves serial comparisons between each item in the memory set and each item in the visual display until a match is achieved or every comparison has been made. In contrast, performance with consistent mapping reflects the use of automatic processes operating independently and in parallel. According to Schneider and Shiffrin (1977), these automatic processes evolve as a result of years of practice in distinguishing between letters and numbers.

The notion that automatic processes develop through practice was tested by Shiffrin and Schneider (1977). They used consistent mapping with the consonants B to L forming one set and the consonants Q to Z forming the other set. As before, items from only one set were always used in the construction of the memory set, and the distractors in the visual display were all selected from the other set. There was a great improvement in performance over 2100 trials, which seemed to reflect the growth of automatic processes.

The greatest problem with automatic processes is their lack of flexibility, which is likely to disrupt performance when the prevailing circumstances change. This was confirmed in the second part of the study. The initial 2100 trials with one consistent mapping were followed by a further 2100 trials with the reverse consistent mapping. This reversal of the mapping conditions greatly disrupted performance. Indeed, it took nearly 1000 trials under the new conditions before performance recovered to its level at the very start of the experiment!

Shiffrin and Schneider (1977) carried out further experiments in which participants initially tried to locate target letters anywhere in a visual display, but were then instructed to detect targets in one part of the display and to ignore targets elsewhere. Participants were less able to ignore part of the visual display when they had developed automatic processes than when they had made use of controlled search processes. As Eysenck (1982, p. 22) pointed out, "Automatic processes function rapidly and in parallel but suffer from inflexibility; controlled processes are flexible and versatile but operate relatively slowly and in a serial fashion."

## Evaluation

Shiffrin and Schneider's (1977) theoretical approach is important, but is open to criticism. There is a puzzling discrepancy between theory and data with respect to the identification of automaticity. The theoretical assumption that automatic processes operate in parallel and place no demands on capacity means there should be a slope of zero (i.e., a horizontal line) in the function relating decision speed to the number of items in the memory set and/or in the visual display when automatic processes are used. In fact, decision speed was slower when the memory set and the visual display both contained several items (see Figure 5.10).

Shiffrin and Schneider's approach is descriptive rather than explanatory. The claim that some processes become automatic with practice is uninformative about what is actually happening. Practice may simply lead to a speeding up of the processes involved, or it may lead to a dramatic change in the nature of the processes themselves. Cheng (1985) used the term "restructuring" to refer to the latter state of affairs. For example, if you are asked to add ten twos, you could do this by adding two and two, and then two to four, and so on. Alternatively, you could short-circuit the process by simplying multiplying ten by two. Thus, simply finding that practice leads to automaticity does not indicate whether the same processes are being performed more efficiently or whether entirely new processes are being used.

Cheng (1985) argued that most of Shiffrin and Schneider's findings on automaticity were actually based on restructuring. She claimed that participants in the consistent mapping conditions did not really search systematically for a match. If, for example, they knew that any consonant in the visual display had to be an item from the memory set, then they could simply scan the visual display looking for a consonant without any regard to which consonants were actually in the memory set. Schneider and Shiffrin (1985) pointed out that some findings could not be explained in terms of restructuring. For example, the finding that participants could not ignore part of the visual display after automatic processes had been acquired does not lend itself to a restructuring explanation.

## Norman and Shallice's theory

Norman and Shallice (1986) distinguised between fully automatic and partially automatic processes. They identified three levels of functioning:

- Fully automatic processing, controlled by schemas (organised plans).
- Partially automatic processing, involving contention scheduling without deliberate direction or conscious control; contention scheduling is used to resolve conflicts among schemas.
- Deliberate control by a supervisory attentional system; Baddeley (1986) argued that this system resembled the central executive of the working memory system (see Chapter 6).

According to Norman and Shallice (1986), fully automatic processes occur with very little conscious awareness of the processes involved. Such automatic processes would often disrupt behaviour if left entirely to their own devices. As a result, there is an automatic conflict resolution process known as contention scheduling. This selects one of the available schemas on the basis of environmental information and current priorities. There is generally more conscious awareness of the partially automatic processes involving contention scheduling than of fully automatic processes. Finally, there is a higher-level supervisory attentional system. This system is involved in decision making and trouble-shooting, and it permits flexible responding in novel situations. The supervisory attentional system may well be located in the frontal lobes (see Chapter 6).

### Section summary

The theoretical approach of Norman and Shallice (1986) includes the interesting notion that there are two separate control systems: contention scheduling and the supervisory attentional system. This contrasts with the views of many previous theorists that there is a single control system. The approach of Norman and Shallice is preferable, because it provides a more natural explanation for the fact that some processes are fully automatic, whereas others are only partially automatic.

## Instance theory

Logan (1988) pointed out that most theories do not indicate clearly how automaticity develops through prolonged practice. He tried to fill this gap by putting forward instance theory based on these assumptions:

- Separate memory traces are stored away each time a stimulus is encountered and processed.
- Practice with the same stimulus leads to the storage of increased information about the stimulus, and about what to do with it.
- This increase in the knowledge base with practice permits rapid retrieval of relevant information when the appropriate stimulus is presented.
- "Automaticity is memory retrieval: performance is automatic when it is based on a single-step direct-access retrieval of past solutions from memory" (Logan, 1988, p. 493).
- In the absence of practice, responding to a stimulus requires thought and the application of rules. After prolonged practice, the correct response is stored in memory and can be accessed very rapidly.

These theoretical views make coherent sense of many characteristics of automaticity. Automatic processes are fast because they require only the retrieval of "past solutions" from long-term memory. Automatic processes have little effect on the processing capacity available to perform other tasks, because the retrieval of heavily over-learned information is relatively effortless. Finally, there is no conscious awareness of automatic processes, because no significant processes intervene between the presentation of a stimulus and the retrieval of the appropriate response.

Logan (1988, p. 519) summarised instance theory as follows: "Novice performance is limited by a lack of knowledge rather than by a lack of resources . . . Only the knowledge base changes with practice." Logan is probably right in his basic assumption that an understanding of automatic, expert performance will require detailed consideration of the knowledge acquired with practice, rather than simply processing changes.

Logan, Taylor, and Etherton (1996) studied auto-maticity. Two words were presented together on each trial, one of which was red or green and the other of which was white. Specific words (e.g., chair) were always presented in the same colour. One group of participants had to make one of three decisions with respect to the coloured word:

1. It does not belong to the target category (e.g., countries).
2. It belongs to the target category and is coloured red.
3. It belongs to the target category and is coloured green.

There were 512 trials of training, and the speeding up of performance over these trials suggested that automatic processes had developed. There were then 32 transfer trials, on which the colour of each word was *reversed* from the training trials. The key finding was that colour reversal disrupted performance, indicating that colour information influenced automatic performance during transfer.

Another group of participants was treated exactly the same during training. However, their task on the transfer trials did *not* require them to attend explicitly to the colour of the words. They had to make one of two decisions with respect to the coloured word:

1. It does not belong to the target category.
2. It belongs to the target category.

Would we expect colour reversal to disrupt performance for these participants? Information about colour had been thoroughly learned during training, and so might produce disruption via auto-matic processes. In fact, there was no disruption. Thus, knowledge stored in memory as a result of prolonged practice may or may not be produced automatically depending on the precise conditions of retrieval.

How did Logan et al. (1996) explain these findings? Their starting point was the notion that automaticity is a memory phenomenon. The rela-tionship between encoding and retrieval is import-ant for an explanation of memory performance (see Chapter 6). According to Logan et al. (1996, p. 621):

Automatic performance depends on both en-coding and retrieval, so evidence that some aspect of a stimulus is important in auto-matic performance suggests that that aspect was encoded in the instance. However, evid-ence that some aspect of a stimulus is not important in automatic performance does not mean that that aspect was not encoded. It may be available to some other retrieval task.

## ACTION SLIPS

In this section, we consider *action slips* (the performance of actions that were not intended). It is clear that attentional failures are usually involved in action slips, and this is recognised at a commonsense level in the notion of "absent-mindedness". However, there are several kinds of action slips, and each one may require its own detailed explanation.

### Diary studies

One way of studying action slip is to via diary studies. Sellen and Norman (1992, p. 317) gave the following example of an action slip from a diary study: "I wanted to turn on the radio but walked past it and put my hand on the telephone receiver instead. I went to pick up the phone and I couldn't figure out why."

Reason (1979) asked 35 people to keep diaries of their action slips over a two-week period. Over 400 action slips were reported, most of which belonged to five major categories. Forty percent of the slips involved *storage failures*, in which intentions and actions were either forgotten or recalled incorrectly. Reason (1979, p. 74) quoted the following example of a storage failure: "I started to pour a second kettle of boiling water into a teapot of freshly made tea. I had no recol-lection of having just made it."

A further 20% of the errors were *test failures* in which the progress of a planned sequence was not monitored sufficiently at crucial junctures. Here is an example of a test failure (Reason, 1979,

p. 73): "I meant to get my car out, but as I passed through the back porch on my way to the garage I stopped to put on my wellington boots and gardening jacket as if to work in the garden." *Subroutine failures* accounted for a further 18% of the errors; these involved insertions, omissions, or re-orderings of the component stages in an action sequence. Reason (1979, p. 73) gave the following example of this type of error: "I sat down to do some work and before starting to write I put my hand up to my face to take my glasses off, but my fingers snapped together rather abruptly because I hadn't been wearing them in the first place."

There were only a few action slips in the two remaining categories of *discrimination failures* (11%) and *programme assembly failures* (5%). The former category consisted of failures to discriminate between objects (e.g., mistaking shaving cream for toothpaste), and the latter category consisted of inappropriate combinations of actions (e.g., Reason, 1979, p. 72): "I unwrapped a sweet, put the paper in my mouth, and threw the sweet into the waste bucket."

*Evaluation*

It would be unwise to attach much significance to the percentages of the various kinds of action slips. The figures are based on those action slips that were detected, and we simply do not know how many cases of each kind of slips went undetected. The number of occurrences of any particular kind of action slip is meaningful only when we know the number of occasions on which that kind of slip might have occurred but did not. Thus, the small number of discrimination failures may reflect either good discrimination or a relative lack of situations requiring anything approaching a fine discrimination.

Another issue is that two action slips may seem similar, and so be categorised together, even though the underlying mechanisms are different. For example, Grudin (1983) conducted videotape analyses of substitution errors in typing involving striking the key adjacent to the intended key. Some of these errors involved the correct finger moving

in the wrong direction, whereas others involved an incorrect key being pressed by the finger that normally strikes it. According to Grudin, the former kind of error is due to faulty execution of an action, whereas the latter is due to faulty assignment of the finger. We would need more information than is generally available in most diary studies to identify such subtle differences in underlying processes.

## Laboratory studies

Several techniques have been used to produce action slips in laboratory conditions. What is often done is to provide a misleading context that increases the activation of an incorrect response. Reason (1992) discussed a study of the "oak–yolk" effect illustraing this approach. Some participants were asked to respond as rapidly as possible to a series of questions (the most frequent answers are given):

Q:  What do we call the tree that grows from acorns?
A:  Oak.
Q:  What do we call a funny story?
A:  Joke.
Q:  What sound does a frog make?
A:  Croak.
Q:  What is Pepsi's major competitor?
A:  Coke.
Q:  What is another word for cape?
A:  Cloak.
Q:  What do you call the white of an egg?
A:  Yolk.

The correct answer to the last question is "albumen". However, 85% of these participants gave the wrong answer, because it rhymed with the previous answers. In contrast, of those participants only asked the last question, a mere 5% responded "yolk".

It is not clear that action slips obtained under laboratory conditions resemble those typically found under naturalistic conditions. As Sellen and Norman (1992, p. 334) pointed out, many naturally occurring action slips occur:

. . . when a person is internally preoccupied or distracted, when both the intended actions and the wrong actions are automatic, and when one is doing familiar tasks in familiar surroundings. Laboratory situations offer completely the opposite conditions. Typically, subjects are given an unfamiliar, highly contrived task to accomplish in a strange environment. Most subjects arrive motivated to perform well and . . . are not given to internal preoccupation . . . In short, the typical laboratory environment is possibly the least likely place where we are likely to see truly spontaneous, absent-minded errors.

This analysis may be too pessimistic. As we will see shortly, Robertson et al. (1997) and Hay and Jacoby (1996) have studied action slips in the laboratory to bring out some of the key aspects of naturally occurring action slips.

### Frontal lobe damage

As Robertson et al. (1997) pointed out, there is convincing evidence that patients with traumatic brain injury causing damage to the frontal lobes and white matter of the brain have severe problems with attention and concentration. Robertson et al. devised a task (the Sustained Attention to Response Task) to assess the tendency of these patients to produce action slips. The task involves presenting a long sequence of random digits, and the task is to respond with a key press to all digits except the digit 3. Failures to withhold responses to the digit 3 are regarded as action slips. Robertson et al. (1997) found that patients produced many more action slips than normal controls (30% vs. 12%, respectively). They also found among the patients that there was a correlation of −.58 between pathological severity of their symptoms and the number of action slips produced.

The findings of Robertson et al. (1997) suggest that sustained attention is needed to avoid action slips. They also suggest that the frontal lobes and the white matter of the brain play an important role in sustained attention, so that damage to these areas makes an individual vulnerable to action slips.

### Theories of action slips

Hay and Jacoby (1996) argued that action slips are most likely to occur when two conditions are satisfied:

1. The correct response is *not* the strongest or most habitual one.
2. Attention is not fully applied to the task of selecting the correct response.

For example, suppose you are looking for your house key. If it is not in its usual place, you are still likely to waste time by looking there first of all. If you are late for an important appointment as well, you may find it hard to focus your attention on thinking about other places in which the key might have been put. As a result, you may spend a lot of time looking in several wrong places.

Hay and Jacoby (1996) tested this theoretical approach in a study in which the participants had to complete paired associates (e.g., knee: b _ n _). Sometimes the correct response on the basis of a previous learning task was also the strongest response (e.g., bend), and sometimes the correct response was *not* the strongest response (e.g., bone). The participants had either 1 second or 3 seconds to respond. Hay and Jacoby (1996) argued that action slips would be most likely when the correct response was *not* the strongest one, and when the response had to be made rapidly. That was what they found (see Figure 5.11).

Why is the research by Hay and Jacoby (1996) of major importance? As they pointed out, "Very little has been done to examine action . . . slips by directly manipulating the likelihood of their occurrence in experimental situations. In the research presented here, we not only manipulated action slips, but also teased apart the roles played by automatic and intentional responding in their production" (p. 1332).

### Schema theory

According to schema theory (Norman, 1981; Sellen & Norman, 1992), actions are determined by hierarchically organised schemas or organised

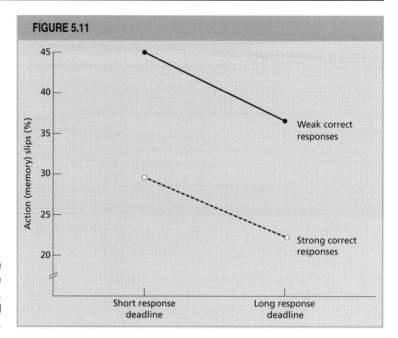

**FIGURE 5.11**

Memory performance as a function of strength of the correct response and time available to respond. Based on data in Hay and Jacoby (1996).

plans. The highest-level schema represents the overall intention or goal (e.g., buying a present), and the lower-level schemas correspond to the actions involved in accomplishing that intention (e.g., taking the train to the nearest shopping centre). A schema determines action when its level of activation is sufficiently high and when the appropriate triggering conditions exist (e.g., getting into the train when it stops at the station). The activation level of schemas is determined by current intentions and by the immediate environmental situation.

According to this schema model, action slips occur for various reasons:

• Errors in the formation of an intention.
• Faulty activation of a schema, leading to activation of the wrong schema or to loss of activation in the correct schema.
• Faulty triggering of active schemas, leading to action being determined by the wrong schema.

Reason's (1979) action slips can be related to this theoretical framework. For example, discrimination failures can lead to errors in the formation of an intention, and storage failures for intentions can produce faulty triggering of active schemas.

*Evaluation*

One of the positive characteristics of recent theories is the notion that errors or action slips should not be regarded as special events produced by their own mechanisms. They emerge from the interplay of conscious and automatic control, and are thus "the normal by-products of the design of the human action system" (Sellen & Norman, 1992, p. 318). On the negative side, the notion that behaviour is determined by either the automatic or conscious mode of control is simplistic. There are considerable doubts about the notion of automatic processing, and it is improbable that there is a unitary attentional system. More needs to be discovered about the factors determining which mode of control will dominate. It is correctly predicted by contemporary theory that action slips should occur most often with highly practised activities, because it is under such circumstances that the automatic mode of control is most likely to be used. However, the incidence of action slips is much greater with trivial actions than with those regarded as important. For example, many circus performers carry out well practised actions, but the danger element ensures they make minimal use of the automatic mode of control. It is not clear that recent theories are equipped to explain such phenomena.

## Behavioural efficiency

It might be argued that people would function more efficiently if they placed less reliance on automatic processes and more on the central processor. However, automated activities can be be disrupted if too much attention is paid to them. For example, it can be harder to walk down a steep spiral staircase if attention is paid to the leg movements involved. Moreover, Reason's diarists produced an average of only one action slip per day, which does not indicate that their usual processing strategies were ineffective. Indeed, most people seem to alternate between the automatic and attention-based modes of control very efficiently.

Action slips result from a failure to shift from automatic to attention-based control at the right time. Although theoretically important, action slips usually have a minimally disruptive effect on everyday life. However, there may be some exceptions, such as absent-minded professors who focus on their own profound inner thoughts rather than on the world around them.

## Section summary

Action slips have been investigated by means of diary studies, in which participants keep daily records of their slips. Various categories of action slip have been identified, but they all involve highly practised activities. Highly practised skills do not require detailed attentional monitoring except at critical decision points. Failures of attention at such decision points cause many action slips. Failure to remember what was done a few seconds previously is responsible for many other action slips.

## CHAPTER SUMMARY

- Introduction. Attention generally refers to selectivity of processing. Access to consciousness is controlled by attentional mechanisms in the same way as what appears on a television screen is determined by which channel is chosen. Attention can be active and based on top-down processes or passive and based on bottom-up processes. It is important to distinguish between focused and divided attention. Most research on attention deals only with external, two-dimensional stimuli and the individual's goals and motivational states are ignored.
- Focused auditory attention. Initial research on focused auditory attention with the shadowing task suggested there was very limited processing of the unattended stimuli. However, there can be extensive processing of unattended stimuli. This is especially the case when the unattended stimuli are dissimilar to the attended ones. There has been a controversy between early- and late-selection theorists as to the location of a bottleneck in processing. Most of the evidence favours early-selection theories. However, there may be some flexibility in the stage of processing at which selection occurs.
- Focused visual attention. Focused visual attention resembles a zoom lens more than a spotlight, as the size of the visual field within focal attention varies as a function of task demands. However, attention is often directed to objects rather than to a given region in space in normals and in neglect and extinction patients. Focused visual attention is more flexible than is implied by the zoom-lens approach. Unattended visual stimuli are typically processed less thoroughly than attended ones, and this conclusion is supported by studies on event-related potentials. However, the use of sensitive measures indicates that normals and neglect patients often process the meaning of unattended visual stimuli. According to Treisman's feature integration theory, visual

search typically involves a rapid initial parallel processing of features followed by a slower serial process in which features are combined to form objects. Visual search is not entirely parallel or serial, and searching for objects is typically faster and more efficient than is predicted by the theory. According to Posner, visual attention involves disengagement of attention from one stimulus, shifting of attention from one stimulus to another, and engagement of attention on the new stimulus.

- Divided attention. Dual-task performance depends on task similarity, practice, and task difficulty. There is a psychological refractory period even when the stimuli and responses involved differ greatly or when there is prolonged practice. This suggests that there is a bottleneck in processing, although extensive parallel processing is also possible. There is evidence for a general central capacity having limited processing powers, and also for modular theories with their emphasis on specific processing resources.

- Automatic processing. Several theorists have argued that practice leads to automatic processing. Automatic processes are fast, they do not reduce the capacity available for other tasks, and there is generally no conscious awareness of them. According to instance theory, increased knowledge about what to do with different stimuli is stored away with practice, and automaticity occurs when this information is retrieved very rapidly. Thus, automaticity is a memory phenomenon that depends on the relationship between encoding and retrieval.

- Action slips. Action slips occur as a result of attentional failure. Individuals run off sequences of highly practised and overlearned motor programmes. Attentional control is not needed while each programme is running, but is needed when there is a switch from one programme to another. Failure to attend at these choice points can lead to the wrong motor programme being activated, especially if it is stronger than the right one. As optimal performance requires frequent shifts between the presence and absence of attentional control, it is perhaps surprising that action slips are not more prevalent.

## FURTHER READING

- Gazzaniga, M.S., Ivry, R.B., & Mangun, G.R. (1998). *Cognitive neuroscience: The biology of the mind*. New York: W.W. Norton. Chapter 6 provides extensive coverage of what is currently known about the neurophysiology of attention.
- Parasuraman, R. (1998). *Attentive brain*. Cambridge, MA: MIT Press. This book contains a series of up-to-date chapters on diverse key topics within attention.
- Parkin, A.J. (1996). *Explorations in cognitive neuropsychology*. Oxford: Blackwell. Chapter 5 contains a detailed account of research on neglect.
- Pashler, H. (1998). *Attention*. Hove, UK: Psychology Press. The chapters in this edited book provide high-level accounts of key contemporary topics in attention.
- Styles, E.A. (1997). *The psychology of attention*. Hove, UK: Psychology Press. This book contains a readable introduction to theory and research in attention.

# 6

# Memory: Structure and Processes

## INTRODUCTION

This chapter and the next two are concerned with human memory. All three chapters deal with normal human memory, but Chapter 7 also considers amnesic patients. Traditional laboratory-based research is the focus of this chapter, with more naturalistic research being the focus of Chapter 8. However, there are important links among these types of research. Many theoretical issues are relevant to brain-damaged and normal individuals, whether tested in the laboratory or in the field.

Theories of memory generally consider both the *structure* of the memory system and the *processes* operating within that structure. Structure refers to the way in which the memory system is organised, and process refers to the activities occurring within the memory system. Structure and process are both important, but some theorists emphasise only one of them in their theoretical formulations.

Learning and memory involve a series of stages. Those stages occurring during the presentation of the learning material are known as "encoding". This is the first stage. As a result of

encoding, some information is stored within the memory system. Thus, storage is the second stage. The third, and final, stage is retrieval, which involves recovering or extracting stored information from the memory system.

We have emphasised the importance of the distinctions between structure and process and among encoding, storage, and retrieval. However, one cannot have structure without process, or retrieval without previous encoding and storage. It is only when processes operate on the essentially passive structures of the memory system that it becomes active and of use. As Tulving and Thomson (1973, p. 359) pointed out, "Only that can be retrieved that has been stored, and . . . how it can be retrieved depends on how it was stored."

## THE STRUCTURE OF MEMORY

### Spatial metaphor

People often liken the mind to a physical space, with memories and ideas contained within that space (e.g., we speak of searching for lost memories). There is general adherence to the *spatial metaphor* (Roediger, 1980), according to which:

- Memories are stored in specific locations within the mind.
- Retrieval of memories involves a search through the mind.

The Greek philosopher Plato compared the mind to an aviary, with the individual memories represented by birds. Technological advances have led to changes in the precise form of analogy used (Roediger, 1980). For many years now, the workings of human memory have been compared to computer functioning (e.g., Atkinson & Shiffrin, 1968).

The spatial metaphor implies that the storage system is rather inflexible. If everything we know is stored within a three-dimensional space, then some kinds of information must be stored closer together than others. Perhaps the organisation of information in human memory is like a library. However, a library's cataloguing system would break down if a novel category of books were requested (e.g., books with red covers). In contrast, retrieval from memory is very flexible. Use of the spatial metaphor leads to an overemphasis on the ways in which information is represented in the memory system, and to an underemphasis on the processes operating on those memorial representations.

According to advocates of connectionist or neural networks (see Chapter 1), information about an individual or event is stored in the form of numerous connections among units and is *not* stored in a single place. According to Haberlandt (1999, p. 167), "In neural network models, there are no specific locations with unique addresses for memory records. Rather, memories are captured by patterns of activation spread over many neuron-like units and links between them."

## Memory stores

Several memory theorists (e.g., Atkinson & Shiffrin, 1968) have described the basic architecture of the memory system, and it is possible to discuss the multi-store approach on the basis of their common features. Three types of memory store were proposed:

- Sensory stores, each of which holds information very briefly and is modality-specific (limited to one sensory modality).
- A short-term store of very limited capacity.
- A long-term store of essentially unlimited capacity which can hold information over extremely long periods of time.

The multi-store model is shown in Figure 6.1. Environmental information is initially received by the sensory stores. These stores are modality-specific (e.g., vision; hearing). Information is held very briefly in the sensory stores, with some being attended to and processed further by the short-term store. Some of the information processed in the short-term store is transferred to the long-term store. Long-term storage of information often depends on rehearsal, with a direct relationship between the amount of rehearsal in the short-term store and the strength of the stored memory trace.

There is much overlap between the areas of attention and memory. Broadbent's (1958) theory of attention (see Chapter 5) was the main precursor of the multi-store approach to memory, and there is a clear resemblance between the notion of a sensory store and his "buffer" store.

Within the multi-store approach, the memory stores form the basic structure, and processes such as attention and rehearsal control the flow of

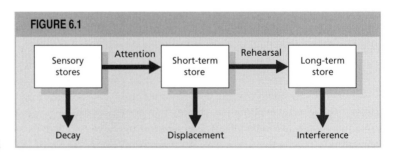

**FIGURE 6.1**

The multi-store model of memory.

information between them. However, the main emphasis within this approach to memory was on structure.

## Sensory stores

Our senses are constantly bombarded with information, most of which does not receive any attention. If you are sitting in a chair as you read this, then tactile information from that part of your body in contact with the chair is probably available. However, you have probably been unaware of that tactile information until now. Information in every sense modality persists briefly after the end of stimulation, aiding the task of extracting its key aspects for further analysis.

### Iconic store

The classic work on the visual or *iconic store* was carried out by Sperling (1960). When he presented a visual array containing three rows of four letters each for 50 milliseconds, his participants could usually report only four or five letters. However, they claimed to have seen many more letters. Sperling assumed that this happened because visual information had faded before most of it could be reported. He tested this by asking his participants to recall only part of the information presented. Sperling's findings supported his assumption, and indicated that information in iconic storage decays within about 0.5 seconds.

How useful is iconic storage? Haber (1983) claimed it is irrelevant to normal perception, except when trying to read in a lightning storm! He argued that "frozen iconic storage of information" may be useful in the laboratory when single stimuli are presented very briefly. In the real world, the icon formed from one visual fixation would be rapidly masked by the next fixation. Haber was mistaken. He assumed the icon is created at the offset of a visual stimulus, but it is actually created at its onset (Coltheart, 1983). Thus, even with a continuously changing visual world, iconic information can still be used. The mechanisms responsible for visual perception always operate on the icon rather than directly on the visual environment.

### Echoic store

The *echoic store* is a transient auditory store holding relatively unprocessed input. For example, suppose someone reading a newspaper is asked a question. The person addressed will sometimes ask, "What did you say?", but then realise that he or she does know what has been said. This "playback" facility depends on the echoic store.

Treisman (1964) asked people to shadow (repeat back aloud) the message presented to one ear while ignoring a second identical message presented to the other ear. When the second or non-shadowed message preceded the shadowed message, the two messages were only recognised as being the same when they were within 2 seconds of each other. This suggests the temporal duration of unattended auditory information in echoic storage is about 2 seconds.

## Short- and long-term stores

The distinction between a short-term and a long-term store is like the one proposed by William James (1890) between primary memory and secondary memory. Primary memory relates to information that remains in consciousness after it has been perceived and forms part of the psychological present. Secondary memory contains information about events that have left consciousness, and are therefore part of the psychological past.

Trying to remember a telephone number for a few seconds is an everyday example of the use of the *short-term store*. It shows two key characteristics usually attributed to this store:

- Very limited capacity (only about seven digits can be remembered).
- Fragility of storage, as any distraction usually causes forgetting.

The capacity of short-term memory has been assessed by span measures and by the recency effect in free recall. Digit span is a span measure, in which participants repeat back a set of random digits in the correct order when they have heard

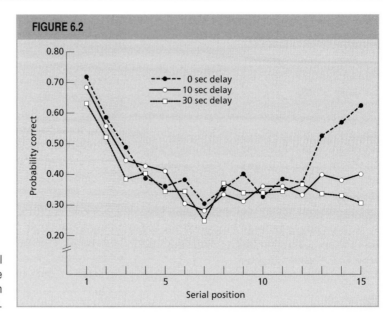

FIGURE 6.2

Free recall as a function of serial position and duration of the interpolated task. Adapted from Glanzer and Cunitz (1966).

them all. The span of immediate memory is usually "seven plus or minus two" whether the units are numbers, letters, or words (Miller, 1956). Miller claimed that about seven chunks (integrated pieces or units of information) could be held in short-term memory. For example, "IBM" is one chunk for those familiar with the company name International Business Machines, but three chunks for everyone else. However, the span in chunks is less with larger chunks (e.g., eight-word phrases) than with smaller chunks (e.g., one-syllable words; Simon, 1974).

The *recency effect* in free recall (recalling the items in any order) refers to the finding that the last few items in a list are usually much better remembered in immediate recall than are the items from the middle of the list. Counting backwards for only 10 seconds between the end of list presentation and the start of recall mainly affects the recency effect (Glanzer & Cunitz, 1966, see Figure 6.2). The two or three words susceptible to the recency effect may be in the short-term store at the end of list presentation, and thus especially vulnerable. However, Bjork and Whitten (1974) found there was still a recency effect in free recall when the participants counted backwards for 12 seconds after each item in the list was

presented. According to Atkinson and Shiffrin (1968) this should have eliminated the recency effect. The findings can be explained by analogy to looking along a row of telephone poles. The closer poles are more distinct that the ones farther away, just as the more recent list words are more discriminable than the others (Glenberg, 1987).

Strong evidence for the distinction between short-term and long-term memory stores comes from the demonstration of a *double dissociation* with brain-damaged patients. Two tasks probably involve different processing mechanisms if there is a double dissociation, i.e., some patients perform normally on task A but poorly on task B, whereas others perform normally on task B but poorly on task A. Amnesic patients have generally poor long-term memory, but intact short-term memory (see Chapter 7). The reverse problem is relatively rare, but a few such cases have been reported. These cases include KF, a patient who suffered damage in the left parieto-occipital region of the brain following a motorcycle accident. KF had no problem with long-term learning and recall, but his digit span was greatly impaired, and he had a recency effect of only one item under some circumstances (Shallice & Warrington, 1970).

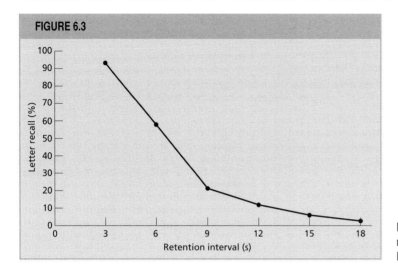

**FIGURE 6.3**

Forgetting over time in short-term memory. Data from Peterson and Peterson (1959).

However, KF did not perform badly on all short-term memory tasks (see next section).

Peterson and Peterson (1959) studied the duration of short-term memory by using the task of remembering a three-letter stimulus for a few seconds while counting backwards by threes. The ability to remember the three-letter stimulus declined to only about 50% after 6 seconds (see Figure 6.3), showing that information is lost rapidly from short-term memory.

Why does counting backwards cause forgetting from short-term memory? Counting backwards may be a source of interference, or it may divert attention away from the information in short-term memory. Interference and diversion of attention both seem to play a part (e.g., Reitman, 1974). Forgetting from the long-term store involves rather different mechanisms. As is discussed later, it depends mainly on *cue-dependent forgetting* (i.e., the memory traces are still in the memory system, but are inaccessible).

## Evaluation

The multi-store model provided a systematic account of the structures and processes involved in memory. The conceptual distinction between three kinds of memory stores (sensory stores, short-term store, and long-term store) makes sense. In order to justify the existence of three qualitatively different types of memory store, we must show major differences among them. Precisely this has been done. The memory stores differ from each other the following ways:

- Temporal duration.
- Storage capacity.
- Forgetting mechanism(s).
- Effects of brain damage.

Many contemporary memory theorists have used the multi-store model as the starting point of their theories. Much theoretical effort has gone into providing a more detailed account of the long-term store than that offered by Atkinson and Shiffrin (1968, 1971; see Chapter 7).

The multi-store model is very oversimplified. It was assumed that both the short-term and long-term stores are unitary, i.e., that each store always operates in a single, uniform way. Evidence that the short-term store is not unitary was reported by Warrington and Shallice (1972). KF's short-term forgetting of auditory letters and digits was much greater than his forgetting of visual stimuli. Shallice and Warrington (1974) then found that KF's short-term memory deficit was limited to verbal materials such as letters, words, and digits, and did not extend to meaningful sounds (e.g., telephones ringing). Thus, we cannot simply argue that KF had impaired short-term memory. According to

Shallice and Warrington (1974), his problems centred on the "auditory-verbal short-term store".

The multi-store model is also oversimplified when it comes to long-term memory. There is an amazing wealth of information stored in our long-term memory, including knowledge that Leonardo di Caprio is a film star, that $2 + 2 = 4$, that we had muesli for breakfast, and perhaps information about how to ride a bicycle. It is improbable that all this knowledge is stored within a single long-term memory store (see Chapter 7).

Logie (1999) pointed out another major problem with the multi-store model. According to the model, the short-term store acts as a gateway between the sensory stores and long-term memory (see Figure 6.1). However, the information processed in the short-term store has already made contact with information stored in long-term memory. For example, our ability to engage in verbal rehearsal of visually presented words depends on prior contact with stored information concerning pronunciation. Thus, access to long-term memory occurs *before* information is processed in short-term memory.

Finally, multi-store theorists assumed that the main way in which information is transferred to long-term memory is via rehearsal in the short-term store. In fact, the role of rehearsal in our everyday lives is much less than was assumed by multi-store theorists. More generally, multi-store theorists can be criticised for focusing too much on structural aspects of memory rather than on memory processes.

## WORKING MEMORY

Baddeley and Hitch (1974) argued that the concept of the short-term store should be replaced with that of working memory. Their working memory system has three components:

- A modality-free *central executive* resembling attention.
- An articulatory loop (now known as *phonological loop*) holding information in a phonological (speech-based) form.

- A visuo-spatial scratch pad (now known as *visuo-spatial sketchpad*) specialised for spatial and/or visual coding.

The key component of working memory is the central executive. It has limited capacity, and deals with any cognitively demanding task. The phonological loop and the visuo-spatial sketchpad are slave systems used by the central executive for specific purposes. The phonological loop preserves the order in which words are presented, and the visuo-spatial sketchpad is used for the storage and manipulation of spatial and visual information.

Every component of the working memory system has limited capacity, and is relatively independent of the other components. Two assumptions follow:

1. If two tasks use the same component, they cannot be performed successfully together.
2. If two tasks use different components, it should be possible to perform them as well together as separately.

Numerous dual-task studies have been carried out on the basis of these assumptions. For example, Robbins et al. (1996) considered the involvement of the three components of working memory in the selection of chess moves by weaker and stronger players. The main task was to select continuation moves from various chess positions while performing one of the following concurrent tasks:

- Repetitive tapping: this was the control condition.
- Random number generation: this involved the central executive.
- Pressing keys on a keypad in a clockwise fashion: this used the visuo-spatial sketchpad.
- Rapid repetition of the word see-saw: this used the phonological loop.

The findings are shown in Figure 6.4. Selecting chess moves involves the central executive and the visuo-spatial sketchpad, but not the phonological loop. The effects of the various concurrent tasks were similar on stronger and weaker players, suggesting that both groups use the working memory system in the same way.

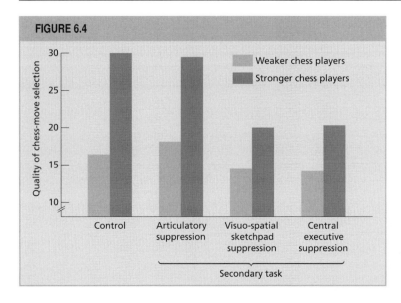

**FIGURE 6.4**

Effects of secondary tasks on quality of chess-move selection in stronger and weaker players. Adapted from Robbins et al. (1996).

## Phonological loop

Baddeley, Thomson, and Buchanan (1975) studied the phonological loop. Participants' ability to reproduce a sequence of words was better with short words than with long words: the *word-length effect*. Participants produced immediate serial recall of as many words as they could read out in 2 seconds. This suggested the capacity of the phonological loop is determined by temporal duration like a tape loop, and that memory span is determined by the rate of rehearsal.

Baddeley et al. (1975) obtained evidence that the word-length effect depends on the phonological loop. The number of visually presented words (out of five) that could be recalled was assessed. Some participants were given the articulatory suppression task of repeating the digits 1 to 8 while performing the main task. The argument was that this task would make use of the phonological loop and prevent it being used on the word-span task. Articulatory suppression eliminated the word-length effect (see Figure 6.5), indicating that the effect depends on the loop.

The phonological loop is more complex than was assumed by Baddeley and Hitch (1974). For example, although Baddeley et al. (1975) found that articulatory suppression eliminated the word-length effect with visual presentation, it did *not*

do so with auditory presentation (see Figure 6.5). Vallar and Baddeley (1984) studied a patient, PV, who did not seem to use the articulatory loop when tested on memory span. Her memory span for visually presented letters remained the same whether or not articulation was prevented by an articulatory suppression task, and there was also evidence that she did not use articulation with spoken letters. However, her memory span for spoken letters was worse when the letters were phonologically similar (i.e., they sounded alike). Thus, PV seemed to be processing phonologically (in a speech-based manner), but *without* making use of articulation.

Baddeley (1986, 1990) drew a distinction between a phonological or speech-based store and an articulatory control process (see Figure 6.6). According to Baddeley, the phonological loop consists of:

- A passive phonological store directly concerned with speech perception.
- An articulatory process linked to speech production that gives access to the phonological store.

According to this revised account, words that are presented auditorily are processed differently from those presented visually. Auditory presentation of

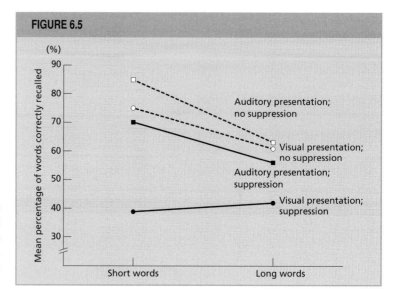

**FIGURE 6.5**

(%)

Auditory presentation;
no suppression

Visual presentation;
no suppression

Auditory presentation;
suppression

Visual presentation;
suppression

Short words          Long words

Mean percentage of words correctly recalled

Immediate word recall as a function of modality of presentation (visual vs. auditory), presence versus absence of articulatory suppression, and word length. Adapted from Baddeley et al. (1975).

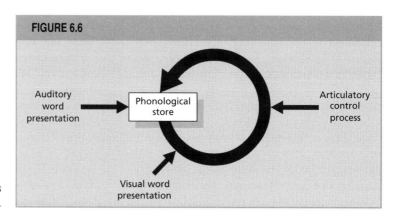

**FIGURE 6.6**

Auditory
word
presentation

Phonological
store

Articulatory
control
process

Visual word
presentation

Phonological loop system as envisaged by Baddeley (1990).

words produces *direct* access to the phonological store regardless of whether the articulatory control process is used. In contrast, visual presentation of words only permits *indirect* access to the phonological store through subvocal articulation (see Chapter 11).

This revised account makes sense of many findings. Suppose the word-length effect observed by Baddeley et al. (1975) depends on the rate of articulatory rehearsal (see Figure 6.5). Articulatory suppression eliminates the word-length effect with visual presentation because access to the phonological store is prevented. It does *not* affect the word-length effect with auditory presentation, because information about the words enters the phonological store directly.

Why was PV's letter span with auditory presentation affected by phonological similarity even though she did not use subvocal articulation? The effects of phonological similarity occurred because the auditorily presented letters entered *directly* into the phonological store even in the absence of subvocal articulation.

Does subvocal articulatory activity within the phonological loop require use of the speech musculature? Baddeley and Wilson (1985) studied patients, all but one of whom suffered from *dysarthria*, in which damage to the system controlling the speech musculature greatly restricts speech. The remaining patient had the even more serious condition of *anarthria*, which totally prevents speech. All the patients engaged in subvocal rehearsal or articulation. Baddeley (1986, p. 107) concluded: "The loop and its rehearsal processes are operating at a much deeper level than might at first seem likely, apparently relying on central speech control codes which appear to be able to function in the absence of peripheral feedback."

Smith and Jonides (1997) used two tasks designed to differ in their demands on the phonological store and the articulatory process. They obtained PET scans during task performance. There was heightened activity in the parietal lobe when the phonological store was being used, and increased activity in Broca's (language) area when the articulatory process was being used. Thus, the two subsystems of the phonological loop depend on different parts of the brain.

## Evaluation

The theory accounts well for the word-length effect, the effects of articulatory suppression, and the performance of various brain-damaged patients. In addition, the theory accounts for two other effects:

1. The irrelevant speech effect: the finding that irrelevant or unattended speech impairs immediate recall is explained by assuming that all spoken material necessarily enters the phonological store.
2. The phonological similarity effect: the finding that immediate recall is impaired when the memorised items are phonologically similar is explained by assuming that this reduces the discriminability of items in the phonological store.

According to the model, irrelevant speech and phonological similarity both affect only the phonological store. This leads to two predictions:

1. Irrelevant speech and phonological similarity should both affect the same brain area.
2. The effects of irrelevant speech and phonological similarity should be *interactive* rather than *independent*.

Martin-Loeches, Schweinberger, and Sommer (1997) tested these predictions. They recorded event-related potentials (ERPs), and obtained evidence against the first prediction: "Irrelevant speech and phonological similarity caused ERP effects with clearly different scalp topographies, indicating that these factors influence different brain systems" (Martin-Loeches et al., 1997, p. 471). They also failed to support the second prediction (as had some previous researchers).

Another problem was identified by Cowan et al. (1998). Memory span was affected by the rate of retrieval from short-term memory as well as by the rate of rehearsal, although only the latter factor is regarded as important within the model. This led Cowan et al. (1998, p. 152) to conclude that, "the leading model of working memory, the phonological loop model . . . has merit, but is an oversimplification."

What is the value of the phonological loop? It increases memory span, but this is far removed from the activities of everyday life. It also aids the reading of difficult material, making it easier for readers to retain information about the order of words in text (see Chapter 12). However, individuals with a severely deficient phonological loop generally cope very well, suggesting that the phonological loop has little practical significance. Baddeley, Gathercole, and Papagno (1998, p. 158) disagreed, arguing that "the phonological loop does have a very important function to fulfil, but it is one that is not readily uncovered by experimental studies of adult participants. We suggest that the function of the phonological loop is not to remember familiar words but to learn new words."

Evidence supporting this viewpoint was reported by Papagno, Valentine, and Baddeley (1991). Native Italian speakers learned pairs of Italian words and pairs of Italian–Russian words. Articulatory suppression (which reduces use of the phonological loop) greatly slowed the learning of foreign vocabulary, but had little effect on the learning of pairs of Italian words.

Trojano and Grossi (1995) studied SC, a patient with extremely poor phonological functioning. SC showed reasonable learning ability in most situations, but was totally unable to learn auditorily presented word–nonword pairs. Presumably SC's poorly functioning phonological loop prevented the learning of the phonologically unfamiliar nonwords.

Which component of the phonological loop is more involved in the learning of new words? According to Baddeley et al. (1998), the phonological store is of more relevance than subvocal rehearsal. Subvocal rehearsal is only used by children to maintain the contents of the phonological store from about the age of 7. However, children as young as 3 years old show a close link between phonological memory performance and vocabulary learning (Baddeley et al., 1998). Such evidence suggests that subvocal rehearsal is not needed for vocabulary learning.

## Visuo-spatial sketchpad

The characteristics of the visuo-spatial sketchpad are less clear than those of the articulatory loop. However, it is used in the temporary storage and manipulation of spatial and visual information. Baddeley et al. (1975) studied the visuo-spatial sketchpad. Participants heard the locations of digits within a matrix described by an auditory message that was either easily visualised or was rather hard to visualise. They then reproduced the matrix. When this task was combined with pursuit rotor (i.e., tracking a light moving around a circular track), performance on the easily visualised message was greatly impaired, but there was no adverse effect on the non-visualisable message.

The most obvious interpretation of these findings is that the pursuit rotor involves visual perception, and thus interferes with performance on the visualisable message. However, Baddeley and Lieberman (1980) found that a specifically visual concurrent task (making brightness judgements) actually disrupted performance *more* on the non-visualisable message. The results were very different when a spatial task with no visual input was performed while the message was being presented. This involved participants trying to point at a moving pendulum while blindfolded, with auditory feedback being provided. This spatial tracking task greatly reduced recall of the visualisable messages, but had little effect on the non-visualisable messages. Thus, recall of visualisable messages of the kind used by Baddeley et al.

(1975) and by Baddeley and Lieberman (1980) is interfered with by spatial rather than by visual tasks, implying that processing of such messages relies mainly on spatial coding.

Visual coding can also be of importance within the visuo-spatial sketchpad. Quinn and McConnell (1996) told their participants to learn a list of words using either visual imagery or rote rehearsal. This learning task was performed either on its own or in the presence of dynamic visual noise (a meaningless display of dots that changed randomly) or irrelevant speech in a foreign language. It was assumed that dynamic visual noise would gain access to the visuo-spatial sketchpad, whereas irrelevant speech would gain access to the phonological loop.

The findings were clear (see Figure 6.7): "Words processed under mnemonic (imagery) instructions are not affected by the presence of a concurrent verbal task but are affected by the presence of a concurrent visual task. With rote instructions, the interference pattern is reversed" (Quinn & McConnell, 1996, p. 213). Thus, imaginal processing used the visuo-spatial sketchpad, whereas rote rehearsal used the phonological loop.

Logie (1995) argued that visuo-spatial working memory memory can be subdivided into two components:

- The *visual cache*, which stores information about visual form and colour.
- The *inner scribe*, which deals with spatial and movement information. It rehearses information in the visual cache, transfers information from the visual cache to the central executive, and is involved in the planning and execution of body and limb movements.

Evidence consistent with this theory was reported by Beschin, Cocchini, Della Sala, and Logie (1997). They studied a man, NL, who had suffered a stroke. He found it very hard to describe details from the left side of scenes in visual imagery, a condition known as unilateral representational neglect. However, NL had no problems with *perceiving* the left side of scenes, so his visual perceptual system was essentially intact. A key finding was that he performed very poorly on

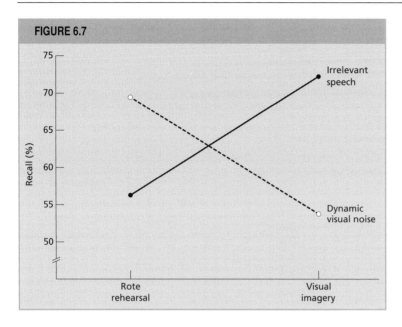

FIGURE 6.7

Percent recall as a function of learning instructions (visual imagery vs. rote rehearsal) and of interference (dynamic visual noise or irrelevant speech). Data from Quinn and McConnell (1996).

tasks thought to require use of the visuo-spatial sketchpad, unless stimulus support in the form of a drawing or other physical stimulus was available. According to Beschin et al. (1997), NL may have sustained damage to the visual cache, so he could only create impoverished mental representations of objects and scenes. Stimulus support was very valuable to NL, because it allowed him to use his intact visual perceptual skills to compensate for the deficient internal representations.

How useful is the visuo-spatial sketchpad in everyday life? Some suggestions about its uses were put forward by Baddeley (1997, p. 82):

The spatial system is important for geographical orientation, and for planning spatial tasks. Indeed, tasks involving visuo-spatial manipulation . . . have tended to be used as selection tools for professions . . . such as engineering and architecture.

There may be important links between the visuo-spatial sketchpad and the spatial medium identified by Kosslyn (e.g., 1983). The spatial medium is used for manipulating visual images, and shares some features with Baddeley's visuo-spatial sketch pad (Brandimonte, Hitch, & Bishop, 1992; see also Chapter 9).

## Evaluation

Is there is a *single* visuo-spatial sketchpad or *separate* visual and spatial systems? The evidence favours the notion of separate systems. Baddeley and Lieberman's (1980) finding that the maintenance of spatial information in working memory was *not* disrupted by a concurrent visual task is consistent with the notion of separate components. Intriguing evidence from a brain-damaged patient (LH), who had been involved in a road accident, was reported by Farah, Hammond, Levine, and Calvanio (1988). He performed much better on tasks involving spatial processing than on tasks involving the visual aspects of imagery (e.g., judging the relative sizes of animals). This evidence is also consistent with the notion of separate visual and spatial systems.

There is also relevant neurophysiological evidence. Smith and Jonides (1997) carried out an ingenious study in which two visual stimuli were presented together, followed by a probe stimulus. The participants had to decide either whether the probe was in the same location as one of the initial stimuli (spatial task) or had the same form (visual task). The stimuli were identical in the two tasks, but there were clear differences in brain activity as revealed by PET. Regions in the right hemisphere (prefrontal cortex; premotor cortex; occipital cortex; and parietal cortex) became active during the spatial task. In contrast, the visual task produced activation in the left hemisphere, especially the parietal cortex and the inferotemporal cortex.

In spite of the evidence discussed here, visual and spatial information becomes interlinked in many situations. This makes the notion of a combined system more attractive (J. Towse, personal communication).

## Central executive

The central executive, which resembles an attentional system, is the most important and versatile component of the working memory system. However, as Baddeley (1996, p. 6) admitted, "our initial specification of the central executive was so vague as to serve as little more than a ragbag into which could be stuffed all the complex strategy selection, planning, and retrieval checking that clearly goes on when subjects perform even the apparently simple digit span task."

Baddeley (1996) argued that damage to the frontal lobes of the cortex can cause impairments to the central executive. Rylander (1939, p. 20) described the classical frontal syndrome as involving "disturbed attention, increased distractibility, a difficulty in grasping the whole of a complicated state of affairs . . . well able to work along old routine lines . . . cannot learn to master new types of task, in new situations." Thus, patients with the frontal system damaged behave as if they lacked a control system allowing them to direct, and to re-direct, their processing resources appropriately. Such patients are said to suffer from *dysexecutive syndrome* (Baddeley, 1996).

It would not be useful to define the central executive as the system that resides in the frontal lobes. As Baddeley (1996, p. 7) pointed out, "If we identify the central executive exclusively with frontal function, then we might well find ourselves excluding from the central executive processes that are clearly executive in nature, simply because they prove not to be frontally located." Baddeley's (1996) preferred strategy is to identify and assess the major functions of the central executive, such as the following:

1. Switching of retrieval plans.
2. Timesharing in dual-task studies.
3. Selective attention to certain stimuli while ignoring others.
4. Temporary activation of long-term memory.

### Evidence

One task Baddeley has used to study the workings of the central executive is random generation of digits or letters. The basic idea is that close attention is needed on this task to avoid producing stereotyped (and non-random) sequences. Baddeley (1996; see also Baddeley, Emslie, Kolodny, & Duncan, 1998) reported a study in which the participants held between one and eight digits in short-term memory while trying to generate a random sequence of digits. It was assumed that the demands on the central executive would be greater as the number of digits to be remembered increased. As predicted, the randomness of the sequence produced on the generation task decreased as the digit memory load increased (see Figure 6.8).

Baddeley (1996) argued that performance on the random generation task might depend on the ability to switch retrieval plans rapidly and so avoid stereotyped responses. This hypothesis was tested as follows. The random digit generation task involved pressing numbered keys. This task was done on its own, or in combination with reciting the alphabet, counting from 1, or alternating numbers and letters (A 1 B 2 C 3 D 4 . . . ). Randomness on the random generation task was reduced by the alternation task, presumably because it required constant switching of retrieval plans. This suggests that rapid switching of retrieval plans is one of the functions of the central executive.

Towse (1998) has argued persuasively that random generation involves various processes, and so is not a pure central executive task. His participants were asked to produce random sequences using the numbers 1–10 or 1–15, and the relevant set of numbers was either visible in front of them or was not presented. Number generation was more random when the numbers were visible, and this was especially the case with the larger set of numbers. Thus, an important factor in random

**FIGURE 6.8**

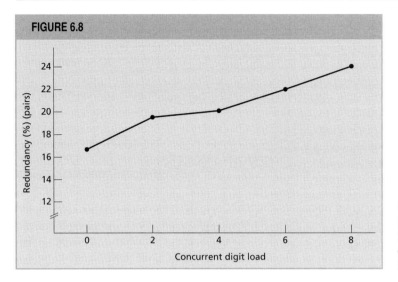

Randomness of digit generation (greater redundancy means reduced randomness) as a function of concurrent digit memory load. Data from Baddeley (1996).

generation is the generation of the potential set of response alternatives, and this is easier when the alternatives are visible.

The notion that the central executive may play an important part in timesharing or distributing attention across two tasks was considered in a number of studies discussed by Baddeley (1996). One study involved patients with *Alzheimer's disease*, which involves progressive loss of mental powers and reduced central executive functioning. First of all, each participant's digit span was established. Then they were given several digit-span trials with that number of digits. Finally, they were given more digit-span trials combined with the task of placing a cross in each of a series of boxes arranged in an irregular pattern (dual-task condition). All the Alzheimer's patients showed a marked reduction in digit-span performance in the dual-task condition, but none of the normal controls did. These findings are consistent with the view that Alzheimer's patients have particular problems with the central executive function of distributing attention between two tasks.

*Evaluation*

There is growing evidence that the central executive is not unitary in the sense of forming a unified whole. For example, Eslinger and Damasio (1985) studied a former accountant, EVR, who had had

a large cerebral tumour removed. He had a high IQ, and performed well on tests requiring reasoning, flexible hypothesis testing, and resistance to distraction and memory interference, suggesting that his central executive was essentially intact. However, he had very poor decision making and judgements (e.g., he would often take hours to decide where to eat). As a result, he was dismissed from various jobs. Presumably EVR's central executive was partially intact and partially damaged. This implies that the central executive is consists of two or more component systems. Such evidence is consistent with the growing body of evidence that the attentional system is not unitary (see Chapter 5).

Shah and Miyake (1996) studied the complexity of the central executive by presenting students with tests of verbal and spatial working memory. The verbal task was the reading span task (Daneman & Carpenter, 1980; see Chapter 12). In this task, the participants read a series of sentences and then recall the final word of each sentence. The reading span is the maximum number of sentences for which they can do this. There was also a spatial span task. The participants had to decide whether each of a set of letters was in normal or mirror-image orientation. After that, they had to indicate the direction in which the top of each letter had been pointing. The spatial span was the maximum number of letters for which they were able to do this.

The correlation between reading span and spatial span was a non-significant +.23, suggesting that verbal and spatial working memory are rather separate. Shah and Miyake's other findings supported this conclusion. Reading span correlated +.45 with verbal IQ, but only +.12 with spatial IQ. In contrast, spatial span correlated +.66 with spatial IQ, and only +.07 with verbal IQ. As Mackintosh (1998, p. 293) concluded, "Within the constraints of this study, and particularly the subject population studied [only university students], . . . verbal and spatial working-memory systems seem relatively independent." Shah and Miyake (1996) favoured a multiple-resource model, and this was developed by Shah and Miyake (1999).

### Overall evaluation

There are several advantages of the working memory system over that of Atkinson and Shiffrin (1968). First, the working memory system is concerned with both active processing and transient storage of information, and so is involved in all complex cognitive tasks (e.g., language comprehension; see Chapter 12).

Second, the working memory model can explain the partial deficits of short-term memory that have been observed in brain-damaged patients. If brain damage affects only one of the three components of working memory, then selective deficits on short-term memory tasks would be expected.

Third, the working memory model incorporates verbal rehearsal as an optional process that within the phonological loop. This is more realistic than the enormous significance of rehearsal within the multi-store model of Atkinson and Shiffrin (1968).

On the negative side, the role played by the central executive remains unclear. The central executive has limited capacity, but it has proved hard to measure that capacity. It is claimed that the central executive is "modality-free" and used in numerous processing operations, but the precise constraints on its functioning are unknown. It has been assumed that the central executive is unitary, but this is becoming increasingly controversial (see Kimberg, D'Esposito, & Farah, 1998). Rather unfairly, Donald (1991, p. 327) argued as follows: "The 'central executive' is a hypothetical entity that sits atop the mountain of working memory and attention like some gigantic Buddha, an inscrutable, immaterial, omnipresent homunculus [miniature man], at whose busy desk the buck stops every time memory and attention theorists run out of alternatives."

## MEMORY PROCESSES

Suppose you were interested in looking at the effects of learning processes on subsequent long-term memory. One method is to present several groups of participants with the same list of nouns, and to ask each group to perform a different activity or orienting task with the list. The tasks used range from counting the number of letters in each word to thinking of a suitable adjective for each word.

If participants were told their memory was going to be tested, they would presumably realise that a task such as simply counting the number of letters in each word would not enable them to remember much, and so they might process the words more thoroughly. As a result, the experimenter does not tell them about the memory test (incidental learning). Finally, all the participants are unexpectedly asked for recall. As the various groups are presented with the same words, any differences in recall reflect the influence of the processing tasks.

Hyde and Jenkins (1973) used the approach just described. Words were either associatively related or unrelated in meaning, and different groups of participants performed each of the following five orienting tasks:

1. Rating the words for pleasantness.
2. Estimating the frequency with which each word is used in the English language.
3. Detecting the occurrence of the letters "e" and "g" in the list words.
4. Deciding on the part of speech appropriate to each word.
5. Deciding whether the list words fitted sentence frames.

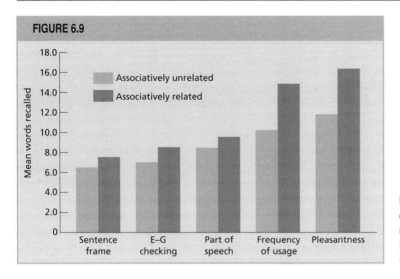

FIGURE 6.9

Mean words recalled as a function of list type (associatively related or unrelated) and orienting task. Data from Hyde and Jenkins (1973).

Half the participants in each condition were told to try to learn the words (intentional learning), whereas the other half were not (incidental learning). There was a test of free recall shortly after the orienting task finished.

The findings are shown in Figure 6.9. Rating pleasantness and rating frequency of usage presumably both involve semantic processing (processing of meaning), whereas the other three orienting tasks do not. Retention was 51% higher after the semantic tasks than the non-semantic tasks on the list of associatively unrelated words, and it was 83% higher with associatively related words. Surprisingly, incidental learners recalled the same number of words as intentional learners. Thus, it is the nature of the processing activity that determines recall.

## Levels-of-processing theory

Craik and Lockhart (1972) proposed a broad framework for memory, arguing that it was too general to be regarded as a theory. However, because they made several specific predictions, it will be treated here as a theory. They assumed that attentional and perceptual processes at the time of learning determine what information is stored in long-term memory. There are various levels of processing, ranging from shallow or physical analysis of a stimulus (e.g., detecting specific letters in words) to deep or semantic analysis. Craik (1973, p. 48) defined depth as "the meaningfulness extracted from the stimulus rather than . . . the number of analyses performed upon it."

The key theoretical assumptions made by Craik and Lockhart (1972) were as follows:

- The level or depth of processing of a stimulus has a large effect on its memorability.
- Deeper levels of analysis produce more elaborate, longer lasting, and stronger memory traces than do shallow levels of analysis.

The findings of Hyde and Jenkins (1973), as well as those of many others, accord with these assumptions.

Craik and Lockhart (1972) distinguished between maintenance and elaborative rehearsal. *Maintenance rehearsal* involves repeating analyses that have previously been carried out, whereas *elaborative rehearsal* involves deeper or more semantic analysis of the learning material. According to the theory, only elaborative rehearsal improves long-term memory. This contrasts with the view of Atkinson and Shiffrin (1968) that rehearsal always enhances long-term memory.

Craik and Lockhart (1972) overstated their position. Maintenance rehearsal typically increases long-term memory, but by less than elaborative rehearsal. For example, Glenberg, Smith, and

Green (1977) found that a nine-fold increase in the time devoted to maintenance rehearsal only increased recall by 1.5%, but increased recognition memory by 9%. Maintenance rehearsal may have prevented the formation of associations among the items in the list, and such associations benefit recall more than recognition.

## Elaboration

Craik and Tulving (1975) argued that elaboration of processing (i.e., the amount of processing of a particular kind) is important. Participants were presented on each trial with a word and a sentence containing a blank, and decided whether the word fitted into the blank space. Elaboration was manipulated by varying the complexity of the sentence frame between the simple (e.g., "She cooked the ____"), and the complex (e.g., "The great bird swooped down and carried off the struggling ____"). Cued recall was twice as high for words accompanying complex sentences, suggesting that elaboration benefits long-term memory.

Long-term memory depends on the kind of elaboration as well as on the amount of elaboration. Bransford et al. (1979) presented either minimally elaborated similes (e.g., "A mosquito is like a doctor because they both draw blood") or multiply elaborated similes (e.g., "A mosquito is like a raccoon because they both have heads, legs, jaws"). Recall was much better for the minimally elaborated similes than for the multiply elaborated ones, indicating that the nature and degree of precision of semantic elaborations need to be considered.

## Distinctiveness

Eysenck (1979) argued that long-term memory is affected by distinctiveness of processing. Thus, memory traces that are distinctive or unique will be more readily retrieved than those resembling other memory traces. Eysenck and Eysenck (1980) tested this theory by using nouns having irregular grapheme–phoneme correspondence (i.e., words not pronounced in line with pronunciation rules, such as "comb" with its silent "b"). Participants performed the non-semantic orienting task of pronouncing such nouns as if they had regular

grapheme–phoneme correspondence, which presumably produced distinctive and unique memory traces (non-semantic, distinctive condition). Other nouns were simply pronounced in their normal fashion (non-semantic, non-distinctive condition), and still others were processed in terms of their meaning (semantic, distinctive and semantic, non-distinctive).

Words in the non-semantic, distinctive condition were much better recognised than those in the non-semantic, non-distinctive condition (see Figure 6.10). Indeed, they were remembered almost as well as the words in the semantic conditions. These findings show the importance of distinctiveness to long-term memory.

## Evaluation

Processes during learning have a major impact on subsequent long-term memory. This may sound obvious, but surprisingly little research pre-1972 involved a study of learning processes and their effects on memory. It is also valuable that elaboration and distinctiveness of processing have been identified as important factors in learning and memory.

On the negative side, it is hard to decide the level of processing being used by learners. The problem is caused by the lack of any independent measure of processing depth. This can lead to the unfortunate state of affairs described by Eysenck (1978, p. 159):

> There is a danger of using retention-test performance to provide information about the depth of processing, and then using the putative [alleged] depth of processing to 'explain' the retention-test performance, a self-defeating exercise in circularity.

However, it is sometimes possible to provide an independent measure of depth (e.g., Parkin, 1979). Gabrieli et al. (1996) argued that functional magnetic resonance imaging (fMRI) could be used to identify the brain regions involved in different kinds of processing. They presented words that were to receive semantic or deep encoding (is the word concrete or abstract?), or that were to

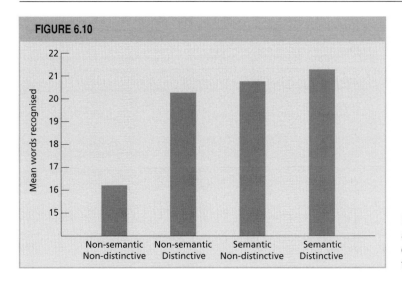

**FIGURE 6.10**

Recognition-memory performance as a function of the depth and distinctiveness of processing. Data from Eysenck and Eysenck (1980).

be processed perceptually or shallowly (upper- or lower-case?). They compared brain activity associated with these two tasks, and concluded: "The fMRI found greater activation of left inferior prefrontal cortex for semantic than for perceptual encoding" (Gabrieli et al., 1996, p. 282).

Morris, Bransford, and Franks (1977) argued that stored information is remembered only if it is of *relevance* to the memory test. Their participants had to answer semantic or shallow (rhyme) questions for lists of words. Memory was tested by a standard recognition test, in which a mixture of list and non-list words was presented, or it was tested by a rhyming recognition test. On this latter test, participants were told to select words that rhymed with list words; note that the list words themselves were not presented.

If one considers only the results obtained with the standard recognition test, then the predicted superiority of deep over shallow processing was obtained (see Figure 6.11). However, the opposite result was obtained with the rhyme test, and this represents an experimental disproof of the notion that deep processing always enhances long-term memory.

Morris et al. (1977) argued that their findings supported a *transfer-appropriate processing theory*. According to this theory, different kinds of processing lead learners to acquire different kinds of information about a stimulus. Whether the stored

information leads to subsequent retention depends on the relevance of that information to the memory test. For example, storing semantic information is essentially irrelevant when the memory test requires the identification of words rhyming with list words. What is required for this kind of test is shallow rhyme information.

The levels-of-processing approach was designed to account for performance on standard memory tests (e.g., recall; recognition) based on conscious and deliberate retrieval of past events. However, there is also *implicit memory* (memory not involving conscious recollection). Tests of implicit memory include *word-fragment completion* and *word-stem completion*, in which participants write down the first word they think of that completes a word fragment (e.g., _ e n _ i _ is a fragment for "tennis") or a word stem (e.g., ten _____), respectively. There is typically a small (and often non-significant) levels-of-processing effect on such tests (see Challis & Brodbeck, 1992).

The levels-of-processing approach describes rather than explains. Craik and Lockhart (1972) did not explain exactly *why* deep processing is so effective.

## Levels-of-processing theory: Update

Lockhart and Craik (1990) accepted that much of their original levels-of-processing theoretical

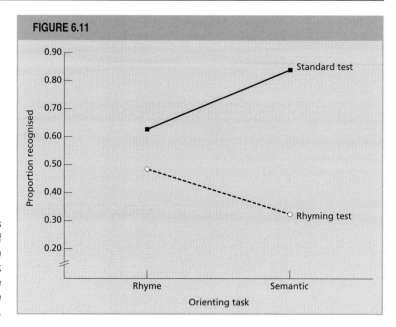

**FIGURE 6.11**

Mean proportion of words recognised as a function of orienting task (semantic or rhyme) and of the type of recognition task (standard or rhyming). Data are from Morris et al. (1977), and are from positive trials only.

framework was oversimplified. For example, the relationship between rehearsal and memory performance is more complex than they had assumed, and they agreed that they had not considered retrieval processes in enough detail.

There were three main ways in which the views of Lockhart and Craik (1990) differed from those of Craik and Lockhart (1972). First, Lockhart and Craik (1990) accepted the notion of transfer-appropriate processing proposed by Morris et al. (1977), but argued that it is possible to reconcile transfer-appropriate processing with the levels-of-processing approach. Transfer-appropriate theory predicts that memory performance depends on interactions between the type of processing at encoding and the type of processing at retrieval (see Figure 6.11). Levels-of-processing theory predicts a main effect of processing depth when transfer appropriateness is held constant. In the study by Morris et al. (1977), there was high transfer appropriateness when semantic processing at learning was followed by a standard recognition test, and when rhyme processing was followed by a rhyming test. In addition, memory performance was much higher in the former condition, as is predicted by levels-of-processing theory (see Figure 6.11).

Second, Lockhart and Craik (1990, pp. 97–98) accepted that their previous theoretical assumption that shallow processing always led to rapid forgetting was not correct: "Since 1972 . . . , a number of results have been reported in which sensory information persists for hours, minutes, and even months . . . sensory or surface aspects of stimuli are not always lost rapidly as we claimed in 1972."

Third, Lockhart and Craik (1990) pointed out that their original theoretical statement had implied that processing of stimuli proceeds in an ordered sequence from shallow sensory levels to deeper semantic levels. They accepted that this was inadequate: "It is likely that an adequate model will comprise complex interactions between top-down and bottom-up processes, and that processing at different levels will be temporally parallel or partially overlapping" (Lockhart & Craik, 1990, p. 95).

## THEORIES OF FORGETTING

Forgetting was first studied in detail by Hermann Ebbinghaus (1885/1913). He carried out numerous studies with himself as the only participant.

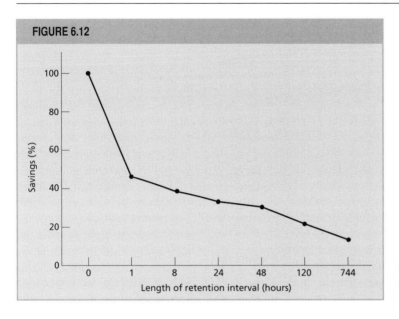

FIGURE 6.12

Forgetting over time as indexed by reduced savings. Data from Ebbinghaus (1885/1913).

Ebbinghaus initially learned a list of nonsense syllables having little or no meaning. At various intervals thereafter, he recalled as many of the nonsense syllables as possible. He then re-learned the list. His basic measure of forgetting was the *savings method*, which involved seeing the reduction or saving in the number of trials during re-learning compared to original learning. Forgetting was very rapid over the first hour or so after learning, with the rate of forgetting slowing considerably thereafter (see Figure 6.12). These findings suggest that the forgetting function is approximately logarithmic.

Rubin and Wenzel (1996) carried out a detailed analysis of the forgetting functions taken from 210 data sets involving many different kinds of learning and memory tests. Rubin and Wenzel (1996, p. 758) found (in line with Ebbinghaus, 1885), that a logarithmic function most consistently described the rate of forgetting: "We have established a law: the logarithmic-loss law." They focused on group data, but it has been confirmed (Wixted & Ebbesen, 1997) that the forgetting functions from individual participants are very similar.

How well did the logarithmic and similar functions fit the data? According to Rubin and Wenzel (1996, p. 752), "One of the biggest surprises . . .

was how well the same functions fit different data sets . . . although there are exceptions, the same functions fit most data sets." The main exception was autobiographical memory (see Chapter 8). Studies on autobiographical memory differ from most memory studies in that the participants are free to produce any memory they want from their lives, and the retention interval can be decades rather than minutes or hours.

According to Baddeley (1997), the forgetting rate is unusually slow for continuous motor skills (e.g., riding a bicycle), in which individuals produce an uninterrupted sequence of responses. For example, Fleishman and Parker (1962) gave their participants extensive training in the continuous motor skills involved in a task resembling flying a plane. Even when they were re-tested after two years, there was practically no forgetting after the first trial.

Why is it important to identify the forgetting function or functions? According to Rubin and Wenzel (1996, p. 757):

There is a circular problem . . . Because no adequate description of the empirical course of retention exists, models of memory cannot be expected to include it. Because no current model predicts a definite form for the retention function, there is no reason for individual model makers to gather retention data to test their models.

Several theories of forgetting are discussed next. However, as Baddeley (1997, p. 176) pointed out, "We know surprisingly little about this most fundamental aspect of human memory."

## Trace decay theory

Various theorists, including Ebbinghaus (1885/1913) have argued that forgetting occurs because there is spontaneous decay of memory traces over time. The main assumption is that forgetting depends crucially on the length of the retention interval rather than on what happens during the time between learning and test.

Jenkins and Dallenbach (1924) tested trace decay theory in a study in which two students were either awake or asleep during the retention interval. According to trace decay theory, forgetting should have been equal in the two conditions. In fact, there was much less forgetting when the students were asleep between learning and test. Jenkins and Dallenbach (1924) concluded that there was more interference with memory when the students were awake during the retention interval.

Hockey, Davies, and Gray (1972) pointed out a confounding of variables in the study by Jenkins and Dallenbach (1924). In the asleep condition, learning always occurred in the evening, whereas it mostly occurred in the morning in the awake condition. Thus, it is not clear whether forgetting depended on what happened during the retention interval or on the time of day at which learning took place. Hockey et al. (1972) unconfounded these variables. The time of day at which learning took place was much more important than whether or the participants slept between learning and test.

Minami and Dallenbach (1946) carried out a study on cockroaches, which learned to avoid a dark box. There was then a retention interval of up to 24 hours, during which the cockroaches were either active or lying inactively in a paper cone. The active cockroaches showed much more

forgetting than the others, which favours an interference explanation. However, trace decay may have happened more slowly in the inactive cockroaches because of their slower metabolic rate.

There is very little direct support for trace decay theory. If all memory traces are subject to decay, it is perhaps surprising how well we can remember many events that happened several years ago and which are rarely thought about. For example, many people remembered in detail for some years what they were doing when they heard the news of Mrs Thatcher's resignation in 1990 (Conway et al., 1994; see Chapter 8).

## Repression

Freud (1915, 1943) emphasised the importance of emotional factors in forgetting. He argued that very threatening or anxiety-provoking material is often unable to gain access to conscious awareness, and he used the term *repression* to refer to this phenomenon. According to Freud (1915, p. 86), "The essence of repression lies simply in the function of rejecting and keeping something out of consciousness." However, Freud sometimes used the concept to refer merely to the inhibition of the capacity for emotional experience (Madison, 1956).

Freud's ideas on repression emerged from his clinical experiences, with the repression he claimed to have observed mostly involving traumatic events that had happened to his patients. Researchers cannot produce such repression in their participants for obvious ethical reasons. However, attempts have been made to study a repression-like phenomenon in the laboratory. The evidence has come from studies on normal individuals known as repressors, having low scores on trait anxiety (a personality factor relating to anxiety susceptibility) and high scores on defensiveness. Repressors describe themselves as controlled and relatively unemotional. According to Weinberger, Schwartz, and Davidson (1979), those who score low on trait anxiety and on defensiveness are the truly low-anxious, those high on trait anxiety and low on defensiveness are the high-anxious, and those high on both trait anxiety and defensiveness are the defensive high-anxious.

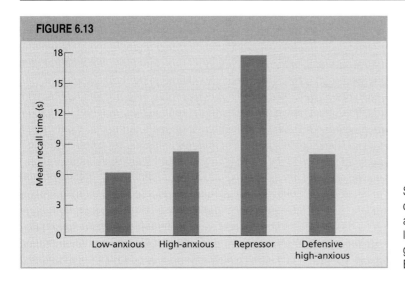

**FIGURE 6.13**

Speed of recall of negative childhood memories by high-anxious, defensive high-anxious, low-anxious, and repressor groups. Data from Myers and Brewin (1994).

All four groups were studied by Myers and Brewin (1994). Repressors were much slower than the other groups to recall negative childhood memories (see Figure 6.13). This did not happen because repressors had enjoyed the happiest childhoods: semi-structured interviews indicated they had experienced the most indifference and hostility from their fathers.

*Childhood trauma*

There is also non-experimental evidence of repression, with large numbers of adults apparently recovering repressed memories of sexual and/or physical abuse they suffered in childhood. There has been a fierce and bitter controversy between those who believe that these recovered memories are genuine and those who argue that such memories are false (see Shobe & Kihlstrom, 1997, and Nadel & Jacobs, 1998, for different views on this issue). The issues are complex, and no definitive conclusion is possible.

Those who believe in repressed memories of childhood traumatic events cite evidence such as that of Williams (1994). She interviewed 129 women who had suffered acts of rape and sexual abuse more than 17 years previously. All of them had been 12 or younger at the time, and 38% had no recollection of the sexual abuse they had suffered. Williams (1994, p. 1174) concluded as follows: "If, as these findings suggest, having no recall of sexual abuse is a fairly common event, later recovery of memories of child sexual abuse by some women should not be surprising." In fact, 16% of those women who recalled being abused said that there had been periods of time in the past when they could remember the abuse. There was one finding that did not fit with Freud's repression hypothesis: he would have expected those women who suffered the most severe abuse to show the worst recall, but the opposite is what was actually found.

Those who believe that recovered memories are false point out that there is often no concrete evidence to confirm their accuracy. They focus on research showing how easy it is for people to be misled into believing in the existence of events that never happened. For example, Ceci (1995) asked preschool children to think about a range of real and fictitious but plausible events over a 10-week period. The children found it hard to distinguish between the real and the fictitious events, with 58% of them providing detailed stories about fictitious events that they falsely believed had occurred. Psychologists who were experienced in interviewing children watched videotapes of the stories, and could not tell which events were real and which were false.

Brewin, Andrews, and Gotlib (1993, p. 94) argued that it was important to consider the ways in which children or adults are asked about traumatic events. According to Brewin et al. (1993, p. 94), "Provided that individuals are questioned about the occurrence of specific events or facts that they were sufficiently old and well placed to know about, the central features of their accounts are likely to be reasonably accurate." However, the final word should go to the American Psychological Association (1995): "At this point it is impossible without further corroborative evidence, to distinguish a true memory from a false one."

## Interference theory

The dominant approach to forgetting during much of the 20th century was based on interference theory. It was assumed that our ability to remember what we are currently learning can be disrupted or interfered with by what we have previously learned or by what we learn in the future. When previous learning interferes with later learning, we have *proactive interference*. When later learning disrupts earlier learning, there is *retroactive interference*. Methods of testing for proactive and retroactive interference are shown in Figure 6.14.

Interference theory can be traced back to Hugo Munsterberg in the 19th century. He had for many years kept his pocket-watch in one particular pocket. When he started keeping it in a different pocket, he often fumbled about in confusion when asked for the time. He had learned an association between the stimulus, "What time is it, Hugo?", and the response of removing the watch from his pocket. Later on, the stimulus remained the same, but a different response was now associated with it. Subsequent research using the methods such as those shown in Figure 6.14 revealed that both proactive and retroactive interference are maximal when two different responses have been associated with the same stimulus; intermediate when two similar responses have been associated with the same stimulus; and minimal when two different stimuli are involved (Underwood & Postman, 1960). Strong evidence for retroactive interference has been obtained in studies of eyewitness testimony, in which memory of an event is interfered with by post-event questioning (see Chapter 8).

It used to be thought that forgetting was due more to retroactive interference than to proactive interference. The position changed, however, with

---

**FIGURE 6.14**

Proactive interference

| Group | Learn | Learn | Test |
|---|---|---|---|
| Experimental | A–B (e.g. Cat–Tree) | A–C (e.g. Cat–Dirt) | A–C (e.g. Cat–Dirt) |
| Control | – | A–C (e.g. Cat–Dirt) | A–C (e.g. Cat–Dirt) |

Retroactive interference

| Group | Learn | Learn | Test |
|---|---|---|---|
| Experimental | A–B (e.g. Cat–Tree) | A–C (e.g. Cat–Dirt) | A–B (e.g. Cat–Tree) |
| Control | A–B (e.g. Cat–Tree) | – | A–B (e.g. Cat–Tree) |

Note: for both proactive and retroactive interference, the experimental group exhibits interference. On the test, only the first word is supplied, and the subjects must provide the second word.

Methods of testing for proactive and retroactive interference.

the publication of an article by Underwood (1957). He reviewed studies on forgetting over a 24-hour retention interval. About 80% of what had been learned was forgotten in one day if the participants had previously learned 15 or more lists in the same experiment, against only 20–25% if no earlier lists had been learned. These findings suggested that proactive interference can have a massive influence on forgetting.

There is a potential problem with many of these studies. The learning of each successive list was equated, in that all lists were learned to the same criterion (e.g., all items correctly recalled on an immediate test), but the participants reached the criterion more rapidly with the later learning lists. Thus, they had less exposure to the later lists than to the earlier ones, and this may explain some of the apparent proactive interference. Warr (1964) equated the amount of exposure to the learning material on all lists, and found the forgetting rate was only modestly affected by the number of lists previously learned. However, Underwood and Ekstrand (1967) obtained substantial proactive interference in a study in which the learning rate did not increase over lists. Thus, proactive interference is a genuine phenomenon.

*Evaluation*

As proactive and retroactive interference have both been shown numerous times, why does interference theory no longer enjoy the popularity it once did? There are three main reasons. First, interference theory is uninformative about the internal processes involved in forgetting. Second, it requires special conditions for substantial interference effects to occur (i.e., the same stimulus paired with two different responses), and these conditions may be fairly rare in everyday life. Third, associations learned outside the laboratory seem less liable to interference than those learned in it. Slamecka (1966) obtained free associates to stimulus words (e.g., colour–red). Then the stimulus words were paired with new associates (e.g., colour–yellow). This should have caused retroactive interference for the original association (e.g., colour–red), but it did not.

## Cue-dependent forgetting and context-change theory

According to Tulving (1974), there are two major reasons for forgetting. First, there is *trace-dependent forgetting*, in which the information is no longer stored in memory. Second, there is *cue-dependent forgetting*, in which the information is in memory, but cannot be accessed. Such information is said to be available (i.e., it is still stored) but not accessible (i.e., it cannot be retrieved).

Tulving and Psotka (1971) compared the cue-dependent approach with interference theory. There were between one and six word lists, with four words in six different categories in each list. After each list had been presented, the participants free-recalled as many words as possible. That was the original learning. After all the lists had been presented, the participants tried to recall the words from *all* the lists that had been presented. That was total free recall. Finally, all the category names were presented, and the participants tried again to recall all the words from all the lists. That was total free cued recall.

There was strong evidence for retroactive interference in total free recall, as word recall from any given list decreased as the number of other lists intervening between learning and recall increased (see Figure 6.15). This finding would be interpreted within interference theory by assuming that there had been unlearning of the earlier lists. However, this interpretation does not fit with the findings from total cued recall. There was essentially *no* retroactive interference or forgetting when the category names were available to the participants. Thus, the forgetting observed in total free recall was basically cue-dependent forgetting.

The studies of cue-dependent forgetting we have considered so far have involved *external* cues (e.g., presenting category names). However, cue-dependent forgetting has also been shown with *internal* cues (e.g., mood state). Information about current mood state is often stored in the memory trace, and there is more forgetting if the mood state at the time of retrieval is different. The notion that there should be less forgetting when the mood state at learning and at retrieval is the same is known as *mood-state-dependent memory* (see

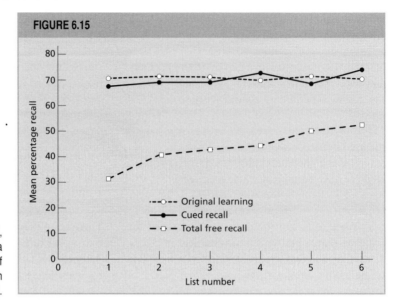

**FIGURE 6.15**

Original learning, total free recall, and total free cued recall as a function of the number of interpolated lists. Data from Tulving and Psotka (1971).

Chapter 18). Ucros (1989) reviewed 40 studies, and concluded there is reasonable evidence for mood-state-dependent memory. The effect is stronger when the participants are in a positive than a negative mood, and it is stronger when they try to remember personal events rather than information lacking personal relevance.

Tulving developed the notion of cue-dependent forgetting in his *encoding specificity principle* (Wiseman & Tulving, 1976, p. 349): "A to-be-remembered (TBR) item is encoded with respect to the context in which it is studied, producing a unique trace which incorporates information from both target and context. For the TBR item to be retrieved, the cue information must appropriately match the trace of the item-in-context." Tulving (1979, p. 408) put forward a more precise formulation of the encoding specificity principle: "The probability of successful retrieval of the target item is a monotonically increasing function of informational overlap between the information present at retrieval and the information stored in memory." For the benefit of any reader wondering what on earth "monotonically increasing function" means, it refers to a generally rising function that does not decrease at any point. Thus, memory performance depends directly on the similarity between

the information in memory and the information available at retrieval. As we will see shortly, there is much support for this principle.

Studies designed to test cue-dependent forgetting and the encoding specificity principle have shown that changes in contextual information between storage and test can produce substantial reductions in memory performance. It is tempting to assume that forgetting over time can be explained in the same way. According to Bouton, Nelson, and Rosas (1999, p. 171):

> Retrieval is best when there is a match between the conditions present during encoding and the conditions present during retrieval . . . ; when there is a mismatch, retrieval failure occurs . . . the passage of time can create a mismatch because internal and external contextual cues that were present during learning may change or fluctuate over time . . . Thus, the passage of time may change the background context and make it less likely that target material will be retrieved . . . We call this approach the *context-change account of forgetting.*

Mensink and Raaijmakers (1988) proposed a version of context-change theory based on the search of associative memory (SAM) model discussed later. They made the following theoretical assumptions:

1. Forgetting over time will occur if the contextual retrieval cues used at time 2 are less strongly associated with the correct memory trace than are the retrieval cues used at time 1.
2. There is a contextual fluctuation process operating over time which can produce forgetting as indicated in (1).
3. Forgetting over time will occur if the strength and number of incorrect memory traces associated with the contextual retrieval cues are greater at time 2 than time 1.

Mensink and Raaijmakers (1988) showed that a mathematical model based on these assumptions could predict a wide range of phenomena, including proactive and retroactive interference. For example, consider proactive interference. Proactive interference is not found when List 2 learning is followed immediately by a memory test, but there is a gradual increase in such interference as the length of the retention interval increases. According to the theory, the contextual fluctuation process weakens the accessibility of the correct memory traces from List 2 over time (assumptions 1 and 2). In addition, the *relative* accessibility of the incorrect memory traces from List 1 increases (assumption 3), in part because of the decreased accessibility of the correct memory traces from List 2 over time. Thus, there is more proactive interference at long retention intervals.

*Evaluation*

Cue-dependent forgetting is of major importance, with the relationship between the external and internal cues available at learning and at test having a great influence on memory performance. The notion that increased forgetting over time can be attributed to a contextual fluctuation process is more speculative. Context-change theories based on this notion provide plausible accounts of forgetting. However, there is little strong

evidence for contextual fluctuation. Mensink and Raaijmakers (1988, p. 453) admitted that they had not tested their context-change theory thoroughly: "All [mathematical] 'fits' were qualitative and it remains to be seen whether the model can predict the correct magnitude of the effects."

## THEORIES OF RECALL AND RECOGNITION

Recognition memory is usually much better than recall, and many theorists have tried to understand why this should be the case. In order to do so, they have focused on the processes involved in recall and recognition. It is to such theories that we now turn.

### Two-process theory

The two-stage or two-process theory makes the following assumptions (see Watkins & Gardiner, 1979), for a review:

- Recall involves a search or retrieval process, followed by a decision or recognition process based on the appropriateness of the retrieved information.
- Recognition involves only the second of these processes.

Two-process theory claims that recall involves two fallible stages, whereas recognition involves only one. As a result, recognition is superior to recall. According to this theory, recall requires an item to be retrieved and then recognised. The notion that the probability of recall is determined by the probability of retrieval multiplied by the probability of recognition was tested by Bahrick (1970) using cued recall (words were presented as cues for to-be-remembered list words). He used the probability of the cue producing the to-be-remembered word in free association as an estimate of the retrievability of the to-be-remembered word, and he ascertained the probability of recognition by means of a standard recognition test. The level of cued recall was predicted well by multiplying together those two probabilities.

Further support for the two-process theory was obtained by Rabinowitz, Mandler, and Patterson (1977). They compared recall of a categorised word list (a list containing words belonging to several categories) under standard instructions and under instructions to generate as many words as possible from the list categories, saying aloud only those that participants thought had actually been presented. Participants given the latter generation–recognition instructions recalled 23% more words than those given standard recall instructions. Thus, the generate–recognise strategy described by the two-process theory can be useful.

Two-process theory also provides an explanation for the frequency paradox (common words are better recalled than rare words, but the opposite is the case for recognition memory; see Kintsch, 1970). Common words have more associative links to other words than do rare words, and so are easier to retrieve. However, the decision process favours rare words over common ones, because it is easier to make decisions about words that have relatively little irrelevant information from previous encounters stored in long-term memory.

*Evaluation*

Two-process theory has attracted much criticism. Recall is sometimes better than recognition, which should not happen according to two-process theory. In a study by Muter (1978), participants were presented with names of people (e.g., DOYLE, FERGUSON, THOMAS) and asked to circle those they "recognised as a person who was famous before 1950". They were then given recall cues in the form of brief descriptions plus first names of the famous people whose surnames had appeared on the recognition test (e.g., author of the Sherlock Holmes stories: Sir Arthur Conan _____; Welsh poet: Dylan _____). Participants recognised only 29% of the names but recalled 42%.

Recognition failure of recallable words also poses problems for two-process theory. This occurs when learning is followed by a recognition memory test and then a test of recall, and some of the items that are not recognised are subsequently recalled (e.g., Tulving & Thomson, 1973). According to two-process theory, recognition failure should practically never happen. This is because recall allegedly requires both retrieval and recognition of the to-be-remembered item.

Another problem with two-process theory is that its account of recognition memory is threadbare. As we will see shortly, recognition memory can involve at least two different kinds of processes (Gardiner & Java, 1993), and the theory simply cannot handle such complexities.

## Encoding specificity

Tulving (1982, 1983) assumed that there are basic similarities between recall and recognition. He also assumed that contextual factors are important, and that what is stored in memory represents a combination of information about the to-be-remembered material and about the context. These notion were incorporated into his *encoding specificity principle*, which was discussed earlier. This principle applies equally to recall and recognition. Attempts to test the encoding specificity principle typically involve two learning conditions and two retrieval conditions. This allows the experimenter to show (as is claimed in the encoding specificity principle) that memory depends on both the information in the memory trace stemming from the learning experience and the information available in the retrieval environment.

A concrete example of this research strategy is a study by Thomson and Tulving (1970). They presented pairs of words in which the first word was the cue and the second word was the to-be-remembered word. The cues were either weakly associated with the list words (e.g., "Train–BLACK") or were strongly associated (e.g., "White–BLACK"). Some of the to-be-remembered items were tested by weak cues (e.g., "Train–?") and others were tested by strong cues (e.g., "White–?"). The results are shown in Figure 6.16. As expected on the encoding specificity principle, recall performance was best when the cues provided at recall were the same as those provided at input. Any change in the cues lowered recall, even when the shift was from weak cues at input to strong cues at recall.

What does Tulving have to say about the relationship between recall and recognition? The general

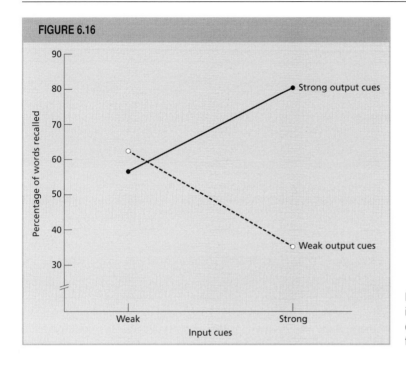

FIGURE 6.16

Mean word recall as a function of input cues (strong or weak) and output cues (strong or weak). Data from Thomson and Tulving (1970).

superiority of recognition over recall is accounted for in two ways. First, the overlap between the information contained in the memory test and that contained in the memory trace will typically be greater on a recognition test (the entire item is presented) than on a recall test. Second, Tulving (1983) argued that a greater amount of informational overlap is required for successful recall than for successful recognition. The reason is that recall involves naming a previous event, whereas recognition involves only a judgement of familiarity.

The encoding specificity principle also predicts that there should be cases in which items that cannot be recognised can be recalled (this is the phenomenon of recognition failure mentioned earlier). Tulving and Thomson (1973) obtained evidence of recognition failure using a complex four-stage design. In the first stage, participants were presented with weakly associated word pairs (e.g., "black–ENGINE") and instructed to learn the second word. In the second stage, they were told to produce associations to a strong associate of each to-be-remembered word (e.g., "steam"). In the third stage, they were asked whether they recognised any of the words generated as

corresponding to list words (e.g., "engine" would normally have been generated). In the fourth stage, they were given the context words presented in the first stage (e.g., "black") and told to recall the to-be-remembered words. In many cases, the to-be-remembered words that were not recognised in stage three were recalled in stage four. Information about the context word (e.g., "black") was stored in the memory trace. Thus, the presentation of this word on the recall test (but not the recognition test) increased the overlap between test information and trace information for recall relative to recognition.

Evidence from the various recognition-failure studies (reviewed by Tulving & Flexser, 1992) indicates that recall performance depends much less on recognition performance than expected by two-process theory. The relationship between recall and recognition is shown in Figure 6.17. The broken line indicates what would be the case if there were no relationship between recall and recognition. The solid line showing the actual weak relationship has been called the "Tulving-Wiseman function".

Flexser and Tulving (1978) provided an explanation of this function based on the encoding

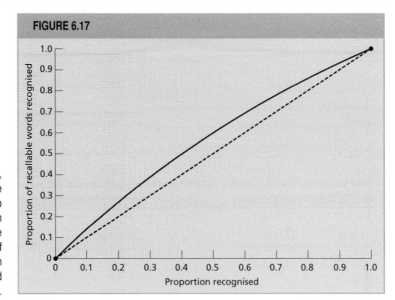

**FIGURE 6.17**

The Tulving-Wiseman function, showing in the solid line that there is only a limited relationship between recall and recognition performance (the broken line indicates what would happen if there were no relationship between recall and recognition). Adapted from Tulving and Flexser (1992).

specificity principle. According to them, there is some relationship between recall and recognition because both tests are directed at the same memory trace. However, the relationship is weak because the information contained in the recognition test is unrelated to that contained in the recall test.

There are numerous exceptions to the Tulving-Wiseman function. According to Lian et al. (1998), "Contrary to the underlying assumption of the TW [Tulving-Wiseman] function, recognition failure is not the norm in the recognition-failure paradigm; rather, it is the exception." For example, recognition failure is almost non-existent when the item to be recognised, "is sufficiently unfamiliar so that it is essentially a novel item" (Lian et al., 1998, p. 701). In one of the studies by Lian et al., this was achieved by asking American students to learn American–Norwegian name pairs. There was practically no recognition failure in this condition, and "the American–Norwegian group showed a remarkable positive deviation from this [i.e., Tulving-Wiseman] function" (Lian et al., 1998, p. 699).

As we have seen, there are some studies (e.g., Muter, 1978) in which recall was actually superior to recognition. According to the encoding specificity principle, this happens when the information in the recall cue overlaps more than the information in the recognition cue with the information

stored in the memory trace. This could explain why, for example, the recall cue "Welsh poet: Dylan ____" produced better memory performance than the recognition cue "Thomas" in the study by Muter (1978).

*Evaluation*

Memory seems to depend jointly on the nature of the memory trace and the information available in the retrieval environment. The emphasis on the role played by contextual information in retrieval is also valuable. Contextual influences were ignored or de-emphasised prior to Tulving's encoding specificity principle, but there is strong evidence that recall and recognition are both affected greatly by the similarity of context at learning and at test.

There is a danger of circularity in applying the encoding specificity principle. Memory is said to depend on "informational overlap", but there is seldom any direct measure of that overlap. It is tempting to infer the amount of informational overlap from the level of memory performance, which produces completely circular reasoning.

Another serious problem associated with Tulving's theoretical position is his view that the information available at the time of retrieval is compared in a simple and direct fashion with the information stored in memory to ascertain the

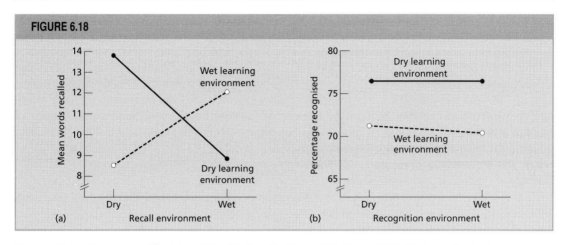

FIGURE 6.18

(a) Recall in the same versus different contexts, data from Godden and Baddeley (1975); (b) Recognition in the same versus different contexts. Data from Godden and Baddeley (1980).

amount of informational overlap. This is implausible if one considers what happens if memory is tested by asking the question, "What did you do six days ago?" Most people answer such a question by engaging in a complex problem-solving strategy to reconstruct the relevant events. Tulving's approach has little to say about how retrieval operates under such circumstances.

A final limitation of Tulving's approach concerns context effects in memory. Tulving assumed that context affects recall and recognition in the same way, but that is not entirely true. Baddeley (1982) proposed a distinction between intrinsic context and extrinsic context. *Intrinsic context* has a direct impact on the meaning or significance of a to-be-remembered item (e.g., strawberry versus traffic as intrinsic context for the word "jam"), whereas *extrinsic context* (e.g., the room in which learning takes place) does not. According to Baddeley (1982), recall is affected by both intrinsic and extrinsic context, whereas recognition memory is affected only by intrinsic context.

Convincing evidence that extrinsic context has different effects on recall and recognition was obtained by Godden and Baddeley (1975, 1980). Godden and Baddeley (1975) asked participants to learn a list of words either on land or 20 feet underwater, and they were then given a test of free recall on land or underwater. Those who had learned on land recalled more on land, and those

who learned underwater did better when tested underwater. Retention was about 50% higher when learning and recall took place in the same extrinsic context (see Figure 6.18). Godden and Baddeley (1980) carried out a very similar study, but using recognition instead of recall. Recognition memory was not affected by extrinsic context (see Figure 6.18).

## Search of associative memory (SAM) model

Raaijmakers and Shiffrin (1981) put forward the search of associative memory (SAM) model. This model, which was developed further by Gillund and Shiffrin (1984), provides an account of recall and recognition. In part, it uses the notion of encoding specificity to develop a detailed mathematical model. Some of the main assumptions of the SAM model are as follows:

- The memory representations or traces formed for each presented item contain information about the item itself, about the learning context, and about other items in the list.
- In recognition memory, each test item plus context forms a compound that activates a memory representation; if that memory representation exceeds a familiarity criterion, the participant identifies the test item as having been presented before.

- In recall, the participant uses contextual information to search repeatedly through long-term memory using associations among items. Selected words that fit the correct context are identified as list words.

The SAM model explains many of the main findings. For example, encoding specificity is accounted for, because changes in context between study and test reduce recall and recognition. Recognition failure of recallable words can also be explained by the SAM model. Recall will be superior to recognition memory when the retrieval cues available at recall overlap more with the stored representations than do the retrievable cues available at recognition (Gillund & Shiffrin, 1984).

As Haberlandt (1999) pointed out, it is especially impressive when models can predict unexpected effects such as recall superiority to recognition. Raaijmakers (1993) showed that the SAM model can explain the part-list cueing effect. In this effect, participants who are given part of a list to assist recall of the remaining items find it *harder* to recall the remaining items than do participants not given this assistance. According to the SAM model, when the experimenter presents list items as cues, this disrupts the participants' normal search processes through long-term memory, and this inhibits access to the remaining list items.

### Evaluation

The SAM model accounts for numerous findings relating to recall and recognition, including counter-intuitive findings such as recall superiority to recognition and the part-list cueing effect. However, Roediger (1993) argued that the success of the SAM model is reduced because it contains a large number of assumptions, which makes it relatively easy to account for most phenomena. Roediger (1993) also argued that some of these assumptions are purely mathematical in nature, and may not be capable of being tested empirically.

## Multiple-route approaches

Most approaches to recall and recognition (including the two-process and encoding specificity theories) are oversimplified. It has often been assumed that there is only one way in which recall occurs, and only one way in which recognition occurs. This is implausible, because it implies that memory operates in a rather inflexible way. In fact, various strategies can be used to recall or recognise stored information. Some of the flavour of these multiple-route approaches will be given here.

### Recall

Jones (e.g., 1982) argued that there are two routes to recall:

- The direct route, in which the cue permits direct accessing of the to-be-remembered information.
- The indirect route, in which the cue leads to recall via the making of inferences and the generation of possible responses.

Jones (1982) showed his participants a list of apparently unrelated cue–target word pairs (e.g., "regal–BEER"), followed by a test of cued recall (e.g., "regal–?"). Some participants were told after learning that reversing the letters of each cue word would produce a new word related to the target word (e.g., "regal" turns into "lager", which in turn suggests "BEER"). Participants who were told about reversing the letters of the cue word recalled more than twice as many words as uninformed participants. According to Jones (1982), uninformed participants made use only of the direct route, whereas informed participants used the direct and indirect routes, and so recalled more words.

We can relate Jones' two recall routes to two of the theories discussed earlier. According to the encoding specificity principle, recall is assumed to occur via the direct route. In contrast, the indirect route closely resembles the recall process as described by two-process theorists.

### Recognition

It has been proposed by several theorists (e.g., Gardiner & Java, 1993) that there are two ways in which recognition memory can occur. Some

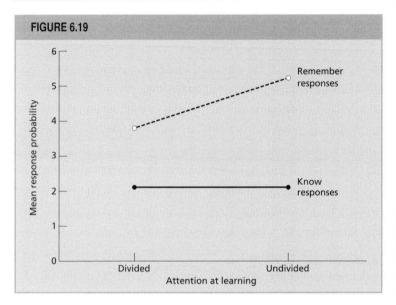

**FIGURE 6.19**

Mean probabilities of remember and know responses on a recognition test as a function of whether attention at learning was divided or undivided. Adapted from Gardiner and Parkin (1990).

indication of what may be involved can be gleaned from the following anecdote. Several years ago, the first author walked past a man in Wimbledon, and felt immediately that he recognised him. However, he was puzzled because it was hard to think of the situation in which he had seen the man previously. After a fair amount of thought about it (this is the kind of thing academic psychologists think about!), he realised the man was a ticket-office clerk at Wimbledon railway station, and this greatly strengthened his conviction that the initial feeling of recognition was correct. Thus, recognition can be based either on familiarity or on remembering relevant contextual information.

Gardiner and Java (1993) distinguished between these two forms of recognition memory. Participants were presented with a list of words followed by a recognition memory test. For each word recognised, participants had to make a "know" or a "remember" response: know responses were made when there were only feelings of familiarity, whereas remember responses were made when retrieval was accompanied by conscious recollection. Gardiner and Java (1993) argued that remember and know responses reflected output from different memory systems.

In order to provide strong evidence for the reality of the know/remember distinction, we need to find experimental manipulations that affect

remember responses but not know responses, and vice versa. This has been done. Gardiner and Parkin (1990) used two learning conditions: (1) attention was devoted only to the list to be remembered (undivided attention); (2) attention had to be divided between the list and another task (divided attention). The attentional manipulation affected only the remember responses (see Figure 6.19).

Rajaram (1993) presented a word below the conscious threshold to participants immediately prior to each test word that was presented for recognition memory. This word was either the same as the test word or different. The relationship between the subliminal word (masked prime) and the test word made a difference to know responses but not to remember responses (see Figure 6.20).

*Evaluation*

The distinction between remembering and knowing may be an important one, and it forms the basis of the distinction between *episodic memory* and *semantic memory* (see Chapter 7). However, there are doubts about the value of the introspective technique just described. Donaldson (1996) argued that the findings can be explained by assuming simply that individuals require more evidence to produce a "remember" response than a "know" response. He carried out a meta-analysis

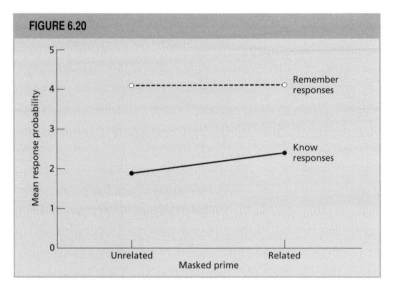

FIGURE 6.20

Mean probabilities of remember and know responses on a recognition test as a function of whether masked primes were related or unrelated. Adapted from Rajaram (1993).

on the published studies that obtained support for his position, and concluded (1996, p. 523):

> Rather than detecting separate memory systems, attempts to distinguish between remembering and knowing are better understood as a division of positive recognition responses into those that lie above a second decision criterion (remember) and those that do not [know].

Evidence consistent with Donaldson's (1996) approach was reported by Dewhurst and Hitch (1999). They presented items as anagrams or as items to be read, followed by a recognition test. The key finding was that the participants' judgements of the source of their memories (word vs. anagram) were much more accurate (80% vs. 24%,

respectively) for remember responses than for know responses. Thus, participants had access to more information about remember items than know items.

## Section summary

One of the implications of the various multi-route approaches is that there is no simple answer to the question of the similarity between the processes involved in recall and recognition. If there are at least two recall processes and two recognition processes, then the degree of similarity clearly depends on which recall process is being compared with which recognition process. One of the issues for the future is to identify more precisely the circumstances in which each process is used.

## CHAPTER SUMMARY

- Structure of memory. According to the multi-store theory, there are separate sensory, short-term, and long-term stores. There is strong evidence to support the notion of various qualitatively different memory stores, but this approach provides a very oversimplified view. For example, multi-store theorists assumed there are unitary short-term and long-term stores, but the reality is more complex.
- Working memory. Baddeley replaced the unitary short-term store with a working memory system consisting of three components: an attention-like central executive; a phonological loop holding

speech-based information; and a visuo-spatial sketchpad specialised for spatial and visual coding. This working memory system is of relevance to non-memory activities such as comprehension and verbal reasoning. It is becoming less clear that the central executive and visuo-spatial sketchpad can be regarded as unitary systems.

• Memory processes. Craik and Lockhart (1972) focused on learning processes in their levels-of-processing theory. They (and their followers) identified depth of processing (i.e., extent to which meaning is processed), elaboration of processing, and distinctiveness of processing as key determinants of long-term memory. Insufficient attention was paid to the relationship between the processes at learning and those at the time of test. Other problems are that the theory is not explanatory, that it is hard to assess the depth of processing, and that shallow processing can lead to very good long-term memory.

• Theories of forgetting. Some theorists have argued that forgetting occurs because of the spontaneous decay of memory traces over time. However, there is very little direct support for this theory. Freud argued for the importance of repression, in which threatening material in long-term memory cannot gain access to consciousness. There is evidence of a repression-like phenomenon in the laboratory, and some adults who suffered childhood abuse seem to recover repressed memories. Strong effects of proactive and retroactive interference have been shown in the laboratory, but it is not clear that the conditions required to show large interference effects occur often in everyday life. Most forgetting is probably cue-dependent, and the cues can be either external or internal (e.g., in mood-state-dependent memory). The cue-dependent approach has been extended to explain forgetting over time in the context-change theory.

• Theories of recall and recognition. Several theories of retrieval have considered recall and recognition. There has been much controversy as to whether the processes involved in recall and recognition are basically similar. Two-process theorists focused on differences between these two kinds of memory tests, whereas Tulving with his encoding specificity principle argued that the informational overlap between retrieval environment and memory is crucial for both recall and recognition. Recall sometimes occurs in a direct fashion, whereas at other times it occurs in an indirect fashion resembling problem solving. In similar fashion, recognition sometimes occurs mainly on the basis of familiarity, and sometimes it involves conscious recollection. There is no simple relationship between recall and recognition.

## FURTHER READING

• Baddeley, A. (1997). *Human memory: Theory and practice (revised edition)*. Hove, UK: Psychology Press. As with Alan Baddeley's other books, this one is very well written and comprehensive in scope.

• Groeger, J.A. (1997). *Memory and remembering: Everyday memory incontext*. Harlow, Essex: Addison Wesley Longman. This book provides a good introduction to most of the topics discussed in this chapter.

• Haberlandt, K. (1999). *Human memory: Exploration and application*. Boston, MA: Allyn & Bacon. There is up-to-date coverage of many of the topics discussed in this chapter.

• Miyake, A., & Shah, P. (1999). *Models of working memory: Mechanisms of active maintenance and executive control*. New York: Cambridge University Press. Various approaches to working memory are discussed by leading theorists in this state-of-the-art book.

# 7

# Theories of Long-term Memory

## INTRODUCTION

We use the information stored in long-term memory in several ways. For example, we recognise the face of a friend across the room, or we recall the main events of our last summer holiday. Some of the processes involved in recall and recognition were considered in Chapter 6. However, we may also use stored information to ride a bicycle, to play the piano, or to realise that the word "toboggan" fits the word fragment _ O _ O _ GA _. Theories of long-term memory used to be rather limited, focusing mainly on recall and recognition. In this chapter, we will consider more recent theories that have considered long-term memory in a broader perspective.

Several contemporary theories of long-term memory are discussed in this chapter. These theories originally seemed to be clearly different from each other. However, the reader should be warned that these theories gradually seem to be coming together. This can be regarded as desirable, because it reflects the natural concerns of the theorists to account adequately for the accumulating data. The disadvantage is that it is becoming harder to discriminate among theories, and to decide which theories are more or less satisfactory than others.

The other main ingredient in this chapter is a consideration of research on amnesia. It is important to identify the precise nature of the problems experienced by amnesic patients, and to try to help them to overcome those problems. Research on amnesia is also important for two other reasons. First, it has provided a good *test-bed* for existing theories of normal memory. In other words, data from amnesic patients can strengthen or weaken the experimental support for memory theories. Second, as we will see, amnesia research has led to new theoretical developments. Studies of amnesia have suggested theoretical distinctions which then proved to be of relevance to an understanding of memory in normal individuals.

## EPISODIC AND SEMANTIC MEMORY

Our long-term memories contain an amazing variety of different kinds of information. As a result, there is a natural temptation to assume there are various long-term memory systems, each of which is specialised for certain types of information. Tulving (1972) argued for a distinction between *episodic memory* and *semantic memory*. According to Tulving, episodic memory refers to the storage (and retrieval) of specific events or episodes occurring in a particular place at a particular time. Thus, memory for what you had for breakfast this morning is an example of episodic memory. In contrast, semantic memory contains information about our stock of knowledge about the world. Tulving (1972, p. 386) defined semantic memory as follows:

> It is a mental thesaurus, organized knowledge a person possesses about words and other verbal symbols, their meanings and referents, about relations among them, and about rules, formulas, and algorithms for the manipulation of these symbols, concepts, and relations.

As a matter of interest, a distinction closely resembling the one proposed by Tulving (1972) had existed for many years beforehand (Liz Valentine, personal communication). For example, in the 1929 edition of *Encyclopaedia Britannica*, there is a reference to an individual's memory knowledge, which is "*personal and is referred to the past*" (p. 233). This is distinguished from other knowledge, which "is not recalled as part of the individual life story. It is *not referred to his past* and it is *impersonal*" (pp. 233–234).

Wheeler, Stuss, and Tulving (1997, p. 333) defined episodic memory differently, arguing that its main distinguishing characteristic was "its dependence on a special kind of awareness that all healthy human adults can identify. It is the type of awareness experienced when one thinks back to a specific moment in one's personal past and consciously recollects some prior episode or state as it was previously experienced." They described this form of awareness as autonoetic or self-knowing. In contrast, retrieval of semantic memories does not possess this sense of conscious recollection of the past. It involves instead noetic or knowing awareness, in which one thinks objectively about something one knows.

How do the definitions of episodic and semantic memory offered by Wheeler et al. (1997) differ from those of Tulving (1972)? According to Wheeler et al. (1997, pp. 348–349):

The major distinction between episodic and semantic memory is no longer best described in terms of the type of information they work with. The distinction is now made in terms of the nature of subjective experience that accompanies the operations of the systems at encoding and retrieval.

In spite of the major differences between episodic and semantic memory, there are also important similarities: "The manner in which information is registered in the episodic and semantic systems is highly similar—there is no known method of readily encoding information into an adult's semantic memory without putting corresponding information in episodic memory or vice versa . . . both episodic and semantic memory obey the principles of encoding specificity and transfer appropriate processing" (Wheeler et al., 1997, p. 333).

## Evidence

The key theoretical assumption made by Wheeler et al. (1997) is that episodic memory depends on various cortical and subcortical networks in which the prefrontal cortex plays a central role. Evidence from brain-damaged patients and from PET scans has been obtained to test this assumption. For example, Janowsky, Shimamura, and Squire (1989) studied memory in frontal lobe patients. They focused especially on *source amnesia*, which involves being unable to remember where or how some piece of factual information was learned. This study is relevant, because it can be argued that source amnesia typically reflects a failure of episodic memory. Janowsky et al. (1989) found that frontal lobe patients showed considerable source amnesia, which is consistent with the view that the frontal cortex is involved in episodic memory. Wheeler et al. (1997, p. 338) summarised the findings from frontal lobe patients as follows: "The overall pattern of results is broadly consistent with the hypothesis that damage localised to the prefrontal cortex causes a selective loss in the episodic memory system . . . The most obvious of the alternative explanations is that the frontal lobes play a critical role in the ability to select and execute complex mental operations."

More convincing evidence comes from PET studies. What was done in these studies was to subtract the image of blood flow in the brain during a semantic memory task from the image of blood flow during a task requiring episodic memory as well as semantic memory. It was assumed that this would reveal those areas of the brain that are active when episodic memory is being used. In 25 out of 26 studies, the right prefrontal cortex was more active during an episodic memory retrieval than during semantic memory retrieval. The same subtraction method was used in 20 studies to identify those brain regions involved in episodic encoding but not in semantic encoding. In 18 out of the 20 studies, the left prefrontal cortex was more active during episodic encoding.

In sum, Wheeler et al. (1997) argued that there are two major differences between episodic and semantic memory. First, episodic memory involves the subjective experience of consciously recollecting personal events from the past whereas semantic memory does not. Second, the prefrontal cortex is much more involved in episodic memory than in semantic memory. Many higher-level cognitive processes take place in the prefrontal cortex, and it is assumed that the "sophisticated form of self-awareness" (Wheeler et al., 1997, p. 349) associated with episodic memory is also a higher-level cognitive process.

## Evaluation

The theoretical views of Wheeler et al. (1997) represent an advance in our understanding of long-term memory. In particular, the notion that there is a major distinction between episodic and semantic memory seems plausible. However, there are some doubts about the strength of the empirical support for the distinction. As Wheeler et al. (1997) themselves pointed out, the finding that patients with damage to the frontal lobes show impaired episodic memory is open to various interpretations. One possibility is that the actual processes involved in episodic memory are *specifically* affected by the brain damage. Another possibility is that the effects of frontal lobe damage are more *general* (e.g., loss of some higher-level cognitive processes). As a result, such brain damage disrupts

the performance of numerous kinds of cognitive tasks, including those involving episodic memory.

What about the findings from PET studies? As Wheeler et al. (1997) pointed out, the validity of the subtraction method used in the PET studies depends on three key assumptions:

1. The two tasks being compared differ with respect to only one component (e.g., presence vs. absence of episodic memory).
2. Subtraction permits the isolation of this component.
3. The brain regions associated with the component can be identified by PET scans.

Unfortunately, there is no easy way to show that these assumptions are justified. However, the great consistency of the findings from the PET studies across several different tasks and measures provides reasonable evidence that the prefrontal cortex is involved in episodic memory.

According to Wheeler et al. (1997), there is an important distinction between autonoetic or self-knowing awareness (found in episodic memory) and noetic or knowing awareness (found in semantic memory). However, there are some doubts about the value of this distinction, especially when applied to amnesic patients (see later in the chapter).

What remains for the future is to consider more closely the relationship between episodic and semantic memory. Research so far has focused on the differences between episodic and semantic memory, in spite of the fact that there are several similarities and interconnections between them.

## IMPLICIT MEMORY

### Definitions

Traditional measures of memory (e.g., free recall; cued recall; and recognition) involve use of direct instructions to retrieve information about specific experiences. Thus, they can all be regarded as measures of explicit memory (Graf & Schacter, 1985, p. 501): "*Explicit memory* is revealed when performance on a task requires conscious recollection of previous experiences." In recent years, researchers have become much more interested in understanding implicit memory (Graf & Schacter, 1985, p. 501): "*Implicit memory* is revealed when performance on a task is facilitated in the absence of conscious recollection." The terms "explicit memory" and "implicit memory" tell us nothing about memory structures, and relatively little about the processes involved. In other words, they are mainly descriptive concepts.

## Evidence

In order to understand what is involved in implicit memory, we will consider a study by Tulving, Schacter, and Stark (1982). Initially, they asked their participants to learn a list of multi-syllabled and relatively rare words (e.g., "toboggan"). One hour or one week later, they were simply asked to fill in the blanks in word fragments to make a word (e.g., _ O _ O _ GA _). The solutions to half of the fragments were words from the list that had been learned, but the participants were not told this. As conscious recollection was not required on the word-fragment completion test, it can be regarded as a test of implicit memory.

There was evidence for implicit memory, with the participants completing more of the fragments

correctly when the solutions matched list words. This is known as a *repetition-priming effect*, and is found when the processing of a stimulus is faster and/or easier when it is presented on more than one occasion. A sceptical reader might argue that repetition priming occurred because the participants deliberately searched through the previously learned list, and thus the test actually reflects explicit memory. However, Tulving et al. (1982) reported an additional finding that goes against that possibility. Repetition priming was no greater for target words that were recognised than for those that were not. Thus, the repetion priming effect was *unrelated* to explicit memory performance as assessed by recognition memory.

This finding suggests that repetition priming and recognition memory involve different forms of memory. Tulving et al. (1982) also found that the length of the retention interval had different effects on recognition memory and fragment completion. Recognition memory was much worse after one week than after one hour, whereas fragment-completion performance was unchanged (see Figure 7.1).

### Process-dissociation procedure

In terms of the definition of implicit memory, it is important to ensure that effects on memory

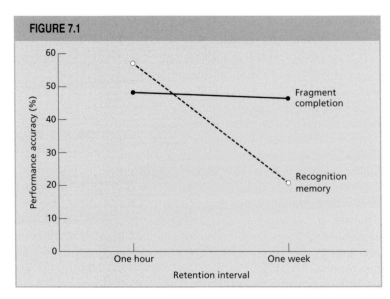

**FIGURE 7.1**

Performance on fragment-completion and recognition memory tests as a function of retention interval. Adapted from Tulving et al. (1982).

performance are shown in the absence of conscious recollection. This is easier said than done. The usual method is to ask the participants at the end of the study about their awareness of any conscious recollection. However, participants may forget, or the questioning may be insufficiently probing. Jacoby, Toth, and Yonelinas (1993) devised the process-dissociation procedure as a way of measuring the respective contributions of explicit and implicit memory processes to performance on a test of cued recall. A list of words was presented (e.g., "mercy"), and there were two conditions at the time of the test:

- Inclusion test: participants were told to complete the cues or word stems (e.g., "mer__") with list words they recollected, or failing that with the first word that came to mind.
- Exclusion test: participants were instructed to complete the word stems (e.g., "mer__") with words that were not presented on the list.

If conscious recollection (explicit memory) were perfect, then 100% of the completions on the inclusion test would be list words compared to 0% on the exclusion test. In contrast, a complete lack of conscious recollection would produce a situation in which participants were as likely to produce list words on the exclusion test as on the inclusion test. This would indicate that the participants could not tell the difference between list and non-list words. Jacoby et al. (1993) assessed the impact of attention on explicit and implicit memory by using full-attention and divided-attention conditions. In the full-attention condition, participants were instructed to remember the list words for a memory test; in the divided-attention condition, they had to perform a complex listening task while reading the list words, and they were not told there would be a memory test.

The findings are shown in Figure 7.2. Most studies of cued recall only use a condition resembling the inclusion test, and inspection of those findings suggests there was reasonable explicit memory performance in both attention conditions. However, the picture looks very different when the exclusion test data are also considered. Participants in the divided-attention condition produced the same level of performance on the inclusion and exclusion tests, suggesting that they were not making any use of conscious recollection or explicit memory. Participants in the full-attention condition did much better on the inclusion test than on the exclusion test, indicating considerable reliance on explicit memory. It also seemed

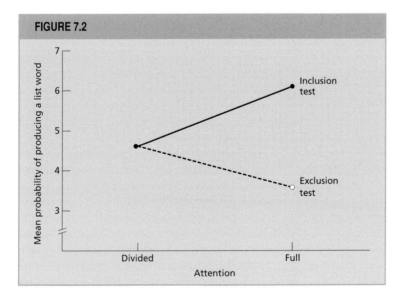

**FIGURE 7.2**

Performance on inclusion and exclusion memory tests as a function of whether attention at learning was divided or full. Adapted from Jacoby et al. (1993).

that implicit memory processes were used equally in the divided-attention and full-attention conditions. Thus, attention at the time of learning may be of crucial importance to subsequent conscious recollection, but is irrelevant to implicit memory.

In sum, these findings confirm that the crucial distinction between explicit and implicit memory is in terms of the involvement of conscious recollection. This poses problems for researchers, because it is often hard to decide whether conscious recollection influences any given memory performance. In spite of this, there is now convincing evidence that the distinction between explicit and implicit memory is both valid and important. Many memory tests (e.g., cued recall; Jacoby et al., 1993) involve a mixture of explicit memory and implicit memory.

Various criticisms have been made of the process-dissociation procedure of Jacoby et al. (1993). Of particular concern is the assumption that implicit or automatic processes and explicit or controlled processes are totally *independent* of each other. If participants are instructed to complete word stems with the first word that comes to mind but to avoid words encountered previously, they are likely to use an implicit or automatic process followed by an explicit or controlled process. Such instructions are likely to lead to use of a generate–recognise strategy in which implicit and explicit processes are *not* independent of each other. Jacoby (1998, p. 10) studied the effects of such a strategy, and admitted that it produced problems: "Participants' reliance on a generate–recognise strategy violates assumptions of the estimation procedure."

## Brain regions

Evidence that different brain regions are involved in explicit and implicit memory was reported by Schacter et al. (1996) in a PET study. When the participants performed an explicit memory task (recall of semantically processed words), there was much activation of the hippocampus. In contrast, when they performed an implicit memory task (word-stem completion), there was reduced blood flow in the bilateral occipital cortex, but the task did not affect hippocampal activation.

## Theoretical considerations

Several theoretical accounts of the differences between explicit and implicit memory have been offered. Some theorists (e.g., Squire, Knowlton, & Musen, 1993) have focused on the underlying brain structures and their associated memory systems. Such theorists typically rely heavily on evidence from amnesic patients, and we will consider this evidence later in the chapter.

## Varieties of implicit memory

Many researchers have discussed implicit memory as if it refers to a single memory system. However, the fact that there are numerous kinds of implicit memory tasks ranging from motor skills to word completion suggests that various memory systems and brain areas are involved. Evidence discussed later in the chapter indicates that different kinds of implicit memory tasks involve brain areas as diverse as the basal ganglia, the cerebellum, and the right parietal cortex.

It has been suggested by several researchers (e.g., Tulving & Schacter, 1990) that there are important differences between *perceptual implicit tests* and *conceptual implicit tests*. On most perceptual implicit tests, the stimulus presented at study is presented at test in a degraded form (e.g., word-fragment completion; word-stem completion; perceptual identification). On conceptual implicit tests, on the other hand, the test provides information conceptually related to the studied information, but there is no perceptual similarity between the study and test stimuli (e.g., general knowledge questions such as "What is the largest animal on earth?"; generation of category exemplars from a category such as "four-footed animals").

Different brain areas are involved in perceptual and conceptual priming. Patients with *Alzheimer's disease* (which involves progressive dementia or loss of mental powers) typically have intact perceptual priming but impaired conceptual priming. In contrast, patients with right occipital lesions have no perceptual priming on visual word-identification tasks but have normal conceptual priming (see Gabrieli, 1998). What we have here is a *double dissociation*, which is generally taken as evidence that separate processes and brain areas are involved in the two types of task.

Neuroimaging studies confirm that different brain areas are involved in perceptual and conceptual priming. As we have seen, PET studies on normals indicate that perceptual priming on visual word-stem completion tasks produces reduced activity in bilateral occipito-temporal areas (e.g., Schacter et al., 1996). In contrast, priming on conceptual priming tasks produces reduced activity in left frontal neocortex (e.g., Wagner et al., 1997). Why is brain activity reduced rather than increased? The most likely reason is because processing is more efficient when a stimulus is re-presented than on its original presentation.

# IMPLICIT LEARNING

Seger (1994, p. 63) defined *implicit learning* as "learning complex information without complete verbalisable knowledge of what is learned". Implicit learning is of relevance here because of its relationship to implicit memory. As Seger (1994, p. 165) pointed out, "there is probably no firm dividing line between implicit memory and implicit learning".

## Evidence

One task used to study implicit learning is artificial grammar learning, in which the participants learn to decide whether strings of letters conform to the rules of an artificial grammar. There is progressive improvement in performance, but participants cannot explain the rules they are using (Reber, 1989).

Berry and Broadbent (1984) studied implicit learning by using a complex task in which a sugar-production factory had to be managed to maintain a specified level of sugar output. Participants learned to perform this task effectively, but most of them could not report the principles underlying their performance. Those participants whose reports revealed good knowledge of these principles tended to perform the task less well than those with poor knowledge. This suggests that the task information available to conscious awareness was of no value to the learners.

Subsequent research on complex control tasks has suggested that people have more conscious access to relevant knowledge about the task than emerged in the study by Berry and Broadbent (1984). For example, McGeorge and Burton (1989) had their participants perform a complex task, and then added the task information they supplied into a computer simulation of the task. For about one-third of the participants, this simulation produced performance comparable to that of the average participant.

A potential problem with the study by Berry and Broadbent (1984) is that the participants may have had conscious access to task-relevant knowledge, but found it hard to express this knowledge in words. Evidence of implicit learning avoiding that problem was reported by Howard and Howard (1992). They used a task in which an asterisk appeared in one of four positions on a screen, under each of which there was a key. The task was to press the key corresponding to the position of the asterisk as rapidly as possible. The position of the asterisk over trials conformed to a complex pattern. The participants showed clear evidence of learning the pattern by responding more and more quickly to the asterisk. However, when asked to predict where the asterisk would appear next, their performance was at chance level. Thus, there seemed to be implicit learning of the pattern.

### Brain regions

Implicit learning can be studied by means of neuroimaging. Grafton, Hazeltine, and Ivry (1995) obtained PET scans from participants engaged in implicit learning of motor sequences. Various brain areas were activated, including the motor cortex and the supplementary motor area. Thus, brain areas that control movements of the limbs are activated during implicit motor learning.

What about explicit learning? Grafton et al. (1995) used the same motor-sequence task under conditions that made it easier for the participants to become consciously aware of the sequence.

They compared the PET scans of participants who were or were not aware of the sequence. The key finding was as follows: "Explicit learning and awareness of the sequences required more activations in the right premotor cortex, the dorsolateral prefrontal cortex associated with working memory, the anterior cingulate, areas in the parietal cortex concerned with voluntary attention, and the lateral temporal cortical areas that store explicit memories" (Gazzaniga et al., 1998, p. 279).

The various findings reported by Grafton et al. (1995) indicate that different brain areas are involved in implicit and explicit learning. This is important evidence for the distinction between these two kinds of learning.

## Theoretical considerations

A key theoretical question is whether learning is possible with little or no conscious awareness of what has been learned. Shanks and St. John (1994) proposed two criteria for learning to be regarded as unconscious:

1. Information criterion: The information that the participants are asked to provide on the awareness test must be the information that is responsible for their improved level of performance.
2. Sensitivity criterion: "We must be able to show that our test of awareness is sensitive to all of the relevant knowledge (Shanks & St. John, 1994, p. 11). The point here is that participants may be consciously aware of more task-relevant knowledge than appears on an insensitive awareness test, and this may lead us to underestimate their consciously accessible knowledge.

The two criteria proposed by Shanks and St. John (1994) may seem reasonable, but are hard to use in practice. However, Shanks and St. John argued that the sensitivity criterion could be replaced provided that the performance and awareness tests resemble each other as closely as possible. This was precisely what was done in the study by Howard and Howard (1992), and their findings provide strong support for implicit

learning. The evidence from neuroimaging also points to the same conclusion.

## TRANSFER APPROPRIATE PROCESSING

Roediger (1990) and Roediger and McDermott (1993) developed a theoretical approach to memory based on *transfer appropriate processing*. The key assumption is that memory performance depends on the extent to which the processes used at the time of learning are the same as those used on the memory test. Performance will be higher when the same (or similar) processes are involved than when the processes differ between learning and retrieval. This approach closely resembles the transfer appropriate processing theory of Morris et al. (1977), and is consistent with the *encoding specificity principle* (both discussed in Chapter 6).

What distinguishes Roediger's approach from previous ones is his assumption that there are two broad types of cognitive processes:

1. Data-driven or perceptual processes, which can be defined as "the analysis of perceptual or surface-level features (but may also include other representations required for stimulus identification)" (Mulligan, 1998, p. 28).
2. Conceptually driven processes, which can be defined as "the analysis of meaning or semantic information" (Mulligan, 1998, p. 28).

There is some overlap between this theoretical approach and the one based on the distinction between explicit and implicit memory. In general terms, data-driven or perceptual processes often underlie performance on tests of implicit memory, whereas conceptually driven processes frequently sustain performance on tests of explicit memory. However, not all implicit tests are perceptual, nor are all explicit tests conceptual.

One of the strengths of Roediger's theoretical approach is that he has identified various criteria for deciding whether any given memory test involves mainly perceptual or conceptual processes (Roediger & McDermott, 1993). The main criteria (and some relevant findings) are as follows:

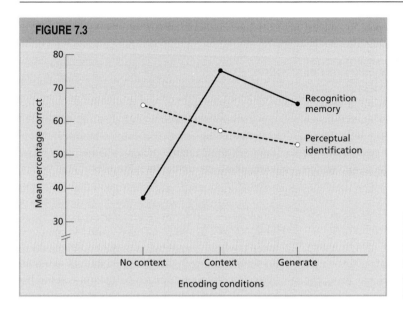

FIGURE 7.3

Performance on recognition memory and perceptual identification tests as a function of conditions at learning (no context; context; or generate). Adapted from Jacoby (1983).

1. The effects of the read–generate study manipulation on performance. Some study words are presented visually to be read, whereas others are not presented, but must be generated from a conceptual cue. It is assumed that there is more perceptual processing in the read condition than in the generation condition, whereas there is more conceptual processing in the generate condition than in the read condition. It follows from the theory that memory tests relying mainly on perceptual processes should be performed better in the read than in the generate condition, whereas the opposite should be the case for memory tests reliant on conceptual processes.

Evidence consistent with these assumptions was reported by Jacoby (1983). He used a read condition (e.g., XXX–COLD) and a generate condition (e.g., hot – ?), in which the participants generated the opposite of the word presented (e.g., cold). There then followed either a test of recognition memory or of perceptual identification identifying rapidly presented words). The findings are shown in Figure 7.3. According to the theory, they indicate that recognition memory mainly involves conceptual processes, whereas perceptual identification relies on perceptual processes.

2. The effects of the levels-of-processing manipulation on performance (see Chapter 6). The essence of this manipulation is that the participants

perform one of two tasks at the time of learning. One requires the processing of stimulus meaning (semantic task), whereas the other requires the processing of physical features of the stimulus (shallow task). Memory tests that involve mainly conceptual processing should be performed better after semantic than shallow processing, but this should not be the case for tests based on perceptual processing.

As we saw in Chapter 6, there is generally a strong levels-of-processing effect with conceptual memory tests such as free recall, cued recall, and recognition memory. What about the findings from perceptual memory tests? Some evidence supporting the distinction between perceptual and conceptual implicit memory tests was reported by Srinivas and Roediger (1990). Manipulation of the level of processing (i.e., semantic vs. non-semantic) at the time of learning affected priming on a conceptual test, but did not affect priming on a perceptual test. There are several other studies reporting that the level of processing had no effect on perceptual priming. However, Challis and Brodbeck (1992) reviewed the literature. They concluded that the level of processing has some effect on implicit perceptual tests (e.g., word-stem completion; word-fragment completion). The effects tended to be smaller than those on implicit conceptual tests. However, the levels-of-processing effect was greater than 10% in 11 out of 35 comparisons, and between 5% and 10% in 12 more comparisons.

**3.** The effects of study-modality manipulation. Suppose that words are presented in the auditory modality at the time of learning, but in the visual modality at the time of test. According to the theory, changing the stimulus modality should reduce performance on memory tests involving perceptual processes (e.g., perceptual identification), but should not do so for tests based on conceptual processes (e.g., recognition memory). There is some support for these predictions (e.g., Blaxton, 1989).

One way of testing the transfer appropriate processing theory is by an attentional manipulation at the time of learning. In one condition (full attention), the participants only have to learn the to-be-remembered material. In the other condition (divided attention), they have to learn the material and perform another task at the same time. It has typically been assumed that dividing attention at study reduces conceptual or semantic processing, but has little or no effect on perceptual processing. If so, then divided attention will reduce memory performance on conceptual tests, but will not affect performance on perceptual tests.

Mulligan (1998) tested these predictions in five experiments using eight perceptual and conceptual tests. As predicted, there were effects of divided attention on conceptual tests involving explicit memory, but no effects on perceptual tests involving implicit memory. However, these findings do not make it clear whether the crucial variable is the perceptual/conceptual one or the explicit/implicit one. This led Mulligan (1998) to use two explicit perceptual tests. These tests were graphemic-cued recall and graphemic recognition, both of which involved non-words resembling words (e.g., "cheetohs" resembles "cheetahs"). In the former test, the participants had to *recall* the list words (e.g., "cheetohs" might cue the list word "cheetah"). In the latter test, the participants had to *recognise* which non-words had a similar appearance to list words.

In spite of the fact that both tests involved perceptual processing, there was a significant effect of the attentional manipulation (see Figure 7.4). These findings are contrary to the transfer appropriate processing framework. As Mulligan (1998, p. 41) concluded, the findings suggest that "performance

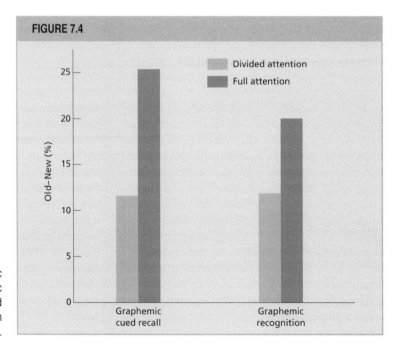

**FIGURE 7.4**

Memory performance on graphemic cued recall and graphemic recognition in full and divided attention conditions. Data from Mulligan (1998).

on explicit tests, whether perceptual or conceptual, is dependent on attention at encoding."

## Evaluation

Roediger's crucial assumption that memory performance depends on the similarity between the processes occurring at learning and at retrieval has proved very useful. Much of the evidence supports this assumption, and it has stimulated a considerable amount of important research. In addition, the evidence generally confirms the value of the distinction between perceptual and conceptual processes. The key limitation of transfer appropriate processing theory is that the distinction between perceptual and conceptual processes (important though it is) is of less fundamental importance than the distinction between explicit and implicit memory. This was shown in the study by Mulligan (1998), and is also revealed in research on amnesia (see later).

## AMNESIA

We can increase our knowledge about human memory by studying brain-damaged patients suffering from amnesia. Such patients generally have extensive memory problems, which can be so great that they cannot remember that they read a newspaper or ate a meal within the previous hour. Over the past 30 years or so, there has been a dramatic increase in the amount of research that cognitive psychologists and cognitive neuropsychologists have carried out on amnesic patients.

Why are amnesic patients of interest? One reason is that the study of amnesia provides a good test-bed for existing theories of normal memory. Data from amnesic patients can strengthen or weaken the support for memory theories. For example, the notion that there is a valid distinction between short-term and long-term memory stores has been tested with amnesic patients. Some patients have severely impaired long-term memory but intact short-term memory, whereas a few patients show the opposite pattern. This is what is known as a double dissociation, and is

good evidence that there are separate short-term and long-term stores.

Another reason for studying amnesic patients is that such research has led to new theoretical developments. Studies of amnesia have suggested theoretical distinctions that have proved relevant to an understanding of memory in normal individuals. Some examples are discussed later in the chapter.

Progress in this area has been slow. Some of the main reasons for this were identified by Hintzman (1990, p. 130):

> The ideal data base on amnesia would consist of data from thousands of patients having no other disorders, and having precisely dated lesions [injuries] of known location and extent, and would include many reliable measures spanning all types of knowledge and skills, acquired at known times ranging from the recent to the distant past. Reality falls near the opposite pole of each dimension of this description.

Amnesic patients often have fairly widespread brain damage. This makes it hard to interpret the findings. It is especially hard to know which brain area is mainly responsible for a given memory deficit if, say, three different brain areas are all damaged.

In order to make sense of the findings from amnesic patients, it is necessary to have some background understanding of the amnesic condition. The reasons why patients have become amnesic are very varied. Bilateral stroke is one factor causing amnesia, but closed head injury is the most common cause. However, patients with closed head injury often have a range of cognitive impairments, and this makes it hard to interpret their memory deficit. As a result, most experimental work has focused on patients who have become amnesic because of chronic alcohol abuse (*Korsakoff's syndrome*). The symptoms of Korsakoff patients tend to become worse over time, whereas those of patients with closed head injury do not. It remains a matter of controversy whether there are enough similarities among these various groups to justify considering them together.

## Amnesic syndrome

Those who think most amnesic patients form a similar or homogeneous group often refer to the "*amnesic syndrome*". Its main features are as follows:

- There is a marked impairment in the ability to remember new information which was learned after the onset of the amnesia; this is *anterograde amnesia*.
- There is often great difficulty in remembering events occurring prior to amnesia; this is known as *retrograde amnesia*, and is pronounced in patients with Korsakoff's syndrome.
- Patients suffering from the amnesic syndrome generally have only slightly impaired short-term memory on measures such as digit span (the ability to repeat back a random string of digits). This is also shown by the fact that it is possible to have a normal conversation with an amnesic patient.
- Patients with the amnesic syndrome have some remaining learning ability after the onset of the amnesia.

The amnesic syndrome can be produced by damage to various brain structures. These structures are in two separate areas of the brain: a sub-cortical region called the diencephalon; and a cortical region known as the medial temporal lobe. It can be hard to pinpoint the precise location of damage in any given patient. Attempts to do so often used to rely on post-mortem examination, but the development of neuroimaging techniques has allowed accurate assessment of the damaged areas while the patient is alive.

Some of the brain areas that can produce the amnesic syndrome when damaged are shown in Figure 7.5. Chronic alcoholics who develop Korsakoff's syndrome have brain damage in the diencephalon, especially the medial thalamus and the mammillary nuclei, but typically the frontal cortex is also damaged. Other amnesics have damage in the medial-temporal region. This can happen as a result of herpes simplex encephalitis, anoxia (lack of oxygen), infarction, or sclerosis (involving a hardening of tissue or organs). There

are other cases in which some of the temporal lobe was removed from epileptic patients to reduce the incidence of epileptic seizures. As a result, many of these patients (including the much-studied HM) became severely amnesic (Scoville & Milner, 1957). The exact extent of HM's brain damage was not known for many years. However, Corkin et al. (1997, p. 3978) carried out MRI on HM. They found that his brain damage was less extensive than had been believed previously. However, they "confirmed that the lesions responsible for the amnesic syndrome in HM are confined to the medial temporal lobe" (Corkin et al., 1997, p. 3978).

In most areas of cognitive neuropsychology, broad categories or syndromes have been replaced by a larger number of more specific categories. Why has this failed to happen with the amnesic syndrome? One possible reason is because nearly all amnesic patients exhibit the same pattern of symptoms. However, this seems very unlikely. As Downes and Mayes (1997, pp. 301–302) argued, "The [amnesic] syndrome almost certainly comprises several functional deficits with their own distinctive neuroanatomies."

A more convincing reason why most theorists have failed to identify sub-types of amnesia is because of the problems of identifying the precise area of brain damage in any given patient. The main brain structures that can be damaged in amnesics are close together, and this has made it hard to associate particular patterns of memory impairment with specific brain structures. However, Parkin and Hunkin (1997, p. 100) divided amnesic patients into those with lesions in the temporal lobe and those with lesions in the diencephalon, and concluded as follows: "We have examined the value of the contextual processing deficit hypothesis [the notion that amnesic patients have special problems in processing contextual information] and have shown that a contextual processing deficit only offers a means of explaining diencephalic amnesia."

Aggleton and Brown (1999) favoured a rather different theoretical position. According to Aggleton and Brown (1999, p. 426), "The traditional distinction between temporal lobe and diencephalic amnesics is misleading; both groups have damage

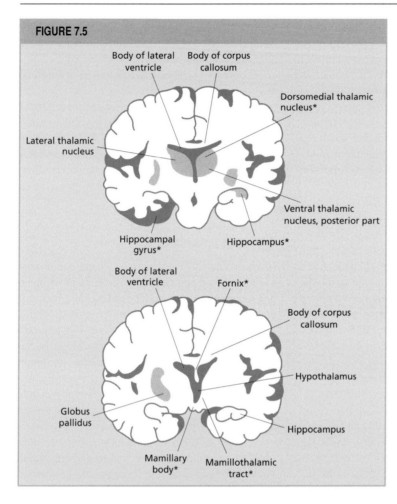

FIGURE 7.5

Some of the brain structures involved in amnesia (indicated by asterisks). Figure from "Clinical symptoms, neuropathology and etiology" by Nelson Butters and Laird S. Cermak in *Alcoholic Korsakoff's syndrome: An information-processing approach to amnesia*. Copyright © 1980 by Academic Press, reproduced by permission of the publisher.

to the same functional system . . . The proposed hippocampal-diencephalic system is required for the encoding of episodic information, permitting the information to be set in its spatial and temporal context." They argued that there is a second system involving the perirhinal cortex of the temporal lobe and the medial dorsal nucleus of the thalamus which is involved in making familiarity judgements on tests of recognition memory. It is difficult to find patients with damage to only one system because, "in the large majority of amnesic cases both the hippocampal-anterior thalamic and the perirhinal-medial dorsal thalamic systems are compromised, leading to severe deficits in both recall and recognition." Various views on this theory are provided in the commentaries that immediately followed the

Aggleton and Brown (1999) article in *Behavioral and Brain Sciences*.

So far there have been relatively few attempts to move beyond the broad notion of an amnesic syndrome. However, the development of increasingly sophisticated brain-scanning techniques (see Chapter 1) means we can now identify the precise regions of brain damage in amnesics more accurately than before. It is likely in the future that theorists will begin to propose various specific categories of amnesia linked to particular damaged brain areas.

## Retrograde amnesia

Retrograde amnesia is the Cinderella of amnesia research, in that it has not received anything like the attention paid to anterograde amnesia. The characteristics of retrograde amnesia vary considerably from patient to patient, sometimes involving severe retrieval problems for memories formed several years before the onset of amnesia, and sometimes involving minor retrieval problems for memories covering a much shorter period. However, there is generally a temporal gradient, with retrieval problems being greater for memories acquired closer to the onset of the amnesia than those acquired longer ago.

Most amnesic patients show evidence of both retrograde and anterograde amnesia, which might suggest that they depend on damage to the same brain structures. The evidence from postmortem analyses indicates that the extent of both retrograde and anterograde amnesia depends on the amount of damage to medial-temporal structures in the brain. In addition, both forms of amnesia share features, such as impaired recall and recognition of factual information (e.g., public events) and of autobiographical information.

There are also important differences between retrograde and anterograde amnesia. Damage restricted to a small part of the hippocampal region known as the CA1 field produces only anterograde amnesia (Gabrieli, 1998). Perhaps as a result, the severity of retrograde amnesia often correlates poorly with the severity of anterograde amnesia. Some patients have focal retrograde amnesia, in which the main deficit is retrograde rather than anterograde. Such patients generally have damage to the anterior temporal lobe, or the posterior temporal lobe, or the frontal lobe. The important point is that these areas are not thought to be directly associated with the amnesic syndrome.

Evidence supporting the involvement of the temporal lobe in producing retrograde amnesia was reported by Reed and Squire (1998) in a study of four amnesic patients. MRI examinations indicated that all four had hippocampal damage, but only two also had temporal lobe damage. The two patients with temporal lobe damage had severe anterograde amnesia for facts and events, whereas the other two patients had limited anterograde amnesia covering only a few years. These findings led Reed and Squire (1998, p. 3953) to conclude: "RA [retrograde amnesia] can be quite limited or

very extensive, depending on whether the damage is restricted to the hippocampal formation or also involves additional temporal cortex."

The precise relationship between retrograde and anterograde amnesia remains unclear. The present state of play was summarised by Mayes and Downes (1997, p. 30): "The evidence is certainly strong enough to suggest that substantial components of AA [anterograde amnesia] and RA [retrograde amnesia] dissociate from one another, but it is still far from conclusively favouring either dissociation or its opposite."

## Korsakoff patients

Many studies on amnesia have made use almost exclusively of Korsakoff patients. How suitable are such patients for understanding the processes underlying amnesia? There are two main problems posed by Korsakoff patients. First, the amnesia usually has a gradual onset. It is caused by an increasing deficiency of the vitamin thiamine, which is associated with chronic alcoholism. As a result, it is often hard to know whether past events occurred before or after the onset of amnesia. Second, brain damage in Korsakoff patients is often rather widespread. Structures within the diencephalon, such as the hippocampus and amygdala, are usually damaged, and these structures seem to be of vital significance to memory. In addition, there is very often damage to the frontal lobes. This may produce a range of cognitive deficits that are not specific to the memory system, but which have indirect effects on memory performance. It would be easier to make coherent sense of findings from Korsakoff patients if the brain damage were more limited.

## Residual learning ability

If we are to understand amnesia, it is important to consider which aspects of learning and memory remain fairly intact in amnesic patients. These aspects are commonly referred to as "residual learning ability". It would be useful to draw up lists of those memory abilities impaired and not impaired in amnesia. By comparing the two lists, it might be possible to identify those processes and/or memory structures that are affected in amnesic patients. Theoretical accounts could then proceed on a solid foundation of knowledge. The available evidence is less extensive than would be desirable, but we will consider it in some detail.

*Short-term memory*

Amnesic patients have a fairly intact short-term memory system, but a severely deficient long-term memory system. Korsakoff patients perform almost as well as normals on the digit-span task (e.g., Butters & Cermak, 1980). Similar results have also been found in non-Korsakoff patients. NA became amnesic as a result of having a fencing foil forced up his nostril and into his brain. This caused widespread diencephalic and medial temporal damage. Teuber, Milner, and Vaughan (1968) found that he performed at the normal level on span measures. HM had an operation that damaged the temporal lobes, together with partial removal of the hippocampus and amygdala, He had intact short-term memory as indexed by immediate span (Wickelgren, 1968).

Span measures are not the only way in which short-term memory can be assessed. Baddeley and Warrington (1970) observed normal performance by amnesic patients on various measures of short-term memory (e.g., *recency effect* in free recall).

*Skill learning*

Skill learning in amnesics can be divided into sensori-motor and perceptual skills. So far as sensori-motor skills are concerned, amnesics have been shown to have normal rates of learning for the pursuit rotor, serial reaction time, and mirror tracing (see Gabrieli, 1998). Each of these skills will be considered in turn.

Corkin (1968) reported that the amnesic patient HM was able to learn mirror drawing and the pursuit rotor, which involves manual tracking of a moving target. His rate of learning was slower than that of normals on the pursuit rotor. In contrast, Cermak et al. (1973) found that Korsakoff patients learned the pursuit rotor as fast as normals. However, the amnesic patients were slower than normals at learning a finger maze.

The typical form of the serial reaction time task involves presenting visual targets in one of four horizontal locations, with the task being to press the closest key as rapidly as possible. The sequence of targets is sometimes repeated over 10 or 12 trials, and skill learning is shown by improved performance on these repeated sequences. This skill learning is generally intact in amnesics (e.g., Nissen & Bullemer, 1987).

Mirror tracing involves tracing a figure with a stylus, with the figure to be traced being seen reflected in a mirror. Performance on this task improves with practice in normals, and the same is true of amnesic patients (e.g., Milner, 1962).

Which brain areas are involved in the acquisition of sensori-motor skills? Sensori-motor skill learning is often impaired in patients with damage to the basal ganglia caused by various diseases (e.g., Parkinson's disease; Huntington's disease; Gilles de la Tourette's syndrome). In addition, patients with cerebellar lesions have impaired mirror-tracing performance (e.g., Sanes, Dimitrov, & Hallett, 1990). Gabrieli (1998, pp. 98–99) put forward a hypothesis to account for the findings: "Closed-loop skill learning, which involves continuous external, visual feedback about errors in movements, depends upon the cerebellum. In contrast, open-loop skill learning, which involves the planning of movements and delayed feedback about errors, depends upon the basal ganglia."

The involvement of the basal ganglia and the cerebellum in sensori-motor skill learning has also been shown in brain-scanning studies. PET studies have shown that serial reaction time skill learning and other tasks involving the learning of specific manual sequences produce increased activation in the basal ganglia (e.g., Hazeltine, Grafton, & Ivry, 1997). The notion that cerebellar activity reflects error correction is supported by the finding that cerebellar activity decreased in line with a decrease in errors on a perceptual-motor task (Friston et al., 1996).

The main perceptual skill learning task studied with amnesic patients is reading mirror-reversed script, in which what is being read can only be seen reflected in a mirror. In these studies, we can distinguish between *general* improvement in speed of reading produced by practice and more *specific*

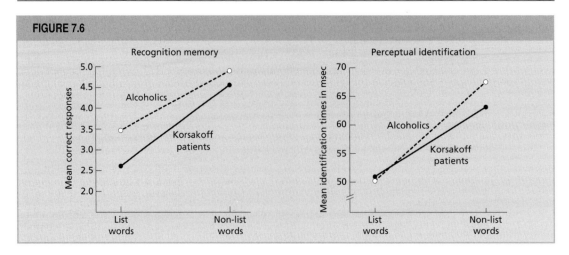

**FIGURE 7.6**

Recognition memory and perceptual identification of Korsakoff patients and non-amnesic alcoholics; delayed conditions only. Data from Cermak et al. (1985).

improvement produced by re-reading the same groups of words or sentences. Cohen and Squire (1980) reported general and specific improvement in reading mirror-reversed script in amnesics, and there was evidence of improvement even after a delay of three months. Martone et al. (1984) also obtained evidence of general and specific improvement in amnesics. However, although the general practice effect was as great in amnesics as in normals, the specific practice effect was not. It may be that normals (but not amnesics) are able to use speed-reading strategies to facilitate reading of repeated groups of words.

The brain areas involved in mirror reading were studied by Poldrack et al. (1996) in a study using functional magnetic resonance imaging (fMRI). Initially, there was much activity in right parietal cortex. However, with practice, this activity decreased, and there was increasing activity in left inferior occipito-temporal cortex. According to Gabrieli (1998, p. 99), "These shifts in activity may represent a change in reliance upon visuospatial decoding of mirror-reversed words in unskilled performance to more direct reading in skilled performance."

*Repetition priming*

The *repetition-priming effect* was discussed earlier in the chapter. As Gabrieli (1998, p. 100) pointed out, "Repetition priming refers to a change in the processing of a stimulus, usually words or pictures, due to prior exposure to the same or a related stimulus." Amnesics generally show normal or nearly normal priming effects on perceptual and conceptual priming tasks.

Cermak et al. (1985) compared the performance of Korsakoff patients and non-amnesic alcoholics on perceptual priming. The patients were presented with a list of words followed by a priming task. This task was perceptual identification, and involved presenting the words at the minimal exposure time needed to identify them correctly. The performance of the Korsakoff patients resembled that of the control participants, with identification times being faster for the primed list words than for the unprimed non-list words (see Figure 7.6). In other words, the amnesic patients showed as great a perceptual priming effect as the controls. Cermak et al. (1985) also used a conventional test of recognition memory for the list words. In line with much previous research, the Korsakoff patients did significantly worse than the controls on this task (see Figure 7.6).

Graf, Squire, and Mandler (1984) studied a different perceptual priming effect. Word lists were presented, with the participants deciding how much they liked each word. The lists were followed by one of four memory tests. Three of the tests were conventional memory tests (free recall;

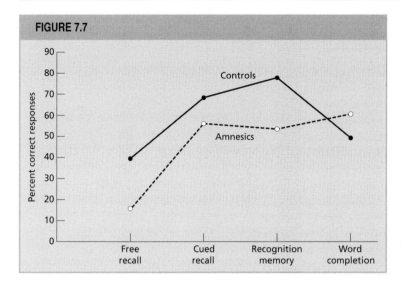

FIGURE 7.7

Free recall, cued recall, recognition memory, and word completion in amnesic patients and controls. Data from different experiments reported by Graf et al. (1984).

recognition memory; cued recall), but the fourth test (word completion) measured a priming effect. On this last test, participants were given three-letter word fragments (e.g., STR __) and simply wrote down the first word they thought of starting with those letters (e.g., STRAP; STRIP). Priming was assessed by the extent to which the word completions corresponded to words from the list previously presented. Amnesic patients did much worse than controls on all the conventional memory tests, but there was no significant difference between the two groups in the size of their priming effect on the word-completion task (see Figure 7.7).

Vaidya et al. (1995) studied perceptual and conceptual priming. Perceptual priming was studied by means of a word-fragment completion task, and conceptual priming was studied with a word-association generation task (e.g., what word goes with KING?). Amnesic patients showed essentially normal priming on both tasks.

Amnesic patients exhibit a variety of repetition-priming effects. Their performance is greatly improved by the prior presentation of stimuli, even when there is an absence of conscious awareness that these stimuli have previously been presented (as indicated by poor recognition memory performance). There has been some controversy as to whether this disparity between performance and conscious awareness on priming tasks is unique to amnesic patients. Some evidence that it is not

was obtained by Meudell and Mayes (1981). They used a task in which cartoons had to be searched for specified objects. When amnesics repeated the task seven weeks later, they found the objects faster than the first time in spite of very poor recognition memory for the cartoons. When normals were tested at the much longer interval of 17 months, they showed the same pattern. Thus, repetition-priming effects in the absence of conscious awareness of having seen the stimuli before can be found in normal individuals as well as in amnesic patients.

## Conditioning

Eyeblink conditioning (a form of classical conditioning) has been studied in amnesic patients. In eyeblink conditioning, a tone is presented shortly before a puff of air is delivered to the eye, and causes an eyeblink. After the tone and puff of air have been presented together several times, the tone alone produces a conditioned eyeblink response. Many amnesic patients show intact eyeblink conditioning. However, Korsakoff patients generally have greatly impaired conditioning because the alcoholism has caused damage to the cerebellum. The involvement of the cerebellum is also indicated by PET studies in which it is activated during the conditioning procedure (see Gabrieli, 1998).

## THEORIES OF AMNESIA

At one time, most theorists tried to apply pre-existing theories of normal memory functioning to amnesics. For example, the evidence of Baddeley and Warrington (1970) and others seemed at one time to provide strong support for the multi-store approach discussed in Chapter 6. Cermak (1979) tried to apply the levels-of-processing approach to amnesia. He argued that amnesics typically fail to process the meaning of to-be-remembered information, and this lack of semantic processing causes the severely impaired long-term memory found in amnesic patients. This theory has been abandoned, because there is strong evidence that amnesic patients are well able to process meaning.

More recent theorists have considered the pattern of deficits shown by amnesic patients, and have then constructed new theories to fit that pattern. Some of these theories have been modified in the light of additional testing on normal individuals. Thus, theorists are increasingly inclined to use memory data from both amnesic patients and normal individuals in the construction and development of their theories.

The assumption that there is a single, unified long-term memory system has been rejected by all the theorists we will be considering. Most theorists have argued that there are at least two major types of processing associated with long-term memory. Other theorists have focused on memory systems, and have tried to identify the underlying brain systems involved. Many of the theories overlap each other. This fact, coupled with the imprecision of many of the theoretical approaches, means it is hard to decide which theoretical approaches are more promising than others.

### Episodic versus semantic memory

As we saw earlier, Tulving (1972) drew a distinction between *episodic memory*, which is concerned with events or episodes happening at a given time in a given place, and *semantic memory*, which is concerned with general knowledge about the world. On the face of it, it seems reasonable to argue that amnesics have a severe deficit in episodic memory but essentially intact semantic memory. Amnesic patients have impaired episodic memory, as this description by Korsakoff (1889) of a typical amnesic patient reveals:

> He does not remember whether he had his dinner, whether he was out of bed. On occasion the patient forgets what happened to him just an instant ago: you came in, conversed with him, and stepped out for one minute; then you come in again and the patient has absolutely no recollection that you had already been with him.

There is also little doubt that major parts of semantic memory are generally intact in amnesics. The most obvious examples of this are their largely unimpaired language skills, including vocabulary and grammar, and their essentially normal performance on intelligence tests.

In fact, there is a serious flaw in this argument, namely that like is not being compared with like. Language and the abilities required to perform well on intelligence tests are nearly always acquired *before* the onset of amnesia, whereas conventional tests of episodic memory are based on information acquired *after* the onset of amnesia. Thus, the findings described so far are consistent with the simple notion that amnesia mainly impairs the ability to acquire new episodic and semantic memories. Evidence that it can be very hard to establish new semantic memories after the onset of amnesia was reported by Gabrieli, Cohen, and Corkin (1988), who found an amnesic patient with an almost complete inability to acquire new vocabulary. In similar fashion, many amnesics do not know the name of the current prime minister or president, and have very poor recognition memory for the faces of people who have become famous fairly recently (Baddeley, 1984). It thus appears that most amnesics are impaired in acquiring new semantic memories as well as new episodic memories.

According to Wheeler et al. (1997), there is an important distinction between autonoetic or self-knowing awareness (found in episodic memory) and noetic or knowing awareness (found in semantic memory). The relevance of this distinction to amnesia was studied by Knowlton and Squire (1995). Amnesics and normal controls were given a test of recognition memory, and asked to divide recognised items into "remember" responses based on conscious recollection and "know" responses based on familiarity only. The amnesic patients performed much worse than the controls on both "remember" and "know" items, suggesting that the memory deficit in amnesia is *not* limited to one level of awareness.

Some recent evidence suggests that the distinction between episodic and semantic memory may have relevance to amnesia. Vargha-Khadem et al. (1997) studied two patients who had suffered bilateral hippocampal damage at an early age before they had had the opportunity to develop semantic memories. Beth suffered brain damage at birth, and Jon did so at the age of 4. Both these patients had very poor episodic memory for the day's activities, television programmes, telephone conversations, and so on. In spite of this, Beth and Jon both attended ordinary schools, and their levels of speech and language development, literacy, and factual knowledge (e.g., vocabulary) were within the normal range.

How can we explain the ability of Beth and Jon to develop fairly normal semantic memory in spite of their grossly deficient episodic memory? According to Vargha-Khadem et al. (1997, p. 376), episodic and semantic memory depend on somewhat different regions of the brain: "Episodic memory depends primarily on the hippocampal component of the larger system [i.e., hippocampus and underlying entorhinal, perihinal, and parahippocampal cortices], whereas semantic memory depends primarily on the underlying cortices." Why do so many amnesics have great problems with episodic and semantic memory? According to Vargha-Khadem et al. (1997), many amnesics (including HM) have damage to the hippocampus *and* to the underlying cortices.

*Evaluation*

Most of the evidence has failed to indicate that the distinction between episodic and semantic memory is of fundamental importance to an understanding of amnesia. The fact that most amnesics have great difficulty in forming new semantic memories poses real problems for this theoretical approach. However, it is possible that partially separate brain systems underlie episodic and semantic memory, but both brain systems are typically damaged in amnesics. The findings reported by Vargha-Kardem et al. (1997) are consistent with this possibility, which should certainly be examined systematically in future research.

## Context processing deficit theory

Long-term memory is generally better when the context at the time of the memory test is the same as that at the time of learning than when it differs (see Chapter 6). Contextual information is also important in allowing us to distinguish between otherwise similar memories Mayes (e.g., 1988) argued that amnesic patients can store information about to-be-remembered information, but find it hard to store and retrieve contextual information. This hypothesis is known as the context processing deficit theory As contextual information about time and place is found with episodic but not with semantic memories, this theory overlaps theories emphasising a deficit in episodic memory in amnesic patients.

Powerful findings related to context processing deficit theory were reported by Huppert and Piercy (1976). They presented a series of pictures on day 1 of their study, and a series of pictures on day 2. Some of the pictures presented on day 2 had been presented on day 1, and some had not. Ten minutes after the day 2 presentation, there was a test of recognition memory. On this test, participants were asked which pictures had been presented on day 2. The normal controls had no problem (see Figure 7.8a). They correctly identified nearly all the pictures that had been presented on day 2, and incorrectly identified very few of the pictures presented only on day 1. Korsakoff patients did much worse, correctly identifying only 70% of the day 2 pictures, and incorrectly identifying 51% of the pictures presented only on day 1.

Huppert and Piercy (1978) found that the recognition-memory ability shown by the amnesic patients was entirely due to the fact that the day

**FIGURE 7.8**

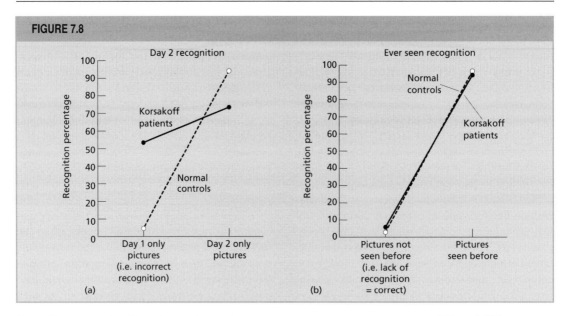

Recognition memory for pictures in Korsakoff patients and normal controls. Data from Huppert and Piercy (1976).

2 pictures were slightly higher in familiarity than the day 1 pictures, rather than to specific memory for the time of learning. Thus, Korsakoff patients showed practically no direct memory for temporal context, i.e., the day on which they had seen any given picture.

The most important finding obtained by Huppert and Piercy (1976) arose when they asked their participants to indicate whether they had *ever* seen the pictures before. With this test, it was not necessary to have stored contextual information about *when* the pictures had been seen in order to show recognition memory. The Korsakoff patients and the normal controls performed this task at a very high level, with the two groups hardly differing in their performance (see Figure 7.8b). Thus, information about the pictures themselves was stored in long-term memory by the Korsakoff patients, but very little (if any) information about the circumstances in which the pictures had been seen previously was available.

Context processing deficit theory has also received support from research on *source amnesia*, in which facts are remembered but not the source of those facts. Source amnesia in amnesic patients was studied by Shimamura and Squire (1987). Amnesic patients were more impaired than normal controls in remembering the source of trivia facts they were able to recall. Thus, amnesic patients have particular problems in remembering contextual information associated with their learning of trivia facts.

*Evaluation*

It is not clear within context processing deficit theory exactly *why* amnesic patients are able to store information about the to-be-remembered stimulus, but cannot store relevant contextual information. After all, what is regarded as the to-be-remembered stimulus and what is regarded as the context is often rather arbitrary and dependent on the researcher's whim. Mayes (1988) suggested that amnesic patients have reduced processing resources, and so can only process to-be-remembered information adequately by ignoring contextual information. However, it is necessary to obtain independent evidence that amnesic patients do actually have reduced processing resources.

At the experimental level, the context processing deficit theory has some problems in accounting for amnesics' poor recognition memory. As we saw in Chapter 6, contextual information is generally less important in recognition memory than in recall, and yet amnesic patients perform poorly on both kinds of memory test. An additional problem is that there is clearer evidence of deficits in contextual processing in amnesic patients with damage to the diencephalon than in those with damage to the temporal lobes (Parkin & Hunkin, 1997).

It could be argued that many of the tasks performed normally by amnesic patients (e.g., motor skills; repetition-priming tasks) share the characteristic that contextual information is not required for successful performance. However, there are substantial differences among these tasks in other ways. Thus, the notion that one should distinguish between memory tasks on which contextual information is important and those on which it is not is an oversimplification.

## Explicit versus implicit memory

The notion that memory performance always depends on conscious awareness has been disproved in studies on normals. There is also compelling evidence from amnesic patients that conscious recollection is often not needed to produce good memory performance. A hackneyed anecdote related by Claparède (1911) illustrates the point. He hid a pin in his hand before shaking hands with one of his amnesic patients. After that, she was understandably reluctant to shake hands with him, but was unable to explain why. The patient's behaviour revealed clearly that there was long-term memory for what had happened, but this occurred without any conscious recollection of the incident.

Schacter (1987) argued that amnesic patients are at a severe disadvantage when tests of explicit memory (requiring conscious recollection) are used, but that they perform at normal levels on tests of implicit memory (not requiring conscious recollection). As would be predicted on this theory, most amnesic patients display impaired performance on tests of recently acquired episodic and semantic memories. Most studies on motor skills and on the various repetition-priming effects are also consistent with Schacter's theoretical perspective, in that they are basically implicit memory

tasks on which amnesic patients perform normally or nearly so.

Particularly striking findings were reported by Graf et al. (1984), in a study that has already been mentioned. One of the tests of explicit memory was cued recall. The first three letters of list words were presented, and the participants retrieved the appropriate list word. The test of implicit memory was word completion. The same initial three letters were presented, but participants were told simply to write down the first word they thought of starting with those letters. The amnesic patients performed as well as normals on the implicit memory test (word completion), but much worse on the explicit memory test (cued recall) (see Figure 7.7).

Another example of intact perceptual priming by amnesic patients was reported by Schacter and Church (1995). In this study, the participants initially heard a series of words spoken in the same voice. After that, they tried to identify the same words passed through an auditory filter; the words were either spoken in the same voice or in an unfamiliar voice. The findings are shown in Figure 7.9 (a). Amnesic patients and normal controls both showed perceptual priming, in that word-identification performance was better when the words were spoken in the same voice.

The notion that perceptual priming depends on different brain systems from those involved in explicit memory would be strengthened if it were possible to obtain a double dissociation. In other words, it would be useful to find patients who had intact explicit memory but impaired perceptual priming. This was achieved by Gabrieli et al. (1995). They studied a patient, MS, who had a right occipital lobe lesion. MS had normal levels of performance on the explicit memory tests of recognition and cued recall, but he had impaired performance on perceptual priming. Gabrieli et al. also tested amnesic patients, and confirmed that they showed the opposite pattern of impaired explicit memory but intact perceptual priming.

### Evaluation

Most of the tasks on which amnesic patients show impaired performance involve explicit memory, and most of those on which they show intact

FIGURE 7.9

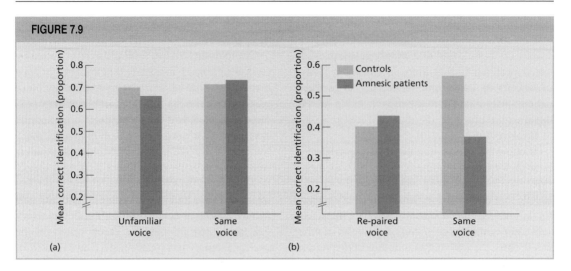

Auditory word identification for previously presented words in amnesics and controls. (a) All words originally presented in the same voice; data from Schacter and Church (1995). (b) Words originally presented in six different voices; data from Schacter et al. (1995).

performance involve implicit memory. An important finding that does not fit is the intact (or nearly intact) short-term memory shown by most amnesic patients, as tests of short-term memory typically involve explicit rather than implicit memory. However, the distinction between explicit and implicit memory is of great value in distinguishing between tests of long-term memory on which amnesic patients do and do not perform poorly.

In spite of the usefulness of the explicit/implicit distinction, the notion that amnesic patients have deficient explicit memory does not in and of itself provide an *explanation* of their memory impairments. As Schacter (1987, p. 501) pointed out, implicit and explicit memory "are descriptive concepts that are primarily concerned with a person's psychological experience at the time of retrieval."

The greatest problem with the theory is that amnesic patients sometimes fail to show intact performance on tests of implicit memory. For example, consider a study on perceptual priming by Schacter, Church, and Bolton (1995). It resembled the study by Schacter and Church (1995), in that perceptual priming based on auditory word identification was investigated. However, it differed in that the words were initially presented in six different voices. On the word-identification

test, half the words were presented in the same voice and half were spoken by one of the other voices (re-paired condition). The normal controls showed more priming for words presented in the same voice, but the amnesic patients did not, as shown in Figure 7.9 (b).

How can we explain these findings? In both the same voice and re-paired voice conditions, the participants were exposed to words and voices they had heard before. The only advantage in the same voice condition was the fact that the pairing of word and voice was the same as before. However, only those participants who had linked or associated words and voices at the original presentation would benefit from that fact. As Curran and Schacter (1997, p. 41) concluded, "Amnesics may lack the necessary ability to bind voices with specific studied words." This view of the major deficit in amnesia is discussed more fully later.

## Data-driven and conceptually driven processes

Roediger (1990) emphasised the distinction between data-driven and conceptually driven processes. He claimed that implicit memory tasks usually depend on data-driven processes, whereas explicit memory tasks generally depend on conceptually driven processes. From this perspective, it could be argued that the reason why amnesic patients typically perform well on implicit memory tasks but poorly on explicit memory tasks is because they have fairly intact data-driven processes but impaired conceptually driven processes.

A key prediction from Roediger's approach is that the memory performance of amnesics depends more on whether data-driven or conceptually driven processes are used than on whether explicit or implicit memory is involved. Amnesics should perform especially well relative to normals when data-driven processes are required at learning and at test, but should perform particularly poorly when conceptually driven processes are needed at learning and test.

Recent evidence has mostly favoured the view that amnesics have impaired explicit memory over Roediger's assumption that the key problem is in conceptually driven processes. For example, Vaidya et al. (1995) made use of four retrieval conditions:

1. Perceptual cues (word fragments); explicit test.
2. Perceptual cues (word fragments); implicit test.
3. Conceptual cues (word associates); explicit test.
4. Conceptual cues (word associates); implicit test.

According to Roediger's theory, the amnesic patients should have been impaired mainly on the two conceptual tests (3 and 4). In fact, the amnesic patients showed impaired performance on the two explicit tests (1 and 3), and intact performance on the two implicit tests (2 and 4). Thus, amnesics' performance was predicted much better by the distinction between explicit and implicit memory than by that between data-driven or perceptual processing and conceptual processing. Similar findings were reported by Cermak, Verfaellie, and Chase (1995). As a result, it seems that Roediger's theory does not provide an adequate account of long-term memory in amnesic patients.

*Evaluation*

Roediger's approach has served the valuable function of focusing on some of the key processes involved in learning and memory. Some evidence (e.g., Blaxton, 1992) supports the application of transfer appropriate processing theory to amnesia, and amnesic patients generally have impaired conceptual rather than perceptual processing. However, there is increasing evidence that impaired long-term memory functioning in amnesics depends more on explicit memory than on conceptual processing.

## Declarative versus procedural knowledge

One of the most influential theoretical approaches to amnesia is based on the notion that there are two or more long-term memory systems. According to Masson and Graf (1993, p. 6), "a memory system is a collection of correlated functions that are served by anatomically distinct brain structures." Cohen and Squire (1980) proposed a memory systems account based on the distinction between *declarative knowledge* and *procedural knowledge*. This distinction is closely related to that made by Ryle (1949) between knowing that and knowing how. Declarative knowledge corresponds to knowing that, and covers both episodic and semantic memory. Thus, for example, we know that we had porridge for breakfast this morning, and we know that Paris is the capital of France. Procedural knowledge corresponds to knowing how, and refers to the ability to perform skilled actions (e.g., how to ride a bicycle; how to play the piano) without the involvement of conscious recollection. Thus, declarative memory corresponds fairly closely to explicit memory and procedural memory to implicit memory.

Cohen (1984, p. 96) provided more formal definitions of declarative and procedural knowledge. Procedural knowledge is involved when "experience serves to influence the organisation of processes that guide performance without access to the knowledge that underlies the performance." Declarative knowledge is represented "in a system . . . in which information is . . . first processed or encoded, then stored in some explicitly accessible form for later use, and then ultimately retrieved upon demand."

## Damage to memory systems

According to Cohen (1984), amnesics have severe impairment of the memory system involved in declarative memory, but they have a relatively intact procedural learning system. In support of this position, we have seen that amnesics cannot readily form new episodic or semantic memories, and declarative knowledge consists (by definition) of episodic and semantic memories. Amnesics acquire many motor skills as rapidly as normals, which is in line with the contention that their procedural learning skills are unimpaired.

Theorists focusing on the distinction between declarative and procedural knowledge have tried to identify the brain structures involved. As we saw earlier in the chapter, amnesia can be produced by damage to various brain structures. Chronic alcoholics who develop Korsakoff's syndrome have damage to the diencephalon, and often also to the frontal lobes. The two principal structures of the diencephalon are the hypothalamus and the thalamus, and the dorsomedial thalamic nucleus seems to be of particular importance in amnesia (see Figure 7.5).

Amnesia following herpes simplex encephalitis or surgery to reduce the incidence of epileptic seizures is caused by damage to the medial temporal lobes, and within them the hippocampus has been especially implicated in memory function (Parkin & Leng, 1993). It should be noted that the diencephalon and the medial temporal lobes are nearby structures within the limbic system.

Squire, Knowlton, and Musen (1993) argued that the major brain structures underlying declarative or explicit memory are located in the hippocampus and anatomically related structures in the medial temporal lobes and the diencephalon, with the neocortex being the final repository of declarative memory. McKee and Squire (1992) found that amnesics with medial temporal lobe lesions showed similar forgetting rates to amnesics with diencephalic lesions at retention intervals of between 10 minutes and one day. These findings led Squire et al. (1993) to argue that the diencephalon and medial lobe structures are of comparable importance to declarative or explicit memory.

Some researchers have used PET scans to study the brain structures involved in declarative or explicit memory. Squire et al. (1992) found that blood flow in the right hippocampus was much higher when participants were performing a declarative memory task (cued recall) than a procedural memory task (word-stem completion). This supports the view that the hippocampus plays an important role in declarative memory. Similar findings were reported by Schacter et al. (1996).

The frontal lobes are also generally damaged in Korsakoff patients, and so it is important to consider their role in declarative memory. Episodic memory seems to depend on the frontal lobes as well as on the diencephalon (Wheeler et al., 1997). An important aspect of episodic memory is temporal discrimination, i.e., remembering when events or episodes occurred. Shimamura, Janowsky, and Squire (1990) found that frontal lobe patients were poor at reconstructing the order in which words in a list had been presented, in spite of having normal recognition memory for those words. However, many patients without frontal lobe damage show poor temporal discrimination.

It is harder to identify the brain structures underlying procedural or implicit memory, because implicit memory consists of several unrelated skills and processes. However, as was discussed earlier, much progress has been made. Sensorimotor skill learning seems to depend on the basal ganglia and the cerebellum, and perceptual skill learning involves the right parietal cortex and the left inferior occipito-temporal cortex. The parts of the brain involved in perceptual priming probably depend on the sense modality involved (e.g., visual; auditory). With visual perceptual priming tasks, bilateral occipito-temporal areas seem to be involved. In contrast, conceptual priming involves left frontal neocortex.

Why are humans equipped with separate brain systems underlying declarative or explicit memory and procedural or implicit memory? Squire et al. (1993, pp. 485–486) argued that each major brain system has its own particular function:

One system involves limbic/diencephalic structures, which in concert with neocortex provides the basis for conscious recollections. This system is fast, phylogenetically recent, and specialised for one-trial learning ... The system is fallible in the sense that it is sensitive to interference and prone to retrieval failure. It is also precious ... giving rise to the capacity for personal autobiography and the possibility of cultural evolution.

Other kinds of memory have also been identified ... Such memories can be acquired, stored, and retrieved without the participation of the limbic/diencephalon brain system. These forms of memory are phylogenetically early, they are reliable and consistent, and they provide for myriad, nonconscious ways of responding to the world ... they create much of the mystery of human experience.

## Synthesis

One of the major developments in theories of amnesia in recent years has been a growing consensus on the key features of amnesia. Similar views have been expressed by Baddeley (1997), Curran and Schacter (1997), and Cohen, Poldrack, and Eichenbaum (1997), as is apparent from the following quotations:

- "What appears to be lost [in amnesia] is ... the record of new links formed in the process of episodic learning ... all conscious links between new experiences are hard to form for amnesics" (Baddeley, 1997, p. 306).
- "The medial temporal lobe [often damaged in amnesia] is critically involved with binding or integrating information that may be stored in separate critical modules" (Curran & Schacter, 1997, p. 42).
- "*The functional deficit in amnesia is the selective disruption of declarative memory*, i.e., of a fundamentally relational representation supporting memory for the relationships among perceptually distinct objects that constitute the outcomes of processing of events" (Cohen et al., 1997).

What is common to these positions is the notion that amnesics find it hard to store integrated or linked information in long-term memory. As Cohen et al. (1997) have the most developed theory (representing a modified form of the theory put forward by Cohen and Squire, 1980), we will focus on it in detail. They argued that declarative memory is impaired in amnesia, whereas procedural memory is not. Declarative memory was defined earlier, and procedural memory "accomplishes experience-based tuning and modification of individual processors, and involves fundamentally inflexible, individual (i.e., nonrelational) representations (Cohen et al., 1997, p. 138).

Evidence that this theoretical approach may be superior to the one based on the explicit/implicit memory distinction was reported by Whitlow, Althoff, and Cohen (1995). They presented amnesic patients and normal controls with real-world scenes, and asked them to respond as rapidly as possible to questions (e.g., "Is there a chair behind the oranges?"). After that, the participants answered questions when presented with three kinds of scenes:

1. Repeated old scenes.
2. New scenes.
3. Manipulated old scenes, in which the positions of some of the objects had been altered.

The participants' eye movements were recorded as they viewed the scenes.

What did Whitlow et al. (1995) find? Both groups answered faster to old scenes (whether repeated or manipulated) than to new scenes. This could be explained on the basis that the task relies on implicit memory, which is intact in amnesic patients. However, normal controls responded faster to *repeated* old scenes than to *manipulated* old scenes, whereas the amnesic patients did not (see Figure 7.10). These findings suggest that amnesic patients did not store information about the relative positions of the objects in the scenes, and so derived no benefit from having the scene repeated. This conclusion was supported by the eye-movement data. The normal controls had numerous eye movements directed to the parts of manipulated old scenes that had changed, whereas the amnesics showed no tendency to fixate on

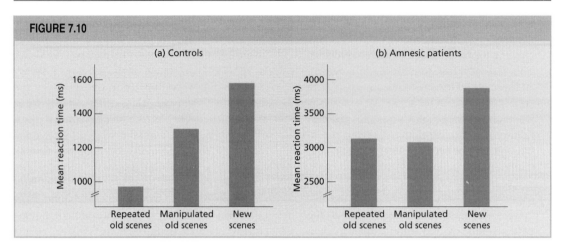

**FIGURE 7.10**

(a) Controls

(b) Amnesic patients

Speed of question answering in three conditions (repeated old scenes; manipulated old scenes; new scenes). Data from Whitlow et al. (1995).

these altered aspects. The failure of amnesics to show intact implicit memory in terms of speed of question answering to repeated old scenes or eye movements to manipulated old scenes cannot readily be accounted for on the explicit/implicit memory distinction.

Additional support for the notion that amnesic patients have great difficulties in storing integrated information was reported by Kroll et al. (1996). They studied conjunction errors, which occur when new objects formed out of conjunctions or combinations of objects seen previously are mistakenly recognised as old. Amnesic patients made numerous conjunction errors, presumably because they remembered having seen the elements of the new objects but did not realise that the combination of elements was novel.

Cohen et al. (1994) used fMRI to identify the brain regions involved in the integration of information. Seven normal participants were presented with three kinds of information at the same time (faces; names; and occupations). On some trials, they were told to learn the associations among these kinds of information, a task involving integrative processes. On other trials, the participants simply made gender decisions about each face, a task not requiring the integration of information. All the participants had more activation in the hippocampus on the task requiring the integration of information. This suggests that

the hippocampus plays a central role in processes of association or integration.

In spite of the important role played by the hippocampus, it cannot be regarded as the seat of consciousness. Damage to the hippocampus still allows conscious access to many memories formed before the onset of amnesia, and large lesions of the hippocampus do not affect consciousness. According to Cohen et al., 1997, p. 148), "The hippocampal system plays only an indirect role in consciousness—it organises the database, so to speak, on which other brain systems may operate and, in so doing, determines the structure and range of conscious recollection."

Curran and Schacter (1997, p. 45) related some of the basic ideas discussed in this section to the implicit/explicit distinction:

Implicit memory reflects primarily the bottom-up, nonconscious effects of prior experience on single brain subsystems, and may also involve interactions between a limited number of brain subsystems. Explicit memory reflects the top-down, simultaneous retrieval of information from multiple information-processing brain mechanisms. This massive integration of information (e.g., perceptual, semantic, temporal, spatial, etc.) may be necessary to support conscious recollection of previous experiences.

According to this viewpoint, information processing typically proceeds through two stages: (1) specific forms of processing in several brain subsystems; (2) integration of information from these brain subsystems. The processing of amnesic patients is essentially normal at the first stage, but severely impaired at the second stage. The various theories we have considered in this chapter are broadly compatible with that viewpoint:

- The conscious recollection of the past involved in episodic memory may depend on the second or integrative stage of processing.
- The context processing deficit theory focuses on the inability of amnesic patients to integrate contextual information with to-be-remembered information, which presumably occurs at the second stage of processing.
- The transfer appropriate processing theory focuses on the problems that amnesics have with conceptual processes, and these conceptual processes generally occur at the second stage of processing.
- As we have seen, Cohen et al. (1997) argued that declarative memory is basically concerned with the integration of information.

## Final thoughts

Neuroimaging has begun to transform research on the brain systems involved in long-term memory. The change this has produced was well expressed by Gabrieli (1998, p. 108): "For nearly a quarter of a century, our understanding of the normal brain organisation depended upon studies of diseased memory. Now, functional neuroimaging studies of healthy brains can begin to illuminate how and why injuries to specific memory systems result in various diseases of memory."

In spite of the successes of the neuroimaging approach, it does not always shed much light on what is happening. For example, Shallice et al. (1994, p. 635) carried out a PET study on normals who learned or retrieved verbal material, and came to the following conclusion: "In common with nearly all relevant functional imaging studies, our study has failed to show selective activation of medial brain structures (apart from the thalamus), damage to which causes amnesia." The fact that the major role of the hippocampus in declarative memory does not always emerge from neuroimaging studies shows very clearly the importance of using a variety of techniques to study human memory.

## CHAPTER SUMMARY

- Introduction. The information stored in long-term memory is used in several ways. Various theories have been put forward to categorise long-term memory, and to explain how it works. These theories have recently become more similar to each other. Research on amnesic patients has been of value in testing existing theories of long-term memory, and in suggesting theoretical developments.
- Episodic and semantic memory. Episodic memory possesses a sense of conscious recollection of the past that is lacking in semantic memory. However, the way in which information is registered in episodic and semantic memory is very similar, and the encoding specificity principles applies to both types of memory. Episodic memory involves the prefrontal cortex to a greater extent than does semantic memory. The left prefrontal cortex is more active during episodic encoding, whereas the right prefrontal cortex is more active during episodic memory retrieval.
- Implicit memory. Implicit memory differs from explicit memory in that there is an absence of conscious recollection. The relative contributions of implicit and explicit memory can be assessed by comparing performance on inclusion and exclusion tests. There is an important distinction between perceptual priming and conceptual priming. Perceptual priming is influenced more by manipulation of study modality than level of processing, whereas the opposite is the case for

conceptual priming. There are probably several kinds of implicit memory, and the term "implicit memory" is often used in a descriptive way.

- Implicit learning. Implicit learning occurs when there is a partial or total inability to verbalise what has been learned. In order to show that there is little or no conscious awareness of what has been learned, it is necessary for participants to be asked to provide the information that is actually responsible for improved performance, and the test of awareness must be sensitive to all of the relevant knowledge.

- Transfer appropriate processing. According to Roediger, there is an important distinction between data-driven or perceptual processes and conceptually driven processes. Memory performance will be better when there is a match between the processes used at study and at test. Various criteria have been proposed to decide whether a memory test involves mainly perceptual or conceptual processes. The distinction between perceptual and conceptual processes is oversimplified, and Roediger's theory cannot account fully for the findings from amnesic patients.

- Amnesia. The study of amnesia has led to new theoretical developments, and has provided a test-bed for existing theories. The amnesic syndrome consists of retrograde amnesia, anterograde amnesia, intact short-term memory, normal intelligence, and residual learning ability. It can be produced by damage to the diencephalon or to the medial temporal lobe. There is usually a temporal gradient with retrograde amnesia, and the extent of retrograde amnesia does not correlate highly with that of anterograde amnesia. Residual learning ability in amnesics typically extends to sensori-motor and perceptual skills, repetition priming (perceptual and conceptual), and some forms of conditioning.

- Theories of amnesia. Amnesic patients often have worse episodic memory than semantic memory. However, they generally have great difficulty in forming new semantic memories even though semantic memories formed before the onset of amnesia are largely intact. There is evidence that amnesic patients have a deficit in contextual processing. However, it is not clear why amnesic patients have particular problems with contextual information. In addition, the context processing deficit theory does not explain amnesics' poor recognition-memory performance. Amnesics generally show impaired explicit memory but essentially intact implicit memory. However, the explicit/implicit distinction describes rather than explains amnesia, and amnesics have impaired performance on some forms of repetition priming that depend on implicit memory.

According to Roediger, amnesic patients have fairly intact data-driven or perceptual processing but impaired conceptual processing, and conceptual processing is generally required on tests of explicit memory. However, amnesics perform poorly on explicit memory tests even when the tests require perceptual or data-driven processes. There is support for the notion that amnesic patients have an intact procedural learning system but an impaired declarative learning system (including episodic and semantic memory). The declarative memory system is based on the hippocampus and anatomically related structures in the medial temporal lobes and the diencephalon. Amnesics find it hard to store integrated or linked information in long-term memory.

## FURTHER READING

- Baddeley, A. (1997). *Human memory: Theory and practice (revised edition)*. Hove, UK: Psychology Press. Alan Baddeley is appropriately sceptical of many of the claimed advances in our theoretical understanding of memory.
- Gabrieli, J.D.E. (1998). Cognitive neuroscience of human memory. *Annual Review of Psychology*, *49*, 87–115. This chapter provides an up-to-date account of research on long-term memory using amnesic patients or brain-scanning techniques.
- Gazzaniga, M.S., Ivry, R.B., & Mangun, G.R. (1998). *Cognitive neuroscience: The biology of the mind*. New York: W.W. Norton & Co. Chapter 7 in this book describes in an interesting but complex way much of the neuroimaging and neuropsychological research on memory.
- Haberlandt, K. (1999). *Human memory: Exploration and applications*. Boston: Allyn & Bacon. Several chapters in this book (e.g., 4, 5, and 10) provide coherent accounts of topics within long-term memory.
- Parkin, A.J. (1996). *Explorations in cognitive neuropsychology*. Oxford: Blackwell. Chapter 9 of this book contains an excellent account of amnesia by one of the leading researchers in the area.

# 8

# Everyday Memory

## INTRODUCTION

When most people think about memory, they consider it in the context of their own everyday experience. They wonder why their own memory is so fallible, or why some people's memories seem much better than others. Perhaps they ask themselves what they could do to improve their own memories. As we saw in Chapters 6 and 7, much research on human memory seems of only marginal relevance to these issues.

This state of affairs has led many researchers to study everyday memory. As Koriat and Goldsmith (1996) pointed out, everyday memory reseachers have tended to differ from other memory researchers in their answers to three questions:

1.  *What* memory phenomena should be studied? According to everyday memory researchers, the kinds of phenomena people experience every day should be the main focus.
2.  *How* should memory be studied? Everyday memory researchers emphasise the importance of *ecological validity* or the applicability of findings to real life, and doubt whether this is achieved in most laboratory research.

3.  *Where* should memory phenomena be studied? Some everyday memory researchers argue in favour of naturalistic settings.

Matters are not actually as neat and tidy as has been suggested so far. As Koriat and Goldsmith (1996, p. 168) pointed out:

> Although the three dimensions—the what, how, and where dimensions—are correlated in the reality of memory research, they are not logically interdependent. For instance, many everyday memory topics can be studied in the laboratory, and memory research in naturalistic settings may be amenable to strict experimental control.

Koriat and Goldsmith (1996) argued that traditional memory research is based on the storehouse metaphor. According to this metaphor, items of information are stored in memory, and what is of interest is the *number* of items that are accessible at retrieval. In contrast, the correspondence metaphor is more applicable to everyday memory research. According to this metaphor, what is important is the correspondence or goodness of fit between an individual's report and the actual event. We can see the difference between these approaches if we consider eyewitness testimony of a crime. According to the storehouse metaphor, what matters is simply how many items of information can be recalled. In contrast, according to the correspondence metaphor, what matters is whether the crucial items of information (e.g., facial characteristics of the criminal) are remembered. In other words, the *content* of what is remembered is important within the correspondence metaphor but not within the storehouse metaphor.

Neisser (1996) identified a crucial difference between memory as it has been studied traditionally and memory in everyday life. The participants in traditional memory studies are generally motivated to be as accurate as possible in their memory performance. In contrast, everyday memory research should be based on the notion that "remembering is a form of purposeful action" (Neisser, 1996, p. 204). This approach involves three assumptions about everyday memory:

1. It is purposeful.
2. It has a personal quality about it, meaning that it is influenced by the individual's personality and other characteristics.
3. It is influenced by situational demands, for example, the wish to impress one's audience.

Some ways in which motivation influences memory in everyday life were studied by Freud (see Chapter 6). He used the term *repression* to refer to motivated forgetting of very anxiety-provoking experiences, and claimed this was common among his patients. More generally, people's accounts of their experiences are often influenced by various motivational factors. They may be motivated to be honest in their recollections. However, they may also want to preserve their self-esteem by exaggerating their successes and minimising their failures. There are occasions in everyday life when people strive for maximal accuracy in their recall (e.g., during an examination; remembering the contents of a shopping list), but accuracy is not typically the main goal. It is unfortunate that these additional motivational factors have not been studied systematically by everyday memory researchers.

There has been much controversy about the respective strengths and weaknesses of traditional laboratory research and everyday memory research. This is no longer the case. As Kvavilashvili and Ellis (1996, p. 200) pointed out, the controversy "is in decline, probably because of the increased versatility of recent research practices, which make it difficult, if not impossible to draw clear distinctions between the ecological and laboratory approaches to the study of memory." The memory phenomena of everyday life need to be submitted to proper empirical test, and this can be done either in naturalistic or laboratory settings.

Kvavilashvili and Ellis (in press) have developed these ideas in interesting ways. They argued that ecological validity consists of two aspects that are frequently confused: (1) *representativeness*; and (2) *generalisability*. Representativeness refers to the naturalness of the experimental situation, stimuli, and task, whereas generalisability refers to the extent to which the findings of a study are applicable to the real world. It is increasingly accepted that generalisability is more important than representativeness.

Kvavilashvili and Ellis (in press) discussed valuable research lacking representativeness but possessing generalisability. For example, Jost (1897) used unrepresentitive stimuli such as nonsense syllables, and found that distributed practice produced much better learning and memory than massed practice. This effect has been repeated many times in studies possessing much more representativeness. For example, Smith and Rothkopf (1984) found that distributed practice produced better memory for the material in lectures on statistics, and Baddeley and Longman (1978) found that distributed practice improved the typing of postcodes by post office workers more than did massed practice.

Before embarking on our review of research on everyday memory, we will briefly mention a study indicating the potential relevance of such research. Conway, Cohen, and Stanhope (1991) tested how much former psychology students could remember about cognitive psychology in terms of research methods, concepts, and names (e.g., Broadbent). These students, who had studied psychology at periods of time up to 12 years previously, were given various memory tests (recognition; sentence verification; and recall). The general level of memory performance was fairly high, which should be encouraging news for students! More specifically, research methods were remembered best, probably because students were exposed to them in several different courses. Concepts were also well remembered, because students could forms schemas or packets of knowledge to connect concepts to each other. Finally, names were worst remembered, but were still remembered at better than chance over a 12-year period.

## AUTOBIOGRAPHICAL MEMORY

According to Conway and Rubin (1993), "autobiographical memory is memory for the events of one's life" (p. 103). There is much overlap between *autobiographical memory* and *episodic memory* (see Chapter 7), in that the recollection of personal events and episodes occurs with both types of memory. However, there can be episodic memory without autobiographical memory (Nelson, 1993, p. 357): "What I ate for lunch yesterday is today part of my episodic memory, but being unremarkable in any way it will not, I am sure, become part of my autobiographical memory—it has no significance to my life story." There can also be autobiographical memory without autobiographical facts "that are not accompanied by a feeling of re-experiencing or reliving the past" (Wheeler, Stuss, & Tulving, 1997, p. 335).

Autobiographical memory relates to our major life goals, our most powerful emotions, and our personal meanings. As Cohen (1989) pointed out, our sense of identity or self-concept depends on being able to recollect our personal history. Individuals (e.g., stroke victims) who cannot recall the events of their lives have effectively lost their identity.

How can we best study autobiographical memory? There are often numerous errors in autobiographical memory when people are asked specific questions. For example, up to 40% of people do not report minor hospitalisations when asked only

one year later! Belli (1998) recommended the use of event-history calendars. Individuals are presented with several major themes (e.g., places of residence; work), and asked to identify the month and the year of all relevant events. A complete pattern of the individual's life over time is gradually constructed. Belli (1998, p. 403) concluded: "Traditional survey questions . . . tend to segment the various themes of respondents' pasts. Event-history calendars, on the other hand, encourage respondents to appreciate the interrelatedness of various themes which serve to cue memories both within and across these themes."

### Structure of autobiographical memory

We have an enormous amount of information stored away in autobiographical memory, ranging from the highly specific to the very general, and from the fairly trivial to the very important. In order to uncover the structure or organisation of autobiographical memory, we can observe the patterns of retrieval of personal information. Conway (1996) used such information to identify three levels of autobiographical memory:

- Lifetime periods: substantial periods of time defined by major ongoing situations (e.g., living with someone; working for a given firm).
- General events: repeated and/or extended events (e.g., a holiday in Austria) covering a period of days to months; general events are related to each other as well as to lifetime periods.
- Event-specific knowledge: images, feelings, and details relating to general events and spanning time periods from seconds to hours.

Each level has its own special value. Every lifetime period contains its own set of themes, goals, and emotions, and indexes a given subset of the autobiographical knowledge base. This applies even to overlapping lifetime periods. Lifetime periods are more effective cues to many kinds of memory retrieval than are other cues. Conway (1996) told participants to retrieve specific events in response to cue words (e.g., restaurant). The participants reported that they often worked through lifetime periods and general events before reporting the details of specific events. The cue words were preceded by a prime referring to the relevant lifetime period (e.g., secondary school) or by a neutral prime. The mean time to retrieve a specific event was 2.7 seconds when a neutral prime was used, compared to only 1.8 seconds when a lifetime period prime was used.

Conway (1996) found in other studies that it took people much longer to retrieve autobiographical memories than other kinds of information. For example, they took about four seconds to retrieve autobiographical memories but only about one second to verify personal information (e.g., name of their bank). According to Conway, it takes longer to produce autobiographical memories because they are constructed rather than reproduced. Conway found that the information contained in autobiographical memories produced on two occasions differed considerably (even when only a few days separated the occasions), which is consistent with the notion that autobiographical memories are constructed.

When people are asked to produce autobiographical memories in a fairly unconstrained way, most of the memories produced consist of general events. Why is this? The information in general events is neither very general (as with lifetime periods) nor very specific (as with event-specific knowledge). Anderson and Conway (1993) studied the relevance of temporal information and distinctive knowledge to the organisation of general events. When participants were asked to provide information about a general event, they typically started with the most distinctive details, and then worked through the event in chronological order.

The importance of distinctive knowledge was also shown in another experiment by Anderson and Conway (1993). The knowledge in general events was accessed more rapidly via distinctive-detail cues than by other cues. According to Conway and Rubin (1993, p. 106), "general events are organised in terms of contextualising distinctive details that distinguish one general event from another, and which also represent the theme or themes of a general event . . . this thematic organisation is also supplemented by temporal organisation, and the order in which action sequences occurred is, at least partly, preserved in general events."

Brewer (1988) studied event-specific knowledge. Participants received randomly timed signals indicating that they should record their current thoughts and actions. They were later tested for their recall of these events by being given a cue. Locations were remembered best, followed by actions and thoughts. Thoughts were best cued by actions, and vice versa. Recall of sensory details was highly predictive of accurate recall of other aspects of the event. When recall of an event was very good, participants generally reported that the sensory re-experience closely resembled the actual experience.

Barsalou (1988), Conway (1996), and others have suggested that autobiographical memories possess a hierarchical structure. Barsalou (1988) suggested that there are hierarchical "partonomies", with event-specific knowledge forming part of a general event, and each general event forming part of a lifetime period. Evidence from brain-damaged patients supports this viewpoint. According to Conway and Rubin (1993), there are no reports of amnesic patients who can retrieve episode-specific knowledge but who cannot retrieve knowledge about general events and lifetime periods, and there are no patients who can retrieve general event knowledge but not lifetime period knowledge. Thus, information at the top of the hierachy (i.e., lifetime period knowledge) is the least vulnerable to loss, and that at the bottom of the hierarchy (i.e., episode-specific knowledge) is the most vulnerable. Presumably the fact that we possess enormous amounts of information about lifetime periods helps to ensure that most forms of brain damage do not prevent access to such knowledge.

*Evaluation*

The notion that autobiographical memory is organised in a hierarchical structure is useful. However, it is not clear that the general-event level is as important as was suggested by Conway. Berntsen (1998) distinguished between *voluntary* and *involuntary* autobiographical memories. Most research has involved presenting cues to elicit autobiographical memories, and thus focuses on voluntary memories. In contrast, an involuntary autobiographical memory is one that "comes to mind without preceding attempts at retrieving this

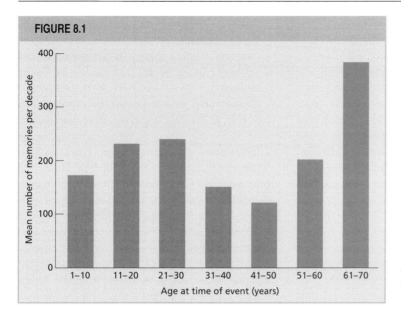

**FIGURE 8.1**

Memory for past events in the elderly as a function of the decade in which the events occurred. Based on Rubin et al. (1986).

memory" (Berntsen, 1998, p. 118). Involuntary autobiographical memories were obtained by asking participants to keep a record of them. A much higher percentage of involuntary than of voluntary memories were of specific events (89% vs. 63%, respectively). As Berntsen (1998, p. 136) pointed out, "The results suggest that we maintain a considerable amount of specific episodes in memory which may often be inaccessible for voluntary retrieval, but highly accessible for involuntary recall."

The key implication of Bernsten's findings is that the hierarchical level that seems to be most important depends on the *methods* used to study autobiographical memory. As Bernsten (1998, p. 138) pointed out:

If autobiographical memory constitutes an hierarchical arrangement . . . it is an hierarchy with no stable "basic" level. What is basic —in the sense of being most accessible— varies with the retrieval strategy employed. Notably, it seems to vary with whether retrieval is voluntary or involuntary.

## Memories across the lifetime

Suppose that we ask 70-year-olds to think of personal memories suggested by cue words (e.g.,

nouns referring to common objects). From which parts of their lives would most of the memories come? Would they tend to think of recent experiences or the events of childhood or young adulthood? Rubin, Wetzler, and Nebes (1986) provided answers to these questions. There are various features about the findings (see Figure 8.1):

- A retention function for memories up to 20 years old, with the older memories being less likely to be recalled than more recent ones.
- A reminiscence bump, consisting of a surprisingly large number of memories coming from the years between 10 and 30, and especially between 15 and 25.
- Infantile amnesia, shown by the almost total lack of memories from the first five years of life.

The reminiscence bump has not generally been found in people younger than 30 years of age, and has not often been observed in 40-year-olds. However, it is nearly always found among older people. Rubin and Schulkind (1997) used far more cue words than had been used in previous studies. They found "no evidence that any aspect of the distribution of autobiographical memories is affected by having close to 1,000 as opposed to close to 100 memories queried" (p. 863). They also found that the reminiscence bump is not simply due to averaging across individuals. They studied five 70-year-olds, and found evidence for the reminiscence bump in each one of them.

Rubin, Rahhal, and Poon (1998) discussed other evidence that 70-year-olds have especially good memories for early adulthood. This effect was found for the following: particularly memorable books; vivid memories; memories the participants would want included in a book about their lives; names of winners of Academy Awards; and memory for current events.

### Theoretical perspectives

How can we interpret these findings? The retention function presumably reflects forgetting over time, but the reasons for the reminiscence bump are less clear. It may be relevant that many new or first-time experiences are associated with adolescence and early adulthood, and such experiences are especially memorable. Cohen and Faulkner (1988) found that 93% of vivid life memories were either of unique events or of first times. Evidence that first-time experiences are very memorable was obtained by Pillemer et al. (1988). Their participants recalled four memories from their first year at college more than 20 years previously, with 41% of them coming from the first month of the course.

Rubin et al. (1998) developed a speculative cognitive theory of the reminiscence bump. According to their theory, "the best situation for memory is the beginning of a period of stability that lasts until retrieval" (pp. 13–14). They argued that most adults have a period of stability starting in early adulthood, because it is then that a sense of adult identity develops. Memories from early adulthood also tend to have the advantage of novelty, in that they are formed shortly after the onset of adult identity. These two factors of novelty and stability produce strong memories for the following reasons:

- Novelty: this causes more effort after meaning.
- Novelty: there is a relative lack of *proactive interference* (interference from previous learning).

- Novelty: this produces distinctive memories (see Chapter 6).
- Stability: events from a stable period of life are more likely to serve as models for future events.
- Stability: this provides a cognitive structure that serves as a stable organisation to cue events.

What about infantile amnesia? The most convincing explanation was provided by Howe and Courage (1997), who related it to the emergence of the self towards the end of the second year of life. Infants at about 20 months show signs of developing a sense of self in the phenomenon of visual self-recognition, which involves responding to their own image in a mirror with self-touching, shy smiling, and gaze aversion. A few months after that, infants start to use words such as I, me, and you. The crucial theoretical assumption made by Howe and Courage (1997, p. 499) is as follows: "The development of the cognitive self late in the second year of life (as indexed by visual self-recognition) provides a new framework around which memories can be organised. With this cognitive advance in the development of the self, we witness the emergence of autobiographical memory and the end of infantile amnesia."

It follows from this theoretical position that the lower limit for people's earliest autobiographical memories should be about 2 years of age, and that is consistent with the evidence. However, it is hard to show that the emergence of a sense of self is the causal factor. Howe and Courage (1997) also assumed that the processes (e.g., rehearsal) used in learning and memory develop during the years of childhood, and so relatively few autobiographical memories should come from the years 2 to 5. This is also in line with the evidence.

### Diary studies

It is often not possible to assess the accuracy of an individual's recollections of the events of his or her own life. Linton (1975) and Wagenaar (1986) resolved this problem by carrying out diary studies, in which they made a daily note of personal events. Both of them later tested their own memory for these events at various retention intervals.

Linton (1975) wrote down brief descriptions of at least two events each day over a six-year period. Every month she selected two of these descriptions at random, and tried to recall as much as possible about the events in question. Forgetting depended substantially on whether or not a given event had been tested before. For example, over 60% of events that had happened $4\frac{1}{2}$ years previously were completely forgotten if they had not been tested, compared to under 40% of events of the same age that had been tested once before. This finding indicates the importance of rehearsal in the prevention of forgetting.

One of the main reasons why events were forgotten was because many events were similar to each other. For example, Linton occasionally attended meetings of a distinguished committee in a distant city. The first such meeting was clearly remembered, but most of the subsequent meetings blended into one another. As Linton (1975) expressed it, her *semantic memory* (or general knowledge) about the meetings increased over time, whereas her *episodic memory* (or memory for specific events) decreased.

It might be imagined that those events that were regarded at the time as important and high in emotionality would be especially well remembered. In fact, the impact of importance and event emotionality on recallability was only modest, perhaps because rated importance and emotionality at retrieval did not correlate highly with each other. Thus, events that seemed at the time to be important and emotional often no longer seemed so with the benefit of hindsight.

What strategies do we use to remember events from our past? Linton (1975) considered how she set about the task of recalling as many events as possible from a given month in the past. When the month in question was under two years previously, the main strategy was based on working through events in the order in which they had occurred. In contrast, there was more use of recall by category (e.g., sporting events attended; dinner parties given) at longer retention intervals.

Wagenaar (1986) recorded over 2000 events over a six-year period. For each event, he noted down information about who, what, where, and when, together with the rated pleasantness,

saliency or rarity, and emotionality of each event. He then tested his memory by using the who, what, where, and when information cues either one at a time or in combination. "What" information provided the most useful retrieval cue, perhaps because our autobiographical memories are organised in categories. "What" information was followed in order of declining usefulness by "where", "who", and "when" information. "When" information on its own was almost totally ineffective. The more cues that were presented, the higher was the resultant probability of recall (see Figure 8.2). However, even with three cues almost half of the events were forgotten over a five-year retention interval. When these forgotten events involved another person, that person was asked to provide further information about the event. In nearly every case, this proved sufficient for Wagenaar to remember the event. This suggests that the great majority of life events may be stored away in long-term memory.

High levels of salience, emotional involvement, and pleasantness were all associated with high levels of recall, especially high salience or rarity. The effects of salience and emotional involvement remained strong over retention intervals ranging from one to five years, whereas the effects of pleasantness decreased over time.

A more complex picture emerged when Wagenaar (1994) carried out a detailed analysis of 120 very pleasant and unpleasant memories from his 1986 study. When someone else played the major role in an event, pleasant events were much better remembered than unpleasant ones. However, the opposite was the case for events in which Wagenaar himself played the major role. Groeger (1997, p. 230) speculated that this latter finding may reflect Wagenaar's personality: "What Wagenaar does not address is the possibility that he may actually have a tendency to be rather self-critical or self-effacing."

The case studies of Linton (1975) and of Wagenaar (1986) are of considerable interest. However, we need to be cautious about assuming that everyone's autobiographical memory system functions in the same way. For example, anxious and depressed individuals recall a disproportionate number of negative events (see Chapter 18), and

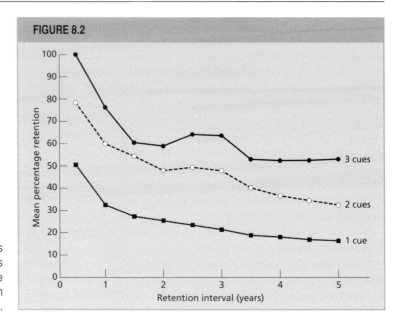

FIGURE 8.2

Memory for personal events as a function of the number of cues available and the length of the retention interval. Adapted from Wagenaar (1986).

this recall bias may colour the way in which they remember their own past. What we remember of our own lives depends in part on our personalities.

## Dating autobiographical memories

Linton (1975) and Wagenaar (1986) both found they were fairly good at dating the events of their lives. How do we remember when past events happened? People often relate the events of their lives to major lifetime periods (Conway & Bekerian, 1987). In addition, we sometimes draw inferences about when an event happened on the basis of how much information about it we can remember. If we can remember very little about an event, we may assume that it happened a long time ago. This idea was tested by Brown, Rips, and Shevell (1985). People were asked to date several news events over a five-year period (1977 to 1982). On average, those events about which much was known (e.g., the shooting of President Reagan) were dated as too recent by over three months, whereas low-knowledge events were dated as too remote by about three months.

In a follow-up study, Brown, Shevell, and Rips (1986) asked participants to date public events that were either political (e.g., the signing of a

major treaty) or non-political (e.g., the eruption of Mount St. Helens). The participants made much use of *landmarks*, i.e., events whose dates they knew well. For example, someone might be able to date the eruption of Mount St. Helens by relating it to the landmark of becoming engaged shortly beforehand (the start and end of lifetime periods are effective landmarks). Landmarks were used about 70% of the time to aid the dating of public events, with the landmarks being either public or personal events. However, over 60% of political events were dated with reference to other political events, compared to only 31% that were related to personal events. In contrast, two-thirds of the landmarks used to date non-political events were personal events.

## Accuracy of autobiographical memories

How accurate are our memories of past events? It is hard to know, because we do not generally have access to objective information about what actually happened. A dramatic exception to this occurred with respect to the Watergate scandal in the early 1970s, in which it emerged that President Nixon and his associates had engaged in a "cover-up" of the White House involvement in the Watergate burglary. The case was of interest to memory researchers, because tape recordings had been made of all the conversations that had taken place in the Oval Office of the White House.

Neisser (1981) compared these tape recordings with the testimony to the Watergate Committee of John Dean, who had been counsel to the President. Of particular interest was Dean's recollection about nine months after it had happened of a conversation involving President Nixon, Bob Haldeman (Nixon's chief of staff), and John Dean on 15 September 1972 to discuss the Watergate situation. According to Neisser (1981, p. 12):

> Dean's account of the opening of the September 15 conversation is wrong both as to the words used and their gist . . . His testimony had much truth in it, but not at the level of "gist". It was true at a deeper level. Nixon was the kind of man Dean described, he had the knowledge Dean attributed to him, there was a cover-up. Dean remembered all of that; he just didn't recall the actual conversation he was testifying about.

It may be unwise to attach too much weight to John Dean's testimony, as he did not know that tape recordings had been made. In order to defend himself effectively, he had to claim he remembered the details of conversations held several months previously. Nevertheless, the notion that our recollections are more likely to be broadly "true" rather than strictly accurate is supported by other evidence. Barclay (1988) used tests of recognition memory to assess the accuracy of people's memories for personal events they had recorded in diaries. These tests were made difficult by using as distractors events resembling actual personal events. The participants made many errors, but their autobiographical memory was truthful in that it corresponded to the gist of their actual experiences.

Our autobiographical memories are sometimes less truthful than has been suggested so far. Dean's memory for the conversations with the President gave Dean too active and significant a role. It is as if Dean remembered the conversations as he wished them to have been. Perhaps people

have a self-schema (organised knowledge about themselves) that influences how they perceive and remember personal information. Someone as ambitious and egotistical as Dean might have focused mainly on those aspects of conversations in which he played a dominant role, and this selective attention may then have affected his later recall. As Haberlandt (1999, p. 226) argued, "The autobiographical narrative . . . does preserve essential events as they were experienced, but it is not a factual report; rather, the account seeks to make a certain point, to unify events, or to justify them."

## Evaluation

Autobiographical memories seem to be stored in categories, and they are organised in a hierarchical way. New or first-time experiences tend to be especially memorable, thus giving rise to the reminiscence bump. Future research should focus more on the relationship between the self-concept or personality and autobiographical memory. People's personalities help to determine what they recall of their lives, and the errors and distinctions they make in their personal recollections. After all, one reason why people read autobiographies is because they believe that what the author remembers, and how he or she remembers it, sheds light on the author's character. The greatest problem with most research in this area is that it is hard to establish the accuracy of autobiographical memories.

## MEMORABLE MEMORIES

There are many reasons why we remember some events much better than others. For example, personal memories with an emotional involvement or possessing rarity value (Wagenaar, 1986) are better remembered than personal memories lacking those characteristics. Attempts to identify other factors associated with very memorable or long-lasting memories have led to the discovery of two interesting phenomena: the *self-reference effect* and *flashbulb memories*.

It seems reasonable that information about oneself should be better remembered than information of a more impersonal kind, because we are especially interested in such information. This intuition defines the self-reference effect. Flashbulb memories are produced by very important, dramatic, and surprising public or personal events, such as the assassination of President Kennedy or the explosion of the space shuttle *Challenger*. Brown and Kulik (1977) coined the term "flashbulb memories", arguing that such memories are generally very accurate and immune from forgetting. As we will see, the crucial issue with both phenomena is whether the processes underlying them are essentially different from those underlying ordinary memories.

## Self-reference effect

Rogers, Kuiper, and Kirker (1977) reported one of the first studies on the self-reference effect. They presented a series of adjectives, and asked some participants to make self-reference judgements (i.e., describes you?). Other participants made semantic judgements (i.e., means the same as . . . ?), phonemic judgements (i.e., rhymes with . . . ?), or structural judgements (i.e., capital letters?). As predicted by levels-of-processing theory (see Chapter 6), later recall of the adjectives was much higher after semantic judgements than either phonemic or structural judgements. However, the key finding was that recall was about twice as high after self-reference than semantic judgements (see Figure 8.3).

The self-reference effect can also be shown by comparing the effects of self-reference against those of other-reference, in which judgements are made about someone known to the participants. Bower and Gilligan (1979) found that other-reference tasks generally produced poorer levels of recall than self-reference. However, memory performance resembling that found with self-reference was obtained when a very well known other person (e.g., one's own mother) was used as a referent.

Symons and Johnson (1997) reviewed 60 studies that had compared the effects of self-reference and semantic encoding, and a further 69 that had compared self-reference tasks against other-reference tasks. *Meta-analyses* (statistical analyses based on combining data from numerous studies) indicated a very clear self-reference effect. This effect was greater when self-reference was compared against semantic tasks than when it was compared against other-reference tasks. However, there was no self-reference effect when the self-reference task involved categories of nouns (e.g., parts of the body) rather than personality

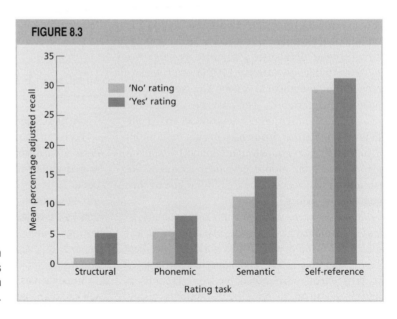

**FIGURE 8.3**

Recall performance as a function of orienting task, and "yes" versus "no" ratings. Based on data in Rogers et al. (1977).

traits. According to Symons and Johnson (1997), "SR [Self-reference] works best to facilitate memory when certain kinds of stimuli are used—stimuli that are commonly organised and elaborated on through SR" (p. 392).

## Theoretical accounts

Why does the self-reference effect occur? According to Rogers et al. (1977), each individual has an extensive self-schema (an organised long-term memory structure incorporating self-knowledge). This self-schema is activated when self-referent judgements are made. At the time of recall, the self-schema activates a network of associations, and thus serves as an effective retrieval cue.

Symons and Johnson (1997) developed that theoretical approach: "the SRE [self-reference effect] results primarily because the self is a well-developed and often-used construct in memory that promotes both elaboration and organisation of encoded information" (p. 372). They reported supporting evidence. The self-reference effect was much smaller than usual in studies in which self-reference was compared against semantic encoding tasks that permitted elaboration and organisation. For example, Klein and Kihlstrom (1986) compared the importance of self-reference and organisation as factors determining memory. Participants were presented with a list of occupations, and had to perform one of four tasks on each word:

1. Semantic, organised: Does this job require a college education?
2. Semantic, unorganised: Different questions for each word (e.g., Does this person perform operations?).
3. Self-reference, organised: Have you ever wanted to be a . . . ?
4. Self-reference, unorganised: Yes–no decisions on different bases for each word (e.g., I place complete trust in my . . . ).

Organisation made a large difference to memory. However, self-reference was no more effective than ordinary semantic processing when the extent to which the information is organised was controlled. In fact, self-reference was associated with poorer recall than normal semantic processing if it failed to encourage organisation. On this line of reasoning, the self-reference reported by Rogers et al. (1977) and by others is found when the self-reference task encourages organisation to a greater extent than does the rival semantic task.

How unique are the effects of self-reference? According to Symons and Johnson (1997, p. 392), "Our evidence suggests that SR [self-reference] is a uniquely efficient process; but it is probably unique only in the sense that, because it is a highly practised task, it results in spontaneous, efficient processing of certain kinds of information that people deal with each day—material that is often used, well organised, and exceptionally well elaborated."

## Flashbulb memories

Brown and Kulik (1977) were impressed by the very vivid and detailed memories that people have of certain dramatic world events (e.g., the assassination of President Kennedy; the resignation of Mrs Thatcher). They argued that a special neural mechanism may be activated by such events, provided that they are seen by the individual as surprising and having real consequences for that person's life. This mechanism "prints" the details of such events permanently in the memory system. According to Brown and Kulik, flashbulb memories are not only accurate and very long-lasting, but also often include the following categories of information:

- Informant (person who supplied the information).
- Place where the news was heard.
- Ongoing event.
- Individual's own emotional state.
- Emotional state of others.
- Consequences of the event for the individual.

Brown and Kulik's (1977) central point was that flashbulb memories are very different from other memories in their longevity, accuracy, and reliance on a special neural mechanism. This view is controversial. Flashbulb memories may be remembered clearly because they have been rehearsed frequently, rather than because of the

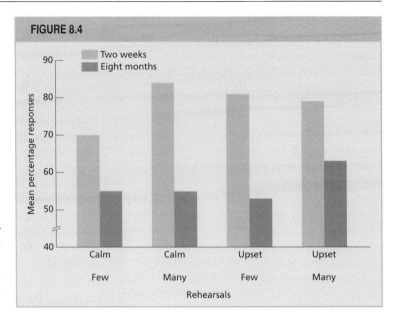

FIGURE 8.4

Memory for the *Challenger* explosion as a function of whether the event upset the participants, the extent of rehearsal, and the retention interval. Based on data in Bohannon (1988).

processing that occurred when learning about the dramatic event. Another problem is checking on the accuracy of reported flashbulb memories. At one time, Neisser (1982) was convinced he was listening to a baseball game on the radio when he heard that the Japanese had bombed Pearl Harbor. However, the bombing took place in December, which is not in the baseball season. In fact, he was almost certainly listening to an American football game, but the location of the match and the names of the teams involved were suggestive of a baseball game.

Bohannon (1988) tested people's memory for the explosion of the space shuttle *Challenger* two weeks or eight months afterwards. Recall fell from 77% at the short retention interval to 58% at the long retention interval, suggesting that flashbulb memories are forgotten in the same way as ordinary memories. However, long-term memory was best when the news had caused a strong emotional reaction, and the event had been rehearsed several times (see Figure 8.4).

Conway et al. (1994) refused to accept that flashbulb memories are simply stronger versions of ordinary memories. According to them, the participants in the study by Bohannon (1988) may not have regarded the explosion of *Challenger* as having consequences for their lives. If they did not,

one of the main criteria for flashbulb memories proposed by Brown and Kulik (1977) was not fulfilled.

Conway et al. (1994) studied flashbulb memories for the resignation of Mrs Thatcher in 1990. This event was regarded as surprising and consequential by most British people, and so should theoretically have produced flashbulb memories. Memory for this event was tested within a few days, after 11 months, and after 26 months. Flashbulb memories were found in 86% of British participants after 11 months, compared to 29% in other countries. Conway et al. (1994, pp. 337–338) concluded: "The striking finding of the present study was the high incidence of very detailed memory reports provided by the U.K. subjects, which remained consistent over an 11-month retention interval and, for a smaller group, over a 26-month retention interval."

Wright and Gaskell (1995, p. 70) pointed out that "The only study that has found a high percentage of subjects reporting what can realistically be considered memories that differ from ordinary memories investigated memories for Margaret Thatcher's resignation (Conway et al., 1994)". Wright, Gaskell, and O'Muircheartaigh (1998) carried out a large population survey in England about 18 months after Mrs Thatcher's resignation, and found that only 12% of those sampled remembered the event vividly. The fact that Conway et al. (1994) used a student sample may help to explain the high percentage of flashbulb memories they reported.

*Theory*

Conway et al. (1994) argued that flashbulb memories depend on three main processes plus one optional process:

1. Prior knowledge: this aids in relating the event to existing memory structures.
2. Personal importance: the event should be perceived as having great personal relevance.
3. Surprise and emotional feeling state: the event should produce an emotional reaction.
4. Overt rehearsal: this is an optional process (some people with flashbulb memories for Mrs Thatcher's resignation had not rehearsed the event). However, rehearsal was generally strongly linked to the existence of flashbulb memories.

Finkenauer et al. (1998) put forward an emotional-integrative model. This extended Conway et al.'s (1994) model by adding the factors of novelty of the event and the individual's affective attitude towards the central person or individuals in the event. They studied flashbulb memories of the unexpected death of the Belgian king Baudouin. Those whose affective attitude towards the royal family was one of strong sympathy were most likely to experience flashbulb memories.

Finkenauer et al. (1998, p. 526) emphasised the fact that their model and that of Conway et al. (1994) agreed on many of the key variables: "(1) the reaction of surprise upon learning about the original event, (2) the appraisal of importance or consequentiality of the original event, (3) an intense emotional feeling state, and (4) rehearsal". However, all these factors can be involved in the formation of *any* memory. This led them to the following conclusion: "FBMs [flashbulb memories] are the result of ordinary memory mechanisms. However, the great number of details constituting FBMs, their clarity, and their durability suggest that a particularly efficient encoding took place" (p. 530).

## EYEWITNESS TESTIMONY

A disturbing feature of the criminal justice system is the fact that many innocent individuals have been put in prison purely on the basis of eyewitness testimony. As Fruzzetti et al. (1992) pointed out, even a very low rate of mistaken identification could lead to several hundreds of innocent people a year being convicted of crimes. Eyewitness testimony, and the factors that influence its reliability, have been the focus of much interest.

One way in which eyewitness testimony can be distorted is via *confirmation bias*. This occurs when what is remembered of an event is influenced by the observer's expectations. For example, students from two universities in the United States (Princeton and Dartmouth) were shown a film of a football game involving both universities. The students showed a strong tendency to report that their opponents had committed many more fouls than their own team.

Does it make any difference to the memory of an eyewitness whether the crime observed by him or her is violent? A study by Loftus and Burns (1982) suggests that the answer is "yes". Participants saw two filmed versions of a crime. In the violent version, a young boy was shot in the face near the end of the film as the robbers were making their getaway. Inclusion of the violent incident caused impaired memory for details presented up to two minutes earlier. Presumably the memory-impairing effects of violence would be even greater in the case of a real-life crime, because the presence of violent criminals might endanger the life of any eyewitness.

### Post-event information

Elizabeth Loftus has shown very clearly that the memory of an incident can be systematically distorted by the questioning that occurs subsequently. To illustrate this point, we will discuss a study by Loftus and Palmer (1974). Participants were shown

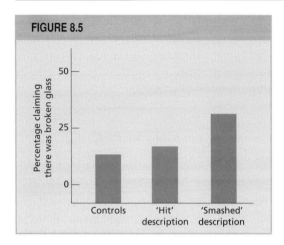

**FIGURE 8.5**

Results from Loftus and Palmer's (1974) study showing how the verb used in the initial description of a car accident affected recall of the incident after one week.

a film of a multiple car accident. After viewing the film, the participants described what had happened, and then answered specific questions. Some were asked, "About how fast were the cars going when they smashed into each other?", whereas for other participants the verb "hit" was substituted for "smashed into". Control participants were not asked a question about car speed. The estimated speed was affected by the verb used in the question, averaging 41 mph when the verb "smashed" was used versus 34 mph when "hit" was used. Thus, the information implicit in the question affected the way in which the accident was remembered.

One week later, all the participants were asked, "Did you see any broken glass?". There was actually no broken glass in the accident, but 32% of the participants who had been asked previously about speed using the verb "smashed" said they had seen broken glass. In contrast, only 14% of the participants asked using the verb "hit" said they had seen broken glass, and the figure was 12% for the control participants who had not been asked a question about speed (see Figure 8.5). Thus, our memory for events is fragile and susceptible to distortion.

Even apparently trivial differences in the way in which a question is asked can have a marked effect on the answers elicited. Loftus and Zanni (1975) showed people a short film of a car accident, and then asked them various questions. Some eyewitnesses were asked, "Did you see a broken headlight?", whereas others were asked, "Did you see the broken headlight?". In fact, there was no broken headlight in the film, but the latter question implied that there was. Only 7% of those asked about a broken headlight said they had seen it, compared to 17% of those asked about the broken headlight.

The tendency for post-event information to distort memory presumably depends in part on individual differences in susceptibility to misinformation. This issue was studied by Tomes and Katz (1997). Those who habitually accepted misinformation possessed the following characteristics:

- Poor general memory for the event for items of information *not* associated with misinformation.
- High scores on imagery vividness.
- High empathy scores, indicating that they were good at identifying with the moods and thoughts of others.

More research is needed to clarify the role of individual differences in susceptibility to misinformation.

The notions that eyewitness memory is fragile and easily distorted were shown strikingly by Schooler and Engstler-Schooler (1990). They presented their participants with a film of a crime. After that, some participants provided a detailed verbal report of the criminal's appearance, whereas others did an unrelated task. Finally, all the participants tried to select the criminal's face on a recognition test. Those who had provided the detailed verbal report performed *worse* than the other participants on this test. This phenomenon (termed verbal overshadowing of visual memories) presumably occurred because the verbal reports interfered with recollection of the purely visual information about the criminal's face.

### Theoretical views

How does misleading post-event information distort what eyewitnesses report? According to Loftus (1979), information from the misleading questions permanently alters the memory representation of the incident: the previously formed memory is "overwritten" and destroyed. In support of this position, Loftus showed that it can be very difficult to retrieve the original memory. In one study, Loftus (1979) offered her participants $25 if their recall of an incident was accurate. This incentive totally failed to prevent their recollections being distorted by the misleading information they had heard.

The notion that the original memory of an event is destroyed by post-event information is *not* generally accepted, because there is evidence that the original information remains in long-term memory. For example, Dodson and Reisberg (1991) used an implicit memory test to show that misinformation had not destroyed the original memories of an event. They concluded that misinformation simply makes these memories inaccessible.

Loftus (1992) argued for a less extreme position than the one she had adopted previously. She emphasised the notion of *misinformation acceptance*: the participants "accept" misleading information presented to them after an event, and subsequently they regard it as forming part of their memory of that event. There is a greater tendency to accept post-event information in this way as the time since the event increases.

Zaragoza and McCloskey (1989) argued for a simpler explanation. According to them, participants do what they think is expected. Suppose, for example, they see slides of an accident involving a man using a hammer, but then read an account of the incident in which the instrument is a screwdriver. They are then asked to decide whether the instrument used was a hammer or a screwdriver. Participants who cannot recollect the instrument used by the man may remember that it was described in the subsequent account as a screwdriver. They may feel they will please the experimenter (and show they were paying attention to the slides) by selecting the screwdriver. Thus, the participants are simply playing along with what they think is expected of them; this is known as responding to the *demand characteristics* of the situation.

Evidence inconsistent with this view was reported by Lindsay (1990). He presented mis-

leading information in a narrative account after showing slides in which a maintenance man stole money and a calculator from an office. After that, the eyewitnesses were told truthfully that any information in the narrative account relating to the subsequent memory test was wrong. These instructions should have prevented distorted memory performance if demand characteristics were operating. In fact, memory for the incident by the misled participants was distorted by the post-event information, suggesting that this information had genuinely affected memory.

The effects of post-event misinformation on eyewitness memory can also be understood within the source monitoring framework (Johnson, Hashtroudi, & Lindsay, 1993). A memory probe (e.g., question) activates memory traces having informational overlap with it; this memory probe may activate memories from various sources. The individual decides on the *source* of any activated memory on the basis of the information it contains. What is of relevance here is the possibility of source misattribution. If the memories from one source resemble those from another source, this will increase the chances of source misattribution. If eyewitnesses falsely attribute the source of misinformation to the original event, then misinformation will form part of their recall of the event. In essence, it is assumed that separate memories are stored of the original event and the misinformation, with potential memory problems occurring at the time of retrieval.

A key prediction from the source monitoring framework is as follows: any manipulation that increases the extent to which memories from one source resemble those from another source increases the likelihood of source misattribution. Support for this prediction was reported by Allen and Lindsay (1998). They presented two narrative slide shows describing two different events with different people in different settings. Thus, the participants knew that the post-event information contained in the second slide show was not relevant to the event described in the first slide show. However, some of the details in the two events were rather similar (e.g., a can of Pepsi vs. a can of Coca-Cola). This caused source misattribution, and led the participants to substitute details from the post-event information for details of the event itself. These findings were obtained with an interval of 48 hours between the two events, but not when there was no time gap. Presumably the participants in the latter condition noticed the resemblances in the details incorporated in the two events, and this helped to reduce source misattribution.

Much research in this area can be interpreted within Bartlett's (1932) theory (see Chapter 12). According to Bartlett, retrieval involves a process of *reconstruction*, in which all of the available information about an event is used to reconstruct the details of that event on the basis of "what must have been true". On that account, new information relevant to a previously experienced event can affect recollection of that event by providing a different basis for reconstruction. Such reconstructive processes may be involved in eyewitness studies on post-event information.

In sum, most of the distorting effects of misleading post-event probably reflect real effects on memory. These effects may involve difficulties of gaining access to the original memory (e.g., because of interference) as was proposed by Loftus (1992), or they may depend on source misattribution. Many distortions may well occur as a consequence of the reconstructive processes emphasised by Bartlett (1932).

An important limitation of most research is its focus on memory for peripheral details of events (e.g., presence or absence of broken glass). As Fruzzetti et al. (1992) pointed out, it is harder to use post-event information to distort witnesses' memory for key details (e.g., the murder weapon) than for minor details.

## Eyewitness identification

Eyewitness identification from identification parades or line-ups is often very fallible (see Wells, 1993, for a review). Shapiro and Penrod (1986) argued that eyewitness identification studies typically produce inferior memory performance to more traditional face recognition studies. One key difference is that the same stimuli (e.g., photographs) are used at acquisition and at test in traditional studies of face recognition, whereas the facial

appearance of someone may differ substantially between a staged incident and the subsequent identification parade.

One factor influencing the likelihood of an incorrect identification is the *functional size* of the line-up. This is the number of people in the line-up matching the eyewitness's description of the culprit. If, for example, the eyewitness recalled only that the culprit was a man, then the functional size of a line-up consisting of three men and two women would be three rather than five. When the actual culprit is absent, low functional size of line-up is associated with a greater probability of mistaken identification (Lindsay & Wells, 1980).

The probability of mistaken identification is also influenced by whether or not the eyewitness is warned that the culprit may not be in the line-up (Wells, 1993). This is probably especially important with real-life line-ups, because eyewitnesses may feel the police would not have set up an identification parade unless they were fairly certain the actual culprit was present.

Wells (1993, p. 560) argued that a small functional line-up and lack of warning that the culprit may be absent produce mistaken identifications because eyewitnesses tend to use *relative judgements*: "The eyewitness chooses the line-up member who most resembles the culprit relative to the other members of the line-up." How can we reduce eyewitnesses' reliance on the relative judgement strategy? One approach is sequential line-ups, in which members of the line-up or identification parade are presented one at a time. Sequential line-ups reduce the effects of functional size and failure to warn of possible culprit absence on mistaken identification (Lindsay et al., 1991).

## Other factors in eyewitness testimony

There has been much research on eyewitness testimony. Those factors that deserve special mention are those that are regarded by eyewitness experts as generally reliable and valid, and which do not correspond to common sense. Kassin, Ellsworth, and Smith (1989) compiled a list of such factors (with percentages of experts believing each statement to be commonsensical in brackets):

- An eyewitness's confidence is not a good predictor of his or her identification accuracy (3%).
- Eyewitnesses tend to overestimate the duration of events (5%).
- Eyewitness testimony about an event often reflects not only what the eyewitness actually saw but information they obtained later on (7.5%).
- There is a conventional forgetting curve for eyewitness memories (24%).
- An eyewitness's testimony about an event can be affected by how the questions are worded (27%).
- The use of a one-person line-up increases the risk of misidentification (29%).

Why is an eyewitness's confidence a poor predictor of identification accuracy? This issue was studied by Perfect and Hollins (1996). The participants were given recognition memory tests for the information contained in a film about a girl who was kidnapped, and for general knowledge questions. Accuracy of memory was not associated with confidence with questions about the film, but it was with the general knowledge questions. Perfect and Hollins (1996, p. 379) explained this difference as follows:

Individuals have insight into their strengths and weaknesses in general knowledge, and tend to modify their use of the confidence scale accordingly . . . So, for example, individuals will know whether they tend to be better or worse than others at sports questions. However, eyewitnessed events are not amenable to such insight: subjects are unlikely to know whether they are better or worse . . . than others at remembering the hair colour of a participant in an event, for example.

Perfect and Hollins (1996) found that eyewitnesses typically had more confidence in their accurate answers than in their inaccurate ones. Thus,

they could discriminate among the quality of their own memories to some extent, even though they did not know whether they were better or worse than others at remembering details of an event.

Psychologists have made a valuable contribution to ensuring that justice is done in criminal cases. For example, John Demjanjuk was convicted of being "Ivan the Terrible", the person who operated the gas chambers at Treblinka concentration camp. The main evidence consisted of eyewitness testimony given by survivors of the camp 40 years after the war. Psychologists warned of the fallibility of eyewitness testimony over such long periods, and their warnings seem to have been justified by the subsequent overturning of the conviction.

## Cognitive interview

The questions asked during a police interview may unwittingly distort an eyewitness's memory and so reduce its reliability. What used to happen was that an eyewitness's account of what had happened was often interrupted repeatedly by police, with the question–answer format being used excessively. The interruptions made it hard for the eyewitness to concentrate, thus reducing recall. In response to psychological research, the Home Office issued guidelines a few years ago recommending that police interviews should proceed from free recall to general open-ended questions, concluding with more specific questions.

According to Fisher and Geiselman (e.g., Geiselman, Fisher, MacKinnnon, & Holland, 1985), interview techniques should be based on the following notions:

- Memory traces are usually complex and contain various kinds of information.
- The effectiveness of a retrieval cue depends on its informational overlap with information stored in the memory trace; this is the *encoding specificity principle* (see Chapter 6).
- Various retrieval cues may permit access to any given memory trace; if one retrieval cue is ineffective, find another one. For example, if you cannot think of someone's name, form an image of that person, or think of the first letter of their name.

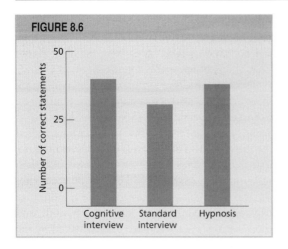

FIGURE 8.6

Number of correct statements using different methods of interview. Based on data in Geiselman et al. (1985).

Geiselman et al. (1985) used these notions to develop the *basic cognitive interview*:

*   The eyewitness tries to recreate the context existing at the time of the crime, including environmental and internal (e.g., mood state) information.
*   The eyewitness reports everything he or she can think of about the incident, even if the information is fragmented.
*   The eyewitness reports the details of the incident in various orders.
*   The eyewitness reports the events from various perspectives, an approach based on the Anderson and Pichert (1978) study (see Chapter 12).

Geiselman et al. (1985) found that the average number of correct statements produced by eyewitnesses was 41.1 using the basic cognitive interview, against only 29.4 using the standard police interview (see Figure 8.6). Hypnosis produced an average of 38.0 correct statements, so it was less effective than the basic cognitive interview.

Fisher et al. (1987) devised an *enhanced cognitive interview*. It incorporates key aspects of the basic cognitive interview, but adds the following recommendations (Roy, 1991, p. 399):

Investigators should minimise distractions, induce the eyewitness to speak slowly, allow a pause between the response and next question, tailor language to suit the individual eyewitness, follow up with interpretive comment, try to reduce eyewitness anxiety, avoid judgmental and personal comments, and always review the eyewitness's description of events or people under investigation.

Fisher et al. (1987) found that the enhanced cognitive interview was more effective than the basic cognitive interview. Eyewitnesses produced an average of 57.5 correct statements when given the enhanced interview, compared to 39.6 with the basic interview. However, there were 28% more incorrect statements with the enhanced interview.

Fisher et al.'s (1987) findings were obtained under artificial conditions. Fisher, Geiselman, and Amador (1990) used the enhanced cognitive interview in field conditions. Detectives working for the Robbery Division of Metro-Dade Police Department in Miami were trained in the techniques of the enhanced interview. Police interviews with eyewitnesses and the victims of crime were tape-recorded and scored for the number of statements obtained, and the extent to which these statements were confirmed by a second eyewitness. Training produced an increase of 46% in the number of statements. Where confirmation was possible, over 90% of the statements proved accurate.

*Evaluation*

The cognitive interview is one of the most successful contributions to society made by cognitive psychologists. Geiselman and Fisher (1997) reviewed the evidence from more than 40 laboratory and field studies, and concluded that 25–35% more correct information was obtained from the cognitive interview than from standard police interviews. They also claimed that this increase in correct information was obtained without any increase in the amount of incorrect information generated.

However, there are some reservations about the general applicability of the cognitive interview.

First, a key ingredient in the cognitive interview is the attempt to recreate the context at the time of the incident. However, context typically has more effect on recall than on recognition memory (see Chapter 6). This led Groeger (1997, p. 250) to argue as follows: "While context might reasonably be expected to enhance a witness's recall, deciding which individuals look familiar among hundreds of mug-shot photographs should not benefit from context reinstatement."

Second, Groeger (1997) pointed out that the cognitive interview may be of more value in increasing recall of peripheral details than of central ones. However, the state of high arousal experienced by many eyewitnesses to crime may prevent them from encoding such peripheral details (e.g., Loftus & Burns, 1982), and so these details will not be available for recall.

Third, the cognitive interview is typically less effective at enhancing recall when it is used at longer retention intervals (Geiselman & Fisher, 1997).

### Section summary

Research on eyewitness testimony has proved very successful. Theoretically, the ways in which human memory can be distorted, and its fragility, are more clearly understood. Practically, psychologists' findings are increasingly influencing various aspects of the legal process (e.g., interviewing techniques; advice given to jurors). The interventions of psychologists have helped to ensure that criminals are arrested and convicted, whereas innocent people are not.

# SUPERIOR MEMORY ABILITY

Much research on human memory has focused on its limitations (omissions; distortions). However, it is useful to study individuals with unusually good memories to understand the principles involved in efficient human learning. The best known mnemonist or memory expert is Shereshevskii, who is usually referred to as S. His amazing powers were studied by the Russian neuropsychologist Luria (1975). After only three minutes' study, S learned a matrix of 50 digits perfectly, and was then able to recall them effortlessly in any direction. More strikingly, he showed almost perfect retention for much of what he had learned several years later. The digits were encoded in the form of visual images. He used a variety of memory strategies in a flexible way. For example, he learned complex verbal information by linking each piece of information to a different, well known location. This is known as the *method of loci*.

S also made frequent use of *synaesthesia*, which is the tendency for one sense modality to evoke another. His usual strategy was to encode all kinds of material in vivid visual terms. For example, S once said to the psychologist Vygotsky, "What a crumbly yellow voice you have" (Luria, 1975, p. 24). Unfortunately, we do not know why S had such strong synaesthesia and such exceptional memory. He did not dedicate much time to improving his memory, which suggests that his abilities were innate. Wilding and Valentine (1991) suggested that S may have had more brain tissue than most people devoted to processing sensory information.

S was unusual among those with superior memory ability in two ways. First, his memory powers were much greater. Second, his superiority seemed to owe little to the use of highly practised memory techniques. More typical is the case of the young man (SF) studied by Ericsson and Chase (1982). He was a student at Carnegie-Mellon University who was paid to practise the digit-span task for one hour a day for two years. The digit span (the number of random digits that can be repeated back in the correct order) is typically about seven items, but this individual eventually attained a span of 80 items.

How did he do it? He reached a digit span of about 18 items by using his extensive knowledge of running times. For example, if the first few digits presented were "3594", he would note that this was Bannister's time for the mile, and so those four digits would be stored away as a single *chunk* or unit. He then increased his digit span to 80 by organising these chunks into a hierarchical structure.

SF's memory had outstanding digit span, but his letter and word spans were only average. A similar pattern was found with Rajan Mahadevan. He managed to produce the first 31,811 digits of *pi* (the ratio of a circle's radius to its circumference) in just under four hours, and this gained him a place in the *Guinness Book of Records*. His exceptional ability to remember digits was also found with digit span: his digit span was 59 for visually presented digits and 63 for heard digits. However, he was below average at remembering the position and orientation of images of various objects (Biederman, Cooper, Fox, & Mahadevan, 1992). The pattern of memory performance showed by individuals such as SF and Rajan led Groeger (1997, p. 242) to conclude: "There is very little evidence that exceptional abilities extend beyond the limits of the particular strategies which the mnemonist has learned to use effectively."

## Theoretical views

Ericsson (1988) proposed that there are three requirements to achieve very high memory skills:

- Meaningful encoding: the information should be processed meaningfully, relating it to pre-existing knowledge; this resembles levels-of-processing theory (see Chapter 6).
- Retrieval structure: cues should be stored with the information to aid later retrieval; this resembles the encoding specificity principle (see Chapter 6).
- Speed-up: there is extensive practice so that the processes involved in encoding and retrieval function faster and faster; this produces automaticity (see Chapter 5).

This theoretical approach was developed by Ericsson and Kintsch (1995). They argued that exceptional memory depends on pre-existing knowledge rather than an enlarged working memory. According to Ericsson and Kintsch (1995, p. 216), the crucial requirements for exceptional memory are as follows: "Subjects must associate the encoded information with appropriate retrieval cues. This association allows them to activate a particular retrieval cue at a later time and thus

partially reinstates the conditions of encoding to retrieve the desired information from long-term memory". The various mnemonic techniques discussed in the next section provide examples of these principles in action.

The theoretical approach of Ericsson (1988) and of Ericsson and Kintsch (1995) might lead one to conclude that those with exceptional memory rely on highly practised memory strategies. However, Wilding and Valentine (1994) found that matters are more complicated. They took advantage of the fact that the World Memory Championships were being held in London to assess the memory performance of the contestants as well as members of the audience who showed outstanding memory abilities.

Wilding and Valentine (1994) classified their participants into two groups: (1) *strategists*, who reported frequent use of memory strategies; and (2) *naturals*, who claimed naturally superior memory ability from early childhood, and who possessed a close relative exhibiting a comparable level of memory ability. They used two kinds of memory tasks:

1. Strategic tasks (e.g., recalling names to faces) that seemed to be susceptible to the use of memory strategies.
2. Non-strategic tasks (e.g., recognition of snow crystals).

There were important differences between the strategists and the naturals (see Figure 8.7). The strategists performed much better on strategic tasks than on non-strategic tasks, whereas the naturals did well on both kinds of memory tasks. The data are plotted in percentiles, so we can see how the two groups compared against a normal control sample (50th percentile = average person's score). Superior ability can depend on either natural ability or on highly practised strategies. However, there was partial support for Ericsson's view of the importance of memory strategies, because easily the most impressive memory performance (surpassing that of more than 90% of the population) was obtained by strategists on strategic tasks.

Some strategists have spent hundreds of hours developing their memory skills. O'Brien devoted

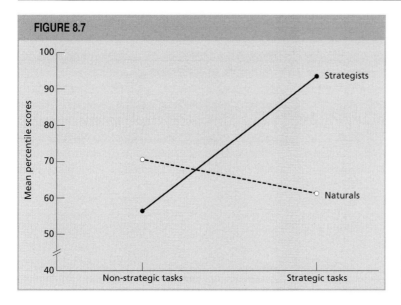

**FIGURE 8.7**

Memory performance strategists and naturals on strategic and non-strategic tasks. Based on data in Wilding and Valentine (1994).

six years of his life to becoming world memory champion in the early 1990s. What motivated him? According to O'Brien (1993, p. 6), "I can now be introduced to a hundred new people at a party and remember all their names perfectly. Imagine what that does for your social confidence. My memory has helped me to lead a more organised life. I don't need to use a diary any more: appointments are all stored in my head. I can give speeches and talks without referring to any notes. I can absorb and recall huge amounts of information (particularly useful if you are revising for exams or learning a new language). And I have used my memory to earn considerable amounts of money at the blackjack table."

## Mnemonic techniques

A basic notion in attempts to improve memory is that relevant previous knowledge is very useful in permitting the efficient organisation and retention of new information. Expert chess players can remember the positions of about 24 chess pieces, provided that the arrangement of the pieces forms a feasible game position (DeGroot, 1966; see Chapter 16). Unskilled amateur players can remember the positions of only about 10 pieces. These findings reflect differences in knowledge of the game rather than in memory ability,

because experts do no better than amateurs when remembering the positions of randomly placed pieces.

Several mnemonic techniques to increase long-term memory have been devised. Most involve some or all of the requirements for superior memory skills identified by Ericsson (1988): meaningful encoding; retrieval structure; and speed-up. There are various peg systems, in which to-be-remembered items are attached to easily memorised items or pegs. The most popular peg system is the "one-is-a-bun" mnemonic based on the rhyme, "one is a bun, two is a shoe, three is a tree, four is a door, five is a hive, six is sticks, seven is heaven . . .". One mental image is formed by associating the first to-be-remembered item with a bun, a second mental image links a shoe with the second item, and so on. The seventh item can be retrieved by thinking of the image based on heaven. This mnemonic makes use of all Ericsson's requirements, and doubles recall (Morris & Reid, 1970). From a scientific rather than a practical perspective, it is unfortunate that we do not know which of Ericsson's three requirements is most responsible for the success of the one-is-a-bun mnemonic.

The keyword method has been applied to the learning of foreign vocabulary. First, an association is formed between each spoken foreign word

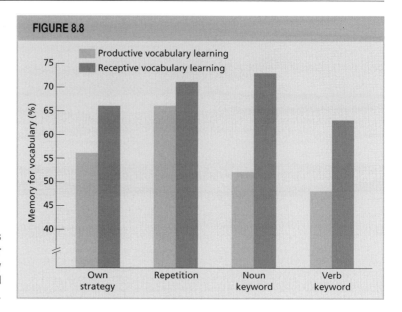

**FIGURE 8.8**

Memory for foreign vocabulary as a function of learning strategy for receptive and productive vocabulary learning. Adapted from Ellis and Beaton (1993).

and an English word or phrase sounding like it (the keyword). Second, a mental image is created with the keyword acting as a link between the foreign word and its English equivalent. For example, the Russian word "*zvonok*" is pronounced "zvah-oak" and means bell. This can be learned by using "oak" as the keyword, and forming an image of an oak tree covered with bells.

The keyword technique is more effective when the keywords are provided than when learners must provide their own. Atkinson and Raugh (1975) presented 120 Russian words and their English equivalents. The keyword method improved memory for Russian words by about 50% over a short retention interval, and by almost 75% at a long (six-week) retention interval.

Ellis and Beaton (1993) pointed out an important limitation in the study by Atkinson and Raugh (1975). It was concerned only with receptive vocabulary learning (being able to produce the appropriate English word when presented with a foreign word), and did not consider productive vocabulary learning (producing the right foreign word when given an English word). Ellis and Beaton (1993) studied receptive and productive vocabulary learning of German words in four conditions: noun keyword; verb keyword; repetition (keep repeating the paired German and English

words); and own strategy. As can be seen in Figure 8.8, the keyword technique (especially with noun keywords) was relatively more successful with receptive than with productive vocabulary learning.

Why was the keyword technique unsuccessful with productive vocabulary learning? As Pressley et al. (1980) pointed out, "There is no mechanism in the keyword method to allow retrieval of the whole word from the keyword." Why was the repetition strategy so successful with productive vocabulary learning? Repetition involves considerable use of the phonological loop, and the phonological loop plays a major role in language learning (Baddeley, Gathercole, & Papagno, 1998; see Chapter 6).

The SQ3R (Survey, Question, Read, Recite, Review) technique can be used for learning complex, integrated material. The initial Survey stage involves skimming through the material while trying to construct a framework to aid comprehension. In the Question stage, learners ask themselves questions based on the headings in the material to make reading purposeful. The material is read thoroughly in the Read stage, with the questions from the previous stage being borne in mind. The material is re-read in the Recite stage, with learners describing the essence of each section to themselves after it has been read. Finally, learners review what has been learned. The general notion is that the Survey stage activates previous knowledge, with the subsequent stages involving active, goal-directed processes designed to integrate that knowledge with the stimulus material.

## Evaluation

Memory researchers have traditionally focused on memory failures, but it is also important to consider situations in which there is very high memory performance. Ericsson and Kintsch (1995) added to our understanding of successful memory strategies, but theoretical progress has been slow. Most mnemonic techniques are effective, but we generally do not know why in detail.

Some of the techniques require time-consuming training, and are often of little applicability. For example, few of us need to learn the order of a list of unrelated words, which is what the one-in-a-bun mnemonic permits us to do. General memory aids (e.g., the SQ3R method of study) are less effective than specific memory aids, but unfortunately it is the general memory aids that have the greatest relevance to everyday life.

## PROSPECTIVE MEMORY

Most studies of human memory have been on retrospective memory. The focus has been on the past, especially on people's ability to remember events they have experienced or knowledge they acquired previously. In contrast, much of everyday life is concerned with *prospective memory*, which involves remembering to carry out intended actions.

One of the few attempts to study prospective memory in an entirely naturalistic way was reported by Marsh, Hicks, and Landau (1998). They found that people reported an average of 15 plans for the forthcoming week. Approximately 25% of these plans were not completed, but the main reasons for these non-completions were rescheduling and reprioritisation. Overall, only about 3% of the plans were not completed because they were forgotten. Forgetting was more common for plans involving an intention to commit or to communicate than it was for commitments or appointments.

There is an important distinction between time-based and event-based prospective memory. *Time-based prospective memory* involves remembering to perform a given action at a particular time (e.g., arriving at the pub at 7.30 pm). In contrast, *event-based prospective memory* involves remembering to perform an action in the appropriate circumstances (e.g., passing on a message when you see someone).

Sellen et al. (1997) compared time-based and event-based prospective memory in a work environment. The participants were equipped with badges containing buttons. They were told to press their button at pre-specified times (time-based task) or when they were in a pre-specified place (event-based task). Performance was better in the event-based task than in the time-based task (52% vs. 33% correct, respectively), in spite of the fact that the participants thought more often about the time-based task. Sellen et al. (1997) speculated that event-based prospective memory tasks are easier than time-based tasks, because the intended actions are more likely to be triggered by external cues.

As Baddeley (1997) pointed out, retrospective and prospective memory do not differ only with respect to their past versus future time orientation. Retrospective memory tends to involve remembering *what* we know about something and can be high in information content. In contrast, prospective memory typically focuses on *when* to do something, and has a low informational content. Another difference is that prospective memory is obviously of relevance to the plans or goals we form for our daily activities in a way that is not true of retrospective memory.

Another difference between prospective and retrospective memory is that there are generally more external cues available in the case of retrospective memory, especially in comparison to time-based prospective memory. If external cues are often lacking, why is prospective memory generally successful? Morris (1992) referred to a study in which there was evidence that cues only marginally related to the to-be-remembered action could sometimes suffice to trigger a prospective memory. For example, a participant who had been told to phone the experimenter as part of an experiment was reminded by seeing a poster for another psychology experiment.

Kvavilashvili (1987) found evidence of differences between prospective and retrospective memory. Participants were told to remind the experimenter to pass on a message. Those who remembered (i.e., showing good prospective memory) were no better than those who did not remind the experimenter at remembering the content of the message. Thus, prospective memory ability may be unrelated to retrospective memory ability.

Common sense indicates that motivation helps to determine whether we remember to do things. It is easier to remember something enjoyable (e.g., visit to the theatre) than something unpleasant (e.g., visit to the dentist). According to Freud (1901, p. 157), the motive behind many of our failures of prospective memory "is an unusually large amount of unavowed contempt for other people." Freud's views (as usual) were over the top, but motivation does make a difference to prospective memory. Meacham and Singer (1977) instructed their participants to post postcards at one-weekly intervals, and performance was better when a financial incentive was offered.

As Cohen (1989) pointed out, prospective memory should be considered with respect to the action plans we form. Action plans can be routine (e.g., have lunch) or novel (e.g., buy a new car); they can be general (e.g., organise a dinner party) or specific (e.g., buy a bottle of wine); they may form part of a network of plans (e.g., organise the arrangements for a business trip) or they may be isolated (e.g., buy a collar for the cat); and they may be high or low in priority. Prospective memory is likely to be best for plans that are routine, high in priority, and relate to a network of plans (see Cohen, 1989). Networks may be of special importance: we rarely forget to carry out actions (e.g., having lunch; catching the 8.00 am train) that are well embedded in our daily plans.

## Theoretical perspectives

Prospective memory depends more than retrospective memory on spontaneous memory retrieval.

This suggests that prospective memory involves top-down or *conceptually driven processes*, a notion that was tested by McDaniel, Robinson-Riegler, and Einstein (1998) in a study on event-based prospective memory. They contrasted conceptually driven processes (depending on the meaning or significance of stimuli) with bottom-up or *data-driven processes* determined by the physical characteristics of stimuli.

In their first experiment, the participants had to press a key when any of three homographic words (words such bat and chest which have more than one distinct meaning) was presented. This prospective memory task was embedded within another task. It was designed to resemble the real world, in which we have to remember to interrupt our ongoing activities to perform some action. Performance on the prospective memory task was worse when the meaning of the homograph changed than when it remained the same. The finding that prospective memory was influenced by meaning rather than purely by the physical stimulus suggests the involvement of conceptually driven processes.

Similar findings were obtained in a second experiment. The stimuli to be detected on the prospective memory task were initially presented as words or pictures, and thereafter they were presented in the *same* form or in the *alternative* form. Prospective memory performance was mostly affected by the meaning of the stimuli rather than by their physical form (word or picture). As McDaniel et al. (1998, p. 130) concluded, "Across a number of manipulations that have been exploited in the retrospective memory literature as markers of conceptually driven and data-driven processes, we obtained convergence for the conclusion that prospective remembering is conceptually based."

In a third experiment, McDaniel et al. (1998) addressed the issue of whether attentional processes are involved in prospective memory. Participants performed a prospective memory task under full or divided attention. In the latter condition, they listened for three odd numbers in a row as well as performing the prospective memory task. Prospective memory performance was much better with full attention than with divided attention, indicating that attentional processes are involved in prospective memory.

Marsh and Hicks (1998) obtained similar findings. Their participants had to remember three words on each trial, and the event-based prospective memory task was to respond whenever a type of fruit was presented. They also had to perform a third task at the same time, and this task involved one of the components of working memory (see Chapter 6). Their key findings were that a task involving the attention-like *central executive* (e.g., random number generation) impaired prospective memory performance, but tasks involving the *phonological loop* or the *visuospatial sketchpad* did not. Marsh and Hicks (1998, pp. 347–348) concluded: "These experiments suggest that event-based prospective memory requires some optimal degree of conscious, central executive processing. This point is non-trivial given people's intuitions that event-based remembering feels spontaneous as evidenced by research participants reporting that the response 'pops to mind' on seeing a target word."

Guynn, McDaniel, and Einstein (1998) developed the theoretical approach of McDaniel et al. (1998). According to their activation theory, what is crucial in event-based prospective memory is the association between the target event and the intended activity. A strong prediction of this theory is that reminders will be ineffective unless they activate this association. They tested this prediction in a study in which the participants' main task was to perform an implicit memory task. The prospective memory task involved detecting certain target words whenever they appeared on the implicit memory task. Reminders either activated the association between target words and action ("Remember what you have to do if you ever see any of those three words") or they did not ("Remember the three words you studied at the beginning of the experiment").

The findings obtained by Guynn et al. (1998) were as predicted. Reminders designed to activate the target–action association produced a significant improvement in prospective memory performance, whereas those not activating the association had no effect. Guynn et al. (1998, pp. 297–298) concluded that, "Effective rehearsal or reminding appears to be that which increases the likelihood that the appearance of a target event automatically evokes remembering of the intended activity, and that appears to be rehearsal or reminding that focuses on both the target event and the intended activity."

## Evaluation

McDaniel et al. (1998) and Guynn et al. (1998) have made progress in understanding the processes involved in event-based prospective memory. As predicted, there are important similarities between event-based prospective memory tasks and conceptually driven retrospective memory tasks involving explicit memory. However, the processes involved in time-based prospective memory remain rather mysterious, because it is generally not possible to identify any obvious external cues that facilitate performance. People sometimes remember to perform an action at a given time because they see a watch or clock shortly beforehand, or they make use of the fact that there is a set pattern to their daily routine (Sellen et al., 1997), but this is probably the exception rather than the rule.

## EVALUATION OF EVERYDAY MEMORY RESEARCH

We can draw up a balance sheet indicating the advantages and limitations of much everyday memory research. However, bear in mind that most everyday memory research has been carried out in the laboratory, and so does not differ hugely from more traditional memory research. The following are some of its major advantages:

- Important, non-obvious phenomena have been discovered, thus enriching the study of human memory.
- There is often more direct applicability to everyday life.
- The functions served by memory in our lives are considered.
- It provides a test-bed for memory theories based on laboratory research.

The following are some of major potential limitations of everyday memory research:

- There is often poor experimental control, especially of the learning stage.
- The *accuracy* of everyday memories often cannot be assessed, because there is incomplete knowledge of the circumstances in which learning occurred.
- Some topics of research (e.g., flashbulb memories; the self-reference effect) have produced relatively few new theoretical insights.

## CHAPTER SUMMARY

- Introduction. The views of some everyday memory researchers differ from those of more traditional memory researchers in terms of *what* should be studied, *how* memory should be studied, and *where* memory should be studied. However, the differences between these two groups of researchers have become less in recent years. According to Neisser, everyday memory is purposeful, it has a personal quality about it, and it is influenced by situational demands.
- Autobiographical memory. Autobiographical memory is memory for the events of one's own life. It may be hierarchically organised into lifetime periods, general events, and event-specific knowledge. Amnesic patients are best able to remember lifetime periods and least able to recall event-specific knowledge. The general-event level has been identified as the most important, but this is more so for voluntary than involuntary memories. A disproportionate number of autobiographical memories come from the years between 15 and 25, coinciding with the development of a stable adult self-concept. Infantile amnesia occurs because infants have no sense of self, and slightly older children have still not developed effective learning strategies. Recall is best for autobiographical memories having high levels of salience, emotional involvement, and pleasantness.
- Memorable memories. Information about oneself (the self-reference effect) and about important, dramatic, and surprising public or personal events (flashbulb memories) is generally well remembered. The self-reference effect may occur because the self-construct aids the elaboration and organisation of information. Brown and Kulik (1977) argued that flashbulb memories differ from other memories in their longevity, accuracy, and reliance on a special neural mechanism. However, the factors associated with the production of flashbulb memories (e.g., novelty; surprise; personal significance; emotional reactions; rehearsal) are also involved in forming ordinary memories, suggesting that flashbulb memories may not differ substantially from other memories.
- Eyewitness testimony. An eyewitness's memory for an incident is rather fragile, and can easily be distorted by misleading post-event information. Some of the findings on post-event information may reflect the demand characteristics of the situation, but most probably depend on misinformation acceptance. Techniques have been devised for increasing the amount of information obtained from eyewitnesses. These techniques are based on the assumption that there are various access routes to memory traces, and that it is useful to use several retrieval cues to maximise recall.
- Superior memory ability. Most individuals with superior memory ability have devoted substantial amounts of time to practising specific memory techniques, but others have a "naturally" good memory. Techniques for improving memory usually involve relating the to-be-learned information in a meaningful way to existing knowledge, storing cues for retrieval, and then devoting considerable practice to speeding up the processes involved. Several mnemonic techniques have been developed for specific purposes (e.g., putting names to faces). These techniques are effective, but have limited practical usefulness. However, some techniques (e.g., the keyword method; the SQ3R method) are of more general relevance.

- Prospective memory. Event-based prospective memory tends to be better than time-based prospective memory, because in the former case the intended actions are more likely to be triggered by external cues. Prospective memory is better for plans that are routine, high in priority, and relevant to a network of plans. Event-based prospective memory involves conceptually driven processes, and depends on attentional processes. The processes involved in time-based prospective memory remain rather mysterious, but partially relevant external cues are sometimes involved.

## FURTHER READING

- Davies, G.M., & Logie, R.H. (1998). *Memory in everyday life*. Amsterdam: Elsevier. There is up-to-date coverage of numerous topics in everyday memory in this book.
- Groeger, J.A. (1997). *Memory and remembering: Everyday memory in context*. Harlow, UK: Addison Wesley Longman. Several of the main topics in everyday memory are dealt with in an accessible way in various places throughout this book.
- Haberlandt, K. (1999). *Human memory: Exploration and application*. Boston: Allyn & Bacon. Chapters 9, 11, and 12 in this book address key issues in everyday memory research.
- Payne, D., & Conrad, F. (1997). *Intersections in basic and applied memory research*. Hillsdale, NJ: Lawrence Erlbaum Associates Inc. Attempts are made by the authors of the various chapters to relate findings on everyday memory to pre-existing theories.

# 9

# Knowledge: Propositions and Images

## INTRODUCTION

For centuries philosophers, linguists, and psychologists have puzzled over how we organise and represent the world "inside our heads". A representation is any notation or sign or set of symbols that "re-presents" something to us, in the absence of that thing. Mental representation deals with the what and how of representation in the mind. Paivio (1986) has proposed that the problem of mental representation might be the most difficult problem to solve in all of the sciences. Of course, topics that experts find difficult, become waking nightmares for students. You should, therefore, read this chapter carefully and thoughtfully.

This chapter and the following one are foundational. For the most part, we deal with research that has been carried out some years ago, but is of fundamental importance to cognitive psychology. In this chapter, we discuss the different ways in which knowledge appears to be organised (i.e., objects, relations, schemata) and how it can be represented in different formats (i.e., images or propositions). In Chapter 10, we look in more detail at objects, concepts, and categories. In subsequent chapters, we consider how this knowledge is used in other mental activities, like reading, speaking, problem solving, and reasoning.

In general, several distinctions can be made between representations (see Figure 9.1). A broad distinction can be made between the external representations of everyday life (e.g., writing, pictures, and diagrams) and our "internal", mental representations. Mental representations can be viewed from two main perspectives: symbolic and analogical representations. However, with the emergence of connectionism, theorists have proposed the notion of sub-symbolic, mental representations; these are "distributed representations" stored as patterns of activation in connectionist networks (see Chapter 1). Most of this chapter presents the traditional symbolic view, but later we review the alternative connectionist position.

### Outline of chapter

In the next section, we consider the key distinction that can be made between propositional and analogical representations using differences in

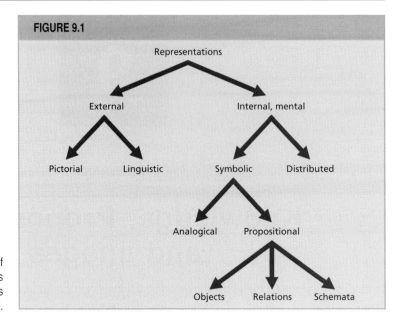

**FIGURE 9.1**

Outline of the different types of representations discussed in this chapter and the distinctions among them.

external representations to illustrate the point. Then, we consider the propositional representations that have been proposed to characterise object concepts, relational concepts, and more complex conceptual structures called schemata. The remainder of the chapter covers analogical representations, mainly visual images, reviewing the evidence and theory in this area. Later we consider neurological evidence on visual imagery before finishing the chapter on connectionist representations. Much of the work reviewed in this chapter is of a historical nature that lays the groundwork for many subsequent chapters.

## WHAT IS A REPRESENTATION?

A representation is any notation or sign or set of symbols that "re-presents" something to us. That is, it stands for some thing in the absence of that thing; typically, that thing is an aspect of the external world or an object of our imagination (i.e., our own internal world). External representations come in many different forms: maps, menus, oil paintings, blueprints, written language, and so on. However, broadly speaking, external representa-

tions are either written notations (typically words) or graphical notations (pictures and diagrams). Consider a practical example how these two types of external representation can be used to achieve the same end.

## External representations: Written versus graphical representations

Imagine you have to work out office allocations for several people. You might draw a diagram of the floor of the building with its corridor, the rooms along it, and the occupants of each room (see Figure 9.2a for one possibility). Essentially the same information can be captured in the description shown in Figure 9.2b. Both of these representations have a critical characteristic that is common to all representations; they only represent *some* aspects of the world. Neither representation shows us the colour of the carpet in the corridor, or the thickness of the walls or the position of fire exits because these things are not relevant to our purpose.

However, the words and diagrams also differ in one important respect; the diagram has a "closer" relationship to the world than the linguistic description. The diagram tells us about the relative

FIGURE 9.2

(a)

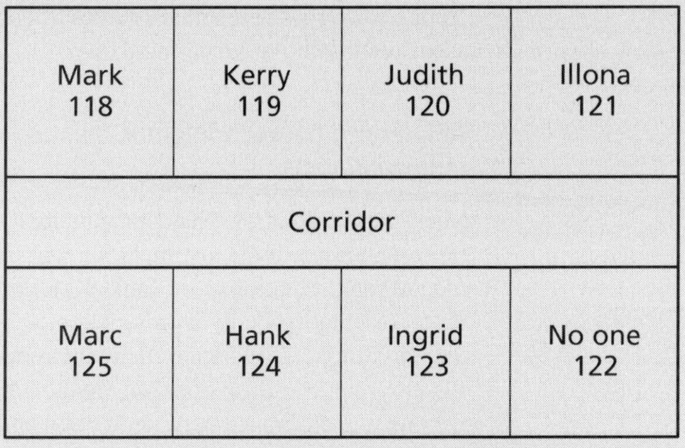

| Mark 118 | Kerry 119 | Judith 120 | Illona 121 |
|----------|-----------|------------|------------|
| Corridor | | | |
| Marc 125 | Hank 124 | Ingrid 123 | No one 122 |

(b)  Mark is in Room 118      No one is in Room 122
     Kerry is in Room 119     Ingrid is in Room 123
     Judith is in Room 120    Hank is in Room 124
     Illona is in Room 121    Marc is in Room 125

An example of the two main types of external representations: (a) a pictorial representation of the occupants of several rooms along a corridor, and (b) a linguistic description of the same information.

spatial position of the rooms. For example, we know that Hank's room faces Kerry's room and that Illona's room is at the opposite end of the corridor to Marc's room. Were the linguistic description to include this information, we would have to include several further sentences.

Pictures and diagrams are "closer" to the world because their structure resembles the structure of the world. In this case, the spatial configuration of the rooms in the diagram is the same as that of the actual rooms in the world. This structural resemblance is often termed *analogical*. Typically, linguistic descriptions do not have this analogical property because the relationship between a linguistic symbol and that which it represents is arbitrary (de Saussure, 1960). There is no inherent reason why small, furry, household pets should be labelled by the word "cats". If the English language had developed along other lines, cats might well have been designated by the word "sprogdorfs". Even onomatopoeic words (like "miaow") that seem to resemble the sound they represent are really arbitrary, as evidenced by their failure to be used in every language. In Irish, for example, the word for "miaow" is "*meamhlach*" (pronounced "me-av-loch").

## Differences between external representations

The critical difference between written and graphical representations just outlined has several specific implications. Consider another example involving two alternative representations of a book on a desk (see Figure 9.3). There are several ways in which these two representations differ (see Kosslyn, 1980, 1983).

First, the linguistic representation is made up of discrete symbols. The words can be broken down into letters but these are the smallest units that can be used. A quarter of the letter "B" is not a symbol that can be used in the language. However, a pictorial representation has no obvious smallest unit. It can be broken up in arbitrary ways and these parts can still be used as symbols (e.g., the corner of the table, half the spine of the book, or even just a single dot from the picture).

Second, a linguistic representation has explicit symbols to stand for the things it represents (e.g., words for the "book" and the "desk" and the relation between them, "on"). The picture does not have distinct symbols for everything it represents. In particular, there is no explicit symbol for the relation between the book and the desk. "On-ness"

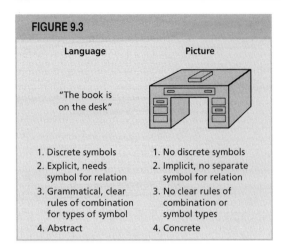

**FIGURE 9.3**

| Language | Picture |
|---|---|
| "The book is on the desk" | |
| 1. Discrete symbols | 1. No discrete symbols |
| 2. Explicit, needs symbol for relation | 2. Implicit, no separate symbol for relation |
| 3. Grammatical, clear rules of combination for types of symbol | 3. No clear rules of combination or symbol types |
| 4. Abstract | 4. Concrete |

Some of the major differences between two external representations of the same situation.

is shown implicitly by the way the book and the desk are placed; that is, "on" cannot be represented by itself but only in a given context.

Third, in the linguistic representation the symbols are organised according to a set of rules (i.e., a grammar). One cannot say "on is table the book" and have a meaningful combination. These rules of combination exploit the fact that there are different classes of symbols (e.g., nouns and verbs). Pictures do not seem to have grammars of the same sort in that (i) they have less distinct classes of symbol, (ii) if there are rules of combination they are less constrained than those in a linguistic representation.

Fourth, the linguistic representation is *abstract* in that the information it characterises could have been acquired from any form of perception (e.g., by touch, by vision) and bears no direct relationship to a given modality. In contrast, the picture

is more *concrete* in the sense that, while the information it represents could have been acquired from a variety of perceptual sources, it is strongly associated with the visual modality.

## Differences between internal, mental representations

Many of the points we have made about external representations have parallels in our internal, mental representations (see Table 9.1). First, mental representations only represent some aspects of the environment (whether that environment be the external world or our own imagined world). Second, the difference between written and graphical representations is paralleled in mental representations, by the difference between propositional and analogical representations. *Propositional representations* are language-like representations that capture the ideational content of the mind, irrespective of the original modality in which that information was encountered. *Analogical representations* tend to be images that may be, for example, visual, auditory, or kinetic.

Propositional and analogical representations also reflect the detailed differences between types of external representations. Propositional representations are discrete, explicit, are combined according to rules, and are abstract. They are abstract in the sense that they can represent information from any modality; but it should also be stressed that, unlike the words of a language, they usually refer to distinct and unambiguous entities. That is, the propositions for the example in Figure 9.3 [represented as *on(book, desk)* to distinguish it from the linguistic representation] refer to a specific book and a specific desk and to a specific relationship

**TABLE 9.1**

Summary of the major differences between propositional and analogical representations

| Propositional | Analogical |
|---|---|
| Discrete | Non-discrete |
| Explicit | Implicit |
| Strong combination rules | Loose combination rules |
| Amodal (abstract) | Modality-specific |

of *on* between them. Analogical representations are non-discrete, can represent things implicitly, have loose rules of combination, and are concrete in the sense that they are tied to a particular sense modality. These differences between propositional and analogical representations are now widely accepted in psychological theory. However, as a counterpoint, you should be aware that some commentators have argued that it is next to impossible to really distinguish between the two forms of representation (for good discussions see Boden, 1988, and Hayes, 1985).

In conclusion, several aspects of external representations have parallels in mental representations. In later sections, we consider the differences between mental representations in some detail. Most of this chapter, and of the literature on analogical representations, concentrates on visual images. More immediately, we now turn to the way in which propositional representations have been used to characterise object concepts, relational concepts, and schemata.

## WHAT IS A PROPOSITION?

As we saw earlier, propositional representations are considered to be explicit, discrete, abstract entities that represent the ideational content of the mind. They represent conceptual objects and relations in a form that is not specific to any language (whether it be it Russian, Serbo-Croat, or Urdu) or to any modality (whether it be vision, audition, olfaction, or touch). Thus, they constitute a universal, amodal, mentalese. By *mentalese*, we mean that propositions are a fundamental language or code that is used to represent all mental information. However, this leaves us with a puzzle. If propositional representations are abstract, language-non-specific, and amodal how do we characterise them? Well, when theorists want to be explicit about the use of propositional representations they use aspects of a logical system called the *predicate calculus*.

One can imagine that the contents of the mind might be object-like entities that are related together in various ways by conceptual relations.

The predicate calculus provides a convenient notation for realising these intuitions; the links on relations are represented as *predicates* and the object-entities as *arguments* of these predicates. By definition, a predicate here is anything that takes an argument or a number of arguments. The terminology sounds daunting but the idea is relatively simple. If you want to express the idea that "the book is on the table"; then the link or relationship between the book and the table is represented by the predicate *on* (where the italics represent the notion that we are dealing with the mental content of on and not the word "on"). The arguments that the on-predicate links are the conceptual entities, the *book* and the *table*. In order to indicate that *on* takes these two arguments, the objects are usually bracketed in the following manner:

*on(book, table)*

Predicates can take any number of arguments; so, the sentence "Mary hit John with the stick and the stick was hard" can be notated as follows:

*hit(mary, john, stick) and*
*hard(stick)*

The predicates *hit* and *hard* are first-order predicates; that is, they take object constants as their arguments. Whenever one has a predicate and a number of arguments combined in this fashion the whole form is called a *proposition*, as can the combination of a number of such forms (i.e., the whole of the above expression is also a proposition).

There are also second-order predicates that take propositions as their arguments. So, in characterising the sentence "Mary hit John with the stick and he was hurt" we can use the second-order predicate *cause* to link the two other propositions:

*cause*[   *hit(mary, john, stick),*
            *hurt(mary, john)*   ]

Cognitive psychologists have used these notations to express *mental, propositional representations*. However, psychologists do not use all the strictures employed by logicians when they use the predicate calculus. In logic, a proposition can be either true or false and this has important consequences for logical systems. Most psychologists are not overly concerned with the formal properties of propositions (one important exception is the work on deductive reasoning described in Chapter 16). In short, typically, theorists merely use the notion that ideational content can be stated in terms of predicates taking one or more arguments.

In an empirical context, the basic properties of propositions are rarely tested directly but are simply assumed. Their characteristics are, however, tested at a more gross level when they are combined to represent knowledge. In this chapter and the next, we review several areas where propositional representations have been used heavily to represent semantic networks and schemata (see e.g., Collins & Quillian, 1969; Rumelhart & Ortony, 1977). Finally, in practical terms propositional representations are very useful for computational modelling. The predicate calculus can be implemented very easily in artificial intelligence computing languages like LISP (Norvig, 1992; Steele, 1990) or PROLOG (Clocksin & Mellish, 1984; Shoham, 1993). This has allowed researchers to be very precise about theories based on propositional representations and to construct and run computer models of cognitive processes.

## PROPOSITIONS: OBJECTS AND RELATIONS

In broad terms, it makes sense to distinguish between objects, relations, and complex combinations of these things (e.g., events and scenes). At the simplest level, an important part of what we know is that there are things or objects; there are specific things, my pet dog Peg, and more general things, pets, dogs, and furniture. An object concept (like *dog*) can be distinguished from relational concepts (like *hit*, *bounce*, and *kiss*). When one combines objects and relations, with some other assumptions, one is starting to characterise schematic structures to characterise events; for example, the dog bit the man causing him to bleed. All of these entities have been characterised using propositional representations.

In object concepts, the meaning of *dog* has tended to be characterised by attribute lists; for instance, a dog is defined by the attributes *four-legs*, *fur*, *barking*, *panting-a-lot*, and so on. The attributes are also propositional representations, and have been variously termed semantic features, semantic primitives, semantic markers by generations of philosphers, linguists, and psychologists. They are viewed as the fundamental meaning units that are used to constitute the meaning of all of our concepts. A particular thing in the world—my dog Peg—can be identified as a dog by virtue of having these attributes; if she had other attributes she might be categorised as a *cat* or a *chinchilla*. These propositional definitions help to define categories of things and are seen to play a crucial role in driving our ability to classify things and organise our conceptual knowledge. Object concepts have been the main focus of research in studies of semantic memory, concepts, and categorisation. For this reason, the next chapter is devoted to a complete review of this literature. We merely mention them here to place them in the wider context of the human conceptual system. Our main concern in this chapter is on this wider context, on how relational concepts and schemata have been characterised from the propositional perspective.

## Representing relational concepts

Relational concepts have, until recently, received much less attention in the literature on knowledge. One reason for this may have been the difficulties inherent in characterising relations in terms of the attribute lists that appeared to work for object concepts (see Chapter 10). One solution, proposed by the linguist Charles Fillmore (1968), is that relational concepts could be represented as a *case grammar*: that is, as predicates taking a number of arguments (see e.g., Kintsch, 1974; Norman & Rumelhart, 1975, and Chapter 10). For example, the representations for the concepts *hit* and *collide* are:

*hit(Agent, Recipient, Instrument)*
*collide(Object1, Object2)*

Here *hit* and *collide* are predicates and Agent, Recipient, and Instrument are the arguments of this predicate. On understanding a sentence about hitting and colliding, people were supposed to construct a mental representation of this sort. So, the sentence:

Karl hit Mark with a champagne bottle.

would be represented as

*hit(Karl, Mark, champagne-bottle)*

People must know which objects can fill the argument slots in the representation; that is, they should be able to determine that Karl is an agent, Mark is a recipient, and that the champagne-bottle is an instrument, and therefore assign them to their proper roles or cases in the situation.

This method of representing relations has been used widely. Most semantic network models of concepts have used this sort of representation; relational concepts, like *hit* and *kick*, were represented as labelled links between the nodes in the network (see Anderson, 1976, 1983; Collins & Loftus, 1975; Norman & Rumelhart, 1975; Quillian, 1966). However, this treatment of relational concepts is not without its critics. Johnson-Laird, Herrmann, and Chaffin (1984) have argued, convincingly, that these propositional representations are not constrained enough to constitute an adequate theory of the meaning of relations; any theory of meaning can be represented by these network representations. In Johnson-Laird et al.'s terms they were "only connections". Johnson-Laird et al. (1984) also pointed out, using the intensional–extensional distinction, that these theories say little about extensional phenomena (see Chapter 10 for a discussion of the intensional–extensional distinction). For example, semantic networks ignore the gap that exists between a linguistic description and a mental representation of that description. The statement "The cat is on the mat" could be mentally represented in many different ways; for instance, the cat in the middle of the mat, the cat on the left corner of the mat, the cat wearing a red-striped, top-hat standing with one foot on the mat. These are alternative mental models of the linguistic description that have

semantic implications (see Johnson-Laird et al., 1984; Johnson-Laird, 1983, on mental models).

## Semantic decomposition of relational concepts

One partial answer to Johnson-Laird et al.'s criticisms is to specify more about the *semantic primitives* that underlie a particular relation (see e.g., Gentner, 1975; Norman & Rumelhart, 1975; Miller & Johnson-Laird, 1976). Roger Schank's *conceptual dependency theory* is one influential attempt to do this in artificial intelligence (see Schank, 1972).

Schank proposed that the core meaning of a whole set of action verbs could be captured by 12 to 15 primitive actions. These primitives were called *acts* and the main ones are listed in Table 9.2. These primitive acts are used in a case-frame fashion to characterise the semantic basis of a whole range of verbs. For example, ATRANS can characterise any verb that involves the transfer of possession:

| | |
|---|---|
| Actor: | person |
| Act: | ATRANS |
| Object: | physical object |
| Direction TO: | person-1 |
| FROM: | person-2 |

This structure is a type of *schema*; it is made up of a series of *variables* (the terms Actor, Act, Object etc.) and in a specific case certain *values* are assigned to these variables. So, "John gave Mary a necklace" would be represented as:

| | |
|---|---|
| Actor: | John |
| Act: | ATRANS |
| Object: | necklace |
| Direction TO: | Mary |
| FROM: | John |

A variable, as its name suggests, can take on any of a number of values. Computer scientists often use the term *slot* for variable and *slot filler* for a value; this taps into a spatial metaphor which suggests that slots are like holes in the schema into which specific objects are put (like necklace). ATRANS can be used to characterise many relations: like receive, take, buy, and sell. In a more

**TABLE 9.2**

The meaning of the main primitive acts in Schank's conceptual dependency theory, with instances of the verbs they are used to characterise

| Primitive | Meaning | Sample verbs |
|---|---|---|
| ATRANS | transfer of possession | give, lend, take |
| PTRANS | physical transfer from one location to another | move, walk, drive |
| MTRANS | transfer of mental information | order, advise |
| MBUILD | build memory structures | remember, understand |
| ATTEND | receive sensory input | see, hear |
| PROPEL | apply force to physical object | push, hit |
| MOVE | move a body part | wave, kick |
| INGEST | intake of food or air | breathe, eat |
| EXPEL | reverse of ingest | vomit, excrete |

complicated fashion, certain verbs can be characterised by a combination of primitives.

Other schemes have been used that are similar to this one, but they all share the characteristic of representing the relational term as a primitive or set of interconnected primitives (see Chapter 10 for a treatment of object concepts from this perspective, in the defining-attribute view).

## Evidence for semantic decomposition

In general, there has been more theoretical analysis of relations than empirical testing of these theories. Some research has examined whether relations are decomposed into their primitives in the course of comprehending a sentence. Some theorists have argued that this *semantic decomposition* does not occur (Kintsch, 1974; Fodor, 1994, 1998; Fodor, Fodor, & Garrett, 1975), but others have taken the opposite view (Gentner, 1975, 1981). Several studies failed to find evidence for semantic decomposition; they showed that complex sentences as opposed to simple sentences (i.e., involving relations with more primitives) did not differ in memorability or take longer to process (see Carpenter & Just, 1977; Kintsch, 1974). However, Gentner (1975, 1981) argued that these studies confounded two distinct types of complex or specific sentences. She maintained that "poorly connected" specific sentences should take less time to process than "well connected" specific sentences

and that previous studies had confounded this difference (see Figure 9.4)

Consider the three main types of materials Gentner (1981) used in her study. First, she distinguished between general and specific sentences: for instance, "Ida *gave* her tenants a clock" was considered to be more general than "Ida *mailed* her tenants a clock" or "Ida *sold* her tenants a clock". This is because *give* involves just a transfer of possession, whereas both *mailed* and *sold* involve a transfer of possession and something else; in *mailed* there are the associated actions of mailing something and in *sold* there is a transfer of goods and of money. However, even though the mailed and sold sentences are both specific, they differ in the degree to which their elements are well connected. Mailing involves Ida as a principal agent who performs a mail routine which causes a transfer of possession to certain recipients (i.e., her tenants). Selling involves Ida as a principal agent who transfers possession of goods to the tenant recipients, but she is also a recipient for the transfer of money from the tenants acting as principal agents. Gentner, therefore, argued that more connections between Ida and the tenants are elaborated in the selling case than in the mailing case; that the former is better connected than the latter (see Figure 9.4). If this hypothesis is true then objects from the well connected, specific sentence should be better recalled than the poorly connected, specific sentence when cued by other

### FIGURE 9.4

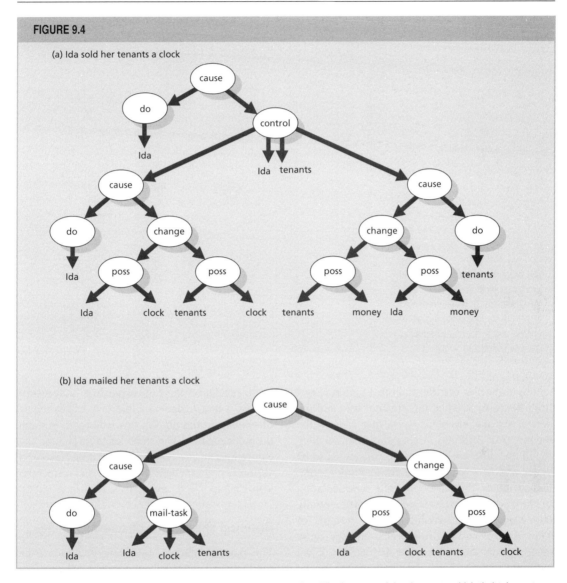

(a) Ida sold her tenants a clock

(b) Ida mailed her tenants a clock

Representations from Gentner (1981) of two complex sentences that differ in terms of the degree to which their elements (e.g. Ida and her tenants) are integrated or connected: (a) the representation of the sentence "Ida sold her tenants a clock", and (b) the representation of the sentence "Ida mailed her tenants a clock".

nouns from the sentence. These predictions were confirmed in her results (see Figure 9.5).

Gentner's research suggests that there are defining primitives for relational concepts. However, Coleman and Kay (1981; also Vaughan, 1985) have shown that these primitives should be treated as characteristic attributes rather than defining attributes (see Chapter 10). Coleman and Kay posited that the verb *to lie* (in the sense of not

telling the truth) had three semantic components or attributes, in which (i) the statement made is false, (ii) the speaker believes the statement is false, and (iii) the speaker intends to deceive the hearer. They then made up stories in which they explicitly cancelled some or all of these attributes and asked subjects to judge the degree to which the incident in the story could be regarded as a lie. For example, a story about a railway porter

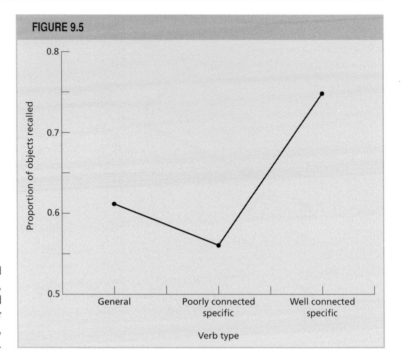

**FIGURE 9.5**

The proportion of objects recalled by subjects in Gentner, 1981, (Experiment 3), when presented with sentences involving either general, poorly connected specific, or well connected specific verbs.

telling a traveller that the train to London leaves from Platform 5, when this was not true and the porter was not aware of its falsity, cancels the second two attributes. Using this method they found that different usages were considered to be better or worse examples of *lying*. Furthermore, the attributes that made up the representation of the verb were considered to be differentially important in characterising a good example of a lie. As we shall see in the next chapter, these results are in line with similar findings for object concepts, which have favoured prototype or exemplar-based theories of categorisation.

## SCHEMATA, FRAMES, AND SCRIPTS

A lot more can be said about human knowledge beyond the characterisation of object and relational concepts. Most of our knowledge is structured in complex ways; concepts are related to one another in ways that reflect the temporal and causal structure of the world. For instance, to represent the notion of an event (e.g., reading your

exam results on the noticeboard) it is necessary to have a knowledge structure that relates the act of reading to the objects involved (e.g., you and the noticeboard). The knowledge structures that can represent this type of information have been variously called schemata, frames, and scripts (see also Chapters 7, 8, and 12).

## Historical antecedents of schema theories

The most commonly used construct to account for complex knowledge organisation is the schema. A *schema* is a structured cluster of concepts; usually, it involves generic knowledge and may be used to represent events, sequences of events, percepts, situations, relations, and even objects. The philosopher Kant (1787/1963) originally proposed the idea of schemata as innate structures used to help us perceive the world. Kant was strongly nativist in his view that innate, a priori structures of the mind allow us to conceive of time, three-dimensional space, and even geometry (even though many school children might disagree).

In the 1930s, the concept of a schema was championed in the work of Sir Frederick Bartlett

**TABLE 9.3**

Part of the original *War of the Ghosts* story and one subject's subsequent recall of it (from Bartlett, 1932)

*The War of the Ghosts*

One night two young men from Edulac went down the river to hunt seals, and while they were there it became foggy and calm. Then they heard war-cries, and they thought: "Maybe this is a war-party". They escaped to the shore, and hid behind a log. Now canoes came up, and they heard the noise of paddles, and saw one canoe coming up to them. There were five men in the canoe, and they said: "What do you think? We wish to take you along. We are going up the river to make war on the people."

... one of the young men went but the other returned home ... [it turns out that the five men in the boat were ghosts and after accompanying them in a fight, the young man returned to his village to tell his tale] ... and said: "Behold I accompanied the ghosts, and we went to fight. Many of our fellows were killed, and many of those who attacked us were killed. They said I was hit, and I did not feel sick."

He told it all and then he became quiet. When the sun rose he fell down. Something black came out of his mouth. His face became contorted ... He was dead. (p.65)

*A subject's recall of the story (two weeks later)*

There were two ghosts. They were on a river. There was a canoe on the river with five men in it. There occurred a war of ghosts ... They started the war and several were wounded and some killed. One ghost was wounded but did not feel sick. He went back to the village in the canoe. The next morning he was sick and something black came out of his mouth, and they cried: "He is dead." (p.76)

at Cambridge University. Bartlett (1932) was struck by how people's understanding and remembrance of events was shaped by their expectations. He suggested that these expectations were mentally represented in a schematic fashion, and carried out experiments illustrating their effects on cognition. In one famous experiment, he gave English subjects a North American Indian folk tale to memorise and recall later at different time intervals. The folk tale had many strange attributions and a causal structure that was contrary to Western expectations. He found that subjects "reconstructed" the story rather than remembering it verbatim and that this reconstruction was consistent with a Western world-view (see Table 9.3 and Chapter 12 for recent replications of this study). Finally, in a developmental context, Piaget (1967, 1970) had also used the schema idea to understand changes in children's cognition.

Schema theories re-emerged as a dominant interest in the 1970s. These theories came in several, superficially different forms: Schank's (1972) conceptual dependency theory essentially uses schemata to represent relational concepts, and "story grammars" were proposed to underlie the comprehension of stories by Rumelhart and

others (Rumelhart, 1975; Stein & Glenn, 1979; Thorndyke, 1977 and Chapter 12). Schemata containing organised sequences of stereotypical actions, called *scripts*, were proposed by Schank and Abelson (1977) to account for people's knowledge of everyday situations. Rumelhart and Ortony (1977; also Rumelhart, 1980) proposed a general theory of schemata and, in artificial intelligence, Marvin Minsky (1975) suggested similar structures called "frames", which he mainly implicated in visual perception (see Alba & Hasher, 1983, Thorndyke & Yekovich, 1980, for reviews).

## Schank and Abelson's script theory

The concept of a schema is a very loose one in many respects. As it is an organising structure for knowledge, it tends to take on ostensibly different forms when representing different sorts of knowledge. However, schemata have certain common characteristics (see Panel 9.1). Earlier, in discussing relational concepts, we saw very simplified schemata in Schank's conceptual dependency representations. More elaborate examples occur in Schank and Abelson's (1977) script theory. Script theory attempts to capture the knowledge we use

---

**Panel 9.1:   Definition of schemata**

- They consist of various relations and variables/slots, and values for these variables.
- The *relations* can take a variety of forms; they can be simple relations (e.g. *is-a, hit, kick*) or they can be more complex, "causal" relations (e.g. *enable, cause, prevent, desire*).
- Variables/slots contain concepts or other sub-schemata; any concept that fills a slot usually has to satisfy some test (e.g. the argument-slot "Agent" in the relation HIT [Agent, Object, Instrument] requires that the concept that fills it is an animate object).
- *Values* refers to the various specific concepts that fill or instantiate slots.
- Schemata, thus, encode general or *generic* knowledge that can be applied to many specific situations, if those situations are instances of the schema; for example, the HIT relation could characterise a domestic dispute (e.g. Harry hit the child) or a car crash (e.g. the van hit the lorry).
- Schemata can often leave slots "open" or have associated with them *default concepts* that are assumed if a slot is unfilled; for instance, we are not told what instrument Harry used (in "Harry hit the child"), but we tend to assume a default value (like a stick or a hand).

---

to understand commonplace events like going to a restaurant.

Schank and Abelson were interested in capturing the knowledge people use to comprehend extended texts, like the following one:

Ruth and Mark had lunch at a restaurant today. They really enjoyed the meal but were worried about its cost. However, when the bill arrived after the ice cream, they were pleasantly surprised to find that it was very reasonable.

In reading this passage, we use our knowledge to infer that the meal (mentioned in the second sentence) was at the restaurant where they had lunch (mentioned in the first sentence), that the meal involved ice-cream and that the bill did not walk up to them but was probably brought by a waiter. Schank and Abelson argued that we must have predictive schemata to make these inferences and to fill in aspects of the event that are left implicit. The specific schemata they proposed were called scripts. *Scripts* are knowledge structures that encode the stereotypical sequence of actions in everyday happenings. For example, if you often eat in restaurants then you would have a script for "eating in restaurants". This "restaurant script" would encode the typical actions that occur in this scenario along with the sorts of objects and actors you would encounter in this context. The restaurant script proposed by Schank and Abelson had four main divisions: entering, ordering, eating, and leaving. Each of these general parts had

sub-actions for what to do: for instance, entering breaks down into walking into the restaurant, looking for a table, deciding where to sit, going to a table, and sitting down (see Table 9.4).

Within this schema the relations are the various actions, like walking or sitting. The slots in the script are either roles (e.g., waiter) or headings for other sub-schemata (e.g., entering). *Role slots* capture the various "parts" in the script like the waiter, the customers and the cook, and are filled by the specific people in the situation (e.g., the tall waiter with the receding hairline). Ordinarily, these roles can only be filled by an object that satisfies the test of being human (e.g., a waiter who is a dog is unexpected and extraordinary). The general components of the script (e.g., entering, ordering) are different types of slots that contain sub-schemata (concerning the various detailed actions of walking, sitting and so on). In this way, it is possible to create structures that characterise people's knowledge of many commonplace situations.

### Evidence for script theory

Several studies have investigated the psychological plausibility of scriptal notions (see Abelson, 1981; Bower, Black, & Turner, 1979; Galambos, Abelson, & Black, 1986; Graesser, Gordon, & Sawyer, 1979; Sanford & Garrod, 1981; Walker & Yekovich, 1984). Bower et al. (1979) asked people to list about 20 actions or events that usually occurred when eating at a restaurant. In spite of the varied restaurant-experiences of their subjects,

**TABLE 9.4**

The components and actions of the restaurant script proposed by Schank and Abelson (1977)

| Script name | Component | Specific action |
|---|---|---|
| Eating at a restaurant | Entering | Walk into restaurant |
| | | Look for table |
| | | Decide where to sit |
| | | Go to table |
| | | Sit down |
| | Ordering | Get menu |
| | | Look at menu |
| | | Choose food |
| | | Waiter arrives |
| | | Give orders to waiter |
| | | Waiter takes order to cook |
| | | Wait, talk |
| | | Cook prepares food |
| | Eating | Cook gives food to waiter |
| | | Waiter delivers food to customer |
| | | Customer eats |
| | | Talk |
| | Leaving | Waiter writes bill |
| | | Waiter delivers bill to customer |
| | | Customer examines bill |
| | | Calculate tip |
| | | Leave tip |
| | | Gather belongings |
| | | Pay bill |
| | | Leave restaurant |

there was considerable agreement in the lists produced. At least 73% of subjects mentioned sitting down, looking at the menu, ordering, eating, paying the bill, and leaving. In addition, at least 48% included entering the restaurant, giving the reservation name, ordering drinks, discussing the menu, talking, eating a salad or soup, ordering dessert, eating dessert, and leaving a tip. So there appear to be at least 15 key events involved in people's restaurant-visiting knowledge. Other evidence from Galambos and Rips (1982) has shown that when subjects have to make a rapid decision about whether or not an action is part of a script (e.g., determining that "getting to a restaurant" is part of a restaurant script), they answer rapidly when the action is part of the script but take longer when it is not a script action. Evidence for script theory has also been found in more applied contexts concerning eyewitness testimony for robberies (see Holst & Pezdek, 1992).

However, in later extensions of this theory (see Schank's, 1982, 1986, dynamic memory theory, in Eysenck & Keane, 1995) the specific organisational structure of scripts was somewhat modified. Psychological evidence had shown that the script idea was wrong in some respects. Bower et al. (1979) found that subjects confused events that, according to script theory, were stored separately and should not have interfered with one another. For example, recognition confusions were found between stories that called on distinct but related scripts; visits to the dentist and visits to the doctor. As scripts had been defined as structures that were specific experiences in specific situations, one clearly could not have a "visit to a health professional" script. In response to these problems, Schank revised script theory, in his dynamic memory theory. Abbot, Black, and Smith (1984) have found support for this new type of organisation proposed in dynamic memory theory by showing that various parts of what were formerly called scripts are hierarchically organised. At the top level is the general goal (e.g., eating at a restaurant), at the intermediate level are scenes that denote sets of actions (e.g., entering, leaving, ordering), and at the lowest level there are the actions themselves.

## General evidence for schemata

There is considerable evidence in several different areas for the operation of schema-like knowledge structures (see e.g., Alba & Hasher, 1983; Graesser, Woll, Kowalski, & Smith, 1980). After Bartlett, many studies have shown that when people have different expectations about a target event they interpret and recall it in different ways (see e.g., Anderson & Pichert, 1978; Bransford & Johnson, 1972; see Chapter 12).

Furthermore, schemata have also been implicated in perception, where they reduce the need to analyse all aspects of a visual scene. When we view everyday scenes, like our bedroom or a lecture theatre, we have clear expectations about what objects are likely to be present. Schemata reduce the amount of processing the perceptual system needs to carry out to identify expected objects (see Chapter 4), thus freeing up resources for processing more novel and unexpected aspects of the scene (like the lecturer's dress-sense). Friedman (1979) has shown this by presenting subjects with detailed line drawings of six different scenes (from a city, a kitchen, a living room, an office, a kindergarten, and a farm). Each picture contained objects you would expect in the setting and a few unexpected objects. Friedman found that the duration of the first look was almost twice as long for unexpected as for expected objects, indicating the role of schemata in processing the latter. The differences between expected and unexpected objects were even more marked on a subsequent recognition memory test. Subjects rarely noticed missing, or partially changed, expected objects even when only those expected objects that had been looked at were considered. In contrast, deletions or replacements of unexpected objects were nearly always detected. As Friedman concluded, "The episodic information that is remembered

about an event is the difference between that event and its prototypical, frame representation in memory" (p. 343).

These effects regarding the recollection of unexpected items have been found repeatedly in a number of different experiments, although they can be modified by conditions that interfere with subjects' attention to the processing of the unexpected objects (see Henderson, 1992; Mäntylä & Bäckman, 1992).

## Fundamental problems with schema theories

Schema theories are not without their problems. While they remain the most overarching set of proposals on the structure and organisation of knowledge in long-term memory, they have a number of faults.

### The unprincipled nature of schema theories

There is a broad consensus among many researchers that schema theories are unprincipled. This stems from the fact that it is often possible to create any particular content for the knowledge structures used, to account for the pattern of evidence found. Schank deals, in part, with this problem by attempting to delimit all the possible structures in long-term memory, but the theory is still underspecified. Problems still remain; for example, what are the specific contents of all of these structures? In general, then, schema theories tend to be good at accounting for results in an ad hoc fashion, but are not as predictive as one would like them to be.

There are two remedies to this situation. First, the theorist could specify the content of structures that *are* used; at least for a definable set of situations. That is, if you were using dynamic memory theory, you could specify all the possible scripts that might be used by a person. Unfortunately, this is probably impossible given the breadth of human knowledge and the possible variability in knowledge structures from one individual to the next. The other option is to be clearer about how these structures are acquired (see Chapter 14). If we knew more about this issue then we could begin to test how different selected experiences might be combined to form hypothetical structures in a more controlled fashion.

## The problem of inflexibility and connectionist schemata

Although dynamic memory theory was developed to overcome many of the inflexibilities of script theory, some prominent theorists still consider that the intuitive flexibility of the schematic approach has not been realised in any of the present schemes (see Rumelhart, Smolensky, McClelland, & Hinton, 1986a). For example, Rumelhart and Ortony (1977) had proposed that the slots/variables in schemata should have two distinct characteristics. First, as stated earlier, they should test to see whether a certain object is an appropriate filler for the slot or provide a default value. Second, there should be interdependencies among the possible slot fillers. That is, if one slot is filled with a particular value then it should initiate changes in the default values of other slots in the schema. For example, assume that you have a schema for rooms that includes slots for the furniture, the small objects found in it and the usual size of the room. So, a kitchen schema would have the following structure and defaults:

| | |
|---|---|
| Furniture: | kitchen table, chairs . . . |
| Small objects: | coffee pot, bread bin . . . |
| Size: | small |

Other rooms would have different defaults; for example a bathroom would also be small but would have a toilet, bath, and sink as furniture and toothbrushes as small objects. Rumelhart and Ortony's proposal was that, when the small-objects slot is filled with coffee pot, there should be an automatic change in the default value for the furniture slot to kitchen table and chairs. However, this second characteristic of schemata was never realised in the schema theories of the 1970s and 1980s.

Rumelhart et al. (1986a) proposed to remedy this state of affairs with a connectionist treatment of schemata. In this view, schemata emerge at the moment they are needed from the interaction of large numbers of parallel processing elements all working in concert with one another (for a treatment of connectionist ideas, see Chapter 1). In this scheme, there is no explicitly represented schema, but only patterns of activation that produce the sorts of effects attributed to schemata in previous research. When inputs are received by a parallel network, certain coalitions of units in the network are activated and others are inhibited. In some cases where coalitions of units tend to work closely together, the more conventional notion of a schema is realised; but where the units are more loosely interconnected the structures are more fluid and less schema-like.

Rumelhart et al. have illustrated the utility of such a scheme by encoding schema-type knowledge in a connectionist network. First, they chose 40 descriptors (e.g., door, small, sink, walls, medium) for five types of rooms (e.g., kitchen, bathroom, and bedroom). To get the basic data to construct the network they asked subjects to judge whether each descriptor characterised an example of a room type they were asked to imagine (e.g., a kitchen). When they built a network that reflected this information, they found that when activation was kept high in the sink unit and then some other unit (e.g., oven), the network settled into a state with high activation in units that corresponded to the typical features of a kitchen (e.g., coffee-pot, cupboard, refrigerator). Similarly, runs starting with other objects resulted in the emergence of descriptors for other prototypical rooms.

This connectionist work could solve the problem of the unprincipled nature of schema theories in that it promises to specify a means by which schemata acquire their contents. Ironically, it does this without having to specify these schematic contents.

## WHAT IS AN IMAGE? SOME EVIDENCE

The first half of this chapter has dealt with propositional representations and the ways they have been used to represent relations and events. In the latter half of the chapter we turn to analogical representations, specifically visual images, to consider how they have been studied in the literature.

Historically, visual imagery has been studied for a long time. Over 2000 years ago, Aristotle regarded imagery as the main medium of thought. Furthermore, orators in ancient Greece used imagery-based, mnemonic techniques to memorise speeches (see Yates, 1966); a technique that is still used today as an aid to improving one's memory. This interest in imagery can be traced in a continuous line through philosophers, like Bishop Berkeley at Trinity College Dublin, to the 19th-century research of Galton (see Mandler & Mandler, 1964). Galton (1883) distributed a questionnaire among his eminent scientific colleagues, asking them to, for example, imagine their breakfast table that morning. Surprisingly enough, several reported no conscious mental imagery at all.

As in Galton's studies, much of this early research relied on the use of introspective evidence. During the behaviourist era, when introspection fell into disrepute and mental representations were in a sense "banned", research on imagery lay fallow for a number of years. However, with the emergence of cognitive science, the study of mental representations once again became respectable. The main motivation behind this push was the perceived necessity to be representationally precise about the possible cognitive mechanisms.

Nowadays, many researchers are working on the structure of imagery. In this section, we report on three sets of studies which illustrate several important properties of mental images. First, studies on *mental rotation* show how people can rotate visual images. Second, studies on *image scanning* give us some idea of how people can "mentally scan" a visual image. Third are studies on *re-interpreting* the images of ambiguous figures.

## Mental rotation

In a series of experiments the mental rotation of a variety of imaged objects has been examined (e.g., Cooper, 1975; Cooper & Podgorny, 1976; Cooper & Shepard, 1973; Shepard, 1978 for a review; Shepard & Metzler, 1971). For example, Cooper and Shepard presented subjects with alphanumeric items in either their normal form or in reversed, mirror-image form (see Figure 9.6). In the experiment subjects were asked to judge whether a test figure was the normal or reversed version of the standard figure. The test figures were presented in a number of different orientations (see Figure 9.6). The main result was that the farther the test figure was rotated from the upright standard

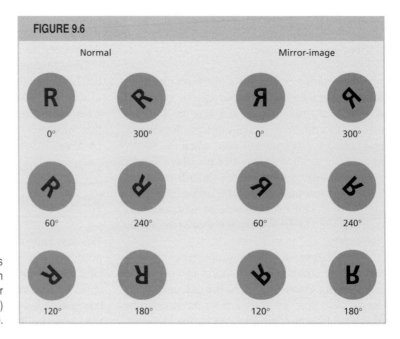

**FIGURE 9.6**

Normal                                          Mirror-image

0°        300°                          0°        300°

60°        240°                          60°        240°

120°        180°                          120°        180°

The different degrees of rotations performed on the materials in Cooper and Shepard (1973) for mirror-imaged letters (on the right) and normal letters (on the left).

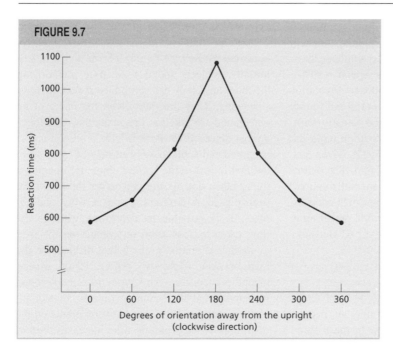

**FIGURE 9.7**

The mean time to decide whether a visual stimulus was in the normal or mirror-image version as a function of orientation. Data from Cooper and Shepard (1973).

figure, the more time subjects took to make their decisions (see Figure 9.7). These experiments have been carried out on a variety of different objects, indicating that there was some generality to the findings; for instance, digits, letters, or block-like forms have been used. (For more recent research on mental rotation see Cohen & Kubovy, 1993; Takano, 1989; Tarr & Pinker, 1989.)

The impression we get from these experiments is that visual images have all the attributes of actual objects in the world. That is, that they take up some form of mental space in the same way that physical objects take up physical space in the world—that these objects are mentally moved or rotated in the same way that objects in the world are manipulated (see later sub-section on re-interpretation). In short, the image seems to be some "quasi-spatial simulacrum of the 3-D object" (see Boden, 1988). This view, however, is not wholly justified as there are conditions under which mental rotation effects differ from physical rotation. If the imagined object becomes more complex subjects are less able to make correct judgements about its appearance when rotated (Rock, 1973). Such a problem would not arise in the physical rotation of a physical object.

Similarly, people's capacity to imagine rotated objects (even simple cubes) depends crucially on the description of the object they implicitly adopt (Hinton, 1979; Boden, 1988, and later section on re-interpreting images). Hinton (1979) provides a practical demonstration of this proposal. You are asked to imagine a cube placed squarely on a shelf with its base level with your eyes. Imagine taking hold of the bottom corner that is nearest your left hand with your left hand, and the top corner that is furthest away from your left hand with your right hand, taking the cube from the shelf and holding it so that your right hand is vertically above your left. What will be the location of the remaining corners? Most subjects tend to reply that they will form a square along the "equator" of the cube. In fact, the middle edge of the cube is not horizontal but forms a zig zag. This occurs because one does not take the image of the cube (as it is in reality) and rotate it, rather one is working off some less elaborate, structural description.

More recently, the focus of research on mental rotation has tended to concentrate on its relationship to visual processing and neurological correlates (see Gill, O'Boyle, & Hathaway, 1998; Harris, Egan, Paxinos, & Watson, 1998). Mental rotation appears to be important in controlling eye movements (saccades) suggesting the interdependence of visual and imagery-based processing (see later section on Kosslyn's theory). de Sperati (1999) instructed subjects to make saccades in directions different from that of a visual stimulus and found that the saccade latency increased linearly with the amount of directional transformation imposed between the stimulus and the response. Given this evidence, it is not surprising to find that motor processes are also implicated in mental rotation, found using a dual task paradigm in which subjects had to mentally rotate an image while performing a motor rotation (Wexler, Kosslyn, & Berthoz, 1998).

## Image scanning

Image scanning studies give us another insight into the nature of mental images. In these studies, subjects usually have to mentally scan an imaged map (e.g., Kosslyn, Ball, & Reiser, 1978).

Typically, in these experiments subjects are given a fictitious map of an island with landmarks indicated by Xs (see Figure 9.8 for an example). Initially, subjects spend some time memorising the map, until they can reproduce it accurately as a drawing. They are then given the name of an object, and are asked to image the map and focus on that object. Five seconds later, a second object is named and subjects are instructed to scan from the first object to the second object by imaging a flying black dot. As the objects on the map have been placed at different distances from one another, it is possible to determine whether the time taken to scan from one object on the map to another is related to the actual distance on the map between these two points. Using experimental procedures of this type, it has been found repeatedly that the scanning time is related linearly to the actual distance between points on the map; that is, the scanning time increases proportionately with the actual distance between two points. This result lends support to the view that

**FIGURE 9.8**

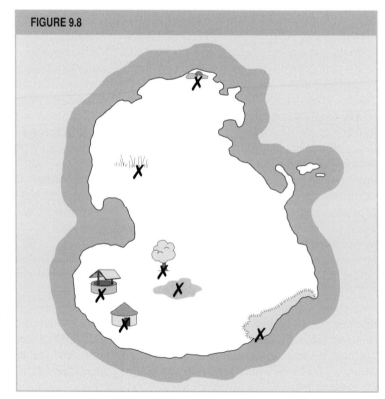

An example of the materials used in mental scanning experiments. Subjects had to image a black dot moving from one point on the map to another (points indicated by the x-ed features). Adapted from *Ghosts in the mind's machine: Creating and using images in the brain* by Stephen Kosslyn. Reproduced by permission of the author. Copyright © 1983 by Stephen M. Kosslyn.

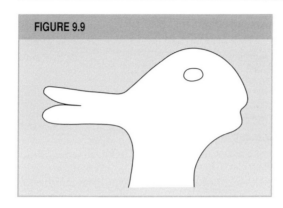

**FIGURE 9.9**

A sample of an ambiguous figure from Chambers and Reisberg's (1985) study. It can be seen as either a duck or a rabbit. Copyright © 1985 by the American Psychological Association. Reprinted with permission.

images have special, spatial properties that are analogous to those of objects and activities in the world.

However, there is a worry about these results (see Baddeley, 1986; Intos-Peterson, 1983). It is expressed succinctly by Baddeley (1986) when he says that "I have a nagging concern that implicitly, much of the experimental work in this field consists of instructing the subject to behave as if he were seeing something in the outside world . . . Whether such results tell us how the system works, or indeed tell us much about the phenomenology, I am as yet uncertain" (p. 130). This matter has been the subject of much debate (see 1999 special issue of *Cahier de Psychologie Cognitive*, 18:4). Although several alternative accounts, such as Baddley's, have been proposed, it has been argued convincingly that there is still a strong empirical basis for accepting that image-scanning experiments do indeed reflect differences in imagery rather than something else (Denis & Cocude, 1999; Denis & Kosslyn, 1999).

### Re-interpreting images of ambiguous figures

Recently, there has been considerable interest in how people re-interpret visual images of ambiguous figures (see Figure 9.9). Chambers and Reisberg (1985) presented subjects with ambiguous figures, like the duck/rabbit, that can be inter-

preted in different ways; for example, as a rabbit facing to the right or a duck facing to the left. Subjects who viewed a figure for five seconds were asked to image it before it was taken away. Then, still imaging it, they were asked to give a second interpretation of the figure. In spite of several different interventions to aid subjects, none of them could produce another interpretation of the figure. However, the same subjects could draw their image of the figure and having drawn it, could produce a re-interpretation of it.

This finding suggests that there is some propositional code that influences the construction of the image, to such an extent that details needed for the re-interpretation are omitted. As Chambers and Reisberg (1992) put it: "What an image depicts depends on what it means" (p. 146). However, these results also show that images do occur in a special medium, a medium that represents images at different levels of resolution. For instance, other research has shown that the definition of the image towards the "face" of the figure is better than at the "back" of the figure (see Brandimonte & Gerbino, 1993; Chambers & Reisberg, 1992; Peterson, Kihlstrom, Rose, & Glinsky, 1992). However, recent work has shown that this conclusion does not always hold, that with specific training and instructions it is impossible to help people re-interpret images (Brandimonte & Gerbino, 1993; Peterson et al., 1992).

## PROPOSITIONS VERSUS IMAGES

Even in our initial description of the nature of imagery, it was hard not to mention the idea that there are propositional aspects to imagery. Some years ago, this conflict between propositions and images became the subject of considerable debate (see Anderson, 1978; Bannon, 1981; Pylyshyn, 1973, 1979, 1981, 1984). We will not rake over the embers of this debate here (see Eysenck & Keane, 1995, Chapter 9, for details; also Kosslyn, 1994). The upshot of this has been that images are a distinct representational format with distinct functional significance over and above propositional representations (later, in Kosslyn's theory

**Panel 9.2:   Paivio's dual-coding theory**

- Two basic independent but interconnected coding or symbolic systems underlie human cognition: a non-verbal system and a verbal system.
- Both systems are specialised for encoding, organising, storing, and retrieving distinct types of information.
- The non-verbal (or imagery) system is specialised for processing non-verbal objects and events (i.e. processing spatial and synchronous information) and thus enters into tasks like the analysis of scenes and the generation of mental images.
- The verbal system is specialised for dealing with linguistic information and is largely implicated in the processing of language; because of the serial nature of language it is specialised for sequential processing.
- Both systems are further sub-divided into several sensorimotor sub-systems (visual, auditory, and haptic).
- Both systems have basic representational units: *logogens* for the verbal system and *imagens* for the non-verbal system that come in modality-specific versions in each of the sensorimotor sub-systems.
- The two symbolic systems are interconnected by referential links between logogens and imagens.

of imagery, we will see how the two might relate). In this section, we will present an empirically driven account for the argument, made by Allan Paivio, that propositions and images are distinct coding systems.

## Paivio's dual-coding theory

Allan Paivio's dual-coding theory (see Paivio, 1971, 1979, 1983, 1986, 1991) is devoted to determining the minimal basic differences between imagistic and propositional representations, grounded in empirical data from a large corpus of experiments. The basic proposals of the theory are shown in Panel 9.2.

Stated simply, the essence of dual-coding theory is that there are two distinct systems for the representation and processing of information. A verbal system deals with linguistic information and stores it in an appropriate verbal form. A separate non-verbal system carries out image-based processing and representation (see Figure 9.10). Each of these systems is further divided into sub-systems that process either verbal or non-verbal information in the different modalities (i.e., vision, audition, tactile, taste, smell). However, it should be noted that there are no corresponding representations for taste and smell in the verbal system (see Table 9.5).

Within a particular sub-system when, for example, a spoken word is processed it is identified by a logogen for the auditory sound of the word. The concept of a logogen comes from Morton's (1969, 1979) theories of word recognition. Paivio

(1986) characterises a *logogen* as a modality-specific unit that "can function as an integrated, informational structure or as a response generator" (p. 66): for example, there may be logogens for the word "snow". Logogens are modality-specific, in the sense that there are separate logogens for identifying the spoken sound "snow" and its visual form (i.e., the letters "s-n-o-w"). The parallel to logogens in the non-verbal system are *imagens*. Imagens are basic units that identify and represent images, in the different sensorimotor modalities. The important point to note about logogens and imagens is that they allow the theorist to posit a processing unit that identifies or represents a particular item (i.e., an image of a dog or a particular word) without having to specify the internal workings of this processing unit or the detailed representation of the item being processed. This lack of specification is one criticism of Paivio's work, although it is a deficit that is compensated for by later computational theories (like Kosslyn's, 1980, 1994).

The verbal and non-verbal systems communicate in a functional fashion via relations between imagens and logogens. The simplest case of such a relation is the referential link between an object and its name. That is, if you see a visual object (e.g., a dog runs by) it would be recognised by an imagen and a link between this imagen and an auditory logogen for the word "dog" may activate the word "dog". Thus, the links between these basic units constitute the fundamental ways in which the sub-parts of the two symbolic systems are interconnected.

**FIGURE 9.10**

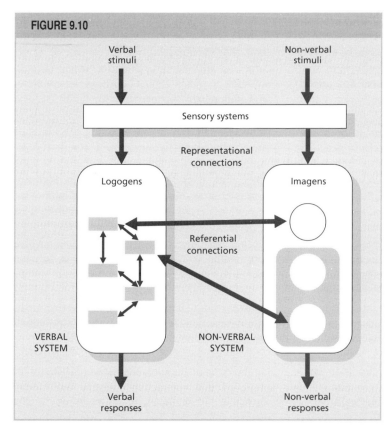

A schematic outline of the major components of dual-coding theory. The two main symbolic systems—the verbal and non-verbal systems—are connected to distinct input and output systems. Within the two systems are associative structures (involving logogens and imagens) that are linked to one another by referential connections. Reproduced with permission from *Mental representations: A dual coding approach*, by Allan Paivio, 1986, Oxford University Press.

**TABLE 9.5**

The relationship between symbolic and sensorimotor systems and examples of the types of information represented in each sub-system in Paivio's dual-coding theory

| | Symbolic systems | |
| Sensorimotor system | Verbal | Non-verbal |
| --- | --- | --- |
| Visual | Visual words | Visual objects |
| Auditory | Auditory words | Environmental sounds |
| Haptic | Writing patterns | 'Feel' of objects |
| Taste | – | Taste memories |
| Smell | – | Olfactory memories |

## Evidence for dual-coding theory

Evidence for dual-coding theory has been provided in a number of distinct task areas: for instance, in memory tasks, in neuropsychological studies, and in problem solving. These studies tend to show that either the two symbolic systems operate in an independent fashion or that they produce joint effects, depending on specific circumstances. For example, an experiment might show that memory for words is quite distinct from memory for pictures, or that memory is enhanced when something is encoded in *both* pictures *and* words. Consider three classic cases from memory experiments designed to test the theory: the differences between recalling pictures and words, the effects of word imaging and concreteness, and repetition effects.

### Effects of dual codes on free recall

Consider an experiment in which subjects are given either a set of pictures or a list of words to memorise. If the pictures are of common objects then subjects are likely to name them spontaneously while memorising them (see Paivio, 1971). So, people should encode them using both verbal and non-verbal systems. In contrast, the words are more likely to be memorised using the verbal system alone (assuming that subjects do not spontaneously image the objects referred to by the words). Memory for pictures should, therefore, be better than that for words because of the joint influence of both systems in the former case. Paivio (1971) found that pictures were remembered, in both free-recall and recognition tasks, more readily than words. In fact, pictures are recalled so much more easily than words that Paivio has proposed that the image code is mnemonically superior to the verbal code, although exactly why this should be so is not clear.

These joint effects are not only found for pictures and words. Initial results indicated that they could also be found between different classes of words. Some words are concrete and evoke images more readily than other words. If words are concrete, in the sense of denoting things that can be perceived by one of the sense modalities, rather than abstract, they appear to be retrieved more easily (see Paivio, Yuille, & Madigan, 1968, for evidence of this). As in the case of the picture–word differences, words that are rated as being high in their image-evoking value or concreteness (or both) are likely to be encoded using two codes rather than just one (for reviews of the results of item-memory tasks see Cornoldi & Paivio, 1982; Richardson, 1999). So, again there seems to be a joint contribution to performance when both systems are involved in the task.

However, there is some controversy on the dual-code explanation of recall differences for concrete and abstract words. Part of the problem is that the results are of a correlational nature, they merely show that the imagibility/concreteness of words *correlates* with good recall performance. They do not show a causal connection between concreteness and recall. We can test for such a causal connection by varying the instructions given to subjects when they are memorising the words. If you employ interactive-imagery instructions (e.g., form images depicting objects interacting in some way), then it is typically found that performance is improved for concrete material but not for abstract materials (see Richardson, 1999). This is perfectly consistent with dual-coding theory because the imagery instructions should involve both coding systems for the concrete words but not for the abstract words.

Unfortunately, similar instructions that do not involve imaging have similar effects; verbal mediation instructions (e.g., form short phrases including the list of items) result in concrete materials being recalled more readily than abstract materials. On the basis of these results, Bower (1970, 1972) proposed that interactive imagery and verbal mediation instructions were both effective in that they increased the organisation and cohesion of the to-be-remembered information. To test this hypothesis, Bower presented subjects with pairs of concrete words using three different types of instructions for different groups: interactive-imagery instructions, separation-imagery instructions (i.e., construct an image of two objects separated in space), or instructions to memorise by rote. On a subsequent cued-recall task, the interactive-imagery subjects performed much better than the separation-imagery subjects, who in turn performed no better than subjects instructed to use rote memorisation. In other words, interactive imagery instructions are effective because they enhance relational organisation. So, recall differences between concrete and abstract words create some difficulties for Paivio's theory. However, we should point out that Paivio has gone some way towards accounting for these results by including organisational assumptions within each of his symbolic systems, which account for differences between interactive-imagery and separation-imagery instructions (see Paivio, 1986, Chapters 4 and

8). Having said this, the issue has not been fully resolved. Recent research has shown that concreteness effects are not due solely to the effects of imagery but may also involve factors like distinctiveness and relational information (see Marschark & Cornoldi, 1990; Marschark & Hunt, 1989; Marschark & Surian, 1992; Plaut & Shallice, 1993). Furthermore, in a review of the literature, Marschark, Richman, Yuille, and Hunt (1987) have rejected the proposal that imaginal codes are stored in long-term memory, arguing instead that verbal and imaginal processing systems operate on a more generic, conceptual memory.

Studies of free recall also support the additivity and functional independence of the two systems (Paivio, 1975; Paivio & Csapo, 1973). In these experiments, subjects were shown a series of concrete nouns and asked to either image to the presented noun or to pronounce it. During the five-second intervals between items they were asked to rate the difficulty of imaging or pronouncing the word. In one manipulation, subjects were presented with a given word repeatedly. In some cases, the repetition encouraged dual coding, in that subjects had to image it on one occurrence and pronounce it on the next. In other cases, the repetition merely promoted encoding in a single code when subjects either imaged or pronounced the word again. After doing this task, without prior warning, subjects were asked to recall the presented words.

Several interesting results were found to support dual-coding theory. First, the probability of imaged words being recalled was twice as high as that for pronounced words, indicating the superiority of non-verbal codes in recall. Second, the imagery-instructions raised the level of recall to the same high level that is normally seen for the encoding of pictures under comparable conditions. Third, in the conditions that predicted dual coding, there was an statistically additive effect on recall relative to recall levels calculated for once-presented items that had been imaged or pronounced. Fourth, in contrast to these results, when a repeated word was encoded in the same way on each presentation, the massed repetitions did not produce similar additive effects (see Figure 9.11).

## Interference within a single system

Paivio's theory sees the routes taken by perception and imagery as basically the same. For example, in talking about the non-verbal system he says that it is responsible both for the cognitive task of forming visual images and the perceptual task of scene-analysis. Therefore, any findings that

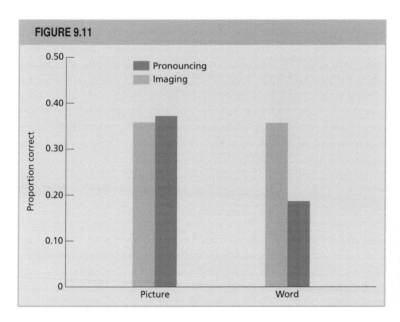

FIGURE 9.11

The relative proportions of correct responses when subjects repeatedly pronounced or imaged pictures or words in a free-recall task. Adapted from Paivio and Csapo (1973).

demonstrate interference between perceptual and imagery tasks are a source of further evidence for the theory. That is, if performance on a perceptual task is disrupted by carrying out an imagery task, and vice versa, it is likely that both tasks are using related processing components. Such interference has been found on a regular basis. For example, Segal and Fusella (1970) asked subjects to form both visual and auditory images and then asked them to perform a visual or auditory detection task. They found that auditory images interfered more with the detection of auditory signals and visual images interfered more with visual detection. As there was some interference in all conditions it seems reasonable to conclude that there is a generalised effect of mental imagery on perceptual sensitivity in addition to a large modality-specific effect.

However, it is not enough to simply demonstrate interference. One needs to pin-point the specific processes that are responsible for the interference and also, if possible, to show how perceptual and image-based processing differ. More detailed evidence of this sort has been found in a task used by Baddeley, Grant, Wight, and Thomson (1975). In this experiment, subjects listened to a description of locations of digits within a matrix and were then asked to reproduce the matrix. The description was either hard or easy to visualise. The interfering task involved a pursuit rotor (i.e., visually tracking a light moving along a circular track). This task results in a distinct type of interference—performance on easily visualised messages is retarded, while the non-visualisable message is unaffected—but the interference is not due specifically to the perceptual processes involved in vision. Baddeley and Lieberman (1980) have shown that if the concurrent task is specifically visual (e.g., the judgement of brightness), rather than visual and spatial (as the pursuit rotor seems to be) then the interference effects disappear. Similarly, when the concurrent task is purely spatial (i.e., when blindfolded subjects were asked to point at a moving pendulum on the basis of auditory feedback) the pattern of interference found reproduces the effects found in the original Baddeley et al. experiment. In summary, it appears that the recall of visualisable (or easily imagined)

messages of the kind used in these experiments is interfered with by spatial processing rather than by visual processing, indicating that these spatial processes are somehow shared by perceptual and image-based processing within the non-verbal system (see Logie & Baddeley, 1989, for a review). However, there are also cases in which interference from purely visual processing can be achieved (see Richardson, 1999, and Wexler et al., 1998, for recent work).

These experiments show that Paivio's interference predictions really rest on the assumption that visual imagery involves visual rather than spatial representations. However, Farah, Hammond, Levine, and Calvanio (1988) have suggested that it is a mistake to argue that imagery is either visual *or* spatial. Rather they have shown, using neuropsychological evidence, that imagery is *both* visual and spatial and taps into distinct visual and spatial representations.

## Neuropsychological evidence for dual coding

A natural question that arises about Paivio's theory is whether there is neuropsychological evidence for the localisation of the two symbolic systems within the brain. For instance, for most people the left hemisphere is implicated in tasks that involve the processing of verbal material. In contrast, the right hemisphere tends to be used in tasks that are of a non-verbal nature (e.g., face identification, memory for faces, and recognising non-verbal sounds). Furthermore, within each hemisphere there seems to be some localisation for the sensorimotor sub-systems: visual, auditory, and tactile (see Cohen, 1983). While dual-coding theory posits distinct symbolic systems, Paivio does not maintain that these distinct systems reside in distinct hemispheres, although the systems are localised to some extent (for evidence against this view see, e.g., Zaidel, 1976).

There is some evidence for localisation differences on concrete and abstract words that disrupt a simple left–right division. Word recognition studies, using tachistoscopes, have shown that there are hemispheric differences in the processing of concrete and abstract words (see Paivio, 1986,

Chapter 12; Johnson, Paivio, & Clark, 1996). Typically, abstract words that are presented to the right-visual-field, and hence are processed by the left hemisphere, are recognised more often than those presented to the left-visual-field (i.e., processed by the right hemisphere). However, concrete words are recognised equally well irrespective of the visual field (and hence the hemisphere) to which they are presented. It should be pointed out that these findings have not been consistent, although there is a tendency for the performance asymmetries to be less consistent for concrete than for abstract words (Boles, 1983). More recently, detailed studies using event-related potentials and fMRI have confirmed many aspects of these proposals (see Holcomb, Kounios, Anderson, & West, 1999; Kiehl et al., 1999).

Converging evidence also comes from so-called deep-dyslexic patients, who have widespread lesions in the left hemisphere. Generally, they have greater difficulty reading abstract, low-imagery words than concrete high-imagery words (see Coltheart, Patterson, & Marshall, 1980; Paivio & te Linde, 1982). Plaut and Shallice (1993) have modelled these concrete–abstract effects by lesioning a connectionist net (see also Hinton & Shallice, 1991). However, the effects were modelled by representing concrete concepts with more features than abstract concepts, rather than using imagery representations. Tyler and Moss's (1997) results present some problems for this proposal because they have found a patient with a selective problem understanding the meaning of abstract words in a specific modality (i.e., auditory modality). We shall see next, in the presentation of Kosslyn's theory, that some more recent evidence presents a clearer picture for what might be happening

in both hemispheres (see Farah, 1984; Kosslyn, 1987).

## KOSSLYN'S COMPUTATIONAL MODEL OF IMAGERY

The work of Stephen Kosslyn and his associates tested and developed a theory that can be viewed as a response to the early criticisms of imagery theory. More recently, Kosslyn has made a strong claim for the overlap between the processes of visual perception and imagery (see also Chapter 4). In his 1994 book, *Image & Brain*, Kosslyn lays out a full theory of visual perception which he then maps onto his earlier 1980 theory of imagery. For the most part, the processes he originally proposed to account for imagery are now re-used (with some minor modifications) to deal with perception too. An important part of this work is the research on the neurological basis of both abilities (see later section on Neuropsychology). For simplicity's sake, we summarise the 1980 theory here (see Kosslyn, 1994, Chapter 11, for more detail).

### The theory and model

Kosslyn's theory has been specified in a computational model and is roughly summarised in Panel 9.3 (see also Figure 9.12; Kosslyn, 1980, 1981, 1987, 1994; Kosslyn & Shwartz, 1977).

Consider the basic task of generating an image of a duck. The theory maintains that several structures and processes are involved: the spatial medium in which the duck is to be represented,

---

**Panel 9.3:  Kosslyn's theory of imagery**
- Visual images are represented in a special, spatial medium.
- The spatial medium has four essential properties: (i) it functions as a space, with limited extent, it has a specified shape and a capacity to depict spatial relations; (ii) its area of highest resolution is at its centre; (iii) the medium has a grain that obscures details on "small" images; (iv) once the image is generated in the medium it begins to fade.
- Long-term memory contains two forms of data structures: image files and propositional files. Image files contain stored information about how images are represented in the spatial medium and have an analogical format. Propositional files contain information about the parts of objects, how these parts are related to one another and are in a propositional format. Propositional files and image files are often linked together.
- A variety of processes use image files, propositional files, and the spatial medium in order to generate, interpret, and transform images.

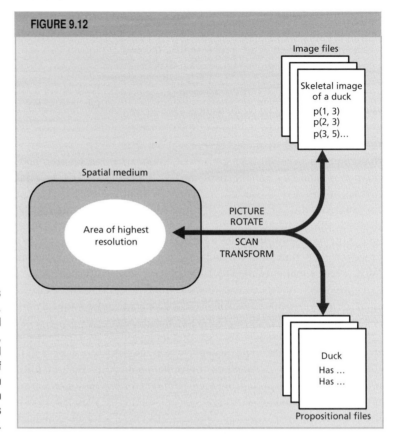

**FIGURE 9.12**

Image files

Skeletal image
of a duck
p(1, 3)
p(2, 3)
p(3, 5)...

Spatial medium

PICTURE
ROTATE

Area of highest
resolution

SCAN
TRANSFORM

Duck
Has ...
Has ...

Propositional files

Schematic diagram of Kosslyn's computational model of imagery. Images are constructed and manipulated (using the PICTURE, ROTATE, SCAN, and TRANSFORM processes) in the highest area of resolution in the spatial medium using the information stored in image files and propositional files in long-term memory.

the propositional and image files that store the knowledge about the duck, and the processes that generate the image in the medium from these files.

## The spatial medium

The spatial medium in which the duck is to be represented is modelled as a television screen in Kosslyn's computational model (see Kosslyn & Shwartz, 1977). That is, the medium has a surface that can be divided up into dots or pixels each of which can be characterised by co-ordinates indicating where a dot is on the screen. The theory mentions four properties of this spatial medium. First, that it functions as a space, in the sense that it preserves the spatial relations of the objects it represents. So, if an object is represented in the extreme top left of this space and another object in the extreme bottom left, then the relative position of the two objects will be preserved (i.e., the

second object will be beneath the first object). The spatial medium is also like a physical space in that it has a limited extent and is bounded. If images move too far in any direction they will overflow the medium, like a slide projected on a screen. Finally, the space has a definite shape; while the central area of highest resolution is roughly circular, the medium becomes more oblong at the periphery.

The second main attribute of this spatial medium is that it does not necessarily represent images at a uniform resolution. Rather, at the centre of the medium, an image is represented at its highest resolution. From there out it begins to get fuzzier. This is akin to the visual field which also has its highest resolution at the centre of the scene being viewed.

Third, the medium has a grain. The grain of a photograph or a VDU refers to the size of the basic dots of colour that make it up. If these dots

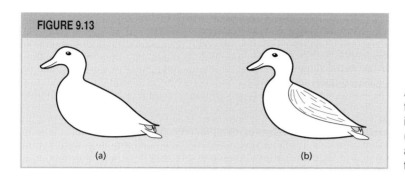

**FIGURE 9.13**

(a)    (b)

According to Kosslyn's theory, images are constructed in parts, so one might first form (a) a skeletal image of a duck, and then (b) add a wing part to this initial skeletal image.

are very large then the detail one can represent is limited, whereas if the dots are very small more detailed images can be represented. A good example of this is the comparison between a conventional Teletype computer screen and a typical PC monitor. The latter has the grain to depict different letter fonts and pictures in a manner that is impossible on the Teletype screen. Thus, the grain of the spatial medium determines what can and cannot be represented clearly. It also means that when an image is reduced in size then parts of it may disappear, because the grain may not be detailed enough to represent these parts. Specifically, a part of the larger image that was represented by a configuration of dots may, when the image is reduced, be represented by a single dot.

Finally, as soon as an image is generated in the medium it begins to fade and so, if the image is to be maintained in the medium, it needs to be regenerated or refreshed. A similar type of fading occurs with after-images in the visual system. When we look at bright lights and then close our eyes, we see after-images caused by the over-stimulation of our retinal cells. Although these after-images are not the same as visual images, they have this same quality of rapidly fading after they first appear.

### Image and propositional files

Returning to our duck, we have a fair idea of where she is represented but not how we come to represent her. In Kosslyn's computational model it is assumed that there are image files that represent the co-ordinates of dot-like points in the spatial medium. These image files can represent a whole object or various parts of an object. Specifically, some image files characterise a *skeletal image* that depicts the basic shape of the object, but lacks many of the object's details. These detailed parts of images may be represented in other image files, for reasons that will become apparent later. In terms of our example, the image in Figure 9.13a is a rough, skeletal image of the duck, while Figure 9.13b shows the addition of one of her parts (i.e., the wings).

The propositional files list the properties of ducks (e.g., HAS_WINGS, HAS_FEET) and the relationships between these properties and a "foundation part" of the duck (i.e., its body). The *foundation part* is that part that is central to the representation of the object and will be linked to the skeletal image file for the object. The propositional file for the duck might, thus, contain entries that relate the wing parts of the duck to the foundation part: for example, WINGS LOCATION ON_EITHER_SIDE BODY indicating that the wings are on either side of the body. Each of these parts would have a corresponding image file that contains the basic material for constructing the image of a given part in the spatial medium. Propositional files also contain more information about the rough size category of the object (e.g., very small, small, large, enormous) and information about superordinate categories of the objects (e.g., in the duck case, that BIRD would be the most likely superordinate; see Kosslyn, 1980, 1983, for details; and Chapter 10).

The information in the propositional files is connected to the image files. So, for example, the foundation part in the propositional file has a link or pointer to the image file that contains the skeletal image of the object. Similarly, the detailed parts of the object have links to image files containing images of these parts. For example, the wings-part is linked to an image file containing co-ordinate information for the construction of an image of a wing.

### Imaging processes

Finally, when someone is asked to image a duck several processes use the propositional and image files to generate an image of the duck in the spatial medium. In the model, the main IMAGE process involves three sub-processes: PICTURE, FIND, and PUT. When asked to image, the IMAGE process first checks to see whether the object (i.e., the duck) mentioned in the instructions has, in its propositional-file definition, a reference to a skeletal-image file. If such a file is present then the PICTURE process takes the information about the co-ordinates of the image and represents it in the spatial medium (see Figure 9.13a). Unless the location or size of the image is specified (e.g., image a giant duck), the image is generated in the part of the spatial medium with the highest resolution and at a size that fills this region. The PUT process directs the PICTURE process to place the remaining image-parts at the appropriate locations on the skeletal image. For example, PUT might use the propositional information about the location of the wings to add them to the side of the skeletal image of the body. PUT, however, must use FIND to locate the objects or parts already in the image to which the new, to-be-imaged parts can be related. When the appropriate size and location of the wings are known they are added to the image (see Figure 9.13b).

In cases where more specific instructions are given, like "Does the duck have a rounded beak?" or "Image a fly on the tip of the duck's wing, up close" or "Rotate the duck 180 degrees", further processes called SCAN, LOOKFOR, PAN, ZOOM, and ROTATE operate on the image (see Kosslyn, 1983, Chapter 7; and Kosslyn, 1980, for more details). The names of these processes are self-explanatory and each one has been modelled as a set of specified procedures in the model that, for instance, SCAN and ROTATE images. These processes are used to explain the results of the mental scanning and mental rotation studies.

## Empirical evidence for Kosslyn's theory

Kosslyn's work has several important and welcome features. First, by specifying computationally the processes and representations involved in imagery, he avoids the vagueness criticism. Second, the claims he makes for the properties of imagery are clear. Third, many of these detailed proposals are supported by empirical evidence. Consider some of the evidence for his proposals on limited extent and granularity, the fading of images and the area of high resolution in the spatial medium.

### The image tracing task

Kosslyn (1975, 1976, 1980) has used an "image tracing task" to test his proposals on the limited extent of the spatial medium and on granularity. As in the duck example, in these experiments subjects were asked to image an object and then to try to "see" some property of the imaged object (e.g., "Can you 'see' the duck's beak?"). The critical manipulation in the experiment was the context in which the animal was imaged. The "target" animal (e.g., a rabbit) was imaged along with another animal that was either much larger or much smaller (i.e., an elephant and a fly, respectively). The rationale here was that in the case where the elephant and the rabbit were imaged together, the elephant would take up most of the space and as a result the rabbit would be represented as being much smaller relative to the elephant. In contrast, in the case where the fly and the rabbit were imaged together, the rabbit would take up most of the space relative to the fly (see Figure 9.14a and b). Given the hypothesis that the spatial medium has granularity, the two different images of the animal-pairs should result in differences in the "visible" properties of the rabbit. In the rabbit–elephant pair many of the rabbit's properties should be hard to "see" whereas in the rabbit–fly pair most of its properties should be easy to "see". This difficulty in "seeing" properties should translate itself into differential response

**FIGURE 9.14**

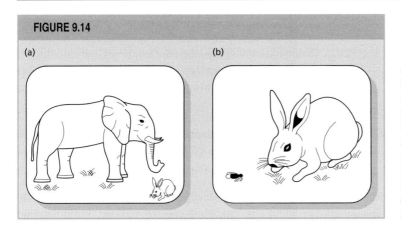

(a)    (b)

A schematic diagram of how the image of (a) an elephant and a rabbit, and (b) a fly and a rabbit might result in the rabbit being imaged at different levels of detail. Adapted from *Ghosts in the mind's machine: Creating and using images in the brain* by Stephen Kosslyn. Reproduced by permission of the author. Copyright © 1983 by Stephen M. Kosslyn.

times in deciding on the presence of a property (e.g., whether the rabbit has a pointed nose).

This is exactly what Kosslyn found in his studies. Subjects take longer to see parts of the rabbit in the rabbit–elephant pair relative to seeing the same parts in the rabbit–fly pair. Furthermore, Kosslyn noted that subjects' introspective reports suggested that they were "zooming in" to see the parts of the subjectively smaller images.

More recently, Kosslyn, Sukel, and Bly (1999) have performed further tests on the resolution of the spatial medium using a task in which subjects either viewed or visualised arrays divided into four quadrants with each quadrant containing stripes. By varying the width of the stripes in the array it was possible to create high- and low-resolution stimuli. Kosslyn et al. found that subjects made more errors in both perception and imagery when evaluating oblique patterns, with more time being taken when imaging. The results suggest that although there are common mechanisms used by both imagery and perception it is more difficult to represent high-resolution information in imagery than in perception (see also Rouw, Kosslyn, & Hamel, 1997).

### Experiments in the spatial medium

A further set of experiments by Kosslyn (1978) examined the idea of the limited spatial extent of the medium. Assume our visual field consists of a 100 degree visual arc in front of us. If we are looking at something in this visual field then at a

given distance, the object will take up a portion of this arc. If we move closer to the object and it is a large object—like a double-decker bus—then eventually it will fill completely the visual arc and may even overflow it. That is, it may stretch beyond our field of view. Kosslyn employed the same idea to test the limited extent of the spatial medium. If one assumes that the spatial medium has a limited extent and has a similar visual-image arc, then one way of measuring the size of an imaged object is in terms of the arc it subtends. At some point an object of a certain size should overflow the medium (see Figure 9.15). To test this prediction, subjects were asked to close their eyes and to image an object (usually an animal again) far away in the distance. They were then asked to "mentally walk" towards the image until they reached a point where they could see *all* the object at once (i.e., the point just prior to overflow). Finally, they were asked to estimate how far away the animal would be if they were seeing it at that subjective size. If the spatial medium has a limited extent of a constant size then the larger the object, the farther away it would seem at the point of overflow. This was the result found by Kosslyn. In general, the estimated distance of the point of overflow increases linearly with the size of the imaged object.

As we have seen throughout this book, one strong test of a theory is to see whether it is consistent with neuropsychological evidence from the study of individuals with brain injuries. As we shall see in the next section, Kosslyn's theory has

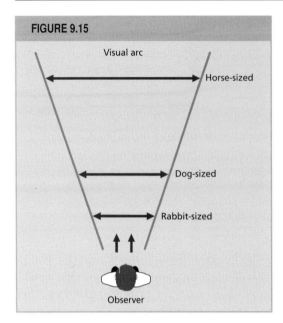

**FIGURE 9.15**

Diagram of the relative amounts of the visual arc that are taken up by different-sized animals. Adapted from *Ghosts in the mind's machine: Creating and using images in the brain* by Stephen Kosslyn. Reproduced by permission of the author. Copyright © 1983 by Stephen M. Kosslyn.

also been applied to understanding the patterns of behaviour manifested by brain-damaged patients.

## THE NEUROPSYCHOLOGY OF VISUAL IMAGERY

Farah (1984) carried out a review of imagery deficits following brain injuries using Kosslyn's theory to understand these deficits. She abstracted the general component processes and structures of the theory and analysed various test tasks in terms of them. She then showed that different deficiencies in brain-damaged patients could be traced to problems with particular components. For instance, Kosslyn's theory posits a process that generates images from long-term memory representations, so if this process is damaged then the patient should not be able to describe the appearance of objects from memory or draw objects from memory. However, the same patient should be able to recognise and draw visually presented objects because these involve component processes other than those used in image generation. Several studies have reported patients with this pattern of behaviour (e.g., Lyman, Kwan, & Chao, 1938; Nielsen, 1946).

Traditionally, imagery has been viewed as being a right hemisphere function (see Ehrlichman & Barrett, 1983, for a review). Farah challenged this view in arguing that at least one component—the imagery generation component—appears to be a left hemisphere function (see Farah, 1984; Farah, Peronnet, Gonon, & Giard, 1988; Kosslyn, 1987; Kosslyn, Holtzmann, Farah, & Gazzaniga, 1985). In a study involving split-brain patients, Farah, Gazzaniga, Holtzman, and Kosslyn (1985) have shown that the disconnected left hemisphere could perform a task requiring image generation when the right hemisphere could not; and that the right hemisphere could be shown to have all the components of the imagery task except for image generation (see also Kosslyn et al., 1985). This work has also dealt with the link between the imagery system and visual system (see Farah, 1988; Farah, Weisberg, Monheit, & Peronnet, 1990).

There has been considerable debate about the lateralisation of imagery processes (see Corballis, 1989; Farah, 1988; Goldberg, 1989; Kosslyn, 1987; Sargent, 1990). Some of this work has questioned the original evidence used by Farah (see Sargent, 1990), whereas other theorists have tried to argue that there are distinct types of imagery information involved in image generation that may arise in both hemispheres (see Kosslyn, 1987). The emerging consensus in this debate appears to be that the left hemisphere has a direct role in the generation of visual images, although the left may not be its sole preserve. Mechanisms in the right hemisphere do seem to play a role in image ROTATION (see Richardson, 1999). Both hemispheres are likely to contribute to image generation but in different ways (see D'Esposito et al., 1997; Farah, 1995; Kosslyn, Thompson, & Alpert, 1997; Tippett, 1992).

Kosslyn et al. (1993) have used PET techniques to investigate the localisation of imagery processing in the brain. They found that when subjects were instructed to close their eyes and evaluate visual mental images of uppercase letters that were either small or large, the small mental images engendered more activation in the posterior portion of the visual cortex whereas the large mental images engendered more activation in anterior portions of the visual cortex (see also Kosslyn, 1994, 1999). Continuing work in this vein has further supported these findings (D'Esposito et al., 1997; Kosslyn et al., 1997).

All of this research represents an important step from psychology into neuropsychology (see Kosslyn, 1999, for more of an overview). Apart from showing how psychological theories can include neuropsychological evidence, it also has important implications for the imagery–propositional debate. Farah (1984) has pointed out that in propositionalist terms there should be no difference between the recall and manipulation of information about the appearances of objects and information about other memory contents (e.g., historical facts or philosophical arguments). Hence, the occurrence of selective impairments to these types of information should be as likely as a selective impairment of imagery. However, specific impairments of historical ability *do not* occur but selective impairments of imagery do; moreover we can identify separate brain areas dedicated to this imagery ability.

## CONNECTIONIST REPRESENTATIONS

In most of this chapter we have concentrated on the traditional symbolic approach to mental representation (see also Chapter 1). The basic view of this approach is that human cognition is centrally dependent on the manipulation of symbolic representations by various rule-like processes. Kosslyn's imagery theory is a prime example of theorising from this viewpoint, in which rule-based processes—like IMAGE and PUT—manipulate various symbols. Even though the symbolic approach has been the dominant one within information processing psychology, some have questioned whether it is ultimately the best way to understand human cognition. These critics have highlighted some of the difficulties in the symbolic approach.

First, as we have seen in this chapter, within a symbolic tradition one has to explicitly state how mental contents are represented (whether they be images or propositions). Moreover, one has to specify how these representations are manipulated by various rules. So, even for relatively simple tasks, symbolic theories can be very complicated. When one moves away from laboratory tasks and looks at everyday tasks (like driving a car) it is sometimes difficult to envisage how such a complicated scheme could work. People can operate quite efficiently by taking multiple sources of information into account at once. Although a symbolic account might be able to account for driving, many feel that this account would be too inelegant and cumbersome. A second worry about the symbolic approach is that it has tended to avoid the question of how cognitive processes are realised in the brain. Granted, it provides evidence for the gross localisation of cognitive processes in the brain, but we are left with no idea of how these symbols are represented and manipulated at the neural level.

In response to these and other issues, in the 1980s a parallel processing approach re-emerged called *connectionism* (see Chapter 1; Ballard, 1986; Feldman & Ballard, 1982; Hinton & Anderson, 1981; Rumelhart, McClelland, & the PDP Research Group, 1986). As we saw in Chapter 1, connectionists use computational models consisting of networks of neuron-like units that have several advantages over their symbolic competitors.

As we shall see, connectionist schemes can represent information without recourse to symbolic entities like propositions; they are said to represent information sub-symbolically in *distributed representations* (see Smolensky, 1988). Second, they have the potential to model complex behaviours without recourse to large sets of explicit, propositional rules (see e.g., Rumelhart et al., 1986c; Holyoak & Thagard, 1989). Third, in their use of neuron-like processing units they suggest a more direct link to the brain (but see Smolensky, 1988). Connectionism clearly provides significant answers to many questions about human cognition. However, it is unclear how much of human cognition can be characterised in this way.

## Distributed representation: The sight and scent of a rose

The concept of a distributed representation can be illustrated by an example involving a simple network called a *pattern associator*. Within the symbolic tradition, the sight and the scent of a rose might be represented as some set of co-ordinates (for the image of the rose) or as a proposition, i.e., ROSE(x). A distributed representation does not have symbols that explicitly represent the rose but rather *stores the connection strengths between units that will allow either the scent or vision of the rose to be re-created* (see Hinton, McClelland, & Rumelhart, 1986). Consider how this is done in the simple network in Figure 9.16a.

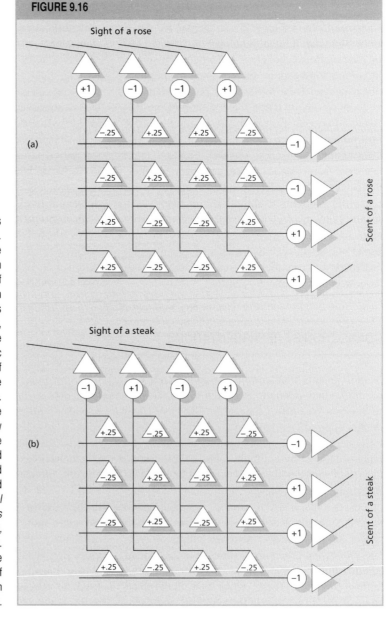

**FIGURE 9.16**

Two simple pattern associators representing different information. The example assumes that the patterns of activation in the vision units, encoding the sight of (a) a rose or (b) a steak, can be associated with the patterns of activation in olfaction units, encoding the smell of (a) a rose or (b) a steak. The synaptic connections allow the outputs of the vision units to influence the activations of the olfaction units. The synaptic weights shown in the two networks are selected to allow the pattern of activation in the olfaction units without the need for any olfactory input. Adapted from David E. Rumelhart and James L. McClelland, *Parallel distributed processing: Explorations in the microstructure of cognition, Volume 1.* The MIT Press. Copyright © 1986 by The Massachusetts Institute of Technology, reproduced with permission.

The sight and scent of the rose can be viewed as being coded in terms of simple signals in certain input cells (i.e., as pluses and minuses, see Figure 9.16). The input cells that take signals from vision are called vision units and those that take signals from the smell senses are called olfaction units. Essentially, the network is capable of associating the pattern of activation that arrives at the vision units with that arriving at the olfaction units. The distributed representation of the sight and scent of the rose is thus represented by the "matrix" of activation in the network; without recourse to any explicit symbol for representing the rose. Consider how this coding of the representation is achieved in more detail.

Figure 9.16a shows the vision and olfaction units. The sight of the rose is represented by a particular pattern of activation on the vision units (characterised by +1, −1, −1, +1), while the pattern of olfactory excitation is shown on the olfaction units (from top to bottom −1, −1, +1, +1). The effect of a single vision unit on an olfaction unit is determined by multiplying the activation of the vision unit times the strength of its link to the olfaction unit. So, all the vision units produce the output of the first olfaction unit in the following fashion:

$$
\begin{aligned}
&\text{1st Vision unit } +1 \times -.25 \text{ (1st link)} = -.25 \\
&\text{2nd Vision unit } -1 \times +.25 \text{ (2nd link)} = -.25 \\
&\text{3rd Vision unit } -1 \times +.25 \text{ (3rd link)} = -.25 \\
&\text{4th Vision unit } +1 \times -.25 \text{ (4th link)} = -.25 \\
\hline
&\text{1st Olfaction unit} \hspace{3.5cm} -1 \\
&\hspace{3cm} \text{(by summation)}
\end{aligned}
$$

In cases where the pattern associator does not learn the association, the links between the vision and olfaction units can be set so that given the vision input of +1, −1, −1, +1 the olfaction output −1, −1, +1, +1 is produced and vice versa (according to the method of combining activation just described). In this way, the pattern associator has represented the association between the sight and scent of the rose in a distributed fashion. We could also represent the sight and smell of another object by a different pattern of activation in the *same network*. For example, the sight and smell of a steak could be characterised by the vision pattern

(−1, +1, −1, +1) and the olfactory pattern (−1, +1, +1, −1); the different pattern of activation for this is shown in Figure 9.16b. Note the differences in the weights of the links in the network.

## Distributed versus local representations

Not all connectionist models use distributed representations. They also use representations similar to those used in the symbolic approach, even though the models still use networks of units. Connectionists call the latter *local representations*. The crucial difference between distributed and local representations is sometimes subtle. A *distributed representation* is one in which "the units represent small feature-like entities [and where] the pattern as a whole is the meaningful unit of analysis" (Rumelhart, Hinton, & McClelland, 1986b, p. 47). The essential tenet of the distributed scheme is that different items correspond to alternative patterns of activity in the same set of units, whereas a *local representation* has a one-unit-one-concept representation in which single units represent entire concepts or other large meaningful units.

To be clear about this distinction, consider two networks that deal with the same task domain; one of which uses a local representation and the other a distributed representation. These networks represent the mappings between the visual form of a word (i.e., c-a-t) and its meaning (i.e., small, furry, four-legged; see Figure 9.17a and 9.17b). The network in this case has three layers. A layer for identifying letters of the word (consisting of *grapheme units*, that indicate the letter and its position in the word), a middle layer, and layer that encodes the semantic units that constitute the meaning of the word (see Chapter 10 for further details on such semantic primitives; here we call them *sememe units*).

In the localist version of the model, the middle layer of the network has units that represent one word. So, a particular grapheme string activates this word unit and this activates whatever meaning is associated with it. In short, there is a one-unit-one-concept representation in the middle layer (see Figure 9.17a). In the distributed version of the network, the grapheme units feed into *word-set*

FIGURE 9.17

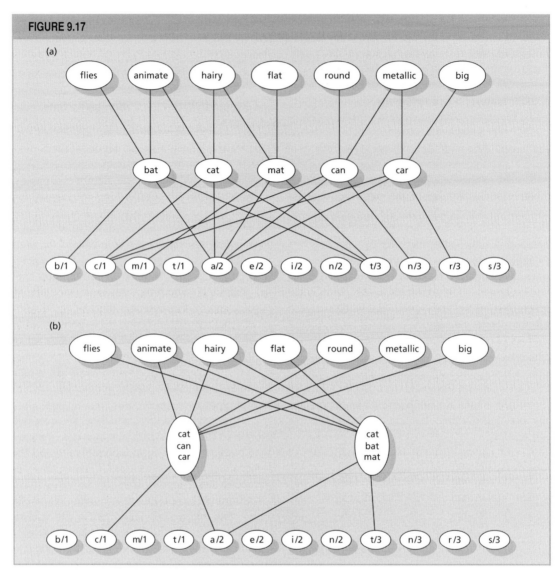

Two examples of a three-layered connectionist network. The bottom layer contains units that represent particular graphemes in particular positions within a word. The middle layer contains units that recognise complete words, and the top layer contains units that represent semantic features of the meaning of the word. Network (a) uses local representations of words in the middle layer, whereas network (b) has a middle layer that uses a more distributed representation. Each unit in the middle layer of network (b) can be activated by the graphemic representation of any one of a whole set of words. The unit then provides input to every semantic feature that occurs in the meaning of any of the words that activate it. Only those word sets containing the word "cat" are shown in network (b). Notice that the only semantic features that receive input from all these word sets are the semantic features of "cat". Adapted from David E. Rumelhart and James L. McClelland, *Parallel distributed processing: Explorations in the microstructure of cognition, Volume 1.* The MIT Press. Copyright © 1986 by The Massachusetts Institute of Technology, reproduced with permission.

*units* that in turn feed into the semantic units. A word-set unit is activated whenever the pattern of the grapheme units activate an item in that set. A set could be something like all the three-letter words beginning with CA or all the words ending in AT. So, in this distributed representation, activation goes from the grapheme units to many different word-set units and these in turn send activation to the sememe layer, to indicate uniquely which set of semantic features is associated with this particular configuration of graphemes. This representation is distributed because each word-set unit participates in the representation of many words. Stated another way, different items correspond to alternative patterns of activity in the same set of units (see Figure 9.17b).

Without wishing to be confusing, it should be noted that the local-distributed representation distinction can often be equivocal. For example, Hinton et al. (1986) admit that semantic networks that use spreading activation (see Chapters 1 and 10) are not very distinguishable from other distributed representations, even though they have units that correspond to single concepts. Similarly, it must be admitted that the word-sets in the distributed representation just described are not very feature-like entities but could be categorised as meaningful wholes. However, until more is known about the characteristics of these networks the distinction is heuristically useful.

## Distributed representations and propositions/images

The sixty-four million dollar question, which we have been ignoring until now, is "What is the relationship between distributed representations and symbolic representations?" Hinton et al. (1986) argue that these views do not contradict one another, but rather are complementary. By this they mean that the high-level representations,

like propositions, may be represented by lower-level distributed representations. However, this complementarity depends on the properties of the lower-level distributed representation being recognised as fundamental aspects of the higher-level representations.

Distributed representations have several properties that make them very attractive relative to symbolic representations. First, distributed representations are *content-addressable*. This property is an important general characteristic of human memory and refers to the fact that apparently any part of a past occurrence or scene can lead to its later retrieval from memory. For instance, you may remember your holiday on the Côte d'Azur on hearing a certain song, on smelling the aroma of ratatouille, or seeing the sun reflected in a certain way on a woman's hair. It seems that any part of the memory can reinstate all of the original memory. Similarly, in distributed representations, a partial representation of an entity is sufficient to reinstate the whole entity. For example, if we present a slight variant of the original scent of the rose (say, $-1, -1, +1, 0$ instead of $-1, -1, +1, +1$) to the network in Figure 9.16a, it will still excite the vision units in roughly the same way. Second, distributed representations allow automatic generalisation. That is, in a manner related to the content-addressibility property, patterns that are similar will produce similar responses.

In conclusion, one can view the symbolic framework as characterising the macro-structure of cognitive representation (i.e., the broad outlines of symbols and their organisation) whereas the distributed representations characterise the micro-structure of cognitive representation (see McClelland et al., 1986; Rumelhart et al., 1986c). However, the full ramifications of the relationship between the two levels requires substantial elaboration.

## CHAPTER SUMMARY

In this chapter, we have tried to cover a broad canvas in painting a picture of the what and how of mental representation and human knowlege. The *what* has concerned itself with the sorts of contents that tend to be represented; objects, relations, events, and so on. The *how* has concerned itself with the format of the representations, whether they be propositional or imagery-based. In the next chapter we delve deeper into the issue of how object concepts and categories have been researched. For now, we conclude this chapter with some summary points:

- A representation is a something that re-presents aspects of our world to us. A broad division is often made between propositional and analogical representations.
- Propositional representations are discrete, explicit, are combined according to rules, and are abstract. They are abstract in the sense that they can represent information from any modality.
- Analogical representations are non-discrete, can represent things implicitly, have loose rules of combination, and are concrete in the sense that they are tied to a particular sense modality (e.g., the visual).
- Object and relational concepts have been captured in propositional terms by predicate calculus representations; more complex structurings of relations in events are often represented as schemata.
- The special properties of imagery have been demonstrated in successive empirical studies of mental rotation, the re-interpretation of ambiguous images, and image scanning.
- Paivio's theory provides detailed account for the distinction between two separate but inter-dependent symbolic systems, one verbally based and one image-based, which have been supported by localisation studies of the brain.
- Kosslyn's theory provides one account of how the imagery system might work in terms of detailed computational processes, an account that he argues overlaps significantly with aspects of visual perception. Various aspects of this system have been supported by empirical studies, for example, on image tracing.
- The neuropsychology of imagery has been extensively examined to determine the hemispheric localisation of imagery process (in both hemispheres).
- Finally, connectionist accounts of representation provide a very different view from the traditional symbolic accounts, one in which representations are characterised as patterns of activation in a network of units (so-called distributed representations)

## FURTHER READING

Several books provide interesting further discussions of the issues raised in this chapter. In particular the following are recommended for further reading.

- Churchland, P.S., & Sejnowski, T.J. (1992). *The computational brain*. Cambridge MA: MIT Press. Chapter 4 of this book provides a fuller context to the issues of representation in connectionist systems.
- Kosslyn, S.M. (1994). *Image & brain: The resolution of the imagery debate*. Cambridge, MA: MIT Press. This is a very readable summary to Kosslyn's research over the years.
- Richardson, J.T.E. (1999). *Imagery*. Hove, UK: Psychology Press. This book gives a more detailed account than we have been able to do here on the psychology of imagery.
- Squire, L.R., & Kosslyn, S.M. (1999). *Findings and current opinion in cognitive neuroscience*. Cambridge, MA: MIT Press. This provides an up-to-date more general overview on developments in neuroscience of relevance to the contents of this chapter.

# 10

# Objects, Concepts, and Categories

## INTRODUCTION

In the previous chapter, we saw how knowledge can be represented and organised. In this chapter, we examine the more circumscribed area of object concepts and categories. Object concepts have been, by far, the most researched topic in the study of concepts. Beyond this chapter, much of the remainder of the book is about how these object concepts and other schematic knowledge is used in the important activities of reading, problem solving, reasoning, and decision making. Before we plunge into this chapter, we should pause to consider why we need knowledge and why that knowledge needs to be organised.

### Constraints on concepts: Economy, informativeness, and naturalness

Why do we need knowledge? We need to know about things to behave and act in the world. In its most general sense our knowledge is all the information that we have inherited genetically or learned through experience. Without this knowledge we simply cannot do certain things. If you have not acquired the knowledge for bicycle

riding, by spending hours falling off bicycles and grazing your knees, then you cannot carry out this behaviour. If you have not studied the recipe for hollandaise sauce, then the likelihood is you will not produce a decent meal using this sauce. In short, knowledge informs and underlies all of our daily activities and behaviour.

Why do we need to organise knowledge? It is not enough just to acquire experience and store it; we need to organise this knowledge in an economic and informative fashion. The South American writer Jorge-Luis Borges (1964, pp. 93–94) describes a fictional character who had a perfect memory of every second of his life, a man called Funes, who had no need to organise or categorise his experience:

> . . . Funes remembered not only every leaf of every tree of every wood, but also every one of the times he had perceived or imagined it . . . He was, let us not forget almost incapable of ideas of a general, Platonic sort. Not only was it difficult for him to comprehend that the generic symbol *dog* embraces so many unlike individuals of diverse size and form; it bothered him that the dog at three fourteen (seen from the side) should have the same name as the dog at three

fifteen (seen from the front). His own face in the mirror, his own hands, surprised him every time he saw them.

No human being is like Funes, because we have to organise our knowledge. We identify categories of things, like dogs, in part to avoid having to remember every individual dog we have seen (or indeed every different angle from which we have seen a specific dog). Our memory systems clearly require a certain *economy* in the organisation of our experience. If we were like Funes, our minds would be cluttered with many irrelevant details. So, we seem to abstract away from our experience to develop general concepts (indeed, Borges suggests that Funes could not think and reason because he lacked abstract categories). *Cognitive economy* is achieved by dividing the world into classes of things to decrease the amount of information we must learn, perceive, remember, and recognise (Collins & Quillian, 1969). Once concepts have been formed they can, in turn, be organised into hierarchies; where *animal* is a superordinate concept (i.e., more general or encompassing) of *dog* and where *living thing* is a superordinate of *animal* and *plant*. However, this sort of cognitive economy has to be balanced by informativeness.

If our minds went too far in applying the economy constraint then we would end up with too many general concepts and lose many important details. If we generalised all of our object concepts to be just three (animals, plants, and everything else) then we would have a very economic conceptual system, but we would not have a very informative system; for instance, we would not have abstractions to distinguish between, say, chairs and tables.

Finally, there is a sense in which some concepts are more "natural" than others. A category that included pints-of-Guinness and birds-that-flew-on-one-wing, does not seem likely or *natural*. Human concepts cohere in certain ways making certain groupings of entities more likely to occur than other groupings. One problem is to specify the basis for this naturalness or cohesiveness.

In short, for reasons of storage and effective use it seems to be necessary to organise and categorise experience. In human memory, this organisation appears to be guided by the principles of cognitive economy, informativeness, and natural coherence. One of the marvels of human memory is that it balances these principles in the acquisition of conceptual knowledge that allows us to get around and understand our world. A marvel whose extent is most horribly revealed when it becomes damaged in brain injury or by a disease like Alzheimer's.

## Outline of chapter

In the next section, we consider some of the main findings in the object concept literature before outlining how the various theoretical perspectives deal with these findings. In the course of reviewing each theory we outline some of the supportive evidence that has been garnered for that specific theoretical approach. Then, in the latter sections of the chapter we consider wider evidential shores against which the various theories should also be tested, by reviewing the literatures on conceptual combination, concept formation, and the cognitive neuropsychological evidence on categorisation.

## EVIDENCE ON CATEGORIES AND CATEGORISATION

Human knowledge consists of everything that we know. In any attempt to characterise this knowledge, a starting point for research is hard to find. As we have seen in Chapter 9, a distinction has been made between "objects" (*dog, cat, dishwasher, spigot*) and the "relations" between things (*above, below, kick, hit*); it is the former we will concentrate on here. Research on object concepts has been heavily influenced by philosophy; especially the British empiricist philosophers (e.g., Locke, 1690) who viewed concepts as being atomic units that were combined in molecule-like ways into more complex structures. We will see that this is a common thread running through research in this area.

In this section, we will review some of the main findings in categorisation before considering the various theoretical accounts of these findings from four positions: the defining-attribute, proto-type, exemplar, and explanation-based views. It is only relatively recently that the multiple functions of categories have been considered to be import-ant, and in line with this trend we review the use of categories from multiple perspectives of usage (Sloman & Rips, 1998). Empirical research on categorisation examines the ways in which con-cepts are used; for example, in making category judgements, making predictions, or explaining dif-fering perspectives on a category. Category judge-ments can be made about whether a particular instance is a member of the category; for instance, whether the mongrel next door and the winner of Crufts are both instances of the category *dog* (n.b., we use the convention of writing dog in italics to indicate that we are discussing the concept *dog* and not the word "dog"). Category judgements can also be used to determine the hierarchical relationship between concepts; for example, how the concepts *dog* and *cat* are subordinates (i.e., more specific versions) of the more general *animal* concept (called the *superordinate*). Traditionally, these two areas have been heavily researched in the categorisation literature. More recently, the empirical attention has shifted to how concepts are used to predict things; for example, how knowing that someone is called Peter is not that inform-ative, but knowing that Peter is a goldfish allows you to predict that he is likely to swim and eat fish food. The fourth and final empirical area we

shall examine is research on the instability of concepts, on how categorisation changes under the influence of differing goals and perspectives.

## Category judgements of membership

Intuitively, one of the basic ways in which we use our concepts is in judging whether something is a specific instance of a category. For example, determining whether the animal running across the lawn is a *dog* or a *deer*. As such, a large body of work has concerned itself with judgements of category membership. The view taken in object-concept research has been that concepts are defined by attributes; for example, a specific dog is categor-ised as a *dog* by virtue of having *four-legs*, *fur*, *barking*, and *panting-a-lot*. In response to behavi-ourist accounts of categorisation, some of the earliest cognitive work tried to show that category judgements were rule-governed based on the con-sideration of such attributes.

### *Category judgements can be rule-governed*

In particular, the influential work of Bruner, Goodnow, and Austin (1956) looked at how people acquire concepts of shapes involving different attributes. In Bruner et al.'s experiments subjects were shown an array of stimuli (see Figure 10.1) that had different attributes (e.g., shape, number of shapes, shading of shapes) with different values (e.g., cross/square, one/three, plain/striped). From

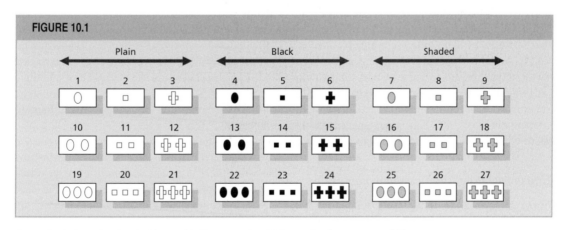

FIGURE 10.1

A sample of the sorts of materials used in Bruner et al.'s (1956) study of concept acquisition.

the experimenter's viewpoint, certain items in the array were instances of a rule; for example, the rule *three, square shapes* identifies items 20, 23, 26 as members of it and all other items as non-members. In one of their tasks, subjects were shown one example of the rule and had to discover the correct rule by asking the experimenter whether other items were instances of the rule.

Bruner et al. identified several different strategies used by subjects in these experiments that could be viewed as possible ways in which people might acquire concepts in everyday life. However, Bruner et al.'s work was carried out in a domain of fairly artificial categories. Can we expect people to operate similarly when making judgements about natural categories, involving the commonplace objects of everyday life? The short answer is "no" (although see Armstrong, Gleitman, & Gleitman, 1983).

### Category judgements reflect typicality gradients

Natural categories do not seem to be as clear-cut as Bruner et al.'s artificial categories; some instances of the category are better examples of the concept than others. For example, Rosch (1973) asked people to rate the typicality of different members of a concept and found that some members were rated as being much more typical than others (see also Rips, Shoben, & Smith, 1973). A *robin* was considered to be a better example of a *bird* than a *canary*. Indeed, the category can be described in terms of a *typicality gradient* of its members; that is, an ordering of the members of the category by their relative typicality scores. Furthermore, this typicality gradient is a good predictor of the time subjects take to make verification judgements. That is, subjects take longer to verify statements involving less typical members (e.g., "A penguin is a bird") than statements involving more typical members (e.g., "A robin is a bird").

### Categories do not have clear boundaries

Some categories are fuzzy, their boundaries are not clear-cut to the extent that some members can slip in and out of the category. That is, even

though some highly typical instances are considered by most people to be category members and less typical instances are considered to be non-members of the category, between these two extremes people differ on whether an object is a member of the category and are also inconsistent in their judgements. That is, sometimes they think the object is a member of the category and other times they think it is not. McCloskey and Glucksberg (1978) found that their subjects were sure about saying that a *chair* was a member of the category furniture and that a *cucumber* was not a member of this category. But they disagreed with one another on whether *book-ends* were a member of the category furniture and differed in their own category judgements from one session to the next (see also Barsalou, 1987; Hampton, 1998; and the later section on concept instability).

### Category judgements with hierarchies

Intuitively, another common category judgement we can make is about the hierarchical relationships between concepts, captured by questions like "Is a chicken a bird?" and "Is a chicken an animal?". Much empirical research has been directed at this question to determine the structure of conceptual hierarchies. One of the key questions has been how many levels of abstraction are used by the human conceptual system. It is easy to think that there may be many levels of abstraction. For example, our hierarchies might start with *things*, below which there are *living* and *non-living things*, below *living things* there might be *animals* and *vegetables*, below *animals* there could be *warm-blooded* and *cold-blooded animals*, below *warm-blooded animals* there could be *land-animals* and *sea-animals*, and so on. For the sake of cognitive economy, it is clear that people must have some efficient scheme for organising hierarchies of concepts.

As we shall see, many studies have revealed that people use about three levels of abstraction and that there is a marked "basic-level" at which categorisation is carried out. The idea of a basic level arose out of anthropological studies of biological and zoological categories (Berlin, 1972; Berlin, Breedlove, & Raven, 1973; Brown et al.,

1976). Berlin (1972) noted that the classification of plants used by the Tzeltal Indians of Mexico corresponded to the categories at a particular level in the scientific taxonomy of plants. For instance, in the case of trees, the cultures studied by Berlin were more likely to have terms for a genus such as beech than for general, superordinate groupings (e.g., deciduous, coniferous) or for individual species (e.g., silver beech, copper beech). The reason Berlin gave for this basic level was that categories such as "beech" and "birch" were naturally distinctive and coherent groupings; that is, the species they include tend to have common patterns of attributes such as leaf shape, bark colour and so on. The basic level was the best level at which to summarise categories. More recent research by Atran (1998; Atran et al., 1999; Lopez et al., 1997) has suggested that these conceptual systems are invariant, for just these categories, across many cultures, suggesting that they may be core domains of human knowledge that have been naturally selected for by evolution.

In psychology, Elanor Rosch and her associates discovered much of the specific evidence on the basic level and the three levels of generality (Rosch et al., 1976a). They found that at the highest level of abstraction, the *superordinate level*, people have general designations for very general categories, like furniture. At the lowest level, the *subordinate level*, there are specific types of objects (e.g., my favourite armchair, a kitchen chair). In between these two extremes is the *basic level*. While we often talk about general categories (that furniture is expensive) and about specific concepts (my new Cadillac), we typically deal with objects at the intermediate, basic level (whether there are enough chairs and desks in the office). Rosch et al. (1976a) asked people to list all the attributes of items at each of the three levels (e.g., furniture, chair, easy chair) and discovered that very few attributes were listed for the superordinate categories (like furniture) and many attributes were listed for the categories at the other two levels. However, at the lowest level very similar attributes were listed for different categories (e.g., easy chair, living-room chair).

Rosch et al. (1976a) also found evidence that basic-level categories have special properties not shared by categories at other levels. First, the basic level is the one at which adults spontaneously name objects and is also the one that is usually acquired first by young children. Furthermore, the basic level is the most general level at which people use similar motor movements for interacting with category members; for instance, all chairs can be sat on in roughly the same way and this differs markedly from the way we interact with tables. Category members at the basic level also have fairly similar overall shapes and so a mental image can capture the whole category. Finally, objects at the basic level are recognised more quickly than objects at the higher and lower levels. It seems that at the basic level there is maximal, within-category similarity relative to between-category similarity. That is, categories that are similar are grouped together in a way that sharpens their differences from other categories.

Theoretically, these organisational properties are proposed to reflect a balance between the principles of informativeness and cognitive economy. The basic-level categories (like chair) are noted by a balance between informativeness (the number of attributes the concept conveys) and economy (a sort of summary of the important attributes that distinguish it from other categories). Informativeness is lacking at the highest level because few attributes are conveyed, and economy is missing at the lowest level because too many attributes are conveyed.

However, it is important to note that basic-level concepts do not always correspond to intermediate terms (e.g., chair in furniture–chair–armchair). In non-biological categories (like furniture) the intermediate term tends to correspond to the basic level. However, in biological categories the superordinate term tends to correspond to the basic level (e.g., "bird", in bird–sparrow–song-sparrow). This difference is seen as being a function of the amount of experience people have with members of biological categories. That is, one's experience with the instances of a category will lead to differences in one's basic level. So, ornithologists would be more likely to consider sparrow to be the basic level for the bird category because, given their expertise, this is the most distinctive level. Similarly, Berlin's findings with the Tzeltal probably reflects their expertise concerning the differences between trees (but see Atran, 1998; see also later section on neuropsychological evidence).

## Using categories for prediction

It is only relatively recently that empirical research on categorisation turned to the arguably more ecologically valid task of prediction (e.g., Corter & Gluck, 1992; Heit, 1992; Lin & Murphy, 1997; Malt, Murphy, & Ross, 1994; Murphy & Ross, 1994; Ross & Murphy, 1996, 1999; Waxman & Markow, 1995; for earlier pieces see Markman, 1989; Rips, 1975; Smith & Medin, 1981). Murphy and Ross (1994) pointed out that categorisation by itself is not very useful; people do not classify things for the sake of classifying them, they classifying things to make predictions about those things. For instance, having decided that a certain object is a dog, you can predict that it might bite, a prediction that would not follow if one had classified it as a cat. This phenomenon is often called inductive inference from categories (see Chapter 15 for more on induction).

Heit (1992) examined how people make predictions from learned instances or from instances that were similar to learned instances (see also Anderson, 1991; Osherson et al., 1990). His subjects memorised a description of 30 individuals who had three potential traits (e.g., Larry is a Jet and liberal, Harry is a Shark and married, Ben is a Jet and unathletic; where Jets and Sharks are clubs; see also later section on similarity). The subjects learned only one trait of a given individual but were told that each individual had two other traits. They were then asked to guess the probability (on a scale of 0 to 100) that a given individual had a proposed trait (e.g., whether Larry was likely to be single). Heit's results showed that people could make one-step and two-step inferences about these unseen traits. In a one-step inference, they inferred a trait based on the similarity of the given individual to other individuals with similar features; so, if one was asked whether Larry was likely to be unathletic, and had been told that Ben and Bill, also members of the Jets, were unathletic, then you might infer that there was a high probability that Larry was unathletic.

In the more complex two-step inferences, Larry might remind you for other reasons of Ben and Bill who, in turn, might remind you of Harry and it is Harry's features that are used to make the inference about Larry. This study shows something of the potential complexity of prediction from category instances.

Other work in this area has examined how predictions are made when there is some uncertainty about the classification of an object; for example, where a far-away object seems to be a dog and may therefore bite (Murphy & Ross, 1994; Ross & Murphy, 1996). A simple model might predict that the object has a feature based on how often that feature occurs in the category (i.e., the inference makes use of a single category); if in your experience 75% of the dogs you know bite, then the probability that a given dog will bite is .75. However, a more complex proposal suggests that if there is uncertainty about the classification then this probability would have to be modified in some way (see Anderson's, 1990, 1991, 1996, rational model). A further proposal made has been that the likelihood of being bitten should be modified by the likelihoods of biting one knows about for other animal categories (i.e., the inference makes use of multiple categories). In short, the inference is sensitive to the base rates for biting in the dog *and* other animal categories (see Chapter 17 on people's treatment of base rates in judgement and decision making). Overall, in an extended series of experiments Murphy and Ross found little evidence for the use of multiple categories in a prediction task, but found that people made use of a single category. Furthermore, this result was the case irrespective of the uncertainty of the initial classification.

## The instability of concepts

It is commonly assumed in theories of concepts that the representations of concepts are relatively static, but Barsalou (1987, 1989) argues convincingly that this assumption may be unwarranted, that concepts are unstable. He points out that the way people represent a concept changes as a function of the context in which it appears. So, for example, when people read "frog" in isolation, "eaten by humans" typically remains inactive in memory. However, "eaten by humans" becomes active when reading about frogs in a French restaurant. Thus, concepts are unstable to the extent that different information is incorporated into the representation of a concept in different situations (see also Anderson & Ortony, 1975). It seems that only a subset of the knowledge about a category becomes active in a given context; what Barsalou (1982) calls *context-dependent information.*

Instability has also been found in the graded structure of category exemplars (see Barsalou, 1985, 1989). As we saw earlier, a category's graded structure is simply the ordering of its exemplars from most to least typical. For instance, in the *bird* category American subjects order the following instances as decreasing in typicality from *robin* to *pigeon* to *parrot* to *ostrich.* Instability shows itself in the rearrangement of this ordering as a function of the population, the individual, or context (see Barsalou, 1989). For example, even though Americans consider a robin to be more typical than a swan, they treat a swan as being more typical than robin when they are asked to take the viewpoint of the average Chinese citizen.

Furthermore, some categories are not well established in memory but seem to be formed on-the-fly (Barsalou, 1983). These, so-called *ad hoc categories*, are constructed by people to achieve certain goals. For example, if you wanted to sell off your unwanted possessions you might construct a category of "things to sell at a garage sale". Barsalou has shown that the associations between instances of these concepts and the concept itself are not well established in memory but can be constructed if required (for more recent work see Ross & Murphy, 1999 and Chapter 9).

## THE DEFINING-ATTRIBUTE VIEW

In turning to consider theories of concepts, there is one initial theory that we have to consider, the classical defining-attribute theory, even though it will be apparent that it is immediately ruled out by the preceding evidence. The defining-attribute view is based on ideas developed in philosophy and logic. This view, elaborated by the logician Gottlob Frege (1952), maintains that a concept can be characterised by a set of *defining attributes* (or semantic features, see Chapter 9). Frege clarified the distinction between a concept's intension and its extension. The *intension* of a concept consists of the set of attributes that define what it is to be a member of the concept and the *extension* is the set of entities that are members of the concept. So, for example, the intension of the concept *bachelor* might be its set of defining attributes (*male, single, adult*), while the extension of the concept is the complete set of all the bachelors in the world (from the Pope to Mr Jones next door). Related ideas have appeared at various times in linguistics and psychology (see e.g., Glass & Holyoak, 1975; Katz & Fodor, 1963; Leech, 1974; Medin & Smith, 1984; Smith & Medin, 1981, for reviews).

The general characteristics of defining-attribute theories are summarised in Panel 10.1. It can be seen that the theory maintains that if defining attributes of the concept *bachelor* are *male, single, adult*, then for Mr Jones to be a bachelor it is necessary for him to have each attribute (i.e., *male, single,* and *adult*) and it is sufficient or enough for him to have all these three attributes together; that is, no other attributes enter into determining whether he is an instance of the concept. So, each of the attributes is singly necessary and all are jointly sufficient for determining whether Mr Jones is a member of the concept *bachelor.* This means that what is and is not a *bachelor* is very clear. If Mr O'Shea is an adult and male but is married then he cannot be considered to be a member of the category bachelor. This theory predicts that concepts should divide up individual objects in the world into distinct classes and that the boundaries between categories should be well defined and rigid. It also predicts that conceptual hierarchies should neatly subsume one another. So, if you have a concept *sparrow* (defined as *feathered, animate, two-legged, small, brown*) and its superordinate, *bird* (defined as *feathered, animate, two-legged*) then the subordinate concept *sparrow* will contain all the attributes of the superordinate, although it will also have many other attributes

---

**Panel 10.1:   Defining-attribute theories of concepts**

- The meaning of a concept can be captured by a conjunctive list of attributes (i.e., a list of attributes connected by ANDs).
- These attributes are atomic units or primitives which are the basic building blocks of concepts.
- Each of these attributes is necessary and all of them are jointly sufficient for something to be identified as an instance of the concept.
- What is and is not a member of the category is clearly defined; thus, there are clear-cut boundaries between members and non-members of the category.
- All members of the concept are equally representative.
- When concepts are organised in a hierarchy then the defining attributes of a more specific concept (e.g., sparrow) in relation to its more general relative (its superordinate; e.g., bird) includes all the defining attributes of the superordinate.

---

**Panel 10.2:   Concept hierarchies**

- People use hierarchies to represent relationships of class inclusion between categories; that is, to include one category within another (e.g., the category of chair within the category for furniture).
- Human conceptual hierarchies have three levels; a superordinate level (e.g., weapons, furniture), a basic level (e.g., guns, chair), and a subordinate level of specific concepts (e.g., hand-guns, rifles, kitchen chairs, armchairs).
- The basic level is the level at which concepts have the most "distinctive attributes" and it is the most cognitively economic; it is the level at which a concept's attributes are *not* shared with other concepts at that level.
- Categories at the basic level are critical to many cognitive activities; for example, they contain concepts that can be interacted with using similar motor movements, they have the same general shape, and they may be associated with a mental image that represents the whole category.
- The position of the basic level can change as a function of individual differences in expertise and cultural differences.

---

(like *brown*), to distinguish it from other subordinate concepts (e.g., *canary*, defined as *feathered, animate, two-legged, small, yellow*). This means that a specific concept will tend to have more attributes in common with its immediate superordinate than with a more distant superordinate. For example, *sparrow* should have more attributes in common with its immediate superordinate, *bird*, than with its more distant superordinate *animal*. Several computational models of this type

of theory have been proposed (Collins & Quillian, 1969, 1970; Quillian, 1966; see also Chapter 1). The details of the Collins and Quillian model are shown in Panel 10.2 (see also Figure 10.2).

## Evidence for the defining-attribute view

Several early studies seemed to support this theory and its particular instantiation as a semantic network model. The early work by Bruner et al.

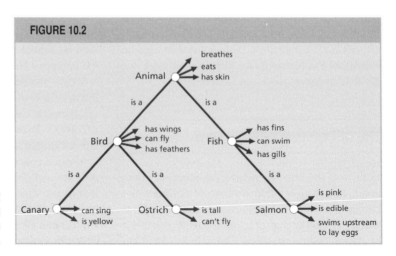

**FIGURE 10.2**

A schematic diagram of the sort of hierarchical, semantic networks proposed by Collins and Quillian (1969).

(1956) using artificial categories clearly assumes this theory. Similarly, Collins and Quillian used sentence-verification tasks to find support for their model of the theory. In these tasks, subjects were asked to say whether simple sentences of two forms were true or false. First, they were asked whether "an INSTANCE was a member of a SUPERORDINATE" (e.g., "Is a canary an animal?" or "Is a canary a fish?"). Second, subjects were asked whether "an INSTANCE had a certain ATTRIBUTE" (e.g., "Can a canary fly?", "Does a canary have skin?"). In both of these cases Collins and Quillian's predictions were confirmed. In the INSTANCE–SUPERORDINATE sentence it was found that the greater the distance between the subject and predicate of the sentence in the hierarchy, the longer it took to verify the sentence. And in the INSTANCE–ATTRIBUTE case the place of the attribute in the hierarchy relative to the instance, predicted the time taken to verify the sentence. However, some of their other predictions were not supported: Reaction times to questions that were false (e.g., a canary is a stone) were very fast even when many links should have been traversed to answer the question.

## Evidence against the defining-attribute view

On the whole the evidence against the defining-attribute view far outweighs that in favour of it. All of the so-called prototype effects outlined earlier go against its basic predictions.

On category judgements, all members of a category are not equally important or representative. In terms of the defining-attribute view, people should list the same attributes for all the members of a category (i.e., the defining set). However, people do not do this but tend to mention non-necessary attributes (Conrad, 1972; Rosch & Mervis, 1975). So, category members are not all equally representative. As Rosch and others have shown, some category members were rated as being much more typical than others (see also Rips, Shoben, & Smith, 1973). For example, a *robin* was considered to be a better example of a *bird* than a *canary*. Even categories that appear to meet the theory, like *bachelor*; show typicality effects. Tarzan is not a good example of a bachelor

because, alone with the apes of the jungle, he did not have the opportunity to marry (see Fillmore, 1982; Lakoff, 1982, 1987). Furthermore, as we have seen, categories do not have clear boundaries but can be fuzzy and changing.

On the issue of conceptual hierarchies, the theory does not specifically predict the three-level structure and the centrality of basic-level categories. Furthermore, contrary to Collins and Quillian's findings, Smith, Shoben, and Rips (1974) have shown that more distant superordinates can be verified faster than immediate superordinates. So, when asked "Is a chicken a bird?" and "Is a chicken an animal?", contrary to Collins and Quillian's node-distance prediction, subjects responded faster to the latter than to the former. Hampton (1982) has shown that the defining-attribute prediction that hierarchies of concepts are transitive is not confirmed (i.e., as "An X is a Y" and "A Y is a Z" are true, "An X is a Z" is also true). Conrad (1972) has also shown that certain attributes of concepts were mentioned more often by subjects than other attributes and, hence, are considered to be more important or salient. For example, the attribute of a salmon *is-pink* is mentioned more often than the attribute *has-fins*. Not only does this suggest that attributes are not given equal weight by subjects but Conrad showed that, in Collins and Quillian's experiments, the fast verifications of some sentences were due to the attribute's salience and not the number of links.

On the predictive use of categories and concept instability, it should be clear that this theory is quite inadequate. It has no notion that attributes may be held in a probabilistic fashion by concepts and takes the view that all the attributes of a concept are equally available and present all of the time.

More generally, the theory suffers from a fundamental problem in determining exactly what are "defining attributes". Several generations of linguists, philosophers, and psychologists have failed to find defining attributes or semantic features for concepts (for examples of the latter see Hampton, 1979, 1995; McNamara & Sternberg, 1983). Some, therefore, argue that the whole enterprise of trying to break concepts down into their necessary and sufficient attributes is fundamentally ill-conceived (Fodor, Garrett, Walker & Parkes, 1980; Wittgenstein, 1958). Some concepts simply do not seem to have defining attributes. Consider Wittgenstein's example of the concept of a *game*. There are clusters of attributes that characterise sets of games (that they involve pieces, involve balls, involve one or more players) but hardly any attribute holds in all the members of the concept. Members of the category *game*, like the faces of the members of a family, bear a *family resemblance* to one another but they do not share a distinct set of necessary and sufficient attributes.

## Saving the defining-attribute view

It is rarely the case that a theory is completely defeated by the evidence. Usually theories make a comeback in some modified form. In this vein, several variants of the defining attribute view have been proposed. One variation, feature comparison theory, admits that there are defining attributes and *characteristic attributes* (Rips et al., 1973; Smith et al., 1974). Using this additional assumption, a variety of effects can be handled (see Eysenck & Keane, 1995, Chapter 10 for details). Another variant on the defining-attribute theme, identified by Smith and Medin (1981) is based on Miller and Johnson-Laird's (1976) distinction between the "core" of a concept and its "identification procedure". The *core* of the concept consists of defining attributes and is important in revealing the relations between a given concept and other concepts. That is, the conceptual core of bachelor (*male, single, adult*) is important to revealing why a *bachelor* and a *spinster* ( *female, single, adult*) are similar or why the terms "bachelor" and a "single male" are considered synonymous. The *identification procedure* plays a role in identifying objects in the real world and is responsive to their characteristic attributes. Thus, the core retains the defining-attribute theory while the identification procedure can account for typicality effects.

Armstrong et al. (1983) carried out a study that suggests evidence for this view. They examined concepts that clearly have defining attributes (e.g., *even number, odd number, plane geometry figure*) and found that members of these categories were judged to be more or less typical of the category. For instance, 22 was rated as being more typical of the concept *even number* than 18 and was also categorised faster. Thus, these concepts seemed to have a conceptual core and yet in categorisation tasks people made use of characteristic attributes. Similarly, McNamara and Sternberg (1983) asked subjects to list the attributes of several different types of nouns (artifacts, natural kinds, and proper names) and to rate the necessity, sufficiency, and importance of each attribute to the word's definition. An inspection of subjects' ratings revealed that they considered some of the words to have defining attributes (i.e., necessary and sufficient attributes) and characteristic attributes. But only half could be defined by the defining attributes produced by subjects. McNamara and Sternberg also showed that these same distinctions were implicated in the real-time processing of the concepts, when read as words.

If we assume that concepts have a conceptual core and then other characteristic features, then one would expect there to be linguistic hedges in the language to take this distinction into account. Lakoff (1973, 1982) has argued that such hedges exist and are signalled by terms like "true" and "technically speaking" or "strictly speaking". These terms qualify assertions we might make about category members. For example, if one says a "a duck is a true bird" the core definition of the concept *bird* is being explicitly marked, whereas the sentence "technically speaking, a penguin is a bird", marks the fact that you know a penguin is a non-representative example of the category but wish to include it within the category.

## THE PROTOTYPE VIEW

As we have seen, the classical defining-attribute view of concepts does not stand up to the evidence found, especially that on the existence of category members with differential typicality, borderline membership, and graded structure of concepts. Most of the research that defeated the defining-attribute view was motivated by the prototype view. This view is named after its fundamental proposal that categories have a central description, a prototype, that in some sense stands for the whole category. However, different theories characterise prototypes in different ways.

In some theories, the prototype is a set of characteristic attributes; there are no defining attributes but rather only characteristic attributes of differential importance within the concept (see e.g., Hampton, 1979; Posner & Keele, 1968; Rosch, 1978). An object is a member of the concept if there is a good match between its attributes and those of the prototype. In other prototype theories, the prototype is captured by a specific instance of the category, the best example of the concept (e.g., Rosch, 1978). So, for example, if *robin* is the best example for the bird category, then it would be the prototype. Another object is a member of the bird category if it shares many attributes with the best example. For the purposes of this chapter, we combine theses two variants of prototype theory in a single treatment that is summarised in Panel 10.3.

## Evidence for the prototype view

Apart from the evidence we have already reviewed, there is a large body of evidence supporting the prototype account of categorisation. One of the most notable and early pieces of evidence came from cross-cultural studies on colour categories.

### Colour categories

There are many different colour terms used in the languages of the world. Some cultures have terms for a wide variety of colours (e.g., in western Europe we have a huge diversity from magenta to sky-blue to red and so on), while other cultures have very few terms (e.g., the Dani of Papua New Guinea have only two colour terms for dark and bright). Berlin and Kay (1969) suggested that this diversity was only apparent if one distinguished between focal colours and non-focal colours. In their studies they identified *basic colour terms* using four criteria: (i) the term must be expressed as one morpheme, so something like sky-blue would be ruled out; (ii) its meaning cannot include that of another term, ruling out scarlet because it cannot be explained without reference to red; (iii) it must not be restricted to a particular domain of objects, ruling out terms like blond which really only apply to hair and possibly furniture; and (iv) it must be a frequently used term, like green, rather than turquoise. Berlin and Kay discovered that all languages draw their basic colour terms from a set of 11 colours. English has words for all of this set and they are black, white, red, green, yellow, blue, brown, purple, pink, orange, and grey.

Using the basic colour terms derived from this analysis, Berlin and Kay set about examining some 20 languages in detail, by performing experiments using a set of over 300 colour chips. In these studies, native speakers of the languages in question were asked two questions about the colour chips. First, they were asked what chips they would be willing to label using a particular, basic colour term. Second, they were asked what chips are the best or most typical examples of a colour term. What Berlin and Kay found was that the speakers of different languages agreed in their identification of focal colours; people consistently agreed on the best example of, say, a red or a blue. This together with the finding that subjects were uncertain about category boundaries, suggested that category membership was judged on the basis of resemblance to focal colours. These results were also found for cultures with a very limited colour terminology like the Dani. Rosch (when her name was Heider, 1972; also Rosch, 1975a) showed that the Dani could remember focal colours better than non-focal colours and that, even though they only had two colour terms, they could learn names of focal colours more quickly than those for non-focal colours. It should be pointed out that Lucy and Schweder (1979) have shown that some of these memory results need to be questioned because the colour array previously used to demonstrate the influence of focality on memory was discriminatively biased in favour of focal chips.

Thus, there seems to be a universality in people's categorisation of certain colours and in the structure of colour categories; in particular, it seems that these categories have a prototype structure. However, it is noteworthy that these categories have a strong physiological basis in the colour vision system (see Gordon, 1989). As such, some of these colour categories may be special cases. So, it is necessary to demonstrate similar effects for other categories.

## Natural and artificial categories

Research on both natural categories (i.e., categories of things in the world, like birds and furniture) and artificial categories (e.g., numbers and dot patterns) has also supported detailed aspects of the prototype view. As we saw earlier, some members of categories are considered to be highly representative or highly typical. Subjects rate the typicality of instances of a concept differentially (Rips et al., 1973; Rosch, 1973). These typicality effects have considerable generality; for instance, they have also been found in psychiatric classifications (Cantor, Smith, French, & Mezzich, 1980), in linguistic categories (Lakoff, 1982, talks of degrees of noun-ness and verb-ness) and in various action concepts (like *to lie*, and *to hope*; see Coleman & Kay, 1981, Vaughan, 1985). Furthermore, the most typical members of a concept play a special role in human categorisation.

First, the typicality gradient of members of a concept is a good predictor of categorisation times. In verification tasks (e.g., "A canary is a bird") typical members, like *robin*, are verified faster than atypical members like *ostrich*. This has proven to be a very robust finding (for reviews see Danks & Glucksberg, 1980; Kintsch, 1980; Smith, 1978; Smith & Medin, 1981). Second, typical members are likely to be mentioned first when subjects are asked to list all the members of a category (Battig & Montague, 1969; Mervis, Catlin, & Rosch, 1976). Similarly, Rosch, Simpson, and Miller (1976b) found that when subjects were asked to sketch the exemplar of a particular category they were more likely to depict the most typical member. Third, the concept members that children learn first are the typical members, as measured by semantic categorisation tasks (Rosch, 1973). Fourth, Rosch (1975b) has found that typical members are more likely to serve as cognitive reference points than atypical members; for example, people are more likely to say "An ellipse is almost a circle" (where circle is the more typical form and occurs in the reference position of the sentence) than a "A circle is almost an ellipse" (where ellipse, the less typical form, occurs in the reference position).

A final important finding is the extent to which estimates of family resemblance correlate highly with typicality. Using Wittgenstein's term *family resemblance*, Rosch and Mervis (1975) have shown that one can derive a family resemblance score for each member of a category by noting all the attributes that that member has in common with all the other members of the category. Rosch and Mervis found that typical members have high family-resemblance scores and share few (if any) attributes in common with related, contrast categories. This is rather direct evidence for the idea that the typicality gradient of a concept's instances is a function of the similarity of those members to the prototype of the category.

## Conceptual hierarchies

Much of the work we have seen on basic-level categories and the three levels of generality (superordinate, basic, and subordinate) was specifically developed in the context of prototype theory. That is, one can think of a basic-level category as being organised around a prototype. So, just as there is a centrality of the prototype in making classification decisions, there is a centrality of the basic level as a focus for the maximally relevant category to consider in making such decisions.

## Evidence against the prototype view

Three main criticisms can be made of the prototype view. First, not all concepts have prototypic characteristics. Hampton (1981) has shown that only some abstract concepts (like "science", "crime", "a work of art", "rule", "belief") exhibit a prototype structure. This difference occurs because of the endless flexibility in membership of some abstract categories, in contrast to concrete categories. For instance, it seems impossible to specify the complete set of possible rules or beliefs. Thus, there are limits to the generality of prototype theory.

The prototype view is also incomplete as an account of the sort of knowledge people have about concepts. People seem to know about the relations between attributes, rather than just attributes alone, and this information can be used in categorisation (Malt & Smith, 1983; Walker, 1975). Consider the following case (see also Holland, Holyoak, Nisbett, & Thagard, 1986). Imagine going to a strange, Galapagos-like island for the first time, accompanied by a guide. On the journey, one sees a beautiful, blue bird fly out of a thicket and the guide indicates that it is called a "warrum". Later in the day, we meet a portly individual and are told that he is a member of the "klaatu" tribe. A day later, wandering without the guide one sees another blue bird, like the first, and considers it to be another warrum; however, on meeting another fat native one does not assume that he is a member of the klaatu tribe. The reason being that we know that colour is a particularly diagnostic and invariant attribute of the bird category but physical weight is not a particularly diagnostic attribute of tribal affiliations and is known to be a highly variable attribute. Hence, we know that some attributes are more likely to vary than others. The fact that people can make

reasonable guesses about the meaning of new terms on the basis of a single exposure to an instance is an important ability that prototype theory is silent about. The research we reviewed earlier on the predictive use of categories has made central use of these ideas and as such stretch beyond the explanatory reach of prototype theory.

Finally, the prototype view does not provide a good account of what makes some categories natural and coherent; what makes us group certain objects together in one category rather than in another. The traditional answer given by the prototype and other views is that similarity is responsible for category cohesion. Stated simply, things form themselves into categories because they all have certain attributes in common. However, similarity cannot be the only mechanism because we often form categories that are only tenuously based on shared attributes but which are nevertheless coherent. In reviewing the evidence on concept instability we saw that people can create categories on the fly, so-called ad hoc categories; from the perspective of prototype theory it is hard to imagine how such categories can cohere, given the lack of overlap between the attributes of category members (e.g., *things-to-sell-in-a-garage-sale*). Murphy and Medin (1985) point to the biblical categories of clean and unclean animals; clean animals include most fish, grasshoppers, and some locusts while unclean animals include camels, ostriches, crocodiles, mice, sharks, and eels (see also Douglas, 1966, Lakoff, 1987).

## THE EXEMPLAR-BASED VIEW

We have seen how prototype theory provides a good antithesis to the failed predictions of the classical theory. However, it is not the only possible explanation of the phenomena of categorisation. There is another view which proposes that specific instances or exemplars lie behind so-called prototype effects; that rather than working from an abstraction of the central tendency of all the instances of a category (i.e., Rosch's prototype), people simply make use of particular instances or exemplars of the category that come to mind in a

> **Panel 10.4:   The exemplar-based view of concepts**
> - Categories are made up of a collection of instances or exemplars rather than any abstract description of these instances (e.g., a prototype summary description).
> - Instances are grouped relative to one another by some similarity metric.
> - Categorisation and other phenomena are explained by a mechanism that retrieves instances from memory given a particular cue.
> - When exact matches are not found in memory the nearest neighbour to the cue is usually retrieved.

given situation (see Panel 10.4) (Brooks, 1978; Erickson & Kruschke, 1998; Estes, 1976, 1993; Hintzman, 1986; Medin, 1975, 1976; Medin & Shaffer, 1978; Nosfosky, 1986, 1988, 1991; Nosofsky, Palmeri, & McKinley, 1994; Shin & Nosofsky, 1992).

As such, the exemplar-based view paints a very different picture of categories from the prototype view. Instead of there being some abstracted description of a bird which acts as a central prototype, the picture is one of a memory that stores millions of specific instances. So, instead of having a prototype for *bird* that is a list of all the characteristic features abstracted away from members of this category (e.g., *has-wings*, *flies*, etc.), one just has a store of all the instances of birds you have encountered in the past (e.g., the robin you see every morning, a crow, a chough, a penguin, etc). As we shall see, all the effects attributed to prototypes can be dealt with by this sort of account depending on what instance(s) come to mind in a specific context.

## Evidence for the exemplar view

Much of the evidence that specifically seemed to support the prototype view can be explained by the exemplar view. Consider the effects of faster categorisation judgements for some members of a category than others. When asked "Is a robin a bird?" you can answer "yes" much faster than when asked "Is a penguin a bird?". Given that you have encountered many robins in the past, there are likely to be a lot more stored instances of robins than penguins. Therefore, a robin instance will be retrieved from memory much faster than a penguin instance, thus giving rise to the differences in judgement times. Similarly, typicality ratings are said to reflect the underlying

pattern of instances in the category; a robin is a more typical instance of a bird than a penguin because there are many more stored instances of robins than penguins. Typicality gradients can be accounted for in similar ways.

The exemplar-based account is also more consistent with the recent research on prediction and conceptual instability. Recall that the research on prediction was really all about comparing one classified target instance with other instances of the category to make appropriate predictions about features of that target instance (e.g., Heit, 1992; Murphy & Ross, 1994). Similarly, effects like those involving changes in perspective and ad hoc categories are easier to explain in the context of a theory where one has instances that can be regrouped in different ways to meet the demands of specific task situation.

There is other more specific evidence that supports the exemplar view in opposition to the prototype view. The exemplar view preserves the variability of instances in the category, whereas a prototype is a type of average over the instances of the category that usually exclude this variability information. Rips and Collins (1993; Rips, 1989a) showed that this variability information could influence classification. Their task involved the categories pizzas and rulers; most pizzas are 12 inches in size but they vary a lot (i.e., anything from 2 inches to 30 inches in width) and rulers are also 12 inches in size but are much less variable (i.e., most of the time they are 12 inches long). Subjects were asked to make a judgement about a new object 19 inches in size, as to whether it was a pizza or a ruler. If people had a prototype then this judgement should reveal a 50–50 split between pizza and ruler, because the prototype average would be 12 inches for both. However, if the variability was used by people, then they should always say that the object was a pizza because it is much more likely to vary in size than a ruler.

The exemplar-based approach also preserves correlational information between instances of a category in ways that a prototype does not. Again, it has been found repeatedly that people use such knowledge in category learning and classification judgements (see Medin, Altom, Edelson, & Freko, 1982; Nosofsky, 1991).

## Evidence against the exemplar view

For the most part, the exemplar view does better than the prototype view on many points. But, like the prototype view, there are some effects that it finds hard to explain. Typicality and category judgements should always co-vary; there should be no dissociation between the two. However, dissociations have been found. As we have seen Armstrong et al. (1983) have shown that people could make typicality judgements even when it was known the category had defining attributes. It is troublesome to the prototype and exemplar approaches to find that the causal link between the definition of a concept and the typicality measures can be called into question (but see Hampton, 1995). Furthermore, like the prototype view, the exemplar view depends on similarity. Hence, difficulties that arise in the treatment of similarity in prototype theory, tend to transfer to exemplar theories. Finally, these theories do not cope easily with class inclusion questions. For example, when people answer questions about the truth of a statement like "All birds are creatures" they seem to rely on general knowledge rather than specific examples. Yet the exemplar view has no good account of how such abstract knowledge comes into being.

## EXPLANATION-BASED VIEWS OF CONCEPTS

The theories we have reviewed so far have been quite successful in accounting for the evidence of typicality effects, prediction effects, and other results involving object concepts. However, these theories still find some pieces of evidence hard to explain (e.g., concept instability effects). One remedy for this deficiency is to suggest that more complex formulations of knowledge than attribute lists are required (see Putnam, 1975a, b, for arguments in philosophy on this point). In Chapter 9, we saw how a variety of more complex, structured representations clearly reside in memory (e.g., schemata and scripts).

Initially, in this chapter, we introduced three guiding constraints for conceptual systems; informativeness, economy, and coherence. In attribute-based theories, concepts cohere because members of a category have similar attributes. However, there are concepts that have little similarity between their attributes. We have already seen how Barsalou's (1983) ad hoc categories upset this view of coherence (e.g., the category of things-to-sell-in-a-garage-sale). As mentioned earlier, Murphy and Medin (1985) point out that in the Bible, the dietary rules associated with the abominations of Leviticus produce the categories of *clean* and *unclean animals*. What is it that makes camels, ostriches, crocodiles, mice, sharks, and eels *unclean*, and gazelles, frogs, most fish, grasshoppers, and some locusts *clean*? Murphy and Medin argued that it was not the similarity of members of the concepts that determined the conceptual distinction but some theory or explanatory framework. The concept of clean and unclean animals rests on a theory of how the features of habitat, biological structure, and form of locomotion should be correlated in various animals (see Douglas, 1966). Roughly speaking, creatures of the water should have fins, scales, and swim, and creatures of the land should have four legs. If a creature conforms with this theory, then it is considered clean. But, any creature that is not equipped for the right kind of locomotion is considered unclean (e.g., ostriches).

Murphy and Medin's notion of a *theory* refers to any of a number of mental "explanations" (rather than a complete scientific account): for example, "causal knowledge certainly embodies a theory of certain phenomena; scripts may contain an implicit theory of entailment between mundane events; knowledge of rules embodies a theory of the relations between rule constituents;

---

book-learned, scientific knowledge certainly contains theories" (p. 290). Murphy and Medin, therefore, argue that even though similarity is important it is not sufficient to determine which concepts will be coherent or meaningful. These arguments have informed a newly emergent view of concepts which has been termed the knowledge-based or explanation-based view.

The explanation-based view of concepts sees concepts as involving more than attribute-lists; concepts also contain causal and other background knowledge that might be represented by schemata (see Chapter 9). For example, living things with wings, feathers, and light bones are seen as forming a natural category because they are, according to a certain theory, manifestations of a single, genetic code; the category coheres because we have a theory that explains the co-occurrence of these attributes. Miller and Johnson-Laird (1976) were among the first to propose that concept representations involved schematic knowledge, although others have made similar proposals (Cohen & Murphy, 1984; Keil, 1989; Lakoff, 1987). For the most part, this view of concepts has been marked by several general statements of the view rather than many concrete realisations of it; see Lakoff (1987) on idealised cognitive models, Johnson-Laird's (1983) mental models account, and Medin and Ortony's (1989) psychological essentialism. Some of the main proposals of the view are shown in Panel 10.5.

## Evidence for explanation-based views

There are several sources of evidence for explanation-based views. Some studies have shown that there is a dissociation between similarity and categorisation judgements, thus showing that similarity could not be the sole mechanism behind categorisation (Rips, 1989a). Other studies have shown how background knowledge (either causal or specific knowledge) can influence the application and learning of categories (see Ahn, Brewer, & Mooney, 1992; Malt, 1994; Medin, Wattenmaker, & Hampson, 1987; Pazzani, 1991; Wisniewski & Medin, 1994).

Rips (1989) has shown a dissociation between similarity judgements and categorisation in a study where one group of subjects were asked whether an object five inches in diameter was more likely to be a coin or a pizza, and a second group were given the same information and asked to judge the similarity of the object to either the coin or the pizza. Although the object's size was roughly midway between a large coin and a small pizza (as determined by prior norms), subjects in the categorisation group tended to categorise it as a pizza. However, the similarity group judged the object to be more similar to the coin. If categorisation was based on similarity alone, subjects' judgements in both groups should have tallied. The fact that they did not indicates that some other variable was at work, namely knowledge (or a theory) about the variability of the sizes of the objects in question. Coins have a size that is mandated by law, whereas pizzas can vary greatly in size (as we have seen earlier there is an alternative exemplar-based account of this effect).

Further evidence comes from Medin et al. (1987) who have shown that conceptual knowledge seems to drive the application of a family resemblance strategy in concept sorting. Recall that within the prototype view the typicality of a concept member is closely related to the family resemblance score for that instance; that is, the score that reflects the extent to which the instance's attributes are the same as those of other instances of the category. Medin et al. (1987) found that, in a sorting task, subjects persisted in sorting on the basis of a single dimension instead of using many dimensions, as a family resemblance account would predict. Medin et al. revealed that subjects abandoned this uni-dimensional sorting strategy in favour of a strategy that used several dimensions when the item had causally related, correlated properties. That is, when subjects were given conceptual knowledge that made inter-property relationships more salient, family resemblance sorting became very common. The moral being that correlated-attribute dimensions are really only used in sorting when there is some background knowledge or theory that connects them together.

Other studies have shown how background knowledge influences the categorisation process. One of the earliest findings in concept formation was that conjunctive concepts were easier to learn than disjunctive concepts (see Bruner et al., 1956). So, for example, it is easier for people to learn a concept called DRAF consisting of the conjoined features—*black and round and furry*—than when its features are disjunctive—*"black OR round OR furry"*. Pazzani (1991) has demonstrated a reversal of this phenomenon when the disjunctive concept is consistent with background knowledge. In this study, groups of subjects were shown pictures of people (adults or children) carrying out actions (stretching or dipping in water) on balloons of different colours and sizes. One set of instructions required subjects to determine whether a given stimulus situation (e.g., a child dipping a large, yellow balloon in water) was an *alpha* situation. Another set of instructions required subjects to predict whether the balloon would *inflate* after the stimulus event. Groups receiving either of these instructions had to learn either a conjunctive concept (size-small and balloon-yellow) or a disjunctive concept (age-adult OR action-stretching-balloon). Pazzani established that most people know that stretching a balloon makes it easier to

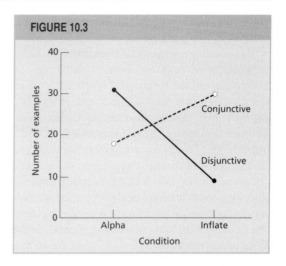

**FIGURE 10.3**

The ease of learning (as measured by number of examples taken to learn a concept) either a conjunctive or disjunctive concept as a function of the instructions given (to classify as alpha, or predict inflation). The disjunctive concept is consistent with the background knowledge on the ease of inflating balloons, whereas the conjunctive concept violates this knowledge. From Pazzani (1991a, Experiment 1).

inflate and that adults can inflate balloons more easily than children (but note that this knowledge does not correspond directly to the disjunctive definition subjects had to learn).

Pazzani found that the alpha groups found the conjunctive concept easier to acquire than the disjunctive concept (see Figure 10.3). As in previous research, this result occurred because the background knowledge about inflating balloons was irrelevant to learning the alpha categorisation. However, in conditions receiving the instructions to predict inflation of the balloon the opposite was found; the group learning the disjunctive concept found it easier to learn than the conjunctive concept. This was due to the fact that subjects' background knowledge informed the formation of the disjunctive concept, but did not support the learning of the conjunctive-inflate concept (see also Pazzani, 1993).

In a similar vein, Wisniewski and Medin (1994) showed subjects children's drawings of people, asking them to form a category rule to describe the set, which could be extended to a new instance of the category. They introduced background knowledge to the task by labelling the pictures meaningfully (i.e., these are drawings by creative or non-creative children) or neutrally (i.e., these drawings were done by Group 1 or Group 2). Subjects given the meaningful labels categorised the drawings in a very different way from those given neutral labels; they tended to use more abstract features of the drawing (e.g., "action", "true to life", "bodily expression") rather than concrete perceptual features (e.g., "arms at the side", "pockets", "curly hair"). In the neutral group, the drawings were predominantly classified according to differences in concrete features. In short, the former group brought intuitive theories to the task, which extracted a very different set of features from the drawing relative to the latter group. This study is just one of a number of recent ones that have shown the extensive influences of background knowledge on classification (e.g., Ahn et al., 1992; Johnson & Mervis, 1998; Keil, Smith, Simons, & Levin, 1998; Lin & Murphy, 1997; Rips & Collins, 1993).

## CONCEPTUAL COMBINATION

The bulk of this chapter has been given over to examining the acquisition and organisation of single concepts. However, new concepts can also be created by combining existing concepts in novel ways. We develop concepts like *pet fish*, *fake gun*, and *blue-striped shirt*. These *conceptual combinations* or *complex concepts* should also be explained by concept theories (Osherson & Smith, 1981). Concept combinations come in a number of different forms: including *adjective–noun combinations* (e.g., red fruit, large bird), *adverb–adjective–noun combinations* (e.g., very red fruit, slightly large bird) and *noun–verb combinations* (e.g., birds eat insects). We will concentrate on the most commonly examined of these; namely, noun–noun and adjective–noun combinations (see Costello & Keane, 1992, 1997, 2000, in press; Hampton, 1983, 1987, 1988; Jones, 1982; Osherson & Smith, 1981, 1982; Smith, 1988; Smith & Osherson, 1984; Smith, Osherson, Rips, & Keane, 1988; Wisniewski, 1996, 1997; Zadeh, 1982).

Defining-attribute theories predict that a combined concept should contain a set of entities that are a conjunction of the members that belong to the two constituent concepts. So, "red apple" should refer to objects that are in both the categories red-things and apples. However, this is nowhere near a complete account. As Lakoff (1982) indicates, a *fake gun* is not a member of the category *gun*. Osherson and Smith (1981, 1982) pointed out several serious problems for any prototype explanation of conceptual combination. They proved formally that the typicality of the member of the conjunction of two concepts could not be a simple function of the two constituent typicalities. Intuitively, a *guppy fish* is a good example of a pet fish, but a guppy is not typical of the category of *pets* (who are generally warm and furry) nor is it typical of the category of fish (who are generally larger; see Hampton, 1988).

Several models have been proposed to account for conceptual combination and to predict the typicality of members of the combined concept (Cohen & Murphy, 1984; Hampton, 1983; Murphy & Medin, 1985; Smith & Osherson, 1984; Thagard, 1984). Hampton's (1983) model talks of the formation of a *composite prototype*, by combining various attributes of the constituent concepts in an interactive fashion. Hampton (1987, 1988) produced evidence in favour of this model which shows that the similarity of an object to the composite prototype of the combined concepts determines the typicality and class membership of that object. Murphy and Medin (1985) maintain that conceptual combination is another case where background conceptual knowledge or theories about the concepts in question play a role. They point out that *ocean drives* are not both *oceans* and *drives*, and *horse races* are not both *horses* and *races*. It is clear from these examples that there are some combinations—intersective combinations—that do conform to prototype accounts (e.g., *orphan girl*), but that many combinations are not intersective in any sense (e.g., *ocean drive*).

More recently, Costello and Keane (1992, 1997, in press) have proposed a theory of conceptual combination for noun–noun compounds that combines aspects of instance-based and explanation-based approaches to categorisation. Costello and

Keane maintain that combinations are interpreted by forming subsets of the attributes and relations in both concepts according to the constraints of informativeness, diagnosticity, and plausibility. When people interpret novel compounds, like "cactus fish", to produce the meaning "a fish with spikes on its skin" they use diagnostic attributes of the cactus (e.g., spiky) rather than non-diagnostic ones (e.g., green), they apply these attributes in a plausible way (e.g., they do not say that it is a fish with spikes on its eyes), and the meaning produced is always informative (e.g., people never say that a cactus fish is a fish that is alive; although alive is an attribute of cacti it conveys no new information about fish). Costello and Keane have produced a computational model of the combination process that uses parallel constraint satisfaction (see also Estes & Glucksberg, in press; Markman & Wisniewski, 1997; Wisniewski, 1996, 1997; Wisniewski & Love, 1998).

# CONCEPTS AND SIMILARITY

Throughout this chapter we have being making implicit use of the notion of similarity without saying much about what it is. In the treatment of prototype theory, we assumed that prototypes were formed by noting the similarity of instances to one another, by finding the attributes they have in common. In the treatment of exemplar theories we saw that instances were retrieved from memory on the basis of similarity. But, how exactly does similarity work? In this section, we outline an important model of similarity and relate recent research that questions this model.

## Tversky's contrast model of similarity

One of the oldest and most successful models in cognitive psychology is Tversky's contrast model (Tversky, 1977). This model accounts for the similarity judgements made by people involving concepts described verbally or diagrammatically. Until recently, it was also the model implicitly or explicitly assumed by many concept theorists (see Smith, 1988). Since 1977, the contrast model has

been developed and tested extensively by Tversky and his colleagues (Tversky, 1977; Tversky & Gati, 1978).

The model maintains that the similarity of two concepts is based on some function of the attributes shared by the concepts less the attributes that are distinctive to both:

$$s(a, b) = \theta \cdot f(A \cap B) - \alpha \cdot f(A - B) - \beta \cdot f(B - A)$$

where $a$ and $b$ are two concepts, $s$ is the similarity of these two concepts, $A$ is the set of attributes of concept $a$ and $B$ is the set of attributes of concept $b$. In this formula, $A \cap B$ gives you the attributes that are common to the two objects, $A - B$ gives you the attributes that are distinctive to $a$, and $B - A$ the attributes that are distinctive to $b$ (note that this is not an absolute distinctiveness, but just what is distinctive in one concept relative to the other). In general, this formula predicts that as the number of common features increases and the number of distinctive features decreases, the two objects $a$ and $b$ become more similar. The function $f$ has a role in weighting certain attributes according to their salience and importance. The parameters $\theta$, $\alpha$, and $\beta$ are used as multipliers to reflect the relative importance of the common and distinctive attribute-sets. For instance, when people judge the similarity of two objects they tend to weight the common-features set as being more important than the distinctive-feature sets, whereas the distinctive-feature sets assume more importance in judgements of difference.

The effects of these $\theta$, $\alpha$, and $\beta$ parameters also appear in the asymmetries that appear in similarity judgements, where it has been found that the similarity of $a$ to $b$ is not equal to the similarity of $b$ to $a$; $s(a, b) \neq s(b, a)$. Tversky points out that in similarity statements there is a subject and a referent, we say that "a (subject) is like b (referent)". Furthermore, the choice of the referent and the subject is in part determined by the most important or salient concept; the more prominent concept being the referent. We say that "North Korea is like China", when China is the more prominent concept in the pair. When we reverse the roles of the concept the similarity of the two concepts

**TABLE 10.1**

Some of the mean similarity judgements for countries from Tversky and Gati (1977) showing the asymmetries between judgements of the form "q is like p" and "p is like q" ( p is the prominent concept)

| p | q | (q is like p) s(q, p) | (p is like q) s(p, q) |
|---|---|---|---|
| United States | Mexico | 7.65 | 6.45 |
| China | Albania | 9.16 | 8.69 |
| United States | Israel | 3.69 | 3.41 |
| Belgium | Luxembourg | 16.14 | 15.54 |
| France | Algeria | 7.94 | 7.86 |
| Germany | Austria | 15.20 | 15.60 |

changes; as in "China is like North Korea". In short, similarity statements are asymmetric.

Tversky and Gati (1978) found evidence for these proposals in a study involving similarity judgements for pairs of countries. They first confirmed that subjects preferred similarity statements in which the prominent country was in the referent rather than the subject position. The *s(q, p)* column of figures in Table 10.1 shows the mean similarity judgements where the prominent country (*p*) was in the referent position (i.e., *q is like p*). The *s(p, q)* column shows the mean similarity judgements when the prominent concept is in the subject position (i.e., *p is like q*). As you can see from Table 10.1, in almost every pair the similarity judgements are asymmetric; with *s(q, p)* forms being judged consistently as being more similar than *s(p, q)* forms.

## Extending similarity models to include relations

The contrast model has stood the test of time well. However, recently, a number of studies have shown that it might have to be adjusted in a number of respects. Tversky's model assumes that concepts can be adequately characterised by attribute lists (as do many of the theories reviewed earlier). Yet, in Chapter 9 we saw that relational concepts might also be important. Traditionally, relations (like *flies*, *on-top-of*, *connected-to*) would be treated as attributes in a concept definition. Running against this treatment, some recent

**FIGURE 10.4**

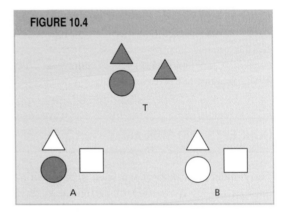

A sample of the materials used by Medin et al. (1990). The sample stimulus T is attributionally similar to A because they both have a shaded circle. B has not got this attributional similarity, but B does share a matching relation—same-colour elements—with T.

research has examined similarity judgements of stimuli where attributes and relations have been separated out (see Davenport & Keane, 1999; Goldstone, Medin, & Gentner, 1991; Markman & Gentner, 1993a, b; Markman & Wisniewski, 1997; Medin, Goldstone, & Gentner, 1990, 1993).

For instance, Medin et al. (1990) gave subjects the stimuli shown in Figure 10.4. In these experiments, subjects had to choose whether the A or B stimulus was more similar to T. In each case, one of the stimulus options always shared a unique attribute with the T stimulus (e.g., in Figure 10.4, A and T share the unique attribute of having a shaded circle) and the other shared a unique relation with T (e.g., in Figure 10.4, B and T share the unique relation *same-colour elements*). They found that the stimulus with the relational similarity tended to be chosen as the more similar of the two, indicating that people were sensitive to relations in their judgements and that they also weighted relational-matches as being more important. Further research along these lines has found support for what Goldstone et al. (1991) call the MAX hypothesis; that attributional and relational similarities are pooled separately and shared similarities affect judged similarity more if the pool that they are in is relatively large.

This research has been used to show that similarity is more like analogy (see Chapter 15), that people map the relational structure of one concept onto that of another, using so-called structural alignment (see Markman & Gentner, 1993a, b; Gentner & Markman, 1997). It is fair to say that this view has now gained considerable currency in the treatment of similarity (but see Davenport & Keane, 1999).

## A connectionist model of concept learning

Most of the computational models of concepts we have mentioned have been semantic networks in the Collins and Quillian style. More recently, several connectionist models have been used to model concepts. Indeed, there is a close relationship between semantic networks and some types of connectionist nets (see the section on localist representations in Chapter 9). Connectionist nets make good concept learners because they can learn from specific instances and implement similarity mechanisms automatically. Their strengths lie in extracting the commonalities between a set of examples. In feedforward networks that use back-propagation of errors (see Chapter 1), the network learns the central tendency of a set of target examples and encodes this as a pattern of activation in the network. Other forms of networks, called interactive activation nets (IAC), can find the commonalities between a set of concepts by the way activation is passed between the nodes of the network. McClelland (1981) provides a neat demonstration of how such networks can manifest many of the properties of human conceptual systems.

McClelland's IAC net was given an attribute description of the individuals in the Jets and Sharks gangs from *West Side Story* (see Table 10.2). In the network, each attribute is represented as a node; so there are nodes for gang names (Jets, Sharks), for education (junior high, college, high school) and jobs (pusher, burglar, bookie). Attributes that are related are grouped into "pools" (see Figure 10.5); so, the pusher, burglar, and bookie nodes are grouped together in a pool because they are all occupations, and all the names of the people are in a "name pool". There is a special "person pool" for each individual in the list. This pool contains nodes, which do not encode any specific attribute, that stand for a particular individual. The links between nodes within a pool are all inhibitory or negative (these links are not explicitly shown in Figure 10.5). This means that the Jets node in the "gang pool" will pass negative activation to the Sharks node and vice versa. So, if one of these nodes has a high activation then it will force the activation of the other node down.

In this network, an individual is encoded by establishing excitatory links between the individual node and the nodes for the attributes of that individual. So, to encode Art, excitatory links are established between the _Art person node and the Art name-node, the Jets node, the 40s age-node, the junior-high education-node, the single marital-status node, and the pusher job-node (see Figure 10.5). This means that if activation is high at one of these nodes it will pass positive excitation to all of its connected nodes. Each of these nodes will then attempt to force down the activation of nodes within its respective pool, via the inhibitory links within the pool.

After the nodes and links have been built in this network it goes through a number of cycles where activation is passed between all the nodes in the network. In this way the activation in one node will interact with the activation in all the other nodes. Typically, after a number of cycles the network will settle into a state where the activation levels in the nodes are relatively unchanging. This network model can be used to demonstrate a number of properties of human conceptual systems. For example, if you want to determine the attributes of a given individual you

## TABLE 10.2

The attributes used to characterise the individual members of two gangs, the Jets and Sharks, from McClelland (1981)

| Person | Name | Age | Education | Marital status | Job | Gang |
|--------|------|-----|-----------|----------------|-----|------|
| _Art | Art | 40s | junior high | single | pusher | Jets |
| _Al | Al | 30s | junior high | married | burglar | Jets |
| _Sam | Sam | 20s | college | single | bookie | Jets |
| _Clyde | Clyde | 40s | junior high | single | bookie | Jets |
| _Mike | Mike | 30s | junior high | single | bookie | Jets |
| _Jim | Jim | 20s | junior high | divorced | burglar | Jets |
| _Greg | Greg | 20s | high school | married | pusher | Jets |
| _John | John | 20s | junior high | married | burglar | Jets |
| _Doug | Doug | 30s | high school | single | bookie | Jets |
| _Lance | Lance | 20s | junior high | married | burglar | Jets |
| _George | George | 20s | junior high | divorced | burglar | Jets |
| _Pete | Pete | 20s | high school | single | bookie | Jets |
| _Fred | Fred | 20s | high school | single | pusher | Jets |
| _Gene | Gene | 20s | college | single | pusher | Jets |
| _Ralph | Ralph | 30s | junior high | single | pusher | Jets |
| _Phil | Phil | 30s | college | married | pusher | Sharks |
| _Ike | Ike | 30s | junior high | single | bookie | Sharks |
| _Nick | Nick | 30s | high school | single | pusher | Sharks |
| _Don | Don | 30s | college | married | burglar | Sharks |
| _Ned | Ned | 30s | college | married | bookie | Sharks |
| _Karl | Karl | 40s | high school | married | bookie | Sharks |
| _Ken | Ken | 20s | high school | single | burglar | Sharks |
| _Earl | Earl | 40s | high school | married | burglar | Sharks |
| _Rick | Rick | 30s | high school | divorced | burglar | Sharks |
| _Ol | Ol | 30s | college | married | pusher | Sharks |
| _Neal | Neal | 30s | high school | single | bookie | Sharks |
| _Dave | Dave | 30s | high school | divorced | pusher | Sharks |

can "clamp" a particular person-node (e.g., _Art); *clamping* is a term used to mean that you keep the activation in this node at a constant level on each cycle—you fix its activation at a given level so it does not change. When this is done, after a number of cycles all of Art's attributes will have high activations, indicating that these are his attributes. Furthermore, because activation passes out from some of these nodes to other instance nodes, all the individuals that share key attributes with Art will be activated to varying degrees. So, for example, the person nodes for _Clyde and _Ralph will also have high activations reflecting their similarity to _Art. More interestingly, the network can form a "generalisation" about the key attributes of different classes of individuals. If we clamp the Jets node, then when the network settles we have a weighted attribute description of the typical attributes of Jets gang-members; namely, that they tend to be single, are in their 20s, and have only been to junior high-school. A generalisation for the Sharks gang can also be determined in this way.

The important point about this model is that you do not have to explicitly encode general knowledge, rather this knowledge emerges from a collection of instances over which certain computations are carried out. Thus, this is one way of implementing

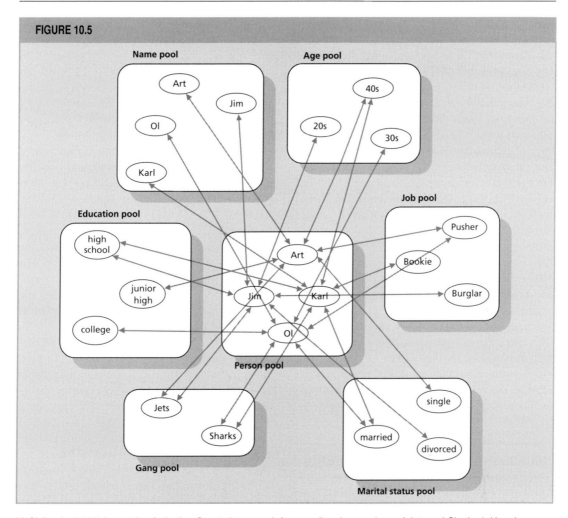

**FIGURE 10.5**

McClelland's (1981) Interactive Activation Constraint network for encoding the members of Jets and Sharks (with only some of the nodes and links shown). There are separate pools of nodes for the different properties (name, age, job, etc.). Within a pool all the nodes are interlinked in an inhibitory fashion (note that these links are not shown here). A particular individual is defined by establishing excitatory links between a given node in the person pool and the attribute nodes that define that individual. Copyright © Cognitive Science Society, Incorporated, used by permission.

exemplar-based models of categorisation reviewed earlier in this chapter (see e.g., Hintzman, 1986; Kruschke, 1992; Nosofsky, 1991).

## EVALUATING THEORIES OF CATEGORISATION

In this chapter, we have reviewed four main accounts of the nature of categorisation and concepts. We have seen that there is considerable diversity in these accounts:

- The classical, defining-attribute view.
- The prototype view.
- The exemplar-based view.
- The explanation-based view.

The truth about categorisation is probably a mixture of aspects of all of these accounts.

For the most part there are really too many evidential problems with the defining-attribute view for it to be properly considered a contender. Although there are some effects that question the dependency between typicality judgements and concept definitions (see e.g., Armstrong et al., 1983) there is so much negative evidence against this theory that it almost seems to be a straw man. As we have seen, the prototype and exemplar views do a much better job of handling the evidence of typicality effects, conceptual hierarchies, and category induction. Of these two, at present, the balance of evidence tips in favour of the exemplar theories, in that their proposal that people work from instances seems to supply a greater flexibility than is delivered by the idea of a central prototype. However, it must be remembered that there are occasions (e.g., in verifying inductive statements) where some abstract description of the members of a category appears to play a role.

However, the exemplar view is not in itself sufficient to account for all of the effects found. There are more rule-governed, theory-based aspects to conceptualisation that appear to depend on a much more relationally structured representation that can use very different processes to determine similarity (e.g., processes like structural alignment).

## NEUROLOGICAL EVIDENCE ON CONCEPTS

Throughout this chapter we have concentrated on attempts to understand the nature of the "normal" knowledge organisation. However, in the last 20 years a parallel research stream has examined impairments in knowledge that arise after neurological damage. This research has revealed a number of interesting and important findings.

First, people with a variety of neurological damage develop specific impairments of their semantic memory. When the cognitive systems involved in reading and speaking remain intact, there is evidence that the storage of knowledge or access to it, or both, can be disrupted. For example, Schwartz, Marin, and Saffran (1979; Schwartz, Saffran, & Marin 1980) studied a patient, WLP, suffering from a severe dementing disease. WLP's ability to read was intact but her comprehension was poor. For example, when she was asked to indicate which one of a set of words

a picture represented (using basic-level words, like "spoon", "apple", "cigarette"), she was poor at selecting the correct word for the picture. Furthermore, when she chose the wrong word, she tended to choose one that was related semantically to the correct choice. So, for example, for a picture of a fork she chose the word "spoon" and for a picture of a brush she chose "comb".

A second noteworthy finding is the way in which knowledge about superordinate concepts seems to be less susceptible to damage than more subordinate information (Warrington, 1975). Warrington (1975; see also Coughlan & Warrington, 1978) studied a patient, EM, also with a dementing illness, using a forced-choice decision task; that is, the patient was given a question like "Is cabbage an animal, a plant, or an inanimate object?" or "Is cabbage green, brown, or grey?" and had to choose one of the alternatives. It was discovered that EM was only wrong in 2% of cases on the former type of question but was wrong 28% of the time on the latter type of question. The point being that more subordinate attribute information about the *cabbage* concept was lost, even though the superordinate classification of a cabbage as a plant was retained (although see Rapp & Caramazza, 1989, for a challenge to this finding). Similar evidence has been found by Martin and Fedio (1983) in the naming errors made by Alzheimer's patients. These patients tend to give superordinates when they name objects wrongly. So, for example, asparagus is named as a vegetable and a pelican as a bird.

A third, and perhaps most surprising, finding from the neurological literature is evidence that patients have deficits in their knowledge of specific categories of objects. For example, Dennis (1976) has reported a patient who had difficulties only with the category "body parts". Warrington and Shallice (1984) have studied patients with similar deficits following damage to the medial temporal lobes, arising from herpes simplex encephalitis. These patients were very good at identifying inanimate objects by either verbal description or picture but were considerably poorer on objects that were living things or foods. More specifically, Hart, Berndt, and Caramazza (1985) have reported a patient, MD, with a deficit specific to the naming and categorisation of fruits and vegetables. Even though lesioned connectionist models manifest these sorts of deficits (see Plaut & Shallice, 1993), some researchers have argued that they may be artefactual (see Funnell & Sheridan, 1992; Parkin & Steward, 1993; Steward, Parkin, & Hunkin, 1992). Funnell and Sheridan (1993) proposed that studies showing category-specific effects did not control for important variables like the familiarity of the objects and their name frequency. In a patient they examined, they found that when they controlled for such factors there was no evidence of category-specific deficits. At this point, although the phenomenon is not at issue, the interpretation of it is the subject of considerable debate (Caramazza, 1998; Forde & Humphreys, 1999).

Many of these effects can be found together in Alzheimer's disease, where there is considerable degradation of patients' abilities in semantic memory tasks (see Nebes, 1989). How are we to understand these findings in the light of the previous theories of concepts? Shallice (1988) suggests that the salience of superordinate information indicates that the Roschian basic level is less important than previously thought. In terms of specific psychological models he suggests that these results favour later network models (e.g., Collins & Loftus, 1975) and distributed memory schemes (McClelland & Rumelhart, 1985). In distributed memory models, patterns of activation encoding superordinate information are less disrupted than patterns of activation representing exemplars.

## CHAPTER SUMMARY

The organisation of knowledge is one of the oldest and most researched areas in cognitive psychology. As such, it should act as a barometer of the state of the discipline. Has progress been made? Well, it is clear that research is not standing still. Researchers have used everything in the cognitive science cupboard (from empirical tests, to formal tests and computational models) to challenge each others' and often their own theories (e.g., Medin appears as the proposer of several different theories). It is clear that certain theoretical views are modified by the evidence found or in some cases wholly defeated. For instance, straight defining-attribute views have had their day, even though they have been the dominant view of conceptualisation for most of the intellectual history of western Europe.

In summary, we have examined the following main points throughout this chapter:

- People need to organise their knowledge into categories and concepts to deal efficiently with the world; conceptual systems need to have cognitive economy, need to be informative, and need to cohere naturally.
- The critical evidence on categorisation comes from category membership judgements showing typicality effects, the different levels of conceptual hierarchies, the fuzziness of category boundaries; prediction tasks showing how people make inductive inferences from categories; and concept instability effects.
- The defining-attribute view characterises concepts in terms of necessary and jointly sufficient attributes. This view asserts that (i) such attributes can be found, (ii) membership of a category is not a matter of degree but is an all-or-nothing affair, (iii) there are clear boundaries between conceptual categories, (iv) a subordinate concept should contain all the attributes of its superordinate concept. However, all of these assumptions are either highly questionable or have not been supported by the evidence found.
- The prototype view characterises concepts as being organised around prototypes, expressed as a central tendency in the attributes of members of the category. This view can account for gradients of typicality, for fuzzy boundaries, and for levels of abstraction in both natural and artificial categories. There are some queries about the generality of the prototype view, as some abstract

concepts do not exhibit prototype structure and it does not account for the use of variability and correlational aspects of concept definitions.

- The exemplar-based view characterises categories as collections of instances and explains the main finding in the literature by the way different example instances come to mind in different task contexts. It has been quite successful in its predictions about human conceptual behaviour.
- Theories of concepts have also been tested by being applied to other phenomena such as conceptual combination; that is, to explain what happens to the typicalities of combined concepts (e.g., red apple, ocean drive).
- Similarity is central to all theories of categorisation. Tversky's contrast model, and variants of it, have been extensively used to account for the judgement of conceptual similarity. Recently, this theory as been modified by research showing that when conceptual representations are characterised as having relations, then an account based on structural alignment or analogy is more appropriate.
- Cognitive neuropsychological accounts of category-specific impairments and other deficits in semantic memory have continued to help constrain the various theories of categorisation.

## FURTHER READING

- Estes, W.K. (1996). *Classification and cognition*. Oxford: Oxford University Press. This book gives a good account of exemplar-based approaches to categorisation, as well as the other theories.
- Fodor, J.A. (1998). *Concepts: Where cognitive science went wrong*. Oxford: Oxford University Press. This book gives a philosophically motivated critique of much of what has been reviewed in this chapter.
- Lamberts, K., & Shanks, D. (Eds.) (1997). *Knowledge, concepts and categories*. Cambridge, MA: MIT Press. This book is a recent collection of articles on prominent areas in concept research.
- McLeod, P., Plunkett, K., & Rolls, E.T. (1998). *Introduction to connectionist modelling of cognitive processes*. Oxford: Oxford University Press. This book provides a very good introduction to various aspects of connectionist modelling, some of which are relevant to theories of categorisation.
- Van Mechelen, I., Hampton, J., Michalski, R.S., & Theuns, P. (Eds.) (1993). *Concepts and categories*. London: Academic Press. This book has a good selection of chapters on key topics.

# Speech Perception and Reading

## INTRODUCTION

Humanity excels in its command of language. Indeed, language is of such enormous importance to human cognition that this chapter and the following two are devoted to it. In this chapter, we will focus on the basic processes involved in listening to speech and in reading. For many purposes, it may not make much difference whether a message is presented to our ears or to our eyes. For example, we would normally understand a sentence such as, "You have done exceptionally well in your cognitive psychology examination", in much the same way regardless of whether we hear or read it. Thus, many comprehension processes are very similar whether we are reading a text or listening to someone talking.

However, speech perception and reading differ in important ways. In reading, each word can be seen as a whole, whereas a spoken word is spread out in time. Speech generally provides a more ambiguous and unclear signal than does printed text. When words were spliced out of spoken sentences and presented on their own, they were recognised only about half the time (Lieberman, 1963). Anyone who has studied a foreign language

will remember the initial shock at being totally unable to understand the very rapid and apparently uninterrupted flow of speech produced by a native speaker of that language.

There are other significant differences. The demands on memory are greater when we are listening to speech than reading a text, because the words that have already been spoken are no longer accessible. So far, we have indicated ways in which listening to speech is harder than reading a text. However, there is one major way in which listening to speech can be easier than reading. Speech usually contains numerous hints to sentence structure and intended meaning via the speaker's pitch, intonation, stress, and timing (e.g., questions have a rising intonation on the last word in the sentence). These various hints are known as *prosodic cues*. In contrast, the main cues to sentence structure specific to text are punctuation marks (e.g., commas; semi-colons). These are often regarded as having the same function as certain aspects of prosody, but are often less informative than the prosodic cues in speech.

The fact that listening to speech and reading are quite different in some ways can be shown by considering children and brain-damaged patients. Young children often have good comprehension of spoken language, but struggle to read even simple stories. Some adult brain-damaged patients can understand spoken language but cannot read, and others can read perfectly well but cannot understand the spoken word.

Basic processes specific to listening to speech are dealt with first in this chapter, followed by basic processes specific to reading. Language comprehension processes common to listening and to reading are discussed in the next chapter.

## LISTENING TO SPEECH

Accurate perception of speech is a more complex achievement than might be imagined, partly because language is spoken at a rate of up to 12 *phonemes* (basic speech sounds) per second. Amazingly, we can understand speech artificially speeded up to 50–60 sounds per minute (Werker & Tees, 1992). In normal speech, phonemes overlap, and there is *co-articulation*, in which producing one speech segment affects the production of the following segment. The "linearity problem" refers to the difficulties for speech perception produced by co-articulation.

Another problem related to the linearity problem is the "non-invariance problem". This arises because the sound pattern for any given speech component such as a phoneme is not invariant. Instead, it is affected by the sound or sounds preceding and following it. This is especially the case for consonants, because their sound patterns often depend on the following vowel.

Speech typically consists of a continuously changing pattern of sound with few periods of silence. This contrasts with our perception of speech as consisting of separate sounds. The continuous nature of the speech signal produces the "segmentation problem", which involves deciding how the continuous stream of sound should be divided up into words.

### Spectrograms and running spectral displays

Much valuable information about the speech signal has been obtained from use of the *spectrograph*. With this instrument, sound enters through a microphone, and is then converted into an electrical signal. This signal is fed to a bank of filters selecting narrow-frequency bands. Finally, the spectrograph produces a visible record of the component frequencies of sound over time; this is known as a *spectrogram* (see Figure 11.1). The spectrogram provides information about *formants*, which are frequency bands emphasised by the vocal apparatus when saying a phoneme. Vowels have three formants; these are numbered first,

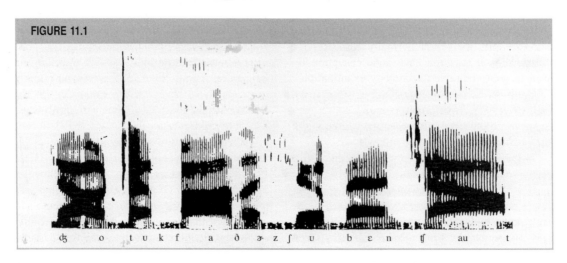

**FIGURE 11.1**

Spectrogram of the sentence "Joe took father's shoe bench out". From *Language Processes* by Vivien C. Tartter (1986, p. 210), reproduced with permission of the author.

second, and third, starting with the formant of lowest frequency. However, vowels can usually be identified on the basis of the first two formants. Most vowel sounds fall below 1200 Hertz (Hz), which is a measure of sound frequency. In contrast, many consonants have sounds falling in the region from 2400 Hz upwards.

Spectrograms may seem to provide an accurate picture of those aspects of the sound wave having the greatest influence on the human auditory system. However, this is not necessarily the case. For example, formants look important in a spectrogram, but this does not prove they are of value in human speech perception. Evidence that the spectrogram *is* of value has been provided by making use of a *pattern playback* or *vocoder*, which allows the spectrograph to be played back. Thus, the pattern of frequencies in the spectrogram was produced by speech, and pattern playback permits the spectrogram to be reconverted into speech again. Liberman, Delattre, and Cooper (1952) constructed "artificial" vowels on the spectrogram based only on the first two formants of each vowel. These vowels were easily identified when they were played through the vocoder, suggesting that formant information is used to recognise vowels.

Sussman, Hoemeke, and Ahmed (1993) asked various speakers to say the same short words starting with a consonant. They found clear differences from speaker to speaker in their spectrograms. How do listeners cope with such differences? Sussman et al. (1993) focused on two aspects of the information contained in the spectrogram record:

1. The sound frequency at the transition point where the second formant starts.
2. The steady frequency of the second formant.

There was relational invariance between these two measures: those speakers who had high frequencies for (1) also had high frequencies for (2), whereas other speakers had low frequencies for both measures. Listeners probably use information about this relational invariance to identify the word being spoken.

An alternative way of turning speech sounds into visual form is by *running spectral displays*.

These displays provide information about changes in sound frequencies that occur in successive brief periods of time. The advantage of running spectral displays over spectrograms is that they show more precisely how much energy is present at each frequency. Kewley-Port and Luce (1984) found their participants were able to identify the voicing and place of articulation of many phonemes with an accuracy of between 80% and 90% on the basis of running spectral displays.

## Categorical speech perception

Speech perception differs from other kinds of auditory perception. For example, there is a definite left-hemisphere advantage for perception of speech but not other auditory stimuli. Speech perception exhibits *categorical speech perception*: speech stimuli intermediate between two phonemes are typically categorised as one phoneme or the other, thus producing a discrimination boundary that is more clear cut than is warranted by the physical stimuli (see Miller & Eimas, 1995, for a review). For example, the Japanese langugage does not distinguish between [l] and [r]. As these sounds belong to the same category for Japanese listeners, it is no surprise that they find it very hard to discriminate between them (see Massaro, 1994). This differs from the case with non-speech sounds, where discrimination between pairs of sounds is superior to the ability to label them as belonging to separate categories.

There is clear evidence for categorical perception in our conscious experience of speech perception. However, that does not necessarily mean that the earlier stages of speech processing are also categorical. In fact, the evidence suggests that they are not (see Massaro, 1994).

The major differences between speech perception and auditory perception in general led Mattingly and Liberman (1990) to argue that speech perception involves a special module or cognitive processor functioning independently of other modules. This issue was addressed by Remez, Rubin, Pisoni, and Carrell (1981). According to them, use of the speech perception module (if it exists) should not be influenced by some quite separate factor such as the listener's belief about the nature of the signal. They played a series of tones to two groups of participants. One group was told that they would be listening to synthetic or artificial speech, and their task was to write down what was said. These participants had no difficulty in carrying out this task. The other group was simply told to describe what they heard. They reported hearing electronic sounds, tape-recorder problems, radio interference, and so on, but they did not perceive any speech. The dependence of speech processing on the manipulation of the listeners' expectations suggests that speech perception does *not* involve a special module.

## Word recognition

A key issue in research on speech perception is to identify the processes involved in spoken word recognition. There are numerous studies on this topic (see Moss & Gaskell, 1999, for a review). We will first consider some of the major processes involved, and will then turn to a discussion of influential theories of spoken word recognition.

### Bottom-up and top-down processes

Spoken word recognition is generally achieved by a mixture of bottom-up or data-driven processes triggered by the acoustic signal, and top-down or conceptually driven processes generated from the linguistic context. However, as we will see, there have been disagreements about precisely how information from bottom-up and top-down processes is combined to produce word recognition.

Spoken language consists of a series of sounds or phonemes incorporating various features. Among the features for phonemes are the following:

- Manner of production (oral vs. nasal vs. fricative, involving a partial blockage of the airstream).
- Place of articulation.
- Voicing: the larynx vibrates for a voiced but not for a voiceless phoneme.

The notion that bottom-up processes in word recognition make use of feature information was supported in a classic study by Miller and Nicely

(1955). They gave their participants the task of recognising consonants presented auditorily against a background of noise. The most frequently confused consonants were those differing on the basis of only one feature.

Evidence that top-down processing based on context can be involved in speech perception was obtained by Warren and Warren (1970). They studied what is known as the *phonemic restoration effect*. Participants heard a sentence in which a small portion had been removed and replaced with a meaningless sound. The sentences that were used were as follows (the asterisk indicates a deleted portion of the sentence):

- It was found that the *eel was on the axle.
- It was found that the *eel was on the shoe.
- It was found that the *eel was on the table.
- It was found that the *eel was on the orange.

The perception of the crucial element in the sentence (i.e., *eel) was influenced by sentence context. Participants listening to the first sentence heard "wheel", those listening to the second sentence heard "heel", and those exposed to the third and fourth sentences heard "meal" and "peel", respectively. The auditory stimulus was always the same, so all that differed was the contextual information.

Samuel (1981) identified two possible explanations for the phonemic restoration effect. First, context may interact directly with bottom-up processes; this would be a sensitivity effect. Second, the context may simply provide an additional source of information; this would be a response bias effect. Participants listened to sentences, and meaningless noise was presented briefly during each sentence. On some trials, this noise was superimposed on one of the phonemes of a word; on other trials, that phoneme was deleted. The task was to decide whether or not the crucial phoneme had been presented. Finally, the word containing this phoneme was predictable or unpredictable from the sentence context.

Performance in Samuel's (1981) study was better when the word was predictable, indicating the importance of context. If context improves sensitivity, then the ability to discriminate between phoneme plus noise and noise alone should be improved by predictable context. If context affects response bias, then participants should simply be more likely to decide that the phoneme was presented when the word was presented in a predictable context. Context affected response bias but not sensitivity, suggesting that contextual information did *not* have a direct effect on bottom-up processing.

Samuel (1990) reported further studies on the phonemic restoration effect. The effect was more likely to occur in long words than in short words, presumably because long words provide additional contextual information. There was more evidence for the phonemic restoration effect when the phoneme that was masked and the masking noise were similar in sound. Samuel (1990) concluded that contextual information influences the listener's expectations in a top-down fashion, but these expectations then need to be confirmed with reference to the sound that is actually presented.

### Prosodic patterns

Spoken speech contains *prosodic cues* in the form of stress, intonation, and so on. This information can be used by the listener to work out the syntactic or grammatical structure of each sentence. For example, in the ambiguous sentence, "The old men and women sat on the bench", the women may or may not be old. If the women are not old, then the spoken duration of the word "men" will be relatively long, and the stressed syllable in "women" will have a steep rise in pitch contour. Neither of these prosodic features will be present if the sentence means that the women are old.

Most studies on listeners' ability to use prosody to interpret ambiguous sentences have only assessed this after an entire sentence has been presented. These studies have shown that prosodic patterns are generally interpreted correctly, but do not indicate *when* prosodic information is used. Beach (1990) presented a sentence fragment, and participants had to decide which of two sentences it had come from. For example, the fragment, "Sherlock Holmes didn't suspect", could be from the sentence, "Sherlock Holmes didn't suspect the beautiful young countess from Hungary", or the

sentence, "Sherlock Holmes didn't suspect the beautiful young countess could be a fraud". Participants were fairly accurate at predicting the overall structure of sentences on the basis of a small fragment, indicating that prosodic information can be used rapidly by listeners.

Doubts about the role of prosodic cues were raised by Allbritton, McKoon, and Ratcliff (1996; see Chapter 13). Trained and untrained speakers were given ambiguous sentences in a disambiguating context, and told to read them out loud. Even the trained speakers only made modest use of prosodic cues to clarify the intended meaning of the ambiguous sentences.

### Lip-reading

Many people (especially those who are hard of hearing) are aware that they use lip-reading to understand speech. However, this seems to happen far more than is generally believed among those whose hearing is normal. McGurk and MacDonald (1976) provided a striking demonstration of the importance of lip-reading. They prepared a video-tape of someone repeating "ba" over and over again. The sound channel then changed so there was a voice saying "ga" repeatedly in synchronisation with the lip movements still indicating "ba". Participants reported that they heard "da", representing a blending of the visual and the auditory information.

The so-called McGurk effect is surprisingly robust. For example, Green, Kuhl, Meltzoff, and Stevens (1991) found the effect even when there was a female face and a male voice. They suggested that information about pitch becomes irrelevant early in speech processing, and this is why the McGurk effect is found even with a gender mismatch between vision and hearing.

Visual information from lip movements is used to make sense of speech sounds because the information conveyed by the speech sounds is often inadequate. Much is now known about the ways in which visual information provided by the speaker is used in speech perception (see Dodd & Campbell, 1986). Of course, there are circumstances (e.g., listening to the radio) in which no relevant visual information is available. We can usually follow what is said on the radio, because broadcasters are trained to articulate clearly.

---

# THEORIES OF WORD RECOGNITION

There are several theories of spoken word recognition, three of which will be discussed here. The first theory (motor theory of speech perception) is of historical importance, and merits inclusion for that reason. The other two theories (cohort theory and the TRACE model) have been very influential in recent years.

## Motor theory

A key issue is to explain how it is that listeners perceive words accurately even though the speech signal provides variable information. Liberman et al. (1967) argued in their motor theory of speech perception that listeners mimic the articulatory movements of the speaker, but this need not involve measurable articulatory responses. The motor signal thus produced was claimed to provide much less variable and inconsistent information about what the speaker is saying than the speech signal itself. Our reliance on the motor signal allows spoken word recognition to be reasonably accurate.

Evidence consistent with the motor theory was reported by Dorman, Raphael, and Liberman (1979). A tape was made of the sentence, "Please say shop", and a 50-millisecond period of silence was inserted between "say" and "shop". As a result, the sentence was misheard as "Please say chop". Our speech musculature forces us to pause between "say" and "chop", but not between "say" and "shop", and so the evidence from internal articulation would favour the wrong interpretation of the last word in the sentence.

The assumption that the motor signal provides invariant information about speech segments is incorrect. There are, for example, as many different motor manifestations of a given consonant as there are acoustic manifestations (MacNeilage, 1972). Such findings rather undermine the main reason for proposing the motor theory in the first place.

It follows from the motor theory that infants with limited expertise in articulation of speech should be very poor at speech perception. In fact, infants perform very well on many tests of speech perception (e.g., Eimas et al., 1987). Thus, the ability to produce and make use of the motor signal is not necessary for good levels of speech perception. Simultaneous translators can listen to speech in one language while producing fluent speech in another language at the same time, and it is hard to see how this could happen on the motor theory.

In spite of experimental disconfirmations, motor theory has influenced contemporary thinking. For example, one of the attractive features of motor theory was that it drew a clear distinction between the processing of speech and the processing of other auditory stimuli. A related position has been adopted by those contemporary theorists (e.g., Mattingly & Liberman, 1990) who argue that there is a separate module for speech perception.

## Cohort theory

One of the most influential theories of spoken word recognition was put forward by Marslen-Wilson and Tyler (1980). The original cohort theory included the following assumptions:

- Early in the auditory presentation of a word, those words known to the listener that conform to the sound sequence that has been heard so far become active; this collection of candidates for the presented word is the "word-initial cohort".
- Words belonging to this cohort are then eliminated because they cease to match further information from the presented word, or because they are inconsistent with the semantic or other context.
- Processing of the presented word continues only until contextual information and information from the word itself are sufficient to eliminate all but one of the words in the word-initial cohort; this is known as the "recognition point" of a word.

According to cohort theory, various knowledge sources (e.g., lexical, syntactic, semantic) *interact*

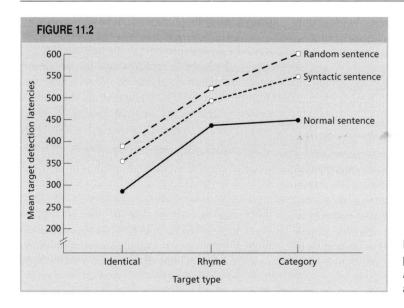

**FIGURE 11.2**

Mean target detection latencies

600
550
500
450
400
350
300
250
200

□ Random sentence
○ Syntactic sentence
● Normal sentence

Identical        Rhyme        Category

Target type

Detection times for word targets presented in sentences. Adapted from Marslen-Wilson and Tyler (1980).

and combine with each other in complex ways to produce an efficient analysis of spoken language. This approach can be contrasted with the notion (e.g., Forster, 1979) that processing proceeds in a serial fashion, with spoken language being analysed in a fairly fixed and invariant series of processing stages.

Marslen-Wilson and Tyler (1980) tested some of their theoretical notions in a word-monitoring task, in which participants had to identify pre-specified target words presented within spoken sentences. There were normal sentences, syntactic sentences (grammatically correct but meaning-less), and random sentences (unrelated words), and the target was a member of a given category, a word that rhymed with a given word, or a word that was identical to a given word. The measure of interest was the speed with which the target could be detected.

It is predicted by cohort theory that sensory information from the target word and contextual information from the rest of the sentence are both used at the same time. In contrast, it is pre-dicted by serial theories that sensory information is extracted prior to the use of contextual informa-tion. The results conformed more closely to the predictions of cohort theory. Complete sensory analysis of the longer words was not needed when there was adequate contextual information (see

Figure 11.2). It was only necessary to listen to the entire word when the sentence context con-tained no useful syntactic or semantic information (i.e., random condition).

Undue significance was given to the initial part of the word in the original cohort theory. It was assumed that a spoken word will generally not be recognised if its initial phoneme is unclear or ambiguous. There is evidence that the meanings of words not sharing an initial phoneme with the presented speech input are not *immediately* activ-ated (e.g., Marslen-Wilson, Moss, & van Halen, 1996, discussed later). However, Connine, Blasko, and Titone (1993) referred to a study in which a spoken word ending in "ent" had an ambiguous initial phoneme between "d" and "t". There was evidence that the words "dent" and "tent" could both be activated at a short delay when the target word was presented.

Marslen-Wilson (1990) and Marslen-Wilson and Warren (1994) revised cohort theory. In the original version, words were either in or out of the word cohort. In the revised version, candidate words vary in their level of activation, and so membership of the word cohort is a matter of degree. Marslen-Wilson (1990) assumed that the word-initial cohort may contain words having similar initial phonemes, rather than being limited only to words having the initial phoneme of the presented word. These, and other, changes to cohort theory allow it to account for findings such as those of Connine et al. (1993).

There is a second major difference between the original and revised versions of cohort theory. In the original version, context influenced word recognition very early in processing. In contrast, the effects of context on word recognition are much more limited in the revised version, occurring only at a fairly late stage of processing. Evidence supporting the revised theory has come from studies on cross-modal priming, in which the participants listen to speech and perform a lexical decision task (deciding whether visual letter strings form words). The key assumption is that only words that have been activated by the speech input will show priming in the form of faster responding on the lexical decision task. Zwitserlood (1989) considered the effects of context on cross-modal priming. Context did not influence the initial activation of words (i.e., contextually inappropriate words as well as appropiate ones were activated), but it did have an effect *after* the point at which a spoken word could be uniquely identified.

*Evaluation*

Cohort theory has proved to be an influential approach to spoken word recognition. The revised version of the theory is generally preferable to the original version for two main reasons:

1. Its assumption that membership of the word cohort is flexible is more in line with the evidence.
2. Contextual effects on spoken word recognition typically occur late rather than early in processing, as proposed within the revised theory.

The major disadvantage with the revised version is that the modifications made to the original theory have made it less precise. As Massaro (1994, p. 244) pointed out, "These modifications are necessary to bring the model in line with empirical results, but they . . . make it more difficult to test against alternative models."

## TRACE model

McClelland and Elman (1986) and McClelland (1991) produced a network model of speech perception based on connectionist principles (see Chapter 1). Their TRACE model of speech perception resembles the original version of cohort theory. For example, it is argued within both cohort theory and the TRACE model that several sources of information combine interactively to achieve word recognition. The TRACE model also resembles the interactive activation model of visual word recognition put forward by McClelland and Rumelhart (1981), which is discussed later.

The TRACE model is based on the following theoretical assumptions:

- There are individual processing units or nodes at three different levels: features (e.g., voicing; manner of production), phonemes, and words.
- Feature nodes are connected to phoneme nodes, and phoneme nodes are connected to word nodes.
- Connections between levels operate in both directions, and are only facilitatory.
- There are connections among units or nodes at the same level; these connections are inhibitory.
- Nodes influence each other in proportion to their activation levels and the strengths of their interconnections.
- As excitation and inhibition spread among nodes, a pattern of activation or trace develops.
- The word that is recognised is determined by the activation level of the possible candidate words.

The TRACE model assumes that bottom-up and top-down processing interact during speech perception. Bottom-up activation proceeds upwards from the feature level to the phoneme level and on to the word level, whereas top-down activation proceeds in the opposite direction from the word level to the phoneme level and on to the feature level. Evidence that top-down processes are involved in spoken word recognition was discussed earlier in the chapter (e.g., Marslen-Wilson & Tyler, 1980; Warren & Warren, 1970).

McClelland and Rumelhart (1986) applied the TRACE model to the phenomenon of categorical speech perception. According to the model, the discrimination boundary between phonemes becomes sharper because of mutual inhibition between phoneme units at the phoneme level. These inhibitory processes produce a "winner takes all" situation, in which one phoneme becomes increasingly activated while at the same time other phonemes are inhibitory. McClelland and Rumelhart (1986) carried out a simulation based on the model that successfully produced categorical speech perception.

Cutler et al. (1987) studied another phenomenon that lends itself to explanation by the TRACE model. They used a phoneme monitoring task, in which participants had to respond immediately to the presence of a target phoneme. They observed a word superiority effect, in that phonemes were detected faster when they were presented in words than in non-words. According to the TRACE model, this phenomenon occurs because of top-down activation from the word level to the phoneme level.

Marslen-Wilson et al. (1996) presented their participants with "words" such as p/blank, in which the initial phoneme was halfway between a /p/ and a /b/. They wanted to see whether this "word" would facilitate lexical decision for words related to plank (e.g., wood) or to blank (e.g., page). The TRACE model predicts that there would be a significant facilitation or priming effect because of spreading activation. In contrast, the original cohort theory assumed that only words matching the initial phoneme of the presented word are activated. Thus, the prediction is that there should be no priming effect. The findings supported the cohort theory and were inconsistent with the prediction of the TRACE model.

## Evaluation

The TRACE model has various successes to its credit. It provides reasonable accounts of phenomena such as categorical speech perception and the word superiority effect in phoneme monitoring. A significant general strength of the TRACE model is its assumption that bottom-up and top-down processes both contribute to spoken word recognition, combined with explicit assumptions about the processes involved. However, the theory predicts that speech perception depends *interactively* on top-down and bottom-up processes, and this was not confirmed by Massaro (1989) on a phoneme-discrimination task. Bottom-up effects stemming from stimulus discriminability and top-down effects stemming from phonological context both influence performance, but they did so in an *independent* rather than interactive way.

There are other problems with the TRACE model. First, it is assumed that words that are phonologically similar to a presented word will be activated immediately, even though they do not match the presented word in the initial phoneme. In fact, this is typically not the case (e.g., Marslen-Wilson et al., 1996).

Second, the theory exaggerates the importance of top-down effects. For example, Frauenfelder, Segui, and Dijkstra (1990) gave their participants the task of detecting a given phoneme. The key condition was one in which a non-word closely resembling an actual word was presented (e.g. "vocabutaire" instead of "vocabulaire"). According to the model, top-down effects from the word node corresponding to "vocabulaire" should have inhibited the task of identifying the "t" in "vocabutaire", but they did not.

Third, the existence of top-down effects depends more on stimulus degradation than is predicted by the model. For example, McQueen (1991) presented ambiguous phonemes at the end of stimuli, and asked participants to categorise these phonemes. Each ambiguous phoneme could be perceived as completing a word or a non-word. According to the model, top-down effects from the word level should have produced a preference for perceiving the phonemes as completing words. This prediction was confirmed *only* when the stimulus was degraded.

Fourth, the model has problems in dealing with issues such as the timing of speech sounds and differences in speech rate from one speaker to another. The TRACE model assumes that there are time slots, with feature, phoneme, and word units or representations being replicated across time slots to allow them to be identified. However, as Ellis and Humphreys (1999, p. 349) pointed out, "The problem with this of course is that it requires massive numbers of units, and of connections between units ... TRACE has local units that are set to a given time slot. There is no guarantee that the speech signal will match the time slots set in the model. As a consequence, the model may fail to generalise its recognition across different speech rates." The consequence of this is that TRACE cannot recognise speech (Protopapas, 1999).

Fifth, tests of the model have relied heavily on computer simulations involving a small number of one-syllable words. As a result, it is not entirely clear whether the model would perform satisfactorily if applied to the vastly larger vocabularies possessed by most people.

Sixth, we learn many aspects of speech perception during the course of development. In contrast, as Protopapas (1999, p. 420) pointed out, TRACE "does not learn anything. It is prewired to achieve all its remarkable results, thus effectively encoding the knowledge and intuition of its designers."

## Section summary

Theories of spoken word recognition are becoming increasingly similar. Most theorists agree that activation of several candidate words occurs early in the process of word recognition. It is also generally assumed that the speed with which word recognition is usually achieved indicates that most of the processes involved proceed in parallel, or at the same time, rather than serially. There is also general agreement that the activation levels of candidate words are graded rather than being either very high or very low. Finally, nearly all theorists agree that bottom-up and top-down processes combine in some way to produce word recognition, although they disagree on how this happens. The revised version of cohort theory and the TRACE model both incorporate all these assumptions.

There are two issues in need of further research. First, there is still very little agreement on the size and number of the basic perceptual units in spoken word recognition, with theorists differing in the importance they attach to features, phonemes, syllables, and so on. Second, there is the issue of precisely how contextual and other forms of top-down information are used in spoken word recognition. As Harley (1995, p. 56) concluded, "It is difficult to draw any definite conclusions about the role of context in spoken word recognition ... we need more detail on the time course of the different stages of word recognition ... it is difficult to be sure that these experiments [on context] are tapping processes before the selection of a unique candidate rather than reflecting post-access effects."

## COGNITIVE NEUROPSYCHOLOGY

Repeating a spoken word immediately after hearing it is an apparently simple task. However, many brain-damaged patients experience difficulties with this task even though audiometric testing reveals they are not deaf. Detailed analysis of these patients suggests there are various processes that can be used to permit repetition of a spoken word.

Information from such patients was used by Ellis and Young (1988) to propose a model of the processing of spoken words (see Figure 11.3 for a modified version). The model consists of five components:

- The *auditory analysis system* is used to extract phonemes or other sounds from the speech wave.
- The *auditory input lexicon* contains information about spoken words known to the listener, but does not contain information about their meaning. The purpose of this lexicon is to recognise familiar words via the activation of the appropriate word units.
- The meanings of words are stored within the *semantic system* (cf. semantic memory, which is discussed in Chapter 7).
- The *speech output lexicon* serves to provide the spoken forms of words.
- The *phoneme response buffer* provides distinctive speech sounds.
- These components can be used in various combinations, so there are three different routes between hearing a spoken word and saying it.

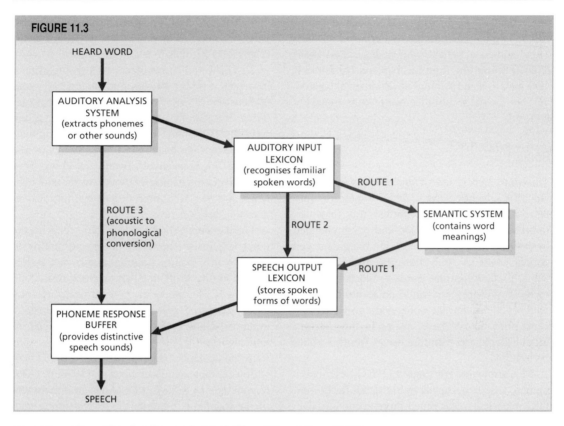

**FIGURE 11.3**

Processing and repetition of spoken words. Adapted from Ellis and Young (1988).

The most striking feature of the model is the notion that saying a spoken word can be achieved using three different routes. It is this feature of the model to which we will devote the most attention. Before doing so, however, we will consider the role of the auditory analysis system in speech perception.

## Auditory analysis system

Suppose that a patient had damage only to the auditory analysis system, thereby producing a deficit in phonemic processing. Such a patient would have impaired speech perception for words and non-words, and this would be especially so for words containing phonemes that are hard to discriminate. However, such a patient would have generally intact speech production, reading, and writing, would have normal perception of non-verbal environmental sounds (e.g., coughs;

whistles), and their hearing would not be impaired. Several patients conforming to this pattern have been identified (see Parkin, 1996), and the term *pure word deafness* has been used to describe their condition.

If patients with pure word deafness have a severe deficit in phonemic processing, then their speech perception should improve when they have access to other kinds of information. This is the case. Okada et al. (1963) studied a patient with pure word deafness who could use contextual information. The patient found it much easier to understand spoken questions when they all referred to the same topic than when they did not. In another study, Auerbach et al. (1982) found that patients with pure word deafness had better speech perception when lip-reading was possible.

A crucial aspect of pure word deafness is that auditory perception problems are highly *selective*, and do not apply to non-speech sounds. Evidence that separate systems deal with speech and non-speech sounds was reported by Fujii et al. (1990). They studied a patient who had suffered brain damage within the right hemisphere. He found it very hard to name familiar environmental sounds, but his language abilities were only modestly affected.

## Route 1

This route makes use of the auditory input lexicon, the semantic system, and the speech output lexicon. It represents the normal way in which familiar words are identified and comprehended by those with no brain damage. If a brain-damaged patient could use only this route (plus perhaps Route 2), then familiar words would be said correctly. However, there would be severe problems with saying unfamiliar words and non-words, because they do not have entries in the auditory input lexicon, and therefore use of Route 3 would be required.

McCarthy and Warrington (1984) described a patient, ORF, who seems to fit the bill fairly well. ORF repeated words much more accurately than non-words (85% vs. 39%, respectively), indicating that Route 3 was severely impaired. However, the fact that he made a fair number of errors in repeating words suggests there was also some impairment to other parts of the system.

## Route 2

If patients could use Route 2, but Routes 1 and 3 were severely impaired, they should be able to repeat familiar words but would often not understand their meaning. In addition, they should have problems with non-words, because non-words cannot be handled through Route 2. Finally, as such patients would make use of the input lexicon, they should be able to distinguish between words and non-words.

Patients suffering from a condition known as *word meaning deafness* fit this description. Unfortunately, very few patients with this condition have been studied, so "the existence of word meaning deafness is still a matter of controversy" (Franklin et al., 1996, p. 1140). However, one of the clearest cases of word meaning deafness, Dr O, was studied by Franklin et al. (1996) themselves, and we will focus on this case.

Dr O showed "no evidence of any impairment in written word comprehension, but auditory comprehension was impaired, particularly for abstract or low-imageability words" (Franklin et al., 1996, p. 1144). His ability to repeat words was dramatically better than his ability to repeat non-words, 80% vs. 7%, respectively. Finally, Dr O was very good at distinguishing between words and non-words: he was 94% correct on an auditory lexical decision task.

Dr O seems to have reasonable access to the input lexicon as shown by his greater ability to repeat words than non-words, and by his almost perfect ability to distinguish between words and non-words. He clearly has some problem relating to the semantic system. However, the semantic system itself does not seem to be damaged, as indicated by the additional finding that his ability to understand written words was intact. These various findings led Franklin et al. (1996, p. 1139) to conclude as follows: "Dr O has an impairment of the mappings between the lexical representations of spoken words and their corresponding semantic representations." Thus, there is damage to parts of Route 1. Tyler and Moss (1997) argued that Dr O may also have problems earlier in processing. They reported some evidence that he may have difficulties in extracting phonemic features from speech. For example, when he was asked to repeat spoken words as rapidly as possible, he made 25% errors.

Hall and Riddoch (1997) reported on KW, a man who had had a stroke, and who suffered from word meaning deafness. He showed impaired auditory comprehension of words even though his ability to understand written words was fairly intact. There was good evidence that KW made use of the input lexicon: (1) he spelled 60% of auditorily presented words correctly, compared to only 35% of non-words; (2) he was 89% accurate in distinguishing between auditorily presented words and non-words. Hall and Riddoch (1997, p. 1161) concluded as follows: "We have clearly demonstrated the use of a lexical nonsemantic spelling route."

## Route 3

If a patient had damage to Route 3 only, he or she would show good ability to perceive and to understand spoken familiar words, but would be impaired at perceiving and repeating unfamiliar words and non-words. This is the case in patients with *auditory phonological agnosia*. Such a patient was studied by Beavois, Dérouesné, and Bastard (1980). Their patient, JL, had almost perfect repetition and writing to dictation of spoken familiar words, but his repetition and writing of non-words was very poor. However, he was very good at *reading* non-words. JL had an intact ability to distinguish between words and non-words, indicating that there were no problems with access to the input lexicon.

## Deep dysphasia

Some brain-damaged patients have extensive problems with speech perception, suggesting that several parts of the speech perception system are damaged. For example, patients with *deep dysphasia* make semantic errors when asked to repeat spoken words (i.e., they say words related in meaning to those spoken). In addition, they find it harder to repeat abstract words than concrete ones, and they have very poor ability to repeat non-words. With reference to the model in Figure 11.3, it could be argued that none of the three routes between heard words and speech is intact. The presence of semantic errors can be explained by assuming there is some impairment in (or near) the semantic system.

Valdois et al. (1995) studied EA, a 72-year-old man who had suffered a stroke. He exhibited all the symptoms of deep dysphasia, including numerous semantic errors when trying to repeat spoken words having a synonym. In addition, EA had very poor short-term memory for auditory and visual verbal material. These latter findings led Valdois et al. (1995, p. 711) to the following theoretical interpretation: "The impairment responsible for both E.A.'s language performance and his short-term memory deficit is rooted in the inability to maintain a sufficiently activated phonological representation [in the response buffer]." They developed a connectionist model to explain the various symptoms of deep dysphasia. For example, the existence of semantic errors may occur because semantic information is often activated for longer than phonological information.

Which theoretical approach is preferable? It is possible that both approaches apply to some (but not all) deep dysphasics. Valdois et al. (1995) reviewed the literature, and discussed six deep dysphasics who had a very severe short-memory memory deficit (memory span of one or two items). These patients conform to the theoretical expectation of Valdois et al. (1995), in that there is evidence of damage to the response buffer. However, they also discussed three other patients who had only slightly impaired short-term memory. As Valdois et al. (1995, p. 719) concluded, "These overall data strongly suggest that different subtypes of repetition disorders of the deep dysphasia type do exist, which probably reflect different underlying deficits."

## Section summary

There has been relatively little research on auditory word recognition and comprehension in brain-damaged patients. However, there are clearly different patterns of impairment in the ability to repeat and to understand spoken words. This encourages the belief that various processes are involved, and that there is more than one route between hearing a word and then saying it. Figure 11.3 represents a possible set of components and their interactions, but its validity will become clear only after much further research.

## BASIC READING PROCESSES

Reading is fairly effortless for most adults. However, it requires several perceptual and other cognitive processes, as well as a good knowledge of language and of grammar. Indeed, most mental activities are related to reading, and it is sometimes referred to as "visually guided thinking".

Why is it important to study reading? Skilled reading has much value in contemporary society, and adults without effective reading skills are at a great disadvantage. Thus, it is important to discover enough about reading processes to be able to sort out the problems of poor readers.

Some reading processes are concerned with identifying and extracting meaning from individual words. Other processes operate at the level of the phrase or sentence, and still others deal with the overall organisation or thematic structure of an entire story or book. However, research has focused on only some of these processes: "Scanning the literature on skilled reading, one could be forgiven for thinking that the goal of reading is to turn print into speech. Of course, it is not: the goal of reading is to understand (perhaps even to enjoy) a piece of text" (Ellis, 1993, p. 35).

## Research methods

Several methods are available for studying reading. Probably the most generally useful method is that of recording *eye movements* during reading. This method has two particular strengths: (1) it provides a detailed on-line record of attention-related processes; and (2) it is unobtrusive. The only major restriction on readers whose eye movements are being recorded is that they should keep their heads fairly still. The main disadvantage is that it is hard to be sure precisely *what* processing occurs during each fixation.

Another method providing an on-line measure of reading involves recordings of people *reading aloud*. This method permits analysis of the type of errors made in reading, and the ways in which readers react to deliberate inaccuracies in the text (e.g., misspellings) can be assessed. However, there are three problems with this method. First, it is unnatural for most adults. Second, the fact that reading aloud is about half as fast as silent reading suggests there are substantial differences between the two forms of reading. Third, the eye–voice span (the distance the eye is ahead of the voice) is about two words, so some errors in reading aloud may reflect memorial errors rather than genuine reading errors.

A third method for studying reading involves a greater diversity of techniques than those considered so far. Rayner and Pollatsek (1989)

referred to these tasks as *word-identification techniques*, because they assess the time taken for word identification. There is the *lexical decision task* (deciding whether a string of letters forms a word) and the *naming task* (saying a word out loud as rapidly as possible). The greatest advantage of word-identification techniques over eye movements is that they ensure that certain processing has been performed on a given word in a given time, whereas identification may not occur while a word is fixated. However, there are clear disadvantages. Normal reading processes are disrupted by the additional task, and it is not clear precisely what processes are reflected in lexical decision or naming times.

Balota, Paul, and Spieler (1999) argued that reading involves several kinds of processing: *orthography* (the spelling of words); *phonology* (the sound of words); word meaning; syntax; and higher-level discourse integration. Reading tasks vary in the emphasis they place on these kinds of processing. According to Balota et al. (1999, p. 47):

In naming, the attentional control system would increase the influence of the computations between orthography and phonology . . . the demands of lexical decision performance might place a high priority on the computations between orthographic and meaning level modules [processors] . . . if the goal . . . is reading comprehension, then attentional control would increase the priority of computations of the syntactic-, meaning-, and discourse-level modules.

It follows that performance on naming and lexical decision tasks may not accurately reflect normal reading processes.

## Eye movements in reading

We feel that our eyes move smoothly across the page while reading. In fact, however, they actually move in rapid jerks (known as *saccades*). Saccades are ballistic (once initiated their direction cannot be changed). There are fairly frequent regressions in which the eyes move backwards in the text, accounting for about 10% of all saccades. Saccades

**FIGURE 11.4**

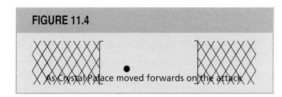

The perceptual span in reading.

take about 10–20 milliseconds to complete, and are separated by fixations lasting for about 200–250 milliseconds. The length of each saccade is about eight letters or spaces. Information is extracted from the text only during each fixation, and not during the intervening saccades (Latour, 1962).

The amount of text from which useful information is obtained in each fixation has been studied by using the "moving window" technique (see Rayner & Sereno, 1994). Most of the text is mutilated except for an experimenter-defined area or window surrounding the reader's point of fixation. Every time the reader moves his or her eyes, different parts of the text are mutilated to permit normal reading only within the window region. The effects of different-sized windows on reading performance can be compared.

The *perceptual span* (effective field of view) is affected by the difficulty of the text and the size of the print. It usually extends three or four letters to the left of fixation and 15 letters to the right (see Figure 11.4). This asymmetry presumably occurs because the most informative text lies to the right of the fixation point. The form of the asymmetry is clearly learned. Readers of Hebrew, which is read from right to left, show the opposite asymmetry (Pollatsek, Bolozky, Well, & Rayner, 1981).

Rayner and Sereno (1994) concluded that there are three different spans:

- The *total perceptual span* (the total area from which useful information is extracted); this is the longest span.
- The *letter-identification span* (the area from which information is obtained).
- The *word-identification span* (the area from which information relevant to word-identification processes is obtained); this is the shortest span.

The size of the perceptual span means that parafoveal information (outside the central or foveal region) is used in reading. Some of the most convincing evidence comes from use of the boundary technique. In this technique, there is a preview word just to the right of the point of fixation. As the reader makes a saccade to this word, it changes into the target word. However, the reader is unaware that it has been changed. The length of fixation on the target word is less when that word is the same as the preview word than when it differs (see Reichle et al., 1998). Reading time on the target word is less when the preview word is visually or phonologically similar to the target word, suggesting that visual and phonological information can be extracted from parafoveal processing. However, the processing of information at the parafoveal level does not reach the semantic level (Rayner & Morris, 1992).

## E-Z Reader model

Reichle et al. (1998) explained the pattern of eye movements during reading in their E-Z Reader model (the name makes more sense in American English, where Z is pronounced "zee"!). About 80% of content words (nouns, verbs, and adjectives) are fixated, and Reichle et al. argued that it is important to identify the factors determining the length of fixation on such words. Only about 20% of function words (articles, conjunctions, prepositions, and pronouns) are fixated, and we need to identify the factors leading some words to be "skipped" or not fixated at all.

It will be useful to start by listing facts the model was designed to explain (see Reichle et al., 1998):

- Rare words are fixated for longer than common words.
- Words that are more predictable in the sentence context are fixated for less time.
- Words that are not fixated tend to be common, short, or predictable.
- The fixation time on a word is longer when it is preceded by a rare word: the "spillover" effect.

What would be the most obvious kind of model? One might assume that readers fixate on a word until they have processed it sufficiently, after which they move their eyes immediately to the next word. However, there are two major problems with such an approach. First, it takes about 150–200 milliseconds to execute an eye-movement program. If readers behaved according to this simple model, they would waste time waiting for their eyes to move. Second, it is hard to see how readers could skip words on this model, because they would know nothing about the next word until they fixate it.

How can we get round these problems? Reichle et al. (1998) argued that the next eye movement is programmed after only *part* of the processing of the currently fixated word has occurred. This greatly reduces the time between completion of processing on the current word and movement of the eyes to the next word. Any spare time is used to start processing the next word. If the processing of the next word is completed rapidly enough, then it is skipped.

Reichle et al. (1998) emphasised several general assumptions in their E-Z Reader model:

1. Readers check the familiarity of the word they are currently fixating.
2. Completion of frequency checking of a word is the signal to initiate an eye-movement program.
3. Readers also engage in the task of *lexical access*, which "refers to the process of identi-fying a word's orthographic and/or phonological pattern so that semantic information can be retrieved" (Reichle et al., 1998, p. 133). This task takes longer to complete than does frequency checking.
4. Completion of lexical access is the signal for a shift of covert (internal) attention to the next word.
5. Frequency checking and lexical access are completed faster for common words than for rare ones, and this is more so for lexical access than for frequency checking.
6. Frequency checking and lexical access are completed faster for predictable than for un-predictable words.

These theoretical assumptions lead to various predictions concerning the effects of word frequency on eye movements (see Figure 11.5). Assumptions (2) and (5) together predict that the time spent fixating common words will be less than the time fixating rare words, which is consistent with the evidence. According to the model, readers spend the time between completion of lexical access to a word and the next eye movement in parafoveal processing of the next word. The amount of time spent in such parafoveal processing is less when the fixated word is rare than when it is common (see Figure 11.5). Thus, the word following a rare word generally needs to be fixated for longer than the word following a common word. This is precisely the spillover effect described earlier.

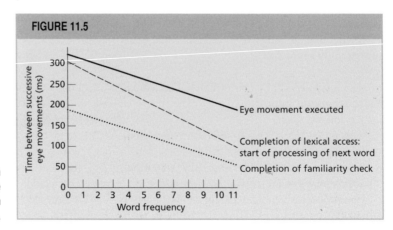

**FIGURE 11.5**

The effects of word frequency on eye movements according to the E-Z Reader model. Adapted from Reichle et al. (1998).

Why are words that are common, predictable, or short more likely than other words to be skipped or not fixated? According to the model, the main reason why the next word in a sentence is skipped is because its lexical access has been completed while the current word is still being fixated. This is most likely to happen for common, predictable, or short words, because lexical access is faster for these words than for others (assumptions 5 and 6).

### Evaluation

The model specifies the major factors determining eye movements in reading. It shows that reading occurs on a word-by-word basis, and that parafoveal processing increases the efficiency of the reading process. The fact that the predictions of the model are generally in good agreement with eye-movement data suggests that its central assumptions are correct.

The E-Z Reader model de-emphasises the impact of higher-level cognitive processes on fixation times. For example, readers generally fixate for an unusually long time on the word "seems" when presented with the sentence, "Since Jay always jogs a mile seems like a short distance" (Frazier & Rayner, 1982; see Chapter 12). They cannot fit "seems" into the syntactic structure they have formed of the sentence, and so there is disruption. This disruption affects eye fixations, but is not explained by the model.

Reichle et al. (1998) identified another problem. According to the model, the motor programming system translates the signal to move to the next word into a saccade. However, it is not clear how this system produces saccades of the appropriate length.

## WORD IDENTIFICATION

College students typically read at about 300 words per minute, thus averaging only 200 milliseconds to identify each word. It has proved hard to decide exactly how long word identification normally takes, in part because of imprecision about the meaning of "word identification". The term can refer to accessing either the name of a word or its meaning. However, reading rate is slowed by only about 15% when a mask appears 50 milliseconds after the start of each eye fixation (Rayner et al., 1981). This suggests that word identification in both senses takes only a little more than 50 milliseconds.

## Automatic processing

Rayner and Sereno (1994) argued that word identification is generally fairly automatic. This makes intuitive sense if you consider that most college students have read between 20 and 70 million words in their lifetimes. It has been argued that automatic processes are unavoidable and unavailable to consciousness (see Chapter 5). Evidence that word identification may be unavoidable comes from the Stroop effect (Stroop, 1935). Participants have to name the colours in which words are printed as rapidly as possible, and naming speed is slowed when the words are conflicting colour names (e.g., the word RED printed in green). The Stroop effect suggests that word meaning is extracted even when participants try not to process it.

Cheesman and Merikle (1984) replicated the Stroop effect. They also found that the effect could be obtained even when the colour name was presented below the level of conscious awareness. This latter finding suggests that word identification does not depend on conscious awareness.

## Context effects

Is word identification influenced by context? This issue was addressed by Meyer and Schvaneveldt (1971) in a study in which the participants had to decide whether letter strings were words. On this lexical decision task, the decision time for a word (e.g., DOCTOR) was shorter when the preceding context or prime was a semantically related word (e.g., NURSE) than when it was an unrelated word (e.g., LIBRARY) or when there was no prime. This is known as the semantic priming effect.

Why does this semantic priming effect occur? Perhaps the context or priming word automatically activates the stored representations of all the words related to it due to massive previous learning. Alternatively, controlled processes may be involved, with a prime such as NURSE leading participants to expect that a semantically related word will follow.

Neely (1977) used an ingenious technique to distinguish between the two explanations of the semantic priming effect. The priming word was the name of a semantic category (e.g., "Bird"), and it was followed by a letter string at one of three intervals: 250, 400, or 700 milliseconds. In the key manipulation, participants expected that a particular category name would usually be followed by a member of a different, pre-specified category (e.g., "Bird" followed by the name of part of a building). There were two kinds of trials with this manipulation:

1. The category name is followed by a member of a different, but expected, category (e.g., Bird–Window).
2. The category name is followed by a member of the same, but unexpected, category (e.g., Bird–Magpie).

The findings are shown in Figure 11.6. There were two priming or context effects. First, there was a rapid, automatic effect based only on semantic relatedness. Second, there was a slower acting attentional effect based only on expectation. Subsequent research has generally confirmed Neely's (1977) findings, except that automatic processes can cause inhibitory effects at short intervals (see Rayner & Pollatsek, 1989).

It is hard to know whether Neely's (1977) findings apply to normal reading, because the situations are so different. However, context does influence reading. For example, Ehrlich and Rayner (1981) found that words fitting the sentential context were fixated for 40 milliseconds less than other words.

We have seen that word identification is affected by context. What is more controversial is whether context effects occur before or after the individual has gained *lexical access* to the stored information contained in the internal *lexicon*. Neely (1977) found that semantic or associative priming had a very rapid effect on word identification, suggesting (but not proving) that this effect of context occurs pre-lexically. He also found that the effects of participants' expectancies were

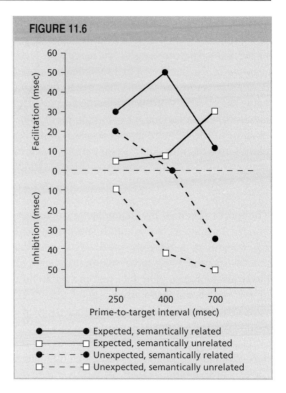

FIGURE 11.6

The time course of inhibitory and facilitatory effects of priming as a function of whether or not the target word was related semantically to the prime, and of whether or not the target word belonged to the expected category. Data from Neely (1977).

slow to develop. This finding suggests that these expectancies (and probably sentence context as well) affect post-lexical processing.

Lucas (1999) carried out a meta-analysis of 17 studies focusing on context effects in lexical access. In most of these studies, each context sentence contained an ambiguous word (e.g., "The man spent the entire day fishing on the *bank*"). The ambiguous word was immediately followed by a target on which a naming or lexical decision task was performed. The target word was either appropriate (e.g., "river") or inappropriate (e.g., "money") to the meaning of the ambiguous word in the sentence context. Overall, the 17 studies in the meta-analysis, "showed a small effect of context on lexical access of about two-tenths of a standard deviation: the appropriate interpretation of a word consistently showed greater priming than the inappropriate interpretation" (Lucas, 1999,

p. 394). The findings from naming and lexical decision tasks were very similar. In view of the different limitations of these two tasks (see earlier), this similarity perhaps offers some reassurance that the findings are valid.

## Letter vs. word identification

Common sense indicates that the recognition of a word on the printed page involves two successive stages:

1. Identification of the individual letters in the word.
2. Word identification.

However, the notion that letter identification must be complete before word identification can begin seems to be wrong. For example, consider the *word superiority effect* (Reicher, 1969). A letter string is presented very briefly followed by a pattern mask. The participant's task is to decide which of two letters was presented in a particular position (e.g., the third letter). The word superiority effect is defined by the fact that performance is better when the letter string forms a word than when it does not.

The word superiority effect suggests that information about the word presented can facilitate identification of the letters of that word. However, there is also a pseudo-word superiority effect: letters are better recognised when presented in pronounceable non-words (e.g., "MAVE") than in unpronounceable non-words (Cole, Rudinsky, Zue, & Reddy, 1980).

## Interactive activation model

McClelland and Rumelhart (1981) put forward an influential interactive activation model of visual word recognition. The key assumptions of this model are as follows: "Visual word recognition involves a process of mutual constraint satisfaction between the bottom-up information gained about the features in the words and the top-down knowledge about word and letter identities" (Ellis & Humphreys, 1999, p. 315). The more detailed theoretical assumptions made by McClelland and Rumelhart (1981) are as follows (see Figure 11.7):

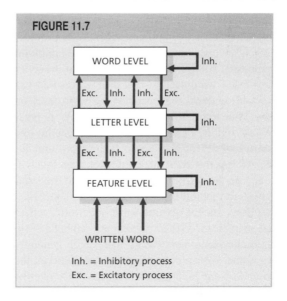

FIGURE 11.7

Inh. = Inhibitory process
Exc. = Excitatory process

McClelland and Rumelhart's (1981) interactive activation model of visual word recognition. Adapted from Ellis (1984).

- There are recognition units at three levels: the feature level at the bottom; the letter level in the middle; and the word level at the top.
- When a feature in a letter is detected (e.g., vertical line at the right-hand side of a letter), activation goes to all the letter units containing that feature (e.g., H, M, N), and inhibition goes to all other letter units.
- Letters are identified at the letter level. When a letter in a particular position within a word is identified, activation is sent to the word level for all four-letter word units containing that letter in that position, and inhibition is sent to all other word units.
- Words are recognised at the word level. Activated word units increase the level of activation in the letter-level units for the letters forming that word (e.g., activation of the word SEAT would increase activation for the four letters S, E, A, and T at the letter level) and inhibit activity of all other letter units.
- At each level in the system, activation of one particular unit leads to suppression or inhibition of competing units.

Bottom-up processes stemming directly from the written word proceed from the feature level through the letter level to the word level by means of activation and inhibition. Top-down processing is involved in the activation and inhibition processes going from the word level to the letter level. The word superiority effect occurs because of the top-down influences of the word level on the letter level. Suppose the word SEAT is presented, and the participants are asked whether the third letter is an A or an N. If the word unit for SEAT is activated at the word level, then this will increase the activation of the letter A at the letter level, and inhibit the activation of the letter N.

How can the pseudo-word superiority effect be explained? When letters are embedded in pronounceable non-words, there will generally be some overlap of spelling patterns between the pseudo-word and genuine words. This overlap can produce additional activation of the letters presented in the pseudo-word and thus lead to the pseudo-word superiority effect.

## Evaluation

The interactive activation model has been very influential. It provides an interesting example of how a connectionist processing system (see Chapter 1) can be applied to visual word recognition. It accounts for various phenomena, including the word superiority effect and the pseudoword superiority effect.

According to the model, letters are coded in terms of their precise locations in the visual field. In fact, however, the evidence suggests that coding is actually based on the *relative* positions of letters rather than their precise positions. For example, Ellis and Humphreys (1999) pointed out that the following letter strings are often misread if seen only briefly:

PSYCHMENT
DEPARTOLOGY

It is hard within the interactive activation model to account for these strings being misread as "PSYCHOLOGY DEPARTMENT". Experimental evidence that the relative positions of words are important in reading was reported by McClelland and Mozer (1986). They found that pairs of words

such as LINK and MINE were sometimes misread as LINE and MINK.

There are some limitations with the model put forward by McClelland and Rumelhart (1981). The most obvious one is that it was only designed to account for performance on four-letter words written in capital letters, although it could probably be applied to longer words.

High-frequency or common words are more readily recognised than low-frequency or rare words. This can be explained by assuming either that stronger connections are formed between the letter and word units of high-frequency words, or that high-frequency words have a higher resting level of activation. It follows that there should be a larger word superiority effect for high-frequency words than for low-frequency words due to more top-down activation from the word level to the letter level. However, the size of the word superiority effect is the same with high- and low-frequency words (Gunther, Gfoerer, & Weiss, 1984).

The model proposed by McClelland and Rumelhart (1981) assumes that lexical access is determined by visual information. However, there has been much controversy on this issue. Frost (1998) claimed that phonological coding is nearly always used prior to lexical access (see later in the chapter).

## Developments of the model

The original interactive activation model predicted *accuracy* of word recognition, but could not predict the *speed* of word reading. This limitation was addressed by Grainger and Segui (1990) and Jacobs and Grainger (1992). They modified the model so that responses were made when activation at the word level reached a variable threshold of activation. With this addition to the model, Jacobs and Grainger (1992) simulated the lexical decision times of human participants. Grainger and Segui (1990) assumed that high-frequency words have a lower activation threshold than low-frequency words. They focused particularly on lexical decision times to low-frequency words (e.g., BLUR) having a similar spelling to a high-frequency word (e.g., BLUE). They predicted (and found) that lexical decision times were slowed down, presumably because activation of the incorrect high-frequency word inhibited activation of the correct low-frequency word.

McClelland (1993) pointed out that the original interactive activation model was a deterministic one, meaning that any given input would always produce the same output. This contrasts with human performance, which is somewhat variable. Accordingly, McClelland (1993) developed the model by including variable or stochastic processes within it. This permitted the model to simulate the response distributions of human participants given various word-recognition tasks.

## ROUTES FROM PRINT TO SOUND -SPEAKING

Suppose you were asked to read out the following list of words and non-words:

CAT FOG COMB PINT MANTINESS FASS

You would probably find it a simple task, but it actually involves some hidden complexities. For example, how do you know that the "b" in "comb" is silent, and that "pint" does not rhyme with "hint"? Presumably you have specific information stored in long-term memory about how to pronounce these words. However, this cannot explain how you are able to pronounce non-words such as "mantiness" and "fass", because you do not have any stored information about their pronunciation. Perhaps non-words are pronounced by analogy with real words (e.g., "fass" is pronounced to rhyme with "mass"). Another possibility is that rules governing the translation of letter strings into sounds are used to generate a pronunciation for non-words.

This description of the reading of individual words is oversimplified. The study of adult patients whose reading skills have been impaired due to brain damage suggests that there are several reading disorders, depending on which parts of the cognitive system involved in reading are damaged. Some of the major findings from the cognitive neuropsychological approach are discussed in the next section.

## Cognitive neuropsychology

Some of the processes and structures that may be involved in reading are shown in Figure 11.8. Ellis and Young (1988) identified these components on the basis of the study of acquired dyslexias (i.e., impairments of reading produced by brain damage in adults who were previously skilled readers). Only selected aspects of the cognitive neuropsychological account of reading will be presented here.

The most important message of Figure 11.8 is that there are three routes between the printed word and speech. All three routes start with the visual analysis system, which has the functions of identifying and grouping letters in printed words. We will consider each of the three routes in turn.

### DUAL-ROUTE MODEL

### Route 1 (grapheme–phoneme conversion)

Route 1 differs from the other routes between the printed word and speech in making use of the process of grapheme–phoneme conversion. This process may well involve working out pronunciations for unfamiliar words and non-words in a piecemeal way by translating letters or letter groups into phonemes by the application of rules. However, not everyone agrees with this view. Kay and Marcel (1981) argued that unfamiliar words and non-words are actually pronounced by analogy with familiar words. They found that the pronunciations of non-words by normal readers were sometimes altered to rhyme with real words that had just been presented. For example, a non-word such as "raste" is generally pronounced to rhyme with "taste", but is more likely to be pronounced to rhyme with "mast" if preceded by the word "caste".

If a brain-damaged patient could use only Route 1 when pronouncing words and non-words, what would one expect to find in their pronunciation performance? The use of grapheme–phoneme conversion rules should permit accurate pronunciation of words having regular spelling–sound correspondences, but not of irregular words. If an irregular word such as "pint" has grapheme–phoneme conversion rules applied to it, it should be pronounced to rhyme with "hint"; this is known as regularisation. Finally, the grapheme–phoneme

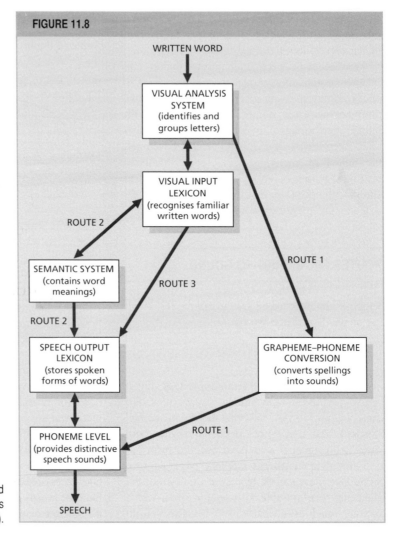

**FIGURE 11.8**

WRITTEN WORD

VISUAL ANALYSIS
SYSTEM
(identifies and
groups letters)

VISUAL INPUT
LEXICON
(recognises familiar
written words)

ROUTE 2

ROUTE 1

SEMANTIC SYSTEM
(contains word
meanings)

ROUTE 3

ROUTE 2

SPEECH OUTPUT
LEXICON
(stores spoken
forms of words)

GRAPHEME–PHONEME
CONVERSION
(converts spellings
into sounds)

PHONEME LEVEL
(provides distinctive
speech sounds)

ROUTE 1

SPEECH

Some of the processes involved
in reading. Adapted from Ellis
and Young (1988).

conversion rules can be used to provide pronunciations of non-words.

Patients who adhere most closely to exclusive use of Route 1 were labelled as surface dyslexics by Marshall and Newcombe (1973). *Surface dyslexia* is a condition in which patients have particular problems in reading irregular words. The surface dyslexic JC, could read 67 out of 130 regular words correctly, but he was successful with only 41 out of 130 irregular words. More striking findings were reported by Bub, Cancelliere, and Kertesz (1985). Their patient, MP, read non-words well, and had a reading accuracy of over 90% with common and rare regular words. In contrast, although common irregular words were read with an accuracy of about 80%, only 40% of rare irregular words were read accurately.

The evidence from surface dyslexics such as JC and MP suggests they have a strong (but not exclusive) reliance on Route 1. If all words were read by means of grapheme–phoneme conversion, then all irregular words would be mispronounced, and this simply does not happen. Presumably surace dyslexics can make some use of routes other than Route 1, even though these other routes are severely damaged.

Finally, surface dyslexics vary considerably in the nature of the impairment that led them to adopt the strategy of grapheme–phoneme conversion. For example, JC had no problem with understanding words that he pronounced correctly, whereas MP often failed to understand words she could pronounce. Thus, the syndrome of "surface dyslexia" may be of limited usefulness.

## Route 2 (lexicon plus semantic system)

Route 2 is the route generally used by adult readers. The basic idea is that representations of thousands of familiar words are stored in a visual input lexicon. Visual presentation of a word leads to activation in the visual input lexicon. This is followed by obtaining its meaning from the semantic system after which the word can be spoken (see Figure 11.8).

How could we identify patients who use Route 2 but not Route 1? Their intact visual input lexicon means that they should experience little difficulty in pronouncing familiar words. However, their inability to use grapheme–phoneme conversion should mean they find it very hard to pronounce relatively unfamiliar words and non-words.

Phonological dyslexics fit this predicted pattern fairly well. *Phonological dyslexia* is a condition in which there are particular problems with reading unfamiliar words and non-words. The first case of phonological dyslexia reported systematically was RG (Beavois & Dérouesné, 1979). In one experiment with 40 words and 40 non-words, RG successfully read 100% of the real words but only 10% of the non-words. Similar findings with patient AM were reported by Patterson (1982). AM had problems in reading function words (e.g., with, if, yet), but was very successful in reading content words (nouns, verbs, and adjectives). In contrast, he managed to read correctly only 8% of a list of non-words.

*Deep dyslexia* is a condition in which there are particular problems in reading unfamiliar words, and in which there are semantic reading errors (e.g., "ship" read as "boat"). It is more severe and mysterious than phonological dyslexia. Deep dyslexics resemble phonological dyslexics in finding it very hard to read unfamiliar words and non-words, suggesting they cannot use grapheme–phoneme conversion effectively. Deep dyslexics

also make semantic errors, in which a word related in meaning to the printed word is read instead of the printed word. Deep dyslexics may mainly use Route 2, but damage within the semantic system itself or in the connections between the visual input lexicon and the semantic system makes this route error-prone.

## Route 3 (lexicon only)

Route 3 resembles Route 2 in that the visual input lexicon and the speech output lexicon are involved in the reading process. However, the semantic system is bypassed in Route 3, so that printed words that are pronounced are not understood. Otherwise, the expectations about reading performance for users of Route 3 are the same as those for users of Route 2: familiar regular and irregular words should be pronounced correctly, whereas most unfamiliar words and non-words should not (see Figure 11.8).

Schwartz, Saffran, and Marin (1980) reported the case of WLP, a 62-year-old woman suffering from senile dementia. She showed a reasonable ability to read familiar words whether they were regular or irregular, but she often indicated that these words meant nothing to her. She was totally unable to relate the written names of animals to pictures of them, although she was fairly good at reading animal names aloud. These findings are consistent with the view that WLP was bypassing the semantic system when reading words. However, it is possible that processing occurred in WLP's semantic system, but she could not use such processing to aid performance on the tasks she was given.

## Evaluation of the dual-route (or triple-route) model

This approach to reading can be regarded as the triple-route model. However, as the fundamental distinction is between reading based on a lexical or dictionary look-up procedure and reading based on a letter-to-sound procedure, the approach is often referred to as the dual-route model. It provides a reasonably good account of normal and brain-damaged reading.

Coltheart et al. (1993) put forward a dual-route computational model of reading based loosely on the processes and structures shown in Figure 11.8. Their focus was on non-lexical reading via Route 1, with the computational system learning the grapheme–phoneme rules embodied in an initial set of words. These rules were later applied to previously unseen letter strings.

Coltheart et al. (1993) trained their computational model on 2897 words. They then tested its performance when reading various non-words on which it had not been trained. It scored 90% correct, which is very close to the figure of 91.5% obtained by human participants.

Coltheart et al. (1993) did not implement the lexical route in reading in their dual-route connectionist model. However, they suggested that a modified version of McClelland and Rumelhart's (1981) interactive activation model (discussed earlier) might account for visual word recognition, with Dell's (1986) spreading activation model (see Chapter 13) being used to account for spoken word production.

According to the dual-route model, normal readers make use of both routes with familiar words, but the direct route will generally be much faster. It was also assumed originally that the main two routes to reading are *independent* of each other. Some evidence is inconsistent with the independence assumption. For example, non-words are supposed to be read by means of grapheme–phoneme correspondence rules without reference to the lexicon. Glushko (1979) tested this prediction by comparing naming times to two kinds of non-words: (1) those having irregular word neighbours (e.g., "have" is an irregular word neighbour of "mave", whereas "gave" and "save" are regular word neighbours); and (2) non-words having only regular word neighbours. Non-words of the former type were named more slowly, suggesting that the lexical route can affect the non-lexical route.

Additional evidence that non-words are not always pronounced according to grapheme–phoneme correspondence rules was reported by Kay and Marcel (1981) in a study mentioned earlier. They found that the pronunciation of non-words was biased by preceding irregular words (e.g., "caste" biasing the pronunciation of "raste").

Simple versions of the dual-route model predict that the naming of familiar words should not be influenced by the regularity of their spelling-to-sound correspondences. In fact, however, irregular words are generally named more slowly than regular ones (see Harley, 1995). Seidenberg, Waters, Barnes, and Tanenhaus (1984) found this regularity effect with low-frequency words but not with high-frequency ones. These findings can be explained by assuming that the direct route operates relatively slowly with low-frequency words, and so allows the indirect route to influence naming performance. As a result, phonological processing (which is crucial to the indirect route) plays an important role in the naming of low-frequency words and in the regularity effect.

Pugh et al. (1997) replicated the findings of Seidenberg et al. (1984) using lexical decision rather than naming as the task. They also obtained fMRI evidence from a different task that the inferior frontal gyrus is activated when people are engaged in phonological processing. Of particular interest, they found that those participants who showed the regularity effect had a relatively greater involvement of the right hemisphere in phonological processing than did those not showing the effect. These findings indicate that phonological processing is involved in the regularity effect, and they shed some light on the brain areas that are active during phonological processing.

## Connectionist approaches

Within the dual-route approach, it is assumed that separate mechanisms are required to pronounce irregular words and non-words. This contrasts with the connectionist approach of Plaut et al. (1996). Their approach

eschews [avoids] separate mechanisms for pronouncing nonwords and exception [irregular] words. Rather, all of the system's knowledge of spelling–sound correspondences is brought to bear in pronouncing all types of letter strings [words *and* non–words]. Conflicts among possible alternative pronunciations of a letter string are resolved . . . by cooperative and competitive interactions based on how the letter string relates to all known words and their pronunciations.

Thus, Plaut et al. (1996) assumed that pronunciation of words and non-words is based on a highly *interactive* system.

The two approaches can be contrasted by considering the distinction between *regularity* and *consistency*. Dual-route theorists divide words into two categories: regular, meaning their pronunciation can be generated by applying rules; and irregular, meaning their pronunciation is not rule-based. Regular words can generally be pronounced more rapidly. In contrast, Plaut et al. (1996) argued that words vary in consistency, meaning the extent to which their pronunciation agrees with those of similarly spelled words. Highly consistent words can generally be pronounced faster and more accurately than inconsistent words, because more of the available knowledge supports the correct pronunciation of such words. Word naming is generally predicted better by consistency than by regularity (e.g., Glushko, 1979).

Plaut et al. (1996) tried various simulations based on two crucial notions:

1.  The pronunciation of a word or non-word is influenced strongly by consistency based on the pronunciations of all those words similar to it.
2.  High-frequency or common words have more influence on pronunciation than do low-frequency or rare words: high-frequency words are encountered more often, and so contribute more to changes in the network.

A successful simulation was based on the architecture shown in Figure 11.9 (hidden units are discussed in Chapter 1). The network learns to pronounce words accurately as connections develop between the visual forms of letters and combinations of letters (grapheme units) and their corresponding phonemes (phoneme units). The network based on this architecture learned by the use of *back-propagation*, in which the actual outputs or responses of the system are compared against the correct ones. The network received prolonged training with a set of 2998 words. At the end of training, the performance of the network closely resembled that of adult readers:

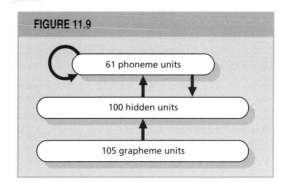

**FIGURE 11.9**

The architecture of the connectionist approach to word reading put forward by Plaut et al. (1996). Copyright © 1986 by the American Psychological Association. Reprinted with permission.

1.  Inconsistent words took longer to name than did consistent words.
2.  Rare words took longer to name than common ones.
3.  There was an interaction between word frequency and consistency, with the effects of consistency being much greater for rare words than for common ones.
4.  The network pronounced over 90% of non-words "correctly", which is comparable with the performance of adult readers; this finding is especially impressive, because the network received no direct training on non-words.

The simulation did not take semantic information into account. However, Plaut et al. (1996, p. 95) argued that, "to the extent that the semantic pathway has learned to derive the meaning and pronunciation of a word, it affords additional input to the phoneme units, pushing them toward their correct activations." They expanded their network model to include semantic information, assuming that such information has more impact on high-frequency words. A network based on this assumption learned to read regular and exception words much faster than a network lacking semantic information.

## Surface dyslexia and phonological dyslexia

Plaut et al. (1996, p. 95) used the notion that semantic information contributes to reading performance to advance the following theory of surface dyslexia: "Partial semantic support for word pronunciations alleviates the need for the phonological pathway to master all words such that, when the support is eliminated by brain damage, the surface dyslexic reading pattern emerges."

Plaut et al. (1996) tested this theory by making "lesions" to the network to reduce or eliminate the contribution from semantics. As has been found with surface dyslexics, the network's reading performance was very good on regular high- and low-frequency words and on non-words, worse on irregular high-frequency words, and worst on irregular low-frequency words.

Further support for the theory comes from the study of patients suffering with *Alzheimer's disease*, which involves progressive dementia or loss of mental powers. Such patients typically have similar reading performance to surface dyslexics, and the severity of the reading impairment is correlated with the extent of semantic deterioration (Patterson, Graham, & Hodges, 1994).

What about phonological dyslexia? Plaut et al. (1996, p. 99) only considered this disorder in general terms: "In the limit of a complete lesion between orthography and phonology, nonword reading would be impossible. Thus, a lesion to the network that severely impaired the phonological pathway while leaving the contribution of semantics to phonology (relatively) intact would replicate the basic characteristics of phonological dyslexia."

## Deep dyslexia

Plaut and Shallice (1993) proposed a network similar to the ones later put forward by Plaut et al. (1996) in order to understand deep dyslexia. This network has four key properties:

- Similar patterns of activation represent similar words in the orthographic and semantic domains.
- Learning alters the strengths of the connections between word spellings and meanings.
- The initial pattern of semantic activity produced by a visually presented word moves towards (or is attracted by) the pattern of the nearest known meaning; this is known as the operation of attractors.

- The semantic representations of most high-imageability words contain many more features than those of low-imageability words.

Plaut and Shallice (1993) studied the consequences of damage to the network. They found that virtually all the main symptoms of deep dyslexia could be simulated. The only important symptom that did not emerge from damage to the connectionist network was impaired writing performance.

Plaut and Shallice's (1993) theory is successful in two main ways. First, it predicts about a dozen symptoms of deep dyslexia from only a few theoretical assumptions. Second, the theory is explicit, in that the processes involved were specified in detail before the simulations proceeded.

## Evaluation

The connectionist approach of Plaut et al. (1996) and Plaut and Shallice (1993) has various advantages over the traditional dual-route approach. First, the apparent non-independence between the two routes of the dual-route approach poses no problems for the connectionist approach, which assumes that the processing system is interactive. Second, the connectionist approach (unlike the dual-route approach) does not draw a sharp distinction between regular and irregular words. This is an advantage, because the evidence does not support the notion of a rigid distinction, and there is no agreement on the rules determining which words belong to each category. Third, the evidence suggests that speed and accuracy of word and non-word pronunciation depend more on consistency than on regularity. Fourth, Plaut et al. (1996) predicted correctly that damage to the semantic system can affect reading performance in surface dyslexics. In contrast, "dual-route theories that include a lexical, nonsemantic pathway (e.g., . . . Coltheart et al., 1993) predict that selective semantic damage should never affect [word] naming accuracy" (Plaut et al., 1996, p. 102).

In spite of its successes, Plaut et al.'s (1996) connectionist approach to the reading of words has various limitations. First, as Plaut et al. (1996, p. 108) admitted, "the nature of processing within the semantic pathway has been characterised in only the coarsest way." Second, the approach has only been tested with one-syllabled words, and clearly needs additional testing with multi-syllabled words. Third, the approach provides only a sketchy account of some key issues, such as the nature of the impairment in phonological dyslexia. Fourth, as Ellis and Humphreys (1999, p. 340) pointed out, "evidence suggests that . . . short words can be named without recourse to sequential letter processing . . . , so the validity of the sequential read-out mechanism might be questioned." Fifth, as Ellis and Humphreys (1999, p. 537) argued:

> Plaut et al. proposed that their second route was semantic in nature; however, they did not attempt to represent semantic knowledge in any plausible manner . . . Hence it may equally be argued that this route was lexical rather than semantic and that, in lesioning the model, they simulate operation of a non-lexical route in isolation from lexical reading processes—much as argued in dual-route accounts of reading.

## Phonological theory of reading

According to the dual-route model, the reading performance of normal individuals is generally little affected by phonological coding. This is because reading via the indirect route (grapheme–phoneme conversion) tends to be much slower than reading via the direct route. Frost (1998) argued that phonological coding is much more important in reading than is implied by the dual-route model. Frost (1998, p. 76) put forward a phonological model of reading based on the following assumption:

> A phonological representation is a necessary product of processing printed words, even though the explicit pronunciation of their phonological structure is not required. Thus, the strong phonological model would predict that phonological processing will be mandatory [obligatory], perhaps automatic.

Two predictions that follow from the phonological model, and that seem inconsistent with the dual-route model, are as follows:

1. Phonological coding will occur even when it impairs performance.
2. Some phonological coding occurs rapidly when a word is presented visually.

A study supporting prediction (1) was reported by Tzelgov et al. (1996). It was based on the Stroop effect (described earlier), in which naming the colours in which words are printed is slowed when the words themselves are different colour names. The participants in the study were English–Hebrew bilinguals, and in the key condition they had to name the colours of non-words in one of the two languages. Each non-word had an unfamiliar printed form, but its phonological translation was a colour name in the other language. Tzelgov et al. (1996) obtained a strong Stroop effect with these non-words. Thus, the participants engaged in phonological coding of the non-words even though it was disadvantageous to do so.

A study supporting prediction (2) was reported by Berent and Perfetti (1995). They used a backward masking technique involving the following stages: (1) a target word was presented very briefly; (2) the target word was masked by a pseudo-word that was presented very briefly; (3) a pattern mask was presented; and (4) the participants wrote down what they had seen. The main measure was the proportion of trials on which the target word was detected. The key finding was that target detection was higher when the non-words were phonemically similar to the target words than when they were graphemically similar. The implication is that basic phonological coding can occur within about 60 milliseconds of the presentation of a word.

### Evaluation

There is reasonable support for the central assumption of the phonological model that phonological coding typically occurs during the processing of printed words. There is evidence for phonological coding even when it disrupts performance. Overall, it seems that phonological coding occurs more often and more rapidly than is assumed by the rival dual-route model.

On the negative side, the phonological model does not provide an explicit and detailed account of the processes involved in reading. In addition, it seems more applicable to reading in normals than in dyslexics. For example, phonological dyslexics have great difficulties with phonological coding, but are reasonably good at reading familiar words. This is puzzling if one assumes that phonological coding is of major importance in reading. As Frost (1998, p. 93) admitted, "Evidence that is . . . damaging to the strong phonological model comes from phonological dyslexia."

## Section summary

There is still some theoretical controversy about the processes involved in reading individual words, in large part because of the inconclusiveness of much of the evidence. There are two main reasons for this inconclusiveness. First, the findings that are obtained depend on the methods that are employed. For example, as Harley (1995, p. 82) pointed out, "Lexical decision and naming do not always give the same results . . . the differences probably arise because while naming times are a relatively pure measure of the time it takes for automatic access to the lexicon, lexical decision times may include a substantial amount of attentional processing." Second, methods such as lexical decision and naming provide measures of the total time taken to complete a series of processes, but are fairly uninformative about those underlying processes. As Frost (1998, p. 95) suggested, "Instead of setting one's experimental camera at the finish line of the cognitive events, one should aim at filming their on-line, step-by-step development."

## CHAPTER SUMMARY

- Listening to speech. Listeners to speech have to confront the linearity, non-invariance, and segmentation problems. There is evidence of categorical speech perception, but this may occur mainly at the level of conscious awareness. It remains unclear whether speech perception involves a special module. Studies on the phonemic restoration effect suggest that contextual information can influence speech perception in a top-down way. Prosodic cues are often used rapidly by listeners, but such cues are sometimes not provided by speakers. The important role played by lip-reading in speech perception is shown by the McGurk effect.
- Theories of word recognition. According to the motor theory of speech perception, listeners mimic the articulatory movements of the speaker, but this need not involve measurable articulatory responses. The ability of infants and of simultaneous translators to show good speech perception is hard to explain by the motor theory. According to the original version of cohort theory, the initial sound of a word is used to construct a word-initial cohort which is reduced to only one word by using additional information from the presented word and from contextual information. Cohort theory has been revised to make it more flexible and in line with the evidence. According to the TRACE model, bottom-up and top-down processes interact during speech perception. This assumption that these processes interact is probably incorrect, and the importance of top-down processes is exaggerated in the TRACE model.
- Cognitive neuropsychology. Patients with pure word deafness have problems with speech perception because of impaired phonemic processing in the auditory analysis system. Patients with word meaning deafness can repeat familiar words without understanding their meaning, but have problems with non-words. Patients with auditory phonological agnosia seem to have damage within Route 3. Deep dysphasia may reflect damage to all three routes involved in the repetition of spoken words, or it may involve damage to the response buffer.
- Basic reading processes. The least obtrusive way of studying reading is by eye-movement recordings. According to the E-Z Reader model, the next eye movement is programmed when only part

of the processing of the currently fixated word has occurred. Completion of frequency checking of a word is the signal to initiate an eye-movement program, and completion of lexical access is the signal for a shift of covert attention to the next word. This model takes insufficient account of the impact of higher-level cognitive processes on fixation times.

- Word identification. According to the interactive activation model, bottom-up and top-down processes are both involved in letter identification and word recognition. This model was only designed to account for performance on four-letter words written in capital letters, and it makes the strong assumption that lexical access is determined by visual information.

- Routes from print to sound. According to the dual-route model, there is an indirect route between the printed word and speech based on grapheme–phoneme conversion, and a direct route based on lexical access. Surface dyslexics seem to have an impaired direct route and so rely mainly on the indirect route. In contrast, phonological dyslexics have an impaired indirect route and so rely on the direct route. Deep dyslexics resemble phonological dyslexics, but also make semantic reading errors. Some patients seem to use a third route based on lexical access but with no use of the semantic system. The direct and indirect routes are less independent than was assumed by dual-route theorists. Connectionist interactive models can simulate adult reading of words and non-words, and "lesioned" networks can mimic the reading performance of surface and deep dyslexics. However, such models have little to say about phonological dyslexia, and their accounts of the semantic system are sketchy. According to the phonological theory, phonological processing is of central importance to reading. It is hard to account for phonological dyslexia within phonological theory.

## FURTHER READING

- Ellis, R., & Humphreys, G.W. (1999). *Connectionist psychology*. Hove, UK: Psychology Press. This book contains detailed accounts of the major connectionist models of word recognition.
- Garrod, S., & Pickering, M.J. (1999). *Language processing*. Hove, UK: Psychology Press. Chapters 2–4 provide thorough accounts of the basic processes involved in speech perception and reading.
- Harley, T.A. (1995). *The psychology of language: From data to theory*. Hove, UK: Psychology Press. The basic processes involved in speech perception and reading are covered in detail in Chapters 2–4 of this enjoyable book.
- Reichle, E.D., Pollatsek, A., Fisher, D.L., & Rayner, K. (1998). Toward a model of eye movement control in reading. *Psychological Review, 105,* 125–157. Most of what is currently known about the role of eye movements in reading is discussed in this long article.

# 12

# Language Comprehension

*¿How do we understand what we read?*

*SENTENCE PROCESSING → PARSING - syntactical (grammatical) structure of the sentence*

*analysing the meaning of the sentence*

## INTRODUCTION

The basic processes involved in the initial stages of reading and listening to speech were discussed in the previous chapter. At the end of that chapter, we had reached the point at which individual words were identified. The main objective of this chapter is to complete our account of reading and listening to speech, dealing with the ways in which phrases, sentences, and entire stories are processed and understood.

In crude terms, the previous chapter dealt with those aspects of language processing that differ between reading and listening to speech. In contrast, the higher-level processes involved in comprehension tend to be rather similar whether a story is being listened to or read. There has been far more research on comprehension processes in reading than in listening to speech, and so the emphasis will be on reading. However, it can usually be assumed that what is true of reading is also true of listening to speech. Any major discrepancies between reading and listening will be specifically dealt with as and when they occur.

*re: once words are recognised auditorily or visually*

## SENTENCE PROCESSING

There are two main levels of analysis in the comprehension of sentences. First, there is an analysis of the syntactical (grammatical) structure of each sentence; this is known technically as *parsing*. What exactly is grammar? It is concerned with the way in which words are combined. However, as Altmann (1997, p. 84) pointed out, "it [the way in which words are combined] is important, and has meaning, only insofar as both the speaker and the hearer (or the writer and the reader) share some common knowledge regarding the significance of one combination or another. This shared knowledge is *grammar*."

Second, there is an analysis of the meaning of the sentence. It is important to note that the intended meaning of a sentence may not be the same as its literal meaning. The study of intended meaning is known as *pragmatics*. Cases in which the literal meaning is not the intended meaning include rhetorical devices such as irony, sarcasm, and understatement. Some of the issues concerning pragmatics are discussed later in the chapter.

The relationship between syntactic and semantic analysis has been a matter of controversy. One possibility is that syntactic analysis generally precedes (and influences) semantic analysis; another possibility is that semantic analysis usually occurs prior to syntactic analysis; and a further possibility is that syntactic and semantic analysis occur at the same time. A final possibility is that syntax and semantics are very closely associated, and have more of a hand-in-glove relationship (Altmann, personal communication). These issues will be addressed shortly.

## Grammar or syntax

An infinite number of sentences is possible in any language, but these sentences are nevertheless systematic and organised in various ways. Linguists such as Chomsky (1957, 1959) have produced rules to take account of the productivity and the regularity of language. A set of rules is commonly referred to as a grammar. Ideally, a grammar should be able to generate all the permissible sentences in a given language, while at the same time rejecting all the unacceptable ones. For example, as Harris (1990) pointed out, our knowledge of grammar allows us to be confident that "Matthew is likely to leave" is grammatically correct, whereas the similar sentence "Matthew is probable to leave" is not.

## Parsing

It might seem that parsing or assigning grammatical structure to sentences would be fairly easy. However, there are numerous sentences in the English language (e.g., "They are flying planes") that pose problems because their grammatical structure is ambiguous. Some sentences are syntactically ambiguous at the *global* level, in which case the whole sentence has two or more possible interpretations. For example, "They are cooking apples" is ambiguous because it may or may not mean that apples are being cooked. Other sentences are syntactically ambiguous at the *local* level, meaning that various interpretations are possible at some point during parsing.

Much research on parsing has focused on sentences that are ambiguous at the global or local level. Why is that the case? Parsing operations generally occur very rapidly, and this makes it hard to study the processes involved. In contrast, observing the problems encountered by readers struggling with ambiguous sentences can provide revealing information about parsing processes. It is conceivable that some of the processes used with ambiguous sentences differ from those used with unambiguous sentences, but there is no clear evidence of that.

There is a major distinction between serial and parallel theories of sentence processing (see Pickering, 1999). According to serial theories, one syntactic analysis of a sentence is selected initially. If this analysis proves unworkable at some point, then a second syntactic analysis is selected, and so on. In contrast, it is assumed within parallel theories that multiple syntactic analyses are all considered at the same time.

Another distinction, which is related to that between serial and parallel, is between modular and interactive: "Possible models range from a highly modular architecture—in which lexical access strictly precedes parsing, which in turn strictly precedes semantic processing . . . —to fully interactive models that claim there is a single process which combines lexical, syntactic, semantic, and world knowledge constraints without distinction" (Crocker, 1999, p. 216). As might be expected, serial theories are nearly always modular, whereas parallel theories are interactive.

There are numerous versions of each kind of theory. For example, as Pickering (1999, p. 127 pointed out, "Parallel models differ, . . . depending on how many analyses are maintained, what kind of ranking [of analyses] is employed, how long the different analyses are considered for, or whether parallelism is only employed under certain conditions." We will consider the most influential serial approach (the garden-path model) and the most influential parallel approach (the constraint-based theory of MacDonald, Pearlmutter, and Seidenberg, 1994). As you read about these theories, bear in mind that "The real issue . . . concerns which knowledge sources are used when" (Crocker, 1999, p. 219).

## Garden-path model

Frazier and Rayner (1982) put forward a garden-path model, which was given that name because readers or listeners can be misled or "led up the garden path" by ambiguous sentences. The model was based on the following notions:

- Only one syntactical structure is initially considered for any sentence.
- Meaning is not involved in the selection of the initial syntactical structure.
- The simplest syntactical structure is chosen, making use of two general principles: minimal attachment and late closure.
- According to the principle of minimal attachment, the grammatical structure producing the fewest nodes (constituent parts of a sentence such as noun phrase and verb phrase) is preferred.
- The principle of late closure is that new words encountered in a sentence are attached to the current phrase or clause if this is grammatically permissible.

The principle of minimal attachment can be illustrated by the following example taken from Rayner and Pollatsek (1989). In the sentences, "The girl knew the answer by heart" and "The girl knew the answer was wrong", the minimal attachment principle leads to a grammatical structure in which "the answer" is regarded as the direct object of the verb "knew". This is appropriate for the first sentence, but not for the second. So far as the principle of late closure is concerned, Rayner and Pollatsek (1989) gave an example of a sentence in which use of this principle would lead to an inaccurate syntactical structure: "Since Jay always jogs a mile seems like a short distance". In this sentence, the principle leads "a mile" to be placed in the preceding phrase rather than at the start of the new phrase. In contrast, the principle of late closure produces the correct grammatical structure in a sentence such as: "Since Jay always jogs a mile this seems like a short distance to him".

There is increasing evidence that is hard to explain within the framework of the garden-path model. According to the garden-path model, prior context should not influence the initial parsing of an ambiguous sentence. However, there are several studies in which initial parsing did seem to be affected by context. For example, Altmann and Steedman (1988) recorded reading times to sentences such as the following:

1. The burglar blew open the safe with the dynamite and made off with the loot.
2. The burglar blew open the safe with the new lock and made off with the loot.

Altmann and Steedman presented a prior context sentence which referred to either one or two safes, and found that the nature of the context made a difference. When the context referred to two safes, this slowed down reading of "with the dynamite" in sentence (1). In contrast, when the context referred to only one safe, this disrupted reading of "with the new lock" in sentence (2). These findings suggest that context may influence initial parsing decisions.

Carreiras and Clifton (1993) studied readers' processing of sentences such as the following: "The spy shot the daughter of the colonel who was standing on the balcony". According to the principle of late closure, readers should interpret this as meaning that the colonel (rather than the daughter) was standing on the balcony. In fact, they did not strongly prefer either interpretation, which is contrary to the garden-path theory. When an equivalent sentence was presented in Spanish, there was a clear preference for assuming that the daughter was standing on the balcony, which is also contrary to theoretical prediction.

Frazier and Clifton (1996) offered an explanation of these findings, but this explanation was "strikingly incompatible with the assumptions of the Garden-Path model" (Pickering, 1999, p. 137).

## Evaluation

The garden-path model has various strengths. In particular, it provides a reasonably simple and coherent account of some of the key processes involved in sentence processing. However, there are various criticisms of the garden-path model, some of which are as follows.

First, it seems inefficient that readers and listeners should often construct incorrect grammatical structures for sentences. However, Frazier and Rayner (1982) claimed that the principles of minimal attachment and late closure are efficient because they minimise the pressure on short-term memory. They measured eye movements while participants read sentences such as those given earlier. Their crucial argument was as follows: if readers construct both (or all) possible syntactic structures, then there should be additional processing time at the point of disambiguation (e.g., "seems" in the first jogging sentence and "this" in the second jogging sentence). In contrast, according to the garden-path model, there should be increased processing time at the point of disambiguation only when the actual grammatical structure conflicts with the one produced by application of the principles of minimal attachment and late closure (e.g., the first jogging sentence). The eye-movement data consistently supported the predictions of the garden-path model.

Second, the assumption that meaning plays no part in the initial assignment of grammatical structure to a sentence seems implausible. For example, context studies (e.g., Altmann & Steedman, 1988) suggest that this assumption is incorrect. According to Pickering (1999, p. 140), "There is good evidence that semantic factors can have very rapid effects on ambiguity resolution. If a restricted account [e.g., garden-path model] is correct, then the initial stage that ignores these factors must be very brief indeed."

Third, it is unlikely that the initial choice of grammatical structure depends only on the principles of minimal attachment and late closure. For example, decisions about grammatical structure are influenced by punctuation when reading and by *prosody* (e.g., rhythm; stress) when listening to speech.

## Constraint-based theory

An approach that has become influential in recent years is the constraint-based theory put forward by MacDonald et al. (1994). This theory is based on a connectionist architecture, and a key assumption is that all relevant sources of information or constraints are available immediately to the parser. Competing analyses of the current sentence are activated at the same time, with the analyses being ranked according to the strength of their activation. According to MacDonald et al. (1994, p. 685), "Ambiguity resolution is . . . a classic example of a constraint satisfaction problem . . . Multiple independent, partially redundant, probabilistic sources of information interact to allow the system to settle on an interpretation at each level."

According to the theory, the processing system makes use of four language characteristics in order to resolve ambiguities in sentences:

1.  Grammatical knowledge constrains possible sentence interpretations.
2.  The various forms of information associated with any given word are typically not independent of each other.
3.  A word may be less ambiguous in some ways than in others (e.g., ambiguous for tense but not for grammatical category).
4.  The various interpretations permissible according to grammatical rules generally differ considerably in frequency and probability on the basis of past experience.

Findings consistent with constraint-based theory were reported by Pickering and Traxler (1998). They presented their participants with sentences such as the following:

1.  As the woman edited the magazine amused all the reporters.
2.  As the woman sailed the magazine amused all the reporters.

These two sentences are identical syntactically, and both are likely to lead readers to identify the wrong syntactic structure initially. However, the semantic constraints favouring the wrong structure are greater in sentence (1) than in sentence (2). These constraints should make it harder for readers of sentence (1) to change their incorrect syntactic analysis when it needs to be abandoned (i.e., when the verb "amused" is reached). As predicted, eye-movement data indicated that eye fixations in the verb and post-verb regions were longer for those reading sentence (1), and there were more regressions.

Some of the findings discussed earlier are also consistent with constraint-based theory. For example, Altmann and Steedman (1988) found that context seemed to affect initial parsing. Constraint-based theory predicts context effects. Context produces activation of relevant information, and this then facilitates or disrupts processing of the following sentence.

*Evaluation*

A valuable feature of the constraint-based theory is the notion that there can be varying degrees of support for different syntactic interpretations of a sentence. As someone reads a sentence, the accumulating syntactic and semantic evidence gradually leads the reader to produce a definite syntactic interpretation. However, McKoon and Ratcliff (1998) pointed out that many of the details of syntactic processing are unspecified by MacDonald et al. (1994). For example, little is said about, "the problem of building syntactic structures for whole sentences when all the processor has to work with are the chunks of syntax stored in the lexicon for individual words. Until a simulation model can be developed to actually produce whole-sentence syntactic structures for a large variety and number of words and constructions, satisfactory evaluation of the constraint-based approach is not possible" (McKoon & Ratcliff, 1998, p. 35). Another problem was identified by Crocker (1999, p. 228): "Parallel models [such as constraint-based theory] predict that alternative, though dispreferred, structures are represented by the language processor. As yet, direct psychological evidence for the existence of such parallel representations has not been forthcoming."

## Pragmatics

As Harley (1995, p. 236) pointed out, "The study of pragmatics looks at how we deal with those aspects of language that go beyond the simple meaning of what we hear and say." Thus, pragmatics is concerned with the ways in which language is actually used for purposes of communication. It is important to consider pragmatics, because the literal meaning of a sentence is often not the one that the writer or speaker intended to communicate. For example, it is usually safe to assume that someone who says "This weather is really great!", when it has been raining almost continuously for several days, actually thinks that the weather is terrible.

Austin (1976) argued that each sentence produced by a speaker has three rather different effects or forces:

1. The *locutionary force*: this is simply the sentence's literal meaning.
2. The *illocutionary force*: this is the speaker's goal in speaking, often called the intended meaning.
3. The *perlocutionary force*: this is the actual effect of the sentence on the listener.

According to this approach, listeners need to take account of the speaker's likely goals and the general context in order to understand what he or she is trying to communicate.

How do listeners or readers construct the intended meaning of a sentence? Clark and Lucy (1975) put forward a two-stage model, according to which the literal meaning is constructed *before* the intended meaning. They obtained support for this model by using sentences such as, "I'll be very happy if you make the circle blue", and "I'll be very sad unless you make the circle blue". These two sentences have the same intended meaning, but it took the participants much longer to understand the second sentence. According to Clark and Lucy, this occurred because the intended meaning of the second sentence differs from its literal meaning, and so both meanings had to be constructed.

Clark and Lucy (1975) used rather artificial sentences to support their two-stage model. More recent research has favoured a one-stage model, according to which people work out the intended meaning instead of (or at the same time as) the literal meaning. This model is supported by the common finding that intended meanings are formed as rapidly as literal meanings (see Taylor & Taylor, 1990, for a review). For example, Gibbs

(1979) found that participants took no longer to process indirect requests (e.g., "Must you open the window?") than to understand literal meanings of the same sentences.

Gibbs (1983) obtained evidence that people can work out the intended meaning of a sentence without processing the literal meaning. Participants interpreted a sentence (e.g., "Can't you be friendly?") in terms of its intended meaning. After that, they were then presented with a similar sentence having a literal interpretation (e.g., "Are you unable to be friendly?"), and had to decide whether it was grammatically correct. The participants did not make this decision any faster than with control sentences, presumably because they had processed the literal meaning of the first sentence.

Cacciari and Glucksberg (1994) argued that much use of language is metaphorical, and involves intended rather than literal meanings (e.g., "My job is a jail"). We often interpret metaphorical language appropriately without being consciously aware of the fact that we are extracting the intended rather than the literal meaning. Why does this happen? Cacciari and Glucksberg (1994, p. 461) argued in favour of "the strong and still controversial claim that the comprehension and interpretive processes people use to understand language are common to literal and figurative [metaphorical] language use. Both types . . . require the application and integration of knowledge from linguistic and nonlinguistic domains."

*Section summary*

It has proved hard to distinguish between different theoretical accounts of ambiguity resolution. As Crocker (1999, p. 229) pointed out, "Each [model] has its own appeal, . . . and each can seemingly be made to account for empirical findings relatively well. Part of this stems from the fact that many models are only partially specified and implemented, if at all." Crocker (1999, p. 213) argued that serial models have certain advantages over parallel models: "Such models have much to recommend them: (1) they are conceptually simpler, (2) they are computationally simpler, in that less processing and memory resources are

required, and (3) . . . they make strong, testable predictions about human behaviour."

An approach such as the garden-path model may have certain advantages, but it also seems to have severe limitations. In particular, MacDonald et al.'s (1994) theory can account for most of the findings more readily than can the garden-path model. As Pickering (1999, p. 145) concluded, "The emerging picture is of a system that integrates different sources of information on-line, in order that its choice of interpretation is based on all the sources of evidence that are available."

## Inner speech

It has sometimes been argued that inner speech is of little or no value to adult readers. Children learn to read out loud before they can read silently, and inner speech while reading may simply be a habit that has persisted from childhood. A very different viewpoint was expressed by Huey (1908):

> The carrying range of inner speech is considerably larger than that of vision . . . It is of the greatest service to the reader or listener that at each moment a considerable amount of what is being read should hang suspended in the primary memory of the inner speech.

One way of studying the role of inner speech in reading comprehension is to take electromyographic (EMG) recordings of some of the muscles used in subvocal articulation. This is of interest, because EMG activity in the speech tract typically increases considerably during reading. Hardyck and Petrinovich (1970) asked their participants to read easy and hard texts while EMG recordings were being made. In the key condition, a tone sounded every time the level of muscle activity in the speech tract was greater than that of a predetermined relaxation level. Participants in this feedback condition were instructed to prevent the tone from being sounded. Reduction of EMG activity in the speech tract (and thus reduction of subvocal articulation) produced a significant impairment of comprehension for the hard text, but had no effect on comprehension of the easy text (see Figure 12.1).

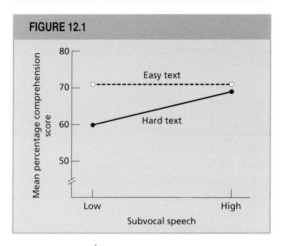

**FIGURE 12.1**

Comprehension for text as a function of text difficulty and opportunity to use subvocal speech. Adapted from Hardyck and Petrinovich (1970).

The role of inner speech in reading has also been studied by means of *articulatory suppression*. Readers are required to say something simple (e.g., "the the the") over and over again reading a text. This requirement prevents them from using the speech apparatus to produce subvocal articulation of the sentences in the text. If subvocal articulation of the text is important for comprehension, then an articulatory suppression task should severely impair comprehension.

Baddeley and Lewis (1981) made use of articulatory suppression on a task in which participants had to decide whether sentences were meaningful or anomalous. Some sentences were anomalous because two words in a meaningful sentence had been switched around (syntactic anomaly), and others were anomalous because a totally inappropriate word replaced one of the words in a sentence (semantic anomaly). Articulatory suppression increased errors on the syntactic anomaly sentences from 15.9% to 35.6%, while also having a modest effect on the semantic anomaly sentences. The powerful effect of suppression on the syntactic anomaly sentences suggests that subvocal articulation is especially useful for retaining information about the order of words, because accurate retention of word order is crucial for successful performance.

Baddeley and Lewis (1981) used a different approach to confirm the role of inner speech in reading. Participants decided whether sentences were syntactically correct with the words in the correct order. Some sentences consisted of phonemically similar words (e.g., "Crude rude Jude chewed stewed food"), whereas other sentences did not contain phonemically similar words. It took longer to make judgements of syntactic correctness with the phonemically similar sentences, indicating the relevance of the sounds of words to the comprehension process. Baddeley and Lewis (1981) also found that articulatory suppression did not influence the size of this phonemic similarity effect, although it led to a general increase in errors. This is an important finding. It suggests that the processes responsible for the phonemic similarity effect are rather different from those responsible for the effects of articulatory suppression.

### Functions of inner speech

Most adults read aloud at about 150–200 words per minute, whereas skilled readers typically have a silent reading rate of about 300 words per minute. How can we explain this difference? Perfetti and McCutchen (1982) argued that normal reading rates are much faster than speech rates, because the phonological specification of words in inner speech is incomplete. Their basic assumption was that the abbreviated phonological representation of inner speech is biased towards key information. Most words are specified more precisely by their consonants than by their vowels, and so consonant sounds are more likely to be included in the phonological representation. However, we do not consciously experience inner speech as having this abbreviated form. An alternative viewpoint was expressed by Rayner and Pollatsek (1989, p. 213): "It is possible that the difference between oral and silent reading rates is because a motor response for actually pronouncing each word need not occur in silent reading."

What functions does inner speech play in reading? Probably the most obvious function is that of holding information about words and about word order in working memory so as to reduce the memory load involved in comprehension. Inner speech preserves temporal order information, and thus may be of particular value when accurate comprehension depends on a precise recollection of word order (e.g., Baddeley & Lewis, 1981).

Support for these ideas comes from a study by Bub, Black, Howell, and Kertesz (1987) on a patient, MV, with very deficient inner speech. When written sentences were presented to her, she had problems with syntactically anomalous sentences in which the word order had been altered, but not with semantically anomalous sentences in which an inappropriate word replaced the correct one. This confirms the view that inner speech serves to preserve word order.

Slowiaczek and Clifton (1980) argued that inner speech may provide the prosodic structure (e.g., rhythm, intonation) lacking in written text but present in spoken language. According to them, inner speech makes it easier to identify the important information within a sentence. The fact that you can sometimes "hear" someone's style of speaking when reading a letter they have written is consistent with this position.

Some of the issues discussed in this section are related to theory and research on working memory (see Chapter 6). Of particular relevance is research indicating that articulation of recently heard speech is of crucial importance in the learning of vocabulary (e.g., Baddeley, Gathercole, & Papagno, 1998).

## CAPACITY THEORY

Just and Carpenter (1992) put forward a theory dealing with some of the constraints on sentence comprehension. Their capacity theory focuses on *working memory*, by which they mean "the part of the central executive in Baddeley's theory that deals with language comprehension" (Just & Carpenter, 1992, p. 123; see Chapter 6). Within the theory, working memory is used for both storage and processing during comprehension. Storage and processing demands can be heavy, and it is assumed that working memory has a strictly limited capacity. Thus, the storage demands

during language processing need to be held to manageable proportions. For example, each word is processed thoroughly when first encountered (this is known as the immediacy assumption), instead of storing it for future processing.

The central assumptions made by Just and Carpenter (1992) are that there are individual differences in the capacity of working memory, and that these individual differences have substantial effects on language comprehension. Working memory capacity is assessed by the reading-span task (Daneman & Carpenter, 1980). On this task, participants read a number of sentences for comprehension, and then try to recall the final word of each sentence. The largest number of sentences from which a participant can recall all the final words more than 50% of the time is defined as his or her *reading span*. It is assumed that the processes used in comprehending the sentences require a smaller proportion of the available working memory capacity of those with a large capacity, and thus they have more capacity for retaining the last words of the sentences.

Reading span is a useful measure. It typically correlates about +0.8 with the ability to answer comprehension questions about a passage, and it correlates about +0.6 with verbal intelligence (see Just & Carpenter, 1992). In addition, those with high reading spans read hard portions of a text much faster than those with low reading spans. Theoretically, Daneman and Carpenter (1980) assumed that reading span measures fairly specific processes relating to reading and other verbal tasks.

### Experimental evidence

Capacity theory has been applied to issues considered earlier in the chapter, such as whether the initial syntactic parsing of a sentence is affected by meaning. Just and Carpenter (1992) studied reading times for sentences such as, "The evidence examined by the lawyer shocked the jury", and "The defendant examined by the lawyer shocked the jury". "The evidence" (an inanimate noun) is unlikely to be doing the examining, whereas "the defendant" (an animate noun) might well be. Accordingly, the actual syntactic structure

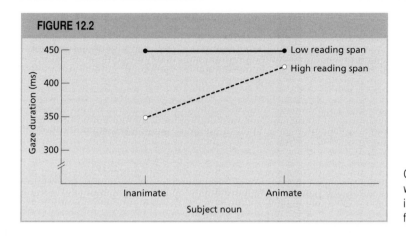

Gaze duration as a function of whether the subject noun was inanimate or animate. Adapted from Just and Carpenter (1992).

of the sentence should come as more of a surprise to readers given the second sentence. However, if meaning does not influence initial syntactic parsing, then the gaze duration on the critical phrase "by the lawyer" should be the same for both sentences.

Just and Carpenter (1992) found that the reading times of participants with a low reading span were unaffected by the animate/inanimate noun manipulation (see Figure 12.2). In contrast, participants with a high reading span made use of the cue of inanimacy, and so their initial parsing was affected by meaning. Presumably only those participants with a high reading span had sufficient working memory capacity available to take the animacy/inanimacy of the subject noun into account. Thus, individual differences need to be taken into account when considering whether meaning affects initial syntactic parsing.

Another area of controversy relates to the processing of sentences containing syntactic ambiguity. One possibility is that those encountering such ambiguity try to retain both (or all) interpretations until disambiguating information is provided. Alternatively, people might select a single interpretation, and retain it unless or until there is invalidating information. Just and Carpenter (1992) discussed a study in which sentences were presented in a self-paced, word-by-word moving window paradigm. Some sentences were syntactically ambiguous until the end (e.g., "The experienced soldiers warned about the dangers before the midnight raid"), but were finally given the more

predictable resolution; others were unambiguous (e.g., "The experienced soldiers spoke about the dangers before the midnight raid").

Participants with a high reading span processed the ambiguous sentences more slowly than the unambiguous ones, especially close to the part of the sentence in which the ambiguity was resolved (see Figure 12.3). These participants incurred a cost in terms of processing time for maintaining two different syntactic interpretations of the ambiguous sentences. In contrast, those with a low reading span did not differ in their processing times for ambiguous and unambiguous sentences, presumably because they treated such sentences as if they were unambiguous.

According to capacity theory, the processes involved in maintaining the last words of sentences in memory in the reading-span task resemble those used in sentence comprehension. Just, Carpenter, and Keller (1996) tested this hypothesis using functional magnetic resonance imaging (fMRI; see Chapter 1). Sentences were presented for comprehension under two conditions: (1) read only; or (2) read and maintain each last word. The brain area of most interest was Wernicke's area, which is involved in language comprehension. There was much more activity in Wernicke's area in the read-and-maintain condition than in the read-only condition. As Just et al. (1996, p. 775) concluded, "the present study supports the argument that the maintenance aspect of the reading-span task draws on processes that overlap with those in sentence comprehension."

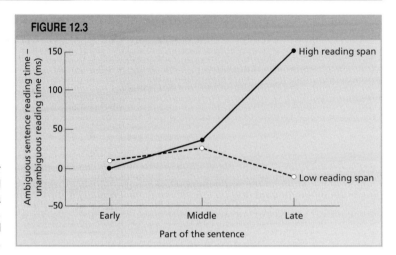

**FIGURE 12.3**

Differences in reading time per word between ambiguous and unambiguous sentences as a function of part of the sentence. Adapted from Just and Carpenter (1992).

The notion in capacity theory that reading span reflects specific reading-related processes was disputed by Turner and Engle (1989), who assessed what they called the operation span. The participants were presented with a series of items such as, "IS $(4 \times 2) - 3 = 5$? TABLE". Their task was to answer each arithmetical question and remember the last word from each item. Their key findings were that operation span (the maximum number of items for which the participants could remember all the last words) correlated as highly with language comprehension as did reading span. These finding would not be expected if reading span is associated with language comprehension because it specifically assesses reading-related processes. The findings of Turner and Engle (1989), when taken together with other similar ones, suggest that "complex tasks such as reading span reflect general, domain-free attentional resources that will be important in any cognitive task requiring controlled processing" (Engle & Conway, 1998, p. 83).

*Aphasia*

The capacity theory has been applied to brain-damaged patients suffering from *aphasia*, in which language abilities are impaired. According to the theory, what is common to all aphasic patients is a reduction in the working memory resources involved in language comprehension. Caspari, Parkinson, LaPointe, and Katz (1994) studied

various patients suffering from aphasia. Performance on a listening-span task correlated +0.82 with an independent measure of text comprehension in these aphasic patients.

Carpenter, Miyake, and Just (1994) discussed a simulation model based on the capacity theory. This model is called CC READER, with the initials standing for Capacity Constrained. According to this model, activation underlies all the activities taking place in working memory: "The constraint on capacity is operationally defined as the maximum amount of activation that the system has available conjointly for maintenance and processing purposes" (Carpenter et al., 1994, p. 1091). Carpenter et al. (1994, p. 1093) argued that this model can readily be applied to aphasia: "The maximum amount of activation available for the storage and processing of linguistic information is far more severely limited in the aphasic system than in the normal system." Haarmann, Just, and Carpenter (1997) used the computational model to observe the effects of reducing activation and working memory resources on comprehension performance. The error rates of the model across various types of sentences resembled those of aphasic patients.

**Evaluation**

Probably the greatest strength of the capacity theory put forward by Just and Carpenter (1992) is the assumption that there are substantial individual differences in the processes used in language comprehension. Some individuals have more processing resources available than others, and so can carry out forms of processing that those with fewer processing resources cannot. This approach has shed important new light on some major controversies (e.g., the role of meaning in the initial parsing of sentences).

On the negative side, it is not clear how to interpret the high correlation between reading span and language comprehension. Just and Carpenter (1992) argued that the efficiency of working memory (as measured by reading span) determines the efficiency of language processing and comprehension. Ericsson and Kintsch (1995) and Ericsson and Delaney (1998) argued for the opposite position, namely, that language processing efficiency determines the efficiency of working memory as assessed by reading span. It is hard to distinguish between these possibilities. According to Ericsson and Delaney (1998, p. 111), "Individual differences in working memory capacity during reading do not reflect innate, fixed capacity differences, in contrast with traditional theories (Just & Carpenter, 1992; Daneman & Carpenter, 1980). Instead, such individual capacity differences primarily reflect differences in the relevant knowledge and acquired memory skills that support encoding of the text." There is also the issue of whether reading span reflects reading-related processes as claimed by Daneman and Carpenter (1980), or whether it reflects more general processing resources (Turner & Engle, 1989).

Waters and Caplan (1996) argued that there are theoretical reasons for doubting whether the processes involved in maintaining the last word of each sentence in the word-span task are the same as those involved in sentence comprehension. According to Waters and Caplan (1996, p. 769):

> [the word-span task] requires conscious retrieval of items held in memory, to an extent not found in processing sentence structure . . . the memory load that is imposed in the [word-span] task is unrelated to the computations of that task, whereas the verbal material that is stored in sentence processing is relevant to the ongoing computations required by that task.

Another issue concerns the importance attached to reading span within capacity theory. As Towse, Hitch, and Hutton (1999, p. 111) pointed out, there are concerns about relying on reading span, "a task requiring sentence comprehension, as the vehicle to explain sentence-comprehension processes."

Finally, the theory emphasises working memory capacity rather than the specific processes involved in comprehension. Thus, Just and Carpenter (1992) do not provide us with a detailed account of comprehension processes. As a result, capacity theory does not provide a comprehensive account of language comprehension in normals or aphasic patients.

## DISCOURSE PROCESSING

We have focused mainly on the processes involved in understanding individual sentences. However, in real life we are generally presented with connected *discourse* (written text or speech). According to Graesser, Millis, and Zwaan (1997, p. 164), there are important differences between the processing of sentences and discourse:

> Connected discourse is . . . much more than a sequence of individual sentences . . . a sentence out of context is nearly always ambiguous, whereas a sentence in a discourse context is rarely ambiguous . . . Both stories and everyday experiences include people performing actions in pursuit of goals, events that present obstacles to these goals, conflicts between people, and emotional reactions.

Most research on discourse comprehension has been based on written texts. Some researchers have used published texts (e.g., articles; books) written by professional writers, whereas others have used specially constructed texts. The former approach has the advantage of *ecological validity* (applicability to real life), but poor control over many variables affecting comprehension. In contrast, the latter approach has the advantage that textual variables can be manipulated in a systematic way, but the resulting texts tend to be artificial and uninteresting. How should researchers proceed? The best solution was proposed by Graesser et al. (1997, p. 166): "Discourse psychologists are on solid footing when a hypothesis is confirmed in a sample of naturalistic texts in addition to properly controlled textoids [experimenter-generated texts]."

## Inference drawing

Comprehension of discourse would be impossible without access to stored knowledge. A simple illustration of the crucial role played by such knowledge is the process of inference or filling-in of gaps. Schank (1976, p. 168) described it as "the core of the understanding process".

Some idea of how readily we make inferences can be formed if you read the following story taken from Rumelhart and Ortony (1977):

1. Mary heard the ice-cream van coming.
2. She remembered the pocket money.
3. She rushed into the house.

You probably made various assumptions or inferences while reading the story. Possible inferences include the following: Mary wanted to buy some ice-cream; buying ice-cream costs money; Mary had some pocket money in the house; and Mary had only a limited amount of time to get hold of some money before the ice-cream van arrived. None of these assumptions is explicitly stated in the three sentences that were presented. It is so natural for us to draw inferences to help understanding that we are often unaware that we are doing so.

A distinction can be drawn between bridging inferences and elaborative inferences. *Bridging inferences* need to be made to establish coherence between the current part of the text and the preceding text, whereas *elaborative inferences* serve to embellish or add details to the text. Most theorists accept that readers generally draw bridging inferences, which are essential for understanding. What is more controversial is the extent to which non-essential or elaborative inferences are drawn.

## Anaphora

Perhaps the simplest form of bridging inference is involved in *anaphora*, in which a pronoun or noun has to be identified with a previously mentioned noun or noun phrase (e.g., "Fred sold John his lawn mower, and then he sold him his garden hose". It requires a bridging inference to realise that "he" refers to Fred rather than to John. How do people make the appropriate anaphoric inference? Sometimes gender makes the task very easy (e.g., "Juliet sold John her lawn mower, and then she sold him her garden hose"), and sometimes the number of the noun provides a useful cue (e.g., "Juliet and her friends sold John their lawn mower, and then they sold him their garden hose").

It seems reasonable that the ease of establishing the appropriate anaphoric inference should depend on the distance between the pronoun and the noun to which it refers: this is the distance effect. However, Clifton and Ferreira (1987) showed that distance is not always important. Their participants presented themselves with passages one phrase at a time, and the reading time for the phrase containing the pronoun was measured. The reading time was fast if the relevant noun was still the topic of discourse, but it was slow otherwise. Distance as such had no effect on reading time. Thus, the distance effect is found normally because greater distance reduces the probability that the noun to which it refers is still the topic of discourse when the pronoun is presented.

## When are inferences drawn?

Consider the following passage from a study by O'Brien, Shank, Myers, and Rayner (1988):

All the mugger wanted was to steal the woman's money. But when she screamed, he stabbed her with his weapon in an attempt to quiet her. He looked to see if anyone had seen him. He threw the knife into the bushes, took her money, and ran away.

O'Brien et al. (1988) were interested in seeing when readers drew the inference that the "weapon" referred to in the second sentence was in fact a knife. They compared reading time on the last sentence in the passage quoted here, and in an almost identical passage in which the word "weapon" was replaced by "knife". There was no difference in the reading time, suggesting that the inference that the weapon was a knife had been drawn immediately by readers.

O'Brien et al. (1988) also considered reading time for the last sentence when the second sentence was altered so that the inference that the weapon was a knife was less clear ("But when she screamed, he assaulted her with his weapon in an attempt to quiet her"). This time, the last sentence took longer to read, presumably because the inference that the weapon was a knife was drawn only while the last sentence was being read.

Other evidence confirms the notion that it is only strong and obvious inferences that are drawn immediately. Singer (1979) asked participants to read pairs of sentences. In some cases, the subject noun of the second sentence had been explicitly mentioned in the first sentence (e.g., "The boy cleared the snow with a shovel. The shovel was heavy."). In other cases, the subject noun had not been specifically referred to before (e.g., "The boy cleared the snow from the stairs. The shovel was heavy."). Singer (1979) found that the time taken to read the second sentence in the pair was greater when the subject noun of the sentence had not been explicitly mentioned before. This suggests that the inference that a shovel was used to clear the snow was not drawn while the first sentence was being read, but was drawn subsequently.

## Which inferences are drawn?

Everyone agrees that various inferences are made while people are reading text or listening to speech. What is of interest theoretically is to understand *why* inferences are made, and to be able to predict which inferences are likely to be made. The constructionist approach originally proposed by Bransford (e.g., Bransford, Barclay, & Franks, 1972) and later developed by others (e.g., Johnson-Laird, 1980; van Dijk & Kintsch, 1983) represents

one very influential theoretical position. Bransford argued that comprehension typically requires our active involvement to supply information that is not explicitly contained in the text. Johnson-Laird (1980) argued that readers typically construct a relatively complete "mental model" of the situation and events referred to in the text (see Chapter 9). A key implication of the constructionist approach is that numerous elaborative inferences are typically drawn while reading a text.

Most early research supporting the constructionist position involved using memory tests to assess inference drawing. For example, Bransford et al. (1972) presented their participants with sentences such as, "Three turtles rested on a floating log, and a fish swam beneath them." They argued that the inference would be drawn that the fish swam under the log. To test this, some participants on a subsequent recognition-memory test were given the sentence, "Three turtles rested on a floating log, and a fish swam beneath it." Most participants were confident that this inference was the original sentence. Indeed, the level of confidence was as high as it was when the original sentence was re-presented on the memory test! Bransford et al. (1972) concluded that inferences from text were typically stored in memory in the same way as information directly presented in the text.

Memory tests provide a rather indirect measure of inferential processes, and there is the ever-present danger that any inferences that are found on a memory test were made at the time of test rather than during reading. This issue has been considered in detail in a number of studies. The findings indicate that many (or most) inferences found on memory tests reflect reconstructive processes occurring during retrieval. As a result, there has been a marked reduction in the use of memory tasks in inference research.

## Minimalist hypothesis

Problems of interpretation with the memory studies (e.g., Bransford et al., 1972) suggested to some theorists that the evidence for the constructionist position is relatively weak. For example, McKoon and Ratcliff (1992, p. 442) reached the following conclusion: "The widely accepted constructionist view of text processing has almost no unassailable empirical support . . . it is difficult to point to a single, unequival piece of evidence in favour of the automatic generation of constructionist inferences." McKoon and Ratcliff (1992, p. 440) proposed an alternative view which they referred to as the *minimalist hypothesis*:

> In the absence of specific, goal-directed strategic processes, inferences of only two kinds are constructed: those that establish locally coherent representations of the parts of a text that are processed concurrently and those that rely on information that is quickly and easily available.

It is important to clarify some of the notions contained in the minimalist hypothesis. In sum, here are the main assumptions made by McKoon and Ratcliff (1992):

- Inferences are either automatic or strategic (goal-directed).
- Some automatic inferences establish local coherence (two or three sentences making sense on their own or in combination with easily available general knowledge); these inferences involve parts of the text that are in working memory at the same time (this is working memory in the sense of a general-purpose capacity rather than the Baddeley multiple-component working memory system discussed in Chapter 6).
- Other automatic inferences rely on information that is readily available either because it forms part of general knowledge or because it is explicitly stated in the text.
- Strategic inferences are formed in pursuit of the reader's goals; they sometimes serve to produce local coherence.

The greatest difference between the minimalist hypothesis and the constructionist position concerns the number of automatic inferences that are formed. Those who support the constructionist view claim that numerous automatic inferences are drawn in reading, whereas those who favour

the minimalist hypothesis argue that there are very definite constraints on the number of inferences that are generated automatically.

McKoon and Ratcliff (1986) tested this discrepancy between the two theories. They argued that a sentence such as "The actress fell from the fourteenth storey" would automatically lead to the inference that she died from the constructionist viewpoint but not from the minimalist hypothesis. Participants read several short texts containing such sentences, followed by a recognition memory test on which they had to decide very rapidly whether or not certain words had been presented in any of the texts. There were critical test words that represented inferences from a presented sentence but which had not actually been presented (e.g., "dead" for the sentence about the actress). The correct response to these critical test words was "No". However, if participants had formed the inference, then this would presumably lead to errors.

McKoon and Ratcliff (1986) found that the number of errors on critical test words was no higher than on control words when they were immediately preceded on the recognition memory test by the neutral word "ready". However, when they were preceded by a word from the relevant sentence (e.g., "actress"), there was an increase in the number of errors to the critical test words. The implication of these slightly complicated findings is that the inferences were not generated fully, which is in line with the minimalist hypothesis. However, the fact that they were formed to a limited extent provides some support for the constructionists.

Evidence opposing the constructionist position and indicating the importance of the distinction between automatic and strategic inferences was obtained by Dosher and Corbett (1982). They used instrumental inferences (e.g., a sentence such as "Mary stirred her coffee" has "spoon" as its instrumental inference). In order to decide whether participants generated these instrumental inferences during reading, Dosher and Corbett made use of a somewhat unusual procedure. It is known from research on the Stroop effect that the time taken to name the colour in which a word is printed is affected if the word has recently been activated.

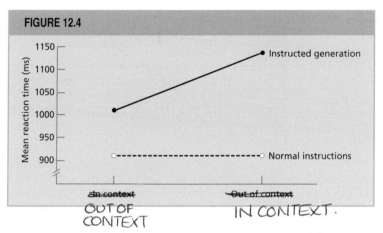

**FIGURE 12.4**

Colour-naming time in the Stroop task as a function of whether or not participants had been asked to guess the instrument in preceding sentences, and as a function of whether the words on the Stroop test were in or out of context with the preceding sentences. Based on data in Dosher and Corbett (1982).

Thus, if presentation of the sentence "Mary stirred her coffee" activates the word "spoon", then this should slow the time taken to name the colour in which the word "spoon" is printed on the Stroop task. In a control (out-of-context) condition, the words presented on the Stroop task bore no relationship to the preceding sentences. There was no evidence that the instrumental inferences had been formed with normal reading instructions (see Figure 12.4). However, when the participants were instructed to guess the instrument in each sentence, then there were effects on the Stroop task.

What do these findings mean? First, they indicate clearly that whether an inference is drawn can depend on the reader's intentions or goals, which is one of the central assumptions made by McKoon and Ratcliff (1992). Second, the findings are very much at variance with the constructionist position. It is necessary to infer the instrument used in stirring coffee to attain full understanding, but the evidence indicates that such instrumental inferences are not normally drawn.

McKoon and Ratcliff (1992) assumed that automatic inferences are drawn to establish local coherence for information contained in working memory, but that global inferences (inferences connecting widely separated pieces of textual information) are not drawn automatically. They tested these assumptions with short texts containing a global goal (e.g., assassinating a president) and one or two local or subordinate goals (e.g., using a rifle; using hand grenades). Active use of global and local inferences was tested by presenting a test word after each text, and instructing the

participants to decide rapidly whether the word had appeared in the text.

There was an important difference between local and global inferences, with the former being drawn automatically but the latter not. These findings are more consistent with the minimalist hypothesis than with the constructionist position, in which no distinction is drawn between local and global inferences.

## Evaluation

One of the greatest strengths of the minimalist hypothesis is that it serves to clarify which inferences are and are not automatically drawn when someone is reading a text. In contrast, constructionist theorists often argue that those inferences that are needed to understand fully the situation described in a text are drawn automatically. This is rather vague, as there obviously could be considerable differences of opinion over exactly what information needs to be encoded for full understanding.

Another strength of the minimalist hypothesis is that it emphasises the distinction between automatic and strategic inferences. The notion that many inferences will be drawn only if they are consistent with the reader's goals in reading is an important one.

On the negative side, it is not always possible to predict accurately from the hypothesis which inferences will be drawn. For example, automatic inferences are drawn if the necessary information is "readily available", but it can be problematic to

## FIGURE 12.5

| | Type of inference | Answers query | Predicted by constructionalists | Predicted by minimalists | Normally found |
|---|---|---|---|---|---|
| 1. | Referential | To what previous word does this apply? (e.g. anaphora) | √ | √ | √ |
| 2. | Case structure role assignment | What is the role (e.g. agent, object) of this noun? | √ | √ | √ |
| 3. | Causal antecedant | What caused this? | √ | √ | √ |
| 4. | Supraordinate goal | What is the main goal? | √ | | √ |
| 5. | Thematic | What is the overall theme? | √ | | ? |
| 6. | Character emotional reaction | How does the character feel? | √ | | √ |
| 7. | Causal consequence | What happens next? | | | × |
| 8. | Instrument | What was used to do this? | | | × |
| 9. | Subordinate goal-action | How was the action achieved? | | | × |

The types of inferences normally drawn, together with the predictions from the constructionist and minimalist perspectives. Adapted from Graesser et al. (1994).

establish the precise degree of availability of some piece of information.

## Search-after-meaning theory

Since the appearance of McKoon and Ratcliff's (1992) minimalist hypothesis, there has been a counter-attack by constructionist theorists. Graesser, Singer, and Trabasso (1994) agreed with McKoon and Ratcliff (1992) that constructionist theories often fail to specify which inferences are drawn during comprehension. They tried to eliminate this omission in their search-after-meaning theory, according to which readers engage in a search after meaning based on the following:

• The reader goal assumption: the reader constructs a meaning for the text that addresses his or her goals.
• The coherence assumption: the reader tries to construct a meaning for the text that is coherent locally and globally.
• The explanation assumption: the reader tries to explain the actions, events, and states referred to in the text.

Graesser et al. (1994) pointed out that the reader will not search after meaning if his or her goals do not necessitate the construction of a meaning representation of the text (e.g., in proofreading); if the text appears to lack coherence; or if the reader does not possess the necessary background knowledge to make sense of the text. Even if the reader does search after meaning, there are several kinds of inference that are not normally drawn according to the search-after-meaning theory. As can be seen in Figure 12.5, these undrawn inferences include ones about future developments (causal consequence); the precise way in which actions are accomplished (subordinate goal-actions); and the author's intent.

Nine different types of inference are described in Figure 12.5. According to Graesser et al. (1994), it is assumed within search-after-meaning theory that six of these types of inference are generally drawn, whereas only three are drawn on the minimalist hypothesis. As can be seen in the last column of Figure 12.5, the evidence seems to be more in line with the predictions of the search-after-meaning theory than those of the minimalist hypothesis.

## Section summary

Inferences are generally drawn during the process of language comprehension. It used to be assumed by constructionist theorists that numerous inferences are made routinely during reading, but some of the studies apparently supporting that view are flawed because of a failure to discriminate between inferences formed during reading and those formed at the time of subsequent testing.

The main goal of recent theories is to identify more precisely which inferences are normally drawn. It may seem that there is a large gap between the minimalist hypothesis and the search-after-meaning theory, because the focus within the minimalist hypothesis is on a narrower set of inferences. However, it should be remembered that McKoon and Ratcliff (1992) accepted that many strategic inferences are formed in addition to the automatic inferences they discussed. All in all, there is a growing consensus on the types of inference that are generally made (e.g., referential; causal antecedent), and on those that are rarely made (e.g., instrumental; causal consequence). Graesser et al. (1997, p. 183) came to the following reasonable conclusion:

> We suspect that each of the . . . models is correct in certain conditions. The minimalist hypothesis is probably correct when the reader is very quickly reading the text, when the text lacks global coherence, and when the reader has very little background knowledge. The constructionist [or search-after-meaning] theory is on the mark when the reader is attempting to comprehend the text for enjoyment or mastery at a more leisurely pace.

Some theorists (e.g., van Dijk & Kintsch, 1983) have argued that readers often construct a mental model or representation of the situation described by the text. The information contained in mental models can go well beyond the information contained in a text, and such information is based on inferences. The notion of situational representations plays an important part in the theory of story processing proposed by Kintsch (1988, 1992, 1994), and so further discussion will be deferred until that theory is considered later in the chapter.

## STORY PROCESSING

If someone asks us to tell them about a story or book that we have read recently, we discuss the major events and themes of the story, and leave out virtually all the minor details. In other words, our description of the story is highly selective, and is determined by its meaning. Indeed, imagine the questioner's reaction if we simply recalled sentences taken at random from the story!

Gomulicki (1956) provided a simple demonstration of the selective way in which stories are comprehended and remembered. One group of participants wrote a précis (abstract or summary) of a story that was visible in front of them, and a second group recalled the story from memory. A third group of participants who were given each précis and recall found it very hard to tell them apart. Thus, story memory resembles a précis, in that people focus mainly on important information.

### Story grammars

Most (or all) stories possess some kind of structure. Some psychologists have argued that all stories share common elements at a very general and abstract level. This led to the notion of a *story grammar*, which is a set of rules from which the structure of any given story can be generated. Thorndyke (1977) considered a story grammar in which there was a hierarchical structure with the major categories of setting, theme, plot, and resolution at the top of the hierarchy. Thorndyke tested this story grammar by presenting a story in which the theme was in its usual place at the start of the story, or it was placed at the end of the story, or it was omitted altogether. Memory for the story was best when the theme had been presented at the start of the story, and it was better when it had been presented at the end rather than not at all.

Other research based on similar notions has supported the view that stories are hierarchically organised. For example, Meyer and McConkie (1973) found that an event low down in the story hierarchy was much more likely to be recalled if the event immediately above it in the hierarchy had been recalled.

## Evaluation

The notion that stories have an underlying structure is reasonable, but the story grammar approach has not proved to be of lasting value. Why is this? One major reason was identified by Harley (1995, p. 233): "There is no agreement on story structure: virtually every story grammatician has proposed a different grammar." Another limitation is that story grammars are not very informative about the processes involved in story comprehension.

## Schema theories

The term *schema* is used to refer to well integrated chunks of knowledge about the world, events, people, and actions. Scripts and frames are relatively specific kinds of schemas. Scripts deal with knowledge about events and consequences of events. Thus, for example, Schank and Abelson (1977) referred to a restaurant script, which contains information about the usual sequence of events involved in going to a restaurant to have a meal. In contrast, frames deal with knowledge about the properties of objects and locations. Schemas are important in language processing, because they contain much of the knowledge that is used to facilitate understanding of what we hear and read.

A crucial function of schemas is that they allow us to form *expectations*. In a restaurant, for example, we expect to be shown to a table, to be given a menu by the waiter or waitress, to order the food and drink, and so on. If any of these expectations is violated, then we usually take appropriate action. For example, if no menu is forthcoming, we try to catch the eye of the waiter or waitress. As our expectations are generally confirmed, schemas help us to make the world a more predictable place than it would be otherwise.

Evidence that schemas can influence story comprehension was reported by Bransford and Johnson (1972, p. 722). They presented a passage in which it was hard to work out which schemas were relevant. Part of it was as follows:

The procedure is quite simple. First, you arrange items into different groups. Of course one pile may be sufficient depending on how much there is to do. If you have to go somewhere else due to lack of facilities that is the next step; otherwise, you are pretty well set. It is important not to overdo things. That is, it is better to do too few things at once than too many. In the short run this may not seem important but complications can easily arise.

The participants who heard the passage in the absence of a title rated it as incomprehensible and recalled an average of only 2.8 idea units. In contrast, those who were supplied beforehand with the title "Washing clothes" found it easy to understand and recalled 5.8 idea units on average. This effect of relevant schema knowledge occurred because it helped comprehension of the passage rather than because the title acted as a useful retrieval cue: participants who received the title after hearing the passage but before recall, produced only 2.6 idea units on average.

### Bartlett's theory

Bartlett (1932) was the first psychologist to argue persuasively that schemas play an important role in determining what we remember from stories. According to him, memory is affected not only by the presented story, but also by the participant's store of relevant prior knowledge in the form of schemas. He had the ingenious idea of presenting his participants with stories that produced a *conflict* between what was presented to them and their prior knowledge. If, for example, people read a story taken from a culture different from their own, then prior knowledge might produce distortions in the remembered version of the story, rendering it more conventional and acceptable from the standpoint of their own cultural background. Bartlett's (1932) findings supported his predictions. In particular, a substantial proportion of the recall errors were in the direction of making the story read more like a conventional English story. He used the term *rationalisation* to refer to this type of error.

Bartlett (1932) assumed that memory for the precise material presented is forgotten over time, whereas memory for the underlying schemas is

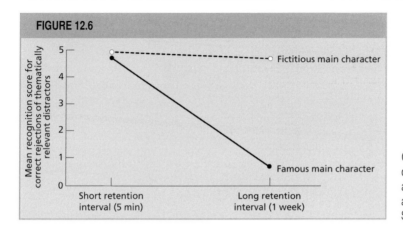

**FIGURE 12.6**

Correct rejection of thematic distractor as a function of main actor (Gerald Martin or Adolf Hitler) and retention interval. Data from Sulin and Dooling (1974).

not. As a result, rationalisation errors (which depend on schematic knowledge) should increase in number at longer retentional intervals. Bartlett (1932) reported findings that supported this prediction. However, his studies are open to criticism. He did not give very specific instructions to his participants (Bartlett, 1932, p. 78): "I thought it best, for the purposes of these experiments, to try to influence the subjects' procedure as little as possible." As a result, some of the distortions observed by Bartlett may have been due to conscious guessing rather than deficient memory. There is some force in this criticism. Gauld and Stephenson (1967) found that instructions stressing the need for accurate recall eliminated almost half the errors usually obtained.

In spite of these problems with Bartlett's procedures, there is evidence from well controlled studies to confirm his major findings. For example, Sulin and Dooling (1974) presented some of their participants with a story about Gerald Martin: "Gerald Martin strove to undermine the existing government to satisfy his political ambitions . . . He became a ruthless, uncontrollable dictator. The ultimate effect of his rule was the downfall of his country" (Sulin & Dooling, 1974, p. 256). Other participants were given the same story, but the name of the main actor was given as Adolf Hitler. Those participants who were told the story was about Adolf Hitler were much more likely than the other participants to believe incorrectly that they had read the sentence "He hated the Jews particularly and so persecuted them." Their

schematic knowledge about Hitler distorted their recollections of what they had read (see Figure 12.6). As Bartlett (1932) predicted, this type of distortion was more frequent at a long than a short retention interval.

There are doubts as to whether some of Bartlett's main findings can be replicated under more naturalistic conditions. Wynn and Logie (1998) tested students' recall of "real-life" events experienced during their first week at university at various intervals of time ranging from 2 weeks to 6 months. What they found was as follows: "The initial accuracy sustained throughout the time period, together with the relative lack of change over time, suggests very limited use of reconstructive processes" (Wynn & Logie, 1998, p. 1). This failure may have occurred in part because the students were only able to make limited use of schema-based processes. Whatever the explanation, these findings suggest that Bartlett's findings may have limited applicability.

Another assumption made by Bartlett (1932) was that memorial distortions occur mainly because of schema-driven reconstructive processes operating at the time of retrieval. As we saw in the study by Bransford and Johnson (1972), schemas often influence comprehension processes rather than retrieval processes. However, schemas do sometimes influence the retrieval of information from long-term memory. Anderson and Pichert (1978) asked participants to read a story from the perspective of either a burglar or someone interested in buying a home. After they had recalled

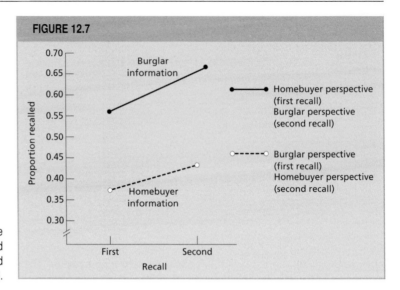

**FIGURE 12.7**

Recall as a function of perspective at the time of retrieval. Based on data from Anderson and Pichert (1978).

the story, they were asked to shift to the alternative perspective, and then to recall the story again. On the second recall, participants recalled more information that was important only to the second perspective or schema than they had done on the first recall (see Figure 12.7).

These findings support the notion of schema-driven retrieval. Further support comes from the participants' own accounts (Anderson & Pichert, 1978, p. 10):

> When he gave me the homebuyer perspective, I remembered the end of the story, you know, about the leak in the roof. The first time through I knew there was an ending, but I couldn't remember what it was. But it just popped into my mind when I thought about the story from the homebuyer perspective.

*Script-pointer-plus tag hypothesis*

The script-pointer-plus-tag hypothesis was put forward by Schank and Abelson (1977). It represents a development of some of Bartlett's ideas, and consists of a number of assumptions about memory for script- or schema-based stories:

- Information from the story is combined with information from the underlying script or schema in memory.

- Actions in a story are either typical (consistent with the underlying script or schema) or atypical (inconsistent with the underlying script).
- Information about atypical actions is tagged individually to the underlying script.
- Recognition memory will be better for atypical than for typical actions, because typical actions present in the story are hard to discriminate from typical actions absent from the story.
- Initial recall for atypical actions should be better than for typical actions, because they are tagged individually in memory.
- Recall for atypical actions at long retention intervals should be worse than for typical actions, because recall increasingly relies on the underlying script or schema.

The evidence generally supports the prediction that recognition memory for atypical actions is better than for typical ones at all retention intervals (Davidson, 1994). However, the findings with respect to recall are more inconsistent. Davidson (1994) shed light on these inconsistencies. She used routine atypical actions that were irrelevant to the story and atypical actions that interrupted the story. For example, in a story about going to the cinema, "Sarah mentions to Sam that the screen is big" belongs to the former category and "Another couple, both of whom are very tall, sits in front of them and blocks their view" belongs to the latter category. Both kinds of atypical actions were better recalled than typical ones at a relatively short retention interval (1 hour), which is in line with prediction. After 1 week, however, the routine, irrelevant atypical actions were less well recalled than typical or script actions, whereas the interruptive atypical actions were better recalled than typical actions. As Davidson (1994, p. 772) concluded, "Part of the problem with existing schema is that they do not specify how different types of atypical actions will be recalled."

*Evaluation*

Our organised knowledge of the world is used in a systematic way to help text comprehension and recall. However, it has proved hard to identify the characteristics of schemas. More importantly, most versions of schema theory are sadly lacking in testability. If we are trying to explain text comprehension and memory in terms of the activation of certain schemas, then we really require independent evidence of the existence (and appropriate activation) of those schemas. However, such evidence is generally not available.

One of the major assumptions of schema theory is that top-down processes lead to the generation of numerous inferences during story comprehension. However, the evidence discussed earlier in the chapter (e.g., McKoon & Ratcliff, 1992) suggests that the number of inferences generated by the average reader is less than is implied by schema theory.

Finally, the reader may have noticed that memory rather than comprehension was the primary focus of the research discussed in this section. Real-world knowledge manifestly affects comprehension processes, but schema theory does not indicate in detail how this happens.

## Kintsch and van Dijk's model

One of the most successful models of discourse processing was put forward by Kintsch and van Dijk (1978). There are two basic units of analysis within their model: the *argument* (the representation of the meaning of a word) and the *proposition* (the smallest unit of meaning to which we can assign a truth value; this is generally a phrase or clause). The text of a story is processed to form structures at two main levels:

- The *micro-structure*: the level at which the propositions extracted from the text are formed into a connected structure.
- The *macro-structure*: the level at which an edited version of the micro-structure (resembling the gist of the story) is formed.

Kintsch and van Dijk (1978) argued that the propositions extracted from a story are entered into a short-term working buffer of limited capacity similar to the working memory system proposed by Baddeley and Hitch (1974; see Chapter 6). Additional propositions are formed from bridging inferences, and added to those formed directly from the text itself. When the buffer contains a number of propositions, the reader tries to link them together in a coherent way. More specifically, propositions that share an argument (i.e., two words having the same meaning) are linked. Linking of propositions occurs only within the buffer, and thus is limited by the capacity of short-term memory. There is a *processing cycle*: at regular intervals, the buffer is emptied of everything but a few key propositions. Propositions are retained in the buffer if they are high-level or central in the evolving structure of the story, or if they were presented recently.

The macro-structure of a story combines schematic information with an abbreviated version of the micro-structure. Various rules are applied to the propositions of the micro-structure:

- Deletion: any proposition not required to interpret a later proposition is deleted.
- Generalisation: a sequence of propositions may be replaced by a more general proposition.
- Construction: a sequence of propositions may be replaced by a single proposition that is a necessary consequence of the sequence.

Memory for the text depends on both the micro-structure and the macro-structure. Higher-level or more central propositions are remembered better than low-level propositions, because they are held longer in the working buffer and are more likely to be included in the macro-structure. This prediction has been confirmed several times (e.g., Kintsch et al., 1975).

## Evidence

Evidence for the importance of propositions was obtained by Kintsch and Keenan (1973). They manipulated the number of propositions in sentences and paragraphs, but equated the number of words. An example of a sentence with four propositions is: "Romulus, the legendary founder of Rome, took the women of the Sabine by force", whereas the following sentence contains eight propositions: "Cleopatra's downfall lay in her foolish trust of the fickle political figures of the Roman world". The reading time increased by about one second for each additional proposition.

Ratcliff and McKoon (1978) provided good evidence for the existence of propositions. They presented sentences (e.g., "The mausoleum that enshrined the czar overlooked the square"). This was followed by a recognition test in which participants had to decide whether test words had been presented before. For the example given, the test word "square" was recognised faster when the preceding test word was from the same proposition (e.g., "mausoleum") than when it was closer in the sentence but from a different proposition (e.g., "czar").

McKoon and Ratcliff (1980) presented participants with a paragraph. This was followed by tests of recognition memory, with participants deciding whether the ideas contained in sentences had been presented in the paragraph. The response times to perform this recognition-memory task were speeded up when a sentence was preceded by another sentence from the paragraph. This speeding up or priming effect was determined more by closeness of the two sentences within the propositional structure of the micro-structure than by closeness in the text, thus providing evidence for the reality of the micro-structure.

Kintsch (1974) distinguished between effects of the micro-structure and of the macro-structure on memory for text using a verification task.

Participants decided whether explicit and implicit inferences were consistent with a text that they had either just read or had read about 15 minutes earlier. Explicitly stated propositions were verified faster than implicitly stated propositions on the immediate test, but there was no difference in verification time between the two kinds of propositions after 15 minutes. According to the theory, explicit propositions are better represented than implicit propositions in the micro-structure, but both are equally well represented in the macro-structure. Information in the micro-structure is much more available immediately than after a delay, and this explains the different pattern of results at the two time intervals.

## Evaluation

There is reasonable evidence for the distinction between micro-structure and macro-structure, and it seems likely that proposition-like representations play a role in text comprehension and memory. The notion that propositions of central importance (e.g., those relating to the main theme) are especially well recalled because they spend a disproportionate amount of time in the working buffer is interesting and plausible.

Most of the major problems with the model proposed by Kintsch and van Dijk (1978) concern what has been omitted from it. For example, the details of how propositions are formed are not spelled out, nor is it indicated exactly how bridging inferences are formed or how schematic knowledge interacts with textual information.

Rayner and Pollatsek (1989, p. 299) pointed out that "coherence and the understanding of discourse entails [sic] more than just tying propositions together with links, and hence . . . other structures are going to be needed besides networks of propositions." For example, Kintsch and van Dijk (1978) were wrong to claim that the coherence of a text depends very largely on the same argument being repeated several times. For example, a series of essentially unrelated statements about the same individual would not be coherent, but would be deemed to be so within the model.

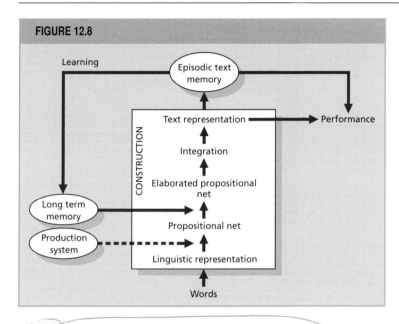

The construction–integration model.
Adapted from Kintsch (1992).

## Kintsch's construction–integration model

Kintsch (1988, 1992, 1994) put forward a construction–integration model that developed and extended his previous model. This model provides more information about the ways in which inferences are formed and stored knowledge interacts with textual information to form the macro-structure.

The basic structure of the construction–integration model is shown in Figure 12.8. According to the model, the following stages occur during the comprehension process:

- Sentences in the text are turned into propositions representing the meaning of the text.
- These propositions are entered into a short-term buffer and form a *propositional net*.
- Each proposition constructed from the text retrieves a few associatively related propositions (including inferences) from long-term memory.
- The propositions constructed from the text plus those retrieved from *long-term memory* jointly form the *elaborated propositional net*; this net will usually contain many irrelevant propositions.

- A spreading activation process is then used to select propositions for the text representation; clusters of highly interconnected propositions attract most of the activation and have the greatest probability of inclusion in the text representation, whereas irrelevant propositions are likely to be discarded: "things that belong together contextually become stronger, and things that do not, die off" (Kintsch, 1994, p. 732): this is the *integration process*.
- The *text representation* is an organised structure which is stored in *episodic text memory*; information about the relationship between any two propositions is included if the two propositions were processed together in the short-term buffer.
- As a result of these processes, three levels of representation are constructed: surface representation (the text itself); propositional representation or textbase (propositions formed from the text); and situational representation (a mental model describing the situation referred to in the text). Schemas can be used as building blocks for the construction of situational representations or models.

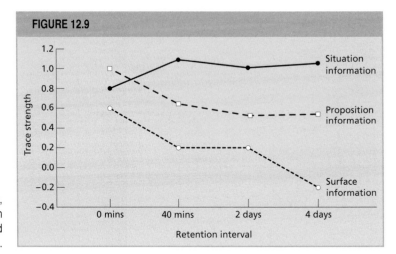

**FIGURE 12.9**

Forgetting functions for situation, proposition, and surface information over a four-day period. Adapted from Kintsch et al. (1990).

One of the most distinctive features of this model is the assumption that the processes involved in the construction of the elaborated propositional net are relatively inefficient, with many irrelevant propositions being included. This is basically a bottom-up approach, in that the elaborated propositional net is constructed without taking account of the context provided by the overall theme of the text. In contrast, as Kintsch, Welsch, Schmalhofer, and Zimny (1990, p. 136) pointed out, "most other models of comprehension attempt to specify strong, 'smart' rules which, guided by schemata, arrive at just the right interpretations, activate just the right knowledge, and generate just the right inferences." According to Kintsch et al. (1990), such strong rules would need to be very complex, and they might prove insufficiently flexible across different situations. In contrast, the weak rules incorporated into the construction–integration model are much more robust, and can be used in virtually all situations.

On the basis of a fairly detailed specification of the model, Kintsch (1988) was able to produce some convincing computer simulations of parts of the model. Further testing of the model was carried out by Kintsch et al. (1990). They tested the assumption that text processing produces three levels of representation ranging from the surface level based directly on the text itself, through the propositional level, to the situational or mental model level (providing a representation that is similar to the one that would result from directly experiencing the situation described in the text). Participants were presented with brief descriptions of very stereotyped situations (e.g., going to see a film), and then their recognition memory was tested immediately or at times ranging up to four days.

The main findings are shown in Figure 12.9. The forgetting functions for the surface, propositional, and situational representations were distinctively different. There was rapid and complete forgetting of the surface representation, whereas information from the situational representation showed no forgetting over four days. Propositional information differed from situational information in that there was forgetting over time, and it differed from surface information in that there was only partial forgetting. As Kintsch et al. (1990) had predicted, the most complete representation of the meaning of the text (i.e., the situational representation) was best remembered, and the least complete representation (i.e., the surface representation) was the worst remembered.

Zwaan (1994) tested the psychological reality of some of the levels of representation identified in the construction–integration model. He argued that the reader's goals influence the extent to which different representational levels are constructed. For example, someone reading an excerpt from a novel might be expected to focus on the text itself (e.g., the wording; stylistic devices), and so form

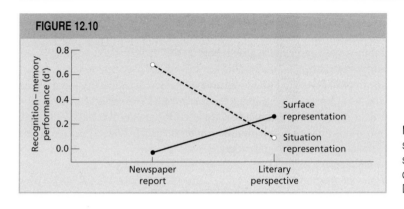

**FIGURE 12.10**

Memory for surface and situation representations for stories described as literary or as newspaper reports. Data from Zwaan (1994).

a strong surface representation. In contrast, someone reading a newspaper article may focus on updating his or her representation of a real-world situation, and so form a strong situation representation. Zwaan (1994) devised texts that were described as literary extracts or news stories. As predicted, memory for surface representations was better for stories described as literary, whereas memory for situation representations was better for stories described as newspaper reports (see Figure 12.10).

The reality of the distinction between textbase and situation representations was studied by McNamara, Kintsch, Songer, and Kintsch (1995). They presented participants who had high or low knowledge about the heart with a technical text about the heart's functioning. There were two versions of the text, one of which was more coherent and easier to read than the other. It would be expected that construction of the textbase and of the situation model would both be facilitated with the more coherent text. This was the case for low-knowledge readers. In contrast, high-knowledge readers showed slightly increased textbase recall with the more coherent text, but constructed a less effective situation model.

What do these findings mean? They suggest that knowledgeable readers benefit from a somewhat incoherent text that makes them fill in the gaps and prevents them from engaging in superficial processing. At a theoretical level, the notion that there are separate textbase and situation representations is supported by the finding that text coherence had opposite effects on these two representations for high-knowledge readers.

*Evaluation*

One of the greatest advantages of the construction–integration model over the Kintsch and van Dijk (1978) theory is the assumption that there is a situational representation or mental model as well as a propositional representation. An interesting study suggesting the superiority of the mental or situation model approach to the propositional approach was conducted by Glenberg, Meyer, and Linden (1987). They presented short passages such as the following:

> John was preparing for a marathon in August. After doing a few warm-up exercises, he (took off/put on) his sweatshirt and went jogging. He jogged halfway round the lake without too much difficulty. Further along the route, however, his muscles began to ache.

The participants were then probed with the word "sweatshirt", and had to decide as rapidly as possible whether it had occurred in the passage. They responded significantly faster with the version of the story in which John put on his sweatshirt than when he took it off. This finding is rather mystifying from the perspective of a propositional theory, because the probe word is represented in only one proposition in both versions of the passage. In contrast, the finding is readily explicable from the mental or situation model approach: if participants construct mental models depicting the events described in the passage, then the sweatshirt has much greater prominence when John puts it on than when he takes it off.

The construction–integration model has the advantage over its predecessors that the ways in which information in the text combines with related knowledge already possessed by the reader are spelled out in much more detail. In particular, the notion that propositions for the text representation are selected on the basis of a spreading activation process operating on propositions drawn from the text and from stored knowledge is an interesting one. This approach seems superior to the previous model's emphasis on integration based on linking together propositions sharing an argument.

Situational representations are not always constructed. Zwaan and van Oostendop (1993) asked their participants to read part of an edited mystery novel describing the details of a murder scene, including the locations of the body and various clues. Most participants did not construct a situational or spatial representation when they read normally. However, such representations were constructed at the cost of a marked increase in reading time when the initial instructions emphasised the importance of constructing a spatial representation. These findings suggest that limited processing capacity may often restrict the formation of situational representations or mental models.

According to Graesser et al. (1997), there are two levels of discourse representation in addition to the three levels identified by Kintsch (1988). There is the *text genre* level, which is concerned with the nature of the text. Text genres include narration, description, jokes, exposition, and persuasion. The kinds of information presented, how the information is presented, and the ways in which the information is to be interpreted differ greatly across genres. There is also the *communication level*, which refers to the ways in which the writer tries to communicate with his or her readers. However, some readers may not form a representation at the communication level. As Graesser et al. (1997, p. 169) pointed out, "The reader of a novel may not construct an invisible, virtual writer or storyteller that communicates with the reader, unless there are explicit features in the text that signal that communication level."

There are two other major problems with the construction–integration model. First, it is assumed within the model that numerous inferences are considered initially, with most of them being discarded before the reader becomes aware of them. This key theoretical assumption has not been tested systematically. Second, the model as a whole has not yet been put to a searching test. Evidence supporting parts of the model has been obtained, but this evidence is insufficiently detailed to be convincing.

## Event-indexing model

The construction–integration model is not specific about the processes involved in the construction of situation models. However, Zwaan, Langston, and Graesser (1995) put forward an event-indexing model to remedy this omission. According to this model, which was further developed by Zwaan and Radvansky (1998), readers monitor five aspects or indexes of the evolving situation model at the same time when they read stories:

1.  The protagonist: the central character or actor in the present event compared to the previous event.
2.  Temporality: the relationship between the times at which the present and previous events occurred.
3.  Causality: the causal relationship of the current event to the previous event.
4.  Spatiality: the relationship between the spatial setting of the current event and that of the previous event.
5.  Intentionality: the relationship between the character's goals and the present event.

Key predictions of the event-indexing model are that discontinuity in any of these aspects (e.g., a change in the spatial setting; a flashback in time) creates difficulties in situation-model construction, and that discontinuities increase reading times for events. Zwaan and Radvansky (1998) referred to an unpublished study of theirs in which the participants rated how well each sentence fitted in with the previous sentences. These ratings were determined by the overlap between the five situational dimensions in the target sentence versus the previous sentences: the greater the overlap, the higher were the ratings.

Additional support for the event-indexing model was reported by Zwaan et al. (1995). They found the reading times for events in a story increased as a function of the number out of the five situational dimensions on which there was discontinuity with the previous event. They also showed that each of the five dimensions had its own influence on reading time.

*Evaluation*

The greatest strength of the event-indexing model is that it identifies some of the most important processes involved in creating and updating situation models. The emphasis of the model on the construction of situation models is probably well placed. As Zwaan and Radvansky (1998, p. 177) argued, "Language can be regarded as a set of processing instructions on how to construct a mental representation of the described situation."

On the negative side, as Zwaan and Radvansky (1998, p. 180) admitted, is the fact that the event-indexing model, "treats the individual dimensions as independent entities." This approach is unlikely to be correct, because the various situational dimensions seem to interact in various ways. Consider the following sentence provided by Zwaan and Radvansky (1998): "Someone was making noise in the backyard; Mike had left hours ago." This sentence provides information about temporality. However, it has relevance to the causality issue, because it permits the causal inference that Mike was not the person making the noise.

## CHAPTER SUMMARY

- Sentence processing. Sentence processing involves parsing and the assignment of meaning. According to the garden-path model, only one grammatical structure is initially considered, and meaning does not influence the selection of this structure. According to content-guided processing theory, meaning *does* play a role in determining the assignment of syntactical structure. According to constraint-based theory, various processes operating in parallel use the constraints imposed by relevant semantic and syntactic information to favour one particular syntactic structure. A limitation of this theory is that many of the details of syntactic processing are not specified. Inner speech is used to preserve information about word order. It may also be used to provide prosodic structure.

- Capacity theory. According to Just and Carpenter's capacity theory, there are individual differences in the capacity of working memory. These individual differences have substantial effects on language comprehension. Working-memory capacity is assessed by the reading-span task. There is evidence based on fMRI to indicate that the various processes involved in the reading-span task use the same areas of the brain as are used in sentence comprehension. It has been argued that what is common to all aphasic patients is a reduction in the working memory resources available for language comprehension. Capacity theory tends to ignore the various specific processes involved in comprehension.

- Discourse processing. According to the minimalist hypothesis, only a few inferences are drawn automatically; additional strategic inferences depend on the reader's goals. This contrasts with the constructionist viewpoint, according to which numerous automatic inferences are drawn. A reasonable compromise is provided by the search-after-meaning theory. This assumes that readers try to construct coherent meaning for texts based on their goals, and they try to explain actions and events in those texts.

- Story processing. According to schema theory, schemas or organised packets of knowledge help to determine what we remember of stories. Recall of texts often includes schematic information that was not presented. Schemas influence comprehension and retrieval processes. There is some support for a specific form of schema theory known as the script-pointer-plus-tag hypothesis. According to Kintsch and van Dijk's model, texts are processed to produce a micro-structure and a macro-structure. According to Kintsch's construction–integration model, three levels of representation of a text are constructed: the surface representation; the propositional representation or textbase; and the situation representation. The surface representation is forgotten most rapidly and the situational representation most slowly. The processes involved in the formation of situation models were identified in the event-indexing model. According to this model, readers monitor five aspects of the evolving situation model: the protagonist; temporality; causality; spatiality; and intentionality. Discontinuity in any of these aspects creates difficulties in situation-model construction and increases reading times.

## FURTHER READING

- Altmann, G.T.M. (1997). *The ascent of Babel: An exploration of language, mind, and understanding*. Oxford: Oxford University Press. This book provides a fascinating account of the role played by language in our lives. It is written in an accessible way.
- Garrod, S., & Pickering, M.J. (1999). *Language processing*. Hove, UK: Psychology Press. Several chapters in this book provide good accounts of areas covered in this chapter. For example, contemporary theoretical approaches to sentence processing are discussed in detail in Chapters 5 and 7.
- Graesser, A.C., Millis, R.A., & Zwaan, R.A. (1997). Discourse comprehension. *Annual Review of Psychology*, *48*, 163–189. There is a detailed account of the main processes involved in discourse comprehension in this paper.
- McKoon, G., & Ratcliff, R. (1998). Memory-based language processing: Psycholinguistic research in the 1990s. *Annual Review of Psychology*, *49*, 25–42. This paper is especially strong on the similarities and differences between research studies on sentence processing and on discourse processing.
- Zwaan, R.A., & Radvansky, G.A. (1998). Situation models in language comprehension and memory. *Psychological Bulletin*, *123*, 162–185. Some interesting new theoretical ideas on discourse comprehension are presented in this article.

# 13

# Language Production

## INTRODUCTION

We know more about language comprehension than language production. Why is this so? It is fairly easy to exercise experimental control over material to be comprehended, whereas it is much harder to constrain an individual's production of language. A further problem in accounting for language production (albeit one that is shared with language comprehension) is that more than a theory of language is needed. Language production is basically a goal-directed activity. People speak and write to impart information, to be friendly, and so on. Thus, motivational and social factors need to be considered.

The two major topics considered within this chapter are speech production and writing. More is known about speech production than about writing. Nearly everyone spends more time talking than writing, and so it is of more practical use to understand the processes involved in talking. However, writing is an important skill in contemporary Western society.

This chapter and the two previous ones are concerned with the processes involved in language.

There are obviously links between language and thought, but there has been much controversy about their precise relationship. Some relevant issues are considered at the end of this chapter.

## SPEECH AS COMMUNICATION

For most people (unless there is something seriously wrong with them) speech nearly always occurs as conversation in a social context. Grice (1967) argued that the key to successful communication is the Co-operative Principle, according to which speakers and listeners must try to be co-operative.

In addition to the Co-operative Principle, Grice proposed four maxims that the speaker should heed:

- Maxim of quantity: the speaker should be as informative as necessary, but not more so.
- Maxim of quality: the speaker should be truthful.
- Maxim of relation: the speaker should say things that are relevant to the situation.
- Maxim of manner: the speaker should make his or her contribution easy to understand.

What needs to be said (maxim of quantity) depends on what the speaker wishes to describe (often called the referent). It is also necessary to know the objects from which the referent must be differentiated. It is sufficient to say, "The boy is good at football", if the other players are all men, but not if some of them are also boys. In the latter case, it is necessary to be more specific (e.g., "The boy with red hair is good at football").

## Common ground

According to Clark and Carlson (1981), the speaker must take account of what they called the "common ground". The common ground between two people consists of their mutual beliefs, expectations, and knowledge. Clark (1994) proposed a distinction between communal common ground and personal common ground. Communal common ground refers to all the knowledge and beliefs universally held in the communities to which the two people belong, whereas personal common ground refers to the mutual knowledge and beliefs that two people have inferred from their dealings with each other. If you overhear a conversation between two friends on a bus or train, it can be very hard to follow, because you lack the personal common ground that they share.

Horton and Keysar (1996) distinguished between two theoretical positions:

1. The initial design model: this is based on the principle of optimal design, in which "the speaker intends each addressee to base his inferences not on just *any* knowledge or beliefs he may have, but only on their *mutual* knowledge or beliefs—their common ground (Clark, 1992, p. 81). Thus, the initial plan for an utterance takes account of the common ground with the listener.
2. The monitoring and adjustment model: according to this model, speakers plan their utterances initially on the basis of information available to them *without* considering the listener's perspective. These plans are then monitored and corrected to take account of the common ground.

Horton and Keysar (1996) tested these models. Their participants were given the task of describing moving objects so the listener (a confederate of the experimenter) could identify them. These descriptions had to be produced either rapidly (speeded condition) or slowly (unspeeded condition). There was a shared-context condition in which the participants knew that the listener could see the same additional objects that they could see. There was also a non-shared-context condition, in which the participants knew the listener could *not* see the other objects. If participants made use of the common ground, they should have used contextual information in their descriptions in the shared-context condition, but not in the non-shared-context condition.

The key findings are shown in Figure 13.1. Participants in the unspeeded condition incorporated common ground with the listener in their descriptions. However, participants in the speeded condition were as likely to include contextual information in their descriptions when it was inappropriate (non-shared-context condition) as when it was appropriate (shared-context condition). These findings fit the predictions of the monitoring and adjustment model better than those of the initial design model. Presumably the common ground was not used properly in the speeded condition because there was insufficient time for the monitoring process to operate.

Would it not be better if we operated on the basis of the initial design model rather than the monitoring and adjustment model? One obvious advantage is that we would communicate more effectively with other people. However, the processing demands involved in always taking account of the listener's knowledge when planning utterances could be excessive. The information available to the speaker often happens to be shared with the listener, and so many utterances will be appropriate for the listener even though the speaker has not devoted processing resources to common ground knowledge.

A possible limitation with the study by Horton and Keysar (1996) is that the listener was a stranger to the participants. Speakers may take much more account of the common ground when they are speaking to friends rather than strangers.

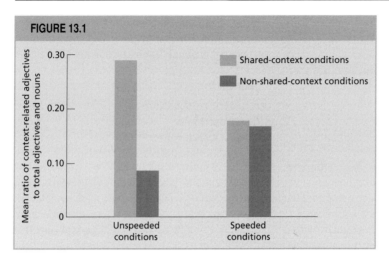

**FIGURE 13.1**

Mean ratio of context-related adjectives of adjectives plus nouns in speeded vs. unspeeded conditions and shared vs. non-shared-context conditions. Adapted from Horton and Keysar (1996).

## Conversational turns

Factors determining who talks when were considered by Brennan (1990). One common way in which the conversation moves from one speaker to another is by means of an *adjacency pair*, in which what the first speaker says provides a strong invitation to the listener to take up the conversation; a question followed by an answer is a very common example of an adjacency pair. If the first speaker completes what he or she intended to say without producing the first part of an adjacency pair, then the next turn goes to the listener who speaks first. If none of the listeners speaks, then the first speaker is free to continue with another turn (known technically as a *turn-constructional unit*).

## SPEECH PRODUCTION PROCESSES

We tend to take the skills involved in speech production for granted. Even young children are usually adept at talking fairly sensibly and grammatically. However, speech is actually a complex activity involving various skills. These include the ability to think of what one wants to say, to select the appropriate words to express it, to organise those words grammatically, and to turn the sentences one wants to say into actual speech.

Speakers use *prosodic cues* in their speech. These cues include rhythm, stress, and intonation, and make it easier for listeners to understand what they are trying to say (see Chapter 12).

Allbritton, McKoon, and Ratcliff (1996) studied the extent to which speakers provide prosodic cues. The participants read short passages containing ambiguous sentences that were disambiguated by the passage context. For example, the sentence "So, for lunch today he is having either pork or chicken and fries" can mean "Either he is having pork alone, or else he is having chicken and fries", or "He is having either pork or chicken, and he is definitely having fries". Very few of the speakers (even trained actors and broadcasters) consistently produced prosodic cues. However, we should not conclude that prosodic cues are rarely used in the real world. Lea (1973) analysed hundreds of naturally occurring spoken sentences, and found that syntactic boundaries (e.g., ends of sentences) were generally signalled by prosodic cues.

A consideration of hesitations and pauses in speech production suggests that speech is planned in phrases or clauses. Pauses in spontaneous speech occur more often at grammatical junctures (e.g., the ends of phrases) than anywhere else. Boomer (1965) found that such pauses last longer on average than those at other locations (1.03 seconds vs. 0.75 seconds, respectively). Pauses coinciding with phrase boundaries tend to be filled with sounds such as "um", "er", or "ah", whereas those occurring within a phrase tend to be silent (Maclay & Osgood, 1959). A major reason for these longish pauses at the end of phrases or clauses is probably to permit forward planning of the next utterance.

## Speech errors

It is hard to identify the processes involved in speech production, partly because they normally occur so rapidly (we produce two or three words per second on average). Many researchers have tried to discover how people normally produce fluent speech by focusing on the errors in spoken language. As Dell (1986, p. 284) pointed out, "The inner workings of a highly complex system are often revealed by the way in which the system breaks down."

There are various collections of speech errors (e.g., Garrett, 1975; Stemberger, 1982). The errors in these collections consist of those personally heard by the researchers concerned. This procedure poses some problems. For example, some kinds of error are more readily detectable than others. Thus, we should be sceptical about percentage figures for the different kinds of speech errors. It is less clear that there are any major problems with the main categories of speech errors that have been identified. The existence of some types of speech errors has been confirmed by experimentation in which errors have been created under laboratory conditions (see Dell, 1986).

Several forms of speech error involve problems with selecting the correct word (lexical selection). A simple kind of lexical selection error is *semantic substitution* (the correct word is replaced by a word of similar meaning, e.g., "Where is my tennis bat?" instead of "Where is my tennis racquet?"). In 99% of cases, the substituted word is of the same form class as the correct word (e.g., nouns substitute for nouns). Verbs are much less likely than nouns, adjectives, or adverbs to undergo semantic substitution (Hotopf, 1980).

*Blending* is another kind of lexical selection error (e.g., "The sky is shining" instead of "The sky is blue" or "The sun is shining"). A further kind of lexical selection error is the *word-exchange error*, in which two words in a sentence switch places (e.g., "I must let the house out of the cat" instead of "I must let the cat out of the house").

The two words involved in a word-exchange error are typically further apart in the sentence than the two words involved in sound-exchange errors (two sounds switching places) (Garrett, 1980).

*Morpheme-exchange errors* involve inflections or suffixes remaining in place but attached to the wrong words (e.g., "He has already trunked two packs"). An implication from morpheme-exchange errors is that the positioning of inflections is dealt with by a rather separate process from the one responsible for positioning word stems (e.g., "trunk"; "pack"). There is some evidence that the word stems are worked out *before* the inflections are added. Smyth et al. (1987) pointed out that inflections are generally altered to fit in with the new word stems to which they are linked. For example, the "s" sound in the phrase "the forks of a prong" is pronounced in a way that is appropriate within the word "forks", but this is different from the "s" sound in the original word "prongs".

One of the best known speech errors is the spoonerism, in which the initial letter or letters of two or more words are switched. The Rev. William Archibald Spooner, after whom the spoonerism is named, is credited with several memorable examples, including "You have hissed all my mystery lectures" and "The Lord is a shoving leopard to his flock". Alas, most of the Rev. Spooner's gems were the result of much painstaking effort.

The study of genuine spoonerisms reveals that consonants always exchange with consonants and vowels with vowels, and that the exchanging phonemes are generally similar in sound (see Fromkin, 1993). Garrett (1976) reported that 93% of the spoonerisms in his collection involved a switching of letters between two words within the same clause, suggesting that the clause is an important unit in speech production.

## THEORIES OF SPEECH PRODUCTION

Several theorists (e.g., Dell, 1986; Dell & O'Seaghdha, 1991; Garrett, 1976) have used evidence from speech errors to construct theories of speech production. These theories have much in common. First, it is assumed that there is a substantial amount of pre-production planning of speech. Second, most theorists agree that there is a series of processing stages in speech production, and there is even agreement that there are four processing stages. Third, it is assumed that the processes proceed from the general (the intended meaning) to the specific (the units of sound to be uttered). The processes in speech production resemble those involved in comprehension, except that the processes are in the opposite order. For example, the goal of comprehension is to understand the meaning of a message, whereas with speech production the meaning of the message is the starting point.

In view of the similarities among theories of speech production, we will consider only two theoretical approaches. First, the spreading-activation theory of Dell (1986) and Dell, Burger, and Svec (1997) will be discussed. It emphasises a psychological process (spreading activation) of general significance within language processing (see Chapter 12). Second, the theoretical approach of Levelt, Roelofs, and Meyer (1999a) is discussed.

## Spreading-activation theory

Dell (1986) and Dell and O'Seaghdha (1991) put forward a spreading-activation theory. It was based on connectionist principles, and consists of four levels. The main assumptions of the theory (including descriptions of the four levels) are as follows:

- Semantic level: the meaning of what is to be said; this level is not considered in detail within the theory.
- Syntactic level: the grammatical structure of the words in the planned utterance.
- Morphological level: the morphemes (basic units of meaning or word forms) in the planned sentence.
- Phonological level: the phonemes or basic units of sound within the sentence.
- A representation is formed at each level.
- Processing during speech planning occurs the same at all four levels, and is both parallel and interactive; however, it is typically more advanced at higher levels (e.g., semantic) than at lower levels (e.g., phonological).

According to spreading-activation theory, there are *categorical rules* at each level. These rules are constraints on the categories of items and on the combinations of categories that are acceptable. The rules at each level define categories appropriate to that level. For example, the categorical rules at the syntactic level specify the syntactic categories of items within the sentence.

In addition to the categorical rules, there is a *lexicon* (dictionary) in the form of a constructionist network. It contains nodes for concepts, words, morphemes, and phonemes. When a node is activated, it sends activation to all the nodes connected to it (see Chapter 1). Finally, *insertion rules* select the items for inclusion in the representation at each level according to the following criterion: the most highly activated node belonging to the appropriate category is chosen. For example, if the categorical rules at the syntactic level dictate that a verb is required at a particular point within the syntactic representation, then that verb whose node is most activated will be selected. After an item has been selected, its activation level immediately reduces to zero; this prevents it from being selected repeatedly.

According to spreading-activation theory, speech errors occur because an incorrect item will sometimes have a higher level of activation than the correct item. The existence of spreading activation means that numerous nodes are all activated at the same time, and this increases the likelihood of errors being made in speech.

What kinds of errors are predicted by the theory? First, errors should belong to the appropriate category (e.g., an incorrect noun replacing the correct noun), because of the operation of the categorical rules. As expected, most errors do belong to the appropriate category (Dell, 1986).

Second, many errors should be anticipation errors, in which a word is spoken earlier in the sentence than is appropriate (e.g., "The sky is in the sky"). This happens because all of the words in the sentence tend to become activated during the planning for speech.

Third, anticipation errors should often turn into exchange errors, in which two words within a sentence are swapped (e.g., "I must write a wife to my letter"). Remember that the activation level of a selected item immediately reduces to zero. Therefore, if "wife" has been selected too early, it is unlikely to compete successfully to be selected in its correct place in the sentence. This allows a previously unselected and highly activated item such as "letter" to appear in the wrong place. Many speech errors are of the exchange variety.

Fourth, anticipation and exchange errors generally involve words moving only a relatively short distance within the sentence. Those words relevant to the part of the sentence that is under current consideration will tend to be more activated than those words relevant to more distant parts of the sentence.

Fifth, it is predicted that speech errors should tend to consist of actual words or morphemes (this is known as the lexical bias effect). This effect was demonstrated by Baars, Motley, and MacKay (1975). Word pairs were presented briefly, and participants had to say both words as rapidly as possible. The error rate was twice as great when the word pair could be re-formed to create two new words (e.g., "lewd rip" can be turned into "rude lip") than when it could not (e.g. "Luke risk" turns into "ruke lisk").

Sixth, the notion that the various levels of processing interact flexibly with each other means that speech errors can be multiply determined. Dell (1986) quoted the example of someone saying "Let's stop" instead of "Let's start". The error is certainly semantic, but it could also be regarded as phonological, because the substitute word shares a common sound with the appropriate word. Detailed investigation of such word-substitution errors reveals that the spoken word and the intended word are more similar in sound than would be expected by chance alone (Dell & O'Seaghdha, 1991; Harley, 1984).

According to spreading-activation theory, most errors are caused by spreading activation. It might appear preferable if activation did not spread so widely through the lexicon, because then there would be fewer speech errors. However, Dell (1986) argued that widespread activation facilitates the production of novel sentences, and so prevents our utterances from becoming too stereotyped.

*Evaluation*

Spreading-activation theory makes various precise and testable predictions about the kinds of errors that should occur most often in speech production. Another strength of the theory is that its emphasis on spreading activation provides links between speech production and other cognitive activities (e.g., word recognition: McClelland & Rumelhart, 1981).

On the negative side, the focus of spreading-activation theory is mainly on individual words or concepts, with broader issues relating to the construction of a message with its intended meaning being de-emphasised. In addition, the theory predicts the nature and number of errors produced in speech, but cannot account for the time taken to produce spoken words. Thus, it is somewhat limited in focus.

## Anticipation and perseveration errors

Dell et al. (1997) developed and extended the spreading-activation theory. The starting point was the notion that most speech errors belong to the following two categories:

1. **Anticipatory:** sounds or words are spoken ahead of their time (e.g., "cuff of coffee" instead of "cup of coffee").
2. **Perseverated:** sounds or words are spoken later than they should have been (e.g., "beef needle" instead of "beef noodle").

Note that Dell et al.'s theory was concerned *only* with these speech errors.

The key assumption was that expert speakers are better able than non-expert speakers to plan ahead when speaking, and so a higher proportion of their speech errors will be anticipatory. Dell et al. (1997, p. 140) expressed this point as follows: "Practice enhances the activation of the present and future at the expense of the past. So, as performance gets better, perseverations become relatively less common." Thus, the activation levels of sounds and words that have already been spoken are little affected by practice. However, the increasing activation levels of present and future sounds

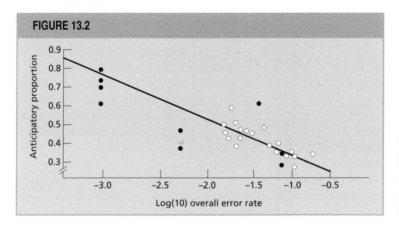

FIGURE 13.2

The relationship between overall error rate and the anticipatory proportion. The filled circles come from studies reported by Dell et al. (1997) and unfilled circles come from other studies. Adapted from Dell et al. (1997).

and words increasingly prevent the past from intruding into present speech.

Dell et al. (1997) assessed the effects of practice on the anticipatory proportion. This is the proportion of total errors (anticipation + perseveration errors) that is anticipatory. In one study, the participants were given extensive practice at saying several tongue twisters (e.g., five frantic fat frogs; thirty-three throbbing thumbs). As expected, the number of errors decreased as a function of practice. However, the anticipatory proportion increased from .37 early in practice to .59 at the end of practice, which was in line with prediction.

Dell et al. (1997) argued that speech errors of all kinds are most likely when the individual speaker has not formed a coherent speech plan. In such circumstances, there will be relatively few anticipatory errors, and so the anticipatory proportion will be low. Thus, the overall error rate (anticipatory + perseverative) should correlate negatively with the anticipatory proportion. Dell et al. (1997) tested this prediction by working out the overall error rate and the anticipatory proportion for several sets of published data. The anticipatory proportion decreased from about .75 with low overall error rates to about .4 with high overall error rates (see Figure 13.2).

This theory has implications for clinical patients having problems with speech production. Patients whose speech is error prone should tend to make relatively more perseverative errors than normals. There is some supporting evidence.

Schwartz et al. (1994) tested a patient, FL, who was classified as suffering from *jargon aphasia* (discussed later). This patient had an anticipatory proportion of .32 (compared to the normal adult figure of about .75), indicating that FL was especially prone to perseverative errors. In addition, Helm-Estabrooks, Bayles, and Bryant (1994) studied patients with *aphasia* (an impairment of speech understanding or production). Aphasic patients whose speech was moderately impaired made many more perseverative errors than did those with mild impairment.

## Levelt's theoretical approach and WEAVER++

The main focus in this section is on the computational model WEAVER++, which was proposed by Levelt, Roelofs, and Meyer (1999a). However, many of the ideas contained within this computational model derive from Levelt (1989). The model is called WEAVER to stand for Word-form Encoding by Activation and VERification. It is based on the following major assumptions:

- There is a feed-forward activation-spreading network, meaning that activation proceeds forwards through the network but not backwards.
- There are three main levels within the network: at the highest level are nodes representing lexical concepts; at the second level are nodes representing lemmas or abstract words from the mental lexicon; at the lowest level are nodes representing word forms in terms of

morphemes (basic units of meaning) and their phonemic segments.

- The network does not contain any inhibitory links.
- Speech production involves a series of processing stages which follow each other in a strictly serial way
- Speech errors are avoided by means of a checking mechanism: "Each node has a procedure attached to it that checks whether the node, when active, links up to the appropriate active node one level up" (Levelt et al., 1999a, p. 7).

A more detailed account of the theory is given in Figure 13.3. There are basically six stages of processing:

1. Conceptual preparation: potential lexical concepts are activated on the basis of meaning.

2. Lexical selection: an abstract word or lemma is selected, together with its syntactic features; a lemma is generally selected because it is more activated than any other lemma.
3. Morphological encoding: the basic word form of the selected lemma is activated.
4. Phonological encoding: during this stage, the syllables of the word are computed: this is syllabilification.
5. Phonetic encoding: speech sounds are prepared, making used a syllabary, "a repository of gestural scores for the frequently used syllables of the language" (Levelt et al., 1999a, p. 5).
6. Articulation: the actual production of the word by the speech musculature.

In addition, there is a self-monitoring process which monitors the speaker's internal speech.

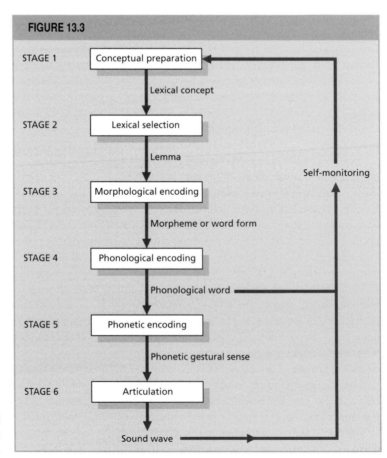

The WEAVER++ computational model. Adapted from Levelt et al. (1999a).

It is easy to get lost in the complexities of this theory. However, it is mainly designed to show how word production proceeds from meaning (lexical concepts and lemmas) to sound (phonological words, phonetic gestural scores, and sound waves). Indeed, Levelt et al. (1999a, p. 2) referred to "the major rift" between a word's meaning and its sound, and argued that crossing this rift is of major importance in speech production. In general terms, the stages of conceptual preparation and lexical selection involve deciding which word is to be produced, and the later stages involve working out the details of its word form, phonological representation, and pronunciation.

## Experimental evidence

*Lexicalisation* is "the process in speech production whereby we turn the thoughts underlying words into sounds: we translate a semantic representation (the meaning) of a content word into its phonological representation or form (its sound)" (Harley, 1995, p. 253). According to Levelt et al. (1999a), lexicalisation is an important process that occurs when the lemma is translated into its word form in terms of morphemes, phonological encoding, and so on.

The "tip-of-the-tongue" state provides evidence generally supportive of the views of Levelt et al. (1999a). We have all had the experience of having a concept or idea in mind, but searching in vain for the right word to describe it. This frustrating situation defines the tip-of-the-tongue state. It was first studied systematically by Brown and McNeill (1966). They stated that a participant in this state, "would appear to be in a mild torment, something like the brink of a sneeze" (Brown & McNeill, 1966, p. 325). Brown and McNeill presented their participants with dictionary definitions of rare words, and asked them to identify the words defined. Thus, for example, "a navigational instrument used in measuring angular distances, especially the altitude of the sun, moon and stars at sea" defines the word "sextant". The tip-of-the-tongue state occurs when the lemma or abstract word has has been activated, but the actual word cannot be accessed. However, this conclusion has been disputed (Caramazza & Miozzo, 1998).

It has been suggested that the tip-of-the-tongue state is more likely to occur for words sounding like other words, on the basis that these other words block or inhibit retrieval of the word being sought. In fact, Harley and Brown (1998) found exactly the opposite. Words sounding unlike nearly all other words (e.g., apron; nectar; vineyard) were much more prone to the tip-of-the-tongue state than were words sounding like several other words (e.g., litter; riddle; pawn). The unusual phonological forms of the former words may make them especially difficult to retrieve.

Levelt et al. (1999a) argued that abstract word or lemma selection is completed before phonological information about the word is accessed. This is an important part of their serial processing model. In contrast, some theorists (e.g., Dell et al., 1997) have argued that phonological processing can start before word selection is completed; in other words, the two stages are *not* totally independent of each other. Theoretical approaches based on this assumption are often termed cascade models.

How can we test these models? According to the cascade model, phonological processing can occur before lemma selection is completed, whereas this is impossible on the alternative model. Suppose that participants are presented with pictures having a dominant name (e.g., rocket) and a non-dominant name (e.g., missile). They are given the task of naming the picture as rapidly as possible. The stage of lemma selection typically produces the dominant name (e.g., rocket). According to the serial processing model, there should be very little phonological processing of the non-dominant name (e.g., missile). According to the cascade model, however, this is not necessarily the case.

Peterson and Savoy (1998) tested these predictions. On some trials, a word appeared in the middle of the picture (e.g., of a rocket or missile), and the participants were to name that word out loud rather than name the picture. As both models would predict, word naming was speeded up or primed when the word was phonologically related to the dominant picture name (e.g., racket). Of more theoretical importance, word naming was also speeded up when the word was phonologically related to the non-dominant picture name (e.g., muscle). As Peterson and Savoy (1998, p. 552) concluded, "We obtained clear evidence for phonological activation of both dominant and secondary picture names during early moments of picture lexicalisation. Thus, in contrast to the serial model's central claim, it appears that multiple lexical candidates do undergo phonological encoding . . . we reject the serial processing view and argue, instead, that the cascade model provides the best account."

How did Levelt et al. (1999a) respond to these findings? They pointed out that multiple phonological encodings have *only* been found for synonyms, and suggested that the findings of Peterson and Savoy (1998) represented only a minor embarrassment for their model.

Studies on brain-damaged patients support some of the theoretical assumptions of Levelt et al. (1999a). According to their theory, the lemma contains syntactic information. Brain-damaged patients who can access the relevant lemma but who cannot carry out the subsequent stages of morphological and phonological encoding should possess syntactic information about words they cannot produce. Badecker, Miozzo, and Zanuttini (1995) studied an Italian patient with *anomia* (an inability to name objects). This patient found it virtually impossible to name pictures, but he was almost perfect at deciding whether the correct word was masculine or feminine (a syntactic feature).

According to Levelt et al. (1999a), morphological encoding precedes phonological encoding. As a result, some brain-damaged patients might possess morphological information about a word (e.g., whether it is a compound word) without being able to gain access to its phonological form. Semenza, Luzzati, and Mondini (1999) discussed studies on aphasic patients who exhibited precisely this pattern of impairment.

Levelt et al. (1998) reported an ambitious magneto-encephalography (MEG) study designed to identify those areas of the brain most active during the successive processing stages involved in naming pictures. The occipital lobes were most active during visual-to-concept mapping, the occipital and parietal areas were most active during lemma selection, there was left-hemisphere activity in Wernicke's area during phonological encoding, and areas in the sensory-motor cortex were especially active during phonetic encoding. These findings provide general support for the serial processing model of Levelt et al. (1999a).

## Evaluation

WEAVER++ has some significant advantages over the theoretical approach of Dell (1986) and Dell et al. (1997). First, it makes detailed predictions about the speed with which words are produced in different situations, whereas Dell has focused on predicting error rates. Second, WEAVER++ with its emphasis on serial processing can be regarded as simpler than Dell's approach based on highly interactive processing. Third, Levelt et al. (1999a) relied much less than Dell (e.g., 1986) on data about speech errors. As Levelt et al. (1991, p. 615) pointed out, "an exclusively error-based approach to . . . speech production is as ill-conceived as an exclusively illusion-based approach in vision research."

There are various limitations with WEAVER++. First, as Levelt, Roelofs, and Meyer (1999b, p. 63) admitted, "WEAVER++ has been designed to account primarily for latency data, not for speech errors . . . in further development of WEAVER++, its error mechanism deserves much more attention." For example, Levelt et al. (1999a) compared the numbers of exchange errors produced by human participants against those produced by WEAVER++. The model produced far fewer than humans.

Second, most of the research carried out by Levelt et al. has involved the production of single words. The problem here was highlighted by Roberts, Kalish, Hird, and Kirsner (1999, p. 54):

Implementation of naming and lexical decision experiments involving isolated words can only yield evidence about the way in which isolated words are produced in response to impoverished experimental conditions. If the way in which a given word is accessed and uttered is sensitive to . . . contextual variables, single-word test procedures will not reveal this.

Third, higher-order cognitive processes probably have more influence on speech production than is assumed in WEAVER++. As Roberts et al. (1999, p. 54) argued, "The processes controlling higher-order processes cannot simply provide conceptual information; they must intrude during the process of lexical formation to define the correct prosodic form." For example, Hird and Kirsner (1993) studied patients with damage to the right cerebral hemisphere who had essentially intact articulation abilities. However, these patients failed to use prosodic cues to indicate the importance of key words in their utterances, suggesting an impaired ability to use higher-order processes to influence speech production.

## COGNITIVE NEUROPSYCHOLOGY: SPEECH PRODUCTION

The cognitive neuropsychological approach to speech production is of importance. However, the syndromes or labels attached to patients having difficulties with speech production often have little meaning. This is perhaps especially the case with Broca's or non-fluent aphasia and Wernicke's or fluent aphasia (both of which are discussed later), which do not form coherent syndromes. In spite of these problems, it is useful for purposes of communication to refer to some of the major syndromes that have been identified.

### Anomia

Some patients suffer from *anomia*, which is an impaired ability to name objects. According to Levelt et al.'s (1999a) theory, there are two main reasons why such patients might have difficulties in naming. First, there could be a problem in lemma selection, in which case errors in naming would tend to be similar in meaning to the correct word. Second, there could be a problem in word-form selection, in which case patients would be unable to find the appropriate phonological form of the word. As we will see, the evidence supports these predictions.

A case of anomia involving a semantic impairment (deficient lemma selection) was reported by Howard and Orchard-Lisle (1984). The patient, JCU, had good object recognition and reasonable comprehension. However, she was very poor at naming the objects shown in pictures unless she was given the first phoneme or sound as a cue. If the cue was the first phoneme of a word closely related to the object shown in the picture, then JCU would often be misled into producing the wrong answer. This wrong answer she accepted as correct 76% of the time. In contrast, if she produced a name quite different in meaning to the object depicted, she rejected it 86% of the time. JCU presumably had access to some semantic information, but this was often insufficient to specify precisely what it was she was looking at.

Problems in lemma selection are especially clear in patients who have problems in naming objects belonging to some categories (e.g., living objects) but not others (e.g., non-living objects). Some of the evidence on such category-specific naming disorders was discussed in Chapter 4. It is hard to interpret the evidence, as is shown by the fact that Forde et al. (1997) identified eight different potential explanations!

Kay and Ellis (1987) studied a patient, EST, who had problems with lemma selection. His performance on a range of tasks was so good that it seemed he had no significant impairment to his semantic system, and thus no real problem with lexeme selection. However, he had a very definite anomia, as can be seen from this attempt to describe a picture (Kay & Ellis, 1987):

> Er . . . two children, one girl one male . . . the . . . the girl, they're in a . . . and their, their mother was behind them in in, they're in the kitchen . . . the boy is trying to get . . . a . . . er, a part of a cooking . . . jar . . . He's standing on . . . the lad, the boy is standing on a . . . standing on a . . . standing on a . . . I'm calling it a seat.

Close inspection of EST's speech indicates that it is reasonably grammatical, and that his greatest problem lies in finding words other than those in very common usage. What are we to make of

EST's anomia? Kay and Ellis (1987) argued that his condition resembles in greatly magnified form that of the rest of us when in the "tip-of-the-tongue" state. The difference is that it is mostly relatively rare words that cause us problems. In contrast, with EST, the problem is present with all but the most common words. However, word frequency correlates highly with age of acquisition, with more common words being acquired earlier in life. Hirsh and Funnell (1997) found that age of acquisition seemed to be the main determinant of anomia, with word frequency also playing a role.

## Agrammatism

It has been assumed within most theories of speech production that there are rather separate stages of working out the syntax or grammatical structure of utterances and producing the content words to fit that grammatical structure (e.g., Dell, 1986). Thus, there should be some brain-damaged patients who can find the appropriate words, but cannot order them grammatically. Such patients are said to suffer from *agrammatism* or non-fluent aphasia. Patients with agrammatism also tend to produce short sentences lacking function words and word endings.

Saffran, Schwartz, and Marin (1980 a,b) studied patients suffering from grammatical impairments. For example, one patient was asked to describe a picture of a woman kissing a man, and produced the following: "The kiss . . . the lady kissed . . . the lady is . . . the lady and the man and the lady . . . kissing." In addition, Saffran et al. found that agrammatic aphasics had great difficulty in putting the two nouns in the correct order when asked to describe pictures containing two living creatures in interaction.

The greatest problem in studying agrammatism is the existence of large individual differences in symptoms. For example, Miceli, Silveri, Romani, and Caramazza (1989) studied the speech productions of 20 patients who could be classified as agrammatic. Some patients omitted many more prepositions than definite articles from their speech, whereas other patients showed the opposite pattern.

Do the syntactic deficiencies of agrammatic aphasics extend to language comprehension? They do in some cases, but not in others. This was established clearly by Berndt, Mitchum, and Haendiges (1996) in a meta-analysis of studies of comprehension of active and passive sentences by agrammatic aphasics. The sentences were constructed so that accurate comprehension required sensitivity to grammatical structure (e.g., "The dog was chased by the cat"). In 34% of the data sets, comprehension performance on both active and passive sentences was at, or close to, chance level. In 30% of the data sets, comprehension was better than chance on both kinds of sentences. In the remaining 36% of data sets, there was good performance on active sentences but chance performance on passive sentences. These findings lead to two conclusions: (1) agrammatic aphasics do not necessarily have major problems with language comprehension; (2) "selection of patients for study on the basis of features of aphasic sentence production does not assure a homogeneous [similar] grouping of patients" (Berndt et al., 1996, p. 298).

## Jargon aphasia

Agrammatic aphasics possess reasonable ability to find the words they want to say, but cannot produce grammatically correct sentences. From most theoretical perspectives, it would be expected that there might be patients who showed the opposite pattern, namely, that they spoke fairly grammatically but had great difficulty in finding the right words. In general terms, this is the case with patients suffering from *jargon aphasia* or fluent aphasia. This is a condition in which the word-finding problems are so great that patients often produce neologisms, which are made-up words.

Ellis, Miller, and Sin (1983) studied a jargon aphasic, RD. He provided the following description of a picture of a scout camp (the words he seemed to be searching for are given in brackets):

A b-boy is swi'ing (SWINGING) on the bank with his hand (FEET) in the stringt (STREAM). A table with orstrum (SAUCE-PAN?) and . . . I don't know . . . and a three-legged stroe (STOOL) and a strane (PAIL)–table, table . . . near the water.

RD, in common with most jargon aphasics, produced more neologisms or invented words when the word he wanted was not a common one.

Most jargon aphasics are largely unaware of the fact that they are producing neologisms and so do not try to correct them. In the case of RD, this may well have been linked to the fact that he could not understand spoken material even though he could understanding written material. However, there are considerable individual differences among jargon aphasics. Maher, Rothi, and Heilman (1994) studied AS, a jargon aphasic who had reasonable auditory word comprehension. AS was better at detecting his own speech errors when listening to someone else speaking than when listening to his own voice. This suggested to Maher et al. (1994) that AS was in a state of denial about his own speech errors.

## Evaluation

Cognitive neuropsychological evidence has provided support for major theories of speech production. Findings from anomic patients have indicate the value of two-stage theories of lexicalisation. Agrammatic aphasics and jargon aphasics provide evidence for separate stages of syntactic planning and content-word retrieval in speech production. As Harley (1995) pointed out, what we have here is a *double dissocation*, which is a particularly powerful kind of evidence that two different sets of processes are involved. This double dissociation is consistent with theories such as those of Dell and of Levelt et al.

## COGNITIVE NEUROSCIENCE: SPEECH PRODUCTION

Are different language functions localised in specific areas of the brain? Several attempts to answer that question have been made over the past 140 years or so. Most of these attempts have been rather inconclusive, but the development of various brain-scanning techniques has led to advances in our understanding of the localisation of language functions. In this section, we will consider only a small fraction of the relevant evidence.

## Non-fluent aphasia

Paul Broca studied a patient, Leborgne, who suffered from great problems with speech production but seemed to understand what was said to him. Postmortem examination of this patient and of other patients with similar speech problems suggested to Broca that damage to certain parts of the left hemisphere of the brain was responsible for the deficient speech. The so-called Broca's area consists mainly of "posterior aspects of the third frontal convolution and adjacent inferior aspects of the precentral gyrus" (Caplan, 1994, p. 1035). Patients with Broca's aphasia are now known as non-fluent aphasics or agrammatic aphasics (see earlier).

The evidence indicates that matters are more complex than was assumed by Broca. For example, Willmes and Poeck (1993) found that only 59% of patients with non-fluent aphasia had lesions or damage in Broca's area, and only 35% of patients with lesions involving Broca's area had non-fluent aphasia. Dronkers (1996) reported that only 10 out of 22 patients with lesions in Broca's area were suffering from non-fluent aphasia. In addition, he found that all of the patients with non-fluent aphasia had damage to the insular cortex, which does not form part of Broca's area.

Various PET studies on normal individuals indicate that Broca's area is involved in speech production. For example, Wise et al. (1991) gave their participants the task of silent generation of verbs as uses for a noun. This task produced activation of Broca's area in the left hemisphere. Chertkow et al. (1993) used the task of silent picture naming, and observed activation of Broca's area. However, as Howard (1997, p. 294) pointed out, "Activations of Broca's area seems less frequently found in tasks involving overt speech production, possibly because activation in this region is masked by the bilateral activation of the adjacent articulatory motor cortex."

## Fluent aphasia

Carl Wernicke studied patients who had great problems in understanding spoken language, but who could speak fluently although not very meaningfully. Postmortem examination led Wernicke to identify damage to part of the left hemisphere of the brain as responsible for the comprehension problems of these patients. Wernicke's area consists of the "posterior half of the first temporal gyrus and possibly adjacent cortex" (Caplan, 1994, p. 1035). The disorder that used to be known as Wernicke's aphasia is now known as fluent aphasia or jargon aphasia (see earlier).

De Bleser (1988) studied 6 very clear cases of fluent aphasia, 7 very clear cases of non-fluent aphasia, and 33 additional aphasic patients. The sites of brain damage were assessed by means of computerised tomography (CT) scans, which allowed the patients to be put into three groups: (1) damage to frontal areas including Broca's area; (2) damage to temporo-parietal areas including Wernicke's area; and (3) large lesions including both Broca's and Wernicke's areas. Four of the six patients with fluent aphasia had damage only to Wernicke's area, but the other two had lesions in Broca's area as well as in Wernicke's area. Of the seven non-fluent aphasic patients, four had damage to Broca's area, but the others had damage to Wernicke's area.

Willmes and Poeck (1993) also used CT scans. They found that 90% of patients with fluent aphasia had lesions in Wernicke's area. However, only 48% of patients with damage in Wernicke's area had fluent aphasia.

PET studies have provided clearer evidence of the involvement of Wernicke's area in speech comprehension. For example, Howard et al. (1992) compared two conditions in which the participants either repeated real words or listened to reversed words and said the same word to each stimulus. As predicted, there was greater activation of Wernicke's area in the former condition.

## Evaluation

Why is there more evidence for localisation of language functions in brain-scanning (e.g., PET) studies on normals than in studies of brain-damaged patients? We can readily observe individual differences in localisation with brain-damaged patients, but similar individual differences are less apparent when information about brain activation is averaged across many people. As Howard (1997, p. 298) pointed out:

> While studies of motor and sensory processes produce changes in rCBF [regional cerebral blood flow] across a group of subjects of up to 30% in specific locations, language studies typically find significant changes of only 5–10%. This is exactly the pattern which one would predict if sensory and motor processes show very consistent localisation across subjects, while there is a great deal of variability of language functions.

What conclusions about speech production can we draw from the findings of cognitive neuroscience? Howard (1997, p. 288) suggested the following answer to that question:

> Language functions, while localised in individual subjects, are not consistently localised in different individuals . . . higher cortical functions such as language may have a certain amount of freedom in the areas of cortex devoted to them.

## WRITING: BASIC PROCESSES

Writing involves the retrieval and organisation of information stored in long-term memory. In addition, it involves complex thought processes. As Kellogg (1994, p. 13) expressed it, "I regard thinking and writing as twins of mental life. The study of the more expressive twin, writing, can offer insights into the psychology of thinking, the more reserved member of the pair." Thus, although writing is an important topic in its own right (no pun intended!), it is not separate from other cognitive activities.

### Theoretical considerations

Hayes and Flower (1986) identified planning, sentence generation, and revising as the key processes in writing:

- The *planning process* involves producing ideas and organising them into a writing plan to satisfy the goals the writer is seeking to achieve.
- The *sentence-generation process* involves turning the writing plan into the actual writing of sentences.
- The *revision process* involves evaluating what has been written; this process can operate at a relatively specific level (e.g., individual words) or at a more general level (e.g., the structural coherence of the writing).
- The natural sequence is planning, sentence generation, and revision, but writers often deviate from this sequence.

Hayes and Flower (1980) used *protocol analysis* to identify the processes involved in writing. This involves tape recordings being made of writers verbalising their thoughts during writing. They studied a writer who was particularly aware of the processes he used while writing. He started by generating information, then proceeded to organisation, and then to sentence generation. There was a definite progression over time from unorganised fragments to more structured items, and then to complete sentences. As expected, the flow of processing was often interrupted by the sentence-generation and revision processes.

Another method is *directed retrospection*. Writers are stopped at various times during the writing process and asked to categorise what they were just doing (e.g., planning; sentence generation; revision). Kellogg (1994) discussed studies involving directed retrospection. On average, writers devoted about 30% of their time to planning, 50% to sentence generation, and 20% to revision.

## Planning

Writing plans depend heavily on the writer's knowledge. Alexander, Schallert, and Hare (1991) identified three kinds of relevant knowledge:

1. Conceptual knowledge: information about concepts and schemas stored in long-term memory.
2. Sociocultural knowledge: information about the social background or context.
3. Metacognitive knowledge: knowledge about what one knows.

There is generally little relationship between the writer's knowledge of the topic (mainly conceptual knowledge) and the quality of the text produced. For example, Kellogg (1987) asked his participants to write a persuasive essay on why the United Nations should remain in New York. Those with much relevant knowledge did not write better essays than those with less knowledge. However, Kellogg (1987) also obtained a measure of cognitive effort by measuring time to respond to an occasional stimulus during the writing process. Participants with more knowledge devoted less effort to writing (see Figure 13.4)

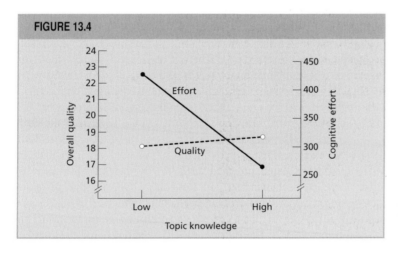

**FIGURE 13.4**

Overall quality of essay writing and cognitive effort as a function of topic knowledge (low vs. high). Data from Kellogg (1987).

According to Hayes and Flower (1986), strategic knowledge also plays a major role in the construction of a writing plan. Strategic knowledge concerns ways of organising the goals and sub-goals of writing to construct a coherent writing plan. Hayes and Flower found that good writers use strategic knowledge very flexibly. The structure of the writing plan often changes as dissatisfaction grows with the original plan.

Adults possessing either a lot of knowledge or relatively little on a topic were compared by Hayes and Flower (1986). The experts produced more goals and sub-goals, and so constructed a more complex overall writing plan. In addition, the various goals of the experts were much more interconnected.

Planning often takes the form of writing notes. Kellogg (1994) identified three types of preliminary note-writing:

1. Clustering or networking ideas and their inter-relationships, sometimes referred to as "mind maps".
2. Listing ideas, with some attempt to place them in the appropriate order.
3. Outlining ideas and how they are related hierarchically.

## Sentence generation

The gap between the writing plan and the actual writing of sentences is usually large. Kaufer, Hayes, and Flower (1986) found that essays were always at least eight times longer than outlines. In some ways, the process going on here is the opposite of that involved in comprehension. Kintsch and van Dijk (1978) argued that comprehension involves extracting the macro-structure from the micro-propositions (see Chapter 12). In contrast, sentence generation can be regarded as generating micro-propositions from the macro-structural plans.

The technique of asking writers to think aloud permitted Kaufer et al. (1986) to explore the process of sentence generation. Here is a typical verbal protocol of a writer engaged in writing, with dots indicating pauses of at least two seconds:

The best thing about it is (1) ................... what? (2) Something about using my mind (3) ................... it allows me the opportunity to (4) ................... uh ................... I want to write something about my ideas (5) ................... to put ideas into action (6) ................... or ................... to develop my ideas into (7) ................... what? (8) ................... into a meaningful form? (9) Oh, Bleh! ...................say it allows me (10) ................... to use (11) ................... Na ................... allows me ................... scratch that. The best thing about it is that it allows me to use (12) ................... my mind and ideas in a productive way (13).

In this protocol, fragments 12 and 13 formed the written sentence, and the earlier fragments 1, 4, 6, 7, 9, and 11 were attempts to produce parts of the sentence.

Kaufer et al. (1986) compared the sentence-generation styles of expert and average writers. Both groups accepted about 75% of the sentence parts they verbalised. The length of the average sentence part was 11.2 words for the expert writers compared with 7.3 words for the average writers. Thus, good writers make use of larger units or "building blocks" than do others.

## Revision

According to Hayes and Flower (1986, p. 110), "the more expert the writer, the greater the proportion of writing time the writer will spend in revision." Why is this? Expert writers focus on the coherence and structure of the arguments expressed, whereas non-expert writers focus on individual words and phrases. It is much more time-consuming to modify the hierarchical structure of a text than to change individual words.

Faigley and Witte (1983) compared the revisions made by writers at different levels of skill. They discovered that 34% of the revisions by experienced adult writers involved a change of meaning, against only 12% of the revisions of inexperienced college writers. This difference probably occurred because experienced writers are more concerned with coherence and meaning.

Further evidence on differences between expert and non-expert writers was obtained by Hayes et al. (1985). Expert writers detected 60% more problems in a text than did non-experts. The expert writers correctly identified the nature of the problem in 74% of cases, against only 42% for the non-expert writers.

One of the greatest problems is make a text more comprehensible to the intended readers. This is a real problem in writing a textbook such as this, where the readers vary considerably in their previous knowledge of the topics being discussed. An interesting way of teaching writers to be more alert to the reader's needs was used by Schriver (1984). Students read an imperfect text, and predicted the comprehension problems a reader would have with it. Then the students read a reader's verbal protocol produced while he or she tried to understand that text. After the students had been given various texts plus reader's protocols, they became better at predicting the kinds of problems readers would have with new texts.

## Evaluation

Hayes and Flower (1980, 1986) have enhanced our understanding of writing processes. However, protocol analysis (on which Hayes and Flower rely heavily) can provide information only about those processes of which there is conscious awareness. Writers are unlikely to be aware of how they search long-term memory for ideas, how they think of inferences, and so on. The requirement to verbalise while writing adds to the writer's processing load, and so may alter the writing process. Rymer (1988) found that only five out of nine scientists approached were willing to try thinking out loud while composing a scientific paper, and only one of them produced useful protocols. Directed retrospection provides less information than protocol analysis, and shares with it a focus on conscious processes. However, it is much less intrusive.

The comparison of writers having more and less skill by Hayes and Flower facilitates the identification of the specific strategies involved in skilled writing. It is also useful in terms of

producing practical advice for those who find it hard to develop adequate writing skills.

On the negative side, the three processes of planning, sentence generation, and revision cannot be neatly separated. In particular, planning and sentence generation are often almost inextricably bound up with each other. A further criticism was raised by Kellogg (1990, p. 376), who argued that writing is more of a social act than was proposed by Hayes and Flower (1986).

## Writing expertise

Why are some writers more skilful than others? Individual differences in writing ability depend most on the processes involved in the planning stage. Bereiter and Scardamalia (1987) identified two major strategies used in the planning stage:

- A knowledge-telling strategy.
- A knowledge-transforming strategy.

The knowledge-telling strategy involves writers simply writing down everything they know about a topic with no planning. The text already generated provides retrieval cues for generating the rest of the text. In the words of a 12-year-old child who used the knowledge-telling strategy (Bereiter & Scardamalia, 1987, p. 9), "I have a whole bunch of ideas and write them down until my supply of ideas is exhausted. Then I might try to think of more ideas up to the point when you can't get any more ideas that are worth putting down on paper."

The knowledge-transforming strategy involves use of a *rhetorical problem space* and a *content problem space*. Rhetorical problems relate to the achievement of the goals of the writing task (e.g., "Can I strengthen the argument?"), and content problems relate to the specific information to be written down (e.g., "The case of Smith vs. Jones strengthens the argument"). There should be movement of information in both directions between the content space and the rhetorical space. However, this happens more with skilled writers using a knowledge-transforming strategy. According to Bereiter and Scardamalia (1987, p. 303):

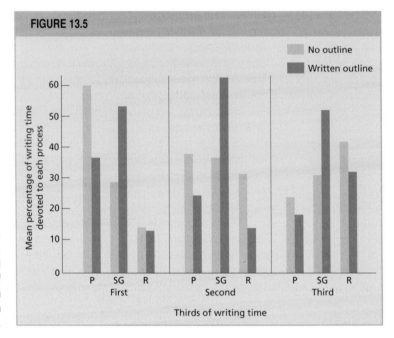

**FIGURE 13.5**

Percentage of writing time devoted to planning (P), sentence generation (SG), and revision (R) as a function of whether an outline had been produced. Based on data in Kellogg (1988).

The key requirement for reflective thought in writing . . . is the translation of problems encountered in the rhetorical space back into subgoals to be achieved in the content space . . . the novice possesses productions for transferring information from the content space to the rhetorical space, but lacks productions for the return trip.

Bereiter, Burtis, and Scardamalia (1988) hypothesised that knowledge-transforming strategists would be more likely than knowledge-telling strategists to produce high-level main points capturing important themes. Children and adults wrote an essay, and thought aloud while planning what to write. Those participants who produced a high-level main point used on average 4.75 different knowledge-transforming processes during planning, whereas those who produced a low-level main point used only 0.23 knowledge-transforming processes.

Are expert writers helped by their use of either rough drafts (an initial version of the text) or outlines (focus on main themes)? Kellogg (1988) asked his participants to learn several facts about a controversy over bussing systems for the handicapped, and then to write a business letter arguing for a particular system. Producing an outline increased the quality of the letter, whereas producing a rough draft did not. The proportion of the time during writing devoted to different processes is shown in Figure 13.5. Outline producers spent more time in sentence generation than did the no-outline participants, but less in planning and reviewing or revising.

What do these results mean? Participants who produced outlines had reduced processing load during the writing of the final text. Planning is the most important and hardest process in writing, and producing an outline has the great advantage that the planning process can be almost complete before starting to write the polished draft.

## Word processing

There has been a large increase in the use of word processors in recent years. Is this a good thing? Kellogg and Mueller (1993) compared text produced by word processor and by writing in longhand. For highly experienced users of word processors, the rate at which text was produced and the quality of what was written did not differ between the two conditions. However, word processing impaired production rate and quality of text for less experienced users of word processors.

Kellogg and Mueller (1993) assessed effortfulness of writing by measuring reaction time to an occasional stimulus. Word processing produced more effortful planning and revision than writing in longhand, but there was no difference for sentence generation. Those using word processors were much less likely than those writing in longhand to make notes (12% vs. 69%, respectively), and this may help to explain the findings.

Kellogg (1994, p. 160) came to the following conclusion: "Studies on writing fluency [speed] and quality generally show no difference between composing on a computer or with pen and paper . . . a writer should select whatever tool he or she finds comfortable and useful." What is important is that the writer has access to all the relevant knowledge needed for the particular writing task. The method of writing rarely influences knowledge accessibility, and so should have only minor effects on writing performance.

## COGNITIVE NEUROPSYCHOLOGY: WRITING

Many brain-damaged patients who have particular problems with spelling and with writing have been studied. The focus here is on two major issues. First, there has been controversy about the role played by inner speech in the writing process. Second, there have been suggestions that the processes involved in spelling can vary. The notion of different "routes" to the writing of words is considered in the light of the relevant cognitive neuropsychological evidence. Cognitive neuropsychologists have focused only on certain limited aspects of writing, especially those concerned with the spelling of individual words (for reasons, see Chapter 19).

### Inner speech and writing

It has often been assumed (e.g., Luria, 1970) that writing depends heavily on inner speech, and that we say words to ourselves before writing them down. This makes intuitive sense, and some spelling mistakes (e.g., "akshun" instead of "action") seem to be based almost entirely on knowledge of word sounds. The key theoretical issue is whether inner speech is *essential* for writing. One approach is to consider brain-damaged patients having little or no inner speech to see whether they can write effectively, and some relevant studies are discussed here.

Levine, Calvanio, and Popovics (1982) reported on the case of EB. He had suffered a stroke, and his overt and inner speech were practically non-existent. In one task, he was given a target picture and four further pictures. His task was to decide which of the four pictures had a name that rhymed with the name of the target picture. He worked out the names and spellings of most of the pictures, but could not use the sounds of the picture names to perform the task accurately. However, EB's writing skills were largely intact. The quality of his written language can be seen in this account (Levine et al., 1982) of his first memories after his stroke:

> Gradually after what seemed days and days, got back enough strength to pull myself up and sit if I held on. I tilted off to the right and had a hard time maintaining my balance . . . The nurse and doctor and an orderly helped me up then.

Most aphasic patients are severely impaired in both writing and speaking, and so lack the marked discrepancy between writing and speaking skills shown by EB. However, there is a potential difficulty in interpreting the findings from EB. He had extensive experience of speed reading, and claimed to be able to read without processing the sounds of words. Thus, what is true of EB may not be true of other patients or normal individuals.

Further evidence that some brain-damaged patients do not rely on inner speech when engaged in writing comes from the study of patients with jargon aphasia (discussed earlier). Their speech is full of non-words which sound similar to the intended words (e.g., "skut" instead of "scout"; "orstrum" instead of "saucepan"). These errors do not seem to be due to problems of articulation, because patients with jargon aphasia can often pronounce common multi-syllabled words accurately.

If jargon aphasics rely on inner speech while writing, then the kinds of errors present in their pronunciation of words should affect their spelling of the same words. Patient RD (Ellis, Miller, & Sin, 1983) was shown various pictures, and called an elephant an "enelust", a screwdriver a "kistro", and a penguin a "senstenz". His spellings of all these words were accurate, but the superiority of writing over speech that RD displayed may not be generally true of jargon aphasics.

## Spelling

In this section, we will consider the various ways in which we spell words that we hear or see. A sketch-map of what may be involved is shown in Figure 13.6. The main points to be noted are as follows:

- There are several routes between hearing a word and spelling it.
- The spelling of known or familiar words involves use of the *graphemic output lexicon* (a store containing information about the written forms of famliar words). Heard words can gain access to the graphemic output lexicon either through the *semantic system* (which stores word meanings), or through the *phonological output lexicon* (which provides information about the spoken forms of words). Both routes can be used by normal individuals.
- The spelling of unknown words or non-words cannot involve use of the grapheme output lexicon, because no information about them is available in the lexicon. Spellings are constructed from the spoken or phonemic forms of words by means of *phoneme–grapheme conversion*, which capitalises on the regularities in the language. This route will produce

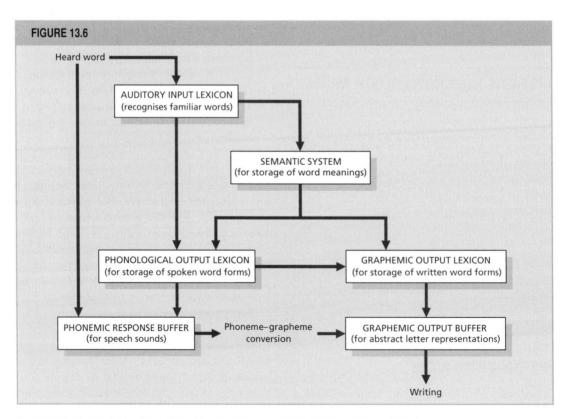

**FIGURE 13.6**

Components of a model for the spelling of heard words. Adapted from Ellis and Young (1988).

plausible but incorrect spellings of irregular words (e.g., "yot" for "yacht").

- It is assumed that there are four lexicons involved in language processing (visual input lexicon; auditory input lexicon; phonological output lexicon; and graphemic output lexicon).

Next we consider some of the evidence relating to the major assumptions incorporated in the model.

## Phonological dysgraphia

What would we expect to find if a patient could make practically no use of phoneme–grapheme correspondence, but the other spelling components or modules were intact? He or she would be able to spell known words accurately, because their spellings would be accessible in the graphemic output lexicon. However, there would be great problems with unfamiliar words and non-words. The term *phonological dysgraphia* is applied to patients with these symptoms.

A patient fitting this description is PR, who was studied by Shallice (1981). He (PR rather than Shallice!) had made a good recovery from a stroke. He wrote over 90% of common words correctly to dictation, and was only slightly worse in his spelling of relatively uncommon words. However, he was extremely poor at producing appropriate spellings for non-words, succeeding less than 20% of the time. On the rare occasions he did spell a non-word accurately, he often reported that he had used a real word to assist him.

Other patients with phonological dysgraphia have been studied (see Parkin, 1996, for a review). The evidence suggests that words can be spelled in the absence of phoneme–grapheme conversion. However, as Barry (1994) pointed out, the fact that patients with phonological dysgraphia can write several non-words correctly suggests they have some residual ability to use phonological information. Evidence against this line of argument was reported by Shelton and Weinrich (1997). Their patient, EA, could not write any of 55 non-words to dictation, but was able to write 50% of regular words and 45% of irregular words correctly. As Shelton and Weinrich (1997, p. 126) concluded, "EA does not appear to be able to do any

phoneme-to-grapheme conversion, yet he can write single words accurately. Thus, his data suggest that writing can be carried out completely independently of sublexical phonological generation, a conclusion contrary to previous arguments (e.g., Barry, 1994)."

## Deep dysgraphia

How do we know that the semantic system is involved in word spelling? If, for some reason, only partial semantic information about a heard word was passed on from the semantic system to the graphemic output lexicon, then a word similar in meaning to the correct word would be written down. Precisely this has been observed in patients with *deep dysgraphia*. Bub and Kertesz (1982) studied a young woman, JC, who made numerous semantic errors, writing "sun" when the word "sky" was spoken, writing "chair" when "desk" was spoken, and so on. However, her reading aloud was very good, and did not contain semantic errors. Thus, the semantic system itself was probably not damaged, but rather the connection between the semantic system and the graphemic output lexicon.

The semantic errors made by deep dysgraphics presumably reflect damage in (or close to) the semantic system. However, Beaton, Guest, and Ved (1997) argued that processes closer to output can also be involved. They studied a female patient, MGK, who suffered from deep dysgraphia and deep dyslexia. She said and wrote down the names of pictures in rapid succession. On 12% of trials, there was a discrepancy between the written and the spoken responses. For example, when a brush was shown, MGK said "comb" and wrote "hair". Beaton et al. (1997, p. 459) concluded: "These discrepancies are interpreted as providing support for the view that semantic errors can arise at the level of selection of items from the . . . orthographic output lexicon (as well as at the level of semantics)."

## Surface dysgraphia

If a patient relied largely on phoneme–grapheme conversion in spelling, what pattern of performance would we expect to see? Apart from producing misspellings sounding like the relevant word, such a patient would have some success in generating spellings of non-words, and would be more accurate at spelling regular words (i.e., those words where the spelling can be worked out from the sound) than irregular words. Patients with these symptoms suffer from *surface dysgraphia.*

All those features characterised the spelling of patient TP, who was studied by Hatfield and Patterson (1983). For example, she wrote "flud" instead of "flood" and "neffue" instead of "nephew". However, she could spell some irregular words correctly (e.g., "sign" and "cough"), suggesting there was some use of the graphemic output lexicon.

Graham, Patterson, and Hodges (1997) studied two patients (SC and FM) with surface dysgraphia. Both patients had a degenerative brain disease, and so other writing abilities deteriorated over time. For example, they became very poor at transcribing upper-case letters into lower-case letters (e.g., seeing "A" and writing "a"), and vice versa. As Graham et al. (1997, p. 996) pointed out, these findings cannot be explained satisfactorily by a model such as the one shown in Figure 13.6: "By this account the association between the deficits arises from the joint disruption of functionally separate subsystems, and is merely coincidental." They argued that interactive connectionist models (e.g., Olson & Caramazza, 1994) provide a better account of their findings.

Phoneme–grapheme conversion is sometimes used in the writing of normals. Unfamiliar and non-words do not have entries in either the graphemic output lexicon or the speech output lexicon. Thus, we must guess at their spelling by using some other strategy, such as phoneme–grapheme conversion. Children often seem to use phoneme–grapheme conversion, producing misspellings sounding like the word in question (e.g., "skool" instead of "school").

## Graphemic and phonological output lexicons

How do we know there are separate graphemic output and phonological output lexicons? If information about the written forms (graphemic output lexicon) and the spoken forms (speech output lexicon) of words were stored in the same lexicon, then presumably patients who had problems with speaking would have problems with writing. We have seen already that this is not always the case. EB was able to write fairly well despite apparently having no inner speech, and RD could write many words he could not say properly. Presumably patients such as EB and RD have a relatively intact graphemic output lexicon, but a severely impaired speech output lexicon (or connections to or from it). The more common pattern among brain-damaged patients is to have a greater problem with writing than with speech (see Parkin, 1996). Such patients presumably have more severe impairment of the graphemic output lexicon than of the speech output lexicon.

## One or two orthographic lexicons?

Knowledge of word spellings (*orthography*) is important in reading and in writing. The simplest theoretical assumption is that a *single* orthographic lexicon is used in both reading and writing. An alternative position (e.g., Weekes & Coltheart, 1996) is that there are two orthographic lexicons, one for reading (visual input lexicon) and one for spelling (graphemic output lexicon; see Figure 13.6).

Evidence in favour of a two-lexicon model has been obtained from patients showing large discrepancies between reading and spelling. Hanley and Kay (1992) studied a patient whose spelling was much worse than his reading. In addition, most of his spelling errors involved making use of phoneme–grapheme correspondence rules (e.g., he wrote "serkel" instead of "circle"), whereas most of his reading errors involved visual confusions (e.g., "feather" was read as "further"). In contrast, Patterson (1986) studied a patient whose spelling was better than his reading. He could spell irregular words (e.g., yacht) as accurately as regular ones (e.g., capsule), but could not read printed words aloud. Thus, his knowledge of spelling did not assist his reading performance.

Weekes and Coltheart (1996) studied a patient, NW, whose main difficulty lay in reading irregularly spelled words. A reading programme produced a significant improvement in his ability to read irregular words, but did not enhance his spelling performance. Weekes and Coltheart (1996,

p. 302) concluded: "We interpret the results we have obtained with NW... as distinctly favouring a two-orthographic-lexicon model." However, as Holmes and Carruthers (1998, pp. 266–267) pointed out, "brain-damaged patients often have deficits that extend beyond their difficulties in reading and spelling... Thus, their reading and spelling behaviour may be affected in multiple ways, with compensatory strategies having little to do with normal reading and spelling determining performance."

Evidence favouring the one orthographic lexicon model was reported by Funnell (1992). A 10-year-old boy was given the task of deciding whether printed words were correctly or incorrectly spelled. He performed this task well *only* for words he could spell accurately.

Holmes and Carruthers (1998) used a modified version of Funnell's procedure. The participants were presented with five versions of each word they could not spell: the correct version; their own misspelling; the most popular misspelling (if that differed from their own misspelling); and two or three other misspellings. The participants showed no ability to select the correct spelling over their own misspelling (see Figure 13.7). As Holmes and Carruthers (1998, p. 284) concluded, "Normal adult readers access the same orthographic representation for both reading and spelling."

In sum, the evidence remains inconclusive. There are no strong reasons at present for rejecting the simple assumption that there is a single orthographic lexicon.

## Phonological output lexicon

There is evidence from normals that the phonological output lexicon is sometimes involved in writing. All of us sometimes write down a word sounding the same as the one we intended to write down. Several examples are given by Hotopf (1980), including "sought" instead of "sort", "their" instead of "there", and "scene" instead of "seen". The fact that actual words are nearly always written down suggests the involvement of the speech output lexicon. If the sounds of words were being used to produce spellings by phoneme–grapheme correspondence, then we would expect numerous non-words to be produced (e.g., "sawt" instead of "sort").

The phonological output lexicon is probably used only rarely by normal individuals. As Parkin (1996, p. 185) pointed out, "Given the extensive presence of homophones in English (e.g., SAIL, SALE) and the relative scarcity of homophonic errors in spelling, it seems unlikely that the phonological output buffer is regularly involved in the generation of spellings."

It has been suggested that some patients produce spellings via a route that uses the phonological output lexicon but avoids the semantic system. For example, Goodall and Phillips (1995) described the findings from a patient, AN. She learned to read non-words, and seemed to do this by treating each one as a whole rather than by using grapheme-to-phoneme correspondence rules. AN was then able to write these non-words

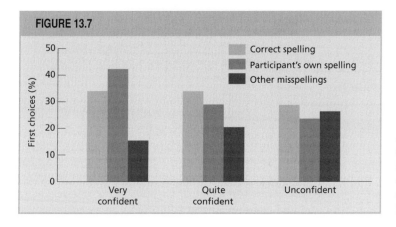

**FIGURE 13.7**

Ability to select the correct spelling of a word from various misspellings as a function of confidence in correctness of decision. Based on data in Holmes and Carruthers (1998).

accurately to dictation, presumably by making use of the phonological output lexicon.

## Graphemic output buffer

Caramazza, Miceli, Villa, and Romani (1987) argued that the graphemic output buffer is a memory store holding graphemic information briefly. If so, what we would expect to find in a patient with damage to the graphemic output buffer? First, the patient should have greater problems with spelling long words than short ones, because long words impose greater demands on memory. Second, if the graphemic output buffer contains only graphemic information, then spelling performance should be similar for words and for non-words. Caramazza et al. (1987) reported findings from a patient, LB, who showed the predicted pattern of results.

## Section summary

There are various ways in which word spellings can be produced, suggesting that several modules or components are involved in the writing process. Ellis and Young's (1988) model seems to be on the right lines. There is reasonable support for the components or modules that Ellis and Young (1988) identified. However, the inter-relationships among the components are probably more complex than they indicated.

The cognitive neuropsychological approach deals with some of the processes involved in sentence generation, but is almost silent on the processes involved in planning and revision. Thus, this approach provides us with a very detailed picture of a small fraction of the processes involved in writing.

# SPEAKING AND WRITING COMPARED

Spoken and written language both have as their central function the communication of information about people and the world, and so it is common-sensical to assume that there are important similarities between speaking and writing. On the other hand, children and adults often find writing much harder than speaking, suggesting there are major differences between the productions of spoken and written language. Speaking and writing will now be compared.

## Similarities

The view that speaking and writing are similar receives some support if we compare the theoretical approach to speech production of Dell et al. (1997) with the theory of writing proposed by Hayes and Flower (1986). In both theories, it is assumed there is an initial attempt to decide on the overall meaning that is to be communicated. At this stage, the actual words to be spoken or written are not considered. This is followed by the production of language, which often proceeds on a clause-by-clause basis.

Gould (1978) compared dictated and written business letters. Even those highly practised at dictation rarely dictated more than 35% faster than they wrote. This is noteworthy, given that people can speak five or six times faster than they can write. Gould (1980) divided the time taken to dictate and to write letters into various component times. His participants were videotaped while composing letters, and the generating, reviewing, accessing, editing, and planning times were calculated. Planning, which was assumed to occur during pauses not obviously devoted to other processes, accounted for more of the total time than any other process. Planning time represented about two-thirds of the total composition time for both dictated and written letters, and this explains why dictation was only slightly faster than writing.

Gould (1978) compared the quality of letter writing across three different response modes: writing; dictating; and speaking. Those who wrote very good letters also tended to dictate and to speak very good letters. The quality of letter writing is determined mainly by internal planning processes, and these processes are essentially the same regardless of the type of response. In addition, the knowledge that someone possesses (e.g., vocabulary; specific knowledge of the topic) is available for use whether that person is writing, speaking, or dictating. However, some of the findings may be specific to business letters. The absence of visual feedback with dictation might be a real disadvantage when composing essays or longer pieces of writing.

## Differences

How do speaking and writing differ? Spoken language makes use of prosody (rhythm, intonation, and so on) to convey meaning and grammatical information, and gesture is also used for emphasis. In contrast, writers have to rely heavily on punctuation to supply the information provided by prosody in spoken language. Writers also make much more use than speakers of words or phrases signalling what is coming next (e.g., but; on the other hand). This helps to compensate for the lack of prosody in written language.

Four of the most obvious differences between speaking and writing are as follows:

* Speakers typically know precisely who is receiving their message.
* Speakers generally receive moment-by-moment feedback from the listener or listeners (e.g., expressions of bewilderment).
* Speakers generally have much less time than writers to plan their language production.
* "Writing is in essence a more conscious process than speaking . . . spontaneous discourse is usually spoken, self-monitored discourse is usually written" (Halliday, 1987, pp. 67–69).

As a result, spoken language is generally fairly informal and simple in structure, with information often being communicated rapidly. In contrast, written language is more formal and complex in structure. Writers need to write clearly because they do not receive immediate feedback, and this slows down the communication rate.

Cognitive neuropsychologists have found that some brain-damaged patients have writing skills that are largely intact in spite of an almost total inability to speak and a lack of inner speech. Others can speak fluently, but find writing very difficult. In addition, there are other patients whose patterns of errors in speaking and in writing differ so much that it is hard to believe that a single system could underlie both language activities. However, these findings do not mean that the higher-level processes involved in language production (e.g., planning; use of knowledge) differ between speaking and writing.

## LANGUAGE AND THOUGHT

The major language processes discussed in this chapter and the two previous ones raise the issue of the relationship between language and thought. For example, speaking and writing are both activities in which thinking about what one wants to say or write (the intended message) is translated into language.

The best known theory about the interrelationship between language and thought was put forward by Benjamin Lee Whorf (1956). He was a fire prevention officer for an insurance company who spent his spare time working in linguistics. According to his hypothesis of linguistic relativity (known as the Whorfian hypothesis), language determines or influences thinking. It is useful to distinguish between the strong and the weak form of the Whorfian hypothesis (Hunt & Agnoli, 1991). According to the strong hypothesis, language *determines* thinking, implying that some thoughts expressible in one language will not be expressible in a second language. This is the issue of *translatability*: can all sentences in one language be translated accurately into sentences in a second language? There is little support for the strong hypothesis.

According to the weak form of the Whorfian hypothesis, language *influences* thought. This is a more reasonable hypothesis. As we will see, it has been tested mainly by studies of the effects of language on memory and perception.

Casual inspection of the world's languages indicates there are significant differences among them. For example, the Hanuxoo people in the Philippines have 92 different names for different varieties of rice, and there are hundreds of camel-related words in Arabic. It is possible that these differences influence thought. A more plausible explanation is that different environmental conditions affect the things people think about, and this in turn affects their linguistic usage. Thus, these differences occur because thought affects language rather than because language affects thought.

## Memory, perception, and language

There has been a fair amount of research concerned with possible cultural differences in memory for colours. Lenneberg and Roberts (1956) found that Zuni speakers made more errors than English speakers in recognising yellows and oranges. The relevance of this finding is that there is only one word in the Zuni language to refer to yellows and oranges. Although the findings of Lenneberg and Roberts suggested that language affects memory, later studies brought this conclusion into doubt.

Heider (1972) used the fact that there are 11 basic colour words in English, and each of these words has one generally agreed best or focal colour. English speakers find it easier to remember focal than non-focal colours, and Heider wondered whether the same would be true of the Dani. The Dani are a Stone-Age agricultural people living in Indonesian New Guinea, and their language has only two basic colour terms: "mola" for bright, warm hues, and "mili" for dark, cold hues. Heider (1972) found that the Dani and Americans both showed better recognition memory for focal colours. However, the overall memory performance of the Dani was much worse than that of Americans, perhaps because of the limited colour terms available to the Dani.

The research of Heider and others on memory for colours suggests that the similarities among cultures are far more pronounced than the dissimilarities. This is in spite of the fact that there are considerable differences from one language to the next in the terms available to describe colours. However, numerous languages have words for the same 11 focal colours, and it seems from work on the physiology of colour vision (DeValois & Jacobs, 1968) that these colours are processed specially by the visual system.

However, some research suggests that language can affect memory for colours. In a study by Schooler and Engstler-Schooler (1990), participants were shown colour chips that were not focal colours, and were or were not asked to label them. Those asked to label the colours did worse than the non-labellers on recognition memory, suggesting that colour memory was distorted by language in the form of labelling. In a study by Stefflre, Castillo Vales, and Morley (1966), memory for colour was compared in Spanish and Mayan speakers. There were significant differences, which were related to differences in linguistic codability (ease of verbal labelling) of the colours between the two languages.

Language can also affect perceptual processes. Miyawaki et al. (1975) compared English and Japanese speakers with respect to their perception of sounds varying between a pure /l/ and a pure /r/. English speakers make a sharp perceptual distinction between similar sounds on either side of the categorical boundary between "l" and "r"; this is known as *categorical speech perception*. No such perceptual distinction is made by Japanese speakers, presumably because there is no distinction between /l/ and /r/ in the Japanese language.

Research on the effects of language on colour perception was reported by Davies et al. (1998), who compared speakers of English and of Setswana, a language spoken in Botswana. They were given the task of deciding which of three colours was least like the other two, and there were crucial trials on which any linguistic influences should have led the two groups to make different choices. The findings were as follows: "Our data show a striking similarity between language groups in their choice of similarities and differences among colours . . . in addition, there are small, but reliable differences between the two samples associated with linguistic differences" (Davies et al., 1998, p. 14).

Similar findings were reported by Davies (1998). Speakers of English, Setswana, and Russian were asked to sort 65 colours into between 2 and 12 groups on the basis of perceptual similarity. English has 11 basic colour terms, Setswana has 5, and Russian has 12, and it was thought that these differences might influence performance. However, "The most striking feature of the results was the marked similarity of the groups chosen across the three language samples" (Davies, 1998, p. 433). In addition, however, there were minor influences of language. For example, Setswana has only one word to describe green and blue, and Setswana speakers were more likely than English and Russian speakers to group blue and green colours together.

In sum, the evidence indicates that language has less impact on cognition than was assumed by Whorf. However, careful research reveals that language exerts modest influences on some perceptual and memorial processes, and so a weak form of the Whorfian hypothesis is tenable.

## Cognitive approach

Hunt and Agnoli (1991) put forward a cognitive account of the Whorfian hypothesis. The essence of their position was as follows (1991, p. 379):

> Different languages lend themselves to the transmission of different types of messages. People consider the costs of computation when they reason about a topic. The language that they use will partly determine those costs. In this sense, language does influence cognition.

Thus, any given language makes it easy to think in certain ways and hard to think in other ways, and this is why thinking is influenced by language.

An especially interesting demonstration of how language can influence thinking was provided by Hoffman, Lau, and Johnson (1986). Bilingual English-Chinese speakers read descriptions of individuals, and were later asked to provide free interpretations of the individuals described. The descriptions conformed to either Chinese or English stereotypes of personality. For example, there is a stereotype of the artistic type in English, consisting of a mixture of artistic skills, moody and intense temperament, and bohemian lifestyle, but this stereotype does not exist in Chinese. Bilinguals

thinking in Chinese made use of Chinese stereotypes in their free impressions, whereas bilinguals thinking in English used English stereotypes. This suggests that the kinds of inferences we draw can be much influenced by the language in which we are thinking.

More evidence consistent with Hunt and Agnoli (1991) was reported by Pederson et al. (1998). They pointed out that space can be coded in either a *relative* system (e.g., left; right; up; down) or an *absolute* system (e.g., north; south). Pederson et al. (1998) gave speakers of 13 languages a non-linguistic spatial reasoning task which could be solved using either a relative or an absolute system. The key finding was that participants' choice of system was determined largely by the dominant system of spatial coding in their native language, presumably because it was easier for them to do this.

### Evaluation

Hunt and Agnoli (1991) have provided a plausible cognitive account of the Whorfian hypothesis, and there is a fair amount of evidence consistent with their account. Most of the evidence supporting this cognitive theory (e.g., Hoffman et al., 1986; Pederson et al., 1998) has used tasks that give the participants flexibility in the approach they adopt, and so provide scope for language to influence performance. What is lacking so far is a systematic programme of research to establish clearly that language influences thought in the ways specified by Hunt and Agnoli (1991). More specifically, Hunt and Agnoli (1991) emphasised the importance of computational costs, but these costs have rarely been assessed.

## CHAPTER SUMMARY

- Speech as communication. A key to successful communication is the Co-operative Principle, according to which speakers and listeners must try to be co-operative. Speakers should take account of the communal and personal common ground they share with their listener(s). A speaker's initial plan for an utterance may be monitored and adjusted in the light of information about common ground. Conversation often involves an adjacency pair, in which what the first speaker says provides a strong invitation to the listener to take up the conversation.

- Speech production processes and theories. Speakers should make use of prosodic cues, but they often fail to do so. There is much pre-planning of speech. This planning involves a series of stages, starting with the intended meaning, proceeding through the formation of a grammatical structure, decisions about the words to be fitted into that structure, and the articulation of the sentence. According to spreading-activation theory, speech errors occur when an incorrect item is more strongly activated than the correct one. Expert speakers are better able than non-expert speakers to plan ahead, and so a higher proportion of their total speech errors is anticipatory. Levelt et al. (1999a) have proposed a six-stage model of speech production, in which the crucial assumption is that a single lemma or abstract word is accessed prior to morphological and phonological encoding. The evidence from tip-of-the-tongue and other studies tends to support the theory. However, the theory focuses on the production of individual words, and is relatively uninformative about the processes responsible for speech errors.

- Cognitive neuropsychology: Speech production. Patients with anomia have an impaired ability to name objects. Some anomic patients have problems with lemma selection, whereas others have problems with word-form selection. Patients with agrammatism generally produce the appropriate words when speaking, but cannot order them grammatically. The syntactic deficiencies of agrammatic aphasics sometimes extend to language comprehension. Patients with jargon aphasia speak fairly grammatically, but have severe problems with word finding, and often produce made-up words. Jargon aphasics are generally unaware that they are producing made-up words, often because of their poor comprehension of spoken material. Agrammatic aphasics and jargon aphasics show a double dissociation between syntactic planning and content-word retrieval.

- Cognitive neuroscience: Speech production. Broca identified areas of the brain that were damaged in patients having mainly speech production problems. Wernicke did the same for patients having severe problems with speech comprehension. There have been recent attempts to relate brain areas to language functions by using CT scans with brain-damaged patients, and by using PET scans with normal individuals performing various language tasks. There is more evidence for localisation of language functions in PET studies on normals. The evidence suggests that there are considerable individual differences in the areas of the brain involved in any given language function.

- Writing: Basic processes. Planning, sentence generation, and revising are the key processes in writing, but they cannot be separated neatly. Methods such as protocol analysis and directed retrospection indicate that more time is spent on sentence generation than on the other processes. Topic knowledge generally has little effect on the quality of written text, but influences the amount of cognitive effort required. Expert writers spend more time on revision than non-expert ones, and focus more on the coherence and structure of the arguments expressed. Expert writers use a knowledge-transforming strategy, whereas non-experts often use a knowledge-telling strategy. Producing an outline reduces planning time during writing, and can improve the quality of the written text. The use of word processors usually has little effect on writing quality, but can make planning and revision more effortful.

- Cognitive neuropsychology: Writing. There is evidence from brain-damaged patients that inner speech is not essential for spelling and writing. Word spelling can be based on information contained in the graphemic output lexicon or on phoneme–grapheme correspondence rules. Patients with phonological dysgraphia rely mainly on the graphemic output lexicon, whereas those with surface dysgraphia mostly use phoneme–grapheme correspondence rules. Deep dysgraphics resemble phonological dysgraphics, but make semantic errors in spelling. There seem to be separate graphemic and phonological output lexicons, but it is not known whether there are one or two orthographic lexicons.

- Speaking and writing compared. The same knowledge base and similar planning skills are used in speaking and in writing, but spoken language is typically more informal than written language. There seem to be separate lexicons containing information about the spoken and the written forms of words. As a result, there are some brain-damaged patients who can speak well although their spelling and writing are poor, and others who can write accurately, but can hardly speak. The processes involved in speaking and writing are most similar during initial planning, although speakers generally have less time for planning. Dissimilarities become increasingly apparent as processing moves towards the end-product of the spoken or written word.
- Language and thought. According to the Whorfian hypothesis, language determines or influences thought. Research indicates that there are some small influences of language on memory and perception. According to Hunt and Agnoli's cognitive theory, language influences thinking by partly determining the computational costs of different kinds of information processing. The available evidence is consistent with this theory, which resembles a weak form of the Whorfian hypothesis.

## FURTHER READING

- Bock, K., & Huitema, J. (1999). Language production. In S. Garrod & M.J. Pickering (Eds.), *Language processing*. Hove, UK: Psychology Press. The main focus of this chapter is on speech production, which is discussed very clearly and coherently.
- Harley, T.A. (1995). *The psychology of language: From data to theory*. Hove, UK: Psychology Press. Chapter 8 in this book provides a very clear introduction to the topic of speech production. The relevant cognitive neuropsychological evidence is also considered.
- Howard, D. (1997). Language in the human brain. In M. Rugg (Ed.), *Cognitive neuroscience*. Hove, UK: Psychology Press. The contributions of cognitive neuroscience to our understanding of language are discussed in detail in this chapter.
- Kellogg, R.T. (1994). *The psychology of writing*. Oxford: Oxford University Press. All aspects of the writing process are covered in a scholarly but approachable way in this useful book.

# 14

# Problem Solving:
# Puzzles, Insight, and Expertise

## INTRODUCTION

Our ability to reflect in a complex way on our lives, to plan and solve problems that arise on a daily basis is the bedrock of thinking behaviour. However, as in all things human, the ways in which we think are many and varied; from solving puzzles in the newspaper to troubleshooting on a car breakdown to developing a new theory of quantum fields. Consider a sample of the sorts of things to which we apply the term "thinking".

First, a fragment of Molly Bloom's sleepy thoughts from James Joyce's *Ulysses* (1922/1960, pp. 871–872), about Mrs Riordan:

> . . . God help the world if all the women in the world were her sort down on bathingsuits and lownecks of course nobody wanted her to wear I suppose she was pious because no man would look at her twice I hope I'll never be like her a wonder she didn't want us to cover our faces but she was a welleducated woman certainly and her gabby talk about

Mr. Riordan here and Mr. Riordan there I suppose he was glad to get shut of her . . .

Next, a person (S) answering an experimenter's (E) question about regulating the thermostat on a home-heating system (Kempton, 1986, p. 83):

E: Let's say you're in the house and you're cold . . . Let's say it's a cold day, you feel cold, you want to do something about it.

S: Oh, what I might do is, I might turn the thing up high to get out, to get a lot of air out fast, then after a little while turn it off or turn it down.

E: Un-huh.

S: So there are also, you know, these issues about, um, the rate at which the thing produces heat, the higher the setting is, the more heat that's produced per unit of time, so if you're cold, you want to get warm fast, um, so you turn it up high.

Finally, a protocol of one of the authors adding 457 and 638 aloud:

Eight and seven is fifteen and then you carry one so, one and three is four and five is nine, and six and four is ten, so the final number is . . . one, nought, nine, five; one thousand and ninety-five.

These three samples illustrate several general aspects of thinking. First, all the pieces involve individuals being *conscious* of their thoughts. Clearly, thinking must involve conscious awareness. However, we tend to be conscious of the products of thinking rather than the processes themselves. For example, we are conscious of taking eight and seven to add, to produce fifteen, but the thought processes responsible for the answer are unconscious and not open to introspection. Furthermore, even when we can introspect on our thoughts, our recollections of them are often inaccurate. Joyce does a good job of reconstructing the character of idle, associative thought in Molly Bloom's internal monologue, but if we interrupted her and asked her to tell us her thoughts from the previous five minutes, little of it would be recalled accurately. Similarly, in psychological experiments retrospective recollections of conscious thoughts are often unreliable. In fact, even the use of concurrent protocols taken as thoughts are being produced is only reliable under some conditions (see Ericsson & Simon, 1980, 1984; for more details see Chapter 1).

 Second, thinking can vary in the extent to which it is directed (Gilhooly, 1995). At one end of the scale it can be relatively undirected and at the other extreme it can be sharply directed towards a specific goal. Molly Bloom's piece is more undirected relative to the other pieces. On the point of slipping into a dream, she is just letting one thought slide into another. If she has any goal it is a very general and ill-defined one (e.g., reflect on the day's happenings). In the other two pieces, the goal is much clearer and well defined. In the addition example, a specific answer must be provided that is known to be either right or wrong (i.e., the goal is clearly defined and can be evaluated easily). As we shall see, most of the research on thinking has been concerned with relatively well defined, goal-driven situations and, hence, these situations will be the main focus of the chapters in this part

of the book (see Gilhooly, 1995, for an exploration of undirected thinking).

Third, the amount and nature of the knowledge used in different thinking tasks can vary enormously. For example, the knowledge required in the addition case is quite limited. It mainly hinges on knowing how to add any number between one and ten and the rule that you carry numbers above ten from one column to the next (see Anderson, 1993, for a production system model of this behaviour). On the other hand, Molly Bloom is using a vast amount of knowledge about the mores of old widows, expectations about what she herself will be like when old, general knowledge about the irony of those who criticise that which they cannot do themselves, and much more besides. Technically, situations that require little knowledge are called *knowledge-poor* whereas those requiring more knowledge are termed *knowledge-rich*. Knowledge-rich situations are much harder to characterise because of the amount of knowledge involved and the variety of ways it is used.

In considering the literature on problem solving, in the first half of this chapter, we will concentrate on research that examines puzzle problems, which tend to be knowledge-poor. In the second half of the chapter, we will consider knowledge-rich types of problem solving: typically, this has been investigated by studying the problem-solving behaviour of experts. The puzzles reviewed here differ considerably from everyday, real-world problems. However, as laboratory tasks they have allowed us to make initial inroads on human problem solving, which have fuelled advances in the understanding of more knowledge-rich situations. Later, we will consider the "ecological validity" of these problems and how they differ from real-world problems.

## Overview of thinking chapters

Thinking research is reviewed in four chapters (Chapters 14–17) covering: (a) puzzle solving, insight, and skilled thinking, (b) creativity and discovery, (c) deductive reasoning, and (d) judgement and decision making. These divisions reflect the way thinking research has developed historically and fundamental distinctions made in this area. These divisions are unlikely to be reflected in everyday thought, which may involve a complex admixture of thinking styles. However, the subject matter is made more manageable by introducing these divisions. All these types of thinking share the property of being directed towards relatively definite goals.

This chapter is broadly structured along historical lines. So, we begin with a review of early problem-solving research—the Gestalt school— before turning to a treatment of the information-processing theories of problem solving that emerged in the 1950s and 1960s. We also consider how these information-processing theories have tried to account for the findings of early research. Then, we follow the subsequent development of these theories in studies of expertise, before reviewing some cognitive neuropsychological research on thinking. In Chapter 15 we consider aspects of creativity and discovery. Chapter 16 deals with reasoning using the conditional (i.e., *if*), and Chapter 17 covers the related area of judgement and decision making. Traditionally, these areas have been dealt with in a quite separate fashion from problem solving. Happily, in recent years, there has been much more convergence in the studies of thinking with an accelerated move towards unified theories that might one day be able to accommodate all of these diverse strands.

## EARLY RESEARCH: THE GESTALT SCHOOL

At the beginning of the 20th century, adherents of the Gestalt school of psychology extended their theories of perception to problem-solving behaviour. These researchers were particularly creative in performing experimental tests of their theories and produced a large corpus of evidence. During the behaviourist period much of this research was re-interpreted in behaviourist terms, even though the basic experimental paradigms remained unchanged (Maltzman, 1955). During much of the 1950s and 1960s this type of problem-solving research became a background activity, although it has been researched actively again more recently, especially when it was re-interpreted in

information-processing terms (see e.g., Bowden & Beeman, 1998; Ohlsson, 1984a, 1992; Raaheim, 1974; Weisberg & Suls, 1973).

## Gestalt research on problem solving in animals

The work of the Gestalt school of psychology had its origins in problem-solving research on animals. Early associationist and behaviourist psychologists had characterised problem solving as the result of either trial-and-error or the reproduction of previously learned responses (Hull, 1930, 1931; Maltzman, 1955; Thorndike, 1911). Following Lloyd Morgan's (1894) observations of his dog, Thorndike's famous experiments on cats were taken as strong evidence for this view.

Thorndike had placed hungry cats in closed cages within sight of a dish of food, outside the cages. The cage-doors could be opened when a pole inside the cage was hit. Initially, the animals thrashed about and clawed the sides of the cage. Inevitably, at some point, the cat hit the pole inside the cage and opened the door. On repeated trials, when the cat was placed in the cage again, similar energetic behaviour ensued but gradually the animal seemed to learn that hitting the pole opened the cage door. Eventually, when placed in the cage it went to the pole, hit it and escaped. So, new problems were initially solved by trial-and-error behaviour and then accidental solutions were amalgamated into responses that were reproduced when the appropriate stimulus was presented.

One of the founders of the Gestalt school, Wolfgang Köhler, disagreed with this formulation and believed that there was more to animal problem solving than trial-and-error and reproductive responses. The Gestalt psychologists had been fairly successful in showing that perception was something more than mere associations (see Chapter 2) and felt that the same ideas could be applied to problem solving. In the perception of illusions, like the Necker cube in Figure 14.1, the corner marked "Y" sometimes appears to be to the front of the figure and other times to the back. In Gestalt terms, the figure is *restructured* to be perceived in one way or the other. In a similar fashion, Gestalt psychologists maintained that one

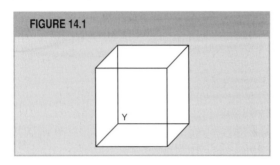

**FIGURE 14.1**

A Necker cube which illustrates the perceptual restructuring in which the corner marked "Y" alternates between being at the back and the front of the figure.

could have "insight" into the problem's structure and "restructure" a problem in order to solve it.

Gestalt theory can be summarised by following points (see e.g., Ohlsson, 1984a; Wertheimer, 1954):

- Problem-solving behaviour is both reproductive and productive.
- Reproductive problem solving involves the re-use of previous experience and can hinder successful problem solving (e.g., as in problem-solving set and functional-fixedness experiments, see later).
- Productive problem solving is characterised by *insight* into the structure of the problem and by productive *restructurings* of the problem.
- Insight often occurs suddenly and is accompanied by an "ah-ha" experience.

The classic example of Gestalt research was Köhler's (1927) study on problem solving in apes. In Köhler's experiments, apes had to reach bananas outside their cages, when sticks were the only objects available. On one occasion, he observed an ape take two sticks and join them together to reach the bananas, and heralded it as an instance of insight. In contemporary terms, Köhler's point was that the animal had acted in a goal-directed way; it was trying to solve the problem using the sticks. He also pointed out that even though the ape had used the sticks initially in a trial-and-error manner, it was only after sitting quietly for a time that the animal produced the insightful solution. Köhler's evidence was not cast-iron because the previous experiences of this once-wild ape were not known. Later, Birch (1945) was to find little evidence of this sort of "insightful" problem solving in apes that were raised in captivity. However, such research set the stage for later Gestalt psychologists to extend their analyses to human problem solving.

---

## Restructuring and insight: The two-string problem

One of the better known Gestalt problems—one that is uncomfortably close to the ape studies—is Maier's (1931) "two-string" or "pendulum problem". In the original version of the problem, human subjects were brought into a room that had two strings hanging from the ceiling and a number of other objects (e.g., poles, pliers, extension cords). They were then asked to tie the two strings together that were hanging from the ceiling. However, they soon found out that when they took hold of one string and went to grab hold of the other, it was too far away for them to reach (see Figure 14.2). Subjects produced several different types of solutions to this problem but the most "insightful" and infrequently produced one was the pendulum solution. This involved taking the pliers, tying them to one of the strings and swinging it. So, while holding one string, it was possible to catch the other on its up-swing and tie the two together. Maier demonstrated a striking example of "problem restructuring" by first allowing subjects to get to a point where they were stuck and then (apparently accidentally) brushing off the string to set it swinging. Soon after this was done subjects tended to produce the pendulum solution, even though few reported noticing the experimenter brush against the string. According to Maier, this subtle hint resulted in a reorganisation or restructuring of the problem so that the solution emerged (recently, Knoblich & Wartenberg, 1998, have made similar observations under more controlled conditions).

## Functional fixedness: The candle problem and nine-dot problem

At around the same time, another young researcher was also expanding Gestalt theory. During his

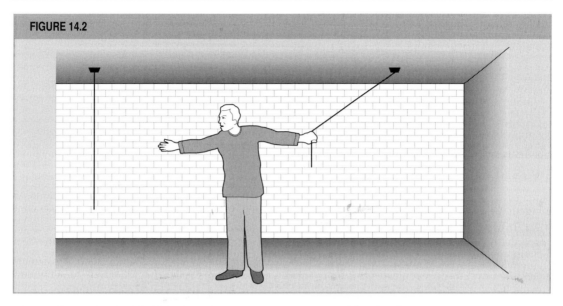

**FIGURE 14.2**

The two-string problem in which it is not possible to reach one string while holding the other.

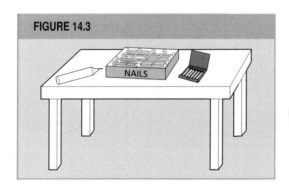

**FIGURE 14.3**

The objects presented to subjects in the candle problem. Adapted from Weisberg and Suls (1973).

twenties, Karl Duncker (1926, 1945) performed experiments on "functional fixedness" or "functional fixity", that continue to be replicated in various guises to this day (see Kubose, Hummel, & Holyoak, in press). He demonstrated this phenomenon in an experiment where subjects were given a candle, a box of tacks, and several other objects, and asked to attach the candle to a wall by a table, so that it did not drip onto the table below (see Figure 14.3). Duncker found that subjects tried to tack the candle directly to the wall or glue it to the wall by melting it, but few thought

of using the inside of the tack-box as a candle holder and tacking it to the wall. In Duncker's terms, subjects were "fixated" on the box's normal function of holding tacks and could not reconceptualise it in a manner that allowed them to solve the problem. Subjects' problem-solving success was hampered by reproductive behaviour (see Weisberg & Suls, 1973, for an information-processing account of the candle problem). Subjects' failure to produce the pendulum solution in the two-string problem can also be seen as a case of functional fixedness because subjects are unable to reconceive of the pliers as a pendulum weight (see Adamson & Taylor, 1954; Keane, 1985a, 1989; Ohlsson, 1992).

Another famous problem from the Gestalt school is Scheerer's (1963) nine-dot problem. As can be seen in Figure 14.4, the problem involves nine dots organised in a three-by-three matrix. In order to solve the problem one must draw four continuous straight lines, connecting all the dots without lifting the pencil from the paper. The correct solution is also shown in Figure 14.4 (although see Adams, 1979, for several wild but valid alternatives). Most people cannot solve the problem because, Scheerer maintained, they assume that the lines must stay within the square

## FIGURE 14.4

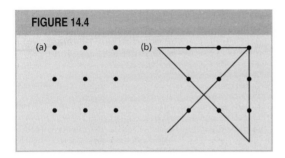

The nine-dot problem (a) and its solution (b).

formed by the dots. In Gestalt terms, subjects had "fixated" on the shape of the dots and could not solve the problem for this reason. We shall see that later research has shown this is not the whole truth.

## Problem-solving set: The water-jug problems

A final set of experiments produced by the Gestalt school that deserve mention are the water-jug experiments of Luchins and Luchins (1959, 1991; Luchins, 1942). These experiments are a special case of the general notion of fixation, where reproductive responses result in problem-solving failure rather than success. The Luchins termed the phenomenon *problem-solving set*. In a typical water-jug problem you have to imagine that you are given an eight-pint jug full of water, and a five-pint jug and three-pint jug that are empty (represented as 8–8, 5–0, 3–0, where the first figure indicates the size of the jug and the second

the amount of water in that jug). Your task is to pour the water from one jug to another until you end up with four pints in the eight-pint jug and four pints in the five-pint jug (i.e., 8–4, 5–4, 3–0). Even though this problem appears straightforward it can take some time to solve (Table 14.1 shows one possible solution).

In order to demonstrate problem-solving set, Luchins and Luchins typically had two groups in their experiments: a set and a control condition. The set condition received a series of problems that could be solved using the same solution method, but the control group received problems that had to be solved using different methods. Then, both groups were given a test problem that could be solved using either a very simple method or the more complex method that the set condition subjects had been applying to all the previous problems. Unsurprisingly, the control group tended to use the simple method but the set group opted for the more complex method. In fact, they did not "see" the simpler method until it was pointed out to them. The set group had, in Gestalt terms, been fixated on the more complex method.

## Evaluating Gestalt theory and its legacy

The Gestalt psychologists attacked associationist views from two sides. First, they tried to show that problem solving was something more than the "mere" reproduction of learned responses; that it involved the productive processes of insight and restructuring. Recall Maier's demonstration of the

## TABLE 14.1

Shortest set of moves to solution in the Luchins water-jug problem ( 8– 8, 5–0, 3– 0)

| States | Jar 1 | Jar 2 | Jar 3 |
|---|---|---|---|
| Initial | 8–8 | 5–0 | 3–0 |
| Intermediate | 8–3 | 5–5 | 3–0 |
| | 8–3 | 5–2 | 3–3 |
| | 8–6 | 5–2 | 3–0 |
| | 8–6 | 5–0 | 3–2 |
| | 8–1 | 5–5 | 3–2 |
| | 8–1 | 5–4 | 3–3 |
| Goal | 8–4 | 5–4 | 3–0 |

effects of the "swing" hint on the solution of the two-string problem. Second, they showed that problem solving that relied solely on past experience often led to failure; recall the demonstrations of problem-solving set (where a routine method is used) and functional fixedness (when the typical function of an object is assumed).

Gestalt theory was based on a perceptual metaphor carried over from their perceptual theories (and everyday life?). This metaphor makes the theory very attractive and comprehensible but it is also its main weakness. The concepts of "insight" and "restructuring" are attractive because they are easily understood and convey something of the mysterious dynamism of human creativity. However, as theoretical constructs they are radically underspecified (see Chapter 1); the conditions under which insight and restructuring occur were unclear and the theory did not really specify the nature of either concept. However, the Gestalt work is not a Jurassic creature to be buried in the cemetery of psychological theory. In many ways the spirit of Gestalt research, with its emphasis on the productive and non-associationistic nature of thinking, informed the information-processing approach that followed some decades later (Holyoak, 1991; Knoblich & Wartenberg, 1998; Ohlsson, 1984a, 1992). The school also left a large corpus of experimental materials (in the form of problems) and evidence that had to be re-interpreted by later information-processing theory (see later sections). The Gestalt legacy was, therefore, substantial.

## NEWELL AND SIMON'S PROBLEM-SPACE THEORY

The problem-solving research of Allen Newell and Herb Simon, of Carnegie-Mellon University, is the very foundation of the information-processing framework. In the late 1950s, they produced the first computational models of psychological phenomena and made milestone discoveries in cognitive psychology and artificial intelligence. Their problem-space theory of problem solving, recounted in their 1972 magnum opus entitled *Human Problem Solving*, remains at the centre of current problem-solving research. In fact, many of the remaining areas reviewed in this chapter and the next are elaborations of Newell and Simon's basic views.

## Problem-space theory

It is very natural to think of problems as being solved through the exploration of different paths to a solution. This is literally the case in finding your way through a labyrinth. You start from a point outside the maze and then progress through it to the centre. On your way, you reach junctions where you have to choose between going straight on, turning to the left or right, or turning back. Each of these alternative paths may branch again and again so that, in the maze as a whole, there are hundreds of alternative paths (only some of which will lead to the centre). Different strategies can be used to find one's way through a labyrinth (e.g., mark your past path, initially always take the left turn). Umberto Eco's (1984) novel *The Name of the Rose* gives a vivid description of using several strategies to pass through a deadly, monastery labyrinth. These strategies provide you with a systematic method for searching the maze and help you to select one from among the many alternative paths.

Newell and Simon used parallels to these basic ideas to characterise human problem-solving behaviour. They suggested that the objective structure of a problem can be characterised as a set of states, beginning from an initial state (e.g., standing outside the maze), involving many intermediate states (e.g., moving through the maze), and ending with a goal state (e.g., being at the centre of the maze). Just as in the labyrinth, actions can be performed or "operators applied" (e.g., turn left, turn right). The application of these operators results in a move from one state to another. In any given state there may be several different operators that apply (e.g., turn left, turn right, go back) and each of these will generate numerous alternative states. Thus, there is a whole space of possible states and paths through this space (only some of which will lead to the goal state). *This problem space describes the abstract structure of a problem.*

Newell and Simon take the further step of proposing that when people solve problems they pass

**Panel 14.1: Problem-space theory**

- For any given problem there are a large number of alternative paths from an initial state to a goal state; the total set of such states, as generated by the legal operators, is called the basic problem space.
- People's problem-solving behaviour can be viewed as the production of knowledge states by the application of mental operators, moving from an initial knowledge state to a goal knowledge state.
- Mental operators encode legal moves that can be made and restrictions that explicitly disallow a move if certain conditions hold.
- People use their knowledge and various heuristic methods (like means–end analysis) to search through the problem space and to find a path from the initial state to the goal state.
- All of these processes occur within the limits of a particular cognitive system; that is, there may be working-memory limitations and limitations on the speed with which information can be stored and retrieved from long-term memory.

*People go through various paths in their head*

through similar *knowledge states* in their heads. They begin at an initial knowledge state and *search through a space of alternative mental states until they reach a goal knowledge state*. Moves from one knowledge state to the next are achieved by the application of *mental operators*. As a given problem may have a large number of alternative paths, people use strategies (or heuristic methods) to move from the initial state to the goal state, efficiently. Search may also be reduced by breaking the initial goal into subgoals which, when achieved, lead to the goals; for instance, if your goal is "to get to the shop before it closes" you might generate the three subgoals of "find a map", "plan the shortest route", and "find a mode of transport faster than walking" to achieve the goal. All in all, the knowledge a person brings to the problem is critical; the person's conception of a problem (i.e., how they represent the initial state) and the knowledge they bring to it (the operators and strategies available to them) critically determine the observed problem-solving behaviour. Problem-space theory is summarised in Panel 14.1 (see Newell, 1990; Newell & Simon, 1972; Simon, 1978):

This theory pins down in explicit representational terms the various hypothetical knowledge states and processes that are used to solve many different problems. It also makes predictions about

what makes a problem difficult; for example, the size of the search space is clearly important to problem-solving success and the interaction between it and the method people use to search this space. Newell and Simon's theory has been implemented in computer programs that usually take the form of production systems (see Chapter 1). In these models, the various knowledge states are held in a working memory, and long-term memory consists of a set of productions that encode the operators that modify these states in working memory. Their now-famous model was called the *General Problem Solver* (GPS; see Newell, Shaw, & Simon, 1958, 1960) which has grown and been developed into the *Soar* cognitive architecture in the 1990s (Newell, 1990; Polk & Newell, 1995). Let us consider a typical problem to which the theory has been applied.

## Problem-space theory and the Tower of Hanoi

In the "Tower of Hanoi" problem, subjects are presented with three vertical pegs in a row, the first of which has a number of disks piled on it in order of size; that is, the largest disk is at the bottom, the next largest on top of it and so on to the smallest at the top (see Figure 14.5). The goal

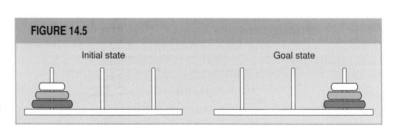

**FIGURE 14.5**

Initial state          Goal state

The initial state and goal state in the Tower of Hanoi problem.

FIGURE 14.6

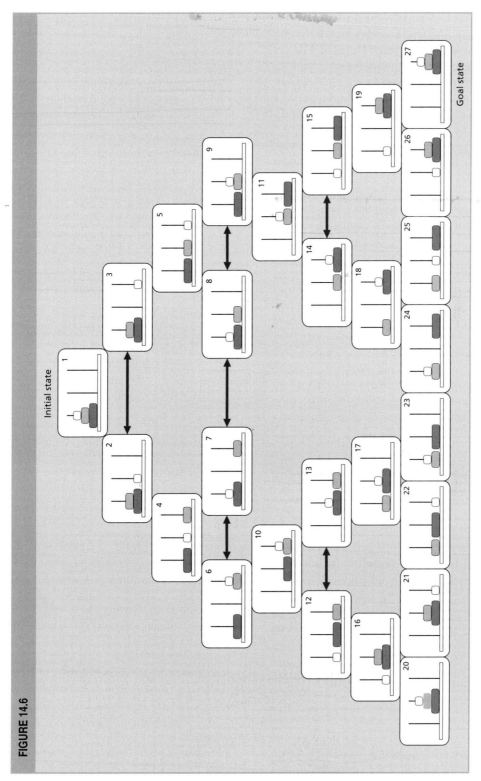

The problem space of legal moves in the Tower of Hanoi problem. If boxes touch each other, or are joined by arrows, this indicates that one can move from one state to the other using a legal operator.

of the problem is to have all the disks piled in the same order on the last peg. However, disks can only be moved in certain ways. Only one disk can be moved at a time and a larger disk cannot be placed on top of a smaller disk. The standard version of the problem uses three disks. Figure 14.6 shows some of the legal states that make up the search space of the problem.

The state described in the problem statement, where all the disks are stacked on the first peg, is the *initial knowledge state*, and the *goal knowledge state* consists of all the disks stacked on the last peg, in order of size. Subjects can use *mental operators* that move disks from one peg to another, with the restriction that no move places a larger disk on a smaller disk. This gives rise to varying numbers of alternative states after each possible move. From the initial state, if one applies the move operation, two alternative new states are possible; moving the small disk from the first peg to either the second or the third peg (i.e., states 2 and 3 in Figure 14.6, respectively). Each of these intermediate states can, in turn, give rise to several alternatives (see Figure 14.6). The number of these alternative states, between the initial and goal state, increases rapidly. In order to solve the problem people have to use a variety of strategies to reduce the number of states they have to pass through to reach the goal. Newell and Simon described several such strategies, which they called *heuristic methods* or *heuristics*.

Heuristics are to be contrasted with algorithms. An *algorithm* is a method or procedure that will definitely solve a problem, if it is applied and if a solution exists. For example, one could use a "check-every-state algorithm" to solve the Tower of Hanoi problem; by starting at the beginning and systematically checking every alternative state until the goal state is encountered. This method will take a long time and be inefficient but it is guaranteed to solve the problem. *Heuristics* are "rules-of-thumb" that do not guarantee a solution to the problem, but more often than not they will succeed and save a lot of time and effort in the process.

One of the most important heuristic methods proposed by Newell and Simon was means–ends

analysis. Means–ends analysis consists of the following steps:

- Note the difference between the current state and the goal state.
- Create a subgoal to reduce this difference.
- Select an operator that will solve this subgoal.

To illustrate means–ends analysis, let us assume that a problem solver is two steps off solving the Tower of Hanoi problem in state 15 in Figure 14.6. At this point, three possible moves can be made (i.e., state 11, 14, 19), but only one of these moves will bring you closer to solving the problem (see state 19 in Figure 14.6). Means–ends analysis proposes that you first note the difference between the current state and the goal state; here the important thing to notice is that the medium disk is on the second peg instead of the third peg. Second, establish the subgoal of reducing this difference; create the new subgoal of moving the medium disk to the third peg. Third, select an operator that solves this subgoal and apply it. So, the medium disk will be moved to the third peg and the problem will move closer to its solution. If you then apply this method again, the goal state will be reached in the next step of the problem. Means–ends analysis can be applied from the initial state of the problem to select a set of operators that will construct a path from this state to the goal state. However, as with any heuristic method, it is not guaranteed to be successful in every case where is it applied.

## Goal–subgoal structures in problem solving

The generation of appropriate subgoals on the way to solving the main goal is important to successful problem solving. So, if you can structure a problem into appropriate subgoals—such as "attempt to get the largest disk onto the third peg"—then problem-solving performance should improve. One possible source of such subgoal structures should be prior experience on related problems.

Several researchers have tested this prediction (Egan & Greeno, 1974; Luger, 1976). For instance,

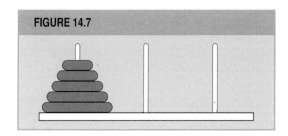

**FIGURE 14.7**

The initial state of the five-disk version of the Tower of Hanoi problem used by Anzai and Simon (1979).

Egan and Greeno (1974) gave different groups of subjects complex five- and six-disk versions of the Tower of Hanoi. Experimental groups received prior experience on three-disk and four-disk problems, whereas controls did not. Egan and Greeno found that subjects with prior experience on the easier problems, which instilled an appropriate goal structure, showed some benefits. Furthermore, the error profiles (as measured by any deviation from the minimal solution path for each problem) indicated that subjects performed better as they neared important goals/subgoals and, conversely, tended to experience more difficulty when they were far from an important goal.

### Learning different strategies

Egan and Greeno's work illustrates the effects that experience can have on subjects' ability to solve the problem. Egan and Greeno's subjects adopted the strategy of partitioning a complex problem into several simpler sub-problems and then solving each of these in turn. Anzai and Simon (1979) examined other strategies adopted by a single subject in four successive attempts to solve a five-disk version of the Tower of Hanoi (see Figure 14.7).

On each of the four attempts the subject used a different strategy, becoming progressively more efficient at solving the problem. Initially, the subject seemed to explore the problem space without much planning of moves. Search at this stage seemed to be guided by avoidance of certain states rather than moves towards definite goal/subgoal states. Anzai and Simon argued that the subject was using general *domain-independent strategies*.

These strategies included a *loop-avoidance strategy* to avoid returning to previously visited states and a heuristic strategy that preferred shorter sequences of moves to achieve a goal, to longer sequences. These general strategies allowed the subject to learn better sequences of moves, and these sequences were carried forward to be used in later attempts to solve the problem. Anzai and Simon developed an adaptive production system model that learned in the same manner. This model could create new production rules that were used to solve the problem on a later attempt. From Anzai and Simon's research, the general course of learning in these situations hinges on the initial use of general, domain-independent heuristics which then allow one to learn domain-dependent or domain-specific heuristics (see also Anderson's, 1993, 1996 ACT-R theory).

### Isomorphic problems: Understanding and problem representation

Clearly, the way you understand a problem should influence your ability to solve it. This intuition is specified in problem-space theory and has been borne out by a variety of findings on solving isomorphic problems. Two things are isomorphic if they have the same form or relational structure. So, in problem-space terms, two problems can be isomorphic if there is a one-to-one correspondence between the states and operators of the problems such that whenever two states are connected by an operator in one problem space, corresponding states are connected by the corresponding operator in the other problem space. Research has shown that slight differences in the way isomorphic problems are presented have significant effects on subjects' problem-solving success, presumably because the presentational differences affect their understanding of the problem. Furthermore, problem-space theory is specific enough to allow one to pinpoint what it is about subjects' understanding of the problem that causes these effects.

Several studies of this type have been performed on variants of the Tower of Hanoi (see Hayes & Simon, 1974, 1977; Simon & Hayes, 1976). In one study, Simon and Hayes (1976) used

**FIGURE 14.8**

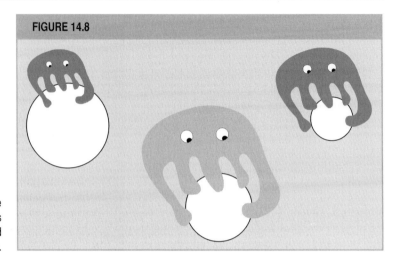

A pictorial representation of the initial state of the monsters-globes problem. Adapted from Simon and Hayes (1976).

problem isomorphs about a tea ceremony involving three different people (corresponding to the three pegs) carrying out three ritual tasks for one another (like the three disks) in differing orders of importance (like disks of different sizes). In other studies, Hayes and Simon used isomorphs to the Tower of Hanoi that involved monsters and globes. In the basic, monster–globe problem there are three monsters of different sizes (small, medium, and large), each holding different-sized globes (that are small, medium, and large). The small monster is holding the large globe; the medium-sized monster the small globe, and the large monster the medium-sized globe. The goal is to achieve a state in which each monster is holding a globe proportionate to its size (e.g., the small monster holding the smallest globe). However, monster etiquette demands that (i) only one globe is transferred at a time, (ii) if a monster is holding two globes, only the larger of the two is transferred, and (iii) a globe may not be transferred to a monster who is holding a larger globe. This monster–globe problem is, thus, a *move* problem with an isomorphic problem space to the Tower of Hanoi problem.

Simon and Hayes also had a *change* version of the monster–globe problem with the same monsters and globes but subjects had to shrink and expand the globes held by the monsters rather than moving them; the rules were that (i) only one globe may be changed (i.e., shrunk

or expanded) at a time, (ii) if two globes have the same size, only the globe held by the largest monster may be changed, and (iii) a globe may not be changed to the same size as the globe of a larger monster.

Hayes and Simon's *rule-application hypothesis* predicted that the move version of the monster–globe problem should be easier than the change version, because the rules in the latter were more difficult to apply (i.e., they involved complex tests to determine legal operations). What they found was that the move problem was twice as easy as the change problem (see Hayes & Simon, 1977; see Figure 14.8). However, apart from Hayes and Simon's rule-application hypothesis, Kotovsky, Hayes, and Simon (1985) proposed that a *rule-learning hypothesis* could also account for the data. That is, that some rules can be learned more easily than others and this contributes to the ease with which the problem is solved. In fact, Kotovsky et al. found evidence, from a task in which subjects simply learned the move and change rules, that they took longer to learn the change rules than the move rules. They also showed that the general ease of rule learning and rule application was likely to be influenced by (i) the extent to which the rules are consistent with real-world knowledge, (ii) the memory load inherent in the problem; that is, how much of the problem solving could be performed in an external memory (e.g., on paper) rather than in working memory, (iii) whether the rules could be easily organised in a spatial fashion or more easily imagined.

Further work on the sources of difficulty in problems has emerged from tests of isomorphism of another problem: the Chinese ring puzzle (see Kotovsky & Simon, 1990). In the original version, this puzzle involves a complex arrangement of five interconnected metal rings on a bar, the task being to remove the rings from the bar (see Afriat, 1982). This puzzle has two important characteristics: (i) what constitutes a move is not immediately obvious, because the rings can be twisted and turned in a number of ways, (ii) the problem space of moves, once found, is linear (i.e., a straight line of moves with no branching). The latter ensures that problem difficulty—which is considerable for this problem—cannot emerge from searching the problem space, but must be due to discovering how to make moves. Kotovsky and Simon developed a digitised version of this puzzle, involving the moving of five balls out of boxes. Their study showed that the major source of difficulty lay in discovering what a legal move was, rather than navigating through the problem space.

## Solving the missionaries and cannibals puzzle

Problem-space theory has also been applied, with some success, to the missionaries–cannibals puzzle. In this problem, you are given the task of transferring three missionaries and three cannibals across a river in a boat. As the boat is fairly small, only two or fewer people can be taken across in it at a time and someone must always accompany the boat back to the other side. Furthermore, at no point in the problem can there be more cannibals than missionaries left on one bank of the river or else the cannibals will have a religious feast. Figure 14.9 shows the legal search space for reaching the goal state. Researchers have argued that people use a variety of heuristics to solve different variants of this problem.

Thomas (1974) used a variant of this problem involving J.R.R. Tolkien's (1966) hobbits and orcs, in which orcs have a proclivity for gobbling up hobbits. He showed that at some points in the

problem—especially states 5 and 8 in Figure 14.9 —subjects took considerably longer and produced more errors than at other points. Thomas maintained that the difficulties experienced at these states had different cognitive sources. In the case of the state 5, the difficulty lies in the many alternative moves that are possible at this point (five in number). Only two of these moves are illegal and of the remaining three legal moves, only one is really helpful. In the case of state 8, subjects are misled because they need to move away from the goal state in order to get closer to it. As can be seen in Figure 14.9, in going from state 8 to state 9, one enters a state that seems further away than closer to the goal. At this point, subjects typically think that they have reached a blind alley and start to backtrack. Figure 14.10 shows the distribution of incorrect responses by Thomas' subjects at each state in the problem.

Thomas also suggested that subjects made three or four major planning decisions in solving the problem, and having made each of these decisions, carried out whole blocks of moves with increasing speed. Then, at the beginning of each planned sequence of moves, there would be a long pause before the next decision was made. Thomas' statistical analysis of the distributions of subjects' times-to-move supported this hypothesis.

Other researchers have looked at more complex versions of the problem and noted strategic changes in subjects' behaviour. Simon and Reed (1976) investigated a version of the missionaries–cannibals problem, involving five missionaries and five cannibals. This problem is more complex in that it has many more legal states even though it can be solved in just 11 moves. However, on average, subjects take 30 moves to solve the problem. Simon and Reed suggested that there were three main strategies used in solving the problem. Initially, subjects adopted a *balancing strategy* whereby they simply tried to ensure that equal numbers of missionaries and cannibals remained on either side of the river. This strategy avoids illegal moves, resulting in more cannibals than missionaries on either bank of the river. At a certain point, subjects become more oriented towards the goal state and adopt a *means–ends strategy*. This strategy is manifested by a tendency to move more people to the goal-side of the river.

**FIGURE 14.9**

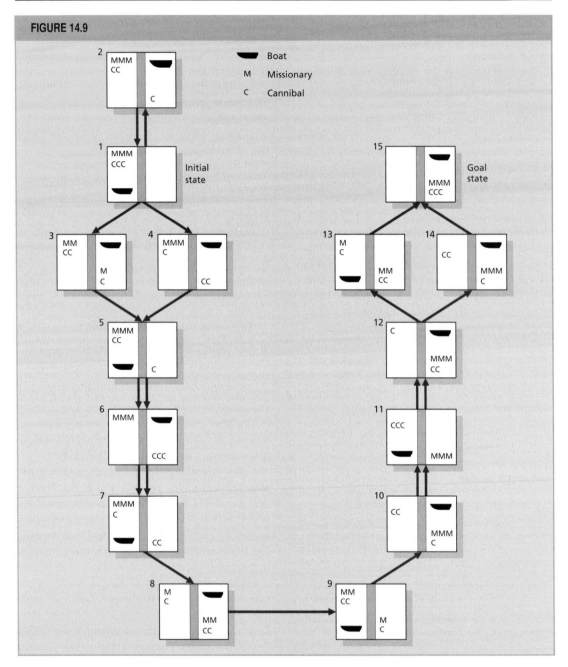

The search space intervening between the initial state and goal state of the missionaries–cannibals problem (M indicates a missionary and C a cannibal).

Finally, subjects use a simple *anti-looping heuristic* to avoid moves that reverse the immediately-preceding move.

Simon and Reed maintained that the key to efficient solution of the problem rested on a *strategy shift* from the balancing strategy to the means–ends strategy. The problem with the balancing strategy is that it leads one into blind-alley states in the problem. Thus, they predicted that any manipulation that increased the probability of a

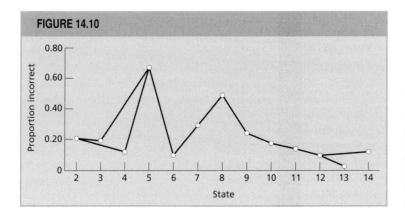

**FIGURE 14.10**

The proportion of incorrect responses in the various states of the hobbits–orcs problem (an isomorph of the missionaries–cannibals problem) from Thomas (1974). It shows the difficulties that subjects experience in states 5 and 8.

strategy shift would result in improved performance on solving the problem. In an experiment designed to test this prediction, a control group of subjects received the problem to solve with no hints, and an experimental group was given, as a hint, a subgoal to achieve on the way to solving the problem. This hint suggested that subjects should work to reach a state where three cannibals were on the goal-side of the river on their own without a boat. As this subgoal involves a state where there are unequal numbers of missionaries and cannibals on either side of the river, it was expected that this subgoal should discourage the use of the balancing strategy early on. This prediction was confirmed. Subjects in the experimental group tended to shift strategies after about four moves, whereas those in the control group only shifted after about 15 moves. Figure 14.11 shows the much better performance of subjects in the subgoal condition versus controls who were not given the subgoal.

## EVALUATING RESEARCH ON PUZZLES

The research on solving puzzles in cognitive psychology has been one of the most successful areas in the discipline. Since it was first proposed in the later 1950s, problem-space theory has been quite successful and has continued to expand steadily to encompass more and more problem-solving phenomena. Later on in this and the next chapter we will look at some further extensions

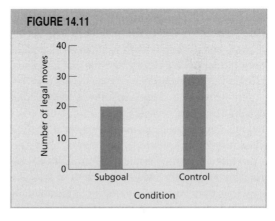

**FIGURE 14.11**

The mean number of legal moves made by subjects in the subgoal and control conditions of Simon and Reed (1976).

of the theory. But before we do this it is perhaps a good idea to review the progress afforded by puzzle problems.

### Benefits of problem-space research on puzzles

Newell and Simon's problem-space theory makes substantial and fundamental contributions to cognitive theory and to our understanding of people's problem-solving abilities. Theoretically, a fundamental contribution of problem-space theory that cannot be overstated, is that it contains a *normative theory* of problem solving. It allows us to specify the structure of problems in an idealised way and to define the best solution to a problem. For most of the puzzles described here we can elaborate the problem space and point to the *correct/best* solution to the problem by tracing the shortest sequence of moves from the initial state to the goal state. Thus, in a normative way, the theory tells us what an ideal thinker should do in this problem. From an empirical standpoint, such a normative theory allows us to look at how and why people's behaviour deviates from the ideal. We can also say what heuristic (or combination of heuristics) are the optimal ones to use to solve the problem successfully. The normative theory also allows us to determine when problems are structurally the same, even when they appear to be very different (i.e., problem isomorphs). Cognitive psychologists often borrow normative theories from other disciplines; for instance, in deductive reasoning, logic is used as the normative theory (see Chapter 16). One of the incredible things about Newell and Simon's work is that they created *both* the normative theory and the psychological research that followed.

Problem-space theory advances our understanding of a very complex, cognitive ability. Even though the research on puzzles is on a specific class of problems, which may be a long way from more everyday problems, it provides a solid foundation for other work. Research always has to start somewhere, and islands of understanding have to be built up. From these islands, our understanding can then extend to more complicated, real-world situations. Problem-space theory provides us with a specific account of the following:

- How people solve puzzles by applying very general rules (heuristics) to reduce the complexity of alternative solutions that are possible.
- The type of learning that can occur in problem solving; namely, the acquisition and development of different strategies for solving problems (see Anzai & Simon, 1979).
- How the understanding of a problem can affect subsequent problem-solving performance (cf. the monster–globe problems).

The problem-space account also has the following features:

- It is general enough to characterise different puzzle problems, showing the theoretical unity in many diverse instances of problem solving.

- It allows us to re-interpret previous research on other problems in an informative fashion (i.e., insight problems).
- It supports the standard model of memory with a limited-capacity working memory, that can retard problem-solving abilities (see Atwood & Polson, 1976, discussed later).

As we shall see in later chapters, these benefits extend outwards to other areas of problem solving and thinking.

## Limitations of problem-space research on puzzles

Having stated the benefits that have followed from puzzle research, it is also important to be clear about the limitations of this research. There is a question mark hanging over the ecological validity of these puzzle problems. They are a special class of problems that have different properties to other problems; indeed, extensions to problem-space theory are needed to extend the generality of the theory to other classes of problems.

Puzzle problems have several contrasting properties with more mundane problems. First, puzzle problems are unfamiliar problems about which we have little knowledge (this is less the case for some insight problems, like the two-string problem). Many of the problems encountered in everyday life require considerable amounts of knowledge. Second, the knowledge required to solve puzzle problems is present in the statement of the problem. In everyday life all the information required to solve problems is often not present. In fact, much of the difficulty in everyday problems may hinge on finding the relevant information in memory or the environment required to solve the problem. If you have to buy a house, you need to know all about mortgages and current houses on sale, and finding this information is a significant part of solving the problem. Third, the requirements in puzzle problems are relatively unambiguous; the start state and goal state are clearly specified and what can and cannot be done in the problems is known (i.e., the legal moves). In everyday problems, the real difficulty may amount to specifying the nature of the goal state. For instance, doing a masters or doctoral thesis is essentially a matter of specifying where you want to end up.

In short, problem-space theory on puzzles concentrates on *well defined* as opposed to *ill defined problems* (Reitman, 1965; Simon, 1973, 1978). In *well defined problems* the operators, initial state, and goal state are well specified and subjects tend to have little *specific knowledge* about the problem. These problems tend to be solved by so-called *general-purpose* or *domain-independent heuristics*. That is, heuristics that can be applied to a wide range of situations and domains. They are rules that do not involve specific knowledge of the domain. In artificial intelligence, heuristics of this type are often called *universal, weak methods*. They are "universal" because they can be applied in many domains and they are "weak" because they are often not very efficient. For instance, solving one of these puzzles takes time using means–ends analysis. However, if one had rules that were specific to the problem-solving domain, the solution could be found more rapidly.

In contrast, *ill defined problems* can be under-specified in many ways and require the use of substantial amounts of *domain-specific knowledge*. The initial state of an ill defined problem may be uncertain; what is and is not part of the initial state may be unclear from the situation. If someone locks their keys inside their car, it is clear that the car and the keys locked in it are part of the initial state, but coat-hangers, brooms, the police, and owners of cars of a same make are also potentially part of the initial state. Second, the operators and operator restrictions may have to be discovered and/or created. You may have to undo some of the implicit constraints in the problem. You may have to dredge your memory for suitable operators (e.g., using a coat-hanger in a certain way, forcing a back window, finding a route into the car through the boot). Finally, the goal state may need definition. On the face of it, getting into the car is a reasonable goal state, but smashing a window to do this does not seem like a good solution; so you may want to define the goal further, to stipulate that you should get into the car without doing much damage. But what constitutes "much damage"? Ill definition and

knowledge go hand in hand because usually ill defined problems are defined through the application of knowledge. Later, we will see how people use domain-specific knowledge when they are experts in an area, based on an extension of problem-space theory. In conclusion, problem-space theory provides an adequate treatment of well defined problems, but has to be extended in order to deal with more ill defined problems.

## RE-INTERPRETING THE GESTALT FINDINGS

We began this chapter by considering the perceptual theories of problem solving proposed by the Gestalt school of psychology. The information-processing approach has inherited the burden of re-interpretation or explanation of the findings of Gestalt research in information-processing terms (see Chapter 1). This re-conception of things past has been carried out since the 1970s (see e.g., Holyoak, 1991; Keane, 1985a, 1989; Knoblich, Ohlsson, Haider, & Rhenius, 2000; Knoblich & Wartenberg, 1998; Metcalfe, 1986a; Newell, 1980; Ohlsson, 1984a, 1985, 1992; Simon, 1986; Weisberg, 1980; Weisberg & Alba, 1981; Weisberg & Suls, 1973).

### Problem-space models of water-jug problems

We saw earlier that water-jug problems were intensively investigated by Gestalt researchers (see Luchins & Luchins, 1959, 1991). These problems are very amenable to a treatment in terms of problem-space theory. In the 8–8, 5–0, and 3–0 problem we encountered earlier (see Table 14.1), the initial state consists of the largest jug being full of water and the other two jugs empty, and the goal state has four pints of water in the largest- and middle-sized jugs with nothing in the smallest. The operators consist of pouring various amounts of water from one jug to another and the operator restrictions are that the water cannot be added to or flung away while solving the problem.

Atwood and Polson (1976) produced a state–space analysis of these problems in the context of a full process model for explaining subjects' behaviour on water-jug problems. They specified the various heuristic methods used by subjects and included assumptions about the limitations on human information processing (i.e., working memory limitations). Their model had the following main points:

- In planning moves, subjects only look ahead to a depth of one move.
- Moves are evaluated using a means–ends analysis method, where subjects look at the difference between the actual and goal quantities in the two largest jugs and see which of the next alternative states will bring them closer to the goal state.
- Subjects tend to avoid moves that return them to immediately preceding states (an anti-looping heuristic).
- There are limitations on the number of possible alternative moves that can be stored in working memory.
- This limitation can be somewhat alleviated by transferring information into long-term memory.

This model makes predictions about the difficulties that people should encounter in solving water-jug problems, which Atwood and Polson (1976) tested. They were particularly interested in two problems: one involving jugs of 8, 5, and 3 units, and one involving jugs of 24, 21, and 3 units. In both cases, the largest jug is filled and the other jugs are empty, and the goal is to distribute the largest jug's contents evenly between the largest and middle jugs. Both problems are isomorphic in the number of moves one needs to consider to solve the problem. Their model predicted that the 8–8, 5–0, 3–0 problem should be harder than the 24–24, 21–0, 3–0, because the latter could be solved by simply applying the means–ends heuristic whereas the former required a violation of this heuristic. Their results showed that the mean number of moves to solve either problem confirmed this prediction.

Atwood, Masson, and Polson (1980) also tested the proposal that subjects only planned one move ahead to avoid overloading working memory.

They assumed that any reduction of the memory load should have the effect of freeing up the problem solver for more long-term planning. To achieve this manipulation they provided subjects with information about all the different moves available from any state in the problem. One group of subjects received even more information in the form of a record of the previous states they had visited. However, although Atwood et al. discovered that the more information subjects received the fewer the number of moves they needed to consider in solving the problem, they did not find the big "planning improvement" they expected. It seems that when the information load is lifted subjects do not use the extra capacity to plan ahead, but rather become more efficient at avoiding states that lead them back to the initial state of the problem.

On the whole, this sort of model has been shown to be very useful. Jeffries, Polson, Razan, and Atwood (1977) and Polson and Jeffries (1982) have extended it to apply to versions of the missionaries–cannibals and Tower of Hanoi problems. So, the model combines predictive specificity with some generality in its applicability.

## Problem-space accounts of insight and restructuring

Weisberg and Alba (1981) re-examined the nine-dot problem (see Figure 14.4). In Scheerer's (1963) original paper on the nine-dot problem, he had argued that subjects failed to solve the problem because they assumed that the lines drawn had to stay within the square shape formed by the dots; they were "fixated" on the Gestalt of the nine dots. To test this Weisberg and Alba gave subjects a hint that they could draw lines outside the square. However, with this hint, only 20% solved the problem. They, therefore, concluded that fixation on the square of dots was not the only factor responsible for subjects' failures. In further experiments, Weisberg and Alba used simpler versions of the problem (a four-dot task) and explored the use of specific hints (e.g., drawing some of the lines that lead to the solution). From these experiments they concluded that in order to solve the problem subjects required highly

**Panel 14.2: Ohlsson's (1992) insight theory**

- The representation of insight problems is a matter of interpretation; so there may be many different mental representations of the same problem (i.e. the problems are ill-defined).
- People have many knowledge operators for solving problems, and therefore operators may have to be retrieved from memory; the retrieval mechanism is spreading activation.
- The current representation of the problem acts as a memory probe for relevant operators in memory.
- Impasses occur because the initial representation of the problem is a bad memory probe for retrieving the operators needed to solve the problem.
- Impasses are broken when the representation of the problem is changed (is re-interpreted, re-represented, or restructured) thus forming a new memory probe that allows the retrieval of the relevant operators.
- This re-representation can occur through (i) elaboration, adding new information about the problem from inference or the environment (e.g. hints), (ii) constraint relaxation, changing some of the constraints on the goal, (iii) re-encoding, changing aspects of the problem representation through re-categorisation or deleting some information (e.g., re-categorising the pliers in the two-string problem as a *building material* rather than a *tool*).
- After an impasse is broken a full or partial insight may occur; a full insight occurs if the retrieved operators bridge the gap between the impasse state and the goal state.

problem-specific knowledge. In their eyes, this undercut the Gestalt concepts of "insight" and "fixation", which they argued were of dubious explanatory value (see also Weisberg, 1986).

However, several other researchers have argued and shown that the notion of "insight" is a key part of problem-solving theory (see Dominowski, 1981; Ellen, 1982; Lung & Dominowski, 1985; Metcalfe, 1986a; Ohlsson, 1992; Simon, 1986). For example, Metcalfe (1986a, 1986b; Metcalfe & Weibe, 1987) asked subjects for their metacognitions—their assessment of their feeling-of-knowing a solution or feelings-of-closeness to a solution—on insight problems and trivia questions they were unable to answer. She found that although people had reasonably accurate metacognitions for the memory/trivia questions they had no predictive metacognitions for the insight problems. This indicates that the insight problems were not solved by an incremental accumulation of information from memory, but by a sudden illumination, which is best described as "insight".

Other theorists, like Ohlsson (1984a, b, 1985, 1992), have tried to re-assess the Gestalt constructs of insight and restructuring in problem-space terms, rather than rejecting them (for related ideas see Keane, 1985b, 1989; Langley & Jones, 1988). Ohlsson's (1992) position is that "insight occurs in the context of an impasse, which is unmerited in the sense that the thinker is, in fact, competent to solve the problem" (p. 4). The impasse is unmerited because the thinker has the knowledge to solve the problem, but for some reason or another cannot use it. Given this definition, Ohlsson maintains that a theory of insight has to explain three things: (i) why the impasse is encountered, (ii) how the impasse is broken, (iii) what happens after it is broken. Ohlsson's theory is summarised in Panel 14.2.

This account is consistent with the known evidence on insight problems and is supported by more recent research (Isaac & Just, 1995; Kaplan & Simon, 1990; Richard, Poitrenaud, & Tijus, 1993; Yaniv & Meyer, 1987). Yaniv and Meyer (1987) have demonstrated in another feeling-of-knowing experiment that unsuccessful attempts to retrieve inaccessible stored information can prime the recognition of later information by a process of spreading activation. Here initial retrieval attempts lead to a spread of activation from some concepts to other concepts in memory. This spread of activation then sensitises the problem solver to other, new information in the environment needed for an insightful solution (e.g., hints, or noticing that the swinging string in the two-string problem provides a solution).

The constraint relaxation proposals of the theory have been more directly tested by Knoblich et al. (1999) using matchstick algebra problems (see Figure 14.12). In these problems, the goal is to move a single stick in such a way that the initial false statement is transformed into a true statement, without discarding any sticks. Therefore, a move consists of moving rotating or sliding

IMPASSE – a situation where progression is blocked.

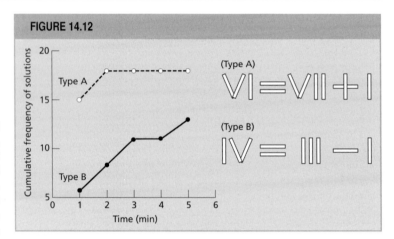

Two of the matchstick problems used by Knoblich et al. (1999), and the cumulative solution rates produced to these types of problems in their study. Copyright © 1999 by the American Psychological Association. Reprinted with permission.

a single stick. For example, the false equation shown as Type A in Figure 14.12 can be changed into a true equation:

$$VII = VI + I$$

by moving the rightmost stick from III and putting it immediately to the right of V. Knoblich et al. (1999) argued that these problems are solved by relaxing the normal constraints of arithmetic; constraints we implicitly adopt about values, functions, and equality signs not usually considered to be arbitrarily modifiable. Furthermore, they proposed that people should find some of these constraints were easier to relax than others, depending to how radically a constraint changed the representation of the equation. For example, removing a stick from a value just changes the value in the equation, but removing a stick in the equality sign changes the whole equation. Based on these assumptions they defined sets of problems that they expected to be harder or easier to solve based on the different constraints that had to be relaxed in them. So, the "VI = VII + I" problem was predicted to be easier than the "IV = III − I" problem, because the former can be solved by relaxing the value of the equation whereas the latter involves relaxing constraints on the function and equality sign. Figure 14.12 shows a plots of the cumulative solution times produced to problems of these two different types, showing a marked difference in the difficulty of the two. Knoblich et al. found

substantial evidence to support a detailed analysis of the impact of different constraints on the solution of these insight problems.

## FROM PUZZLES TO EXPERTISE

We have seen that the key issue posed by the Gestalt school of psychology was whether problem solving was *productive* or *merely reproductive*, as the associationists claimed. Problem-space accounts of puzzle research can be read as support for the productive claim, as they show us that people have general heuristics that they can apply to situations about which they have little prior knowledge. Hence, they are not merely recollecting solutions to problems but actively and dynamically constructing solutions by applying different heuristics.

However, it is also true to say that there are many different ways to conceptualise reproductive problem solving, ways that are much richer and productive than the associationists ever imagined. More recent problem-solving research has shown that there are important reproductive components to problem solving. People can recall partial solutions and use prior knowledge to classify and define problems. Human problem solving seems to rely on a lot of specific knowledge about particular situations. Even though this is strictly-speaking "reproduced knowledge" it is not "mere reproduced knowledge" because of the amazing variety of this knowledge, the complexity of the mechanisms used to acquire it, and the flexibility of the ways in which it is used.

In much of the remainder of this chapter we turn to a consideration of this research, as it is represented by studies of expertise in thinking. Puzzle solving is only one branch of a large tree of problem types. Indeed, one could argue that puzzles are a fairly marginal type of problem. Many jobs in everyday life are concerned with solving specific problems based on expertise in an area. Most of the puzzles we have met were well defined, in the sense that the initial states, goal states, and operators were well specified. However, real-world problems tend to be ill defined rather than well defined.

In the next few sections, we consider how experts solve ill defined problems in specific domains like chess, physics, and computer programming. The keynote of this work is the importance of knowledge to the solution of ill defined problems. Problem-solving expertise hinges on having considerable knowledge of the problem domain; by definition, expertise means being good at specific problems in a specific domain. In the domain of physics, an undergraduate student has less knowledge than a lecturer. Even though both of them may have equivalent intellectual abilities, the differences in their knowledge makes one a *novice* and the other an *expert problem solver.* Many of the domains studied in expertise research have enormous practical significance and represent a major move in cognitive psychology away from laboratory-based puzzles and towards everyday, ecologically valid problems. We review chess, physics, and computer programming because they manifest several important theoretical and practical aspects of expertise research.

We have already seen the importance of problem representation in determining the difficulty of a problem. We also see that in expertise a major source of difficulty is the representation/definition of problems. Expert problem solvers have the right sorts of knowledge to encode problems easily and represent them optimally, whereas novices often lack this knowledge.

## The skill of chess masters

Differences in problem-solving expertise were first studied in the domain of chess. One view is that chess masters are masters because they have much specific knowledge about the game. Chess fits nicely into problem-space theory. The initial state of a game consists of all the pieces on the board in their starting positions, and the goal state is some specific checkmate against an opponent. Many alternative moves are possible from any state; from the initial state one can move legally any of the pawns or either of the knights. For each possible turn, a player can make one of a large number of replies and an opponent can counter each of these replies with many more moves and so on. In computational terms, one faces a "combinatorial explosion" of possibilities. The sheer number of possible paths is overwhelming; the problem space is truly vast. From the initial state after 2 ply (i.e., a turn each by both sides), given the 20 possible moves by both White and Black there are 400 possible positions. At only 6 ply from the opening position there are more than 9 million distinct board positions.

Most chess-playing computer programs search through a considerable number of alternatives and evaluate each alternative. For example, Newell and Simon (1972) reported a program called MANIAC, developed at Los Alamos in the 1950s, that explored nearly 1,000,000 moves at each turn. Even so MANIAC only considered each alternative move to a depth of four turns (an initial move, an opponent's reply, a reply to this move, and the opponent's counter move). Even with this brute-force computation, it did not play chess well and occasionally made serious mistakes. Current chess programs do almost unimaginable amounts of search. The current state-of-the-art, Deep Blue, considers 90 billion moves at each turn, at a rate of 9 billion a second; using this amount of search it beat the World Chess Champion, Gary Kasparov, in May 1997. People do not appear to (want to) search this much, so *something else* seems to underlie the expertise of chess masters.

## DeGroot's chess studies

DeGroot (1965, 1966; DeGroot & Gobet, 1996) provided the first indication of what this "something else" might be. DeGroot compared the performance of five grand masters and five expert players on choosing a move from a particular board position. He asked his subjects to think aloud and then determined the number and type of different moves they had considered. He found that grand masters did not consider more alternative moves than less expert players and did not search any deeper than expert players, although they took slightly less time to make a move. However, independent raters judged the final moves made by the masters to be better than those of expert players.

In contrast to chess programs, the human players manifested a paradoxical mix of laziness and efficiency. They tended to consider only around thirty alternative moves and about four alternative first-moves. At most, they searched to a depth of six turns although frequently they searched a lot less (see Charness, 1981a; Saariluoma, 1990, 1994). Wagner and Scurrah (1971) examined this behaviour in further detail and found evidence that chess players used a *progressive deepening* strategy (proposed by DeGroot). Players only check a small number of alternative first moves. These moves are then returned to repeatedly and explored to a greater depth each time that they are re-examined.

So, where do the essential differences lie between grand masters and experts, and between human players and computer players? DeGroot proposed that experts and masters differed in their knowledge of different board positions. Chess players study previous games and can recall their own games in detail. Therefore, good chess players recognise previous board positions and remember good moves to make from these positions. This use of prior knowledge excludes the need to entertain irrelevant moves and a host of alternatives. DeGroot argued that if chess players had stored previous board positions in some schematic fashion (see Chapter 9) then this knowledge should be reflected in tasks that measure memory.

Therefore, DeGroot gave subjects brief presentations of board positions from actual games (i.e., ranging from 2 to 15 seconds) and, after taking the board away, he asked them to reconstruct the positions. The main finding was that chess masters could recall the positions very accurately (91% correct), whereas less expert players made many more errors (41% correct). Thus, chess masters were better at recognising and encoding the various configurations of pieces than less expert players. Researchers working with DeGroot also found that when the pieces were randomly arranged on the board (i.e., were not arranged in a familiar configuration), both groups of players did equally badly. Neither group had the knowledge available to encode the unfamiliar configurations, although recent evidence has called this particular finding into question (Gobet & Simon, 1996a, b).

## Chunking in chess

Simon and his associates extended DeGroot's findings (see Figure 14.13; Chase & Simon, 1973a, b; Simon & Barenfeld, 1969; Simon & Gilmartin, 1973; but see Vincente & Brewer, 1993, on mistakes surrounding the uptake of DeGroot's work). Chase and Simon proposed that players "chunked" the board (see Miller, 1956; and Chapter 6); that they memorised board positions by breaking them down into seven or so familiar units in short-term memory. The essential difference between chess masters and expert players lay in the size of the chunk that they could encode. So, the seven chunks in a master's short-term memory contained more information than the seven chunks in a poorer player's memory.

Chase and Simon tested this hypothesis using a modified version of DeGroot's task. Chase and Simon asked their three subjects (a master, a class A player, and a beginner) to reconstruct a board position on a second chess board with the first board still in view. They recorded the number and type of pieces subjects placed on the second board after a glance at the first board, where successive trials (glances) were made to build up the full board of pieces. The chunking hypothesis predicts that players should only place a few

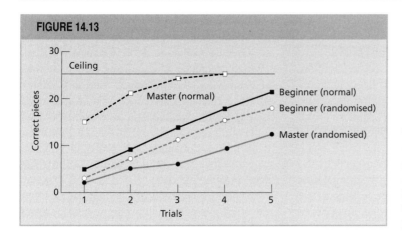

**FIGURE 14.13**

The number of pieces correctly recalled by masters and beginner chess players, from Chase and Simon (1973b), when they were presented with "normal" as opposed to randomised board positions.

pieces after each glance and that they should form some coherent whole. In each of the three players studied, Chase and Simon found that the average number of pieces taken in at a glance was small in number (i.e., about three) and similar in content. However, better players used significantly shorter glances to encode a chunk. Chase and Simon also discovered systematic differences in the number of pieces encoded in a chunk as a function of expertise. The strongest player encoded about 2.5 pieces per chunk, whereas the weakest player encoded only 1.9 pieces per chunk. Recent research suggests that this may have been an underestimate of the chunk-size of masters (Gobet & Simon, 1998b). So, Chase and Simon's results showed that expert players can recognise chunks in a board position more quickly and can encode more information in these chunks than novice players.

Chase and Simon also found similar effects to those of DeGroot on the encoding of random board positions; using a presentation time of 5 seconds there was no difference between their three subjects. However, recently, this finding has been questioned in a review of similar studies. Gobet and Simon (1996a) showed that across a dozen or so studies there is a correlation between skill level and recall performance of random positions, although it is rarely statistically significant. They maintained that strong players do have a superiority in recalling random positions but that it has been overlooked by the lack of statistical power in most experiments because the sample size is so small (e.g., three subjects). This proposal does not defeat the chunking hypothesis, it merely suggests that portions of even random positions may be encoded by the chunks possessed by experts.

*Theories and models of chess expertise*

These results have acted as an important target for theories of expert memory and the computational modelling of thinking. Simon and Gilmartin (1973) produced one of the earliest instantiations of the chunking theory, called the Memory-Aided Pattern Perceiver (MAPP). The model contained a large number of different board patterns and encoded a "presented" board configuration into its short-term memory, by recognising various chunks of the total configuration. Simon and Gilmartin produced one version of the program with more patterns than another version (1114 patterns vs. 894 patterns) and ran both versions on board-reconstruction tasks. They found that the version with fewer patterns performed the poorest. Thus, the model provided concrete support for the proposal that board-position knowledge was the key to understanding novice–expert differences in these tasks. Extrapolating from the model, Simon and Gilmartin estimated that master-level performance required a long-term memory of between 10,000 and 100,000 patterns.

Beyond chunking theory there are currently three other theories of chess expertise (see Ericsson & Lehmann, 1996; Gobet, 1998a, for reviews):

the SEEK theory (Holding, 1985, 1992), the long-term working memory theory (Ericsson & Staszewski, 1989; Ericsson & Kintsch, 1995) and the template theory (Gobet & Simon, 1996b, 1998a, 1998b, in press). The SEEK theory proposes that three elements are central to chess expertise: search, evaluation, and knowledge. Masters search more and better than weaker players, produce better evaluations of positions, and have much more knowledge. Although many aspects of the theory are ill specified (it has not been modelled computationally) there is evidence to support the importance of evaluative knowledge, as opposed to just board-position knowledge (see Charness, 1981b, 1991; Holding, 1985, 1989). Holding and Reynolds (1982) presented players, rated as being of high- or low-ability, with random board positions for 8 seconds and then again for 3 minutes to evaluate the strength of the position and decide on the next best move to make. They found that high-ability players produced better quality moves. So, even though the subjects had no specific schemata for these random board positions, they had other knowledge that allowed them to generate and evaluate potential moves from that position.

Ericsson and Kintsch's (1995) long-term working memory theory, which was reviewed earlier as a general account of many memory effects (see Chapter 6), critically makes use of similar assumptions to template theory (Gobet & Simon, 1996b). Both theories propose the idea that board-position knowledge is mediated by schematic retrieval structures; these are structures that are more general than actual board positions. In template theory these schemas, called *templates*, are an abstraction of a whole set of similar positions; the template encodes some invariant pieces and slots for other pieces that can change for this type of position (see Chapter 9). Importantly, the schema would also have associated knowledge on possible moves and general plans that follow from this type of position. These two theories are quite successful in dealing with a wide range of evidence in chess expertise; specifically, their proposed retrieval structures help to account for chess players' ability to give high-level accounts of the nature of a board position.

The mix of knowledge proposed in these theories (i.e., board positions, abstract schema,

evaluation knowledge) shows that expertise is not just about memory for routine problem solving (see Green & Gilhooly, 1992). Hatano and Inagaki (1986) have made a crucial distinction between different types of expertise; routine and adaptive expertise (see also Holyoak, 1991; Lamberts & Pfeifer, 1992). *Routine expertise* manifests itself in the ability to solve familiar, standard problems in an efficient manner; and probably relies on schemata that encode the routine, like standard board-position knowledge. *Adaptive expertise* works best on non-standard, unfamiliar problems and allows experts to develop *ad hoc* procedures and strategies for solving such problems. Evaluation knowledge seems to underlie adaptive expertise. It comes into play when a problem situation deviates from a known situation. In general, board-position knowledge allows the player to find out what parts of the board are relevant, whereas evaluation knowledge helps to develop moves from these positions and evaluate the consequences of these moves.

## Physics expertise

Anyone who has studied physics will recall (possibly with dread) problems like the following one:

A block of mass M is dropped from a height $x$ onto a spring of force constant $K$. Neglecting friction, what is the maximum distance the spring will be compressed?

People solve physics problems by selecting appropriate principles from the physics domain and deriving a solution through the application of these principles. A problem solver must analyse the problem, build some cognitive representation of it that cues relevant principles, and then strategically apply these principles to solve it. Clearly, if someone represents the problem incorrectly they are less likely to solve it. If we follow the hypotheses from chess research, we should expect experts to have a larger repertoire of problem-solving knowledge than novices. In physics, this knowledge takes the form of schemata that link problem situations to principles (see Chapter 9). Without this knowledge both groups should fall back on more heuristic knowledge similar to that used in puzzle problems (e.g., means–ends analysis; see earlier).

## Evidence of novice–expert differences in physics

It has been proposed that expert physicists build better representations of the problem than novices based on their schematic knowledge (Heller & Reif, 1984; Larkin, 1983, 1985). Chi, Feltovich, and Glaser (1981) asked novices and experts to sort problems into related groups and found that the two groups classified problems differently. Novices tended to group problems together that had the same *surface features*; they grouped two problems together if they used pulleys or ramps. Novices were led by the keywords and the objects in the problem. However, experts classified problems in terms of their *deep structure*. That is, they grouped problems together that could be solved by the same principles, even though these problems had different surface features (Chi, Glaser, & Rees, 1983; see Figure 14.14).

Chi et al. (1981) also discovered that even though experts solved the problems four times

faster than novices, they spent more time than novices analysing and understanding the problems. Unlike the novices who waded into the problem immediately applying equations, the experts elaborated the representation of the problem by selecting the appropriate principles that applied to it. Experts carried out a complex categorisation of the problem situation using their available knowledge.

Strategic differences have also been found between experts and novices. Experts tend to *work forwards* to a solution whereas novices tend to *work backwards* (Larkin, McDermott, Simon, & Simon, 1980). When they have analysed the problem, experts apply the principles they have selected to the given quantities in the problem. These principles generate the unknown quantities needed to solve the problem. This planned working-forward strategy is both efficient and powerful. Novices, in contrast, have an impoverished repertoire of available principles. Typically, they take the goal (e.g., what is the maximum distance the spring will be compressed?), and find a principle that contains the desired quantity and usually no more than one other unknown quantity. They then try to find this new unknown quantity and hence work backwards to the givens of the problem statement.

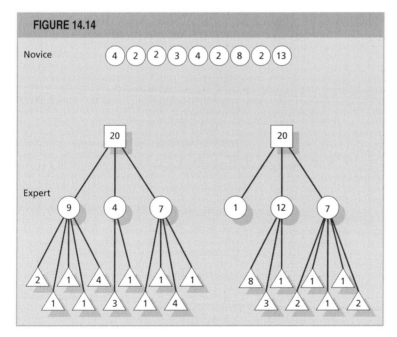

**FIGURE 14.14**

A schematic diagram of the sortings of physics problems by a novice and expert, adapted from Chi, Glaser, and Rees (1983). The squares indicate higher-order categories which organise lower-order groupings (circles). The conceptual groups represented by circles can be further subdivided into smaller groupings (triangles). The numbers indicate the number of problems in the category. Note how the expert's categorisation reveals a hierarchical organisation that is missing from the novice's categorisation, which is completely flat.

## Symbolic and connectionist models of physics skills

Several computational models of physics problem solving have been produced to model physics experts and the shift in expertise from novices to experts (Elio & Sharf, 1990; Lamberts, 1990; Lamberts & Pfeifer, 1992; Larkin, 1979; Priest, 1986). Most of these models are conventional symbolic models, like production systems (see Chapter 1). However, recently Lamberts (1990) has produced an interesting *hybrid model* that mixes connectionist and production-system ideas. Lamberts noted that physics expertise seems to be a mix of knowledge of previous problems and strategic reasoning (e.g., forward reasoning). In his model, a connectionist memory encodes previous problem-solving experience and a production system handles the strategic reasoning.

The model's long-term memory is a distributed memory that encodes previous problem situations (see Chapters 1 and 9). This memory has input units that are divided into three types: data units, final goal units, and subgoal units. The *data units* can encode different sorts of symbols in problem statements (e.g., the explicitly mentioned objects and variables), while the *final goal units* encode the required quantity to be found in the problem. Problems are encoded in memory using these two sets of units. From experience of solving previous problems, the memory learns an association between a particular set of problem statements (including their goals) and a set of useful subgoals (see Figure 14.15).

The model goes through four main processing stages when solving a problem. First, the problem to be solved is encoded by both the distributed memory system and the production system. In the distributed memory, the problem statement is encoded as activations to the appropriate data and final goal units (it should be noted that no encoding of subgoals occurs). The production system

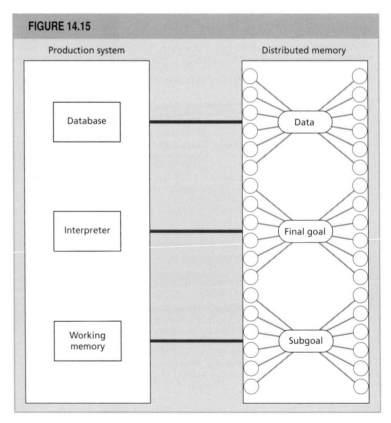

FIGURE 14.15

Production system

Database

Interpreter

Working memory

Distributed memory

Data

Final goal

Subgoal

A schematic diagram of Lamberts' (1990) hybrid system for modelling physics expertise.

encodes the problem as a structured representation in its working memory. Second, the encoded problem is processed by the distributed memory until it settles into a stable state, at which point one or more of the units in the subgoal set achieve a high activation. Third, the production system then comes into play and uses its sets of inference rules on the problem representation and the subgoals generated by the distributed memory. These inference rules are used to reach the goals of the problem using forward inference. If forward inference fails, then the system starts backward inference. Fourth, if a solution is learned in the third stage then the subgoals that were found to be useful are used along with the problem statement and goal to put the network through a learning cycle that encodes the association between these three entities. So, in the future, if the same or a similar problem is met, the network will produce a certain set of suitable subgoals to be adopted. Lamberts has shown that the system, when trained, can produce solutions that closely correspond to those generated by human experts.

A number of theorists have suggested that connectionist models should form the basis of future accounts of expertise (see Holyoak, 1991; Lamberts & Pfeifer, 1992). Their argument rests on the claim that connectionist models easily capture adaptive expertise, rather than just routine expertise (see Hatano & Inagaki, 1986). A case in point is the type of adaptive expertise manifested in solving problems by analogy, which we encounter in the next chapter (see Holyoak & Thagard, 1989).

## Computer programming skills

With developments in information technology many people, other than computer scientists, have had to learn to program computers. Three unassailable facts have emerged from this experience. First, people do not find programming languages easy to learn. Second, even expert programmers frequently make mistakes. Third, all of this takes time and costs money. From a research perspective, the interest lies in fundamental questions about the cognitive demands of computer programming; about the features of programming languages that

make them difficult to learn and use (see e.g., Anderson, Boyle, & Reiser, 1985; Eisenstadt, Keane, & Rajan, 1992; Kahney, 1989; Kahney & Eisenstadt, 1982; Soloway & Spohrer, 1989).

### Plans in programming

Like chess masters and expert physicists, the expert programmer appears to have developed elaborated schemata or abstract plans for programming tasks (Chapter 9). Soloway and his associates argue that expert programmers have script-like plans that are stereotypical chunks of code. For example, a programmer might have an "averaging plan", which contains the knowledge that an average is a sum divided by a count (see Rist, 1989, 1995; Spohrer, Soloway, & Pope, 1985). These plans are seen as being "natural" in the sense that programmers possess them before they learn to program. According to this view, programmers plan a program at an abstract level, by co-ordinating and sequencing these chunks to achieve the required task (see Erlich & Soloway, 1984).

Evidence for this theory has been found by Adelson (1981). She has shown, using a recall task, that expert programmers can recall more lines of code than novices and have a larger chunk size for encoding this information than novices (see also McKeithen, Reitman, Rueter, & Hirtle, 1981). Soloway and Erlich (1984) have supported the theory with evidence from a different fill-in-the-blanks task, in which subjects have to add missing statements to a program. Expert programmers have less difficulty in filling in the blanks than novices. Skilled programmers appear to be able to select appropriate plans from memory and adapt them to the local requirements of a specific programming task. Soloway, Bonar, and Erlich (1983) have found direct evidence for the existence of such programming plans when the requirements of the programming language conflict with programmers "natural" plans from everyday life. Programmers order program statements according to the dictates of everyday knowledge, even when this ordering leads to bugs in their programs. For example, the process/read loop construct in PASCAL is a major source of bugs because it mismatches the normal course of events in the real world; in the real world we get an object (read it), and then do something with it (process it), but in the PASCAL loop-world items are processed first and then read.

However, Gilmore and Green (1988) have argued against the view that programming plans are necessarily natural and general. They asked skilled programmers in two languages—PASCAL and BASIC—to carry out plan-related and plan-unrelated tasks, when the plan structure of a program was highlighted. They reasoned that if plans were being used, then highlighting the structure of these plans should facilitate subjects in a plan-related task, but not in a plan-unrelated task. This prediction was only confirmed for PASCAL programs. Gilmore and Green therefore proposed that the contents of programming plans do not generalise across languages (even though they admitted that BASIC programmers may use other plans). In particular, they maintained that plans emerge from notational aspects of the programming language in question. So, the notation of PASCAL makes it easier to form plans than the notation of BASIC (see Davies, 1990a). Interestingly, as an aside, it appears that when programmers learn a new language, the structure of plans in the first language is transferred to the second, irrespective of whether they are appropriate or not (Scholtz & Wiedenbeck, 1993).

Davies (1990a, b) has produced a synthesis to heal the conflict between these findings and earlier work. His position is that natural plans exist but they may be harder to express in one language than in another. Furthermore, programmers may find it easier to express natural plans in a particular language after being trained in program design. Davies pointed out that Gilmore and Green's results could be due to the PASCAL programmers' previous training in design. He therefore performed a similar study looking at novice BASIC programmers with or without design experience. In contrast to Gilmore and Green's results, he found that BASIC programmers *could* benefit from the cues to plan structures in programs, but only when they had training in program design. So, to characterise the knowledge involved in programming expertise we need to consider three distinct factors: the structures in

the problem domain (i.e., natural plans), the structures in the particular programming language domain (to do with the notation of the language), and the mapping between the former and the latter (see Rist, 1995, for a computational model that simulates design in programming). Education in program design is seen as providing the basis for this mapping.

All the aforementioned studies have concentrated on the comprehension and recall of programs, rather than on the debugging and coding of programs. More recently, some studies have addressed code-generation, showing that there are systematic changes in the strategies used by programmers as they move from being novices to experts (see Davies, 1991; Green, 1989, 1990; Rist, 1989, 1995). There is also some work on debugging which shows that it can be usefully understood as a form of situated action, involving little planning (Law, 1998). As such, it is clear that there are significant differences between the different tasks carried out when people do what is generally called programming. Theories of programming expertise now take into account the many ingredients that go into making up the skill; the programming language used, the background education of the programmer, the knowledge structures acquired, and the strategies employed to write the code.

## EVALUATION OF EXPERTISE RESEARCH

Problem-solving expertise relies on acquiring knowledge structures and strategies appropriate to a particular problem situation. Green and Gilhooly (1992) summarise the results of expertise research in five maxims, which we paraphrase as:

- Experts remember better.
- Experts employ different problem-solving strategies.
- Experts have better and more elaborated problem representations.
- Experts' superiority is based on knowledge, not on some basic capacity.
- Experts become expert through extensive practice.

We have seen these maxims reflected in the three areas of expertise research that have been reviewed. The consensus on these maxims is some indication of the success of this research area. Expertise research has been marked by success in several respects. First, it is an area where computational modelling has proved to be very informative. We now have very well developed models of skill acquisition and expert problem solving. Indeed, both Anderson (1996) and Newell (1990) consider these production system models to be candidate, cognitive architectures; that is, general theoretical frameworks for characterising all of cognition. Second, this research has considerable significance to everyday cognition; in particular, it is important in education, where one view of the task of educators is to create experts.

## LEARNING TO BE AN EXPERT

Thus far, we have seen some of the differences that exist between novices and experts in several different domains. We have not said how these differences come about; how novices become experts. Theoretically, we need an account of how people start as novices with little domain knowledge, using weak methods to solve problems, and end up as experts with elaborate, domain-specific knowledge structures and efficient problem-specific

strategies. In this section, we review some explanations of how people become experts.

### Practice makes perfect

Common-sense suggests that one way to become an expert is to practice something. Chase and Simon (1973a) estimated that most grand masters had studied for at least 9 to 10 years to reach their level of expertise. The relationship between practice and performance in perceptual-motor skills has been captured by one of the few "laws" in cognitive psychology; the Power Law of Practice (see Figure 14.16). This law states that if the time per trial and number of trials are graphed on log–log co-ordinate axes, then a straight line results (Fitts & Posner, 1967). It is now generally accepted that the power law also holds for purely cognitive skills, so much so that Logan (1988, p. 495) has said that "the power-function speed-up has been accepted as . . . a law, a benchmark prediction that theories of skill acquisition must make to be serious contenders". Not surprisingly several researchers have suggested a number of mechanisms to explain these effects of practice and the acquisition of expertise: chunking, proceduralisation, and compression (see Chapter 1; Anderson, 1993, 1996; Newell, 1990; Rosenbloom & Newell, 1986). Most of these techniques have been developed in the context of production system models of cognition (Chapter 1).

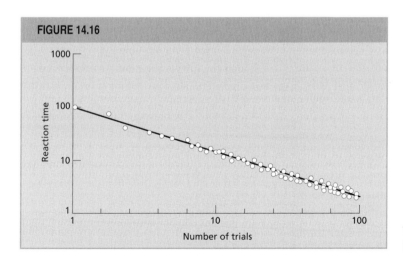

**FIGURE 14.16**

Typical log–log plot for the Power Law of Practice.

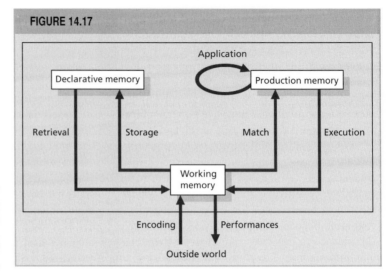

**FIGURE 14.17**

A schematic diagram of the major components and interlinking processes used in Anderson's (1983, 1993) ACT models. Reprinted by permission of the author.

## Practice makes chunks

One proposal is that a form of *chunking* underlies practice effects (this is a very specific sense of the term, to be distinguished from Miller's, 1956, memory formulation; see Chapter 6). Rosenbloom and Newell (1986, 1987) have argued that when a series of production rules is applied to solve a particular problem, a new rule can be created that does away with the chain of rules (moves) to get to the solution. For example, suppose an problem solver encounters a problem situation, *state-a*, and needs to reach a goal state, *state-f*. In solving the problem a chain of rules might be applied: rule 1 changes state-a to state-b, rule 2 changes state-b to state-e, and rule 3 changes state-e to state-f. Stated simply, chunking would create a new rule that contains the relevant conditions that led to the goal state; a new rule that will change state-a to state-f in one step. An immediate implication of chunking is that the problem is solved in one step rather a succession of steps, allowing the time taken to solve the problem to decrease significantly. The idea of a chunk of knowledge has become a standard in many cognitive architectures (e.g., Anderson, 1996; Newell, 1990) and, as we have seen, proves to be a very useful concept in characterising chess expertise.

## Learning from problem-solving attempts and instruction: Proceduralisation

Anderson (1982, 1983, 1987a, 1990, 1993, 1996; Anderson & Lebiere, 1998) has proposed another mechanism called knowledge compilation in his theory of skill learning within his ACT cognitive architecture (*Adaptive Control of Thought*). Among other phenomena, his ACT models— successively named ACTE, ACT*, and ACT-R— have modelled the learning of geometry (Anderson, Greeno, Kline, & Neves, 1981), computer programming (Anderson & Reiser, 1985; Pirolli & Anderson, 1985), serial list learning (Anderson & Matessa, 1997; Anderson, Bothell, Lebiere, & Matessa, 1998), and computer text-editing (Singley & Anderson, 1989). The main components of the ACT architecture have remained fairly invariant over the years although representational and processing details have changed (see Figure 14.17):

- A *declarative memory*, that is a semantic network of interconnected concepts that have different activation strengths (see Chapters 1 and 9).
- A *procedural memory*, of production rules.
- A *working memory* that contains currently active information.

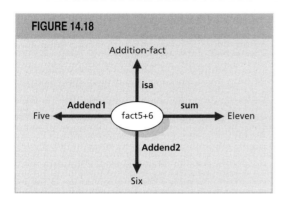

**FIGURE 14.18**

A network representation of a declarative chunk from Anderson's ACT architecture. This chunk represents a piece of knowledge encoding the fact that 5 and 6 add up to 11.

Declarative knowledge is represented as chunks, which are just schema-like structures encoding a small bundle of knowledge (see Figure 14.18). Declarative knowledge can be reported and is not tied to the situation in which it can be used (e.g., a memorised textbook procedure to apply a statistical test), whereas procedural knowledge often cannot be expressed, is applied automatically, and is specifically tuned to specific situations (e.g., the knowledge we use when adding numbers). Information can be *stored* and *retrieved* from declarative memory by a number of methods. Information in the production memory takes the form of production rules, which are *executed* when they *match* the contents of working memory. Production memory can also be applied to itself by *application processes*; new productions can be learned by examining existing productions. For the most part, Anderson explains skill acquisition as *knowledge compilation*; as a move from the use of declarative knowledge to procedural knowledge. Knowledge compilation has two sub-processes: proceduralisation and composition.

*Proceduralisation* is the process that transforms declarative knowledge into production knowledge. Usually, problem solvers initially attempt to solve, say, a maths or programming problem, from a textbook. In these solution attempts, the novice will generate a number of subgoals using a combination of weak methods (like hill climbing or means–ends analysis) and declarative knowledge

from instruction. During repeated problem-solving episodes, a particular piece of declarative knowledge will occur repeatedly in the context of a particular subgoal. When this happens, a new production rule is created that has the declarative knowledge as a pattern (its IF-part) and the executed action as its action (its THEN-part). This declarative–procedural change should result in a concurrent reduction in verbalisation by the problem solver. Correlatively, there is an increase in the automaticity of the problem-solving behaviour (see also Chapter 5). Reductions in verbalisation have been demonstrated repeatedly in the literature (Anderson, 1982; Sweller, 1983; Sweller, Mawer, & Ward, 1983).

Stated simply, Anderson's view of learning is based on the accrual and tuning of small units of knowledge—knowledge that combines to produce complex cognition. The environment plays a critical role in the learning process, in that it establishes the configuration of simple objects that aid the learning of chunks and also drives the formation of production rules. The importance of this step is that it re-emphasises the importance of analysing the nature of the environment as an essential step to understanding cognition, an emphasis that has been somewhat lost since the demise of behaviourism in the cognitive revolution (Anderson, 1990).

## Learning from your mistakes

Finally, intuitively, we also learn from our mistakes. Most theories of skill learning stress the importance of successful problem solving to the learning process. However, we also learn from episodes in which we fail. Ohlsson (1996) has proposed a theory of skill learning from performance errors. In this theory, errors occur because people use knowledge that is overly general; their encoded knowledge does not capture a distinction that is in the task environment. So, novice chess players may have so general a conception of threatening board positions that they miss many situations when they are under attack. The theory also stresses the subjective nature of errors, characterising them as conflicts between what the learner believes ought to be true and what is perceived to be the case. The learning that occurs results in a specialisation of the knowledge structures being used, so that they come to be applied under more appropriate conditions in the future.

## COGNITIVE NEUROPSYCHOLOGY OF THINKING

Until relatively recently there has been little research on the cognitive neuropsychology of thinking (Shallice, 1988). This gap in the field must have been due to the complexity of thought in its reliance on many diverse lower-level systems (e.g., attention, working memory, and language). Because thinking violated many of the assumptions of modularity some theorists ruled it out as a meaningful area of study from the neuroscience perspective (Fodor, 1983). Happily, the development of more advanced neuroimaging techniques combined with the better understanding of lower-level processes has led to rapid advances in our understanding.

For some time it has been proposed that the prefrontal cortex was implicated in higher-level activities like thinking. While people with prefrontal damage often show no obvious decrease in IQ measures, they have obvious difficulties in managing and planning their lives; they fail to plan for future events, and meet difficulties in carrying out routine plans like shopping for food. Recent research has confirmed the importance of the prefrontal cortex in different forms of thinking, from problem solving to reasoning, planning, and analogical thinking (Duncan et al., 1996; Halford, Wilson, & Phillips, 1998; Johnson-Laird, 1995a, b; Shallice, 1988; Wharton & Grafman, 1998).

One argument that has been made is that the prefrontal cortex, which has greatly expanded in human evolution (Benson, 1993), is the seat of processes that manipulate and integrate complex relational representations, a fundamental process that underlies diverse forms of reasoning, problem solving, and planning (Holyoak & Kroger, 1995; Robin & Holyoak, 1995). Whether one is doing means–ends analysis with problem states,

combining the premises of a logical argument, planning a meal, or making analogical inferences, a fundamental step is this ability to integrate complex, relational representations. There appears to be a big developmental and evolutionary step from understanding the single relation "Bill is taller than Charles" to integrating multiple relations; integrating "Bill is taller than Charles" and "Abe is taller than Bill" to form the transitive inference that "Abe is taller than Charles" (Halford, 1992; Halford & Wilson, 1980; Halford et al., 1998). In children, the integration of multiple relations to make a transitive inference reliably only appears after the age of 5 (Halford, 1984). In animals, the abilities of the brightest chimps to reason relationally severely trails human abilities (Tomasello & Call, 1997). In later chapters, we will return to the specific results for analogical thinking (Chapter 15) and reasoning (Chapter 16). In this section, we will consider some of the findings on puzzles and insight problems.

Shallice (1982) made use of a variant of the Tower of Hanoi problem, called the Tower of London problem, to assess planning and problem-solving impairments in brain-damaged patients. Typically, instructions were given to pre-plan the whole sequence of moves to be carried out mentally before executing the sequence. Thus, the poor performance of frontal-lobe patients on these is usually interpreted as the inability to pre-plan effectively (Owen, 1997; Owen et al., 1990; Shallice, 1982). However, recently aspects of this simple pre-planning account have become more complex (Owen, 1997; Phillips et al., 1999; Ward & Allport, 1997). Ward and Allport (1997) have emphasised the importance of conflicts that occurred between goals and subgoals in the problem, where they characterised a subgoal as a set of moves that were essential to the solution of the problem but which did not place a disk in its final goal position. Several studies have shown that goal–subgoal conflicts are particularly difficult for frontal-lobe patients (Goel & Grafman, 1995; Morris et al., 1997). Other research has suggested that pre-planning may be less important than the on-line planning of moves—planning of moves during the execution of a solution rather than pre-planning (Phillips et al., 1999). Phillips et al.

looked at working memory effects on the task by using verbal and visuospatial executive secondary tasks (see Chapter 6) and found that pre-planning was less important than executive processing involving the execution and monitoring of on-line planning.

Unfortunately, there has been a lot less work on the cognitive neuropsychology of insight problems. The studies that have been done have also been considered successful from this perspective in assessing the hemispheric difference of relevance to them, supporting some of the theoretical proposals made about spreading activation and insight. Most notably, Bowden and Beeman (1998) have shown hemispheric differences when hints to the solutions of insight problems are presented to the left or right visual field, hence being processed by either the right or left hemisphere, respectively. Specifically, priming of the solution was more effective when the presented information was processed by the right rather than the left hemisphere, a result they explained as being due to the coarse-coded nature of semantic information in this hemisphere.

## CHAPTER SUMMARY

In this chapter, we have considered several aspects of skilled thinking. The emphasis in this chapter has been on the role that various forms of specific knowledge play in problem solving.

- The Gestalt school argued in opposition to associationist psychologists that thinking was productive rather than merely reproductive. They performed many experiments to demonstrate that problem solving could be productively successful and reproductively a failure; making use of concepts like insight, restructuring, and fixation.
- Newell and Simon's (1972) problem-space theory emerged from the information-processing revolution. At base, it characterises problem solving as a constrained and guided search through a space of alternative mental possibilities. This search is guided by various heuristic methods or rules of thumb that co-ordinate the application of various operators (moves) used for transforming one state into another. This theory has been used successfully to predict problem-solving behaviour in puzzle problems, like the Tower of Hanoi, the missionaries–cannibals problem, and water-jug problems. Computational models have been constructed for many of these problems that simulate subjects' behaviour.
- From an evaluative standpoint, the strength of the problem-space approach has been its predictive success, but its main weakness has been the narrowness of the problem situations to which it has been applied. Fortunately, later research has widened the scope of the theory.
- Problem-space theory has been extended to re-interpret the findings of the Gestalt school. Some puzzles, like the Luchins' water-jugs problems, can be dealt with quite directly using problem-space theory. Other problems, like the two-string problem and the candle problem, have required some extension of the theory to characterise notions like insight, restructuring, and fixation.
- Chess expertise appears to depend on knowledge about specific board positions, about how to evaluate such positions, and schemas encoding types of board position. Expert players have more of this knowledge than novices and this accumulated wisdom is manifest in the speed with which they can encode board positions (normal or random) and how they treat such positions.
- In physics, expertise again depends on schemata that encode the important theorems in the discipline. There are also strategic differences in the way expert physicists deploy this knowledge, working forward from a problem statement to a solution rather than backwards from a solution to the givens in the problem statement.

- In programming, people develop schemata that encode programming plans depending on the specific programming language they are learning. These domain-specific plans can sometimes conflict with existing plans about how we do things in the world and may be transferred to be applied in learning a second programming language.
- Overall, expertise research has been a successful research area. It has developed many specific accounts of important thinking skills, which have been used in education. It has also delivered a consistent story that fits in well with accounts of other thinking behaviour and which can be captured readily in several cognitive architectures.
- Novices learn to be experts by forming chunks of knowledge, by developing declarative knowledge, and moving from declarative to procedural knowledge. The ACT theory is an integrated cognitive architecture that has been used to simulate these types of learning.
- Until recently, cognitive neuropsychological accounts of thinking behaviour were not well developed (see Eysenck & Keane, 1995). However, considerable advances have been made in localising various types of thinking in the prefrontal cortex. The current suggestion is that several regions in this area are responsible for the fundamental task of integrating complex relational information, a process that is basic to all higher thought processes.

## FURTHER READING

- Anderson, J.R., & Lebiere, C. (1998). *Atomic components of thought.* Hillsdale, NJ: Lawrence Erlbaum Associates Inc. This book provides the most up-to-date treatment of the ACT theory.
- Ericsson, K.A., & Lehmann, A.C. (1996). Expert and exceptional performance: Evidence of maximal adaptation to task constraints. *Annual Review of Psychology, 47*, 273–305. A recent review of expertise.
- Gazzaniga, M.S. (Ed.) (1999). *The cognitive neurosciences* (2nd Edn). Cambridge, MA: MIT Press. This monumental tome reviews a wide range of cognitive neuroscience topics by the foremost researchers in the field.
- Gilhooly, K.J. (1996). *Thinking: Directed, undirected and creative* (3rd Edn). London: Academic Press. This provides more detail on some of the research covered here and explores other areas too.
- Gilhooly, K.J., & Hoffman, R. (Eds.) (1998). *Expert thinking.* Hove, UK: Psychology Press. This book is a good collection of recent papers on aspects of expertise.

# 15

# Creativity and Discovery

## INTRODUCTION

In the previous chapter, we looked at relatively mundane forms of thinking, in our examination of problem solving in puzzles, insight problems, and expertise. In this chapter, we explore creative thinking. Creativity is hard to define but roughly speaking it concerns the production of novel ideas that are in some sense useful or an advance beyond previous conceptions. According to one view, creativity is distinguished from other forms of thinking by being less mundane and more exceptional. Is this an accurate view?

The traditional view has been that there are a small number of "great" individuals who are responsible for what we call "creative thoughts"; these are people of talent, the Einsteins and Mozarts of this world, who have intellectual abilities that stretch far beyond those of the mass of humanity (otherwise known as *us*). In contrast to this view, there is an emerging perspective that talent may be more a matter of hard work, that we are all a little bit creative, and that the cognitive processes used to produce Nobel prize ideas might not be radically different from those used

to produce a joke over coffee (Finke, Ward, & Smith, 1992; Holyoak & Thagard, 1995; Koestler, 1964; Weisberg, 1993). It is very much this latter perspective that will be unfolded in the following pages. Many of the processes we review—like mental simulation, analogy, and hypothesis testing —are quite mundane and unexceptional, although they may be used to produce creative products.

This chapter is divided into distinct parts. In the first two sections, we consider general perspectives on creativity and the issue of whether talent exists. We then review three cognitive processes that have been implicated in creativity; mental simulation using mental models, the use of analogy, and methods for hypothesis testing in scientific discovery. Finally, we evaluate the whole of problem-solving research as it has been reviewed in this and the previous chapter.

## GENIUS AND TALENT

Traditionally, the dominant view of genius has been that it is a product of an innate talent that singles out creative individuals from everyone else (Gardner, 1984; Winner, 1996). The existence of child prodigies appears to support this view. In music, from the age of 6 Mozart was composing and performing in public. Some young children have been shown to possess "perfect" or "absolute" pitch; that is, they can both name and sing specified pitches without being given any reference pitch (Takeuchi & Hulse, 1993). In language skills, Fowler (1981) has reported the case of a boy who was said to have begun speaking at five months, who had developed a 50-word vocabulary by six months and a speaking knowledge of five languages by the age of 3. But, what indeed is the basis for talent and is there a causal dependence between genius and talent?

Howe, Davidson, and Sloboda (1998) have addressed this question in a wide-ranging review of the literature. They begin by attempting to pin down the sometimes slippery notion of talent with a five-point definition:

- It originates in genetically transmitted structures and is, at least partly, innate.
- Although its full effects may not be evident at an early age, there will be advance indications of the talent.
- These early indications provide a predictive basis for deciding who is likely to excel.
- Only a minority of children are talented.
- Talents are relatively domain-specific.

Howe et al. call into question the accuracy of anecdotal and autobiographical reports like those mentioned earlier. In general they argue that, on closer inspection, there is evidence that the parents and child have often put a good deal of work into the exceptional ability. For example, Howe, Davidson, Moore, and Sloboda (1995) studied the type and frequency of early signs of musical ability in 257 children, only a few of whom became superior performing musicians. Parents were asked when the child first sang, moved to music, showed a liking for music, was attentive to and showed a liking for musical activities. Howe et al. found some indication that the most successful musicians displayed a slight tendency to begin singing at an earlier age. However, in most of these cases there were other grounds for the early onset, such as a parent singing to the infant well before the

infant began to sing. In many other studies, from mathematics to swimming, there has been little evidence of early innate indicators that reliably predict later success. So, if raw talent does not exist, what does account for exceptional ability? Howe et al. advance all the other cognitive factors that are recognised to be important, such as motivation, persistence, interests, and competitiveness, to name just a few (Howe, 1990).

On a more social note, there are important implications that follow from rejecting the view that genius is based on innate talents. If no such talent exists then the classification of some children as talented and others as untalented is discrimination without foundation. The no-talent view supports an educational system that promotes a more egalitarian approach to the encouragement of excellence.

## GENERAL APPROACHES TO CREATIVITY

In the past, accounts of creativity have often been descriptive rather than explanatory. The classic example of this descriptive approach is Wallas's (1926) classification of the broad stages of the creative process into:

- Preparation, where the problem under consideration is formulated and preliminary attempts are made to solve it.
- Incubation, where the problem is left aside to work on other tasks.
- Illumination, where the solution comes to the problem solver as a sudden insight.
- Verification, in which the problem solver makes sure that the solution really works.

This classification appears to be supported by the reports of creative scientists. One such famous report is by the French mathematician Henri Poincaré (1913), who reported working intensively on the development of Fuchsian functions for 15 days. At the end of this time he reported that:

I wanted to represent these functions by the quotient of two series; this idea was perfectly conscious and deliberate; the analogy with elliptic functions guided me. I asked myself what properties these series must have if they existed, and succeeded without difficulty in forming the series I have called theta-Fuchsian.

Just at that time I left Caen, where I was living, to go on a geologic excursion under the auspices of the school of mines. The changes in travel made me forget my mathematical work. Having reached Coutances, we entered an omnibus to go some place or other. At the moment when I put my foot on the step the idea came to me, without anything in my former thoughts seeming to have paved the way for it, that the transformations I had used to define Fuchsian functions were identical to those of non-Euclidean geometry. I did not verify the idea; I should not have had time, as, upon taking my seat in the omnibus, I went on with a conversation already commenced, but I felt a perfect certainty.

Poincaré's report fits Wallas's framework perfectly, with illumination following an incubation period after extensive preparation. However, even though Wallas's analysis provides us with a broad framework, it is really too general and descriptive. Fortunately, some attempts have been made to specify these stages; for example, incubation and illumination have been treated in Gestalt research on insight (see Chapter 14).

## Incubation and illumination

Few studies have been carried out on incubation, although on balance they support the existence of the phenomenon (see Ohlsson, 1992, and Kaplan & Simon, 1990). Incubation can be explained within problem-space theory as a special type of forgetting (see Simon, 1966). Simon (1966) makes the distinction between control information about a problem (e.g., a record of the subgoals tried in a problem) and factual information (e.g., some property of an object or substantive aspect of the problem). For example, in Maier's (1931) two-string problem, control knowledge might include the subgoal "try to reach something that is far

away" and substantive information would be that "the string is a flexible object" (see Chapter 14 and Keane, 1989). Factual information discovered in the context of one subgoal will not be available to other goals. However, during incubation, control information decays faster than factual information. Therefore, after the problem has been set aside for a time, subgoal information will be lost but the factual information will still be present. This factual information will thus be available to newly generated subgoals of the problem, increasing the likelihood of the problem being solved. Several other recent studies support this sort of account. In cognitive neuroscience studies, Bowden and Beeman (1998) have shown hemispheric differences in the priming of hints to insight problems. Similarly, Yaniv and Meyer (1987) have shown that unsuccessful attempts to retrieve inaccessible stored information can prime the recognition of later information by a process of spreading activation.

Ohlsson (1992) maintains that there is very little empirical support for illumination; the literature on it seems to rely on two anecdotal reports by von Helmholtz and Poincaré (see Hadamard, 1945). If we are to relate the phenomenon to any literature, it is that on the use of hints in problem solving. Again, much of this work has been carried out within the Gestalt tradition (see Chapter 14). The current favoured account seems to be that any new information introduced into the problem or met in the environment may activate related concepts in memory and result in the sudden emergence of a solution. For example, in the case of the two-string problem, Maier reported that when the experimenter brushed off the string, setting it swinging in the line of sight of subjects, many of them suddenly produced the solution of swinging the string and catching it on the upswing, while holding the other string.

## Recent accounts of creativity

Even though Wallas's stages of creativity have been very influential, his formulation is not the final word on creativity. More recently, several cognitive scientists have made a number of proposals about aspects of the phenomenon. None of these proposals is at variance with the theoretical proposals of this and the previous chapter and many of the ideas have been modelled computationally already.

Boden's (1991, 1994) account of creativity makes the distinction between improbabilistic creativity and impossibilistic creativity. Improbabilistic discoveries involve novel combinations of familiar ideas; hence, they are discoveries that have a low probability of occurring. Boden sees this type of creativity as being the product of associationistic or analogical thinking (see later section). Impossibilistic discoveries are more radical, in that ideas are generated that, in some sense, could not have been generated before. Boden argues that ideas are always generated within a conceptual space, like a problem space, which is generated by some set of rules or constraints. People explore these conceptual spaces using various conceptual maps, which characterise typical routes through the space. Some forms of creativity are linked to exploring new parts of the space, or in showing the limits of the space. Other forms of creativity emerge when the fundamental rules of the space are violated or modified. When the space itself changes, ideas *that could not have been generated before* emerge. For example, James Joyce's *Ulysses* could be viewed as an exploration and extension of the space of literary styles used in the novel. This conceptual space is explored by writing different sections of *Ulysses* in widely differing styles (e.g., as a Middle-English, Chaucerian tale or a threepenny-terrible, romantic novel). The space of styles used in the novel is extended by introducing the style of *streaming consciousness*, which is designed to mimic the flow of an individual's thoughts (see beginning of Chapter 14 for an example). Any computer program that changes its own rules and hence its conceptual space can be said to manifest impossibilistic creativity (Boden, 1991).

Finke, Ward, and Smith (1992) have outlined another general model of creativity, the so-called Geneplore model, which divides creativity into a generative phase and an exploratory phase (Smith, Ward, & Schumacher, 1993; Ward, Smith, & Finke, 1995). In the generative phase, people are said to construct mental representations, called *preinventive structures* which have certain properties that

promote creative discovery. In the exploratory phase, these properties are exploited to make sense of the preinventive structures. If these explorations are successful then a creative product might result, if not then one cycles back to the generative phase to either produce new preinventive structures or to modify the original structure. In this cycling process, various constraints are applied or even discovered on the creative product, gradually refining and improving it. The Geneplore model is very general and can be used to account for everything from conceptual combination (see Chapter 9), to imagination to fixation in insight problems.

One of the Geneplore model's most well known applications has been in the area of *structured imagination*. The preinventive structures built during the generative processes should be founded on people's prior knowledge; hence, it was predicted that when people were given imagination tasks they would tend to generate products that were structured in various ways. Ward (1992) asked subjects to draw imaginary creatures on a planet somewhere else in the galaxy; subjects were asked to draw their initially imagined animal, another animal of the same species, and a member of a different species (see Figure 15.1). Ward found that the "majority of imagined creatures were structured by properties that are typical of animals on earth: bilateral symmetry, sensory receptors and appendages" (see Figure 15.2). In a similar study, Bredart (1998) found that when a feature was not included (e.g., an eye) a novel structure with the same function was included (e.g., some sensor for extracting sensory information). Ward (1992) has shown that people dealt with the task by first retrieving exemplars of known earth animals (i.e., the preinventive structure) and then modified these representations according to instructions and task constraints (i.e., exploration of the preinventive structure under the guidance of constraints). Furthermore, when some subjects were asked to produce "wildly different" animals they still retained symmetry and such properties in their drawings relative to controls given the standard instructions, although they tended to produce more novel variations (e.g., in the number of eyes or limbs; Ward & Sifonis, 1997).

**FIGURE 15.1**

One subject's (a) initial creation, (b) same-species variant, and (c) different-species variant. Reproduced with permission from T.B. Ward (1992), "Structured imagination" in R.A. Finke, T.B. Ward, and S.M. Smith (Eds.), *Creative cognition: Theory, research and applications.* Cambridge, MA: MIT Press.

**FIGURE 15.2**

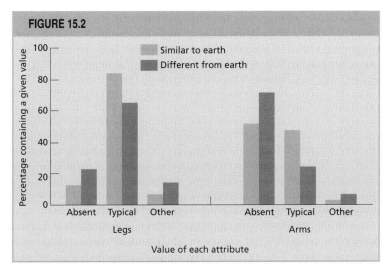

The percentages of imaginary creatures with no legs, two or four legs, or some other number of legs, no arms, two arms, or some other number of arms, when people imagined a planet similar to or completely unlike earth. Reproduced with permission from T.B. Ward (1992), "Structured imagination" in R.A. Finke, T.B. Ward, and S.M. Smith (Eds.), *Creative cognition: Theory, research and applications.* Cambridge, MA: MIT Press.

## DISCOVERY USING MENTAL MODELS

In the previous sections, we have dealt with some general approaches to creativity. In the rest of the chapter, we consider some specific cognitive processes that play a key role in creative thinking and discovery. We begin with the issue of simulation using mental models. Many creative thinkers have reported imagining or simulating various states of the world or situations in the generation of new ideas. Einstein reported thought experiments about riding on light beams and standing in

plummeting lifts in developing his ideas on relativity. In this section, we consider some research that has been done on trying to characterise this form of simulation using the idea of mental models.

It has been proposed that people understand the world and simulate aspects of it using "naive theories", "folk theories", or "mental models" (see Brewer, 1987; Gentner & Stevens, 1983; Gilhooly, 1995; Norman, 1983; Rips, 1986; Vosniadou & Brewer, 1992). The theory of *mental models* is used to account for a variety of aspects of behaviour in novel, problem-solving situations (see Johnson-Laird & Byrne, 1991, and Chapter 16 for a slightly different conception used in reasoning research).

In the present sense, mental models refer to mostly imagined, dynamic models that we use in every-day life to think about the world. For example, if you are trying to cross a raging torrent without the aid of a bridge, you might imagine trying to jump across at some point or swing on a rope. This simulation of crossing the river is achieved by a mental model.

## Mental models of home heating

Kempton's (1986) work is a prime example of the use of mental models. She proposed that when people regulated their thermostats to heat their houses they used one of two models of how a heating system works: a "feedback model" or a "valve model".

According to the *feedback model*, the thermostat turns the furnace on and off depending on the room temperature. So, when the room is too cold, the thermostat turns the furnace on and when the room is warm enough, it turns the furnace off. The temperature at which the furnace is turned on, is determined by the setting on the thermostat's dial. This model posits that the furnace runs at a constant rate and so the only way that the thermostat can control the amount of heat in a room is by the length of time that the furnace is on. If the dial is adjusted upward only a little bit, the furnace will run for a short time and turn off; if it is adjusted upward a large amount, the furnace must run for a longer period to heat the house sufficiently. Left at one setting, the thermostat will switch the furnace off and on as necessary to maintain the temperature on the dial setting.

In contrast, in the *valve model*, the thermostat controls the rate at which the furnace generates heat, rather than having a feedback function. So, the furnace runs at variable rates depending on the setting on the dial. To maintain a constant temperature in the house the setting is adjusted so that the amount of heat generated balances the amount being lost. In this model, the thermostat has no specific role as a regulator of heat; indeed, in one sense, it is the person adjusting the thermostat that acts as the regulator. Several other common physical devices operate in a similar manner and are used as analogies for the valve model. For example, as you turn a tap, more water comes out.

These models make different predictions about how heating systems work and about how energy can be saved in the home. However, even though they are elaborate and intriguing, neither of them is technically accurate. The valve model predicts that more fuel is consumed at higher settings than at lower settings. This prediction is correct but for the wrong reasons; the higher fuel consumption is not the result of the valve opening wider, but is due to higher internal temperatures in the house resulting in greater heat loss through walls, windows, and ceilings. Hence, people using the valve model tend to re-adjust their thermostats more frequently and be more efficient energy users. In contrast, the feedback model can, under certain circumstances, lead to fuel wastage. People using the feedback model tend to leave their thermostat settings at a set, often high, level for long periods of time; they assume that the thermostat will turn the heating off when the required temperature is reached. So, the heating is on more than is necessary. In an ecology-conscious world, the importance of these findings is enormous. Kempton estimates that if people had an appropriate and accurate model of home heating then the saving for all US households in a single year could be around $5 billion.

Home heating models illustrate some of the main properties of mental models. First, mental models are predictive; they suggest different ways in which physical mechanisms operate. Second, they simulate physical mechanisms and phenomena, and are often accompanied by visual imagery. For example, someone using the valve model could easily imagine a signal going from the dial on the wall to the furnace causing the valve to open, stoking the flames of the boiler. Third, people can have multiple models to deal with different aspects of the same system; Kempton identified two different models but admitted that many people may have a mixture of both. Fourth, mental models can be volatile; they can undergo sudden changes depending on the knowledge used to construct them and an individual's conception of the task situation. Finally, it is also possible that people's protocols, which appear to reflect model use, include ad-hoc rationalisations to account for actions that have been taken. So, some of the information that people report may not be part of the model at all.

## Naive models of motion

Similar evidence for the use of mental models has been found in studies of people's naive theories of object motion (see Caramazza, McCloskey, & Green, 1981; McCloskey, 1983). These models are fairly consistent across individuals and can be applied to many different situations; however, they differ markedly from the fundamental principles of classical physics (interestingly enough, they parallel early pre-Newtonian physics). McCloskey and his colleagues examined these naive theories by looking at subjects' answers to problems like the following one (see Figure 15.3):

> In the diagram, an airplane is flying along at a constant speed. The plane is also flying at a constant altitude, so that the flight path is parallel to the ground. The arrow shows the direction in which the plane is flying. When the plane is in the position shown in the diagram a large metal ball is dropped from the plane. The plane continues flying at the same speed in the same direction and at the same altitude. Draw the path the ball will follow from the time it is dropped until it hits the ground. Ignore wind or air resistance. Also show as well as you can the position of the plane at the moment that the ball hits the ground.

Only one of the diagrams in Figure 15.3 is correct (the first). When the ball is dropped it will describe a parabolic arc and the plane will be above the ball when it hits the ground. The total velocity of the ball is made up of two independent velocities; a horizontal and a vertical velocity. Before the ball is dropped, it has a horizontal velocity equal to that of the plane and a vertical velocity of zero. After the ball is released, it undergoes a constant vertical acceleration due to gravity, and thus acquires a constantly increasing vertical velocity. The ball's horizontal velocity, however, does not change; it continues to move

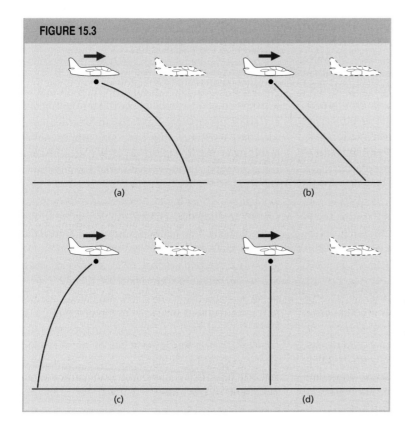

**FIGURE 15.3**

(a)

(b)

(c)

(d)

The correct response (a) and incorrect responses (b–d) for the aeroplane problem. Reproduced from *Mental models* (edited by D. Gentner & A. Stevens) published by Lawrence Erlbaum Associates Inc., © 1983 Lawrence Erlbaum Associates Inc.

horizontally at the same speed as the plane. It is the combination of the constant horizontal velocity and the continually increasing vertical velocity that produces a parabolic arc. Because the horizontal velocity of the ball equals that of the plane, it hits the ground directly beneath the plane.

However, few subjects appear to think about the problem in this way. Only 40% of subjects drew diagrams with parabolic arcs and not all of these placed the plane above the ball as it hit the ground. The remaining 60% produced the other variants shown in Figure 15.3. According to McCloskey (1983) these responses arise from a simple model of motion that he calls impetus theory. In deference to classical physics, *impetus theory* proposes that (i) the act of setting an object in motion imparts to the object an internal force or "impetus" that serves to maintain the motion, and (ii) that a moving object's impetus gradually dissipates. McCloskey argued that this mental model was useful in predicting object motions in everyday life. However, the model is not true in general and leads to incorrect predictions in many contexts.

Many of these experiments were carried out on university-level subjects and so illustrate surprising misconceptions in educated people. More recently, several investigators have questioned the generality of these findings and their explanation. It now seems that the results found are, in part, due to the use of paper-and-pencil tests. Kaiser, Jonides, and Alexander (1986) asked subjects to reason about similar problems in familiar contexts and found that the majority of people produced correct predictions. Cooke and Breedin (1994) have also shown that aspects of the display and response instructions also affect the results found (but see Ranney, 1994). Furthermore, if subjects are asked to make judgements about object motions as part of a dynamic simulation of ongoing events, then they rarely make errors (see Kaiser, Proffitt, & Anderson, 1985). It has also been shown that when people have made erroneous predictions on a picture-based task, they frequently view simulations of their predictions as being anomalous. So, people are not as poor at predicting particle motions as the McCloskey studies suggested. However, it does appear that people are quite poor

at judgements of more complex events, like the dynamics of wheels, under many testing contexts (see Kaiser, Proffitt, Whelan, & Hecht, 1992; Proffitt, Kaiser, & Whelan, 1990).

Yates et al. (1988) have challenged the theoretical basis of McCloskey's work. They have argued that people do not have abstract theories about motion, but rather rely on imagery-based, prototypical motion events to construct specific "enactments" of the motions of objects. This theory predicts that the more "realistic" or familiar the testing scenario, the greater the likelihood that such prototypes would be cued and used to generate appropriate predictions. Ironically, the conception of mental models is wide enough to include both intuitive theories or prototypic motion events as instances of mental models. In conclusion, it should be noted that whatever mental model we *do* use, may be entirely appropriate for making predictions about the motions of everyday objects, even though it may be at variance with the predictions of classical physics (see Hecht, 1996; Springer, 1990; Yates, 1990).

## DISCOVERY BY ANALOGY

Analogical thinking has often been identified as a core method in creativity. Koestler (1964) gives accounts of creativity in disparate domains—including literature, the arts, and science—that result from the juxtaposition of two sets of very different ideas. Various creative individuals report solutions to unfamiliar problems based on deep analogies. For example, Rutherford used a solar system analogy to understand the structure of the atom; viewing the electrons as revolving around the nucleus in the same way that the planets revolve around the sun (see Gentner, 1983, and Figure 15.4). So, when people do not have knowledge that is directly relevant to a problem, they apply knowledge indirectly, *by analogy* to the problem.

Analogical thought involves a mapping of the conceptual structure of one set of ideas (called a base domain) into another set of ideas (called a target domain). Technically, there are two key processes in the ability; analogue retrieval and

**FIGURE 15.4**

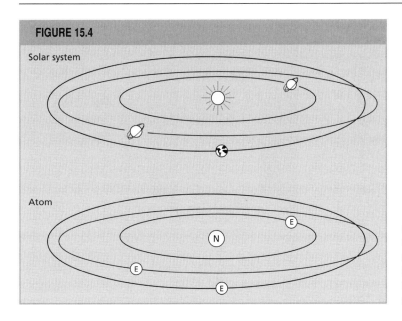

Solar system

Atom

A diagram of the solar system–atom analogy. The planets are attracted to the sun and revolve around it, just as the electrons (Es) are attracted to and revolve around the nucleus (N).

analogical mapping. In retrieval, the thinker must somehow recall a domain (or analogue) that corresponds to the problem they face. In mapping, the two domains or analogues are matched against one another to find corresponding concepts in each, usually to find corresponding relational structure (see Gentner, 1983; Holyoak & Thagard, 1995; Keane, 1985a, 1988). For example, at some point Rutherford had to retrieve or recognise that the solar system could be used to understand the atom, and then map the two together to make the revolution of the planets around the sun correspond to the revolution of the electrons around the nucleus. In essence, analogies involve similarities in the relational structure of two things, rather than in their superficial appearances (e.g., the solar system and atom are relationally similar although they involve very different sets of objects). As such, the causal, relational structure of the domain plays an important role in supporting this mapping process.

Gick and Holyoak (1980, 1983) demonstrated analogical problem solving by giving subjects analogous stories to Duncker's (1945) "radiation problem". The radiation problem involves a doctor's attempt to destroy a malignant tumour using rays. The doctor needs to use high-intensity rays to destroy the tumour, but these high-intensity rays will destroy the healthy tissue surrounding the tumour. If the doctor uses low-intensity rays then the healthy tissue will be saved but the tumour will remain unaffected too. This dilemma can be solved by a "convergence solution" which proposes that the doctor send low-intensity rays from a number of different directions so that they converge on the tumour, summing to a high intensity to destroy it. However, only about 10% of subjects produce this solution if they are given the problem on its own.

Gick and Holyoak (1980) gave subjects a story about a general attacking a fortress. The general could not use his whole army to take the fortress because the roads leading to it were mined to explode if large groups of men passed over them. He therefore divided his army up into small groups of men and sent them along different roads to the fortress so that they converged on it. When subjects were given this analogous story to memorise and later asked if they could use it to solve the radiation problem the rates of convergence solutions rose to about 80% (see Figure 15.5). So, people could use the analogous story to solve the problem. However, without a specific hint to use the analogy subjects did not tend to notice it (Holyoak & Koh, 1987; Keane, 1987; but see Schunn & Dunbar, 1996, for evidence of priming influences without analogue retrieval).

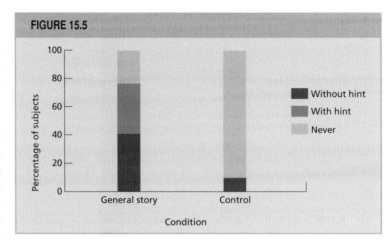

**FIGURE 15.5**

Some of the results from Gick and Holyoak (1980, Experiment 4) showing the percentage of subjects who solved the radiation problem when they were given an analogy (general-story condition) or were just asked to solve the problem (control condition). Note that just under half of the subjects in the general-story condition had to be given a hint to use the story analogue before they solved the problem.

Apart from the difficulties involved in retrieving remote analogues, Gentner, Ratterman, and Forbus (1992) have shown that subjects tend to retrieve analogues that *only* share superficial features (so-called mere appearance matches). In other words, people are more likely to retrieve a story about doctors using rays, even if that story involves events that are irrelevant to the radiation problem. These results support the intuition that one reason why acts of creativity involving remote analogies are fairly rare is that most people have difficulties retrieving potentially relevant experiences from memory (Keane, 1987; Ripoll, 1998, 1999). However, Wharton et al. (1994) have shown that people may not be as poor at retrieval as they first seem. They found that subjects can retrieve deep analogues, once they are distinct from competing analogues stored in memory.

## Theories and models of analogical thinking

There is now considerable theoretical agreement about the basis for analogical mapping and about what should be explained by models based on this theory (Holyoak & Thagard, 1995; Hummel & Holyoak, 1997). Table 15.1 shows the set of phenomena that a model should manifest. The phenomena outline the important psychological properties of analogy. For instance, that it involves finding a one-to-one (isomorphic) mapping between ideas on two domains, and that the similarity of the concepts plays an important role in helping to find these correspondences.

However, the specific models instantiating this theory differ in their success at accounting for these phenomena: the Structure-Mapping Engine (SME; Falkenhainer, Forbus, & Gentner, 1986; 1989), the Incremental Analogy Machine (IAM; see Keane & Brayshaw, 1988; Keane, Ledgeway, & Duff, 1994), the Analogical Constraint Mapping Engine (ACME; Holyoak & Thagard, 1989), and LISA (Hummel & Holyoak, 1997). At present, the LISA model is probably the most adequate model, followed by IAM, SME, and ACME, at dealing with these key phenomena.

For instance, Keane (1997) has reported one key result that was predicted by the IAM model. IAM attempts to find analogies in an incremental fashion; that is, the basic proposal realised in the model is that people try to break an analogy up into chunks of knowledge and map each chunk in a consistent way one after the other. Using so-called "unnatural analogies", Keane gave subjects mapping problems that had a non-thematic or thematic base domain (see Figure 15.6 and Table 15.2). The non-thematic and thematic problems were structurally identical in their written form, but the thematic version told a vignette about a love-triangle. Using his IAM model, Keane predicted that subjects would infer causal relations for the thematic problem, and that this extra relational structure would form a chunk of knowledge that would make the problem easier to map. IAM (and LISA) predicts that causal structure in the base domain alone (i.e., A list) is sufficient to improve mapping, but all other models require relational

**TABLE 15.1**

**Seven core phenomena of analogical thinking proposed by Hummel and Holyoak (1997)**

- *Isomorphism.* People use relational structure to find one-to-one (or isomorphic) mappings between corresponding objects in two domains when such objects are dissimilar or non-corresponding objects are (misleadingly) similar (Ross, 1977, 1989).

- *Semantic similarity.* In general, similarity between domains eases mapping (Gentner & Toupin, 1986; Keane et al., 1994).

- *Pragmatic centrality.* When parts of a domain are emphasised (e.g., by instructions) or deemed important they are more likely to be used in a mapping (Spellman & Holyoak, 1996; but see Keane, 1988, 1996).

- *Many mappings for one analogy.* For any two domains there may be several different analogies drawn (Clement & Genter, 1991; Keane 1997; Spellman & Holyoak, 1996).

- *Incrementality.* The order in which parts of two domains are incrementally matched can effect the analogy that is found for two domains (Keane, 1997; Keane et al., 1994).

- *Unnatural analogies are difficult.* Certain mapping problems which involve analogical mapping but lack semantic similarities — so-called unnatural analogies — are much more difficult for people to solve (Keane et al., 1994).

- *Mapping predicates with different arguments.* In some cases, people can match predicates with different numbers of arguments.

**FIGURE 15.6**

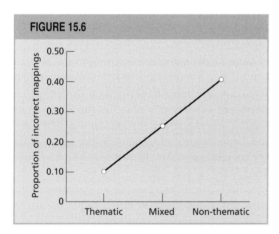

The mean proportion of incorrect mappings produced by participants in the different conditions of Keane's (1997) Experiment 3. Copyright © 1997 by the American Psychological Association. Reprinted with permission.

structure to be shared between domains (i.e., matching causal relations should be present in both the A and B lists). The results showed that subjects in the thematic conditions made significantly fewer mapping errors than subjects in the non-thematic problems; a result that has been subsequently replicated (Kubose, Hummel, & Holyoak, in press).

## Cognitive neuropsychology of analogical thinking

Analogical thinking is one of the few areas in thinking research where computational models have become tightly constrained by evidence from neurological studies (Hummel & Holyoak, 1997). The LISA model has a restricted short-term memory based on neurological constraints about the number of relations that can be represented and mapped in a given time-step. As in other forms of

**TABLE 15.2**

| Examples of the mapping problems used in Experiment 3 (Keane, 1997) | | | |
| --- | --- | --- | --- |
| Thematic | | Non-thematic | |
| List A | List B | List A | List B |
| Jim kisses Mary. | Ruth motivates Debra. | Jim hugs Mary. | Ruth motivates Debra. |
| Jim loves Mary. | Ruth knows Debra. | Jim sees Mary. | Ruth knows Debra. |
| Bill loves Mary. | Laura motivates Debra. | Bill sees Mary. | Laura motivates Debra. |
| Bill is jealous of Jim. | Laura waves to Ruth. | Bill is beside Jim. | Laura waves to Ruth. |

thought, the prefrontal cortex has been implicated in analogical thinking. Recent PET studies have shown, using proportional analogies with geometrical shapes, that analogical mapping is localised in the left prefrontal cortex and left inferior parietal cortex (Wharton, et al., 1998). Wharton et al.'s task involved identifying source–target pairs of geometrical shapes that were analogous or identical. This is further support for the proposal that analogy, like other forms of thinking, is essentially about the integration of multiple relations, a task that appears to be localised in the dorsolateral prefrontal cortex (Grafman, 1995; Robin & Holyoak, 1995). Interestingly, Baddeley (1992) has identified the same region as being responsible for working memory and executive functions (see Chapter 6) suggesting that relational integration may be essentially what working memory does (Waltz et al., 1999).

## SCIENTIFIC DISCOVERY BY HYPOTHESIS TESTING

Although analogies may be used to make new discoveries and develop new hypotheses, they are not the only means available to scientists. Other cognitive processes have been implicated in hypothesis formation and entirely different processes are involved in the testing of hypotheses. In the philosophy of science, Karl Popper (1968, 1969, 1972; see also Magee, 1973) argued that hypotheses could never be shown to be logically true by simply generalising from *confirming* instances (i.e., induction). As the philosopher Bertrand Russell pointed out, a scientist turkey might form the generalisation "Each day I am fed" because this hypothesis has been confirmed every day of his life. However, the generalisation provides no *certainty* that the turkey will be fed tomorrow, and if tomorrow is Christmas Eve then it is likely to be proven false. Popper concluded that the hallmark of science is not confirmation but *falsification*. Scientists attempt to form hypotheses that can be shown to be untrue by experimental tests. According to Popper, falsification separates scientific from unscientific activities, like religion

and pseudo-science (e.g., psychoanalysis). Against Popper's dictates, most ordinary people and scientists often seek confirmatory rather than disconfirmatory evidence when testing their hypotheses (see Evans, 1989; Gorman, 1992; Mitroff, 1974; Mynatt, Doherty, & Tweney, 1977; Tweney, 1998). For instance, Mitroff (1974) carried out a study of NASA scientists which revealed that they tended to seek confirmation of their hypotheses more often than disconfirmation.

## Confirmation bias in the 2–4–6 task

A number of key tasks have been used in the hypothesis-testing literature, most notably the 2–4–6 task (see Wason, 1960, 1977, and Chapter 16 on the Wason selection task). In the 2–4–6 task, subjects have to discover a rule known to the experimenter, starting with the hint that the number triple 2–4–6 is an instance of it. The experimenter's rule is that the numbers are "an ascending sequence". Subjects have to write down additional triples along with their reason for suggesting them. So, a subject might write 6–8–10, giving "numbers ascending by twos" as the rationale, to which the experimenter would answer that "yes, this triple is also an instance of the rule". After the subject has generated a number of such triples (e.g., 20–22–24, 45–47–49) and has received the positive feedback that they are all instances of the rule, they can declare what they think the rule to be (e.g., "numbers ascending by twos"). However, this is not the experimenter's rule, and after they are informed of this they must continue generating triples and proposing other rules until they guess correctly. The task allows subjects to generate an infinite variety of hypotheses and tests. Unfortunately, most of these alternatives are not the rule that is required. Wason (1960) found that subjects tended to gather evidence that confirmed their hypothesised rules, rather than generating examples that would falsify their hypotheses (like 33–31–32). He called this tendency a *confirmation bias*, subjects sought confirmation for hypotheses rather than resorting to falsification. Mahony (1976) also found that scientists fared no better on the task than other groups (indeed, clergymen proved to be better at abandoning their hypotheses).

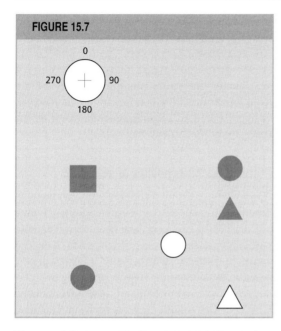

**FIGURE 15.7**

The type of display used by Mynatt et al. (1977) to study confirmation bias. Subjects had to direct a particle that was fired from the upper left part of the screen, by selecting the direction of its path. The relative shading of the objects indicates the two levels of brightness at which objects were presented.

Confirmation bias appears to be quite prevalent. Mynatt, Doherty, and Tweney (1977) found similar results in a simulation world that was closer to real scientific testing. In this computer world, subjects fired particles at circles and triangles that were presented at two brightness levels (low and high). The world had other features but all of these were irrelevant to the task (see Figure 15.7). Subjects were not told that the lower-brightness shapes had a 4.2 cm invisible boundary around them that deflected particles. At the beginning of the experiment, they were shown arrangements of shapes which suggested the initial hypothesis that "triangles deflect particles". They were then presented with pairs of screens, where one screen contained similar features to those that deflected particles and the other screen contained novel features. Subjects were divided into three groups that were instructed to adopt either a confirmatory strategy, a disconfirmatory strategy, or no particular strategy (i.e., a control). Again, as in the 2–4–6

task, subjects tended to confirm their hypotheses by picking the confirming screen 71% of the time. Furthermore, the strategy instructions did not deflect subjects from this confirmation bias. Mynatt, Doherty, and Tweney (1978) found similar results using an interactive version of this simulation world. They also found that subjects tended to ignore falsificatory evidence when it occurred. More recently, Garavan, Doherty, and Mynatt (1997) have proposed that attempts to falsify in such complex environments are just too difficult for people to do, although they also proposed that a new classification for types of hypothesis tests needed to be developed. More generally, one of the things that should be remembered about falsification and confirmation is that either may be appropriate at different times. Chalmers (1982) has pointed out that established theories should be falsifiable, but that it will often be more beneficial to a scientist to seek confirmatory evidence during the development of a new theory.

The failure of instructions to undo people's confirmation bias led subsequent researchers to try a number of different manipulations to encourage disconfirmation. Tweney et al. (1980) used a manipulation that increased subjects' disconfirmatory responses by using either confirmatory instructions (it was pointed out that given a hypothetical triple 3–3–3 and the rule "three equal numbers", this rule could be tested with triples like 8–8–8 to confirm the hypothesis) or disconfirmatory instructions (given a hypothetical triple 3–3–3 and the rule "three equal numbers", subjects were told that if triples like 5–7–9 were correct then the rule would be wrong). However, even though subjects changed their strategy, Tweney et al. did not find any improvement in their success on the problem. Gorman and Gorman (1984) observed greater success, along with an increase in the use of disconfirmation on the 2–4–6 task, when they instructed subjects to use a disconfirmatory strategy and did not give subjects feedback as to the correctness of their hypotheses (see Gorman, 1992, for other related studies).

All these studies indicate that confirmation bias is difficult to modify by instruction. However, some researchers have argued that the studies fail to prove that subjects have *the intention to confirm their hypotheses* (see Evans, 1983; Klayman & Ha, 1987; Poletiek, 1996; Wetherick, 1962). They point out that subjects are led to induce a hypothesis that is a specific version of the experimenter's rule (e.g., "numbers ascending by twos" is more specific than "any ascending sequence"). As the subject's rule is a restricted version of the experimenter's rule, any triple that fits the subject's hypothesis will also fit the experimenter's. Thus, they fail to produce triples that do not fit their rule, but do conform to the experimenter's. In other situations, an attempt to test a hypothesis with a triple could result in a falsification (which could be intended by subjects). However, in the 2–4–6 problem falsification can only be achieved by explicitly trying negative tests of the hypothesis.

There is one manipulation that has been surprising successful at improving subjects' performance on the 2–4–6 task; this involved indicating to subjects that there were two distinct rules to be considered. Tweney et al. (1980) told subjects that the experimenter had two rules in mind; one of these rules generated DAX triples and the other generated MED triples. They were also told that 2–4–6 was a DAX triple. The DAX rule was intended to be what has been called the experimenter's rule (i.e., "any ascending sequence"), whereas the MED rule characterised the rule that generated any other triple. Thus, instead of being told that their triples were right or wrong, subjects were told that they were DAX or MED. This manipulation led to the striking result that the majority of subjects generated the correct rule on their first attempt. Furthermore, this success occurred even though subjects continued to make "confirmatory" tests of their hypothesis. In this version of the task subjects succeed because they do not have to disconfirm the DAX hypothesis, rather they can alternatively test the MED hypothesis in a confirmatory fashion. Wharton, Cheng, and Wickens (1993) have ruled out a number of other explanations for the DAX–MED effects, such as the information quantity in this version of the task (e.g., the greater number of tests performed before the rule is announced) and the possible influence of positive labels. Their results supported the proposal that the effect follows

from being given two complementary goals to test involving the DAX and MED hypotheses. However, Vallée-Tourangeau, Austin, and Rankin (1995) have shown that these results are not specifically due to the complementarity of the hypotheses but rather arise from the breadth of hypotheses that subjects generate based on the specific testing strategy they adopt.

## Problem-space accounts of scientific discovery

Traditionally, for the most part, hypothesis testing and discovery have not been formulated in problem-space terms (see Chapter 14). Kulkarni and Simon (1988, 1990) adopted a historical perspective by simulating Hans Kreb's discovery of the urea cycle in biochemistry in a system called KEKDA. One of the key phenomena modelled in this system is how surprising new results can lead to new hypotheses and theories. Klahr and Dunbar (1988; Klahr, Fay, & Dunbar, 1993) have also looked at discovery in different task situations. In one task, they asked subjects to discover the function of a mystery button (labelled "RPT") for controlling a toy vehicle called Big Trak. Subjects tested the function of the button by including it in brief sets of instructions they had to write to make the toy move. Subjects, therefore, propose hypotheses about the function and then experimentally test them by seeing whether they work. Initially, subjects adopt a positive test strategy reasoning that "If Big Trak does X then my hypothesis is correct", although they are often forced to revise their theories by negative evidence.

Using problem-space theory, Klahr and Dunbar characterised scientific discovery as a *dual-space search*; one space contains the experimental possibilities in the situation and the other contains a space of possible hypotheses. These ideas are very similar to the ideas proposed by Ohlsson (1992) to explain insight problem solving (see Chapter 14). In searching the *hypothesis space* the initial state is some knowledge of the domain and the goal state is a hypothesis that can account for that knowledge in a more concise, universal form. Hypothesis generation in this space may be the result of a variety of mechanisms (e.g., memory search, analogical mapping, or remindings). Search in the *experiment space* is directed towards experiments that will discriminate between rival hypotheses and yield interpretable outcomes. On the basis of protocol analysis, Klahr and Dunbar distinguished two groups of subjects, *theorists* who preferred to search the space of hypotheses and *experimenters* who preferred to search the space of experiments (see Van Joolingen & DeJong, 1997, for a further elaboration of this approach). Gorman (1992) has suggested that much previous research has concentrated on the experiment space, ignoring the hypothesis space. The latter is important, as is illustrated in the DAX–MED study which shows how subjects' representation of hypothesis goals can be very important to their subsequent success on a task. Finally, it should be pointed out that all these studies were based on individual problem solving, when most scientific discoveries are collaborative efforts between groups of individuals. Unfortunately, the cognitive processes in discovery appear to change when more than one individual is involved (see Dunbar, 1997; Okada & Simon, 1997).

## EVALUATING PROBLEM-SOLVING RESEARCH

Problem-solving research is important to cognitive psychology because it is a testbed for the methodology of cognitive science. Since the advent of information-processing psychology, problem-solving research has been at the forefront in combining the use computational techniques and empirical testing (cf. Newell & Simon, 1972). During this time, the area has made steady progress and is quite unified in embracing a common theoretical stance, based on problem-space theory. To conclude these chapters on problem solving, we consider a number of core issues that are posed by this research. First, we consider what problem-space theory says about what makes problems difficult. Second, we broach the question of the ecological validity of problem-solving research. Finally, we consider the extent to which thinking

phenomena can be modelled using connectionist techniques.

## Why are problems difficult?

Given 30 or so years of problem-solving research, we should be able to say something about what influences the ease of problem solving. First, problems are made more difficult if people have to memorise and search through a large problem space to find a solution. Stated more simply, problems get difficult when people have to "hold more in their heads" (for "heads" read "working memory"). Second, search difficulties can be alleviated by knowledge of the problem; whole parts of the problem can be chunked and routine strategies used, all of which lightens the load on working memory. In short, the more familiar a problem the easier it becomes. Third, problems can be difficult because they are ill defined; again, the ability to define problems hinges on having the right sort of knowledge available. Problems may be difficult because it is not clear what they are about or how they can be solved.

The constant theme that emerges from this research is that problems are difficult because of two main limitations; resource limitations and limitations of knowledge. The major resource limitations lie in a working memory that can only process a certain quantity of information at a certain rate. Knowledge limitations can give rise to a wide range of difficulties. Furthermore, there is an interaction between these two limitations; the probability of being affected by resource limitations can decrease the more knowledge one has of a problem (because of chunking). In Chapter 14 we saw that the essential difference between expert problem solvers and novice problem solvers hinges on the amount and type of knowledge they have available about a domain; this knowledge may take the form of "facts" about the domain or "rules" about what to do in the domain. Knowledge is the key to unlocking difficult problems.

Indeed, many of the problem-solving methods we have encountered in these two chapters can be classified in terms of the amount and specificity of their domain knowledge (see Carbonell, 1986, and Figure 15.8).

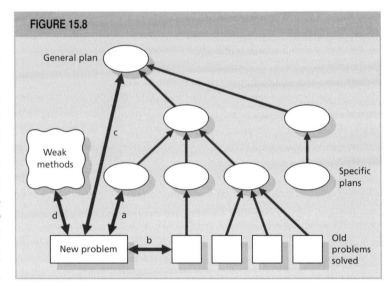

**FIGURE 15.8**

Problem solving may involve the following: (a) instantiating specific plans, (b) using analogical transformation to a known solution of a similar problem, (c) applying general plans to reduce the problem, (d) applying weak methods to search heuristically for a possible solution, or using a combination of these approaches. Reproduced with the permission of the publishers from *Machine learning: An artificial intelligence approach*, Volume 2, edited by R.S. Michalski, J.G. Carbonell, and T.M. Mitchell. Copyright © by Morgan Kaufmann.

- In knowledge-poor, puzzle situations where we have little useful past experience, the only useful methods are universal, weak methods (e.g., means–ends analysis).
- A problem may be relatively familiar but we may lack specific plans to solve it, in which case general plans may be applied; these plans will break the problem down into sub-problems, in a divide-and-conquer fashion, even though these sub-problems will not suggest immediate solutions (cf, in successive problem-solving attempts on the Tower of Hanoi problem).
- With more familiar problems we may have various specific plans or schemata about how to solve them (e.g., the expert physicist or programmer); in these cases, we can instantiate such schemata and solve any sub-problems that arise with other instantiated schemata.
- Finally, if problem solvers have no specific or general schemata, they may choose a specific past experience (e.g., a specific previously encountered problem) and apply it by analogy to solve the problem they face, or they may modify some past instances using structured imagination.

These four situations lay out the main ways in which researchers have proposed that different types of knowledge are used. Clearly, we would not want to maintain that the application of these approaches is mutually exclusive; people may use a combination of all four at different points in solving a particular problem. The key point, however, is that different methods of problem solving can be distinguished by the amount and types of knowledge they use.

## Is problem-solving research ecologically valid?

Earlier we encountered the criticism that problem-solving research was not ecologically valid because it only considered well defined, puzzle-like problems. This criticism certainly held water in the early history of the area, but is less true now.

We have seen that the research on expertise and mental models has broadened research to consider problem solving in the classroom and other everyday, real-world situations. Investigations of physics expertise have important implications for the teaching of this discipline in schools. Research on programming expertise tackles a very important ability for technological development and suggests better ways to design programming languages and the computers that use such languages. Some expert–novice research, which we have not reviewed here, has been applied to everyday tasks in other domains. For example, Lesgold and his associates (Lesgold et al., 1988; see also Lesgold, 1988) have examined expertise in the reading of X-rays by radiologists. Patel and his associates (Patel & Groen, 1986, 1993; Patel, Groen, & Arocha, 1993) have examined the expertise under-lying medical diagnosis. This work has taken cognitive psychology out into the world and indeed, has led some to argue that the everyday world is the most important context in which to test cognitive theories (see Anderson, 1987b; Anderson & Lebiere, 1998).

## Connectionism and thinking

The rise of the modelling techniques associated with connectionism appears to be at variance with the character of thinking and the classical, sym-bolic models that have tended to be used in this area. The argument that theorists often make is that thinking is inherently serial and therefore is not amenable to a parallel processing treatment. Intuitively, this looks like a reasonable proposal, but it does not stand up to much scrutiny. If one examines carefully the models of thinking in the literature, connectionist techniques are used repeatedly.

Consider Anderson's (1983, 1993, 1996; Anderson & Lebiere, 1998) ACT models. Even though they use a production-rule system, the models also have a declarative memory, that is a network of concepts through which activation passes in parallel (indeed, it is a precursor of localist, connectionist nets; see Chapters 1 and 9). More recently, we have seen that connectionist models have been produced to model aspects of skill (see e.g., Lamberts, 1990). Indeed, Holyoak (1991) has suggested that the next generation of expertise models will all have a connectionist char-acter. In analogical thinking, parallel constraint satisfaction has been used with some success; such methods seem central to analogue retrieval (see Thagard et al. 1990) and are an elegant solution to some aspects of analogical mapping (Holyoak & Thagard, 1989, 1995). Holyoak and Spellman (1993) have argued that these techniques have a wider applicability in a range of problem-solving situations. Finally, Shastri and Ajjanagadde's (1993) work on dynamic binding suggests a gen-eral solution to modelling problems of seriality in many thinking phenomena. They have been used with some success in modelling analogical thinking (Hummel & Holyoak, 1997) and have the added benefit that they are explicitly designed with neurological constraints in mind.

## CHAPTER SUMMARY

In this chapter, we have reviewed several aspects of creativity broadly organised into general approaches followed by a consideration of three specific treatments of possible cognitive processes involved in different expressions of creativity. The other main piece of work has been an evaluation of problem solving in general, as it has been reviewed over these two chapters. To summarise:

- The idea that creativity is a function of innate talents is not as straightforward as it first seems; not only is the idea of a talent hard to define but, once defined, there is little evidence to support the idea that such innate talent exists.
- There are varying degrees of support for the proposal of different stages of creativity—notably, incubation and illumination. More productively, the Geneplore model has a high-level account of creativity—as generation and exploration—that is more easily specified as detailed cognitive processes.
- People often make discoveries by using mental models to simulate aspects of the world, an ability that appears to depend on domain-specific knowledge based on experiences in the world.

- Analogy is another method often used in discovery, whereby people use the relational structure of one domain of knowledge (e.g., the solar system) to understand or make inferences about a new domain/problem (e.g., the atom). There are a number of computational models of analogical thinking, some of which include explicit neurological constraints.
- Both trained scientists and ordinary people have a tendency to confirm their hypotheses rather than disconfirm them, even though logically the latter is the only valid strategy. This finding has been a constant of laboratory hypothesis-testing tasks (like the 2–4–6 task) as well as more realistic, simulated environment tasks.
- The most important dimension to understanding problem-solving behaviour is the amount and type of knowledge that people bring to bear in the situation; this factor will determine the problem-solving strategies used and the likelihood of success. Problem-solving research can be criticised for lacking ecological validity, although this is less true today. Finally, thinking research has been increasingly influenced by connectionist-type models.

## FURTHER READING

Gilhooly, K.J. (1996). *Thinking: Directed, undirected and creative* (3rd Edn). London: Academic Press. This book provides more detail on some of the research covered here and explores other areas too.

Gorman, M.E. (1992). *Simulating science: Heuristic, mental models and technoscientific thinking.* Bloomington, IN: Indiana University Press. This volume is a good source on scientific discovery and hypothesis testing.

Holyoak, K.J., Gentner, D., & Kokinov, B. (Eds.) (2000). *Analogy: A cognitive science perspective.* Cambridge, MA: MIT Press. This book is the most up-to-date treatment of the main work being done on analogy.

Ward, T.B., Smith, S.M., & Finke, R.A. (1995). *The creative cognition approach.* Cambridge, MA: MIT Press. This book is a good account of a very interesting practical and empirically testable approach to creativity.

# 16

# Reasoning and Deduction

## INTRODUCTION

Reasoning, as one of the oldest research areas in psychology, has concerned itself with a key question about human nature: "Are human beings rational?". Philosophers have tended to answer this question with a resounding "yes", with arguments that the laws of logic *are* the laws of thought (Boole, 1854; Mill, 1843). This basic idea has been used, albeit in more sophisticated forms, in the psychology of reasoning. The psychology of reasoning covers both deductive and inductive reasoning. When people carry out deductive reasoning they usually determine what conclusion, if any, *necessarily* follows when certain statements or premises are assumed to be true. In inductive reasoning, people make a generalised conclusion from premises that describe particular instances (see e.g. Chapters 10 and 15).

Johnson-Laird and Byrne (1991, p. 3) point out that deductive reasoning is a central intellectual ability, which is necessary:

in order to formulate plans; to evaluate alternative actions; to determine the con-

sequences of assumptions and hypotheses; to interpret and formulate instructions, rules and general principles; to pursue arguments and negotiations; to weigh evidence and to assess data; to decide between competing theories; and to solve problems. A world without deduction would be a world without science, technology, laws, social conventions and culture.

Deductive reasoning research makes central use of logical systems—especially the propositional calculus—to characterise the abstract structure of reasoning problems. So, we will review the logic of deduction in some detail before considering the psychological research. If you are not familiar with logic then you may find that a little extra effort with this section will improve your understanding of later sections.

In this chapter, we focus on deductive reasoning with conditionals or, more simply, reasoning with "if". The propositional calculus and reasoning based on it involve the use of a number of logical operators: *or*, *and*, *if . . . then*, *if and only if* (see Evans, Newstead, & Byrne, 1993b, for a full account of propositional reasoning). In research on conditional reasoning the question "Are people rational?" is re-cast as "Are they logical?". In other words, do people conform to the logical interpretation of *if . . . then*, make valid inferences and reject the invalid inferences dictated by the propositional calculus (see section on logic). As we shall see later on, the simple answer is "No".

## The use of logic in reasoning research

Newell and Simon's problem-space theory uses the notion of an idealised problem space to characterise the abstract structure of a problem, quite independently of any psychological proposals (see Chapters 14 and 15). In reasoning research, some logics—usually, the propositional calculus—have been used in a similar manner. These logics are used to characterise the abstract structure of reasoning problems and to determine categories of responses (i.e., incorrect and correct answers). So, a clear understanding of this sub-section is essential to make sense of large portions of reasoning research.

In mathematical systems we use symbols to stand for things (e.g., let *h1* be the height of the Empire State building and *h2* be the height of the Eiffel Tower) and then apply mathematical operators to these symbols to manipulate them in various ways to produce a new statement (the combined height of both buildings should be *h1 plus h2*, where *plus* is the operator used). In an analogous fashion, logical systems use symbols to stand for sentences and apply logical operators to them to reach conclusions. So, in the propositional calculus, we might use *P* to stand for the verbally expressible proposition "It is raining" and *Q* to stand for "Alicia gets wet", and then use the logical operator *if . . . then* to relate these two propositions: *if P then Q*. It is very important to remember that even though logical operators use common words (such as *or, and, if . . . then*) in logic these terms have very different meanings. The logical meaning of the conditional (i.e., *if . . . then*) is well specified and differs markedly from everyday conceptions of the words "If . . . then". In the next subsection, we attempt to explain how logicians specify the meaning or semantics of these operators.

## Truth tables and the "meaning" of logical operators

The propositional calculus has a small number of logical operators: *not, and, or, if . . . then, if and only if*. In this logical system, propositions can only have one of two truth-values, they are either true or false. For instance, if *P* stands for "it is raining" then *P* is either true (in which case it *is* raining) or *P* is false (it is not raining). The calculus does not admit any uncertainty about the truth of *P* (where it is not really raining but is so misty you could almost call it raining), although there are other multi-valued logics that do.

Logicians use a system of *truth tables* to lay out the possibilities for a proposition (i.e., whether it is true or false) and to explain how a logical operator acts on that proposition. For example, a single proposition *P* can be either true or false. In truth tables, this is notated by putting *P* as a heading and showing the two values of it, as follows:

*P*
T
F

If we want to indicate the effects of *not* on *P*, then we get the following truth table:

| *P* | *not P* |
| --- | --- |
| T | F |
| F | T |

This new column shows the effects of *not* on *P*, when *P* is true or false. So, when *P* is true the result of negating *P* will make that proposition false, and when *P* is false, negation will make *P* true. This truth table defines the "meaning" of *not*.

Consider the more complicated case of the conditional, which unlike negation involves two propositions (P, Q): *if P then Q*. On their own *P* and *Q* can each be true or false; when they are combined there are four possible states of affairs (see Table 16.1): both *P* and *Q* can be true, *P* can be true when *Q* is false and vice versa, and both can be false.

Now consider what happens when *if . . . then* is applied to these propositions. First, when *P* and *Q* are true then clearly *if P then Q* is true. If we

**TABLE 16.1**

The truth tables for the conditional and the biconditional

|  |  | Conditional | Biconditional |
|---|---|---|---|
| P | Q | if P then Q | if and only if P then Q |
| T | T | T | T |
| T | F | F | F |
| F | T | T | F |
| F | F | T | T |

know that "it is raining" and that "Alicia is wet" then we can be confident that the assertion "If it is raining, Alicia gets wet" is true. However, if it is raining (*P* is true) and Alicia is not wet (*Q* is false) then clearly the assertion "If it is raining, Alicia gets wet" is false.

The next two cases are somewhat trickier. Imagine that it is not raining (*P* is false) and Alicia still gets wet (*Q* is true), then, psychologically, one may feel uncertain whether the statement *if P then Q* is true or false. You might want to say, "Well, the statement might be true" or "We don't know whether it's true or not". However, in the context of the logic, we are dealing with a world in which everything is either true or false. Hence, the logicians' choice has been to maintain that the assertion is true, when *P* is false and *Q* is true; something else may have made Alicia wet—someone may have thrown a bucket of water over her—so we have no grounds for saying that "If it is raining, Alicia gets wet" is false; therefore, it is true. Again, when *P* and *Q* are false—when "it is not raining" and "Alicia is not wet"—the assertion is also considered to be true. This then is the logician's conception of the meaning of *if . . . then* (see Table 16.1 for the truth table).

Furthermore, logicians distinguish this treatment of *if . . . then* (called *material implication* in logic) from *if and only if*, the *biconditional* (or in logic *material equivalence*). The biconditional (notated as ↔) has a similar truth table to the conditional except for the *P* is false and *Q* is true case; it characterises this case as making the assertion false. The reason for this is that the biconditional rules out other states of affairs (like the bucket of water); that is, P ↔ Q is read as "if and only if *P* is true, then *Q* is true".

We shall see later that people often deviate from these logical interpretations in their reasoning. Using these truth tables it is possible to define valid and invalid inferences (see later section). For example, the inference of *Q* from the true premises *If P then Q* and *P* is a valid inference, called *modus ponens*, and the inference of *not-P* from the true premises *If P then Q* and *not-Q* is a valid inference, called *modus tollens*. However, although most people make the modus ponens inference readily, a lot fewer people are willing to make the modus tollens one. As we shall see, these deviations from the dictates of the logic become the evidential bread-and-butter of theories of reasoning (outlined in the next section). The importance of the logical analysis presented here is that it allows us to characterise the abstract structure of reasoning problems and gives us a criterion for determining whether a certain conclusion is valid or invalid, correct or in error.

## THEORETICAL APPROACHES TO REASONING

Deductive reasoning research covers a wide variety of tasks from syllogistic reasoning, to reasoning with spatial connectives, to reasoning with propositional connectives (e.g., *if, or,* and *not*). Any adequate theory of deduction should be able to explain the phenomena arising from this research. At this point there are probably only two real candidate theories to meet this challenge (the abstract rule and mental models theories), although there are other accounts that cover smaller sets of phenomena. Each of these are briefly outlined next and then some of them are expanded on in subsequent sections.

## Abstract rule theories of deduction

The abstract rule theory generally takes logical notions of validity as its normative model of reasoning (see previous section). It assumes that people reason validly by applying abstract, content-free rules of inference, in a manner that is similar to the derivation of proofs in logic. In short, people employ a form of *mental logic* to derive conclusions from premises. However, people can make mistakes because some derivations are more complex than others (and exceed working memory) or because they misunderstand the premises of a given deductive problem. The main proponents of this view are Braine and O'Brien (1991; Braine, 1990; O'Brien, 1993, 1995; O'Brien, Braine, & Yang, 1994) and Rips (1994).

## Mental models theory

The mental models theory also, in essence, assumes logical notions of validity as its normative model (Johnson-Laird, 1999; Johnson-Laird & Byrne, 1991). It assumes that people reason by manipulating mental models of a set of premises, in a manner akin to semantic methods of proof in logic. In short, people construct mental models that represent possible states-of-affairs in the world, and then they describe and verify these models to reach valid conclusions. A conclusion is valid if there are no counterexamples to it; that is, if there is no state of affairs in which the premises are true but the conclusion is false. Again, however, people may make mistakes if they have to represent a large number of models that exceed their working memory. The main exponents of this view are Johnson-Laird and Byrne (1991, 1996; Johnson-Laird, 1983, 1995a, b, 1999).

## Domain-specific rule theories

Most domain-specific rule theories are essentially dual-process theories. They assume that some basic logical competence is handled by some core mechanism (be it an abstract rule or mental models one), but that there is a second mechanism using domain-specific rules that handles certain effects. Thus, reasoning is, in part, based on rules that are sensitive to the content of different situations; rules that are encoded in domain-specific schemata (see Chapter 9). There is a wide variety of such theories that propose different flavours of rules from pragmatic reasoning schemata (Cheng & Holyoak, 1985; Cheng, Holyoak, Nisbett, & Oliver, 1986; Politzer & Nguyen-Xuan, 1992) to social exchange schemata (Cosmides, 1989; Cosmides & Tooby, 1992).

## Heuristics and bias accounts

Most heuristic/bias accounts are also essentially dual-process theories. They assume that people have a basic logical competence, which is sometimes over-ridden by various heuristics or biases. Reasoning is seen as being, in part, due to non-logical tendencies based on a response to superficial aspects of a task situation (e.g., the presence of matching negatives, the position of an item on a test screen). We have called these accounts rather than theories, as they are a loose collection of ideas rather than a coherent theory. They also carry a theoretical health warning in that they can involve reified phenomena as cognitive processes; that is, the tendency to turn the description of a phenomenon into a theory. For example, one might find in a particular reasoning problem that people always choose the conclusion on the top left of the screen and then "explain" this by saying that people have a left-bias heuristic, when we really should be seeking a deeper explanation of why such a bias might occur. Evans (1989, 1995; Wason & Evans, 1975) has been most active in exploring this approach in a reasoning context.

## Probabilistic theory

Unlike all the aforementioned theories, the probabilistic theory does not rely on logic for its normative model, but rather draws on probability theory (e.g., Bayesian probability theory). Reasoning is not about validity but is about maximising information gain to reduce uncertainty. A maximally informative statement is one that tells you something improbable or surprising, relative to your prior knowledge. People have the cognitive goal of reducing uncertainty by increasing informativeness, and they make conclusions designed to maximise informativeness. Oaksford and Chater (1994, 1995, 1996; Chater & Oaksford, 1999a, b) have developed this theory.

# HOW PEOPLE REASON WITH CONDITIONALS

Before giving an overview of the various theories of reasoning, we saw how truth tables are used to define the meaning of *if*. Using these truth tables it is possible to define what inferences are valid (or correct) and invalid (incorrect) according to logic. This definition of valid and invalid inferences is critical to the empirical treatment of reasoning because it defines the dependent measures used in most experiments. In this section, we show how the validity of inferences is determined and then review some of the standard evidence on conditional inference found in the literature. Our review focuses on inference tasks using conditional premises and on tasks about testing conditional rules (i.e., Wason's selection task).

## Conditional inferences: Valid and invalid forms

Earlier, we saw how propositions, like *P* and *Q*, were acted upon by logical operators. When a number of propositions are related together by a given logical operator we have a premise (e.g., *If P then Q*). Logics define a variety of rules of inference that can be used to make logically valid conclusions from premises. Consider the inference rules used on premises involving the conditional. Two valid inferences that can be made using conditionals are: *modus ponens* and *modus tollens*. An argument of the modus ponens form is as follows (it may help to keep the truth table in Table 16.1 close by, to understand the following discussion):

*Valid: Modus ponens*

*Premises*
If it is raining, then Alicia    *If P then Q,*
gets wet
It is raining.                   *P,*

*Conclusion*
Therefore, Alicia gets wet.    *Therefore, Q*

So, if you are given the conditional about it raining and Alicia getting wet, and are then told that it is raining, you can validly conclude that "Alicia gets wet". To understand this conclusion, note that there is only one line in the truth table where *P* is true and *if P then Q* is true, and this is the one where *Q* is also true (see Table 16.1).

It is important to remember that *logical validity* is not about the actual truth or falsehood of statements but about possibilities; that is, for a valid argument there is no possibility, as represented by lines on a truth table, in which all the premises are true and the conclusion false. So, even premises and conclusions we know to be patently ridiculous can be logically valid:

*Valid: Modus ponens*

*Premises*
If he is a cowboy, then    *If P then Q,*
he is a chair
He is a cowboy.            *P,*

*Conclusion*
Therefore, he is a chair.    *Therefore, Q*

The modus ponens form is obvious and most people readily make it when the content is sensible. However, the other valid inference made from the conditional—*modus tollens*—is not as intuitively obvious. This rule states that, if we are given the proposition *If P then Q* and that *Q* is false, then we can infer that *P* is false. Thus, the following argument is valid:

*Valid: Modus tollens*

*Premises*
If it is raining, then Alicia    *If P then Q,*
gets wet
Alicia does not get wet.    *not Q,*

*Conclusion*
Therefore, it is not raining.    *Therefore, not P*

Again, this inference is consistent with the truth table (in Table 16.1). The line where *If P then Q* is true and *Q* is false, is that one in which *P* is false.

**TABLE 16.2**

Valid and invalid inferences for the conditional

| *Valid* | | |
|---|---|---|
| | Modus ponens | If P then Q, P, Therefore, Q |
| | Modus tollens | If P then Q not Q Therefore, not P |
| *Invalid* | | |
| | Affirmation of the consequent | If P then Q Q, Therefore, P |
| | Denial of the antecedent | If P then Q, not-P Therefore, not-Q |

Modus ponens and modus tollens are the two valid inferences that can be drawn from simple conditional arguments. Two other inferences can be drawn but they are invalid (even though people often think them plausible). They are called the "affirmation of the consequent" and the "denial of the antecedent".

In the *affirmation of the consequent*, if *P then Q* is true and *Q* is true, for instance:

*Invalid: Affirmation of the consequent*

*Premises*
If it is raining, then Alicia    *If P then Q,*
gets wet
Alicia is wet.                   *Q,*

*Conclusion*
Therefore, it is raining.        *Therefore, P*

One can see where this form gets its name, because the consequent of the conditional premise (i.e., *Q*) has been affirmed. But why is it considered to be invalid? If you examine the truth table for the lines where *If P then Q* is true and *Q* is true, you can see that there are two lines that meet this description. On one of these lines, *P* is true and on the other *P* is false. This means that logically speaking the most we can conclude is that "no conclusion can be made". So, a conclusion which asserts that *P* is true is considered invalid.

A similar explanation can be made for the other invalid form, the *denial of the antecedent*; for example:

*Invalid: Denial of the antecedent*

*Premises*
If it is raining, then Alicia    *If P then Q,*
gets wet
It is not raining.               *not P,*

*Conclusion*
Therefore, Alicia does           *Therefore, not Q*
not get wet.

Here one has denied the antecedent of the conditional (i.e., the *P*). There are two lines in the truth table where *If P then Q* is true and *P* is false. In one of these lines, *Q* is false and in the other *Q* is true. Therefore, again, no firm conclusion can be made. So, to conclude that *not-Q* is the case is invalid (these forms are summarised in Table 16.2). If you think that these two invalid forms yield plausible conclusions, you are not alone.

## Making valid and invalid inferences

The literature on conditional reasoning in cognitive science is vast, as are the range of findings on how people reason with conditionals (see Evans et al., 1993b; Johnson-Laird & Byrne, 1991;

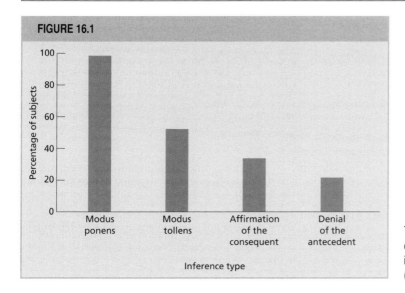

**FIGURE 16.1**

The percentage of subjects endorsing the various conditional inferences from Marcus and Rips (1979, Experiment 2).

Manktelow, 1999). We consider just some of these findings; the patterns of valid and invalid inferences made by subjects, the effects of context, and testing a conditional rule (i.e., the selection task). Later, during our review of the various theories we introduce further empirical tests that are based on the predictions made by specific theories.

As we hinted earlier, it is not the case that people automatically make the valid modus ponens and modus tollens inferences and resist the invalid denial of the antecedent and affirmation of the consequence inferences. Sometimes people fail to make valid inferences and consider invalid inferences to be acceptable. These results have been found in experiments where subjects are presented with a conditional statement (e.g., "if she gets up early, she will go for a run") and a premise (e.g., "she gets up early") and are asked to either evaluate a conclusion, draw a conclusion, or choose from a list of possible conclusions.

Figure 16.1 charts the characteristic pattern of inferences for each of the four forms (from Experiment 2 by Marcus & Rips, 1979). Typically, nearly 100% of subjects make the valid modus ponens inference, but most people find the modus tollens inference much harder, about 50% or so of subjects do not make this inference. On the other hand, many subjects accept the invalid inferences; the rates for making the denial of the antecedent and affirmation of the consequent inferences can increase to around 70%. In the Marcus and Rips' (1979) study 21% of subjects make the denial of the antecedent inference and 33% make the affirmation of the consequent inference (although the difference is not always in this direction; see Evans, 1993a, and Evans et al., 1993b, p. 36, for a composite table showing the results from several different experiments). As we will see, this pattern of inferences should be explained by any adequate theory of deductive reasoning.

## Context effects on inference with "if . . ."

In some contexts people do *not* make the inferences outlined earlier, what are called *context effects*. The rates of invalid or fallacious inferences can be modified by contexts in which further information is given (Rumain, Connell, & Braine, 1983). For example, if alternative antecedents to the conditional are provided then people avoid making the fallacious inferences (Markovits, 1984, 1985; Rumain et al., 1983). For example, the following argument explicitly indicates *alternative antecedents* to the consequent:

If it is raining then she will     *If P then Q,*
get wet,
If it is snowing then she will     *If R then Q,*
get wet,
She got wet,                       *Q,*
Therefore, ?                       *Therefore, ?*

The data show that people are more likely to produce the correct answer (i.e., no conclusion can be made) than the fallacious *P* conclusion they usually make in the affirmation of the consequent. So, when people are told about an explicit alternative to the consequent (the woman getting wet), they can use this extra information to generate the logically appropriate inference. On the face of it this suggests that extra information can help people to improve their logical reasoning.

However, Byrne (1989a) has found, using a similar paradigm to Rumain et al., that the provision of extra information can suppress the *valid* inferences as well as the invalid inferences. Byrne replicated the alternative-antecedents effect but also showed that *additional antecedents* reduced the frequency of valid modus ponens and modus tollens inferences (see Figure 16.2).

So, when subjects were given:

If she has an essay to write     *If P then Q,*
then she will study late
in the library,
If the library stays open        *If R then Q,*
then she will study late
in the library,
She has an essay to write         *P,*
Therefore, ?                      *Therefore, ?*

which contained the additional requirement of the "library staying open", people typically did not make the modus ponens inference to conclude that "she will study late in the library" (i.e., *Q*). This result has become important in the debate between different theoretical positions (Bach, 1993; Byrne, 1991, 1997; Fillenbaum, 1993; Politzer & Braine, 1991; Savion, 1993). Byrne, Espino, and Santamaria (1999) have explored the effects further to rule out a number of possible alternative explanations raised in these discussions (see later section on mental models).

There have also been several extensions of the work examining a group of related factors like causality, saliency, and uncertainty. Cummins, Lubart, Alksnis, and Rist (1991; Cummins, 1995) have examined causality effects on suppression by getting subjects to generate disabling conditions or alternative causal conditions:

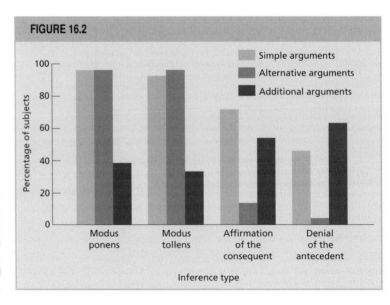

**FIGURE 16.2**

The percentage of subjects endorsing the various conditional inferences from Byrne (1989a) when they are given simple (standard conditional) arguments, alternative arguments, and additional arguments.

*Premise*:    If a student gets under 40% the exam is failed.

Disabling Condition:    The student was sick.

Alternative Cause:    The student did no coursework.

In general, the more disabling and alternative causes that are present the greater the implicit suppression of the valid inferences. Indeed, it seems that the more additional conditions people can think of, the greater the suppression of the inferences (Elio, 1997; Thompson, 1994, 1995). In a similar vein, Chan and Chua (1994) have shown that, based on background knowledge, additional requirements can have a differential impact on suppression depending on their relative saliency or strength. For example, given:

If Steven is invited then he will attend the dance party.    (Standard Premise)

If Steven knows the host well he will attend the dance party.    (Weak Additional)

If Steven is invited he will attend the dance party.    (Strong Additional)

then it seems as if all additional premises are not equal; suppression of the valid inferences is less with weak additional relative to strong additional premises (see Byrne et al., 1999, for further work on this finding).

Stevenson and Over (1995) have also shown that introducing a degree of uncertainty regarding the additional premises can undo the suppression effect. So, when subjects were presented with:

If John goes fishing, he will have a fish supper    (Standard Premise)

If John catches a fish, he will have a fish supper    (Additional Premise)

John is * lucky when he goes fishing    (Qualification)

John goes fishing

Therefore, ?

* One of the following words was used: *always, usually, rarely, never.*

Stevenson and Over found that, when *always* was used in the qualifying sentence, the suppression of modus ponens disappeared, but that it gradually increased as it moved from *always* to *never*.

## Evidence from Wason's selection task

Another strand of evidence on reasoning with conditionals comes from research on Wason's selection task, which is not purely a deductive reasoning task, but concerns hypothesis testing using a conditional rule (see Evans, 1982, 1989; Evans et al., 1993b; Wason, 1966 for reviews). The original findings on the task were taken as evidence of people's tendency to confirm hypotheses in reasoning situations (see Chapter 15 on hypothesis testing). Although the task has now assumed a special place in reasoning research, there is still some controversy about its utility as an instrument to examine human reasoning (Sperber, Cara & Girotto, 1995).

The selection task, first proposed by Wason (1966), looks like an innocuous puzzle but it hides a multitude of difficulties. In the original version, subjects are shown four cards face-down with letters or numbers on each of them (see Figure 16.3). They are told that each of these cards has a letter on one side and a number on the other side and they have to name the cards that *need* to be turned over to test the following rule:

> *If there is a vowel on one side of a card, then there is an even number on the other side of the card.*

Because you can turn over any of the four cards, there are four possible choices. However, subjects are asked to turn over only those cards that need to be turned over. The correct answer is to turn over just two cards, the E-card and the 7-card; but few subjects spontaneously pick these cards on this abstract version of the task. To understand why this is the correct answer, first consider why the 4-card and K-card choices are wrong (and keep the truth table for *if . . . then* in Table 16.1 handy).

In logic, the rule in the selection task is a conditional *if P then Q*; *P* here is the statement that

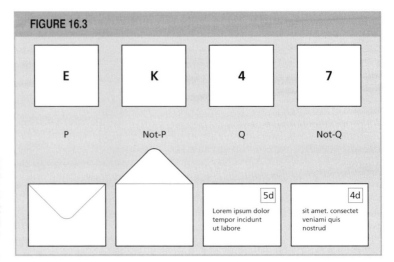

**FIGURE 16.3**

Examples of the abstract and concrete (postal) versions of Wason's selection task, with an indication of how the different cards/envelopes are labelled for the classification of subjects' choices in experiments.

"there is a vowel on one side of the card" and $Q$ is "there is an even number on the other side of the card". So, each of the cards can be re-expressed as follows: the E-card is $P$, the K-card is *not-P*, the 4-card is $Q$, and the 7-card is *not-Q* (see Figure 16.3). It is not a good idea to pick the $Q$ card (i.e., 4-card) because when $Q$ is true and the rule *if P then Q* is true, $P$ can be either true or false (see the truth table in Table 16.1); irrespective of what is on the other side of the 4-card (a vowel or a consonant), the rule will be true. Thus, turning over this card will tell you very little logically (cf. Oaksford & Chater, 1994). Of course, many people who turn over the $Q$ card may be making the fallacious affirmation of the consequent inference; they assume the rule *If P then Q* is true, they know $Q$ to be true and so they can conclude that $P$ must be on the other side (see Table 16.2). So, if *not-P* is on the other side they feel they can conclude that the rule is not true. The same sort of reasoning may account for turning over the K-card, except that in this case one is making an inference similar to the denial of the antecedent fallacy.

In contrast, the choices of the E-card (i.e., $P$) and the 7-card (i.e., *not-Q*) are correct because one is making logically valid inferences that may falsify the rule. When $P$ is true and we turn over this card, then what we find on the other side will indicate whether the rule is true or false (see Table 16.1). If $Q$ is on the other side then the rule

is true, if *not-Q* then the rule is false (this is similar to a modus ponens inference). Similarly, if one turns over *not-Q* then a $P$ on the other side will make the rule false and a *not-P* on the other side will make the rule true (see Table 16.2).

### Effects in the abstract selection task

The difficulty of reasoning in this problem should be apparent. Typically, in abstract versions of the task (i.e., ones involving vowels and consonants) very few subjects make the correct choices. In Johnson-Laird and Wason's (1970) study only 5 subjects out of 128 chose the $P$ and *not-Q* cards alone. The overwhelming majority of subjects choose either the $P$ and $Q$ cards (59 out of 128) or the $P$ card alone (42 out of 128).

Originally, it was thought that subjects were trying to confirm rather than falsify the rule (see e.g., Wason & Johnson-Laird, 1972; and Chapter 15); they turned over the *P*-card to see if there is a $Q$ (i.e., an even number) on the other side and the $Q$-card to see if there is a $P$ (i.e., a vowel) on the other side. If they had wanted to falsify the rule they would have chosen the *P*-card to see if there is *not-Q* on the other side (i.e., a consonant) and *not-Q* to see if there is $P$ (i.e., a vowel) on the other side of it. However, as we shall see, variants of the task involving more realistic materials lead to very different behaviour.

## Matching bias effects in the selection task

Evans has suggested that in such abstract versions of the task subjects manifest a non-logical, *matching bias* (Evans 1984 , 1998; Evans & Lynch, 1973; Wason & Evans, 1975). That is, subjects select those cards showing the symbols that are mentioned in the rule. So, when subjects are given another variant of the rule (i.e., "If there is a B on one side, there is not a 3 on the other side") they choose the B (*P*) and the 3 (*not-Q*) card because they are mentioned in the rule. In a separate conditional, truth-table task, Evans (1983) found that matching bias depended on the way the "negative cards" are presented; the negative cards, *not-P* and *not-Q*, can be presented as "explicit negatives" (e.g., *not-P* can presented as "not an A"), or as "implicit negatives" (e.g., *not-P* presented as "K"). Evans found that the use of explicit negatives reduced matching bias and facilitated subjects' performance on the task.

## Effects in thematic selection tasks

One of most researched effects on performance in the selection task is the change in subjects' performance when they are given "concrete" or "realistic" or "thematic" content in the task (see Bracewell & Hidi, 1974; Gilhooly & Falconer, 1974; Wason & Shapiro, 1971). Johnson-Laird, Legrenzi, and Sonino-Legrenzi (1972) used realistic materials; they asked subjects to imagine that they worked in a post office and had to detect violations in a rule, given letters of different types (in the pre-decimalisation days when unsealed letters were cheaper to send):

*If a letter is sealed, then it has a 5d. stamp on it.*

The envelopes provided were either sealed or unsealed and had a 4d. or a 5d. stamp on the side that was showing (see Figure 16.3). Again, subjects had to make just those choices needed to determine if the rule had been violated. Johnson-Laird et al. also used an abstract version of the task involving an abstract rule (i.e., "If there is a D is on one

side, then there is a 5 on the other side"). They found that, of the 24 subjects who attempted the tasks, 92% (22) produced the correct choices on the realistic version and only 8% (2) were successful on the abstract version.

This result led to an extended discussion about the role of specific experience in facilitating performance on the selection task, the so-called *memory-cueing hypothesis* (see Griggs, 1983; Griggs & Cox, 1982; Manktelow & Evans, 1979; Reich & Ruth, 1982; see Eysenck & Keane, 1995, and Manktelow, 1999 for reviews), which eventually has shown that neither realistic content nor specific experience *per se* is behind the effects. For example, D'Andrade found that subjects could also solve tasks that involved realistic content, when they lacked direct experience (reported in Rumelhart, 1980; replicated by Griggs & Cox, 1983). He used a realistic version of the task in which subjects had to imagine they were Sears' store managers responsible for checking sales. Subjects had to detect violations of the rule: "If a purchase exceeds $30, then the receipt must be approved by the department manager". They were then shown four receipts: one for $15, one for $45, one signed, and one not signed. Even without direct experience of this situation, subjects made the correct choices about 70% of the time. So, what is indeed the root cause of such effects? The emerging view is that thematic versions of the task admit some form of reasoning with regulations, so-called deontic reasoning (Manktelow & Over, 1991). All the realistic versions that facilitate reasoning use deontic forms rather than indicative forms of the conditional:

| | |
|---|---|
| Indicative form: | "If there is a p then there is a q" |
| Deontic form: | "If you do p then you *must* do q" |

The difficult abstract version of the task always has an indicative form of the rule whereas realistic versions have used deontic forms (but see Platt & Griggs, 1993, for further tests of this). For when the task is given in some deontic form then facilitation is found, even for abstract versions of the task.

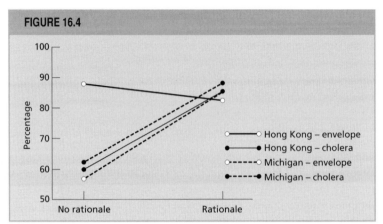

**FIGURE 16.4**

The percentage of subjects who solved Wason's selection task correctly in each condition as a function of provision of a rationale. Figure from Cheng and Holyoak "Pragmatic reasoning schemas" in *Cognitive Psychology, Volume 17,* 391–416. Copyright © 1985 by Academic Press, reproduced by permission of the publisher.

The crucial test was carried out by Cheng and Holyoak (1985) who gave subjects in Hong Kong and Michigan a version of the Johnson-Laird et al. postal problem and a variant about checking passengers' forms at an airport. The latter involved the testing of the following rule:

*If the form says "ENTERING" on one side, then the other side includes cholera among the list of diseases.*

Again, each problem had the appropriate *P*, *Q*, *not-P*, and *not-Q* cases. Neither group of subjects had direct experience of the airport problem, but the Hong Kong subjects were expected to be familiar with the postal rule. So, a memory-cueing hypothesis would predict that, on the airport problem, subjects in both Hong Kong and Michigan should be equivalent. However, Hong Kong subjects should do better than Michigan subjects on the postal version because of their prior experience. Cheng and Holyoak also gave half the subjects a rationale on both the postal and airport tasks. The stated rationale for the postal task was that a sealed envelope indicated first-class mail, for which the post office received more revenue; the rationale for the airport task was that a cholera inoculation was required to protect the entering passengers from the disease. The rationale casts the rule in a deontic light. Specifically, Cheng and Holyoak predicted that the rationale would cast the problems as a permission situation, in which

some action/precondition must be carried out before another action is permitted, and that this would result in facilitation. As such, all subjects should improve on both versions of the task (accepting that there may be a ceiling effect for the Hong Kong group on the postal task with the rationale).

Figure 16.4 shows the results of the experiment. They indicate that the memory-cueing hypothesis has some validity but is clearly not the whole story. The Hong Kong subjects did do better on the postal task with no rationale relative to the comparable Michigan group. However, irrespective of prior experience, all subjects produced uniformly high rates of correct responses when the rationale was provided. More conclusively, Cheng and Holyoak also found facilitation in performance for abstract materials, when the selection task was presented as an abstract description of a permission situation (i.e., If one is to take action A, then one must satisfy precondition P). Subjects in the abstract-permission version fared better (61% correct) than those in the usual version of the abstract task (19%). This finding is significant because such facilitation had never been observed for any other abstract version of the standard selection task (Jackson & Griggs, 1990). Although there has been some empirical questioning of these findings, the consensus seems to support the original result (see Evans, 1983; Girotto, Mazzocco, & Cherubini, 1992; Griggs & Cox, 1993; Kroger, Cheng & Holyoak, 1993).

# ABSTRACT-RULE THEORY

The evidence on conditional reasoning suggests that people are not wholly rational; they fail to make valid inferences and often make invalid inferences. Abstract-rule theories maintain that people are inherently rational, that they use a *mental logic* (although, as we shall see later, one could argue that this is a very narrow definition of rationality). According to this account, people only make invalid inferences because they misunderstand or misrepresent the reasoning task. After their initial misunderstanding the reasoning itself is logical (Henle, 1962).

*Abstract-rule theories* propose that humans reason using a set of very abstract, logic-like rules that can be applied to any domain of knowledge (e.g., rules like modus ponens). These abstract rules do not take the content of the premises into account (see e.g., Braine, 1990; Johnson-Laird, 1975; O'Brien, 1995; Osherson, 1975; Rips, 1983, 1990, 1994). From this theoretical perspective, people construct proofs to reach conclusions in a manner similar to logical proofs. For example, Rips (1983, p. 40) says that "the sequence of applied rules forms a mental proof or derivation of the conclusion from the premises, where these implicit proofs are analogous to the explicit proofs of elementary logic." Although there are several variants of this theoretical position, we concentrate on a representative case: Braine and O'Brien's abstract-rule theory.

## Braine and O'Brien's abstract-rule theory

Braine and O'Brien's theory maintains that deductive reasoning is mediated by basic, abstract rules or schemata (see Chapter 9). People comprehend the premises of an argument and encode them into abstract rules from which they make inferences. The theory is summarised in Panel 16.1 (see also Braine, 1978, 1990; Braine & O'Brien, 1991; Braine, Reiser, & Rumain, 1984; Braine & Rumain, 1983; Lea et al., 1990; O'Brien, 1995; O'Brien, Braine, & Yang, 1994; Rumain, Connell, & Braine, 1983). In this view people are natural logicians who are slightly fallible at the edges. When reasoning directly, people always reason validly, except for extraneous influences from the comprehension of premises or the inherent limitations of working memory. In the following sections, we elaborate how the theory accounts for the different inferences made by people.

## Valid and invalid inferences

Consider the abstract-rule account of how a conclusion is drawn for the following premises:

---

**Panel 16.1:  Braine and O'Brien's abstract-rule theory**

- Natural language premises are encoded by comprehension mechanisms, which are sensitive to conversational implications (e.g., Grice, 1975), into a mental representation of the premises in working memory.
- In *direct reasoning*, abstract-rule schemas are applied to these premises to derive conclusions. *Core schemas* encode fundamental reasoning rules (like *modus ponens*) and *feeder schemas* are auxiliary schemas that are applied to produce intermediate conclusions for core schemas. *Incompatibility rules* also examine the contents of working memory for incompatible inferences, such as contradictions (e.g., inferring *P* and *not-P*).
- The application of these schemata is controlled by a reasoning program (in essence, a production system, see Chapter 1).
- In *indirect reasoning*, problems that are beyond the bounds of "normal" reasoning problems are handled (e.g., the abstract selection task). People can learn other non-logical schemas that may be applied to solve such problems (like the domain-specific rules of other problem-solving systems), but they may result in bias-type responses.
- Even within direct reasoning, people can draw invalid conclusions or errors of three types: (a) comprehension errors, where the premises or conclusion are misconstrued in some fashion, (b) heuristic inadequacy errors, where a conclusion to a problem fails to be reached because the strategies for co-ordinating the application of the reasoning schemas are inadequate, (c) processing errors, resulting from lapses of attention or a failure to hold relevant information in working memory.

| If I get hungry, then I will go for a walk, | *If P then Q,* |
| If I go for a walk, I will feel much better, | *If Q then R,* |
| I am hungry | *P* |

Most abstract-rule theories have a reasoning rule that corresponds to modus ponens; theorists assume that because people find this inference so easy, there must be an appropriate mental rule to deal with it. A conclusion to the example here can be derived by the repeated application of this modus ponens rule. First, the rule is applied to the first premise (If I get hungry then I will go for a walk) and third premise (I am hungry) to produce the intermediate conclusion of "I will go for a walk"; then the rule is applied again to the second premise "If I go for a walk, I will feel much better" and the intermediate conclusion "I will go for a walk" to produce the final conclusion "I will feel much better" (see Byrne, 1989b, for explicit tests of these chains of inferences). The rules are applied successively to the set of premises until a conclusion is derived.

The existence of a modus ponens rule accounts nicely for why people find this argument so easy, but why do they find the other valid form, modus tollens, so hard? In the abstract-rule theory, modus tollens is a harder inference to make because no single rule can be applied to it. Rather, a proof involving several different rules has to be formed to reach a conclusion. In general, the longer a derivation, the greater the likelihood that errors will occur or no conclusion will be reached.

In abstract-rule theories, people make the fallacious inferences, like the invalid denial of the antecedent and affirmation of the consequent inferences, as a result of comprehension errors. One account maintains that people make the conversational assumptions used in everyday life thus causing a re-interpretation of the premises (O'Brien, 1995). So, people still apply their logically valid rules but because the input to the rules is erroneous, the output is often erroneous too. Consider the detailed explanation for why people make the fallacious denial of the antecedent inference:

## Invalid: Denial of the antecedent

*Premises*

| If it is raining, then Alicia gets wet | *If P then Q,* |
| It is not raining. | *not P,* |

*Conclusion*

| Therefore, Alicia does not get wet. | *Therefore, not Q* |

Rumain et al. (1983) maintained that the conditional premise of this argument, *If P then Q,* was re-interpreted as *If not-P then not-Q*. As Geis and Zwicky (1971) have pointed out, the statement "if you mow the lawn I will give you five dollars" invites the inference "If you don't mow the lawn, I won't give you five dollars". If one starts with this as the conditional premise then by the application of the modus ponens rule one reaches the conclusion *not-Q*. For example:

*Premises*

| If it is not raining, then Alicia does not get wet | *If not P then not Q,* |
| It is not raining. | *not P,* |

*Conclusion*

| Therefore, Alicia does not get wet. | *Therefore, not Q* |

So, valid rules are still being applied, but to re-interpreted premises (note that this is not the only account of this effect, when one considers that the Geis & Zwicky sentence is deontic, namely a conditional promise). A similar explanation can be made for the affirmation of the consequent fallacy.

This switch in the interpretation of the premise is said to occur because of Grice's (1975) *co-operative principle*. This principle maintains that a speaker tells a hearer exactly what they think the other needs to know. For example, if a speaker says "If it is raining, then Alicia will get wet", the hearer will assume, in the context of the conversation, that rain is the only likely event that will lead to Alicia getting wet. The hearer assumes that no other alternative *P*s will play a role. So, during comprehension people make a reasonable assumption that modifies the premises. Having made this comprehension error, reasoning continues normally through the application of the various reasoning rules (see O'Brien, 1995).

## Context effects

The context effects reviewed earlier are also explained in terms of these conversational assumptions. Rumain et al. (1983) predicted that alternative antecedents undo these conversational assumptions resulting in the suppression of the invalid inferences. Braine et al. (1984) took these results as evidence that there could not be rules for invalid inferences of the denial of the antecedent and the affirmation of the consequent. However, this conclusion is upset by the other context effects showing the suppression of the valid inferences by the provision of additional antecedents (see Byrne, 1989a). If the same argument is applied to Byrne's results, then abstract-rule theorists would also have to conclude that there are no mental inference rules for the valid inferences. Politzer and Braine (1991) have therefore challenged these results; they argued that Byrne's materials led subjects to doubt the truth of one of the premises because one premise was inconsistent with the other premises (see also George, 1995; O'Brien, 1993). If subjects doubted the premises then Byrne's manipulation was radically different from Rumain et al.'s. However, in reply, Byrne (1991) has shown that the conclusions drawn by subjects in her experiments were not those predicted by Politizer and Braine's account. Furthermore, Byrne et al. (1999) have explicitly tested this proposal and found no evidence that people doubt the truth of the premises (or, indeed, that they are viewed as inconsistent).

The abstract-rule theory does not do much better on the other aspects of these context effects. On the effects of uncertainty, Stevenson and Over (1995) point out that no existing abstract-rule theory (and indeed, mental model theory) can account for these effects and would have to be supplemented with a probability theory (see later section on probabilistic theory) in order to do so. This would lead to a rather baroque and psychologically

implausible model. Similarly, the effects of causality (Cummins et al., 1991) and saliency (Chan & Chua, 1994) do not sit easy with the theory, as they are background knowledge effects that suggest a role for domain-specific schemata. Of course, such schemata could be entertained in Braine and O'Brien's indirect reasoning route, but this has the uncomfortable result of placing these tasks outside of reasoning proper (which would not be a generally agreed assessment).

## The selection task

Braine and O'Brien also see abstract versions of the selection task as falling outside the operation of their direct reasoning routine; that is, they do not view it as a reasoning problem proper (O'Brien, 1995). As such, the theory predicts that people should not reveal much rational competence at the task, which is essentially what one finds in their behaviour. However, they do predict that people should be better on deontic versions of the task (e.g., thematic materials) because these versions have a simpler logical structure. In deontic versions of the task people are asked to judge possible violations in a regulation whose truth status is not in question, whereas in non-deontic versions they are asked for "judgements of cases that could potentially falsify descriptive statements whose truth status is uncertain" (Manktelow & Over, 1991, 1993, p. 184).

## Other evidence supporting the theory's predictions

There is considerable evidence for the proposals of abstract-rule theory (see also Braine, 1990; Lea et al., 1990). For example, Braine et al. (1984) examined several predictions from the theory in a series of experiments. In one experiment, subjects were given a simple reasoning task about the presence or absence of letters on an imaginary blackboard (from Osherson, 1975). So, on being given a problem such as:

If there is a T, there is an L,
There is a T
? There is an L ?

subjects were asked to evaluate whether the provided conclusion was true. These problems were designed to be solved in a single step by one of the 16 rules proposed by the theory. The results showed that reasoning on these problems was essentially error-free. Difficulty measures were derived from subjects' performance on these problems that were then used to predict behaviour on problems that involved short chains of reasoning (on the assumption that the difficulty measures for single rules would be additive in more complex tasks). A variety of measures were used to determine problem difficulty, including subjective ratings of difficulty, times taken to solve a problem and the number of errors made. Braine et al. found high correlations between the difficulty measures of problems and the number of predicted inferences, from the repertoire of rules, required to solve the problems.

## Evaluation of abstract-rule theories

The abstract-rule approach is very attractive in its promise to account for conditional reasoning with recourse to a limited set of reasoning rules. It also has the benefit of being consistent with models developed in problem-solving research, suggesting a unified account of problem solving and reasoning. For example, the Braine and O'Brien model can be viewed as a production system model that uses very abstract operators, rather than domain-specific ones (see also Rips, 1994).

The one main problem facing this approach is that abstract-rule theories achieve their elegance at the price of a considerable underspecification of the accompanying comprehension component. The core reasoning system is well specified and makes predictions about what inferences people will and will not make. However, some predictions are grounded in a comprehension component that is considerably less specified (e.g., predictions on invalid inferences). Although O'Brien (1995) has taken steps to specify further aspects of this component, more remains to be done. Hence, in general, its treatment of context effects leaves a lot to be desired. Furthermore, depending on one's

perspective, it could be said that the theory's treatment of the selection task is weak, as it does so by excluding it from the set on explanatory phenomena to be considered.

## MENTAL MODELS THEORY

Like the abstract-rule theory, the mental models theory, or more simply the model theory, proposes that people have a modicum of rationality, but that this rationality can be hampered by processing limitations (e.g., limited working memory; Johnson-Laird, 1983, 1995a, b, 1999; Johnson-Laird & Byrne, 1991, 1993a, 1996). Unlike the abstract-rule theory, the model theory gives comprehension a central role in reasoning; people build models when they comprehend linguistic descriptions and then their reasoning relies on these models. Indeed, the distinction between these two theories is paralleled by a distinction in logic, between logics based on syntactic methods using proofs and semantic methods using models. Abstract-rule theorists developed their ideas from proof systems, whereas model theorists have developed their ideas from logical, semantic systems. The proponents of this theory do not maintain that people use truth tables when they reason, but rather they see truth tables as containing a kernel of psychological truth (Johnson-Laird & Byrne, 1993b, p. 324).

Stated simply, the model theory maintains that people reason by constructing a representation or model of the state of affairs described in the premises, based on the meanings of the premises and general knowledge. They then describe this model in a parsimonious manner to generate a conclusion, before validating the model. Validation is carried out by searching for alternative models or counterexamples that refute the conclusion drawn. If no such counterexamples are found then subjects view the inference as being valid (Johnson-Laird & Byrne, 1991, 1993a). The basic idea can be illustrated easily in simple spatial problems (see Byrne & Johnson-Laird, 1989; Erlich & Johnson-Laird, 1982; Mani & Johnson-Laird, 1982).

Consider the representation or model one might build from the following set of premises, given the instructions to imagine the state of affairs described in them:

The lamp is on the right of the pad
The book is on the left of the pad
The clock is in front of the book
The vase is in front of the lamp

Spatially, these objects can be viewed as being arranged in the following manner:

book    pad    lamp
clock          vase

So, one could make the novel inference from this model that "the clock is to the left of the vase". A novel inference or conclusion is any statement that follows from the premises and was not explicitly stated in them (so, many more could be made). If we try to refute this conclusion then we need to discover another layout or model of the objects that is consistent with the description in the premises, but is not consistent with the conclusion of "the clock is on the left of the vase" (i.e., we need to find a counterexample). In fact, there is no such model.

But consider the following premises:

The lamp is on the right of the pad
The book is on the left of the lamp
The clock is in front of the book
The vase is in front of the pad

This is consistent with two distinct models (see Byrne & Johnson-Laird, 1989):

book    pad    lamp        pad    book    lamp
clock   vase                vase    clock

In this case, the conclusion that we might make from the first model, that "the clock is to the left of the vase", is inconsistent with an alternative model of the premises in which "the clock is to the right of the vase" (i.e., a counterexample can be found). Thus, in this case, one would have to admit that "there is no valid conclusion" to be made about the relationship of the vase and the clock on their own.

Several variants of the model theory have been proposed, which represent models in distinct ways; like Euler circles (Erickson, 1974; Guyote & Sternberg, 1981) or Venn diagrams (Newell, 1981). We will concentrate on a more general scheme initially proposed by Johnson-Laird (1983) and extended by Johnson-Laird and Byrne (1991, 1993a) which is summarised in Panel 16.2. We have already seen, in a rough

---

**Panel 16.2: The model theory of reasoning**

- Reasoning involves three processes: the *comprehension* of premises to form a model (or set of models); the *combining* and *description* of models to produce a conclusion; and the *validation* of this conclusion by eliminating alternative models of the premises that show the putative conclusion to be false (i.e., the search for counterexamples).

- In *comprehending* premises, semantic procedures are used to construct models taking background knowledge into account; the models are specific (they do not contain variables but specific mental tokens) and can be visually imagined, although they are not necessarily visual images.

- The models of premises are *combined* to form an integrated model (or set of models) and then this model is *described* in a parsimonious fashion to arrive at a conclusion.

- The *validation* of this conclusion involves a search for counterexamples or alternative models in which all the premises are true and the putative conclusion false; if there are no such models, the conclusion is valid; if a model is found that falsifies the conclusion, then the ideal reasoner should attempt to discover whether there is any conclusion that is true in all the constructed models.

- Given the limited nature of working memory, several assumptions are made: (i) an inference will be more difficult if it can only be generated using several explicit models, (ii) an inference that can be made from initial models will be easier than one that can only be made from "fleshing out" implicit models, (iii) it takes time to detect inconsistencies between elements in a model.

- Errors may arise when conclusions are made from (i) initial models that have not been rigorously evaluated, or (ii) implicit models that have not been fleshed out sufficiently.

fashion, how this theory is applied to spatial reasoning. Consider how it has been applied to conditional reasoning.

## Valid inferences in the model theory

Johnson-Laird and Byrne (1991; Byrne & Johnson-Laird, 1992; Johnson-Laird, Byrne, & Schaeken, 1992) have proposed a model theory of conditional reasoning. In this theory, a conditional premise like "If there is a circle then there is a triangle" is represented *explicitly* by the following three models:

    O     Δ
    ¬O    Δ
    ¬O   ¬Δ

In this notation, each line represents a new model. These three models represent all those situations where the premise is true, but not the situation when the premise is false (compare it to the truth table in Table 16.1). The "¬" symbol is a propositional tag in the model, used to indicate "not". Intuitively, this means that when people understand the premise—"if there is a circle then there is a triangle"—they represent it by states of affairs described by this sentence; namely, a situation where there is a circle and a triangle, a situation where there is not a circle and there is a triangle, and a situation where there is neither a circle nor a triangle.

However, people attempt to represent as little information as possible because of their processing limitations and so they build representations that indicate the various alternative situations *implicitly*. So, Johnson-Laird and Byrne suggest that when people understand this premise they build the following initial models:

    [O]   Δ
    . . .

This representation contains just two models, one representing a situation where there is a circle and a triangle and one (indicated by the three dots or ellipsis) indicating that there are other alternative models (i.e., the two other explicit models

shown earlier). These explicit models can be added or "fleshed out" later. The square brackets around the circle mean that the circle has been represented "exhaustively" in the model; that is, the alternative models will not contain a circle because in any other model where a circle occurs, there has to be a triangle (see Johnson-Laird & Savary, 1996, for a notational variant called *footnotes*). When reasoners are given a second premise—"There is a circle"—they construct a model in which there is just a circle:

    O

and when they combine this model and the original models, they get the following:

    O    Δ

a single model, with the implicit (ellipsis) model eliminated. The implicit model can be removed because all the other models it implicitly indicates are ones in which there is not a circle.

To form a conclusion this model is described in a parsimonious fashion with the sentence: "there is a triangle". This is how the model theory accounts for the valid, modus ponens inference. This inference can be made readily from the initial representation of the conditional, without any need to make the implicit information explicit. In the more difficult modus tollens inference, subjects are given the extra premise "There is not a triangle" represented by the model:

    ¬Δ

To combine this model with the initial models:

    [O]   Δ
    . . .

a lot more work must be carried out. First, the implicit aspects of the initial models must be fleshed out with the explicit models, for example:

    O     Δ
    ¬O    Δ
    ¬O   ¬Δ

and then these models must be combined with the model of the second premise (i.e., $\neg\Delta$), to get the following model:

$$\neg O \quad \neg\Delta$$

which can be described by the conclusion: "There is not a circle". Thus, modus tollens is more difficult than modus ponens because people have to flesh out the models and keep multiple alternatives in mind.

## Invalid inferences in the model theory

Invalid inferences arise for two reasons: people can have different interpretations of the conditional premise and they may fail to flesh out the explicit models for their interpretation. First, people can interpret the original premise—"If there is a circle, there is a triangle"—as a biconditional; "if and only if there is a circle, there is a triangle".

In the minimal set of models adopted by people, this interpretation of the premise would be represented implicitly as:

$$[O] \quad [\Delta]$$
$$\cdots$$

where both components are exhaustively represented; indicating that no other models will contain circles or triangles. Invalid inferences arise from these initial models. When subjects are given the extra information that "There is a triangle" ($\Delta$), the second model will be eliminated, leaving the affirmation of the consequent inference: "There is a circle".

When subjects are given the information "There is not a circle", they can get the right answer for the wrong reason; that is, they may say that "nothing follows", simply because they cannot combine the model ($\neg O$) with the initial set of models, regardless of whether those models are for the conditional or biconditional interpretation. However, if subjects flesh out the explicit models for the biconditional (see Table 16.2):

$$O \quad \Delta$$
$$\neg O \quad \neg\Delta$$

then when they combine these models with the model of the second premise ($\neg O$), the first model will be ruled out and they will draw the denial of the antecedent inference: "There is not a triangle". In this way the theory explains why the denial of the antecedent inference is made less often than the affirmation of the consequent inference, as people can get the right answer for the wrong reason (although see Evans et al., 1993, and Evans, 1993a).

## Context effects

Regarding context effects, Byrne (1989a) has proposed that extra information leads to a different interpretation of the premises. Premises that contain alternatives as opposed to additionals result in different sets of models being constructed. The validation procedures that revise the models find that alternative antecedents act as counterexamples to the invalid inferences, whereas additional antecedents act as counterexamples to the valid inferences. Indeed, Byrne et al. (1999) have shown that combined additional *and* antecedent premises can suppress all of four inferences. Byrne et al. (1999; Byrne, 1991) propose that the effects of causality and saliency are due to the immediate availability of counterexamples based on background knowledge. So, for example, Chan and Chua's (1994) saliency effects are attributed to the differential effectiveness of the counterexamples called to mind for the weak and strong saliency premises. Similarly, Stevenson and Over (1995) discuss extensions to the model theory that would account for their uncertainty effects. Although such accounts are not fully worked out, it is clear that several feasible proposals are on the table.

## The selection task

The model theory has also been applied to account for the results of the selection task (Johnson-Laird, 1995; Johnson-Laird & Byrne, 1991). The explanation is based on three key points:

- People consider only those cards that are represented explicitly in their models of the rule.
- Different contexts (e.g., deontic ones) can affect what comes to be represented explicitly in the model.

• People then select those cards for which the hidden value could have a bearing on the truth or falsity of the rule.

It may be remembered that people typically choose the *P* and *Q* cards on this task, when the *P* and *not-Q* cards are the optimal choices. The model representation of the conditional "if there is a vowel on one side of the card, then there is an even number on the other side" (instantiated with E and 4, see Figure 16.3) would be represented by the following models:

[E]   4

. . .

which given the aforementioned proposals suggests that *P* (E-card) and *Q* (4-card) should be chosen. Furthermore, this account suggests that any manipulation that makes the *not-Q* card explicit in the model should facilitate performance on the task. The suggestion, therefore, is that effects due to a deontic reading of the task achieve just this sort of explicit representation. Matching bias effects are also explained in terms of how rules with negations are represented as explicit models, although there has been some debate on exactly what form these models might take (see Evans, 1993a; Johnson-Laird, 1995; Johnson-Laird & Byrne, 1991). In short, the model theory also has a story to tell about the selection task.

## Further evidence for the model theory

The model theory accounts for other evidence and many novel predictions from it have been confirmed (see Evans et al., 1993, Chapter 2 for a review). Johnson-Laird, Byrne, and Schaeken (1992) have shown that the difficulty data, which abstract-rule theorists propose to be due to length of the mental derivation, can be explained in an alternative manner by the model theory. They have shown that the simpler problems involved inferences that could be made from initial models, whereas the difficult problems required more models to be constructed. Furthermore, they also tested a novel prediction from the model theory, that modus tollens inferences should be easier from a biconditional than a conditional interpretation

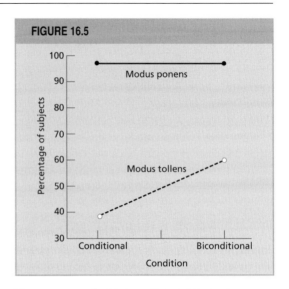

**FIGURE 16.5**

The percentage of subjects making modus ponens and modus tollens inferences when given two-premise conditional or biconditional problems from Johnson-Laird, Byrne, and Schaeken (1992, Experiment 2).

of the premises, whereas the rate of modus ponens inferences should remain constant (abstract-rule theories predict no difference in either case). This result is predicted because modus ponens can be made from just one explicit model from either interpretation, whereas modus tollens requires three explicit models to be considered for the conditional and just two explicit models for the biconditional. This prediction was confirmed (see Figure 16.5).

Furthermore, Byrne and Johnson-Laird (1992) found evidence that people represent conditionals by an explicit model in which the events occur and an implicit model in which alternative events may occur. They gave subjects different versions of three assertions:

| *With Modal* | *Without Modal* |
| --- | --- |
| John hires a gardener. | John hires a gardener. |
| John does some gardening. | John does some gardening. |
| John can get the grass cut. | John gets the grass cut. |

in which a modal (e.g., can) was present or absent, and asked subjects to paraphrase the assertions in a single sentence. As predicted by the model theory, they found that subjects tended to use a conditional-like paraphrase to combine the three assertions when the outcome contained a modal (e.g., John can get the grass cut; 36%) rather than when it does not (e.g., John gets the grass cut, 5%). The modal cues people to think, at least implicitly, of alternative situations in which the events do not occur.

## Evaluation of the model theory

The model theory is a well specified theory that has been applied to a wide range of phenomena in conditional reasoning and beyond. There have been a large number of commentaries and criticisms of the theory (see Eysenck & Keane, 1995, for an earlier summary; Andrews, 1993; Bonatti, 1994; Bundy, 1993; Evans & Over, 1996; Goldman, 1986; O'Brien, Braine, & Yang, 1994; Rips, 1984, 1986). Many of these criticisms are answered by Johnson-Laird and Byrne (1993a) in a published debate in the journal, *Behavioral & Brain Sciences* (see also Johnson-Laird, Byrne, & Schaeken, 1992). We will concentrate on the main outstanding theoretical and empirical criticisms.

Theoretically, Bonatti (1994) pointed out that there were several different formulations of the number of models that might be constructed for a given problem. This is a significant criticism because most of the predictions made by the model theory are based on the number of models required by a given problem (see the spatial models described earlier). If one can pick and choose the number of different models for a given problem, then the basis on which the theory makes predictions is considerably weakened. However, Johnson-Laird et al. (1994) have asserted that the number of models is based on those required to represent and evaluate the conclusion. A computer program to automatically generate the appropriate number of models for any given set of premises has also been written, which should settle this issue (Johnson-Laird & Savary, 1996).

The other main theoretical criticism is that the model theory is incomplete. First, the comprehension component of the theory is underspecified, especially with respect to the effects of background knowledge and uncertainty. Model theorists have maintained that background knowledge plays a role in constructing models of premises but they do not have a detailed account of this process. So, although they have computational models that simulate what happens in human reasoning with premises such as "if there is a circle, there is a triangle", they do not have similar models for context effects (see Byrne, 1989a). Second, they have no detailed account of how people validate models by searching for counterexamples because there is little available evidence on how people carry out this validation (see Polk, 1993; Polk & Newell, 1995; Rips, 1990). However, it should be noted that Byrne et al. (1999) have proposed that the suppression-effect experiments can be used to explore this aspect of the theory.

From an empirical perspective, the coverage of the model theory is quite good. The main outstanding criticisms seem to hinge on its ability to explain bias type effects in reasoning tasks beyond conditionals (see Evans & Over, 1996).

## DOMAIN-SPECIFIC RULE THEORIES

Relative to the other theories we have just reviewed, the domain-specific rule theories have considerably less coverage. Recall, that most of these theories espouse a dual-process view of reasoning; namely, that some reasoning component handles deductive competence which is supplemented by domain-specific rules (Cosmides' theory is one exception to this view). Thus, in this section, we will not discuss how these theories explain the basic conditional inference patterns and context effects (because they are silent on these) but rather deal solely with the selection-task effects they have been specifically designed to explain. Of course, on parsimony grounds, these theories are at a disadvantage relative to a single-process account that can explain these and other phenomena.

## The selection task and domain-specific rules

Domain-specific-rule theories are a family of theories that have arisen to explain the various thematic or deontic effects in the selection task.

These theories differ in the content of the domain-specific rules they posit. Some theories maintain that the content is very specific prior experience used by analogy (see Griggs, 1983; and Chapter 15), but most of these theories hinge on the use of schemata that are specific to classes of situations (e.g., permission situations or various contractual situations). Even though these schematic rules are relatively abstract, they are more specific than the content-free, abstract rules we met earlier. We consider two variants of domain-specific-rule theories.

### Pragmatic reasoning schemata: Domain-specific rules for permissions and obligations

Cheng and Holyoak (1985; Cheng, Holyoak, Nisbett, & Oliver, 1986) call their domain-specific rules *pragmatic reasoning schemata* because they are sensitive to the pragmatics of the situation (see Chapter 9 on schemata). Permission situations are one class of such situations that occur regularly in everyday life; for example, to gain permission to enter university you must satisfy the precondition of achieving a certain exam result. The schemata for such situations are abstract in that they potentially apply to a wide range of content domains, but unlike abstract rules they are constrained by particular inferential goals and event relationships of certain broad types (see Holland et al., 1986).

Pragmatic reasoning theory proposes that:

- People have specific rules that deal with particular types of situation; for instance, permission schemata and obligation schemata.
- Rules in the permission schemata take the form "If an action is to be taken, then a precondition must be satisfied"; if you are asked to test a rule that elicits a permission schema then the appropriate rule from this schema is applied (its logic is like that of the conditional in Table 16.1).
- Obligation schemata have also been elaborated for situations in which one is obliged to do something.

In this theory, errors occur when situations cannot be mapped easily into pragmatic schemata, or errors may arise directly from the inferences generated by schemata (because the rules in the schema may not conform to those sanctioned by propositional logic). Cheng and Holyoak have also suggested that in situations where the schemata do not apply (e.g., abstract content) abstract rules and other strategies may come into play.

### Social contract theory: Domain-specific rules encoding contracts

Cosmides (1989) has an alternative domain-specific-rule theory based on an evolutionary approach to cognition. She suggests that people have rules—called Darwinian algorithms—that maximise their ability to achieve their goals in social situations. She concentrates on situations involving social exchange, where two people must co-operate for mutual benefit. The social contract theory proposes that people have schemata pertaining to these sorts of social contracts, such as schemata that encode the following rules:

> Standard social contract:
> "If you take a benefit then you must pay the cost"
> Switched social contract:
> "If you pay the cost then you take the benefit"

Along with these schemata, for evolutionary reasons, people must have a mechanism for detecting those who might break a contract: a "look for cheaters" algorithm. If the standard contract schema is applied to the selection task, along with the cheater-detection algorithm, then people should make the correct selections (of $P$ and *not-Q*), but when the switched-contract schema is applied they will make less optimal selections (taking the logical view of rationality). Social contract situations are a subset of permission situations, so those permission situations that are social contracts will show facilitation, but permission situations that are not social contracts will not. The postal rules used in some realistic contents (see earlier) can be viewed as reified social contracts, as can the rules about ages at which people can legally drink alcohol, which have been used in some realistic-content studies. Furthermore, instructions to find violators of the rule can be viewed as a means to facilitate the application of the cheater-detection algorithm (see also Gigerenzer & Hug, 1992, for a further elaboration of this theory; and Cummins, 1996).

Following on Cheng and Holyoak's (1985) results, Cosmides examined cases of permission situations that were not social contracts and found less facilitation than in permission situations that were social contracts (see also Gigerenzer & Hug, 1992). However, the levels of correct responses in permission cases that were not social contracts were still higher than the usual levels on the abstract task. So, while social contract situations appear to be highly facilitating, there is also some facilitation for pure permission situations. Although many of Cosmides' results have been replicated and further clarified (see Platt & Griggs, 1993), some researchers contested her claims. For example, some have disputed her interpretation that some realistic-content versions of the task are, in fact, social contracts; for example, the Sears' receipts version of the task (see earlier) seems to have no obvious contractual component to it (see Cheng & Holyoak, 1989; Gigerenzer & Hug, 1992). As we saw earlier, there is a growing consensus that these effects are due to the deontic aspects of the tasks, rather than whether they are specifically permissions or contracts, although this does not completely invalidate these theories as accounts of such deontic effects.

### Evaluation of domain-specific-rule theories

In general, domain-specific-rule or schema theories are an interesting addition to the theoretical corpus of research on the selection task. They have been used to generate new predictions about the underlying basis of subjects' performance on the task and many of these predictions have been confirmed.

The major criticism of this view is that they are not complete theories of reasoning; they can characterise some versions of the selection task, but do not go far beyond this point. For example,

they make no predictions for other logical connectives (e.g., *and* and *or*) and have no account of the pattern of selections on the abstract task. In other words, these theories are silent on what people are doing when they are *not* using domain-specific rules. Cheng and Holyoak suggest that some responses may be due to non-logical biases but they do not elaborate this further. O'Brien (1993) has suggested a marriage between the abstract-rule account and Cheng and Holyoak's theory.

Finally, the theories themselves have many underspecified components. Both pragmatic-rule and social-contract theory do not specify how natural language is parsed into the rules used for reasoning. So many aspects of their predictions could be open to ad-hoc interpretation.

## PROBABILISTIC THEORY

Oaksford and Chater's (1994, 1995, 1996; Chater & Oaksford, 1999a, b) probabilistic theory takes quite a different tack from the theories reviewed earlier. Unlike the other theories, it takes its normative model from probability theory rather than from logic. The core idea of the theory is that people are not reasoning *per se* but are attempting to maximise information gain. That is, people make choices that reduce the uncertainty of their situation and that maximise information gain about the world. So, in the selection task, people make card choices that are the most informative; they choose cards that on balance of probabilities convey the most. A hint as to the further details of the theory are shown in Panel 16.3.

Typically, this theory is applied by performing some analysis of the premises of a reasoning problem in terms of probability theory. From this analysis one can predict the information gain of all possible conclusions/choices for the problem and predict a rank ordering of which responses people are likely to make based on the information gain of each; that is, the conclusion/choice with the highest information gain should come first, the next highest being the next most likely and so on.

---

**Panel 16.3:   Oaksford and Chater's probabilistic theory**

- The probabilistic theory deals with assessing the optimal hypothesis (H) to select from among $n$ mutually exclusive and exhaustive hypotheses (H$i$); in short, with assessing the uncertainty of these hypotheses, $I$(H$i$):

$$I(\text{H}i) \text{ is } - \sum_{i=1}^{n} P(\text{H}i) \log_2 P(\text{H}i)$$

- After some data D have been found (e.g., by turning a card), the probability of the hypotheses, P(H$i$) is undated relative to D, P(H$i$ | D), giving a new uncertainty measure $I$(H$i$ | D):

$$I(\text{H}i \mid \text{D}) \text{ is } - \sum_{i=1}^{n} P(\text{H}i \mid \text{D}) \log_2 P(\text{H}i \mid \text{D})$$

- The P(H$i$ | D) terms are computed from Bayes' theorem:

$$P(\text{H}i \mid \text{D}) = \frac{P(\text{D} \mid \text{H}i)P(\text{H}i)}{\sum\limits_{j=1}^{n} P(\text{D} \mid \text{H}j)P(\text{H}j)}$$

which specifies the posterior probability of a hypothesis H$i$ given some data D can be found from the prior probability of each hypothesis H$i$ and the likelihoods of D given each H$j$. Choosing the prior probabilities of a hypothesis can be a contentious issue; in a simple case, if there are four possible choices in a situation then the prior probability of each occurring is .25. In their analysis, Oaksford and Chater make an important assumption about the P and Q cases (the so-called *rarity assumption*) that their prior probabilities are low.

- Assuming this formula, the information gain in a situation is the amount of reduction in uncertainty that follows from the arrival of a new datum:

$$Ig = I(\text{D} \mid \text{H}i) - I(\text{H}i)$$

although, in the theory a more precise measure, the Expected Information Gain E(Ig), is computed; this is the uncertainty after making a choice weighted by the probability of each possible choice outcome, less the prior uncertainty.

---

## Probabilistic theory applied to the selection task

The analysis of probabilistic theory can be made clear by showing how it concretely applies to the selection task (Oaksford & Chater, 1994; Oaksford, Chater, Grainger, & Larkin, 1997). Using an example proposed by these theorists, imagine that you are testing hypotheses about eating tripe and getting sick, the hypothesis being "if you eat tripe," (*P*) "then you feel sick" (*Q*). To test this hypothesis you might investigate groups of people who have eaten tripe (*P*), not eaten tripe (*not-P*), become sick (*Q*), and not become sick (*not-Q*); these being the equivalent of the four cards in the task. The question is, what are the most informative groups to check? First, asking people who have eaten tripe (*P*) should provide some information gain, because if you find that they have not been sick then you know the hypothesis is false. Second, asking people who have never eaten tripe

(*not-P*) has little or no information gain, because the hypothesis says nothing about people who have not eaten tripe. Third, in contrast, it makes sense to ask someone who is feeling sick (*Q*) whether they have eaten tripe; if they have eaten tripe then there is considerable information gain, although if they have not eaten tripe then no conclusion can be drawn. Fourth, asking someone who is not feeling sick (*not-Q*) may be informative; if they have eaten tripe then the hypothesis is falsified, but if they have not eaten tripe then no conclusion can be made. In short, it seems that choosing *P* is certain to be informative, choosing *not-P* is definitely not informative, and *Q* and *not-Q* are somewhere in between (i.e., they may or may not be informative).

Behind this loose description of information gain is an elaborate Bayesian probability model that specifies exactly how to compute the information gain for the various cards (see Panel 16.3). This computation of probabilities, combined with a further assumption (the *rarity assumption*, that properties that figure in causal relations are rare) leads to the proposal that the best selections, in order of optimal information gain, are the *P*, *Q*, *not-Q*, and *not-P* items. In a meta-analysis of research in the area, Oaksford and Chater show that the frequency of occurrence of the difference card-choices exactly follows this pattern. It is interesting to note that this probabilistic account sanctions the choices of *P* and *Q* as being rational, in contrast to the logical account which viewed them as irrational.

With additional assumptions, this model can be used to account for other effects in the selection task, like the effects in deontic versions of the task and the effects of negations (see Oaksford & Chater, 1994, 1996).

## Context effects and conditional inference

This theory has been mainly applied to an analysis of versions of the selection task. Thus far it has not been applied to conditional inference *per se* and so it has little to say about the typical patterns of inference and suppression effects of conditional inference. However, it is clear that the theory should be applicable to manipulations of uncertainty in conditional inference (e.g., Cummins et al., 1991; Stevenson & Over, 1995) and work in this area has been promised for the future.

## Evaluation of probabilistic theory

As a new arrival on the scene in an area where theories are relatively long-standing, the probabilistic theory has attracted a lot of attention and excitement (Almor & Sloman, 1996; Evans & Over, 1996; Klauer, 1999; Laming, 1996). One of the big promises of the theory is that it suggests a way to unite research on reasoning with that on judgement and decision making, bringing two previously disparate fields together.

Having said this, like domain-specific-rule theories, the probabilistic theory has a way to go theoretically and empirically before it really challenges the abstract-rule and mental models

theories. Theoretically, it is important to realise that the theory lacks a performance component (Johnson-Laird, 1999). The probabilistic theory is a computational-level theory (see Marr, 1982, and Chapter 1) which specifies what needs to be computed in a reasoning task (namely, factors like information gain). It does not propose a performance mechanism that shows which reasoning processes produce the candidate set of choices/conclusions and which memory processes retrieve past experiences to compute the probabilities for these items. In the absence of such a mechanism, the theory has little to say about reasoning *per se* (i.e., how specific conclusions are generated from premises). Indeed, it may end up being a dual-process theory which proposes that reasoning is carried out by either abstract rules or mental models over which probabilities are computed.

Empirically, the theory needs to be tested much more extensively. There has been a tendency to carry out meta-analyses on the existing literature rather than to test novel predictions of the theory (but see Oaksford et al., 1997). With meta-analyses there is always the worry that the theory is being shaped to the data in an ad hoc fashion rather than standing on its own predictive legs. For example, in the selection task, the theory's consistency with the typical choices made is carried heavily by the rarity assumption. This assumption is not well founded on grounds other than the fact that it delivers the sorts of results that are typically found in the literature.

## COGNITIVE NEUROPSYCHOLOGY OF REASONING

In the other chapters on thinking, we have seen that there has been a considerable amount of new activity in the cognitive neuropsychology area. Similar developments have occurred in reasoning research. This research has confirmed the importance of the frontal lobes, and has gone further to distinguish hemispheric specialisations in deductive reasoning (see e.g., Goel, Gold, Kapur, & Houle, 1997).

In this chapter, we have reported marked differences in people's responses to logical problems when they are couched in abstract versus thematic content. There is evidence to suggest that this distinction has a grounding in hemispheric differences. Golding (1981) used a circles and colours version of the selection task to test subjects that had either no cerebral brain lesions, right hemisphere lesions, or left hemisphere lesions. This abstract version of the task was found to be particularly difficult for those patients with left hemisphere damage, whereas the right-hemisphere-damaged patients did much better (better indeed than controls). The left hemisphere has also been implicated in studies showing that aphasics, with left posterior lesions, have severe difficulties understanding simple logical statements, whereas right-hemisphere-lesioned subjects have no general difficulties with logical reasoning (Wharton & Grafman, 1998).

Johnson-Laird (1995) has emphasised the right hemisphere's contribution to deduction based on the proposals of mental models theory. He reports an experiment by Whitaker et al. (1991) on conditional reasoning in group of patients who had undergone a unilateral anterior temporal lobectomy to relieve epilepsy, either to the right or left hemispheres. Those with right hemisphere damage were poorer at reasoning from false conditional premises than those with left hemisphere damage. Thus given: "If it rained the streets will be dry" and the categorical assertion: "It rained" the right-hemisphere-damaged group had a reliable tendency to conclude: "The streets will be wet". In other words, these patients were unable to carry through the process of deduction in isolation from their knowledge of reality.

Finally, Waltz et al. (1999) have used deductive and inductive problems to show that the underlying basis for the localisation in the prefrontal cortex is specifically the integration of multiple relations. They gave three groups of subjects who were matched in terms of their IQ—patients with prefrontal damage, patients with anterior lobe damage, and controls—versions of problems that could be solved by using one relation or two relations. They found that the prefrontal patients showed a very specific, catastrophic deficit in their ability to deal with the multiple-relation problems, although they paralleled people in the other groups on single-relation problems. On the multiple-relation problems they exhibited a level of performance normally seen in pre-school children. In short, the picture emerging from these studies and others on problem solving and analogy is a very consistent one (see Chapters 14 and 15).

# RATIONALITY AND EVALUATION OF THEORIES

## Are we rational?

Given the evidence we have seen on people's reasoning abilities, one might be forgiven for thinking that we are all massively irrational. From the literature we have reviewed there are perhaps three main stances on this question.

The view that emerges from the long-standing theories in the area—the abstract-rule and mental models theories—is that people are rational, that they operate in accordance with a rational principle, in trying to deduce valid conclusions from the premises of an argument. Johnson-Laird and Byrne (1991, Johnson-Laird, 1999) frame this as a *modicum* of rational competence, which is important to everyday goals and essential for the development of expertise in logic. This is not to rule out irrational responses altogether; such responses clearly occur and will continue to occur.

A second, more recent, view changes the question slightly, in proposing that people are adaptive to their environment. This is clearly the view motivating domain-specific-rule theories and probabilistic theory. The proposal is that people act in accordance with another rational principle—maximising goal achievement or maximising information gain—rather than one derived from logic. For instance, on evolutionary grounds Cosmides (1989) argues that there are specialised inferential mechanisms for "checking for cheaters" which were specifically adaptive for our hunter-gather forebears. Oaksford and Chater argue for the maximisation of information gain and the reduction of uncertainty as the guiding principle. More widely, this view is taken by Anderson (1990) in his "rational analysis" technique to characterise many diverse areas of cognition from memory to problem solving.

The final position, which is more a meta-analysis of the problem, is to distinguish between different forms of rationality. Evans and Over (1996, 1997) distinguish between the unfortunately named rationality$_1$ and rationality$_2$. Rationality$_1$ is the adaptive goal-directed form of reasoning and problem solving that helps us achieve our goals in the world. Rationality$_2$ is a more reflective form of reasoning that is consistent with the normative models of logic. It is possible for someone to be make an inference that is fine from the rationality$_1$ perspective but completely at variance with the rationality$_2$ view (for commentaries see Cummins, 1997; Hertwig, Ortmann, & Gigerenzer, 1997; Noveck, 1997; Ormerod, 1997; Stanovich, 1999). However, beyond labelling two interpretations of rationality, it is not clear how this distinction brings us closer to any conclusions about human rationality. Ideally, we should have a definition of rationality that is both adaptive and normative.

In summation, it is clear that there is general agreement that people are, for the most part, adaptive or rational in some way. What is at issue is the exact rational principle at work.

## Assessing competing theories

In this chapter, we have examined empirical work that centres on reasoning with conditionals. It is important to note that this is just one area of research in deductive reasoning. There are large literatures on syllogistic reasoning (see Evans et al., 1993; Eysenck & Keane, 1995, Chapter 17; Manktelow, 1999), on spatial reasoning (Johnson-Laird & Byrne, 1991), and reasoning with logical connectives other than *if . . . then* (e.g., *and*, *or*, *not*). We have only peeked through a small window at the theories of concern. With this in mind, we can tentatively broach the question "What is the current best account of reasoning?". Usually, science seeks a single unified theory, rather than a cluster of alternative theories. So, we will assume that the answer to this question should be a single candidate theory.

The domain-specific rule and probabilistic theories probably come off the worst in terms of the generality of their coverage. Domain-specific rules really only apply to selection task problems and rely on some other theory (e.g., abstract rules) to deal with a wide set of phenomena. Probabilistic theory has also been applied to the selection task and more recently to syllogistic reasoning (Chater & Oaksford, 1999b) but, as we saw earlier, has a way to go in developing a performance theory of reasoning. The remaining theories—the abstract-rule and mental model theories—have the best overall coverage of the field.

Abstract-rule theories have been applied to propositional reasoning. They can generate precise predictions about subjects' judgements of validity (Braine et al., 1984; Osherson, 1974, 1975; Rips, 1983), about the reaction times of subjects on tasks (Braine et al., 1984), and about inter-subject differences on problems (Rips & Conrad, 1983). They have also been applied to syllogistic reasoning (Braine & Rumain, 1983; Osherson, 1976; Rips, 1994). The results of research on the selection task are more embarrassing. Some abstract-rule theorists have proposed that formal inference rules can be supplemented by domain-specific rules or by the addition of modal logics and non-logical operators (see Braine & O'Brien, 1991; Rips 1989). However, the problem with this proposal is that it begins to move away from a unified account of a variety of reasoning phenomena (see also Manktelow & Over's, 1991, criticisms of this proposition).

Finally, the model theory scores highly on generality. It has well developed accounts of conditional and syllogistic reasoning. Johnson-Laird and Byrne (1991) have proposed an account of all of the effects found on the selection task, although this proposal requires some fleshing out. The theory has also been spread wider to explain aspects of imagination in counterfactual reasoning (Byrne, 1997; Byrne & Tasso, 1999), spatial reasoning (Johnson-Laird & Byrne, 1991), creativity (Johnson-Laird, 1989), and probabilistic reasoning (Johnson-Laird et al., 1999). At present, it looks like the most complete theory of human reasoning, although its opponents continue to challenge many of its foundations.

## CHAPTER SUMMARY

In this chapter, we have reviewed some of the major theories of deductive reasoning as they apply to reasoning with conditionals.

- The evidence on reasoning with conditionals shows that people do not consistently make inferences sanctioned as being valid by propositional logic, and sometimes make invalid inferences. Context effects have shown that these patterns of valid and invalid inferences are sensitive to other factors like the provision of additional conditions, alternative conditions, uncertain premises, salient premises, and causal conditions.
- The evidence on the selection task shows that people do not make the logically appropriate falsifying choices in abstract versions of the task, but do better on deontic versions of the task (using thematic, realistic, or permission materials).
- The abstract-rule theory proposes that people construct mental proofs of conclusions from premises using abstract, content-free rules. It thus relies on a normative theory from logic. This theory can account for the different patterns of inferences with conditionals, some context effects, and some aspects of the selection task.
- The mental models theory proposes that people construct models of the premises from which conclusions are drawn and validated by a search for counterexamples. It also relies on a normative theory from logic. This theory can account for the different patterns of inferences with conditionals, most context effects, and many of the findings in the selection task.
- The domain-specific-rule theory proposes that people have specific schemata for classes of situations like permissions, obligations, and contracts. This theory has been applied to explain thematic or deontic versions of the selection task. It requires an additional theory (either abstract-rule or mental models) to account for reasoning with more abstract materials; hence, it argues for a dual process account.
- The probabilistic theory proposes that people act to maximise information gain by making the most informative choices/conclusions. It relies on a normative model from probability theory. This theory has been extensively applied to the findings on the selection task.
- Cognitive neuropsychological research on reasoning has implicated the left frontal lobes although background knowledge influences are apparent in the right hemisphere.
- In general, it is clear that people are rational in some sense. What is not yet clear is whether they are rational in a purely adaptive, goal-directed sense or whether they can be said to be truly rational in a normative sense (e.g., relative to a logical model).

## FURTHER READING

- Braine, M., & O'Brien, M. (1998). *Mental logic.* Cambridge, MA: MIT Press. This book provides a recent account of a major abstract-rule theory.
- Evans, J.St.B.T., Newstead, S.E., & Byrne. R.M.J. (1993). *Human reasoning: The psychology of deduction.* Hove, UK: Psychology Press. This text provides a comprehensive review of recent reasoning research, covering some of the areas reviewed here, but in more detail.
- Johnson-Laird, P.N., & Byrne, R.M.J. (1991). *Deduction.* Hove, UK: Psychology Press. This work provides the most comprehensive statement of the mental models theory.

- Manktelow, K.I. (1999). *Reasoning & thinking*. Hove, UK: Psychology Press. This is an advanced text on reasoning and is quite excellent in the comprehensiveness of its coverage and the balance of its criticism.
- Oaksford, M., & Chater, N. (Eds.) (1998). *Rational models of cognition*. Oxford: Oxford University Press. This book has a collection of chapters on the probabilistic approach to reasoning.
- Stanovich, K.E. (1999). *Who is rational?: Studies of individual differences in reasoning*. Hillsdale, NJ: Lawrence Erlbaum Associates Inc. Gives much needed attention to a topic not reviewed here, namely the existence of individual differences in reasoning.

# 17

# Judgement and Decision Making

## INTRODUCTION

In this chapter, we will be focusing on judgement and decision making. The two areas of research are similar (and also resemble human reasoning in some ways, see Chapter 16), but can be distinguished. In essence, judgement research is concerned with the processes used in drawing conclusions from the knowledge and evidence available to us. In contrast, decision making is concerned with choosing among options, and can involve choices of personal significance.

Research on judgement and decision making has been concerned largely with statistical judgements. For example, many judgements are based on uncertain or ambiguous information, and so we necessarily deal with probabilities rather than with certainties. Most of the early research on judgements of utility and intuitive statistics was led by theories of optimal decision making and statistics developed by philosophers and economists (e.g., Coombs, Dawes, & Tversky, 1970; Edwards, 1954). These normative theories describe how one should go about determining the best possible course of action, given one's knowledge about the world and what one wants. They

describe, given certain strong assumptions, how we can make optimal judgements and decisions.

An important reason why decision making is often difficult is because we live in a world full of uncertainty. For example, you might want to choose a career in which you would be well paid. However, the fact that it is well paid now does not guarantee that that will still be the case in 20 years' time. As a result of such uncertanties, accounts of decision making (whether involving optimal decision making or not) typically emphasise the role of subjective probabilities.

An approach based on optimal judgements and decisions does not generally apply well to human reasoning. There are many reasons for this. First, people often do not have access to all the information needed to make optimal judgements or decisions. Second, they may exaggerate the importance of some of the available information and minimise the importance of other information. Third, individuals who are very anxious or depressed are unlikely to make optimal decisions, because their emotional state makes it difficult for them to think clearly about the various options available to them. However, emotional factors can readily be incorporated into theories of optimal decision making. For example, if someone is deciding whether or not to sell their old car, it is entirely appropriate for theories of decision making to take full account of any emotional attachment the owner has to his or her car.

## JUDGEMENT RESEARCH

Much of the judgement research we will review has its origins in our everyday experience of revising our opinions in the light of new information or evidence. For example, suppose that you believe that it is very likely that someone has lied to you. If you then discover that another person supports their story, your confidence in your original belief is likely to decrease (this example was suggested by Peter Ayton, personal communication). Changes in beliefs can often be expressed in terms of probabilities. For example, we may initially be 90% confident that the other person is lying, but when their story is confirmed by another person, the probability may be reduced to 60%. The Rev. Thomas Bayes went still further, and produced a mathematical formula which shows how we can combine probabilities in order to calculate the impact of new evidence on a pre-existing probability. More specifically, he focused on situations in which there are two beliefs or hypotheses (e.g., X is lying vs. X is not lying), and he showed how new data or information alter the probabilities of these two hypotheses. The approach adopted by Bayes has been applied to conditional reasoning (see Chapter 16).

According to Bayes' theorem, we need to take account of the relative probabilities of the two hypotheses before the data were obtained (prior odds), and the relative probabilities of obtaining the data under each hypothesis (posterior odds). Bayesian methods evaluate the probability of observing the data, D, if hypothesis A is correct, written $p(D/H_A)$, and if hypothesis B is correct, written $p(D/H_B)$. Bayes' theorem itself can be expressed in the form of an odds ratio as follows:

$$\frac{p(H_A/D)}{p(H_B/D)} = \frac{p(H_A)}{p(H_B)} \times \frac{p(D/H_A)}{p(D/H_B)}$$

On the left of the equation, we have the relative probabilities of hypotheses A and B, which is what

we are trying to find out. On the right of the equation, we have the prior odds of each hypothesis being correct before the data are collected, followed by the posterior odds involving the probability of the data given each hypothesis.

In order to clarify what is involved in Bayes' theorem, we will consider the taxi-cab problem used by Tversky and Kahneman (1980):

> A taxi-cab was involved in a hit-and-run accident one night. Two cab companies, the Green and the Blue, operate in the city. You are given the following data: (a) 85% of the cabs in the city are Green, and 15% are Blue, and (b) in court a witness identified the cab as a Blue cab.
>
> However, the court tested the witness's ability to identify cabs under appropriate visibility conditions. When presented with a series of cabs, half of which were Blue and half of which were Green, the witness made the correct identification in 80% of the cases, and was wrong in 20% of cases.
>
> What was the probability that the cab involved in the accident was Blue rather than Green? . . . per cent.

We will refer to the hypothesis that the cab was Blue as $H_A$, and the hypothesis that it was Green as $H_B$. The prior probabilities are 0.15 for $H_A$ and 0.85 for $H_B$. The probability of the witness saying the cab was Blue when it was Blue, i.e., $p(D/H_A)$, is .80, and the probability of the witness saying the cab was Blue when it was Green, i.e., $p(D/H_B)$, is .20. If we enter these values in the formula, we obtain the following ratio:

$$\frac{.15}{.85} \times \frac{.80}{.20} = \frac{.12}{.17}$$

Thus, the odds ratio is 12:17, meaning that there is a 41% probability that the taxi cab was Blue versus a 59% probability that it was Green.

### Neglecting base rates

What we have done so far is to describe how people's estimates of the probability of certain hypotheses might vary in the light of new evidence.

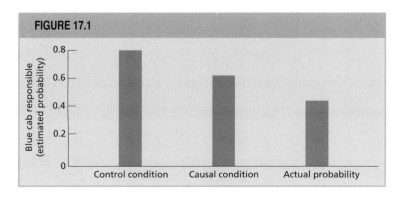

FIGURE 17.1

Estimated probability in the taxi-cab problem that a Blue cab was responsible for the accident in causal and control conditions. Data from Tversky and Kahneman (1980).

In fact, people often take much less account of the prior odds or the base-rate information than they should if they were following the principles of Bayes' theorem. *Base-rate information* was defined by Koehler (1996, p. 16) as "the relative frequency with which an event occurs or an attribute is present in the population." There are many situations in which participants seem to neglect base rates. For example, consider the taxi-cab problem discussed earlier. Tversky and Kahneman (1980) found that most participants ignored the base-rate information about the relative numbers of Green and Blue cabs. They concentrated on the evidence of the witness, and maintained that there was an 80% likelihood that the taxi was Blue rather than Green (see Figure 17.1). In fact, as we have seen, the correct answer based on Bayes' theorem is 41%.

Tversky and Kahneman (1980) also used an alternative condition in which people *did* take base-rate information into account. They changed the (a) part of the problem to:

Although the two companies are roughly equal in size, 85% of cab accidents in the city involve Green cabs, and 15% involve Blue cabs.

In this version of the problem, a clear *causal* relation is drawn between the accident record of a cab company and the likelihood of there being an accident. In the original version of the problem, in contrast, the population difference for the two cab companies is given no causal significance. Thus, the base-rate information was predicted to

be of more significance in this new problem, and to play a greater part in participants' assessments. This prediction was confirmed, with most participants producing estimates of a 60% likelihood (see Figure 17.1). It appears that base rates may be ignored, but various factors (e.g., the presence of a causal relation) can partially reverse this behaviour.

Additional evidence about the circumstances in which people do and do not use base-rate information emerges from studies by Casscells, Schoenberger, and Graboys (1978) and by Cosmides and Tooby (1996). Casscells et al. (1978) presented the following problem to members of staff and to students at Harvard Medical School:

If a test to detect a disease whose prevalence is 1/1000 has a false positive rate of 5%, what is the chance that a person found to have a positive result actually has the disease, assuming that you know nothing about the person's symptoms or signs?

The base-rate information is that 999 people out of every 1000 do not suffer from the disease. However, 50 out of every 1000 people tested would give a false positive finding (5% is the false positive rate). Thus, 50 times as many people give a false positive result as give a true positive result (the one person in 1000 who had the disease), and so there is only a 2% chance that a person testing positive actually has the disease. The correct answer was given by 18% of the participants, but 45% ignored the base-rate information and gave the wrong answer of 95%.

Cosmides and Tooby (1996) used a rather similar problem. However, they emphasised the *frequencies* of individuals in the various categories relevant to the problem. In addition, they told the participants to construct an active pictorial representation. More specifically, the participants had to colour in different squares to represent those individuals with and without the disease. In these circumstances, 92% used the base-rate information and gave the correct answer.

## Evaluation

Koehler (1996) reviewed findings on use of base-rate information. He concluded that this literature, "does not support the conventional wisdom that people routinely ignore base rates. Quite the contrary, the literature shows that base rates are almost always used and that their degree of use depends on task structure and representation" (p. 1).

Koehler (1996) argued that there are three main reasons for not concluding that base-rate information is typically ignored. First, the most common finding is that individuals pay less attention than they should to base-rate information. However, it does have some influence on their decision making, and so cannot be said to have been ignored altogether.

Second, there are typically major differences between the laboratory and the real world in terms of how we obtain base-rate information. In the laboratory, this information is generally provided directly by the experimenter. In the real world, in contrast, such information is typically obtained indirectly (if at all) via numerous experiences. There is some evidence suggesting that this difference is important. For example, consider the real-world research carried out by Christensen-Szalanski and Bushyhead (1981). They found that doctors were sensitive to the predictive value of various symptoms associated with pneumonia, and argued that the doctors were sensitive to base rates. However, of those patients estimated by the doctors to have a 90% chance of having pneumonia, under 20% actually had pneumonia (Clare Harries, personal communication). Thus, the doctors were not actually very sensitive to base-rate information.

The notion that doctors typically make effective use of base-rate information was disproved by Bergus, Chapman, Gjerde, and Elstein (1995). Doctors were presented with the case history of a man who reported a 1-hour episode of weakness in the right arm and leg. Some of the doctors were informed initially that he had had treatment for lung cancer, whereas the others were only told this at the end of the experiment. Those who were told initially about the lung cancer gave a mean probability of 48% that the correct diagnosis was brain cancer that had spread from the lungs. In fact, however, the correct probability is 99.5%, and so their estimate of the base rate was incorrect. All the doctors were then told that the patient had been given a CAT scan which had not revealed any abnormality. This additional information reduces the likelihood that the correct diagnosis is brain cancer spreading from the lungs to 93%. Those who had just learned of the previous lung cancer produced an average probability estimate of 79%, compared to only 11% for those doctors who had been given that information initially. Thus, the doctors were more likely to neglect information relevant to base rate if it had been provided some time previously.

The effects of experience on usage of base-rate information can be complex. For example, Gluck and Bower (1988) carried out a study in which the participants had 250 learning trials. On each trial, combinations of four symptoms were displayed, and the participants had to decide which of two diseases was present. One disease was present 75% of the time and the other disease was present 25% of the time. The participants' performance on the last 50 trials indicated that they were using base-rate information about the relative frequencies of the diseases. However, when asked questions at the end of the experiment, their answers did not reflect accurate knowledge of base-rate information. According to Spellman (1996), base-rate information that has been acquired via *implicit learning* (complex learning in the absence of conscious recollection of what has been learned) can be accessed more readily on implicit memory tests (e.g., performance) than on explicit memory tests (e.g., direct questioning).

To return to the third of Koehler's points, in most real-world situations, base-rate information is either unavailable or of limited usefulness. According to Koehler (1996, p. 14), "When base rates in the natural environment are ambiguous, unreliable, or unstable, simple normative rules for their use do not exist. In such cases, the diagnostic value of base rates may be substantially less than that associated with many laboratory experiments." There are often several competing base rates in the real world. Suppose you are trying to work out the probability that a given professional golfer will score under 70 in his next round on a given course. What is the relevant base rate? Is it his previous scores on that course during his career, or his general level of performance that season, or his performance over his entire career, or the average performance of other professionals? As Connolly (1996, p. 19) pointed out, "In any reasonably complex informational environment, it is essentially arbitrary to select some part of the information as relevant to the estimation of a base rate." As a result of these uncertainties, our everyday experiences may have indicated that there is little value in base-rate information, and so we are reluctant to make use of such information when it is available.

## Representativeness heuristic

Why do we often fail to make much use of base-rate information? Tversky and Kahneman and their associates argued that we typically utilise a simple heuristic or rule of thumb known as the *representativeness heuristic*. When people use this heuristic, "events that are representative or typical of a class are assigned a high probability of occurrence. If an event is highly similar to most of the others in a population or class of events, then it is considered representative" (Kellogg, 1995, p. 385). The representativeness heuristic is studied in situations in which people are asked to judge the probability that an object or event A belongs to a class or process B. If someone is given a description of an individual and asked to guess the probability that this individual has a certain occupation, it is typically found that they judge probabilities in terms of the similarity of

the individual to their stereotype for that occupation. In a study by Tversky and Kahneman (1974), the participants were given the following description of Steve:

> . . . very shy and withdrawn, invariably helpful, but with little interest in people, or in the world of reality. A meek tidy soul, he has a need for order and structure and a passion for detail . . .

The participants were then asked to determine the probability that Steve was a farmer, pilot, doctor, or librarian. As expected, many people chose librarian as a high-probability job for Steve, because he is a good match to the stereotype for this occupation.

Kahneman and Tversky (1973) carried out a study in which use of the representativeness heuristic produced faulty assessments of probability. The participants were provided with a brief description, which they were told had been selected at random from a total of 100 descriptions. Half of the participants were told that the total consisted of descriptions of 70 engineers and 30 lawyers, whereas the others were told that there were 70 lawyers and 30 engineers. Their task was to decide the probability that the person described was an engineer (or lawyer). A sample description was as follows (Kahneman & Tversky, 1973, p. 241):

> Jack is a 45-year-old man. He is married and has four children. He is generally conservative, careful, and ambitious. He shows no interest in political and social issues and spends most of his free time on his many hobbies which include home carpentry, sailing, and mathematical puzzles.

The participants decided that there was a .90 probability that Jack was an engineer, and this was so regardless of whether most of the 100 descriptions were of lawyers or engineers. Thus, the participants did not take base-rate information (i.e., the 70:30 split of descriptions) into account.

The representativeness heuristic is also used in a more striking way to produce what is known

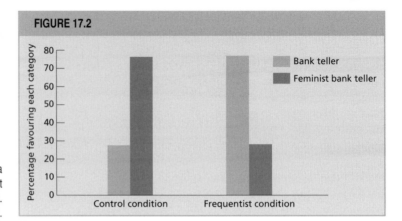

**FIGURE 17.2**

Performance on the Linda problem in the frequentist and control conditions. Data from Fiedler (1988).

as the *conjunction fallacy*. This is the mistaken belief that a conjunction of two events (A and B) is more likely than one of the two events (A or B). Tversky and Kahneman (1983) informed their participants that Linda was a former student activist, very intelligent, single, and a philosophy graduate. They then estimated the likelihood that Linda was a bank teller, a feminist, or a feminist bank teller. The estimated probability that Linda was a feminist bank teller was higher than the probability that she was a bank teller. This cannot be correct, because all feminist bank tellers belong to the larger category of bank tellers.

Some studies have obtained inconsistent evidence for the conjunction fallacy. Fiedler (1988) used two versions of the Linda problem. Of those participants who had to decide whether it was more likely that Linda was a bank teller or a feminist bank teller, 75% incorrectly chose the latter alternative, and so showed the conjunction fallacy (see Figure 17.2). However, other participants were given a frequentist version of the problem. They were asked to estimate how many out of 100 Lindas would be bank tellers and how many would be feminist bank tellers. In this condition, 75% of the participants decided correctly that more of them would be bank tellers.

### Availability heuristic

Tversky and Kahneman (1974) found that people often make use of the *availability heuristic*. This involves estimating the frequencies of events on the basis of how easy or difficult it is to retrieve relevant information from long-term memory. Tversky and Kahneman (1974) asked participants the following question:

If a word of three letters or more is sampled at random from an English text, is it more likely that the word starts with "r" or has "r" as its third letter?

Tversky and Kahneman (1974) found that most participants reported that a word starting with "r" was more likely to be picked out at random than a word with "r" in its third position. In reality, the reverse is the case. However, words starting with "r" can be retrieved more readily from memory (i.e., are more available) than words with "r" as their third letter. As a result, participants make the wrong judgement about the relative frequency of the two classes of words.

In this case, availability was based on the effectiveness of retrieval of instances from long-term memory. Availability can also be based on frequency of occurrence. In other words, we tend to recall those things that have been encountered most frequently in the past. This strategy often leads to effective judgements. However, availability can also be affected by the relative salience of instances, i.e., happenings or objects that have been encountered recently or have become salient for some reason can be temporarily more available. If you are a US citizen trying to decide where to go on holiday, and there is a sudden rash of terrorist incidents in Europe against US citizens, it is highly likely that you will be swayed into taking a holiday in the United States (even though the probability of getting killed in, say, Florida may be comparable to Europe or higher). Lichtenstein et al. (1978) have shown how causes of death attracting more publicity (e.g., murder) are judged more likely than those attracting less publicity (e.g., suicide), contrary to the true state of affairs.

An issue that is very relevant to the use of the availability heuristic concerns the strategies that people use to judge the frequency of events. Brown (1995) presented his participants with category–exemplar pairs (e.g., Country–Greece). Each category was presented a number of times, and it was either accompanied by the same exemplar each time (same context) or by a different exemplar (different context). The task was to decide how frequently each category name had been presented, and then to indicate the strategy that had been used. About 60% of the responses produced by different-context participants were based on enumeration (retrieving and counting the relevant items), whereas 69% of the responses produced by same-context participants were uninformative (e.g., "There weren't too many of those"). The implication of these findings is that availability is merely one among several strategies for estimating event frequency.

## Support theory

Tversky and Koehler (1994) put forward a support theory of subjective probability, which was subsequently developed by Rottenstreich and Tversky (1997). The key insight lying behind this theory is that any given event may seem more or less likely depending on the way in which it is described, and so we must distinguish between events and descriptions of events. For example, you would undoubtedly argue that the probability that you will die on your next summer holiday is very low indeed. However, the probability of that event occurring might seem somewhat higher if it were described as follows: "What is the probability that you will die on your next summer holiday from a disease, a sudden heart attack, an earthquake,

terrorist activity, a civil war, a car accident, a plane crash, or from any other cause?" According to support theory, "Probability judgements are attached not to events but to descriptions of events . . . the judged probability of an event depends on the explicitness of its description" (Tversky & Koehler, 1994, p. 548).

The most striking prediction of support theory is that a more explicit description of an event will typically be regarded as having greater subjective probability than precisely the same event described in less explicit terms. Why is this prediction made? There are two main reasons:

1. An explicit description may draw attention to aspects of the event that are less obvious in the non-explicit description.
2. Memory limitations may mean that people do not remember all of the relevant information if it is not supplied.

Evidence consistent with support theory was provided by Johnson, Hershey, Meszaros, and Kunreuther (1993). Some participants were offered hypothetical health insurance covering hospitalisation for any reason, whereas others were offered health insurance covering hospitalisation for any disease or accident. These offers are the same, but participants were prepared to pay a higher premium in the latter case. Presumably the explicit references to disease and accident made it seem more likely that hospitalisation would be required, and so increased the value of being insured.

It might seem reasonable to assume that the phenomenon of higher subjective probability for an event when it is explicitly described would not be found among those possessing relevant expertise. After all, experts provided with a non-explicit description can presumably fill in the details from their own knowledge. In fact, however, the phenomenon has proved to be surprisingly robust. For example, Redelmeier, Koehler, Liberman, and Tversky (1995) presented doctors at Stanford University with a description of a woman suffering from abdominal pain. Half of them were asked to decide the probabilities of two specified diagnoses (gastroenteritis and ectopic pregnancy) and of a residual category of everything else. The other half assigned probabilities to five specified diagnoses (including gastoenteritis and ectopic pregnancy) and the residual category of everything else. The key comparison was between the subjective probability of the residual category for the former group and the combined probabilities of the three additional diagnoses plus the residual category in the latter group. The former probability was .50, and the latter probability was .69, indicating that subjective probabilities are higher for explicit descriptions even with experts.

In sum, support theory provides an interesting development of earlier ideas about heuristics. More specifically, some of the assumptions within support theory extend the notion of an availability heuristic in various ways.

## Overall evaluation

Tversky, Kahneman and others have shown that several general heuristics or rules of thumb (e.g., representativeness heuristic; availability heuristic) underlie judgements in many different contexts. Considerable research has been carried out on these biases, and they seem to be of great practical importance. Heuristics are also of relevance in understanding aspects of human reasoning (see Chapter 16).

Gigerenzer (1996) claimed that there are five main limitations of the theoretical approach adopted by Kahneman and Tversky (e.g., 1996). First, Gigerenzer (1996) claimed that Kahneman and Tversky had failed to provide process models that specified in detail when and how the various heuristics are used. According to Gigerenzer (1996, p. 594), "The two major surrogates [substitutes] for modeling cognitive processes have been (a) one-word-labels such as representativeness that seem to be traded as explanations, and (b) explanations by redescription." In other words, we have very limited understanding of what is involved in use of these heuristics.

Second, Gigerenzer (1996) argued that Kahneman and Tversky generally focus on the statistical principles relevant to a problem at the expense of any proper consideration of its real-world content. The dangers of doing this can be seen with reference to the taxi-cab problem discussed earlier.

Tversky and Kahneman (1980) claimed there was only one correct answer to this problem. In contrast, Birnbaum (1983) focused on the cognitive processes that might be used by an eyewitness. He found that there are several possible answers to the taxi-cab problem, depending on the theory of eyewitness processing that one favours. For example, the eyewitness was 80% correct when asked to identify a series of cabs, 50% of which were Blue and 50% of which were Green. In those circumstances, there was no advantage in systematically saying Blue or Green when the eyewitness was unsure. However, when 85% of the cabs are Green and only 15% are Blue, it would have made sense for the eyewitness to say Green whenever he/she was unsure.

Third, most of the problems used by Kahneman and Tversky involved the presentation of probability information, and led to apparently error-prone judgements. However, as we have seen, people are sometimes more likely to follow logical or statistical principles when the relevant numerical information is represented by frequencies rather than by probabilities (e.g., Cosmides & Tooby, 1996; Fiedler, 1988). Gigerenzer (1996) has obtained evidence that this occurs more often when absolute frequencies (actual numbers of events or individuals falling into different categories) are used rather than relative frequencies or probabilities. Why is there this difference? According to Gigerenzer (1996, p. 594), "cognitive algorithms [computational procedures] designed to do Bayesian reasoning with absolute frequencies . . . involve fewer steps of mental computation." However, it should be noted that the use of absolute frequencies does *not* usually lead to full use of base-rate information (see Gigerenzer, 1996).

Gigerenzer and Hoffrage (1999) developed the theoretical position of Gigerenzer (1996). They emphasised the notion of natural sampling, which is "the process of encountering instances in a population sequentially" (Gigerenzer & Hoffrage, 1999, p. 425). Natural sampling is what typically happens in everyday life, and it allows us to work out absolute frequencies of different kinds of events. According to Gigerenzer and Hoffrage (1999, p. 430), "Humans seem to be developmentally and evolutionarily prepared to handle natural frequencies. In contrast, many of us go through a considerable amount of mental agony to learn to think in terms of fractions, percentages, and other forms of normalised counts."

Fourth, Gigerenzer (1996) argued that some of the biases in judgements reported in the literature owe much to misunderstandings of parts of the problem by the participants. For example, consider the Linda problem discussed earlier. Gigerenzer and others have found that between 20% and 50% of people interpret "Linda is a bank teller" as implying that she is not active in the feminist movement (see Gigerenzer, 1996). Thus, the conjunction fallacy can be obtained for reasons other than use of the representativeness heuristic.

Fifth, there has been a controversy about whether it makes sense to assign probabilities to unique events, as is done in many of the problems used by Kahneman and Tversky. They interpret probability as a subjective measure of belief, and so are willing to attach a probability value to a unique event. In contrast, Gigerenzer and other frequentists interpret probability as being determined by the relative frequencies of different events over time, and so argue that it is meaningless to assign probability to unique events. The complex issues here are discussed by Kahneman and Tversky (1996) and by Gigerenzer (1996).

## DECISION MAKING

When we are confronted by a choice that affects us personally (e.g., going to France or to Spain for a holiday), there are nearly always benefits and costs associated with each choice. How do we decide what to do? A fairly straightforward approach was proposed by von Neumann and Morgenstern (1947). According to their utility theory, we try to maximise *utility*, which is the subjective value we attach to an outcome. When we need to choose between simple options, we assess the expected utility or expected value of each one by means of the following formula:

Expected utility = (probability of a given outcome)
× (utility of the outcome)

In the real world, there will typically be various factors associated with each option. For example, one holiday option may be preferable to a second holiday option, because it is in a more interesting area and the weather is likely to be better. However, the first holiday is more expensive and more of your valuable holiday time would be spent in travelling. In such circumstances, people are supposed to calculate the expected utility or disutility (cost) of each factor in order to work out the overall expected value or utility of each option.

When the choice is an easy one, then people do seem to behave in line with utility theory. For example, if given the choice between two holidays, one of which is in a more interesting place with better weather than the other, and is also cheaper and involves less travelling time, then virtually everyone will choose that holiday. However, as is discussed next, people's choices are often decided by factors other than simply utility. Readers interested in finding out about contemporary versions of utility theory should consult Luce (1996) or Mellers, Schwartz, and Cooke (1998).

## Loss aversion

In many situations, people demonstrate a phenomenon known as *loss aversion*, that is, they are much more sensitive to potential losses than to potential gains. For example, consider a study by Kahneman and Tversky (1984). Participants were given the chance to toss a coin, winning $10 if it came up heads and losing $10 if it came up tails. Most of them declined this offer, even though it is a fair bet. More surprisingly, most participants still refused to bet when they were offered $20 if the coin came up heads, with a loss of only $10 if it came up tails. They showed loss aversion, in that they were unduly concerned about the potential loss. In terms of utility theory, they should have accepted the bet, because it provides an average expected gain of $10 per toss. In real life, however, loss aversion may often be desirable (Trevor Harley, personal communication).

A phenomenon that resembles loss aversion is the *sunk-cost effect*, in which additional resources are expended to justify some previous commitment.

Dawes (1988) discussed a study in which two people had paid a $100 non-refundable deposit for a weekend at a resort. On the way to the resort, both of them became slightly unwell, and felt they would probably have a more pleasurable time at home than at the resort. Should they drive on or turn back? Many participants argued that the two people should drive on to avoid wasting the $100: this is the sunk-cost effect. The implications of this decision are that more money will be needed in order to spend the weekend at the resort, even though it is less preferred than being at home!

## Framing

Many of our decisions are influenced by irrelevant aspects of the situation (e.g., the precise way in which an issue is presented). This phenomenon is known as *framing*. Tversky and Kahneman (1987) provided an interesting example of framing in the Asian disease problem. The participants were told that there was likely to be an outbreak of an Asian disease in the United States, and that it was expected to kill 600 people. Two programmes of action had been proposed: Programme A would allow 200 people to be saved; programme B would have a 1/3 probability that 600 people would be saved, and a 2/3 probability that none of the 600 would be saved. When the issue was expressed in this form, 72% of the participants favoured programme A, although the two programmes (if implemented several times) would on average both lead to the saving of 200 lives.

Other participants in the study by Tversky and Kahneman (1987) were given the same problem, but this time it was negatively framed. They were told that programme A would lead to 400 people dying, whereas programme B carried a 1/3 probability that nobody would die, and a 2/3 probability that 600 would die. In spite of the fact that the problem was the same, 78% chose programme B. The various findings obtained by Tversky and Kahneman (1987) can be accounted for in terms of loss aversion in the sense of avoiding certain losses.

Wang (1996) carried out a series of studies using different versions of the Asian disease problem in which the total number of people in the patient group varied between 600 and 6. He replicated the findings of Tversky and Kahneman (1987) when the group size was 600. However, the key findings were as follows:

1. There was no framing effect when the size of the patient group was 60 or 6.
2. With the smaller patient groups, there was a clear preference for the probabilistic outcome (1/3 probability that nobody would die, and a 2/3 probability that everyone would die).

What do these findings mean? The most common reason that participants gave for choosing the probabilistic outcome is that they wanted to give everyone an equal chance to survive. In other words, they were concerned about fairness, and this concern was greater in a small-group context than in a large-group context.

Wang (1996) then tested the importance of fairness by asking participants to choose between two options: (1) one-third of the group is saved; (2) one-third of the group is selected to be saved. When the group size was 600, 60% of the participants chose the option with the non-selected survivors; this rose to 80% when the group size was 6. These findings strengthen the notion that concerns about fairness are greater when dealing with small groups than with large ones.

In a final study, Wang (1996) asked participants to choose between definite survival of two-thirds of the patients (deterministic option) or a one-third probability of all patients surviving and a two-thirds probability of none surviving (probabilistic option). They were told that the group size was 600, 6, or 3 patients unknown to them, or 6 patients who were close relatives of the participant. According to utility theory, the participants should have chosen the definite survival of two-thirds of the patients. In fact, the decision was greatly affected by group size and by the relationship between the participants and the group members (see Figure 17.3). Presumably the increased percentage of participants choosing the probabilistic option with small group size (especially for relatives) occurred because the social context and psychological factors relating

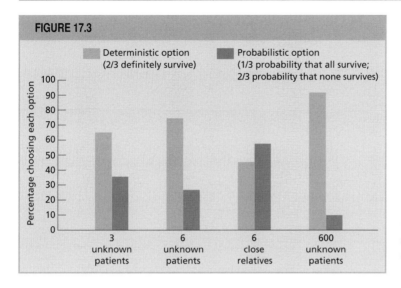

Effects of fairness manipulation on choice of the option with selected or with non-selected survivors. Data from Wang (1996).

to fairness were regarded as more important in those conditions. Their apparently "irrational" behaviour becomes immediately explicable when one takes account of this social context.

## Perceived justification

When people choose one option over another, they generally want to be able to justify their decision to themselves and to other people. One of the clearest demonstrations of the influence of perceived justification on choice making was reported by Tversky and Shafir (1992). Their participants were asked to imagine that they had the chance to buy a very cheap holiday in Hawaii, but the special offer expired tomorrow. They had three choices: (1) buy the holiday; (2) decide not to buy the holiday; (3) pay a $5 non-refundable fee to retain the opportunity to buy the holiday the day after tomorrow. All the participants were asked to assume that they had just taken a difficult examination. In one version of the problem, they knew that they had passed the examination. In a second version, they knew they had failed. In the third version, they would find out whether they had passed or failed the day after tomorrow.

What do you think the three groups of participants decided to do? Of those who had passed, a majority decided to buy the holiday, as did most

of those who had failed (see Figure 17.4). However, only 32% of those who did not know their examination result decided to buy the holiday immediately. These findings can be explained in terms of perceived justification. Those who have passed an examination "deserve" a holiday, and those who have failed "deserve" some kind of consolation. If someone does not know whether or not they have passed an examination, there seems to be no compelling justification for going on holiday. The participants' use of perceived justification sounds rational, but actually violates utility theory.

## Anticipated regret

The choices we make are often affected by the anticipated emotions that will be produced by each choice. More specifically, anticipated regret influences choices between consumer products, sexual practices, gambles, and medical decisions (see Mellers et al., 1998). Thus, choices that seem generally desirable are avoided if they produce anticipated regret.

Baron (e.g., 1997) predicted that anticipated regret can produce an *omission bias*, in which individuals prefer inaction over action. For example, Ritov and Baron (1990) studied a situation in which people had to choose whether or not to

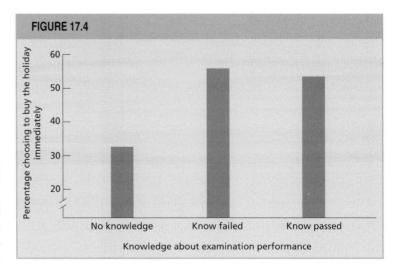

**FIGURE 17.4**

Percentage choosing to buy a holiday immediately as a function of having passed an examination, failed an examination, or not knowing whether the examination has been passed or failed. Data from Tversky and Shafir (1992).

have their child vaccinated. When the vaccine had potentially fatal side effects, many people chose not to have their child vaccinated, even though the likelihood of the vaccine causing death was much lower than the death rate from the disease against which the vaccine protects. This omission bias occurred because parents naturally anticipated enormous regret at the possibility of causing their child's death, but their inaction had the effect of increasing their child's risk of death.

### Self-esteem

Decision making undoubtedly depends in part on individual differences in personality. There has been disappointingly little relevant research, but a study by Josephs, Larrick, Steele, and Nisbett (1992) is an exception. Individuals high and low in self-esteem were invited to choose between two options of equal utility but differing in risk (e.g., a sure win of $10 versus a 50% chance of winning $20 on a gamble). The key finding was that individuals low in self-esteem were 50% more likely than those high in self-esteem to choose the sure gain.

Why were those low in self-esteem reluctant to take risks? People of low self-esteem seem to focus on self-protection, and are concerned that negative or threatening events will reduce still further their self-esteem (see Wood et al., 1994).

## HOW FLAWED ARE JUDGEMENT AND DECISION MAKING?

Most of the evidence discussed in this chapter indicates that people's judgements and decision making are error-prone. As Reisberg (1997, pp. 469–470) concluded his discussion of research on various heuristics:

> We have painted an unflattering portrait of human reasoning. We have discussed several sources of error, and we have suggested that these errors are rather widespread. These studies have been run on many different campuses, including some of the world's most prestigious colleges and universities. Thus, the subjects are, presumably, talented and intelligent. The errors occur nonetheless . . . One might draw rather cynical conclusions from these findings: Human reasoning is fundamentally flawed; errors are appallingly common.

There are, in fact, several reasons for not being unduly pessimistic about human decision making. If people's decision making in everyday life were as flawed as it appears to be in the laboratory, then it seems very unlikely that the human race would have been as successful as it has. According to numerous experts (e.g., Oaksford, 1997), there are important differences between decision making in the real world and in the laboratory. People often have to make decisions on the basis of very incomplete information, whereas this is typically not the case in laboratory studies. There are other situations in the real world in which people are exposed to a considerable amount of redundant information, which is also not true of most laboratory studies. It is likely that people have developed decision-making strategies that work reasonably well in everyday life, but may not work so well in the laboratory. As Oaksford (1997, p. 260) argued, "Many of the errors and biases seen in people's reasoning are likely to be the result of importing their everyday probabilistic strategies into the lab."

This line of argument can be applied to the various heuristics or rules of thumb used in making judgements. The use of heuristics can lead to error, but they serve a valuable function in our lives. As Reisberg (1997, p. 471) pointed out:

Heuristics provide efficiency. A heuristic is therefore valuable if this gain in efficiency is worth more to us than the cost . . . our lives are filled with countless occasions requiring a judgment of one sort or another. If we took too much time in each of these judgments, we would spend our days frozen in thought, unable to move forward in any

way . . . it might be madness *not* to use the heuristics, even if they do, on occasion, lead us astray.

Another important point is that the emphasis on people as inadequate users of logic and statistical information may be unduly limited. According to Mellers et al. (1998, p. 450), "Early metaphors for decision makers posited human beings as intuitive scientists, statisticians, and economists . . . Depending on the situation, people may be better understood as intuitive politicians who balance pressures from competing constituencies, intuitive prosecutors who demand accountability, or intuitive theologians who protect sacred values from contamination." For example, the importance of taking account of social factors was shown clearly by Wang (1996). Even Kahneman (1994) has argued that we need to move beyond simple logical analyses of problems. For example, he proposed that we should assess decision outcomes in terms of the benefits and costs to the individual as well as in terms of their match or mismatch to Bayes' theorem or some other form of statistical inference.

Finally, most people have a need to be able to justify the choices they make to themselves and to others. It is likely that the perceived justification of any given choice is a significant factor in many of the phenomena of decision making, including the framing effect, loss aversion, the sunk-cost effect, and omission bias.

## CHAPTER SUMMARY

- Introduction. Early approaches to decision and choice making were strongly influenced by normative theories of optimal decision making and by statistical theories such as Bayesian probability theory. It soon became apparent that people often fail to make optimal decisions, in part because they exaggerate the importance of some of the available evidence and minimise the importance of other evidence.
- Judgement research. People often seem to neglect base-rate information, but this is less likely when such information has clear causal relevance. Base-rate information may be neglected because it is often unavailable or of limited usefulness in the real world. Probability decisions often involve the use of various rules of thumb, such as the representativeness and availability heuristics. There is a lack of process models to explain when and how the various heuristics are used. There has been too much concern about the statistical principles relevant to problems at the

expense of their real-world content. Judgements tend to be more accurate when the relevant numerical information is presented in the form of absolute frequencies rather than probabilities.

- *Decision making*. According to utility theory, we try to maximise utility or subjective value. However, decisions are also determined by other factors such as framing, the social context, perceived justification, anticipated regret, loss aversion, the sunk-cost effect, and individual differences in personality (e.g., self-esteem). There is no general theory that accounts for all these diverse findings.
- How flawed are judgement and decision making? Most of the available evidence indicates that people's judgements and decision making are error-prone. However, most people have developed decision-making strategies that work reasonably well in everyday life even though they do not work so well in the laboratory. For example, heuristics permit rapid and efficient decision making, and these benefits probably outweigh the possible costs of inaccuracy. In the real world, considerations such as being able to justify decisions to ourselves and to others may be more important than optimising utility.

## FURTHER READING

- Gigerenzer, G., Todd, P.M., & the ABC Research Group. (1999). *Simple heuristics that make us smart*. Oxford: Oxford University Press. This book provides up-to-date coverage on the role of heuristics or rules of thumb in human thinking and reasoning.
- Kahneman, D., & Tversky, A. (1996). On the reality of cognitive illusions. *Psychological Review*, *103*, 582–591. This article, and the response by Gigerenzer immediately after it in the same issue of *Psychological Review*, discuss many of the strengths and weaknesses of the Kahneman-Tversky approach to decision and choice making.
- Koehler, J.J. (1996). The base rate fallacy reconsidered: Descriptive, normative, and methodological challenges. *Behavioral and Brain Sciences*, *19*, 1–53. Koehler's article, the open peer commentary, and Koehler's response provide a comprehensive overview of theory and research on base rates.
- Mellers, B.A., Schwartz, A., & Cooke, A.D.J. (1998). Judgment and decision making. *Annual Review of Psychology*, *49*, 447–477. This article considers a range of contemporary theoretical approaches to decision making.
- Reisberg, D. (1997). *Cognition: Exploring the science of the mind*. Chapters 11 and 12 contain accessible coverage of many of the topics discussed in this chapter.

# Cognition and Emotion

## INTRODUCTION

Much of contemporary cognitive psychology is dominated by the computer analogy or metaphor. This has led to an emphasis on information-processing models. However, this approach does not lend itself readily to an examination of the relationship between cognition and emotion, in part because it is hard to think of computers as having emotional states.

Most cognitive psychologists have chosen to ignore the issue of the effects of emotion on cognition by trying to keep the emotional states of their participants constant. Why do they take this evasive action? In the words of Gardner (1985, p. 6), emotion is a factor "which may be important for cognitive functioning but whose inclusion at this point would unnecessarily complicate the cognitive-scientific enterprise."

In spite of this negative attitude, there is a growing volume of research on cognition and emotion. Some of that research, such as the role of emotional states in eyewitness testimony and autobiographical memory, was discussed earlier in the book (see Chapter 8). Probably the most common approach adopted by cognitive psychologists wishing to study the effects of emotion on cognition has involved manipulating participants' emotional states in a systematic way. In contrast, some researchers (e.g., Smith & Lazarus, 1993) have studied the effects of cognition on emotion. As there are almost constant interactions between cognition and emotion in everyday life, any attempt to provide an adequate theory of cognition that ignores emotion is likely to be inadequate.

Before proceeding, it is worth considering some definitions. The term "affect" is very broad, and has been used to cover a wide variety of experiences such as emotions, moods, and preferences. In contrast, the term "emotion" tends to be used to refer to fairly brief but intense experiences, although it is also used in a broader sense. Finally, "mood" or "state" describe low-intensity but more prolonged experiences.

## DOES AFFECT REQUIRE COGNITION?

Suppose that a stimulus (e.g., a spider) is presented to someone, as a result of which his or her affective response to that stimulus changes. Is it essential for the stimulus to be processed cognitively for the changed affective response to occur? This issue is of theoretical importance. If affective responses to all stimuli depend on cognitive processing, it follows that theories of emotion should have a distinctly cognitive flavour. In contrast, if cognitive processing is *not* necessary in the development of affective responses to stimuli, then a specifically cognitive approach to emotion may be less necessary.

Zajonc (1980, 1984) argued that the affective evaluation of stimuli can occur independently of cognitive processes. According to Zajonc (1984, p. 117), "affect and cognition are separate and partially independent systems and . . . although they ordinarily function conjointly, affect could be generated without a prior cognitive process." In contrast, Lazarus (1982, p. 1021) claimed that some cognitive processing is an essential prerequisite for an affective reaction to a stimulus to occur: "Cognitive appraisal (of meaning or significance) underlies and is an integral feature of all emotional states."

## Zajonc's position

Zajonc (1980) claimed in his affective primacy hypothesis that we often make affective judgements about people and objects even though we have processed very little information about them. Zajonc discussed several studies supporting the notion of affective primacy. In these studies, stimuli such as melodies or pictures were presented either very briefly below the level of conscious awareness or while the participant was involved in a task. Even though these stimuli could not subsequently be recognised, participants were still more likely to choose previously presented stimuli than comparable new ones when asked to select the ones they preferred. Thus, there was a positive affective reaction to the previously presented stimuli (as assessed by their preference judgements), but no evidence of cognitive processing (as assessed by recognition-memory performance). This phenomenon is known as the *mere exposure effect*.

Studies on the mere exposure effect do not have much obvious relevance to ordinary emotional states. Participants make superficial preference judgements about fairly meaningless stimuli unrelated to their lives, and so no more than minimal affect is involved.

Another major limitation with these studies is that the conclusion that the stimuli had not been processed cognitively was based on a failure of recognition memory. This may make sense if one equates cognition with consciousness, but very few cognitive psychologists would do so. The data do not rule out the possibility that there was extensive pre-conscious processing involving automatic and other processes. Murphy and Zajonc (1993, p. 724) have accepted that the term "cognitive" can be used to refer to non-conscious processes: "We do not require either affect or cognition to be accessible to consciousness."

According to the affective primacy hypothesis, simple affective qualities of stimuli can be processed much faster than more cognitive ones. Murphy and Zajonc (1993) provided some support for this hypothesis in a series of priming studies. In these studies, a priming stimulus was presented for either 4 milliseconds or 1 second, and was followed by a second stimulus. In one study, the priming stimuli consisted of happy and angry faces, and there was a no-priming control condition. The priming stimuli were followed by Chinese ideographs which were given liking ratings. The findings are shown in Figure 18.1. The liking ratings were influenced by the affective primes when they were presented for only 4 milliseconds, but not when they were presented for 1 second. Presumably participants in the latter condition realised that their affective reaction was produced by the priming stimulus, and so that reaction did not influence their rating of the second stimulus.

In another study, Murphy and Zajonc (1993) required participants to make a cognitive judgement. Male or female priming faces were followed by Chinese ideographs, which were rated for femininity. These ratings were influenced by the priming faces when they were presented for 1 second, but not when they were presented for 4 milliseconds (see Figure 18.1). The various findings obtained by Murphy and Zajonc (1993) suggest the following conclusions:

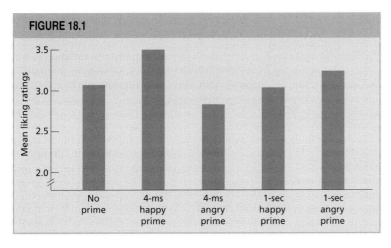

**FIGURE 18.1**

Liking ratings for Chinese ideographs following the presentation of a happy or angry priming stimulus for 4 msec or 1 second. Based on data in Murphy and Zajonc (1993).

1.  Affective processing can sometimes occur faster than cognitive processing.
2.  The initial affective processing of a stimulus is very different from the later cognitive processing.

## Lazarus's position

Lazarus (1982) argued that *cognitive appraisal* plays a crucial role in emotional experience. Cognitive appraisal can be subdivided into three more specific forms of appraisal:

*   Primary appraisal: an environmental situation is regarded as being positive, stressful, or irrelevant to well-being.
*   Secondary appraisal: account is taken of the resources that the individual has available to cope with the situation.
*   Re-appraisal: the stimulus situation and the coping strategies are monitored, with the primary and secondary appraisals being modified if necessary.

The importance of cognitive appraisal in determining emotional experience has been shown in several studies by Lazarus and his associates (e.g., Speisman, Lazarus, Mordkoff, & Davison, 1964). One approach involves presenting an anxiety-evoking film under various conditions. One film showed a Stone Age ritual in which adolescent boys had their penises deeply cut, and another film showed various workshop accidents. The most

dramatic of these accidents involves a board caught in a circular saw which rams with tremendous force through the midsection of a worker, who dies writhing on the floor. Cognitive appraisal was manipulated by varying the accompanying soundtrack, and then comparing the stress experienced against a control condition without a soundtrack. Denial was produced by indicating that the incision film did not show a painful operation, or that those involved in the workshop film were actors. Intellectualisation was produced in the incision film by considering matters from the perspective of an anthropologist viewing strange native customs, and was produced in the workshop film by telling the viewer to consider the situation in an objective way. Various psychophysiological measures of arousal or stress (e.g., heart rate; galvanic skin response) were taken continuously during the viewing of the film.

The major finding of Lazarus's studies was that denial and intellectualisation both produced substantial reductions in stress as indexed by the psychophysiological measures. Thus, manipulating an individual's cognitive appraisal when confronted by a stressful event can have a significant impact on physiological stress reactions. However, it has not always proved easy to replicate these findings (e.g., Steptoe & Vogele, 1986).

Smith and Lazarus (1993) adopted a rather different approach. They argued that there are six appraisal components, two of which involve primary appraisal and four of which involve secondary appraisal:

- Primary: motivational relevance (related to personal commitments?).
- Primary: motivational congruence (consistent with the individual's goals?).
- Secondary: accountability (who deserves the credit or blame?).
- Secondary: problem-focused coping potential (can the situation be resolved?).
- Secondary: emotion-focused coping potential (can the situation be handled psychologically?).
- Secondary: future expectancy (how likely is it that the situation will change?).

Smith and Lazarus (1993) argued that different emotional states can be distinguished on the basis of which appraisal components are involved. Thus, for example, anger, guilt, anxiety, and sadness all possess the primary appraisal components of motivational relevance and motivational incongruence (these emotions only occur when goals are blocked), but differ in terms of secondary appraisal components. Guilt involves self-accountability, anxiety involves low or uncertain emotion-focused coping potential, and sadness involves low future expectancy for change.

Smith and Lazarus (1993) used scenarios in which the participants were told to identify with the central character. In one scenario, the central character has performed poorly in an important course, and he appraises the situation. Other-accountability was produced by having him put the blame on the unhelpful teaching assistants; self-accountability was produced by having him argue that he made a lot of mistakes (e.g., doing work at the last minute); low emotion-focused coping potential was produced by thinking that there was a great danger that he would finish with a poor academic record; and low future expectancy for change was produced by having him think that it was impossible to succeed with his chosen academic path. The appraisal manipulations generally had the predicted effects on the emotional states reported by the participants, indicating that there are close links between appraisal on the one hand and experienced emotion on the other hand.

Lazarus (e.g., 1982) has argued consistently that cognitive appraisal always precedes any affective reaction, but that such appraisal may not be at the conscious level. However, the notion that pre-conscious cognitive processes determine affective reactions is often no more than an article of faith. However, the literature on subliminal perception suggests that there are important pre-conscious cognitive processes.

## Evaluation

Appraisal processes are important in determining our emotional reactions to stimuli. However, the notion of appraisal is rather broad and vague, and so it can be hard to assess an individual's appraisals. For example, Lazarus (1991, p. 169) referred to "two kinds of appraisal processes— one that operates automatically without awareness or volitional control, and another that is conscious, deliberate, and volitional."

Parkinson and Manstead (1992) argued that there are several problems of interpretation with studies such as the one by Speisman et al. (1964). In essence, the soundtrack manipulations may not have had a direct impact on the appraisal process. Changing the soundtrack changed the stimulus information presented to the participants, and different soundtracks may have influenced the direction of attention rather than the interpretive process itself. More generally, Parkinson and Manstead (1992, p. 146) argued that Lazarus's approach represents a rather limited view of emotion: "Appraisal theory has taken the paradigm [model] of emotional experience as an individual passive subject confronting a survival-threatening stimulus." Thus, Lazarus's approach de-emphasises the social context in which emotion is normally experienced.

## Conclusions

Zajonc (1980) and others have provided evidence that affective responses can occur in the absence of any conscious awareness of cognitive processing, and Lazarus (1982) does not dispute that this is possible. As Williams, Watts, MacLeod, and Mathews (1997, p. 3) pointed out, "There would ... be fairly wide support for a reformulated version of Zajonc's thesis that emotion can be independent of *conscious* cognitive processes."

Several theorists have argued that this dispute between Zajonc and Lazarus is based on a false assumption. In the words of Power and Dalgleish (1997, p. 67), "The distinction presupposed in the Zajonc–Lazarus debate between cognition and emotion is a false one . . . The 'emotion' and the 'cognition' are integral and inseparable parts of each other and though it is useful to use different names for different aspects of the generation of emotion, the parts are no more separable than are waves from the water on which they occur." This view may exaggerate the similarities between emotion and cognition.

## Multi-level theories

Progress in understanding how stimuli produce emotional reactions is most likely to occur when we have theories specifying the intervening processes. Two recent multi-level theories (those of LeDoux, 1992, 1996, and of Power & Dalgleish, 1997) are of value in this regard.

LeDoux (e.g., 1992, 1996) has focused exclusively on anxiety in his research. He has emphasised the role of the amgydala, which he regards as the brain's "emotional computer" for working out the emotional significance of stimuli. According to LeDoux, sensory information about emotional stimuli is relayed from the thalamus simultaneously to the amgydala and to the cortex. Of key relevance here, LeDoux (1992, 1996) argues that there are two different emotion circuits in anxiety:

1. A slow-acting thalamus-to-cortex-to-amygdala circuit involving detailed analysis of sensory information.
2. A fast-acting thalamus-amygdala circuit based on simple stimulus features (e.g., intensity); this circuit bypasses the cortex.

LeDoux (1992, p. 275) related his theory to the Zajonc–Lazarus debate:

The activation of the amygdala by inputs from the neocortex is . . . consistent with the classic notion that emotional processing is postcognitive, whereas the activation of the amygdala by thalamic inputs is consistent with the hypothesis, advanced by Zajonc (1980), that emotional processing can be preconscious and precognitive.

Why do we have two emotion circuits? The thalamus-amygdala circuit allows us to respond rapidly in threatening situations, and thus can be valuable in ensuring our survival. In contrast, the cortical circuit produces a detailed evaluation of the emotional significance of the situation, and so allows us to respond to situations in the most appropriate fashion.

Power and Dalgleish (1997) put forward a Schematic Propositional Associative and Analogical Representational Systems (SPAARS) approach, which is shown in Figure 18.2. The various components of the model are as follows:

- Analogical system: this is involved in basic sensory processing of environmental stimuli.
- Propositional system: this is an essentially emotion-free system which contains information about the world and about the self.
- Schematic system: within this system, facts from the propositional system are combined with information about the individual's current goals to produce an internal model of the situation. This will lead to an emotional response if the current goals are being thwarted.
- Associative system: its workings were described by Dalgleish (1998, p. 492): "If the same event is repeatedly processed in the same way at the schematic level, then an associative representation will be formed such that, on future encounters of the same event, the relevant emotion will be *automatically* elicited."

The SPAARS approach has some relevance to the Zajonc–Lazarus debate. According to Power and Dalgleish (1998), there are two main ways in which emotion can occur. First, it can occur as a result of thorough cognitive processing when the schematic system is involved. Second, it occurs automatically and without the involvement of conscious processing when the associative system is involved.

How does the schematic system use information about current goals to decide on the precise

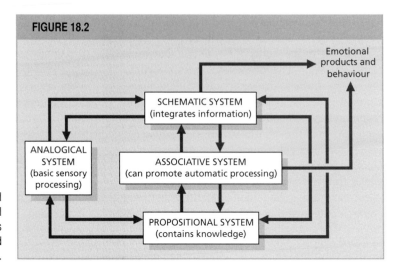

**FIGURE 18.2**

The Schematic Propositional Associative and Analogical Representational Systems (SPAARS) approach put forward by Power and Dalgleish (1997).

emotion that is appropriate in a given situation? Power and Dalgleish (1997) made use of an earlier theory of Oatley and Johnson-Laird (1987), according to which there are five basic emotions. Each of these emotions occurs at a key juncture with respect to a current goal or plan:

1. Happiness: progress has been made on a current goal.
2. Anxiety:  the goal of self-preservation is threatened.
3. Sadness:  the current goal cannot be achieved.
4. Anger:    the current goal is frustrated or blocked.
5. Disgust:  a gustatory [taste] goal is violated.

There is reasonable evidence from cross-cultural studies of facial expressions of emotion, emotional development in children, and so on that these are indeed the five most basic emotions (see Power & Dalgleish, 1997). Complex emotions involve different combinations of these basic emotions.

*Evaluation*

Multi-level theories of emotion have the advantage that they can provide explanations for emotional conflict. For example, individuals with spider phobia become very frightened when they see a spider even though they may "know" that most

spiders are harmless. LeDoux could explain this conflict by assuming that the fear is produced by the fast-acting system, whereas the conflicting knowledge is produced by the slow-acting system. In the SPAARS approach, fear could be generated by the associative system, and the conflicting knowledge could come from the propositional and schematic systems.

## THEORIES OF EMOTIONAL PROCESSING

We have seen that there may well be five basic emotions. However, theory and research on emotional processing have focused mainly on anxiety and depression, with some attention being paid to happiness, and practically none to anger and disgust. This imbalance is reflected in our discussion of emotional processing.

Some theories of emotional processing have focused on the effects of *mood* on emotional processing, whereas others deal with the effects of *personality* on emotional processing. However, there is overlap between the two types of theory. For example, we might want to consider the influence of *trait anxiety* (a personality dimension related to individual differences in susceptibility to anxiety). If we carry out a study, then those participants who are high in trait anxiety will probably be in a more anxious mood state than those

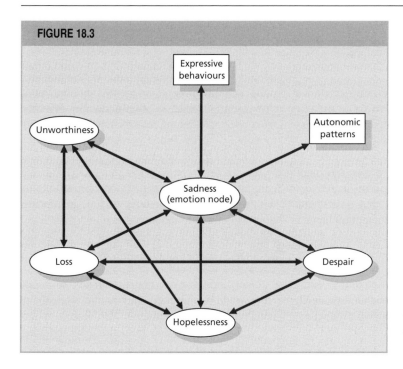

FIGURE 18.3

Bower's semantic network theory. The ovals represent nodes or units within the network. Adapted from Bower (1981).

low in trait anxiety. In such a case, it is hard to disentangle the effects of personality from those of mood.

In this section, we consider theories put forward by Bower (1981), by Beck (1976), and by Williams, Watts, MacLeod, and Mathews (1988, 1997). Bower's network theory has been influential within the area of mood and emotional processing, Beck's schema theory has dominated research on personality and emotional processing, and the theory of Williams et al. builds on these earlier theories.

## Bower's network theory

Some of the key features of the network theory proposed by Bower and his associates (e.g., Bower, 1981; Gilligan & Bower, 1984) are shown in Figure 18.3. The theory as expressed by Gilligan and Bower (1984) makes six assumptions:

- Emotions are units or nodes in a semantic network, with numerous connections to related ideas, to physiological systems, to events, and to muscular and expressive patterns.
- Emotional material is stored in the semantic network in the form of propositions or assertions.

- Thought occurs via the activation of nodes within the semantic network.
- Nodes can be activated by external or by internal stimuli.
- Activation from an activated node spreads to related nodes. This assumption is crucial, because it means that activation of an emotion node (e.g., sadness) leads to activation of emotion-related nodes or concepts (e.g., loss; despair) in the semantic network.
- "Consciouness" consists of a network of nodes activated above some threshold value.

These assumptions lead to the following hypotheses:

- Mood-state-dependent recall: recall is best when the mood at recall matches that at the time of learning.
- Mood congruity: emotionally toned information is learned best when there is correspondence between its affective value and the learner's current mood state.
- Thought congruity: an individual's free associations, interpretations, thoughts, and judgements tend to be thematically congruent with his or her mood state.

- Mood intensity: increases in intensity of mood cause increases in the activation of associated nodes in the associative network.

How exactly do the four hypotheses relate to the six theoretical assumptions? So far as mood-state-dependent recall is concerned, associations are formed at the time of learning between the activated nodes representing the to-be-remembered items and the emotion node or nodes activated because of the participant's mood state. At the time of recall, the mood state at that time leads to activation of the appropriate emotion node. Activation then spreads from that emotion node to the various nodes associated with it. If there is a match between the mood state at learning and at recall, then this increases activation of the nodes of to-be-remembered items, and leads to enhanced recall. However, the associative links between the to-be-remembered stimulus material and the relevant emotion node are likely to be relatively weak. As a result, mood-state-dependent effects are likely to be greater when the memory test is a difficult one offering few retrieval cues (e.g., free recall) than when it provides strong retrieval cues (e.g., recognition memory).

Mood-state-dependent effects are also predicted by other theories. According to Tulving's encoding specificity principle (see Chapter 6), the success of recall or recognition depends on the extent to which the information available at the time of retrieval matches the information stored in memory. If information about the mood state at the time of learning is stored in memory, then being in the same mood state at the time of retrieval increases this information matching. Theoretically, this should increase both recall and recognition.

Thought congruity occurs for two reasons. First, the current mood state leads to activation of the corresponding emotion node. Second, activation spreads from that emotion node to other, associated related nodes, which will tend to contain information emotionally congruent with the activated emotion node.

Mood congruity occurs when people in a good mood learn and remember emotionally positive material better than those in a bad mood, whereas the opposite is true for emotionally negative material. According to Gilligan and Bower (1984), mood congruity depends on the fact that emotionally loaded information tends to be associated more strongly with its congruent emotion node than with any other emotion node. For example, those nodes containing information about sadness-provoking events and experiences are associatively linked to the emotion node for sadness (see Figure 18.3). To-be-remembered material that is congruent with the current mood state links up with this associative network of similar information. This leads to extensive or elaborative encoding of the to-be-remembered material. As we saw in Chapter 6, elaborative encoding is generally associated with superior long-term memory.

One might assume that the effects described here would become stronger as the intensity of the current mood increases. The reason is that the spread of activation from the activated emotion node to other related nodes would increase in line with the intensity with which emotion was experienced. However, a very sad mood may lead to a focus on internal information relating to failure, fatigue, and so on, and this may inhibit processing of all kinds of external stimuli whether or not they are congruent with the sad mood state.

## Mood states

It is hard to ensure that participants are in the appropriate mood state. One method is to try to induce the required mood state under laboratory conditions, and another is to make use of naturally occurring mood states (e.g., in patients with mood disorders).

The most popular mood-induction approach is based on the procedure introduced by Velten (1968). Participants read a set of sentences designed to induce increasingly intense feelings of elation or depression. Participants typically report that their mood has altered as expected, but they may simply be responding as they believe the experimenter wants them to. A further problem is that this mood-induction procedure usually produces a blend of several mood states rather than just the desired one (Polivy, 1981).

Bower (e.g., Bower, Gilligan, & Monteiro, 1981; Bower & Mayer, 1985) has used hypnosis combined with self-generated imagery. When in the hypnotic state, participants are asked to think of images of a past happy or sad emotional experience, using those images to produce the appropriate mood state. This approach produces strong and long-lasting moods. However, it is necessary to use participants who score highly on tests of hypnotic susceptibility, and it may be unwise to generalise from such participants to other people.

### Evaluation

Bower's network theory is clearly oversimplified. Emotions or moods and cognitive concepts are both represented as nodes within a semantic network. In reality, however, moods and cognitions are very different. For example, moods tend to change slowly in intensity, whereas cognitions tend to be all-or-none, and there is often rapid change from one cognition to another. As Power and Dalgleish (1997, p. 74) pertinently remarked, "A theory that gives emotion the same status as individual words or concepts is theoretically confused."

### Beck's schema theory

Beck (1976) put forward a different theoretical approach to that of Bower, and this approach was developed by Beck and Clark (1988). The essence of this approach is that some individuals have greater vulnerability than others to developing depressive or anxiety disorders. Such vulnerability depends on the formation in early life of certain *schemas* or organised knowledge structures (see Chapter 9). According to Beck and Clark (1988, p. 26):

> The schematic organisation of the clinically depressed individual is dominated by an overwhelming negativity. A negative cognitive trait is evident in the depressed person's view of the self, word and future . . . In contrast the maladaptive schemas in the anxious patient involve perceived physical or psychological threat to one's personal domain as well as an exaggerated sense of vulnerability.

Beck and Clark (1988) assumed that schemas influence most cognitive processes such as attention, perception, learning, and retrieval of information. Schemas produce processing biases in which the processing of schema-consistent or emotionally congruent information is favoured. Thus, individuals with anxiety-related schemas should selectively process threatening information, and those with depressive schemas should selectively process emotionally negative information. While Beck and Clark (1988) emphasised the role of schemas in producing processing biases, they claimed that schemas would only become active and influence processing when the individual is an anxious or depressed state.

Beck's schema theory was originally intended to provide a framework for understanding clinical anxiety and depression. However, it can readily be applied to personality research. For example, Eysenck (1992, 1997) argued that normal individuals high in trait anxiety possess danger or vulnerability schemas leading them to favour the processing of threat-related information, especially when they are feeling anxious.

### Evaluation

The notion that some individuals have schemas that predispose them towards clinical anxiety or depression is a valuable one. However, it has proved hard to show that such schemas play a *causal* role in the development of anxiety disorders or depression. Some weaknesses in Beck's approach were identified by Eysenck (1997, pp. 95–96):

> First, the central theoretical construct of 'schema' is amorphous [vague], and often seems to mean little more than 'belief'. Second, the evidence for the existence of specific schemas is often based on a circular argument. Behavioural evidence of a cognitive bias in anxious patients is used to infer the presence of a schema, and then that schema is used to 'explain' the observed cognitive bias. In other words, there is generally no direct or independent evidence of the existence of a schema.

## Comparison of approaches

On the face of it, Bower's network theory and Beck's schema theory are very different. For example, the emphasis within network theory is on the transient effects of mood on information processing via low-level processes in long-term memory, whereas the focus in schema theory is on the semi-permanent effects of schemas on information processing via high-level processes in long-term memory. However, as MacLeod (1990, p. 15) pointed out, the two theories or models

> make parallel predictions concerning the relationship between emotion and cognition . . . Both the schema model and the network model of emotion and cognition predict the existence of pervasive processing biases, associated with both anxiety and depression, affecting the encoding, comprehension and retrieval of emotionally valenced [loaded] information. Such biases should operate to favour consistently the processing of emotionally congruent information.

## Williams et al. (1988, 1997)

Williams et al. (1988) focused on the effects of anxiety and depression on emotional processing. Their starting point was the distinction between priming and elaboration originally proposed by Graf and Mandler (1984). Priming is an automatic process in which a stimulus word produces activation of its various components in long-term memory, whereas elaboration is a later strategic process involving the activation of related concepts. According to the theory, anxious individuals show initial priming of threat-related stimuli, and so have an attentional bias towards threat. In contrast, depressed individuals show elaboration of threat-related stimuli, and so have a memory bias in which they find it easier to retrieve threatening than neutral material.

Some of the main predictions made by Williams et al. (1988) concern the effects of anxiety and depression on explicit and implicit memory. *Explicit memory* involves conscious recollection of past events, and presumably involves elaborative

processes. In contrast, *implicit memory* does not involve conscious recollection, and may depend mainly on priming or automatic processes (see Chapter 7). Depressed individuals should show an explicit memory bias favouring retrieval of threatening material, whereas anxious individuals should show an implicit memory bias for threatening material.

Williams et al. (1997) developed their previous theory in various ways. They argued that the different functions of anxiety and depression have implications for information processing. Anxiety has the function of anticipating danger. As a result, it is "associated with a tendency to give priority to processing threatening stimuli; the encoding involved is predominantly perceptual rather than conceptual in nature" (Williams et al., 1997, p. 307). In contrast, if depression involves the replacement of failed goals, "then the conceptual processing of internally generated material related to failure or loss may be more relevant to this function than perceptual vigilance" (Williams et al., 1997, p. 315).

Williams et al. (1997) made use of Roediger's (1990) distinction between perceptual and conceptual processes (see Chapter 7). Perceptual processes are essentially *data-driven processes*, and are typically involved in basic attentional processes and in implicit memory. In contrast, conceptual processes are *top-down processes*, and are typically involved in explicit memory. Suppose we assume that anxiety facilitates the perceptual processing of threat-related stimuli, whereas depression facilitates the conceptual processing of threatening information. This would lead to the prediction of an implicit memory bias associated with anxiety and an explicit memory bias associated with depression.

### Evaluation

The greatest strength of the Williams et al. approach is that it is based on an analysis of the functional differences between anxiety and depression. This leads Williams et al. to predict that the pattern of cognitive biases will differ between anxious and depressed individuals. This contrasts with the approaches of Beck and of Bower, both of whom predict the existence of global cognitive

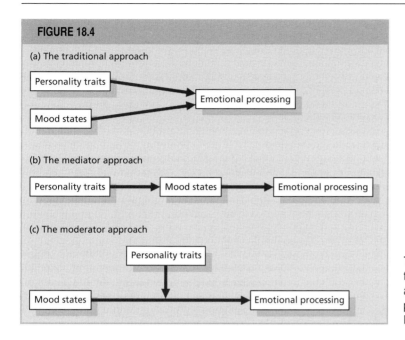

**FIGURE 18.4**

(a) The traditional approach

Personality traits → Emotional processing

Mood states → Emotional processing

(b) The mediator approach

Personality traits → Mood states → Emotional processing

(c) The moderator approach

Personality traits

Mood states → Emotional processing

Three theoretical approaches to the effects of personality traits and mood states on emotional processing. Adapted from Rusting (1998).

biases applying to all emotional states. As we will see, the evidence is more supportive of the Williams et al. view. However, the differences in cognitive biases between anxious and depressed individuals are less clear-cut than predicted theoretically. Thus, even the revised theory of Williams et al. is oversimplified.

## Rusting's approach

Rusting (1998) distinguished between mood-state and trait approaches, with Bower's network theory exemplifying a mood-state theory and Beck's schema theory being a prominent trait theory. She argued that there are three main ways in which emotional processing may be affected by traits and mood states (see Figure 18.4):

1.  The traditional approach: personality traits and mood states have separate or independent effects on emotional processing.
2.  The mediator approach: apparent effects of personality on emotional processing are indirect: personality affects mood state, and mood state influences emotional processing.
3.  The moderator approach: the effects of mood states on emotional processing are moderated

or influenced by personality traits. There should be significant *interactions* between traits and states in determining emotional processing, indicating their joint influences. This approach was adopted by Williams et al. (1988, 1997), and a similar approach was favoured by Beck and Clark (1988).

Two points need to be made here. First, most studies have been concerned with personality traits or with mood states, but not with both together. Thus, such studies cannot provide direct evidence on the mediator or moderator approaches. Second, studies on mood and emotional processing have mostly focused on learning and memory, whereas studies on personality and emotional processing have often focused on attention and perception. Our review of the evidence reflects these imbalances.

## EMOTION AND MEMORY

There is some support for all four hypotheses put forward by Gilligan and Bower (1984, see earlier). The strongest support has been for mood

**FIGURE 18.5**

Design for a study of mood-state-dependent memory together with the predicted results on Bower's (1981) theory.

| Mood state at learning | Mood state at recall | Predicted level of recall |
|---|---|---|
| Happy | Happy | High |
| Happy | Sad | Low |
| Sad | Happy | Low |
| Sad | Sad | High |

congruity (i.e., learning is best when the participant's mood matches the emotional tone of the to-be-learned material). However, there have been several failures to show mood-state-dependent recall, thought congruity, mood congruity, and effects of mood intensity.

## Mood-state-dependent memory

Experimental studies testing for mood-state-dependent memory typically make use of learning either one or two lists of words. Learning occurs in one mood state (e.g., happy or sad), and recall occurs in the same mood state or in a different one (see Figure 18.5). When two lists are presented (e.g., Bower, Monteiro, & Gilligan, 1978; Schare, Lisman, & Spear, 1984), one list is learned in one mood and the other list is learned in a different mood. Subsequently participants are put back into one of these two moods, and instructed to recall only the list learned first. It is predicted that recall should be higher when the mood state at the time of recall is the same as that at the time of learning.

Schare et al. (1984) and Bower et al. (1978) obtained mood-state-dependent recall with the two-list design but not with the one-list design. Perhaps participants trying to recall the first list with the mood appropriate to the second list thought of some of the words from the second list, and this interfered with the task of recalling first-list words.

Eich, Macaulay, and Lam (1997) reported interesting evidence of mood-state-dependent memory in patients suffering from bipolar disorder. They were initially given the task of thinking of autobiographical events to cues when in a depressed or manic mood. They were then asked to recall as many as possible of these events a few days later.

When the patients' mood was the same on both occasions, an average of 33% of the autobiographical events could be recalled. This compared to only 23% when there had been a mood change between testing sessions.

Ucros (1989) reviewed 40 published studies of mood-state-dependent memory. The evidence revealed a moderate tendency for people to remember material better when there is a match between the mood at learning and at retrieval. However, the effects are generally stronger when participants are in a positive mood rather than a negative one. They are also greater when people try to remember personal events than when the learning material lacks personal relevance. Possible explanations for these effects are discussed later.

Kenealy (1997) noted various problems with research on mood-state-dependent memory. First, the level of learning was not established in most studies. As a result, it is not clear whether poor performance reflects deficient memory or deficient learning. Second, there was no check in some studies that the mood manipulations had been successful. Third, only one memory test was used in most studies. However, the extent of any mood-state-dependent effects on memory may depend on the nature of the memory test. For example, Kihlstrom (1991) suggested that the effects of mood state will be weaker when rich and informative cues are provided within the retrieval environment.

Kenealy (1997) addressed all these issues in a series of experiments producing strong evidence for mood-state-dependent memory. In one study, the participants looked at a map and learned a set of instructions concerning a particular route until their learning performance exceeded 80%. The following day they were given tests of free

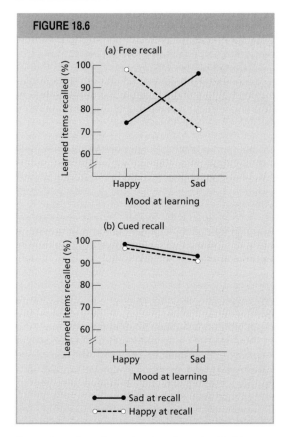

**FIGURE 18.6**

(a) Free recall

(b) Cued recall

● ━━━━● Sad at recall
○ ----- ○ Happy at recall

Free and cued recall as a function of mood state (happy or sad) at learning and at recall. Based on data in Kenealy (1997).

recall and cued recall (the visual outline of the map). There were strong mood-state-dependent effects in free recall, but not in cued recall (see Figure 18.6). Thus, mood state can affect memory even when learning is controlled, but does so only when no other powerful retrieval cues are available.

Most studies have focused on *explicit memory* involving conscious recollection of previous events. However, Macaulay, Ryan, and Eich (1993) found that mood-state-dependent effects can also be obtained on tests of implicit memory, on which conscious recollection is not required. Relevant evidence was reported by Nissen et al. (1988). They studied explicit and implicit memory in a 45-year-old woman suffering from multiple personality disorder, each of whose separate

personalities can be regarded as corresponding to a different mood state.

The woman studied by Nissen et al. (1988) showed 22 different personalities ranging in age from 5 to 45. One of her personalities was Alice, who was 39 years old, studying to be a ministerial counsellor, and who worked as a nurses' assistant. Another of her personalities was Charles, who was 45 years old and an aggressive heavy drinker, and a third personality was Bonnie, 36, who was very social and whose main interests were in the theatre. There were striking personality-dependent effects on some tasks. The same story was read to five of the personalities in turn, with each personality providing almost immediate recall. There was no systematic improvement in recall across personalities (see Figure 18.7). On another task, memory for words was tested by means of an implicit memory test (word completion) and an explicit memory test (recall). Performance on both tests was much worse when the personality at the time of test was different from the personality at learning. In contrast, recognition memory for faces was almost as good when the personality changed between learning and test as when it remained the same (42% vs. 52%, respectively). Finally, there was an implicit task in which repeated and non-repeated words had to be identified from very brief presentations. Donna performed this task, then Charles, and then Donna again. Donna's performance on the repeated words was much better after Charles had performed the task than beforehand.

The findings from this woman produced evidence of strong personality-dependent effects with some explicit and implicit memory tasks, but weak or non-existent personality-dependent effects with other explicit and implicit memory tasks. Nissen et al. (1988, p. 131) accounted for the findings as follows:

Material that allows a variety of different interpretations or whose encoding is significantly guided by strategic processing, or whose interpretation might be expected to depend on one's mood and beliefs and biases is relatively inaccessible across personalities.

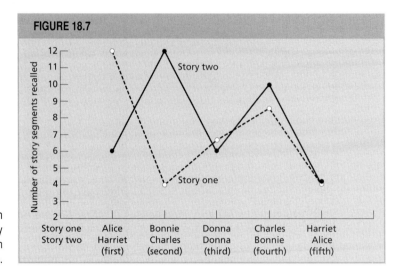

**FIGURE 18.7**

Memory performance in a woman suffering from multiple personality disorder. Based on data in Nissen et al. (1988).

## Mood congruity

There is more experimental support for mood congruity than for any of the other hypotheses put forward by Gilligan and Bower (1984). The usual procedure is that a mood is induced, followed by the learning of a list or the reading of a story containing emotionally toned material. There is then a memory test for the list or the story after the participant's mood has returned to normal. Mood congruity is shown by recall being greatest when the affective value of the to-be-learned material matches the participant's mood state at the time of learning.

Bower et al. (1981) studied mood congruity. Participants who had been hypnotised to feel happy or sad read a story about two college men, Jack and André. Jack is very depressed and glum, because he is having problems with his academic work, with his girl-friend, and with his tennis. In contrast, André is very happy, because things are going very well for him in all three areas. Participants identified more with the story character whose mood resembled their own while they were reading the story, and recalled more information about him. Unfortunately, it has proved difficult to replicate these findings (Bower, 1987).

Kwiatkowski and Parkinson (1994) compared memory performance in naturally depressed participants and in participants who received a depressed mood induction but were not naturally depressed. Mood congruity occurred *only* in the naturally depressed group. As Kwiatkowski and Parkinson (1994, p. 232) concluded, "The present study suggests important qualitative differences between the two types of depression."

Perrig and Perrig (1988) instructed their participants to behave as if they were depressed or happy, but no attempt was made to induce any mood state. These instructions were followed by a word list containing positive, negative, and neutral words, which then had to be recalled. Those participants indicating an awareness of mood-congruity effects produced results very similar to those obtained by Bower et al. (1981), whereas those who did not showed no evidence of selective learning.

One interpretation of Perrig and Perrig's findings is that the participants were simply behaving as they thought the experimenter wanted them to behave. Perhaps the mood-congruity effects obtained in mood-induction studies merely reflect a desire on the part of participants to do what is expected. A more plausible interpretation was offered by Perrig and Perrig (1988, p. 102): "Mood

It should be noted in conclusion that the whole notion of multiple personality disorder remains controversial. More research is needed to prove (or disprove) its existence.

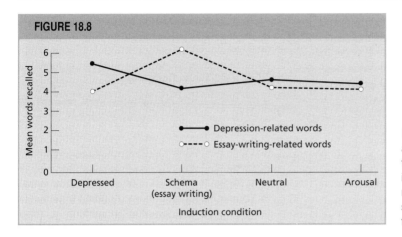

**FIGURE 18.8**

Free recall of depression-related and essay-writing-related words in four conditions: depressed mood induction; arousal induction; neutral mood induction; and schema induction. Adapted from Varner and Ellis (1998).

may be a sufficient but not a necessary condition to produce the mood-congruity effect of selective learning." Thus, mood-congruity effects can be produced either by genuine mood induction or by mood simulation.

Mood states produce changes in physiological arousal as well as in cognitive activity. Bower (1981) assumed that the cognitive changes were responsible for mood congruity, but it is possible that mood congruity actually depends on the arousal changes. Varner and Ellis (1998) compared these possibilities in two experiments in which the participants were presented with a list of words, some of which were associated with being depressed and the rest of which were related to the organisation of skills when writing an essay. There were four conditions: depressed mood induction; arousal induction (stepping up and down on a wooden platform); neutral mood induction; and schema induction (reading statements relevant to writing an essay). After the list had been presented, there was a test of free recall.

What were the findings? Mood congruity was found in the depressed mood induction condition, but not in the arousal induction condition (see Figure 18.8). Evidence that cognitive processes in the absence of physiological arousal can produce selective recall was found in the schema induction condition. Varner and Ellis (1998) obtained similar findings in a second experiment, in which the various induction procedures were used after learning but before recall. Thus, mood

congruity can affect retrieval as well as learning. Varner and Ellis (1998, p. 947) concluded as follows: "Taken as a whole, the findings indicate that cognitive activity is of central import to the occurrence of mood-congruent processing and that arousal has little or no impact on the selective processing of mood-related information."

## Thought congruity

Thought congruity has been studied in various ways. One method is to present participants with a list of pleasant and unpleasant words prior to mood induction, and then to test for recall after mood induction. The prediction is that pleasant words will be recalled better after pleasant mood induction than after unpleasant mood induction, with the opposite being the case for unpleasant words. Another method is to ask participants to recall autobiographical memories following mood induction. Pleasant moods should increase the number of pleasant memories recalled, and perhaps the speed with which they are recalled, and unpleasant moods should do the same for unpleasant memories.

Thought congruity has been shown in various studies using both of the methods just described (see Blaney, 1986, for a review). For example, Clark and Teasdale (1982) tested depressed patients on two occasions, with the depth of the depression being more severe on one occasion than on the other. More depressing or unhappy memories and fewer happy memories were recalled on the more depressed occasion, with the opposite being the case on the less depressed occasion. These findings are consistent with the notion of a vicious circle in depressed patients: depressed mood state leads to recall of depressing memories, and the recall of depressing memories exacerbates the depressed mood state.

## Mood intensity

There has been relatively little work on the mood intensity hypothesis. However, Rinck, Glowalla, and Schneider (1992) considered a related issue, namely, the emotional intensity of the stimulus material. Participants who were put into a happy or sad mood rated words in terms of their pleasantness–unpleasantness. There was a mood-congruency effect for the intensely emotional words (i.e., strongly pleasant or unpleasant) on a later unexpected recall test, but this effect was not found for the weakly emotional words.

## Evaluation

Bower's network theory has provided a focus for research on mood and memory. Although the findings are somewhat inconsistent, the effects of mood on learning and memory generally resemble those predicted. However, the findings pose some problems for the theory. First, negative moods have often failed to enhance the learning and recall of negative material. This was shown most strikingly by Williams and Broadbent (1986) in a study on thought congruity. They studied the retrieval of autobiographical memories to positive and negative cue words by individuals who had recently attempted suicide by overdose. The suicide attempters were slower than normal controls to retrieve personal memories to the positive cue words, but were no faster than normals in thinking of negative personal experiences. Presumably it was so painful for the suicide attempters to retrieve unpleasant personal memories that they inhibited the retrieval of such memories. Second, mood-state effects are strongest when participants learn and remember personal events (Ucros, 1989).

It is not clear on Bower's (1981) original network theory why this should be so.

## Other theoretical perspectives

In the years since Bower (1981) put forward his network theory, there have been various attempts to provide more adequate theoretical accounts of mood and memory. Bower (1992) offered an explanation of why mood-state effects are greatest when personal events are learned and remembered. He argued for a causal belongingness hypothesis. According to this hypothesis, memory is only affected by mood state when participants believe that their emotional state at learning is *caused* by the to-be-learned stimuli. Causal attribution leads to an effective association between the stimulus and the emotional state. This is much more likely to occur with personal events (e.g., feeling delighted after succeeding in an important examination) than when an emotional state is induced before presenting the learning task.

Eich and Metcalfe (1989) argued that mood state has more effect on *internal* events such as reasoning or imagination than on events that are more closely determined by *external* factors. Thus, memory for internal events is more susceptible to mood effects than is memory for external events. They tested this hypothesis in two ways. First, participants who had been put into a happy or sad mood were given either a read task or a generate task. The read task involved reading a category name followed by two exemplars (e.g., precious metals: silver–*gold*), whereas the generate task required participants to complete the last word (e.g., precious metals: silver–g . . . ?). It was assumed that internal events would be more important with the generate task than with the read task. Second, memory was tested with either free recall or recognition, and it was assumed that free recall would place more demands on internal events than would recognition memory. Thus, it was predicted that mood-state-dependent effects would be greater with the generate condition than with the read condition and with free recall than with recognition memory.

The main findings were in line with the predictions (see Figure 18.9). Mood-state-dependent

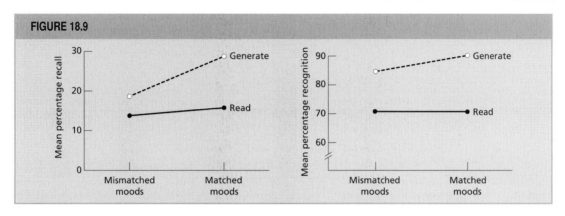

**FIGURE 18.9**

Memory performance (recall and recognition) as a function of learning conditions (generate vs. read) and match vs. mismatch of moods at learning and test. Based on data in Eich and Metcalfe (1989).

effects were observable with free recall but not with recognition, which resembles the findings of Kenealy (1997). In addition, the effects on free recall were greater following the generate task than following the read task. Other similar studies provide additional support for the notion that mood-state effects are greater when internal events (rather than external events) are involved at learning and/or test (Macaulay et al., 1993).

## EMOTION, ATTENTION, AND PERCEPTION

Most research concerned with mood effects on attention and perception has focused on anxiety or depression. One reason is that they can be studied at both normal and clinical levels. However, a problem with trying to compare the effects of anxiety and depression on cognitive functioning is that individuals who are high in anxiety tend to be high in depression, and vice versa. This is true of both normal and clinical populations.

Research in this area has been strongly influenced by Beck's schema theory, which predicts that there should be facilitated processing of schema-congruent information in attention and perception. However, Bower's (1981) network theory is also relevant. It has mainly been applied to memory, but has implications for other aspects of cognitive functioning. According to network

theory, whenever the node corresponding to an emotion is activated, activation spreads out to all of the related nodes. If someone is happy, then nodes relating to happy personal experiences and similar concepts to happiness (e.g., euphoria, joy, contentment, and so on) will be activated. This widespread activation should facilitate performance across a wide range of tasks involving processing of happiness-related information.

The focus in this section will be on two main cognitive biases. First, there is *attentional bias*, which is selective attention to threat-related rather than neutral stimuli. Second, there is *interpretive bias*, which is the tendency to interpret ambiguous stimuli in a threatening rather than an innocuous fashion.

Before proceeding to discuss the effects of anxiety and depression on attention and perception, it is worth mentioning their effects on memory. The main focus of the research has been on two memory biases:

1. Explicit memory bias, in which negative or threatening information is retrieved relatively better than positive or neutral information on a test based on conscious recollection.

2. Implicit memory bias, in which memory performance for negative information is relatively better than that for neutral information on a test in which conscious recollection is not involved.

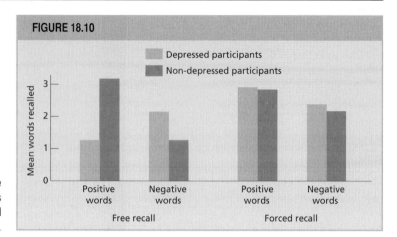

Free and forced recall for positive and negative words in individuals high and low in depression. Based on data in Murray et al. (1999).

Williams et al. (1997, pp. 285–288) reviewed the relevant studies, and came to the following conclusions:

Out of nine studies using indirect [implicit] tests of memory in anxious subjects or patients, seven have found significant bias towards negative material . . . no study has yet found word congruent bias in implicit memory in depression . . . all published studies appear to find explicit memory biases in depression, yet only a third of the studies on trait anxiety or GAD [generalised anxiety disorder] find explicit memory biases.

More recently, it has proved hard to replicate the finding of an implicit memory bias in anxiety. For example, Richards et al. (1999, p. 67) reported three experiments on implicit memory, and came to the following conclusion: "None of the experiments offered any support for the prediction of a threat-related implicit memory bias in high-trait anxiety."

There may also be problems in interpreting the consistent finding of an explicit memory bias in depression (see Burt, Zembar, & Niederehe, 1995, for a review). Murray, Whitehouse, and Alloy (1999) showed that the typical explicit memory bias in depression disappeared in certain conditions. They asked high and low scorers on Beck's Depression Inventory to perform a self-referential task ("Describes you?") on a series of positive and negative words. Then the participants provided free recall or forced recall, in which they were required to write down a large number of words. There was the usual explicit memory bias in depression with free recall, but no bias at all with forced recall (see Figure 18.10).

What do these findings mean? According to Murray et al. (1999, p. 175), they "implicate an important contribution of diminished motivation and/or conservative report criterion in the manifestation of depression-related biases and deficits in recall."

## Anxiety

The effects of anxiety on attention and perception have been studied in normal and clinical populations. Among normal individuals, those high and low in anxiety have been identified on questionnaires measuring trait anxiety (e.g., the Spielberger State–Trait Anxiety Inventory). Clinical studies have used patients suffering from various anxiety disorders, including generalised anxiety disorder, social phobia, panic disorder, and obsessive-compulsive disorder. In general terms, similar findings have been obtained from normal and clinical populations.

### Attentional bias

The existence of *attentional bias* in anxious individuals has been shown in several studies (see

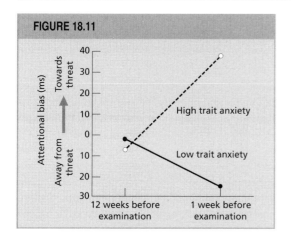

**FIGURE 18.11**

Attentional bias for examination-relevant stress words as a function of trait anxiety and proximity of an important examination. Based on data in MacLeod and Mathews (1988).

Eysenck, 1997), many of which used the dot-probe task. In this task, two words are presented at the same time, one to an upper and the other to a lower location on a computer screen. On critical trials, one of these words is threat-related and the other is neutral. The allocation of attention is measured by recording speed of detection of a dot which can replace either word. It is assumed that detection latencies are shorter in attended areas.

MacLeod and Mathews (1988) used the dot-probe task. Attentional bias was affected by state anxiety as well as by trait anxiety, in line with the expectations of the moderator approach discussed earlier. High and low trait-anxious students showed no attentional bias towards or away from examination-relevant stress words a long time prior to an important examination (see Figure 18.11). In the week before the examination, when state anxiety levels were elevated, the high trait-anxious students showed attentional bias to the threat-related stimuli, whereas those low in trait anxiety showed bias away from the same stimuli.

Attentional bias has also been studied by the emotional Stroop task. The participants have to name the colours in which words are printed as rapidly as possible. Some of the words are emotional (e.g., stupid; inadequate) whereas others are neutral. The key prediction is that participants will take longer to name the colours of emotion-congruent words, because such words will be attended to more than will neutral words. Most of the studies using normals high in trait anxiety or clinically anxious patients have supported the prediction. In some studies (e.g., Mogg, Kentish, & Bradley, 1993), the threat-related words were presented subliminally (below the conscious threshold). The emotional Stroop effect was still found, suggesting that attentional bias may involve more or less automatic processes operating below the level of conscious awareness.

There has been some dispute about the appropriate interpretation of findings with the emotional Stroop. As De Ruiter and Brosschot (1994, p. 317), "The increased Stroop interference might . . . be the result of an attempt to avoid processing the stimulus because it contains emotionally valenced [loaded] information . . . Attentional bias occurs in the early stages, and cognitive avoidance at later stages."

### Interpretive bias

There is convincing evidence that anxious individuals possess an *interpretive bias*. For example, Eysenck et al. (1987) asked participants to write down the spellings of auditorily presented words. Some of the words were homophones having both a threat-related and a neutral interpretation (e.g., die, dye; pain, pane). They reported a correlation of +0.60 between trait anxiety and the number of threatening homophone interpretations.

A potential problem with the homophone task is that the participants may think of both spellings. In that case, their decision as to which word to write down may involve response bias (e.g., which spelling is more socially desirable?). Eysenck et al. (1991) assessed response bias using ambiguous sentences (e.g., "The doctor examined little Emily's growth"). Patients with generalised anxiety disorder were more likely than normal controls to interpret such sentences in a threatening way, and there were no group differences in response bias.

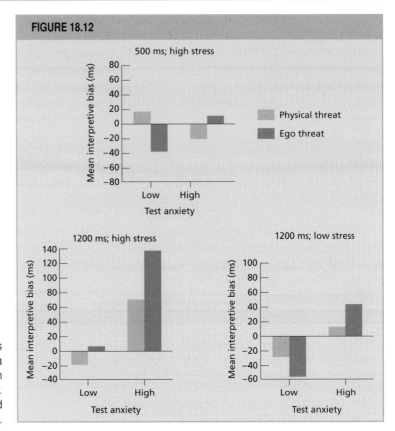

Interpretive bias in high-anxious and low-anxious participants as a function of stress condition (high or low) and context–target delay. Adapted from Calvo and Castillo (1997).

More detailed information about interpretive bias was reported by Calvo and Castillo (1997). They presented ambiguous sentences concerned with ego threat, physical threat, or neutral events under low or high stress conditions. Each sentence was followed by a disambiguating sentence containing a target word confirming or disconfirming the consequence implied by the ambiguous sentence. The target word was presented either 500 (short delay) or 1200 milliseconds (long delay) after the preceding context, and the task was to name the target word as rapidly as possible.

Interpretive bias was shown when the target word was named faster when it confirmed a threatening interpretation than when it disconfirmed such an interpretation. The high-anxious participants showed strong interpretive bias at the long delay under high stress conditions, but not at the short delay or with low stress (see Figure 18.12). What do these findings mean? Interpretive bias

depends on state anxiety or anxiety as a mood state as well as on anxiety as a personality dimension. In addition, interpretive bias does not occur rapidly and automatically, but rather involves subsequent strategic processes.

## Depression

The effects of depression on emotion-congruent processing have been studied in various attentional and perceptual tasks. Normal and clinical depression have been considered. Depression in normals has often been assessed by questionnaires such as the Beck Depression Inventory.

### Attentional bias

There is little convincing evidence for the existence of attentional bias among depressed individuals. In a study using the dot-probe task, MacLeod et al. (1986) found that anxious patients showed an attentional bias when a threatening and a neutral word were presented together. However, depressed patients showed no attentional bias.

Gotlib, McLachlan, and Katz (1988) used a modified version of the task employed by MacLeod et al. (1986), but presented emotionally positive words as well as emotionally negative and neutral words. There was an effect of depression on attention, in that the non-depressed participants attended selectively to positive stimuli. However, Gotlib et al. (1988) did not establish whether the attentional bias was due to anxiety rather than to depression. Mogg et al. (1991) carried out a replication of the Gotlib et al. (1988) study, and found that the attentional bias was due to state anxiety rather than to depression.

Most studies on attentional bias in depression have probably measured fairly automatic attentional processes. An exception is a study by Matthews and Antes (1992) on controlled attentional processes. They measured the eye movements of depressed and non-depressed individuals who were presented with slides containing "sad" and "happy" regions. The depressed participants focused relatively more on the sad regions and less on the happy regions.

*Interpretive bias*

The effects of depression on interpretation of ambiguity have been assessed in several studies. The evidence consistently indicates that there is an interpretive bias in depressed individuals. Various studies (discussed by Rusting, 1998) have made use of the Cognitive Bias Questionnaire. Events are described briefly, with participants having to select one out of four possible interpretations of each event. Depressed patients consistently select more negative interpretations than controls.

Pyszczynski, Holt, and Greenberg (1987) carried out a study in which depressed and non-depressed students rated various possible future events. The depressed participants rated negative future events as more likely to happen than did the non-depressed participants, whereas the opposite was the case for positive future events.

## CONCLUSIONS ON EMOTIONAL PROCESSING

### General evaluation

Rusting (1998) reviewed the relevant research literature more thoroughly than has been possible here. As a result, we will start with one of her main conclusions (1998, pp. 189–190):

> Most of the traditional emotion-congruency literature has examined the effects of moods and traits on the processing of emotional stimuli separately. However, this literature has yielded mixed findings across perception, attention, interpretation/judgement, recall and recognition, and autobiographical memory tasks. Although many studies do obtain evidence for mood-congruency and trait-congruency, some studies have found mood-incongruency effects, and others have found no effects of mood or personality at all.

There are several possible reasons why the findings have been somewhat inconsistent. First, participants who are in a negative mood state may use various strategies (e.g., thinking about positive events) to improve their mood. If these strategies succeed, they will weaken any findings. Second, some studies of mood congruity may have produced non-significant findings because of discrepancies between the emotional state of the participants and the specific emotional content of the learning material. For example, participants in a depressed mood may be asked to learn anxiety-related words. Relevant evidence was reported by Ingram et al. (1987). Depressed but non-anxious participants had enhanced recall of depression-relevant words, whereas anxious but non-depressed participants had greater recall of anxiety-relevant words. Third, there have generally been more significant findings when the participants had to process the learning material with reference to themselves. Why is this? According to Rusting (1998, p. 183), "studies that incorporate self-referent processing tasks may actually be tapping into stable structures in memory, rather than producing effects that are purely dependent on temporary mood states."

There is only limited support for the traditional approach, in which it was assumed that personality and mood have independent effects on emotional processing. What about the mediator and moderator approaches? There have been practically no attempts to assess the mediator approach. The evidence is most consistent with the moderator approach. According to Rusting (1998, p. 188), the evidence for this approach, "is fairly consistent across attention, interpretation/judgement, recall and recognition, and autobiographical memory tasks. In each of these areas there is some evidence indicating that certain personality traits moderate whether mood-congruency or mood-incongruency effects are obtained."

It makes sense that emotional processing should depend interactively on traits and mood states. Any given personality trait is associated with a richly interconnected network of relevant emotional information and knowledge. However, there is a huge amount of information in long-term memory, and so this trait-relevant information is only likely to influence emotional processing when it is activated by the appropriate mood state. Thus, maximal effects on emotional processing will be obtained when individuals possess the relevant knowledge structures (personality traits), and when these knowledge structures are fully activated (mood states).

## Theories of emotional processing

The research findings provide more support for the theoretical approach of Williams et al. (1988, 1997) than for Bower's network theory or Beck's schema theory. For example, there is strong evidence that anxiety is associated with an attentional bias, but the evidence is much weaker so far as depression is concerned. According to network and schema theories, individuals in a depressed mood should have facilitated processing of (and attention to) mood-congruent stimuli, and should thus show attentional bias. In contrast, Williams et al. (1997) argued that depressed individuals do not engage in excessive perceptual processing of threat-related stimuli, and so they should not have an attentional bias.

The theory of Williams et al. is also better equipped to handle the findings on explicit and implicit memory biases. Network and schema theories predict that anxious and depressed individuals should show both kinds of memory bias. However, it follows from the Williams et al. theory that anxiety should tend to produce an implicit memory but not an explicit memory bias, whereas the opposite should be the case with depression. There is some support for these predictions, but anxiety is often associated with an explicit memory bias.

Network and schema theories also have difficulties with the findings from studies on perceptual word recognition of emotional and neutral words. In most of these studies, words were presented very briefly but for progressively longer until they were identified correctly. As Niedenthal, Setterlund, and Jones (1994, p. 93) concluded, "Research designed to explore emotional influences in perception has revealed little systematic evidence for changes in the efficiency of word recognition as a function of emotional state." For example, Gerrig and Bower (1982) put hypnotised participants into a happy or angry mood, and then presented positive, negative, and neutral words. There was no evidence of any emotion-congruent effects in two experiments, although this is what is predicted by network theory.

Why have most studies failed to obtain evidence for facilitated processing of emotion-congruent information in perceptual word recognition? *Selective* attention was not involved, in that the participants were presented with only one stimulus at a time. If mood states influence selective attentional processes, as is proposed by Williams et al. (1988, 1997), this would explain why there is evidence for attentional bias but not for emotion-congruent effects in word recognition.

What of the future? Theoretically, there is a need to develop the approach of Williams et al. They have made good use of the distinction between perceptual and conceptual processes to shed light on differences between anxious and depressed individuals in the processing of threat. However, most tasks involve a mixture of perceptual and conceptual processes, and it is often hard to identify their respective contributions. Human information processing is very complicated, and so much more complex theories will be required, which may attach less importance to the imprecise distinction between perceptual and conceptual processes.

Experimentally, there has been too much emphasis on the processing of threat-related environmental stimuli (e.g., words). Anxious individuals often exhibit cognitive biases for *internal* stimuli. For example, patients with panic disorder catastrophically misinterpret their own physiological activity (Clark, 1986), and patients with social phobia have an interpretive bias for the adequacy of their own social behaviour (Stopa & Clark, 1993), assuming it to be much less adequate than is actually the case.

Finally, it is important to emphasise the potential relevance of research on emotional processing for an understanding of the anxiety disorders and clinical depression. For example, attentional, interpretive, and memory biases can all produce increased levels of anxiety or depression in individuals who are already anxious or depressed. Eysenck (1997, p. 100) discussed some of the implications so far as anxiety is concerned:

> Cognitive biases applied to the processing of threat-related information increase the level of state anxiety, and elevated state anxiety exaggerates the cognitive biases. This can create a positive feedback loop which eventually creates extremely high levels of uncontrollable experienced anxiety. Anxious patients often have more pronounced cognitive biases than normals high in trait anxiety, and so may be especially likely to become trapped in such positive feedback loops.

## CHAPTER SUMMARY

- Does affect require cognition? Affective responses can occur without any conscious awareness of cognitive processing. However, pre-conscious cognitive processing generally precedes any affective reaction when there is no conscious awareness of cognitive processing. LeDoux has shown the existence of a fast, non-conscious emotion circuit and a slow, cortical emotion circuit. Power and Dalgleish have put forward a multi-level theory in which emotion can be produced either automatically or via conscious processes.

- Theories of emotional processing. Bower's network theory applies to mood and emotional processing, and Beck's schema theory applies to personality and emotional processing. Network theory predicts mood-state dependent recall, mood congruity, thought congruity, and mood intensity. Mood states can be induced by means of the Velten procedure. According to Beck's schema theory, schemas or knowledge structures (when activated) produce processing biases, in which the processing of schema-consistent or emotionally congruent information is favoured. The two theories can be combined in the moderator or mediator approaches. Williams et al. have proposed a theory, according to which anxiety enhances perceptual processing of threat-related stimuli and depression increases conceptual processing of such stimuli.

- Emotion and memory. There is experimental support for mood congruity and mood-state-dependent recall. Bower has proposed a causal belongingness theory, according to which memory is best when the learner perceives that his or her mood state has been caused by the learning material. Eich and Metcalfe argued that mood has stronger effects on memory for internal events than for external events.

- Attention and perception. Anxious individuals have attentional and interpretive biases, and these biases are greater in stressful conditions. Interpretive bias depends on strategic rather than automatic processes, whereas the opposite is the case with attentional bias. Depressed individuals mostly show an interpretive bias, but no attentional bias. Anxiety has the function of detecting potential dangers, and this leads to enhanced perceptual processing of threatening stimuli. Depression is involved in replacing failed goals, and this leads to increased conceptual processing of threat-related information.

- Conclusions on emotional processing. There is reasonable support for the moderator approach, which claims that emotional processing depends interactively on personality and mood state. Network and schema theories mistakenly assume the following: (1) there will be facilitated processing of emotion-congruent information in virtually all situations; and (2) different emotional states have the same effects on cognitive processing. The theory of Williams et al. accounts for the differences in cognitive biases between anxious and depressed individuals better than network or schema theory.

## FURTHER READING

- Eysenck, M.W. (1997). *Anxiety and cognition: A unified theory*. Hove, UK: Psychology Press. This book presents a new cognitive theory designed to integrate research on anxiety as an emotion, anxiety as a personality dimension, and the major anxiety disorders.
- Power, M., & Dalgleish, T. (1997). *Cognition and emotion: From order to disorder*. Hove, UK: Psychology Press. This excellent book contains comprehensive coverage of theories and research linking cognition and emotion.
- Rusting, C.L. (1998). Personality, mood, and cognitive processing of emotional information: Three conceptual frameworks. *Psychological Bulletin*, *124*, 165–196. This article provides a competent and detailed account of research on emotion and cognition.
- Williams, J.M.G., Watts, F.N., MacLeod, C., & Mathews, A. (1997). *Cognitive psychology and emotional disorders (2nd Edn)*. Chichester, UK: Wiley. Research on cognitive biases in patients suffering from anxiety and mood disorders is discussed in detail in this informative book.

# 19

# Present and Future

## INTRODUCTION

The various approaches within contemporary cognitive psychology have been discussed at length in the previous chapters of this book. Cognitive psychologists have made much theoretical and empirical headway in making sense of human cognition, especially in recent years. Some of this progress is negative, in the sense that we now know that certain theoretical approaches are actually dead ends. Of course, eliminating erroneous approaches is not the same as discovering the best approach. However, the history of science reveals that it is usually an important step along the way.

Most of the emphasis in this book has been on specific theories and bodies of research. In contrast, the primary aims of this chapter are to provide more global evaluations of the entire approach of cognitive psychology and of its four main perspectives: experimental cognitive psychology; cognitive neuropsychology; cognitive science; and cognitive neuroscience.

## EXPERIMENTAL COGNITIVE PSYCHOLOGY

### Strengths

The recent dramatic increase in the impact of cognitive neuropsychology, cognitive science, and cognitive neuroscience has led many people to de-emphasise the contribution made by the more traditional experimental cognitive approach. In fact, all three of the newer approaches owe much to experimental cognitive psychology. For example, cognitive neuropsychology became a significant discipline about 20 years after cognitive psychology. It was only when cognitive psychologists had developed reasonable accounts of normal human cognition that the performance of brain-damaged patients could be understood fully. Before that, it was very hard to decide which patterns of cognitive impairment were of theoretical importance. In a similar way, the computational modelling activities of cognitive scientists are often informed to a major extent by pre-computational psychological theories. Finally, the tasks selected by cognitive neuroscientists for their neuroimaging studies are determined by the theoretical and empirical efforts of experimental cognitive psychologists.

A striking success of experimental cognitive psychology has been the way its approach has influenced several areas of psychology. For example, social, developmental, and clinical psychology have all become decidedly more "cognitive" in recent years. Many of the experimental paradigms used by researchers in those areas were initially developed in the research laboratories of experimental cognitive psychologists.

Finally, the methodological contribution of experimental cognitive psychology should not be underemphasised. In cognitive science and the neurosciences, the methodologies for studying phenomena are still being developed. Cognitive modellers are often accused of being unprincipled in their use of models (Cooper & Shallice, 1995), and in brain imaging there are still many issues about the methods used to rule out noise and exclude activation in brain regions that are merely by-products of the focus of a study. In all of this methodological flux, experimental cognitive psychology is the bedrock with its well worked-out empirical methods built up over 100 years of experimentation.

## Limitations

A recurring criticism of experimental cognitive psychology is that it lacks *ecological validity*, i.e., the findings cannot readily be generalised to the "real" world (see Chapter 8). For example, the participants in most cognitive experiments are well motivated, undistracted, have no other goals competing with that of task completion, and know exactly what they are supposed to do with the task stimuli. The near-optimal conditions in which cognitive psychologists usually assess cognition can be contrasted with those prevailing in the workplace: many office workers have multiple work goals to satisfy, they have to devote time and effort to prioritising goals, they are distracted by phone calls and by people knocking on their door, and their behaviour is greatly affected by social pressures.

The $64,000 question is whether this really matters. That it may do so can be illustrated by an analogy. We could study the limits of people's mobility by having them run races of different

distances on a fast running track wearing running spikes, singlet, and shorts. Measures of some of the processes involved could be obtained by recording heart rate, respiration rate, and so on. However, we would not expect that the information obtained would be of much value when predicting people's speeds while laden down with shopping or walking with their children, nor would we expect to be able to make accurate predictions of their heart rate or respiration rate under those conditions.

In the real world, people are constantly behaving in ways that will have an impact on the environment (e.g., turning on the television to watch a favourite programme). Thus, the responses that people make often change the stimulus situation. In contrast, most of the research of cognitive psychologists involves what Wachtel (1973) referred to as the "implacable [unyielding] experimenter". That is to say, the sequence of stimuli that the experimenter presents to the participant is *not* influenced by his or her behaviour, but is determined by the experimenter's predetermined plan.

As a result of the implacable experimenter, cognitive psychology is unduly limited in various respects. Consider what cognitive psychologists have discovered about attention (see Chapter 5). Many of the characteristics of divided and focused attention have been identified, but it could be argued that fundamental aspects of attention have been de-emphasised. The focus of attention in most research is determined by the experimenter's instructions. As a result, relatively little is known of the factors that normally influence the focus of attention (but see Chapter 18): relevance of stimuli to current goals; unexpectedness of stimuli; threateningness of stimuli; intensity of stimuli; and so on. This is an important limitation, because it would be impossible to predict someone's cognitive processes and behaviour in most situations without detailed knowledge of the factors determining attentional focus.

Another issue related to ecological validity is what has been called the "decoupling" problem. If a researcher wants to explore some aspect of, say, human memory, then an attempt is usually made to decouple the memory system from other cognitive systems, and to minimise the impact of motivational and emotional factors on performance. Even if it is possible to study the memory system in isolation, it is clear that it usually operates in interaction with other functional systems. Accordingly, the more successful we are in examining part of the cognitive system in isolation, the less our data are likely to tell us about cognition in everyday life. For example, there are influences of emotional states on cognition, and of cognition on emotional states (see Chapter 18). The usual strategy of ignoring emotional factors cannot be recommended if we want to generalise from the relatively unemotional states found in the laboratory to the much stronger emotional states of everyday life.

The key point can be expressed by referring to the distinction between *internal validity* (the validity of research within the context in which it is carried out) and *external validity* (the validity of research outside the research situation). Much of cognitive psychology is higher in internal than in external validity. However, this criticism has lost some of its force in recent years. There are several examples in this book of the increased willingness of experimental cognitive psychologists to move closer to "real life". For example, researchers have become more interested in perceptual processing of the human face, which is a very significant stimulus in everyday life (see Chapter 4). In Chapter 5, there is a discussion of attentional and automatic processes in connection with the "real-world" phenomenon of absent-mindedness. Chapter 8 is devoted to everyday memory, Chapter 14 deals with instances of skilled thinking in everyday life, and much of Chapters 11 and 12 is concerned with the important everyday activity of reading.

Some authorities have expressed scepticism about this increased focus on naturalistic research. For example, consider research on everyday memory (see Chapter 8). According to Banaji and Crowder (1989, p. 1190):

We have not been able to see any new principles of memory emerging from the everyday memory studies. Again and again, what seem at first like new, dramatic, emergent principles turn out to be everyday manifestations of laboratory wisdom.

Although many experimental cognitive psychologists are aware that their research may be somewhat lacking in ecological validity, they are rightly sceptical of a wholesale abandonment of experimental rigour and control in favour of a totally naturalistic approach. There are so many variables influencing behaviour in the real world, and it is so hard to manipulate them systematically, that it can become almost impossible to assess the relative importance of each variable in determining behaviour. It is hard to achieve the desirable combination of experimental rigour and ecological validity, but some of the more successful endeavours in that direction have been discussed throughout this book.

A puzzling feature of experimental cognitive psychology is the reluctance to take individual differences seriously. The typical research strategy involves using analysis of variance to assess statistically the effects of various experimental manipulations on cognitive performance, with individual differences being relegated to the error term. Cognitive psychologists who adopt this strategy seem to assume implicitly that individual differences are unimportant, and do not interact with any of the experimental manipulations.

The reality is very different. Bowers (1973) considered 11 studies in which the percentages of the variance accounted for by individual differencs, by situational factors, and by their interaction could be assessed. On average, individual differences accounted for 11.3% of the variance, the situation for 10.2%, and the interaction between individual differences and situation for 20.8%. In the light of such evidence, it seems perverse to ignore individual differences altogether!

A final problem with experimental cognitive psychology is that the emphasis has been on relatively specific theories that are applicable to only a narrow range of cognitive tasks. What has been lacking is an overarching theoretical architecture. Such an architecture would clarify the interrelationships among different components of the cognitive system. Various candidate cognitive architectures have been proposed, including Newell's (1990) SOAR architecture, and Anderson's (1993) ACT* model. Both of these cognitive architectures are based on production systems. These architectures have been applied to a wide range of tasks. However, the research community has not abandoned specific theories in favour of using these architectures, because researchers are not convinced that either of them is the "one true cognitive architecture". As long as there is no overarching, accepted architecture, experimental cognitive psychology will always suffer from a certain lack of theoretical integration.

# COGNITIVE NEUROPSYCHOLOGY

## Strengths

The cognitive neuropsychological approach has become much more influential over the past 25 years. There are two main reasons for this. First, theoretical developments within cognitive psychology have helped to guide the research efforts of cognitive neuropsychologists. Second, the development of techniques such as MRI and computed tomography (CAT scans) has allowed much more precise identification of the areas of brain damage.

Cognitive psychologists often need experimental evidence to decide whether two mechanisms, structures, or processes are really separate from each other. Two examples are as follows: Are there separate short-term and long-term memory systems? Are there separate explicit and implicit memory systems? Some of the clearest evidence on such issues has come from research by cognitive neuropsychologists which has led to the discovery of *double dissociations*. For example, there is accumulating evidence that separate areas of the brain are involved in explicit and implicit memory (see Chapter 7).

One of the greatest strengths of cognitive neuropsychology is that it provides a good test-bed for evaluating theories originally based on the performance of normal individuals. For example, some of the most powerful evidence that there are at least two different routes involved in reading has come from studying brain-damaged patients largely lacking one route or the other (see Chapter 11).

The contribution of cognitive neuropsychology does not consist only of testing pre-existing theories. Consider, for example, the study of amnesic patients (see Chapter 7). It became increasingly clear that they could display good memory performance provided that conscious recollection of previous events was not required, and this finding was instrumental in establishing the key theoretical distinction between explicit and implicit memory. Thus, findings within cognitive neuropsychology have been used to generate new theories as well as to test existing ones.

The cognitive neuropsychological approach has been applied successfully to several areas, including perception, attention, memory, and language. However, there has probably been more research devoted to language than to any other area. Why is this? It seems that language lends itself especially well to the cognitive neuropsychological approach. The comprehension and production of language involve various skills (i.e., those of reading, listening, writing, and speaking), and cognitive neuropsychologists have shown that each of these skills has various modules or cognitive processes associated with it.

The study of brain-damaged individuals has also proved of value in establishing the functions supported by different areas of the brain. In essence, the cognitive functioning of patients having overlapping areas of brain damage is studied. A full consideration of the evidence thus obtained can reveal which part or parts of the brain are most closely associated with specific cognitive impairments.

## Limitations

In spite of the successes of the cognitive neuropsychological approach, it has several limitations. First, patients, even those with the same *syndrome* or set of symptoms, typically have rather different lesions (see Chapter 1). There is no simple answer as to what to do about the variations from one patient to another. However, the key point was expressed clearly by Knight (1998, p. 110):

People often make the mistake that a large number of patients is by definition better than a smaller one. However, as in all experimental work, the variance of the group under investigation is paramount. Your interpretations are only as reliable as the variance in your group of interest.

Second, there are often large differences among individuals having broadly similar brain damage. As Banich (1997, p. 55) pointed out, such individuals "typically vary widely in age, socioeconomic status, and educational background. Prior to brain damage, these individuals may have had diverse life experiences. Afterward, their life experiences likely vary too, depending on the type of rehabilitation they receive, their attitudes toward therapy and recovery and their social support network."

Third, as a general rule of thumb, more is likely to be learned about cognitive functioning from patients with lesions of limited extent than from those with more extensive lesions. Thus, for example, total destruction of the cortex would prevent the person affected from performing any cognitive tasks at all, but all this would tell us is that the cortex is necessary for all cognitive functions. The actual brain damage suffered by many patients is too great to permit clear inferences about cognitive functions.

Fourth, there are various important cognitive activities (e.g., creative thought; organisational planning) that seem resistant to a modular approach. For example, Fodor (1983, p. 119) argued that there was little reason to believe that advances could be made on the neuropsychology of thinking, because "in the case of central processes you get an approximation to universal connectivity, hence no stable neural architecture." However, more recently, some progress has been made (see Chapters 6, 14 and 15). For example, there have been attempts (e.g., Eslinger & Damasio, 1985; Shallice & Burgess, 1993) to apply a modular approach to the functions of the central executive of the working memory system. There is nevertheless a danger that the modular approach exaggerates the extent to which cognitive functions are localised within the brain (Farah, 1994b). As Banich (1997, p. 52) noted, "we must not forget that the brain is comprised of about 50 billion *interconnected* neurons. Therefore, even complex

cognitive functions for which a modular description seems apt rely on a number of interconnected brain regions or systems."

Fifth, even though the study of language may be regarded as the "jewel in the crown" of cognitive neuropsychology, there are significant limitations in that research. There has been a substantial amount of work on the reading and spelling of individual words by brain-damaged patients, but rather little on larger units of language. Many important language processes are involved in reading and spelling single words, but equally there are important additional factors (e.g., contextual influence; structural themes) which are only of relevance to larger units of language (see Chapter 13). In similar fashion, cognitive neuropsychology has been uninformative about the planning processes involved in speaking and writing.

Sixth, the study of brain-damaged patients can lead to *underestimates* of the brain areas involved in performing any given cognitive function. The lesion method generally only permits identification of those brain areas of crucial importance to a cognitive function, but not of those that may be partially involved. Another reason is that damage to an area that is normally used to perform a cognitive function may lead the patient to develop an alternative strategy that does not rely on the damaged area. In that case, his or her cognitive performance may be normal.

Seventh, the study of brain-damaged patients can lead to *overestimates* of the areas of the brain directly involved in certain aspects of cognitive functioning. This can happen when the damaged region contains axons known as fibres of passage which connect the brain areas crucially involved in performing a certain cognitive function.

Eighth, the task of relating areas of brain damage to specific cognitive functions is complicated because there are clear individual differences in the localisation of some functions. Some of the clearest evidence was reported by Ojemann (1991; see Chapter 14). He studied 117 epileptic patients undergoing surgery. They named pictures while a small electric current was applied to the exposed cortex. The current interfered with picture naming, and was thus like a temporary cortical lesion. The findings indicated that the parts of the brain

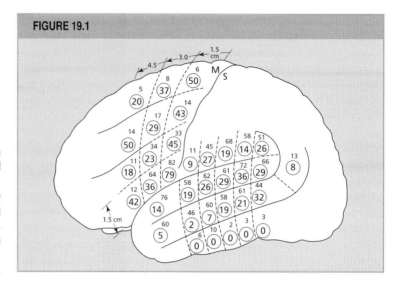

**FIGURE 19.1**

Areas of the brain in which electrical stimulation was found to interfere with picture naming. The numbers represent the percentage of participants showing interference in each brain area. Reproduced with permission from Ojemann (1991). Copyright © 1991 by the Society for Neuroscience.

associated with interference varied considerably from patient to patient (see Figure 19.1).

## COGNITIVE SCIENCE

### Strengths

The computational modelling of psychological theories provides a strong test of their adequacy, because of the need to be explicit about every theoretical assumption in a computational model. Many theories from traditional cognitive psychology have been found to be inadequate, because crucial aspects of the human information-processing system were not spelled out computationally. For example, Marr (1982) found that previous theoretical assumptions about feature detectors in visual perception were oversimplified when he began to construct programs to specify precisely how feature extraction might occur (see Chapter 2). Alternatively, it can be shown that a particular theory is unfeasible in principle, because it proposes processes that would take forever to compute. For example, early analogy models suggested computationally intractable processes to underlie analogy-making that took people a matter of seconds to complete (Veale & Keane, 1998; see Chapter 15).

A second advantage of computational modelling is that it supports the development of more complex theories in cognitive psychology. In many cognitive theories, theorists can rapidly reach a point where the complexity of the theory makes it very hard to say what the theory might predict. If you have developed a computational model, then the predictions can be generated rapidly and easily by simply running the model with the target stimuli. In short, the model can be a significant crutch to the theorist's thinking.

A third advantage of computational modelling is the clarity it can bring to the comparison of theories. First, it is very hard to maintain differences between theories that really do not exist when both theories have been elaborated in computational models. Second, computational models have clarified the distinctions between theories and models. Two theorists commonly present statements about a phenomenon that mix theoretical proposals with specific assertions based on a model. Often, when this situation is clarified, it becomes clear that both theories agree at the computational level (see Marr, 1982, and Chapter 1), but merely differ in the added assumptions made in their specific model instantiating the theory. For example, Keane et al. (1994) showed that what appeared to be three different theories of analogy were in fact three variations on an agreed theoretical scheme.

A fourth advantage is that computational models have been proposed as general cognitive architectures that can be applied to the understanding of all cognitive functioning (see, for example, Newell, 1990; Rumelhart et al., 1986). Such widely applicable theoretical notions have emerged less often from the work of traditional cognitive psychologists and cognitive neuropsychologists. They also offer a remedy to the fragmentation that dogs psychological theorising arising from specific empirical paradigms.

Many theorists have argued that connectionism and models based on parallel-distributed processing offer the prospect of providing better accounts of human cognition than previous approaches within cognitive science (see Chapters 2, 3, and 12). Some of the potential advantages of the newer approach can be seen with reference to the following quotation from Churchland (1989, p. 100):

> The brain seems to be a computer with a radically different style. For example, the brain changes as it learns, it appears to store and process information in the same places . . . Most obviously, the brain is a parallel machine, in which many interactions occur at the same time in many channels.

Connectionist models with their parallel-distributed processing resemble brain functioning more closely than do traditional computer models based on serial processing. Furthermore, with their modifiable connections and distributed representations, such models provide very elegant and convincing models of human learning (see Chapter 1). For instance, when some of these models are "lesioned", they produce systematic errors that parallel the behaviour of brain-damaged patients (e.g., Plaut & Shallice, 1993).

## Limitations

Cognitive science is perhaps the fullest expression of the computational metaphor for the mind (Von Eckardt, 1993). Although some commentators refuse to accept the validity of this metaphor (Still & Costall, 1991), 40 or so years of success

in cognitive psychology are hard to ignore given the practicalities of paradigm-driven science. We will not enter the fray on the computational metaphor, but rather concentrate on the more revealing limitations arising from within when you accept this metaphor.

First, it can be argued that cognitive science is just "fancy" cognitive psychology. Originally, cognitive science was touted as a great bringing together of diverse disciplines like philosophy, linguistics, neuroscience, anthropology, and psychology (Gardner, 1985). However, the reality is more limited. Hardcastle (1996) argued that it is just experimental psychology "with bells and whistles". Concrete evidence for Hardcastle's view was forthcoming from an analysis of papers published in the journal *Cognitive Science* and the *Proceedings of the Cognitive Science Society's Annual Conference* (Schunn, Crowley, & Okada, 1998). Schunn et al. (1998) found that almost two-thirds of the authors of *Cognitive Science* articles came from either psychology or computer science departments, with the remainder coming from a sprinkling of linguistics and philosophy schools or from industry. Few published articles combined a true interdisciplinary mix; that is, most articles were straight experimental psychology or straight artificial intelligence, with few combining empirical and computational aspects. Furthermore, while many of these articles referred to papers in other disciplines, like linguistics or philosophy, these disciplines did not reciprocate by referring to work in cognitive science. Thus, it could be argued that the interdisciplinary claims for cognitive science are unfounded. The only plus to counter this argument is Schunn et al.'s (1998) finding that in recent years a rising number of articles come from "departments of cognitive science", suggesting that the area is maturing into a distinct discipline.

Second, it can be argued that computational models are rarely used to make predictions; they are produced as a prop for a theory, but have no real predictive function. For any given theory, there are a huge number of possible models (probably an infinite number), and these variations are rarely explored. To quote Gazzaniga et al. (1998, p. 102), "Unlike experimental work which by its nature is cumulative, modelling research tends to occur in isolation. There may be lots of ways to model a particular phenomenon, but less effort has been devoted to devising critical tests that pit one theory against another." The root of this complaint is that cognitive scientists develop one model of a phenomenon rather than exploring many models, which could then be distinguished by critical empirical testing. However, for some exceptions refer to Hummel and Holyoak (1997), Keane (1997), and Gentner and Markman (in press). In short, models are rarely used to make real predictions.

One of the reasons for this state of affairs may be the lack of any definite methodology for relating a computational model's behaviour to human behaviour. As Costello and Keane (2000) have pointed out, there are many levels of detail at which a model can simulate people. For example, a model can capture the direction of a difference in correct responses between two groups of people in an experiment, the specific correct and error responses of groups, general trends in response times for all response types, response times and types for specific individuals, and so on. Many models operate at the more general end of these possible parallels. This suggests that such models are, and may always be, predictively weak. In some cases, there are in-principle obstacles to them becoming more specific (Costello & Keane, 2000).

A third criticism of cognitive science is that models tend to be limited in diverse ways. The models often lack neural plausibility, they fail to capture the scope of cognitive phenomena, and the biological context in which cognition occurs. Connectionist models that are claimed to have neural plausibility do not really resemble the human brain. First, connectionist models typically use thousands or tens of thousands of connected units to model a cognitive task that might be performed by tens of millions of neurons in the brain. Second, there is little evidence that the pattern of connectivity between units and the learning rules (like backprop) used in connectionist models have parallels in the human brain. Third, numerous models can generally be found to "explain" any sets of findings. As Carey and Milner (1994, p. 66) pointed out, "any neural net

which produces a desired output from a specified input is hugely under-constrained; an infinitely large number of solutions can be found for each problem addressed." In short, these models need to be much more constrained by what has been found at the neurological level.

Computational models often fail to capture the scope of cognitive phenomena. Human cognition is influenced by a multiplicity of potentially conflicting motivational and emotional factors, many of which may be operative at the same time. Most models do not try to capture these wider aspects of cognition. For example, most language processing models tend to focus on the process of understanding a sentence or phrase—for instance, a metaphor like "surgeons are butchers"—without considering its emotional import. However, if you were a surgeon, and this was said to you by a patient, the pejorative implications of the metaphor would be your main concern (see Veale & Keane, 1994). Similar arguments have been made about the failure to capture the moral and social dimensions of cognitive behaviour (Shotter, 1991).

Computational models also tend to model cognition independently of its biological context. Norman (1980) pointed out that human functioning involves an interplay between a cognitive system (which he called the Pure Cognitive System) and a biological system (which he called the Regulatory System). Much of the activity of the Pure Cognitive System is determined by the various needs of the Regulatory System, including the need for survival, for food and water, and for protection of oneself and one's family. Cognitive science, in common with most of the rest of cognitive psychology, focuses on the Pure Cognitive System and virtually ignores the key role played by the Regulatory System.

A fourth limitation of connectionist models was identified by Ellis and Humphreys (1999), who pointed out that most computational models have been designed to simulate human performance on single tasks. That obviously limits what they can tell us about human cognition. It is also limiting in less obvious ways, as was pointed out by Ellis and Humphreys (1999, p. 623): "Double dissociations based on evidence from different tasks . . .

cannot be captured in models that perform only single tasks. To begin to address such evidence, multi-task models are needed."

A fifth limitation of cognitive science is that it may fail to deliver on its greatest promise, namely the provision of a general unified theory of cognition to weld the fragmentary theories of cognitive psychology together. Throughout the 1990s, one of the greatest developments in cognitive science was the proposal and elaboration of unified theories of cognition like Newell's SOAR model (Newell, 1990), Anderson's (1993) ACT* model, and the more amorphous connectionist framework (Shephard, 1989). Apart from the practical realities of these models being adopted by researchers in the field, there has been some criticism of the fundamental potential of these models. Cooper and Shallice (1995) have argued that SOAR is no better than the grand theories of the 1930s because it has insecure methodological foundations, an ill-specified computational/ psychological theory, and inadequate empirical tests. Ironically, for it to work as an adequate unified theory, it has been proposed that it needs to be more clearly specified in a language like that used in everyday life (Cooper et al., 1996).

---

## COGNITIVE NEUROSCIENCE

---

### Strengths

One of the strengths of the cognitive neuroscience approach is that it allows us to obtain detailed information about the brain *structures* involved in different kinds of cognitive processing. Techniques such as MRI and CAT scans have proved of particular value when used on patients to discover which brain areas are damaged. Previous cognitive neuropsychological research on patients with conditions such as amnesia or various language disorders was hampered by the fact that the precise areas of brain damage could only be established by postmortem examination (see Chapters 7 and 13).

Why is it useful to know precisely which brain areas are damaged in each patient? One important reason is because such information has led to more realistic views of brain organisation. For example, the earlier assumption that any given language function is located in the same brain region for everyone has been replaced by the assumption that there are great individual differences in the localisation of language functions (see Chapter 13).

As was pointed out in Chapter 1, the various neuroimaging techniques differ considerably in their temporal and spatial resolution of cognitive processes. For example, two of the most popular techniques (PET and fMRI) both have fairly poor temporal resolution but good spatial resolution, whereas event-related potentials have good temporal resolution but poor spatial resolution. As Gazzaniga et al. (1998, p. 118) pointed out, the best way of achieving the desirable goal of good temporal and spatial resolution is by *combining* information from different techniques: "Researchers have opted to combine the temporal resolution of evoked potentials with the spatial resolution of PET or fMRI for a better picture of the physiology and anatomy of cognition."

Clear examples of the value of good temporal resolution are to be found in attention research (see Chapter 5). It has long been known that there are important differences in the processing of attended and unattended stimuli. However, it has proved very hard to distinguish empirically between theories based on the assumption that these differences occur early in processing versus those that assume they occur only late in processing. Studies using event-related potentials have found strong evidence for early processing differences between attended and unattended stimuli in the visual and auditory modalities (see Chapter 5).

A clear example of the value of good spatial resolution comes in research on episodic and semantic memory (see Chapter 7). Most brain-damaged patients with amnesia have poor episodic and semantic memory, which suggests that they both depend on the same brain areas. However, evidence from cognitive neuroscience suggests that episodic and semantic memory depend on adjacent brain structures that are typically both damaged in amnesic patients (see Vargha-Khadem et al., 1997).

Another strength of the cognitive neuroscience approach is that it can help to demonstrate the reality of theoretical distinctions. For example, it has been argued by many theorists (e.g., Roediger, 1990) that implicit memory can be divided into perceptual and conceptual implicit memory. Support for that view has come from PET studies by Schacter et al. (1996) and by Wagner et al. (1997). In these studies, perceptual and conceptual priming tasks affected different areas of the brain.

## Limitations

It is very easy to be impressed by the ever-increasing number of neuroimaging techniques available to researchers. However, it is important not to be over-impressed. As Tulving (1998, p. 275) pointed out:

> The single most critical piece of equipment is still the researcher's own brain. All the equipment in the world will not help us if we do not know how to use it properly . . . What is badly needed now, with all those scanners whirring away, is an understanding of exactly what we are observing, and seeing, and measuring.

In most neuroimaging studies, data are collected from several individuals and then averaged. Some concern has been expressed about such averaging because of the existence of significant individual differences. This issue was illustrated by Howard (1997, p. 298) in the following hypothetical (but plausible) example: "If, for instance, some 50% of subjects recognise words in Wernicke's area . . . and show increased rCBF [regional cerebral blood flow] there in a task, while the other 50% show no change, over the whole group there will probably be a significant increase."

How serious are the problems associated with averaging neuroimaging data? A reasonable answer to that question was provided by Raichle (1998, p. 115): "One only has to inspect individual human brains to appreciate that they do differ. However, general organising principles emerge that transcend these differences." Such organising principles do not necessarily apply to all the individuals tested.

It is a matter of some concern that findings obtained from neuroimaging studies sometimes seem inconsistent with those obtained by cognitive neuropsychologists with brain-damaged patients. For example, studies on amnesic patients have indicated clearly that the hippocampus is of central importance in declarative or explicit memory (see Chapter 7). In contrast, most neuroimaging studies using PET or fMRI have failed to find evidence of high levels of activation in normals performing declarative memory tasks (see Chapter 7).

There are various reasons for differences between neuroimaging studies and studies on brain-damaged patients. First, PET and fMRI show all the areas that are active during a task, including those that are essential to the performance of that task. In contrast, damage to a given area of the brain will only lead to impaired performance when that area is essential for the task and when non-damaged parts of the brain have not taken over the functions of the damaged area. Second, as Knight (1998, p. 110) pointed out, there are age differences between the participants in the two types of study: "Except for a few aging and lesion studies the metabolic techniques [PET, fMRI] are limited to young normal subjects. Conversely, lesion studies typically involve older populations who now have a superimposed brain lesion."

The techniques for measuring brain activity used by cognitive neuroscientists have become progressively more sophisticated and sensitive. These advances have sometimes had the paradoxical effect of making it harder to decide which areas of the brain are most involved in specific functions. For example, Price, Wise, and Frackowiak (1996) gave their participants the simple task of deciding whether words contained an ascender (a letter such as b, d, or f rising above the body of the word). PET revealed activation in large areas of the brain, including the posterior part of the temporal lobe, the frontal lobe, and the posterior parieto-occipital junction. Such findings make it very hard to identify the brain areas *crucially* involved in task performance.

## PRESENT AND FUTURE DIRECTIONS

The four approaches of experimental cognitive psychology, cognitive neuropsychology, cognitive science, and cognitive neuroscience differ in their strengths and weaknesses. As a result, what is needed in order to maximise our understanding of human cognition is to use the *method of converging operations*. This method involves making use of a variety of approaches to consider any given issue from different perspectives. When this method is applied with two approaches, there are two possible outcomes:

1. The findings obtained are broadly comparable.
2. The findings differ significantly.

When the findings from two approaches are similar, this increases our confidence in the validity of the findings and in the usefulness of both approaches. When the findings are dissimilar, this indicates the need for further research to clarify what is happening. Thus, the method of converging operations can help to prevent researchers from drawing incorrect conclusions on the basis of limited findings from a single approach.

There are various examples in this book of cases in which the method of converging operations has produced comparable findings from different approaches. For example, there is the issue of whether implicit memory should be divided into perceptual and conceptual implicit memory (considered earlier in the chapter). PET studies have indicated that visual perceptual priming affects the bilateral occipito-temporal areas, whereas conceptual priming affects left frontal neocortex (see Chapter 7). The distinction between perceptual and conceptual priming is also supported by research within cognitive neuropsychology. Intact perceptual priming but impaired conceptual priming is shown by Alzheimer patients, and the opposite pattern is shown by patients with right occipital lesions (see Chapter 7).

Some cases in which the findings from two approaches are different have been discussed in this chapter. Such differences are probably most common when findings from cognitive neuropsychology and cognitive neuroscience are compared. There is a general tendency for the cognitive neuropsychological approach to *underestimate* the brain areas necessary to perform a given cognitive function, whereas the cognitive neuroscience approach tends to *overestimate* them. An awareness of these tendencies makes it easier to reconcile the findings of cognitive neuropsychology and cognitive neuroscience.

Rugg (1997) has identified some of the key ways in which the present approach to human cognition differs from those used in the past. As he pointed out, the historical emphasis within cognitive psychology, "is placed on models of cognitive function that make no reference to their possible biological substrates, and the idea that biological data might constrain or inform functional models is treated with scepticism" (Rugg, 1997, p. 5). In contrast, the current (and probably future) approach is based on the following key assumption: "The mapping between physical activity in the brain and its functional state is such that when two experimental conditions are associated with different patterns of neural activity, it can be assumed that they have engaged distinct cognitive functions . . . this assumption opens the way for physiological data to play a role in the development of functional models of cognition" (Rugg, 1997, pp. 5–6).

Marr (1982) provided a more complete theoretical framework. According to him, information-processing theories should be characterised at three levels (see Table 19.2). The computational level contains a specification of what needs to be computed for a given task to be carried out. It is also concerned with the purpose or function of the computation. At the algorithmic level, the exact nature of the computation is specified. This level should capture the detailed processing steps that intervene between the inputs and outputs, and it should take account of the mechanisms people actually use. Finally, the hardware level is the brain. The brain imposes limitations on the kinds

**TABLE 19.2**

| Marr's (1982) framework for theories | |
| --- | --- |
| Computational level | The goal of the computation, why it is appropriate, what the logic of the strategy carried out might be. |
| Algorithmic level | How can the computational theory be implemented, the representation for the input, and the algorithm for the transformation. |
| Hardware level | How can the representation and the algorithm be realised physically. |

of representations and algorithms that can actually be used. A crucial point is that "a complete psychological explanation of any task performance must invoke all three levels of analysis" (Oaksford, 1994, p. 76). The research discussed in this book has made substantial progress in this direction. However, complete psychological explanations still lie in the future.

## CHAPTER SUMMARY

- Experimental cognitive psychology. The experimental cognitive approach has had a major impact on cognitive neuropsychology and cognitive neuroscience, as well as on other areas within psychology (e.g., social psychology; abnormal psychology). Experimental cognitive psychology has made significant contributions across the whole range of human cognition. Its limitations include a lack of ecological validity, the implacable experimenter, the decoupling problem, the relative neglect of emotional factors, the de-emphasis of individual differences, and the construction of fairly specific theories.

- Cognitive neuropsychology. The cognitive neuropsychological approach provides a good test-bed for evaluating theories of normal cognition. It has also produced findings that have been used to generate new theories. The approach has proved successful in understanding language, which seems to be organised in a modular way. The limitations of cognitive neuropsychology include the following: patients vary in the extent of brain damage, their symptoms, and their personal characteristics and experiences; lesions are often too large in extent to permit clear inferences about cognitive functions; the modular approach works less well with higher-level processes; and the areas of brain involved in performing a given cognitive function can be overestimated or underestimated.

- Cognitive science. The cognitive science approach has the advantage of encouraging explictness that can rule out computationally infeasible theories, facilitate the comparison of theories, and support the making of predictions when theories become complex. It also offers a possible solution to the fragmentary nature of theories in cognitive psychology in its proposal of cognitive architectures to accommodate diverse cognitive phenomena. However, cognitive science lacks a sufficient inter-disciplinary mix and may just be "fancy" cognitive psychology. It has been argued that computational models are used more to decorate theories than as strongly predictive models. Computational models tend to be limited in scope, ignoring the wider context of cognition (e.g., emotional, social, and biological contexts), and focusing on single tasks. Finally, the promise that cognitive architectures will deliver unified theories may not be delivered.

- Cognitive neuroscience. Cognitive neuroscience provides detailed information about the brain areas that are damaged in the patients studied by cognitive neuropsychologists. In combination, neuroimaging techniques allow us to achieve good temporal and spatial resolution of cognitive processes. The cognitive neuroscience approach can help to show the reality of theoretical distinctions. Neuroimaging data are typically averaged across individuals, which may obscure important individual differences. It can be hard with brain scanning to distinguish between those active brain areas that are more and less crucial for successful task performance.
- Present and future directions. There is increased use of the method of converging operations, which involves addressing any given issue with various approaches. When the findings from different approaches are comparable, this increases our confidence in the validity of the findings. The cognitive neuropsychological and cognitive neuroscience approaches sometimes produce different findings because the brain areas essential for task performance tend to be underestimated in the former approach and overestimated in the latter approach. The key assumption for present and future research is that there are important links between brain activity and cognitive functions. Complete psychological accounts of cognitive functioning require consideration of the computational, algorithmic, and hardware or brain levels.

## FURTHER READING

- Banich, M.T. (1997). *Neuropsychology: The neural bases of mental function*. New York: Houghton Mifflin. Chapter 2 of this book provides clear and detailed evaluations of most of the methods and approaches dealt with in this chapter.
- Ellis, R., & Humphreys, G. (1999). *Connectionist psychology: A text with readings*. Hove, UK: Psychology Press. Chapter 9 in this book provides an assessment of the connectionist approach to cognition.
- Gazzaniga, M.S., Ivry, R.B., & Mangun, G.R. (1998). *Cognitive neuroscience: The biology of the mind*. New York: W.W. Norton. Several methods used in cognitive neuroscience are discussed and evaluated in Chapter 3.
- Wilson, R.A., & Keil, F. (1999). *The MIT encyclopaedia of the cognitive sciences*. Cambridge, MA: MIT Press. Research and theory across the whole range of cognitive psychology are evaluated by numerous experts.

# Glossary

**Accommodation**: one of the **binocular cues** to depth, based on the variation in optical power produced by a thickening of the lens of the eye when focusing on a close object.

**Achromatopsia**: this is a brain-damaged condition in which there is little or no colour perception, but form and motion perception are sometimes intact.

**Action slips**: actions that are performed in ways that were not intended.

**Affirmation of the consequent**: an invalid argument form in conditional reasoning where one concludes *P*, given the true statements *If P then Q* and *Q*.

**Affordances**: the potential uses of an object, which Gibson claimed are directly perceived.

**Agrammatism**: a condition in which speech productions lack grammatical structure and many function words and word endings are omitted.

**Akinetopsia**: this is a brain-damaged condition in which objects in motion cannot be perceived, whereas stationary objects are perceived fairly normally.

**Alexia**: a condition in which there are great problems with reading even though speech is understood.

**Algorithmic method**: a specified set of steps for solving a problem, which guarantees the solution of the problem.

**Alzheimer's disease**: a disease involving progressive dementia or loss of mental powers.

**Amnesic syndrome**: a condition in which there is substantial impairment of long-term memory; the condition includes both **anterograde amnesia** and **retrograde amnesia**.

**Analogical representation**: a mental **representation** that somehow parallels the structure of the thing it represents in the world, e.g., the way visual images parallel the spatial organisation of things in the world (see **propositional representation**).

**Analogy**: a figurative comparison between two **domains** of knowledge that allows you to make some inferences that may or may not be correct (e.g., the atom is like a minature solar system).

**Anaphora**: the use of a pronoun or noun to represent some previously mentioned noun or noun phrase.

**Anarthria**: a condition caused by brain damage in which the patient cannot speak in spite of having intact general language knowledge; see **dysarthria**.

**Anecdotal evidence**: evidence that has more the status of hearsay, rather than that gathered by controlled observation or experimental testing.

**Anomia**: a condition caused by brain damage in which there is an impaired ability to name objects.

**Anterograde amnesia**: reduced ability to remember information acquired after the onset of amnesia.

**Aphasia**: impaired language abilities as a result of brain damage.

**Apparent motion**: the illusion of motion created by the rapid presentation of still images.

**Apperceptive agnosia**: this is a form of **visual agnosia** in which there is impaired perceptual analysis of familiar objects.

**Articulatory suppression**: rapid repetition of some simple sound (e.g., the the the) which uses the articulatory control process of the **phonological loop**.

**Associationism**: philosophical approach that stressed the associative character of perception, memory, and thought (originally inspired by so-called British Empiricists, Hume, Locke, and Berkeley).

**Associative agnosia**: this is a form of **visual agnosia** in which perceptual processing is fairly normal but there is an impaired ability to derive the meaning of objects.

**Attentional bias**: selective attention to threat-related stimuli when presented at the same time as neutral stimuli.

**Auditory phonological agnosia**: a condition in which there is poor perception of unfamiliar words and non-words, but not familiar words.

**Autobiographical memory**: memory for the events of one's own life.

**Availability heuristic**: the assumption that the frequencies of events can be estimated accurately by the accessibility in memory.

**Back-propagation**: a learning mechanism in **connectionist networks** based on comparing actual responses to correct ones.

**Balint's syndrome**: a brain-damaged condition in which some patients find it hard to shift visual attention.

**Base-rate information**: the relative frequency of an event within a population.

**Basic cognitive interview**: an approach to improving the memory of eyewitnesses based on the assumption that memory traces contain many features.

**Basic level**: an intermediate level of abstraction in a **conceptual hierarchy**, usually corresponding to a maximally informative category, like chairs and desks (see **superordinate level** and **subordinate level**).

**Between-category similarity**: the similarity of categories to one another, organised by some **superordinate** concept (see **within-category similarity**).

**Bias**: used in reasoning research to indicate a tendency to respond in a certain way that is often, in some sense, incorrect.

**Biconditional**: the logical operator that is sometimes notated as "*if*" or "*if and only if*", as in the statement "if and only if there is a circle there is a triangle".

**Binding problem**: issues arising when different kinds of information need to be integrated to produce object recognition.

**Binocular cues**: cues to depth that require both eyes to be used together.

**Blindsight**: the ability to respond appropriately to visual stimuli in the absence of conscious vision in patients with damage to the primary visual cortex.

**Blobs**: areas in the primary visual cortex forming part of the P pathway and responding strongly to contrast and to colour; see **interblobs**.

**Bottom-up processing**: processing that is directly influenced by environmental stimuli; see **top-down processing**.

**Bridging inferences**: inferences that are drawn to increase the coherence between the current and preceding parts of a text.

**Case grammar**: a **schema**-like representation for relational concepts proposed by Fillmore (1968) which makes use of case-categories [e.g., Agent, Object, Recipient, as in hit(Agent, Recipient, Instrument)].

**Categorical speech perception**: classification of ambiguous speech sounds as representing specific phonemes in an all-or-none way.

**Category-specific anomia**: a condition in which there is selective impairment in the ability to name objects belonging to certain categories in spite of good access to semantic information about objects.

**Central executive**: a modality-free, limited-capacity, component of **working memory**.

**Centre of moment**: the reference point in the upper body around which the shoulders and hips swing.

**Characteristic attributes**: **semantic features** of a concept that are not necessary but merely occur in many instances of the concept (see **defining attributes**).

**Chromatic adaptation**: reduced sensitivity to light of a given colour after lengthy exposure.

**Chunk**: a stored unit formed from integrating smaller pieces of information.

**Co-articulation**: slight distortion in speech when the production of one speech segment is influenced by the production of the previous speech segment.

**Code generation**: the writing of computer programs.

**Cognitive economy**: the principle, mainly applied in categorisation theory, that human knowledge is organised to maximise the distinctions between categories while minimising the number of knowledge items to be stored.

**Cognitive neuropsychology**: it involves studying cognitive functioning in brain-damaged patients in order to increase our understanding of normal human cognition.

**Cognitive neuroscience**: it involves using various techniques to study the functioning of the human brain.

**Cognitive science**: it involves constructing computational models in order to understand human cognition.

**Cohesion**: a property of categories whereby their members seem to coalesce into a natural grouping.

**Colour constancy**: the tendency for any given object to be perceived as having the same colour under widely varying viewing conditions.

**Combinatorial explosion**: a description of how the number of possibilities in a task or problem increases rapidly as more items have to be processed or more decisions have to be made.

**Competence**: the idea that people have a basic ability in some task (e.g., linguistic competence or logical competence) that may or may not be realised in their performance of the task for a variety of reasons (e.g., working memory load).

**Conceptual hierarchies**: the inclusive relationships between categories at different levels of abstraction (e.g., that "living things" includes "animals" which, in turn, includes dogs and cats).

**Conceptual implicit tests**: memory tests on which the information provided is conceptually related to the studied information and conscious recollection is not required; see **perceptual implicit tests**.

**Conceptual spaces**: a **domain** of knowlege or set of ideas defined by some semantic parameters, often conceived of as a multi-dimensional space.

**Conceptually driven processes**: processes initiated by the individual in a top-down way; see **data-driven processes**.

**Conditionals**: the name given to if . . . then statements in logic and reasoning by **deduction**.

**Confirmation:** technique used in hypothesis testing that, according to Popper (1968), is logically incorrect, whereby one attempts to find supportive evidence for your hypotheses rather than **falsify** them.

**Confirmation bias**: memory that is distorted by being influenced by the individual's expectations rather than what actually happened.

**Connectionism**: the school of thought that propounds the use of **connectionist networks** or **neural networks** as computational models of the mind.

**Connectionist networks**: a computational modelling technique, based on an analogy to neurons, which uses elementary units or nodes that are connected together; each network has various structures or layers (e.g., input; intermediate or hidden; output); also called neural networks.

**Contrast sensitivity function**: an assessment of an individual's ability to detect targets of various spatial frequencies.

**Control knowledge**: knowledge about the subgoal structure of a problem, knowledge about how a problem is to be solved.

**Convergence**: one of the **binocular cues**, based on the inward focus of the eyes with a close object.

**Covert attention**: attention to an object or sound in the absence of overt movements of the relevant receptors (e.g., looking at an object out of the corner of one's eye).

**Creativity**: the product of a thinking process that is, in some sense, novel and productive, in that it goes beyond what has been previously known by an individual or group of people.

**Cue-dependent forgetting**: forgetting in which the information is stored in memory but cannot be retrieved because of inadequate retrieval cues; see **trace-dependent forgetting**.

**Darwinian algorithms**: rules proposed to be used in reasoning about social contract situations that enable one to maximise one's goals, and are considered to have adaptive significance.

**Data-driven processes**: processes triggered directly by external stimuli in a bottom-up way; see **conceptually driven processes**.

**Declarative knowledge**: it is concerned with knowing that something is the case (e.g., that London is the capital of England). It covers **episodic memory** and **semantic memory**; see **procedural knowledge**.

**Deduction**: deduction or deductive reasoning concerns the reasoning to a conclusion from some set of premises, where that conclusion necessarily follows from the assumption that the premises are true (see **induction**).

**Deep dysgraphia**: a condition in which there are semantic errors in spelling and non-words are incorrectly spelled.

**Deep dyslexia**: a condition in which reading of unfamiliar words is impaired, and there are semantic reading errors (e.g., reading "missile" as "rocket").

**Deep dysphasia**: a condition in which there is poor ability to repeat spoken non-words and there are semantic errors in repeating spoken words.

**Defining attributes**: **semantic features** of a concept that are necessary and sufficient to instances of the concept (see **characteristic attributes**).

**Demand characteristics**: those aspects of the experimental situation leading participants to draw inferences about the behaviour expected of them.

**Denial of the antecedent**: an invalid argument form in conditional reasoning where one concludes *not-Q*, given the true statements *If P then Q* and *not-P*.

**Differential motion parallax**: the perception that objects nearer than the point of fixation

are moving in the opposite direction to those beyond the point of fixation.

**Directed retrospection**: a method of studying writing in which writers are asked to categorise their immediately preceding thoughts while writing.

**Discourse**: connected text or speech.

**Divided attention**: a situation in which two tasks are performed at the same time.

**Domain-specific knowledge**: a relatively self-contained collection of knowledge about a particular topic; e.g., knowledge of car engines or of the solar system would be distinct domains of knowledge.

**Domain-specific strategy**: a problem-solving method that can be used in many different **domains** of knowledge.

**Double dissociation**: the finding that some individuals (often brain-damaged) do well on task A and poorly on task B, whereas others show the opposite pattern.

**Dual-space search**: the theoretical proposal that in scientific discovery there are two distinct **problem spaces**, one that is **searched** for hypotheses and one that is **searched** for experiments.

**Dysarthria**: a condition caused by brain damage in which the patient has a severe motor speech impairment; see **anarthria**.

**Dysexecutive syndrome**: a condition in which damage to the frontal lobes causes impairments to the **central executive** component of **working memory**.

**Ecological approach**: perspective in vision research proposed by Gibson, that the environment supplies many factors that simplify the processing problems faced by humans.

**Ecological validity**: the extent to which the findings of laboratory studies are applicable to everyday settings.

**Elaborative inferences**: inferences that add details to a text that is being read.

**Elaborative rehearsal**: processing that involves a deeper or more semantic analysis of the learning material; see **maintenance rehearsal**.

**Empiricism**: philosophical perspective which maintains that most knowledge is acquired through experience in the world (see Locke, Hume, and Berkeley); the "nurture" part of the nature versus nurture debate, often contrasted with **nativism**.

**Encoding specificity principle**: the notion that retrieval depends on the overlap between the information available at retrieval and the information within the memory trace.

**Enhanced cognitive interview**: an approach to improving the memory of eyewitnesses based on developing the **basic cognitive interview** to improve its effectiveness.

**Episodic memory**: a form of long-term memory concerned with personal experiences or episodes that happened in a given place at a specific time; see **semantic memory**.

**Event-based prospective memory**: remembering to perform some action when the circumstances are suitable; see **time-based prospective memory**.

**Exemplar**: an instance (or best example) of a category.

**Experimental cognitive psychology**: it involves carrying out traditional experiments on normal human participants, generally under laboratory conditions.

**Expertise**: the specific knowledge that an expert has about a particular domain; e.g., that an engineer might have about bridges, or a software engineer might have about programming (see **domain**).

**Explicit memory**: memory that involves conscious recollection; see **implicit memory**.

**Explicit memory bias**: the tendency to retrieve relatively more negative or unpleasant information than positive or neutral information on a test of **explicit memory**.

**Extension**: the set of entities in the world that are the members of a category (e.g., all the bachelors in the world making up the bachelor category; see **intension**).

**External validity**: the validity of research findings outside the situation in which they were obtained; see **internal validity**.

**Extinction**: a disorder of visual attention in which a stimulus presented to the side opposite the brain damage is not detected when another stimulus is presented at the same time.

**Extrinsic context**: context that does not affect the meaning of to-be-remembered information; see **intrinsic context**.

**Face inversion effect**: the finding that faces that are inverted (turned upside down) are harder to recognise than faces viewed in their normal orientation.

**Falsification**: the logically correct means by which science is meant to work, proposed by Popper (1968), whereby one proposes hypotheses from a theory and attempts to falsify them by experimental tests (see **confirmation**).

**Family resemblance**: Wittgenstein's term for the type of similarity that seems to hold between members of a category, later used to derive family resemblance scores by Rosch and Mervis (1975).

**Feed-forward network**: a type of connectionist model that has a large number of connected units organised in layers, which is usually trained with a learning rule (like **back-propagation of errors**).

**Figure–ground segregation**: the perceptual organisation of the visual field into a figure (object of central interest) and a ground (less important background).

**Flashbulb memories**: vivid and detailed memories of dramatic events.

**Focus of expansion**: this is the point towards which someone who is in motion is moving; it is the only part of the visual field that does not appear to move.

**Focused attention**: a situation in which individuals try to attend to only one source of stimulation while ignoring other stimuli.

**Folk theory**: a mental representation of a commonsense explanation of some aspect of the world (e.g., about how objects fall, bounce, or break) which may be at variance with what actually occurs; also sometimes called **mental models** or **naive theories**.

**Frame**: an organised packet of information about the world, events, or people, stored in long-term memory (also called a **schema**).

**Framing**: the influence of irrelevant aspects of a situation on decision making.

**Functional fixedness**: the **Gestalt School**'s term for the inflexible use of the usual funcion of an object in problem solving.

**Fuzzy categories**: categories that do not have clear boundaries, derived from Zadeh's fuzzy logic.

**Gestalt School**: a largely German school of perception and thinking researchers from the early 20th century, who proposed theories that stressed the active, productive nature of cognition rather than its passive associationist nature.

**Heuristic method**: a rule-of-thumb technique for solving a problem, which does not guarantee the solution of the problem but is highly likely to solve the problem.

**Hybrid model**: a computational model that combines standard symbolic modelling techniques (e.g., **production systems**) with a connectionist modelling technique (like **feed-forward networks**).

**Iconic store**: a sensory store in which visual information is held very briefly.

**Ill defined problem**: a problem in which the definition of the problem statement is ill specified; it may not be clear what constitutes the initial state, goal state, and methods to be used to solve the problem (see also **well defined problem**).

**Impasse**: block or obstacle in achieving a goal in a problem-solving episode.

**Implicit learning**: learning complex information without the ability to provide conscious recollection of what has been learned.

**Implicit memory**: memory that does not depend on conscious recollection; see **explicit memory**.

**Implicit memory bias**: the tendency to show relatively better performance for negative than for neutral information on a test of **implicit memory**.

**Impossibilistic creativity**: a type of creative thinking, proposed by Boden (1991), which produces radically new ideas based on changing the fundamental conventions/rules in a particular **domain** of knowledge.

**Improbabilistic creativity**: a type of creative thinking, proposed by Boden (1991), which produces unlikely or low-probability ideas based on novel combinations of familiar ideas.

**Incubation**: a phase in creative thinking, proposed by Wallas (1926), in which a problem is left to one side, during which time some unconscious processing occurs that eventually yields an **insight**.

**Induction**: the name given to the process, which may be formalised logically or statistically, by which generalisations are formed from examples or sample phenomena (see **deduction**).

**Infantile amnesia**: the inability of adults to recall autobiographical memories from early childhood.

**Innate**: generally, an ability that is strongly genetically determined.

**Inner scribe**: according to Logie, the part of the **visuo-spatial sketchpad** which deals with spatial and movement information.

**Insight**: the experience of suddenly realising how to solve a problem or of understanding the structure of a problem (see **incubation**).

**Intension**: the definition of a concept usually characterised as a set of necessary and sufficient semantic features (see **extension**).

**Interblobs**: areas in the primary visual cortex forming part of the P pathway and responding strongly to contrast, location, and orientation; see **blobs**.

**Internal validity**: the validity of research findings within the research situation itself; see **external validity**.

**Interpretive bias**: the tendency to interpret ambiguous stimuli and situations in a threatening way.

**Intrinsic context**: context that influences the meaning of to-be-remembered information.

**Introspection**: examination or observation of one's own mental processes.

**Isomorphic**: a one-to-one correspondence between two entities or systems (e.g., our left and right hands are isomorphic to one another, one can be placed directly on top of the other to form a one-to-one correspondence).

**Isomorphism**: the assumption that the organisation of the mind closely matches that of the physical brain.

**Jargon aphasia**: a brain-damaged condition in which speech is reasonably correct grammatically, but there are great problems in finding the right words.

**Kinetic depth effect**: the accurate perception of three-dimensional structure when a two-dimensional image of an object is rotated.

**Knowledge-poor problem**: a problem that can be solved without the use of much prior knowledge, most of the information required is given in the problem statement (see also **knowledge-rich problem**).

**Knowledge-rich problem**: a problem that can only be solved through the use of considerable amounts of prior knowledge, e.g., problems requiring expertise in an area (see also **knowledge-poor problem**).

**Knowledge state**: a mental representation of a possible state-of-affairs either real or imagined.

**Korsakoff's syndrome**: amnesia (impaired long-term memory) caused by chronic alcoholism.

**Landmarks**: key public or personal events that can be used to date less significant political or personal events.

**Lexical access**: entering the **lexicon** with its store of detailed information about words.

**Lexical decision task**: a task in which participants have to decide as rapidly as possible whether a letter string forms a word.

**Lexicalisation**: the process of translating the meaning of a word into its sound representation during speech production.

**Lexicon**: a store of detailed information about words, including orthographic, phonological, semantic, and syntactic knowledge.

**Logical operator**: the name given to the basic functions in a logical system, usually including *and, or, not, if . . . then* and *if and only if.*

**Loop-avoidance strategy**: a problem-solving strategy that avoids repeating a step already taken in a problem, used to avoid repeating a sequence of solution steps over and over again.

**Loss aversion**: the tendency to be more sensitive to potential losses than to potential gains.

**Magneto-encephalography (MEG)**: a non-invasive brain-scanning technique based on recording the magnetic fields generated by brain activity.

**Maintenance rehearsal**: processing that involves simply repeating analyses which have already been carried out.

**Means–ends analysis**: a **heuristic method** for solving problems based on noting the difference between a current and goal state, and creating a subgoal to overcome this difference.

**Mental logic**: the proposal that people use some form of proof-derivation system when they reason.

**Mental model:** a mental representation of a state-of-affairs in the world that may be descriptive (e.g., some characterisation of a set of individuals) or an explanation for a particular phenomenon (see also **naive theory**).

**Mere exposure effect**: an effect in which stimuli that have been presented before (even when not perceived consciously) are preferred to new stimuli.

**Meta-analyses**: statistical analyses based on data from numerous studies on a given issue.

**Metacognition**: a person's assessment of their own thought processes, e.g., their feeling-of-knowing how close they are to the solution of a problem.

**Method of converging operations**: an approach to psychology based on using a variety of methods to study any given issue.

**Method of loci**: a mnemonic technique in which the to-be-remembered items are associated with locations (e.g., places along a walk).

**Microspectrophotometry**: a technique that allows measurement of the amount of light absorbed at various wavelengths by individual cone receptors.

**Modal logic**: a type of logic that involves statements that take into account necessity and sufficiency (e.g., statements involving *can* and *must*).

**Modularity**: the assumption that the cognitive system consists of several fairly independent processors or modules.

**Modus ponens**: a valid argument form in conditional reasoning where one concludes *Q*, given the true statements *If P then Q* and *P.*

**Modus tollens**: a valid argument form in conditional reasoning where one concludes *not-P*, given the true statements *If P then Q* and *not-Q.*

**Monocular cues**: cues to depth that can be used with one eye, but can also be used with both eyes.

**Mood-state-dependent memory**: the finding that memory is better when the mood state at retrieval is the same as that at learning than when the two mood states differ.

**Naive theory**: a mental representation of a commonsense explanation of some aspect of the world (e.g., about how objects fall, bounce, or break) which may be at variance with what actually occurs; also called **mental models** or **folk theories**.

**Naming task**: a task in which visually presented words have to be pronounced aloud as rapidly as possible.

**Nativist**: philosophical perspective that maintains that most knowledge is innate and given to the organism at birth (see Kant, 1787); the "nature" part of the nature versus nurture debate, often contrasted with empiricism.

**Negative afterimage**: the illusory perception of the complementary colour to the one that has just been fixated for several seconds; green is the complementary colour to red, and blue to yellow.

**Negative priming**: inhibited processing of a target stimulus when that stimulus was a distractor on the previous trial.

**Neglect**: a disorder of visual attention in which stimuli or parts of stimuli presented to the side opposite the brain damage are undetected and not responded to; the condition resembles **extinction**, but is more severe.

**Normative theory**: a theory about how a particular task is achieved, which is not necessarily a psychological theory; that is, it is not necessarily an account of what people actually do, but rather an abstract analysis of the task.

**Omission bias**: the tendency to prefer inaction over action when engaged in decision making.

**Operators**: the mental representation of "actions in the mind" that can be carried out in a given cognitive act, usually in **searching** a **problem space**.

**Optic aphasia**: a condition in which there is a severe impairment in the ability to name visually presented objects even though their use can be mimed and they can be named when handled.

**Optic array**: the structured pattern of light falling on the retina.

**Optic ataxia**: a condition in which there are problems with making visually guided limb movements.

**Optic flow pattern**: the structured pattern of light intensity created when there is movement of the observer and/or aspects of the environment.

**Optical trajectory**: the flight path of an object (e.g., ball) as seen by an observer.

**Orthography**: information about the spellings of words.

**Paradigm**: according to Kuhn, a general theoretical orientation that is agreed upon by most scientists working in a given discipline.

**Parietal cortex**: part of the parietal lobe bordering the frontal lobe, concerned with integrating and interpreting sensory information from different modalities.

**Parsing**: an analysis of the syntactical or grammatical structure of sentences.

**Pattern recognition**: identification or classification of visually presented two- and three-dimensional objects.

**Perceived causality**: the impression that one object has caused movement of a second object.

**Perceptual implicit tests**: memory tests on which the stimuli that are presented are degraded versions of the stimuli presented at study, and on which conscious recollection is not required; see **conceptual implicit tests**.

**Perfect pitch**: the ability to name and sing specified pitches without being given any reference pitch.

**Phonemes**: basic speech sounds conveying meaning.

**Phonemic restoration effect**: the finding that listeners are unaware that a phoneme has been deleted from an auditorily presented sentence.

**Phonological dysgraphia**: a condition in which familiar words can be spelled reasonably well but non-words cannot.

**Phonological dyslexia**: a condition in which familiar words can be read but there is impaired ability to read unfamiliar words and non-words; see **surface dyslexia**.

**Phonological loop**: a component of **working memory**, in which speech-based information is held and subvocal articulation occurs.

**Phonology**: information about the sounds of words and parts of words.

**Pragmatics**: the study of the ways in which language is used, including a consideration of its intended meaning.

**Pragmatic schema**: rules or **schemata** that are proposed to be used in reasoning about situations involving permissions or obligations.

**Predicate calculus**: a type of logic in which predicates are used, i.e. statements consisting of a predicate relation and a number of arguments [e.g., red(x), put-on(book table)].

**Prefrontal cortex**: generally used to indicate the entire frontal lobes of the brain, concerned with the make-up of the individual's personality, resulting from the input of many cortical and subcortical sources, and specialisms in handling information needed to guide action.

**Problem-solving set**: the **Gestalt School**'s term for the inflexible use of a particular problem-solving technique.

**Problem space**: an abstract description of all the possible states-of-affairs that can occur in a problem situation.

**Procedural knowledge**: it is concerned with knowing how, and includes the ability to perform skilled actions; see **declarative knowledge**.

**Production systems**: they consist of numerous IF. . . THEN rules and a working memory containing information.

**Productive thinking**: thinking behaviour that is based on prior knowledge which has been adapted or modified in some way to be applicable to a problem situation (see **reproductive thinking**).

**Progressive deepening**: a strategy used in chess for progressively looking farther and farther ahead in a set of moves, in determining the best move to take.

**Proportional analogies**: **analogies** often used in intelligence tests presented in the proportional form, A:B::C:D, described as "A is to B as C is to D" (e.g., Red is to Stop as Green is to Go).

**Propositional calculus**: a logic in which propositions are manipulated using a small set of logical operators (e.g., *if . . . then*).

**Propositional representation**: language-like mental **representation** that characterises the conceptual content of ideas (see **analogical representation**).

**Prosodic cues**: features of spoken language, such as stress and intonation.

**Prosopagnosia**: a condition caused by brain damage in which the patient cannot recognise familiar faces but can recognise familiar objects.

**Prospective memory**: remembering to carry out intended actions.

**Protocol analysis**: a method of studying cognitive processes in which tape recordings are made of a person's verbalisations, called the protocol, while carrying out some cognitive task (e.g., problem solving, writing).

**Psychological refractory period**: the slowing of response to the second of two stimuli when they are presented close together in time.

**Pure word deafness**: a condition in which there is severely impaired speech perception combined with good speech production, reading, writing, and perception of non-speech sounds.

**Rationalisation**: in Bartlett's theory, the tendency in recall of stories to produce errors that conform to the cultural expectations of the rememberer.

**Reading span**: the largest number of sentences read for comprehension from which an individual can recall all the final words more than 50% of the time.

**Recency effect**: the finding that only recall of the last few items in a list is severely impaired by introducing a short task between list presentation and recall.

**Reminiscence bump**: the tendency of older people to recall a disproportionate number of autobiographical memories from the years of adolescence and early adulthood.

**Repetition-priming effect**: the finding that stimulus processing is faster and easier on the second and successive presentations.

**Representation**: any notation or sign or set of symbols that "re-presents" something to us, usually in the absence of that thing (see **propositional** and **analogical representation**).

**Representativeness heuristic**: the assumption that representative or typical members of a category are encountered most frequently.

**Repression**: motivated forgetting of traumatic or other threatening events.

**Reproductive thinking**: thinking behaviour that is based on the rote-like use of prior knowledge (see **productive thinking**).

**Resonance**: the process of automatic pick-up of visual information from the environment in Gibson's theory.

**Resource limitations**: limitations on cognitive processing usually caused by the limited size of working memory.

**Restructuring**: the **Gestalt School**'s proposed process by which perceptual scenes or problem situations were changed to produce some new interpretation of the perceptual or problem situation (see **insight**).

**Retrograde amnesia**: impaired memory for events occurring before the onset of amnesia.

**Running spectral displays**: visual displays of changes over time in the frequencies contained within the speech signal.

**Savings method**: a measure of forgetting introduced by Ebbinghaus, in which the number of trials for re-learning is compared against the number for original learning.

**Schema**: an organised packet of information about the world, events, or people, stored in long-term memory.

**Scripts**: a type of schema for representing typical events (e.g., going to a restaurant) proposed by Schank and Abelson (1977).

**Search**: the systematic mental exploration of a **problem space** during problem solving.

**Self-reference effect**: the finding that memory is especially good after self-reference judgements.

**Semantic decomposition**: the breaking down of a concept into its component **semantic features** or attributes.

**Semantic features**: the fundamental meaning units that constitute the basis of the meaning of all concepts (also called semantic markers, semantic primitives, and semantic attributes).

**Semantic memory**: a form of long-term memory consisting of general knowledge about the world, language, and so on; see **episodic memory**.

**Semantic networks**: they consist of concepts linked to other concepts by means of various kinds of relations (e.g., is-similar-to).

**Semantic priming effect**: the finding that word identification is facilitated when there is priming by a semantically related word.

**Simultanagnosia**: a brain-damaged condition in which only one object can be seen at a time.

**Single-unit recording**: an invasive technique permitting the study of activity in single neurons.

**Sinusoidal gratings**: patterns of alternating dark and light bars in which there are gradual intensity changes between bars.

**Situated action**: the proposal that a lot of cognition about how to act is held in the environment rather than in the head (akin to Gibson's ecological approach in vision research).

**Size constancy**: objects are perceived to have a given size regardless of the size of the retinal image.

**Source amnesia**: retention of a fact combined with an inability to remember where or how the fact was learned.

**Spatial connectives**: **logical operators** dealing with spatial relations (like *on* or *above*).

**Spectrograph**: an instrument that is used to produce visible records of the sound frequencies in speech.

**Stereopsis**: one of the binocular cues, based on the disparity in the retinal images of the two eyes.

**Story grammar**: a set of rules permitting the structure of any story to be generated.

**Stroop effect**: the finding that naming of the colours in which words are printed is slower when the words are conflicting colour-words (e.g., the word RED printed in green).

**Subgoal**: a subsidary goal that must be satistfied on the way to reaching the main goal of a problem.

**Subordinate level**: a low, if not the lowest, level of abstraction in a **conceptual hierarchy**, usually corresponding to a very specific category, like kitchen chairs (see **basic level** and **subordinate level**).

**Sunk-cost effect**: expending additional resources to justify some previous commitment (i.e., throwing good money after bad).

**Superordinate level**: a high level of abstraction in a **conceptual hierarchy**, usually corresponding to a very general category, like animals (see **basic level** and **superordinate level**).

**Surface dysgraphia**: a condition in which there is poor spelling of irregular words and non-words, but not of regular words.

**Surface dyslexia**: a condition in which regular words can be read but there is impaired ability to read irregular words; see **phonological dyslexia**.

**Syllogism**: a logical argument consisting of two premises and a conclusion, usually involving statements of the "all X are Y" or "some X are Z" form; syllogisms formed the basis for one of the first logical systems attributed to Aristotle.

**Symbols**: a sign that stands for something usually in the absence of that thing.

**Synaesthesia**: the tendency for one sense modality to evoke another.

**Syndromes**: labels used to categorise brain-damaged and other patients on the basis of co-occurring symptoms.

**Time-based prospective memory**: remembering to carry out a future action at the right time; see **event-based prospective memory**.

**Top-down processing**: stimulus processing that is affected by factors such as the individual's past experience and expectations.

**Trace-dependent forgetting**: forgetting that occurs because the information contained in memory traces has been lost; see **cue-dependent forgetting**.

**Trait anxiety**: a personality dimension concerned with individual differences in susceptibility to anxiety.

**Truth tables**: logical method for laying out the truth conditions of some logical statement, whereby all the logical possibilities are elaborated and shown.

**Typicality gradient**: the ordering of the members of a category in terms of their typicality ratings (e.g., that "robin" is a more typical instance of "bird" than "canary", and that "canary" is, in turn, more typical than "penguin").

**Unilateral visual neglect**: a condition in brain-damaged patients in which half of the visual field is neglected or ignored.

**Universal weak method**: a problem-solving technique that is **domain-independent**, which is "universal" because it can be applied in any domain and "weak" because it can be very inefficient.

**Utility**: subjective value of a given outcome.

**Visual agnosia**: a condition in which there are great problems in recognising objects presented visually even though visual information reaches the visual cortex.

**Visual cache**: according to Logie, the part of the **visuo-spatial sketchpad** which stores information about visual form and colour.

**Visuo-spatial sketchpad**: a component of **working memory** which is involved in visual and spatial processing of information.

**Weapon-focus effect**: the finding that eyewitnesses pay so much attention to some crucial aspect of the situation (e.g., the weapon) that they tend to ignore other details.

**Well defined problem**: a problem that is fully defined in its problem statement, in that the nature of its initial state, goal state, and methods to be used to solve it are clearly laid out (see also **ill defined problem**).

**Within-category similarity**: the similarity of instances within a category to one another (see **between-category similarity**).

**Word-fragment completion**: a task on which participants try to think of a word based on a few letters (e.g., f _ ag _ _ _ t); a **perceptual implicit test**.

**Word-length effect**: the finding that word span is greater for short words than for long words.

**Word meaning deafness**: a condition in which there is a selective impairment of the ability to understand spoken (but not written) language.

**Word-stem completion**: a task on which participants try to think of a word based on its first few letters (e.g., fra _ _ _ _ ); a **perceptual implicit test**.

**Word superiority effect**: a target letter is more readily detected in a letter string when the string forms a word than when it does not.

**Working memory**: according to Baddeley, a system consisting of three components: **central executive**, **phonological loop**, and **visuo-spatial sketchpad**; also used more generally to refer to a general-purpose limited-capacity system by other theorists (e.g., Just & Carpenter).

# References

Abbot, V., Black, J.B., & Smith, E.E. (1984). The representation of scripts in memory. *Journal of Memory & Language, 24,* 179–199.

Abelson, R.P. (1981). Psychological status of the script concept. *American Psychologist, 36,* 715–729.

Abramov, I., & Gordon, J. (1994). Colour appearance: On seeing red, or yellow, or green, or blue. *Annual Review of Psychology, 45,* 451–485.

Adams, J.L. (1979). *Conceptual blockbusting: A guide to better ideas (2nd Edn).* New York: W.W. Norton.

Adamson, R.E., & Taylor, D.W. (1954). Functional fixedness as related to elapsed time and set. *Journal of Experimental Psychology, 47,* 221–226.

Adelson, B. (1981). Problem solving and the development of abstract categories in programming languages. *Memory & Cognition, 9,* 422–433.

Afriat, S.N. (1982). *The ring of linked rings.* London: Duckworth.

Aggleton, J.P., & Brown, M.W. (1999). Episodic memory, amnesia, and the hippocampal–anterior thalamic axis. *Behavioral & Brain Sciences, 22,* 425–489.

Aglioti, S., Goodale, M.A., & DeSouza, J.F.X. (1995). Size-contrast illusions deceive the eye but not the hand. *Current Biology, 5,* 679–685.

Ahn, W.-K., Brewer, W., & Mooney, R.J. (1992). Schema acquisition from a single example. *Journal of Experimental Psychology: Learning, Memory, & Cognition, 18,* 391–412.

Alba, J.W., & Hasher, L. (1983). Is memory schematic? *Psychological Bulletin, 93,* 203–231.

Alexander, P.A., Schallert, D.L., & Hare, U.C. (1991). Coming to terms: How researchers in learning and literacy talk about knowledge. *Review of Educational Research, 61,* 315–343.

Allbritton, D.W., McKoon, G., & Ratcliff, R. (1996). Reliability of prosodic cues for resolving syntactic ambiguity. *Journal of Experimental Psychology: Learning, Memory, & Cognition, 22,* 714–735.

Allen, B.P., & Lindsay, D.S. (1998). Amalgamations of memories: Intrusion of information from one event into reports of another. *Applied Cognitive Psychology, 12,* 277–285.

Allport, D.A. (1989). Visual attention. In M.I. Posner (Ed.), *Foundations of cognitive science.* Cambridge, MA: MIT Press.

Allport, D.A. (1993). Attention and control: Have we been asking the wrong questions? A critical review of twenty-five years. In D.E. Meyer & S.M. Kornblum (Eds.), *Attention and performance, Vol. XIV.* London: MIT Press.

Allport, D.A., Antonis, B., & Reynolds, P. (1972). On the division of attention: A disproof of the single channel hypothesis. *Quarterly Journal of Experimental Psychology, 24,* 225–235.

Almor, A., & Sloman, S.A. (1996). Is deontic reasoning special? *Psychological Review, 103,* 374–380.

Altmann, G.T.M. (1997). *The ascent of Babel: An exploration of language, mind, and understanding*. Oxford: Oxford University Press.

Altmann, G.T.M., & Steedman, M.J. (1988). Interaction with context during human sentence processing. *Cognition, 30*, 191–238.

American Psychological Association (1995). *Can a memory be forgotten and then remembered?* Washington, DC: Office for Public Affairs.

Andersen, R.A., Snyder, L.H., Bradley, D.C., & Xing, J. (1997). Multimodal representation of space in the posterior parietal cortex and its use in planning movements. *Annual Review of Neuroscience, 20*, 303–330.

Anderson, J.R. (1976). *Language, memory & thought*. Hillsdale, NJ: Lawrence Erlbaum Associates Inc.

Anderson, J.R. (1978). Arguments concerning representations from mental imagery. *Psychological Review, 85*, 249–277.

Anderson, J.R. (1982). Acquisition of cognitive skill. *Psychological Review, 89*, 396–406.

Anderson, J.R. (1983). *The architecture of cognition*. Harvard: Harvard University Press.

Anderson, J.R. (1987a). Skill acquisition: Compilation of weak-method problem solutions. *Psychological Review, 94*, 192–210.

Anderson, J.R. (1987b). Methodologies for studying human knowledge. *Behavioral & Brain Sciences, 10*, 467–505.

Anderson, J.R. (1990). *The adaptative character of thought*. Hillsdale, NJ: Lawrence Erlbaum Associates Inc.

Anderson, J.R. (1991). The adaptive nature of human categorisation. *Psychological Review, 98*, 409–429.

Anderson, J.R. (1993). *Rules of the mind*. Hillsdale, NJ: Lawrence Erlbaum Associates Inc.

Anderson, J.R. (1996). ACT: A simple theory of complex cognition. *American Psychologist, 51*, 355–365.

Anderson, J.R., Bothell, D., Lebiere, C., & Matessa, M. (1998). An integrated theory of list memory. *Journal of Memory & Language, 38*, 341–380.

Anderson, J.R., Boyle, C.F., & Reiser, B.J. (1985). Intelligent tutoring systems. *Science, 228*, 456–462.

Anderson, J.R., Greeno, J.G., Kline, P.J., & Neves, D.M. (1981). Acquisition of problem solving skill. In J.R. Anderson (Ed.), *Cognitive skills and their acquisition*. Hillsdale, NJ: Lawrence Erlbaum Associates Inc.

Anderson, J.R., & Lebiere, C. (1998). *Atomic components of thought*. Hillsdale, NJ: Lawrence Erlbaum Associates Inc.

Anderson, J.R., & Matessa, M. (1997). A production system theory of serial memory. *Psychological Review, 104*, 728–748.

Anderson, J.R., & Reder, L.M. (1999). The fan effect: New results and new theories. *Journal of Experimental Psychology: General, 128*, 186–197.

Anderson, J.R., & Reiser, B.J. (1985). The LISP tutor. *Byte, 10*, 159–175.

Anderson, R.C., & Ortony, A. (1975). On putting apples in bottles: A problem of polysemy. *Cognitive Psychology, 7*, 167–180.

Anderson, R.C., & Pichert, J.W. (1978). Recall of previously unrecallable information following a shift in perspective. *Journal of Verbal Learning & Verbal Behavior, 17*, 1–12.

Anderson, S.A., & Conway, M.A. (1993). Investigating the structure of autobiographical memories. *Journal of Experimental Psychology: Learning, Memory, & Cognition, 19*, 1178–1196.

Anderson, S.J., Holliday, I.E., Singh, K.D., & Harding, G.F.A. (1996). Localization and functional analysis of human cortical area V5 using magneto-encephalography. *Proceedings of the Royal Society London B, 263*, 423–431.

Andrews, A.D. (1993). Review of "Deduction". *Behavioral & Brain Sciences, 16*, 334.

Anzai, Y., & Simon, H.A. (1979). The theory of learning by doing. *Psychological Review, 86*, 124–180.

Armstrong, S.L., Gleitman, L.R., & Gleitman, H. (1983). What some concepts might not be. *Cognition, 13*, 263–308.

Ashby, F.G., Prinzmetal, W., Ivry, R., & Maddox, W.T. (1996). A formal theory of feature binding in object perception. *Psychological Review, 103*, 165–192.

Ashley, W.R., Harper, R.S., & Runyon, D.L. (1951). The perceived size of coins in normal and hypnotically induced economic states. *American Journal of Psychology*, *64*, 564–572.

Atkinson, R.C., & Raugh, M.R. (1975). An application of the mnemonic keyword method to the acquisition of a Russian vocabulary. *Journal of Experimental Psychology: Human Learning & Memory*, *104*, 126–133.

Atkinson, R.C., & Shiffrin, R.M. (1968). Human memory: A proposed system and its control processes. In K.W. Spence & J.T. Spence (Eds.), *The psychology of learning and motivation (Vol. 2)*. London: Academic Press.

Atkinson, R.C., & Shiffrin, R.M. (1971). The control of short-term memory. *Scientific American*, *225*, 82–90.

Atkinson, R.L., Atkinson, R.C., Smith, E.E., & Bem, D.J. (1993). *Introduction to psychology (11th Edn)*. New York: Harcourt Brace.

Atran, S. (1998). Folk biology and the anthropology of science: Cognitive universals and cognitive particulars. *Behavioral & Brain Sciences*, *21*, 547–569.

Atran, S., Medin, D.L., Ross, N., Lynch, E., Coley, J., Ek, E.U., & Vapnarsky, V. (1999). Folkecology and commons management in the Maya Lowlands. *Proceedings of the National Academy of Sciences of the United States of America*, *96*, 7598–7603.

Atwood, M.E., Masson, M.E., & Polson, P.G. (1980). Further exploration with a process model for water jug problems. *Memory & Cognition*, *8*, 182–192.

Atwood, M.E., & Polson, P.G. (1976). A process model for water jug problems. *Cognitive Psychology*, *8*, 191–216.

Auerbach, S.H., Allard, T., Naeser, M., Alexander, M.P., & Albert, M.L. (1982). Pure word deafness: An analysis of a case with bilateral lesions and a defect at the prephonemic level. *Brain*, *105*, 271–300.

Austin, J.L. (1976). *How to do things with words (2nd Edn)*. Oxford: Oxford University Press.

Ayers, M.S., & Reder, L.M. (1998). A theoretical review of the misinformation effect: Predictions from an activation-based memory model. *Psychonomic Bulletin & Review*, *5*, 1–21.

Baars, B.J. (1997). Consciousness versus attention, perception, and working memory. *Consciousness and Cognition*, *6*, 363–371.

Baars, B.J., Motley, M.T., & MacKay, D.G. (1975). Output editing for lexical status from artificially elicited slips of the tongue. *Journal of Verbal Learning & Verbal Behavior*, *14*, 382–391.

Bach, K. (1993). Getting down to cases. *Behavioral & Brain Sciences*, *16*, 334–335.

Baddeley, A.D. (1982). Domains of recollection. *Psychological Review*, *89*, 708–729.

Baddeley, A.D. (1984). Neuropsychological evidence and the semantic/episodic distinction. *Behavioral & Brain Sciences*, *7*, 238–239.

Baddeley, A.D. (1986). *Working memory*. Oxford: Clarendon Press.

Baddeley, A.D. (1990). *Human memory: Theory and practice*. Hove, UK: Psychology Press.

Baddeley, A.D. (1992). Working memory. *Science*, *255*, 556–559.

Baddeley, A.D. (1996). Exploring the central executive. *Quarterly Journal of Experimental Psychology*, *49A*, 5–28.

Baddeley, A.D. (1997). *Human memory: Theory and practice (revised edition)*. Hove, UK: Psychology Press.

Baddeley, A.D., Emslie, H., Kolodny, J., & Duncan, J. (1998). Random generation and the executive control of working memory. *Quarterly Journal of Experimental Psychology*, *51A*, 819–852.

Baddeley, A.D., Gathercole, S., & Papagno, C. (1998). The phonological loop as a language learning device. *Psychological Review*, *105*, 158–173.

Baddeley, A.D., Grant, S., Wight, E., & Thomson, N. (1975). Imagery and visual working memory. In P.M.A. Rabbitt & S. Dornic (Eds.), *Attention & performance, Vol. V.* London: Academic Press.

Baddeley, A.D., & Hitch, G.J. (1974). Working memory. In G.H. Bower (Ed.), *The psychology of learning and motivation (Vol. 8)*. London: Academic Press.

Baddeley, A.D., & Lewis, V.J. (1981). Inner active processes in reading: The inner voice, the inner ear and the inner eye. In A.M. Lesgold & C.A.

Perfetti (Eds.), *Interactive processes in reading.* Hillsdale, NJ: Lawrence Erlbaum Associates Inc.

Baddeley, A.D., & Lieberman, K. (1980). Spatial working memory. In R.S. Nickerson (Ed.), *Attention & performance, Vol. VIII.* Hillsdale, NJ: Lawrence Erlbaum Associates Inc.

Baddeley, A.D., & Longman, D.J.A. (1978). The influence of length and frequency of training sessions on the rate of learning to type. *Ergonomics, 21,* 627–635.

Baddeley, A.D., Thomson, N., & Buchanan, M. (1975). Word length and the structure of short-term memory. *Journal of Verbal Learning & Verbal Behavior, 14,* 575–589.

Baddeley, A.D., & Warrington, E.K. (1970). Amnesia and the distinction between long- and short-term memory. *Journal of Verbal Learning & Verbal Behavior, 9,* 176–189.

Baddeley, A.D., & Wilson, B. (1985). Phonological coding and short-term memory in patients without speech. *Journal of Memory & Language, 24,* 490–502.

Badecker, W., Miozzo, M., & Zanuttini, R. (1995). The two-stage model of lexical retrieval: Evidence from a case of anomia with selective preservation of grammatical gender. *Cognition, 57,* 193–216.

Bahrick, H.P. (1970). Two-phase model for prompted recall. *Psychological Review, 77,* 215–222.

Baird, J.C., Wagner, M., & Fuld, K. (1990). A simple but powerful theory of the moon illusion. *Journal of Experimental Psychology: Human Perception and Performance, 16,* 675–677.

Ballard, D.H. (1986). Cortical connections and parallel processing. *Behavioral & Brain Sciences, 9*(1), 68–120.

Balota, D.A., Paul, S., & Spieler, D. (1999). Attentional control of lexical processing pathways during word recognition and reading. In S. Garrod & M.J. Pickering (Eds.), *Language processing.* Hove, UK: Psychology Press.

Banaji, M.R., & Crowder, R.G. (1989). The bankruptcy of everyday memory. *American Psychologist, 44,* 1185–1193.

Banich, M.T. (1997). *Neuropsychology: The neural bases of mental function.* New York: Houghton Mifflin.

Bannon, L.J. (1981). An investigation of image scanning: Theoretical claims and empirical evidence. *Unpublished PhD Dissertation, University of Western Ontario, Canada.*

Barclay, C.R. (1988). Truth and accuracy in autobiographical memory. In M.M. Gruneberg, P.E. Morris, & R.N. Sykes (Eds.), *Practical aspects of memory: Current research and issues: Vol. 1. Memory in everyday life.* Chichester, UK: John Wiley.

Baron, J. (1997). Biases in the quantitative measurement of values for public decisions. *Psychological Bulletin, 122,* 72–88.

Barry, C. (1994). Spelling routes (or roots or rutes). In G.D.A. Brown & N.C. Ellis (Eds.), *Handbook of spelling: Theory, process and intervention.* New York: Wiley.

Barsalou, L.W. (1982). Context-independent and context-dependent information in concepts. *Memory & Cognition, 10,* 82–93.

Barsalou, L.W. (1983). Ad hoc categories. *Memory & Cognition, 11,* 211–227.

Barsalou, L.W. (1985). Ideals, central tendency, and frequency of instantiation as determinants of graded structure in categories. *Journal of Experimental Psychology: Learning, Memory, & Cognition, 11,* 629–654.

Barsalou, L.W. (1987). The instability of graded structure: Implications for the nature of concepts. In U. Neisser (Ed.), *Concepts and conceptual development: Ecological and intellectual factors in categorisation.* Cambridge: Cambridge University Press.

Barsalou, L.W. (1988). The content and organization of autobiographical memories. In U. Neisser & E. Winograd (Eds.), *Remembering reconsidered: Ecological and traditional approaches to the study of memory.* New York: Cambridge University Press.

Barsalou, L.W. (1989). Intra-concept similarity and its implications for inter-concept similarity. In S. Vosniadou & A. Ortony (Eds.), *Similarity and analogical reasoning.* Cambridge: Cambridge University Press.

Bartlett, F.C. (1932). *Remembering*. Cambridge: Cambridge University Press.

Battig, W.F., & Montague, W.E. (1969). Category norms for verbal items in 56 categories. *Journal of Experimental Psychology Monograph, 80*, 1–46.

Bauer, R.M., & Verfaellie, M. (1988). Electrodermal recognition of familiar but not unfamiliar faces in prosopagnosia. *Brain & Cognition, 8*, 240–252.

Beach, C.M. (1990). The interpretation of prosodic patterns at points of syntactic structure ambiguity: Evidence for cue trading relations. *Journal of Memory & Language, 30*, 644–663.

Beasley, N.A. (1968). The extent of individual differences in the perception of causality. *Canadian Journal of Psychology, 22*, 399–407.

Beaton, A., Guest, J., & Ved, R. (1997). Semantic errors of naming, reading, writing, and drawing following left-hemisphere infarction. *Cognitive Neuropsychology, 14*, 459–478.

Beauvois, M.-F., & Dérouesné, J. (1979). Phonological alexia: Three dissociations. *Journal of Neurology, Neurosurgery & Psychiatry, 42*, 1115–1124.

Beauvois, M.-F., Dérouesné, J., & Bastard, V. (1980). *Auditory parallel to phonological alexia*. Paper presented at the Third European Conference of the International Neuropsychological Society, Chianciano, Italy, June.

Beck, A.T. (1976). *Cognitive therapy and the emotional disorders*. New York: International Universities Press.

Beck, A.T., & Clark, D.A. (1988). Anxiety and depression: An information processing perspective. *Anxiety Research, 1*, 23–36.

Beckers, G., & Zeki, S. (1995). The consequences of inactivating areas V1 and V5 on visual motion perception. *Brain, 118*, 49–60.

Behrmann, M., Moscovitch, M., & Winocur, G. (1994). Intact visual imagery and impaired visual perception in a patient with visual agnosia. *Journal of Experimental Psychology: Human Perception & Performance, 20*, 1068–1087.

Behrmann, M., Nelson, J., & Sekuler, E.B. (1998). Visual complexity in letter-by-letter reading: "Pure" alexia is not pure. *Neuropsychologia, 36*, 1115–1132.

Belli, R.F. (1998). The structure of autobiographical memory and the event history calendar: Potential improvements in the quality of retrospective reports in surveys. *Memory, 6*, 383–406.

Benson, D.F. (1993). Prefrontal abilities. *Behavioral Neurology, 6*, 75–81.

Bereiter, C., Burtis, P.J., & Scardamalia, M. (1988). Cognitive operations in constructing main points in written composition. *Journal of Memory & Language, 27*, 261–278.

Bereiter, C., & Scardamalia, M. (1987). *The psychology of written composition*. Hillsdale, NJ: Lawrence Erlbaum Associates Inc.

Berent, I., & Perfetti, C.A. (1995). A rose is a REEZ: The two-cycles model of phonology assembly in reading English. *Psychological Review, 102*, 146–184.

Berg, W.P., Wade, M.G., & Greer, N.L. (1994). Visual regulation of gait in bipedal locomotion: Revisiting Lee, Lishman, and Thomson (1982). *Journal of Experimental Psychology: Human Perception & Performance, 20*, 854–863.

Bergus, G.R., Chapman, G.B., Gjerde, C., & Elstein, A.S. (1995). Clinical reasoning about new symptoms despite preexisting disease: Sources of error and order effects. *Family Medicine, 27*, 314–320.

Berlin, B. (1972). Speculations on the growth of ethnobiological nomenclature. *Language in Society, 1*, 51–86.

Berlin, B., Breedlove, D.E., & Raven, P.H. (1973). General principles of classification and nomenclature in folk biology. *American Anthropologist, 75*, 214–242.

Berlin, B., & Kay, P. (1969). *Basic colour terms: Their universality and evolution*. Berkeley, CA: University of California Press.

Berndt, R.S., Mitchum, C.C., & Haendiges, A.N. (1996). Comprehension of reversible sentences in "aggrammatism": A meta-analysis. *Cognition, 58*, 289–308.

Berntsen, D. (1998). Voluntary and involuntary access to autobiographical memory. *Memory, 6*, 113–141.

Berry, D.C., & Broadbent, D.E. (1984). On the relationship between task performance and associated verbalisable knowledge. *Quarterly Journal of Experimental Psychology*, *36*A, 209–231.

Bertamini, M., Yang, T.L., & Proffitt, D.R. (1998). Relative size perception at a distance is best at eye level. *Perception and Psychophysics*, *60*, 673–682.

Beschin, N., Cocchini, G., Della Sala, S., & Logie, R.H. (1997). What the eyes perceive, the brain ignores: A case of pure unilateral representational neglect. *Cortex*, *33*, 3–26.

Biederman, I. (1987). Recognition-by-components: A theory of human image understanding. *Psychological Review*, *94*, 115–147.

Biederman, I. (1990). Higher-level vision. In D.N. Osherson, S. Kosslyn, & J. Hollerbach (Eds.), *An invitation to cognitive science: Visual cognition and action*. Cambridge, MA: MIT Press.

Biederman, I., Cooper, E.E., Fox, P.W., & Mahadevan, R.S. (1992). Unexceptional spatial memory in an exceptional memorist. *Journal of Experimental Psychology: Learning, Memory, & Cognition*, *18*, 654–657.

Biederman, I., & Gerhardstein, P.C. (1993). Recognising depth-rotated objects: Evidence for 3-D viewpoint invariance. *Journal of Experimental Psychology: Human Perception & Performance*, *19*, 1162–1182.

Biederman, I., Ju, G., & Clapper, J. (1985). *The perception of partial objects*. Unpublished manuscript, State University of New York at Buffalo.

Birch, H.G. (1945). The relationship of previous experience to insightful problem solving. *Journal of Comparative Psychology*, *38*, 267–383.

Birnbaum, M.H. (1983). Base rates in Bayesian inference: Signal detection analysis of the cab problem. *American Journal of Psychology*, *96*, 85–94.

Bisiach, E., & Luzzatti, C. (1978). Unilateral neglect of representational space. *Cortex*, *14*, 129–133.

Bjork, R.A., & Whitten, W.B. (1974). Recency-sensitive retrieval processes in long-term free recall. *Cognitive Psychology*, *6*, 173–189.

Blaney, P.H. (1986). Affect and memory: A review. *Psychological Bulletin*, *99*, 229–246.

Blaxton, T.A. (1989). Investigating dissociations among memory measures: Support for a transfer-appropriate processing framework. *Journal of Experimental Psychology: Learning, Memory, & Cognition*, *15*, 657–668.

Blaxton, T.A. (1992). Dissociations among memory measures in memory-impaired subjects: Evidence for a processing account of memory. *Memory & Cognition*, *20*, 549–562.

Blaxton, T.A., Bookheimer, S.Y., Zeffiro, T.A., Figlozzi, C.M., William, D.D., & Theodore, W.H. (1996). Functional mapping of human memory using PET: Comparisons of conceptual and perceptual tasks. *Canadian Journal of Experimental Psychology*, *50*, 42–56.

Boden, M. (1988). *Computer models of mind*. Cambridge: Cambridge Univeristy Press.

Boden, M. (1991). *The creative mind: Myths and mechanisms*. London: Abacus.

Boden, M. (1994). *Dimensions of creativity*. Cambridge, MA: MIT Press.

Bohannon, J.N. (1988). Flashbulb memories for the space shuttle disaster: A tale of two theories. *Cognition*, *29*, 179–196.

Boles, D.B. (1983). Dissociated imagibility, concreteness, and familiarity in lateralized word recognition. *Memory & Cognition*, *11*, 511–519.

Bonatti, L. (1994). Propositional reasoning by model? *Psychological Review*, *101*, 725–733.

Boole, G. (1854). *An investigation of the laws of thought on which are founded the mathematical theories of logic and probabilities*. London.

Boomer, D. (1965). Hesitation and grammatical encoding. *Language & Speech*, *8*, 145–158.

Borges, J.-L. (1964). *Labyrinths*. London: Penguin.

Bourke, P.A., Duncan, J., & Nimmo-Smith, I. (1996). A general factor involved in dual-task performance decrement. *Quarterly Journal of Experimental Psychology*, *49*A, 525–545.

Bouton, M.E., Nelson, J.B., & Rosas, J.M. (1999). Stimulus generalisation, context change, and forgetting. *Psychological Bulletin*, *125*, 171–186.

Bowden, E.M., & Beeman, M.J. (1998). Getting the right idea: Semantic activation in the right hemisphere may help to solve insight problems. *Psychological Science*, *9*, 435–440.

Bower, G.H. (1970). Imagery as a relational organizer in associative learning. *Journal of Verbal Learning & Verbal Behavior, 9,* 529–533.

Bower, G.H. (1972). Mental imagery and associative learning. In L. Gregg (Ed.), *Cognition in learning and memory.* New York: Wiley.

Bower, G.H. (1981). Mood and memory. *American Psychologist, 36,* 129–148.

Bower, G.H. (1987). Commentary on mood and memory. *Behaviour Research & Therapy, 25,* 443–455.

Bower, G.H. (1992). How might emotions affect learning? In S.-A. Christianson (Ed.), *The handbook of emotion and memory: Research and theory.* Hillsdale, NJ: Lawrence Erlbaum Associates Inc.

Bower, G.H., Black, J.B., & Turner, T.S. (1979). Scripts in memory for text. *Cognitive Psychology, 11,* 177–220.

Bower, G.H., & Gilligan, S.G. (1979). Remembering information related to one's self. *Journal of Research in Personality, 13,* 420–432.

Bower, G.H., Gilligan, S.G., & Monteiro, K.P. (1981). Selectivity of learning caused by affective states. *Journal of Experimental Psychology: General, 110,* 451–473.

Bower, G.H., & Mayer, J.D. (1985). Failure to replicate mood dependent retrieval. *Bulletin of the Psychonomic Society, 23,* 39–42.

Bower, G.H., Monteiro, K.P., & Gilligan, S.G. (1978). Emotional mood as a context for learning and recall. *Journal of Verbal Learning & Verbal Behavior, 17,* 573–585.

Bowers, K.S. (1973). Situationism in psychology: An analysis and a critique. *Psychological Review, 80,* 307–336.

Bracewell, R.J., & Hidi, S.E. (1974). The solution of an inferential problem as a function of stimulus materials. *Quarterly Journal of Experimental Psychology, 26,* 480–488.

Braddick, O.J. (1980). Low-level and high-level processes in apparent motion. *Philosophical Transactions of the Royal Society of London, B, 209,* 137–151.

Brainard, D.H., & Wandell, B.A. (1986). Analysis of the retinex theory of colour vision. *Journal of the Optical Society of America, 3,* 1651–1661.

Braine, M.D.S. (1978). On the relationship between the natural logic of reasoning and standard logic. *Psychological Review, 85,* 1–21.

Braine, M.D.S. (1990). The "natural logic" approach to reasoning. In W.F. Overton (Ed.), *Reasoning, necessity and logic.* Hillsdale, NJ: Lawrence Erlbaum Associates Inc.

Braine, M.D.S., & O'Brien, D.P. (1991). A theory of If: A lexical entry, reasoning program and pragmatic principles. *Psychological Review, 98,* 182–203.

Braine, M.D.S., Reiser, B.J., & Rumain, B. (1984). Some empirical justification for a theory of natural propositional logic. In G.H. Bower (Ed.), *The psychology of learning & motivation, 18.* New York: Academic Press.

Braine, M.D.S., & Rumain, B. (1983). Logical reasoning. In J.H. Flavell & E.M. Markman (Eds.), *Handbook of child psychology, Vol. 3: Cognitive development (4th Edn).* New York: Wiley.

Bramwell, D.I., & Hurlbert, A.C. (1996). Measurements of colour constancy by using a forced-choice matching technique. *Perception, 25,* 229–241.

Brandimonte, M.A., & Gerbino, W. (1993). Mental image reversal and verbal recoding. *Memory & Cognition, 21,* 23–33.

Brandimonte, M.A., Hitch, G.J., & Bishop, D.V. (1992). Mental image reversal and verbal recoding. *Memory & Cognition, 20,* 449–455.

Bransford, J.D., Barclay, J.R., & Franks, J.J. (1972). Sentence memory: A constructive versus interpretive approach. *Cognitive Psychology, 3,* 193–209.

Bransford, J.D., Franks, J.J., Morris, C.D., & Stein, B.S. (1979). Some general constraints on learning and memory research. In L.S. Cermak & F.I.M. Craik (Eds.), *Levels of processing in human memory.* Hillsdale, NJ: Lawrence Erlbaum Associates Inc.

Bransford, J.D., & Johnson, M.K. (1972). Contextual prerequisites for understanding. *Journal of Verbal Learning & Verbal Behavior, 11,* 717–726.

Bredart, S. (1998). Structured imagination of novel creatures' faces. *American Journal of Psychology, 111,* 607–626.

Brennan, S.E. (1990). *Seeking and providing evidence for mutual understanding*. Unpublished PhD thesis. Stanford University, Stanford, CA.

Brewer, W.F. (1987). Schemas versus mental models in human memory. In P.E. Morris (Ed.), *Modelling cognition*. Chichester, UK: Wiley.

Brewer, W.F. (1988). Memory for randomly sampled autobiographical events. In U. Neisser & E. Winograd (Eds.), *Remembering reconsidered: Ecological and traditional approaches to the study of memory*. New York: Cambridge University Press.

Brewin, C.R., Andrews, B., & Gotlib, I.H. (1993). Psychopathology and early experience: A reappraisal of retrospective reports. *Psychological Bulletin, 113*, 82–98.

Broadbent, D.E. (1958). *Perception and communication*. Oxford: Pergamon.

Broadbent, D.E. (1982). Task combination and selective intake of information. *Acta Psychologica, 50*, 253–290.

Broadbent, D.E., & Broadbent, M. (1988). Anxiety and attentional bias: State and trait. *Cognition & Emotion, 2*, 165–183.

Brooks, L. (1978). Non-analytic concept formation and memory for instances. In E. Rosch & B.B. Lloyd (Eds.), *Cognition and categorisation*. Hillsdale, NJ: Lawrence Erlbaum Associates Inc.

Brown, C.H., Kolar, J., Torrey, B.J., Truong-Quang, T., & Volkman, P. (1976). Some general principles of biological and non-biological folk classification. *American Ethologist, 3*, 73–85.

Brown, N.R. (1995). Estimation strategies and the judgement of event frequency. *Journal of Experimental Psychology: Learning, Memory, & Cognition, 21*, 1539–1553.

Brown, N.R., Rips, L.J., & Shevell, S.K. (1985). The subjective dates of news events in very-long-term memory. *Cognitive Psychology, 17*, 139–177.

Brown, N.R., Shevell, S.K., & Rips, L.J. (1986). Public memories and their personal context. In D.C. Rubin (Ed.), *Autobiographical memory*. Cambridge: Cambridge University Press.

Brown, R., & Kulik, J. (1977). Flashbulb memories. *Cognition, 5*, 73–99.

Bruce, V., Green, P.R., & Georgeson, M.A. (1996). *Visual perception: Physiology, psychology, and ecology (3rd Edn)*. Hove, UK: Psychology Press.

Bruce, V., & Valentine, T. (1986). Semantic priming of familiar faces. *Quarterly Journal of Experimental Psychology, 38*A, 125–150.

Bruce, V., & Valentine, T. (1988). When a nod's as good as a wink: The role of dynamic information in face recognition. In M. Gruneberg, P. Morris, & R. Sykes (Eds.), *Practical aspects of memory: Current research and issues (Vol. 1)*. Chichester, UK: John Wiley.

Bruce, V., & Young, A.W. (1986). Understanding face recognition. *British Journal of Psychology, 77*, 305–327.

Bruner, J.S. (1957). On perceptual readiness. *Psychological Review, 64*, 123–152.

Bruner, J.S., & Goodman, C.D. (1947). Value and need as organising factors in perception. *Journal of Abnormal & Social Psychology, 42*, 33–44.

Bruner, J.S., Goodnow, J.J., & Austin, G.A. (1956). *A study of thinking*. New York: John Wiley.

Bruner, J.S., Postman, L., & Rodrigues, J. (1951). Expectations and the perception of colour. *American Journal of Psychology, 64*, 216–227.

Bruno, N., & Cutting, J.E. (1988). Mini-modularity and the perception of layout. *Journal of Experimental Psychology: General, 117*, 161–170.

Brunswik, E. (1956). *Perception and the representative design of psychological experiments*. Berkeley, CA: University of California Press.

Bub, D., Black, S., Howell, J., & Kertesz, S. (1987). Speech output processes and reading. In M. Coltheart, G. Sartori, & R. Job (Eds.), *The cognitive neuropsychology of language*. Hove, UK: Psychology Press.

Bub, D., Cancelliere, A., & Kertesz, A. (1985). Whole-word and analytic translation of spelling to sound in a nonsemantic reader. In K.E. Patterson, J.C. Marshall, & M. Coltheart (Eds.), *Surface dyslexia: Neuropsychological and cognitive studies of phonological reading*. Hove, UK: Psychology Press.

Bub, D., & Kertesz, A. (1982). Deep agraphia. *Brain and Language, 17*, 146–165.

Bundy, A. (1993). "Semantic procedure" is an oxymoron. *Behavioral & Brain Sciences*, *16*, 339–340.

Burt, D.B., Zembar, M.J., & Niederehe, G. (1995). Depression and memory impairment: A meta-analysis of the association, its pattern, and specificity. *Psychological Bulletin*, *117*, 285–305.

Burton, A.M., & Bruce, V. (1993). Naming faces and naming names: Exploring an interactive activation model of person recognition. *Memory*, *1*, 457–480.

Butters, N., & Cermak, L.S. (1980). *Alcoholic Korsakoff's syndrome: An information-processing approach*. London: Academic Press.

Byrne, R.M.J. (1989a). Suppressing valid inferences with conditionals. *Cognition*, *31*, 61–83.

Byrne, R.M.J. (1989b). Everyday reasoning with conditional sequences. *Quarterly Journal of Experimental Psychology*, *41*A, 141–166.

Byrne, R.M.J. (1991). Can valid inferences be suppressed. *Cognition*, *39*, 61–83.

Byrne, R.M.J. (1997). Cognitive processes in counterfactual thinking about what might have been. *Psychology of Learning & Motivation*, *37*, 105–154.

Byrne, R.M.J., Espino, O., & Santamaria, C. (1999). Counterexamples and the suppression of inferences. *Journal of Memory & Language*, *40*, 347–373.

Byrne, R.M.J., & Johnson-Laird, P.N. (1989). Spatial reasoning. *Journal of Memory & Language*, *28*, 564–575.

Byrne, R.M.J., & Johnson-Laird, P.N., (1990). Models and deductive reasoning. In K.J. Gilhooly, M.T. Keane, R. Logie, & G. Erdos (Eds), *Lines of thinking: Reflections on the psychology of thought, Vol. 1*. Chichester, UK: John Wiley.

Byrne, R.M.J., & Johnson-Laird, P.N. (1992). The spontaneous use of propositional connectives. *Quarterly Journal of Experimental Psychology*, *44*A, 89–110.

Byrne, R.M.J., & Tasso, A. (1999). Deductive reasoning from factual, possible, and counterfactual conditionals. *Memory & Cognition*, *27*, 726–740.

Cacciari, C., & Glucksberg, S. (1994). Understanding figurative language. In M.A. Gernsbacher (Ed.), *Handbook of psycholinguistics*. San Diego, CA: Academic Press.

Calvo, M., & Castillo, M.D. (1997). Mood-congruent bias in interpretation of ambiguity: Strategic processes and temporary activation. *Quarterly Journal of Experimental Psychology*, *50*A, 163–182.

Campbell, F.W., & Robson, J.G. (1968). Application of Fourier analysis to the visibility of gratings. *Journal of Physiology*, *197*, 551–566.

Cantor, N., Smith, E.E., French, R.D., & Mezzich, J. (1980). Psychiatric diagnosis as prototype categorisation. *Journal of Abnormal Psychology*, *89*, 181–193.

Caplan, D. (1994). Language and the brain. In M.A. Gernsbacher (Ed.), *Handbook of psycholinguistics*. San Diego, CA: Academic Press.

Caramazza, A. (1998). The interpretation of semantic category-specific deficits. *Neurocase*, *4*, 265–272.

Caramazza, A., McCloskey, M., & Green, B. (1981). Naive beliefs in "sophisticated" subjects: Misconceptions about trajectories of objects. *Cognition*, *9*, 117–123.

Caramazza, A., Miceli, G., Villa, G., & Romani, C. (1987). The role of the graphemic buffer in spelling: Evidence from a case of acquired dysgraphia. *Cognition*, *26*, 59–85.

Caramazza, A., & Miozzo, M. (1998). More is not always better: A response to Roelofs, Meyer, and Levelt. *Cognition*, *69*, 231–241.

Carbonell, J.G. (1986). Derivational analogy: A theory of reconstructive problem solving and expertise acquisition. In R.S. Michalski, J.G. Carbonell, & T.M. Mitchell (Eds.), *Machine learning II: An artificial intelligence approach*. Los Altos, CA: Morgan Kaufmann.

Carey, D.P., Harvey, M., & Milner, A.D. (1996). Visuomotor sensitivity for shape and orientation in a patient with visual form agnosia. *Neuropsychologia*, *34*, 329–338.

Carey, D.P., & Milner, A.D. (1994). Casting one's net too widely? *Behavioral & Brain Sciences*, *17*, 65–66.

Carpenter, P.A., & Just, M.A. (1977). Reading comprehension as eyes see it. In M.A. Just & P.A. Carpenter (Eds.), *Cognitive processes in comprehension.* Hillsdale, NJ: Lawrence Erlbaum Associates Inc.

Carpenter, P.A., Miyake, A., & Just, M.A. (1994). Working memory constraints in comprehension: Evidence from individual differences, aphasia, and aging. In M.A. Gernsbacher (Ed.), *Handbook of psycholinguistics.* New York: Academic Press.

Carreiras, M., & Clifton, C. (1993). Relative clause interpretation preferences in Spanish and English. *Language & Speech, 36,* 353–372.

Caspari, I., Parkinson, S.R., LaPointe, L.L., & Katz, R.C. (1994). *Working memory and aphasia.* Paper presented at the Clinical Aphasiology Conference, Tranverse City, MI.

Casscells, W., Schoenberger, A., & Graboys, T.B. (1978). Interpretation by physicians of clinical laboratory results. *New England Journal of Medicine, 299,* 999–1001.

Cavallo, V., & Laurent, M. (1988). Visual information and skill level in time-to-collision estimation. *Perception, 17,* 623–632.

Cavanaugh, P., Tyler, C.W., & Favreau, O.E. (1984). Perceived velocity of moving chromatic gratings. *Journal of the Optical Society of America A, 1,* 893–899.

Ceci, S.J. (1995). False beliefs: Some developmental and clinical considerations. In D.L. Schacter (Ed.), *Memory distortions.* Cambridge, MA: Harvard University Press.

Cermak, L.S. (1979). Amnesic patients' level of processing. In L.S. Cermak & F.I.M. Craik (Eds.), *Levels of processing in human memory.* Hillsdale, NJ: Lawrence Erlbaum Associates Inc.

Cermak, L.S., Lewis, R., Butters, N., & Goodglass, H. (1973). Role of verbal mediation in performance of motor tasks by Korsakoff patients. *Perceptual & Motor Skills, 37,* 259–262.

Cermak, L.S., Talbot, N., Chandler, K., & Wolbarst, L.R. (1985). The perceptual priming phenomenon in amnesia. *Neuropsychologia, 23,* 615–622.

Cermak, L.S., Verfaellie, M., & Chase, K.A. (1995). Implicit and explicit memory in amnesia: An analysis of data-driven and conceptually driven processes. *Neuropsychology, 22,* 85–97.

Challis, B.H., & Brodbeck, D.R. (1992). Level of processing affects priming in word fragment completion. *Journal of Experimental Psychology: Learning, Memory, & Cognition, 18,* 595–607.

Chalmers, A.F. (1982). *What is this thing called science?* Milton Keynes, UK: Open University Press.

Chambers, D., & Reisberg, D. (1985). Can mental images be ambiguous? *Journal of Experimental Psychology: Human Perception & Performance, 11,* 317–328.

Chambers, D., & Reisberg, D. (1992). What an image depicts depends on what an image means. *Cognitive Psychology, 24,* 145–174.

Chan, D., & Chua, F. (1994). Suppression of valid inferences: Syntactic views, mental models, and relative salience. *Cognition, 53,* 217–238.

Charness, N. (1981a). Search in chess: Age and skill differences. *Journal of Experimental Psychology: Human Perception & Performance, 7,* 467–476.

Charness, N. (1981b). Aging and skilled problem solving. *Journal of Experimental Psychology: General, 110,* 21–38.

Charness, N. (1991). Expertise in chess: The balance between knowledge and search. In A. Ericsson & J. Smith (Eds.), *Toward a general theory of expertise.* Cambridge: Cambridge University Press.

Chase, W.G., & Simon, H.A. (1973a). Perception in chess. *Cognitive Psychology, 4,* 55–81.

Chase, W.G., & Simon, H.A. (1973b). The mind's eye in chess. In W.G. Chase (Ed.), *Visual information processing.* London: Academic Press.

Chater, N., & Oaksford, M.R. (1999a). Information gain and decision-theoretic approaches to data selection: Response to Klauer (1999). *Psychological Review, 106,* 223–227.

Chater, N., & Oaksford, M.R. (1999b). The probability heuristic model of syllogistic reasoning. *Cognitive Psychology, 38,* 191–258.

Cheesman, J., & Merikle, P.M. (1984). Priming with and without awareness. *Perception & Psychophysics, 36,* 387–395.

Cheng, P., Holyoak, K.J., Nisbett, R.E., & Oliver, L.M. (1986). Pragmatic versus syntactic approaches to training deductive reasoning. *Cognitive Psychology, 18*, 293–328.

Cheng, P.W. (1985). Restructuring versus automaticity: Alternative accounts of skills acquisition. *Psychological Review, 92*, 414–423.

Cheng, P.W., & Holyoak, K.J. (1985). Pragmatic reasoning schemas. *Cognitive Psychology, 17*, 391–416.

Cheng, P.W., & Holyoak, K.J. (1989). On the natural selection of reasoning theories. *Cognition, 33*, 285–314.

Cherry, E.C. (1953). Some experiments on the recognition of speech with one and two ears. *Journal of the Acoustical Society of America, 25*, 975–979.

Chertkow, H., Bub, D., Evans, E., Meyer, S., & Marrett, S. (1993). Neural correlates of picture processing studied with positron emission tomography. *Brain & Language, 44*, 460.

Chi, M.T.H., Feltovich, P.J., & Glaser, R. (1981). Categorization and representation of physics problems by experts and novices. *Cognitive Science, 5*, 121–152.

Chi, M.T.H., Glaser, R., & Rees, E. (1983). Expertise in problem solving. In R.J. Sternberg (Ed.), *Advances in the psychology of human intelligence, Vol. 2*. Hillsdale, NJ: Lawrence Erlbaum Associates Inc.

Chomsky, N. (1957). *Syntactic structures*. The Hague: Mouton.

Chomsky, N. (1959). Review of Skinner's "Verbal behaviour". *Language, 35*, 26–58.

Christensen-Szalanski, J.J.J., & Bushyhead, J.B. (1981). Physicians' use of probabilistic information in a real clinical setting. *Journal of Experimental Psychology: Human Perception & Performance, 7*, 928–935.

Churchland, P.S. (1989). From Descartes to neural networks. *Scientific American, July*, 100.

Churchland, P.S., & Sejnowski, T.J. (1991). Perspectives on cognitive neuroscience. In R.G. Lister & H.J. Weingartner (Eds.), *Perspectives on cognitive neuroscience*. Oxford: Oxford University Press.

Churchland, P.S., & Sejnowski, T.J. (1992). *The computational brain*. Cambridge, MA: MIT Press.

Cicerone, C.M., & Nerger, J.L. (1989). The relative number of long-wavelength-sensitive to middle-wavelength-sensitive cones in the human fovea centralis. *Vision Research, 29*, 115–128.

Claparède, E. (1911). Recognition et moitié. *Archives de Psychologie, 11*, 75–90.

Clark, D.M. (1986). A cognitive approach to panic. *Behaviour Research & Therapy, 24*, 461–470.

Clark, D.M., & Teasdale, J.D. (1982). Diurnal variation in clinical depression and accessibility of memories or positive and negative experiences. *Journal of Abnormal Psychology, 91*, 87–95.

Clark, H.H. (1992). *Arenas of language use*. Chicago: University of Chicago Press.

Clark, H.H. (1994). Discourse in production. In M.A. Gernsbacher (Ed.), *Handbook of psycholinguistics*. London: Academic Press.

Clark, H.H., & Carlson, T.B. (1981). Context for comprehension. In J. Long & A. Baddeley (Eds.), *Attention and performance, Vol. IX*. Hillsdale, NJ: Lawrence Erlbaum Associates Inc.

Clark, H.H., & Lucy, P. (1975). Understanding what is meant from what is said: A study in conversationally conveyed requests. *Journal of Verbal Learning & Verbal Behavior, 14*, 56–72.

Clifton, C., & Ferreira, F. (1987). Discourse structure and anaphora: Some experimental results. In M. Coltheart (Ed.), *Attention and performance (Vol. XII)*. Hove, UK: Psychology Press.

Clocksin, W.F., & Mellish, C.S. (1984). *Programming in prolog (2nd Edn)*. Berlin: Springer-Verlag.

Cohen, B., & Murphy, G.L. (1984). Models of concepts. *Cognitive Science, 8*, 27–58.

Cohen, D., & Kubovy, M. (1993) Mental rotation, mental representation and flat slopes. *Cognitive Psychology, 25*, 351–382.

Cohen, G. (1983). *The psychology of cognition (2nd Edn)*. London: Academic Press.

Cohen, G. (1989). *Memory in the real world*. Hove, UK: Psychology Press.

Cohen, G. (1990). Why is it difficult to put names to faces? *British Journal of Psychology, 81*, 287–297.

Cohen, G., & Faulkner, D. (1988). Life span changes in autobiographical memory. In M.M. Gruneberg, P.E. Morris, & R.N. Sykes (Eds.), *Practical aspects of memory: Current research and issues (Vol. 1)*. Chichester, UK: John Wiley.

Cohen, N.J. (1984). Preserved learning capacity in amnesia: Evidence for multiple memory systems. In L.R. Squire & N. Butters (Eds.), *Neuropsychology of memory*. New York: Guilford Press.

Cohen, N.J., Poldrack, R.A., & Eichenbaum, H. (1997). Memory for items and memory for relations in the procedural/declarative memory framework. *Memory, 5*, 131–178.

Cohen, N.J., Ramzy, C., Hut, Z., Tomaso, H., Strupp, J., Erhard, P., Anderson, P., & Ugurbil, K. (1994). Hippocampal activation in fMRI evoked by demand for declarative memory-based bindings of multiple streams of information. *Society for Neuroscience Abstracts, 20*, 1290.

Cohen, N.J., & Squire, L.R. (1980). Preserved learning and retention of pattern-analysing skill in amnesia using perceptual learning. *Cortex, 17*, 273–278.

Cole, R.A., Rudnisky, A.I., Zue, V.W., & Reddy, W. (1980). Speech as patterns on paper. In R.A. Cole (Ed.), *Perception and production of fluent speech*. Hillsdale, NJ: Lawrence Erlbaum Associates Inc.

Coleman, L., & Kay, P. (1981). Prototype semantics. *Language, 57*, 26–44.

Collins, A.M., & Loftus, E.F. (1975). A spreading activation theory of semantic processing. *Psychological Review, 82*, 407–428.

Collins, A.M., & Quillian, M.R. (1969). Retrieval time from semantic memory. *Journal of Verbal Learning & Verbal Behavior, 8*, 240–248.

Collins, A.M., & Quillian, M.R. (1970). Does category size affect categorisation time. *Journal of Verbal Learning & Verbal Behavior, 9*, 432–438.

Coltheart, M. (1983). Ecological necessity of iconic memory. *Behavioral & Brain Sciences, 6*, 17–18.

Coltheart, M., Curtis, B., Atkins, P., & Haller, M. (1993). Models of reading aloud: Dual-route and parallel-distributed-processing approaches. *Psychological Review, 100*, 589–608.

Coltheart, M., Patterson, K., & Marshall, J.C. (Eds.). (1980). *Deep dyslexia*. London: Routledge & Kegan Paul.

Connine, C.M., Blasko, P.J., & Titone, D. (1993). Do the beginnings of spoken words have a special status in auditory word recognition? *Journal of Memory & Language, 32*, 193–210.

Connolly, T. (1996). Are base rates a natural category of information? *Behavioral & Brain Sciences, 19*, 19–20.

Conrad, C. (1972). Cognitive economy in semantic memory. *Journal of Experimental Psychology, 92*, 148–154.

Conway, M.A. (1996). Autobiographical knowledge and autobiographical memories. In D.C. Rubin (Ed.), *Remembering our past: Studies in autobiographical memory*. Cambridge: Cambridge University Press.

Conway, M.A., Anderson, S.J., Larsen, S.F., Donnelly, C.M., McDaniel, M.A., McClelland, A.G.R., & Rawles, R.E. (1994). The function of flashbulb memories. *Memory & Cognition, 22*, 326–343.

Conway, M.A., & Bekerian, D.A. (1987). Organisation in autobiographical memory. In A.F. Collins, S.E. Gathercole, M.A. Conway, & P.E. Morris (Eds.), *Theories of memory*. Hove, UK: Psychology Press.

Conway, M.A., Cohen, G., & Stanhope, N. (1991). On the very long-term retention of knowledge acquired through formal education: Twelve years of cognitive psychology. *Journal of Experimental Psychology: General, 120*, 395–409.

Conway, M.A., & Rubin, D.C. (1993). The structure of autobiographical memory. In A.F. Collins, S.E. Gathercole, M.A. Conway, & P.E. Morris (Eds.), *Theories of memory*. Hove, UK: Psychology Press.

Cooke, N.J., & Breedin, S.D. (1994). Constructing naive theories of motion on the fly. *Memory & Cognition, 22*, 474–493.

Coombs, C.H., Dawes, R.M., & Tversky, A. (1970). *Mathematical psychology*. Englewood Cliffs, NJ: Prentice-Hall.

Cooper, L.A. (1975). Mental rotation of random two-dimensional shapes. *Cognitive Psychology, 7*, 20–43.

Cooper, L.A., & Podgorny, P. (1976). Mental transformations and visual comparison processes. *Journal of Experimental Psychology: Human Perception & Performance, 2,* 503–514.

Cooper, L.A., & Shepard, R.N. (1973). Chronometric studies of the rotation of mental images. In W.G. Chase (Ed.), *Visual information processing.* New York: Academic Press.

Cooper, R., & Shallice, T. (1995). SOAR and the case for unified theories of cognition. *Cognition, 55,* 115–149.

Corballis, M.C. (1989). Laterality and human evolution, *Psychological Review, 96,* 492–505.

Coren, S., & Girgus, J.S. (1972). Visual spatial illusions: Many explanations. *Science, 179,* 503–504.

Corkin, S. (1968). Acquisition of motor skill after bilateral medial temporal-lobe excision. *Neuropsychologia, 6,* 255–265.

Corkin, S., Amaral, D.G., Gonzalez, R.G., Johnson, K.A., & Hyman, B.T. (1997). H.M.'s medial temporal lobe lesion: Findings from magnetic resonance imaging. *Journal of Neuroscience, 17,* 3964–3979.

Cornoldi, C., & Paivio, A. (1982). Imagery value and its effects on verbal memory: A review. *Archivio de Psicologia Neurologia e Psichiatria, 2,* 171–192.

Corter, J.E., & Gluck, M.A. (1992). Explaining basic categories: Feature predictability and information. *Psychological Bulletin, 111,* 291–303.

Coslett, H.B., & Saffran, E. (1991). Simultanagnosia: To see but not two see. *Brain, 113,* 475–486.

Cosmides, L. (1989). The logic of social exchange: Has natural selection shaped how humans reason? *Cognition, 31,* 187–276.

Cosmides, L., & Tooby, J. (1992). Cognitive adaptations for social change. In J.H. Barkow, L. Cosmides, & J. Tooby (Eds.), *The adapted mind.* Oxford, UK: Oxford University Press.

Cosmides, L., & Tooby, J. (1996). Are humans good intuitive statisticians after all? Rethinking some conclusions from the literature on judgement under uncertainty. *Cognition, 58,* 1–73.

Costello, F., & Keane, M.T. (1992). Concept combination: A theoretical review. *Irish Journal of Psychology, 13,* 125–140.

Costello, F., & Keane, M.T. (1997). Polysemy in conceptual combination: Testing the constraint theory of combination. In *Proceedings of the Nineteenth Annual Conference of the Cognitive Science Society.* Hillsdale, NJ: Lawrence Erlbaum Associates Inc.

Costello, F., & Keane, M.T. (in press). Efficient creativity: Constraint guided conceptual combination. *Cognitive Science, 23.*

Costello, F., & Keane, M.T. (in press). Alignment and diagnosticity. *Journal of Experimental Psychology: Learning, Memory, & Cognition.*

Coughlan, A.K., & Warrington, E.K. (1978). Word-comprehension and word-retrieval in patients with localised cerebral lesions. *Brain, 101,* 163–185.

Cowan, N., Wood, N.L., Wood, P.K., Keller, T.A., Nugent, L.D., & Keller, C.V. (1998). Two separate verbal processing rates contributing to short-term memory span. *Journal of Experimental Psychology: General, 127,* 141–160.

Craik, F.I.M. (1973). A "levels of analysis" view of memory. In P. Pliner, L. Krames, & T.M. Alloway (Eds.), *Communication and affect: Language and thought.* London: Academic Press.

Craik, F.I.M., & Lockhart, R.S. (1972). Levels of processing: A framework for memory research. *Journal of Verbal Learning & Verbal Behavior, 11,* 671–684.

Craik, F.I.M., & Tulving, E. (1975). Depth of processing and the retention of words in episodic memory. *Journal of Experimental Psychology: General, 104,* 268–294.

Crocker, M.W. (1999). Mechanisms for sentence processing. In S. Garrod & M.J. Pickering (Eds.), *Language processing.* Hove, UK: Psychology Press.

Crutcher, R.J. (1994). Telling what we know: The use of verbal report methodologies in psychological research. *Psychological Science, 5,* 241–243.

Cumming, B. (1994). Motion-in-depth. In A.T. Smith & R.J. Snowden (Eds.), *Visual detection of motion.* London: Academic Press.

Cummins, D.D. (1995). Naive theories and causal deduction. *Memory & Cognition, 23,* 646–658.

Cummins, D.D. (1996). Evidence for the innateness of deontic reasoning. *Mind & Language, 11,* 160–190.

Cummins, D.D. (1997). Rationality: Biological, psychological, and normative theories. *Current Psychology of Cognition, 16,* 78–86.

Cummins, D.D., Lubart, T., Alksnis, O., & Rist, R. (1991). Conditional reasoning and causation. *Memory & Cognition, 19,* 274–282.

Curran, T., & Schacter, D.L. (1997). Implicit memory: What must theories of memory explain? *Memory, 5,* 37–47.

Cutler, A., Mehler, J., Norris, D., & Segui, J. (1987). Phoneme identification and the lexicon. *Cognitive Psychology, 19,* 141–177.

Cutting, J.E. (1978). Generation of synthetic male and female walkers through manipulation of a biomechanical invariant. *Perception, 7,* 393–405.

Cutting, J.E. (1986). *Perception with an eye to motion.* Cambridge, MA: MIT Press.

Cutting, J.E., & Kozlowski, L.T. (1977). Recognising friends by their walk: Gait perception without familiarity cues. *Bulletin of the Psychonomic Society, 9,* 353–356.

Cutting, J.E., Proffitt, D.R., & Kozlowski, L.T. (1978). A biomechanical invariant for gait perception. *Journal of Experimental Psychology: Human Perception & Performance, 4,* 357–372.

Cutting, J.E., Springer, K., Braren, P.A., & Johnson, S.H. (1992). Wayfinding on foot from information in retinal, not optical, flow. *Journal of Experimental Psychology: General, 121,* 41–72.

Dalgleish, T. (1998). Emotion. In M.W. Eysenck (Ed.), *Psychology: An integrated approach.* Harlow, Essex: Addison Wesley Longman.

Damasio, H., Grabowski, T., Frank, R., Galaburda, A.M., & Damasio, A.R. (1996). A neural basis for lexical retrieval. *Nature, 380,* 499–505.

Daneman, M., & Carpenter, P.A. (1980). Individual differences in working memory and reading. *Journal of Verbal Learning & Verbal Behavior, 19,* 450–466.

Danks, J.H., & Glucksberg, S. (1980). Experimental psycholinguistics. *Annual Review of Psychology, 31,* 391–417.

Dartnall, H.J.A., Bowmaker, J.K., & Mollon, J.D. (1983). Human visual pigments: Microspectrophotometric results from the eyes of seven persons. *Proceedings of the Royal Society of London Series B, 220,* 115–130.

Davenport, J., & Keane, M.T. (1999). Similarity and structural alignment: You can have one without the other. In *Proceedings of the Twenty-First Annual Conference of the Cognitive Science Society.* Hillsdale, NJ: Lawrence Erlbaum Associates Inc.

Davidson, D. (1994). Recognition and recall of irrelevant and interruptive atypical actions in script-based stories. *Journal of Memory & Language, 33,* 757–775.

Davies, G.M., & Logie, R.H. (1998). *Memory in everyday life.* Amsterdam: Elsevier.

Davies, I.R.L. (1998). A study of colour grouping in three languages: A test of the linguistic relativity hypothesis. *British Journal of Psychology, 89,* 433–452.

Davies, I.R.L., Sowden, P.T., Jerrett, D.T., Jerrett, T., & Corbett, G.G. (1998). A cross-cultural study of English and Setswana speakers on a colour triads task: A test of the Sapir-Whorf hypothesis. *British Journal of Psychology, 89,* 1–15.

Davies, S.P. (1990a). The nature and development of programming plans. *International Journal of Man–Machine Studies, 32,* 461–481.

Davies, S.P. (1990b). Plans, goals and selection rules in the comprehension of computer programs. *Behaviour & Information Technology, 10,* 173–190.

Davies, S.P. (1991). The role of notation and knowledge representation in the determination of programming strategy. *Cognitive Science, 15,* 547–573.

Dawes, R.M. (1988). *Rational choice in an uncertain world.* San Diego, CA: Harcourt Brace Jovanovich.

De Bleser, R. (1988). Localisation of aphasia: Science or fiction? In G. Denese, C. Semenza, & P. Bisiacchi (Eds.), *Perspectives on cognitive neuropsychology.* Hove, UK: Psychology Press.

DeGroot, A.D. (1965). *Thought and choice in chess.* The Hague: Mouton.

DeGroot, A.D. (1966). Perception and memory versus thought. In B. Kleinmuntz (Ed.), *Problem solving*. New York: Wiley.

DeGroot, A.D., & Gobet, F. (1996). *Perception and memory in chess: Heuristics of the professional eye*. Assen: Van Gorcum.

De Haan, E.H.F., Young, A.W., & Newcombe, F. (1987). Faces interfere with name classification in a prosopagnosic patient. *Cortex, 23*, 309–316.

De Haan, E.H.F., Young, A.W., & Newcombe, F. (1991). A dissociation between the sense of familiarity and access to semantic information concerning familiar people. *European Journal of Cognitive Psychology, 3*, 51–67.

de Jong, B.M., Shipp, S., Skidmore, B., Frackowiak, R.S.J., & Zeki, S. (1994). The cerebral activity related to the visual perception of forward motion in depth. *Brain, 117*, 1039–1054.

Delk, J.L., & Fillenbaum, S. (1965). Differences in perceived colour as a function of characteristic colour. *American Journal of Psychology, 78*, 290–293.

Dell, G.S. (1986). A spreading-activation theory of retrieval in sentence production. *Psychological Review, 93*, 283–321.

Dell, G.S., Burger, L.K., & Svec, W.R. (1997). Language production and serial order: A functional analysis and a model. *Psychological Review, 104*, 123–147.

Dell, G.S., & O'Seaghdha, P.G. (1991). Mediated and convergent lexical priming in language production: A comment on Levelt et al. (1991). *Psychological Review, 98*, 604–614.

Dell, G.S., Schwartz, M.F., Martin, N., Saffran, E.M., & Gagnon, D.A. (1997). Lexical access in aphasic and nonaphasic speakers. *Psychological Review, 104*, 801–838.

DeLucia, P.R., & Hochberg, J. (1991). Geometrical illusions in solid objects under ordinary viewing conditions. *Perception & Psychophysics, 50*, 547–554.

Denis, M., & Cocude, M. (1999). On the metric properties of visual images generated from verbal descriptions: Evidence for the robustness of the mental scanning effect. *European Journal of Cognitive Psychology, 9*, 353–379.

Denis, M., & Kosslyn, S.M. (1999). Scanning visual mental images: A window on the mind. *Cahier de Psychologie, 18*, 409–465.

Dennis, M. (1976). Dissociated naming and locating of body parts after left anterior lobe resection: An experimental case study. *Brain & Language, 3*, 147–163.

Derakshan, N., & Eysenck, M.W. (1997). Interpretive biases for one's own behaviour and physiology in high trait-anxious individuals and repressors. *Journal of Personality & Social Psychology, 73*, 816–825.

De Ruiter, C., & Brosschot, J.F. (1994). The emotional Stroop interference effect in anxiety: Attentional bias or cognitive avoidance? *Behaviour Research & Therapy, 32*, 315–319.

de Saussure, F. (1960). *Course in general linguistics*. London: Peter Owen.

de Sperati, C. (1999). Saccades to mentally rotated targets. *Experimental Brain Research, 126*, 563–577.

D'Esposito, M., Detre, J.A., Aguirre, G.K., Stallcup, M., Alsop, D.C., Tippet, L.J., & Farah, M.J. (1997). A functional MRI study of mental image generation. *Neuropsychologia, 35*, 725–730.

Deutsch, J.A., & Deutsch, D. (1963). Attention: Some theoretical considerations. *Psychological Review, 93*, 283–321.

Deutsch, J.A., & Deutsch, D. (1967). Comments on "Selective attention: Perception or response?" *Quarterly Journal of Experimental Psychology, 19*, 362–363.

DeValois, R.I., DeValois, K.K. (1975). Neural coding of colour. In E.C. Carterette & M.P. Friedman (Eds.), *Handbook of perception, Vol. 5*. New York: Academic Press.

DeValois, R.L., & Jacobs, F.H. (1968). Primate colour vision. *Science, 162*, 533–540.

Dewhurst, S.A., & Hitch, G.J. (1999). Cognitive effort and recollective experience in recognition memory. *Memory, 7*, 129–146.

Dodd, B., & Campbell, R. (1986). *Hearing by eye: The psychology of lip reading*. Hove, UK: Psychology Press.

Dodson, C., & Reisberg, D. (1991). Indirect testing of eyewitness memory: The (non) effect of misinformation. *Bulletin of the Psychonomic Society, 29*, 333–336.

Dominowski, R.L. (1981). Comment on "An examination of the alleged role of 'fixation' in the solution of several insight problems" by Weisberg & Alba. *Journal of Experimental Psychology: General, 110*, 199–203.

Donald, M. (1991). *Origins of the modern mind: Three stages in the evolution of culture and cognition*. Cambridge, MA: Harvard University Press.

Donaldson, W. (1996). The role of decision processes in remembering and knowing. *Memory & Cognition, 24*, 523–533.

Dorman, M.F., Raphael, L.J., & Liberman, A.M. (1979). Some experiments on the sound of silence in phonetic perception. *Journal of the Acoustical Society of America, 65*, 1518–1532.

Dosher, B.A., & Corbett, A.T. (1982). Instrument inferences and verb schemata. *Memory & Cognition, 10*, 531–539.

Douglas, M. (1966). *Purity and danger*. London: Routledge & Kegan Paul.

Downes, J.J., & Mayes, A.R. (1997). Concluding comments: Common themes, disagreements, and future directions. *Memory, 5*, 301–311.

Driver, J. (1998). The neuropsychology of spatial attention. In H. Pashler (Ed.), *Attention*. Hove, UK: Psychology Press.

Driver, J., & Tipper, S.P. (1989). On the nonselectivity of "selective seeing": Contrast between interference and priming in selective attention. *Journal of Experimental Psychology: Human Perception & Performance, 15*, 304–314.

Dronkers, N. (1996). A new brain region for coordinating speech articulation. *Nature, 384*, 159–161.

Duhamel, J.-R., Colby, C.L., & Goldberg, M.E. (1992). The updating of the representation of visual space in parietal cortex by intended eye movements. *Science, 255*, 90–92.

Dunbar, K. (1997). "On-line" inductive reasoning in scientific laboratories: What it reveals about the nature of induction and scientific discovery. In M.G. Shafto, & P. Langley (Eds.), *Proceedings of the Nineteenth Annual Conference of the Cognitive Science Society*. Hillsdale, NJ: Lawrence Erlbaum Associates Inc.

Duncan, J. (1979). Divided attention: The whole is more than the sum of its parts. *Journal of Experimental Psychology: Human Perception, 5*, 216–228.

Duncan, J., Emslie, H., Williams, P., Johnson, R., & Freer, C. (1996). Intelligence and the frontal lobe: The organization of goal-directed behaviour. *Cognitive Psychology, 30*, 257–303.

Duncan, J., & Humphreys, G.W. (1989). A resemblance theory of visual search. *Psychological Review, 96*, 433–458.

Duncan, J., & Humphreys, G.W. (1992). Beyond the search surface: Visual search and attentional engagement. *Journal of Experimental Psychology: Human Perception & Performance, 18*, 578–588.

Duncker, K. (1926). A qualitative (experimental and theoretical) study of productive thinking (solving of comprehensible problems). *Journal of Genetic Psychology, 68*, 97–116.

Duncker, K. (1945). On problem solving. *Psychological Monographs, 58* (Whole No. 270).

Ebbinghaus, H. (1885/1913). *Uber das Gedächtnis* (Leipzig: Dunker) [translated by H. Ruyer & C.E. Bussenius]. New York: Teacher College, Columbus University.

Eco, U. (1984). *The name of the rose*. London: Picador.

Edwards, W. (1954). The theory of decision making. *Psychological Bulletin, 51*, 380–417.

Edwards, W. (1968). Conservatism in human information processing. In B. Kleinmuntz (Ed.), *Formal representations of human judgement*. New York: Wiley.

Egan, D.W., & Greeno, J.G. (1974). Theories of rule induction: Knowledge acquired in concept learning, serial pattern learning and problem solving. In W.G. Gregg (Ed.), *Knowledge and cognition*. Hillsdale, NJ: Lawrence Erlbaum Associates Inc.

Ehrlich, S.F., & Rayner, K. (1981). Contextual effects on word perception and eye movements during reading. *Journal of Verbal Learning & Verbal Behavior, 20*, 641–655.

Ehrlichman, H., & Barrett, J. (1983). Right hemispheric specialisation for mental imagery: A review of the evidence. *Brain & Cognition, 2*, 55–76.

Eich, E., Macaulay, D., & Lam, R.W. (1997). Mania, depression, and mood dependent memory. *Cognition & Emotion, 11*, 607–618.

Eich, E., & Metcalfe, J. (1989). Mood dependent memory for internal versus external events. *Journal of Experimental Psychology: Learning, Memory, & Cognition, 15*, 443–455.

Eimas, P.D., Miller, J.L., & Jascyzyk, P.W. (1987). On infant speech perception and the acquisition of language. In S. Harnad (Ed.), *Categorical perception: The groundwork of cognition*. New York: Cambridge University Press.

Eisenstadt, M., Keane, M.T., & Rajan T. (Eds.) (1992). *Novice programming environments*. Hove, UK: Psychology Press.

Elio, R. (1997). What to believe when inferences are contradicted. In *Proceedings of the Nineteenth Annual Conference of the Cognitive Science Society*. Hillsdale, NJ: Lawrence Erlbaum Associates Inc.

Elio, Y., & Sharf, P. (1990). Modeling novice-to-expert shifts in problem solving strategy and knowledge organization. *Cognitive Science, 14*, 579–639.

Ellen, P. (1982). Direction, past experience and hints in creative problem solving: A reply to Weisberg & Alba. *Journal of Experimental Psychology: General, 111*, 316–325.

Ellis, A.W. (1987). Intimations of modularity, or, the modularity of mind: Doing cognitive neuropsychology without syndromes. In M. Coltheart, G. Sartori, & R. Job (Eds.), *The cognitive neuropsychology of language*. Hove, UK: Psychology Press.

Ellis, A.W. (1993). *Reading, writing and dyslexia (2nd Edn)*. Hove, UK: Psychology Press.

Ellis, A.W., Miller, D., & Sin, G. (1983). Wernicke's aphasia and normal language processing: A case study in cognitive neuropsychology. *Cognition, 15*, 111–144.

Ellis, A.W., & Young, A.W. (1988). *Human cognitive neuropsychology*. Hove, UK: Psychology Press.

Ellis, H.D., Shepherd, J.W., & Davies, G.M. (1975). An investigation of the use of the Photofit technique for recalling faces. *British Journal of Psychology, 66*, 29–37.

Ellis, J.A. (1988). Memory for future intentions: Investigating pulses and steps. In M.M. Gruneberg, P.E. Morris, & R.N. Sykes (Eds.), *Practical aspects of memory: Current research and issues, Vol. 1. Memory in everyday life*. Chichester, UK: John Wiley.

Ellis, N., & Beaton, A. (1993). Factors affecting the learning of foreign language vocabulary: Imagery keyword mediators and phonological short-term memory. *Quarterly Journal of Experimental Psychology, 46*A, 533–558.

Ellis, R., & Humphreys, G. (1999). *Connectionist psychology: A text with readings*. Hove, UK: Psychology Press.

Encyclopaedia Britannica. (1929). Memory. In *Encylopaedia Britannica (14th Edn)*. London: Encyclopaedia Britannica Ltd.

Engel, A.K., Koenig, P., & Kreiter, A.K. (1992). *Trends in Neurosciences, 15*, 218–226.

Engle, R.W., & Conway, A.R.A. (1998). Working memory and comprehension. In R.H. Logie & K.J. Gilhooly (Eds.), *Working memory and thinking*. Hove, UK: Psychology Press.

Enns, J.T., & Rensick, R.A. (1990). Sensitivity to three-dimensional orientation from line drawings. *Psychological Review, 98*, 335–351.

Erickson, J.R. (1974). A set analysis theory of behaviour in formal syllogistic reasoning tasks. In R. Solso (Ed.), *Loyola symposium, vol. 2*. Hillsdale, NJ: Lawrence Erlbaum Associates Inc.

Erickson, M.A., & Kruschke, J.K. (1998). Rules and exemplars in category learning. *Journal of Experimental Psychology: General, 127*, 107–140.

Ericsson, K.A. (1988). Analysis of memory performance in terms of memory skill. In R.J. Sternberg (Ed.), *Advances in the psychology of human intelligence, Vol. 4*. Hillsdale, NJ: Lawrence Erlbaum Associates Inc.

Ericsson, K.A., & Chase, W.G. (1982). Exceptional memory. *American Scientist, 70*, 607–615.

Ericsson, K.A., & Delaney, P.F. (1998). Working memory and expert performance. In R.H. Logie & K.J. Gilhooly (Eds.), *Working memory and thinking*. Hove, UK: Psychology Press.

Ericsson, K.A., & Kintsch, W. (1995). Long-term working memory. *Psychological Review, 102*, 211–245.

Ericsson, K.A., & Lehmann, A.C. (1996). Expert and exceptional performance: Evidence of maximal adaptation to task constraints. *Annual Review of Psychology, 47*, 273–305.

Ericsson, K.A., & Simon, H.A. (1980). Verbal reports as data. *Psychological Review, 87*, 215–251.

Ericsson, K.A., & Simon, H.A. (1984). *Protocol analysis: Verbal reports as data.* Cambridge, MA: MIT Press.

Ericsson, K.A., & Staszewski, J.J. (1989). Skilled memory and expertise. In D. Klahr, & K. Kotovsky (Eds.), *Complex information processing: The impact of Herbert A. Simon.* Hillsdale, NJ: Lawrence Erlbaum Associates Inc.

Eriksen, C.W., & St. James, J.D. (1986). Visual attention within and around the field of focal attention: A zoom lens model. *Perception & Psychophysics, 40*, 225–240.

Erlich, K., & Johnson-Laird, P.N. (1982). Spatial descriptions and referential continuity. *Journal of Verbal Learning & Verbal Behavior, 21*, 296–306.

Erlich, K., & Soloway, E. (1984). An empirical investigation of tacit plan knowledge in programming. In J.C. Thomas & M.L. Schneider (Eds.), *Human factors in computing systems.* Norwood, NJ: Ablex.

Eslinger, P.J., & Damasio, A.R. (1985). Severe disturbance of higher cognition after bilateral frontal lobe ablation: Patient EVR. *Neurology, 35*, 1731–1741.

Estes, W. (1976). Structural aspects of associative models of memory. In C.N. Cofer (Ed.), *The structure of human memory.* San Francisco, CA: Freeman.

Estes, W. (1993). Concepts, categories and psychological science. *Psychological Science, 4*, 143–153.

Estes, W.K. (1996). *Classification and cognition.* Oxford: Oxford University Press.

Estes, Z., & Glucksberg, S. (in press). Interactive property attribution in concept combination. *Memory & Cognition.*

Evans, J.St.B.T. (1982). *The psychology of deductive reasoning.* London: Routledge & Kegan Paul.

Evans, J.St.B.T. (1983). Linguistic determinants of bias in conditional reasoning. *Quarterly Journal of Experimental Psychology, 35*A, 635–644.

Evans, J.St.B.T. (1984). Heuristic and analytic processes in reasoning. *British Journal of Psychology, 75*, 451–458.

Evans, J.St.B.T. (1989). *Bias in human reasoning.* London: Psychology Press.

Evans, J.St.B.T. (1993a). The mental model theory of conditional reasoning: Critical appraisal and revision. *Cognition, 48*, 1–20.

Evans, J.St.B.T. (1993b). On rules, models and understanding. *Behavioral & Brain Sciences, 16*, 345–346.

Evans, J.St.B.T. (1995). Relevance and reasoning. In S.E. Newstead & J.St.B.T. Evans (Eds.), *Perspectives on thinking and reasoning: Essays in honour of Peter Wason.* Hove, UK: Psychology Press.

Evans, J.St.B.T. (1998). Matching bias in conditional reasoning: Do we understand it after 25 years. *Thinking & Reasoning, 4*, 45–82.

Evans, J.St.B.T., & Lynch, L.S. (1973). Matching bias in the selection task. *British Journal of Psychology, 64*, 391–397.

Evans, J.St.B.T., Manktelow, K.I., & Over, D. (1993a). Reasoning, decision making and rationality. *Cognition, 49*, 156–187.

Evans, J.St.B.T., Newstead, S.E., & Byrne, R.M.J. (1993b). *Human reasoning: The psychology of deduction.* Hove, UK: Psychology Press.

Evans, J.St.B.T., & Over, D.E. (1996). Rationality in the selection task: Epistemic utility versus uncertainty reduction. *Psychological Review, 103*, 356–363.

Evans, J.St.B.T., & Over, D.E. (1997). Rationality in reasoning: The problem of deductive competence. *Current Psychology of Cognition, 16*, 3–38.

Eysenck, M.W. (1978). Verbal remembering. In B.M. Foss (Ed.), *Psychology survey, No. 1.* London: Allen & Unwin.

Eysenck, M.W. (1979). Depth, elaboration, and distinctiveness. In L.S. Cermak & F.I.M. Craik (Eds.), *Levels of processing in human memory.* Hillsdale, NJ: Lawrence Erlbaum Associates Inc.

Eysenck, M.W. (1982). *Attention and arousal: Cognition and performance.* Berlin: Springer.

Eysenck, M.W. (1992). *Anxiety: The cognitive perspective.* Hove, UK: Psychology Press.

Eysenck, M.W. (1997). *Anxiety and cognition: A unified theory.* Hove, UK: Psychology Press.

Eysenck, M.W., & Eysenck, M.C. (1980). Effects of processing depth, distinctiveness, and word frequency on retention. *British Journal of Psychology, 71*, 263–274.

Eysenck, M.W., & Keane, M.T. (1995). *Cognitive psychology: A student's handbook (3rd Edn)*. Hove, UK: Psychology Press.

Eysenck, M.W., MacLeod, C., & Mathews, A. (1987). Cognitive functioning and anxiety. *Psychological Research*, *49*, 189–195.

Eysenck, M.W., Mogg, K., May, J., Richards, A., & Mathews, A. (1991). Bias in interpretation of ambiguous sentences related to threat in anxiety. *Journal of Abnormal Psychology*, *100*, 144–150.

Faigley, L., & Witte, S. (1983). Analysing revision. *College Composition and Communication*, *32*, 400–414.

Falkenhainer, B., Forbus, K.D., & Gentner, D. (1986). Structure-mapping engine. *Proceedings of the Annual Conference of the American Association for Artificial Intelligence*. Los Altos, CA: Morgan Kaufmann.

Falkenhainer, B., Forbus, K.D., & Gentner, D. (1989). Structure-mapping engine. *Artificial Intelligence*, *41*, 1–63.

Farah, M.J. (1984). The neurological basis of mental imagery: A componential analysis. *Cognition*, *18*, 245–272.

Farah, M.J. (1988). Is visual imagery really visual? Overlooked evidence from neuropsychology. *Psychological Review*, *95*, 307–317.

Farah, M.J. (1989). The neuropsychology of mental imagery. In F. Boller & J. Grafman (Eds.), *Handbook of neuropsychology, Vol. 2*. Amsterdam: Elsevier.

Farah, M.J. (1990). *Visual agnosia: Disorders of object recognition and what they tell us about normal vision*. Cambridge, MA: MIT Press.

Farah, M.J. (1994a). Specialisation within visual object recognition: Clues from prosopagnosia and alexia. In M.J. Farah & G. Ratcliff (Eds.), *The neuropsychology of high-level vision: Collected tutorial essays*. Hillsdale, NJ: Lawrence Erlbaum Associates Inc.

Farah, M.J. (1994b). Neuropsychological inference with an interactive brain: A critique of the "locality" assumption. *Behavioral & Brain Sciences*, *17*, 43–104.

Farah, M.J. (1995). Current issues in the neuropsychology of image generation. *Neuropsychologia*, *33*, 1455–1471.

Farah, M.J., & Aguirre, G.K. (1999). Imaging visual recognition: PET and fMRI studies of the functional anatomy of human visual recognition. *Trends in Cognitive Sciences*, *3*, 179–186.

Farah, M.J., Gazzaniga, M.S., Holtzman, J.D., & Kosslyn, S.M. (1985). A left-hemisphere basis for visual mental imagery? *Neuropsychologia*, *23*, 115–118.

Farah, M.J., Hammond, K.M., Levine, D.N., & Calvanio, R. (1988). Visual and spatial mental imagery: Dissociable systems of representation. *Cognitive Psychology*, *20*, 439–462.

Farah, M.J., & McClelland, J.L. (1991). A computational model of semantic memory impairment: Modality specificity and emergent category specificity. *Journal of Experimental Psychology: General*, *120*, 339–357.

Farah, M.J., O'Reilly, R.C., & Vecera, S.P. (1993). Unconscious perception of extinguished visual stimuli: Reassessing the evidence. *Neuropsychologia*, *29*, 949–958.

Farah, M.J., Peronnet, F., Gonon, M.A., & Giard, M.H. (1988). Electrophysiological evidence for a shared representational medium for visual images and visual percepts. *Journal of Experimental Psychology: General*, *117*, 248–257.

Farah, M.J., & Wallace, M.A. (1992). Semantically-bounded anomia: Implications for the neural implementation of naming. *Neuropsychologia*, *30*, 609–621.

Farah, M.J., Weisberg, L.L., Monheit, M., & Peronnet, F. (1990). Brain activity underlying mental imagery: Event-related potentials during mental image generation. *Journal of Cognitive Neuroscience*, *1*, 302–316.

Farah, M.J., Wilson, K.D., Drain, M., & Tanaka, J.N. (1998). What is "special" about face perception? *Psychological Review*, *105*, 482–498.

Feldman, J.A., & Ballard, D.H. (1982). Connectionist models and their properties. *Cognitive Science*, *6*, 205–254.

Fendrich, R., Wessinger, C.M., & Gazzaniga, M.S. (1992). Residual vision in a scotoma: Implications for blindsight. *Science*, *258*, 1489–1491.

ffytche, D.H., Guy, C., & Zeki, S. (1995). The parallel visual motion inputs into areas V1 and V5 of the human cerebral cortex. *Brain*, *118*, 1375–1394.

Fiedler, K. (1988). The dependence of the conjunction fallacy on subtle linguistic factors. *Psychological Research*, *50*, 123–129.

Fillenbaum, S. (1993). Deductive reasoning: What are taken to be the premises and how are they interpreted? *Behavioral & Brain Sciences*, *16*, 348–349.

Fillmore, C.J. (1968). The case for case. In E. Bach & R.T. Harms (Eds.), *Universals of linguistic theory.* New York: Holt, Rinehart & Winston.

Fillmore, C.J. (1982). Frame semantics. In Linguistic Society of Korea (Eds.), *Linguistics in the morning calm.* Seoul: Hanshin.

Finke, R.A., Ward, T.B., & Smith, S.M. (1992). *Creative cognition: Theory, research and applications.* Cambridge, MA: MIT Press.

Finkenauer, C., Luminet, O., Gisle, L., El-Ahmadi, A., & van der Linden, M. (1998). Flashbulb memories and the underlying mechanisms of their formation: Toward an emotional-integrative model. *Memory & Cognition*, *26*, 516–531.

Fisher, R.P., Geiselman, R.E., & Amador, M. (1990). A field test of the cognitive interview: Enhancing the recollections of actual victims and witnesses of crime. *Journal of Applied Psychology*, *74*, 722–727.

Fisher, R.P., Geiselman, R.E., Raymond, D.S., Jurkevich, L.M., & Warhaftig, M.L. (1987). Enhancing enhanced eyewitness memory: Refining the cognitive interview. *Journal of Police Science and Administration*, *15*, 291–297.

Fitts, P.M., & Posner, M.I. (1967). *Human performance.* London: Prentice-Hall.

Fleishman, E.A., & Parker, J.F. (1962). Factors in the retention of perceptual-motor skill. *Journal of Experimental Psychology*, *64*, 215–226.

Flexser, A.J., & Tulving, E. (1978). Retrieval independence in recognition and recall. *Psychological Review*, *85*, 153–171.

Flude, B.M., Ellis, A.W., & Kay, J. (1989). Face processing and name retrieval in an anomic aphasia: Names are stored separately from semantic information about people. *Brain & Cognition*, *11*, 60–72.

Fodor, J.A. (1983). *The modularity of mind.* Cambridge, MA: MIT Press.

Fodor, J.A. (1994). *The ELM and the expert: Mentalese and its semantics.* Cambridge, MA: MIT Press.

Fodor, J.A. (1998). *Concepts: Where cognitive science went wrong.* Oxford: Clarendon Press.

Fodor, J.A., Garrett, M.F., Walker, E.C.T., & Parkes, C.H. (1980). Against definitions. *Cognition*, *8*, 263–367.

Fodor, J.A., & Pylyshyn, Z.W. (1981). How direct is visual perception? Some reflections on Gibson's "ecological approach". *Cognition*, *9*, 139–196.

Fodor, J.D., Fodor, J.A., & Garrett, M.F. (1975). The psychological unreality of semantic representations. *Linguistic Inquiry*, *4*, 515–531.

Forde, E.M.E., Francis, D., Riddoch, M.J., Rumian, R.I., & Humphreys, G.W. (1997). On the links between visual knowledge and naming: A single case study of a patient with a category-specific impairment for living things. *Cognitive Neuropsychology*, *14*, 403–458.

Forde, E.M.E., & Humphreys, G.W. (1999). Category-specific recognition impairments: A review of important case studies and influential theories. *Aphasiology*, *13*, 169–193.

Forster, K. (1979). Levels of processing and the structure of the language processor. In W.E. Cooper & E.C.T. Walker (Eds.), *Sentence processing: Psycholinguistic studies presented to Merrill Garrett.* Hillsdale, NJ: Lawrence Erlbaum Associates Inc.

Fowler, W. (1981). Case studies of precocity: The role of exogenous and endogenous stimulation in early mental development. *Journal of Applied Developmental Psychology*, *2*, 319–367.

Fox, E. (1993). Allocation of visual attention and anxiety. *Cognition & Emotion*, *7*, 207–215.

Fox, R., & McDaniel, C. (1982). The perception of biological motion by human infants. *Science*, *218*, 486–487.

Francolini, C.N., & Egeth, H.E. (1980). On the non-automaticity of automatic activation: Evidence of selective seeing. *Perception & Psychophysics*, *27*, 331–342.

Franklin, S., Turner, J., Ralph, M.A.L., Morris, J., & Bailey, P.J. (1996). A distinctive case of word meaning deafness? *Cognitive Neuropsychology*, *13*, 1139–1162.

Frauenfelder, U.H., Segui, J., & Dijkstra, T. (1990). Lexical effects in phonemic processing: Facilitatory or inhibitory? *Journal of Experimental Psychology: Human Perception & Performance, 16*, 77–91.

Frazier, L., & Clifton, C. (1996). *Construal*. Cambridge, MA: MIT Press.

Frazier, L., & Rayner, K. (1982). Making and correcting errors in the analysis of structurally ambiguous sentences. *Cognitive Psychology, 14*, 178–210.

Frege, G. (1952). On sense and reference. In P. Geach & M. Black (Eds.), *Translations from the philosophical writings of Gottlob Frege*. Oxford: Basic Blackwell.

Freud, S. (1901). *The psychopathology of everyday life*. New York: W.W. Norton.

Freud, S. (1915). Repression. In *Freud's collected papers (Vol. IV)*. London: Hogarth.

Freud, S. (1943). *A general introduction to psychoanalysis*. New York: Garden City.

Friedman, A. (1979). Framing pictures: The role of knowledge in automatised encoding and memory for gist. *Journal of Experimental Psychology: General, 108*, 316–355.

Friedman-Hill, S.R., Robertson, L.C., & Treisman, A. (1995). Parietal contributions to visual feature binding: Evidence from a patient with bilateral lesions. *Science, 269*, 853–855.

Frisby, J.P. (1986). The computational approach to vision. In I. Roth & J.P. Frisby (Eds.), *Perception and representation: A cognitive approach*. Milton Keynes, UK: Open University Press.

Frisby, J.P., & Mayhew, J.E.W. (1976). Rivalrous texture stereograms. *Nature, 264*, 53–56.

Friston, K.J., Frith, C.D., Passingham, R.E., Liddle, P.F., & Frackowiak, R.S.J. (1996). Motor practice and neurophysiological adaptation in the cerebellum: A positron tomography study. *Proceedings of the Royal Society of London, Series B Biological Sciences, 248*, 223–228.

Fromkin, V.A. (1993). Speech production. In J.B. Gleason & N.B. Ratner (Eds.), *Psycholinguistics*. Orlando, FL: Harcourt Brace.

Frost, R. (1998). Toward a strong phonological theory of visual word recognition: True issues and false trails. *Psychological Bulletin, 123*, 71–99.

Fruzzetti, A.E., Toland, K., Teller, S.A., & Loftus, E.F. (1992). Memory and eyewitness testimony. In M. Gruneberg & P. Morris (Eds.), *Aspects of memory: The practical aspects*. London: Routledge.

Fry, G.A., Bridgman, C.S., & Ellerbrock, V.J. (1949). The effect of atmospheric scattering on binocular depth perception. *American Journal of Optometry, 26*, 9–15.

Fujii, T., Rukatsu, R., Watabe, S., Ohnura, A., Teramura, K., Kimura, I., Saso, S., & Kogure, K. (1990). Auditory sound agnosia without aphasia following a right temporal lobe lesion. *Cortex, 26*, 263–268.

Funnell, E. (1992). On recognising misspelled words. In C.M. Sterling & C. Robson (Eds.), *Psychology, spelling and education*. Clevedon, UK: Multilingual Matters.

Funnell, E., & Sheridan, J. (1992). Categories of knowledge: Unfamiliar aspects of living and non-living things. *Cognitive Neuropsychology, 9*, 135–154.

Gabrieli, J., Fleischman, D., Keane, M., Reminger, S., & Morell, F. (1995). Double dissociation between memory systems underlying explicit and implicit memory in the human brain. *Psychological Science, 6*, 76–82.

Gabrieli, J.D.E. (1998). Cognitive neuroscience of human memory. *Annual Review of Psychology, 49*, 87–115.

Gabrieli, J.D.E., Cohen, N.J., & Corkin, S. (1988). The impaired learning of semantic knowledge following bilateral medial temporal-lobe resection. *Brain, 7*, 157–177.

Gabrieli, J.D.E., Desmond, J.E., Demb, J.B., Wagner, A.D., Stone, M.V., Vaidya, C.J., & Glover, G.H. (1996). Functional magnetic resonance imaging of semantic memory processes in the frontal lobes. *Psychological Science, 7*, 278–283.

Gaffan, D., & Heywood, C.A. (1993). A spurious category-specific visual agnosia for living things in normal human and nonhuman primates. *Journal of Cognitive Neuroscience, 5*, 118–128.

Galambos, J.A., Abelson, R.P., & Black, J.B. (1986). *Knowledge structures*. Hillsdale, NJ: Lawrence Erlbaum Associates Inc.

Galambos, J.A., & Rips, L.J. (1982). Memory for routines. *Journal of Verbal Learning & Verbal Behavior*, *21*, 260–281.

Galton, F. (1883). *Inquiries into human development and its development*. London: Macmillan.

Garavan, H., Doherty, M.E., & Mynatt, C.R. (1997). When falsification fails. *Irish Journal of Psychology*, *18*, 267–292.

Gardiner, J.M., & Java, R.I. (1993). Recognising and remembering. In A.F. Collins, S.E. Gathercole, M.A. Conway, & P.E. Morris (Eds.), *Theories of memory*. Hove, UK: Psychology Press.

Gardiner, J.M., & Parkin, A.J. (1990). Attention and recollective experience in recognition. *Memory & Cognition*, *18*, 579–583.

Gardner, H. (1984). *Frames of mind*. New York: Heinemann.

Gardner, H. (1985). *The mind's new science*. New York: Basic Books.

Garrett, M.F. (1975). The analysis of sentence production. In G.H. Bower (Ed.), *The psychology of learning and motivation, Vol. 9*. San Diego, CA: Academic Press.

Garrett, M.F. (1976). Syntactic processes in sentence production. In R.J. Wales & E. Walker (Eds.), *New approaches to language mechanisms*. Amsterdam: North-Holland.

Garrett, M.F. (1980). Levels of processing in sentence production. In B. Butterworth (Ed.), *Language production: Vol. 1. Speech and talk*. San Diego, CA: Academic Press.

Garrod, S., & Pickering, M.J. (1999). *Language processing*. Hove, UK: Psychology Press.

Gauld, A., & Stephenson, G.M. (1967). Some experiments relating to Bartlett's theory of remembering. *British Journal of Psychology*, *58*, 39–50.

Gazzaniga, M.S., Ivry, R.B., & Mangun, G.R. (1998). *Cognitive neuroscience: The biology of the mind*. New York: W.W. Norton & Co.

Geis, M., & Zwicky, A.M. (1971). On invited inferences. *Linguistic Inquiry*, *2*, 561–566.

Geiselman, R.E., & Fisher, R.P. (1997). Ten years of cognitive interviewing. In D.G. Payne & F.G. Conrad (Eds.), *Intersections in basic and applied memory research*. Mahwah, NJ: Lawrence Erlbaum Associates Inc.

Geiselman, R.E., Fisher, R.P., MacKinnon, D.P., & Holland, H.L. (1985). Eyewitness memory enhancement in police interview: Cognitive retrieval mnemonics versus hypnosis. *Journal of Applied Psychology*, *70*, 401–412.

Gentilucci, M., Chieffi, S., Daprati, E., Saetti, M.C., & Toni, I. (1996). Visual illusion and action. *Neuropsychologia*, *34*, 369–376.

Gentner, D. (1975). Evidence for the psychological reality of semantic components: The verbs of possession. In D.A. Norman & D.E. Rumelhart (Eds.), *Explorations in cognition*. San Francisco, CA: Freeman.

Gentner, D. (1981). Verb structures in memory for sentences: Evidence for componential representation. *Cognitive Psychology*, *13*, 56–83.

Gentner, D. (1983). Structure-mapping: A theoretical framework for analogy. *Cognitive Science*, *7*, 155–170.

Gentner, D., & Markman, A.B. (1997). Structure mapping in analogy and similarity. *American Psychologist*, *52*, 45–56.

Gentner, D., & Markman, A.M. (in press). Why syntactic graph matches are not analogies. *Journal of Experimental Psychology: Language, Memory & Cognition*.

Gentner, D., Rattermann, M.J., & Forbus, K. (1992). The role of similarity in transfer. *Cognitive Psychology*, *25*, 431–467.

Gentner, D., & Stevens, A.L. (1983). *Mental models*. Hillsdale, NJ: Lawrence Erlbaum Associates Inc.

Gentner, D., & Toupin, C. (1986). Systematicity and surface similarity in the development of analogy. *Cognitive Science*, *10*, 227–300.

George, C. (1995). The endorsement of premises: Assumption-based or belief-based reasoning. *British Journal of Psychology*, *86*, 93–111.

Georgopoulos, A.P. (1997). Voluntary movement: Computational principles and neural mechanisms. In M.D. Rugg (Ed.), *Cognitive neuroscience*. Hove, UK: Psychology Press.

Gernsbacher, M.A., Varner, K.R., & Faust, M. (1990). Investigating differences in general comprehension skill. *Journal of Experimental Psychology: Learning, Memory, & Cognition*, *16*, 430–445.

Gerrig, R.J., & Bower, G.H. (1982). Emotional influences on word recognition. *Bulletin of the Psychonomic Society, 21,* 175–178.

Gibbs, R.W. (1979). Contextual effects in understanding indirect requests. *Discourse Processes, 2,* 1–10.

Gibbs, R.W. (1983). Do people always process the literal meaning of indirect requests? *Journal of Experimental Psychology: Learning, Memory, & Cognition, 9,* 524–533.

Gibson, J.J. (1950). *The perception of the visual world.* Boston: Houghton Mifflin.

Gibson, J.J. (1966). *The senses considered as perceptual systems.* Boston: Houghton Mifflin.

Gibson, J.J. (1979). *The ecological approach to visual perception.* Boston: Houghton Mifflin.

Gick, M.L., & Holyoak, K.J. (1980). Analogical problem solving. *Cognitive Psychology, 12,* 306–355.

Gick, M.L., & Holyoak, K.J. (1983). Schema induction in analogical transfer. *Cognitive Psychology, 15,* 1–38.

Gigerenzer, G. (1996). On narrow norms and vague heuristics: A reply to Kahneman and Tversky (1996). *Psychological Review, 103,* 592–596.

Gigerenzer, G., & Hoffrage, U. (1999). Overcoming difficulties in Bayesian reasoning: A reply to Lewis and Keren (1999) and Mellers and McGraw (1999). *Psychological Review, 106,* 425–430.

Gigerenzer, G., & Hug, K. (1992). Domain specific reasoning: Social contracts, cheating and perspective change. *Cognition, 43,* 127–171.

Gigerenzer, G., Todd, P.M., & the ABC Research Group (1999). *Simple heuristics that make us smart.* Oxford: Oxford University Press.

Gilhooly, K.J. (1995). *Thinking: Directed, undirected and creative (2nd Edn).* London: Academic Press.

Gilhooly, K.J., & Falconer, W. (1974). Concrete and abstract terms and relations in testing a rule. *Quarterly Journal of Experimental Psychology, 26,* 355–359.

Gill, H.S., O'Boyle, M.W., & Hathaway, J. (1998). Cortical distribution of EEG activity for component processes during mental rotation. *Cortex, 34,* 707–718.

Gilligan, S.G., & Bower, G.H. (1984). Cognitive consequences of emotional arousal. In C. Izard, J. Kagen, & R. Zajonc (Eds.), *Emotions, cognition, and behaviour.* New York: Cambridge University Press.

Gillund, G., & Shiffrin, R.M. (1984). A retrieval model for both recognition and recall. *Psychological Review, 91,* 1–67.

Gilmore, D.J., & Green, T.R.G. (1988). Programming plans and programming expertise. *Quarterly Journal of Experimental Psychology, 40*A, 423–442.

Ginsburg, A.P., Evans, D.W., Sekuler, R., & Harp, S.A. (1982). Contrast sensitivity predicts pilots' performance in aircraft simulation. *American Journal of Optometry & Physiological Optics, 59,* 105–108.

Girotto, V., Mazzacco, A., & Cherubini, P. (1992). Judgements of deontic relevance in reasoning: A reply to Jackson & Griggs. *Quarterly Journal of Experimental Psychology, 45*A, 547–574.

Glanzer, M., & Cunitz, A.R. (1966). Two storage mechanisms in free recall. *Journal of Verbal Learning & Verbal Behavior, 5,* 351–360.

Glass, A.L., & Holyoak, K.J. (1975). Alternative conceptions of semantic memory. *Cognition, 3,* 313–339.

Glenberg, A.M. (1987). Temporal context and recency. In D.S. Gorfein & R.R. Hoffman (Eds.), *Memory and learning: The Ebbinghaus centennial conference.* Hillsdale, NJ: Lawrence Erlbaum Associates Inc.

Glenberg, A.M., Meyer, M., & Linden, K. (1987). Mental models contribute to foregrounding during text comprehension. *Journal of Memory & Language, 26,* 69–83.

Glenberg, A.M., Smith, S.M., & Green, C. (1977). Type I rehearsal: Maintenance and more. *Journal of Verbal Learning & Verbal Behavior, 16,* 339–352.

Gluck, M., & Bower, G.H. (1988). From conditioning to category learning: An adaptive network model. *Journal of Experimental Psychology: General, 117,* 227–247.

Glushko, R.J. (1979). The organisation and activation of orthographic knowledge in reading aloud. *Journal of Experimental Psychology: Human Perception & Performance, 5,* 674–691.

Gobet, F. (1998a). Expert memory: A comparison of four theories. *Cognition, 66,* 115–152.

Gobet, F. (1998b). Memory for the meaningfulness: How chunks help. *Proceedings of the 20th Annual Conference of the Cognitive Science Society.* Mahwah, NJ: Lawrence Erlbaum Associates Inc.

Gobet, F., & Simon, H.A. (1996a). Recall of rapidly presented random board positions is a function of skill. *Psychonomic Bulletin & Review, 3,* 159–163.

Gobet, F., & Simon, H.A. (1996b). Templates in chess memory: A mechanism for recalling several boards. *Cognitive Psychology, 31,* 1–40.

Gobet, F., & Simon, H.A. (in press). Five seconds or sixty: Presentation time in expert memory. *Cognitive Science.*

Godden, D.R., & Baddeley, A.D. (1975). Context-dependent memory in two natural environments: On land and under water. *British Journal of Psychology, 66,* 325–331.

Godden, D.R., & Baddeley, A.D. (1980). When does context influence recognition memory? *British Journal of Psychology, 71,* 99–104.

Goel, V., Gold, B., Kapur, S., & Houle, S. (1997). The seats of reason? An imaging study of deductive and inductive reasoning. *Neuroreport, 8,* 1305–1310.

Goel, V., & Grafman, J. (1995). Are the frontal lobes implicated in planning functions: Interpreting data from the Tower of Hanoi. *Neuropsychologia, 33,* 623–642.

Goldberg, G. (1989). The ability of patients with brain damage to generate mental visual images. *Brain, 112,* 305–325.

Golding, E. (1981). The effect of unilateral brain lesion on reasoning. *Cortex, 17,* 31–40.

Goldman, A.I. (1986). *Epistemology and cognition.* Cambridge, MA: Harvard University Press.

Goldstein, E.B. (1996). *Sensation and perception (4th Edn).* New York: Brooks/Cole.

Goldstone, R.L., Medin, D.L., & Gentner, D. (1991). Relational similarity and the nonindependence of features in similarity judgements. *Cognitive Psychology, 23,* 222–262.

Gomulicki, B.R. (1956). Recall as an abstractive process. *Acta Psychologica, 12,* 77–94.

Goodale, M.A., & Humphrey, G.K. (1998). The objects of action and perception. *Cognition, 67,* 181–207.

Goodale, M.A., & Milner, A.D. (1992). Separate visual pathways for perception and action. *Trends in Neuroscience, 15,* 22–25.

Goodall, W.C., & Phillips, W.A. (1995). Three routes from print to sound: Evidence from a case of acquired dyslexia. *Cognitive Neuropsychology, 12,* 113–147.

Gordon, I.E. (1989). *Theories of visual perception.* Chichester, UK: John Wiley & Sons.

Gorman, M.E. (1992). Experimental simulations of falsification. In M.T. Keane & K.J. Gilhooly (Eds.), *Advances in the psychology of thinking.* London: Harvester Wheatsheaf.

Gorman, M.E., & Gorman, M.E. (1984). A comparison of disconfirmation, confirmation and control strategy on Wason's 2−4−6 task. *Quarterly Journal of Experimental Psychology, 36*A, 629–648.

Gotlib, I.H., McLachlan, A.L., & Katz, A.N. (1988). Biases in visual attention in depressed and nondepressed individuals. *Cognition & Emotion, 2,* 185–200.

Gould, J.D. (1978). An experimental study of writing, dictating, and speaking. In J. Requin (Ed.), *Attention and performance, Vol. VII.* Hillsdale, NJ: Lawrence Erlbaum Associates Inc.

Gould, J.D. (1980). Experiments on composing letters: Some facts, some myths, and some observations. In L.W. Gregg & E.R. Sternberg (Eds.), *Cognitive processes in writing.* Hillsdale, NJ: Lawrence Erlbaum Associates Inc.

Graesser, A.C., Gordon, S.E., & Sawyer, J.D. (1979). Recognition memory for typical and atypical actions: Tests of a script pointer + tag hypothesis. *Journal of Verbal Learning & Verbal Behavior, 18,* 319–332.

Graesser, A.C., Millis, K.K., & Zwaan, R.A. (1997). Discourse comprehension. *Annual Review of Psychology, 48,* 163–189.

Graesser, A.C., Singer, M., & Trabasso, T. (1994). Constructing inferences during narrative text comprehension. *Psychological Review, 101,* 371–395.

Graesser, A.C., Woll, S.B., Kowalski, D.J., & Smith, D.A. (1980). Memory for typical and atypical actions in scripted activities. *Journal of Experimental Psychology: Human Learning & Memory, 6*, 503–515.

Graf, P., & Mandler, G. (1984). Activation makes words more accessible, but not necessarily more retrievable. *Journal of Verbal Learning & Verbal Behavior, 23*, 553–568.

Graf, P., & Schacter, D.L. (1985). Implicit and explicit memory for new associations in normal and amnesic subjects. *Journal of Experimental Psychology: Learning, Memory, & Cognition, 11*, 501–518.

Graf, P., Squire, L.R., & Mandler, G. (1984). The information that amnesic patients do not forget. *Journal of Experimental Psychology: Learning, Memory, & Cognition, 10*, 164–178.

Grafman, J. (1995). Similarities and distinctions among current models of prefrontal cortical functions. In J. Grafman, K.J. Holyoak, & F. Boller (Eds.), Structure and functions of the human prefrontal cortex. *Annals of the New York Academy of Sciences, 769*, 337–368.

Grafton, S., Hazeltine, E., & Ivry, R. (1995). Functional mapping of sequence learning in normal humans. *Journal of Cognitive Neuroscience, 7*, 497–510.

Graham, N.L., Patterson, K., & Hodges, J.R. (1997). Progressive dysgraphia: Co-occurrence of central and peripheral impairments. *Cognitive Neuropsychology, 14*, 975–1005.

Grainger, J., & Segui, J. (1990). Neighbourhood frequency effects in visual word recognition: A comparison of lexical decision and masked identification latencies. *Perception & Psychophysics, 47*, 191–198.

Gray, J.A., & Wedderburn, A.A. (1960). Grouping strategies with simultaneous stimuli. *Quarterly Journal of Experimental Psychology, 12*, 180–184.

Graziano, M.S.A., Andersen, R.A., & Snowden, R.J. (1994). Tuning of MST neurons to spiral motions. *Journal of Neuroscience, 14*, 54–67.

Green, A.J.K., & Gilhooly, K.J. (1992). Empirical advances in expertise research. In M.T. Keane & K.J. Gilhooly (Eds.), *Advances in the psychology of thinking*. London: Harvester Wheatsheaf.

Green, K.P., Kuhl, P.K., Meltzoff, A.N., & Stevens, E.B. (1991). Integrating speech information across talkers, gender, and sensory modality: Female faces and male voices in the McGurk effect. *Perception & Psychophysics, 50*, 524–536.

Green, T.R.G. (1989). Cognitive dimensions of notation. In A. Sutcliffe & L. Macaulay (Eds.), *People and computers (vol. 5)*. Cambridge: Cambridge University Press.

Green, T.R.G. (1990). Programming languages as information structures. In J.-M. Hoc, T.R.G. Green, R. Samurçay, & D.J. Gilmore (Eds.), *Psychology of programming*. London: Academic Press.

Greeno, J.G. (1994). Gibson's affordances. *Psychological Review, 101*, 336–342.

Gregory, R.L. (1970). *The intelligent eye*. New York: McGraw-Hill.

Gregory, R.L. (1972). Seeing as thinking. *Times Literary Supplement*, 23 June.

Gregory, R.L. (1973). The confounded eye. In R.L. Gregory & E.H. Gombrich (Eds.), *Illusion in nature and art*. London: Duckworth.

Gregory, R.L. (1980). Perceptions as hypotheses. *Philosophical Transactions of the Royal Society of London, Series B, 290*, 181–197.

Grice, H.P. (1967). Logic and conversation. In P. Cole & J.L. Morgan (Eds.), *Studies in syntax, Vol. III*. New York: Seminar Press.

Grice, H.P. (1975). Logic and conversation. In P. Cole & J.L. Morgan (Eds.), *Syntax and semantics, III: Speech acts*. New York: Seminar Press.

Griggs, R.A. (1983). The role of problem content in the selection task and THOG problem. In J.St.B.T. Evans (Ed.), *Thinking and reasoning: Psychological approaches*. London: Routledge & Kegan Paul.

Griggs, R.A., & Cox, J.R. (1982). The elusive thematic-material effect in Wason's selection task. *British Journal of Psychology, 73*, 407–420.

Griggs, R.A., & Cox, J.R. (1983). The effects of problem content and negation on Wason's selection task. *Quarterly Journal of Experimental Psychology, 35*A, 519–533.

Griggs, R.A., & Cox, J.R. (1993). Permission schemas and the selection task. *Quarterly Journal of Experimental Psychology, 46*A, 637–652.

Groeger, J.A. (1997). *Memory and remembering.* Harlow, UK: Addison Wesley Longman.

Grudin, J.T. (1983). Error patterns in novice and skilled transcription typing. In W.E. Cooper (Ed.), *Cognitive aspects of skilled typewriting.* New York: Springer.

Gunther, H., Gfoerer, S., & Weiss, L. (1984). Inflection, frequency, and the word superiority effect. *Psychological Research, 46,* 261–281.

Guynn, M.J., McDaniel, M.A., & Einstein, G.O. (1998). Prospective memory: When reminders fail. *Memory & Cognition, 26,* 287–298.

Guyote, M.J., & Sternberg, R.J. (1981). A transitive-chain theory of syllogistic reasoning. *Cognitive Psychology, 13,* 461–524.

Haarmann, H., Just, M.A., & Carpenter, P.A. (1997). Aphasic sentence comprehension as a resource deficit: A computational approach. *Brain & Language, 59,* 76–120.

Haber, R.N. (1983). The impending demise of the icon: A critique of the concept of iconic storage in visual information processing. *Behavioral & Brain Sciences, 6,* 1–11.

Haberlandt, K. (1999). *Human memory: Exploration and application.* Boston, MA: Allyn & Bacon.

Hadamard, J. (1945). *A essay on the psychology of invention in the mathematical field.* New York: Dover.

Haffenden, A.M., & Goodale, M.A. (1998). The effect of pictorial illusion on prehension and perception. *Journal of Cognitive Neuroscience, 10,* 122–136.

Halford, G.S. (1984). Can young children integrate premises in transitivity and serial-order tasks? *Cognitive Psychology, 16,* 65–93.

Halford, G.S. (1992). Analogical reasoning and conceptual complexity in cognitive development. *Human Development, 35,* 193–217.

Halford, G.S., & Wilson, W.H. (1980). A category theory approach to cognitive development. *Cognitive Psychology, 16,* 65–93.

Halford, G.S., Wilson, W.H., & Phillips, S. (1998). Processing capacity defined by relational complexity: Implications for comparative, developmental and cognitive psychology. *Behavioral & Brain Sciences, 21,* 803–829.

Hall, D.A., & Riddoch, M.J. (1997). Word meaning deafness: Spelling words that are not understood. *Cognitive Neuropsychology, 14,* 1131–1164.

Halliday, M.A.K. (1987). Spoken and written modes of meaning. In R. Horowitz & S.J. Samuels (Eds.), *Comprehending oral and written language.* New York: Academic Press.

Hampson, P.J. (1989). Aspects of attention and cognitive science. *The Irish Journal of Psychology, 10,* 261–275.

Hampton, J.A. (1979). Polymorphous concepts in semantic memory. *Journal of Verbal Learning & Verbal Behavior, 18,* 441–461.

Hampton, J.A. (1981). An investigation of the nature of abstract concepts. *Memory & Cognition, 9,* 149–156.

Hampton, J.A. (1982). A demonstration of intransitivity in natural categories. *Cognition, 12,* 151–164.

Hampton, J.A. (1983). *A composite prototype model of conceptual conjunction.* Unpublished manuscript, The City University, London.

Hampton, J.A. (1987). Inheritance of attributes in natural concept conjunctions. *Memory & Cognition, 15,* 55–71.

Hampton, J.A. (1988). Overextension of conjunctive concepts. *Journal of Experimental Psychology: Language, Memory, & Cognition, 14,* 12–32.

Hampton, J.A. (1995). Testing the prototype theory of concepts. *Journal of Memory & Language, 34,* 686–708.

Hampton, J.A. (1998). Similarity-based categorisation and fuzziness of natural categories. *Cognition, 65,* 137–165.

Hanley, J.R., & Kay, J. (1992). Does letter-by-letter reading involve the spelling system? *Neuropsychologia, 30,* 237–256.

Hardcastle, V.G. (1996). *How to build a theory in cognitive science.* Albany, NY: State University of New York Press.

Hardyck, C.D., & Petrinovich, L.F. (1970). Subvocal speech and comprehension level as a function of the difficulty level of reading material. *Journal of Verbal Learning & Verbal Behavior, 9,* 647–652.

Harley, T. (1984). A critique of top-down independent levels models of speech production: Evidence from non-plan-internal speech errors. *Cognitive Science, 8,* 191–219.

Harley, T.A. (1995). *The psychology of language: From data to theory*. Hove, UK: Psychology Press.

Harley, T.A., & Brown, H.E. (1998). What causes a tip-of-the-tongue state? Evidence for lexical neighbourhood effects in speech production. *British Journal of Psychology, 89*, 151–174.

Harris, I.M., Egan, G.F., Paxinos, G., & Watson, J.D.G. (1998). Functional activation in the right parietal lobe during mental rotation of letters. *European Journal of Neuroscience, 10*, 9913.

Harris, M. (1990). Language and thought. In M.W. Eysenck (Ed.), *The Blackwell dictionary of cognitive psychology*. Oxford: Blackwell.

Hart, J., Berndt, R.S., & Caramazza, A. (1985). Category-specific naming deficit following cerebral infarction. *Nature, 316*, 439–440.

Harvey, L.O., Roberts, J.O., & Gervais, M.J. (1983). The spatial frequency basis of internal representations. In H.-G. Geissler, H.F.J.M. Buffart, E.L.J. Leeuwenberg, & V. Sarris (Eds.), *Modern issues in perception*. Rotterdam: North-Holland.

Hatano, G., & Inagaki, K. (1986). Two courses of expertise. In H. Stevenson, H. Azuma, & K. Hatuka (Eds.), *Child development in Japan*. San Francisco, CA: Freeman.

Hatfield, F.M., & Patterson, K.E. (1983). Phonological spelling. *Quarterly Journal of Experimental Psychology, 35*A, 451–468.

Haxby, J.V., Horwitz, B., Ungerleider, L.G., Maisog, J.M., Pietrini, P., & Grady, C.L. (1994). The functional organisation of human extrastriate cortex: A PET-rCBF study of selective attention to faces and locations. *Journal of Neuroscience, 14*, 6336–6353.

Hay, J.F., & Jacoby, L.L. (1996). Separating habit and recollection: Memory slips, process dissociations, and probability matching. *Journal of Experimental Psychology: Learning, Memory, & Cognition, 22*, 1323–1335.

Hayes, J.R., & Flower, L.S. (1980). Identifying the organisation of writing processes. In L.W. Gregg & E.R. Sternberg (Eds.), *Cognitive processes in writing*. Hillsdale, NJ: Lawrence Erlbaum Associates Inc.

Hayes, J.R., & Flower, L.S. (1986). Writing research and the writer. *American Psychologist, 41*, 1106–1113.

Hayes, J.R., Flower, L.S., Schriver, K., Stratman, J., & Carey, L. (1985). *Cognitive processes in revision* (Technical Report No. 12). Pittsburgh, PA: Carnegie Mellon University.

Hayes, J.R., & Simon, H.A. (1974). Understanding written problem instructions. In R.L. Gregg (Ed.), *Knowledge and cognition*. Hillsdale, NJ: Lawrence Erlbaum Associates Inc.

Hayes, J.R., & Simon, H.A. (1977). Psychological differences among problem isomorphs. In N.J. Castellan, D.B. Pisoni, & G.R. Potts (Eds.), *Cognitive theory, vol. 2*. Hillsdale, NJ: Lawrence Erlbaum Associates Inc.

Hayes, P.J. (1985). Some problems and non-problems in representational theory. In R.J. Brachman & H.J. Levesque (Eds.), *Readings in knowledge representation*. Los Altos, CA: Morgan Kaufmann.

Hazeltine, E., Grafton, S.T., & Ivry, R. (1997). Attention and stimulus characteristics determine the locus of motor-sequence encoding: A PET study. *Brain, 120*, 123–140.

Hebb, D.O. (1949). *The organisation of behaviour*. New York: John Wiley.

Hecht, H. (1996). Heuristics and invariants in dynamic event perception: Immunized concepts or nonstatements? *Psychonomic Bulletin & Review, 3*, 61–70.

Heider, E. (1972). Universals in color naming and memory. *Journal of Experimental Psychology, 93*, 10–20.

Heinze, H.J., Mangun, G.R., Burchert, W., Hinrichs, H., Scholz, M., Munte, T.F., Gos, A., Scherg, M., Johannes, S., Hundeshagen, H., Gazzaniga, M.X., & Hillyard, S.A. (1994). Combined spatial and temporal imaging of brain activity during visual selective attention in humans. *Nature, 372*, 543–546.

Heit, E. (1992). Categorisation using chains of examples. *Cognitive Psychology, 24*, 341–380.

Heller, J., & Reif, F. (1984). Prescribing effective human problem solving: Problem description in physics. *Cognition & Instruction, 2*, 191–203.

Helm-Estabrooks, N., Bayles, K., & Bryant, S. (1994). Four forms of perseveration in dementia and aphasia patients and normal elders. *Brain & Language, 47*, 457–460.

Helmholtz, H. von (1866). *Treatise on physiological optics*, Vol. III. New York: Dover [translation published 1962].

Henderson, J.M. (1992). Object identification in context: The visual processing of natural scenes. *Canadian Journal of Psychology, 46*, 319–341.

Henle, M. (1962). On the relation between logic and thinking. *Psychological Review, 69*, 366–378.

Hering, E. (1878). *Zur Lehre vom Lichtsinn*. Vienna: Gerold.

Hertwig, R., Ortmann, A., & Gigerenzer, G. (1997). Deductive competence: A desert devoid of content and context. *Current Psychology of Cognition, 16*, 102–107.

Heywood, C.A., Cowey, A., & Newcombe, F. (1994). On the role of parvocellular P and magnocellular M pathways in cerebral achromatopsia. *Brain, 117*, 245–254.

Hillis, A.E., & Caramazza, A. (1995). Cognitive and neural mechanisms underlying visual and semantic processing: Implications from optic aphasia. *Journal of Cognitive Neuroscience, 7*, 457–478.

Hinton, G.E. (1979). Some demonstrations of the effects of structural descriptions in mental imagery. *Cognitive Science, 3*, 231–251.

Hinton, G.E., & Anderson, J.A. (1981). *Parallel models of associative memory*. Hillsdale, NJ: Lawrence Erlbaum Associates Inc.

Hinton, G.E., McClelland, J.L., & Rumelhart, D.E. (1986). Distributed representations. In D.E. Rumelhart, J.L. McClelland, & the PDP Research Group (Eds.), *Parallel distributed processing: Volume 1, foundations*. Cambridge, MA: MIT Press.

Hinton, G.E., & Shallice, T. (1991). Leisoning an attractor network: Investigations of acquired dyslexia. *Psychological Review, 98*, 74–95.

Hintzman, D.L. (1986). "Schema abstraction" in a multiple-trace memory model. *Psychological Review, 93*, 411–428.

Hintzman, D.L. (1990). Human learning and memory: Connections and dissociations. *Annual Review of Psychology, 41*, 109–139.

Hird, K., & Kirsner, K. (1993). Dysprosody following acquired neurogenic impairment. *Brain & Language, 45*, 46–60.

Hirst, W., Spelke, E.S., Reaves, C.C., Caharack, G., & Neisser, U. (1980). Dividing attention without alternation or automaticity. *Journal of Experimental Psychology: General, 109*, 98–117.

Hitch, G.J., & Ferguson, J. (1991). Prospective memory for future intentions: Some comparisons with memory for past events. *European Journal of Cognitive Psychology, 3*, 285–295.

Hockey, G.R.J., Davies, S., & Gray, M.M. (1972). Forgetting as a function of sleep at different times of day. *Quarterly Journal of Experimental Psychology, 24*, 386–393.

Hoffman, C., Lau, I., & Johnson, D.R. (1986). The linguistic relativity of person cognition. *Journal of Personality & Social Psychology, 51*, 1097–1105.

Hoffman, D.D., & Richards, W.A. (1984). Parts of recognition. *Cognition, 18*, 65–96.

Holcomb, P.J., Kounios, J., Anderson, J.E., & West, W.C. (1999). Dual-coding, context-availability, and concreteness effects in sentence comprehension: An electrophysiological investigation. *Journal of Experimental Psychology: Learning, Memory, & Cognition, 25*, 721–742.

Holding, D.H. (1985). *The psychology of chess*. Hillsdale, NJ: Lawrence Erlbaum Associates Inc.

Holding, D.H. (1989). *Human skills (2nd Edn)*. Chichester, UK: Wiley.

Holding, D.H. (1992). Theories of chess skill. *Psychological Research, 54*, 10–16.

Holding, D.H., & Reynolds, J.R. (1982). Recall or evaluation of chess positions as determinants of chess skill. *Memory & Cognition, 10*, 237–242.

Holland, J.H., Holyoak, K.J., Nisbett, R.E., & Thagard, P. (1986). *Induction: Processes in inference, learning and discovery*. Cambridge, MA: MIT Press.

Hollands, M.A., Marple, H., Dilwyn, E., Henkes, S., & Rowan, A.K. (1995). Human eye movements during visually guided stepping. *Journal of Motor Behavior, 27*, 155–163.

Holmes, V.M., & Carruthers, J. (1998). The relation between reading and spelling in skilled adult readers. *Journal of Memory & Language, 39*, 264–289.

Holst, V.F., & Pezdek, K. (1992). Scripts for typical crimes and their effects on memory for eyewitness testimony. *Applied Cognitive Psychology, 6*, 573–587.

Holway, A.F., & Boring, E.G. (1941). Determinants of apparent visual size with distance variant. *American Journal of Psychology, 54*, 21–37.

Holyoak, K.J. (1991). Symbolic connectionism: Toward third-generation theories of expertise. In A. Ericsson & J. Smith (Eds.), *Toward a general theory of expertise*. Cambridge: Cambridge University Press.

Holyoak, K.J., & Koh, K. (1987). Surface and structural similarity in analogical transfer. *Memory & Cognition, 15*, 332–340.

Holyoak, K.J., & Kroger, J.K. (1995). Forms of reasoning. Insight into prefrontal functions? In J. Grafman, K.J. Holyoak, & F. Boller (Eds.), *Structure and functions of the human prefrontal cortex* (pp. 253–263). New York, NY: New York Academy of Sciences.

Holyoak, K.J., & Spellman, B.A. (1993). Thinking. *Annual Review of Psychology, 44*, 265–315.

Holyoak, K.J., & Thagard, P. (1989). Analogical mapping by constraint satisfaction. *Cognitive Science, 13*, 295–355.

Holyoak, K.J., & Thagard, P. (1995). *Mental leaps.* Cambridge, MA: MIT Press.

Horton, W.S., & Keysar, B. (1996). When do speakers take into account common ground? *Cognition, 59*, 91–117.

Hotopf, W.H.N. (1980). Slips of the pen. In U. Frith (Ed.), *Cognitive processes in spelling*. London: Academic Press.

Howard, D. (1997). Language in the human brain. In M.D. Rugg (Ed.), *Cognitive neuroscience*. Hove, UK: Psychology Press.

Howard, D., & Orchard-Lisle, V. (1984). On the origin of semantic errors in naming: Evidence from the case of a global aphasic. *Cognitive Neuropsychology, 1*, 163–190.

Howard, D., Patterson, K.E., Wise, R.J.S., Brown, W.D., Friston, K., Weiller, C., & Frackowiak, R.S.J. (1992). The cortical localisation of the lexicons: Positron emission tomography evidence. *Brain, 115*, 1769–1782.

Howard, D.V., & Howard, J.H. (1992). Adult age differences in the rate of learning serial patterns: Evidence from direct and indirect tests. *Psychology & Aging, 7*, 232–241.

Howard, I.P., Bergstrøm, S.S., & Masao, O. (1990). Shape from shading in different frames of reference. *Perception, 19*, 523–530.

Howe, M.J.A. (1990). *The original of exceptional abilities*. London: Blackwell.

Howe, M.J.A., Davidson, J.W., & Sloboda, J.A. (1998). Innate talents: Reality or myth? *Behavioral & Brain Sciences, 21*, 399–415.

Howe, M.J.A., Davidson, J.W., Moore, D.G., & Sloboda, J.A. (1995). Are there early childhood signs of musical ability? *Psychology of Music, 23*, 162–176.

Howe, M.L., & Courage, M.L. (1997). The emergence and early development of autobiographical memory. *Psychological Review, 104*, 499–523.

Huang, T., & Lee, C. (1989). Motion and structure from orthographic projections. IEEE Transactions on Pattern Analysis and functional architecture in the cat's visual cortex. *Journal of Physiology, 160*, 106–154.

Hubel, D.H., & Wiesel, T.N. (1962). Receptive fields, binocular interaction and functional architecture in the cat's visual cortex. *Journal of Physiology, 160*, 106–154.

Hubel, D.H., & Wiesel, T.N. (1968). Receptive fields and functional architecture of monkey striate cortex. *Journal of Physiology, 148*, 574–591.

Hubel, D.H., & Wiesel, T.N. (1979, September). Brain mechanisms of vision. *Scientific American, 249*, 150–162.

Huey, E.B. (1908). *The psychology and pedagogy of reading*. New York: Macmillan.

Hull, C.L. (1930). Knowledge and purpose as habit mechanisms. *Psychological Review, 37*, 511–525.

Hull, C.L. (1931). Goal attraction and directing ideas conceived as habit phenomena. *Psychological Review, 38*, 487–506.

Hummel, J.E., & Holyoak, K.J. (1997). Distributed representations of structure: A theory of analogical access and mapping. *Psychological Review, 104*, 427–466.

Humphreys, G.W., & Bruce, V. (1989). *Visual cognition: Computational, experimental and neuropsychological perspectives*. Hove, UK: Psychology Press.

Humphreys, G.W., Lamote, C., & Lloyd-Jones, T.J. (1995). An interactive activation approach to object processing: Effects of structural similarity, name frequency and task in normality and pathology. *Memory, 3*, 535–586.

Humphreys, G.W., & Müller, H.J. (1993). Search via recursive rejection (SERR): A connectionist model of visual search. *Cognitive Psychology, 25*, 43–110.

Humphreys, G.W., & Riddoch, M.J. (1984). Routes to object constancy: Implications from neurological impairments of object constancy. *Quarterly Journal of Experimental Psychology, 36*A, 385–415.

Humphreys, G.W., & Riddoch, M.J. (1985). Author corrections to "Routes to object constancy". *Quarterly Journal of Experimental Psychology, 37*A, 493–495.

Humphreys, G.W., & Riddoch, M.J. (1987). *To see but not to see: A case study of visual agnosia*. Hove, UK: Psychology Press.

Humphreys, G.W., & Riddoch, M.J. (1993). Interactions between object and space systems revealed through neuropsychology. In D.E. Meyer & S.M. Kornblum (Eds.), *Attention and performance, Vol. XIV*. London: MIT Press.

Humphreys, G.W., & Riddoch, M.J. (1994). Visual object processing in normality and pathology: Implications for rehabilitation. In M.J. Riddoch & G.W. Humphreys (Eds.), *Cognitive neuropsychology and cognitive rehabilitation*. Hove, UK: Psychology Press.

Humphreys, G.W., Riddoch, M.J., & Quinlan, P.T. (1985). Interactive processes in perceptual organization: Evidence from visual agnosia. In M.I. Posner & O.S.M. Morin (Eds.), *Attention and performance, Vol. XI*. Hillsdale, NJ: Lawrence Erlbaum Associates Inc.

Humphreys, G.W., Riddoch, M.J., & Quinlan, P.T. (1988). Cascade processes in picture identification. *Cognitive Neuropsychology, 5*, 67–103.

Humphreys, G.W., Riddoch, M.J., Quinlan, P.T., Price, C.J., & Donnelly, N. (1992). Parallel pattern processing in visual agnosia. *Canadian Journal of Psychology, 46*, 377–416.

Hunt, E., & Agnoli, F. (1991). The Whorfian hypothesis: A cognitive psychological perspective. *Psychological Review, 98*, 377–389.

Huppert, F.A., & Piercy, M. (1976). Recognition memory in amnesic patients: Effect of temporal context and familiarity of material. *Cortex, 4*, 3–20.

Huppert, F.A., & Piercy, M. (1978). The role of trace strength in recency and frequency judgements by amnesic and control subjects. *Quarterly Journal of Experimental Psychology, 30*, 346–354.

Hurvich, L.M. (1981). *Colour vision*. Sunderland, MA: Sinauer.

Hyde, T.S., & Jenkins, J.J. (1973). Recall for words as a function of semantic, graphic, and syntactic orienting tasks. *Journal of Verbal Learning & Verbal Behavior, 12*, 471–480.

Ingram, R.E., Kendall, P.C., Smith, T.W., Donnell, C., & Ronan, K. (1987). Cognitive specificity in emotional distress. *Journal of Personality & Social Psychology, 53*, 734–742.

Intos-Peterson, M.J. (1983). Imagery paradigms: How vulnerable are they to experimenters' expectations? *Journal of Experimental Psychology: Human Perception & Performance, 9*, 394–412.

Isaac, K., & Just, M.A. (1995). Constraints on thinking in insight and invention. In R.J. Sternberg & J.E. Davidson (Eds.), *The nature of insight*. Cambridge, MA: MIT Press.

Ittelson, W.H. (1951). Size as a cue to distance: Static localisation. *American Journal of Psychology, 64*, 54–67.

Ittelson, W.H. (1952). *The Ames demonstration in perception*. New York: Hafner.

Jackson, S.L., & Griggs, R.A. (1990). The elusive pragmatic reasoning schemas effect. *Quarterly Journal of Experimental Psychology, 42*A, 353–374.

Jacobs, A.M., & Grainger, J. (1992). Testing a semi-stochastic variant of the interactive activation model in different word recognition experiments. *Journal of Experimental Psychology: Human Perception & Performance, 18*, 1174–1188.

Jacoby, L.L. (1983). Remembering the data: Analysing interactive processes in reading. *Journal of Verbal Learning & Verbal Behavior, 22*, 485–508.

Jacoby, L.L. (1998). Invariance in automatic influences of memory: Toward a user's guide for the process-dissociation procedure. *Journal of Experimental Psychology: Learning, Memory, & Cognition, 24*, 3–26.

Jacoby, L.L., Toth, J.P., & Yonelinas, A.P. (1993). Separating conscious and unconscious influences of memory: Measuring recollection. *Journal of Experimental Psychology: General, 122*, 139–154.

Jakobsson, T., Bergstrøm, S.S., Gustafsson, K.A., & Fedorovskaya, E. (1997). Ambiguities in colour constancy and shape from shading. *Perception, 26*, 531–541.

James, W. (1890). *Principles of psychology.* New York: Holt.

Janowsky, J.S., Shimamura, A.P., & Squire, L.R. (1989). Source memory impairment in patients with frontal lobe lesions. *Neuropsychologia, 27*, 1043–1056.

Jeffries, R., Polson, P., Razran, L., & Atwood, M.E. (1977). A process model for missionaries–cannibals and other river-crossing problems. *Cognitive Psychology, 9*, 412–440.

Jenkins, J.G., & Dallenbach, K.M. (1924). Obliviscence during sleep and waking. *American Journal of Psychology, 35*, 605–612.

Johansson, G. (1973). Visual perception of biological motion and a model for its analysis. *Perception & Psychophysics, 14*, 201–211.

Johansson, G. (1975). Visual motion perception. *Scientific American, 232*, 76–89.

Johansson, G., von Hofsten, C., & Jansson, G. (1980). Event perception. *Annual Review of Psychology, 31*, 27–64.

Johnson, C.J., Paivio, A., & Clark, J.M. (1996). Cognitive components of picture naming. *Psychological Bulletin, 120*, 113–139.

Johnson, E.J., Hershey, J., Meszaros, J., & Kunreuther, H. (1993). Framing, probability distortions, and insurance decisions. *Journal of Risk & Uncertainty, 7*, 5–51.

Johnson, K.E., & Mervis, C.B. (1998). Impact of intuitive theories on feature recruitment throughout the continuum of expertise. *Memory & Cognition, 26*, 382–401.

Johnson-Laird, P.N. (1975). Models of deduction. In R.J. Falmagne (Ed.), *Reasoning: Representation and process in children and adults.* Hillsdale, NJ: Lawrence Erlbaum Associates Inc.

Johnson-Laird, P.N. (1977). Procedural semantics. *Cognition, 5*, 189–214.

Johnson-Laird, P.N. (1980). Mental models in cognitive science. *Cognitive Science, 4*, 71–115.

Johnson-Laird, P.N. (1983). *Mental models.* Cambridge: Cambridge University Press.

Johnson-Laird, P.N. (1989). Mental models. In M. Posner (Ed.), *Foundations of cognitive science.* Cambridge, MA: MIT Press.

Johnson-Laird, P.N. (1995a). Inference and mental models. In S.E. Newstead & J.St.B.T. Evans (Eds.), *Perspectives on thinking and reasoning: Essays in honour of Peter Wason.* Hove, UK: Psychology Press.

Johnson-Laird, P.N. (1995b). Mental models, deductive reasoning and the brain. In M.S. Gazzaniga (Ed.), *The cognitive neurosciences* (pp. 987–1008). Cambridge, MA: MIT Press.

Johnson-Laird, P.N. (1999). Deductive reasoning. *Annual Review of Psychology, 50*, 109–135.

Johnson-Laird, P.N., & Byrne, R.M.J. (1991). *Deduction.* London: Psychology Press.

Johnson-Laird, P.N., & Byrne, R.M.J. (1993a). Multiple book review of "Deduction". *Behavioral & Brain Sciences, 16*, 323–380.

Johnson-Laird, P.N., & Byrne, R.M.J. (1993b). Models and deductive rationality. In K.I. Manktelow & D. Over (Eds.), *Rationality: Psychological and philosophical perspectives.* London: Routledge.

Johnson-Laird, P.N., & Byrne, R.M.J. (1996). Mental models and syllogisms. *Behavioral & Brain Sciences, 19*, 543–546.

Johnson-Laird, P.N., Byrne, R.M.J., & Schaeken, W. (1992). Propositional reasoning by model. *Psychological Review, 99*, 418–439.

Johnson-Laird, P.N., Herrmann, D.J., & Chaffin, R. (1984). Only connections: A critique of semantic networks. *Psychological Bulletin, 96*(2), 292–315.

Johnson-Laird, P.N., Legrenzi, P., Girotto, V., Legrenzi, M.S., & Caverni, J.P. (1999). Naive probability: A mental model theory of extensional reasoning. *Psychological Review, 106*, 62–88.

Johnson-Laird, P.N., Legrenzi, P., & Sonino-Legrenzi, M. (1972). Reasoning and a sense of reality. *British Journal of Psychology, 63*, 395–400.

Johnson-Laird, P.N., & Savary, F. (1996). Illusionary inferences about probabilities. *Acta Psychologia, 93*, 69–90.

Johnson-Laird, P.N., & Wason, P.C. (1970). A theoretical analysis of insight into a reasoning task. *Cognitive Psychology, 1*, 134–148.

Johnson, M.K., Hashtroudi, S., & Lindsay, D.S. (1993). Source monitoring. *Psychological Bulletin, 114*, 3–28.

Johnston, W.A., & Heinz, S.P. (1978). Flexibility and capacity demands of attention. *Journal of Experimental Psychology: General, 107*, 420–435.

Johnston, W.A., & Wilson, J. (1980). Perceptual processing of non-targets in an attention task. *Memory & Cognition, 8*, 372–377.

Jones, G.V. (1982). Stacks not fuzzy sets: An ordinal basis for prototype theory of concepts. *Cognition, 12*, 281–290.

Jones, G.V. (1982). Tests of the dual-mechanism theory of recall. *Acta Psychologica, 50*, 61–72.

Joseph, J.E., & Proffitt, D.R. (1996). Semantic versus perceptual influences of colour in object recognition. *Journal of Experimental Psychology: Learning, Memory, & Cognition, 22*, 407–429.

Josephs, R.A., Larrick, R.P., Steele, C.M., & Nisbett, R.E. (1992). Protecting the self from the negative consequences of risky decisions. *Journal of Personality & Social Psychology, 62*, 26–37.

Jost, A. (1897). Die Assoziationsfestigkeit in ihrer Abhängigkeit von der Verteiling der Wiederholungen. *Zeitschrift für Psychologie, 14*, 436–472.

Joyce, J. (1922/1960). *Ulysses*. London: Bodley Head.

Julesz, B. (1971). *Foundations of cyclopean perception*. Chicago: University of Chicago Press.

Julesz, B. (1975). Experiments in the visual perception of texture. *Scientific American, 212*, 38–48.

Juola, J.F., Bowhuis, D.G., Cooper, E.E., & Warner, C.B. (1991). Control of attention around the fovea. *Journal of Experimental Psychology: Human Perception & Performance, 15*, 315–330.

Just, M.A., & Carpenter, P.A. (1992). A capacity theory of comprehension. *Psychological Review, 99*, 122–149.

Just, M.A., Carpenter, P.A., & Keller, T.A. (1996). The capacity theory of comprehension: New frontiers of evidence and arguments. *Psychological Review, 103*, 773–780.

Kahneman, D. (1973). *Attention and effort*. Englewood Cliffs, NJ: Prentice Hall.

Kahneman, D. (1994). New challenges to the rationality assumption. *Journal of the Institute of Theoretical Economics, 150*, 18–36.

Kahneman, D., & Henik, A. (1979). Perceptual organisation and attention. In M. Kubovy & J.R. Pomerantz (Eds.), *Perceptual organisation*. Hillsdale, NJ: Lawrence Erlbaum Associates Inc.

Kahneman, D., & Tversky, A. (1973). On the psychology of prediction. *Psychological Review, 80*, 237–251.

Kahneman, D., & Tversky, A. (1984). Choices, values and frames. *American Psychologist, 39*, 341–350.

Kahneman, D., & Tversky, A. (1996). On the reality of cognitive illusions. *Psychological Review, 103*, 582–591.

Kahney, H. (1989). What do novice programmers know about recursion? In E. Soloway & J.C. Spohrer (Eds.), *Studying the novice programmer*. Hillsdale, NJ: Lawrence Erlbaum Associates Inc.

Kahney, H., & Eisenstadt, M. (1982). Programmers' mental models of their programming tasks. *Proceedings of the Fourth Annual Conference of the Cognitive Science Society*. Ann Arbor, MI: Cognitive Science Society.

Kaiser, M.K., Jonides, J., & Alexander, J. (1986). Intuitive reasoning about abstract and familiar physics problems. *Memory & Cognition, 14*, 308–312.

Kaiser, M.K., Proffitt, D.R., & Anderson, K. (1985). Judgements of natural and anomalous trajectories in the presence and absence of motion. *Journal of Experimental Psychology: Learning, Memory, & Cognition, 11*, 795–803.

Kaiser, M.K., Proffitt, D.R., Whelan, S.M., & Hecht, H. (1992). Influence of animation on dynamic judgements. *Journal of Experimental Psychology: Human Perception & Performance*, *18*, 669–689.

Kaneko, H., & Uchikawa, K. (1997). Perceived angular and linear size: The role of binocular disparity and visual surround. *Perception*, *26*, 17–27.

Kanizsa, G. (1976). Subjective contours. *Scientific American*, *234*, 48–52.

Kant, E. (1963). *Critique of pure reason (2nd Edn)*. London: Macmillan [original work published 1787].

Kanwisher, N., McDermott, J., & Chun, M.M. (1997). The fusiform face area: A module in human extrastriate cortex specialised for face perception. *Journal of Neuroscience*, *9*, 605–610.

Kaplan, G.A., & Simon, H.A. (1990). In search of insight. *Cognitive Psychology*, *22*, 374–419.

Kassin, S.M., Ellsworth, P.C., & Smith, U.L. (1989). The "general acceptance" of psychological research on eyewitness testimony. *American Psychologist*, *44*, 1089–1098.

Katz, J.J., & Fodor, J.A. (1963). The structure of a semantic theory. *Language*, *39*, 170–210.

Kaufer, D., Hayes, J.R., & Flower, L.S. (1986). Composing written sentences. *Research in the Teaching of English*, *20*, 121–140.

Kay, J., & Ellis, A.W. (1987). A cognitive neuropsychological case study of anomia: Implications for psychological models of word retrieval. *Brain*, *110*, 613–629.

Kay, J., & Marcel, T. (1981). One process not two in reading aloud: Lexical analogies do the work of nonlexical rules. *Quarterly Journal of Experimental Psychology*, *39*A, 29–41.

Keane, M. (1985a). Restructuring revised: A theoretical note on Ohlsson's mechanism of restructuring. *Scandinavian Journal of Psychology*, *26*, 363–365.

Keane, M. (1985b). On drawing analogies when solving problems: A theory and test of solution generation in an analogical problem solving task. *British Journal of Psychology*, *76*, 449–458.

Keane, M. (1987). On retrieving analogues when solving problems. *Quarterly Journal of Experimental Psychology*, *39*A, 29–41.

Keane, M.T. (1988). *Analogical problem solving*. Chichester, UK: Ellis Horwood (New York: Wiley).

Keane, M.T. (1989). Modelling "insight" in practical construction problems. *Irish Journal of Psychology*, *11*, 201–215.

Keane, M.T. (1997). What makes an analogy difficult?: The effects of order and causal structure in analogical mapping. *Journal of Experimental Psychology: Language, Memory, & Cognition*, *23*, 946–967.

Keane, M.T., & Brayshaw, M. (1988). The Incremental Analogical Machine: A computational model of analogy. In D. Sleeman (Ed.), *European Working Session on Machine Learning*. London: Pitman.

Keane, M.T., Ledgeway, T., & Duff, S. (1994). Constraints on analogical mapping: A comparison of three models. *Cognitive Science*, *18*, 287–334.

Keil, F.C. (1989). *Concepts, kinds and conceptual development*. Cambridge, MA: MIT Press.

Keil, F.C., Smith, W.C., Simons, D.J., & Levin, D.T. (1998). Two dogmas of conceptual empiricism: Implications for hybrid models of the structure of knowledge. *Cognition*, *65*, 103–135.

Kellogg, R.T. (1987). Effects of topic knowledge on the allocation of processing time and cognitive effort to writing processes. *Memory & Cognition*, *15*, 256–266.

Kellogg, R.T. (1988). Attentional overload and writing performance: Effects of rough draft and outline strategies. *Journal of Experimental Psychology: Learning, Memory, & Cognition*, *14*, 355–365.

Kellogg, R.T. (1990). Writing. In M.W. Eysenck (Ed.), The *Blackwell dictionary of cognitive psychology*. Oxford: Blackwell.

Kellogg, R.T. (1994). *The psychology of writing*. Oxford: Oxford University Press.

Kellogg, R.T. (1995). *Cognitive psychology*. Thousand Oaks, CA: Sage.

Kellogg, R.T., & Mueller, S. (1993). Performance amplification and process restructuring in computer-based writing. *International Journal of Man–Machine Studies, 39*, 33–49.

Kempton, W. (1986). Two theories used of home heat control. *Cognitive Science, 10*, 75–91.

Kenealy, P.M. (1997). Mood-state-dependent retrieval: The effects of induced mood on memory reconsidered. *Quarterly Journal of Experimental Psychology, 50A*, 290–317.

Kewley-Port, D., & Luce, P.A. (1984). Time-varying features of initial stop consonants in auditory running spectra: A first report. *Perception & Psychophysics, 35*, 353–360.

Kiehl, K.A., Liddle, P.F., Smith, A.M., Mendrek, A., Forster, B.B., & Hare, R.D. (1999). Neural pathways involved in the processing of concrete and abstract words. *Human Brain Mapping, 7*, 225–233.

Kihlstrom, J.F. (1991). On what does mood-dependent memory depend? In D. Kuiken (Ed.), *Mood and memory: Theory, research and applications*. London: Sage.

Kilpatrick, F.P., & Ittelson, W.H. (1953). The size–distance invariance hypothesis. *Psychological Review, 60*, 223–231.

Kimberg, D.Y., D'Esposito, M., & Farah, M.J. (1998). Cognitive functions in the prefrontal cortex—Working memory and executive control. *Current Directions in Psychological Science, 6*, 185–192.

Kimchi, R. (1992). Primacy of wholistic processing and global/local paradigm: A critical review. *Psychological Bulletin, 112*, 24–38.

Kinchla, R.A., & Wolfe, J.M. (1979). The order of visual processing: "Top-down", "bottom-up", or "middle-out". *Perception & Psychophysics, 25*, 225–231.

Kintsch, W. (1970). Models for free recall and recognition. In D.A. Norman (Ed.), *Models of human memory*. London: Academic Press.

Kintsch, W. (1974). *The representation of meaning in memory*. Hillsdale, NJ: Lawrence Erlbaum Associates Inc.

Kintsch, W. (1980). Semantic memory: A tutorial. In R.S. Nickerson (Ed.), *Attention & performance, vol. VIII*. Hillsdale, NJ: Lawrence Erlbaum Associates Inc.

Kintsch, W. (1988). The role of knowledge in discourse comprehension: A construction–integration model. *Psychological Review, 95*, 163–182.

Kintsch, W. (1992). A cognitive architecture for comprehension. In H.L. Pick, P. van den Broek, & D.C. Knill (Eds.), *Cognition: Conceptual and methological issues*. Washington, DC: American Psychological Association.

Kintsch, W. (1994). The psychology of discourse processing. In M.A. Gernsbacher (Ed.), *Handbook of psycholinguistics*. London: Academic Press.

Kintsch, W., & Keenan, J.M. (1973). Reading rate and retention as a function of the number of propositions in the base structure of sentences. *Cognitive Psychology, 5*, 257–274.

Kintsch, W., Kozminsky, E., Streby, W.J., McKorn, G., & Keenan, J.M. (1975). Comprehension and recall of text as a function of content variables. *Journal of Verbal Learning & Verbal Behavior, 14*, 196–214.

Kintsch, W., & van Dijk, T.A. (1978). Toward a model of text comprehension and production. *Psychological Review, 85*, 363–394.

Kintsch, W., Welsch, D., Schmalhofer, F., & Zimny, S. (1990). Sentence memory: A theoretical analysis. *Journal of Memory & Language, 29*, 133–159.

Klahr, D., & Dunbar, K. (1988). Dual space search during scientific reasoning. *Cognitive Science, 12*, 1–55.

Klahr, D., Fay, A.L., & Dunbar, K. (1993). Heuristics for scientific experimentation: A developmental study. *Cognitive Psychology, 25*, 111–146.

Klauer, K.C. (1999). On the normative justification for information gain in Wason's selection task. *Psychological Review, 106*, 216–223.

Klayman, J., & Ha, Y.-W. (1987). Confirmation, disconfirmation, and information in hypothesis testing. *Psychological Review, 94*, 211–228.

Klein, F.B., & Kihlstrom, J.F. (1986). Elaboration, organisation and the self-reference effect in memory. *Journal of Experimental Psychology: General, 115*, 26–38.

Knight, R.T. (1998). An interview with Robert T. Knight. In M.S. Gazzaniga, R.B. Ivry, & G.R. Mangun (Eds.), *Cognitive neuroscience: The biology of the mind*. New York: W.W. Norton.

Knoblich, G., Ohlsson, S., Haider, H., & Rhenius, D. (1999). Constraint relaxation and chunk decomposition in insight problem solving. *Journal of Experimental Psychology: Learning, Memory, & Cognition*, *25*, 1534–1555.

Knoblich, G., & Wartenberg, F. (1998). Unnoticed hints facilitate representational change in problem solving. *Zeitschrift für Psychologie*, *206*, 207–234.

Knowlton, B.J., & Squire, L.R. (1995). Remembering and knowing: Two different expressions of declarative memory. *Journal of Experimental Psychology: Learning, Memory, & Cognition*, *21*, 699–710.

Koehler, J.J. (1996). The base rate fallacy reconsidered: Descriptive, normative, and methodological challenges. *Behavioral & Brain Sciences*, *19*, 1–17.

Koestler, A. (1964). *The act of creation*. London: Picador.

Koffka, K. (1935). *Principles of Gestalt psychology*. New York: Harcourt Brace.

Köhler, W. (1927). *The mentality of apes (2nd Edn)*. New York: Harcourt Brace.

Køhler, S., & Moscovitch, M. (1997). Unconscious visual processing in neuropsychological syndromes: A survey of the literature and evaluation of models of consciousness. In M.D. Rugg (Ed.), *Cognitive neuroscience*. Hove, UK: Psychology Press.

Køksal, F. (1992). *Anxiety and narrowing of visual attention*. Unpublished manuscript, Bogazici University, Istanbul, Turkey.

Koriat, A., & Goldsmith, M. (1996). Memory metaphors and the real-life/laboratory controversy: Correspondence versus storehouse conceptions of memory. *Behavioral & Brain Sciences*, *19*, 167–188.

Korsakoff, S.S. (1889). Uber eine besondere Form psychischer Storung, kombiniert mit multiplen Neuritis. *Archiv für Psychiatrie und Nervenkrankheiten*, *21*, 669–704.

Kosslyn, S.M. (1975). Information representation in visual images. *Cognitive Psychology*, *7*, 341–370.

Kosslyn, S.M. (1976). Can imagery be distinguished from other forms of internal representation?: Evidence from studies of information retrieval time. *Memory & Cognition*, *4*, 291–297.

Kosslyn, S.M. (1978). Measuring the visual angle of the mind's eye. *Cognitive Psychology*, *10*, 356–389.

Kosslyn, S.M. (1980). *Image and mind*. Cambridge, MA: Harvard University Press.

Kosslyn, S.M. (1981). The medium and the message in mental imagery: A theory. *Psychological Review*, *88*, 44–66.

Kosslyn, S.M. (1983). *Ghosts in the mind's machine: Creating and using images in the brain*. New York: W.W. Norton & Co.

Kosslyn, S.M. (1987). Seeing and imagining in the cerebral hemispheres: A computational approach. *Psychological Review*, *94*, 148–175.

Kosslyn, S.M. (1994). *Image & brain: The resolution of the imagery debate*. Cambridge, MA: MIT Press.

Kosslyn, S.M. (1999). If neuroimaging is the answer, what is the question? *Philosophical Transactions of the Royal Society of London, Series B*, *354*, 1283–1294.

Kosslyn, S.M., Alpert, N.M., Thompson, W.L., Maljkovic, V., Weise, S.B., Chabris, C.F., Hamilton, S.E., Rauch, S.L., & Buonanno, F.S. (1993). Visual mental imagery activates topographically organized visual cortex: PET investigations. *Journal of Cognitive Neuroscience*, *5*, 263–287.

Kosslyn, S.M., Ball, T.M., & & Reiser, B.J. (1978). Visual images preserve metric spatial information: Evidence from studies of image scanning. *Journal of Experimental Psychology: Human Perception & Performance*, *4*, 47–60.

Kosslyn, S.M., Flynn, R.A., Amsterdam, J.B., & Wang, G. (1990). Components of high-level vision: A cognitive neuroscience analysis and accounts of neurological syndromes. *Cognition*, *34*, 203–277.

Kosslyn, S.M., Holtzmann, J.D., Farah, F., & Gazzinga, M.S. (1985). A computational analysis of mental image generation: Evidence from functional dissociations in split-brain patients. *Journal of Experimental Psychology: General*, *114*, 311–341.

Kosslyn, S.M., & Shwartz, S.P. (1977). A simulation of visual imagery. *Cognitive Science*, *1*, 265–295.

Kosslyn, S.M., Sukel, K.E., & Bly, B.M. (1999). Squinting with the mind's eye: Effects of stimulus resolution on imaginal and perceptual comparisons. *Memory & Cognition, 27*, 276–287.

Kosslyn, S.M., Thompson, W.L., & Alpert, N.M. (1997). Neural systems shared by visual imagery and visual perception: A positron emission tomography study. *Neuroimage, 6*, 320–334.

Kotovsky, K., Hayes, J.R., & Simon, H.A. (1985). Why are some problems hard?: Evidence from the Tower of Hanoi. *Cognitive Psychology, 17*, 248–294.

Kotovsky, K., & Simon, H.A. (1990). What makes some problems really hard. *Cognitive Psychology, 22*, 143–183.

Kozlowski, L.T., & Cutting, J.E. (1978). Recognising the gender of walkers from point-lights mounted on ankles: Some second thoughts. *Perception & Psychophysics, 23*, 459.

Kroger, J.K., Cheng, P.W., & Holyoak, K.J. (1993). Evoking the permission schema: The impact of explicit negation and a violation-checking context. *Quarterly Journal of Experimental Psychology, 46A*, 615–636.

Kroll, N.E., Knight, R.T., Metcalfe, J., Wolf, E.S., & Tulving, E. (1996). Cohesion failure as a source of memory illusions. *Journal of Memory & Language, 35*, 176–196.

Kruk, R., & Regan, D. (1983). Visual test results compared with flying performance in telemetry-tracked aircraft. *Aviation, Space, & Environmental Medicine, 54*, 906–911.

Kruschke, J.K. (1992). ALCOVE: An exemplar-based connectionist model of category learning. *Psychological Review, 99*, 22–44.

Kubose, T.T., Hummel, J.E., & Holyoak, K.J. (in press). Strategic use of working memory in analogical mapping. *Journal of Experimental Psychology: Learning, Memory, & Cognition*.

Kuhn, T.S. (1970). *The structure of scientific revolutions*. Chicago: Chicago University Press.

Kulkarni, D., & Simon, H.A. (1988). The processes of scientific discovery: The strategy of experimentation. *Cognitive Science, 12*, 139–175.

Kulkarni, D., & Simon, H.A. (1990). Experimentation in machine discovery. In J. Shrager & P. Langley (Eds.), *Computational models of scientific discovery and theory formation*. San Mateo, CA: Morgan Kaufmann.

Kunnapas, T.M. (1968). Distance perception as a function of available visual cues. *Journal of Experimental Psychology, 77*, 523–529.

Kvavilashvili, L. (1987). Remembering intention as a distinct form of memory. *British Journal of Psychology, 78*, 507–518.

Kvavilashvili, L., & Ellis, J. (1996). Let's forget the everyday/laboratory controversy. *Behavioral & Brain Sciences, 19*, 199–200.

Kvavilashvili, L., & Ellis, J. (in press). Ecological validity and twenty years of real-life/laboratory controversy in memory research: A critical review.

Kwak, H.-W., Dagenbach, D., & Egeth, H. (1991). Further evidence for a time-independent shift of the focus of attention. *Perception & Psychophysics, 49*, 473–480.

Kwiatkowski, S.J., & Parkinson, S.R. (1994). Depression, elaboration, and mood congruence: Differences between natural and induced mood. *Memory & Cognition, 22*, 225–233.

LaBerge, D. (1983). The spatial extent of attention to letters and words. *Journal of Experimental Psychology: Human Perception & Performance, 9*, 371–379.

LaBerge, D., & Buchsbaum, J.L. (1990). Positron emission tomography measurements of pulvinar activity during an attention task. *Journal of Neuroscience, 10*, 613–619.

Lachman, R., Lachman, J.L., & Butterfield, E.C. (1979). *Cognitive psychology and information processing*. Hillsdale, NJ: Lawrence Erlbaum Associates Inc.

Lakoff, G. (1973). Hedges: A study of meaning criteria and the logic of fuzzy concepts. *Journal of Philosophical Logic, 2*, 458–508.

Lakoff, G. (1982). Categories and cognitive models. *Berkeley Cognitive Science Report No. 2*, November.

Lakoff, G. (1987). *Women, fire and dangerous things*. Chicago: Chicago University Press.

Lamberts, K. (1990). A hybrid model of learning to solve physics problems. *European Journal of Cognitive Psychology, 2*, 151–170.

Lamberts, K., & Pfeifer, R. (1992). Computational models of expertise. In M.T. Keane & K.J.

Gilhooly (Eds.), *Advances in the psychology of thinking*. London: Harvester Wheatsheaf.

Laming, D. (1996). On the analysis of irrational data selection: A critique of Oaksford & Chater (1994). *Psychological Review*, *103*, 364–373.

Land, E.H. (1977). The retinex theory of colour vision. *Scientific American*, *237*, 108–128.

Land, E.H. (1986). Recent advances in retinex theory. *Vision Research*, *26*, 7–21.

Land, M.F., & Lee, D.N. (1994). Where we look when we steer. *Nature*, *369*, 742–744.

Langley, P., & Jones. R. (1988). A computational model of scientific insight. In R.J. Sternberg (Ed.), *The nature of creativity: Contemporary psychological approaches.* Cambridge, MA: Cambridge University Press.

Larkin, J.H. (1979). Information processing models and science instructions. In J. Lochhead & J. Clement (Eds.), *Cognitive process instructions.* Philadelphia, PA: Franklin Institute Press.

Larkin, J.H. (1983). The role of problem representation in physics. In D. Gentner & A.L. Stevens (Eds.), *Mental models.* Hillsdale, NJ: Lawrence Erlbaum Associates Inc.

Larkin, J.H. (1985). Understanding problem representations and skill in physics. In S.F. Chipman, J.W. Segal, & R. Glaser (Eds.), *Thinking and learning skills: Vol. 2; Research and open questions.* Hillsdale, NJ: Lawrence Erlbaum Associates Inc.

Larkin, J.H., McDermott, J., Simon, D., & Simon, H.A. (1980). Expert and novice performance in solving physics problems. *Science*, *208*, 1335–1342.

Lashley, K.S., Chow, K.L., & Semmes, J. (1951). An examination of the electrical field theory of cerebral integration. *Psychological Review*, *58*, 123–136.

Latour, P.L. (1962). Visual threshold during eye movements. *Vision Research*, *2*, 261–262.

Law, L.C. (1998). A situated cognition view about the effects of planning and authorship on computer program debugging. *Behaviour & Information Technology*, *17*, 325–337.

Lazarus, R.S. (1982). Thoughts on the relations between emotion and cognition. *American Psychologist*, *37*, 1019–1024.

Lazarus, R.S. (1991). *Emotion and adaptation.* Oxford: Oxford University Press.

Lea, R.B., O'Brien, D.P., Noveck, I.A., Fisch, S.M., & Braine, M.D.S. (1990). Predicting propositional logic inferences in text comprehension. *Journal of Memory & Language*, *29*, 361–387.

Lea, W.A. (1973). An approach to syntactic recognition without phonemics. *IEEE Transactions on Audio & Electroacoustics*, *AU-21*, 249–258.

LeDoux, J.E. (1992). Emotion as memory: Anatomical systems underlying indelible neural traces. In S.-A. Christianson (Ed.), *The handbook of emotion and memory: Research and theory.* Hillsdale, NJ: Lawrence Erlbaum Associates Inc.

LeDoux, J.E. (1996). *The emotional brain: The mysterious underpinnings of emotional life.* New York: Simon & Schuster.

Lee, D.N. (1976). A theory of visual control of braking based on information about time-to-collision. *Perception*, *5*, 437–459.

Lee, D.N. (1980). Visuo-motor coordination in space–time. In G.E. Stelmach & J. Requin (Eds.), *Tutorials in motor behaviour.* Amsterdam: North-Holland.

Lee, D.N., Lishman, J.R., & Thomson, J.A. (1982). Regulation of gait in long-jumping. *Journal of Experimental Psychology: Human Perception & Performance*, *8*, 448–459.

Lee, D.N., Young, D.S., Reddish, P.E., Lough, S., & Clayton, T.M.H. (1983). Visual timing in hitting an accelerating ball. *Quarterly Journal of Experimental Psychology*, *35*A, 333–346.

Leech, G. (1974). *Semantics.* Harmondsworth, UK: Penguin.

Leibowitz, H., Brislin, R., Permutter, L., & Hennessy, R. (1969). Ponzo perspective illusions as a manifestation of space perception. *Science*, *166*, 1174–1176.

Lenneberg, E.H., & Roberts, J.M. (1956). *The language of experience, memoir 13.* Indiana: University of Indiana, Publications in Anthropology and Linguistics.

Lesgold, A.M (1988). Problem solving. In R.J. Sternberg & E.E. Smith (Eds.), *The psychology of human thought.* Cambridge: Cambridge University Press.

Lesgold, A.M., Rubinson, H., Feltovich, P., Glaser, R., Klopfer, D., & Wang, Y. (1988). Expertise in a complex skill: Diagnosing X-ray pictures. In M.T.H. Chi, R. Glaser, & M. Farr (Eds.), *The nature of expertise*. Hillsdale, NJ: Lawrence Erlbaum Associates Inc.

Leslie, A.M., & Keeble, S. (1987). Do six-month-old infants perceive causality? *Cognition, 25*, 265–288.

Levelt, W.J.M. (1989). *Speaking: From intention to articulation*. Cambridge, MA: MIT Press.

Levelt, W.J.M., Praamstra, P., Meyer, A.S., Helenius, P., & Salmelin, R. (1998). A MEG study of picture naming. *Journal of Cognitive Neuroscience, 10*, 553–567.

Levelt, W.J.M., Roelofs, A., & Meyer, A.S. (1999a). A theory of lexical access in speech production. *Behavioral & Brain Sciences, 22*, 1–38.

Levelt, W.J.M., Roelofs, A., & Meyer, A.S. (1999b). Multiple perspectives on word production. *Behavioral & Brain Sciences, 22*, 61–75.

Levine, D.N., Calvanio, R., & Popovics, A. (1982). Language in the absence of inner speech. *Word, 15*, 19–44.

Lian, A., Glass, A.L., & Raanaas, R.K. (1998). Item-specific effects in recognition failure: Reasons for rejection of the Tulving-Wiseman function. *Memory & Cognition, 26*, 692–707.

Liberman, A.M., Cooper, F.S., Shankweiler, D.S., & Studdert-Kennedy, M. (1967). Perception of the speech code. *Psychological Review, 74*, 431–461.

Liberman, A.M., Delattre, P.C., & Cooper, F.S. (1952). The role of selected stimulus variables in the perception of the unvoiced stop consonants. *American Journal of Psychology, 65*, 497–516.

Lichten, W., & Lurie, S. (1950). A new technique for the study of perceived size. *American Journal of Psychology, 63*, 280–282.

Lichtenstein, S., Slovic, P., Fischhoff, B., Layman, M., & Combs, J. (1978). Judged frequency of lethal events. *Journal of Experimental Psychology: Human Learning & Memory, 4*, 551–578.

Lieberman, P. (1963). Some effects of semantic and grammatical context on the production and perception of speech. *Language & Speech, 6*, 172–187.

Lin, E.L., & Murphy, G.L. (1997). Effects of background knowledge on object categorisation and part detection. *Journal of Experimental Psychology: Human Perception & Performance, 23*, 1153–1169.

Lindsay, D.S. (1990). Misleading suggestions can impair eyewitnesses' ability to remember event details. *Journal of Experimental Psychology: Learning, Memory, & Cognition, 16*, 1077–1083.

Lindsay, P.H., & Norman, D.A. (1977). *Human information processing (2nd Edn)*. New York: Academic Press.

Lindsay, R.C.L., Lea, J.A., Nosworthy, G.J., Fulford, J.A., Hector, J., LeVan, V., & Seabrook, C. (1991). Biased lineups: Sequential presentation reduces the problem. *Journal of Applied Psychology, 76*, 741–745.

Lindsay, R.C.L., & Wells, G.L. (1980). What price justice? Exploring the relationship of lineup fairness to identification accuracy. *Law & Human Behavior, 4*, 303–314.

Linton, M. (1975). Memory for real-world events. In D.A. Norman & D.E. Rumelhart (Eds.), *Explorations in cognition*. San Francisco, CA: Freeman.

Locke, J. (1690). *Essay on human understanding*. Oxford: Clarendon Press [1924].

Lockhart, R.S., & Craik, F.I.M. (1990). Levels of processing: A retrospective commentary on a framework for memory research. *Canadian Journal of Psychology, 44*, 87–112.

Loftus, E.F. (1979). *Eyewitness testimony*. Cambridge, MA: Harvard University Press.

Loftus, E.F. (1992). When a lie becomes memory's truth: Memory distortion after exposure to misinformation. *Current Directions in Psychological Science, 1*, 121–123.

Loftus, E.F., & Burns, H.J. (1982). Mental shock can produce retrograde amnesia. *Memory & Cognition, 10*, 318–323.

Loftus, E.F., & Palmer, J.C. (1974). Reconstruction of automobile destruction: An example of the interaction between language and memory. *Journal of Verbal Learning & Verbal Behavior, 13*, 585–589.

Loftus, E.F., & Zanni, G. (1975). Eyewitness testimony: The influence of the wording of a question. *Bulletin of the Psychonomic Society*, *5*, 86–88.

Logan, G.D. (1988). Toward an instance theory of automatization. *Psychological Review*, *95*, 492–527.

Logan, G.D., Taylor, S.E., & Etherton, J.L. (1996). Attention in the acquisition and expression of automaticity. *Journal of Experimental Psychology: Learning, Memory, & Cognition*, *22*, 620–638.

Logie, R., & Baddeley, A.D. (1989). Imagery and working memory, In P.J. Hampson, D.F. Marks, & J.T.E. Richardson (1989). *Imagery: Current developments*. London: Routledge.

Logie, R.H. (1995). *Visuo-spatial working memory*. Hove, UK: Psychology Press.

Logie, R.H. (1999). State of the art: Working memory. *The Psychologist*, *12*, 174–178.

Logvinenko, A.D., & Belopolskii, V.I. (1994). Convergence as a cue for distance. *Perception*, *23*, 207–217.

Lopez, A., Atran, S., Coley, J.D., Medin, D.L., & Smith, E.E. (1997). The tree of life: Universal and cultural features in folkbiological taxonomies and inductions. *Cognitive Psychology*, *32*, 251–295.

Lucas, M. (1999). Context effects in lexical access: A meta-analysis. *Memory & Cognition*, *27*, 385–398.

Luce, L.L. (1996). When four distinct ways to measure utility are the same. *Journal of Mathematical Psychology*, *40*, 297–317.

Luchins, A.S. (1942). Mechanisation in problem solving. The effect of Einstellung. *Psychological Monographs*, *54*, (248).

Luchins, A.S., & Luchins, E.H. (1959). *Rigidity of behaviour*. Eugene, Oregon: University of Oregon Press.

Luchins, A.S., & Luchins, E.H. (1991). Task complexity and order effects in computer presentation of water jar problems. *Journal of General Psychology*, *118*, 45–72.

Luck, S.J. (1998). Neurophysiology of selective attention. In H. Pashler (Ed.), *Attention*. Hove, UK: Psychology Press.

Lucy, J., & Schweder, R. (1979). Whorf and his critics: Linguistic and non-linguistic influences on colour memory. *American Anthropologist*, *81*, 581–615.

Lueck, C.J., Zeki, S., Friston, K.J., Deiber, M.-P., Cope, P., Cunningham, V.J., Lammertsma, A.A., Kennard, C., & Frackowiak, R.S.J. (1989). The colour centre in the cerebral cortex of man. *Nature*, *340*, 386–389.

Luger, G.F. (1976). The use of the state space to record the behavioural effects of sub-problems and symmetries in the Tower of Hanoi problem. *International Journal of Man–Machine Studies*, *8*, 411–421.

Lung, C.T., & Dominowski, R.L. (1985). Effects of strategy instructions and practice on nine-dot problem solving. *Journal of Experimental Psychology: Learning, Memory & Cognition*, *11*, 804–811.

Luria, A.R. (1970). *Traumatic aphasia*. The Hague: Mouton.

Luria, A.R. (1975). *The mind of a mnemonist*. New York: Basic Books.

Lyman, R.S., Kwan, S.T., & Chao, W.H. (1938). Left occipito-parietal brain tumor with observations on alexia and agraphia in Chinese and English. *Chinese Medical Journal*, *54*, 491–516.

Macaulay, D., Ryan, L., & Eich, E. (1993). Mood dependence in implicit and explicit memory. In P. Graf & M.E.J. Masson (Eds.), *Implicit memory: New directions in cognition, development, and neuropsychology*. Hillsdale, NJ: Lawrence Erlbaum Associates Inc.

MacDonald, M.C., Pearlmutter, N.J., & Seidenberg, M.S. (1994). Lexical nature of syntactic ambiguity resolution. *Psychological Review*, *101*, 676–703.

Mackintosh, N.J. (1998). *IQ and human intelligence*. Oxford: Oxford University Press.

Maclay, H., & Osgood, C.E. (1959). Hesitation phenomena in spontaneous English speech. *Word*, *15*, 19–44.

MacLeod, C. (1990). Mood disorders and cognition. In M.W. Eysenck (Ed.), *Cognitive psychology: An international review*. Chichester, UK: Wiley.

MacLeod, C., & Mathews, A. (1988). Anxiety and the allocation of attention to threat. *Quarterly Journal of Experimental Psychology*, *38*A, 659–670.

MacLeod, C., & Mathews, A. (1991). Cognitive-experimental approaches to the emotional disorders. In P.R. Martin (Ed.), *Handbook of behaviour therapy and psychological science: An integrative approach*. Oxford: Pergamon.

MacLeod, C., Mathews, A., & Tata, P. (1986). Attentional bias in emotional disorders. *Journal of Abnormal Psychology, 95*, 15–20.

MacNeilage, P.F. (1972). Speech physiology. In J.H. Gilbert (Ed.), *Speech and cortical functioning*. New York: Academic Press.

Madison, P. (1956). Freud's repression concept: A survey and attempted clarification. *International Journal of Psychoanalysis, 37*, 75–81.

Magee, B. (1973). *Popper*. London: Fontana.

Maher, L.M., Rothi, L.J.G., & Heilman, K.M. (1994). Lack of error awareness in an aphasic patient with relatively preserved auditory comprehension. *Brain & Language, 46*, 402–418.

Mahony, M.J. (1976). *Scientist as subject: The psychological imperative*. Cambridge, MA: Ballinger.

Maier, N.R.F. (1931). Reasoning in humans II: The solution of a problem and its appearance in consciousness. *Journal of Comparative Psychology, 12*, 181–194.

Malone, D.R., Morris, H.H., Kay, M.C., & Levin, H.S. (1982). Prosopagnosia: A double dissocation between the recognition of familiar and unfamiliar faces. *Journal of Neurology, Neurosurgery, & Psychiatry, 45*, 820–822.

Malt, B. (1994). When water is not $H_2O$. *Cognitive Psychology, 27*, 41–70.

Malt, B.C., Murphy, G.L., & Ross, B.H. (1994). Predicting features for members of natural categories when categorisation is uncertain. *Journal of Experimental Psychology: Language, Memory, & Cognition, 21*, 646–661.

Malt, B.C., & Smith, E.E. (1983). Correlated properties in natural categories. *Journal of Verbal Learning & Verbal Behavior, 23*, 250–269.

Maltzman, I. (1955). Thinking: From a behaviouristic point of view. *Psychological Review, 62*, 275–286.

Mandler, J.M., & Mandler, G. (1964). *Thinking: From association to gestalt*. New York: Wiley.

Mani, K., & Johnson-Laird, P.N. (1982). The mental representation of spatial descriptions. *Memory & Cognition, 10*, 181–187.

Manktelow, K.I. (1999). *Reasoning and thinking*. Hove, UK: Psychology Press.

Manktelow, K.I., & Evans, J.St.B.T. (1979). Facilitation of reasoning by realism: Effect or non-effect? *British Journal of Psychology, 70*, 477–488.

Manktelow, K.I., & Over, D.E. (1991). Social role and utilities in reasoning with deontic conditionals. *Cognition, 43*, 183–186.

Manktelow, K.I., & Over, D.E. (1993). *Rationality: Psychological and philosophical perspectives*. London: Routledge.

Mäntylä, T., & Bäckman, L. (1992). Aging and memory for expected and unexpected objects in real world settings. *Journal of Experimental Psychology: Learning, Memory, & Cognition, 18*, 1298–1309.

Mapelli, D., & Behrman, M. (1997). The role of colour in object recognition: Evidence from visual agnosia. *Neurocase, 3*, 237–247.

Marcus, S.L., & Rips, L.J. (1979). Conditional reasoning. *Journal of Verbal Learning & Verbal Behavior, 18*, 199–233.

Markman, A.B., & Gentner, D.R. (1993a). Splitting the differences: A structural alignment view of similarity. *Journal of Memory & Language, 32*, 517–535.

Markman, A.B., & Gentner, D.R. (1993b). Structural alignment during similarity comparisons. *Cognitive Psychology, 26*, 356–397.

Markman, A.B., & Wisniewski, E.J. (1997). Same and different: The differentiation of basic-level categories. *Journal of Experimental Psychology: Language, Memory, & Cognition, 23*, 54–70.

Markman, E.M. (1989). *Categorization and naming in children: Problems of induction*. Cambridge, MA: MIT Press.

Markovits, H. (1984). Awareness of the "possible" as a mediator of formal thinking in conditional reasoning problems. *British Journal of Psychology, 75*, 367–376.

Markovits, H. (1985). Incorrect conditional reasoning among adults: Competence or performance? *British Journal of Psychology, 76*, 241–247.

Marr, D. (1976). Early processing of visual information. *Philosophical Transactions of the Royal Society (London)*, *B275*, 483–524.

Marr, D. (1982). *Vision: A computational investigation into the human representation and processing of visual information.* San Francisco, CA: W.H. Freeman.

Marr, D., & Hildreth, E. (1980). Theory of edge detection. *Proceedings of the Royal Society of London*, *B207*, 187–217.

Marr, D., & Nishihara, K. (1978). Representation and recognition of the spatial organisation of three-dimensional shapes. *Philosophical Transactions of the Royal Society, Series B*, 269–294.

Marr, D., & Poggio, T. (1976). Cooperation computation of stereo disparity. *Science*, *194*, 283–287.

Marschark, M., & Cornoldi, C. (1990). Imagery and verbal memory. In C. Cornoldi & M. McDaniel (Eds.), *Imagery & cognition.* New York: Springer-Verlag.

Marschark, M., & Hunt, L. (1989). A reexamination of the role of imagery in learning and memory. *Journal of Experimental Psychology: Learning, Memory, & Cognition*, *15*, 710–720.

Marschark, M., & Surian, L. (1992). Context effects in free recall: The role of imaginal and relational processing. *Memory & Cognition*, *20*, 612–620.

Marschark, M., Richman, C.L., Yuille, J.C., & Hunt, R.R. (1987). The role of imagery in memory: On shared and distinctive information. *Psychological Bulletin*, *102*, 28–41.

Marsh, R.L., & Hicks, J.L. (1998). Event-based prospective memory and executive control of working memory. *Journal of Experimental Psychology: Learning, Memory, & Cognition*, *24*, 336–349.

Marsh, R.L., Hicks, J.L., & Landau, J.D. (1998). An investigation of everyday prospective memory. *Memory & Cognition*, *26*, 633–643.

Marshall, J.C., & Halligan, P.W. (1988). Blindsight and insight in visuo-spatial neglect. *Nature*, *336*, 766–767.

Marshall, J.C., & Halligan, P.W. (1994). The yin and yang of visuo-spatial neglect: A case study. *Neuropsychologia*, *32*, 1037.

Marshall, J.C., & Newcombe, F. (1973). Patterns of paralexia: A psycholinguistic approach. *Journal of Psycholinguistic Research*, *2*, 175–199.

Marslen-Wilson, W.D. (1990). Activation, competition, and frequency in lexical access. In G.T.M. Altmann (Ed.), *Cognitive models of speech processing: Psycholinguistics and computational perspectives.* Cambridge, MA: MIT Press.

Marslen-Wilson, W.D., Moss, H.E., & van Halen, S. (1996). Perceptual distance and competition in lexical access. *Journal of Experimental Psychology: Human Perception & Performance*, *22*, 1376–1392.

Marslen-Wilson, W.D., & Tyler, L.K. (1980). The temporal structure of spoken language comprehension. *Cognition*, *6*, 1–71.

Marslen-Wilson, W.D., & Warren, P. (1994). Levels of perceptual representation and process in lexical access: Words, phonemes, and features. *Psychological Review*, *101*, 653–675.

Martin, A., & Fedio, P. (1983). Word production and comprehension in Alzheimer's disease: The breakdown of semantic knowledge. *Brain & Language*, *19*, 121–141.

Martin, G.N. (1998). *Human neuropsychology.* London: Prentice Hall.

Martin-Loeches, M., Schweinberger, S.R., & Sommer, W. (1997). The phonological loop model of working memory: An ERP study of irrelevant speech and phonological similarity effects. *Memory & Cognition*, *25*, 471–483.

Martone, M., Butters, N., Payne, M., Becker, J.T., & Sax, D.S. (1984). Dissociations between skill learning and verbal recognition in amnesia and dementia. *Archives of Neurology*, *41*, 965–970.

Massaro, D.W. (1989). Testing between the TRACE model and the fuzzy logical model of speech perception. *Cognitive Psychology*, *21*, 398–421.

Massaro, D.W. (1994). Psychological aspects of speech perception: Implications for research and theory. In M.A. Gernsbacher (Ed.), *Handbook of psycholinguistics.* San Diego, CA: Academic Press.

Masson, M.E.J., & Graf, P. (1993). Introduction: Looking back and into the future. In P. Graf & M.E.J. Masson (Eds.), *Implicit memory:*

*New directions in cognition, development, and neuropsychology.* Hillsdale, NJ: Lawrence Erlbaum Associates Inc.

Mather, G. (1994). Motion detector models: Psychophysical evidence. In A.T. Smith & R.J. Snowden (Eds.), *Visual detection of motion.* London: Academic Press.

Mather, G. (1997). The use of image blur as a depth cue. *Perception, 26,* 1147–1158.

Mather, G., & Murdoch, L. (1994). Gender discrimination in biological motion displays based on dynamic cues. *Proceedings of the Royal Society of London, B,* 273–279.

Matin, L., Picoult, E., Stevens, J., Edwards, M., & MacArthur, R. (1982). Oculoparalytic illusions: Visual-field dependent spatial mislocations by humans partially paralysed with curare. *Science, 216,* 198–201.

Matlin, M.W., & Foley, H.J. (1997). *Sensation and perception (4th Edn).* Bostyn: Allyn & Bacon.

Matthews, G., & Antes, J.R. (1992). Visual attention and depression: Cognitive biases in the eye fixation of the dysphoric and the non-depressed. *Cognitive Therapy & Research, 16,* 359–371.

Mattingley, I.G., & Liberman, A.M. (1990). Speech and other auditory modules. In G.M. Edelman, W.E. Gall, & W.M. Cowan (Eds.), *Signal and sense: Local and global order in perceptual maps.* New York: Wiley.

Mayes, A.R. (1988). *Human organic memory disorders.* Cambridge: Cambridge University Press.

Mayes, A.R., & Downes, J.J. (1997). What do theories of the functional deficit(s) underlying amnesia have to explain? *Memory, 5,* 3–36.

Mayhew, J.E.W., & Frisby, J.P. (1981). Psychophysical and computational studies towards a theory of human stereopsis. *Artificial Intelligence, 17,* 349–385.

McBeath, M.K., Shaffer, D.M., & Kaiser, M.K. (1995). How baseball outfielders determine where to run to catch fly balls. *Science, 268,* 569–573.

McCarthy, R., & Warrington, E.K. (1984). A two-route model of speech production. *Brain, 107,* 463–485.

McClelland, J.L. (1981). Retrieving general and specific information from stored knowledge of specifics. *Proceedings of the Third Annual Meeting of the Cognitive Science Society.* Ann Arbor, MI: Cognitive Science Society.

McClelland, J.L. (1991). Stochastic interactive processes and the effect of context on perception. *Cognitive Psychology, 23,* 1–44.

McClelland, J.L. (1993). The GRAIN model: A framework for modelling the dynamics of information processing. In D.E. Meyer & S. Kornblum (Eds.), *Attention and performance, Vol. XIV.* Hillsdale, NJ: Lawrence Erlbaum Associates Inc.

McClelland, J.L., & Elman, J.L. (1986). The TRACE model of speech perception. *Cognitive Psychology, 18,* 1–86.

McClelland, J.L., & Mozer, M.C. (1986). Perceptual interactions in two-word displays: Familiarity and similarity effects. *Journal of Experimental Psychology: Human Perception & Performance, 12,* 18–35.

McClelland, J.L., & Rumelhart, D.A. (1985). Distributed memory and the representation of general and specific information. *Journal of Experimental Psychology: General, 114,* 159–188.

McClelland, J.L., & Rumelhart, D.E. (1981). An interactive activation model of context effects in letter perception. Part 1. An account of basic findings. *Psychological Review, 88,* 375–407.

McClelland, J.L., Rumelhart, D.E., & The PDP Research Group (1986), *Parallel distributed processing: Vol. 2. Psychological and biological models.* Cambridge, MA: MIT Press.

McCloskey, M. (1983). Intuitive physics. *Scientific American, 24,* 122–130.

McCloskey, M.E., & Glucksberg, S. (1978). Natural categories: Well-defined or fuzzy sets. *Memory & Cognition, 6,* 462–472.

McCloskey, M., Wible, C.G., & Cohen, N.J. (1988). Is there a special flashbulb-memory mechanism? *Journal of Experimental Psychology: General, 117,* 171–181.

McCulloch, W.S., & Pitts, W. (1943). A logical calculus of the idea imminent in nervous activity. *Bulletin of the Mathematical Biophysics, 5,* 115–133.

McDaniel, M.A., Robinson-Riegler, B., & Einstein, G.O. (1998). Prospective remembering: Perceptually driven or conceptually driven processes? *Memory & Cognition*, *26*, 121–134.

McGeorge, P., & Burton, M. (1989). The effects of concurrent verbalisation on performance in a dynamic systems task. *British Journal of Psychology*, *80*, 455–465.

McGlinchey-Berroth, R., Milber, W.P., Verfaellie, M., Alexander, M., & Kilduff, P.T. (1993). Semantic processing in the neglected visual field: Evidence from a lexical decision task. *Cognitive Neuropsychology*, *10*, 79–108.

McGurk, H., & MacDonald, J. (1976). Hearing lips and seeing voices. *Nature*, *264*, 746–748.

McKee, R., & Squire, L.R. (1992). Equivalent forgetting rates in long-term memory for diencephalon and medial temporal lobe amnesia. *Journal of Neuroscience*, *12*, 3765–3772.

McKeithen, K.B., Reitman, J.S., Rueter, H.H., & Hirtle, C. (1981). Knowledge organization and skill differences in computer programmers. *Cognitive Psychology*, *13*, 307–325.

McKoon, G., & Ratcliff, R. (1980). Priming in item recognition: The organization of propositions in memory for text. *Journal of Verbal Learning & Verbal Behavior*, *19*, 369–386.

McKoon, G., & Ratcliff, R. (1986). Inferences about predictable events. *Journal of Experimental Psychology: Learning, Memory, & Cognition*, *12*, 82–91.

McKoon, G., & Ratcliff, R. (1992). Inference during reading. *Psychological Review*, *99*, 440–466.

McKoon, G., & Ratcliff, R. (1998). Memory-based language processing: Psycholinguistic research in the 1990s. *Annual Review of Psychology*, *49*, 25–42.

McClelland, J.L. (1981). Retrieving general and specific information from stored knowledge of specifics. *Proceedings of the Third Annual Meeting of the Cognitive Science Society*. Cognitive Science Society.

McLeod, P. (1977). A dual-task response modality effect: Support for multiprocessor models of attention. *Quarterly Journal of Experimental Psychology*, *29*, 651–667.

McLeod, P., & Dienes, Z. (1996). Do fielders know where to go to catch the ball or only how to get there? *Journal of Experimental Psychology: Human Perception & Performance*, *22*, 531–543.

McLeod, P., Plunkett, K., & Rolls, E.T. (1998). *Introduction to connectionist modelling of cognitive processes*. Oxford: Oxford University Press.

McNamara, D.S., Kintsch, E., Songer, N.B., & Kintsch, W. (1995). Text coherence, background knowledge and levels of understanding in learning from text. *Cognitive Instruction*, *3*, 455–468.

McNamara, T.P., & Sternberg, R.J. (1983). Mental models of word meaning. *Journal of Verbal Learning & Verbal Behavior*, *22*, 449–474.

McNeil, J.E., & Warrington, E.K. (1993). Prosopagnosia: A face-specific disorder. *Quarterly Journal of Experimental Psychology*, *46*A, 1–10.

McQueen, J.M. (1991). The influence of the lexicon on phonetic categorisation: Stimulus quality in word-final ambiguity. *Journal of Experimental Psychology: Human Perception & Performance*, *17*, 433–443.

Meacham, J.A. (1988). Interpersonal relations and prospective remembering. In M.M. Gruneberg, P.E. Morris, & R.N. Sykes (Eds.), *Practical aspects of memory: Current research and issues, Vol. 1. Memory in everyday life*. Chichester, UK: John Wiley.

Meacham, J.A., & Singer, J. (1977). Incentive in prospective remembering. *Journal of Psychology*, *97*, 191–197.

Medin, D. (1975). A theory of context in discrimination learning. In G.H. Bower (Ed.), *The psychology of learning and motivation*. New York: Academic Press.

Medin, D. (1976). Theories of discrimination learning and learning set. In W.K. Estes (Ed.), *Handbook of learning and cognitive processes*. Hillsdale, NJ: Lawrence Erlbaum Associates Inc.

Medin, D.L., Altom, M.W., Edelson, S.M., & Freko, D. (1982). Correlated symptoms and simulated medical classification. *Journal of Experimental Psychology: Language, Memory, & Cognition*, *8*, 37–50.

Medin, D.L., Goldstone, R.L., & Gentner, D. (1990). Similarity involving attributes and relations: Judgements of similarity and difference are not inverses. *Psychological Science*, *1*, 64–69.

Medin, D.L., Goldstone, R.L., & Gentner, D. (1993). Respects for similarity. *Psychological Review*, *100*, 254–278.

Medin, D., & Ortony, A. (1989). Psychological essentialism. In S. Vosniadou & A. Ortony (Eds.), *Similarity and analogical reasoning*. Cambridge: Cambridge University Press.

Medin, D.L., & Shaffer, M.M. (1978). Context theory of classification learning. *Psychological Review*, *85*, 207–238.

Medin, D.L., & Smith, E.E. (1984). Concepts and concept formation. *Annual Review of Psychology*, *35*, 113–138.

Medin, D.L., Wattenmaker, W.D., & Hampson, S.E. (1987). Family resemblance, conceptual cohesiveness and category construction. *Cognitive Psychology*, *19*, 242–279.

Mellers, B.A., Schwartz, A., & Cooke, A.D.J. (1998). Judgement and decision making. *Annual Review of Psychology*, *49*, 447–477.

Mensink, G.-J., & Raaijmakers, J.G.W. (1988). A model for interference and forgetting. *Psychological Review*, *95*, 434–455.

Menzel, E.W. (1978). Cognitive mapping in chimpanzees. In S.H. Hulse, F. Fowler, & W.K. Honig (Eds.), *Cognitive processes in animal behaviour*. Hillsdale, NJ: Lawrence Erlbaum Associates Inc.

Mervis, C.B., Catlin, J., & Rosch, E. (1976). Relationships among goodness-of-example, category norms, and word frequency. *Bulletin of the Psychonomic Society*, *7*, 283–284.

Metcalfe, J. (1986a). Feeling of knowing in memory and problem solving. *Journal of Experimental Psychology: Learning, Memory, & Cognition*, *12*, 288–284.

Metcalfe, J. (1986b). Premonitions of error predict impending insight. *Journal of Experimental Psychology: Learning, Memory, & Cognition*, *12*, 623–634.

Metcalfe, J., & Weibe, D. (1987). Intuition in insight and noninsight problem solving. *Memory & Cognition*, *15*, 238–246.

Meudell, P.R., & Mayes, A.R. (1981). The Claparède phenomenon: A further example in amnesics, a demonstration of a similar effect in normal people with attenuated memory, and a reinterpretation. *Current Psychological Research*, *1*, 75–88.

Meyer, B.J.F., & McConkie, G.W. (1973). What is recalled after hearing a passage? *Journal of Educational Psychology*, *65*, 109–117.

Meyer, D.E., & Schvaneveldt, R.W. (1971). Facilitation in recognising pairs of words: Evidence of a dependence between retrieval operations. *Journal of Experimental Psychology*, *90*, 227–234.

Miceli, G., Silveri, M.C., Romani, C., & Caramazza, A. (1989). Variation in the pattern of omissions and substitutions of grammatical morphemes in the spontaneous speech of so-called agrammatic patients. *Brain & Language*, *36*, 447–492.

Michotte, A. (1946). *The perception of causality* [1963 translation by T. & E. Miles]. London: Methuen.

Mill, J.S. (1843). *A system of logic*. London: Longman.

Miller, G.A. (1956). The magic number seven, plus or minus two: Some limits on our capacity for processing information. *Psychological Review*, *63*, 81–93.

Miller, G.A., & Johnson-Laird, P.N. (1976). *Language and perception*. Cambridge: Cambridge University Press.

Miller, G.A., & Nicely, P. (1955). An analysis of perceptual confusions among some English consonants. *Journal of the Acoustical Society of America*, *27*, 338–352.

Miller, J.L., & Eimas, P.D. (1995). Speech perception: From signal to word. *Annual Reviews in Psychology*, *46*, 467–492.

Milner, A.D., & Goodale, M.A. (1995). *The visual brain in action*. Oxford: Oxford University Press.

Milner, A.D., & Goodale, M.A. (1998). The visual brain in action. *Psyche*, *4*, 1–14.

Milner, A.D., Perret, D.I., Johnston, R.S., Benson, P.J., Jordan, T.R., Heeley, D.W., & Bettuci, D. (1991). Perception and action in "visual form agnosia". *Brain*, *114*, 405–428.

Milner, B. (1962). Les troubles de la mémoire accompagnant des lésions hippocampiques bilaterales. In P. Passouant (Ed.), *Physiologie de l'hippocampe*. Paris: Centre des Recherches Scientifiques.

Minami, H., & Dallenbach, K.M. (1946). The effect of activity upon learning and retention in the cockroach. *American Journal of Psychology*, *59*, 1–58.

Minsky, M. (1975). A framework for representing knowledge. In P.H. Winston (Ed.), *The psychology of computer vision*. New York: McGraw-Hill.

Minsky, M., & Papert, S. (1988). *Perceptrons (2nd Edn)*. Cambridge, MA: MIT Press.

Mishkin, M., & Ungerleider, L.G. (1982). Contribution of striate inputs to the visuospatial functions of parieto-preoccipital cortex in monkeys. *Behavioral Brain Research*, *6*, 57–77.

Mitchell, D. (1994). Sentence parsing. In M.A. Gernsbacher (Ed.), *Handbook of psycholinguistics*. London: Academic Press.

Mitroff, I. (1974). *The subjective side of science.* Amsterdam: Elsevier.

Miyake, A., & Shah, P. (1999). *Models of working memory: Mechanisms of active maintenance and executive control*. New York: Cambridge University Press.

Miyawaki, K., Strange, W., Verbrugge, R., Liberman, A.M., Jenkins, J.J., & Furjima, O. (1975). An effect of linguistic experience. The discrimination of [r] and [l] by native speakers of Japanese and English. *Perception & Psychophysics*, *18*, 331–340.

Mogg, K., Kentish, J., & Bradley, B.P. (1993). Effects of anxiety and awareness on colour-identification latencies for emotional words. *Behaviour Research & Therapy*, *31*, 559–567.

Mogg, K., Mathews, A., May, J., Grove, M., Eysenck, M.W., & Weinman, J. (1991). Assessment of cognitive bias in anxiety and depression using a colour perception task. *Cognition & Emotion*, *5*, 221–238.

Moray, N. (1959). Attention in dichotic listening: Affective cues and the influence of instructions. *Quarterly Journal of Experimental Psychology*, *11*, 56–60.

Morgan, L. (1894). *An introduction to comparative psychology*. London: Scott.

Morris, C.D., Bransford, J.D., & Franks, J.J. (1977). Levels of processing versus transfer appropriate processing. *Journal of Verbal Learning & Verbal Behavior*, *16*, 519–533.

Morris, P.E. (1992). Prospective memory: Remembering to do things. In M. Gruneberg & P. Morris (Eds.), *Aspects of memory: Vol. 1. The practical aspects*. London: Routledge.

Morris, P.E., & Reid, R.L. (1970). The repeated use of mnemonic imagery. *Psychonomic Science*, *20*, 337–338.

Morris, R.G., Miotto, E.C., Feigenbaum, J.D., Bullock, P., & Polkey, C.E. (1997). Planning ability after frontal and temporal lobe lesions: The effects of selection equivocation and working memory load. *Cognitive Neuropsychology*, *14*, 1007–1027.

Morton, J. (1969). Interaction of information in word recognition. *Psychological Review*, *76*, 165–178.

Morton, J. (1979). Facilitation in word recognition: Experiments causing change in the logogen model. In P.A. Kolers, M. Wrolstead, & H. Bouma (Eds.), *Processing of visible language (Vol. 1)*. New York: Plenum Press.

Moscovitch, M., Winocur, G., & Behrmann, M. (1997). What is special about face recognition? Nineteen experiments on a person with visual object agnosia and dyslexia but normal face recognition. *Journal of Cognitive Neuroscience*, *9*, 555–604.

Moss, H.E., & Gaskell, M.G. (1999). Lexical semantic processing during speech comprehension. In S. Garrod & M.J. Pickering (Eds.), *Language processing*. Hove, UK: Psychology Press.

Müller, H.J., Humphreys, G.W., & Donnelly, N. (1994). Search via recursive rejection (SERR): Visual search for single and dual form-conjunction targets. *Journal of Experimental Psychology: Human Perception & Performance*, *20*, 235–258.

Mulligan, N.W. (1998). The role of attention during encoding in implicit and explicit memory. *Journal of Experimental Psychology: Learning, Memory, & Cognition*, *24*, 27–47.

Murphy, G.L., & Medin, D.L. (1985). The role of theories in conceptual coherence. *Psychological Review*, *92*, 289–316.

Murphy, G.L., & Ross, B.H. (1994). Predictions from uncertain categorisations. *Cognitive Psychology*, *27*, 148–193.

Murphy, S.T., & Zajonc, R.B. (1993). Affect, cognition, and awareness: Affective priming with optimal and suboptimal stimulus exposures. *Journal of Personality & Social Psychology*, *64*, 723–739.

Murray, L.A., Whitehouse, W.G., & Alloy, L.B. (1999). Mood congruence and depressive deficits in memory: A forced-recall analysis. *Memory*, *7*, 175–196.

Muter, P. (1978). Recognition failure of recallable words in semantic memory. *Memory & Cognition*, *6*, 9–12.

Myers, L.B., & Brewin, C.R. (1994). Recall of early experiences and the repressive coping style. *Journal of Abnormal Psychology*, *103*, 288–292.

Mynatt, C.R., Doherty, M.E., & Tweney, R.D. (1977). Confirmation bias in a simulated research environment. *Quarterly Journal of Experimental Psychology*, *29*, 85–95.

Mynatt, C.R., Doherty, M.E., & Tweney, R.D. (1978). Consequences of confirmation and disconfirmation in a simulated research environment. *Quarterly Journal of Experimental Psychology*, *30*, 395–406.

Nadel, L., & Jacobs, W.J. (1998). Traumatic memory is special. *Current Directions in Psychological Science*, *7*, 154–157.

Navon, D. (1977). Forest before trees: The precedence of global features in visual perception. *Cognitive Psychology*, *9*, 353–383.

Nealey, T.A., & Maunsell, J.H.R. (1994). Magnocellular and parvocellular contributions to the responses of neurons in macaque striate cortex. *Journal of Neuroscience*, *14*, 2069–2079.

Nebes, R.D. (1989). Semantic memory in Alzheimer's disease. *Psychological Bulletin*, *106*, 380–408.

Neely, J.H. (1977). Semantic priming and retrieval from lexical memory: Roles of inhibitionless spreading activation and limited capacity attention. *Journal of Experimental Psychology: General*, *106*, 226–254.

Neisser, U. (1964). Visual search. *Scientific American*, *210*, 94–102.

Neisser, U. (1967). *Cognitive psychology*. New York: Appleton-Century-Crofts.

Neisser, U. (1976). *Cognition and reality*. San Francisco, CA: W.H. Freeman.

Neisser, U. (1981). John Dean's memory: A case study. *Cognition*, *9*, 1–22.

Neisser, U. (1982). *Memory observed*. San Francisco, CA: Freeman.

Neisser, U. (1996). Remembering as doing. *Behavioral & Brain Sciences*, *19*, 203–204.

Neisser, U., & Becklen, R. (1975). Selective looking: Attending to visually specified events. *Cognitive Psychology*, *7*, 480–494.

Nelson, K. (1993). Explaining the emergence of autobiographical memory in early childhood. In A.F. Collins, S.E. Gathercole, M.A. Conway, & P.E. Morris (Eds.), *Theories of memory*. Hove, UK: Psychology Press.

Newell, A. (1981). Reasoning, problem solving and decision processes. In R.S. Nickerson (Ed.), *Attention & performance, Vol VIII*. Hillsdale, NJ: Lawrence Erlbaum Associates Inc.

Newell, A. (1990). *Unified theories of cognition*. Cambridge, MA: Harvard University Press.

Newell, A., Shaw, J.C., & Simon, H.A. (1958). Elements of a theory of human problem solving. *Psychological Review*, *65*, 151–166.

Newell, A., Shaw, J.C., & Simon, H.A. (1960). Report on a general problem solving program for a computer. In *Information processing: Proceedings of the International Conference on Information Processing*. Paris: UNESCO.

Newell, A., & Simon, H.A. (1972). *Human problem solving*. Englewood Cliffs, NJ: Prentice-Hall.

Niedenthal, P.M., Setterlund, M.B., & Jones, D.E. (1994). Emotional organisation of perceptual memory. In P.M. Niedenthal & S. Kitayama (Eds.), *The heart's eye: Emotional influences in perception and attention*. New York: Academic Press.

Nielsen, J.M. (1946). *Agnosia, apraxia, aphasia: Their value in cerebral localization*. New York: Paul B. Hoeber.

Nisbett, R.E., & Wilson, T.D. (1977). Telling more than we can know: Verbal reports on mental processes. *Psychological Review*, *84*, 231–259.

Nissen, M., Ross, J., Willingham, D., Mackenzie, T., & Schacter, D. (1988). Memory and amnesia in a patient with multiple personality disorder. *Brain & Cognition*, *8*, 117–134.

Nissen, M.J., & Bullemer, P. (1987). Attentional requirements of learning: Evidence from performance measures. *Cognitive Psychology*, *19*, 1–32.

Norman, D.A. (1980). Twelve issues for cognitive science. *Cognitive Science*, *4*, 1–32.

Norman, D.A. (1981). Categorisation of action slips. *Psychological Review*, *88*, 1–15.

Norman, D.A. (1983). Some observations on mental models. In D. Gentner & A.L. Stevens (Eds.), *Mental models*. Hillsdale, NJ: Lawrence Erlbaum Associates Inc.

Norman, D.A., & Rumelhart, D.E. (1975). *Explorations in cognition*. San Francisco, CA: Freeman.

Norman, D.A., & Shallice, T. (1986). Attention to action: Willed and automatic control of behaviour. In R.J. Davidson, G.E. Schwartz, & D. Shapiro (Eds.), *The design of everyday things*. New York: Doubleday.

Norvig, R. (1992). *Paradigms for artificial intelligence programming*. Los Altos, CA: Morgan Kaufmann.

Nosofsky, R.M. (1986). Attention, similarity, and the identification–categorisation relationship. *Journal of Experimental Psychology: General*, *115*, 39–57.

Nosofsky, R.M. (1988). Exemplar-based accounts of relations between classification, recognition and typicality. *Journal of Experimental Psychology: Learning, Memory, & Cognition*, *14*, 700–708.

Nosofsky, R.M. (1991). Tests of an exemplar model for relating perceptual classification and recognition memory. *Journal of Experimental Psychology: Learning, Memory, & Cognition*, *17*, 3–27.

Nosofsky, R.M., Palmeri, T.J., & McKinley, S.C. (1994). Rule-plus-exception model of classification learning. *Psychological Review*, *101*, 53–79.

Noveck, I.A. (1997). Deductive competence need not be problematic. *Current Psychology of Cognition*, *16*, 162–172.

Oakes, L.M. (1994). Development of infants' use of continuity cues in their perception of causality. *Developmental Psychology*, *30*, 869–879.

Oaksford, M. (1994). Computational levels again. *Behavioral & Brain Sciences*, *17*, 76–77.

Oaksford, M. (1997). Thinking and the rational analysis of human reasoning. *The Psychologist*, *10*, 257–260.

Oaksford, M.R., & Chater, N. (1994). A rational analysis of the selection task as optimal data selection. *Psychological Review*, *101*, 608–631.

Oaksford, M.R., & Chater, N. (1995). Information gain explains relevance which explains the selection task. *Cognition*, *57*, 97–108.

Oaksford, M.R., & Chater, N. (1996). Rational explanation of the selection task. *Psychological Review*, *103*, 381–391.

Oaksford, M.R., Chater, N., Grainger, B., & Larkin, J. (1997). Rational explanation of the selection task. *Journal of Experimental Psychology: Learning, Memory, & Cognition*, *23*, 441–458.

Oatley, K., & Johnson-Laird, P.N. (1987). Towards a cognitive theory of emotions. *Cognition & Emotion*, *1*, 29–50.

O'Brien, D. (1993). *How to develop a perfect memory*. London: Pavilion Books.

O'Brien, D., Braine, M.D.S., & Yang, Y. (1994). Propositional reasoning by mental models? Simple to refute in principle and in practice. *Psychological Review*, *101*, 701–724.

O'Brien, D.P. (1993). Mental logic and irrationality. In K.I. Manktelow & D. Over (Eds.), *Rationality: Psychological and philosophical perspectives*. London: Routledge.

O'Brien, D.P. (1995). Finding logic in human reasoning requires looking in the right places. In S.E. Newstead & J.St.B.T. Evans (Eds.), *Perspectives on thinking and reasoning: Essays in honour of Peter Wason*. Hove, UK: Psychology Press.

O'Brien, E.J., Shank, D.M., Myers, J.L., & Rayner, K. (1988). Elaborative inferences during reading: Do they occur on-line? *Journal of Experimental Psychology: Learning, Memory, & Cognition*, *14*, 410–420.

Ohlsson, S. (1984a). Restructuring revisited I: Summary and critique of Gestalt theory of problem solving. *Scandinavian Journal of Psychology*, *25*, 65–76.

Ohlsson, S. (1984b). Restructuring revisited II: An information processing theory of restructuring and insight. *Scandinavian Journal of Psychology*, *25*, 117–129.

Ohlsson, S. (1985). Retrieval processes in restructuring: Answer to Keane. *Scandinavian Journal of Psychology*, *26*, 366–368.

Ohlsson, S. (1992). Information processing explanations of insight and related phenomena. In M.T. Keane & K.J. Gilhooly (Eds.), *Advances in the psychology of thinking*. London: Harvester Wheatsheaf.

Ohlsson, S. (1996). Learning from performance errors. *Psychological Review*, *103*, 241–262.

Ojemann, G.A. (1991). Cortical organisation of language. *Journal of Neuroscience*, *11*, 2281–2287.

Okada, S., Hanada, M., Hattori, H., & Shoyama, T. (1963). A case of pure word deafness. *Studia Phonologica*, *3*, 58–65.

Okada, T., & Simon, H.A. (1997). Collaborative discovery in a scientific domain. *Cognitive Science*, *21*, 109–146.

Olson, A., & Caramazza, A. (1994). Representation and connectionist models: The NETspell experience. In G.D.A. Brown & N.C. Ellis (Eds.), *Handbook of spelling: Theory, process and intervention*. Chichester, UK: Wiley.

Ormerod, T.C. (1997). Rationalities 1 and 2: Dual processes or different task demands? *Current Psychology of Cognition*, *16*, 181–189.

Osherson, D.N. (1974). *Logical abilities in children, vol. 2*. Hillsdale, NJ: Lawrence Erlbaum Associates Inc.

Osherson, D.N. (1975). *Logical abilities in children, vol. 3*. Hillsdale, NJ: Lawrence Erlbaum Associates Inc.

Osherson, D.N. (1976). *Logical abilities in children, vol. 4*. Hillsdale, NJ: Lawrence Erlbaum Associates Inc.

Osherson, D.N., & Smith, E.E. (1981). On the adequacy of prototype theory as a theory of concepts. *Cognition*, *9*, 35–58.

Osherson, D.N., & Smith, E.E. (1982). Gradedness and conceptual conjunction. *Cognition*, *12*, 299–318.

Osherson, D.N., & Smith E.E. (Eds.) (1990). *Thinking: An invitation to cognitive science*. Cambridge, MA: MIT Press.

Osherson, D.N., Wilkie, O., Smith, E.E., Lopez, A., & Shafir, E. (1990). Category-based induction. *Psychological Review*, *97*, 185–200.

Oudejans, R.R.D., Michaels, C.F., Bakker, F.C., & Dolne, M.A. (1996). The relevance of action in perceiving affordances: Perception of catchableness of fly balls. *Journal of Experimental Psychology: Human Perception & Performance*, *22*, 879–891.

Owen, A.M. (1997). Cognitive planning in humans: Neuropsychological, neuroanatomical, and neuropharmacological perspectives. *Progress in Neurobiology*, *53*, 431–450.

Owen, A.M., Downes, J.J., Sahakian, B.J., Polkey, C.E., & Robbins, T.W. (1990). Planning and spatial working memory following frontal lobe lesions in man. *Neuropsychologia*, *28*, 1021–1034.

Paivio, A. (1971). *Imagery and verbal processes*. New York: Holt, Rinehart & Winston [reprinted by Lawrence Erlbaum in 1979].

Paivio, A. (1975). Coding distinctions and repetition effects in memory. In G.H. Bower (Ed.), *The psychology of learning & motivation (Vol. 9)*. New York: Academic Press.

Paivio, A. (1979). Psychological processes in the comprehension of metaphor. In A. Ortony (Ed.), *Metaphor and thought*. New York: Cambridge University Press.

Paivio, A. (1983). The empirical case for dual coding. In J.C. Yuille (Ed.), *Imagery, memory & cognition: Essays in honor of Allan Paivio*. Hillsdale, NJ: Lawrence Erlbaum Associates Inc.

Paivio, A. (1986). *Mental representations: A dual coding approach*. Oxford: Oxford University Press.

Paivio, A. (1991). Dual coding theory: Retrospect and current status. *Canadian Journal of Psychology*, *45*, 255–287.

Paivio, A., & Csapo, K. (1973). Picture superiority in free recall: Imagery or dual coding? *Cognitive Psychology*, *5*, 176–206.

Paivio, A., & te Linde, J. (1982). Imagery, memory and brain. *Canadian Journal of Psychology*, *36*, 243–272.

Paivio, A., Yuille, J.C., & Madigan, S.A. (1968). Concreteness, imagery and meaningfulness values for 925 nouns. *Journal of Experimental Psychology Monographs*, *78* (1, Pt. 2).

Palmer, S.E. (1975). The effects of contextual scenes on the identification of objects. *Memory & Cognition*, *3*, 519–526.

Palmer, S.E., & Kimchi, R. (1986). The information processing approach to cognition. In T. Knapp & L.C. Robertson (Eds.), *Approaches to cognition: Contrasts and controversies*. Hillsdale, NJ: Lawrence Erlbaum Associates Inc.

Papagno, C., Valentine, T., & Baddeley, A.D. (1991). Phonological short-term memory and foreign-language learning. *Journal of Memory & Language, 30*, 331–347.

Parasuraman, R. (1998). *Attentive brain*. Cambridge, MA: MIT Press.

Parkin, A.J. (1979). Specifying levels of processing. *Quarterly Journal of Experimental Psychology, 31*, 175–195.

Parkin, A.J. (1996). *Explorations in cognitive neuropsychology*. Oxford: Blackwell.

Parkin, A.J., & Hunkin, N.M. (1997). How should a database on human amnesia evolve? Comments on Mayes and Downes "What do theories of the functional deficit(s) underlying amnesia have to explain?" *Memory, 5*, 99–104.

Parkin, A.J., & Leng, N.R.C. (1993). *Neuropsychology of the amnesic syndrome*. Hove, UK: Psychology Press.

Parkin, A.J., & Steward, F. (1993). Category-specific imparments?: Yes. *Quarterly Journal of Experimental Psychology, 46*A, 505–510.

Parkin, A.J., & Williamson, P. (1986). Cerebral lateralisation at different stages of facial processing. *Cortex, 26*, 23–42.

Parkinson, B., & Manstead, A.S.R. (1992). Appraisal as a cause of emotion. In M.S. Clark (Ed.), *Review of personality and social psychology (Vol. 13)*. New York: Sage.

Pashler, H. (1990). Do response modality effects support multiprocessor models of divided attention? *Journal of Experimental Psychology: Human Perception & Performance, 16*, 826–842.

Pashler, H. (1993). Dual-task interference and elementary mental mechanisms. In D.E. Meyer & S. Kornblum (Eds.), *Attention and performance, Vol. XIV*. London: MIT Press.

Pashler, H. (1998). *Attention*. Hove, UK: Psychology Press.

Pashler, H., & Johnston, J.C. (1998). Attentional limitations in dual-task performance. In H. Pashler (Ed.), *Attention*. Hove, UK: Psychology Press.

Pashler, H., Luck, S.J., Hillyard, S.A., Mangun, G.R, & Gazzaniga, M. (1994). Sequential operation of disconnected cerebral hemispheres in split-brain patients. *Neuroreport, 5*, 2381–2384.

Patel, V.L., & Groen, G.J. (1986). Knowledge-based solution strategies in medical reasoning. *Cognitive Science, 10*, 91–116.

Patel, V.L., & Groen, G.J. (1993). Confusing apples and oranges: Some dangers in confusing frameworks with theories. *Cognitive Science, 17*, 135–141.

Patterson, K.E. (1982). The relation between reading and phonological coding: Further neuropsychological observations. In A.W. Ellis (Ed.), *Normality and pathology in cognitive functions*. London: Academic Press.

Patterson, K.E. (1986). Lexical but non-semantic spelling? *Cognitive Neuropsychology, 3*, 341–367.

Patterson, K., Graham, N., & Hodges, J.R. (1994). Reading in Alzheimer's type dementia: A preserved ability? *Neuropsychology, 8*, 395–412.

Payne, D., & Conrad, F. (1997). *Intersections in basic and applied memory research*. Hillsdale, NJ: Lawrence Erlbaum Associates Inc.

Pazzani, M.J. (1991a). Influence of prior knowledge on concept acquisition: Experimental and computational results. *Journal of Experimental Psychology: Learning, Memory, & Cognition, 15*, 416–432.

Pazzani, M.J. (1991b). A computational theory of learning causal relationships. *Cognitive Science, 15*, 401–424.

Pazzani, M.J. (1993). Learning causal patterns. *Machine Learning, 11*, 173–194.

Pederson, E., et al. (1998). Semantic typology and spatial conceptualisation. *Language, 74*, 557–589.

Peper, C.E., Bootsma, R.J., Mestre, D.R., & Bakker, F.C. (1994). Catching balls: How to get the hand to the right place at the right time. *Journal of Experimental Psychology: Human Perception & Performance, 20*, 591–612.

Perenin, M.-T., & Vighetto, A. (1988). Optic ataxia: A specific disruption in visuomotor mechanisms. 1. Different aspects of the deficit in reaching for objects. *Brain, 111*, 643–674.

Perfect, T.J., & Hollins, T.S. (1996). Predictive feeling of knowing judgements and postdictive confidence judgements in eyewitness memory and general knowledge. *Applied Cognitive Psychology, 10*, 371–382.

Perfetti, C.A., & McCutchen, D. (1982). Speech processes in reading. In N. Lass (Ed.), *Speech and language: Advances in basic research and practice (Vol. 7)*. New York: Academic Press.

Perrig, W.J., & Perrig, P. (1988). Mood and memory: Mood-congruity effects in absence of mood. *Memory & Cognition, 16*, 102–109.

Petersen, S.E., Corbetta, M., Miezin, F.M., & Shulman, G.L. (1994). PET studies of parietal involvement in spatial attention: Comparison of different task types. *Canadian Journal of Experimental Psychology, 48*, 319–338.

Peterson, L.R., & Peterson, M.J. (1959). Short-term retention of individual verbal items. *Journal of Experimental Psychology, 58*, 193–198.

Peterson, M.A., Kihlstrom, J.F., Rose, P.M., & Glinsky, M.L. (1992). Mental images can be ambiguous: Reconstruals and reference frame reversals. *Memory & Cognition, 20*, 107–123.

Peterson, R.R., & Savoy, P. (1998). Lexical selection and phonological encoding during language production: Evidence for cascaded processing. *Journal of Experimental Psychology: Learning, Memory, & Cognition, 24*, 539–557.

Phillips, L.H., Wynn, V., Gilhooly, K.J., Della Sala, S., & Logie, R.H. (1999). The role of memory in the Tower of London task. *Memory, 7*, 209–231.

Phinney, R.E., & Siegel, R.M. (1999). Stored representations of three-dimensional objects in the absence of two-dimensional cues. *Perception, 28*, 725–737.

Piaget, J. (1967). *The child's conception of the world*. Totowa, NJ: Littlefield, Adams.

Piaget, J. (1970). Piaget's theory. In J. Mussen (Ed.), *Carmichael's manual of child psychology, Vol. 1*. New York: Basic Books.

Pickering, M.J. (1999). Sentence comprehension. In S. Garrod & M.J. Pickering (Eds.), *Language processing*. Hove, UK: Psychology Press.

Pickering, M.J., & Traxler, M.J. (1998). Plausibility and recovery from garden paths: An eye-tracking study. *Journal of Experimental Psychology: Learning, Memory, & Cognition, 24*, 940–961.

Pillemer, D.B., Goldsmith, L.R., Panter, A.T., & White, S.H. (1988). Very long-term memories of the first year in college. *Journal of Experimental Psychology: Learning, Memory, & Cognition, 14*, 709–715.

Pinel, J.P.J. (1997). *Biopsychology (3rd Edn)*. Boston: Allyn & Bacon.

Pirolli, P.L., & Anderson, J.R. (1985). The role of learning from examples in the acquisition of recursive programming skill. *Canadian Journal of Psychology, 39*, 240–272.

Platt, R.D., & Griggs, R.A. (1993). Darwinian algorithms and the Wason selection task: A factorial analysis of social contract selection task problems. *Cognition, 48*, 163–192.

Plaut, D.C., McClelland, J.L., Seidenberg, M.S., & Patterson, K. (1996). Understanding normal and impaired word reading: Computational principles in quasi-regular domains. *Psychological Review, 103*, 56–115.

Plaut, D.C., & Shallice, T. (1993). Deep dyslexia: A case study of connectionist neuropsychology. *Cognitive Neuropsychology, 10*, 377–500.

Poincaré, H. (1913). Mathematical creation. In H. Poincaré, *The foundations of science*. New York: Science Press.

Poldrack, R.A., Desmond, J.E., Glover, G.H., & Gabrieli, J.D.E. (1996). The neural bases of visual skill: An fMRI study of mirror reading. *Society of Neuroscience, 22*, 719.

Poletiek, F.H. (1996). Paradoxes of falsification. *Quarterly Journal of Experimental Psychology, 49A*, 447–462.

Politzer, G., & Braine, M.D.S. (1991). Responses to inconsistent premises cannot count as suppression of valid inferences. *Cognition, 38*, 103–108.

Politzer, G., & Nguyen-Xuan, A. (1992). Reasoning about conditional promises and warnings. *Quarterly Journal of Experimental Psychology, 44A*, 401–412.

Polivy, J. (1981). On the induction of emotion in the laboratory: Discrete moods or multiple affect states? *Journal of Personality & Social Psychology, 41*, 803–817.

Polk, T. (1993). Mental models, more or less. *Behavioral & Brain Sciences*, *16*, 362–363.

Polk, T.A., & Newell, A. (1995). Deduction as verbal reasoning. *Psychological Review*, *102*, 533–566.

Pollatsek, A., Bolozky, S., Well, A.D., & Rayner, K. (1981). Asymmetries in the perceptual span for Israeli readers. *Brain & Language*, *14*, 174–180.

Polson, P., & Jeffries, R. (1982). Problem solving as search and understanding. In R.J. Sternberg (Ed.), *Advances in the psychology of human intelligence, vol. 1*. Hillsdale, NJ: Lawrence Erlbaum Associates Inc.

Pomerantz, J.R., & Garner, W.R. (1973). Stimulus configuration in selective attention tasks. *Perception & Psychophysics*, *14*, 157–188.

Popper, K.R. (1968). *The logic of scientific discovery*. London: Hutchinson.

Popper, K.R. (1969). *Conjectures and refutations*. London: Routledge & Kegan Paul.

Popper, K.R. (1972). *Objective knowledge*. Oxford: Oxford University Press.

Posner, M.I. (1980). Orienting of attention. The VIIth Sir Frederic Bartlett lecture. *Quarterly Journal of Experimental Psychology*, *32*A, 3–25.

Posner, M.I. (1995). Attention in cognitive neuroscience: An overview. In M.S. Gazzaniga (Ed.), *The cognitive neurosciences*. Cambridge, MA: MIT Press.

Posner, M.I., & Keele, S.W. (1968). On the genesis of abstract ideas. *Journal of Experimental Psychology*, *77*, 353–363.

Posner, M.I., & Petersen, S.E. (1990). The attention system of the human brain. *Annual Review of Neuroscience*, *13*, 25–42.

Posner, M.I., Rafal, R.D., Choate, L.S., & Vaughan, J. (1985). Inhibition of return: Neural basis and function. *Cognitive Neuropsychology*, *2*, 211–228.

Posner, M.I., Walker, J.A., Friedrich, F.J., & Rafal, R.D. (1984). Effects of parietal lobe injury on covert orienting of visual attention. *Journal of Neuroscience*, *4*, 1863–1874.

Power, M., & Dalgleish, T. (1997). *Cognition and emotion: From order to disorder*. Hove, UK: Psychology Press.

Pressley, M., Levin, J.R., Hall, J.W., Miller, G.E., & Berry, J.K. (1980). The keyword method and foreign word acquisition. *Journal of Experimental Psychology: Human Learning & Memory*, *6*, 163–173.

Price, C.J., Wise, R.J.S., & Frackowiak, R.S.J. (1996). Obligatory word processing: A direct demonstration. *Cerebral Cortex*, *6*, 62–70.

Priest, A.G. (1986). Inference strategies in physics problem-solving. In A.G. Cohn & J.R. Thomas (Eds.), *Artificial intelligence and its applications*. Chichester, UK: Wiley.

Proffitt, D.R., Kaiser, M.K., & Whelan, S.M. (1990). Understanding wheel dynamics. *Cognitive Psychology*, *22*, 342–373.

Protopapas, A. (1999). Connectionist modeling of speech perception. *Psychological Bulletin*, *125*, 410–436.

Pugh, K.R., Shaywitz, B.A., Shaywitz, S.E., Shankweiler, D.P., Katz, L., Fletcher, J.M., Skudlarski, P., Fulbright, R.K., Constable, R.T., Bronen, R.A., Lacadie, C., & Gore, J.C. (1997). Predicting reading performance from neuroimaging profiles: The cerebral basis of phonological effects in printed word identification. *Journal of Experimental Psychology: Human Perception & Performance*, *23*, 299–318.

Putnam, H. (1975a). Is semantics possible? In H. Putnam (Ed.), *Philosophical papers, Vol. 2*. Cambridge: Cambridge University Press.

Putnam, H. (1975b). The meaning of 'meaning'. In H. Putnam (Ed.), *Philosophical papers, Vol. 2*. Cambridge: Cambridge University Press.

Pylyshyn, Z. (1973). What the mind's eye tells the mind's brain. *Psychological Bulletin*, *80*, 1–24.

Pylyshyn, Z. (1979). Imagery theory: Not mysterious—just wrong. *Behavioral & Brain Sciences*, *2*, 561–563.

Pylyshyn, Z. (1981). The imagery debate: Analogue media versus tacit knowledge. *Psychological Review*, *88*, 16–45.

Pylyshyn, Z. (1984). *Computation and cognition*. Cambridge, MA: MIT Press.

Pyszczynski, T., Holt, K., & Greenberg, J. (1987). Depression, self-focused attention, and expectancies for positive and negative future life events for self and others. *Journal of Personality & Social Psychology*, *52*, 994–1001.

Quillian, M.R. (1966). *Semantic memory.* Unpublished PhD Dissertation, Carnegie Institute of Technology, Pittsburgh, PA.

Quinlan, P.T., & Wilton, R.N. (1998). Grouping by proximity or similarity? Competition between the Gestalt principles in vision. *Perception, 27,* 417–430.

Quinn, J.G., & McConnell, J. (1996). Irrelevant pictures in visual working memory. *Quarterly Journal of Experimental Psychology, 49*A, 200–215.

Raaheim, K.J. (1974). *Problem solving and intelligence.* Bergen: Universitetforlaget.

Raaijmakers, J.G. (1993). The story of the two-store model of memory: Past criticisms, current status and future directions. In D.E. Meyer & S. Kornblum (Eds.), *Attention and performance, Vol. XIV.* Cambridge, MA: Bradford/MIT.

Raaijmakers, J.G., & Shiffrin, R.M. (1981). SAM: Search of associative memory. *Psychological Review, 88,* 93–134.

Rabinowitz, J.C., Mandler, G., & Patterson, K.E. (1977). Determinants of recognition and recall: Accessibility and generation. *Journal of Experimental Psychology: General, 106,* 302–329.

Rafal, R., Smith, J., Krantz, J., Cohen, A., & Brennan, C. (1990). Extrageniculate vision in hemianopic humans: Saccade inhibition by signals in the blind field. *Science, 250,* 118–121.

Rafal, R.D., & Posner, M.I. (1987). Deficits in human visual spatial attention following thalamic lesions. *Proceedings of the National Academy of Science, 84,* 7349–7353.

Raichle, M.E. (1994a). Images of the mind: Studies with modern imaging techniques. *Annual Review of Psychology, 45,* 333–356.

Raichle, M.E. (1994b). Visualizing the mind. *Scientific American, 270,* 36–42.

Raichle, M.E. (1998). An interview with Marcus E. Raichle. In M.S. Gazzaniga, R.B. Ivry, & G.R. Mangun, *Cognitive neuroscience: The biology of the mind.* New York: W.W. Norton.

Rajaram, S. (1993). Remembering and knowing: Two means of access to the personal past. *Memory & Cognition, 21,* 89–102.

Ramachandran, V.S. (1988). Perception of shape from shading. *Nature, 331,* 163–166.

Ramachandran, V.S., & Anstis, S.M. (1986). The perception of apparent motion. *Scientific American, 254,* 80–87.

Ranney, M. (1994). Relative consistency and subjects theories in domains such as naive physics: Common reseach difficulties illustrated by Cooke and Breedin. *Memory & Cognition, 22,* 494–502.

Rapp, B.C., & Caramazza, A. (1989). General to specific access in word meaning: A claim re-examined. *Cognitive Neuropsychology, 6,* 251–272.

Ratcliff, R., & McKoon, G. (1978). Priming in item recognition: Evidence for the propositional structure of sentences. *Journal of Verbal Learning & Verbal Behavior, 20,* 204–215.

Rayner, K., Inhoff, A.W., Morrison, R.E., Slowiaczek, M.L., & Bertera, J.H. (1981). Masking of foveal and parafoveal vision during eye fixations in reading. *Journal of Experimental Psychology: Human Perception & Performance, 7,* 167–179.

Rayner, K., & Morris, R.K. (1992). Eye movement control in reading: Evidence against semantic preprocessing. *Journal of Experimental Psychology: Human Perception & Performance, 18,* 163–172.

Rayner, K., & Pollatsek, A. (1989). *The psychology of reading.* London: Prentice-Hall.

Rayner, K., & Sereno, S.C. (1994). Eye movements in reading: Psycholinguistic studies. In M.A. Gernsbacher (Ed.), *Handbook of psycholinguistics.* New York: Academic Press.

Reason, J.T. (1979). Actions not as planned: The price of automatisation. In G. Underwood & R. Stevens (Eds.), *Aspects of consciousness: Vol. 1. Psychological issues.* London: Academic Press.

Reason, J.T. (1992). Cognitive underspecification: Its variety and consequences. In B.J. Baars (Ed.), *Experimental slips and human error: Exploring the architecture of volition.* New York: Plenum Press.

Reber, A.S. (1989). Implicit learning and tacit knowledge. *Journal of Experimental Psychology: General, 118,* 219–235.

Redelmeier, D., Koehler, D.J., Liberman, V., & Tversky, A. (1995). Probability judgment in medicine: Discounting unspecified alternatives. *Medical Decision Making.*

Reed, J.M., & Squire, L.R. (1998). Retrograde amnesia for facts and events: Findings from four new cases. *Journal of Neuroscience, 18,* 3943–3954.

Regan, D., Beverley, K.I., & Cynader, M. (1979). The visual perception of motion in depth. *Scientific American, 241,* 136–151.

Reich, S.S., & Ruth, P. (1982). Wason's selection task: Verification, falsification and matching. *British Journal of Psychology, 73,* 395–405.

Reicher, G.M. (1969). Perceptual recognition as a function of meaningfulness of stimulus material. *Journal of Experimental Psychology, 81,* 274–280.

Reichle, E.D., Pollatsek, A., Fisher, D.L., & Rayner, K. (1998). Toward a model of eye movement control in reading. *Psychological Review, 105,* 125–157.

Reisberg, D. (1997). *Cognition: Exploring the science of the mind.* New York: W.W. Norton.

Reitman, J.S. (1974). Without surreptitious rehearsal, information in short-term memory decays. *Journal of Verbal Learning & Verbal Behavior, 13,* 365–377.

Reitman, W. (1965). *Cognition and thought.* New York: Wiley.

Remez, R.E., Rubin, P.E., Pisoni, D.B., & Carrell, T.D. (1981). Speech perception without traditional speech cues. *Science, 212,* 947–950.

Restle, F. (1979). Coding theory of the perception of motion configuration. *Psychological Review, 86,* 1–24.

Richard, J.-F., Poitrenaud, S., & Tijus, C. (1993). Problem solving restructuration: Elimination of implicit constraints. *Cognitive Science, 17,* 497–529.

Richards, A., French, C.C., Adams, C., Eldridge, M., & Papadopolou, E. (1999). Implicit memory and anxiety: Perceptual identification of emotional stimuli. *European Journal of Cognitive Psychology, 11,* 67–86.

Richardson, J.T.E. (1999). *Imagery.* Hove, UK: Psychology Press.

Riddoch, M.J., & Humphreys, G.W. (1993). The smiling giraffe: An illustration of a visual

memory disorder. In R. Campbell (Ed.), *Mental lives.* Oxford: Blackwell.

Rinck, M., Glowalla, U., & Schneider, K. (1992). Mood-congruent and mood-incongruent learning. *Memory & Cognition, 20,* 29–39.

Ripoll, T. (1998). Why this makes me think of that. *Thinking & Reasoning, 4,* 15–43.

Ripoll, T. (1999). Discussion—A comparison between Keane (1987) and Ripoll (1998): Studies in the retrieval phase of reasoning by analogy. *Thinking & Reasoning, 5,* 189–190.

Rips, L.J. (1975). Inductive judgements about natural categories. *Journal of Verbal Learning & Verbal Behavior, 14,* 665–681.

Rips, L.J. (1983). Cognitive processes in propositional reasoning. *Psychological Review, 90,* 38–71.

Rips, L.J. (1984). Reasoning as a central intellective ability. In R.J. Sternberg (Ed.), *Advances in the study of intelligence.* Hillsdale, NJ: Lawrence Erlbaum Associates Inc.

Rips, L.J. (1986). Mental muddles. In M. Brand & R.M. Harnish (Eds.), *Problems in the representation of knowledge and belief.* Tucson, AZ: University of Arizona Press.

Rips, L.J. (1989a). Similarity, typicality and categorisation. In A. Ortony & S. Vosniadou (Eds.), *Similarity and analogical reasoning* Cambridge: Cambridge University Press.

Rips, L.J. (1989b). The psychology of knights and knaves. *Cognition, 31,* 85–116.

Rips, L.J. (1990). Reasoning. *Annual Review of Psychology, 41,* 321–353.

Rips, L.J. (1994). *The psychology of proof: Deductive reasoning in human thinking.* Cambridge, MA: MIT Press.

Rips, L.J., & Collins, A. (1993). Categories and resemblance. *Journal of Experimental Psychology: General, 122,* 468–486.

Rips, L.J., & Conrad, F.J. (1983). Individual differences in deduction. *Cognition & Brain Theory, 6,* 259–285.

Rips, L.J., Shoben, E.J., & Smith, E.E. (1973). Semantic distance and the verification of semantic relations. *Journal of Verbal Learning & Verbal Behavior, 12,* 1–20.

Rist, R.S. (1989). Schema creation in programming. *Cognitive Science, 13,* 389–414.

Rist, R.S. (1995). Program structure and design. *Cognitive Science, 19,* 507–562.

Ritov, J., & Baron, J. (1990). Reluctance to vaccinate: Omission bias and ambiguity. *Journal of Behavioral Decision Making, 3,* 263–277.

Robbins, T.W., Anderson, E.J., Barker, D.R., Bradley, A.C., Fearnyhough, C., Henson, R., Hudson, S.R., & Baddeley, A. (1996). Working memory in chess. *Memory & Cognition, 24,* 83–93.

Roberts, B., Kalish, M., Hird, K., & Kirsner, K. (1999). Decontextualised data IN, decontextualised theory OUT. *Behavioral & Brain Sciences, 22,* 54–55.

Robertson, I.H., Manly, T., Andrade, J., Baddeley, B.T., & Yiend, J. (1997). "Oops!" Performance correlates of everyday attentional failures in traumatic brain injured and normal subjects. *Neuropsychologia, 35,* 747–758.

Robin, N., & Holyoak, K.J. (1995). Relational reasoning and the functions of the prefrontal cortex. In M.S. Gazzaniga (Ed.), *The cognitive neurosciences* (pp. 987–997). Cambridge, MA: MIT Press.

Rock, I. (1973). *Orientation and form.* New York: Academic Press.

Rock, I., & Palmer, S. (1990). The legacy of Gestalt psychology. *Scientific American,* December, 48–61.

Roediger, H.L. (1980). Memory metaphors in cognitive psychology. *Memory & Cognition, 8,* 231–246.

Roediger, H.L. (1990). Implicit memory: Retention without remembering. *American Psychologist, 45,* 1043–1056.

Roediger, H.L. (1993). Learning and memory: Progress and challenge. In D.E. Meyer & S. Kornblum (Eds.), *Attention and performance, Vol. XIV.* Cambridge, MA: Brad/MIT.

Roediger, H.L., & McDermott, K.B. (1993). Implicit memory in normal human subjects. In H. Spinnler & F. Boller (Eds.), *Handbook of neuropsychology, Vol. 8.* Amsterdam: Elsevier.

Rogers, B.J., & Collett, T.S. (1989). The appearance of surfaces specified by motion parallax and binocular disparity. *Quarterly Journal of Experimental Psychology, 41*A, 697–717.

Rogers, B.J., & Graham, M.E. (1979). Motion parallax as an independent cue for depth perception. *Perception, 8,* 125–134.

Rogers, T.B., Kuiper, N.A., & Kirker, W.S. (1977). Self-reference and the encoding of personal information. *Journal of Personality & Social Psychology, 35,* 677–688.

Rolls, E.T., & Tovée, M.J. (1995). Sparseness of the neuronal representation of stimuli in the primate temporal visual cortex. *Journal of Neurophysiology, 73,* 713–726.

Rosch, E. (1973). Natural categories. *Cognitive Psychology, 4,* 328–350.

Rosch, E. (1975a). The nature of mental codes for colour categories. *Journal of Experimental Psychology: General, 104,* 192–233.

Rosch, E. (1975b). Cognitive reference points. *Cognitive Psychology, 7,* 532–547.

Rosch, E. (1978). Principles of categorisation. In E. Rosch & B.B. Lloyd (Eds.), *Cognition and categorisation.* Hillsdale, NJ: Lawrence Erlbaum Associates Inc.

Rosch, E., & Mervis, C.B. (1975). Family resemblances: Studies in the internal structure of categories. *Cognitive Psychology, 7,* 573–605.

Rosch, E., Mervis, C.B., Gray, W.D., Johnson, D.M., & Boyes-Braem, P. (1976a). Basic objects in natural categories. *Cognitive Psychology, 8,* 382–439.

Rosch, E., Simpson, C., & Miller, R.S. (1976b). Structural bases of typicality effects. *Journal of Experimental Psychology: Human Perception & Performance, 2,* 491–502.

Rosenbloom, P., & Newell, A. (1986). The chunking of goal hierarchies: A generalised model of practice. In R.S. Michalski, J.G. Carbonell, & J.M. Mitchell (Eds.), *Machine learning II: An artificial intelligence approach.* Los Altos, CA: Morgan Kaufmann.

Rosenbloom, P.S., & Newell, A. (1987). Learning by chunking: A production system model of practice. In D. Klahr, P. Langley, & R. Neches (Eds.), *Production system model of learning and development.* Cambridge, MA: MIT Press.

Ross, B.H., & Murphy, G.L. (1996). Category-based predictions: Influence of uncertainty and feature associations. *Journal of Experimental*

*Psychology: Language, Memory, & Cognition, 22*, 736–753.

Ross, B.H., & Murphy, G.L. (1999). Food for thought: Cross-classification and category organization in a complex real-world domain. *Cognitive Psychology, 38*, 495–553.

Roth, I. (1986). An introduction to object perception. In I. Roth & J.P. Frisby (Eds.), *Perception and representation: A cognitive approach*. Milton Keynes, UK: Open University Press.

Rottenstreich, Y., & Tversky, A. (1997). Unpacking, repacking, and anchoring: Advances in support theory. *Psychological Review, 104*, 406–415.

Rouw, R., Kosslyn, S.M., & Hamel, R. (1997). Detecting high-level and low-level properties in visual images and visual percepts. *Cognition, 63*, 209–226.

Roy, D.F. (1991). Improving recall by eyewitnesses through the cognitive interview: Practical applications and implications for the police service. *The Psychologist, 4*, 398–400.

Rubin, D.C., Rahhal, T.A., & Poon, L.W. (1998). Things learned in early childhood are remembered best. *Memory & Cognition, 26*, 3–19.

Rubin, D.C., & Schulkind, M.D. (1997). The distribution of autobiographical memories across the lifespan. *Memory & Cognition, 25*, 859–866.

Rubin, D.C., & Wenzel, A.E. (1996). One hundred years of forgetting: A quantitative description of retention. *Psychological Bulletin, 103*, 734–760.

Rubin, D.C., Wetzler, S.E., & Nebes, R.D. (1986). Autobiographical memory across the life span. In D.C. Rubin (Ed.), *Autobiographical memory*. Cambridge: Cambridge University Press.

Rugg, M.D. (1997). *Cognitive neuroscience*. Hove, UK: Psychology Press.

Rumain, B., Connell, J., & Braine, M.D.S. (1983). Conversational comprehension processes are responsible for reasoning fallacies in children as well as adults: IF is not the biconditional. *Developmental Psychology, 19*, 471–481.

Rumelhart, D.E. (1975). Notes on a schema for stories. In D.G. Bobrow & A. Collins (Eds.), *Representation and understanding: Studies in cognitive science*. New York: Academic Press.

Rumelhart, D.E. (1980). Schemata: The basic building blocks of cognition. In R. Spiro, B. Bruce, & W. Brewer (Eds.), *Theoretical issues in reading comprehension*. Hillsdale, NJ: Lawrence Erlbaum Associates Inc.

Rumelhart, D.E., Hinton, G.E., & McClelland, J.L. (1986b), A general framework for parallel distributed processing. In D.E. Rumelhart, J.L. McClelland, & the PDP Research Group (Eds.), *Parallel distributed processing: Volume 1, foundations*. Cambridge, MA: MIT Press.

Rumelhart, D.E., McClelland, J.L., & The PDP Research Group (Eds.) (1986c). *Parallel distributed processing, Volume 1: Foundations*. Cambridge, MA: MIT Press.

Rumelhart, D.E., & Ortony, A. (1977). The representation of knowledge in memory. In R.C. Anderson, R.J. Spiro, & W.E. Montague (Eds.), *Schooling and the acquisition of knowledge*. Hillsdale, NJ: Lawrence Erlbaum Associates Inc.

Rumelhart, D.E., Smolensky, P., McClelland, J.L., & Hinton, G.E. (1986a). Schemata and sequential thought processes in PDP models. In J.L. McClelland, D.E. Rumelhart, & the PDP Research Group (Eds.), *Parallel distributed processing, Volume 2: Psychological & biological models*. Cambridge, MA: MIT Press.

Runeson, S., & Frykholm, G. (1983). Kinematic specifications of dynamics as an informational basis for person-and-action perception: Expectation, gender recognition, and deceptive intention. *Journal of Experimental Psychology: General, 112*, 585–615.

Rusting, C.L. (1998). Personality, mood, and cognitive processing of emotional information: Three conceptual frameworks. *Psychological Bulletin, 124*, 165–196.

Rylander, G. (1939). Personality changes after operations on the frontal lobes. *Acta Psychiatrica Neurologica* (Supplement No. 30).

Ryle, G. (1949). *The concept of mind*. London: Hutchinson.

Rymer, J. (1988). Scientific composing processes: How eminent scientists write journal articles.

In D.A. Jollife (Ed.), *Advances in writing research, Vol. 2: Writing in academic disciplines*. Norwood, NJ: Ablex.

Saariluoma, P. (1990). Apperception and restructuring in chess players' problem solving. In K.J. Gilhooly, M.T.G. Keane, R. Logie, & G. Erdos (Eds.), *Lines of thinking: Reflections on the psychology of thought (Vol. 2)*. Chichester, UK: John Wiley.

Saariluoma, P. (1994). Location coding in chess. *Quarterly Journal of Experimental Psychology, 47A*, 607–630.

Saffran, E.M., Schwartz, M.F., & Marin, O.S.M. (1980a). Evidence from aphasia: Isolating the components of a production model. In B. Butterword (Ed.), *Language production, Vol. 1*. London: Academic Press.

Saffran, E.M., Schwartz, M.F., & Marin, O.S.M. (1980b). The word order problem in agrammatism: II. Production. *Brain & Language, 10*, 249–262.

Salzman, C.D., Murasugi, C.M., Britten, K.H., & Newsome, W.T. (1992). Microstimulation in visual area MT: Effects on direction discrimination performance. *Journal of Neuroscience, 12*, 2331–2355.

Samuel, A.G. (1981). Phonemic restoration: Insights from a new methodology. *Journal of Experimental Psychology: General, 110*, 474–494.

Samuel, A.G. (1990). Using perceptual-restoration effects to explore the architecture of perception. In G.T.M. Altmann (Ed.), *Cognitive models of speech processing*. Cambridge, MA: MIT Press.

Sanes, J.N., Dimitrov, B., & Hallett, M. (1990). Motor learning in patients with cerebellar dysfunction. *Brain, 113*, 103–120.

Sanford, A.J., & Garrod, S.C. (1981). *Understanding written language*. New York: Wiley.

Sanocki, T., Bowyer, K.W., Heath, M.D., & Sarkar, S. (1998). Are edges sufficient for object recognition? *Journal of Experimental Psychology: Human Perception & Performance, 24*, 340–349.

Sargent, J. (1990). The neuropsychology of visual image generation. *Brain & Cognition, 13*, 98–129.

Sary, G., Vogels, R., & Orban, G.A. (1993). Cue-invariant shape selectivity of macaque inferior temporal neurons. *Science, 260*, 995–997.

Savelsbergh, G.J.P., Pijpers, J.R., & van Santvoord, A.A.M. (1993). The visual guidance of catching. *Experimental Brain Research, 93*, 148–156.

Savelsbergh, G.J.P., Whiting, H.T.A., & Bootsma, R.J. (1991). Grasping tau. *Journal of Experimental Psychology: Human Perception & Performance, 17*, 315–322.

Savion, L. (1993). Review of "Deduction". *Behavioral & Brain Sciences, 16*, 364–365.

Schacter, D.L. (1987). Implicit memory: History and current status. *Journal of Experimental Psychology: Learning, Memory, & Cognition, 13*, 501–518.

Schacter, D.L., Alpert, N.M., Savage, C.R., Rauch, S.L., & Albert, M.S. (1996). Conscious recollection and the human hippocampal formation: Evidence from positron emission tomography. *Proceedings of the National Academy of Science, USA, 93*, 321–325.

Schacter, D.L., & Church, B.A. (1995). Implicit memory in amnesic patients: When is auditory priming spared? *Journal of the International Neuropsychological Society, 1*, 434–442.

Schacter, D.L., Church, B.A., & Bolton, E. (1995). Implicit memory in amnesic patients: Impairment of voice-specific impairment priming. *Psychological Science, 6*, 20–25.

Schafer, R., & Murphy, G. (1943). The role of autism in visual figure–ground relationship. *Journal of Experimental Psychology, 32*, 335–343.

Schank, R.C. (1972). Conceptual dependency: A theory of natural language understanding. *Cognitive Psychology, 3*, 552–631.

Schank, R.C. (1976). *Conceptual information processing*. Amsterdam: North-Holland.

Schank, R.C. (1982). *Dynamic memory*. Cambridge: Cambridge University Press.

Schank, R.C. (1986). *Explanation patterns*. Hillsdale, NJ: Lawrence Erlbaum Associates Inc.

Schank, R.C., & Abelson, R.P. (1977). *Scripts, plans, goals and understanding*. Hillsdale, NJ: Lawrence Erlbaum Associates Inc.

Schare, M.L., Lisman, S.A., & Spear, N.F. (1984). The effects of mood variation on state-dependent retention. *Cognitive Therapy & Research, 8*, 387–408.

Scheerer, M. (1963). Problem-solving. *Scientific American, 208*(4), 118–128.

Schiff, W., & Detwiler, M.L. (1979). Information used in judging impending collision. *Perception, 8*, 647–658.

Schiffman, H.R. (1967). Size estimations of familiar objects under informative and reduced conditions of viewing. *American Journal of Psychology, 80*, 229–235.

Schill, T., & Althoff, M. (1968). Auditory perceptual thresholds for sensitizers, defensive and non-defensive repressors. *Perceptual & Motor Skills, 27*, 935–938.

Schiller, P.H., & Lee, K. (1991). The role of primate extrastriate area V4 in vision. *Science, 251*, 1251–1253.

Schiller, P.H., Logothetis, N.K., & Charles, E.R. (1990). Functions of the colour-opponent and broad-band channels of the visual system. *Nature, 343*, 68–70.

Schinder, A., Benson, D.F., & Scharre, D.W. (1994). Visual agnosia and optic aphasia: Are they anatomically distinct? *Cortex, 30*, 445–458.

Schlottmann, A., & Anderson, N.H. (1993). An information integration approach to phenomenal causality. *Memory & Cognition, 21*, 785–801.

Schlottmann, A., & Shanks, D.R. (1992). Evidence for a distinction between judged and perceived causality. *Quarterly Journal of Experimental Psychology, 44*A, 321–342.

Schneider, W., & Shiffrin, R.M. (1977). Controlled and automatic human information processing: 1. Detection, search, and attention. *Psychological Review, 84*, 1–66.

Schneider, W., & Shiffrin, R.M. (1985). Categorisation (restructuring) and automatisation: Two separable factors. *Psychological Review, 92*, 424–428.

Scholtz, J., & Wiedenbeck, S. (1993). An analysis of novice programmers learning a second language. In C.R. Cook, J.C. Scholtz, & J.C. Spohrer (Eds.), *Empirical studies of programmers.* Norwood, NJ: Ablex.

Schooler, J.W., & Engstler-Schooler, T.Y. (1990). Verbal overshadowing of visual memories: Some things are better left unsaid. *Cognitive Psychology, 22*, 36–71.

Schriver, K. (1984). *Revised computer documentation for comprehension: Ten lessons in protocol-aided revision* (Tech. Rep. No. 14). Pittsburgh, PA: Carnegie Mellon University.

Schunn, C.D., Crowley, K., & Okada, T. (1998). The growth of multidisciplinarity in the Cognitive Science Society. *Cognitive Science, 22*, 107–130.

Schunn, C.D., & Dunbar, K. (1996). Priming, analogy, and awareness in complex reasoning. *Memory & Cognition, 24*, 271–284.

Schwartz, M.F., Marin, O.S.M., & Saffran, E.M. (1979). Dissociation of language function in dementia: A case study. *Brain & Language, 7*, 277–306.

Schwartz, M.F., Saffran, E.M., Bloch, D.E., & Dell, G.S. (1994). Disordered speech production in aphasic and normal speakers. *Brain & Language, 47*, 52–88.

Schwartz, M.F., Saffran, E.M., & Marin, O.S.M. (1980). Fractionating the reading process in dementia: Evidence for word-specific print-to-sound associations. In M. Coltheart, K.E. Patterson, & J.C. Marshall (Eds.), *Deep dyslexia.* London: Routledge & Kegan Paul.

Scoville, W.B., & Milner, B. (1957). Loss of recent memory after bilateral hippocampal lesions. *Journal of Neurology, Neurosurgery, & Psychiatry, 20*, 11–21.

Searcy, J.H., & Bartlett, J.C. (1996). Inversion and processing of component and spatial-relational information in faces. *Journal of Experimental Psychology: Human Perception & Performance, 22*, 904–915.

Segal, S.J., & Fusella, V. (1970). Influence of imaged pictures and sounds on detection of visual and auditory signals. *Journal of Experimental Psychology, 83*, 458–464.

Seger, C.A. (1994). Implicit learning. *Psychological Bulletin, 115*, 163–196.

Seidenberg, M.S., Waters, G.S., Barnes, M.A., & Tanenhaus, M. (1984). When does irregular spelling or pronunciation influence word recognition? *Journal of Verbal Learning & Verbal Behavior, 23*, 383–404.

Sejnowski, T.J., & Rosenberg, C.R. (1987). Parallel networks that learn to pronounce English text. *Complex Systems, 1*, 145–168.

Sekuler, R., & Blake, R. (1994). *Perception (3rd Edn)*. New York: McGraw-Hill.

Sellen, A.J., Lowie, G., Harris, J.E., & Wilkins, A.J. (1997). What brings intentions to mind? An *in situ* study of prospective memory. *Memory, 5*, 483–507.

Sellen, A.J., & Norman, D.A. (1992). The psychology of slips. In B.J. Baars (Ed.), *Experimental slips and human error: Exploring the architecture of volition*. New York: Plenum Press.

Semenza, C., Luzzatti, C., & Mondini, S. (1999). Lemma theory and aphasiology. *Behavioral & Brain Sciences, 22*, 56.

Shaffer, L.H. (1975). Multiple attention in continuous verbal tasks. In P.M.A. Rabbitt & S. Dornic (Eds.), *Attention and performance, Vol. V.* London: Academic Press.

Shah, P., & Miyake, A. (1996). The separability of working memory resources for spatial thinking and language processing: An individual differences approach. *Journal of Experimental Psychology: General, 125*, 4–27.

Shah, P., & Miyake, A. (1999). Models of working memory: An introduction. In A. Miyake & P. Shah (Eds.), *Models of working memory: Mechanisms of active maintenance and executive control*. New York: Cambridge University Press.

Shallice, T. (1981). Phonological agraphia and the lexical route in writing. *Brain, 104*, 413–429.

Shallice, T. (1982). Specific impairments of planning. *Philosophical Transactions of the Royal Society London [Biol.], 298*, 199–209.

Shallice, T. (1988). *From neuropsychology to mental structure*. Cambridge: Cambridge University Press.

Shallice, T. (1991). From neuropsychology to mental structure. *Behavioral & Brain Sciences, 14*, 429–439.

Shallice, T., & Burgess, P. (1993). Supervisory control of action and thought selection. In A. Baddeley & L. Weiskrantz (Eds.), *Attention: Selection, awareness and control*. Oxford: Clarendon Press.

Shallice, T., Fletcher, P., Frith, C.D., Grasby, P., Frackowiak, R.S.J., & Dolan, R.J. (1994). Brain regions associated with acquisition and retrieval of verbal episodic memory. *Nature, 368*, 633–635.

Shallice, T., & Warrington, E.K. (1970). Independent functioning of verbal memory stores: A neuropsychological study. *Quarterly Journal of Experimental Psychology, 22*, 261–273.

Shallice, T., & Warrington, E.K. (1974). The dissociation between long-term retention of meaningful sounds and verbal material. *Neuropsychologia, 12*, 553–555.

Shanks, D.R., & St. John, M.F. (1994). Characteristics of dissociable human learning systems. *Behavioral & Brain Sciences, 17*, 367–394.

Shapiro, P.N., & Penrod, S. (1986). Meta-analysis of facial identification studies. *Psychological Bulletin, 100*, 139–156.

Shastri, L., & Ajjanagadde, V. (1993). From simple associations to systematic reasoning: A connectionist representation of rules, variables and dynamic bindings. *Behavioral & Brain Sciences, 16*, 417–194.

Shelton, J.R., & Weinrich, M. (1997). Further evidence of a dissociation between output phonological and orthographic lexicons: A case study. *Cognitive Neuropsychology, 14*, 105–129.

Shepard, R.N. (1978). The mental image. *The American Psychologist, 33*, 125–137.

Shepard, R.N., & Metzler, J. (1971). Mental rotation of three-dimensional objects. *Science, 191*, 701–703.

Shephard, R.N. (1989). Internal representation of universal regularities: A challenge for connectionism. In L. Nadel, L.A. Cooper, P. Culicover, & R.M. Harnish (Eds.), *Neural connections, mental computation*. Cambridge, MA: MIT Press.

Sheridan, J., & Humphreys, G.W. (1993). A verbal-semantic category-specific deficit. *Cognitive Neuropsychology, 10*, 143–184.

Shiffrar, M. (1994). When what meets where. *Current Directions in Psychological Science, 3*, 96–100.

Shiffrar, M., & Freyd, J.J. (1990). Apparent motion of the human body. *Psychological Science, 1*, 257–264.

Shiffrin, R.M., & Schneider, W. (1977). Controlled and automatic human information processing: II. Perceptual learning, automatic attending, and a general theory. *Psychological Review, 84*, 127–190.

Shimamura, A.P., Janowsky, J., & Squire, L.R. (1990). Memory for temporal order of events in patients with frontal lobe lesions and amnesic patients. *Neuropsychologia, 28*, 803–813.

Shimamura, A.P., & Squire, L.R. (1987). A neuropsychological study of fact memory and source amnesia. *Journal of Experimental Psychology: Learning, Memory, & Cognition, 13*, 464–473.

Shin, H., & Nosofsky, R. (1992). Similarity-scaling studies of dot-pattern classification and recognition. *Journal of Experimental Psychology: General, 121*, 278–304.

Shipp, S., de Jong, B.M., Zihl, J., Frackowiak, R.S.J., & Zeki, S. (1994). The brain activity related to residual activity in a patient with bilateral lesions of V5. *Brain, 117*, 1023–1038.

Shobe, K.K., & Kihlstrom, J.F. (1997). Is traumatic memory special? *Current Directions in Psychological Science, 6*, 70–74.

Shoham, Y. (1993). *Prolog programming*. Cambridge, MA: MIT Press.

Shotter, J. (1991). The rhetorical-responsive nature of mind: A social constructionist account. In A. Still & A. Costall (Eds.), *Against cognitivism: Alternative foundations for cognitive psychology*. Hemel Hempstead, UK: Harvester Wheatsheaf.

Shuren, J.E., Brott, T.G., Schefft, B.K., & Houston, W. (1996). Preserved colour imagery in an achromatopsic. *Neuropsychologia, 34*, 485–489.

Simon, H.A. (1966). Scientific discovery and the psychology of problem solving. In *Mind and cosmos: Essays in contemporary science and philosophy*. Pittsburgh, PA: University of Pittsburgh Press.

Simon, H.A. (1973). The structure of ill-structured problems. *Artificial Intelligence, 4*, 181–201.

Simon, H.A. (1974). How big is a chunk? *Science, 183*, 482–488.

Simon, H.A. (1978). Information-processing theory of human problem solving. In W.K. Estes (Ed.), *Handbook of learning and cognitive processes, vol. 5*. Hillsdale, NJ: Lawrence Erlbaum Associates Inc.

Simon, H.A. (1980). Cognitive science: The newest science of the artificial. *Cognitive Science, 4*, 33–46.

Simon, H.A. (1986). The information processing explanation of Gestalt phenomena. *Computers in Human Behaviour, 2*, 241–255.

Simon, H.A. (1995). Artificial intelligence: An empirical science. *Artificial Intelligence, 77*, 95–127.

Simon, H.A., & Barenfeld, M. (1969). Information processing analysis of perceptual processes in problem solving. *Psychological Review, 76*, 473–483.

Simon, H.A., & Gilmartin, K. (1973). A simulation of memory for chess positions. *Cognitive Psychology, 5*, 29–46.

Simon, H.A., & Hayes, J.R. (1976). The understanding process: Problem isomorphs. *Cognitive Psychology, 8*, 165–190.

Simon, H.A., & Kaplan, C.A. (1989). Foundations of cognitive science. In M.I. Posner (Ed.), *Foundations of cognitive science*. Cambridge, MA: MIT Press.

Simon, H.A., & Reed, S.K. (1976). Modelling strategy shifts on a problem solving task. *Cognitive Psychology, 8*, 86–97.

Singer, M. (1979). Processes of inference during sentence encoding. *Memory & Cognition, 7*, 192–200.

Singley, M.K., & Anderson, J.R. (1989). *The transfer of cognitive skill*. Cambridge, MA: Cambridge University Press.

Slamecka, N.J. (1966). Differentiation versus unlearning of verbal associations. *Journal of Experimental Psychology, 71*, 822–828.

Sloman, S.A., & Rips, L.J. (1998). Similarity as an explanatory construct. *Cognition, 65*, 87–101.

Slowiaczek, M.L., & Clifton, C. (1980). Subvocalisation and reading for meaning. *Journal of Verbal Learning & Verbal Behavior, 19*, 573–582.

Smith, C.A., & Lazarus, R.S. (1993). Appraisal components, core relational themes, and the emotions. *Cognition & Emotion, 7*, 233–269.

Smith, D.E., & Hochberg, J.E. (1954). The effect of "punishment" (electric shock) on figure–ground perception. *Journal of Psychology, 38,* 83–87.

Smith, E.E. (1978). Theories of semantic memory. In W.K. Estes (Ed.), *Handbook of learning and cognitive processes, Vol. 6.* Hillsdale, NJ: Lawrence Erlbaum Associates Inc.

Smith, E.E. (1988). Concepts and thought. In R.J. Sternberg & E.E. Smith (Eds.), *The psychology of human thought.* Cambridge: Cambridge University Press.

Smith, E.E., & Jonides, J. (1997). Working memory: A view from neuroimaging. *Cognitive Psychology, 33,* 5–42.

Smith, E.E., & Medin, D.L. (1981). *Categories and concepts.* Harvard: Harvard University Press.

Smith, E.E., & Osherson, D.N. (1984). Conceptual combination with prototype concepts. *Cognitive Science, 8,* 337–361.

Smith, E.E., Osherson, D.N., Rips, L.J., & Keane, M. (1988). Combining prototypes: A modification model. *Cognitive Science, 12,* 485–528.

Smith, E.E., Shoben, E.J., & Rips, L.J. (1974). Structure and process in semantic memory: A featural model for semantic decisions. *Psychological Review, 81,* 214–241.

Smith, S.M., & Rothkopf, E.Z. (1984). Contextual enhancement and distribution of practice in the classroom. *Cognition & Instruction, 1,* 341–358.

Smith, S.M., Ward, T.B., & Schumacher, J.S. (1993). Constraining effects of examples in a creative generation task. *Memory & Cognition, 21,* 837–845.

Smolensky, P. (1988). On the proper treatment of connectionism. *Behavioral & Brain Sciences, 11,* 1–74.

Smyth, M.M., Morris, P.E., Levy, P., & Ellis, A.W. (1987). *Cognition in action.* Hove, UK: Psychology Press.

Soloway, E., Bonar, J., & Erlich, K. (1983). Cognitive strategies and looping constructs: An empirical study. *Communications of the ACM, 26,* 853–860.

Soloway, E., & Erlich, K. (1984). Empirical studies of programming knowledge. *IEEE Transactions of Software Engineering, 5,* 595–609.

Soloway, E., & Spohrer, J. (1989). *Studying the novice programmer.* London: Psychology Press.

Speisman, J.C., Lazarus, R.S., Mordkoff, A.M., & Davison, L.A. (1964). Experimental reduction of stress based on ego-defence theory. *Journal of Abnormal Psychology, 68,* 367–380.

Spelke, E.S., Hirst, W.C., & Neisser, U. (1976). Skills of divided attention. *Cognition, 4,* 215–230.

Spellman, B.A. (1996). The implicit use of base rates in experiential and ecologically valid tasks. *Behavioral & Brain Sciences, 19,* 38.

Sperber, D., Cara, F., & Girotto, V. (1995). Relevance theory explains the selection task. *Cognition, 57,* 31–95.

Sperling, G. (1960). The information that is available in brief visual presentations. *Psychological Monographs, 74* (Whole. No. 498), 1–29.

Spohrer, J.C., Soloway, E., & Pope, E. (1985). A goal-plan analysis of buggy Pascal programs. *Human–Computer Interaction, 1,* 163–207.

Springer, K. (1990). In defence of theories. *Cognition, 35,* 293–298.

Squire, L.R., Knowlton, B., & Musen, G. (1993). The structure and organisation of memory. *Annual Review of Psychology, 44,* 453–495.

Squire, L.R., Ojemann, J.G., Miezin, F.M., Petersen, S.E., Videen, T.O., & Raichle, M.E. (1992). Activation of the hippocampus in normal humans: A functional anatomical study of memory. *Proceedings of the National Academy of Science, USA, 89,* 1837–1841.

Srinivas, K., & Roediger, H.L. (1990). Classifying implicit memory tests: Category association and anagram solution. *Journal of Memory & Language, 29,* 389–412.

Stanovich, K.E. (1999). *Who is rational?: Studies of individual differences in reasoning.* Hillsdale, NJ: Lawrence Erlbaum Associates Inc.

Steele, G.L. (1990). *Common lisp: The language (2nd Edn).* Bedford MA: Digital Press.

Stefflre, V., Castillo Vales, V., & Morley, L. (1966). Language and cognition in Yucatan: A cross-cultural replication. *Journal of Personality & Social Psychology, 4,* 112–115.

Stein, N.L., & Glenn, C.G. (1979). An analysis of story comprehension in elementary school children. In R. Freedle (Ed.), *Multidisciplinary perspectives in discourse comprehension.* Norwood, NJ: Ablex.

Stemberger, J.P. (1982). The nature of segments in the lexicon: Evidence from speech errors. *Lingua, 56*, 235–259.

Steptoe, A., & Vogele, C. (1986). Are stress responses influenced by cognitive appraisal? An experimental comparison on coping strategies. *British Journal of Psychology, 77*, 243–255.

Stevens, J.K., Emerson, R.C., Gerstein, G.L., Kallos, T., Neufield, G.R., Nichols, C.W., & Rosenquist, A.C. (1976). Paralysis of the awake human: Visual perceptions. *Vision Research, 16*, 93–98.

Stevenson, R., & Over, D. (1995). Deduction from uncertain premises. *Quarterly Journal of Experimental Psychology, 48*A, 613–643.

Steward, F., Parkin, A.J., & Hunkin, N.M. (1992). Naming impairments following recovery from herpes simplex encephalitis: Category-specific? *Quarterly Journal of Experimental Psychology, 44*A, 261–284.

Stewart, D., Cudworth, C.J., & Lishman, J.R. (1993). Misperception of time-to-collision by drivers in pedestrian accidents. *Perception, 22*, 1227–1244.

Stewart, F., Parkin, A.J., & Hunkin, N.M. (1992). Naming impairments following recovery from herpes-simplex encephalitis: Category specific? *Quarterly Journal of Experimental Psychology, 44*A, 261–284.

Still, A., & Costall, A. (Eds.) (1991). *Against cognitivism: Alternative foundations for cognitive psychology.* Hemel Hempstead, UK: Harvester Wheatsheaf.

Stopa, L., & Clark, D.M. (1993). Cognitive processes in social phobia. *Behaviour Research & Therapy, 31*, 255–267.

Stroop, J.R. (1935). Studies of interference in serial verbal reactions. *Journal of Experimental Psychology, 18*, 643–662.

Stuss, D.T., Toth, J.P., Franchi, D., Alexander, M.P., Tipper, S., & Craik, F.I.M. (1999). Dissociation of attentional processes in patients with focal frontal and posterior lesions. *Neuropsychologia, 37*, 1005–1027.

Styles, E.A. (1997). *The psychology of attention.* Hove, UK: Psychology Press.

Sulin, R.A., & Dooling, D.J. (1974). Intrusion of a thematic idea in retention of prose. *Journal of Experimental Psychology, 103*, 255–262.

Sullivan, L. (1976). Selective attention and secondary message analysis: A reconsideration of Broadbent's filter model of selective attention. *Quarterly Journal of Experimental Psychology, 28*, 167–178.

Sussman, H.M., Hoemeke, K.A., & Ahmed, F.S. (1993). A cross-linguistic investigation of locus equations as a phonetic descriptor for place of articulation. *Journal of the Acoustical Society of America, 94*, 1256–1268.

Sweller, J. (1983). Control mechanisms in problem solving. *Memory & Cognition, 11*, 32–40.

Sweller, J., Mawer, R.F., & Ward, M.R. (1983). Development of expertise in mathematical problem solving. *Journal of Experimental Psychology: General, 112*, 639–661.

Symons, C.S., & Johnson, B.T. (1997). The self-reference effect in memory: A meta-analysis. *Psychological Bulletin, 121*, 371–394.

Takano, Y. (1989). Perception of rotated forms. *Cognitive Psychology, 21*, 1–59.

Takeuchi, A.H., & Hulse, S.H. (1993). Absolute pitch. *Psychological Bulletin, 113*, 245–361.

Tanaka, K. (1992). Inferotemporal cortex and higher visual functions. *Current Opinion in Neurobiology, 2*, 502–505.

Tarr, M.J. (1995). Rotating objects to recognise them: A case study of the role of viewpoint dependency in the recognition of three-dimensional objects. *Psychonomic Bulletin & Review, 2*, 55–82.

Tarr, M.J., & Bülthoff, H.H. (1995). Is human object recognition better described by geon structural descriptions or by multiple views? Comment on Biederman and Gerhardstein (1993). *Journal of Experimental Psychology: Human Perception & Performance, 21*, 1494–1505.

Tarr, M.J., & Bülthoff, H.H. (1998). Image-based object recognition in man, monkey and machine. *Cognition, 67*, 1–20.

Tarr, M.J., & Pinker, S. (1989). Mental rotation and orientation-dependence in shape recognition. *Cognitive Psychology, 21*, 233–282.

Tarr, M.J., Williams, P., Hayward, W.G., & Gauthier, I. (1998). Three-dimensional object recognition is viewpoint-dependent. *Nature Neuroscience*, *1*, 195–206.

Tartter, V. (1986). *Language processes*. New York: Holt, Rinehart & Winston.

Taylor, I., & Taylor, M.M. (1990). *Psycholinguistics: Learning and using language*. Englewood Cliffs, NJ: Prentice-Hall International.

Teuber, H.-L., Milner, B., & Vaughan, H.G. (1968). Persistent anterograde amnesia after stab wound of the basal brain. *Neuropsychologia*, *6*, 267–282.

Thagard, P. (1984). Conceptual combination and scientific discovery. In P. Asquith & P. Kitcher (Eds.), *PSA (Vol. 1)*. East Lansing, MI: Philosophy of Science Association.

Thagard, P., Holyoak, K.J., Nelson, G., & Gochfeld, D. (1990). Analogue retrieval by constraint satisfaction. *Artificial Intelligence*, *46*, 259–310.

Thomas, J.C. (1974). An analysis of behaviour in the hobbits–orcs problem. *Cognitive Psychology*, *6*, 257–269.

Thompson, V.A. (1994). Interpretational factors in conditional reasoning. *Memory & Cognition*, *22*, 742–758.

Thompson, V.A. (1995). Conditional reasoning: The necessary and sufficient conditions. *Canadian Journal of Experimental Psychology*, *49*, 1–60.

Thomson, D.M., & Tulving, E. (1970). Associative encoding and retrieval: Weak and strong cues. *Journal of Experimental Psychology*, *86*, 255–262.

Thorndike, E.L. (1911). *Animal intelligence*. New York: Macmillan.

Thorndyke, P.W. (1977). Cognitive structures in comprehension and memory of narrative discourse. *Cognitive Psychology*, *9*, 77–110.

Thorndyke, P.W., & Yekovich, F.R. (1980). A critique of schema-based theories of human memory. *Poetics*, 9, 23–49.

Tipper, S.P., Lortie, C., & Baylis, G.C. (1992). Selective reaching: Evidence for action-centred attention. *Journal of Experimental Psychology: Human Perception & Performance*, *18*, 891–905.

Tippett, L.J. (1992). The generation of visual images: A review of neuropsychological research and theory. *Psychological Bulletin*, *112*, 415–432.

Todd, J.T., & Akerstrom, R.A. (1987). Perception of three-dimensional form from patterns of optical texture. *Journal of Experimental Psychology: Human Perception & Performance*, *13*, 242–255.

Todd, J.T., & Norman, J.F. (1991). The visual perception of smoothly curved surfaces from minimal apparent motion sequences. *Perception & Psychophysics*, *50*, 509–523.

Tolkien, J.R.R. (1966). *The hobbit (3rd Edn)*. London: Allen & Unwin.

Tomasello, M., & Call, J. (1997). *Primate cognition*. Oxford: Oxford University Press.

Tomes, J.L., & Katz, A.N. (1997). Habitual susceptibility to misinformation and individual differences in eyewitness memory. *Applied Cognitive Psychology*, *11*, 233–251.

Tootell, R.B.H., Reppas, J.B., Dale, A.M., Look, R.B., Sereno, M.I., Malach, R., Brady, T.J., & Rosen, B.R. (1995b). Visual motion aftereffect in human cortical area MT revealed by functional magnetic resonance imaging. *Nature*, *375*, 139–141.

Tootell, R.B.H., Reppas, J.B., Kwong, K.K., et al. (1995a). Functional analysis of human MT and related visual cortical areas using magnetic-resonance-imaging. *Journal of Neuroscience*, *15*, 3215–3230.

Tovée, M.J. (1996). *An introduction to the visual system*. Cambridge: Cambridge University Press.

Towse, J.N. (1998). On random generation and the central executive of working memory. *British Journal of Psychology*, *89*, 77–101.

Towse, J.N., Hitch, G.J., & Hutton, U. (1999). The Resource King is dead! Long live the Resource King! *Behavioral & Brain Sciences*, *22*, 111.

Trabasso, T., & Sperry, L.L. (1985). Causal relatedness and importance of story events. *Journal of Memory & Language*, *24*, 595–611.

Treisman, A.M. (1960). Contextual cues in selective listening. *Quarterly Journal of Experimental Psychology*, *12*, 242–248.

Treisman, A.M. (1964). Verbal cues, language, and meaning in selective attention. *American Journal of Psychology*, *77*, 206–219.

Treisman, A.M. (1988). Features and objects: The fourteenth Bartlett memorial lecture. *Quarterly Journal of Experimental Psychology*, *40*A, 201–237.

Treisman, A.M. (1992). Spreading suppression or feature integration? A reply to Duncan and Humphreys (1992). *Journal of Experimental Psychology: Human Perception & Performance*, *18*, 589–593.

Treisman, A.M. (1993). The perception of features and objects. In A. Baddeley & L. Weiskrantz (Eds.), *Attention: Selection, awareness, and control*. Oxford: Clarendon Press.

Treisman, A.M., & Davies, A. (1973). Divided attention to ear and eye. In S. Kornblum (Ed.), *Attention and performance, Vol. IV.* London: Academic Press.

Treisman, A.M., & Geffen, G. (1967). Selective attention: Perception or response? *Quarterly Journal of Experimental Psychology*, *19*, 1–18.

Treisman, A.M., & Gelade, G. (1980). A feature integration theory of attention. *Cognitive Psychology*, *12*, 97–136.

Treisman, A.M., & Riley, J.G.A. (1969). Is selective attention selective perception or selective response: A further test. *Journal of Experimental Psychology*, *79*, 27–34.

Treisman, A.M., & Sato, S. (1990). Conjunction search revisited. *Journal of Experimental Psychology: Human Perception & Performance*, *16*, 459–478.

Treisman, A.M., & Schmidt, H. (1982). Illusory conjunctions in the perception of objects. *Cognitive Psychology*, *14*, 107–141.

Tresilian, J.R. (1994a). Approximate information sources and perceptual variables in interceptive timing. *Journal of Experimental Psychology: Human Perception & Performance, 20*, 154–173.

Tresilian, J.R. (1994b). Two straw men stay silent when asked about the "direct" versus "inferential" controversy. *Behavioral & Brain Sciences*, *17*, 335–336.

Tresilian, J.R. (1995). Perceptual and cognitive processes in time-to-contact estimation: Analysis of prediction–motion and relative judgement tasks. *Perception and Psychophysics*, *57*, 231–245.

Trojano, L., & Grossi, D. (1995). Phonological and lexical coding in verbal short-term memory and learning. *Brain & Cognition*, *21*, 336–354.

Tulving, E. (1972). Episodic and semantic memory. In E. Tulving & W. Donaldson (Eds.), *Organisation of memory*. London: Academic Press.

Tulving, E. (1974). Cue-dependent forgetting. *American Scientist*, *62*, 74–82.

Tulving, E. (1982). Synergistic ecphory in recall and recognition. *Canadian Journal of Psychology*, *36*, 130–147.

Tulving, E. (1983). *Elements of episodic memory*. Oxford: Oxford University Press.

Tulving, E. (1998). An interview with Endel Tulving. In M.S. Gazzaniga, R.B. Ivry, & G.R. Mangun, *Cognitive neuroscience: The biology of the mind*. New York: W.W. Norton.

Tulving, E., & Flexser, A.J. (1992). On the nature of the Tulving-Wiseman function. *Psychological Review*, *99*, 543–546.

Tulving, E., & Psotka, J. (1971). Retroactive inhibition in free recall: Inaccessibility of information available in the memory trace. *Journal of Experimental Psychology*, *87*, 1–8.

Tulving, E., & Schacter, D.L. (1990). Priming and human memory. *Science*, *247*, 301–306.

Tulving, E., Schacter, D.L., & Stark, H.A. (1982). Priming effects in word-fragment completion are independent of recognition memory. *Journal of Experimental Psychology: Learning, Memory, & Cognition*, *17*, 595–617.

Tulving, E., & Thomson, D.M. (1973). Encoding specificity and retrieval processes in episodic memory. *Psychological Review*, *80*, 352–373.

Turner, M.L., & Engle, R.W. (1989). Is working-memory capacity task dependent? *Journal of Memory & Language*, *28*, 127–154.

Tversky, A. (1977). Features of similarity. *Psychological Review*, *84*, 327–352.

Tversky, A., & Gati, I. (1978). Studies of similarity. In E. Rosch & B.B. Lloyd (Eds.), *Cognition and categorisation*. Hillsdale, NJ: Lawrence Erlbaum Associates Inc.

Tversky, A., & Kahneman, D. (1973). Availability: A heuristic for judging frequency and probability. *Cognitive Psychology*, *5*, 207–232.

Tversky, A., & Kahneman, D. (1974). Judgement under uncertainty: Heuristics and biases. *Science*, *185*, 1124–1131.

Tversky, A., & Kahneman, D. (1980). Causal schemas in judgements under uncertainty. In M. Fishbein (Ed.), *Progress in social psychology*. Hillsdale, NJ: Lawrence Erlbaum Associates Inc.

Tversky, A., & Kahneman, D. (1983). Extensional versus intuitive reasoning: The conjunction fallacy in probability judgement. *Psychological Review, 91*, 293–315.

Tversky, A., & Kahneman, D. (1987). Rational choice and the framing of decisions. In R. Hogarth & M. Reder (Eds.), *Rational choice: The contrast between economics and psychology*. Chicago: University of Chicago Press.

Tversky, A., & Koehler, D.J. (1994). Support theory: A nonextensional representation of subjective probability. *Psychological Review, 101*, 547–567.

Tversky, A., & Shafir, E. (1992). The disjunction effect in choice under uncertainty. *Psychological Science, 3*, 305–309.

Tweney, R.D. (1998). Toward a cognitive psychology of science: Recent research and its implications. *Current Directions in Psychological Science, 7*, 150–154.

Tweney, R.D., Doherty, M.E., Worner, W.J., Pliske, D.B., Mynatt, C.R., Gross, K.A., & Arkkelin, D.L. (1980). Strategies for rule discovery in an inference task. *Quarterly Journal of Experimental Psychology, 32*, 109–123.

Tyler, L.K., & Moss, H.E. (1997). Imageability and category-specificity. *Cognitive Neuropsychology, 14*, 293–318.

Tzelgov, J., Henik, A., Sneg, R., & Baruch, O. (1996). Unintentional reading via the phonological route: The Stroop effect with cross-script homophones. *Journal of Experimental Psychology: Learning, Memory, & Cognition, 22*, 336–339.

Ucros, C.G. (1989). Mood state-dependent memory: A meta-analysis. *Cognition & Emotion, 3*, 139–167.

Underwood, B.J. (1957). Interference and forgetting. *Psychological Review, 64*, 49–60.

Underwood, B.J., & Ekstrand, B.R. (1967). Word frequency and accumulative proactive inhibition. *Journal of Experimental Psychology, 74*, 193–198.

Underwood, B.J., & Postman, L. (1960). Extra-experimental sources of interference in forgetting. *Psychological Review, 67*, 73–95.

Underwood, G. (1974). Moray vs. the rest: The effect of extended shadowing practice. *Quarterly Journal of Experimental Psychology, 26*, 368–372.

Vaidya, C.J., Gabrieli, J.D.E., Keane, M.M., & Monti, L.A. (1995). Perceptual and conceptual memory processes in global amnesia. *Neuropsychology, 10*, 529–537.

Valdois, S., Carbonnel, S., David, D., Rousset, S., & Pellat, J. (1995). Confrontation of PDP models and dual-route models through the analysis of a case of deep dysphasia. *Cognitive Neuropsychology, 12*, 681–724.

Valentine, T. (1988). Upside-down faces: A review of the effect of inversion upon face recognition. *British Journal of Psychology, 79*, 471–491.

Vallar, G., & Baddeley, A.D. (1984). Phonological short-term store, phonological processing and sentence comprehension: A neuropsychological case study. *Cognitive Neuropsychology, 1*, 121–141.

Vallée-Tourangeau, F., Austin, N.G., & Rankin, S. (1995). Inducing a rule in Wason 2–4–6 task: A test of the information quantity and goal-complementarity hypotheses. *Quarterly Journal of Experimental Psychology, 48*A, 895–914.

van Dijk, T.A., & Kintsch, W. (1983). *Strategies of discourse comprehension*. New York: Academic Press.

Van Essen, D.C., & Gallant, J.L. (1994). Neural mechanisms of form and motion processing in the primate visual system. *Neuron, 13*, 1–10.

Van Joolingen, W.R., & DeJong, T. (1997). An extended dual space search model of scientific discovery learning. *Instructional Science, 25*, 306–346. —

Van Mechelen, I., Hampton, J., Michalski, R.S., & Theuns, P. (1993). *Concepts and categories*. London: Academic Press.

Vargha-Khadem, F., Gadian, D.G., Watkins, K.E., Connelly, A., Van Paesschen, W., & Mishkin, M. (1997). Differential effects of early hippocampal pathology on episodic and semantic memory. *Science, 277*, 376–380.

Varner, L.J., & Ellis, H.C. (1998). Cognitive activity and physiological arousal: Processes that mediate mood-congruent memory. *Memory & Cognition, 26*, 939–950.

Vaughan, J. (1985). *Hoping and commanding: Prototype semantics demonstrated.* Unpublished BA Thesis, Department of Psychology, Trinity College, Dublin, Ireland.

Vecera, S.P., & Farah, M.J. (1997). Is visual image segmentation a bottom-up or an interactive process? *Perception & Psychophysics, 59,* 1280–1296.

Velten, E. (1968). A laboratory task for induction of mood states. *Behaviour Research & Therapy, 6,* 473–482.

Vera, A., & Simon, H.A. (1994). Reply to Touretsky and Pomerleau: Reconstructing physical symbol systems. *Cognitive Science, 18,* 355–360.

Verfaellie, M., Gabrieli, J.D.E., Vaidya, C.J., & Croce, P. (1996). Implicit memory for pictures in amnesia: Role of aetiology and priming task. *Neuropsychology, 10,* 517–537.

Vincente, K.J., & Brewer, W.F. (1993). Reconstructive remembering of the scientific literature. *Cognition, 46,* 101–128.

Von Eckardt, B. (1993). *What is cognitive science?* Cambridge, MA: MIT Press.

Von Neumann, J., & Morgenstern, O. (1947). *Theory of games and economic behaviour.* Princeton, NJ: Princeton University Press.

Von Wright, J.M., Anderson, K., & Stenman, U. (1975). Generalisation of conditioned G.S.R.s in dichotic listening. In P.M.A. Rabbitt & S. Dornic (Eds.), *Attention and performance, Vol. V.* London: Academic Press.

Vosniadou, S., & Brewer, W. (1992) Mental models of the earth: A study of conceptual change in childhood. *Cognitive Psychology, 24,* 535–585.

Wachtel, P. (1973). Psychodynamics, behaviour therapy and the implacable experimenter: An inquiry into the consistency of personality. *Journal of Abnormal Psychology, 82,* 324–334.

Wagenaar, W.A. (1986). My memory: A study of autobiographical memory over six years. *Cognitive Psychology, 18,* 225–252.

Wagenaar, W.A. (1994). Is memory self-serving? In U. Neisser & R. Fivush (Eds.), *The remembering self: Construction and accuracy in the self-narrative.* Cambridge: Cambridge University Press.

Wagner, A.D., Desmond, J.E., Demb, J.B., Glover, G.H., & Gabrieli, J.D.E. (1997). Semantic memory processes and left inferior prefrontal cortex: A functional MRI study of form specificity. *Journal of Cognitive Neuroscience.*

Wagner, D.A., & Scurrah, M.J. (1971). Some characteristics of human problem solving in chess. *Cognitive Psychology, 2,* 451–478.

Walker, C.H., & Yekovich, F.R. (1984). Script-based inferences: Effects of text and knowledge variables on recognition memory. *Journal of Verbal Learning & Verbal Behavior, 23,* 357–370.

Walker, J.H. (1975). Real-world variability, reasonableness judgements, and memory representations for concepts. *Journal of Verbal Learning & Verbal Behavior, 14,* 241–252.

Wallach, H., & O'Connell, D.N. (1953). The kinetic depth effect. *Journal of Experimental Psychology, 45,* 205–217.

Wallas, G. (1926). *The art of thought.* London: Cape.

Waltz, J.A., Knowlton, B.J., Holyoak, K.J., Boone, K.B., Mishkin, F.S., de Menezes Santos, M., Thomas, C.R., & Miller, B.L. (1999). A system for relational reasoning in human prefrontal cortex. *Psychological Science, 10,* 119–125.

Wandell, B.A. (1995). *Foundations of vision.* Sunderland, MA: Sinauer.

Wang, X.T. (1996). Domain-specific rationality in human choices: Violations of utility axioms and social contexts. *Cognition, 60,* 31–63.

Wann, J.P. (1996). Anticipating arrival: Is the tau margin a specious theory? *Journal of Experimental Psychology: Human Perception & Performance, 22,* 1031–1048.

Wann, J.P., & Rushton, S.K. (1995). Grasping the impossible: Stereoscopic virtual balls. In B.G. Bardy, R.J. Bootsma, & Y. Guiard (Eds.), *Studies in perception and action, Vol. III.* Hillsdale, NJ: Lawrence Erlbaum Associates Inc.

Ward, G., & Allport, A. (1997). Planning and problem solving using the 5-disc Tower of London task. *Quarterly Journal of Experimental Psychology, 50,* 49–78.

Ward, R., Goodrich, S., & Driver, J. (1994). Grouping reduces visual extinction: Neuropsychological evidence for weight-linkage in visual selection. *Visual Cognition*, *1*, 101–129.

Ward, T.B. (1992). Structured imagination. In R.A. Finke, T.B. Ward, & S.M. Smith (Eds.), *Creative cognition: Theory, research and applications*. Cambridge, MA: MIT Press.

Ward, T.B., & Sifonis, C.M. (1997). Task demands and generative thinking: What changes and what remains the same? *Journal of Creative Behaviour*, *31*, 245–259.

Ward, T.B., Smith, S.M., & Finke, R.A. (1995). *The creative cognition approach*. Cambridge, MA: MIT Press.

Warr, P.B. (1964). The relative importance of proactive interference and degree of learning in retention of paired associate items. *British Journal of Psychology*, *55*, 19–30.

Warren, R. (1976). The perception of egomotion. *Journal of Experimental Psychology: Human Perception & Performance*, *2*, 448–456.

Warren, W.H., & Hannon, D.J. (1988). Direction of self-motion is perceived from optical flow. *Nature*, *336*, 162–163.

Warren, W.H., Morris, M.W., & Kalish, M.L. (1988). Perception of translational heading from optical flow. *Journal of Experimental Psychology: Human Perception & Performance*, *14*, 646–660.

Warren, R.M., & Warren, R.P. (1970). Auditory illusions and confusions. *Scientific American*, *223*, 30–36.

Warren, W.H., Young, D.S., & Lee, D.N. (1986). Visual control of step length during running over irregular terrain. *Journal of Experimental Psychology: Human Perception & Performance*, *12*, 259–266.

Warrington, E.K. (1975). The selective impairment of semantic memory. *Quarterly Journal of Experimental Psychology*, *27*, 635–657.

Warrington, E.K., & McCarthy, R.A. (1994). Multiple meaning systems in the brain: Case for visual semantics. *Neuropsychologia*, *32*, 1465–1473.

Warrington, E.K., & Shallice, T. (1972). Neuropsychological evidence of visual storage in short-term memory tasks. *Quarterly Journal of Experimental Psychology*, *24*, 30–40.

Warrington, E.K., & Shallice, T. (1984). Category-specific semantic impairment. *Brain*, *107*, 829–853.

Warrington, E.K., & Taylor, A.M. (1978). Two categorical stages of object recognition. *Perception*, *7*, 695–705.

Wason, P.C. (1960). On the failure to eliminate hypotheses in a conceptual task. *Quarterly Journal of Experimental Psychology*, *12*, 129–140.

Wason, P.C. (1966). Reasoning. In B.M. Foss (Ed.), *New horizons in psychology*. Harmondsworth, UK: Penguin.

Wason, P.C. (1977). On the failure to eliminate hypotheses . . . A second look. In P.N. Johnson-Laird & P.C. Wason (Eds.), *Thinking: Readings in cognitive science*. Cambridge: Cambridge University Press.

Wason, P.C., & Evans, J.St.B.T. (1975). Dual processes in reasoning? *Cognition*, *3*, 141–154.

Wason, P.C., & Johnson-Laird, P.N. (1972). *The psychology of reasoning: Structure and content*. Cambridge, MA: Harvard University Press.

Wason, P.C., & Shapiro, D. (1971). Natural and contrived experience in reasoning problems. *Quarterly Journal of Experimental Psychology*, *23*, 63–71.

Waters, G.S., & Caplan, D. (1996). The capacity theory of sentence comprehension: Critique of Just and Carpenter (1992). *Psychological Review*, *103*, 761–772.

Watkins, M.J., & Gardiner, J.M. (1979). An appreciation of generate–recognise theory of recall. *Journal of Verbal Learning & Verbal Behavior*, *18*, 687–704.

Watt, R.J. (1988). *Visual processing: Computational, psychophysical, and cognitive research*. Hove, UK: Psychology Press.

Waxman, S.R., & Markow, D.B. (1995). Words as invitations to form categories: Evidence from 12- to 13-month-old infants. *Cognitive Psychology*, *29*, 257–302.

Weekes, B., & Coltheart, M. (1996). Surface dyslexia and surface dysgraphia: Treatment studies and their theoretical implications. *Cognitive Neuropsychology*, *13*, 277–315.

Weinberger, D.A., Schwartz, G.E., & Davidson, J.R. (1979). Low-anxious, high-anxious, and repressive coping styles: Psychometric patterns and behavioural and physiological responses to stress. *Journal of Abnormal Psychology*, *88*, 369–380.

Weisberg, R.W. (1980). *Memory, thought and behaviour*. Oxford: Oxford University Press.

Weisberg, R.W. (1986). *Creativity, genius and other myths*. New York: W.H. Freeman.

Weisberg, R.W. (1993). *Creativity: Beyond the myth of genius*. San Francisco, CA: W.H. Freeman.

Weisberg, R.W., & Alba, J.W. (1981). An examination of the alleged role of "fixation" in the solution of several insight problems. *Journal of Experimental Psychology: General, 110*, 169–192.

Weisberg, R.W., & Suls, J. (1973). An information-processing model of Duncker's candle problem. *Cognitive Psychology, 4*, 255–276.

Weiskrantz, L. (1980). Varieties of residual experience. *Quarterly Journal of Experimental Psychology, 32*, 365–386.

Weiskrantz, L. (1986). *Blindsight: A case study and implications*. Oxford: Oxford University Press.

Weiskrantz, L. (1995). Blindsight—not an island unto itself. *Current Directions in Psychological Science, 4*, 146–151.

Weiskrantz, L., Barbur, J.L., & Sahraie, A. (1995). Parameters affecting conscious versus unconscious visual discrimination with damage to the visual cortex V1. *Proceedings of the National Academy of Sciences, USA, 92*, 6122–6126.

Weiskrantz, L., Warrington, E.K., Sanders, M.D., & Marshall, J. (1974). Visual capacity in the hemianopic field following a restricted occipital ablation. *Brain, 97*, 709–728.

Weisstein, N., & Harris, C.S. (1974). Visual detection of line segments: An object-superiority effect. *Science, 186*, 752–755.

Weisstein, N., & Wong, E. (1986). Figure–ground organisation and the spatial and temporal responses of the visual system. In E.C. Schwab & H.C. Nusbaum (Eds.), *Pattern recognition by humans and machines, Vol. 2*. New York: Academic Press.

Welford, A.T. (1952). The psychological refractory period and the timing of high speed performance. *British Journal of Psychology, 43*, 2–19.

Wells, G.L. (1993). What do we know about eyewitness identification? *American Psychologist, 48*, 553–571.

Werker, J.F., & Tees, R.C. (1992). The organisation and reorganisation of human speech perception. *Annual Review of Neuroscience, 15*, 377–402.

Wertheimer, M. (1912). Experimentelle Studien über das Sehen von Bewegung. *Zeitschrift für Psychologie, 61*, 161–265.

Wertheimer, M. (1954). *Productive thinking*. New York: Harper & Row.

Wetherick, N.E. (1962). Eliminative and enumerative behaviour in a conceptual task. *Quarterly Journal of Experimental Psychology, 14*, 246–249.

Wexler, M., Kosslyn, S.M., & Berthoz, A. (1998). Motor processes in mental rotation. *Cognition, 68*, 77–94.

Wharton, C.M., Cheng, P.W., & Wickens, T.D. (1993). Hypothesis-testing strategies: Why two goals are better than one. *Quarterly Journal of Experimental Psychology, 46*A, 753–758.

Wharton, C.M., & Grafman, J.G. (1998). Reasoning and the brain. *Trends in Cognitive Science, 2*, 54–59.

Wharton, C.M., Grafman, J., Flitman, S.K., Hansen, E.K., Brauner, J., Marks, A., & Honda, M. (1998). The neuroanatomy of analogical reasoning. In K.J. Holyoak, D. Gentner, & B. Kekinar (Eds.), *Analogy 98*. Sofia, Bulgaria: New University of Bulgaria.

Wharton, C.M., Holyoak, K.J., Downing, P.E., Lange, T.E., Wickens, T.D., & Melz, E.R. (1994). Below the surface: Analogical similarity and retrieval competition in reminding. *Cognitive Psychology, 26*, 64–101.

Wheatstone, C. (1838). Contributions to the physiology of vision. Part 1: On some remarkable and hitherto unobserved phenomena of binocular vision. *Philosophical Transactions of the Royal Society of London, 128*, 371–394.

Wheeler, M.A., Stuss, D.T., & Tulving, E. (1997). Toward a theory of episodic memory: The frontal lobes and autonoetic consciousness. *Psychological Bulletin, 121*, 331–354.

Whitaker, H.A., Savary, F., Markovits, H., & Grou, C. (1991). Inference deficits after brain damage. *Annual INS Meeting*, San Antonio, Texas.

Whitlow, S.D., Althoff, R.R., & Cohen, N.J. (1995). Deficit in relational (declarative) memory in amnesia. *Society for Neuroscience Abstracts, 21*, 754.

Whorf, B.L. (1956). *Language, thought, and reality: Selected writings of Benjamin Lee Whorf.* New York: John Wiley.

Wickelgren, W.A. (1968). Sparing of short-term memory in an amnesic patient: Implications for strength theory of memory. *Neuropsychologia, 6*, 235–244.

Wickens, C.D. (1984). Processing resources in attention. In R. Parasuraman & D.R. Davies (Eds.), *Varieties of attention.* London: Academic Press.

Wilding, J., & Valentine, E. (1991). Superior memory ability. In J. Weinman & J. Hunter (Eds.), *Memory: Neurochemical and abnormal perspectives.* London: Harwood.

Wilding, J., & Valentine, E. (1994). Memory champions. *British Journal of Psychology, 85*, 231–244.

Wilkins, M.C. (1928). The effect of changed material on the ability to do formal syllogistic reasoning. *Archives of Psychology, 16*, no. 102.

Williams, J.M.G., & Broadbent, K. (1986). Autobiographical memory in suicide attempters. *Journal of Abnormal Psychology, 95*, 144–149.

Williams, J.M.G., Watts, F.N., MacLeod, C., & Mathews, A. (1988). *Cognitive psychology and emotional disorders.* Chichester, UK: Wiley.

Williams, J.M.G., Watts, F.N., MacLeod, C., & Mathews, A. (1997). *Cognitive psychology and emotional disorders (2nd Edn).* Chichester, UK: Wiley.

Williams, L.M. (1994). Recall of childhood trauma: A prospective study of women's memories of childhood abuse. *Journal of Consulting & Clinical Psychology, 62*, 1167–1176.

Willmes, K., & Poeck, K. (1993). To what extent can aphasic syndromes be localised? *Brain, 116*, 1527–1540.

Wilson, R.A., & Keil, F. (1999). *The MIT encyclopaedia of the cognitive sciences.* Cambridge, MA: MIT Press.

Winner, E. (1996). The rage to master: The decisive role of talent in the visual arts. In K.A. Ericsson (Ed.), *The road to excellence.* Hillsdale, NJ: Lawrence Erlbaum Associates Inc.

Wise, R.J.S., Chollet, F., Hadar, U., Friston, K., Hoffner, E., & Frackowiak, R.S.J. (1991). Distribution of cortical neural networks involved in word comprehension and word retrieval. *Brain, 114*, 1803–1817.

Wiseman, S., & Tulving, E. (1976). Encoding specificity: Relations between recall superiority and recognition failure. *Journal of Experimental Psychology: Human Learning & Memory, 2*, 349–361.

Wisniewski, E.J. (1996). Construal and similarity in conceptual combination. *Journal of Memory & Language, 35*(3), 434–453.

Wisniewski, E.J. (1997). Conceptual combination: Possibilities and esthetics. In T.B. Ward, S.M. Smith, & J. Vaid (Eds.), *Creative thought: An investigation of conceptual structures and processes.* Washington, DC: American Psychological Association.

Wisniewski, E.J., & Love, B.C. (1998). Relations versus properties in conceptual combination. *Journal of Memory & Language, 38*, 177–202.

Wisniewski, E.J., & Medin, D. (1994). On the interaction of theory and data in concept learning. *Cognitive Science, 18*, 221–281.

Wittgenstein, L. (1958). *Philosophical investigations (2nd Edn).* Oxford: Blackwell.

Wixted, J.T., & Ebbeson, E.B. (1997). Genuine power curves in forgetting: A quantitative analysis of individual subject forgetting functions. *Memory & Cognition, 25*, 731–739.

Woldorff, M.G., Gallen, C.C., Hampson, S.A., Hillyard, S.A., Pantev, C., Sobel, D., & Bloom, F.E. (1993). Modulation of early sensory processing in human auditory cortex during auditory selective attention. *Proceedings of the National Academy of Sciences, 90*, 8722–8726.

Wolfe, J.M. (1998). Visual search. In H. Pashler (Ed.), *Attention.* Hove, UK: Psychology Press.

Wong, E., & Mack, A. (1981). Saccadic programming and perceived location. *Acta Psychologia, 48*, 123–131.

Wood, J.V., Giordano-Beech, M., Taylor, K.L., Michela, J.L., & Gaus, V. (1994). Strategies of social comparison among people with low self-esteem: Self-protection and self-enhancement. *Journal of Personality & Social Psychology, 67*, 713–731.

Woodworth, R.S., & Schlosberg, H. (1954). *Experimental psychology (2nd Edn)*. New York: Holt, Rinehart, & Winston.

Woodworth, R.S., & Sells, S.B. (1935). An atmosphere effect in formal syllogistic reasoning. *Journal of Experimental Psychology*, *18*, 451–460.

Wright, D.B., & Gaskell, G.D. (1995). Flashbulb memories: Conceptual and methodological issues. *Memory*, *3*, 67–80.

Wright, D.B., Gaskell, G.D., & O'Muircheartaigh, C.A. (1998). Flashbulb memory assumptions: Using national surveys to explore cognitive phenomena. *British Journal of Psychology*, *89*, 103–121.

Wynn, V.E., & Logie, R.H. (1998). The veracity of long-term memories—Did Bartlett get it right? *Applied Cognitive Psychology*, *12*, 1–20.

Yaniv, I., & Meyer, D.E. (1987). Activation and metacognition of inaccessible information. Potential bases for incubation effects in problem solving. *Journal of Experimental Psychology: Learning, Memory, & Cognition*, *13*, 187–205.

Yantis, S. (1998). Control of visual attention. In H. Pashler (Ed.), *Attention*. Hove, UK: Psychology Press.

Yates, F.A. (1966). *The art of memory*. London: Routledge & Kegan Paul.

Yates, J. (1990). What is a theory? A response to Springer. *Cognition*, *36*, 91–96.

Yates, J., Bessman, M., Dunne, M., Jertson, D., Sly, K., & Wendelboe, B. (1988). Are conceptions of motion based on a naive theory or on prototypes? *Cognition*, *29*, 251–275.

Young, A.W., & de Haan, E.H.F. (1988). Boundaries of covert recognition in prosopagnosia. *Cognitive Neuropsychology*, *5*, 317–336.

Young, A.W., Hay, D.C., & Ellis, A.W. (1985). The faces that launched a thousand slips: Everyday difficulties and errors in recognising people. *British Journal of Psychology*, *76*, 495–523.

Young, A.W., Hellawell, D., & Hay, D.C. (1987). Configural information in face perception. *Perception*, *16*, 747–759.

Young, A.W., McWeeny, K.H., Hay, D.C., & Ellis, A.W. (1986a). Naming and categorisation latencies for faces and written names. *Quarterly Journal of Experimental Psychology*, *38*A, 297–318.

Young, A.W., McWeeny, K.H., Hay, D.C., & Ellis, A.W. (1986b). Matching familiar and unfamilar faces on identity and expression. *Psychological Research*, *48*, 63–68.

Young, A.W., Newcombe, F., de Haan, E.H.F., Small, M., & Hay, D.C. (1993). Face perception after brain injury: Selective impairments affecting identity and expression. *Brain*, *116*, 941–959.

Young, M.P. (1995). Open questions about the neural mechanisms of visual pattern recognition. In M.S. Gazzaniga, *The cognitive neurosciences*. Cambridge, MA: MIT Press.

Zadeh, L. (1982). A note on prototype theory and fuzzy sets. *Cognition*, *12*, 291–297.

Zaidel, E. (1976). Auditory vocabulary of the right hemisphere following brain bisection or hemidecortication. *Cortex*, *12*, 191–211.

Zajonc, R.B. (1980). Feeling and thinking: Preferences need no inferences. *American Psychologist*, *35*, 151–175.

Zajonc, R.B. (1984). On the primacy of affect. *American Psychologist*, *39*, 117–123.

Zaragoza, M.S., & McCloskey, M. (1989). Misleading postevent information and the memory impairment hypothesis: Comment on Belli and reply to Tversky and Tuchin. *Journal of Experimental Psychology: General*, *118*, 92–99.

Zeki, S. (1983). Colour coding in the cerebral cortex: The reaction of cells in monkey visual cortex to wavelengths and colour. *Neuroscience*, *9*, 741–756.

Zeki, S. (1992). The visual image in mind and brain. *Scientific American*, *267*, 43–50.

Zeki, S. (1993). *A vision of the brain*. Oxford: Blackwell.

Zeki, S., Watson, J.D.G., Lueck, C.J., Friston, K.J., Kennard, C., & Frackowiak, R.S.J. (1991). A direct demonstration of functional specialisation in human visual cortex. *Journal of Neuroscience*, *11*, 641–649.

Zihl, J., von Cramon, D., & Mai, N. (1983). Selective disturbance of movement vision after bilateral brain damage. *Brain*, *106*, 313–340.

Zihl, J., von Cramon, D., Mai, N., & Schmid, C. (1991). Disturbance of movement vision after bilateral posterior brain damage, further evidence and follow up observations. *Brain, 114,* 2235–2252.

Zwaan, R.A. (1994). Effects of genre expectations on text comprehension. *Journal of Experimental Psychology: Learning, Memory, & Cognition, 20,* 920–933.

Zwaan, R.A., Langston, M.C., & Graesser, A.C. (1995). The construction of situation models in narrative comprehension: An event-indexing model. *Psychological Science, 6,* 292–297.

Zwaan, R.A., & Radvansky, G.A. (1998). Situation models in language comprehension and memory. *Psychological Bulletin, 123,* 162–185.

Zwaan, R.A., & van Oostendop, U. (1993). Do readers construct spatial representations in naturalistic story comprehension? *Discourse Processes, 16,* 125–143.

Zwitserlood, P. (1989). The locus of the effects of sentential–semantic context in spoken-word processing. *Cognition, 32,* 25–64.

# Author index

# Subject index

Entries given in **bold** indicate glossary terms.